THE PRACTICAL GUIDE TO SOFTWARE LICENSING and Cloud Computing

Eighth Edition

H. WARD CLASSEN

ABA
AMERICAN BAR ASSOCIATION
Business Law Section

Cover design by Catherine Zaccarine.

Printed in the United States of America.

28 27 26 25 24 5 4 3 2 1

ISBN: 978-1-63905-436-7

Contents

Acknowledgments

It has been said that it takes a village to raise a child, and so it is with writing a book. *The Practical Guide to Software Licensing and Cloud Computing* would not exist without the assistance and support of a great many people.

This Eighth Edition is the collective effort of many talented people who lent their time and expertise to make this book a success. Chris Falkowski imparted his encyclopaedic knowledge of the ever-changing world of patent law while Matt Homyk provided his unparalleled copyright expertise to confirm my understanding of copyright law was correct. Erika Moore, CPA, of Marcum LLP spent countless hours reviewing my summation of revenue recognition rules to ensure that my summary correctly reflects the nuances of this complex area, while Matt Jacobs provided his invaluable insights on free and open-source software. Anthony Ramirez's probing questions and suggestions ensured I comprehensively addressed cloud computing and hosting. I am grateful for Hank Jones' invaluable expertise and counsel on software licensing, not to mention his editing skills.

Dan Roffman, a leading expert in software audits, provided many insightful comments on software audits while Christiana State's practical perspectives on mobile applications were invaluable. Rita M. Piel generously allowed me to include her comprehensive SaaS agreement (Form D.3.8) in the online forms. Allie Tobian's strong grasp of grammar as well as her proof reading skills made this book much easier to read.

Finally, I am indebted to Ali Kille, Shanna Whitley, Tom Maguire, Anne Madden, Darina Byrne, Robin Kynaston, Cristian Luna Chandia, Rich Kent, Jaytonious Perkins, Jay Shah, Jonathan Savage, Shari Wilkozek, Tamzin Evershed and my many talented and gifted colleagues at Honeywell International who have been extremely supportive of my efforts to write this book and never hesitated to answer my endless questions.

I am also grateful for the opportunity and support provided by the American Bar Association. Without the encouragement of Eric Goldman, this book would not have been written. I am especially indebted to Richard Paszkiet and Katrina Krause for their tireless efforts to bring this book to fruition.

Finally, the unending support of Sibley, Keena, and Pierce made a difficult and seemingly endless task possible.

CHAPTER **1**

Introduction

This book examines some of the fundamental issues that both vendors and customers may confront in the negotiation of software licenses and cloud computing agreements. This includes related issues such as software development, professional services, as well as maintenance and support. It also discusses ancillary issues such as software development kits (SDKs), application program interfaces (APIs), service level agreements (SLAs), and escrow agreements. The book focuses primarily on non-mass-market production licenses, as most "retail" or mass-market "off-the-shelf" software is governed by non-negotiable "shrink-wrap," "browse-wrap," and "click-wrap" licenses. Nonetheless, the principles of software licensing are generally the same for shrink-wrap, browse-wrap, click-wrap, and custom-developed software.

This book does not discuss software transactions with the government, as the laws relating to government contracting are beyond the scope of this treatise. For an overview of intellectual property rights related to government contracting, see *Nash, Intellectual Property in Government Contracts* (6th ed).

The structure and context of every software license, and cloud agreement differs depending on the nature of the transaction. While this book discusses some of the most important issues, including numerous forms, D.C. Toedt III, Esq., in conjunction with the Computer Programs Committee of the Information Division of the Section of Intellectual-Property Law of the American Bar Association, created a model license that, although voluminous, is quite thorough and educational. Toedt's license was created to be a resource but is not commercially viable due to its complexity and length. It is included as Form B.8.1. For a detailed discussion of this license, see Toedt, *The Model Software License Provisions: Precursor to a Gap-Filling Uniform License Statute*, 18 Rutgers Computer & Tech. L.J. 521 (1992).

Finally, the nature of software licensing is trending toward access, and delivery through the cloud, commonly referred to as cloud computing. Chapter 14 discusses several of the most common alternative delivery methods, and the principal issues associated with each. Further, Chapter 20 examines licenses, and issues arising from the marketing, and distribution of software through third parties.

CHAPTER **2**

The Negotiation and Contracting Process

Negotiations for software licenses are unique in many respects. Most importantly, the parties will often be entering into a long-term relationship for potentially complex software that may be extremely important to the success of the customer's business. As such, it may be difficult for the customer to switch vendors in the event of an unsuccessful implementation. Further, the individuals negotiating the license agreement on the customer's behalf may not fully understand the underlying technology of the software and how it may impact the customer's legacy systems. At the same time, the vendor may possess significant negotiating leverage over the customer and may be unwilling to make material concessions to the terms of its license agreement. Interestingly, some vendors charge a higher price to those customers who seek to negotiate the terms of their software license, claiming the increased risk to the vendor from modifying its standard terms justifies a higher price. *See, e.g.*, https://www.solver.com/pricing-standard-versus-custom-terms-and-conditions.

A. The Traditional Negotiation Process

Traditionally, a customer evaluates potential solutions and narrows the field to a single vendor. The customer then proceeds to negotiate on an exclusive basis with the selected vendor until an agreement is reached. If an impasse arises, the customer has little recourse but to either accede to the vendor's demands or terminate the negotiations and select a new vendor, which requires a significant amount of duplicative time, effort, and cost.

In the selection process, a vendor is focused on eliminating its competition to gain significant leverage in the negotiation process. When the customer seeks particular commitments or guarantees, the vendor typically is free to accept or reject the customer's demands without fear of losing the business, knowing the customer is negotiating only with it. Single-vendor negotiations also provide an incentive for the vendor to defer the more contentious issues to the end of the negotiations, a time when the customer is least likely to terminate the negotiations. Further, the vendor can use the threat of time to leverage its position—especially if the customer is under a tight timeline to implement the software or system.

The basis for negotiation is usually the vendor's template agreement, which naturally favors the vendor. The customer usually accepts the vendor's agreement as a starting point because it does not want to expend the time, effort, or cost to create its own single-transaction contract. The vendor often insists on using the vendor's template contract arguing that its expertise in software makes it advantageous for both parties to use its contract in an effort to save time and obtain a comprehensive agreement. While there is nothing wrong with using the vendor's template as a basis for negotiation, the customer should realize that it is often slanted, whether overtly or discreetly, to the vendor's advantage, and further, the types of protections sought by savvy technology buyers are typically not found in the vendor's form. Nonetheless, starting with the vendor's template may speed the time to contract given the template is most likely tailored to the vendor's solution.

Regardless of who creates the initial draft, a party should seek to control or at least share responsibility for drafting the agreement. Many lawyers fail to realize the importance of controlling the draft and the ability to craft the agreement. There are many ways of stating the same concept. By controlling the drafting process, a party can provide its interpretation of each issue using the language that best represents its interests. This is especially important for licensees; as often when the vendor controls the draft, the full extent of the vendor's concessions fail to be included in the resulting draft, or the language is slanted to minimize the vendor's concession. If the vendor insists on controlling the draft, drafting the language of any concession at the negotiating table can minimize the vendor's drafting advantage.

See Forms Q.1 and Q.2 for examples of definitions and clauses that present the same concept but are drafted to benefit a particular party.

B. The Competitive Negotiation Process

1. Overview

Unlike a traditional negotiation discussed above, an increasing number of customers, especially in IT outsourcing transactions, utilize a competitive bidding process for software purchases for large systems and negotiating their software licenses as part of the bidding process. While a competitive bidding process can assume different forms, the procurement and negotiation process is different than the traditional software vendor-customer negotiations process.

A competitive bidding process begins with the customer sending a Request For Information (RFI), a Request For Proposal (RFP), or other qualification document to interested vendors. The process, start to finish, can take three to four months from initiation through the selection of the chosen vendor.

For a general discussion of the issues that should be considered by a licensee before entering into a software transaction, *see* Willret & Ketler, *10 Questions to Ask Before Software License Transactions,* 27 ACC DOCKET 38 (Sept. 2009).

2. Requests for Information ("RFI")

If a customer is unsure of the approach to take in addressing its technology needs, it should submit a Request for Information to interested vendors to solicit their ideas. RFIs usually describe the customer's existing IT infrastructure, the challenges the customer is facing, and how the customer hopes to benefit from the contemplated project. The RFI may include the customer's own ideas on how to address its technology needs.

The RFI should solicit the vendors' ideas and thoughts on how to address the issues, as well as their insights on the customer's thought process and plans. Some customers will invite vendors to meet with them to further exchange ideas. This may include having the vendors suggest information and selection criteria to be included in the subsequent RFP. Utilizing an RFI approach, however, will most likely add four to six weeks to the selection process.

From the customer's perspective, the customer will want the ability to use any ideas generated from the RFI process, regardless of whether a vendor is ultimately selected for the project. From the vendor's perspective, a vendor wants to avoid having the customer use its ideas without retaining the vendor to perform the contemplated services. To protect itself, a vendor may want to either insist on executing a nondisclosure agreement with the customer or submit only very general concepts to the customer. See Form A.2.4 § 2 for a nondisclosure agreement that expressly permits the customer to disclose/use the information submitted by the vendor in a vendor's RFI/RFP response.

See Forms A.1.1 and A.1.2 for model RFIs.

3. *Requests for Proposal ("RFP")*

(a) Customer Perspective

Once the customer has received the responses to its RFI and conducted any desired vendor meetings, it should utilize the information obtained from the RFI process to draft the RFP.

(i) Customer Requirements

In most cases, the RFP sets forth the customer's requirements for the new software or solution it intends to purchase. Although a significant effort is often required to capture the customer's technical and functional requirements, the RFP is critical to provide sufficient detail for the vendor to provide a detailed proposal and accurately price its response. Ambiguities and missing information increase a vendor's risk and may impact the quoted pricing. Despite their best intentions, individuals who draft RFPs often omit a detailed focus on the buying process itself (i.e., how the customer intends to purchase the system). Important contractual terms such as testing criteria, payment terms, and warranties are usually not identified, or if they are identified, they are not tailored to the specifics of the proposed technology purchase.

(ii) Requesting Detailed Information

The customer should ask direct questions related to the potential vendors' capabilities, which will allow the customer to make an informed decision. It should avoid asking non-critical questions or requesting tangential data solely for the purpose of obtaining all possible information.

In general, customers should request detailed information on the proposed solution/application including:

- Can the solution be scaled and have functionality added?
- Is the solution highly/easily configurable?

- Can the application be provided as a service (ASP, SAAS, hosted)?
- Is the potential vendor developing new technology that will make the proposed solution obsolete in the near future?
- How large is the vendor's support organization?
- Where is the support organization located?
- What are the hours of operation for the support organization?
- What quality assurance standards does the vendor meet? (ISO 9001, SOC II)
- How is the pricing determined?
- A list of current customers utilizing the proposed solution?

(iii) Requiring Detailed Responses

Many customers seek to obtain competitive business intelligence on the potential vendor by asking the vendor to disclose previous litigation and security breaches, representative customers, consistent skill sets, regulatory compliance and potential merger and acquisition activity. Many vendors will not respond with detailed answers but instead prefer to provide a general answer that can be expanded upon during negotiations. See Form A.2.8 for model RFP questions and vendor responses.

Sophisticated customers purchasing large-scale systems identify in the RFP specific contractual requirements and how the customer intends to conduct the negotiation process. Increasingly, to avoid a "non-response" as discussed in the previous paragraph, customers break their contracts down, paragraph by paragraph, in matrix form and require vendors to comment on each contract provision. This approach, once seen only in outsourcing transactions, is becoming more prevalent in software licensing transactions. For instance, the customer would set forth contractual language for its proposed payment terms and require the bidders to state whether they will comply with such language. If the bidder does not accept the customer's language, they must state why they do not accept such language and supply alternative language or a counterproposal. The structure of the RFP is intended to prevent the vendor from later changing its position once it has been down-selected. Vendors submit their responses in a matrix format so they can be easily compared and contrasted. This approach allows customers to evaluate each vendor's technical and functional capabilities, as well as their flexibility and willingness to contract on terms that are acceptable to the customer. See Form A.2.2 for an example of an RFP Response Matrix.

To avoid a "bait and switch" by a vendor, the customer should include language in the RFP that the risks of a misunderstanding falls squarely on the vendor and that the vendor is responsible for standing behind its bid.

The Vendor or its authorized representatives are expected to fully inform themselves fully as to the conditions, requirements, circumstances, prerequisites, qualifications, and/or specifications before submitting their proposal/bid. A Vendor's failure to become fully informed is at the Vendor's sole and complete risk of loss. The Vendor shall have no right to any damages, cost and/or any other remedy at law or equity against Customer for any miscalculation, misunderstanding, error (either omissions or commissions), mistake, misinterpretation, and/or the failure by the Vendor to obtain an award of bid, award of contract and/or profits, fees or money from Customer when the Vendor failed to fully inform themselves. In the case of error in extension of prices, the percentages markup(s)/

discount(s) indicated, the unit price(s) shall govern or the entire bid may be declared non-responsive.

(iv) The Customer Contract

Historically, many customers have attached their proposed agreements and asked potential vendors to identify any provisions the vendor considers objectionable, to provide an explanation of the provision is considered objectionable, and provide alternative language while providing that doing so will not be interpreted as prohibiting either party from proposing additional contract terms during the negotiation period.

Many RFPs also include the customer's template license agreement, which the vendor is advised "must be accepted" as the document governing the licensed software or purchased services. Including the customer's contract with the RFP and seeking the vendor's comments as well as any proposed additional terms, will reduce the time needed to negotiate a contract after the successful vendor is selected. A prudent customer will negotiate a complete contract prior to selection of the successful vendor, as the customer will lose significant leverage once the successful vendor has been selected.

> *For the purpose of facilitating the contract documentation process and setting expectations for both parties, Customer has attached its standard Software License Agreement (the "Contract"). Your submission of a Proposal shall constitute your agreement to use the attached Contract as the first draft of the document. Customer believes that the Contract is fair to both Customer and its vendors, but is willing to consider your comments to the Contract. You are entitled to mark-up the Contract and submit such mark-up with your Proposal. DO NOT ATTACH YOUR STANDARD CONTRACT OR REFER TO SECTIONS OF YOUR STANDARD CONTRACT.* ***Please note that the extent and nature of any changes made by you will be an important consideration in the evaluation of your Proposal.*** *By submitting a Proposal, you will thereby be representing to Customer that any such mark-up contains substantially all the changes and comments you have to the Contract and that otherwise the Contract is acceptable to you. Customer will be relying upon this representation in making its determination on which party to award the Project and incurring costs in the negotiation of the definitive legal documents. Customer's attachment of the Contract is not intended to legally bind Customer, and Customer reserves the right to make such changes in the Contract as it deems necessary and/or appropriate.*

Many vendors are hesitant to commit to specific terms during early negotiations and often reply with a "non-response" to allow the vendor maximum flexibility in negotiating the contract, similar to the following:

> *Vendor has reviewed the Master License and Services Agreement (MLA) attached to this RFP and believes that at such time as more business details are agreed upon, including with respect to the information to be contained in the various schedules, that the parties will be able to readily come to satisfactory closure on all of the terms contained in the MLA. Vendor reserves the right to comment in greater detail on the MLA terms at such time as is appropriate based on the availability of such details and any down-selection of Vendor as may occur.*

> See Form Q.2 § PP for more expansive language.

(v) The Selection of Vendors to Participate

The customer should carefully consider which vendors it invites to participate in the RFP process and should include a wide variety of vendors, from its existing vendors to large industry leaders to small, cutting-edge companies. By soliciting a large cross-section of vendors, the customer will hopefully receive a variety of creative responses that in turn will allow it to develop the best possible solution for its needs.

Prior to the deadline for submitting vendor responses, the customer should hold a telephonic bidder's conference to discuss any issues that may have arisen after the RFP was issued and to allow the vendors to ask any questions they may have. All questions should be asked anonymously, and vendor questions and the customer's answers should be posted to a website accessible by all vendors so no vendor has a competitive advantage. The customer may also request that vendors make a presentation to the customer's project team. After evaluating the first round of responses and "down selecting" several potential vendors, the customer may occasionally solicit a second round of proposals, allowing the customer to obtain a solution that is more closely tailored to the customer's needs at a more favorable price.

From the time the RFP is submitted to the time vendors are down selected for negotiations, including bidders' conferences and scoring the vendors' proposals, the process will likely take six to eight weeks.

(vi) Simultaneous Negotiations

Many customers are hesitant to walk away from a deal after a long negotiation because they are uncertain they can obtain more advantageous terms with another vendor while potentially delaying an important project. If a customer, however, establishes a competitive negotiation process where there are two or more vendors competing for the business, the leverage shifts in favor of the customer.

By negotiating simultaneously with several vendors, the customer can maximize its leverage and play each vendor against the others. If one vendor makes a concession, the customer can directly or indirectly signal to the second vendor that it is not competitive on the particular negotiation point, and that if the second vendor will not agree to the point, it will be viewed as a "negative" when the final bids are evaluated. By negotiating simultaneously, the customer has the advantage of negotiating the most favorable terms it can with each vendor and then selecting the best overall deal at the end of the negotiation process. Knowing the terms agreed to by the other vendor creates an incentive for each vendor to be flexible in response to the customer's requested terms. Further, large system vendors have sales cycles of six months or longer, creating an incentive not to drop out of the bidding process.

(vii) Technology Consultants

For a very large project, the customer may retain a consultant or technology vendor to draft the RFI/RFP as the customer may lack the experience/knowledge to create a detailed requirements document. A common concern is that if the consultant also provides technology services, the consultant may draft the RFI/RFP in a manner that favors the consultant if it responds to the RFI/RFP. In such situations, the consultant who drafts the RFP should be excluded from responding to the RFP to avoid a conflict of interest (i.e., the vendor could potentially draft the RFP in such a way that the vendor is the only party to meet the selection criteria).

Thus, prudent customers prohibit the consultant drafting the RFI/RFP from submitting a bid. Model language follows:

> *The Consultant agrees that it and its parent, its affiliates and subsidiaries, if any, waive the right to bid on any procurement contracts, of any tier, resulting from the services to be provided under this Agreement.*

If the consultant drafting the RFI/RFP is permitted to bid, those employees involved in drafting its RFP response should be excluded from responding to the RFP, and the vendor should certify that there was no actual conflict of interest. See Form A.2.10 for a model certificate.

(viii) Nondisclosure Agreements

To ensure fairness in the negotiation process, each vendor should enter into a mutual nondisclosure agreement with the customer prohibiting the customer from disclosing a vendor's pricing and methodologies to other vendors. Otherwise, a vendor may simply become a stalking horse to drive the preferred vendor to the customer's desired terms and price. Further, under U.S. law, if a party publicly discloses confidential information (i.e., without a non-disclosure agreement in place), such disclosure will prevent that party from obtaining a patent on such information and trade secret protection will be lost. When entering into a nondisclosure agreement, the vendor should ensure that any information it disclosed prior to entering into the agreement is protected, as many agreements only protect information disclosed from the date the agreement is signed.

Many customers will argue that there is no need to enter into a mutual nondisclosure agreement because only the customer, not the vendor, is disclosing confidential information. The customer usually offers that it will enter into a mutual nondisclosure agreement with the winning bidder once the vendor has been selected. This reasoning is flawed; the vendor's methodology and approach to addressing the issue as well as its pricing—both of which are proprietary—are the most important types of information supplied by the vendor and are the differentiating factors in an RFP process. See Form A.2.3 for an example of a unilateral nondisclosure agreement used in an RFP process.

At a minimum, the vendor should attach a proprietary notice to its RFP response similar to the following:

> *Confidentiality/Proprietary Notice: This proposal contains the confidential and proprietary information of Vendor and shall not be disclosed by Company other than to its employees with a need to know for the purpose of evaluating this proposal.*

Note, however, that including a footer or notice with a confidentiality statement may not be sufficient to protect the confidentiality of the information disclosed. See *Hill Holliday Connors Cosmopolos, Inc. v. Greenfield*, 433 Fed. Appx. 207 (4th Cir. 2011). A confidentiality obligation may also arise implicitly through the relationship and interactions of the parties. *See e.g. Burten v. Milan Bradley Co.* 763 F.3d 463 (1st Cir. 1985); *Daniels Health Sci., LLC v. Vascular Health Sci., LLC*, 710 F.3d 579 (5th Cir. 2013).

See Chapter 25 for a detailed discussion of nondisclosure agreements. *See* Forms A.2.3 and A.2.4 for model RFP nondisclosure agreements.

(b) Vendor Perspective

(i) Responding to the RFP

Before responding to an RFP, the vendor should ensure it has executed an NDA with the customer sufficient to protect any confidential information the vendor will disclose in its response including its pricing, methodologies, the names of its personnel etc. At the same time, it should copyright notices and proprietary marking on every page of its response. While the customer will most likely be deemed to have an implied license to use the vendor's materials, the response should include a license grant conveying to the customer a license to use the materials in the vendor's response.

Many customer RFPs include detailed requests regarding the vendor's data security policies and procedures. Some vendors will not comply with these requests because they do not want to publicly disclose their security practices, putting their systems at risk, or because it is too time consuming to respond to the request. Alternatively, they may provide an overview of their security practices or respond that they have achieved certain security certifications such as ISO 27001 or FedRamp certification.

In responding to an RFP, a vendor must be careful to accurately respond to the questions presented and to clearly indicate those responses to which it does not intend to be bound. Many RFPs provide that if the vendor fails to take issue with a proposed contractual provision, the customer will consider the vendor to be bound by the provision. If the vendor later indicates that it cannot accept that provision, the customer will often eliminate the vendor from consideration. Occasionally, the customer will require the vendor to certify that it will enter into an agreement with the customer if it is selected and require each vendor to submit a performance bond to ensure that it will actually do so.

To avoid these issues, the vendor should include language in its RFP response reserving the right to negotiate the contractual terms in the underlying agreement, especially those that were not included in the customer's proposed agreement. Furthermore, the vendor should list any assumptions it has made in responding to the RFP or any dependencies on which its response is conditioned. This is especially important if the deliverables have not been definitively determined at the time of the RFP response. Model language the vendor may want to include in its RFP response is as follows:

> *Vendor has set forth below its principal concerns with the General Terms and Conditions (Section _ of the RFP), including but not limited to the absence of terms that are standard in contracts for software licensing, such as a limitation of liability and disclaimer of implied warranties. Notwithstanding the exceptions set forth below, Vendor reserves the right to negotiate all contract terms and conditions in the context of the work that is actually awarded. Vendor will work with Customer to successfully resolve any outstanding matters.*

(ii) Avoiding Sales Puffery and Overselling

Failed software projects usually arise as a result of the licensed software failing to meet the expectations of the customer. This failure is often due to a combination of the customer not understanding what it purchased and the vendor's sales puffery. Although a customer may have a number of legal claims against the vendor, litigation does not benefit either party, as the customer will not receive the software system it contracted for and the licensor may suffer financial and reputational damage. Thus, both parties should carefully manage the sales and negotiation process to avoid a lose-lose situation.

From the vendor's perspective, the vendor should ensure that any statements it makes are factually accurate and can be supported in the event of a dispute, preferably with written documentation. The vendor should not make any forward-looking statements that it cannot keep. While sales puffery is present in all sales cycles, the vendor must ensure that such puffery cannot be considered a misrepresentation or even fraud. The nature of software sales, with every installation requiring some level of customization, lends itself to sales puffery and has given rise to the term "vaporware" to describe software functionality that had been sold but does not exist at the time of the sale. See Chapter 31 for a further discussion of marketing and drafting best practices.

Prudent vendors should never make statements as to the functionality or suitability of the software beyond what is set forth in the vendor's written documentation. Any documentation provided to the customer regarding the software should include a disclaimer that such documentation is subject to change without notice and that the customer should rely only on the technical specifications set forth in the parties' statement of work. Communications between the parties should be limited to a few, specifically identified individuals to avoid providing inconsistent positions to the other party and to reduce the possibility of misinformation being provided to the customer.

Prudent vendors should include a disclaimer to the following effect:

> *Disclaimer: Vendor has prepared this proposal in good faith based on information made available to it by Company and it is intended only for Company's review. Except as expressly agreed in a subsequent signed agreement, nothing in this proposal or any related discussions or correspondence should be considered as a representation that should be relied upon.*

Vendors should strictly limit the type of information its sales force can provide to the customer and limit oral presentations to pre-approved talking points and PowerPoint® presentations. The vendor's sales force should not make misleading or incomplete statements regarding the software and should not answer any technical questions, instead referring such questions to the vendor's technical team. To the extent the vendor is aware that a salesperson has made misleading or inaccurate statements, the vendor should discipline the salesperson and correct any misimpression with the potential customer. By understanding the risks associated with sales puffery not only to the vendor but also to their own careers, members of the sales team will be less likely to engage in unacceptable behavior.

Any software used in customer demonstrations should be retained by the vendor to protect against claims that the software delivered to the customer was less robust than the version demonstrated by the vendor. Finally, prudent vendors should encourage the customer to conduct its own due diligence and make any inquiries the customer believes appropriate and include an acknowledgment to that effect in the parties' agreement.

(iii) Vendor Business Considerations

From the vendor's perspective, the vendor should consider four questions when formulating its response to the customer's RFP to ensure that the vendor will successfully deliver the project if it is awarded to it:

(w) Does the vendor want the business?

The vendor must first determine why it wants to win the business. There are many reasons for seeking business but unless a party can clearly articulate its reason for doing so it is unlikely to win the business or successfully deliver the business. Reasons for pursuing the business may include:

- The potential customer will provide the vendor access to a new revenue stream or a new industry.
- The account will be very profitable.
- The customer will fund the further development of the vendor's software.
- The customer is extremely prestigious and will provide the vendor increased visibility/stature in the customer's industry, assisting in future sales efforts.
- The vendor will be able to maintain or increase its market share.

Only by understanding its own reasons for submitting a bid will the vendor's efforts be successful. Without a clearly defined reason, the vendor will be unable to focus its RFP response on the customer's needs.

(x) Can the vendor win the business?

The vendor must clearly understand the customer's reasons for issuing an RFP and must also be able to clearly communicate the vendor's value proposition. To win the business, the vendor must be able to provide tangible benefits to the customer, focusing its RFP response on the customer's needs and desires. The vendor's value proposition may include:

- Improving the quality of the services the customer receives. Can the vendor improve the quality of the customer's existing software and services?
- Reducing/controlling the customer's operating costs. Can the vendor effectively control or reduce the customer's costs? Being able to fix and/or lower the customer's costs provides a clear benefit to the customer which is easily measurable.
- Creating operational flexibility/agility on the customer's behalf. Can the vendor create economic flexibility by converting fixed costs to volume-sensitive operating costs that will allow the customer to operate its business with greater agility and flexibility, i.e., through cloud computing?
- Reducing IT costs/times. Can the vendor reduce costs by migrating the customer to the cloud for certain aspects of the customer's IT environment?
- Reducing risk. Can the vendor reduce the customer's IT risks?
- Transforming the customer's business. Can the vendor's proposed solution transfer the customer's business by providing the customer with the ability to differentiate itself in the marketplace, thereby generating increased revenue and profitability for the customer?

(y) Can the vendor deliver the solution/services?

The vendor must carefully consider whether it can successfully meet its contractual obligations from a technical standpoint. It must avoid entering into agreements for which it lacks the technical skill or ability to successfully deliver or for which it will be unable to deliver on time due to aggressive delivery dates established by the customer. Agreeing to deliverables that require an aggressive delivery schedule or the development of new or unproved technology creates significant risk for the vendor.

It has been said that there are three variables in IT development: time, money, and functionality. To an extent, each aspect is dependent on the others. Thus, a prudent vendor must carefully balance a customer's desire to reduce its costs against delivery time and the desired functionality. Common sense provides that it is difficult to obtain the most robust functionality in the shortest delivery time at the lowest cost. The more robust functionality a solution possesses, the more it will usually increase cost while requiring longer delivery times.

(z) Can the vendor make money on the proposed transaction?

Equally important is the ability of the vendor to deliver the contracted work profitably. The vendor must ensure that it understands the scope of the deliverables and the effort required to profitably deliver the deliverables in a timely manner. It must avoid misinterpreting the scope of work and failing to deliver the work within budget. To that end, the vendor should avoid making aggressive assumptions as to development times and the level of effort associated with the contracted deliverables.

PRACTICE POINT:

When responding to an RFP, a prudent vendor should:

- **Never make promises regarding the benefits of using the vendor's products and/or services.** The vendor should never make promises or predictions of:
  - "lower costs,"
  - "increased revenues,"
  - "higher ROI,"
  - "larger profits" or
  - "improved operating efficiencies," especially when dealing with dependencies the vendor cannot control.
- **Caveat all statements** by use of words such as:
  - "designed to,"
  - "may,"
  - "assist,"
  - "help,"
  - "can,"
  - "could,"
  - "one of the,"

and other words that soften strong sales messages (e.g., "may reduce software total cost of ownership" or "designed to efficiently manage ownership of software").

- **Never provide a "road map" of a product's/solution's future functionality.** Doing so may impact the timing of the vendor's ability to recognize revenue. *See* Chapter 5.J.4 for a more detailed discussion.
- **Always confirm that all statements within its RFP response are true, correct, and accurate.**
- **State all assumptions and dependencies** on which the proposal is founded.
- **Reserve the right to make additional comments**, take additional exceptions, or revise its response if it receives new information from the customer.
- **State the time period for which its RFP response is valid**.

See Form A.2.1 for an example of a model RFP.

4. *Procedures and Rules for a Competitive Negotiation*

To ensure an orderly and equitable process, the customer should establish clear procedures and rules on how the negotiation process will be conducted. This includes not only the selection criteria but also rules on how information will be disseminated and how prospective vendors may communicate with the customer team. To avoid undue influence and the dissemination of insider information to a preferred vendor, most RFPs require that all communications be in writing through a single point of customer contact. Any violation of this process should result in the vendor's disqualification. All questions and the customer's response are then posted on a website allowing all potential bidders to view.

Setting out the rules at the initiation of the process can significantly benefit the customer. More vendors are likely to participate if they believe the process is free of favoritism and undue influence. No vendor wants to expend a significant amount of time and money only to serve as a stalking horse for "pre-selected" vendors. Some vendors seek to circumvent the selection process by contacting friendly customer executives to ask them to lobby their colleagues to select the vendor. The threat of being eliminated from consideration should discourage this behavior, but employees not on the customer's project team should be reminded not to discuss the project either inside or outside of the company. Finally, because the vendors are all receiving the same (limited) information from a single source (which should always offer encouragement), they are incented to remain in the bidding process and offer their best terms and pricing.

It is also important that the customer adhere to its own rules. Vendors can spend millions of dollars in responding to an RFP and engaging in negotiations with a customer. If a customer gains a reputation as an entity that does not treat vendors fairly, it may have difficulty getting the best qualified vendors to participate in future procurements.

To ensure a successful procurement, the customer should:

- Draft the RFP in a non-adversarial manner, as the successful vendor will become a valued business partner.
- Provide vendors all information they need to develop an accurate, well-reasoned, and insightful response (i.e., the number of present and expected

users of the system, the customer's existing software platform, the customer's global footprint, expected maintenance and support standards, any unique technical challenges).

- Provide a process for the customer to respond to the vendors' questions.
- Share all information including the vendors' questions and the customer's responses to all vendors participating in the process.
- Request information from the vendors that the customer needs to make an informed decision. Do not require vendors to compile reams of data that provides little insight into their capabilities.
- Identify those aspects of the RFP that the customer considers to be most important.
- Provide an overview and time line for completing the RFP process.
- Ensure the free flow of information necessary for vendors to create informed responses.

See Forms A.2.6 and A.2.7 for model procedures and rules for responding to an RFP.

5. *Responding to an RFI/RFP.*

In responding to an RFI, vendors usually provide high-level information without significant detail, including marketing materials for their relevant products, a list of the vendor's installed customer base along with several references. The intent is to provide enough information to be down-selected to receive the RFP and to remain a viable candidate.

Many customers include their template agreement in their RFP and ask potential vendors to redline the agreement with their comments. The RFP usually provides that: the vendor's failure to comment on the agreement will be interpreted as the vendor accepting the agreement "as is", the vendor may not make additional comments to the template once it submits its response, and the extent of the potential vendor's comments will be a factor in selecting the successful vendor. The intent is to encourage the vendor to accept the customer's terms to the greatest extent possible.

Often the customer's template is long and complex, requiring a significant effort on the potential vendor's behalf to provide comprehensive comments. Further, the template agreement may not be tailored to the software and services that will be provided by the vendor. Thus, many vendors submit their own template as an alternative or respond that they will provide comments only after being selected as the successful vendor. While there is a risk of being disqualified for the failure to submit comments or responding with its own template, most customers will not do so, especially if the vendor's product is the industry leader or the vendor has the significant market share.

6. *Structuring the Transaction*

Prior to beginning negotiations with the vendor, the customer should determine the structure of the transaction, as the structure can have a significant impact if a dispute arises. Many transactions have a number of components, including hardware, software, and services. Each of these components can potentially receive disparate treatment under the law in the event of a dispute. For example, the sale of hardware usually has a four-year statute of limitations under the UCC while the statute of limitations for a claim of a breach of contract can be up to ten years.

Before entering into a turnkey system, a prudent vendor should ensure that it understands the risks associated with the project. For example, it will be responsible for the performance of all work provided by its subcontractors, including third-party vendors who may be providing their proprietary software and hardware. Further, there is significant risk that the combination of the third-party hardware and software, when integrated, may not work as initially contemplated. Finally, fixed price contracts create greater risk on the vendor's behalf.

Thus, a prudent customer should consider whether to address each of these components in a separate agreement or address them in a single master agreement. If addressed together, many courts will utilize a "predominant purpose" test to ascertain whether goods, services, or software were the "predominant purpose" for the parties entering into the contract. *Smart Online, Inc. v. Opensite Technologies, Inc.*, 5 UCC Rep. Serv. 2d 47 (N.C. Super. Ct. 2003). Other courts will utilize a "Gravamen of the Action" test which "asks whether the underlying action is brought because of alleged defective goods or because of the quality of the service rendered." *In re Trailer and Plumbing Supplies*, 578 A.2d 343, 345 (N.H. 1990). By addressing each aspect in a contract separately, a customer can take advantage of certain protections established under the law. *See, e.g., Bruel & Kjaer v. The Village of Bensenville*, 969 N.E.2d 445 (Ill. 2012) (provision of software, hardware, and software development services primarily a contract for goods; thus, customer's claim was time-barred).

7. Documenting the Negotiations/Term Sheet/Letters of Intent

As the negotiation process progresses, the parties should carefully document the agreed-upon positions. Some parties prefer to enter into a Letter of Intent (LOI), term sheet, or Memorandum of Understanding (MOU) to document their positions prior to executing the definitive agreement to ensure the parties truly have an agreement on the principal terms. Others prefer to negotiate the definitive agreement and not bother with an LOI or MOU under the belief that they are a waste of time that could be better used to negotiate of the definitive agreement. While either approach may be appropriate depending on the situation, most parties will negotiate only a definitive agreement.

MOUs and LOIs are most often used to establish the parties' agreement on the principal terms of the contemplated transaction, such as: the software to be licensed, services to be provided, term and termination, indemnity, IP ownership, the license fee, the scope of the license grant, warranties, limitation of liability, etc., prior to negotiating the definitive agreement. They should be used to memorialize only the principal terms of the agreement and not all potential outcomes. When drafting an MOU, the parties should use clear, simple language and avoid using complex sentences full of legalese. MOUs/LOIs are most often used for confirming that the parties have reached agreement on the principal terms of the transaction. MOUs/ LOIs, however, can delay the consummation of the definitive agreement if the parties try to resolve minor points that are best addressed during the negotiation of the definitive agreement.

Careful consideration should be given to whether the MOU/LOI will incorporate binding provisions. Some parties prefer to include at least some binding provisions in their MOU/LOIs—most often the parties' confidentiality obligations, but also exclusivity, noncompetition, and non-solicitation provisions.

Most parties, however, elect not to negotiate a binding MOU/LOI and thus must be careful to ensure that neither party is bound until all terms of the master/final agreement have been agreed upon. It is exactly because most LOI/MOUs are nonbinding that most parties do not feel the need to enter into such agreements.

It cannot be overemphasized that any document signed by the parties must clearly state that there is no agreement until the definitive contract has been signed. A number of courts have found the existence of a contract in the absence of a signed writing. *See, e.g., Latiivafter Liquidating Trust v. Clear Channel Communications*, 345 Fed. Appx. 46 (6th Cir. 2009) (jury found existence of an "agreement" despite lack of signed document.); *Hermosilla v. Coca-Cola Company*, 446 Fed. Appx. 201 (11th Cir. 2011) (copyright transferred through exchange of e-mails which were deemed to constitute a binding agreement even though the parties intended to enter into a written agreement); *Republic Bank, Inc. v. West Penn Allegheny Health Systems, Inc.*, 475 Fed. Appx. 692 (10th Cir. 2012) (binding contract created through exchange of e-mails). *Wal-Mart Stores Texas, LLC v. Shirey*, 2020 WL 548323 (Ct. App. Tex 2020) (exchange of emails created binding agreement because emails had material terms); *Copano Energy, LLC v. Bujnoch*, 593 S.W.3d 721 (Tex. 2020) (exchange of emails insufficient to form a contract because they lacked material terms).

At least one court has found a letter of intent that was marked on each page with the words "NON-BINDING TERMS" could be enforceable if it was subject to an express obligation to negotiate in good faith. *SIGA Technologies, Inc. v. PharmAthene, Inc.*, 67 A.3d 330 (Del. 2013). An implied covenant of good faith has been held to obligate the parties to negotiate any remaining open terms, precluding a party from simply ending the negotiations. *See, e.g., Teachers Ins. and Annuity Ass'n v. Tribune Co.*, 670 F. Supp.2d 491 (S.D.N.Y. 1987); *Channel Home Centers v. Grossman*, 795 F.2d 291 (3d Cir. 1986); *but see Budget Marketing, Inc. v. Centronics Corp.*, 927 F.2d 421 (8th Cir. 1991). In certain circumstances, a court may use a MOU/LOI to interpret the definitive agreement to which it pertains. Some courts have found MOUs/LOIs to be binding agreements when a definitive agreement has not been executed but all the major substantive provisions regulating the parties' relationship have been agreed in principle. *See, e.g., Teachers Ins. and Annuity Ass'n v. Tribune Co.*, 670 F. Supp. 2d 491 (S.D.N.Y. 1987); *Channel Home Centers v. Grossman*, 795 F.2d 291 (3d Cir. 1986).

If the successful bidder is going to commence work while the parties are negotiating the definitive agreement, the vendor may want to enter into an interim agreement to document its ownership of any intellectual property it creates prior to the execution of the agreement. This is important if the vendor wants to protect itself in the event the parties are unable to reach agreement on the definitive agreement and the customer later seeks to utilize the intellectual property the vendor developed. The parties should be careful to avoid acting in such a manner as to give rise to an oral agreement. To the extent the parties perform in accordance with an unsigned license agreement, a court may find the existence of a binding oral agreement. *See In re Golden Books Family Entertainment, Inc.*, 269 B.R. 300 (Bankr. D. Del. 2001) (license drafts were "binding oral agreements . . . demonstrated by parties' course of conduct."). *See* Forms C.1.5 and C.1.6 for model Interim Services Agreements.

In *Turner Broadcasting System, Inc. v. McDavid*, 693 S.E.2d 873 (Ga. App. 2010), the parties entered into a letter of intent for the purchase and sale of two sports franchises that provided "neither party nor any of [their] affiliates [would] be bound . . . unless and until such party (or affiliate) has executed the Definitive Agreements" and that "[n]o such binding agreement shall exist or arise unless and until the parties have negotiated, executed and delivered to each other Definitive Agreements." *Id.* at 879. The letter of intent expired, and the parties continued to negotiate. McDavid brought suit after Turner later sold the franchises to a third party. The Georgia Court of Appeals found the existence of an oral contract concluding that the statement contained within the letter of intent that neither party would be bound until the execution of a definitive agreement expired with the letter of intent. *Id.* at 881. Thus, the parties' oral agreement was sufficient to bind both parties despite the contemplation of a subsequent written agreement.

In deciding whether a binding agreement has been formed, courts will look to a number of indicia:

- the wording of any written documents;
- the nature of the negotiations;
- whether the parties have fully or partially performed their obligations;
- whether any issues remain to be negotiated; and
- whether industry custom is to enter into a definitive agreement.

See Teachers Ins. and Annuity Ass'n v. Tribune Co., 670 F. Supp. 2d. 491 (S.D.N.Y. 1987). Courts will place the greatest emphasis on the actual language used in the letter of intent. Parol evidence can be used to successfully rebut any language within the document providing that the letter of intent is nonbinding. *See Computer Sys. of Am., Inc. v. IBM Corp.*, 795 F.2d 1086 (1st Cir. 1986) (letter and lease could be read together to satisfy requirements of the statute of frauds); *but see Reprosystem, B.V. v. SCM Corporation*, 727 F.2d 257 (2d Cir. 1984) (testimony and written documentation clearly showed intent of parties was not to be bound). To communicate the intent of the parties not to be bound until a definitive agreement has been executed, the parties should use words such as "nonbinding," "intent," and "proposal" and they should avoid using "agreement," "contract," and "obligation."

To protect its interests, a party should insert language to the following effect.

THIS DOCUMENT IS NOT INTENDED TO BIND [PARTY] OR ANY OF ITS AFFILIATES

There shall be no agreement between the parties relating to this document unless and until the parties have executed and delivered definitive agreement(s) containing the agreement of the parties. Nothing herein is intended to, or does, bind either party and is not intended to waive, nor does it waive, any rights, remedies and/or defenses of Licensor or any of its affiliates, whether legal and/or equitable, under any existing agreement, all of which are expressly reserved.

Alternative language providing that some provisions will be binding is as follows:

This Letter of Intent is intended for discussion purposes only to facilitate the negotiation process and, except for Section _ ("Confidentiality"), shall not create a binding obligation on either party. The definitive agreement between the parties, in addition to the matters specifically set forth in this Letter of Intent, shall contain additional material terms relating to the license grant, pricing, representations and warranties, indemnities, termination, governing law and venue, among others.

In summary, if the parties clearly intend not to be bound until a definitive agreement is reached, the court will recognize such intent, even if all open issues have been resolved. *See R.G. Group, Inc. v. Horn & Hardart Co.*, 751 F.2d 69 (2d Cir. 1984). The parties should avoid using "agreement," "contract," and "obligation" and should consider referring to the document as an "outline." At the same time, if parties include within the letter of intent an obligation to negotiate in good faith to consummate the contemplated transaction, the courts will enforce this obligation. *Itek Corp. v. Chicago Aerial Industries, Inc.*, 248 A.2d 625 (Del. 1968).

For a general overview, *see* Jaskolka & Strnad, *A Letter of Intent Should Not Spoil the Venture*, 38 ACC DOCKET 47 (Oct. 2020); *Letter of Intent Case Law Update*, 354 COMM. L. ADV. 1 (June 2017).

8. *Negotiating the Agreement*

The ability of a party to negotiate meaningful concessions for the other party is usually dependent on the market power of the party, the size of the transaction, and the parties' respective desires to reach agreement. In negotiating the underlying agreement, prudent parties should seek to shorten the negotiation process and develop a strong relationship of trust with the other party. Negotiations and contracting are built on trust. The parties should avoid bluffing or making false statements which may lead to a loss of trust in the event such statements are found to be false. For example, vendors should never state that the price will increase if the contract is not signed by the end of the quarter if the price will not increase. Similarly, vendors should never tell the customer that the agreement must close by quarter end as it may cause the customer to hold out for a better price. Instead, the vendor should state that the agreement needs to be signed in the current quarter to meet the customer's delivery schedule.

Licensing and technology contracts are unique in that they often entail a long-term relationship where each party is dependent on the other. This is especially true for the customer purchasing missing critical software and services and dependent on the vendor for long-term support and maintenance. Disputes and litigation benefit neither party, while termination may not be practical for the customer. As such, using the right "touch and tone" in negotiating with the counter-party is very important. Today there is less support for long negotiations, as customers want to contract and implements the solution immediately. The parties should not seek to win every point at the expense of the other party, but rather seek a win-win outcome.

Before beginning the negotiation process, it is important for the vendor to understand the process. Some customers will down-select two vendors and negotiate simultaneously with both to play each against the other. Given the significant time and money vendors may invest in a large RFP/negotiation process, a prudent vendor should confirm that the customer is seriously considering it as opposed to using the vendor as a stalking horse for the vendor it prefers.

(a) Controlling the Draft

Perhaps the most important aspect of the negotiation process is to control the creation of the initial draft of the contract. By creating the initial draft, a party can ensure the agreement reflects all of the salient points of the transaction important to the drafting party while at the same time having the opportunity to utilize language favorable to the drafting party. Some parties seek to lower their legal fees by allowing the opposing party to create the initial draft, but this approach is often shortsighted. A party that chooses to let the other party draft the agreement will potentially have to respond to a one-sided, onerous draft and will most likely spend a significant amount of time, effort, and legal fees to revise it.

(b) Agree on the Principal Terms before Starting to Draft the Agreement

To avoid creating and negotiating endless drafts, the parties should agree on the principal terms as well as structure of the agreement before drafting begins. By ensuring the parties have a meeting of the minds prior to the start of the negotiations, the parties will be able to save a significant amount of time and effort. Important terms that should be resolved prior to entering into detailed negotiations include price, functionality, term, and performance metrics.

(c) Produce a Balanced Initial Draft

A savvy party will produce a reasonable, balanced draft that will not shock the conscience of the other party while reducing the time to contract. A balanced draft will go a long way toward developing trust between the parties and will strengthen the parties' relationship. Creating an onerous, one-sided document will only alienate the other party and extend the length of the negotiations. Prudent parties should remember that the contract negotiations are only the beginning of the relationship and that the negotiations often set the tone for the future relationship of the parties. To that end, both parties should strive to be courteous and respectful during the negotiations. Confrontational arguments should raise questions as to whether the relationship will be successful going forward. If the parties cannot conduct the negotiations in a positive, constructive manner, it is unlikely they will have a mutually beneficial relationship during the term of the agreement.

(d) Locking the Document

Some parties password-protect or "pdf" their draft agreements before sending them to the other party in an effort to prevent the receiving party from making their proposed revisions directly in the agreement. Parties who lock their agreements often argue that locking a document is necessary to: (i) ensure that non-negotiable provisions are included in a document, especially when required as a "pass-through" by a third party; (ii) ensure uniform terms across all customers, especially when providing commodity services such as SaaS services; or (iii) protect against the other party making unauthorized changes to the agreement.

The benefit of doing so is questionable, however, as locked documents are often circumvented, defeating the intent of the party that locked the agreement while alienating the other party. Locking a document sends the message that the other party cannot be trusted to fully and accurately mark its proposed changes. In addition, doing so is counterproductive if the other party is reduced to inserting its proposed changes by hand into the agreement, preventing it from communicating its comments in a prompt and efficient manner. The original party is never at risk, as it can use the "Compare" function in its word-processing software to compare the other party's changes to the original document, limiting the possibility of the other party making surreptitious changes. In short, locking the agreement is unlikely to produce any tangible benefit, while potentially slowing down the negotiation process and alienating the other party.

(e) Be Well Prepared

To ensure a smooth negotiation, each party should be well prepared for the start of the negotiations and should understand the important issues as well as why they are of significance. The parties should remain flexible and should consider many different options for resolving an issue. Maintaining an open dialogue and a cordial relationship with the other party is important to conducting a successful negotiation and maintaining a strong working relationship. Above all, no matter how contentious the negotiations become, the parties should remain cordial, separating their professional differences from their personal relationships.

Being prepared also requires understanding how the underlying technology works, how it interacts with the customer's other software solutions and systems as well as the importance of the software/services to the customer's ecosystem.

(f) Beware Electronic Communications

In negotiating the agreement, the parties should be careful that their electronic communications do not inadvertently create a binding agreement, as courts are increasingly being asked to determine whether an email or text created a binding agreement among the parties. *See St. John's Holdings, LLC v. Two Electronics, LLC*, 2016 WL 1460477 (Mass. Land Ct. April 14, 2016) (text messages among parties could create binding agreement); *APB Realty, Inc. v. Georgia-Pacific, LLC*, 889 F.3d 26 (1st Cir. 2018) (contract could be formed via email).

Prudent parties should include a disclaimer clearly stating that their email does not create a binding obligation. *Dhillon v. Zions First Nat' l Bank*, 462 Fed. Appx. 880 (11th Cir 2012); *McCoy v. Gamesa Tech. Corp., Inc.*, 2012 WL 983747 (N. D. Ill. Mar. 22, 2012).

9. Inclusion of the RFI and RFP Response in the Final Agreement

Both the vendor and the customer should be wary of incorporating the customer's RFP and the vendor's RFP response into the contract. Often the parties incorporate these documents in the final agreement in an ill-fated attempt to incorporate each party's understanding of the other party's obligations. The customer often wants to include the RFP to hold the vendor to the requirements set forth in the RFP and the standards the customer expects the vendor to meet. Further, the customer may want to include the vendor's RFP response to hold the vendor to any statements (including any sales puffery) set forth in the vendor's RFP response. The vendor often desires to incorporate its RFP response for its own protection, as it will often reject some of the RFP's requirements in its RFP response.

A problem arises, however, when the delivery requirements set forth in the RFP and RFP response differ from each other and from the specifications included in the negotiated contract. Further, disputes often arise in trying to resolve any differences between the RFP and the RFP response and what the parties agreed to. To avoid these potential issues, it is preferable to agree on and attach functional specifications negotiated after the successful bidder has been selected. The importance of accuracy, clarity, and completeness in the specifications cannot be overemphasized. The specifications are the vendor's contractual obligations to the customer. If they do not provide significant detail to hold the vendor to the intended obligations, then the entire negotiation process is undermined. The RFP and RFP response in turn should then be negated by the contract's "integration" or "entire agreement" clause. See Chapter 6.T. The vendor should also resist the customer's demands to represent and warrant that all statements made by the vendor during the RFI and RFP process are true and correct as of the date the parties entered into the license agreement. See Chapter 5.A.1.(a).(ii) for a more detailed discussion.

The courts are unlikely to hold a vendor liable for the typical statements made in the sales process including sales puffery or opinions of future performance. Sales puffery will be viewed in light of the facts of the matter to determine if it exceeds the bounds of fairness. *See I-Conn. Healthcare Solutions, LLC v. Advanced Internet Technologies, Inc.*, 689 S.E.2d 600 (N.C. App. 2010) (Claim of being "The World Leader in Dedicated and Shared Web Hosting" does not constitute fraud in the inducement as sophisticated, knowledgeable purchaser would not make purchasing decision solely based on such statement). To be actionable, such statements must relate to a past or present fact. *American Computer v. Jack Farrell Implet. Co.*, 763 F. Supp. 1473 (D. Minn. 1991); *Shema Kolainu — Hear Our Voices v. Providersoft, LLC*, 832 F. Supp.2d 194 (E.D.N.Y. 2010) (licensor representations regarding software functionality supported claim of fraudulent inducement). Nonetheless, the vendor should make sure to include an integration clause and the customer should make sure to include all statements it has relied on in making its decision in the license agreement. See Chapter 6.T.1 for a more detailed discussion of the importance of integration clauses.

At the conclusion of the RFP process, there is occasionally the temptation to substitute the RFP and RFP response to serve as the Statement of Work. This philosophy often leads to a poor result. The RFP and RFP response usually lack the required detail to deliver a quality product that meets the customer's needs. Further, the parties frequently fail to resolve any inconsistencies between the RFP and RFP response.

Often the customer's RFP will include language similar to the following:

> *It is a firm requirement that Vendor's responses to this RFP shall be included either in their entirety or by reference in the final contract.*

The vendor's response should be carefully crafted to avoid any commitment that may create ambiguity in the vendor's obligations, the deliverable, or make any commitment that may be superseded by any subsequent negotiations. A model vendor response is as follows:

> *Vendor's response to the RFP is a general overview of the ______ System (the "System") and provides general answers to the questions asked. Items in this response to the RFP may be ambiguous and open to differing interpretations because a Requirements Study has not been performed to define Customer's needs. During the Requirements Study, Vendor and Customer will discuss Customer's needs and determine if modifications are needed to completely satisfy Customer's requirements. Although certain functionality may be designated in this response as included in the System, modifications may be required for the System to provide such functionality as required by Customer. Thus, this response is not a specific, technical, or legal document and, therefore, any inconsistencies, questions, uncertainties, or contradictions as to the System shall be controlled by the System's documentation. Further, it is Vendor's intention to be totally responsive to the Request for Proposal ("RFP"). This response is based on the information that you have provided to Vendor concerning your needs. Consequently, while we believe that our response is sound, it cannot constitute express or implied warranties, including, without limitation, the implied warranties of merchantability, fitness, and fitness for a particular purpose. Vendor has reviewed the RFP and it is Vendor's intention that any award resulting there from shall be based on the Software License Agreement and Master Services Agreement to be negotiated between the parties.*

If the parties nevertheless decide to include the RFP and/or the RFP response, they should clearly set forth the order of precedence among the various provisions and exhibits of the agreement in the event of a conflict.

10. Concerns for Lawyers

Lawyers representing the customer in a dual negotiation process must be careful to abide by the ABA Model Rules of Professional Conduct. Rule 4.1 (Truthfulness in Statements to Others) provides that a lawyer cannot knowingly "make a false statement of material fact or law to a third person." Formal opinion 06-432 (Apr. 12, 2006). A lawyer must be careful not to represent that another party has accepted a provision when in fact it has not done so. Rule 4.1 differentiates "puffery" from "lying" recognizing that puffery is part of any sales process but forbidding any outright misstatements of the truth. *Rubin v. Schottenstein, Zox & Dunn,* 143 F.3d 263 (6th Cir. 1998) (fraud claim brought against attorney for statements made during negotiations); *Trust Company of Louisiana v. N.H.P. Inc.,* 104 F.3d 1478 (5th Cir. 1997) (fraud claim brought against attorney for misrepresentations made to investors).

Further, lawyers must be cognizant of the laws of professional responsibility that may apply when negotiating with non-lawyers. *See* Seger, *Coming to Terms when Negotiating with a Non-Lawyer,* 30 ACC DOCKET 70 (Nov. 2012).

For a general overview, *see* Burnham, *Ethical Issues in Negotiating Contracts,* Bus. L. Today (December 2012), www.americanbar.org/groups/business_law/resources/business-law-today/2012-December/training-for-tomorrow-ethical-issues-in-negotiating-contracts/; Young, *Where Deception Is Still King,* ADVOCATE - J. OF CONSUMER ATTYS. ASSOC. S. CAL. (Aug. 2012).

11. Metadata

Metadata refers to the data contained within a document. Often Metadata is revealed or hidden through common commands such as "track data." Metadata has been defined as "information which a computer generates to identify relevant facts about a saved file." Himmelrich, *Metadata: Data About Data,* 43 MD. B.J. 34, 35 (May/June 2010). In its most common form, metadata provides information as to the author of the document, when it was created, who reviewed and commented on the document and the subsequent revisions made to it.

A party can avoid inadvertently disclosing metadata by sending all files in a pdf format or accepting all changes in a document and resaving it prior to sending the document to another party. Alternatively, software applications that remove metadata are commercially available and should be used as a matter of course.

There is a dichotomy among the states as to how to treat metadata. Alabama, Arizona, Florida, and New York have adopted the position that a lawyer should not try to obtain information from metadata if he or she knows the sending party did not intend for the receiving party to review it. New York Bar Association Committee on Professional Ethics Opinion 749. The American Bar Association ("ABA") and Maryland are in the minority having adopted a contrary position in that they do not prohibit a receiving party from accessing metadata. Maryland State Bar Association Committee on Ethics, Ethics Docket 2007-09; ABA Standing Committee on Ethics and Professional Responsibility, Formal Opinion 06-422. The District of Columbia prohibits mining metadata if the receiving lawyer has actual knowledge that the metadata was sent inadvertently. District of Columbia Bar Legal Ethics Committee Opinion 341. Pennsylvania leaves it to the individual lawyer to determine the appropriateness of mining metadata.

For a detailed discussion of metadata, *see* Twiford & Rouse, *A Primer on Metadata: To Scrub or Not to Scrub?,* EXECUTIVE COUNS. 33 (Aug./Sept. 2011); Coyle, *"Metadata" Mining Vexes Lawyers, Bars,* NAT'L L.J., Feb. 18, 2008 at 1; Himmelrich, *Metadata: Data About Data,* 43 MD. B.J. 34 (May/June 2010).

12. *PRACTICE POINT*: Negotiation insights.

All negotiations can be summarized by the following insights:

- Even the best forms and tools are only as good as the user implementing them. Training and mentorship remain an invaluable part of the process that should not be neglected in the hope that templates alone will be an adequate substitute.
- A vendor form can be the best starting place. Ask: are the terms of the vendor's agreement so product-driven and unique that any attempt at substitution with a generic form will provide a less efficient path to closure?
- Do not lose sight of the need to facilitate the business. Wasting weeks negotiating extremely remote risks is pointless.
- Almost every contractual issue is a business decision. The go/no-go decision rests with the combined negotiating team and the business stakeholder(s). That said, lawyers do their job best when they act as trusted advisors, and do not simply defer any decision.
- Do not try to win every point and instead seek a win-win solution. A bankrupt vendor will not provide the customer with the software system it needs, while exploiting the customer will hurt the vendor's reputation.
- Any engagement is subject to three variables: scope, schedule/time, and price. These interrelated constraints are dependent on one another. Important to any engagement, but critical to large-scale and complex engagements, is an agreement among all parties to the weight placed on the competing constraints of scope, schedule, and price. The customer should understand the relationship among these three constraints and ensure that the underlying agreement reflects the customer's priority.
- Parties tend to focus not only on the individual positions taken on issues but also on the sheer number and extent of the proposed changes. Avoid marking up language where there is not a material issue and avoid too many "reasonably"s.
- A party can improve its position by contacting the other party's lawyer in advance of submitting its comments to obtain insight into the other party's willingness to entertain significant changes to the agreement and the other party's timeline for signing the agreement.
- Unreasonably failing to resolve an open issue can potentially taint the parties' relationship. Do not draw out negotiations over meaningless issues. Customers view the negotiation process as part of the relationship-building process and remember difficult negotiations.
- Always explain the rationale for a party's position and offer reasonable solutions that will resolve the issue and meet the other party's needs. To that end, statements to the effect that something is "against Company policy" will not convince a party to concede an issue but will only serve to alienate the other party. Make sure there is always a valid rationale behind every position and that the party has a reasonable fallback position.

- Determine if there are existing agreements between the parties from which they can draw language that has already been agreed to, avoiding potentially difficult negotiations.
- Discuss any open issues with the client beforehand to understand the importance of each issue to the client and where you can concede points.
- Make sure the negotiators have the authority to make definitive decisions.
- Establish your priorities and identify the other side's priorities.
- Remain flexible, as your priorities will likely change as the negotiations progress.
- Take the lead on addressing difficult issues and get ahead of the issue.
- Be prepared to suggest viable solutions and compromises to resolve an issue.
- Never underestimate the impact that personalities can have on the negotiation process.
- Face-to-face meetings can be much more productive and can allow the parties to develop a stronger sense of trust from the personal relationships that will be developed.
- Be creative – create and offer solutions to potential sticking points. Do not remain stuck on your position without offering a path forward.
- Avoid disagreeing or contradicting your team in front of the counter party. Fanning, Zhao &d Fishel, *Five Secrets to Successfully Negotiating with Your Own Side*, 36 ACC DOCKET 32 (Oct 2018).
- Always remember the goal is to obtain a mutually beneficial agreement, not to "win" the negotiation.

For an overview of how to quickly and successfully bring an agreement to closure, *see* Kleinberger, *Contracts and Disputes: Winning the War or Waging the Peace?* Bench & B. Minn. 15 (Oct. 1987); Kelly & Jaramillo, *Business Decision Expedition: Don't Get Turned Around During Contract Negotiations*, 38 ACC DOCKET 40 (Jan./Feb. 2020).

C. Successful Procurement

Regardless of which approach a customer adopts, the customer should seek to incorporate a number of best practices in its procurement process. To ensure a successful negotiation, the customer should focus on five issues: establishing the customer's goals, vendor selection, the negotiation process, allocating and quantifying risk, and managing the customer-vendor relationship.

For a more detailed discussion, *see* Mangan & Hines, *Beating Vendor Lockdown: Negotiating Software Licenses for Your Organization,* 24 ACC DOCKET 45 (Feb. 2006); Boudreau, *The Insider's Guide to Technology Procurement: 20 Practical Ways to Make Large Procurements a Success,* 23 ACC DOCKET 28 (July/Aug. 2005).

1. Establishing Each Party's Needs and Goals

The most important aspect of the procurement from the customer's perspective is determining and establishing the customer's goals, as without a clear understanding of what the customer needs, the procurement and final result will likely be considered a failure. The first step in determining the customer's needs is for the customer's project lead to discuss the needs of the business team driving the purchasing decision and with the customer's internal technology team. Preferably, the internal drivers and customer can complete an "intake" document indicating:

- What the business team hopes to accomplish through the contemplated technology purchase;
- The desired functionality;
- Who will access and use the solution (employees, contractors, affiliates customers);
- How is the solution accessed: On prem or in the cloud?;
- How the software/service will be used?
  - By the customer for internal use or with its customers
  - Stand-alone usage; or
  - Incorporated into another third-part software/platform;
- What rights does the customer require to achieve these uses? i.e., the right to host, display, modify, maintain, sublicense
  - Where the software/service will be used;
  - The period for which the software will be used; and
- Does the customer want the right to move the software from on premises to the cloud.

It is important that the customer identify not only its current need but also anticipate its future needs. For example, prior to COVID, many customers sought on-premises licenses but as working remotely has gained greater acceptance, customers have increasingly sought to transition to a distributed/cloud environment.

Once the customer's attorneys understand their client's needs, they will be able to assist in drafting an RFI/RFP and have the knowledge necessary to negotiate an agreement that will meet the customer's needs.

2. *Vendor Selection*

To be successful, the customer must have a clear understanding of its business goals. Key stakeholders in the customer's organization should be consulted both to establish the entity's collective goals and to obtain buy-in on the procurement. The "user" representative should be open-minded and not wedded to the customer's legacy system. These goals should drive the content of the RFP and the evaluation criteria. For example, if the purpose of the RFP is to acquire a new system to reduce costs, care should be taken not to include technical and functional "requirements" that greatly exceed current operations and that will require increased pricing on the part of the vendor.

Prudent customers should conduct in-depth due-diligence on all potential vendors as contract terms are not a substitute for due diligence on a vendor.

The successful vendor should be selected on the totality of the vendor's response. At a minimum, the vendor's response should address in a comprehensive manner:

- The scope and functionality of the proposed solution;
- A discussion of evolution of the proposed solution as well as any innovations proposed by the vendor;
- Service levels;
- A proposed governance structure;
- Key personnel and proposed subcontractors; and
- A proposed process for coordinating the development and delivery of the solution with other vendors and suppliers.

3. The Negotiation Process—Build a Well-Rounded Team

It is important that the customer and vendor each assemble a well-rounded team to participate in the negotiations. In addition to the attorney and business sponsor, the team should include members of the information technology, security, data privacy, finance, and procurement departments. In some instances, especially in large IT outsourcing transactions and large systems integration projects, it may be appropriate for the customer to retain an independent, third-party consultant. Utilizing a comprehensive team will help achieve a productive, liveable agreement that ensures the customer's goals will be reached. In addition, a broad-based team will likely assure corporate-wide support and avoid "second guessing" if problems arise.

Once the desired number of vendors has been "down selected," the customer should ask to review the vendors' error logs for the system the customer is seeking to license. Error logs are maintained by all vendors to track product defects and errors and subsequent corrections. By examining a vendor's error logs, the customer can ascertain the extent of any problems with the vendor's system and hopefully avoid selecting the wrong vendor.

Even after the customer has identified a preferred vendor, it should inform the preferred vendor that the customer is also negotiating with its second-choice vendor, which should motivate the preferred vendor to negotiate a mutually beneficial agreement with the customer.

During the negotiations, the customer should ensure it understands the vendor's pricing. If the customer is purchasing a license through an ASP model, it should clearly understand what part of the price is attributable to the software license and what part is attributable to the accompanying services. By bifurcating the pricing, the customer will better be able to compare prices and will hopefully be able to better understand the nature of the services that will be provided.

Today, there is less support for long negotiations. To ensure that the parties quickly conclude a contract, both parties should have representatives present at the negotiations that have the authority to make a decision. Further, both parties should include their subject matter experts (SMEs) in their negotiations to discuss and agree on the technical specifications of the software and any third-party products or software necessary to operate the software. Attorneys can prepare for the negotiation by studying the product's "About" or "Product" page to familiarize themselves with the product.

4. The Type and Structure of the Agreement

Once the vendor(s) has been selected, the parties should determine the type and structure of agreement based on the likely relationship of the parties. For example, if the parties are likely to have a long-term relationship with multiple work streams such as licensing, service, maintenance and support, the parties may want to consider negotiating a master services agreement under which many work orders can be attached. Under a master agreement, comprehensive legal terms are agreed in the master agreement with each SOW falling under the agreement containing the terms specific to the particular work stream. Alternatively, some parties prefer to use a framework agreement which contains fewer legal terms and under which there are stand-alone agreements allowing for greater flexibility in the legal terms.

One agreement cannot fit every transaction. The initial draft should be closely tailored to the underlying products and services to ensure the transaction is closed quickly and efficiently. Further, savvy attorneys will temper their comments based on the importance of the agreement and their client's timeline for closing the agreement.

The type and structure of the agreement will depend on many factors including:

- The reasons for the transaction
- How the agreement fit into the larger business organization
- The importance of the transaction
- What terms are important to the respective parties
- Each party's culture and risk tolerance
- The importance of the product being contracted for. Is it mission critical for the long term future of the client or something that will not materially impact the customer's business?
- The size of the parties relative to each other

5. Quantifying and Allocating Risk

Contracts are a means of allocating risk among the parties. Before agreeing to accept a particular risk, a prudent party should quantify and understand the likelihood of a particular risk occurring. Once identified and quantified, the party can allocate and manage the risk.

(a) Quantifying Risk

Contracts are the basis for allocating risk among the parties. Risk, in turn, is determined by the likelihood of an issue arising, and if it does, what is the likely severity of the issue. In short, is the issue likely to happen and if it does, how large are the consequences.

Once these questions are answered, a party can quantify its risk and seek to mitigate the risk. In discussing open issues with the business team, an attorney should assist the business team in better understanding the issues by, to the extent possible, quantifying the risks associated with a particular issue. For example (from the vendor's perspective):

- **The cost of fixing bugs:** Assume during the one-year warranty period, the customer proposes language requiring the vendor to pay to fix all "bugs" in the software even if they are minor or unimportant. Although this is usually never agreed to in a license agreement, if the vendor is willing to assume the expense of fixing all software bugs and understands the corresponding impact on the vendor's financial model, the vendor may concede this point.
- **Agreement termination and damages:** Assume the agreement provides that if the vendor does not or cannot fix a bug, even a small one, within 30 days, the customer may terminate the license agreement and sue the vendor for damages. Prudent vendors will allow the customer only to terminate (and sue) if the bug prevents the customer from utilizing the functionality of the software or creates material problems (a "demonstrated material failure"). Because all software has bugs to some degree, and some are hard to fix, if the vendor concedes this point, it essentially provides the customer the ability to terminate for convenience and to sue the vendor for damages over minor issues.
- **Regulatory risk:** What is the likely cost if the vendor is unable to charge the customer for any regulatory changes/changes in the law occurring during the term of the agreement?

(b) Allocating Risk

One of the most important aspects of commercial contracting is allocating the risk among the parties, as it is unrealistic to believe that one party will assume all risk inherent in a relationship. Rather, through negotiation the parties will allocate risk between themselves. Risk allocation infuses almost all provisions in an agreement. While most parties focus on disclaimer of warranties, limitation of liability, and indemnities, risk is also allocated through insurance provisions, payment terms, guarantees, and force majeure provisions (as shown by the recent COVID 19 pandemic). Prudent parties should evaluate each provision in their agreement to identify and understand the risk being allocated by the provision as well as their comfort in assuming that risk.

Based on this review, the party can prioritize which terms it cannot accept, which terms it can accept if modified, and which terms it can accept as is. Prioritizing its willingness to accept different risks will allow the party to enter its negotiations prepared to make concessions based on this prioritization. A party's risk tolerance will, in most cases, not mirror the other party's. Thus, the parties may be forced to make difficult decisions and accept risks they would prefer not to assume.

Vendors should avoid the tendency to accept greater risk or lower their prices at the end of the fiscal quarter in an effort to meet their financial goals. Too often vendors

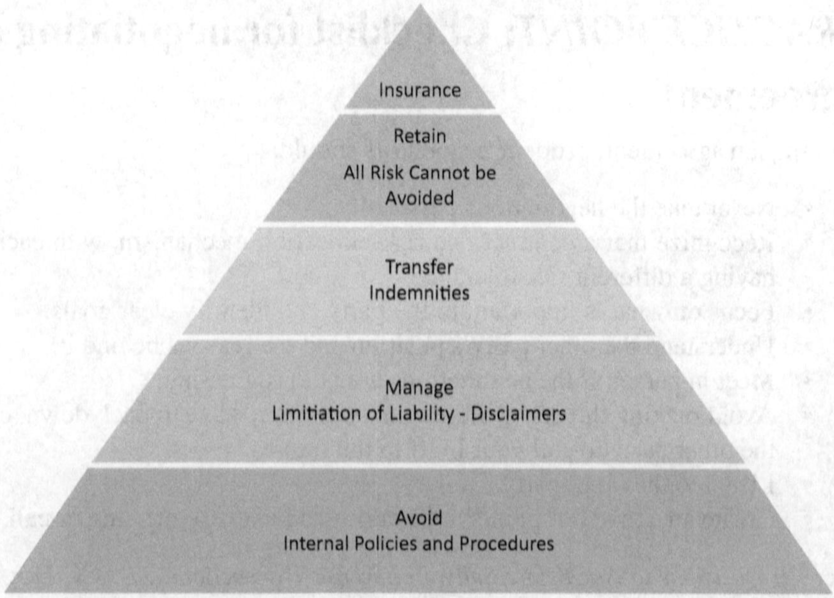

are focused on short-term financial goals and not the long-term implications of doing so. Resisting the temptation to meet quarterly sales goals at any cost, allows vendors to focus on long-term goals and their ability to successfully deliver the contracted solution.

The illustration above illustrates how contractual risk may be managed through the parties' contractual terms, internal actions and third party insurance. See Chapter 31 for a more detailed discussion of reducing risk.

6. *Managing the Customer-Vendor Relationship*

Successful procurement does not end with contract signature; rather, the parties enter the most critical stage of their relationship upon contract signature. Upon contract signature, the parties must focus on managing the relationship to ensure each party meets its contractual obligations in a timely manner. The parties must work together to avoid scope creep and undocumented changes in scope. They must ensure that best practices are implemented to avoid potential problems, including the use of change-control methodologies, the creation of audit trails, and the prompt escalation of potential issues. See Chapter 31 for a more detailed discussion of best practices in contracting.

The parties should interact at all levels to ensure a seamless development, delivery, and implementation. Functional towers such as technical, finance, contracts, operations, and strategic planning should all work in close coordination. The failure to fully integrate the teams of both parties will likely lead to serious problems in the future.

D. *PRACTICE POINT*: Checklist for negotiating an agreement.

In negotiating an agreement, prudent negotiators should:

- Never take the negotiations personally.
- Recognize that a contract is a risk-allocation mechanism, with each party having a different risk tolerance.
- Focus on what is important to the party and identify clear goals.
- Understand the other party's position and the reasons behind it.
- Meet in person if the negotiations are not progressing.
- Avoid making threats or ultimatums (you may have to back down, causing the other party to call your bluff in the future).
- Listen to the other party.
- Create an agenda of points to be addressed in every meeting or call.

See Keller, *10 Questions to Ask Before Software License Transactions,* 27 ACC Docket 39 (Sept. 2009); Boudreau, *The Insider's Guide to Technology Procurement,* 23 ACC Docket 29 (July/August 2005).

For a general overview of contracting considerations and the contracting process, *see* Borris, *How to Be a Commercial Attorney in a Growing Sales-Focused IT Company,* 28 ACC Docket 70 (Mar. 2010); Okray, *Conquering Corporate Contracts* 30 ACC Docket 29 (Oct. 2012); Feldman, *Contracts Illustrated,* 23 ACC Docket 30 (Sept. 2005).

CHAPTER 3

Licensing Software

A. Overview

1. *The Concept of Licensing*

A license can be thought of as the permission of the owner of property to use that property. A more precise understanding, however, can be gained by using the old law school example of comparing property ownership to a bundle of sticks. The owner of the property possesses all of the sticks, which can be separated, subdivided by time and place, transferred outright or licensed, and licensed exclusively or nonexclusively. If the owner grants a license, the property owner is giving some of the sticks from the owner's bundle to the licensee. Thus, to understand software licensing it is necessary to understand the sticks, or intellectual property rights, contained in the software owner's bundle.

2. *Intellectual Property Rights Applicable to Software*

Software is a unique technology, in that it comprises rights that are protectable under copyright law, patent law (including both utility and design patents), and trade secret law. These multiple protections arise because software can be a work of authorship as well as a business process or the key "component" in the functionality of a machine. Set forth below is a brief overview of the three primary types of intellectual property rights provided for under U.S. law that are applicable to software.

(a) Patents

(i) What Is a Utility Patent?

In most contexts, the word "patent" is used in the context of utility patents. Utility patents are granted on "any new and useful process, machine, manufacture, or composition of matter, or any new and useful improvement thereof." 35 U.S.C. § 101. A patent is a time limited exclusive right to practice an invention granted by the government. Anyone else who practices the invention within the jurisdiction of the patent without a license from the patent holder is infringing the patent. 35 U.S.C. § 121.

In return for granting a patent, the government requires the inventor to disclose the invention to the public in full, clear, and exact terms. 35 U.S.C. § 112. While the inventor has the exclusive right to practice the invention, anyone can examine the patent and understand the invention. Such third parties can develop improvements to the technologies disclosed in the issued patents and file their own patent applications attempting to cover those improvements to the technology patented by prior inventors.

(ii) What Is a Design Patent?

Although not as prominent as utility patents, software-related inventions can also be subject to design patent protection. Under 35 U.S.C. § 171, "[w]hoever invents any new, original, and ornamental design for an article of manufacture may obtain a [design] patent." User interfaces, icons, fonts, menus, patterns, and other ornamental subject matter used in computer software can be patented. Many of the patents asserted in the 2011 to 2018 patent litigation between Apple and Samsung regarding their respective smartphone and tablet computers were design patents, not utility patents. Design patents tend to be narrower in scope than utility patents, but they benefit from (i) high success rates at the United States Patent and Trademark Office ("USPTO"); (ii) quicker pendency periods at the USPTO; and (iii) being less expensive relative to utility patents.

(iii) Software Patents

The USPTO issued the world's first software patent in 1963 with U.S. Patent Number 3,380,029 directed to a sorting system. Nonetheless, the patenting of software was considered controversial and unsettled for many years, with the validity of the patent often depending on the degree to which the software was couched in terms of hardware or the degree to which the software was considered transformational. *Compare Gottchalk v. Benson*, 405 U.S. 63, 72 (1972) (patent invalidated because "in practical effect" the patent covered a "mathematical formula") with *In re Alappat*, 33 F.3d 1526, 1545 (Fed. Cir. 1994) ("[w]e have held that such programming creates a new machine, because a general purpose computer in effect becomes a special purpose computer once it is programmed to perform particular functions pursuant to instructions from program software.").

The U.S. Supreme Court in *Diamond v. Chakrabarty* famously held that "anything under the sun that is made by man" is patentable subject matter. 447 U.S. 303, 315 (1980). That broad rule is subject to important exclusions for "laws of nature, natural phenomena and abstract ideas." *Diamond v. Diehr*, 450 U.S. 175, 185 (1981). The physicality of the claimed subject matter became an important requirement under the *Freeman-Walter-Abele* test. *See In re Freeman*, 573 F.2d 1237 (C.C.P.A. 1978); *In re Walter*, 618 F.2d 758 (C.C.P.A. 1980); *In re Abele*, 684 F.2d 902 (C.C.P.A. 1982).

The difference between an unpatentable "manipulation of abstract ideas" (*see In re Warmerdam*, 33 F.3d 1354, 1360 (Fed. Cir. 1994)) and "a specific machine to produce a useful, concrete, and tangible result" (*see In re Alappat* at 1544) was often difficult for even seasoned patent practitioners to discern. Further complicating matters was the "business method exception" of *Hotel Security Checking Co. v. Lorraine Co.*, 160 F. 467 (2d Cir. 1908). In *Hotel Security Checking*, the Second Circuit Court of Appeals held that systems for transacting business, such as a bookkeeping system, were unpatentable.

The business method exception was eliminated in 1998, when the Federal Circuit issued its opinion in *State Street Bank & Trust Co. v. Signature Financial Group, Inc.*, 149 F.3d 1368 (Fed. Cir. 1998). In *State Street*, the district court granted summary judgment invalidating a patent governing a data processing system, relying in part on the "business method" exception to patentable subject matter. *Id.* at 1375. The theory behind the "business method" exception was that merely doing business did not qualify as patentable subject matter. *Id.* The Federal Circuit reversed the district court's decision that a data processing system did not qualify as patentable subject matter and it eliminated the business method exception, opening the floodgates on software patents.

Although the *State Street Bank* opinion did a lot to open the doors for future software and business method patents, business method patents have been around in one form or another going back to at least 1840. *See O'Reilly v. Morse,* 56 U.S. 52 (1854).

Many commentators have complained that the Supreme Court in *Bilski v. Kappos,* 561 U.S. 593 (2010) further complicated the patentable subject matter requirements for software and business method patents when it held that the "machine-or-transformation test is a useful and important clue . . . but is not the sole test for deciding whether an invention is a patent-eligible 'process.'" The *Bilski* opinion never even attempts to provide a comprehensive definitive test for patentability. To the contrary, it repudiates the exclusive applicability of various Federal Circuit formulations without repudiating the formulations themselves. The ultimate impact of *Bilski* may be best evaluated by the language below:

> *Today, the Court once again declines to impose limitations on the Patent Act that are inconsistent with the Act's text. The patent application here can be rejected under our precedents on the unpatentability of abstract ideas. The Court, therefore, need not define further what constitutes a patentable "process," beyond pointing to the definition of that term provided in § 100(b) and looking to the guideposts in Benson, Flook, and Diehr.*
>
> *And nothing in today's opinion should be read as endorsing interpretations of § 101 that the Court of Appeals for the Federal Circuit has used in the past. See, e.g., State Street, 149 F.3d at 1373; AT&T Corp., 172 F.3d at 1357. It may be that the Court of Appeals thought it needed to make the machine-or-transformation test exclusive precisely because its case law had not adequately identified less extreme means of restricting business method patents, including (but not limited to) application of our opinions in Benson, Flook, and Diehr. In disapproving an exclusive machine-or-transformation test, we by no means foreclose the Federal Circuit's development of other limiting criteria that further the purposes of the Patent Act and are not inconsistent with its text.*

Id. at 612.

Software is considered to be patentable if the claims are not directed at an abstract idea. *Alice Corp. Pty. Ltd. V. CLS Bank Intern.,* 573 U.S. 208, 134 S. Ct. 2347 (2014). In *Alice,* the United States Supreme Court upheld the longstanding exceptions that "[l] aws of nature, natural phenomenon, and abstract ideas are not patentable." *Id.* at 2350. It stated:

> *We have described the concern that drives this exclusionary principle as one of pre-emption. Laws of nature, natural phenomena, and abstract ideas are "the basic tools of scientific and technological work." "[M]onopolization of those tools through the grant of a patent might tend to impede innovation more than it would tend to promote it," thereby thwarting the primary object of the patent laws. We have "repeatedly emphasized this . . . concern that patent law not inhibit further discovery by improperly tying up the future use of" these building blocks of human ingenuity.*

Alice, 134 S. Ct. at 2354 (citations omitted).

To avoid being characterized as merely the computer implementation of an "abstract idea" a software-related invention must be "transformative." The Court explained:

> *At the same time, we tread carefully in construing this exclusionary principle lest it swallow all of patent law. At some level, "all inventions . . . embody, use, reflect, rest upon, or apply laws of nature, natural phenomena, or abstract ideas." Thus, an invention is not rendered ineligible for patent simply because it involves an abstract concept. "[A]pplication[s]" of such concepts "'to a new and useful end,'" we have said, remain eligible for patent protection.*
>
> *Accordingly, in applying the § 101 exception, we must distinguish between patents that claim the "'buildin[g] block[s]'" of human ingenuity and those that integrate the building blocks into something more, thereby "transform[ing]" them into a patent-eligible invention. The former "would risk disproportionately tying up the use of the underlying" ideas, and are therefore ineligible for patent protection. The latter pose no comparable risk of pre-emption, and therefore remain eligible for the monopoly granted under our patent laws.*

Alice, 134 S. Ct. at 2354–55 (citations omitted).

To provide clarity to the test set forth by the Supreme Court in *Alice*, the United States Patent and Trademark Office issued the 2019 Revised Patent Subject Matter Eligibility Guidelines ("Guidelines"). The Guidelines set forth an expanded process for determining patentability:

- Step 1: Is the claim to a process, machine, manufacture, or composition of matter?
- Step 2: *Alice* two-part analysis:
  - Step 2A: Determine whether a claim is "directed to" an exception.
    - Prong 1: Does the claim recite an abstract idea, law of nature or natural phenomenon?
    - Prong 2: Does the claim recite additional elements that integrate the judicial exception into a practical application?
  - Step 2B: Evaluate whether the claim recites additional elements that amount to an inventive concept (aka "significantly more") than the recited judicial exception.

The citation of *Alice* has been ubiquitous in the litigation of software patents, but the application of *Alice* is often inconsistent and thus difficult to predict. Former Federal Circuit Chief Judge Paul Michel testified before a Senate committee in 2019 that *Alice* has resulted in "excessively incoherent, inconsistent, and chaotic" case law. Former USPTO Director David Kappos similarly testified that the current state of patent eligibility "truly is a mess" and that courts "are spinning their wheels on decisions that are irreconcilable, incoherent and against our national interest." Time will tell if Congress decides to enact legislation that addresses the apparent randomness of post-*Alice* decisions. Patents issued by the USPTO post-*Alice* will presumably be less vulnerable to invalidity challenges under 35. U.S.C. § 101.

(iv) Period of Protection

In the United States, the term of a patent depends upon when it was filed. For patents issued before June 8, 1995, and patent applications that were pending on that date, the patent term is the longer of either 17 years from the issue date or 20 years from the earliest claimed filing date, the longer term applying. 35 U.S.C. § 154. For applications filed on or after June 8, 1995, the patent term is 20 years from the earliest claimed filing date. *Id.* Generally, a patent holder may not enforce a patent license beyond the term of the patent. *Brulotte v. Thys Co.*, 379 U.S. 29 (1964). Thus, theoretically, a software licensor could have difficulty enforcing a license to its patented software after the expiration of the patent term. Pragmatically, however, a licensor can also protect its software via copyright. As discussed above, the patentability of software is subject to a significant degree of confusion and scrutiny.

(v) Ownership

Under U.S. patent law, the inventor owns the right to patent any invention, even if the invention was created within the scope of their employment. Unlike copyright law, there is no "work for hire" doctrine for patents, and thus employers should be proactive in having employees execute written assignments of patent rights before starting work. Joint ownership arises if there is more than one inventor and each owner may unilaterally exploit the patent by licensing it to a third party without having account to the other owner(s). All owners, however, must participate in any action to enforce an infringement claim against a third party. Conversely, even one fractional owner of an issued patent is free to license the patent to an infringer, negating the possibility of the other owners collecting any monies from the infringer. Under copyright law, each copyright co-owner has a duty to account to the other co-owners for any profits made. *Ashton-Tate Corp. v. Ross*, 916 F.2d 516, 522 (9th Cir. 1990). Patent law does not impose such a duty to account on co-owners of a patent. *See* 35 U.S.C. § 262.

For an overview of the history of patenting software, see *The History of Software Patents*, http://www.bitlaw.com/software-patent/history.html. *See also* Walden & Dennhardt, *Copyright and Patent Protection for Computer Software: How Has the Landscape Changed?*, INTELL. PROP. TODAY 32 (Apr. 2015).

(b) Trade Secrets

(i) What Is a Trade Secret?

Trade secrets are another form of intellectual property that can be used to protect software. Trade secrets are protected under the relevant state trade secret laws, almost all of which are derived from the Uniform Trade Secret Act (UTSA), which has been adopted in 49 states and the District of Columbia. Only New York has not adopted the Uniform Trade Secret Act.

Under the UTSA, a trade secret is information, including a formula, pattern, compilation, program device, method, technique, or process, that: (1) derives independent economic value, actual or potential, from not being generally known to, and not being readily ascertainable by proper means by other persons who can obtain economic value from its disclosure or use, and (2) is the subject of efforts that are reasonable under the circumstances to maintain its secrecy. As set forth above, the scope of trade secrets overlaps patents but is also potentially applicable to information that does not meet the standard of patentability. Thus, trade secret protection is potentially broader than that available under patent law. However, a program that is solely functional in nature, i.e., the program's function is readily available or ascertainable, is not protectable under the UTSA. Unlike patent protection, trade secret protection does not protect against a party independently developing the same invention.

The UTSA defines "misappropriation" to mean the (1) acquisition of a trade secret by a person who knows or has reason to know the trade secret was acquired by improper means, or (2) disclosure or use of a trade secret without express or implied consent by a person who improperly acquired knowledge of the trade secret or, who at the time of disclosure or use, knew or had reason to know that the trade secret had been improperly acquired, and there was an obligation to maintain its confidentiality. UTSA § 1(2); *see, e.g.*, MD. CODE ANN., COM. LAW § 11-201(c).

For a further discussion of the UTSA, see Chapter 25.B.2.

A fundamental distinction between patent protection and trade secret protection is the requirement that the owner of a trade secret use reasonable efforts to maintain the secrecy of information. This is in sharp contrast to the duty of disclosure and enablement under patent law. Thus, a licensor seeking to protect software should include confidentiality provisions in the license agreement. Special care should be taken to protect the confidentiality of source code. See Chapter 25 for a detailed discussion of the issues involved in confidentiality provisions.

(ii) Advantages of Trade Secret Protection

Trade secret protection offers several advantages over other types of protection for intellectual property law, principally the perpetual protection offered for trade secrets (for example, the formula for Coke) and initially the minimal cost to obtain such protection. These benefits are often outweighed by the fluid nature of such protection and the immediate loss of trade secret status even in the event of an inadvertent disclosure. The disclosure of the protected information in a patent or copyright application will also cause a loss of protection. *See BondPro Corp. v. Siemens Power Generation, Inc.*, 463 F.3d 702 (7th Cir. 2006). Further, a competitor who is able to reproduce a trade secret without use of illegal means is free to do so. In short, trade secrets generally retain their value so long as they remain secret. Not all categories of technology are easy or even possible to effectively monetize while being protected as trade secrets. Many famous examples of trade secrets are recipes for food or beverage products such as the recipe for Coca-Cola's coke syrup formula or McDonald's special sauce used in its Big Mac® burger. In the world of information technology, complex algorithms such as Google's search algorithm are sustained as trade secrets, but many software products and processes can be definitively reverse engineered by competitors, effectively ending their status as trade secrets.

State trade secret laws offer broader protection than copyright laws because the trade secret laws apply to concepts and information, which are both excluded from protection under federal copyright law. *See* 17 U.S.C. § 102(b). Information eligible for protection includes computer code, *Trandes Corp. v. Guy F. Atkinson Co.*, 996 F.2d 655 (4th Cir.), *cert. denied*, 510 U.S. 965 (1993); *University Computing Co. v. Lykes-Youngstown Corp.*, 504 F.2d 518 (5th Cir.), *reh'g denied*, 505 F.2d 1304 (5th Cir. 1974); *Integrated Cash Management Servs., Inc. v. Digital Transactions, Inc.*, 732 F. Supp. 370 (S.D.N.Y. 1989), *aff'd*, 920 F.2d 171 (2d Cir. 1990); program architecture, *Trandes*, 996 F.2d at 661; *Computer Assocs. Int'l, Inc. v. Bryan*, 784 F. Supp. 982 (E.D.N.Y. 1992); information content including order, structure, and sequence, *Q-Co. Indus., Inc. v. Hoffman*, 625 F. Supp. 608, 617 (S.D.N.Y 1985); and algorithms, *Vermont Microsystems, Inc. v. Autodesk, Inc.*, 88 F.3d 142 (2d Cir. 1996); *Micro Consulting, Inc. v. Zubeldia*, 813 F. Supp. 1514 (W.D. Okla. 1990), *aff'd without opinion*, 959 F.2d 245 (10th Cir. 1992). Mathematical algorithms are also protectable under patent law, *Arrhythmia Research Technology v. Corazonix Corp.*, 958 F.2d 1053 (Fed. Cir.) *reh'g denied*, 958 F.2d 1053 (Fed. Cir. 1992); *In re Iwashi*, 888 F.2d 1370 (Fed. Cir. 1989).

Courts are divided as to the application of trade secret protection for customer lists. *See Morlife, Inc. v. Perry*, 56 Cal. App. 4th 1514 (Cal. App. 1997) (file of customer business cards maintained by sales manager are trade secrets); *Fireworks Spectacular, Inc. v. Premier Pyrotechnics, Inc.*, 147 F. Supp. 2d 1057 (D. Kan. 2001) (customer lists constitute trade secrets, applying Kansas law), and *In re American Preferred Prescription, Inc.*, 186 B.R. 350 (Bankr. E.D.N.Y. 1995) (client list is trade secret). *See also DeGiorgio v. Megabyte Int'l., Inc.*, 468 S.E.2d 367 (Ga. 1996) (only tangible customer lists are subject to protection as a trade secret), and *Ed Nowogroski Insurance v. Rucker*, 944 P.2d 1093 (Wash. 1997) (memorized client list constitutes trade secret); *but see Vigoro Indus. v. Cleveland Chem. of Ark.*, 866 F. Supp. 1150 (E.D. Ark. 1994) (customer lists alone not considered a trade secret), and *WMW Machinery Co., Inc. v. Koerber A.G.*, 658 N.Y.S.2d 385 (App. Div. 1997) (customer lists are not trade secrets where lists are readily ascertainable from sources outside employee's business). Further, at least one court has held that the execution of a nondisclosure agreement by an employee does not in and of itself create trade-secret status for the employer's customer lists. *Equifax Servs., Inc. v. Examination Management Servs., Inc.*, 453 S.E.2d 488 (Ga. App. 1994). For a further discussion, *see Intellectual Property Issues in the Employment Setting*, 119 Intell. Prop. Couns. 1, 4 (Nov. 2006).

(iii) Pre-emption

A majority of courts have held that claims based on state trade secret laws are not pre-empted by federal copyright law (§ 301 of Federal Copyright Act). *Dun & Bradstreet Software Services, Inc. v. Grace Consulting, Inc.*, 307 F.3d 197 (3d Cir. 2002); *Nat'l Car Rental Sys., Inc. v. Computer Assocs. Intl., Inc.*, 991 F.2d 426 (8th Cir. 1993); *Bishop v. Wick*, 1998 WL 166652, 11 U.S.P.Q.2d 1360 (N.D. Ill. 1988); *Brignoli v. Balch, Hardy and Scheinman*, 645 F. Supp. 1201 (S.D.N.Y. 1986), *but see Computer Associates Int'l v. Atari*, 775 F. Supp. 544 (E.D.N.Y. 1991); *Enhanced Computer Solutions, Inc. v. Rose*, 927 F. Supp. 738 (S.D.N.Y. 1996); *Benjamin Capital Investors v. Cossey*, 867 P.2d 1388 (Or. Ct. App. 1994). *See also Lennon v. Seaman*, 63 F. Supp.2d 428, 437 (S.D.N.Y. 1999), which discusses in detail the dichotomy among the different courts. At the same time, two commentators have suggested that trade secret laws may be the only method of protection for the ideas incorporated in the functionality of mass distributed commercial software. Johnston & Grogan, *Trade Secret Protection for Mass Distributed Software*, 11 Computer Law. 1 (Nov. 1994).

(iv) Examples of Trade Secrets

Matters of public knowledge, general knowledge of an industry, routine or small skill and knowledge readily ascertainable, and differences in procedures or methodology are not considered to be trade secrets. *Anaconda Co. v. Metric Tool & Die Co.*, 485 F. Supp. 410, 421–22 (E.D. Pa. 1996). Furthermore, any skill or experience learned during the course of employee's employment is not considered to be a trade secret. *Rigging Int'l Maintenance Co. v. Gwin*, 128 Cal. App. 3d 594 (1981); *American Red Cross v. Palm Beach Blood Bank, Inc.*, 143 F.3d 1407 (11th Cir. 1998) (employer may not preclude former employees from utilizing contacts and expertise gained during employment), but *see Air Products and Chemicals, Inc. v. Johnson*, 442 A.2d 1114 (Pa. Super. 1982) (details of research and development, projected capital spending, and marketing plans are trade secrets); *Den-Tal-Ez, Inc. v. Siemens Capital Corp.*, 566 A.2d 1214 (Pa. Super. 1989) (detailed unit costs, profit margin date, and pricing methods are trade secrets).

(v) Remedies for Misappropriation

An owner of trade secrets is entitled to receive injunctive relief and damages for the misappropriation of its trade secrets. UTSA § 3. Such damages include the actual loss caused by the misappropriation and any unjust enrichment arising as a result of the misappropriation that is not taken into account in computing any actual loss. UTSA § 3; *see, e.g.*, Md. Code Ann. Com. Law § 11-1203. A court may also award attorney's fees if wilful and malicious misappropriation exists. UTSA § 4(iii); *see, e.g.*, Md. Code Ann., Com. Law § 11-1204.

Section 7 of the UTSA provides that except for contractual remedies, whether or not based upon the misappropriation of a trade secret or other civil remedies that are not based upon the misappropriation of a trade secret, the UTSA "displaces conflicting tort, restitutionary and other laws . . . providing civil remedies for misappropriation of a trade secret." *See, e.g., Auto Channel, Inc. v. Speedvision Network, LLC*, 144 F. Supp. 2d 784 (W.D. Ky. 2001) (Kentucky Uniform Trade Secrets Act replaces all conflicting civil state law regarding misappropriation of trade secrets, except for those relating to contractual remedies); *Boeing Co. v. Sierracin Corp.*, 738 P.2d 665 (Wash. 1987) (UTSA merely displaces conflicting tort, restitutionary, and other law regarding civil liability for misappropriation and does not displace claims for breach of contractual and confidential relationship).

(vi) Importance of State Laws

Given the differences in state trade secret laws, the choice of governing law is very important. For example, South Carolina has enacted legislation providing that written agreements not to disclose trade secrets will be enforced without limitation on duration or geographic scope when the employee knows or has reason to know of the trade secret's existence, S.C. Code Ann. § 39-8-30(d) (Law Co-op. 1997), while the Wisconsin Court of Appeals in an unpublished decision declined to enforce a nondisclosure provision in an agreement because it was unlimited as to time and overly broad. *Williams v. Northern Technical Services, Inc.*, 568 N.W.2d 784 (Wis. App. 1997).

For a general overview of trade secret issues, *see* Rodgers & Marrs, *Trade Secrets and Corporate Espionage: Protecting Your Company's Crown Jewels*, 22 ACC Docket 60–78 (April 2004); O'Brien, *Trade Secret Reclamation: An Equitable Approach in a Relative World*, 21 J. Computer & Information Law 227 (2003); Peterson, *Trade Secrets in an Information Age*, 32 Hous. L. Rev. 385 (1995); Dodd, *Rights in Information: Conversion and Misappropriation Causes of Action in Intellectual Property Cases*, 32 Hous. L. Rev. 459

(1995); Gross, *What Is Computer "Trade Secret" Under State Law,* 53 A.L.R.4th 1046 (1987); Gulbis, *Disclosure or Use of Computer Application Software as Misappropriation of Trade Secret,* 30 A.L.R.4th 1250 (1984); Pooley, TRADE SECRETS, Law Journal Press (2023).

For a discussion of trade secret laws as they apply to employees, see Chapters 25.A.5 and 25.B.

(c) Copyrights

(i) What Is a Copyright?

Copyright law protects "works of authorship fixed in any tangible medium of expression, now known or later developed, from which they can be perceived, reproduced, or otherwise communicated, either directly or with the aid of a machine or device." 17 U.S.C. § 102. Copyright protection, however, does not "extend to any idea, procedure, process, system, method of operation, concept, principle, or discovery, regardless of the form in which it is described, explained, illustrated, or embodied in such work." *Id.*

Software is eligible for protection under the Copyright Act. *Apple Computer, Inc. v. Franklin Computer Corp.*, 714 F.2d 1240 (3d Cir. 1983). Thus, copyright only protects the expression, not the underlying ideas or concepts. Software is a work of authorship that is fixed in a tangible medium of expression. As such, it is entitled to protection under copyright law. Copyright protection does not extend, however, to the processes that software performs or the ideas that it implements. Instead, only the expression itself is protected. This is a fundamental distinction between the protection offered by copyright law and that potentially offered by patent and trade secret law. In a nutshell, copyright law prevents anyone from copying source code without the owner's permission, but it does not prevent third parties from independently writing software that performs the same functions as the copyrighted software.

It is important to note that a copyright does not provide the copyright holder rights similar to those held by patent owners. A copyright grants the holder the exclusive right to duplicate the copyrighted material and make derivative works. 17 U.S.C. § 106(1), (2); *CMAX/Cleveland, Inc. v. UCR, Inc.*, 804 F. Supp. 337 (M.D. Ga. 1992). A patent grants the holder the right to prevent others from using, making, or selling the patented subject matter. 35 U.S.C. § 154 (1994). A copyright does not protect against another entity creating similar or even identical software independent from the copyrighted work. For example, it does not protect against the creation of similar screen displays, icons, the method of operation of the software, or the key commands. *See, e.g., Lotus Development Corp. v. Borland International, Inc.*, 49 F.3d 807, 815–18 (1st Cir. 1995), *aff'd per curiam,* 516 U.S. 233 (1996) (menu-command hierarchy was an uncopyrightable method of operation) and *Engineering Dynamics, Inc. v. Structural Software, Inc.*, 26 F.3d 1335, 1342-43 (5th Cir. 1994) (user interface, input formats, and output reports are protectable), *but see Whelen v. Jaslow,* 797 F.2d 1222 (3d Cir. 1986) (concept of program's content not copyrightable but all functions used for implementing the program are protectable).

See Chapter 7.K for a more in-depth discussion of the creation of copies of software by independent service organizations (ISOs).

(ii) Period of Protection

In general, for a work created after January 1, 1978, a copyright endures for a period equal to the life of the author and for 70 years after the author's death. 17 U.S.C § 302(a). For works made for hire, a copyright endures for a term of 95 years from the year of its first publication or for a term of 120 years from the year of its creation, whichever expires first. 17 U.S.C § 302(c).

(iii) The Importance of Registration

Copyright registration establishes a public record and legal presumption of exclusive ownership of the underlying intellectual property. Confusion often arises, however, as to the role of registration in copyright law. A work of authorship is protected when it is fixed in a tangible medium. *See In re World Auxiliary Power Co.*, 303 F.3d 1120, 1125 (9th Cir. 2002). It is not mandatory, however, that copyright owners include a copyright notice on the work or that the work be published to receive protection. 17 U.S.C. § 401(a); *Data General Corp. v. Grumman Systems Support Corp.*, 36 F.3d 1147 (1st Cir. 1994).

Copyright protection arises as a matter of law without registration. An author need not affirmatively apply for a federal copyright registration in order for that work to be protected under U.S. copyright laws. However, a U.S. copyright holder must register the work before bringing an infringement action. 17 U.S.C. § 411(a). Further, owners of registered copyrights who prevail in litigation may receive an award of lawyer's fees and, at their election, statutory damages if the infringement occurs after registration or if the copyrights are registered within three months of publication. 17 U.S.C. § 412. Registering a work within five years of the first publication of the work constitutes prima facie evidence of the validity of the copyright and the facts stated in the certificate. 17 U.S.C. § 410(c).

A copyright owner must register its copyright, as opposed to filing an application to register a copyright, before it may sue for infringement. *Fourth Estate Public Benefit Corp. v. Wall-Street, LLC,* 139 S. Ct. 881 (2019). Registration allows an owner to avail itself of the protections under federal copyright law, as without registration, an owner would have to rely on trade secret, breach of contract, and tort theories to enforce its ownership rights in the work.

Registration within three months of the publication of the work permits a copyright holder to obtain up to $150,000 in statutory damages for intentional infringement without proof of an actual loss and the right to obtain attorney's fees and costs. 17 U.S.C. §§ 504(c), 412. If the work is published within five years from the date of creation, the registration is prima facie evidence of the validity of the copyright, shifting the burden of proof to the other party. 17 U.S.C. § 410(c); *Gates Rubber Co. v. Bando Chem. Ind., Ltd.*, 9 F.3d 823 (10th Cir. 1993). Registration also allows the copyright owner to record its registration with the U.S. Customs Service to protect against infringing copies being imported into the United States. 17 U.S.C. § 602; 19 U.S.C. § 1595(a)(1)(C).

The ability to obtain statutory damages and attorney's fees is important as the copyright owner's actual damages and the infringer's profits may be less than the cost of the litigation. The award of attorney's fees is made at the discretion of the court and not automatically to the prevailing party, however, in copyright infringement suits, there is a strong presumption that the prevailing defendants may recover their costs. *Design*

Basics, L.L.C. v. Kerstein Home & Designs, Inc., 1 F.4th 502 (9th Cir. 2021); *Fogerty v. Fantasy, Inc.*, 510 U.S. 517, 537 (1994). Courts are free to award legal fees in excess of the amount of damages awarded. *See, e.g., Spooner v. EEN, Inc.*, 644 F.3d 62 (1st Cir. 2011) (Court upheld award for $98,745.80 in legal fees, which were twice the damages award of $40,000.) Prevailing defendants are also entitled to recover their legal fees. *See T-Peg, Inc., et al. v. Vermont Timber Works, Inc. et al.*, 669 F.3d 59 (1st Cir. 2012). Note, however, that statutory damages are not available where a work is not registered at the time of infringement. 17 U.S.C. § 412 ("...no award of statutory damages or of attorney's fees, as provided by sections 504 and 505, shall be made for - (1) any infringement of copyright in an unpublished work commenced before the effective date of its registration; or (2) any infringement of copyright commenced after first publication of the work and before the effective date of its registration, unless such registration is made within three months after the first publication of the work....").

For a general overview, *see* Hanovice, Bruzzone, Vayner & Findley, *Copyright, Licenses and Avoiding the Perils of Infringement*, 35 ACC Docket 69 (Oct. 2017).

(iv) Director and Officer Liability

If willful infringement can be proven, a copyright owner can obtain personal recourse against the officers and directors of the entity willfully infringing. *See Warner Bros., Inc. v. Lobster Pot, Inc.*, 582 F. Supp. 478, 482 (N.D. Ohio 1984); *Asher Worldwide Enterprises, LLC v. Housewaresonly. com, Inc.*, 2013 WL 5953825 (N.D. Ill. Aug. 26, 2013) (Corporate officers may be held personally liable for willful and knowing copyright infringement.); *Perfect 10, Inc. v. Amazon.com, Inc.*, 508 F.3d 1146, 1173–74 (9th Cir. 2007); *Ellison v. Robertson*, 357 F.3d 1072, 1076 (9th Cir. 2004) ("A defendant is vicariously liable for copyright infringement if he enjoys a direct financial benefit from *another's* infringing activity and 'has the right and ability to supervise' the infringing activity." (citation omitted)); *Symantec Corp. v. CD Micro, Inc.*, 286 F. Supp. 2d 1265, 1275 (D. Or. 2003) (CEO held vicariously liable on summary judgment for company's copyright infringement where "[i]n addition to his salary, [the CEO] is also the majority shareholder and would thus have a direct financial benefit if the infringing sales raise the value of the company's stock"); *Broad. Music, Inc. v. Blueberry Hill Family Rests., Inc.*, 899 F. Supp. 474, 480 (D. Nev. 1995) (director and shareholder of corporation "jointly [and severally] liable with his corporation for the copyright infringement" where he "had the power to control the conduct of the 'primary' copyright infringers").

Further, directors may be liable for contributory infringement if they (i) knew of or had reason to know of the infringing activity and (ii) intentionally induced or materially contributed to the infringing activity such as by directly supervising and controlling the development efforts related to the infringing software. *Perfect 10, Inc. at* 1170–73.

(v) Copyright Infringement vs. Breach of Contract Claims

Copyright infringement arises when the licensee acts outside the scope of the license. *Sun Microsystems v. Microsoft Corp.*, 188 F.3d 1115 (9th Cir. 1999). To recover for copyright infringement based on the breach of a license agreement, (1) the copying must exceed the scope of the defendant's license, and (2) the copyright owner's complaint must be grounded in an exclusive right of copyright (e.g., unlawful reproduction or distribution).

An infringement "claim fails if the challenged use of the work falls within the scope of a valid license . . . . " *Great Minds v. Office Depot, Inc.*, 945 F.3d 1106, 1110 (9th Cir. 2019). "[w]hen a licensee exceeds the scope of the license granted by the copyright holder, the licensee is liable for infringement." *LGS Architects, Inc. v. Concordia Homes of Nev.*, 434 F.3d 1150, 1156 (9th Cir. 2006).

The existence of a contractual agreement gives rise to the question as to whether a claim lies with a breach of contract claim or a copyright infringement claim.

Whether a claim falls under contract or copyright depends on whether a party breached a "condition" as opposed to a "covenant." *MDY Indus, LLC. v. Blizzard Entm't., Inc.*, 629 F.3d 928, 939 (9th Cir. 2011). The answer depends on whether a "term is a condition that limits the scope of the license or is merely a covenant." *BitManagement Software GmBH v. United States*, 989 F.2d 938, 950 (Fed Cir. 2021). Courts will presume the terms of a copyright license are covenants unless the agreement clearly indicates a condition precedent was intended. *Id.* at 950.

Conditions are "contractual terms that limit a license's scope . . . the breach of which constitute[s] copyright infringement." *Id.*

"A covenant is a contractual promise, i.e., a manifestation of intention or promise to act or refrain from acting in a particular way . . . ." *Id.* Over deployment or breaching a true up provision is a covenant as they are unrelated to the scope of the license. *Quest Software, Inc., v. DirecTV Operations*, LLC, 2011 WL 4500922 (C.D. Cal. Sept. 26, 2011); *Broad Vision, Inc. v. Medical Protective, Co.*, 2010 WL 5158129 (S.D.N.Y. Nov 23, 2010). Courts tend to interpret contractual obligations as covenants instead of conditions. *See e.g., Jacobsen v. Katzer*, 535 F.3d 1373 (Fed Cir. 2008) (Open-source license agreement made "provided that" user insert notice in each changed file, found to be a condition).

A copyright claim allows a plaintiff to receive injunctive relief and potentially recover significant penalties as well as its legal fees. A recovery under a breach of contract claim is limited to the actual loss suffered by the breach. Richard A. Lord, 24 WILLISTON ON CONTRACTS § 65:1 (4th ed. 2007), Normally, legal fees are not recoverable in a breach of contract claim. *Alyeska Pipeline Svc. Co. v. Wilderness Soc'y*, 421 U.S. 240, 247 (1975).

Courts will carefully evaluate any efforts to restyle a breach of contract claim as a copyright infringement claim. *See generally Eastern Broadcasting Am. Corp. v. Universal Video, Inc.*, 2006 WL 767871 (E.D.N.Y. Mar. 24, 2006); *Marshall v. New Kids on the Block Partnership*, 782 F. Supp. 1008 (S.D.N.Y. 1991). Exceeding the scope of a license gives rise to a copyright infringement claim not a breach of contract claim. *Harrell v. Van der Plas*, 2009 WL 3756327 (S.D.N.Y. Nov. 9, 2009).

To bring a successful action for copyright infringement, a plaintiff must establish that the rights violated were a condition not a covenant. *Sun Microsystems, Inc., v. Microsoft Corp.*, 188 F.3d 1115 (9th Cir. 1999); *MDY Indus., LLC v. Blizzard Entm't. Inc.*, 629 F.3d 928, 939 (9th Cir. 2011) (conditions are contractual terms that limit a license's scope that when breached constitute copyright infringement.) A dispute over the payment of license fees and the limitation of one user per license are not limitations on the scope of the license, but rather separate contractual covenants and are not the basis for a copyright claim. *Netbula, LLC v. Storage Technology Corp.*, 2008 WL 228036 (N.D. Cal. Jan.

18, 2008); *BroadVision, Inc. v. Medical Protective Co.*, 2010 WL 5158129 (S.D.N.Y. Nov. 23, 2010) (provisions establishing additional fees in event number of licenses granted is exceeded are covenants not conditions.)

(vi) Statute of Limitations

A copyright holder must bring a claim for copyright infringement "within three years after the claim accrued." 17 U.S.C. § 507(b). A split of authority has arisen, however, over whether the three-year period begins on the date of the injury (the "Injury Rule") or the date the copyright holder knows or should have known of the injury giving rise to the claim (the "Discovery Rule"). Presently, a majority of circuits have recognized the Discovery Rule as the correct interpretation. The Supreme Court will resolve this dichotomy with its decision in *Nealy et. al. v. Warner Chappell Music Inc. et al.* which is expected to be issued during the spring term of 2024.

(vii) *De minimis* Infringement

Although a *de minimis* defense exists under copyright law, there is not a set standard that allows small portions of computer code to be copied. *See Sandoval v. New Line Cinema Corp.*, 147 F.3d 215 (2d. Cir. 1998) quoting *Ringgold v. Black Ent'ment Television, Inc.*, 126 F.3d 70, 74 (2d Cir. 1997) (*de minimis* defense requires that "the copying of the protected material is so trivial 'as to fall below' the quantitative threshold of substantial similarity."); *See also Dun & Bradstreet Software Services, Inc. v. Grace Consulting, Inc.*, 307 F.3d. 197 (3d Cir. 2002) (*de minimis* defense may not be invoked; 27 out of 525,000 lines of code not relevant where qualitative value of copied material is material); *Veritas Operating Corp., v. Microsoft Corp.*, 2008 WL 474248 (W.D. Wash. Feb. 4, 2008) (copying 54 lines of code out of 160,000 lines (0.03%) may constitute copyright infringement); *Marketing Technology Solutions, Inc. v. Medizine LLC.*, 2010 WL 2034404 (S.D.N.Y. May 18, 2010) (rejecting *de minimis* defense where 437 lines of code out of 1,187,363 lines of code in the program were allegedly similar). In general, courts look to the quantitative and qualitative significance of the copied materials in comparison to the completed work. *Dun & Bradstreet Software Servs., Inc. v. Grace Consulting, Inc.*, 307 F.3d 197, 208 (3d Cir 2002) ("A *de minimis* defense does not apply where the qualitative value of the copying is material."); *LeHererse v. World Institute of Scientology Enterprises, Int'l.*, 533 F.3d. 1287 (11th Cir. 2008). See also 17 U.S.C. § 106 (11). Downloading but not installing unlicensed software may constitute copyright infringement, as at least one court has found such actions do not fall within the *de minimis* exception to copyright infringement. *Design Data Corp. v. Unigate Enterprise, Inc.*, 847 F.3d 1169 (9th Cir. 2017).

(viii) Copyright Notices

Inclusion of a copyright notice abrogates a defendant's claim of innocent infringement in mitigation of actual or statutory damages. 17 U.S.C. § 401 (d). Thus, prudent copyright owners should include a copyright notice. Copyright notices are usually included in the software's documentation (which protects the documentation rather than the software), the label of the CD by which the software is distributed or the page from which the software can be downloaded in an app store, the software's initial or landing screen, and in the software's source code.

A copyright notice usually consists of three elements:

(1) the © symbol (or, if the character codes do not allow the use of the © character, then the word "Copyright");
(2) the first year of publication of the work and any subsequent years of publication; and
(3) the owner's name—XYZ Software Corporation.

For example: "Copyright 2025, 2026, XYZ Software Corporation. All rights reserved."

For an overview of software copyrights, see Bruno & Loganzo, *Software Copyrightability: Where We Are and What's to Come*, INTELL. PROP. & TECH. L. J. 1 (May 1, 2021); copyright protection for software see Buckman, *Copyright Protection of Computer Programs,* 180 A.L.R. FED. 1 (2002). For an overview of copyright infringement, *see* Hannay & Parkhurst, 47 LAW. BRIEF 1 (Mar 15, 2017 and Mar. 31, 2017); Copyright Infringement Basics, 183 INTELL. PROP. COUNS. 1 (Mar. 2012).

B. The First Sale Doctrine

1. In General

The theory of the First Sale Doctrine under the Copyright Act 17 U.S.C. § 101 *et seq.* is that an individual who *purchases* an authorized copy may use and resell that particular copy free of any restraint by the copyright owner. 17 U.S.C. § 109(a) (emphasis supplied). *See Bobbs Merrill Co. v. Straus,* 210 U.S. 339 (1908). A copyright owner's sale of an authorized copy "exhausts" the copyright owner's exclusive distribution and display rights, such that the purchaser may use, resell, or display that copy free of any claim of infringement. 17 U.S.C. § 109(a).[1] In short, the First Sale Doctrine addresses a *copy owner's rights* as opposed to the *copyright owner's* rights.

The First Sale Doctrine does not apply, however, to the separate exclusive rights of copying, derivative work preparation, and public display or performance. *See* 17 U.S.C. § 106 (which sets forth five separate and distinct rights). *See, e.g., Red Baron-Franklin Park, Inc. v. Taito Corp.,* 883 F.2d 275, 280 (4th Cir. 1989), and *Columbia Pictures Industries, Inc., v. Aveco, Inc.,* 800 F.2d 59, 64 (3d Cir. 1986). *See also* 17 U.S.C. § 109(e) (which, to legislatively overrule *Red Baron,* permits display of copyrighted video games in coin-operated equipment). The First Sale Doctrine only applies to the *copyright owner's* exclusive rights of distribution and display in its copyrighted work, which are "automatically" conveyed to the buyer or the copy owner upon sale. 17 U.S.C. § 109(a) and (c). The owner of a copyright embodying the copyright work receives only the right to display that physical copy where it is located. 17 U.S.C. § 109(a).

Section 106(3) provides that the copyright owner has the exclusive right to distribute and to authorize distribution of copies or phonorecords of the copyrighted

1. Section 109(a) codifies the First Sale Doctrine, which provides "Notwithstanding the provisions of Section 106(3), the owner of a particular copy or phonorecord lawfully made under this title, or any person authorized by such owner, is entitled, without the authority of the copyright owner, to sell or otherwise dispose of that copy or phonorecord."

work to the public by sale or other transfer of ownership or by rental, lease, or lending. Section 106(4) and (5) give the copyright owner the exclusive right to publicly perform or display a literary, musical, dramatic, or choreographic work or a pantomime, motion picture, or other audiovisual work. Section 106(6) gives the copyright owner the exclusive right to perform a sound recording work publicly by means of a digital audio transmission. To prove infringement, the copyright holder must demonstrate only that it possesses a valid copyright, that the copyrighted material was registered for copyright, and that there was unauthorized copying. The principal means of showing unauthorized copying is through access and substantial similarity. *Ford Motor Co. v. Summit Motor Products*, 930 F.2d 277, 290–91 (3d Cir. 1990) (copying is shorthand for violating any of the five exclusive rights of copyright owners).

The First Sale Doctrine acts as a defense to a claim of infringement. At least one court has held that the defense is available "only to copies legally made and sold in the United States" *Omega S.A., v. Costco Wholesale Corp.*, 541 F.3d 982, 986 (9th Cir. 2008), *aff'd per curium*, 562 U.S. 40 (2010) Interestingly, several courts have held that overseas purchases of software manufactured outside of the United States are not entitled to invoke the first sale defense, 17 U.S.C. § 109(a), to a claim of infringement. *Microsoft Corp. v. Big Boy Distribution, LLC*, 589 F. Supp. 2d 1308 (S.D. Fla. 2008); *Microsoft Corp. v. Intrax Group, Inc., d/b/a Surplus Computers*, 2008 WL 4500703 (N.D. Cal. Oct. 6, 2008) (rejecting first sale defense for software manufactured and licensed outside of U.S.); *Microsoft Corp. v. Software Wholesale Club, Inc.*, 129 F. Supp. 2d 995, 1006 (S.D. Tex. 2000) ("first sale doctrine does not apply to admittedly counterfeit unit").

Software developers, in order to avoid application of the First Sale Doctrine and retain control over redistribution of their programs, have typically distributed even mass-market software under license, rather than through an outright sale, to prevent the First Sale Doctrine from severing control over redistribution. *See Microsoft Corp. v. Software Wholesale Club, Inc.*, 129 F. Supp. 2d 995 (S.D. Tex. 2000) (first sale doctrine not applicable to licensed software); *Adobe Systems, Inc. v. One Stop Micro, Inc.*, 84 F. Supp. 2d 1086, 1089 (N.D. Cal. 2000) ("First sale doctrine is only triggered by an actual sale."); *Allen-Myland, Inc. v. Int'l. Business Mach. Corp.*, 746 F. Supp. 520 (E.D. Pa. 1990) (first sale doctrine does not apply to computer programs).

For computer software, Section 109(b) limits the First Sale Doctrine and the rights of copy owners in three ways. First, adaptations may not be transferred without permission of the copyright owner. This is true even under the First Sale Doctrine as there is no right to create derivative works. Second, under Section 117 the owner of a program may make an archival copy or an adaptation of the program if such adaptation is essential to the use of the original program by a computer, and that the creator of the copy may only transfer it as part of lease, sale, or other transfer of rights in the underlying program. Exact copies authorized to be made under Section 117 may be transferred without permission of the copyright owner only as part of a transfer of all rights in the underlying program. The distribution right conveyed to the buyer does not, for example, include the right to make further copies for resale.

Third, it provides that the owner of a copy of computer software cannot lend or rent that copy to third parties without permission from the copyright owner. *See Microsoft v. Harmony Computers & Electronics, Inc.*, 846 F. Supp. 208 (E.D.N.Y. 1994) (unauthorized distributor of a copy of software not entitled to protection under First Sale Doctrine because owner licensed not sold software to distributor's supplier); *Triad Systems Corp. v. Southeastern Express Co.*, 64 F.3d 1330 (9th Cir. 1995), *cert. denied*, 516 U.S. 1145 (1996) (software sold to customers is subject to 17 U.S.C. § 117 protection while copies that are licensed are not); and *Stenograph LLC v. Sims*, 2000 WL 964748, 55 U.S.P.O.2d 1436 (E.D. Pa. 2000) (first sale doctrine does not apply to gifts).

Known as the Computer Software Rental Amendments Act of 1990, Section 109(b) also addresses computer software rentals. It provides that, unless authorized by the owner of the copyright in a software program (including any tape, disk, or other medium embodying such program), no person in possession of a particular copy of a software program (including any tape, disk, or other medium embodying such program) may, for the purposes of direct or indirect commercial advantage, dispose of or authorize the disposal of the possession of that computer software (including any tape, disk, or other medium embodying such program) by rental, lease, or lending, or any similar act. Section 109(b) specifically excludes nonprofit libraries and nonprofit educational institutions from its prohibitions on renting, leasing, or lending copies of copyrighted software. In short, Section 109 prohibits the rental of a copy of a computer program by the owner of a copy without the permission of the licensor. 17 U.S.C. § 107. *See, generally, Central Point Software, Inc v. Global Software & Access, Inc.*, 880 F. Supp. 957 (E.D.N.Y. 1995).

Section 109(d) further limits the scope of application of the First Sale Doctrine by providing that, unless authorized by the copyright owner, the provisions of 17 U.S.C. §§ 109 (a) and (c) do not extend to any person who has acquired possession of the copy or phonorecord from the copyright owner, by rental, lease, loan, or otherwise, without also acquiring ownership of it.

For a general discussion, *see* Robins, *Anticipating the First Sale and Essential Step Doctrines in Software Licensing*, 30 COMPUTER & INTERNET LAW. 9 (Oct. 2013), and Carver, *Why License Agreements Do Not Control Copy Ownership: First Sales and Essential Copies*, 25 BERKELEY TECH L.J. 1887 (2010).

2. Applicability to Software

A software owner must consider how it will protect its software. It may be able to protect methods and processes by either trade secret or patent. Patents, however, require revealing the protected process to the public, while trade secret protection requires keeping it confidential. Thus, the same process cannot be protected by both methods although it possible to patent and copyright aspects of software while keeping other aspects a secret. The process for submitting source code to the U.S. Copyright Office affirmatively provides avenues for copyrighting software that includes trade secret elements within the software. *See US Copyright Office Circular 61: Copyright Registration of Computer Programs.* By writing the software, the owner receives copyright protection on the actual expression. This protection does not, however, prevent third parties from independently developing software that performs the same function.

When granting a license to a licensee, a vendor needs to consider what protections it has in the software, and what rights (or sticks in the bundle) it wishes to convey to the licensee. The scope of the license granted will govern the licensee's use. Only if the licensee exceeds the scope may the licensor seek damages or other remedies from a licensee under any intellectual property regimen. Thus, the license grant should be drafted broadly enough to permit use by the licensee, but narrowly enough to enable the intellectual property holder to use copyright, patent, or trade secret law to stop or prevent infringement by the licensee.

There is no uniform test for ascertaining whether a transaction is a sale or a license. In *Vernor v. Autodesk, Inc.*, 621 F.3d 1102 (9th Cir. 2010), the Ninth Circuit established a three-prong test to determine whether the user is an owner or licensee of the software:

[A] software user is a licensee rather than an owner of a copy where the copyright owner

1. *specifies that the user is granted a license;*
2. *significantly restricts the user's ability to transfer the software; and*
3. *imposes notable use restrictions.*

Id. at 1111. The first two prongs will usually be satisfied in any dispute, making the third prong the determinative issue. The *Vernor* court cited the governing agreement's restrictions on the transfer of the software and the retention of ownership by Autodesk. The agreement also contained prohibitions "against modifying, translating, or reverse-engineering the software, removing any proprietary marks from the software or documentation, or defeating any copy protection device." *Id.* Thus, it appears, at least in the Ninth Circuit, that language to this effect will satisfy the third prong and allow a court to find the existence of a license and not a sale.

In general, the label placed on the transaction by the parties is not determinative. "[I]n determining whether a transaction is a sale, a lease or a license, courts look to the economic realities of the exchange." *SoftMan Products Co., LLC v. Adobe Systems, Inc.*, 171 F. Supp. 2d 1075, 1084 (C.D. Cal. 2001). Courts will look to the nature of the transaction itself to reach a decision and will examine such factors as to whether the underlying agreement reserves title with the owner, transfers "limited rights," allows the "purchaser" to permanently retain possession for a single up-front payment or contains restrictions on any future transfers of the software, prohibits resale, or simply requires the payment of an additional fee. *UMG Recordings, Inc. v. Augusto*, 558 F. Supp.2d 1055 (C.D. Cal 2008) (permanent possession without further benefit to copyright owner indicative of sale). Restrictions on the number of users and the number of computers within the licensed entity are indicative of a license. Finally, a court will look to extrinsic evidence to reach a decision. *United States v. Wise*, 550 F.2d 1180 (9th Cir. 1977); *Adobe Systems Incorporated v. One Stop Micro., Inc.*, 84 F. Supp. 2d 1086 (N.D. Cal. 2000) (software licensed not sold despite use of terms "purchase," "owned" and "repurchase" in underlying agreement).

In *UMG*, the court found the software had been sold not licensed despite the copyright owners structuring the transactions as a license. In concluding the defendant had not misappropriated the owner's rights under copyright law, the court focused on the fact that the defendants had not made a copy of the copyrighted work prior to reselling their copies. Because the defendant had not made copies, the defendant was simply exercising its rights under the First Sale Doctrine to transfer the single copy in their possession.

For a discussion of several different types of intellectual property protections available for software, *see* Neelakantan & Armstrong, *Source Code, Object Code, and the Da Vinci Code: The Debate on Intellectual Property Protection for Software Programs,* 23 COMPUTER & INTERNET LAW 1 (Oct. 2006).

C. The Transfer of Intellectual Property Rights

In general, there are two means of conveying intellectual property rights: assignments and licenses. In an assignment, the property owner conveys all of the sticks in the owner's bundle, while in a license the property owner only transfers certain sticks, and retains the rest. Under copyright law, a license applies to *intangible* property rights while a "sale" applies to the transfer of *tangible* property. 17 U.S.C. § 202; *see also Chamberlain v. Cocola Assoc.*, 958 F.2d 282 (9th Cir. 1992).

The First Sale Doctrine, which applies to the sale of a tangible *copy* of software, provides that such sale conveys certain rights to the buyer in the purchased tangible copy of the software, namely the buyer's right to resell the software copy. 17 U.S.C. § 109(a). This right is in derogation of the overall copyright and it is also "automatically" transferred to a new buyer if the copy is resold. 17 U.S.C. § 117. Any transfer of ownership in a copyright must be through an unambiguous written agreement. *Davis v. Meridian Films, Inc.*, 2001 WL 758765 (4th Cir. July 5, 2001). Although 17 U.S.C. § 117 provides that any assignment must be in writing, the Fourth Circuit in *Metropolitan Regional Info. Sys. v. American Home Health Network,* 722 F.3d 591 (4th Cir. 2013), held that a copyright may be validly assigned via an electronic agreement.

Typically, the sale of software is not a "sale" of a copy (or anything else) within the meaning of Section 109. The only thing that is sold when software is "sold" at retail is the media on which the copyrighted work is fixed. Certain rights inherent in the work are licensed in conjunction with the sale. A copyright owner who grants a nonexclusive license to use copyrighted material generally waives the right to sue the licensee for a copyright infringement to the extent of the license granted. *Sun Microsystems, Inc. v. Microsoft Corp.*, 188 F.3d 1115 (9th Cir. 1999).

An assignment is an absolute conveyance of the intangible rights and equates to a "sale," with the caveat that a sale typically only conveys the absolute right of distribution and, subject to certain exceptions, the right to display and use. *MacLean Assoc., Inc. v. William M. Mercer-Meidinger-Hanson, Inc.*, 952 F.2d 769 (3d Cir. 1991). A "sale" does not include, for example, the rights of performance or preparation of derivative works rights.

Similar to an assignment, an exclusive license, even if limited in time or place of effect, can amount to a "transfer of copyright ownership." 17 U.S.C. § 201(d)(2). Under the Copyright Act, transfer of an exclusive license is considered to be a conveyance of copyright ownership to the extent granted in the license. 17 U.S.C. § 201(d)(2). In short, entering into a license agreement in which the licensor reserves title is not a "sale" for purposes of the Copyright Act. For example, a licensee cannot distribute the licensor's software without the licensor's authorization, because the licensor is still the owner of the intellectual property. *Relational Design & Technology, Inc. v. Brock*, 1993 WL 191323 (D. Kan. May 25, 1993).

See Chapter 4.H for a more detailed discussion.

CHAPTER **4**

Terminology of a License Grant (§ 3.1)

Unless otherwise indicated, all section references (§) refer to the corresponding sections of the Annotated Software License and Services Agreement set forth in Form B.3.1.

A typical grant of a license favoring the licensor is as follows:

> *Subject to the provisions of this Agreement, Licensor grants to Licensee a perpetual, personal, non-assignable, non-transferable, nonexclusive object code license to use the Software solely for Licensee's internal business purposes in the United States.*

Savvy licensees often seek a broader license grant that tracks the language of 35 U.S.C. § 271(a):

> *Licensor hereby grants to Licensee a non-exclusive, royalty-free, transferable, irrevocable, perpetual, worldwide, fully paid-up license (with rights to sublicense through multiple tiers of sublicensees) to fully use, practice and exploit those non-assignable rights, title and interest, including, but not limited to, the right to make, use, sell, offer for sale, import, have made, and have sold, the Software.*

Each of the terms set forth in the above license grants have a specific meaning that fundamentally impacts the rights of the licensor and licensee. Set forth below is a discussion of these terms.

The language of the license grant should reflect the licensee's intended use of the software. For example, the licensee may seek a license: (i) for its internal use on behalf of itself; (ii) for use by the licensee on behalf of its customers; or (iii) for use by the licensee in a cloud environment. Each of these uses requires specific language in the license grant to provide the licensee the rights necessary to achieve its needs.

> *Subject to the terms and conditions of this Agreement, Licensor grants to Customer a non-exclusive and non-transferable license to use the Licensed Software in the territory during the Term of this Agreement, subject to the following limitations:*
>
> (a) *Customer shall use the Licensed Software for its internal purposes only. In no event shall the Licensed Software be disclosed, made available to or used for the benefit of any third-party; sold, assigned, leased or otherwise disposed of; or commercially exploited or marketed in any way, with or without charge, by Customer or any of Customer's employees or agents;*
>
> (b) *The license granted hereunder shall be limited to the number of concurrent users as specificized in the Products/Pricing Schedule and for which the appropriate license fees have*

been paid. The total number of users accessing the Licensed Software at any given time may not exceed the total number of concurrent users licensed for the applicable Licensed Software.

Licensees who plan to utilize the licensed software to provide services to their own customers should carefully consider the terms of the license grant to distinguish between the right to use the software on the licensee's clients' behalf and the right to sublicense the software to the licensee's clients. This distinction usually arises through the licensee's provision of outsourcing services, hosting services, and cloud services.

Most licensors include a statement to make it clear that the licensee's rights are limited to those expressly stated in the license grant and that the licensee is not receiving any implied rights.

Except for the rights expressly granted herein, Licensor does not grant, license or transfer to Licensee or other third party any ownership or other rights to the Software. No implied licenses are granted herein and all rights not expressly granted to Licensee herein are reserved by Licensor.

See Chapter 14 for a more detailed discussion of license grants for use in cloud computing and Chapter 20 for license agreements related to resellers.

A. Important Definitions

The use of "Definitions" is an accepted means of defining terms that will be used throughout the agreement to ensure the parties have agreement on the meaning of the defined terms. The definitions should not be limited to defining the particular term and should not include any contractual obligations or provisions or the defined term. Further, the definition of the defined term should not include the term itself.

Prudent parties should carefully review and understanding the implications of how a particular term is defined, as the definition can have a significant impact on the parties' obligations. *See e.g., Cellport Systems, Inc. V. Peiker Acustic GmbH & Co. KG*, 762 F.3d 1016 (10th Cir. 2014) (Expansive definition of "Licensed Products" allows patent holder to recover royalties on products not covered by its patents).

Most agreements set forth the definitions at the beginning of the agreement or in an attachment to the agreement. See e.g., Form B.3.1.

1. *"Licensor"*

The definition of "Licensor" is important from the licensee's perspective, as the licensee needs to ensure that the licensor has the financial ability to deliver the software/services contracted for and, in the event of a breach, the ability to pay for any damages. If the "Licensor" is a subsidiary and lacks the significant assets of its parent, the licensee may seek to have the licensor's parent guaranty the financial performance of the subsidiary. See the Heading and Signature line of Form B.3.1, and Form O.1 for a model guaranty.

The licensee should also ensure that the entity granting any applicable license actually owns the underlying intellectual property or has the right to grant a license, and that ownership of the intellectual property is not held by the granting entity's parent, thus preventing a valid license from being granted.

Some licensors prefer to license their software through resellers who often disclaim all warranties and indemnities. Since the licensee is not in contractual privity with the licensor, the licensee has few remedies if there is an issue with the software. Licensees should require that resellers either provide appropriate remedies or pass them through from the licensor or seek to be a third-party beneficiary to the licensor-reseller agreement.

2. *"Licensee"*

The definition of "Licensee" is important for both financial and legal reasons. Defining "Licensee" to include its affiliates and subsidiaries may allow such entities to utilize the software under the license grant or even be considered licensees, while under a master agreement their inclusion in the definition of "Licensee" will allow them to purchase their own licenses under the agreement.

See Section 4.A.4 below for a discussion of affiliates and subsidiaries purchasing licenses under a master agreement.

Financially, the broader the definition of the "Licensee," the greater the number of entities or individuals who will have access to and use of the licensed software, potentially negatively impacting the potential license fees a licensor may receive based on the pricing mechanism while imposing upon the licensor additional obligations and potential liabilities. A narrow definition potentially acts to restrict the licensee's use of the software, including preventing third parties, potentially the licensor's competitors, from accessing the software.

By defining "Licensee" to include the licensee's affiliates or subsidiaries, the affiliates and subsidiaries may utilize the licensed software as well as the parent. *See* § 1.4. From the licensor's perspective, it is important that the license distinguish between allowing a subsidiary or affiliate to utilize the software *and* granting a subsidiary or affiliate a right to use the software. To the extent the affiliates are authorized to utilize the software, the licensor should ensure that the license grant does not grant licenses to affiliates, only a right to use. Granting each affiliate a license creates obligations on the licensor's behalf to numerous entities when the intent was to grant a single license to the parent.

In formulating the definition of "Licensee," the licensee should consider its potential future needs and ensure that the definition is broad enough to encompass its needs. The licensee should consider not only the acquisition or divestiture of a business unit but also the outsourcing of certain functions, the retention of third-party consultants, the need to relocate its businesses, the need for third-party entities such as joint ventures and strategic alliance partners to access the software, as well as the need for its customers to access or use the software.

A licensee can seek access to the software by its third-party consultants by including third-party consultants in the license grant or by including third-party consultants in the definition of "Licensee." The licensee may have a better chance of having the licensor accept access by third-party consultants if it includes them in the definition of "Licensee," rather than granting them use rights in the license grant. Courts will read the license provisions governing third party access and use strictly; thus, the licensee must ensure it is explicitly granted the usage rights it requires. *See, e.g., The Compliance Source Inc. v. GreenPoint Mortgage Funding, Inc.*, 624 F.3d 252 (5th Cir. 2010) (use of licensed software by lawyers acting on behalf of licensee breached license agreement). *Geoscan, Inc. v. Geotrace Technologies Inc.*, 226 F.3d 387 (5th Cir. 2000) (third-party access to licensed software did not violate license terms as license provided that software may be used by third parties "by and on behalf of licensee"); *Hogan Systems, Inc. v. Cybresource Int'l, Inc.*, 158 F.3d 319 (5th Cir. 1998) (licensee did not breach license by providing third party access to the software as license allowed access and use by other persons during the period such other persons who are on licensee's premises for purposes specifically relating to licensee's authorized use of the software.) See Form B.6.1 § 2.1 for an example of a license grant allowing third-party consultants to access the software.

The licensee's greatest negotiating leverage is at the time of contract signature. Once the license has been signed, the licensor will have little incentive other than a financial incentive to expand the scope of the license. If the licensee's enterprise is to be included in the license, and the license fee is paid at the start of the license, the licensor will need to consider the potential impact if the licensee either acquires or is acquired by a large corporation. If the licensor is concerned about the possible lost sales opportunity involved in such an acquisition, the licensor should seek to exclude a potential purchaser from the definition of "Licensee" as outside the scope of the license. This position protects the licensor in the event a large corporation acquires or is acquired by the licensee and permits the licensor to price the enterprise license in accordance with the licensee's size. However, normal growth of the licensee's business can be included in the scope of the license and the licensor's pricing established accordingly. If the license fee is annual and based upon the number of seats or concurrent users, or another volume-based measure that will increase in the event of an acquisition, the licensor may not need to seek an exclusion.

Drafting a broad definition of "Licensee" to include affiliates can create a privity issue as to the licensee's ability to bind the affiliate to the terms of the license. If the licensee lacks such authority, the licensor should create a mechanism by which the "affiliate" acknowledges that it is bound by the terms of the license. The licensor will want to have the licensee guaranty the performance of the affiliate. Further, if the license is a global license, tax issues may arise from foreign affiliates' license payments to the licensor.

The parties must also consider the ramifications, if any, of United States export laws. If a licensee and its affiliates are granted simultaneous use of the licensed software, or the licensee has the unencumbered right to assign the license, and/or use is not restricted to the United States, the licensee's or its affiliates' use of the software outside of the United States may violate U.S. export laws if the appropriate export licenses have not been obtained. Furthermore, the laws of a foreign jurisdiction with which the licensor is unfamiliar, and which may not afford the licensor the same benefits and protections as the laws of the United States, may govern use of the licensed software outside of the United States.

International licenses require the licensor to consider a number of additional issues, such as U.S. export laws (see Chapter 7.L, § 43), import duties and taxes (Chapter 7.L.7), payments, and intellectual property indemnification, as well as moral rights (Chapter 7.A.1 and Form C.3.3 § 8). Additionally, local counsel should be consulted in each jurisdiction to verify that the license complies with and is enforceable under local law. See Chapter 26.E for a more detailed discussion.

Additionally, the licensor should consider the implications of permitting affiliates and/or third parties to use the software in the event of any dispute related to the software. In the event of a dispute related to the software, the licensor could be sued by each of these parties separately, each asserting that they are third party beneficiaries of the license agreement. The licensor should consider including an express statement that there are no third-party beneficiaries to the agreement. In the event that the licensor permits affiliates to be third-party beneficiaries, the licensor should include terms requiring the licensee to consolidate all suits by affiliates. See Chapter 6.K for a more detailed discussion of third-party beneficiaries.

3. *"Affiliates" (§1.2)*

Many license agreements either define "Affiliates" and "Subsidiaries" as entities at least 51 percent owned by a party or, alternatively, as those entities controlled by or controlling a party similar to the definition used in securities transactions. *See* § 1.4.A. Using the concept of "control" allows the licensee flexibility in operating its business and reflects the reality that companies are often continually acquiring or divesting business units. A third, more conservative approach is to specifically identify in an appendix the licensee's affiliates and subsidiaries that are authorized to use the software or purchase under the parties' agreement. From the licensor's perspective, this approach provides certainty and limits a court's ability to possibly interpret "affiliate" in an unintended manner. *See PWP Xerion Holdings III LLC v. Red Leaf Resources, Inc.*, 2019 WL 5424778 (Del. Ch. Oct. 23, 2019) (officers and directors can be considered an "affiliate.")

Licensors should be careful to limit the definition of "Affiliates" and "Subsidiaries" to those affiliates and subsidiaries in existence at the time the license agreement is executed and only for as long as they continue to be 51 percent or more owned by the licensee or under the control of the licensee. Otherwise, the licensor runs the risk that the subsidiaries and affiliates acquired after the execution, or even the expiration, of the license agreement may be covered under the license as well as those that are divested during the term. From the vendor's perspective, divested entities can be problematic especially if they are acquired by a competitor. *See, e.g., Imation Corp. v. Koninklijke Philips Electronics N.V.*, 586 F.3d 980 (Fed. Cir. 2009) (license extends to subsidiaries acquired after expiration of license agreement); *but see Ellington v. EMI Music, Inc.*, 24 N.Y.3d 239 (2014) (absent express language to the contrary, "affiliates" in an agreement only refers to affiliates in existence at the time the agreement was executed); *nQueue v. Control Systems (USA)*, CV 12-01365 BRO (RNBx) (C.D. Cal. Nov. 27, 2013). *See also* Singer, *Defining Affiliate: Pay Attention to the "Boilerplate,"* 35 LICENSING J. 1 (Feb. 2015).

It is important to note that from the licensor's perspective, to avoid potentially having multiple licensees, the license grant should provide that affiliates who purchase licenses under another party's license agreement, are "users" of the software, not individual licensees.

Many vendors will allow affiliates to use the licensed software/services but will not permit affiliates to be licensees, which would grant them additional rights and remedies under the underlying agreement. From the customer's perspective, many practitioners recommend against allowing affiliates to purchase under an agreement as the agreement usually provides that the customer/contracting party is responsible for the actions of its affiliates, creating potential liability on the customer's behalf. Further, by including "affiliates" the affiliates may become liable for the actions of the parent and vice versa. In the event of a breach each affiliate can proceed against the vendor individually, each with a separate of limit of liability and must the vendor pursue each affiliate separately in the event they breach the agreement. Further, does the parent have the authority to sign an agreement on behalf of each affiliate?

Many vendors avoid the issue of authority by requiring affiliates to purchase through the parent such that the parent is responsible for the actions of its affiliates. Conversely, some parents include language in the master agreement stating that the vendor will look solely to the affiliate if the affiliates breaches the agreement.

Regardless of the definitional approach taken, the licensor should contractually require the licensee to assume financial responsibility for the acts of the licensee's subsidiaries and affiliates or at least to be jointly and severally liable. In many cases, licensees seek the right for their affiliates to license/purchase under the agreement but do not want to assume responsibility for any breaches arising from the acts of their affiliates. Given that a parent can, in most cases, control the actions of its affiliates, the parent should assume responsibility for its affiliates. Unless a plaintiff is able to pierce the corporate veil, a parent corporation is not liable for any act or breach by its subsidiary. *Dow Jones v. Ablaise*, 606 F.3d. 1338 (Fed. Cir. 2010). The following language illustrates the concept of holding the parent liable for the actions of its affiliates.

> *The benefits, obligations and privileges of the Agreement shall extend to all entities that constitute "Customer," including all Affiliates, even though each such entity is not specifically named as a party to the Agreement. As such,* ***the undersigned customer and its successors and assigns will be and remain liable for all of the obligations of all entities that constitute "Customer" under the Agreement, including all Affiliates, and Vendor will look to the undersigned Customer and its successors and assigns for enforcement of Vendor's rights under the Agreement.***

> *For purposes of the Agreement, "Affiliate" means each legal entity that is directly or indirectly controlled by the undersigned customer* ***on or after the Effective Date and for so long as such entity remains directly or indirectly controlled by the undersigned customer*** *(where "controlled" means the ownership of, or the power to vote, directly or indirectly, a majority of any class of voting securities of a corporation or limited liability company, or the ownership of any general partnership interest in any general or limited partnership),* ***excluding any entity that is a party to a written agreement with Vendor for the same Software that is the subject of the Agreement.***

Some practitioners argue against having a party's affiliates being parties to the agreement. For example, *Chelsea Pharmaceuticals, Inc. together with its Affiliates, (collectively "Company")*. Doing so creates many potential issues including:

- Does the parent have the authority to execute the agreement on behalf of its affiliates?
- Does the agreement include signature lines for each affiliate to indicate they agree to be bound by the terms of the agreement?
- How is any potential liability apportioned among the various affiliates and the parent, is there joint and several liability?
- Is the agreement enforceable against those affiliates outside the jurisdiction in which the agreement is signed?
- Do the representations and warranties flow from all of the affiliates to the counter-party?
- Does the limitation of liability apply to all affiliates in the aggregate or is each affiliate liable for the limitation of liability?

One means to avoid these issues is to allow affiliates to order under the agreement with the parent fully liable for any breach by its affiliates.

4. "Software"

The definition of "Software" usually references a specific product and version. It should also state that the term "Software" includes all updates etc to make it clear that any such updates are licensed to the licensee subject to the term of the license grant. . This wording protects both parties, as the licensor wants to ensure that any enhancements are protected by the license terms and the licensee wants to ensure it receives all enhancements and updates.

"***Licensed Software***" *means the applications and tools as set forth more specifically in Exhibit A together with Upgrades and Updates.*

5. "User"

The definition of "User" or "Authorized User" is perhaps the most important term in the agreement as determines who may "use" the software or services.

Prudent customers should contemplate who will need to use the software and services, not only now, but also in the future. This is especially important in a post-COVID world where a significant portion of the work force is working remotely but many customers failed to anticipate that their use needs would morph from on premise use in their offices to distributed use in their employees remote work locations.

From the customer's perspective, at a minimum, "users" should include employees, consultants, contractors and customers. Many vendors will push back on the inclusion of contractors as they want to avoid allowing potential competitors access to their trade secrets/software, potentially depriving the vendor of providing maintenance and support services to its customers. Which are very profitable. Vendors can limit the potential impact by limiting how contractors may access the software, i.e., to perform a particular function in a particular location.

The failure to anticipate and ensure the customer obtains the rights it needs can have a significant operational and financial impact on its business. *See SAP U.K. Limited v. Diageo Great Britain Ltd.*, [2017] EWHC 189 (TCC) Case No. HT-2015-000340. To avoid ambiguity, product licensors should affirmatively state those actions a licensee is prohibited from undertaking such as:

- Using the software to provide services to its own customers
- Allowing the licensee's customers to access the software's functionality; and
- Using the software to process third party data

> ***"User"*** *means any* ***individual natural human being*** *(a) who is an active employee, consultant, contractor or agent of Customer, (b) who is authorized by Customer to use the Software solely on behalf of Customer for Customer's internal business purposes, (c) whom Customer has designated as a User of the Software in accordance with Section ___ (Users) and (d) to whom Customer has supplied a single-user (i.e., named user) log-in account, user ID and password for the Software.*

Many vendors utilize a license grant that mirrors the language of the Copyright Act:

> *Vendor hereby grants to Customer an exclusive, royalty-free, transferable, irrevocable, perpetual, worldwide, fully paid-up license (with rights to sublicense through multiple tiers of sublicensees) to fully use, practice and exploit those non-assignable rights, title and interest, including, but not limited to, the right to make, use, sell, offer for sale, import, have made, and have sold, the Created Materials.*

B. Term of the License (§ 4.2)

1. Overview

The term of the license should begin on delivery of the licensed software, rather than acceptance of the licensed software, to avoid any uncertainties regarding the licensee's obligations or restrictions as to the use of the software prior to acceptance. While many licensees are concerned with the concept of the license beginning upon delivery, the license should clearly state that although the license may begin to protect the licensor's interests upon delivery, acceptance of the software or an obligation of the licensee to pay for the license does not occur until the licensee accepts the licensed software. For the licensee, this issue takes added importance if the term is for a set period of years rather than a perpetual license.

While shrink-wrapped software licenses traditionally have had a perpetual term, historically other software licenses often have a more limited term, such as 5 or 10 years. Today, the distinction is less important, as most software is obsolete within 10 years, and licensors routinely grant perpetual licenses in recognition of the rapid obsolescence of software in general. *But see Apple Computer, Inc. v. Microsoft Corp.*, 35 F.3d 1435 (9th Cir. 1994) (in 1985, Apple granted, in effect, a perpetual license of its Windows visual displays to Microsoft). The term of the license is often linked to price, with the licensor's pricing model closely aligned to the "value proposition" of the software. Some lawyers, however, are hesitant to enter into perpetual licenses in the belief they are unenforceable and instead insist on a 99-year license term. *See generally* NIMMER, LAW OF COMPUTER TECHNOLOGY §§ 7:94–7:98 (2005). Use of the software beyond the term of the license constitutes copyright infringement. *Clinical Insight v. Louisville Cardiology Med. Group*, 2013 WL 3713414 (W.D.N.Y. July 12, 2013).

Interestingly, at least one court, applying New York law, has voided a software license and exclusive distribution agreement as violating the Rule against Perpetuities. *McAllister Software Systems, Inc. v. Henry Schein, Inc.*, 2008 WL 922328 (E.D. Mo. April 2, 2008); *but see Ultracts, Ltd. v. Wal-Mart Stores, Inc.*, 16 S.W.3d 265, 270 (Ark. Ct. App. 2000).

Finally, it is important to remember that the term of the license is separate and distinct from the term of the license agreement and they are not always co-terminus.

2. A Fixed Term

Many licenses provide for a specific term, for example 5 years. Licensees should avoid entering into a license for a fixed term unless they are certain they will not need to use the software after the license terminates. Otherwise, the licensor will have a significant advantage in negotiating a license extension as it knows the licensee needs to continue using the software and the licensee's only alternative is to migrate to anew software product which likely involves significant time and expense.

From the licensee's perspective, one alternative is to negotiate several option periods (i.e., several 5 year extensions) which the licensee can exercise at its option. The pricing for the option periods should be established at the time of contract signature to limit the licensor's leverage and avoid the licensor quoting an unreasonable price.

3. Perpetual and Irrevocable Licenses

Licensors should carefully consider the use of terms such as "perpetual" and "irrevocable" in the license grant as the licensor will likely want the right to terminate the license upon the licensee's breach of the license terms or breach of the agreement by the licensee. "Perpetual" licenses refer to the passage of time and are generally interpreted as "of indefinite duration." While an irrevocable license cannot be terminated, depending on the language of the agreement/license grant, a perpetual license may be terminated.

Prudent licensors should seek to avoid any dispute over the interpretation of these terms and whether these terms will prevail over any implied right to terminate the agreement upon the licensee's breach by carefully tailoring the language of the license grant. *See Nano-Proprietary, Inc. v. Canon, Inc.*, 537 F.3d 394, 400-01 (5th Cir. 2008) (An irrevocable and perpetual license "could not be terminated, notwithstanding a material breach of the agreement [because] [o]therwise the terms 'irrevocable' and 'perpetual' would be rendered superfluous in contravention of established rules of contract interpretation."). Licensors should preface the license grant with the phrase "*Subject to the terms of this Agreement, Licensor grants Licensee . . .* ." This phrase clarifies any potential ambiguity as to the ability of the licensor to terminate the license. Further, the licensor should also include a definitive statement that any license grant may be terminated in the event of the licensee's breach of the license or contract.

From the licensee's perspective, if the licensee wants to prevent the license from being terminated, it should seek to include "non-terminable" or "irrevocable" in the license grant and include the license grant in the survival clause or otherwise provide that the license grant survives the termination of the agreement for any reason. Doing so will also likely limit the licensor's remedy to monetary damages.

A perpetual license, however, does not infer that the licensee will receive unlimited maintenance, support or updates or that the licensor will continue to maintain and support the software. *See Software AG, Inc. v. Consist Software Solutions, Inc.*, 2008 WL 563449 (S.D.N.Y. Feb. 21, 2008). The licensor also may terminate any support or other services the licensor provides the licensee without terminating the license if the licensee fails to pay for such services or otherwise breaches its contractual obligations.

Perpetual licenses allow a licensee to use only those versions of the software created prior to the termination of the license. *Gene Codes Forensics Inc. v. The City of New York*, 2012 WL 1506166 (S.D.N.Y. Apr. 26, 2012) (licensor had no obligation to provide software upgrades after termination of the license). For a more detailed discussion, see Chapter 4.G.

4. *Evergreen (Autorenewal) Term*

Some licensors seek to include language in their licenses providing that the license/agreement will automatically renew for an additional period of years unless the licensee provides the licensor 60 or 90 days' written notice prior to the expiration of the then existing term. If the licensee fails to do so, the license automatically renews for an additional term. Occasionally, licensors will provide that notice of termination cannot be provided more than 90 days prior to the expiration of the existing term and not less than 60 days, creating a very short window in which the licensee may terminate the license/agreement.

Prudent licensees should think carefully before agreeing to accept an "evergreen" provision in their licenses and ask why an evergreen provision is necessary/how it benefits the customer. At a minimum, the licensor should be required to provide the licensee notice of the upcoming renewal and provide an easy and convenient method to cancel the renewal. If a licensee accepts an evergreen provision, it should implement a calendaring system to automatically notify the licensee of the window in which it may terminate the license.

Licensors should be aware that many states regulate the use of evergreen clauses, especially in consumer transactions. For example, New York's statute prohibits the automatic renewal of a contract for services, maintenances, or repair to or for any real or personal property unless the service provider gives prior written notice of the automatic renewal to the customer personally or via certified mail. At least one court has found that the New York statute applies to intellectual property services agreements. *See Aimee Mann* v. *MediaNet Digital, Inc.*, 2013 WL 12141398 (C.D.C.A. Nov. 27, 2013). *See also* N.Y. Gen. Oblio Law, § 5-903(2); *Ovitz v. Bloomberg*, 77 A.D.3d 515, 516 (1st Dep't. 2010), *aff'd*, 18 N.Y.3d 753 (2012).

For a 50-state survey of state evergreen laws, see https://www.faegrebd.com/webfiles/50-State%20Survey%20Automatic%20Renewal%20Laws.pdf.

5. *The Failure to State a Term*

Generally, if the license for a copyrighted work that is not a work made for hire fails to state a term or contains a term of greater than 35 years, the license will be terminable after 35 years from execution under the Copyright Act, unless state law provides for the license to be terminable in less than 35 years, in which case state law would apply. 17 U.S.C. § 203 (There is a split between the Ninth Circuit with *Rano v. Sipa Press*, 987 F.2d 580 (9th Cir. 1993) on the one hand and the Seventh and Eleventh Circuits on the other with *Walthal v. Rusk*, 172 F.3d 481 (7th Cir. 1999) and *Korman v. HBC Florida, Inc.*, 182 F.3d 1291, 1294–95 (11th Cir. 1999) concerning whether the 35-year provision of Section 203 preempts state law and is therefore a minimum term for contracts). Most commentators, including Nimmer, think *Rano* is wrongly decided. See 3 Melville B. Nimmer & David Nimmer, Nimmer on Copyright § 11.01 [B] at 11-4–11-9 (2005) and § 10.10[F] at 10-98 (1998) ("Where an assignment or license does not expressly prescribe the period or term of its duration, it will generally be construed (in the absence of evidence of a contrary intent) to be effective for the duration of the then existing copyright term of the work"). *Accord P.C. Films Corp. v. MGM/VA Home Videos, Inc.*, 138 F.3d 453 (2d Cir. 1998); 2 Howard Abrams, The Law of Copyright § 13.15 at 13–59 n.28 (2004).

After the 35-year period expires, the license is terminable at will by the author for a period of five years. 17 U.S.C. § 203(3). The licensor must give the licensee, however, advance written notice of at least two but not more than 10 years before such termination. 17 U.S.C. § 203(a)(4)(A). Material breach of the license will also give rise to a right of rescission, which allows the non-breaching party to terminate the license. *Costello Publishing Co. v. Potell*, 670 F.2d 1035 (D.C. Cir. 1981); 3 Melville B. Nimmer & David Nimmer, Nimmer on Copyright § 10.15[A] at 10-118-10-120 (2005). If the license is not terminated, it will continue in effect for the remaining term of the copyright protecting the licensed software. (17 U.S.C. § 203(b)(6)). Assuming it is an anonymous work or work made for hire, the term of the copyright will be either 95 years from the date of the software's first publication or 120 years from the date of the software's creation, whichever expires first. 17 U.S.C. § 302(c). Under § 2-309 of the Uniform Commercial Code (UCC), however, a contract (license) without a fixed term is valid for a reasonable time and unless otherwise agreed is terminable at will. See Chapter 15.A for a discussion of the applicability of the UCC to software licensing.

C. Use (§ 3.1)

1. General

Most licensors place restrictions on the licensee as to how the licensed software may be used. Except in the case of open-source software, the principal reason is financial, causing most restrictions to be strictly an element of price. A licensor may have other, nonfinancial business motives; it may want to restrict the license agreement in the event the licensee is a competitor, or the licensor is concerned that the licensee may later be acquired by another company.

To avoid problems of interpretation, the parties should always define "use." *See, e.g.*, § 1.17. Parties who fail to define "use" often later have different interpretations of what it means to "use" the software. *See, e.g., S&H Computer Systems, Inc. v. SAS Institute, Inc.*, 568 F. Supp. 416, 421 (D. Tenn. 1983) (the meaning of "use" as contemplated by the computer industry (i.e., execute a program) differs from its "normal meaning"); *Kennedy v. Nat'l Juvenile Detention Association*, 187 F.3d 690, 694-95 (7th Cir. 1999) ("use" as used in applicable consulting agreement included the right to creative derivative works; dissent: "use" as used in applicable consulting agreement was ambiguous, as the license agreement utilized statutory language of the Copyright Act, i.e., right to reproduce and publish).

By tracking the statutory language of the Copyright Act in defining "use," the licensor will likely avoid the types of disputes set forth in *S&H Computer Systems* and *Kennedy*. The following definition when used with the grant of an object code license (with the right to use source in the event of a triggering event) protects the licensor's interest by clearly delineating the licensee's rights:

> *"'Use" shall mean the ability to use, load, run, execute, store, transmit, display, copy, maintain, duplicate, and distribute internally the Licensed Software in its Object Code form. In the event that the Source Code for the Licensed Software is released from escrow, then "Use" shall also mean the right to modify, enhance, create derivative works, make and have made copies of the Licensed Software.*

For a web-based application, the definition might be amended as follows:

> *"'Use" shall mean the ability to access, run, execute, and display the Remote Software.*

In drafting the language of the license grant, the licensor and licensee should undertake a three-step process to ensure such language meets their needs. First, the parties should consider the fundamental rights a copyright owner is granted: (1) to reproduce the copyrighted work, (2) to prepare derivative works, and (3) to distribute copies of the derivative work. 17 U.S.C. § 106; *Kennedy*, 187 F.3d at 694. Second, they should consider whether there are any rights that are unique to the system such as "access" for a website. Finally, they should consider whether they need to include any industry-specific language such as the right to "create with," in the case with tools.

A corresponding license grant is as follows:

> *Licensor grants to Licensee a transferable, nonexclusive right to Use the Licensed Software during the Term and any renewal period.*

The licensor should ensure that license restrictions are part of the license grant rather than separate covenants in the agreement. While the breach of a separate covenant is still a breach of contract, such a breach will not constitute a violation of the scope of the license sufficient to support injunctive relief for copyright infringement. *Sun Microsystems, Inc. v. Microsoft Corp.*, 81 F. Supp. 2d 1026, 1031 (N.D. Cal. 2001).

To avoid disputes over the scope of use, the licensee should consider future potential changes in its business requirements or those of its customer, as well as the need for third party consultants and its customers, for access to the software. *See, e.g., SMC Promotions, Inc. v. SMC Promotions, et al.*, 355 F. Supp. 1127, 1132 (C.D. Cal. 2005) (limited license allowing wholesaler's retail customers to download copyrighted product images was not broad enough to encompass wholesaler's practice of engaging a third party vendor to download images). The licensee should also establish an audit mechanism to track the terms and limitations of the license agreement to ensure the licensee's compliance with the license terms. See Chapter 23 for a more detailed discussion of software use audits.

At the same time, licensors should include specific prohibitions to ensure that the licensee's permitted uses are clearly defined. For example, licensors may want to specifically prohibit use of the software for third-party data processing, service bureaus, outsourcing, etc.

2. *Scope of Use*

Other common limitations include limiting use of the software to a particular central processing unit (CPU), to one class or brand of computer only, to a specific geographic site (§§ 8.B, 8.C), to a specific number of seats or concurrent users, or to a specific time period. This allows the licensor to charge the licensee a fee if the licensee expands or changes its use of the software. *See Equinox Software Sys., Inc. v. Airgas, Inc.*, 1996 WL 278841 (E.D. Pa. May 23, 1996) (soft copies made in violation of license restricting use on a particular CPU constituted copyright infringement); *Apple, Inc. v. Psystar Corp.*, 673 F. Supp. 2d 931 (N.D. Cal. 2009) (use of software on computers not manufactured by copyright owner constituted copyright infringement). CPU licenses are increasingly less common as software is licensed to an entity/licensor, not a particular machine. Many licensors are moving to subscription-based licenses because they provide for an annual license fee for the life of the software. Some licensees prefer this model, even though they may pay more in the long run, because it reduces the up-front cost associated with licensing the software. Further, a licensee should carefully consider any limitation on the license it receives. It must contemplate future needs to avoid limiting itself in the future as a court will likely strictly enforce any agreed to license terms. *See, e.g., McRoberts Software, Inc. v. Media 100, Inc.*, 329 F.3d 557 (7th Cir. 2003) (license limited licensee's use of copyrighted software to Macintosh software and licensee exceeded the scope of license by distributing of source code in Windows hardware).

A smart licensee will seek to ensure the license provides a reasonable degree of flexibility as the licensee's needs change. It should seek to anticipate its potential needs and bargain for them at the time the license is entered into. Once the license is executed, the licensee's bargaining power often dissipates. For a discussion of site licenses, *see Software Site Licensing Overview*, 229 COM. L. ADV. 1 (Jan. 2007).

In *Wall Data, Inc. v. Los Angeles County Sheriff's Dept.*, 447 F.3d 769 (9th Cir. 2006), the Ninth Circuit Court of Appeals found that a licensee who purchased 3,663 licenses but installed the software on 6,007 computers was in breach of the license even though it had configured its computers to limit the total number of users that could access the software to the number of licenses the licensee had purchased. In essence, the court held that the mere presence of a software copy on a computer is an infringement even though the software is not accessible to a user.

The decision emphasizes the importance of clearly defining "use" and "seats." In entering into a license, the licensee should clearly understand whether the number of purchased licenses limits the number of users who can access the software concurrently at the same time or the number of users authorized to access the system during the license term.

The *Wall Data* case was also interesting because the court excluded evidence that the licensee's purchase agreement with the software reseller may have allowed such use because the copyright owner was unaware of the reseller's license terms with the licensee. *Id.* at 782-83. This decision creates significant concern for any company that purchases its software through a reseller. For a more detailed discussion, *see Sheriffs' Over-Installation of Licensed Software Was Copyright Infringement, Despite Limited Access or Use of Software*, 23 COMPUTER & INTERNET LAW. 24 (Aug. 2006). Similarly, in *Thoroughbred Software, Int'l v. Dice Corp., et al.*, the court found a software distributor liable for all unpaid license fees for all unauthorized copies made even though some copies were not accessible to or used by its customers. 488 F.3d 352 (6th Cir. 2007).

One exception is the licensee's right to make one backup or archival copy or transfer the software to an alternative backup site for a limited period of time (60-90 days) in the case of a catastrophic failure (§ 20). Some licensors also allow the backup or archival copy to be used at a remote source for disaster recovery and disaster recovery training. Often licensors seek to limit the licensee to a single backup copy for archival purposes. Section 117 of the Copyright Act, which applies only to copy owners (and not licensees), grants the purchaser of a copy of software the right to make archival copies and adapt the software to operate on its computer. This position may be viewed as overly pro-licensor, which may create unnecessary friction with the potential licensee. A more balanced approach takes into account the legitimate needs of the licensee without negatively impacting pricing or the licensor's need for intellectual property protection, ensuring the greater likelihood of entering into an agreement. Note, however, that if the licensee is not a purchaser of the software, such copying may constitute copyright infringement. *See DSC Communications Corp. v. DGI Technologies, Inc.*, 81 F.3d 597 (5th Cir. 1996) (downloading software to hard disk by licensee for compatibility modifications was infringement where licensee had not purchased software).

Some licensors base their license fee on the application involved, while other licensors restrict the number of users who can access their software at any one time. This type of restriction is common in a client-server network environment. If the licensee's use is tied to a set number of users, the parties should clearly describe how those users will be calculated. For example, is use restricted by seats (users who may access the software, concurrent users, or some other means of measurement)? The failure to clearly define usage can lead to litigation. *See Accusoft Corporation v. Quest Diagnostics Inc. and Medplus, Inc.*, Civil Action No. 4:12-cv-40007-TSH (D. Mass. 2012) (dispute over meaning of "concurrent user").

In the event of a dispute regarding a permitted use, the licensor bears the burden of proof that the licensee exceeded the scope of the license agreement. *Netbula, LLC v. Bindview Development Corp.*, 516 F. Supp. 2d 1137 (N.D. Cal. 2007).

In negotiating the license grant, prudent licensees should clearly understand how the underlying software/technology functions and who requires access to or use of the software's functionality. A United Kingdom case, *SAP UK Ltd. v. Diageo Great Britain Ltd.* [2017] EWHC 189 (TCC) Case No: HT-2015-000340, emphasizes the importance of understanding how the licensed software will be used and ensuring that the license grant provides the licensee the rights to use the licensed software in the manner contemplated by the licensee.

In *Diageo*, Deloitte developed two systems for Diageo based on Salesforce software. One system, "Connect," permitted customers to place orders directly through an online portal instead of through a call center. Diageo licensed SAP's Process Integration (PI) software to allow Connect users/Diageo customers to access and process certain data stored in mySAP ERP, which was licensed to Diageo on a "named user" basis.

SAP brought suit seeking approximately $68M in damages, claiming:

1. Connect used SAP's PI software engine to indirectly access data in mySAP ERP, and
2. Diageo's customers who used Connect to order through the online portal were not "named users" for mySAP ERP, and thus did not have a license to access the data.

The court considered the plain meaning of the recitals in the license and the license grant and found "The plain and obvious meaning . . . is that ***only Named Users are authorised to use or access the mySAP ERP software*** . . . ." (emphasis supplied). Further,

- ". . . the interactions . . . between the Connect customer and mySAP ERP constitute use of, or access to, the mySAP ERP software."
- "if a call center employee submitting an order to the mySAP ERP system was required to be a "named user," a customer submitting an order to the mySAP ERP system should also be a "named user."

It concluded that usage by Connect customers was not authorized under the mySAP ERP license agreement, entitling SAP to additional license and maintenance fees.

For a discussion on limiting potential claims for the misuse of a licensor's software, *see* Hershkowitz & Carroll, *10 Simple Steps to Ensure Software Licensing Compliance*, 37 Law. Brief 13 (No. 16, 2007).

PRACTICE POINT:

Given the increasingly competitive technology market, it is likely that vendors will be more aggressive in claiming licensees have exceeded the scope of their license and seeking additional license fees. To reduce the possibility of a potential claim by a vendor, prudent customers should undertake the following steps prior to negotiating the license grant with a vendor:

- Understand the software's functionality and how it will be used.
- Determine who will need to access and use the software's functionality. (i.e., will the licensee's customers or vendors need to access the software's functionality)?
- Understand the terms and extent of the license grant.
- Ensure that the license grant explicitly addresses indirect access.
- Ensure that the license clearly grants the licensee and its customers, if appropriate, the rights they need.
- Avoid ambiguous language in the license grant.
- Consider using vendors with customer-friendly terms.
- Exclude any language in the agreement's recitals that impacts the interpretation of the license.

3. *Nonexclusive/Exclusive Licenses*

The term "nonexclusive" is necessary to indicate that the licensor reserves the right to license the same software to other licensees. This is important as some licensees seek exclusive use of the licensed software if they believe the software provides a competitive advantage. This is especially likely if the licensee paid for the development of the software or educated the licensor about the need for such software in a particular industry. Exclusivity may be for a set period of time, a particular use or industry, or, in the case of distribution rights, for a specific geographic location.

A nonexclusive license can be granted orally or can be implied from the conduct of the parties. *Korman v. HBC Florida, Inc.*, 182 F.3d 1291 (11th Cir. 1999); *Effects Assoc. Inc. v. Cohen*, 908 F.2d 555, 558 (9th Cir. 1990) (nonexclusive copyright licenses do not need to be in writing). An implied license may be created where the author of a work created at the request of a third party provides the work to such party knowing it intends to copy and distribute it. *See MacLean Assoc, v. Wm. M. Mercer-Meidinger-Hansen*, 952 F.2d 769, 779 (3d Cir. 1991), citing *Effects Assoc. Inc. v. Cohen*, 908 F.2d 555, 558–59 (9th Cir. 1990).

A nonexclusive licensee lacks the ability to sue or be joined in a suit. *Ortho Pharmaceutical Corp. v. Genetics Institute, Inc. and Amgen, Inc.*, 52 F.3d 1026 (Fed. Cir.), *cert. denied*, 516 U.S. 907 (1995) (citing *Overman Cushion Tire Co. v. Goodyear Tire and Rubber Co.*, 59 F.2d 998, *cert. denied*, 287 U.S. 651 (1932) (nonexclusive licensee has no right to sue or be joined in a suit)); and *Philadelphia Brief Case Co. v. Specialty Leather Products Co., Inc.*, 145 F. Supp. 425, 429-30 (D.N.J. 1956) (contract clause cannot give right to sue where licensee would otherwise have no such right). Furthermore, the licensor cannot grant such a right where one does not already exist.

Subject to the terms and conditions of the particular license, a copyright owner who grants a licensee a nonexclusive license to use the copyrighted material generally may not sue for copyright infringement and is limited to bringing a claim for breach of contract. *Sun Microsystems, Inc. v. Microsoft Corp.*, 188 F.3d 1115, 1121 (9th Cir. 1999). If the license is limited in scope and the licensee exceeds the scope, a claim of copyright infringement may be brought. *S.O.S., Inc. v. Payday, Inc.*, 886 F.2d 1081, 1087 (9th Cir. 1989).

When the licensor is licensing to the licensee an existing product, in contrast to a custom solution, the licensor should not agree to limit future sales of the software by granting the licensee exclusivity, as the licensee is not paying the licensor its full development cost. The ability to develop and sell a repeatable solution is critical to maintaining high margins. Granting exclusivity to a single licensee will likely severely impact the licensor's margins and potentially require the licensor to create a new solution for each licensee, which would likely be prohibitively expensive and impractical given there are a finite number of approaches to creating a software solution. In evaluating whether to grant an exclusive license, the licensor should consider its lost opportunity costs and the licensor's investment in its software.

On occasion a licensor may grant an exclusive license. The exclusivity may go to a geographic region, a specific industry, a set time period, or the use of the entire product itself. Exclusive licenses are uncommon in that they prevent the licensor from relicensing the software and receiving additional license fees to the extent of the exclusivity. If the licensor does grant the licensee an exclusive license, the underlying license agreement should clearly provide whether the exclusive license extinguishes the licensor's own right to use the software. Further, the license agreement should state whether the exclusivity is perpetual or expires after some period of time.

Under the Copyright Act, exclusive licenses must be in writing. 17 U.S.C. §§ 101, 204(a); *MacLean Assoc. v. Wm. M. Mercer-Meidinger-Hansen*, 952 F.2d 769, 778 (3d Cir. 1991). *See generally I.A.E., Inc. v. Sharer*, 74 F.3d 768 (7th Cir. 1996) (a nonexclusive copyright license is granted when (1) the licensee requests creation of a work, (2) the creator/licensor delivers the work to the licensee, and (3) the licensor intends the licensee to copy and distribute the work); *Korman v. HBC Florida, Inc.*, 182 F.3d 1291, 1293 (11th Cir. 1999). Note that an oral exclusive license creates an implied nonexclusive license. 17 U.S.C. § 204(a); *Gracen v. Bradford Exchange*, 698 F.2d 300, 303 (7th Cir. 1983). Before granting an exclusive license, a licensor must consider whether it needs to reserve any rights. For example, if an exclusive license to distribute is being granted for a particular jurisdiction, a licensor that also distributes via the Internet should consider whether Internet sales should be excluded from the exclusive license.

If the licensor does agree to some element of exclusivity, the restriction should be narrowly defined and for a limited time period. From a financial perspective, if the licensor agrees to restrict future sales of the software, the licensor's licensee fees should equal the licensor's lost future sales from granting the licensee an exclusive license as well as the full amount of the licensor's development costs.

PRACTICE POINT:

In deciding whether to grant an exclusive license, the licensor should consider:

- The value and profitability of the overall transaction.
- The product or services should be narrowly defined and should not be broader than actual services, deliverables and software being delivered to the customer.

- The increased fee the customer willing to pay for the exclusivity.
- The impact on the licensor's future sales.
- The software or solutions is the licensor prohibited from providing to other customers.
- The potential customers the licensor is restricted from offering its software.
- The geographic scope of exclusivity which should not be broader than where the client is going to use the deliverables.
- The duration of the exclusivity period. Some customers demand the period of exclusivity not start until the software solution "goes live," but prudent vendors will reject this provision, as the customer has significant control over that date and can significantly delay the go-live date.

4. Internal Use

Many license grants provide that the licensed software may be used for the licensee's "internal use" or "internal business purposes only." The primary objective of this wording is to limit the licensee's use of the licensed software to the licensee's specific business needs and to prevent the licensee from using the software to operate a service bureau or data processing center or from allowing a third-party to access and use the software in the event of outsourcing. It is prudent to state this prohibition clearly in the license agreement to avoid a subsequent dispute over the interpretation of the license *grant. See, e.g., National Car Rental Sys., Inc. v. Computer Associates. Intl., Inc.*, 991 F.2d 426, 427 (8th Cir. 1993).

Although many licenses utilize the concept of "internal use," many practitioners believe this term by its nature is inherently ambiguous as almost all software is used to directly or indirectly sell the licensee's products or services. This ambiguity is especially apparent when the software is utilized in a networked environment. For example, does an "internal use" grant allow the licensee to operate the software on the licensee's servers and provide access to the software to its customers in a cloud environment or over the web? If the licensee operates a service bureau business or operates an outsourcing business and provides access to the software's functionality to third parties, is that an "internal business purpose"? Is there a difference in the meaning of "internal use" versus "internal business purposes"?

The parties can avoid any potential issues related to interpretation by explicitly stating the limits on the software's use (e.g., "Licensee may not use the Software to provide services directly or indirectly to any third party including, but not limited to, via a service bureau or though outsourced services.") instead of making a general, amorphous statement regarding the software's use for the licensee's "internal use." Some licensors utilize broader, less specific language to achieve the same result by seeking to contractually prohibit third parties from "accessing the software's functionality" as a means to prevent outsourcing or the use of the software in a service bureau. If the licensee contemplates using third parties or contractors to operate or maintain the software, it should ensure that the license grant affirmatively gives it the right to do so. Regardless of the approach taken, the parties should seek to clearly define how the software may be used or seek other wording to codify this concept.

In evaluating whether the licensee's use constitutes "internal use," some licensors utilize a three-prong test:

- Will the licensee offer the licensor's products as a "service bureau" where the licensee's clients directly access and use the licensor's products?
- Will the licensee charge separately for the licensor's products on any invoice? (i.e., will there be a line item for the licensor's software on any invoice?); and
- Will the licensee "resell" or "transfer" the software object code to the licensee's clients?

If the answer to any of these questions is yes, the licensee's use will likely be found to not constitute internal use.

For a greater discussion of the issues involved, *see* Marenberg & Brown, *"Scope of Use" Restrictions in Software Licenses,* 10 COMPUTER LAW. 1 (Dec. 1993).

5. *Creation of Derivative Works (§ 3.4)*

"Disassembly," "decompilation," and "translation" of software requires making copies of the software program itself and creating "derivative works" in the process based upon the original software. Section 101 of the Copyright Act defines a "derivative work" as:

> *a work based upon one or more pre-existing works, such as a translation, musical arrangement, dramatization, fictionalization, motion picture version, sound recording, art reproduction, abridgment, condensation, or any other form in which a work may be recast, transformed, or adapted. A work consisting of editorial revisions, annotations, elaborations, or other modifications, which, as a whole, represent an original work of authorship, is a "derivative work".*

17 U.S.C. § 101.

Section 106(2) of the Copyright Act prohibits the creation of derivative works without the copyright owner's permission. An author of a derivative work cannot obtain a copyright on any such work if it lacked the permission of the copyright owner to make a derivative work. *Gracen v. Bradford Exchange,* 698 F.2d 300, 303 (7th Cir. 1983); *CMAX/Cleveland, Inc. v. UCR, Inc.,* 804 F. Supp. 337 (M.D. Ga. 1992).

In certain situations, the alteration of an original work may create a copyrightable derivative work. To receive copyright protection, a work must be sufficiently original, requiring more than a "modicum of originality." *Waldman Pub. Corp. v. Landoll, Inc.,* 43 F.3d 775, 782 (2d Cir. 1994); *Simon v. Birraporetti's Restaurants, Inc.,* 720 F. Supp. 85 (S.D. Tex. 1989). A derivative work must be substantially different from the underlying work to be copyrightable, *Gracen v. Bradford Exchange,* 698 F.2d 300 (7th Cir. 1983), but yet must be substantially copied from [based on the expression of] prior work. *Apple Computer, Inc. v. Microsoft Corp., 759* F. Supp. 1444 (N.D. Cal. 1991), on reconsideration, 779 F. Supp. 133, *aff'd,* 35 F.3d 1435 (9th Cir. 1994); *Litchfield v. Spielberg,* 736 F.2d 1352 (9th Cir.), *cert. denied,* 470 U.S. 1052 (1984). Although the derivative work refers to the entire work, not just the modifications, the copyright in a derivative work applies only to the new work contributed by the author and not to the preexisting material. The new copyright does not imply any exclusive rights in the preexisting copyright. 17 U.S.C. § 103(b); *Moore Pub., Inc. v. Big Sky Marketing, Inc.*, 756 F. Supp. 1371 (D. Idaho 1990). Further, if a derivative work is created using preexisting copyrighted material, copyright protection will not extend to any part of the work in which such preexisting copyrighted material has been used unlawfully. 17 U.S.C. § 103(a).

The right to claim a copyright on a non-infringing, derivative work arises by operation of law, not by the granting of such right by the owner of the original work. Melville B. Nimmer & David Nimmer, Nimmer on Copyright, § 3.06 n.14 (2005). Copyright law does allow, however, the copyright owner of the original work to establish restrictions on preparing any derivative works, and prudent licensors should include a prohibition on the creation of derivative works in their license agreements. *Stewart v. Abend*, 495 U.S. 207, 223 (1990) (It is an "axiomatic copyright principle that a person may exploit only such copyrighted literary material as he either owns or is licensed to use"); *EyePartner, Inc. v. Kor Media Group LLC*, 2013 WL 3733434 (S.D. Fla. July 15, 2013) (preliminary injunction granted against licensee who created derivative work in contravention of software license terms). Any use of copyrighted material in a derivative work that exceeds the scope of the license constitutes an infringement. *NLFC, Inc. v. Devcom Mid-America, Inc.*, 45 F.3d 235 n.5 (7th Cir. 1995).

Thus, a licensor may contractually require a licensee to assign to the licensor copyright ownership in a derivative work. Any licensee that claims ownership in contravention of a contractual prohibition (i.e., a license) may infringe on the original work. Interestingly, it is not an infringement of copyright to falsely claim ownership of copyright in a derivative work. It may not even be a violation of Lanham Act § 43(a) since copyright ownership does not mean the owner is the source or author of a work. It could be a violation of a license if the license contains a specific restriction regarding attribution.

A license does not always need to explicitly state that a copyright in a derivative work will be the property of the owner of the original work, and the license does not have to be in writing. *Gracen v. Bradford Exchange*, 698 F.2d 300, 303 (7th Cir. 1983); *see also* 1 Melville B. Nimmer & David Nimmer, Nimmer on Copyright § 3.06 at 3-34 23 n.14 (Perm. Ed. 2000) ("a license may contractually preclude the licensee from obtaining a copyright in a licensed derivative work"). This position is similar to the laws governing a work made for hire that allow an employer to contractually require an independent contractor who is the author of a work to execute an assignment transferring ownership of the work to the employer. See Chapter 7.A.1.

If a licensor is considering granting a licensee the right to modify and adapt the software, it should do so solely under the provisions of Section 117 of the Copyright Act ("as an essential step in the utilization of the computer program"). The licensor must carefully consider whether the sum of any such modifications will rise to the level of a derivative work. In an abundance of caution, licensors should seek to obtain the copyright for all such modifications and adaptations even if they do not constitute a derivative work. Given that the copyright for a derivative work vests in the author immediately upon the creation of a work, the licensor should contractually require that the author assign the copyright in any derivative it creates to the licensor. *See S.O.S., Inc.*

v. Payday, Inc., 866 F.2d 1081, 1085 (9th Cir. 1989) ("Copyright protection subsists from the moment the work is 'fixed in a tangible medium of expression.'"). This will ensure the sanctity of the licensor's software and avoid any disputes regarding ownership if its licensees were to later claim ownership of different portions of the licensor's software.

Conversely, at least one court, without deciding the ownership issue, has rejected the contention that a licensee may not obtain an enforceable copyright on a derivative work unless there was an express authorization in the governing license agreement. *Liu v. Price Waterhouse LLP*, 1999 WL 47025 (N.D. I11. Jan. 25, 1999).

Further, "a derivative work prepared under authority of the grant [to prepare a derivative work] before its termination may continue to be utilized under the terms of the grant after its termination." 17 U.S.C. § 203(b). Thus, termination only serves to prohibit the licensee from creating future derivative works based on the original work and does not prevent the licensee from creating additional derivative works based on a derivative work made lawfully during the license agreement. 17 U.S.C. § 304(c)(6)(A) recognizes this right as it grants the copyright owner of the derivative work all the rights of a copyright owner. *See also* 17 U.S.C. § 203(b). To avoid problems arising from the creation of derivative works, the licensor should contractually restrict the licensee from utilizing any derivative works in any manner that may be competitive with the licensee.

Finally, prudent licensors should carefully consider the language of the license grant to avoid inadvertently granting the licensee the right to create derivative works. *Edgenet, Inc. v. Home Depot U.S.A.*, 658 F.3d 662 (7th Cir. 2011) (License grant to all "right, title and interest in and to" allowed licensee to create derivative works.).

6. *Prohibition of Reverse Engineering*

Most licensors are very concerned with the licensee reverse engineering the object code provided to the licensee under its license. To alleviate this concern, prudent licensors should include a clause in their licenses stating that the licensee is prohibited from reverse engineering, decompiling, or recompiling the licensed software. In *Bowers v. Baystate Technologies, Inc.*, 320 F.3d 1317 (Fed. Cir. 2003) the court upheld the validity of a contractual clause prohibiting reverse engineering and found that the Copyright Act does not narrow or pre-empt any such contractual provisions. This decision is consistent with the findings of many other circuits. *Wrench LLC v. Taco Bell Corp., 256* F.3d 446, 457 (6th Cir. 2001) (state law contract claim not pre-empted by federal copyright law); *Nat'l Car Rental Sys., Inc. v. Computer Assocs. International, Inc.*, 991 F.2d 426, 433 (8th Cir. 1993); *Taquino v. Teledyne Monarch Rubber*, 893 F.2d 1488, 1501 (5th Cir. 1990); *Edelman v. N2H2*, 263 F. Supp.2d 137 (D. Mass. 2003) (There is no right or privilege to reverse-engineer software in violation of license terms.), but see *Lipscher v. LRP Publications, Inc.*, 266 F.3d 1305, 1312 (11th Cir. 2001) ("Copyright Act pre-empts only those state law rights that may be abridged by an act which, in and of itself, would infringe one of the exclusive rights provided by federal copyright law." *Foley v. Luster*, 249 F.3d 1281, 1285 (11th Cir. 2001) (quoting *Computer Assoc. Int'l, Inc. v. Altai, Inc.*, 982 F.2d 693, 716 (2d Cir. 1992)). The right plaintiff "is attempting to protect in its acquisition misconduct claims are copyright rights" and thus pre-empted.)

Nonetheless, Section 117 of the Copyright Act permits licensees to make a copy of the software for backup and archival purposes. 17 U.S.C. 117.

The *Bowers* court specifically stated that its opinion "left untouched" its decision in *Atari Games Corp. v. Nintendo of America, Inc.*, 975 F.2d 832 (Fed. Cir. 1992), and those "expressly defined circumstances in which infringement is not copyright infringement under 17 U.S.C. § 1201(f) (section of the Digital Millennium Copyright Act) and 17 U.S.C. § 906." *Id.* at 1325. In *Davidson R. Associates v. Jung*, 422 F.3d 630, 639 (8th Cir. 2005), the Eighth Circuit recognized the *Bowers* holding that a party can waive its right to reverse engineer to obtain interoperability through the fair use exception.

Surprisingly, one court has held that the ability to create derivative works may be inferred from the language of the license grant. *Kennedy v. Nat'l Juvenile Detention Ass'n.*, 197 F.3d 690 (7th Cir. 1999) (Language permitting licensee to "reproduce, publish and use" any copyright material infers the right to create derivative works).

The Digital Millennium Copyright Act (DMCA), while providing limited exceptions, prohibits reverse engineering. 17 U.S.C. § 1201(a)(1)(A) (prohibiting circumvention of "a technological measure that effectively controls access to a [copyrighted] work.") The DMCA provides three limited exceptions:

1. "[F] or the sole purpose of . . . interoperability" of an independently created computer program. 17 U.S.C. § 1201 (f) (1);
2. To develop and employ a technological means to enable interoperability, 17 U.S.C. § 1201 (f) (2); and
3. To provide information or means for interoperability to others, 17 U.S.C. § 1201 (f) (3).

Model language prohibiting reverse engineering except as permitted by law follows:

> *Licensee will not reverse engineer, decompile, disassemble or otherwise attempt to derive the source code, techniques, processes, algorithms, know-how or other information from the binary code portions of the Software (collectively, "**Reverse Engineering**") or permit or induce any Reverse Engineering. Only if permitted by directly applicable law, Licensee may engage in Reverse Engineering solely for purposes of obtaining such information as is necessary to achieve interoperability of independently created software with the Software, or as otherwise and to the limited extent permitted by directly applicable law, but only if:*
>
> *(a) Reverse Engineering is strictly necessary to obtain such information; and*
> *(b) Licensee has first requested such information from Licensor and Licensor failed to make such information available (for a fee or otherwise) under reasonable terms and conditions.*
>
> *Any information supplied to or obtained by Licensee under this Section is confidential information of Licensor subject to the obligations of Section __ (Confidentiality), which may only be used by Licensee for the purpose described in this Section, and Licensee shall not disclose any such confidential information to any third party or create any software which is substantially similar to the expression of the Software.*

For an overview of the DMCA, see Lee, *Reverse Engineering Under the DMCA: Recognizing a "Fair Access" Defense*, 20 COMPUTER LAW ASSOC. BULL. 135 (No. 4, 2005);

Davidson & Axtell, *Reverse Engineering: The DMCA and the Reverse Engineering of Suspected Infringing Products,* 23 Computer & Internet Law. 1 (Feb. 2006). For a more detailed discussion of the DMCA, see Chapter 7.K.3.

Any prohibition on reverse engineering is not absolute, as several courts have found that a licensee who makes an intermediate copy of software to the extent necessary to determine how such software works—in order to interface the licensee's or another party's proprietary software to the licensor's software—may fall under the "Fair Use" doctrine of the Copyright Act. *See Sega Enterprises, Ltd. v. Accolade, Inc.,* 977 F.2d 1510 (9th Cir. 1992); *Atari Games Corp. v. Nintendo of America, Inc.,* 975 F.2d 832 (Fed. Cir. 1992). In *Sony Computer Entertainment v. Connectix Corp.,* 203 F.3d 596 (9th Cir. 2000), *cert denied,* 531 U.S. 871 (2000), the court held that the fair use doctrine allows public access to the functional elements and ideas contained in copyright software. If reverse engineering is the only method to access the ideas and functional elements embedded in the software and there is a legitimate reason for such access, reverse engineering/disassembly will constitute fair use of the copyrighted work. *Sega Enterprises Ltd. v. Accolade, Inc.,* 977 F.2d 1510, 1527-28 (9th Cir. 1992) (amended opinion). Thus, in certain situations the fair use doctrine allows the reverse engineering of software. However, any licensee planning to rely upon the fair use doctrine should understand that it is an affirmative defense to a claim of copyright infringement. *Wall Data, Inc. v. Los Angeles County Sheriff's Dept.,* 447 F.3d 769, 776 (9th Cir. 2006). Thus, the burden is on the defendant to prove that the use was fair.

Additionally, the standard to be met for "fair use" is somewhat subjective. In determining whether a particular use is fair use, courts consider factors including the following: (1) the purpose and character of the use, including whether such use is of a commercial nature or is for nonprofit educational purposes; (2) the nature of the copyrighted work; (3) the amount and substantiality of the portion used in relation to the copyrighted work as a whole; and (4) the effect of the use upon the potential market for or value of the copyrighted work. *Madison River Management Co. v. Business Management Software Corp.,* 387 F. Supp.2d 521, 536 (M.D.N.C. 2005). Thus, a licensee cannot be certain in advance that its actions will constitute a fair use. *Id.* (declining to find a fair use when the defendant copied software to "run reports," which took advantage of copyrighted data structure rather than to discover unprotected raw data). *See also, SAS Institute, Inc. v. World Programming Limited,* 874 F.3d 370 (4th Cir. 2017) (licensee breached reverse engineering prohibition where it analyzed licensor's software's design to improve licensee's own software products even though licensee did not access licensor's software's source code).

Another limit on reverse engineering prohibitions is that a licensee may modify a software program in order to make the program operate more efficiently for the licensee's internal use, including creating a derivative work. *Aymes v. Bonelli,* 47 F.3d 23 (2d Cir. 1995).

In general, in a negotiated contract a licensee can contractually bind itself not to undertake acts of infringement that others would be able to perform under the fair use doctrine. It is still up in the air whether waivers of fair use rights in click-wrap and shrink-wrap agreements for mass-market software are enforceable. See *Bowers v. Baystate Technologies, Inc.,* 320 F.3d 1317, 1323 (Fed. Cir.), *cert. denied,* 539 U.S. 928 (2003).

In *Bowers,* the Federal Circuit, over a strong dissent, held that a click-wrap waiver of the right to reverse engineer mass-market software (one of the rights generally considered to fall within fair use) was enforceable, even though the agreement was a classic contract of adhesion.

Similarly, European Community (EC) Directive 91/250 allows licensees to reverse engineer software to the extent necessary to create interfaces to the licensor's software. For a more detailed discussion of E.C. Directive 91/250, see Chapter 26.F.

The courts have justified these decisions under the "Fair Use" doctrine of copyright law. Under the fair use doctrine, use of a copyrighted work, including use by reproduction of copies for purposes such as criticism, comment, teaching, scholarship, or research, is not an infringement of the owner's copyright. 17 U.S.C. § 107. Factors to be used in determining fair use include the purpose and character of the use, the nature of the copyrighted work, whether the entity possessed an authorized copy of the software, the amount and substantiality of the portion used in relation to the whole, whether the copying was necessary to gain access to the functional elements of the software, whether the reproduction exceeded what was necessary to understand the protected elements, and the effect of the use upon the potential market for or value of the copyrighted work. *Id.* In most situations, verbatim copying of software made for commercial purposes is not fair use. *See, e.g., Compaq Computer Corp. v. Procom Tech., Inc.*, 908 F. Supp. 1409, 1419-21 (S.D. Tex. 1995); *Allen-Myland, Inc. v. Int'l Bus. Machs. Corp.*, 746 F. Supp. 520, 533-35 (E.D. Pa. 1990). *See also Princeton Univ. Press v. Mich. Document Servs.*, 99 F.3d 1381, 1385-92 (6th Cir. 1996) (verbatim copying of college "course packs" was not fair use). For an overview of the fair use doctrine, see Hooper & Frame, *Can I Make a Copy of That? A Primer on Copyright's Doctrine of Fair Use*, 34 COMP. & INTERNET LAW. 27 (May 2017).

At the same time, however, an entity will usually not be allowed to reverse engineer software for the purpose of directly competing with the owners of the software. *See Triad Systems Corp. v. Southeastern Express Co.*, 64 F.3d 1330 (9th Cir. 1995), *cert. denied,* 516 U.S. 1145 (1996); *MAI Systems Corp. v. Peak Computer, Inc.*, 991 F.2d 511 (9th Cir. 1993), *cert. denied,* 510 U.S. 1033 (1994). *Triad* did not, however, overrule *Sega.* Reverse engineering remains a fair use even where the defendant displaces sales by the plaintiff, as long as the use is transformative. *See Sony Computer Entertainment v. Connectix Corp.*, 203 F.3d 596 (9th Cir. 2000), *cert denied,* 531 U.S. 871 (2000) distinguishing *Triad.*

For a general discussion, see, *Reverse Engineering,* 35 CORP. COUNS. Q. 168 (Jan. 2019); Note, *Locked Out: The Hazards of Reverse Engineering,* 21 J. COMPUTER & INFO. LAW 591 (2003); For a general discussion, see Rowles, *Reverse Engineering—Can Software Owners License Against It?*, E-COM. ADVISOR, July 2001.

7. Reservation of Rights Clauses

"Reservation of rights" clauses do not alter the interpretation of the license grant as they simply provide that the licensor retains all rights that it did not grant. *Boosey & Hawkes Music Publishers, Ltd. v. The Walt Disney Co.*, 145 F.3d 481, 488 (2d Cir. 1998) (A reservation of rights clause "contributes nothing to the definition of the boundaries of the license.").

D. Geographic Restrictions (§ 3.1)

Most licensors seek to limit the use of the licensed software to a specific country or site; for example, the United States or "Licensee's Wilmington, Delaware site" to allow the licensor to charge additional license fees for each additional geography or site. Specifically stating any geographic limitations benefits both parties by avoiding any unintended consequences of having the geographic restrictions determined by a dispute resolution process. *Mid-West Conveyor Co. v. Jervis B. Webb Co.*, 92 F.3d 992 (10th Cir 1996) (license limited to the United States); *Micro Data Base Systems, Inc. v. State Bank of India*, 177 F. Supp. 2d 881 (N.D. Ind. 2001) (licensee may use software both within and outside India where license did not contain a geographic limitation.). To the extent the parties intend the license grant to provide "world-wide" use, the license should specifically state "world-wide" as after the fact, silence may be interpreted differently.

Geographic limitations allow the licensor to grant exclusive rights in a particular or geographic area, potentially segmenting its markets. *See, e.g., Elliott Co. v. Legonda Mfg. Co.*, 205 F. 152 (W.D. Pa. 1913) (license to sell to others for "use" in United States held to limit defendant sales for "use" in United States.)

The failure to limit the use of the licensed software to a particular country may also give rise to a number of export issues. For example, licensing software to a Mexican company that has a subsidiary or affiliate in Cuba would violate the Trading with the Enemy Act if such software were used in Cuba. Furthermore, the use of such software outside of the United States may be governed by the laws of a foreign jurisdiction with which the licensor is unfamiliar and/or which does not grant the same protections to the licensor as the laws of the United States. To protect the licensor's interests, the licensor should insist on receiving a written assurance from the licensee that the licensee will not violate the export laws.

Limitation of geographic scope is closely tied to intellectual property rights indemnification. The intellectual property rights indemnification provision in the license agreement is another important concern. As discussed in Chapter 5.C, a domestic licensor should limit the licensor's indemnification to intellectual property infringement of a U.S. intellectual property right and those of the country in which the licensed software will be used. Failure to include a geographic restriction as to the use of the software may expand the scope of indemnification granted by the licensor. If a license is worldwide, the licensor should consider limiting its potential risk by indemnifying the licensee for infringement arising in countries that are signatories to the Berne Convention.

E. Paid Up (§ 3.1)

"Paid up" refers to the concept that the license is fully paid and that the licensor may not charge the licensee additional license fees to use the software. While licensees seek assurance that they will not be charged additional amounts to use the software, licensors should carefully define how the phrase is used to avoid any claims by the licensee that it is entitled to maintenance, support and other services without charge.

F. Object Code Licenses and Source Code Licenses (§ 3.1)

"Object code" is the binary, machine-readable version of the software. Object code allows the licensee to operate the software but does not enable the licensee to make enhancements or modifications to the software or create derivative works. "Source code" is the human-readable statement in a computer language that, when processed by a compiler, assembler, or interpreter, becomes executable by a computer. Source code allows the licensee to maintain the software, to make modifications and enhancements to the software, and to create derivative works.

If a licensee purchases a source code license it *theoretically* does not need further assistance from the licensor as the licensee itself has the ability to maintain, as well as to modify and enhance the software, or create derivative works from it. The licensing of source code creates a significant risk of misappropriation and piracy. With the source code, a licensee can become a competitor or intentionally or unintentionally make the source code available to a competitor. Further, routinely granting source code licenses may make it more difficult to maintain trade secret protection for the source code. Consequently, most licensors refuse to sell source code licenses. Those who do sell source code licenses usually charge a significant premium for a source code license over the cost of an object code license.

In granting a source code license, the licensor should restrict the licensee from creating derivative works, enhancements, or modifications. If the licensee obtains the right to do so, it should be prohibited from licensing any such derivative works, enhancements, or modifications. It is important to note that derivative works will generally be owned by the copyright owner unless conveyed. 17 U.S.C. §§ 201(d)(2) and 103(a). The licensor should restrict use of the source code to one physical location and limit access to the source code to the licensee's employees and contractors who have a need for access. The licensee should also be restricted from making additional copies of the source code. Maintaining the confidentiality of the source code is the licensor's most important concern, and the licensor should place strict limitations on the licensee to protect its confidentiality. Finally, the standard limitations on use of the software discussed in Chapter 4.C, above, should be imposed on the licensee.

Licensees should carefully consider whether purchasing a source code license makes sense, especially if the licensee is not a software company, as maintaining source code can be difficult, expensive, and time-consuming. In evaluating whether to purchase a source code license, the licensee should consider whether the source code is stable, maintainable, reliable, and secure. If not, it may be more cost-effective to purchase an object code license and purchase maintenance and support from the licensor.

See Form B.4.1 for a model Source Code License.

PRACTICE POINT:

When considering granting a source code license, a prudent licensor should consider:

- Will there be geographic or other limitations to the license?
- Will the licensee have the right to create derivative works?

- If so, who will own the derivative works?
- If the licensee will own the derivative works, is there an obligation to license the newly created intellectual property back to the licensor?
- Will there be an acceptance testing period?
- Does the licensor have an obligation to provide ongoing improvements or modifications to the licensed software?
- Does the licensor have an obligation to provide support for the licensed software?

G. Irrevocable/Non-Terminable Licenses (§ 3.1)

Licensees often want the terms "irrevocable" or "non-terminable" included in the license grant to ensure that, after they accept the software and pay for the license, the licensor cannot revoke the license. The terms "irrevocable" and "non-terminable" imply permanency, however, and as such they cause concern for licensors. Licensors are concerned that the licensee may later violate the terms of the license and that the licensor will lack the ability to terminate the license. This concern is alleviated by prefacing the license grant with the phrase "*Subject to the provisions of this Agreement, . . .*" This wording conditions any permanency on the licensee meeting the terms of the license, eliminating the licensor's concerns.

In *Nano-Proprietary, Inc. v. Canon. Inc.*, 537 F.2d 394 (5th Cir. 2008), the Fifth Circuit Court of Appeals held that a court must give effect to the plain meaning of the terms, "fully paid-up," "irrevocable," and "perpetual" finding that the patent license granted in this case was non-terminable even in the event of the licensee's material breach. Further, such language may prevent the licensor from recovering damages for a breach of the license. *Id.* at 400. If a license is non-terminable, the licensor's remedies for breach will lie in damages and equitable relief.

Even though the license may unequivocally grant the licensee an "irrevocable" license without any limiting language, the license may be terminable at will by the author after 35 years for a period of five years under the Copyright Act. 17 U.S.C. § 203(3). See Chapter 4.B, above, for a more detailed discussion of this issue.

H. Assignment of the License (§ 3.1, § 22)

1. *By Licensee*

Depending on the type of license granted, a licensee may or may not be able to assign its license.

(a) Nonexclusive Licenses

In general, a nonexclusive software license is not assignable unless the license agreement expressly provides that it may be assigned. *See, e.g., Cincom Systems, Inc. v. Novelis Corp.*, 581 F.3d 431 (6th Cir. 2009) (intellectual property licenses non-assignable unless specifically provided for in license agreement); *SQL Solutions, Inc. v. Oracle Corp.*, 1991 WL 626458 (N.D. Cal. Dec. 18, 1991) (assignment of software license by operation of law/merger violates license terms prohibiting assignment); *Harris v. Emus*

Records Corp., 734 F.2d 1329 (9th Cir. 1984) (as to copyright license). *See also Verson Corp. v. Verson International Group PLC,* 899 F. Supp. 358 (N.D. I11. 1995) (nonexclusive licensee may not assign patent license unless the right of assignment is expressly provided for in the license agreement). This principle is based upon the reasoning that a nonexclusive license is merely a contractual promise not to sue the licensee, which is personal to the licensee and cannot be transferred. RAYMOND T. NIMMER, THE LAW OF COMPUTER TECHNOLOGY § 7.78 (2005). Nonexclusive licenses are not required to be in writing. *Effects Assocs., Inc. v. Cohen,* 908 F.2d 555, 558 (9th Cir. 1990).

Silence as to assignability will be interpreted in light of federal copyright law prohibiting assignment without the express authorization to make such transfer.

(b) Exclusive Licenses

Courts are divided over the ability to assign an exclusive license without consent. *Gardner v. Nike, Inc.*, 279 F.3d 774, 780–81 (9th Cir. 2002) held that exclusive copyright licenses are only assignable with the consent of the copyright owner as a matter of law. It further held that federal law would govern the interpretation of a license where state law conflicts with federal copyright law and policy. *Id. citing S.O.S., Inc. v. Payday, Inc.*, 886 F.2d 1081, 1088 (9th Cir. 1989).

Several courts, however, have held that an exclusive license is assignable by the exclusive licensee, unless the license agreement expressly provides otherwise. The Federal District Court for the Southern District of Indiana took exception to *Gardner,* stating "Exclusive licensees, as copyright owners of their exclusive rights, are free under the [Copyright] Act to transfer those rights to third parties." *Traicoff v. Digital Media, Inc.*, 439 F. Supp.2d 872, 877 (S.D. Ind. 2006). *See also Golden Books Family Entertainment Inc.*, 269 B.R. 311 (Bankr. D. Del. 2001); *In re Sentry Data, Inc.*, 87 B.R. 943 (Bankr. N.D. I11. 1988); *In re Valley Media, Inc.*, 279 B.R. 105, 135 (Bankr. D. Del. 2002) ("Exclusive licenses grant the licensee a property right in the copyright that is freely transferable . . . .")

This view is shared by the principal treatise on copyrights, *Nimmer on Copyright,* which reasons that an exclusive licensee is considered to be the copyright owner to the extent of the exclusive rights granted by the license and may re-convey such rights absent a contractual restriction. 3 MELVILLE B. NIMMER & DAVID NIMMER, NIMMER ON COPYRIGHT § 10.02 [B][4] at 10-25–10-28 (2005). Another noted expert, Jay Westermeier, believes, however, that exclusive licenses are not assignable without the copyright owner's consent, as a licensor still retains ownership of the copyright even though it has granted the licensee an exclusive license. The transfer of an ownership interest or exclusive right in a copyright must be in writing. 17 U.S.C. § 204(a).

An exclusive license that does not resemble an assignment (e.g., an exclusive license to market the software) is arguably a non-assignable license. *See In re Sentry Data, Inc.*, 87 B.R. 943 (Bankr. N.D. I11. 1988). Therefore, an exclusive license may convey only certain rights to the licensee, which is similar to the buyer's rights to resell and use the software under the First Sale Doctrine. 17 U.S.C. § 117. See Chapter 3.A.

Several courts, however, have held that a nonexclusive copyright or patent license cannot be transferred without the consent of the licensor. *In re Catapult Entertainment, Inc.*, 165 F.3d 747 (9th Cir. 1999); *Everex Systems, Inc. v. Cadtrak Corp.*, 89 F.3d 673 (9th Cir. 1996); *Harris v. Emus Records Corp.*, 734 F.2d 1329 (9th Cir. 1984); *Unarco Indus.*,

Inc. v. Kelley Co., Inc., 465 F.2d 1303 (7th Cir. 1972); *In re Patient Education Media, Inc.*, 210 B.R. 237 (Bankr. S.D.N.Y. 1997).

The federal policy on transfers arises in part from the fact that a nonexclusive license is a personal contractual privilege that does not create a property interest. It is also embedded in policies of encouraging innovation and reserving to the owner of the rights in question the ability to determine to whom and when a license is granted. *See, e.g., Everex Systems, Inc. v. Cadtrak Corp.*, 89 F.3d 673 (9th Cir. 1996).

This area of the law is uncertain, however, as copyright law would appear to conflict with general contract law in this matter. Under Article 2 of the UCC, unless otherwise agreed, contract rights are freely assignable so long as such assignment does not materially change the duty of the other party or materially increase such party's risk or burden. UCC Article 2 § 2-210(2). Similarly, the Restatement (Second) of Contracts provides that a contract is not assignable if it could materially reduce the value received by the obligor, materially increase its burden or risk, materially impair its ability to obtain return performance, or materially reduce the value of the transaction to him. RESTATEM ENT (SECOND) OF CONTRACTS, § 317(2)(a).

For a more detailed discussion, see Ziff, *The Effect of Corporate Acquisitions on the Target Company's License Rights*, 57 BUS. LAW. 767 (2002). A related issue in outsourcing is allowing third party contractors to access and maintain the software. See Chapters 21.D and 25.A.3 for a discussion of this issue.

(c) Prohibition on Assignment

Given the potential uncertainty as to assignment, from the licensor's standpoint, the license should clearly state that the license is not assignable or transferable whether by merger, consolidation, operation of law, or otherwise, and any attempt to do so is void. See § 22.1. For clarity, the assignment clause should provide that the phrase "operation of law" will include any change of control of the ownership structure of the licensee. See § 22.1. This will potentially allow the licensor to prevent a transfer or in the alternative charge a transition fee if the licensee is acquired by another company or the customer seeks to outsource the licensor's technology. See *Meso Scale Diagnostics, LLC v. Roche Diagnostics GmbH*, 2011 WL 1348438 (Del. Ch. April 8, 2011) (contractual provision prohibiting assignment "by operation of law" may require the other party's consent prior to transferring contract to the surviving party in merger.) If the licensor is willing to allow the assignment of the agreement/license to an "affiliate" of the licensee, the licensor should ensure that the licensee remains liable for the affiliate's subsequent breach of the agreement/license.

In *Cincom Systems, Inc. v. Novelis Corp.*, 581 F.3d 431 (6th Cir. 2009), the Sixth Circuit Court of Appeals held that a nonexclusive, non-transferable license could not be transferred by merger when an affiliate was merged into a sister entity and out of existence as part of a corporate reorganization. The underlying license agreement licensed the software for use on a designated computer and prohibited the transfer of the license without the licensor's consent. The court emphasized that under federal law, a copyright is unassignable absent express language to the contrary. *Id.* at 437. Further, it stated "[a] transfer is no less a transfer because it takes place by operation of law rather than by a particular act of the parties." *Id.* at 438, *citing PPG Industries v. Guardian Industries Corp.*, 597 F.2d

1090, 1096 (6th Cir. 1979). *See also SQL Solutions, Inc. v. Oracle Corp.*, 1991 WL 626458 (N.D. Cal. Dec. 18, 1991) (assignment of software license by operation of law/merger violates license terms prohibiting assignment). *But see Evolution, Inc. v. Prime Rate Premium Finance Corp., Inc.*, 2004 WL 1824389 (D. Kan. Aug. 13, 2004) ("whether a merger effectuates an automatic assignment or transfer of license rights is a matter of state law.")

If the license agreement does not contain explicit language defining assignment to include mergers, consolidations, and operation of law, a court may not interpret such actions as an assignment because the assignment arose through the operation of law and not a formal written agreement. In such event, the court may allow the assignment to be concluded and award the licensor monetary damages. *See Rumbin v. Utica Mutual Ins. Co. et al., 757* A.2d 526 (Conn. 2000) (Anti-assignment clause did not render assignment ineffective but gave other party right to recover damages for breach). See § 22.1. *See also* Restatement (Second) of Contracts § 322(2) and comment b (1979).

Some licensees seek to avoid this issue by including language in the license agreement by which the licensor consents to any future outsourcing provided the outsourcer complies with the terms of the license. *See* § 41. A licensor should carefully consider accepting this type of clause, as the outsourcer may be a competitor and may have no incentive to maintain the confidentiality of the licensor's trade secrets.

Farsighted licensees should seek to include language to protect their future business needs, such as in the event that a business unit using the software is sold or otherwise transferred. *See* § 22.3. Similarly, prudent licensees should also seek the right to use the software on a "beneficial" basis to provide transition services to a third-party purchaser of one of its business units to support the transferred assets. *See* § 42.2.

Licensors should seek to limit assignability to ensure the sanctity of their software. The failure to do so may result in the licensee assigning the software license to a competitor of the licensor or to a party who is much larger than the licensee, preventing the licensor from realizing a larger license fee. Further, the new licensee may lack the creditworthiness of the existing licensee. Finally, when considering the right of assignment, the parties need to distinguish licenses from other ancillary contracts such as software development agreements and support and maintenance agreements when the agreement lacks a limitation on assignment. These ancillary agreements may be governed by common law, not copyright law, potentially resulting in different outcomes for different types of agreements.

Licensors should also include a prohibition on transferring the license as well as prohibiting assignment. A transfer refers to the transfer of the software itself, i.e., a transfer of the physical asset. Including such a prohibition eliminates any potential ambiguity, further protecting the licensor's interests.

See Chapter 4.G, above, and Chapter 3.C for further discussions of this issue.

PRACTICE POINT:

Under the Delaware Limited Liability Company Act (6 Del. C. § 18-217(1)(8)), for contracts entered into after August 1, 2018, divisions of LLCs cannot be prevented by anti-assignment clauses from assigning an agreement unless stated explicitly in the contract.

Accordingly, when licensing to an LLC, prudent licensors should ensure those licenses subject to Delaware law specifically address transfers effected by division, or the allocation of assets and liabilities by division of an LLC. Potential model language is as follows:

> ***Assignment.*** *If Licensor assigns or sells or otherwise transfers its rights to a business or product line or substantially all its assets and provided such Party agrees to perform the obligations under the Agreement, then Licensor may transfer its rights and obligations under the Agreement upon written notice to Licensee. Licensee may not transfer, whether by (i) operation of law, (ii) transfer of its rights to a business, product line or substantially all of its assets to a separate entity <u>(including but not limited to divisions, re-allocations and transfers of assets, liabilities and obligations amongst LLC divisions),</u> (iii) change of control, or otherwise, the Agreement without prior written consent of Licensor, and consent shall not be unreasonably withheld. Attempts to transfer in contravention of this section shall be deemed null and void. The Agreement shall be binding on the Parties hereto and their respective successors and assigns.*

2. *By Licensor*

The licensee should also be concerned with the assignment of the license agreement by the licensor. Specifically, the licensee wants to ensure that any assignee possesses the technical competence and formal resources to support, maintain, and enhance the software. To protect its interests, the licensee should prohibit any assignment of the agreement by merger, consolidation, operation of law, or otherwise without the prior written consent of the licensee. While this right may be qualified by the caveat that the licensee's consent will not be unreasonably withheld or delayed, the licensee should seek the right to immediately terminate the license in the event its consent is not obtained. This will protect the licensee from those assignees who plan to "sunset" the licensed software or seek to contractually exploit the licensee's dependence on the software. Before consenting to any assignment, the licensee should insist on receiving written guarantees that the assignee will continue to support the software at agreed-upon levels and at an agreed-upon pricing for a set period of years.

PRACTICE POINT:

When drafting an assignment provision, the parties should consider:

- How is "assignment" defined?
  - Transfer to an affiliate
  - Change of control
  - Consolidation
  - Merger
  - Operation of law
  - A successor in interest to all of a party's business or assets
- Under what circumstances is assignment permitted, if any?
- Is consent required under all circumstances?

    - To an "affiliate"?
    - Only to a competitor?
    - In connection with a change in control?
    - To a successor in interest to all of the licensee's business or assets?
- If consent is required, under what conditions?
    - Must a request for assignment be in writing?
    - Is the licensor required to reply to a request to assign within a stated time period?
- What if the licensor does not reply within such period?
    - Consent is deemed granted
    - Consent is deemed rejected
- What is the standard for review? i.e., consent will not be unreasonably withheld
- Will the assignor remain liable for any breach?
- How is transfer of the agreement effected? (i.e., written consent?)
- What are the ramifications of a breach of the assignment provision?
    - The assignment is null and void
    - The other party may seek damages
    - Injunctive relief

3. Transfer

Software licenses encompass two groupings of rights—the intangible rights and the tangible personal property rights. The intangible rights are separate and distinct from the tangible personal property in which the intangible rights are embodied. As such, the concepts of "transfer" and "assignment" in relation to software differ. A "transfer" refers to the physical movement of the software tangible property itself from the licensee to a third party whereas an "assignment" refers to the transfer of the ownership of the license from the licensee to a third party unless the assignment relates to the transfer of ownership rights by the licensor. If the "transfer" is a distribution under the copyright laws, then the transfer requires the permission of the copyright owner/licensor. Thus, from the licensor's perspective, it is prudent to include express prohibitions against both transfers and assignments in the license agreement.

I. Implied Licenses

While most licenses arise though an affirmative grant, an implied license arises by implication which causes another party to believe they have the right to use the copyrighted materials. *See Field v. Google, Inc.*, 412 F. Supp. 2d 1106 (D. Nev. 2006). An implied license usually arises when an entity (the licensor) creates a work for a party (the licensee) and the creator/licensor intends for the requesting party/licensee to use and distribute the created work. *See Bitmanagement Software GmbH v. United States*, 989 F.3d 938 (Fed. Cir 2021); *Asset Marketing Systems, Inc. v. Gagnon*, 542 F.3d 748 (9th Cir. 2008). Implied licenses are often used as a defense to copyright infringement. *Numbers Licensing LLC v. bVisual USA Inc.*, 643 F. Supp. 2d 1245 (E.D. Wash. 2009).

See Chapter 7.A for a discussion of the work made for hire doctrine, which often gives rise to implied licenses if the requesting party does not obtain an assignment of ownership rights for the created work. For a more detailed discussion see, Hornick, *Implied Licenses in Software Licensing*, The Licensing J. (May 2010).

CHAPTER 5

Ancillary Clauses

Unless otherwise indicated, all section references (§) refer to the corresponding sections of the Annotated Software License and Services Agreement set forth in Form B.3.1.

A. Representations, Warranties, Covenants, and Disclaimers (§ 16)

1. *Representations and Warranties (§§ 16.1, 16 A-AE, 16.2)*

(a) General

It is generally held that a representation is a statement of a present or past fact as such fact exists at the given time, and a warranty is a promise that certain existing or future facts will be or are true. *Krys v. Henderson,* 69 S.E.2d 635, 637 (Ga. Ct. App. 1952). Representations and warranties are not always mutually inclusive and can have different consequences in terms of liability. Thus, the parties should carefully consider the impact of making a representation versus a warranty.

Some commentators, however, argue that there is no practical distinction between a representation and a warranty. *See, e.g.,* Adams, *A Manual of Style for Contract Drafting,* ABA PRESS (5th ed. 2023).

(i) Representations

A false representation gives rise to a breach of contract claim for damages and potentially having the contract voided if the false representation was made knowingly and the fact was material to the risk. "A false representation may be implied as well as actual." *Dunn Appraisal Co. v. Honeywell Information Systems Inc.*, 687 F.2d 877, 882 (6th Cir. 1982). "[F]raud is established when misrepresentation is knowingly made with intent to induce reliance, and justifiable reliance results, causing plaintiff damages." *Glovatorium, Inc. v. NCR Corp.*, 684 F.2d 658 (9th Cir. 1982).

A "representation" creates a legal risk that the licensor's sales puffery may lead to a claim of fraud in the inducement. *See* RESTATEMENT (SECOND) OF TORTS §§ 525, 526, and 552C. The Ninth Circuit has defined "sales puffery" as "exaggerated advertising, blustering and boasting upon which no reasonable buyer would rely." *Southland Sod Farms v. Stover Seed Co.*, 108 F.3d 1134 (9th Cir. 1997). *See also Castrol Inc. v. Pennzoil Co.*, 987 F.2d 939 (3d Cir. 1993). In general, sales puffery is not actionable.

An action for a fraudulent misrepresentation must be predicated upon a statement relating to a past or an existing fact. Future promises are contractual and do not constitute fraud. *Central On Line Data Systems, Inc. v. Filenet Corp.*, 99 F.3d 1138 (table), 1996 WL 483031 (6th Cir. Aug. 23, 1996) (unpublished disposition). If the plaintiff is successful in proving fraud in the inducement, the contract's limitation of liability will be void. *Accusystems, Inc. v. Honeywell Information Systems, Inc.*, 580 F. Supp. 474 (S.D.N.Y. 1984) (statute of limitations does not apply to claims for fraud in the inducement).

Damages for such fraud may include the amount paid under the contract minus any benefits obtained; the cost of cover; extra labor expenses; the expense related to obtaining different computer services; the costs associated with installing and removing hardware; program conversion costs; and the costs of equipment maintenance, as well as the risk of the rescission of the license agreement without the necessary legal protections for the licensor. *See Applied Data Processing, Inc. v. Burroughs Corp.*, 394 F. Supp. 504 (D. Conn. 1975); *Clements Auto Co. v. Service Bureau Co.*, 298 F. Supp. 115 (D. Minn. 1969), *aff'd as modified*, 444 F.2d 169 (8th Cir. 1971).

In the event of fraud in the inducement, the license agreement's integration clause may be voided allowing previously excluded statements to be considered. *See Financial Times Publications, Inc. v. Compugraphic Corp.*, 873 F.2d 936, 943–44 (8th Cir. 1990). Further, a party may not escape liability for misrepresentation by invoking a contract's limitation of liability clause. *Vmark Software, Inc. v. EMC Corp.*, 642 N.E.2d 587 (Mass. App. Ct. 1994).

The failure to satisfy a representation does not necessarily give rise to a fraud claim. "[F]raud may not be based on representations of future conduct, on broken promises, or representations of existing intent that are not executed." *Digitech Computer, Inc. v. Trans-Care, Inc.*, 583 F. Supp. 2d 984 (S.D. Ind. 2008).

Given that most licensees are willing to accept only a warranty and not require the licensor to provide a representation in the belief one is as good as the other, the licensor should refrain from making any representations in its license.

For a general overview of liability for misrepresentations in the sale or lease of computer systems, see Leahy, *Misrepresentation in Sale or Lease of Computer Systems*, 20 AM. JUR. 3D *Proof of Facts* 621 (1993).

(ii) Warranties

Unlike a representation, a beneficiary does not have to rely on a warranty to recover damages. *Rogath v. Siebermann*, 129 F.3d 261 (2d Cir. 1997); *CBS, Inc. v. Ziff Davis Publishing Co.*, 553 N.E.2d 997 (N.Y. 1990). Further, a party's knowledge that a warranty is false does not prevent the party from bringing a claim for breach of warranty unless the party making the warranty informed the beneficiary of such falsehood. *Rogath v. Siebermann*, 129 F.3d 261, 264 (2d Cir. 1997). The remedy for a breach of a warranty gives rise to a claim for damages but not termination of the agreement.

(iii) Contract vs. Tort Claims

A breach of contract does not give rise to a cause of action under tort law. A duty under tort law arises from circumstances extraneous to and not constituting elements of the contract, even though it may be related to and dependent on the contract. *Bristol-Meyers Squibb, Industrial Division v. Delton- Star, Inc.*, 620 N.Y.S.2d 196, 197 (N.Y.A.D. 1994).

In short, tort actions arise from the breach of duties imposed by law (e.g., a duty of care) regardless of the contractual terms defining the parties' relationship. Consequently, a claim of fraud will not be allowed where the only alleged fraud arises from the breach of the contract. *Jackson Heights Medical Group v. Complex Corp.*, 634 N.Y.S.2d 721, 722 (1995). By clearly stating or warranting the standard of care or duty in the agreement (e.g., a workmanlike manner; see, e.g., § 16.C) and/or providing for service levels (see, e.g., § 16.B), the licensor should be able to establish the duty it owes the licensee and avoid the implementation of a standard outside the four corners of the license.

In the case of solely economic losses, recovery is limited to contract claims and not tort claims. *Transport Corp. of Amer., Inc. v. International Business Machines Corp.*, 30 F.3d 953, 957 (8th Cir. 1994); *Huron Tool and Engineering Co. v. Precision Consulting Services, Inc.*, 532 N.W.2d 541 (Mich. App. 1995) (fraudulent representations alleged by plaintiff were indistinguishable from terms of contract and warranties, thus plaintiff limited to contractual remedies). *See also Word Management Corp. v. AT&T Info. Sys., Inc.*, 525 N.Y.S.2d 433 (1988).

Courts have used two tests, the "economic loss doctrine" and the "gist of the action" test, to determine whether tort claims that accompany contract claims should be allowed or rejected as a wrongful attempt to recover additional contract damages. *Bohler v. Uddeholm America, Inc.*, 247 F.3d 79, 103 (3d Cir. 2001). The economic loss doctrine is a judicially created doctrine to preclude a commercial purchaser of a product from suing in negligence (tort) for a loss that is solely economic under the belief that recovery should be had under contract law, warranty, and the UCC. *Prent Corp. v. Martek Holdings, Inc.*, 618 N.W.2d 201 (Wis. 2000). It is unclear, however, whether the doctrine would apply in the case of fraud. A trend has begun to emerge that claims of fraud involving a breach of contract claim will be precluded by the economic loss doctrine. *Werwinski v. Ford Motor Car Co.*, 286 F.3d 661 (3d Cir. 2002) (court refused to recognize an exception to the economic loss doctrine where intentional fraud was alleged). A fraud claim that is distinct from a breach of contract claim may survive. *See, e.g., AKA Distributing Co. v. Whirlpool Corp.* 137 F.3d 1086 (8th Cir. 1998) (fraud claim barred by economic loss doctrine); *Huron Tool & Engineering Co. v. Precision Consulting Services, Inc.*, 532 N.W.2d 541 (Mich. App. 1995) (not all fraud claims precluded by the economic loss doctrine). For a more detailed discussion, *see* Sanford, *Fraud and the Economic Loss Doctrine,* COM. L. NEWSL. 3 (Dec. 2000).

Similarly, under the "gist of the action" test, courts have sought to preclude recharacterizing breach of contract claims as tort claims. The doctrine seeks to determine whether the "gist" of the plaintiff's claim lies in contract or tort and bars "plaintiffs from bringing a tort claim that merely replicates a claim for breach of an underlying contract." *Fish Net, Inc. v. Profitcenter Software, Inc.*, 2011 WL 1235204 (E.D. Pa. Mar. 31, 2011); *Phico Insurance Co. v. Presbyterian Medical Services Corp.*, 663 A.2d 753, 757 (Pa. 1995). At least one court has held that the "gist of the action" test even bars tort claims based upon allegations of intentional fraud. *eToll, Inc. v. Elias/Savion Advertising, Inc.*, 811 A.2d 10 (Pa. Super. 2002).

For a discussion of the use of representations and warranties, *see* Adams, *A Lesson in Drafting Contracts: What's Up with 'representations and warranties'?*, 15 BUS. L. TODAY 32 (Nov./Dec. 2005) (author argues that drafters would be better served by using only representation/represents and not warranty/warrants as the term "representation" has a broader meaning), *but see* Stark, *Another View on Reps and Warranties*, 16 BUS. L. TODAY 8 (Jan./Feb. 2006).

(b) Licensor Warranties

Although it has not been definitively determined whether the UCC applies to the licensing of software, many courts have looked to the UCC for guidance in determining warranty issues. See Chapter 15.A for a discussion of the applicability of the UCC to software licensing.

The UCC recognizes two types of warranties: express warranties and implied warranties. "Express warranties are affirmative promises about the quality and features of the goods being sold. They [can] also include descriptions of the goods being sold or samples shown to the buyer." Cadden & Fuller LLP, *Commercial Law: Express and Implied Warranties Under the Uniform Commercial Code*, http://www.caddenfuller.com/CM/Articles/Articles34.asp. Express warranties are statements of facts or promises which are expressly part of the transaction. UCC § 2-313(a)(1). Implied warranties are warranties [which] rest so clearly on a common factual situation . . . [that] they will arise in such a situation unless unmistakably negated" (UCC § 2-313 comment 1) and are presumed to have been made in the sale of a good regardless of whether the seller made any written or verbal affirmative assurances.

For a general overview of warranties, *see* Kelley & Allgeyer, *Warranties, Remedies and Related Peccadilloes: Steps to a Successful Contract Negotiation*, 29 ACC DOCKET 44 (March 2011).

(i) Implied Warranties under Article 2 of the UCC

The UCC provides for two implied warranties: (1) the implied warranty of merchantability (UCC § 2-314) and (2) the implied warranty of fitness for particular purpose. UCC § 2-315. Implied warranties are made whether or not they are affirmatively stated.

(A) Merchantability

The warranty of merchantability is "a warranty that the goods shall be merchantable and is implied in a contract for their sale if the seller is a merchant with respect to goods of that kind." UCC § 2-314. The goods must (i) pass without objection in the trade under the contract description; (ii) in the case of fungible goods, be of fair average quality within the description; (iii) be fit for the ordinary purposes for which such goods are used; (iv) run, within the variations permitted by the agreement, of even kind, quality and quantity within each unit and among all units involved; (v) be adequately contained, packaged, and labeled as the agreement may require; and (vi) conform to the promise or affirmations of fact made on the container or label if any. *Id.* In essence, the warranty requires that a good meet a consumer's reasonable expectations for a good of that kind. Fitness for ordinary purposes is often considered to be part of merchantability but is usually discussed separately to contrast it with fitness for a particular purpose (see below).

The implied warranty of merchantability assures the purchaser that the product falls within the general standards of fitness for ordinary purposes under the product's description. *Vision Graphics, Inc. v. E.I. du Pont de Nemours*, 41 F. Supp. 2d 93 (D. Mass. 1999). It does not guarantee that the product will be ideal or ever optimal for a particular use. *Id.*

Use of the phrase "AS IS" is sufficient to disclaim a warranty of merchantability; however, implied warranty disclaimers will not be upheld in the presence of fraud. *Sorchaga v. Ride Auto, LLC*, 893 N.W.2d 360 (Minn. App. 2017).

For a more detailed discussion, *see The Implied Warranty of Merchantability*, 44 LAW. BRIEF 1 (Oct. 2014).

(B) Fitness for Particular Purpose

Whereas the warranty of merchantability implies that the goods are fit for the purpose for which they are ordinarily sold in the marketplace, the warranty of fitness for a particular purpose guarantees that the goods are suitable for a specific purpose that may be different from their ordinary purpose. The warranty of fitness for a particular purpose "applies if the seller knows or has reason to know that the buyer will be using the goods he is buying for a certain purpose." Cadden & Fuller LLP, *Commercial Law: Express and Implied Warranties Under the Uniform Commercial Code*, http://www.caddenfuller.com/CM/Articles/Articles34.asp.

"AS IS" eliminates the warranty of fitness for a particular purpose.

(ii) Other Warranties under Article 2 of the UCC

Under the UCC, two other warranties are read into every contract: (1) the warranty of title, and (2) the warranty of non-infringement. UCC § 2-312. Unlike the implied warranties of merchantability and fitness for a particular purpose (collectively "Implied Warranties"), these warranties are treated somewhat differently. Arguably, the warranties of title and infringement cannot be classified as implied warranties as they are not identified as such under the UCC and cannot be negated by a general disclaimer of implied warrants. Because the UCC does not identify the warranties of good title and infringement as implied warranties, these warranties may not be disclaimed or modified.

(A) Good Title

In a contract for the sale of goods, a seller is deemed to warrant that (i) the title conveyed is good, and its transfer rightful; and (ii) the goods shall be delivered free from any security interest or other lien or encumbrance of which the buyer at the time of contracting has no knowledge. UCC § 2-312. It implies that the seller of goods has the right to sell those goods.

Stating that a good is provided "AS IS" does not disclaim a warranty of title.

(B) Non-infringement

The warranty of infringement provides that "the goods shall be delivered free of the rightful claim of any third person by way of infringement." UCC § 2-312.

As with good title, "AS IS" does not disclaim the warranty of infringement.

(iii) Express Warranties

For software licenses, there are a number of "standard" express warranties that a licensor typically might make and a number that the licensee should seek. Which warranties to include is dependent on the nature of the transaction and the risk tolerance of the parties. The licensor's willingness to provide warranties will be a function of the size of the transaction but may also be influenced by other factors, such as the licensor's ability to recognize revenue. For example, a licensor that provides a licensee with a warranty based on licensee-defined criteria may find that a right of cancellation is imputed to the licensee, and therefore the licensor may have difficulty recognizing the revenue under the agreement.

General (§ 16.1)

At a minimum, a licensor should warrant that:

(i) it has valid title to the software it is licensing,
(ii) the licensor has the right to grant the license, including a license to any third-party software incorporated into the licensed software,
(iii) the software will operate in all material respects with the functional specifications and current documentation; and
(iv) the software does not infringe on any third party intellectual property rights.

It is customary, however, for the licensor to state that the operation of the licensed software will not be uninterrupted or error free (§ 16.1.2).

Licensors should avoid making broad statements, usually made in the course of the sales process, to prevent the licensee from claiming such statements were express warranties. *See, e.g., Wojcik v. Borough of Manville*, 71 U.C.C. Rep. Serv. 2d 19 (Sup. Ct. N.J. App. 2010) (statement that helmet was the "best" is not an express warranty); *John F. Ruggles, Jr., Inc. v. Ventex Technology, Inc.*, 75 U.C.C. Rep. Serv. 2d 136 (E.D. Ky. 2011) (vendor statements that technology is so advanced no other product comes close to performance was sales puffery, not express warranty).

To limit its risk, a licensor should consider limiting its warranties with a materiality or knowledge qualifier. From the licensee's perspective, however, such qualifiers are, in most cases, inappropriate, as the licensor should stand behind its product without qualification.

Prudent licensors should never warrant that the software is fit for the licensee's intended use or that it will allow the licensee comply with any regulatory obligations applicable to the licensee.

> *Licensor warrants all products/goods provided under this Agreement shall (i) be of good quality (ii) be fit for their ordinary purpose, (iii) conform to the agreed upon specifications, (iv) be delivered free of any claim of any third party for infringement and (v) perform substantially in accordance with the accompanying documentation, when unmodified and used in the manner specified in such documentation.*

System Warranty (§ 16.A)

When purchasing a software system, the licensee should require the licensor to represent and warrant that the system as a whole will operate within the parameters of certain service levels. A system warranty limits the problems that may arise when each of the individual system components operates properly but when they are combined the resulting performance is less than desired.

Where the software is part of an integrated system being installed by the licensor (i.e., a system integration project), or a group of different vendors, the licensee should require the licensor to expressly warrant that once installed, the system as a whole (versus the independent components) will operate in conformance with certain performance metrics. (Note: UCITA contains an implied warranty regarding integration. *See* UCITA § 405; Chapter 15.B.3(i),(iv)).

Licensors should carefully consider any warranty they make as to the software's performance when operated in conjunction with any third-party software or certain hardware configurations as they may negatively influence the performance or operation of the licensor's software. Licensees, however, should insist on the inclusion of such a warranty to ensure they receive what they have paid for. If the licensee fails to do so, it may be unable to determine which third-party product or service caused the noncompliance and unwittingly assumes the risk of the integrated system being noncompliant with the licensee's needs. The licensee should always seek to have one entity or vendor be responsible for the performance of the integrated product, usually through a prime/subcontract relationship.

The customer should insist on the inclusion of detailed performance metrics that set forth the levels to which the individual components and the system as a whole will perform. This usually is done through a warranty. (See § 16.B.)

Software (§ 16.B)

A licensor should warrant that all software will meet certain written performance standards such as the user manuals, user notes, or new release notes. For example, "The Software will at all times perform in accordance with the published specifications." (See §§ 16B, E and § 3.B.) At the same time, the licensor should avoid making broad or exaggerated statements about its software's performance or capabilities. In the extreme, any misrepresentation may void a license agreement's limitation of liability. *Vmark Software, Inc. v. EMC Corp.*, 642 N.E.2d 587 (Ct. App. Mass. 1994). Software by its nature is imperfect. Thus, a licensor should never warrant that the software will operate uninterrupted or error-free, as software will always contain "bugs."

Alternatively, many licensees seek to have the licensor warrant that the software is free from defects in design, materials and workmanship. Licensees should carefully consider whether language to this effect is acceptable, as at least one court had held that such a disclaimer excuses the licensor from any obligation to fix all errors. *Info Systems Technology, Inc. v. Logical Software, Inc.*, 835 F.2d 874 (4th Cir. 1987). Further, the term "materials" is ambiguous and arguably is inapplicable to software as software is intangible. The licensor should be willing, however, to give a warranty as to the media on which the software is contained. See the discussion below and § 16.N. Such a warranty creates little risk for the licensor, given that most software is delivered electronically and in the event of a breach, the media can be immediately replaced. The term "design" is also ambiguous although one court has interpreted a warranty as to design to mean the software will have the ability to perform the required functions within a reasonable time frame. *USM Corp. v. Arthur D. Little Systems, Inc.*, 546 N.E.2d 888 (Mass. 1989).

Licensees should seek a warranty period sufficient to address any inherent problems that may arise after acceptance. Although many licensees seek a warranty of one year, 30 to 90 days is more common. Some practitioners equate an extended warranty to "free" maintenance. It is not free, however, as a prudent licensor will build the cost of any extended warranty into its pricing. From the licensor's perspective, it is better to provide a shorter warranty period and have the licensee execute a separate maintenance agreement under which the licensor can provide free services. See Chapter 21 for a discussion of the benefits of a separate maintenance agreement.

By having the licensor commit to certain service levels, the licensee is in essence guaranteed that minimum level of performance, and such service level will become the standard of care/duty in the event of any subsequent negligence action. The licensor should ensure that it is excused from liability if the licensor follows the licensee's designated specifications and such specifications do not produce the performance levels the licensee desires or are otherwise set forth in their contract. See Chapter 12 for a more detailed discussion of service levels.

Usually, the remedy for the breach of this warranty is the provision of pre-agreed service level credits or liquidated damages to the licensee, most likely a small amount. This remedy is also usually accompanied by language stating that if the service credits or liquidated damages reach a certain level, the licensor will be deemed to be in material breach of the underlying agreement and the licensee may terminate the agreement. The licensor has some protection in that the licensor's failure to meet the service levels does not immediately result in a material breach but rather the licensor has some period of time to correct its non-performance while providing the licensee financial compensation during the period it tries to correct its breach. Most licensors will insist on providing credits instead of actually making a cash payment to the licensee.

The license should include language that the service level credits, or liquidated damages are the exclusive remedy of the licensee, to preclude the licensee from also bringing an action for breach. The licensee should insist that there not be separate limitations of liability throughout the contract to ensure the licensee is able to obtain the benefit of the bargain.

Services (§ 16.C)

Where the agreement contemplates a services component, such as for development, support, or maintenance, the licensor should warrant that all services will be rendered in a professional and workmanlike manner. Some practitioners argue against making such a warranty believing they are two different standards and both cannot be satisfied at the same time. They believe "professional" is a looser standard that implies a standard of care or quality as well as the qualifications of the people performing the work.

If, however, a vendor is providing only staff augmentation services and the contracted labor is working at the direction of the customer, it is inappropriate for the vendor to provide a services warranty. The majority of states hold that under common law there are no implied warranties for the provision of services. FELDMAN & NIMMER, DRAFTING EFFECTIVE CONTRACTS § 5.05[A][2] (2d ed. 2007); *Pearl Investments, LLC v. Standard I/O, Inc.*, 257 F. Supp. 2d 326 (D. Me. 2003) (no warranty implied in software development contract); *Gilbert Const. Co. v. Gross*, 129 A.2d 518, 520 (Md. 1957); *Craig v. American Dist. Tel. Co.*, 399 N.Y.S.2d 164, 165 (1977) (implied warranties do not arise from the performance of a service). *But see Adobe Masters, Inc. v. Downey*, 883 P.2d 133, 134 (N.M. 1994); *Continental Dredging, Inc. v. De-Kaizered, Inc.*, 120 S.W.3d 380,

390 n.6 (Tex. 2003). Such licensees should include language in the underlying license agreement that all services will be performed in a "first class manner" or "consistent with the licensor's status as an industry leader." *See also* RESTATEMENT (SECOND) OF TORTS (1965) § 299A (those who provide professional services will be "required to exercise the skill and knowledge normally possessed by members of that profession or trade in good standing in similar communities."). While no standard is perfect, a more desirable standard from the licensor's perspective is to use a "commercially reasonable manner."

Many lawyers representing licensors believe these standards are ambiguous and can later lead to disputes in interpretation. As such, they seek to avoid these terms in favor of clearly defined standards. Further, the use of the term "professional" raises the issue of whether service personnel are "professionals" and need to be licensed. If so, what professional codes are imported into the license? Similarly, licensors should be careful not to hold themselves out as possessing special skills to avoid creating implied warranties. *Data Processing Services, Inc. v. L.H. Smith Oil Corp.*, 492 N.E.2d 314 (Ind. 1986) (programmer who held self out as possessing ability and qualification to design and develop computer programs implied by representation possession of skill and diligence possessed by well-informed member of computer programming trade).

Several enterprising plaintiffs have sought to create a higher standard to which all computer services companies and professionals should be held when providing computer services. To date, these attempts have been rejected by the courts. *See Chatlos Systems, Inc. v. Nat'l. Cash Register Corp.*, 479 F. Supp. 738 (D.N.J. 1979) (court declined to create a new tort of "computer malpractice"); *RKB Enterprises, Inc. v. Ernst & Young*, 582 N.Y.S.2d 814 (1992) (there is no cause of professional malpractice in the provision of computer services); *Metpath, Inc. v. IDS Corp.*, 1991 WL 39617 (Conn. Super. Mar. 12, 1991) (allegation of negligence against computer services company does not spawn tort of "computer malpractice").

Documentation (§ 16.D)

The licensor should warrant that the documentation accurately describes the functional and operational characteristics of the software as delivered to the licensee and that the documentation is detailed and complete. Some licensees seek to include language that the documentation will allow a "reasonably skilled" operator to use and operate the software. The use of the term "reasonably skilled" or a similar term is ambiguous and creates significant risk to the licensor. Thus, the licensor should resist including language to this effect.

During the warranty period and in any subsequent support agreement, the licensor should agree to promptly provide all updates and enhancements to the software as well as any accompanying documentation to the licensee. Further, all documentation should be contemporaneously updated to reflect any enhancements to the software. Without proper documentation, the licensee will not be able to fully utilize the software. Thus, it is important that the requirements of the documentation are explicitly detailed.

A common question arises as to what is an "update" or "enhancement" as opposed a new version. A vendor will often claim that a customer is not entitled to receive a free copy of a particular improvement to the software, as the improvement constitutes a new version not an enhancement or update. At least two courts have acknowledged that the term "enhancement" is ambiguous and does not have a standard meaning in the technology industry. *Infosystems Technology, Inc. v. Logical Software, Inc.*, 1987 WL 24433 (4th Cir. Nov. 27, 1987); *PRC Reality Systems, Inc. v. Nat'l Ass'n of Realtors*, 766 F. Supp. 972 (E.D. Va. 1991), *aff'd in part, vacated in part*, 972 F.2d. 341 (4th Cir. 1992).

Defects in Design, Materials, and Workmanship (§ 16.E)

Many licensees seek to have the licensor warrant that the software is free from defects in materials and workmanship. A licensee may also ask the licensor to warrant defects in design as well. A licensor should think carefully before granting a warranty as to design, as software by its nature is imperfect, creating a potentially significant risk. Defects in materials usually relates to the physical media rather than the intangible software.

The licensor should clarify any warranty regarding "materials" to ensure it is clear that the licensor is only warranting the disk that contains the software to avoid a "bootstrap" argument that a warranty as to materials equates to a "design" warranty. *See, for example*, the discussion regarding Media below § 16.N. Similarly, the licensor should also clarify the meaning of "workmanship" in any warranty, which arguably includes the design of the software. See the discussion regarding Services above § 16.C.

Interface (§ 16.F)

The licensor should warrant/agree that it will assist the licensee in the licensee's development of any application programming interfaces (APIs) between third-party systems and the software. Further, the licensor should provide any industry standard APIs that the licensor is evaluating. The licensee should also seek to have the licensor use as many industry-standard protocols as possible. This warranty ensures that the licensee will have the licensor's support in developing APIs. Without the licensor's support, it could be quite difficult and potentially very expensive to develop the necessary interfaces.

If a licensor does not create or publish APIs, the licensee should seek the right to reverse engineer, disassemble, or decompile for the purpose of facilitating interoperability between the licensor's software and third-party software products. Without this right, the licensee is at the mercy of the licensor, which could significantly impact the licensee's ability to efficiently operate the licensee's IT systems. Under existing law, the licensee most likely already has this right, but the licensee should seek to have the licensor explicitly acknowledge this right. *See* Chapter 4.C.6.

Open Architecture/Open System Warranty (§ 16.G)

Licensor should also warrant that the software is designed in an "Open Architecture" environment such that the licensor should publish all external interface specifications. Again, this will allow the licensee to create interfaces in a quicker, more cost-effective manner.

Compatibility (§§ 16.H, 16.I)

A prudent licensee should include a warranty that any enhancements to the software will be compatible with the licensee's existing version of the software. The license should also seek a warranty that any enhancement will not degrade the functionality of the existing system. A licensor should be careful about making an open-ended warranty. Rather, the licensor should limit its compatibility obligations to the two most recent versions of the software to avoid the liability of making updated versions compatible with earlier versions in perpetuity.

If the licensor is providing the licensee a complete, integrated system or hardware with the software, the licensor should warrant the compatibility and interoperability of the individual components without modification and with all third-party software. A licensor, however, should be hesitant to make such broad open-ended statements.

Alternatively, the licensor should warrant that all software and hardware sold by the licensor will be compatible with those third-party components set forth in an exhibit attached to the underlying agreement. To the extent the licensor has claimed certain compatibility in its marketing materials, product documentation or RFP response, those products should be included in the attached exhibit.

Data Integrity (§ 16.J)

As part of an ancillary services agreement, a licensee may request that the licensor convert its existing data and have the licensor warrant that the data will be converted accurately and completely. A licensor should think carefully before agreeing to undertake such a conversion or make such a warranty without fully understanding the risk involved. Most prudent licensors will not agree to perform or be responsible for any data conversion as there is significant risk and expense involved in the process.

Software Obsolescence (§ 16.K)

The licensee should seek to obtain a representation and warranty that the licensor is committed to enhancing the software in the future and that the licensor has no plans to discontinue the development, marketing, maintenance, or support of the software. This is especially important if the software will be mission critical to the operation of the licensee's business and the software will be used for a significant period of time. While it is unlikely that a licensor will agree to such a broad commitment, licensors are more receptive to committing to provide maintenance and support services for a set period of time. A more aggressive position is to require the licensor to represent and warrant that it will actually market and license the software for a set period of time. Again, licensors cannot predict changing market demands and thus should be hesitant to do so.

Occasionally, a licensee will seek to have a licensor commit to investing a certain percentage of revenues/profits into the product each year (See § 3.A). A licensor should be hesitant to make this type of commitment as it limits the licensor's flexibility in operating the licensor's business and could significantly reduce its profits. At the same time, however, a licensee has a legitimate interest in knowing that the software/system is not going to be "sunsetted" shortly after the transaction is consummated. An alternate position is to have the licensor covenant that (1) if it ceases to market the licensed software and introduces a new, functionally equivalent software program within a set number of years of the license date or (2) introduces a new software product with a certain percentage of the functionality of the licensed software within a set period of time from the license date, (a) the new software will be licensed free of charge to the licensee, and (b) the licensor will port the licensee to the new product without charge or provide a functionally equivalent third-party product. For mission-critical software, however, it is most likely impractical to migrate to a new platform.

In addition, the licensee should seek to have the licensor represent and warrant that it will issue a minimum of two updates per year which will address and correct all errors and bugs in the software as of the date of the release. Again, the licensor should be hesitant to commit in writing to an action for which it may lack the resources, finances or business justification to comply.

In addition, the licensee may want the licensor to warrant that the version of the software being delivered to the licensee is the most current version of the software. The intent of this warranty is to ensure the licensor is delivering the licensee the same version of the software it is delivering to its other and perhaps larger customers, and to avoid having the licensee purchase an updated version within a short period of time after it licenses the software.

Any provision capturing this intent should reflect the specifics of the underlying transaction, including the nature and use of the particular software, the cost and useful life of the software, the cost of implementing a new software solution and converting any data, and the general availability of functionally equivalent software.

Model language favoring the licensor is as follows:

Licensor will ***use commercially reasonable efforts to notify*** *Licensee six (6) months in advance of the effective date of the Discontinued Availability ("DA") of Licensor's Software, or Services that are provided under this Agreement. Notwithstanding the provision of Section ____ ("Notices"), such notice may be provided by posting on Licensor's website. Such obligation to provide notice will be waived in the event that a functionally equivalent software product is available when Licensor ceases to offer the Software. From such effective date, Licensor shall have no further obligation to support, repair, replace, provide spare parts for or maintain a discontinued software, provided, however, that Licensor shall not be excused from any warranty obligations remaining on the DA effective date. In the case of items supplied by third-party licensors, Licensor will notify Licensee of the discontinuance of availability of hardware, software, or support provided by the Licensor as soon as practical after Licensor receives notice from such licensor. Licensee's right to notice herein shall be Licensee's sole and exclusive right upon DA of the Software.*

This language requires that the licensor exert only "reasonable efforts" to notify the licensee and allows the licensor to post such notice on its website, where it may go unnoticed by the licensee. Licensors will argue that, due to a rapidly changing business environment, they cannot make an absolute commitment to notify the licensee unless the licensor agreed to provide maintenance and support for a longer period of time during the sales process. These arguments ring hollow, as the annual budgeting and the pre-payment of maintenance and support service annually in advance dictates that these decisions be made well in advance to allow for the reallocation of the licensor's resources. Thus, from the licensee's perspective, notice should be provided at least 12 months in advance.

To the extent the parties have agreed on a source code escrow, many licensees seek to include the licensor's failure to maintain and support the software as a release event. As discussed in Chapter 24, escrow agreements and the subsequent release of the source code is not a panacea to the licensee's issues, as it will be very difficult for the licensee to support and maintain the software itself.

Disabling Code, Trap Doors, Viruses, and the Like (§ 16.L)

It is common to warrant that, except as documented, there are no trap doors, time bombs, or disabling devices. The failure of a licensee to obtain such a warranty may give the licensor significant leverage in the event of any dispute, as some licenses specifically state that the licensor may disable the software in case of a breach. *See American Computer Trust Leasing v. Jack Farrell Implement Co.*, 763 F. Supp. 1473 (D. Minn. 1991), *aff'd*, 967 F.2d 1208 (8th Cir. 1992) (license permitted licensor to disable software for licensee's nonpayment). As such, the licensee should always seek to include a statement that the licensor will not engage in electronic self-help. A prudent licensor may seek to limit its risk by instituting the caveat "to the knowledge of licensor" under the reasoning that it cannot control the actions of a rogue employee.

> *Licensor warrants to Licensee that the Software provided under this Agreement shall be free of any master access key (worms, ID, password, trap door, Trojan Horse, back door, etc.) computer virus or other destructive code, device or expiration date. This warranty shall include all upgrades to the Software, maintenance performed, and any modifications made by to the Software by Licensor.*

At the same time, however, a licensor who disables software without contractual authority may be guilty of an intentional tort and be liable to punitive damages, *see, e.g., Clayton X-Ray Co. v. Professional Systems Corp.*, 812 S.W.2d 565 (Mo. Ct. App. 1991), and may potentially be in violation of the Computer Fraud and Abuse Act (CFAA), 18 U.S.C. § 1030. *See North Texas Preventative Imaging, L.L.C. v. Eisenberg*, 1996 WL 1359212 (C.D. Cal. Aug. 19, 1996) (surreptitious inclusion of time bomb could lead to violation of CFAA). *YourNet Dating, Inc. v. Mitchell*, 88 F. Supp. 2d 870 (N.D. Ill. 2000) (unauthorized entry into computer system was violation of CFAA). Courts have interpreted the CFAA broadly. Data Security and Privacy Law: Combating Cyberthreats § 8.42 (Kevin P. Cronin and Ronald N. Weikers eds. 2005).

Because demonstration licenses usually provide the licensee a limited time period during which the licensee may use the software for testing purposes, most demonstration software and term based software include an internal mechanism that terminates the licensee's access upon expiration of the term. To avoid potential problems, prudent licensors should ensure that the automatic termination of the license is clearly disclosed in the license. Depending on the specific security measures contained within the software (e.g., IP tracking, nonuser triggered "phone home" features, automatic termination), a licensor may have to disclose and may even be required to obtain the licensee's consent in the European Union and in those countries with similar laws addressing data privacy. This is particularly true if it is not self-evident from the nature of the software that such features have been incorporated.

Subject to the nature and type of license, licensees should seek to include an express prohibition in the license prohibiting the vendor from incorporating any "lock-out" mechanisms in the software. Vendors should reject this position if the licensee is receiving a license limited to a specific time period or if the licensor is using a SaaS model and thus requires the ability to terminate access upon expiration of the license term or a breach of the license terms.

Model language to this effect favoring the licensee is as follows:

> *Licensor further represents and warrants that if the Works or other deliverables include any computer programs or software code ("Software"): (a) the Software and its media shall contain no computer instructions or inappropriate functions whose purpose or result is to disrupt, damage or interfere with Licensee's or its Affiliates' use of or access to the Software or any of their data, programs, systems, or telecommunications or broadcast equipment, software or services; and (b) unless expressly authorized in writing by Licensee, such Software shall not contain (i) any mechanism which electronically notifies Licensor of any fact or event, nor (ii) any key, node lock, time-out, login bomb or other function, implemented by any means, which may restrict Licensee or its Affiliates' use of or access to the Software or any other data, programs, computers, systems or telecommunications or broadcast equipment, software or services.*

Licensees should also insist on a virus warranty. Virus detection and removal is reactive as opposed to proactive, with virus detection software responding with a "cure" only once a virus has been identified. Thus, it is impossible for the licensor ever to be completely sure the software is virus-free. As such, many licensors will seek to give a "knowledge" warranty with respect to viruses or worms or warrant that they will use commercially reasonable efforts to screen the software and media for viruses prior to the delivery of the software to the licensee. *See generally* Robbins, *Vendor Liability for Computer Viruses and Undisclosed Disabling Devices in Software*, 10 COMPUTER LAW. 20 (July 1993). Licensors should avoid providing an absolute warranty as to the existence of viruses, as viruses are difficult to detect and may enter the software through no fault of the licensor. Model language is as follows:

> *Licensor has and will maintain industry-standard quality assurance and virus protection procedures designed to ensure that all Deliverables and Services, as applicable, are free of viruses, contaminants, and other malicious code that may harm Customer systems.*

Further, some licensors seek an additional level of protection by requiring the licensee to run the software through the licensee's own virus detection software prior to installing the software on the licensee's systems and seek to have the licensee warrant to the licensor that the licensee will not infect the licensor's system. In the event of an infection, the party causing the infection should agree to assume all costs of removing the virus and restoring any corrupted data from the affected party's computer systems.

Compliance with Laws/Regulatory Requirements (§ 16.M)

A prudent licensee should require the licensor to represent and warrant that it is in compliance with all applicable laws, including federal, state, and local labor and employment laws. The licensor should seek to make the representation and warranty mutual, especially if the licensor's employees will be working on the licensee's premises. Prudent licensors will ensure that the warranty clearly delineates which laws the licensor must comply with. Licensors should agree to comply with only those laws directly affecting the licensor and perhaps its industry. The licensor should not agree to comply with those laws applying to the licensee's business or industry unless those laws have been identified, and the licensor has quantified the risk and is compensated to assume such risk.

To the extent the licensee operates in a regulated industry with which the software interrelates, the licensee will often seek to have the licensor warrant that the software meets all applicable regulatory requirements as specified by the licensee. The licensor should strictly limit the extent of any such warranty, and if the licensor agrees to make such a warranty it should specifically identify the regulatory requirements the software will meet. Further, such warranty should be limited to the regulatory requirements in existence at the time of the contract execution. The licensee should seek to include language stating that the licensor will make the software comply with any new requirements if the licensee pays for such enhancements. Any warranties made by the licensor should be narrowly drawn to avoid unintended liability as the licensee should know the regulatory rules obligation much better than the licensor. See § 1.17 and Form Q.1 for definitions of "Regulatory Requirements," which could have a significant impact on the strength and meaning of this warranty.

See Chapter 6.I for a more detailed discussion of the issues arising from Compliance with Laws provisions.

Media (§ 16.N)

In commercial licenses, the licensor should warrant that the media on which the software is delivered is free from defects. This warranty does not create significant risk to the licensor, provided the license states that the remedy for breach is to provide the licensee with a new disk or tape. *See* Chapter 5.A.3(b) below, for a discussion of the applicability of the Magnuson-Moss Act.

Intellectual Property Infringement (§ 16.O)

Historically, licensors have warranted that the software will not infringe on any third-party intellectual property rights including patents, copyrights and trade secrets. An increasing number of licensors have ceased giving such broad warranties in light of the ever-increasing number of software patents and the accompanying risk of patent infringement claims. In doing so, they argue that there is no need to provide a warranty because the licensee's risk is mitigated by the licensor's agreement to indemnify the licensee in the event of an infringement claim. An indemnity only provides a licensee with rights equivalent to a representation and warranty if the indemnification covers the same intellectual property, i.e. patents, copyrights, trade secrets, etc., and the indemnification is not limited to indemnifying the licensee for intellectual property infringement. Further, breach of a representation or warranty usually provides the licensee a right of termination with the ability to recover its license fee, while an indemnity usually provides only for a financial recovery. *See* Chapter 5.C, below.

Representations and warranties, as well as indemnities, are means to allocate risk. Representations and warranties look retrospectively while indemnities look prospectively. Thus, it is reasonable for a licensee to seek both a representation/warranty and an indemnity. If the licensor is willing to provide a strong indemnity, however, a licensee may not need a representation and/or warranty. The licensor has no liability until it is sued, which is a remote possibility. While limiting the licensor's risk, this philosophy does not benefit the licensee. While the licensor's indemnity in theory protects the licensee from third-party claims, it does not give the licensee the right to declare a breach of the license, terminate the license as a result of the breach, and sue for direct damages. Even if the licensor defends the suit, the licensee may not want to continue using the software for a number of business and legal reasons. From the licensee's perspective, it should have the right to notice a breach, require a cure, and be able to sue for damages.

It is also possible that a licensee may become aware that the licensor does not have good title or infringes a third party's intellectual property rights without having been sued. In that case, the licensee should be able to confront the licensor without having to wait to be sued. Practically, a licensee does not want to be reliant on a software solution when it is possible that the licensee will have to switch or accept a less capable version in the future.

In essence, the licensor seeks to allocate the risks of the unknown. The licensee should think carefully before accepting this position and make sure that it is willing to forgo these claims. This is especially important where the indemnification language allows the licensor to simply refund the licensee's license fee where it is impracticable to obtain a license or make the software non-infringing. (See § 14.B.1.) The licensee may want to consider inserting language to allow the licensee to recover its "switching/transition costs" if there is a comparable product the licensee can migrate to. Further, what if a claim is never made against the licensee but the licensee knows the software infringes? Does it have a means to terminate the license?

To the extent the licensor agrees to provide a representation and/or warranty relating to intellectual property infringement, the licensee should reject limiting qualifications of the representation or warranty, as the licensor owns the underlying intellectual property and is in a better position to assume and mitigate any risk. Common qualifications sought by licensors include:

- The licensor's knowledge (actual or constructive);
- Unites States patents issued as of the date of the license agreement;
- Claims made by the licensor's competitors; or
- Limiting a licensee's recovery to a set dollar amount.

In some situations, a "reason to know" or even an "actual knowledge" qualifier may be appropriate for representations and warranties relating to intellectual property. Such qualifiers are more appropriate in the context of patent infringement than they are in the context of trademark infringement, and more appropriate in the context trademark infringement than they are in the context of copyright infringement or trade secret misappropriation. For example, while it is possible to "subconsciously" copy something, *see Abkco Music, Inc. v. Harrisongs Music, Inc.*, 944 F.2d 971 (2d Cir. 1991) (former Beatle George Harrison found liable for copyright infringement in which he "subconsciously" copied the song "He's So Fine" in composing "My Sweet Lord"), it is, generally speaking, easier to avoid infringing a trademark than it is to avoid infringing a patent, and it is generally easier to avoid infringing a copyright or misappropriating a trade secret than it is to avoid infringing a trademark.

Alternatively, the risk to the licensor by including a warranty can be mitigated to a degree by stating that the licensee's "sole and exclusive" remedy for the breach of such warranty is limited to the rights contained in the indemnification provision (see § 14.A.5). Stating that it is the "sole and exclusive" remedy seeks to make the warranty a limited warranty and thereby eliminate the licensor's risk from excluding intellectual property infringement from the limitation of liability. Alternatively, the licensor can explicitly state that the licensee's remedy for the breach of the representation and/or warranty is the same as the licensor's indemnification obligations. For this strategy to be successful, the licensor must ensure that the indemnification language is clearly written to limit the licensor's liability.

Under the UCC, a purchaser receives an implied warranty that title to the software will be delivered free of any third-party claim of infringement. UCC § 2-312. Thus, even if the licensee fails to obtain a warranty of title and against infringement in those states that recognize that UCC Article 2 governs software licensing, the licensee will still theoretically be able to bring a claim against the licensor unless the licensor specifically excluded or modified such warranty in writing or by the circumstances of the sale. UCC § 2-312(2). The warranties of title and infringement must be disclaimed separately. The "AS IS" or "all express and implied warranty" disclaimers are not sufficient. UCC § 2-312(3). In those states where the UCC does not apply, the licensee should seek to obtain an affirmative warranty of title and against infringement.

From the licensee's perspective, the licensee will want to avoid any "sub" limitations from being included through the various provisions of the license. The licensee's ability to recover damages is most likely already limited by any disclaimer of consequential damages and limits on direct damages within the license.

Some licensees may seek to include a "back door" intellectual property infringement representation and warranty by having the licensor represent and warrant that the licensed software provides the technology necessary to undertake a particular action, i.e., process the licensee's billing function. Prudent licensors should avoid giving broad, generalized representations and warrants to that effect as a patent infringement claim would breach the licensor's representation and warranty. *See, e.g., In re Paragon Trade Brands, Inc.*, 324 B.R. 797, 817 (Bankr. N.D. Ga. 2002) (transferor breached warranty that the intellectual property services "are adequate for the continuation of the [b]usiness as currently conducted" when third party filed patent infringement claim.)

See Chapter 5.C for a further discussion of this issue.

Third-Party Warranties and Indemnities (§ 16.P)

The licensee should require the licensor to assign to the licensee all end-user warranties and indemnities related to any third-party software to ensure that the licensee receives the benefit of what it has paid for. To the extent the licensor is unable to assign any such warranties or indemnities, or they do not run to the end-user licensee, the licensor should agree to enforce all such warranties and indemnities on behalf of the licensee or for its benefit.

Quality (§ 16.Q)

Many licensees require the licensor to certify that the licensor is ISO 9000 compliant, that the software will be developed in compliance with ISO 9000 or that the software will meet certain quality assurance standards. The licensee should insist on the right to inspect the licensor's quality assurance processes and interview its quality assurance team. A few licensees actually seek to insert their own employees into the development process to ensure a quality product. *See* § 10.

Authority (§ 16.R)

The licensor should warrant that it has the authority to enter into the license agreement, that the individual executing the license is authorized to do so, and that the grant of the license does not violate any third-party agreements. Further, if the licensor is providing third-party software, it should warrant that it has the right to grant the third- party license and pass through all benefits of the third-party license.

Pending Litigation (§ 16.S)

The licensee should ask the licensor to warrant that there is no pending or threatened litigation regarding the software of which the licensor has knowledge. This will force the licensor to disclose any existing litigation, which in turn will allow the licensee to learn of any potential defects or claims by other licensees alleging the software is defective. Regardless of whether this representation or warranty is included in the license agreement, the licensee should explore this issue as part of its due diligence.

Change in Control (§ 16.T)

The licensee should insist that the licensor represent and warrant that no "change of control" with the respect to the licensor is being considered, planned, or pending. This protects the licensee from entering into an agreement with the licensor based on the licensor's reputation, size, experience, or the like, and then having the license agreement transferred to a third party—a party that the licensee might otherwise not have been interested in contracting with. A licensor may not be able to make this warranty as the selective disclosure of a potential acquisition/merger may violate any applicable securities laws. Further, the parties negotiating the license for the licensor may be unaware of any potential merger.

In certain rare instances, some licenses contain a provision that to the extent a particular entity may acquire the licensor, the licensee may terminate the license for its convenience without penalty. *See* § 4.1.B.

Material Misstatements (§ 16.U)

Licensees occasionally seek a representation and a warranty similar to the representations and warranties contained in acquisition agreements that the licensor has not failed to disclose any "material fact" to the licensee or that any of the warranties contained in the agreement are misleading by omission. *See, e.g.*, 17 C.F.R § 240.10b-5. This protects the licensee from the licensor misleading the licensee by omission, but it creates a significant risk for the licensor, as the licensor is obligated to disclose any fact that a reasonable licensee would consider to be "material." From the licensor's perspective, this type of warranty should not be included as it is appropriate only in securities transactions and not software licensing. It potentially creates significant liability and a question of fact as to what was and was not known by the licensor, as well as what is "material."

Interestingly, a warranty of this type raises the issue of whether the licensor is required to disclose any facts of which the licensor has knowledge that would prevent the software from conforming to the stated warranty. A minority of states impose a duty of good faith when entering into a contract. *See, e.g.*, Del.: *Merrill v. Crothall-American, Inc.*, 606 A.2d 96, 102 (Del. 1992); Ill.: *Cuerton v. Abbott Laboratories, Inc.*, 443 N.E.2d 1069, 1071 (Ill. App. 1982) ("As a member of [Illinois] law, every contract includes a duty of good faith and fair dealing."; Mass.: *Anthony's Pier Four, Inc. v. HBS Associates*, 583 N.E.2d 806 (Mass. 1991) ("Neither party shall do anything that will have the effect of destroying or injuring the right of the other party to receive the fruits of the contract."); Mo.: *Insurance & Consulting Assoc. v. ITT Hartford Ins.*, 48 F. Supp. 2d 1181, 1191 (W.D. Mo. 1999) ("[C]ovenant of good faith and fair dealing is implied in every Missouri contract."); N.Y.: *Jaffe v. Paramount Communications, Inc.*, 644 N.Y.S.2d 43, 47 (1996) ("Implied in every contract is a covenant of good faith and fair dealing. . . .").

At the same time, the licensor must be careful that any statements regarding the performance or capabilities of the software are not misleading. Whether a statement arises to the level of a misrepresentation is a matter of fact and is subjective. Courts generally recognize that the sales process includes a degree of "puffery" and demonstrate some restraint in finding misrepresentation. *See, e.g., Hodell-Natco Industries, Inc. v. SAP America, Inc.*, 13 F. Supp. 3d 786, 811 n.13 (N.D. Ohio 2014) (rejecting SAP's argument that SAP's representations as to the number of users its software could support was "puffery" that no reasonable person would rely on); *Teragram Corp. v. MarketWatch.com, Inc.*, 2004 WL 3086883 (D. Mass. Dec. 29, 2004) (licensor's conduct in promoting the capabilities of its products did not constitute misrepresentations; "superior" is sales puffery, not a misrepresentation); *Moses.com Securities, Inc. v. Comprehensive Software Systems, Inc.*, 406 F.3d 1052 (8th Cir. 2005) (general statements made by software developer indicating there would be no problem in meeting launch date for new software system did not establish specific promise respecting system completion or system capabilities).

Fitness for a Particular Purpose (§ 16.V)

Licensors should avoid making statements about future performance or fitness for a particular purpose, as they may unintentionally create an express warranty. If the licensee relied on certain statements by the licensor as to the applicability of the software to the licensee's business needs, the licensee should insist that the licensor warrant that the software is fit for the particular purpose. In *L.S. Heath & Son, Inc. v. AT&T Info. Sys., Inc.*, 9 F.3d 561 (7th Cir. 1993), the court held that a statement that a computer system could meet the buyer's needs induced the buyer to purchase the system, creating an express warranty and becoming part of the bargain. *Id.* at 570.

Data Privacy, Data Breach and Data Transfer (§ 16.X)

In conjunction with the provision of ancillary services to the software license, prudent licensees should have the licensor disclose/warrant whether it has experienced a data breach as well as it will comply with certain standards in transferring data. With the increased focus on data security, a prudent licensee should insist on the adoption of certain data protection standards (which should be attached to the agreement as an exhibit) and require the licensor to comply with such standards.

> *To the Company's Knowledge, it has not experienced any type of security breach regarding data (wherever located regardless of media) it has an obligation to protect (either under state, federal or international law) and/or to report on. If a breach has occurred, Company warrants it has complied with all relevant data breach notification laws and taken reasonable measures to ensure appropriate security to prevent further breaches. Company will provide for inspection of any and all audits of its enterprise security program, indicating specifically any material issues.*

See Chapter 22 for a more detailed discussion of the issues related to data privacy and protection.

Gifts and Gratuities (§§ 16.Y, 45)

Both parties may want to include a warranty that gifts and gratuities were not exchanged by either party in consideration of entering into a contract. This is especially important in international contracts to avoid the ramifications of the Foreign Corrupt Practices Act. *See* § 45. This warranty assumes special importance when dealing with a governmental entity or a client that is publicly regulated such as utilities or the healthcare industry. For a more detailed discussion of the Foreign Corrupt Practices Act, see Chapter 26.H.

Customer Complaints (§ 16.Z)

The licensee may want to include a warranty that the licensor has not received a systemic number of customer complaints related to the product in question or one aspect of the product in question. This warranty is similar to the warranty set forth in § 16.S, which provides that there has been no material litigation relating to the product in question. This "belt and suspenders" approach seeks to identify those situations where the licensor settled complaints about the software's performance prior to the initiation of litigation.

Open Source Software (§ 16.AA)

Historically, many licensees sought to prohibit licensors from incorporating open source software into the licensor's product, however, given the presence of open source software in almost all software, licensees are less focused on open source in general and more focused on prohibiting the incorporation of copyleft open source software into the deliverables. To that end, these licensees seek to require the licensor to obtain the licensee's consent prior to incorporating copyleft open source software into the deliverables or to notify the licensee of any copyleft open source software incorporated into the licensor's software. Notification should not be an issue for the licensor, as under the right of attribution in all open source licenses, the licensor is required to provide the licensee with a copy of the applicable open source license.

For an overview of the issues involved with open source software, *see* Falkowski, *An Innovation in Contract Drafting: Open Source*, MICH. B.J. 30 (May 2005) and Kalina & Czyzcki, *The Ins and Outs of Open Source*, 36 LAW. BRIEF 2 (No. 14, July 2006). *See also* Davidson, *Open Source Technical Due Diligence*, 23 COMPUTER & INTERNET LAW. 1 (Aug. 2006).

See also Chapter 10 for a discussion of open source software.

Location of Performance (§ 16.AB)

With the increasing political instability throughout the world, some licensees seek a warranty that all services and work will be performed in the United States or that work cannot be performed offshore without the licensee's consent. The licensee may want to expand its warranty to provide that in the event work is performed overseas, the individuals performing such services may not work from home. *See* Form Q.2.GG.4. This warranty is usually related to the provision of services and may be especially important if the licensee is a governmental entity or the work involves sensitive information, such as health or financial records. Some licensors are willing to accept this warranty, as it simply is an element of the price charged to the licensee while others, whose development centers are off-shore, are unwilling to do so. The licensee should realize that utilizing U.S. labor will increase the cost. Regardless of whether the licensee includes such a warranty, the licensee should always require that the licensor will comply with all U.S. export laws. *See* Chapter 7.L. See also Form Q.2.GG for additional language regarding the use of foreign labor.

Representations Made in RFI and RFP (§ 16.AE)

Occasionally, licensees seek to have the licensor represent and warrant that all statements made by the licensor during the RFI and RFP process are true and correct as of the date the parties entered into the license agreement. The licensor should never make this representation and warranty, as the product delivered is almost always different from the product requested in the RFI or RFP. The inclusion of a representation of this nature undercuts the validity of the agreement's integration clause. Are the licensee's RFI and RFP, as well as the licensor's RFI response and RFP response, now incorporated into the license agreement? Such language creates ambiguity that in turn increases the likelihood the parties will later enter into a dispute resolution process. As such, the licensee is better off including those statements on which it relied in the agreement, instead of referencing documents that may no longer be valid and may create ambiguity.

Security (See, e.g., §§ 16.AD)

A prudent licensor should disclaim any warranty that the licensor's security methods will protect against a data breach or that the software is compliant with data protection laws. No system is immune to a determined hacker. At best, a prudent licensor should only warrant that it will use commercially reasonable security procedures and that it will review such procedures on a semi-annually basis to ensure they remain current. See Chapter 22 for a more detailed discussion of data privacy and security-related issues.

Other Warranties (See, e.g., §§ 16.AF, AG, AH)

The licensee should also consider whether the nature of the transaction dictates that the licensor make other specialized representations and warranties to the licensee. See, e.g., §§ 16.AF, AG, AH.

Training (§ 16.AI)

Some licensees seek to have the licensor represent and warrant that the training provided by the licensor is sufficient to allow the licensee and its employees to "understand, operate and use" the software. Prudent licensors should be hesitant to make such a representation and warranty as the training provided by the licensor may be sufficient, but the licensee's employees are not technically competent. An alternative position is to warrant that technically competent employees will be able to understand and operate the software but doing so creates an ambiguity as to the meaning of "technically competent" employees.

Existing Installation (§ 16.AJ)

To avoid the issue of sales puffery and vaporware, the licensor should be required to represent that the software is successfully operating in similar production environments at a certain number of customer sites with the same or greater computing requirements as the licensee.

Hardware (§ 16.AK)

To the extent the licensor is supplying hardware as part of the contracted solution, the licensor should represent and warrant that the recommended hardware configuration will meet the needs of the licensee and the requirements of the contracted solution. Further, the licensor should also represent and warrant that the recommended hardware configuration has the ability to meet a given percentage increase in the licensee's present computing requirements.

The proper sizing of hardware is extremely challenging, as it difficult to predict how a software application will operate a particular hardware configuration especially when the software may have not been fully developed. Further, performance metrics often depend on the individual characteristics of the user. Thus, the licensor should avoid making any such warranties unless it is extremely confident in its methodology for sizing the hardware.

(c) Licensee Warranties (§ 16.1.2)

The licensor should seek to have the licensee make a number of warranties to the licensor. First, the licensee should warrant that it is a company in good standing in the state in which it is incorporated and that the individual executing the license on behalf of the licensee is authorized to do so (§ 16.2.1). The licensee should warrant that the execution of the license agreement does not violate any other agreement to which the licensee is a party (§ 16.2.2). Further, the licensee should warrant that it has the ability to pay the license fee and its debts as they come due (§ 16.2.3).

If the licensor is developing software to the licensee's specifications, the licensee should warrant that the software will not infringe on any third-party intellectual property rights. See § 14.C. The licensor should also consider whether the nature of the transaction dictates that the licensee make other specialized representations and warranties to the licensor. See, e.g., §§ 16.AC, 16.AD, AE.

For a general discussion of computer warranties, *see* McKenzie & Roach, *Negotiating Software License Agreements in an Economic Downturn*, 18 COMPUTER & INTERNET LAW 9 (Dec. 2001) and Feldman, *Warranties and Computer Services: Past, Present and Future*, 10 COMPUTER LAW. 1 (1993).

2. Covenants

A covenant is an agreement by a party to undertake or not undertake a particular act. *Vierk v. Ritenour*, 172 N.E.2d 679 (Ind. App. 1961). An affirmative covenant is one where the parties agree to take an action, such as obtaining consent before assigning an agreement, while a negative covenant is one where the parties agree to refrain from taking an action, such as not hiring the other party's employees. In the event of a breach of a covenant, the remedy is an action for damages and potentially specific performance. *Globe American Corp. v. Miller Hatcheries*, 110 S.W.2d 393 (Mo. 1937).

A covenant may be an express covenant or an implied covenant. Express covenants arise from the specific terms of an agreement, while an implied covenant is inferred from the words of the agreement. *Mercury Inv. Co. v. F.W. Woolworth Co.*, 706 P.2d 523 (Okla. 1985). Implied covenants, however, are not favored in the law. *Id.*

The most common implied covenant is the covenant of good faith and fair dealing implied in all contracts. *Collard v. Incorporated Village of Flower Hill*, 427 N.Y.S.2d 301, *aff'd*, 421 N.E.2d 818 (N.Y. 1981).

3. Disclaimer of Representations and Warranties (§ 16.1.4)

(a) In General

As permitted under UCC § 2-316, the licensor should disclaim all warranties except those expressly made in the license agreement including all implied warranties. If the licensor does not disclaim all other warranties, under UCC §§ 2-313 (express warranties), 2-314 (implied warranty of merchantability), and 2-315 (implied warranty of fitness for a particular purpose), the licensor could be potentially liable for the failure of the licensed software to be merchantable or fit for the purpose for which it is intended by the licensee. Under UCC § 2-316, to disclaim an implied warranty of merchantability, the underlying agreement must include a conspicuous disclaimer that expressly identifies merchantability or a statement that the good in question is sold "AS IS" or "with all faults." Arguably, the warranties of title and infringement cannot be classified as implied warranties as the UCC does not identify the implied warranties and thus they may not be disclaimed or modified.

Interestingly, Mississippi does not allow a party to disclaim the warranties of merchantability and fitness for a particular purpose (MISS. CODE ANN. § 11-7-18 (2018)) except for sales of computer hardware and software between two merchants. § 75-2-719(4)(2013).

Under the Uniform Computer Information Transactions Act (UCITA), specialized warranty disclaimers are established to better reflect the "service" and "non-goods" nature of software, but UCITA also allows UCC Article 2 disclaimers to suffice. See Chapter 15.B.3(i)(v) for a more detailed discussion and § 16.1.4.A for an example of a UCITA warranty disclaimer. In electing the governing law of the agreement, the parties should carefully consider the implications of UCITA and UCC Article 2, as well as the common law, on the outcome of any potential dispute.

In disclaiming such representations and warranties, the license should specifically identify the sections that contain the representations and warranties to strengthen the disclaimer. Doing so prevents the licensee from claiming that a particular provision in the license acts as a representation or warranty. See § 16.1.4 for model language. Finally, the license should contain a non-reliance acknowledgment to the effect that the licensee has not relied on any facts, statements, representations or warranties, written or oral, other than those set forth specific sections of the license.

All prior agreements, representations, warranties, statements, negotiations, understandings, and undertakings are superseded hereby ***and Customer hereby represents and acknowledges that in entering into this Agreement it did not rely on any representations or warranties other than those explicitly set forth in Section __ (Warranties) of this Agreement.***

(b) Magnuson-Moss

Although the Magnuson-Moss Warranty-Federal Trade Commission Improvement Act (the "Act"), 15 U.S.C. § 2301 et seq; 16 C.F.R. § 701, primarily addresses consumer products and would appear to be inapplicable to commercial transactions, the Act also applies to products normally used for consumer purposes even if the purchaser plans to use the product exclusively for a commercial use. *Najran Co. v. Fleetwood Enterprises, Inc.*, 659 F. Supp. 1081 (S.D. Ga. 1986).

Further, if the software is to be supplied to consumers who will utilize the software for personal, family, or household purposes (i.e., a "consumer product"), and the license contains any written warranties, the supplier may have to comply with the Act. The Act does not apply if the supplier does not make any express warranties. It is unclear, however, if the Act applies to software at all: the Act applies to "consumer products"— tangible products that are sold. Software is typically intangible and licensed.

The Act broadly defines warranties to include any written affirmations of fact or written promises made in connection with the sale that relate to the nature of the workmanship and that affirm or promise that the material or workmanship is defect free or will meet a specified level of performance over a specified period of time. 15 U.S.C. § 2301(6) (A). It also includes any written undertakings to repair, replace, refund the license, or take other corrective actions if the software fails to meet certain stated functionality. 15 U.S.C. § 2301(6)(B). Functional specifications or a right to return the software are not considered warranties under the Act. The Act requires full and conspicuous disclosure of a warranty's terms and conditions in simple and readily understood language. Furthermore, the Act lists thirteen items whose inclusion may be required by Federal Trade Commission rules. 15 U.S.C. § 2302 (1996).

Under the Act, certain consumer product warranties made in writing must clearly and conspicuously designate the warranty as either a "limited warranty," that is, one that does not meet federal minimum standards set forth in Section 2304 of the Act, or a "full warranty," one that meets minimum federal standards set forth in Section 2304 of the Act. 15 U.S.C. § 2303 (1996). If a full warranty is made, the supplier must correct defects within a reasonable time and without charge and may not limit the duration of implied warranties. Further, after a reasonable number of attempts to remedy a defect, the consumer may elect to receive a refund or replacement. 15 U.S.C. § 2304 (1996). Most companies, however, provide limited, not full, warranties regardless of the industry they are in.

In any case, unlike the UCC and UCITA, the Act prohibits a supplier from disclaiming or modifying any implied warranties of merchantability and fitness for the purpose intended if the supplier makes a written warranty as defined under the Act or the supplier enters into a service contract with the consumer within 90 days of the date of sale. 15 U.S.C. § 2308 (1996). In addition, the Act allows the supplier to limit the duration of these implied warranties only to "the duration of a written warranty of reasonable duration." 15 U.S.C. § 2308(b) (1996).

It is believed the Act applies only to the physical media on which software resides, as opposed to the software program itself, although there has been no judicial decision on this issue as of this writing. Nevertheless, written warranties as to the workings of the software itself may be covered and thus from the licensor's perspective should be avoided. Moreover, warranties as to turnkey systems may fall under the Act, in which case both hardware and software would be covered as a single product. Thus, the careful licensor of software to be licensed to consumers should make no written warranties and should not provide service contracts that become effective less than 91 days from the date of sale.

For a more detailed discussion on the effects of representations and warranties on software licensing, *see* Dutton, *Warranties, Time-Bombs and Other Risk Allocation Issues*, 69 Com. L. Adv. 69–102 (Sept. 1993); Friedman & Hildebrand, *Computer Litigation: A Buyer's Theories of Liability*, 4 Computer Law. 34 (Dec. 1987); Philips, *When Software Fails: Emerging Standards of Vendor Liability Under the Uniform Commercial Code*, 50 Bus. Law. 151 (1994). *See also* Hammond, *Limiting and Dealing with Liability in Software Controls*, 9 Computer Law. 22 (June 1992).

(c) Specific Disclaimers (§ 16.5)

Section 2-316(2) of the UCC requires that any warranty disclaimers related to merchantability must mention the word "merchantability," and if in a writing, it must be conspicuous. *See, e.g., Estey. v. Mackenzie Eng'g., Inc.*, 902 P.2d 1220 (Or. 1995). While "conspicuous" is defined under UCC § 1-201(10), whether or not a particular disclaimer is conspicuous is subject to the interpretation of the courts. Printing a disclaimer in block letters has been held to be sufficient. *Window Headquarters, Inc. v. MAI Basic Four, Inc.*, 1994 WL 673519 (S.D.N.Y. Dec. 1, 1994), *but see Sierra Diesel Inj. Service v. Burroughs Corp.*, 656 F. Supp. 426 (D. Nev. 1987), *aff'd*, 874 F.2d 653 (9th Cir. 1989) (disclaimer in bold type not conspicuous when it appeared on reverse of contract).

Those disclaimers relating to fitness for a particular purpose must be in writing and conspicuous. UCC § 2-316.

When disclaiming warranties, the licensor should ensure that the disclaimer clause identifies those sections that set forth the agreement's warranties; for example, "Except as set forth in *Sections 12 and 13*, Licensor disclaims all other express and implied warranties. . . ." The reason for doing so is to definitively identify those warranties that the licensor is making and limit the licensee from claiming the licensor made other warranties in the agreement. If a warranty is not set out in the identified sections it is disclaimed and is of no effect. Of course the licensee should insist on more general language: "Except as set forth in this Agreement, the parties disclaim all other express or implied warranties . . ." as the licensee should be concerned about failing to list all warranties contained in the agreement and thus losing the benefit of its bargain.

The licensor should specifically provide that all warranties are voided by any misuse of the software, modification of the software by the licensee, or the failure to operate the software in the specified environment. Software is temperamental by nature, and its performance can be adversely affected by the failure to run it in the specified environment. Further, the licensee should not be held responsible for misuse of the software or for modifications made by the licensee. The licensor needs to control the integrity of its software to ensure the software meets the stated functional specifications.

4. Length of Warranty (§ 16.1)

The length of the warranty period for the licensed software is an element of price. Industry standard is to provide a warranty of 30-90 days, effective on the date of delivery or date of acceptance of the software. It is important to understand when the warranty begins. Many licensors state that the warranty begins on the date of installation or shipment. This is potentially troublesome for the licensee as the warranty may expire prior to acceptance and thus should not be agreed to by the licensee. The equitable solution is to have the warranty run from the date of acceptance. If the licensee requires a warranty longer than the standard warranty offered by the licensor, the licensor can provide one for an increased price. Generally, 12 months of maintenance is priced at an amount equal to 18 to 20 percent of the license fee plus the cost of any enhancements. Some licensors include the first year's maintenance in the initial license fee or require the licensee to purchase maintenance for the first year.

Licensors must be careful to limit the length of any warranty they give. Many licensees request a one-year warranty. This creates a hidden risk for the licensor as, during the warranty period, the licensee may terminate the license agreement and seek a refund if the licensor is in material breach. During a maintenance period provided under a properly worded and separate maintenance agreement, however, the licensee would only receive a refund of the maintenance fee if the licensor was in material breach. Thus, a potential solution is for the licensor to grant, for example, a 60-day warranty and 10 months free maintenance under a separate maintenance agreement. At least one major software company does not provide a warranty and instead gives the licensee a 90-day period in which to evaluate and test the software prior to acceptance. At the end of the 90-day period, the potential licensee can either accept the software "as is" without a warranty or reject the software without obligation.

5. *Third-Party Warranties*

Licensors often incorporate third-party software and hardware into their solutions. In such cases, the licensee should insist that the licensor pass through to the licensee any warranties the licensor receives from such third parties on the basis that the licensee most likely paid for the warranty and thus should receive its benefit. Licensors should not resist these requests provided the licensee will look to the third party and not the licensor for any warranty issues related to such software or hardware. Model language follows:

> *For any Third-Party Software provided by Vendor to Customer, Vendor hereby assigns to Customer all end-user warranties and indemnities relating to such Third-Party Software. To the extent that Vendor is not permitted to assign any of such end-user warranties and indemnities through to Customer, Vendor shall enforce such warranties and indemnities on behalf of Customer to the extent Vendor is permitted to do so under the terms of the applicable Third-Party agreements.*

B. General Indemnification (§ 15)

1. *Overview*

General indemnification is a risk-shifting mechanism transferring a loss from the legally responsible party (the "indemnitee") to another party (the "indemnitor") which historically has been limited to third-party claims. *Oliver B. Cannon & Sons, Inc. v. Dorr-Oliver, Inc.*, 394 A.2d 1160, 1165 (Del. 1978) (indemnity clauses normally only apply to third party claims). It is an attempt to transfer the burden of risk to the party who creates the risk or liability to the other party/party best able to eliminate or control the risk. Indemnification is appropriate where the indemnified party may incur a loss or receive a claim arising from the actions or omission of the other party or a loss or casualty the result of which was under the control of the other party. "Generally, indemnity agreements do not apply claims between the parties; rather they apply to claims made by the others who are not parties to the agreement." *Claybar v. Samson Exploration, LLC*, 2018 WL 651258 *2 (Tex. Feb 1, 2018) and are narrowly construed. *Stephens Inc. v. Flexiti Financial Inc.*, 2019 WL 2725627 (S.D.N.Y. July 1, 2019).

Indemnification is usually limited to particular types of third-party claims, such as personal bodily injury or tangible property damage caused by one of the parties to a third party, including the other party's employees or contractors, as well as violations of the law, willful misconduct and gross negligence, data and security breaches, and intellectual property infringement. It also allows a party to recover costs that might not be otherwise recoverable, such as attorney's fees and court costs. Except to permit recovery for liability arising from a disclosed liability, indemnification is not an appropriate remedy for claims between two contracting parties who have a direct claim against the other, i.e., for breach of contract.

Indemnification clauses traditionally encompass two distinct obligations: (i) the obligation to defend the claim and (ii) the obligation to pay all costs associated with any lawsuit and to indemnify or reimburse the indemnified party for its obligations to the third-party claimant. *Trust One Mortgage Corp. v. Invest America Mortgage Corp.*, 134 Cal. App. 4th 1302 (Cal. 2005). Indemnification differs from a warranty and a representation in that the entity making the representation or warranty must pay the other party's damages including legal fees arising from the facts not being as stated while recovery under an indemnity provision can be much broader.

Indemnification is governed by state contract law and may arise under statute, common law or contractually. *See, e.g., Mims Crane Service, Inc. v. Insley Mfg. Corp.*, 226 So. 2d 836, 839 (Fla. 1969) ("The obligation to indemnify need not be based upon express contract of indemnification but may arise out of implied contractual relations or out of liability imposed by law."). Although the right of indemnification may arise under common law, indemnification clauses are a common means to contractually allocate risk between the parties. *See, e.g., Novak v. BASF Corp.*, 869 F. Supp. 113, 119 (N.D.N.Y. 1994). A correctly worded indemnification provision will also allow for the recovery of legal's fees that traditionally are not recoverable in a legal action. In most situations, the indemnification provisions contained in a license agreement should be mutual for the protection of both parties.

2. *Relevant Language*

Usually, the parties will incorporate language into their agreement to the following effect:

> Licensor shall **defend, indemnify** and **hold harmless** Licensee and its Affiliates and their respective officers, directors, agents, lawyers and representatives (collectively the "Indemnified Parties") from and against any and all damages, losses, liabilities, judgments, awards, costs, and expenses of any nature whatsoever, including reasonable attorney's fees and court costs **finally awarded**, incurred by any Indemnified Party **to the extent arising out of or relating to** any nonaffiliated **third-party claims** for: (i) any loss or damage to real property or tangible personal property, or any bodily injury, including death, to the extent caused by the intentional or negligent acts or omissions of Licensor; or (ii) claims, actions, or proceedings brought by any third party alleging infringement by any Software provided to Licensee by Licensor. Any liability limitations set forth in this Agreement shall not apply to these indemnification obligations.

Often, however, a party may not understand the true meaning of the language contained in an indemnification clause which is important given a savvy indemnitor seeks to grant as narrow an indemnity as possible. The three most important terms are:

> ***Defend*** *– to mount a defense and pay the indemnitee's legal costs in defending a claim, an ongoing obligation which arises when a claim is made regardless of whether the claim has merit.*
>
> ***Indemnify*** *– to reimburse a party for any damage or loss incurred, after the fact.*
>
> ***Hold Harmless*** *– to protect the indemnitee against harm.*

An obligation to provide indemnification against liability creates a duty when the liability matures. *Williams v. Johnston*, 442 P.2d 178 (Idaho 1968). In the event of an ambiguity, an indemnity provision will be strictly construed against the drafter, or if mutually negotiated, against the indemnitee. *Topp Copy Prods., Inc. v. Singletary*, 626 A.2d 98 (Pa. 1993); (ambiguity construed against indemnitee); *Hooper Assocs., Ltd. v. AGS Computers, Inc.*, 548 N.E.2d 903 (N.Y. 1989).

The interaction between the license's indemnification clause and the indemnifying party's insurance policies should be closely scrutinized as the waiver of indemnifying party's insurance company's right of subrogation may raise the indemnifying party's insurance rates. *See* Gesellschap & Hicks, *The Interplay Between Indemnification Provisions and Insurance Clauses in Contracts for Goods and Services*, 32 ACC DOCKET 47 (Mar. 2014).

Some indemnitors seek to limit their obligation to defending the indemnitee and paying those damages finally awarded in an effort to limit their liability. They seek to avoid holding the indemnitee harmless as "hold harmless" may include other costs not directly related to the indemnity claim such as inhouse counsel fees Before agreeing to such language, prudent indemnitees should understand the impact of removing "hold harmless" from the operative language.

Some practitioners advocate that indemnitors should avoid including language to "reimburse" the indemnitee as such language may infer that the indemnitee has the right to select counsel, control the defense and have the indemnitor pay all legal fees.

(a) "Defend" vs. "Indemnify"

The duty to defend and the duty to indemnify are considered to be distinct and separate duties. From the licensor's perspective, to limit its obligations and financial risk, the licensor should seek only to defend but not to indemnify the licensee.

A duty to defend is broader than an indemnity and, unlike an indemnity obligation, is not dependent on the outcome of a claim or suit. The duty of defend arises at the time a potential claim may be subject to indemnification. *Alpha Constr. and Eng'g. Corp. v. Ins. Co. of State of Pennsylvania*, 601 F. Supp. 2d 684 (D. Md. 2009) and is not dependant on a claim being meritorious. *Crawford v. Weather Shield Mfg. Inc.*, 79 Cal. Rptr. 3d 721 (2008). An indemnitor must defend the indemnitee until a court determines the claim does not fall under the indemnity or the indemnitor did not cause the basis for the claim. *Westlake Vinyls, Inc. v. Goodrich Corp.*, 518 F. Supp. 2d 918 (W.D. Ky. 2007).

An obligation to indemnify but not defend is narrower, requiring the indemnifying party to act only when the indemnitee has suffered an actual loss. *Larson Mach., Inc. v. Wallace*, 600 S.W.2d (Ark. 1980). In some situations, states have statutorily required indemnitors to defend indemnitees. *See, e.g.*, CAL. CIV. CODE § 2778(4); OKLA. STAT. ANN. TIT. 15, 427(4). In New York, the courts will look to the language of the indemnity provision to determine if there is a duty to defend. *Klock v. Grosodonia*, 674 N.Y.S.2d 187 (N.Y. App. 1998). It is important from the licensee's perspective that the licensor indemnify *and* defend the licensee, as defense costs will likely be significant, potentially exceeding any damages that are awarded.

The term "defend" obligates the indemnitor to manage (and directly pay for) the legal defense against the claim, *Crawford v. Weather Shield Mfg. Inc.*, 38 Cal. Rptr. 3d 787,

806 (Cal. 2006) while the term "indemnify" may be interpreted as merely an indemnitor by the licensor to pay at some later time the loss or damage incurred by the indemnitee. *Id.* at 805. Unless the underlying agreement provides otherwise, indemnitees are generally entitled to recover their reasonable attorneys' fees in defending claims by third parties. *Jones v. Calvin B. Taylor Banking Co.*, 253 A.2d 742 (Md. 1969). Unless expressly provided in the agreement, indemnitees are usually not entitled to recover their legal fees incurred in their claims against the indemnitor to enforce an indemnity obligation. *Nova Research, Inc. v. Penske Truck Leasing Co., L.P.*, 952 A.2d 275 (Md. 2008).

The licensor/indemnitor generally seeks to assume control of the defense of the claim, as it bears the risk of loss although the licensee often seeks the right to control the defense. In some situations, the right to control any defense may be more important to the licensee than avoiding the need to mount the licensee's own defense. In such situations, the licensee should delete the word "defend" along with the corresponding language granting the licensor right to control the suit. Note that the licensor may argue that it is superfluous to include "defend" because the obligation to defend is part of the obligation to indemnify in many jurisdictions. Because this may not be true in all jurisdictions, the licensee should insist on retaining "defend" as appropriate and respond to the argument that if "defense" is encompassed already, then there is no harm in making it explicit.

An obligation to indemnify runs only to claims that are covered by a contractual provision, while the duty to defend extends to claims that are potentially covered. *Crawford v. Weather Shield Mfg. Inc.*, 187 P.3d 424 (Cal. 2008); *Trinity Universal Ins. Co. v. Cowan*, 945 S.W.2d 819 (Tex. 1997); *Heyden Newport Chemical Corp. v. Southern General Ins. Co.*, 387 S.W.2d 22 (Tex. 1965). "The duty to defend does not depend upon the outcome of the suit, as it does where the purported source of the duty is an indemnity agreement; rather, where the pleadings disclose 'even a possibility of liability' under the contract, the duty is triggered." *Suire v. Lafayette City-Parish Consolidated Government*, 907 So.2d 37 (La. 2005). *See also Servidone Construction Corp. v. Security Insurance Co. of Hartford*, 64 N.Y.2d 419 (1985) ("The duty to indemnify is, however, distinctly different. The duty to defend is measured against the allegations of pleadings but the duty to pay is determined by the actual basis for the insured's liability to a third person.").

For a further discussion, *see* Brocato, *Drafting Indemnification Clauses*, 1 Transactional Law. 1 (Oct. 2011).

(b) "Indemnify" vs. "Hold Harmless"

There is a difference of opinion as to whether "indemnify" and "hold harmless" are synonymous. "The terms 'indemnify' and 'hold harmless' refer to slightly different legal remedies." *Martin v. American Optical Co.*, 184 F.2d 528 (5th Cir. 1950); *U.S. v. Contract Management, Inc.*, 912 F.2d 1045 (9th Cir. 1990); *Queen Villas Homeowners Ass'n v. TCB Property Mgmt.*, 56 Cal. Rptr. 3d 528 (Cal. Dist. Ct. App. 2007); *Majkowski v. American Imaging Mgmt. Servs. LLC*, 913 A.2d 572, 592 n.55 (Del. Ch. Ct. 2006) ("The word 'indemnify' generally grants rights, and the phrase 'hold harmless' generally limits liability.") Other courts have held differently. *See Paniaguas v. Aldon Cos., Inc.*, 2006 WL 2788585 (N.D. Ind. Sept. 26, 2006); *Consult Urban Renewal Dev. Corp. v. T.R. Arnold & Assoc., Inc.*, 2007 WL 1175742 (D.N.J. Apr. 19, 2007).

The term "indemnify" is considered to be an offensive right allowing a party to seek indemnification for an actual loss while the term "hold harmless" is considered defensive, protecting the indemnified party against claims made by the indemnifying party, i.e., the risk of loss as well as actual loss. *Queen Villas Homeowners Ass'n. v. TCB Property Mgmt.*, 56 Cal. Rptr. 3d 528 (Cal. Dist. Ct. App. 2007).

Many licensors resist the licensee's demand to indemnify the licensee for all losses, damages, liabilities, settlements, costs, and expenses. However, in addition to covering amounts paid to third parties as a result of claims against the licensee (e.g., attorney's fees and damage awards), the licensee should seek to have the licensor cover the licensee's own costs. For example, addressing an infringing licensor deliverable may require the licensee to incur expenses, such as retraining. For this reason, a prudent licensee should avoid limiting the licensor's indemnification obligations.

(c) "To the Extent Arising From" and "Solely Related to"

In drafting and negotiating a contract, a party's liability can turn on only a few words. Indemnification provisions are no different, and prudent parties should draft their indemnification provisions tightly to limit their potential liability. Broad, all-encompassing language should be avoided. Each party should be responsible only for those damages that flow directly from their actions.

As such, the language of the indemnity should be tied to the indemnitor's actions. A party should be responsible for claims "to the extent such claims arise from the indemnitor's actions" and not "all claims related to or arising from" the indemnitor's actions. Another option is to limit a party's liability to those claims "solely related to" the party's action.

(d) Finally Awarded

Many party's seek to indemnify the indemnitee from all damages, liabilities, costs, and expenses "finally awarded" by a court of competent jurisdiction. Doing so limits the indemnitor's potential liability and delays any potential payment to the indemnitee. From the indemnitee's perspective, "finally awarded" will likely delay the indemnitee's recovery for many years until the matter has been fully litigated and all appeals exhausted, leaving the indemnitee out of pocket for the monies it has expended during that time period.

(e) Recoverable Losses

The parties should carefully consider the potential implications of the indemnitor's obligation to indemnify the indemnitee for all "claims, damages, losses, liabilities, and causes of action" as each term has a unique and distinct meaning under the law which can significantly expand the indemnitor's potential liability. Most important is the intent of the parties as it relates to the scope of the indemnification.

Is the indemnitor obligated to cover:

- Direct damages and third-party losses only
- Consequential damages

- Punitive damages? (UCC § 2-717 permits indemnification for punitive damages)
- Losses from alleged wrongdoing or actual wrongdoing as determined by a court or arbiter
- Losses caused by unrelated third parties
- Losses related to third parties such as affiliates
- Fines, penalties, judgments, interest, taxes, awards, assessments, investigations, consultants, enforcement costs, lost profits
- Attorney's fees and expenses for claims between the parties
- Claims between the indemnitee and the indemnitee's affiliates

Each of these issues must be considered and resolved with language carefully crafted to reflect the parties' allocation of risk. Arguably, the breadth of any indemnity is an element of price and if the indemnitee is willing to pay for a broader indemnity, the indemnitor will likely be willing to offer a broader indemnity. Set forth below is a brief discussion of the meaning and impact of each of these terms.

(i) Claim

Assuming responsibility for damages resulting from a "claim" requires the indemnitor to make the indemnitee whole for all costs and losses incurred as a result of a claim without requiring any culpability on behalf of the indemnitee including losses resulting from a third-party lawsuit. Liability arises at the time a lawsuit is filed. Thus, the risks to the indemnitor are potentially great.

(ii) Liability

The term "liability" is interpreted more narrowly than the term "claim." Responsibility for a liability arises when the liability has been imposed on the indemnitee but prior to any monies being paid. "Liability" is less inclusive than "claim" as it requires that a liability actually be incurred.

(iii) Loss

"Loss" is even more restrictive than the terms "claim" or "liability" as it requires that the indemnitee actually satisfy an obligation to a third party prior to the indemnitor being legally obligated to reimburse the indemnitee.

"Losses" can be read broadly to include judgments, attorney's fees, court fees, as well as expenses and costs associated with a settlement. It may also include losses such as the loss in value of a party's intellectual property such as its trademarks.

Generally, unless the language of the indemnity provides otherwise, the indemnitee is entitled to recover its legal fees because they arise from the defense of claims by a third party. *Jones v. Calvin B. Taylor Banking Co.*, 253 A.2d 742, 748 (Md. 1969). Depending on the jurisdiction, an indemnitee may be unable to recover its legal fees incurred in establishing its right to indemnity against the indemnitor unless the language of the indemnity expressly permits the recovery of such fees. *Pike Chiropractic Center, P.A. v. Robinson*, 637 A.2d 418 (Del. 1994) (indemnity covering legal fees allowed indemnitee to recover its legal fees expended in lawsuit to establish right to indemnity); *Maule v. Phila Media Holdings, LLC*, 2010 WL 3859613 (E.D. Pa. Oct. 1, 2010); *Nova Research, Inc. v. Penske Truck Leasing Co., L.P.*, 952 A.2d 275 (Md. 2008) (indemnity must expressly provide for the recovery of legal fees incurred to establish a right to indemnity for legal fees).

For a further discussion, *see* Brocato, *Drafting Indemnification Clauses*, 1 TRANSACTIONAL LAW. 1 (Oct. 2011).

(iv) Causes of Action

Liability for a "cause of action" arises when the indemnitee's right to bring a claim accrues. Liability includes losses arising from the indemnitee's right to seek relief.

(f) Connection of "Recoverable Losses" and "Indemnified Acts"

The indemnitor should carefully focus on the language "connecting" the extent of its obligations to the indemnitee and the actions for which it will indemnify the indemnitee to limit the breadth of its obligations and limit the accompanying risk.

Most indemnitees will seek broad wording to ensure the indemnitee is protected to the greatest extent possible by using "to the extent arising from", "solely arising from" and "directly arising from". Indemnitors seek to narrowly craft the language to limit their potential exposure. Indemnitees prefer broad language such as "related to" and "arising from" while prudent indemnitors should insist on more narrow language such as "directly caused by," "directly resulting from," "solely resulting from," or "to the extent directly caused by." The actual language agreed to by the parties should reflect the allocation of risk.

(g) Sole Remedy/Cumulative Remedy

From the indemnitor's perspective, the indemnification provision should clearly provide that the indemnitor's indemnification obligations are the indemnitee's sole remedy in the event of a claim under the indemnification provision. Failure to include a "sole remedy" provision may allow the indemnitee to seek an additional recovery under another provision of the agreement.

Similarly, the indemnitor should ensure that the underlying agreement does not contain a "cumulative remedies" clause allowing the indemnitee to recover damages beyond those contemplated in the indemnification clause, which may include terminating the agreement or making a claim under the indemnitor's insurance policies if the indemnitee has been named an additional insured.

(h) Indemnified Parties

Both parties should carefully consider who, outside of the contracting parties, will be covered by the indemnity. Often the indemnification language includes a long list of different groups, including all present, past, and future employees, officers, directors, subsidiaries, affiliates, representatives, contractors, agents, and customers of the parties. The list of indemnified parties should represent those parties whose activities are directly related to the indemnified event. In most cases, it is not appropriate to indemnify a party's representatives, consultants, and agents. Further, most licensors will argue that it is inappropriate to indemnify the licensee's customers, as the licensee can contractually limit its liability in its contract with its customer.

(i) Common Claims for Indemnification

The following claims are often addressed in general indemnification provisions:

- Personal bodily injury and death;
- Damage to tangible personal property;
- Breach of representations and warranties;
- Failure to comply with applicable laws;
- Employee claims made by the indemnitor's employees;
- Failure to comply with applicable data privacy and data security obligations;
- Negligence;
- Intentional behavior;
- Gross negligence or willful misconduct;
- Failure to pay any taxes due, including worker's compensation and payroll taxes;
- Breach of confidentiality obligations;
- Breach of contract; and
- Negligence.

From the vendor's perspective, indemnification for breach of contract and negligence is never appropriate as in the event of the vendor's negligence or breach of contract, the customer's recovery lies in a breach of contract claim. Negligence can underlie almost any claim, significantly expanding the vendor's potential liability; as many customers seek to exclude the vendor's indemnity obligations from the agreement's limitation of liability. Some vendors will also not agree to an indemnity for gross negligence believing the term is ill-defined, exposing the vendor to liability for an act that is subjectively defined. Further, most indemnity provisions allow the indemnified party to recover its legal and court costs, costs that otherwise would not be recoverable in a breach of contract claim.

3. Exclusions

Most licensors will seek to negotiate a number of exclusions from their indemnification obligations. The most common exclusion is for claims arising when the licensed software is used in connection with another product that causes the software to infringe on a third party's intellectual property. This qualification is not always appropriate, as software is designed to operate with hardware, software interfaces, power supplies, etc. Thus, if a combination exclusion is included, the licensee may be left without a viable remedy.

A compromise is to exclude combinations except where a combination is necessary to utilize the functionality of the software. If the licensor is aware of certain risks inherent in the software's functionality, it can seek to exclude those specific combinations. The licensee can attempt to limit its risk by asking the licensor whether there have been any prior claims and if not, seek a representation and warranty to that effect.

Other common qualifiers include the indemnified party's acts or omissions; intentional, willful, or negligent misconduct by the indemnified party; and the indemnified party's failure to mitigate its losses. In addition, parties should avoid indemnifying the other party for fines and penalties, as fines and penalties are usually not covered by insurance and can be difficult to negotiate with a governmental agency. From the indemnitee's perspective, the fines and penalties should not be excluded, especially if they result from the indemnitor's actions or omissions.

Some indemnitors seek to include a "knowledge" qualifier to their indemnification obligation. Because "knowledge" applies retroactively, it is imprudent for an indemnitee to accept for a knowledge qualifier.

4. Contributory vs. Comparative Negligence

The failure to include an indemnification provision may limit an injured party's recovery under the laws of those states that have not adopted the doctrine of comparative negligence and still recognize the doctrine of contributory negligence. The principle of indemnification seeks to ensure that the standard for the allocation of risk is on a comparative risk basis versus a contributory risk basis. Without an indemnification provision, the parties are subject to the uncertainty of where the action is brought and whether that state utilizes a contributory negligence standard. By including an indemnification provision, the parties can create certainty and eliminate any benefit a party may achieve by bringing a claim in a state whose laws are favorable to its potential claim.

As of November 1, 2023, only Alabama, the District of Columbia, Maryland, North Carolina, and Virginia apply the doctrine of pure contributory negligence.

Some licensees seek to avoid the impact of comparative fault by specifically stating that the obligation to indemnify is absolute, regardless of any comparative fault. See the illustrative language below.

> *"Comparative Fault" shall mean the attribution of fault of each party on a percentage of fault basis where both parties contributed to the cause of the injury.*
>
> *The duty of the Licensor to defend, indemnify and hold harmless the Licensee, its agents and employees under this Section shall exist regardless of whether or not the act giving rise to this duty is caused or claimed to have been caused, in part, by a party indemnified hereunder and such duty shall be determined without regard to any apportionment of liability under the laws relating to Comparative Fault; however, this provision does not apply to claims arising out of or caused by the sole negligence or willful misconduct of any indemnities.*

Another approach is to state that the obligation to indemnify exists except to the extent that the indemnified party's injury arose from the indemnified party's *sole* negligence. The inclusion of the word "sole" addresses the issue of why the indemnifying party should pay for injuries resulting from the indemnified party's own negligence. Often, however, the vendor must accept such language to win the transaction.

5. Equitable and Implied Indemnification

An indemnification obligation may arise not only through contract but also through equity. *Smoketree-Lake Murray, Ltd. v. Mills Concrete Construction Co., Inc.*, 234 Cal. App. 3d 1724 (1991). The creation of an equitable indemnification obligation arises as a result of language contained in an agreement unrelated to the indemnification clause or "by the equities of the particular case." *Id.* at 1736. Implied indemnities are a form of equitable indemnities. In its most common form, equitable indemnities are applied "to proportion loss among tortfeasors in proportion to their relative culpability so there will be an equitable sharing of the loss." *Id.*

A majority of jurisdictions that have addressed the issue of implied indemnification obligations have found that a contractual relationship under the UCC, with its implied warranties, provides a sufficient basis for an implied indemnity claim when the buyer incurs liability to a third party as a result of a defect in goods that would constitute a breach of the seller's implied or express warranties. Majority: California, Maine, Michigan, Minnesota, Missouri, Nebraska, New Hampshire, New York, North Carolina, Pennsylvania, Virginia, Washington. *See, e.g., Central Washington Refrigeration, Inc. v. Barbee*, 946 P.2d 760, 764 (Wash. 1997); *Carrier Corp. v. Detrex Corp.*, 6 Cal. Rptr. 2d 565, 569 (1992); *Cyr v. Michaud*, 454 A.2d 1376, 1385 (Me. 1983). Minority: Idaho, South Dakota, Utah. *See, e.g., Sheehan v. Morris Irrigation, Inc.*, 460 N.W.2d 413 (S.D. 1990); *Perry v. Pioneer Wholesale Supply Co.*, 681 P.2d 214, 219 (Utah 1984).

6. *Limits on Liability for Indemnification Obligations*

Many licensors seek to limit their liability arising from indemnity claims. Such caps are often tied to the value of the license or the value of the services being rendered. In addition, licensors often seek to limit the types of damages that they are responsible for, by excluding indirect, or punitive damages, etc., arguing that direct damages make the indemnitee whole and other damages are speculative. Indemnitees respond that excluding consequential damages prevents the indemnitee from recovering damages that were reasonably foreseeable.

Usually, indemnification for personal bodily injury or personal property damages is excluded from the contract's limit of liability. To the extent an indemnitee is willing to accept a cap on indemnification, the agreement should carefully provide whether the cap is for liability only or both liability and defense costs. Prudent indemnitees should not agree to a cap on defense costs to avoid having the indemnitor abandon its defense of the indemnitee when the cap is reached. In consumer goods transactions, any limit of consequential damages in the event of personal bodily injury is prima facie unconscionable. UCC § 2-719(3). As such, the limitation of liability clause discussed in Section I.1 below often contains " carve-out provisions" excluding the license agreement's indemnification provisions from any limit of liability.

7. *Direct vs. Third-Party Indemnification Claims*

"Generally, indemnity agreements do not apply to claims between the parties; rather they apply to claims made by the others who are not parties to the agreement. *Claybar v. Samson Exploration, LLC*, 2018 WL 651258 (Tex. Feb. 1. 2018). In *Hooper Assocs., Ltd.*

v. AGS Computers, Inc., 548 N.E.2d 903, 905 (N.Y. 1989), the New York Court of Appeals found that an indemnification covered by New York law will be construed to apply solely to claims brought by third parties and not claims brought by the contracting parties against each other unless the agreement is "unmistakably clear" that the parties intended the indemnification provisions to apply. Parties seeking an indemnity for direct claims should include language in their indemnity provision allowing the parties to seek indemnification against each other: ". . . . *any Loss an Indemnified Person may incur whether directly or as a result of third party claims, ...*" *But see, Metex Mfg. Corp. v. Manson*, 2008 WL 877870 (D.N.J. Mar. 28, 2008) (Indemnity provision deemed to include claims between the parties unless explicitly excluded).

From the indemnitor's perspective, indemnity for claims brought by the contracting parties against each other is unnecessary as the parties are in contractual privity and each can bring a breach of contract claim against the other. Indemnification does, however, potentially allow the indemnitee to recover costs it would otherwise be unable to recover such as legal fees and costs.

8. *Indemnifying a Party for Its Own Negligence*

Increasingly, some licensors are seeking to limit their indemnity and other liability to third-party claims arising from the licensor's gross negligence and even have the licensee indemnify the licensor for the licensor's own negligence. Most licensees argue that this is unreasonable, and this point most likely will be viewed as a deal killer. Gross negligence is a very difficult standard to meet and would likely leave the licensee without a remedy except in the most egregious cases. See Section B.7.(a)(ii)(y), below for a more detailed discussion of gross negligence. The licensor controls its own actions not the licensee, thus the licensee cannot be expected to insure the actions of the licensor.

Further, there is a dichotomy of opinion as to whether a provision requiring a party to indemnify a second party for the second party's own negligence is enforceable. Permitted: *Levine v. Shell Oil Co.*, 269 N.E.2d 799 (N.Y. Ct. App. 1971); *Estes Express Lines, Inc. v. Chopper Express, Inc.*, 641 S.E.2d 476, 480 (Va. 2007). Not permitted: *Northwest Airlines, Inc. v. Alaska Airlines, Inc.*, 351 F.2d 253 (9th Cir. 1965) (exculpatory and indemnity provision that excuses party from liability for its own negligence is against public policy and invalid); *City of Santa Barbara v. Superior Court*, 161 P.3d 1095 (Cal. 2007) (release for future gross negligence or intentional misrepresentation is unenforceable); Cal. Civ. Code § 2273. *See also Feed Management Systems, Inc. v. Comco Systems, Inc.*, 823 F.3d 488 (8th Cir. 2016) (court will "strictly construe indemnification agreements that shift liability for the indemnitee's own negligence"); *Burns v. N&L Realty Corp.*, 160 F. Supp. 203 (W.D. Pa. 1958) (contract provisions indemnifying lessor for lessor's negligence will be construed strongly against lessor and in favor of lessee).

To be enforced, the language of the indemnity provision must clearly provide that it is the intent of the parties to have one party indemnify the second party for the second party's own negligence. *United States v. Seckinger*, 397 U.S. 211 (1970). Some jurisdictions permit such an indemnification under the express negligence rule, requiring only that any indemnification that releases a party from all liability from its own future negligence "must be expressed in unambiguous terms within the four corners of the contract" and must also be "conspicuous." *Griffin Industries, Inc. v. Foodmaker, Inc.*, 22 S.W.3d 33, 37 (Tex. 2000). *See also Iowa*: *Maxim Technologies, Inc. v. City of Dubuque*, 690 N.W.2d 896 (Iowa 2005) (indemnification of party for its own negligence must be expressed in unambiguous terms and will be strictly construed). Conn: *Dow-Westbrook, Inc. v. Candlewood Equine Practice LLC*, 989 A.2d 1075 (Conn. App. 2010) (indemnity clause releasing a party from its own negligence is not unusual in commercial contracts and should be viewed as a means to allocate risk); Maryland: *Mass. Transit Admin. v. CSX Transp.*, 349 Md. 299, 308-09 (Md. App. 1998) ("The general rule is the contracts will not be construed to indemnify a person against his own negligence unless an intention to do so is expressed in those very words or in other unequivocal terms.").

Similarly, New York allows indemnification for a party's own negligence, except to the extent the underlying damages arise from the intentional causation of injury. *Austro v. Niagara Mohawk Power Corp.*, 487 N.E.2d 267 (N.Y. 1985). Any indemnity for an act known to be unlawful at the time of such indemnification, however, is void. *Lemat v. American Basketball Assn.*, 51 Cal. App. 3d 267 (1975). *But see* California Civ. Code § 2773 (a party can be indemnified for past wrongful act unless a felony).

9. *When an Indemnification Event Arises*

When an event arises for which a party is indemnified, the indemnitee should:

- Immediately place the indemnitor on notice of the claim (even if the indemnitor is a party to the litigation).
- Immediately place its insurance carrier on notice of a potential claim.
- In its notice to the indemnitor and its insurance carrier, cite the specific clause in the relevant agreement that requires the indemnitor to indemnify, defend, and hold the indemnitee harmless.
- Request that the indemnitor acknowledge the demand and state that it will indemnify the indemnitee.
- Determine whether under the agreement the indemnitee has the right to select counsel and lead the defense. If not, the indemnitee may want to retain its own counsel to assist in the defense of the case, such as defending depositions, assisting in discovery, etc.
- When appropriate, discuss settlement parameters and how that settlement will be agreed upon.
- If appropriate, discuss the need to enter into a joint defense agreement so the parties and their counsel can freely communicate while retaining the attorney-client privilege.
- Remember that as a defendant it may have to pay out any damages before it can recover its costs from the indemnitor.
- Ensure that the indemnitor has the financial resources to stand behind its indemnity.

10. General Drafting Considerations

Indemnification usually covers only third-party claims and not the indemnitee's own damages, as the indemnitee is in contractual privity with the indemnitor and can bring a breach of contract claim against the indemnitor. From the licensor's perspective, the indemnification should not cover all third-party claims but only those claims arising from intellectual property infringement (see Chapter 5.B.3 for a more detailed discussion) and those arising from damage to tangible personal property and personal bodily injury, including death. A licensee should seek an indemnity for any claim, loss, costs, and damages arising from the licensor's negligence or willful misconduct in performing under the agreement. The licensee should reject any attempt by the licensor to limit its indemnification obligations to specified acts to avoid assuming liability arising outside of the identified actions. Further, it is inappropriate for the licensor to limit its indemnification obligations with a knowledge qualifier.

A party should indemnify the officers, directors, and employees of the indemnified party but should resist indemnifying a party's contractors and agents as well as doing so creates a much larger obligation. The indemnitor should ensure that the indemnity is tightly drafted and should resist indemnifying the other party for "any act or omission," the indemnitor's general negligence, or for damages arising from the breach of the license/agreement, as an injured party always has the right to bring a contract claim in the event of a breach of contract. From the indemnitor's perspective, if the indemnitor is willing to indemnify another party for any "act or omissions," such indemnification should be limited to the indemnitor's grossly *negligent* acts and omissions. Further, the indemnitor should ensure that it has disclaimed all liability for all third-party claims except those for which it is specifically indemnifying the indemnitee. See, e.g., § 16.1. The underlying reasoning for this position is that the indemnitee can limit its liability through its contracts with its own customers.

Similarly, the indemnitor should limit its indemnification obligations solely to third-party claims and claims for tangible personal property for damage and personal bodily injury. Some parties also require a representation or warranty of non-infringement to retain a direct cause of action against the licensor. A licensee may object to limiting the indemnification to tangible personal property in software information/technology agreements as the underlying software is usually of greater importance to the parties.

Every indemnification provision should require the indemnitee to give the indemnitor prompt notice of any claim, to cede control of the defense to the indemnitor and to assist the indemnitor in the defense of the claim. What constitutes prompt notice is dependent on the facts of the matter. *Am. Transtech Inc. v. U.S. Trust Corp.*, 933 F. Supp. 1193, 1200 (S.D.N.Y. 1996) (prompt notice in an indemnification provision requires the indemnitor to be given sufficient notice to participate in the defense); *Avaya, Inc. v. Charter Communications Holding Co., LLC*, 2014 WL 6675750 (Del. Super. Nov. 10, 2014) (denying summary judgment motion that claim for indemnity was not prompt when made 10 months after indemnitee was sued for infringement).

Unless set forth in the agreement, notice is not a condition precedent to providing indemnification. *ELRAC, Inc. v. Cruz*, 699 N.Y.S.2d 647 (1999) (notice not required); *Am. Home Assur. Co. v. Int'l Ins. Co.*, 684 N.E.2d 14 (N.Y. 1997) (failure to comply with notice provision may void indemnity obligation). *But see Morris v. Schlumberger, Ltd.*, 445 So.2d 1242 (La. 1984).

The indemnification clause should provide that if the indemnitor fails to accept control of the dispute or settle the claim in a reasonable manner, the indemnitee may settle the matter on a reasonable basis without the consent of the indemnitor. *ELRAC*, 699 N.Y.S.2d at 647. Any action or inaction by the indemnitee which prejudices the indemnitor will negate the indemnitor's obligations to the extent its interests have been prejudiced. *New Amsterdam Cas. Co. v. Lundquist*, 198 N.W.2d 543 (Minn. 1972). Finally, the strength of an indemnity is dependent on the financial strength of the indemnitor. If the indemnitee is concerned about the indemnitor's ability to meet its obligations, it should require the indemnitor to purchase sufficient insurance to cover its obligations.

The indemnitor should ensure that the agreement clearly provides that the indemnitor will control and lead the defense of any claim. Given that the indemnitor is responsible for paying the cost of the defense and any settlement, it should control the defense. The indemnitee may protect its interests by requiring the indemnitor to obtain the indemnitee's consent prior to settling the matter if the settlement would financially impact the indemnitee.

The statute of limitations on an indemnity claim begins to run when the claim is settled, even if the statute on the underlying warranty has already expired. *Central Washington Refrigeration Inc. v. Barbee*, 946 P.2d 760, 765 (Wash. 1997).

To the extent the parties provide mutual indemnities, each parties' indemnification obligations should be set forth in separate paragraphs as each party's obligations will likely be different.

Finally, within the agreement, the indemnity should be conspicuous. *Martin K. Eby Construction Company v. One Beacon Insurance Company*, 777 F.3d 1132 (10th Cir. 2015).

11. PRACTICE POINT: Checklist for drafting an indemnity provision.

When reviewing/drafting an indemnity provision, the parties should address the following points:

- Who are the indemnified parties Carefully consider the definitions of the "Indemnified Party" and the "Indemnifying Party" to ensure that the definitions reflect the nature of the specific transaction. Include those parties that should be included and exclude those who should be excluded. Are directors, officers, employees, contractors, agents, distributors, and customers indemnified?
- What is the scope of the indemnity (e.g., defend, hold harmless)?
- What is the breadth of the indemnity (e.g., third-party claims, licensor's negligence, intellectual property infringement claims, personal bodily injury, tangible personal property damage)?
- Is there a time limitation in which the indemnitee must bring its claim?
- What claims are included/excluded (e.g., use of the software, in breach of agreement, licensee modifications to software)?

- What triggers the indemnitor's indemnification claims?
  - A complaint?
  - A suit?
  - An administrative hearing?
- What is the obligation of the indemnitee to notify the indemnitor of any claim?
  - How must notice be given?
  - Promptly in writing?
- What if the indemnitor is not given notice promptly?
- Must the indemnitor admit liability to defend the claim and assume control of the claim?
- Who controls the defense of any claim?
- Who selects counsel to defend the claim?
- Is there an enforcement mechanism if the indemnitor fails to assume defense of the claim?
- What happens if the indemnitor refuses to accept a demand for indemnification? Does the indemnitee have the right to assume control of the defense?
- What costs are indemnified?
  - Judgments?
  - Penalties?
  - Interest?
  - Legal fees? Reasonable legal fees?
  - Expert fees?
  - Arbitration fees?
  - The indemnitee's internal costs?
- When does the indemnitor's obligation to pay/reimburse the indemnitee arise? As incurred, upon award of a judgment, or when finally awarded?
- Can the indemnitee participate in the defense?
  - At its own cost?
  - With counsel of its choice?
- Is indemnification the indemnitee's exclusive remedy? If there is an alternative, which party selects the alternative?
- Are there any limits or caps on the indemnitor's indemnity obligations?
- If there is a cap on the indemnity, do legal costs count toward the indemnity?
- What happens when the cap is exceeded?
- What is the obligation of the indemnitee to cooperate in the defense of the claim at the indemnitee's own cost?
- Who controls the settlement of any claim? Can the indemnitor settle the claim without the indemnitee's consent?
- What is the term of the indemnity?

From the indemnitor's perspective:

- Indemnification should be conditioned on the indemnitor:
  - receiving prompt notice of the claim;
  - controlling the dispute; and
  - the indemnitee's cooperation.

- The indemnity obligation should be limited to third-party claims.
- The indemnitor's liability should be limited to the extent the indemnitor caused the harm, thus confirming comparative liability rather than contributory liability. Use "to the extent arising from" or "solely resulting from." Avoid "arising from or related to."
- The indemnitor should have the right to select and control counsel.
- The indemnitor should limit the basis for its indemnification obligations and exclude causes such as improper use of the software or issues arising from the indemnitee's negligence, i.e., use of the software in violation of the license grant, modifications to the software made by the indemnitee.
- The indemnity should cover only those reasonable costs, expenses, and damages finally awarded against the indemnitee.
- The indemnitor should not be responsible for penalties and fines which generally are not covered by insurance.
- The indemnitor should have the right to lead the defense of the claims against the indemnitee.

From the indemnitee's perspective:

- The indemnitee should have the right to defend the matter if the indemnitor does not promptly acknowledge its indemnification obligation once it has received notice of the claim.
- The indemnitor should not have the right to settle any claim, other than a monetary settlement, without the indemnitee's consent, if such settlement;
  - contains a stipulation to or admission or acknowledgement of, any liability or wrongdoing on the part of the indemnitor,
  - involves the incurrence of any costs or expenses on the part of the indemnifying party, or
  - imposes any obligation upon the indemnifying party.
- The indemnitee should have the right to retain its own counsel at its own expense to participate in the defense of the claim.
- The indemnitor's obligations should not be limited by any cap on liability.

For an excellent discussion of indemnities, see Tollen, *The Tech Indemnities Pocket Guide: Indemnities in Software and Other IT Contracts for Lawyers and Business people* (ABA Press 2020). *See also*, Wolfson, *Language Issues In Drafting Indemnification Clauses in High-Tech Contracts*, 3 PLI Current: The Journal of PLI Press 321 (Spring 2019); Jaskolka & Strnad, *The 5 W's and 1 H of Drafting Indemnity Provisions in Energy Contracts*, 38 ACC DOCKET 32 (Nov. 2020).

C. Intellectual Property Indemnification (§ 14)

Many of the concepts governing general indemnification provisions apply equally to intellectual property indemnification. In an effort to avoid repetition, the discussions set forth in the previous section are not repeated here. As such, readers should also consult the previous section.

1. Overview

Intellectual property indemnification protects a licensee if a third party brings a claim that the licensee's use of the licensed software violates such third party's intellectual property rights. Usually, these intellectual property rights are copyright, patent, trademark, and trade secrets. An intellectual property indemnity is important because the licensee cannot control the risk, as the intellectual property that is the genesis of any claim is usually created and owned by the licensor.

From the licensor's perspective, intellectual property indemnities should be viewed as being in the licensor's self-interest. Indemnities allow the licensor to assume responsibility for third-party infringement claims and protect its intellectual property, as the licensee is not going to defend the licensor's product against an infringement claim with the same level of intensity and importance as the licensor. Thus, a licensor may want to exclude most, if not all, forms of liability under an evaluation license, but still assume control of any infringement claim that may arise.

Most licensees argue that the licensor should bear the risk of third-party claims alleging that the licensor's software or services infringe the third party's intellectual property rights, and that licensees should not bear any risk irrespective of the amount of the license fee paid by the licensee. Given the increasing number of infringement claims arising in the software arena, a prudent licensee should seek comprehensive warranties and indemnification provisions from the licensor whether negotiating an evaluation license or a production license.

From the licensor's perspective, any indemnification should be closely tailored to the intended use of the software and should cover only patents, copyrights, and trade secrets, as trademarks are not an integral part of a software license unless the licensee is distributing the software under the licensor's marks. Some licensors such as Amazon and SAP will not give an intellectual property indemnity and will only agree to defend the licensee due to concerns related to potential patent infringement and the difficulty of identifying potentially infringing patents.

Typical licensor indemnity provisions provide for mutual indemnification. While a two-way indemnification is theoretically preferable to a unilateral indemnity obligation by the licensor to the licensees, mutual indemnities often result in broad indemnities in both directions. Because the most likely use of this provision is an indemnity claim against the licensor and it is unlikely that the licensor will receive any benefit from the two-way indemnity, it is often prudent to forego the two-way indemnity in favor of a narrowly drafted unilateral indemnity. Some licensors seek to only defend but not indemnify the licensee. The obligation to defend but not indemnify provides little comfort to the licensee, especially in the event of a judgment against the licensee. As a concession, some licensors seek to indemnify the licensee from all damages, liabilities, costs, and expenses "finally awarded" by a court of competent jurisdiction.

If the licensor is providing goods or services to the licensee, the licensor should indemnify the licensee against intellectual property infringement claims without any limits on liability. Further, the indemnification should survive the termination or expiration of the underlying agreement for any reason. Savvy parties should remember that the value of any indemnification depends on the other party's size, financial health, and overall ability to satisfy its indemnity obligations.

If the licensee intends to incorporate the licensor's software into its own product and license that product to third parties, the licensee should seek to have the licensor indemnify the licensee for not only third-party claims made against the licensee, but also claims made against the licensee's clients. Many licensors refuse to expand their indemnification obligations by indemnifying the licensee for claims against the licensee's customers, arguing that the licensee can protect itself by disclaiming liability for third-party software in the licensee's contracts with its customers. Depending on the wording of the indemnity, another, less favorable approach would be to have the licensee's customer bring a claim against the licensee and then have the licensee seek indemnification from the licensor.

Trade secrets create the greatest risk for the licensor as they are not usually recorded in any location where the licensor would be able to determine whether the intellectual property in question infringed upon a third party's trade secrets. Similarly, some licensors are hesitant to provide patent indemnification for software given the recent proliferation of business method patents, as well as the inability of licensors to know what inventions are disclosed in competitors' patent applications that can take two years or more to issue and become publicly available. In response to the ever-increasing number of claims bought by "patent trolls," some licensors have sought to transfer the burden of proof of patent infringement claims from the licensor to the licensee. Licensees should strongly resist such change, as the licensor should have a much more thorough understanding of its owned intellectual property and thus, can better understand and mitigate the risk. Trademark infringement is not as serious a concern in software licensing, as only infrequently will the licensee be using the licensor's trademarks.

Traditionally, the liability associated with a licensor's obligation to indemnify the licensee is uncapped. The implementation of a cap will depend on the contract size and the potential profitability of the agreement from the licensor's perspective. If the contract value is small and the licensor's profit margin is small, it is unreasonable to expect the licensor to assume unlimited liability. The United States, Canada, Mexico and Europe have robust patent systems allowing a licensor to justify accepting a larger cap. Outside these countries and the Berne Convention jurisdictions, prudent licensors should insist on more modest caps given the uncertainty of the local patent systems and the local judiciary.

Some large software vendors seek to limit their liability for intellectual property indemnities based on the argument that the risk of software patent litigation should be shared between the vendor and customer, rather than the licensor's failure to fulfill an express covenant. There is typically some symmetry between (i) the likelihood that the vendor will attract claims (directly and via its customers) on account of its size and ubiquity, including the resources and inclination to aggressively defend such claims, and (ii) the leverage the vendor possesses to have its customers agree to a cap or other limits on liability for third-party intellectual property claims. The justification for the limits diminishes to the extent that the licensed software is unlikely to be the target of trolling and/or is being licensed for specific, proprietary purposes by the licensee.

From the customer's perspective, in considering whether to accept a cap on the licensor's indemnity obligations, it should consider the vendor's ability and desire to meet its indemnity obligations, the likelihood of an infringement claim being made, and the customer's ability to limit its exposure by discontinuing use of the software in the event a claim is made. Another risk is the possibility the vendor will abandon its defense of the claim once it reaches the cap on its liability.

For a discussion of the issues unique to multi-party indemnification obligations, *see* Bloch, Molono, Bucigross & Ramachanduan, *Ground Satellite Litigation, IP Indemnification Provisions Implicating Multiple Suppliers*, 34 ACC Docket 51 (Sept. 2016).

2. Implied Indemnification under UCC § 2-312

Upon granting a license to the licensee, a licensee may argue that the licensor is assumed to have made an implied warranty of title under UCC § 2-312(2). Section 2-312(2) of the UCC provides that unless otherwise agreed, a seller who is a merchant regularly dealing in goods of the kind sold, warrants that the goods delivered will be free of any rightful claim of infringement by any third party. It also provides that a buyer who furnishes the specifications must likewise indemnify the seller for any claim arising from the seller complying with the buyer's specifications. UCC § 2-312(2); *Bonneau Co. v. AG Industries, Inc.*, 116 F.3d 155 (5th Cir. 1997). This indemnity is limited to third-party rights existing at the time of delivery. *Yttro Corp. v. X. Ray Imaging Assoc., Inc.*, 559 A.2d 3, 5 (N.J. 1989). Any disclaimer of this warranty must specifically disclaim the warranty of infringement such that the buyer has reason to know that the seller does not claim title or that a third party may have a claim of infringement. Disclaimers of UCC § 2-312 have been upheld. *Landis & Staefa (UK) Ltd. v. Flair Int'l Corp.*, 60. F. Supp. 2d 14 (E.D.N.Y. 1999) (denying buyer's indemnification claims against seller based on seller's contractual warranty disclaimers). However, general disclaimers such as "AS IS" are insufficient to disclaim the warranties of title and infringement. UCC § 2-312(3).

Although a licensor is likely to argue that software is not a good and the software is licensed, not sold, thus, UCC 2-312(2) would be inapplicable a majority of courts will apply the applicable UCC provisions. *But see DSC Communications Corp. v. Pulse Communications, Inc.*, 170 F.3d 1354 (Fed. Cir. 1999) (court applies common law and does not refer to UCC).

A patent license, however, does not usually contain an implied warranty of non-infringement. Deller, Deller's Walker on Patents 406 (1981). *See Motorola, Inc. v. Varo, Inc.*, 656 F. Supp. 716 (N.D. Tex. 1986), and *Chevron, Inc. v. Aqua Products*, 830 F. Supp. 314 (E.D. Va. 1993) (under the doctrine of federal preemption, UCC § 2-312(3) does not impose an indemnity obligation on a party that would not otherwise bear infringement liability under federal patent law). *But see Cover v. Hydramatic Packing Co.*, 83 F.3d 1390 (7th Cir. 1996) (UCC § 2-312(3), which is not preempted by federal law).

3. Limits on Indemnification

The defense of intellectual property indemnification suits can be costly even if the licensor eventually prevails, and during their pendency a licensee may be prohibited from using the software it needs to operate its business. As such the licensor/indemnitor should carefully craft the indemnity it offers, while the licensee should make sure it obtains the protection it needs to operate its business.

Some licensors believe the indemnification clause should be limited to existing U.S. intellectual property rights or registered copyrights at the time the license agreement is executed. This eliminates any right to indemnification for intellectual property rights created subsequent to the grant of the license. At the same time, it limits indemnification only to those U.S. intellectual property rights significantly limiting the licensor's risk. However, a limited intellectual property rights indemnity by the licensor may be shortsighted. If the licensee is sued for intellectual property infringement outside the scope of the licensor's indemnification, the licensee will be forced to defend the suit. The licensee's interest in defending the suit, however, may be greatly different from the licensor's in that the licensee may be motivated to settle the suit on terms favorable to the licensee, but which have a disastrous impact on the licensor's business if the decision voids the licensor's intellectual property rights or otherwise creates a negative precedent for the licensor that impacts its business in the future.

With foreign transactions, indemnification should be limited to the United States and the country in which the software will be used. If the license is worldwide, the licensor should seek to limit its indemnification to those countries that are signatories to the Berne Convention. Prudent licensees should seek indemnification against claims in any country in which they are exploiting the licensed software in accordance with the license. The model language below, which favors the licensee by not limiting the licensor's indemnification obligations to a definitive list of international agreements, is illustrative:

> *Licensor hereby agrees to indemnify, defend and hold harmless Licensee from any claim brought against Licensee that the Software infringes any third party's intellectual property rights issued, honored or enforceable under U.S. laws or international convention(s) (including but not limited to the Berne Convention, Paris Convention, Universal Copyright Convention, Patent Cooperation Treaty) including but not limited to patents, copyrights, trademarks, trade names and trade secrets.*

4. Qualifications to Limit the Licensor's Risk

The licensor may offer a number of qualifications to reduce its risk as it relates to possible patent infringement. The following may be offered in order of preference:

- U.S. patents issued as of the effective date of the agreement,
- U.S. patents issued as of the date of delivery,
- U.S. patents,
- Patents issued as of the effective date of the agreement in the United States, United Kingdom, Canada, European Union, and Australia.

If the underlying license agreement does not contemplate use outside of the United States or in all of these countries, reference to all such countries should be removed. If the underlying license agreement contemplates sale or use in additional countries, these countries may be added after an analysis of the risks and benefits has been performed, taking into account the license fees paid, the strategic nature of the transaction, the software being licensed (i.e., what is the likelihood of an infringement claim being brought), and the relative bargaining power of the parties. In evaluating the risks, licensors should remember that in some countries, the scope of patent protection and potential remedies may be very difficult to evaluate.

From the licensee's perspective, the indemnity should cover all intellectual property rights. If the licensor insists on limiting its indemnity, several fallback positions may be acceptable. The first is to cap the licensor's indemnity liability in countries which do not represent a large area where the licensee will be using the software. For example, under this fallback, the licensor's indemnity liability for U.S. patents would not be subject to a cap, but the licensor's indemnity liability for patents issued in China would be capped. The negotiation rationale is that this limits licensor's exposure in countries in which intellectual property protection may be poorly defined, inconsistently applied, or subject to political whims, while still covering the majority of the licensee's operations. The amount of the cap can be defined in many ways, such as a fixed amount or a percentage of sales derived from the country in which the liability arises.

At the same time, any foreign indemnification should be granted only after sufficient due diligence has been performed with respect to the product market in the particular foreign country, and even then it should be limited solely to patent and copyright indemnification, since a number of foreign jurisdictions have "first to file" trademark laws that encourage manipulation of the rights of foreign trademark owners. Including the phrase "finally awarded" limits the licensor's obligation to make payments to the licensee until all appeals have been exhausted. The licensor should also be careful to limit indemnification to a specific licensee and not a broad class of entities, such as "the licensee and its affiliates" or "the licensee and its customers." Obviously limiting the jurisdictions covered by the indemnification has a similar risk to the other scope restrictions discussed above. However, this may be outweighed by the risk of providing legal resources in foreign jurisdictions.

Even if the licensee is willing to agree to a limited intellectual property indemnification, the licensee should reject any attempt to limit indemnification to only U.S. intellectual property rights. Copyright infringement, for example, should not be limited solely to U.S. copyrights, as under the Berne Convention a foreign copyright holder may enforce its copyrights in the United States. Berne Convention for the Protection of Literary and Artistic Works art. 4, July 24, 1971, S. Treaty Doc. No. 99–27 at 39 (1986).

If the licensor agrees to allow the licensee's contractors to access to its intellectual property, the licensee should indemnify the licensor for any misuse of the licensor's intellectual property by the licensee's contractors.

An indemnification obligation can be characterized by its "front-end" obligations and its "back-end" obligations. Front-end obligations include the right of the indemnitor to receive notice of a claim and the right to develop a work around or obtain a license for the indemnitee. The back end includes the indemnitor's right to control any lawsuit and the right of the indemnity to participate in the lawsuit. In drafting the provision, to the extent the licensee lacks other remedies (such as a breach of contract claim if there is a warranty of non-infringement), the licensor/indemnitor should clearly state that the remedy is the exclusive remedy for a claim of intellectual property infringement.

This is especially important if the licensor has also provided a representation of non-infringement.

5. Conditions Precedent to Indemnification

Indemnification by the licensor should be predicated on several requirements. First, the licensee must promptly notify the licensor of any claim. Second, the licensor must control the defense and settlement of the suit as the licensor ultimately bears the financial responsibility of any settlement or loss. Prudent licensees will qualify the licensor's right to settle a matter requiring the licensee's approval for any settlement that impacts the licensee's right to use the software in question or the scope of the licensee's license grant. Third, the licensee must assist and cooperate in the claim's defense (at the licensor's expense).

6. Mitigation by Licensor

Many intellectual property provisions provide that upon notice of a claim, the licensor may, at its option:

- make the licensed software non-infringing,
- obtain a license to use such software from the party trying to enforce its rights, or
- provide functionally equivalent software.

Alternatively, if these options are impracticable, at the licensor's option, the licensor may refund the license fee to the licensee. Often this refund is calculated based on a three-to five-year depreciation schedule to reflect the benefit the licensee received prior to the software's removal. Although the period of depreciation may vary, most licensors seek to provide that this remedy is in full satisfaction of the licensor's liability to the licensee.

Many licensors seek to depreciate any refund amount provided to the licensee over time to reflect the end user's use of the software in the intervening years before an infringement claim arose. The period of time over which the licensee fee will be amortized is subject to negotiation by the parties, with the licensor generally seeking a shorter period and the licensee a longer period, as a longer period extends the time the licensor is at risk for a refund. Another alternative is to tie the period to the term of the license agreement.

A licensee must be sure it is comfortable with language that allows a licensor to refund the licensee's license fee, especially if the software is important to the operation of the licensee's business, as the licensee may receive only a refund of its license fee in the event of a claim of infringement. Similarly, if the licensee insists on removing the licensor's option to refund the license fee in full satisfaction of an infringement claim, the licensor must be comfortable with the concept that it may be forced to expend a significant amount of money to create work-around or a license for a functionally similar software package. The final solution will usually be an element of price, as the licensor will usually expand its indemnification for an increased license fee.

Many licensees will resist any attempt by the licensor to "depreciate" the value of the software. Although the licensee may have had use of the software prior to its removal, the licensee will have to obtain new software and, in the process, may incur potentially significant disruptions of its business, as well as the costs incurred in migrating to a new application or solution. As such, many licensees seek to recover the full cost of the software and any implementation and maintenance costs. If the software was fully depreciated, some licensors will refund fees paid by the licensee starting when the software has been fully depreciated.

Licensees should ensure that a licensor's obligation to repair/replace/refund is in addition to and not in place of its indemnity obligations, as some license agreements are drafted such that the repair/replace/refund option is an election of remedies. The underlying agreement should clearly provide that the licensor's efforts and right to refund any license fee is in addition to the indemnity obligations and that the licensor remains responsible for any losses incurred by the licensee prior to any modification or substitution. In the event of an infringement, the licensee wants the licensor to both indemnify the licensee and provide a remedy to allow the licensee to continue to use the software. Some licensors seek to include language providing that the indemnity and/or licensor's efforts are the licensee's sole remedy. In the absence of such language, under common law the remedies set forth in the underlying agreement are considered to be in addition to any other remedies that might be available to the licensee under the law. From the licensee's perspective, provided the licensor's indemnity and mitigation obligations are broadly worded, a sole remedy provision is acceptable.

To the extent the licensor modifies the software so that it is non-infringing or substitutes functionally equivalent software, the licensee should ensure that the modified or new software conforms to all requirements of the software license, including those related to functionality as well as performance, and the scope of the license grant is the same as the original license grant and that maintenance and support are available for the new software.

7. *Exclusions*

All agreements should void the licensor's indemnification obligations to the extent that:

- the licensor acts on the licensee's direct instructions,
- the licensee fails to use the latest version of the software or incorporate the latest updates and upgrades,
- the licensee uses the software in violation of the license terms,
- the licensee uses the licensor's software in conjunction with third-party software that has not been approved by the licensor,
- the claim arises from derivative works, enhancement or modifications made by the licensee without the licensor's consent,
- the claim arises from compliance with technical or commercial standards adopted by industry consortia, such as the International Organization for Standardization ("ISO"), the World Wide Web Consortium (W3C), or similar organization,

- a patent, copyright or other intellectual property claim in which the licensee or an affiliate of the licensee has an interest, or
- the licensee fails to assist in the defense.

If the licensor utilizes any of the licensee's intellectual property in the licensor's development efforts, the licensee should indemnify the licensor for any claims that the licensee's intellectual property infringes on a third party's intellectual property rights.

As mentioned above, licensors often seek to exclude from their indemnification obligations any infringement caused by the combination of their software with any data, software, or hardware not provided by the licensor arguing that any such infringement is outside their control. The practical effect of such an exclusion is to eliminate all indemnification obligations for patents that include a computer or a computer memory as an element of the claim. Software by its nature is intended to be used with third-party products, whether hardware or other software. Frequently, infringement claims will be directed to a system or solution composed of multiple products provided by both the licensor and the licensee. The licensor's indemnity should extend to these combinations such that the licensor is liable for its proportionate amount of the costs.
This carveout is illustrated by the following language:

> *We will have no obligation to indemnify you under this section to the extent that the alleged infringement (i) involves any intellectual property rights issued by any country other than the United States, or (ii) is caused by (a) any modification of the Software by any person that is not approved by us, or (b)* ***any combination of the Software with any program, data, product, device or service not provided by us or specified by us as required for use of the Software if such infringement claim would have been avoided by use of the Software alone.***

From the licensor's perspective, the licensor seeks to eliminate any risk outside of its control. For example, if the licensee interfaces the licensor's software with a third-party open-source tool and the open-source tool infringes a third-party intellectual property right, the licensor would be responsible for any intellectual property infringement claims against the licensee even though the licensor had no control over the use of the third-party open-source software.

From the licensee's perspective, while the exclusion of infringement claims caused by a combination of the licensor's software with other third-party hardware or software is not unreasonable, the exclusion should not be absolute. Any such exclusion should be qualified to exclude:

- any combination of the licensor's application with third-party software or hardware that could have been reasonably anticipated including, but not limited to, any third-party software or hardware that is referenced in the licensor's applicable product literature, marketing materials, instructions or documentation;
- any infringement that would have occurred without such combination; and
- arguably, those situations where the licensor is providing integration services.

Even in these situations, the carveout should be limited "to the extent" that the combination infringes on a third party's intellectual property rights.

A prudent licensee should seek to require the licensor to warrant that the software will be non-infringing, whether standing alone or in conjunction with the hardware or software with which it was designed to operate. Licensors, however, may be hesitant to make such a warranty as it is difficult to predict how the licensor's software will perform in conjunction with third-party products. Licensors should not agree to a warranty that permits combinations unnecessary for the use of the software to be covered by the indemnification.

Another issue that arises from a multiple vendor scenario is the right to control the defense and settlement. If there are multiple vendors whose products and services are involved in the claim, it is impractical to provide each vendor an "exclusive right to control and direct" the defense. The most practical solution is for the licensee to defend the claim and for each vendor to contribute to the defense proportionately. While it may be difficult to determine what amount each vendor should contribute, this concept provides a structure to allocate costs.

Given the ever-increasing litigation involving intellectual property, software vendors will likely seek to reduce their indemnification obligations around intellectual property infringement. Some vendors no longer provide an indemnity for claims of patent infringement. As such, licensees will be forced to assume greater risk.

8. *Assumption of the Defense*

Finally, the licensee should insist on including language allowing the licensee to assume its own defense at the licensor's cost if the licensor fails to promptly assume any defense. While a reasonable requirement from the licensee's perspective, this creates a significant risk from the licensor's perspective, both in its potential cost and in that the licensee's interests in defending and settling the suit may be vastly different than the licensor's. See the detailed discussion of the parties' different interests earlier in this Section 4.C.

For a more in-depth discussion of the issues surrounding intellectual property indemnification and model clauses, *see* Neumeyer, *Responding to Patent License and Indemnification Demands*, 27 ACC DOCKET 45 (Oct. 2009). Ocampo, Curtin & Moss, *Infringement Indemnity*, 14 ACCA DOCKET 64 (July/August 1996).

D. Acceptance and Acceptance Test Procedures (§§ 1.14, 7)

1. *Software*

The concept of acceptance and the corresponding acceptance test procedures are extremely important in both software and custom software development agreements. With custom software, the concept of acceptance is not difficult to understand, but in practicality it is difficult to quantify. Too often, the license agreement is unclear as to the standard to which the software must conform to be accepted by the customer. Will the software conform to the contractual specifications, the operational documentation, the acceptance test procedures, or some other standard? Must the software strictly comply with all requirements or simply comply in all material respects to the functional specifications? Further, what differentiates a "bug" from an "error"? What level of bugs is acceptable? It is difficult, if not impossible, to agree on the acceptance tests if the parties do not know what aspects of the software will be tested, much less know the functional specifications of the completed software.

The acceptance test procedures should be objective in nature such that an independent third party should be able to determine whether the licensed software has satisfied the tests. Any acceptance test procedures should be mutually agreed upon by the parties to ensure fairness. The licensor usually drafts the test procedures protocol document, given its familiarity with its own software, and submits this document to the licensee for approval. The licensee then either accepts the document or suggests potential modifications. To ensure that there is mutual agreement as to what constitutes "acceptance," the term should be carefully defined. Otherwise, a court itself may determine what is "acceptable." *See Sha-I Corp. v. City and County of San Francisco*, 612 F.2d 1215 (9th Cir. 1980) (satisfactory completion of 95 percent of acceptance requirements constituted acceptance). In the event the software fails to pass the acceptance test procedures, the contract should provide a set period of time for the licensor to fix the errors and submit the software to the licensee for retesting. The license should then have a set period of time to retest the software. See § 7.2 for model language.

To avoid disputes as to whether or not the software has been accepted, the licensor should have the customer execute an acceptance certificate, formally accepting the software. Execution of the certificate should be contractually required if the software meets the acceptance test procedures. The certificate should also provide formal notice of the start of the warranty. *See* the model Certificate of Acceptance, Forms E.3.1 and E.3.2.

Software by its nature is considered imperfect, and bugs will always exist in a program's code. Acceptance testing will not eliminate all bugs but will hopefully identify any material problems. Consequently, most agreements contain language to the effect that the software will "substantially conform" to the functional specifications or "comply in all material respects" to avoid claims of breach or default. Thus, many agreements classify and delineate the levels of errors and then quantify how many of each level are acceptable. For an example of the classification of errors, see Appendix A to the Software Maintenance and Services Agreement in Form J.1.

2. Deemed Acceptance

Like off-the-shelf software, custom software contracts should include a provision that the use of the software in a commercial context shall be deemed acceptance. Otherwise, the licensee may have an incentive not to accept the software while receiving the commercial benefits of using the software without paying for the software, starting the warranty period or having to pay for maintenance. *See* § 7.3. Many licensees, however, seek to include specific language that the software can be accepted only through the acceptance test procedures, and that use of the software in a live operational environment does not constitute acceptance. *See* § 7.3 (alternative language).

Smart licensees will require that acceptance of any new releases or enhancements are subject to acceptance testing. New releases or enhancements are just as important to the licensee's system as the core software, and these need to be tested prior to being incorporated in the licensee's existing software or system.

For an overview of the issues involved with acceptance from a UCC perspective, *see* Vizy, *Managing Acceptance*, 226 Com. L. Adv. 1 (Oct. 2006).

3. *Shrinkwrap Software*

Off-the-shelf shrink-wrap licenses are deemed "accepted" when the cellophane packaging of the software has been opened or, alternatively, with the use of the software. While there is a split among the federal circuit courts, the enforceability of off-the-shelf acceptance is the majority rule. *See ProCD, Inc. v. Zeidenberg*, 86 F.3d 1447 (7th Cir. 1996); *but see Step-Saver Data Systems, Inc. v. Wyse Technology*, 939 F.2d 91 (3d Cir. 1991) (shrink-wrap license not enforceable under Section 2-207 of UCC as license terms mutually altered the contract between the parties). See Chapter 15 for a more detailed discussion of the validity of shrink-wrap licenses.

Finally, the customer should ensure that the license clearly states that payment does not constitute acceptance. Any payments made by the customer should be considered an advance payment toward the delivery of an accepted deliverable. See Form B.3.1 § 8.2 for model language.

4. *Professional Services (§ 16.C)*

If professional services are a distinct component of the deliverables, the licensee should ensure that the agreement contains a representation and warranty as to the quality of services delivered. Many licensees insist that the services should be delivered in accordance with the highest industry standards. Prudent licensors should not accept this standard, as it is impossible to ascertain what this language would require without conducting continuous surveys as to what the highest standard in the industry entails. A more measured approach is to require the services to be provided in a professional and workmanlike manner in accordance with industry standards. *See D.B. Feedyards v. Environmental Sciences*, 745 N.W.2d 593, 606 (Neb. App. 2008) (consulting service "owed a duty to perform its services as a reasonable . . . consultant with specialized knowledge, skill, training and expertise would under similar circumstances.")

E. Term of the Agreement

When evaluating a license agreement, it is important to differentiate between the term of the over-arching agreement and the term of the license grant itself. They are two distinct concepts, but ones that are often confused. Some agreements and the licenses granted within the agreement are co-terminus, while master agreements may have many individual licenses granted under the terms of the master agreement, each expiring at different times.

1. *Fixed Term*

Most agreements provide for a fixed term for a set number of years that is renewable upon the mutual agreement of the parties. To the extent that there are outstanding Statements of Works (SOWs) or licenses outstanding at the time of termination, most agreements provide that the agreement shall continue until all licenses or SOWs have expired. A fixed term reduces the risk of the parties, as the contract termination date is known at the time of contract signature and cannot be extended without the affirmative act of the parties.

2. *Evergreen Term*

"Evergreen" agreements set forth an initial term and provide that the agreement shall automatically renew on the anniversary of the contract's effective date unless one party provides notice to the other, within a set period prior to the anniversary date (i.e., 90 days), that it is terminating the agreement. If a party fails to give notice within the stated window, the agreement and its accompanying financial obligation renew for another year. Unless a party carefully tracks the contractual requirements to terminate the agreement and establishes a "tickler" calendar, it may end renewing an agreement that it wanted to terminate and having to pay for an unneeded software or services.

Given the increasing prevalence of evergreen agreements and the propensity of parties to fail to remember to opt out, many states have enacted laws requiring vendors to notify customers that their agreement will automatically renew for another term unless the customer opts out of the agreement. *See, e.g.*, CAL. BUS & PROF CODE. § 17602; WIS. STAT. § 134.49. For a 50-state survey of the validity of evergreen clauses see: https://www.faegredrinker.com/en/insights/publications/2018/8/automatic-renewal-laws-in-all-50-states-an-updated-guide.

F. Breach and Cure (§ 5)

A license's breach and cure provisions are extremely important from both the licensor's and licensee's perspective's as each has different concerns about the ability to terminate the license agreement and the rights of each party upon such termination.

The parties should consider the ramifications of not only a breach arising from negligence but also a willful breach. In most cases, the parties will want to establish a carve out from the agreement's limitation of liability in the event of a willful breach to the extent the governing law does not recognize that a willful breach voids a contract's limitation of liability. *Khulusi v. Southwestern Yellow Pages, Inc.*, 916 S.W.2d 227 (Mo. 1995) (willful and wanton conduct voids contract's limitation of liability). Further, in the event of a willful breach or default, the breaching party is not entitled to receive damages from the other party's breach of contract. *Ficara v. Belleau, et al.*, 117 N.E.2d 287 (Mass. 1954). Similarly, the parties may want to create a carveout from the licensee's limitation of liability provision for gross negligence. See, e.g., Form B.3.7 §17.2

1. Breach

(a) Licensee's Breach (§ 5.2)

Most license agreements set forth a number of criteria that allow the licensor to terminate the agreement and the underlying license. The most common are breach of the license grant, nonpayment of any amounts due the licensor, and breach of the licensee's confidentiality obligations. Aggressive licensors often seek to include other triggers such as a change in the licensee's financial status. In the event of a breach, the courts will enforce a license's termination provisions, and licensees should not expect a court to issue an injunction due to undue hardship on the licensee's behalf arising from its inability to use the licensed software. *Complex Systems, Inc. v. ABN AMRO Bank, N.V.*, 2014 WL 1883474 (S.D.N.Y. May 9, 2014). Licensees should avoid accepting broad subjective language, such as the language below, as it grants the licensor the unfettered ability to terminate the agreement or license.

> *Licensor may terminate this Agreement if in Licensor's reasonable judgment, Customer's financial condition does not justify the terms of payment specified herein, unless Customer immediately pays for all Software and Services which have been delivered, and pays in advance for the balance of Software and Services remaining to be delivered during the term of this Agreement.*

Many licensors include language allowing the licensor to terminate the agreement in the event the licensee declares bankruptcy, becomes insolvent or is unable to pay its debts as they become due. These conditions, known as *ipso facto* clauses, are unenforceable under the U.S. bankruptcy laws. 11 U.S.C. § 365(e).

See Chapter 27 for a more detailed discussion of the impact of bankruptcy on software licenses.

(b) Licensor's Breach (§ 5.1)

A licensee should also ensure the license agreement allows it to terminate the agreement in the event of the licensor's breach. The most common justifications are the failure of the software to comply with the software's functional specifications, a breach of the agreement's representations or warranties and a breach of the licensor's confidentiality obligations. Some licensees will also seek to include a number of other triggers including changes in the licensor's financial status, the failure to meet agreed upon service levels, as well as the failure of the licensor to meet any other material terms of the agreement.

Some licensees seek to include language in the license that if they terminate the licensor for breach and it is later found that they wrongfully terminated the licensor, the termination shall be treated as a termination for convenience, not breach. This provision should be rejected by the licensor as it seeks to excuse the licensee from any liability for wrongfully terminating the license and removes any element of risk from wrongful termination.

(c) Material Breach

Many agreements provide that the agreement may be terminated in the event of a party's material breach that is not cured within a set period of time. While it is generally understood that "material" means an action that is so substantial that it defeats the purpose of entering into the agreement, prudent parties will list those events they consider to be material to eliminate any potential ambiguity. The failure to do so allows for different interpretations of "materiality" and the possibility of a dispute. Two different approaches to achieve the same result are illustrated below.

> *Vendor may terminate this License, effective immediately, if Customer fails to pay the License Fee when due or commits a material breach of this Agreement, including, but not limited to, any breach of the provisions of Sections 1, 3, 4, 5, 8, 12, 13 and 17 hereunder which adversely affects Vendor's rights.*

> *Vendor and Customer acknowledge and agree that the following shall constitute events of default ("Events of Default") and that the occurrence of one (1) or more of such Events of Default shall constitute a material breach of this Agreement, which shall allow a party, as applicable, to seek the rights and remedies set forth in this Article: . . . [LIST EVENTS THAT CONSTITUTE A DEFAULT]*

2. Notice

The failure of a party to comply with its contractual obligations should immediately trigger the issuance of a breach notice from the non-breaching party to the party in breach. The failure to provide notice is, in most cases, a prerequisite to bringing a breach claim and may bar a party from remedy. *See Samia Companies LLC v. MRI Software LLC*, 53 F. Supp. 3d 385 (D. Mass 2014); *Emanuel Law Outlines, Inc. v. Multi-State Legal Studies, Inc.*, 899 F. Supp. 1081 (S.D.N.Y. 1995). Under the UCC, a buyer who accepts a tender must notify the seller within a reasonable time if any breach has been discovered or should have been discovered. *See, e.g.*, UCC § 2-607; *Peavey Electronics Corp. v. Baan U.S.A., Inc.*, 10 So. 3d 945 (Miss. Ct. App. 2009). Further, an unjustified notice of breach can itself constitute a breach. *Bridger del Sol, Inc. v. VincentView LLC*, 406 P.3d 460 (Mont. 2017).

3. Cure

(a) Cure and Cure Periods (See, e.g., § 5.1 (e), (f), (g), (i), (j))

Both parties should ensure that the agreement contains a cure period allowing the party in breach a period of time during which to cure its performance before the other party may terminate the agreement. Except for a breach of the agreement's confidentiality provisions, almost all breaches by a party should be subject to a cure period, usually no less than 30 days. To avoid a dispute, the agreement should stipulate a definitive cure period such as 30 days from receipt of a notice of breach and avoid subjective language giving the breaching party a "reasonable" amount of time to cure the breach. The parties should make sure that the agreed upon time period is sufficient to allow a resolution to be reached without impacting the other party's business. For example, the licensor will likely need at least thirty days to fix any software problems. The licensee should also avoid accepting language that prohibits the licensee from terminating the agreement as long as the licensor is trying to cure the breach.

Any breach notice should be delivered in accordance with the agreement's notice provision and the notice should set forth in detail the nature of the breach in order to allow the breaching party to cure. *See Jasting v. Wright Medical Technology, Inc.*, 528 F.3d 28, 36 (1st Cir. 2008) ("notice of contract termination must state with reasonable certainty the essential facts required by law or by contract."); *Valspar Refinish, Inc. v. Gaylord's Inc.*, 764 N.W.2d 359 (Minn. 2009) (failure of buyer to provide supplier written notice of supplier's breach, setting forth the nature of the alleged breach, barred buyer's breach of contract claim.). *SVS, Inc. v. Rabbit Ears Productions, Inc.*, 1992 WL 91183 (S.D.N.Y. Dec. 12, 1991). See § 52.

In New York, a party's failure to comply with a condition precedent for asserting a claim for breach of contract may constitute a breach itself and, in turn, preclude recovery. *Sweetser v. Netsmart Technologies., Inc.*, 558 F. Supp. 2d 108, 113 (D. Me. 2008) (citing *Filmline (Cross Country) Prods., Inc. v. United Artists Corp.*, 865 F.2d 513, 518 (2d Cir. 1989)); *Bausch & Lomb Inc. v. Bressler*, 977 F.2d 720 (2d Cir. 1992) (manufacturer committed material breach by terminating agreement with two days' notice in contravention of agreement's 30-day notice requirement); *Inter-Americas Ins. Corp., Inc. v. Imaging Solutions Co.*, 185 P.3d 963 (Kan. App. 2008) (buyer breached agreement by terminating agreement without providing seller notice and opportunity to cure). Thus, it is imperative that a party seeking to terminate an agreement know the terms of the agreement and abide by them.

Express provisions establishing a requirement of notice and opportunity to cure before commencing legal action must be followed. Typically, a party claiming non-performance must provide any contractually secured opportunity to cure prior to terminating the contract. *Sea Tow Int'l, Inc. v. Pontin*, 607 F. Supp. 2d 378, 388 (E.D.N.Y. 2009) (citing *Point Prods. A.G. v. Sony Music Entm't, Inc.*, 2000 WL 1006236, at *3 (S.D.N.Y. July 20, 2000). Thus, if the contract stipulated that notice and a period of days must be given for an opportunity to cure, the party bringing the claim must perform the contract pursuant to that provision in order to avoid the preclusive effect of noncompliance.

(b) Implied Right to Cure

It is unclear, however, whether there is an implied right to cure a breach in the absence of a contractual provision granting such a right. Some commentators have stated that, at least in construction law, a right to cure "is a fundamental common law right implied in every contract as a matter of law." PHILLIP BRUNER & PATRICK J. O'CONNOR, JR., 5 BRUNER & O'CONNOR ON CONSTRUCTION LAW § 18.41 (May 2008). Outside of construction law, there is very little case law on the matter. At least one commentator has stated that no such right exists for services contracts. *The Seller's Right to Cure*, 270 COMM. L. ADV. 1, 2 (June 2010) ("there is no right to cure in service contracts.") Other commentators believe that the right to cure is implied within the Restatement (Second) of Contracts and UCITA but there appears to be no case law addressing the issue. RAYMOND T. NIMMER & JEFF DODD, MODERN LICENSING § 11.8. In contracts that do not expressly require an opportunity to cure, the failure to provide one will most likely constitute a preclusive breach. In *Delvecchio v. Bayside Chrysler Plymouth Jeep Eagle, Inc.*, a New York court evaluated an employment contract without a provision requiring an opportunity to cure. 271 A.D.2d

636, 639, 706 N.Y.S.2d 724, 726 (App. Div. 2000). The contract provision required only notice of termination, not a specified chance to cure. *Id.* As a result, and in light of the underlying assertion that the plaintiff employee had been terminated for cause, the court held that the required notice was not a material term of the contract and the termination for cause remained effective. *Id.* The fact that the court reached this conclusion indicates that it is likely that New York does not imply a right to an opportunity to cure. If such a right were implied, the court would have found the failure to provide an opportunity as a breach by the defendant, and the plaintiff's termination would have been rendered ineffective. While the *Delvecchio* holding pertains to employment contracts, it is probable that an implied right to an opportunity to cure does not exist in commercial services contracts as well.

(c) Cure Provisions

Most contracts include the right to cure a breach upon receipt of notice of such breach from the non-breaching party. The underlying contract should require the non-breaching party to notify the party in breach setting forth in detail that nature of the breach. Usually, the parties agree on a 30-day cure period. In those instances where the breach is of an egregious nature, such as a violation of laws, the parties may agree on a much shorter time frame. In some situations, such as the breach of a confidentiality obligation, the non-breaching party may have the right to immediately terminate the agreement without providing the breaching party a period in which to cure.

(d) Practical Considerations in Providing a Notification of Breach

To avoid potential problems and the cost of unnecessary litigation, a party terminating agreement should follow the terms of the contract's termination provision and not only give the required notice and cure period, but also describe the nature of the breaching party's breach in sufficient detail. *See, e.g., Computrol, Inc. v. Newtrend, L.P.*, 203 F.3d 1064 (8th Cir. 2000) (failure to significantly specify nature of breach and provide cure period was breach of contract).

The failure of a party to provide the breaching party a contractually required notice and cure period is itself a breach of the contract. A provision in a contract for the termination thereof upon certain conditions can be enforced only in strict compliance with the terms of these conditions. *Blaine Econ. Dev. Auth. v. Royal Elen. Co., Inc.*, 520 N.W.2d 473, 479 (Minn. Ct. App. 1994) (plaintiff wrongfully terminated contract by failing to provide written notice to cure pursuant to contract); *Nat'l Bankcard Services, Inc. v. Family Express Corp.*, 2006 WL 2480479 (D. Minn. April 29, 2006) (failure to give notice to plaintiff of its alleged breach and provide contractually mandated cure period was breach of contract).

(e) Incurable Breaches and Futility

Some states allow a party to terminate a contract immediately, without affording the breaching party notice and an opportunity to cure, if the breach is incurable or the cure is futile. *Needham v. Candie's, Inc.*, 2002 WL 1896892, at *4 (S.D.N.Y. Aug. 16, 2002) (citing *Wolff & Munier, Inc. v. Whiting-Turner Contracting Co.*, 946 F.2d 1003, 1009 (2d Cir. 1991)); *AAMCO Industries, Inc. v. DeWolf*, 250 N.W.2d 835 (Minn. 1977) (failure to give plaintiff controlling mandated 24-hour cure period would have been futile gesture). Courts have also held that a material breach going to "the root of the matter or the essence of the contract" would excuse the obligation of a period for cure. *Sea Tow Int'l, Inc. v. Pontin*, 607 F. Supp. 2d 378, 389 (E.D.N.Y. 2009) (quoting *Southland Corp. v. Froelich*, 41 F. Supp. 2d 227, 246 (E.D.N.Y. 1999)). However, the applied scope of what is futile in New York courts is relatively narrow in order to avoid judicial removal of core provisions from contracts. *Annecca Inc., Lexent, Inc.*, 307 F. Supp. 2d 999, 1010 (N.D. Ill. 2004) (citing *Petracca v. Petracca*, 756 N.Y.S.2d 587, 588 (App. Div. 2003)). Therefore, a party will not be in breach if it does not provide an opportunity to cure as long as the situation conforms to the narrow scope of the futility exception.

(f) Breaches for Which a Cure Period Is Not Reasonable

Some breaches should not be subject to a cure period if it is clear the breach is incurable. These events include misappropriation or breach of a party's confidentiality obligations or breach of the law. In these events, the agreement should be clear that the non-breaching party may immediately seek injunctive relief or otherwise terminate the agreement without prior notice.

Licensors are very concerned with the protection of their intellectual property and, to a lesser degree, receiving payment. While a "cure period" of 30 days is standard for most breaches by a licensee, most licensors seek to include a provision allowing the licensor to immediately terminate the license or obtain an injunction if the licensee violates any of the terms of the license grant or the license agreement's confidentiality provisions. The basis for immediate termination stems from the licensor's desire to immediately stop the misuse of its software or confidential information, as these breaches cannot be cured. Other issues such as payment, which are not so critical and can be easily cured, are subject to a standard 30-day cure period.

At the same time, the licensee wants to make sure the licensor can only terminate the license and take possession of the software for a material breach. In addition, the licensee should carefully consider any self-help measures the licensor seeks to include in the license and any language regarding the licensor's ability to disable the software without liability. For a more detailed discussion of the issues involved with self-help, see Section B.6.(b)(iii)(z), below.

Many licensees insist that the license contain a provision allowing the licensee to use the software until any dispute is resolved. Licensees should negotiate to obtain the right to utilize the software for a reasonable time after termination to allow the licensee to migrate to another product. In most cases, the licensor's damages will be monetary, and the licensor will not be further damaged by the licensee's continueduse of the software for a limited period of time. In certain situations, such as breach of the license's confidentiality provisions, an injunction, temporary restraining order and termination without the right of further use would be appropriate.

(g) Step-in Agreements (Form E.5.3)

A "step-in" agreement allows a party to "step in" in the event another party fails to meet its contractual obligations and assume the breaching party's rights and/or obligations. In essence, a step-in agreement allows a party to reduce its risks when dealing with its vendors or in a high-risk transaction. One common example is the ability of a customer to contact a vendor's subcontractors in the event the vendor fails to meet its delivery obligations to the customer. Although the customer lacks contractual privity with the vendor's subcontractors, the step-in agreement grants the customer the right to contract directly with the subcontractors and perhaps even assume the vendor's agreement with the sub-contractor. Another potential scenario would allow a vendor to assume certain rights in the event of the subcontractor's breach. For example, if a systems integrator is dependent on a small software licensor for a large systems integration project, the systems integrator may insist on the right to "step in" and assume control of the licensor's software and its employees in the event of the licensor's breach.

G. Expiration, Termination, and Cancellation

The expiration/termination provisions in a license are extremely important from both the licensor's and licensee's perspectives, as each has different concerns about the termination of the license agreement and the rights of each party upon such termination.

1. *Expiration*

Well-drafted license agreements should set forth the parties' obligations upon expiration of the license. At a minimum the agreement should address the licensee's certification that it has stopped using the software and returned all copies of the object code and source code, any transition services, a final accounting, return of all confidential information, and the licensor's right to audit the licensee to confirm its compliance with the licensee's termination-related obligations.

2. *Termination for Breach*

(a) Material Breach

A party's right to terminate a license agreement for breach should be for a *material* breach only. Common law recognizes that unless the agreement provides otherwise, an agreement can only be terminated for a material breach and not a minor deviation from a contractual obligation. *Rano v. Sipa Press, Inc.*, 987 F.2d 580 (9th Cir. 1993) (material breach required to rescind/terminate license).

Although the phrase "material" is subject to interpretation and varies depending upon state law, it has been defined as "affect[ing] the purpose of a contract in an important or vital way." *K&K Management, Inc. v. Lee*, 557 A.2d 965 (Md. 1989). See also *Village of Fox Lake v. Aetna Casualty & Surety Co.*, 534 N.E.2d 133 (Ill. 1989) (a material breach is one that defeats the objects of the parties in making the agreement); WILLISTON ON CONTRACTS § 866. The parties will often seek to include a definitive list of "material" breaches in the contract. Licensees should resist this approach, as it may limit their ability to terminate the agreement if the licensor's non-performance does not fall into one of the enumerated breaches.

Software, especially customized software, is often very complex. Thus, in the event of a failure to meet the functional specifications, it may require quite some time to duplicate and diagnose a problem, code the solution, and then install and test the software. The licensee can protect itself from the resulting late delivery by including a provision for liquidated damages, should the licensor fail to deliver the software in a timely manner or if the software fails to operate in accordance with the functional specifications. However, the amount of liquidated damages must not be so high as to be considered unconscionable or the agreement will be unenforceable. *See* UCC § 2-718, comment 1.

Licensees are often hesitant to terminate the agreement for the licensor's *material* breach as it creates a dilemma for the licensee. Even though the licensor has not delivered a working product, if the licensee terminates the agreement, its business may be severely affected, and it will be forced to restart the procurement process. Therefore, many licensees seek the option of either receiving the software's source code to complete the project itself, the right to receive monetary damages, or both. To ensure that they receive the source code when licensors breach the license agreement, most licensees insist on the execution of an escrow agreement. While this ensures the release of the software's source code to the licensee, receipt of the source code does not necessarily solve the licensee's problems. See Chapter 24 for a more in-depth discussion of this issue.

Licensees should also seek to include language requiring the licensor to correct any nonconformance and prohibiting the licensor from walking away from a contract if it becomes unprofitable to perform. At least one court has recognized that a licensor's failure to perform due to a contract's unprofitability is not an intentional breach of contract that would void the contract's limit of liability. *Metropolitan Life Ins. Co. v. Noble Lowndes Int'l Inc.*, 643 N.E.2d 504 (N.Y. 1994). In essence, the licensee seeks to ensure a form of specific performance.

Some licensees question the need to include "material" before "breach" as it infers the agreement cannot be terminated in the event of a non-material breach, leaving the licensee without a remedy. These licensees argue that every obligation should be material, but many licensors reply that an uncured breach of a "*de minimis*" obligation should not trigger termination. In response, some licensees seek to include language, often in the service level agreement, providing that multiple breaches during a stated period of time (i.e., 12 months) will justify termination even if cured. Model language follows:

> *If Supplier fails to adhere to any Service Level in any three (3) consecutive calendar months, Customer may terminate the Agreement or the applicable Statement of Work, regardless of any term remaining on the Agreement, or Statement of Work, without liability for penalties or damages associated with such termination, and upon thirty (30) days prior written notice. In such event Supplier shall refund any prepaid fees for periods after termination.*

(b) Termination vs. Seeking Damages for Breach

Even if an opportunity to cure is afforded, it may not apply to every claim arising under the contract. In *Sweetser v. Netsmart Technologies, Inc.*, the court, applying New York law, drew a distinction between a suit for termination of the contract and one for its breach. 558 F. Supp. 2d 108, 115 (D. Me. 2008). The underlying agreement provided that termination could be sought on written notice to the defaulting party if that party had not commenced cure within ten days and effected cure within 30 days of receipt of notice of default. *Id.* at 113. The provision did not require a party to terminate before seeking any legal remedies for breach or default. *Id.* After considering the provision in relation to the entire contract, the court held that the notice and cure requirement of the termination provision did not act as a prerequisite to bringing an action for damages from breach. *Id.* at 115. Thus, the terms of the contract providing for an opportunity to cure must be analyzed to see if the requirement pertains to both a claim for breach of contract and termination. If it does not, then failure to provide an opportunity to cure may not constitute a breach for the party commencing legal action.

A termination provision can preclude a claim for breach. *Needham v. Candie's, Inc.*, 2002 WL 1896892 (S.D.N.Y. Aug. 16, 2002) (a party was precluded from suing for breach of contract even though only the termination provision provided for an opportunity to cure because the breach consisted of nonpayment of severance after termination).

3. *Termination for Reasons Unrelated to Performance*

(a) An Adverse Change in a Licensor's Financial Condition

Some licensees seek the contractual right to terminate the licensor in the event the licensor's financial stability, such as its debt rating, is downgraded. A typical provision provides:

> Licensee may terminate this Agreement by providing Licensor with notice of termination in the event that Licensor's Senior Unsecured Debt Rating falls to or below [xx] from Standard & Poor's Rating Group or [xx] from Moody's Investors Service.

This provision is unacceptable from the licensor's perspective, as the licensee is asking for an absolute right of termination in the event of a downgrade of the licensor's debt rating regardless of the strength of the licensor's balance sheet or the reason for the downgrade. A downgrade in the licensor's debt rating might not result from any action or inaction on the part of the licensor but rather from changes in the U.S. and global economies. Further, the licensor may be in full compliance with all of its obligations under the agreement and the licensee has not been harmed by such downgrade.

Alternatively, some licensees see the right to terminate the agreement in the event of a "material adverse change" in the licensor's financial condition or in the event the licensee has "reasonable grounds" for questioning the licensor's ability to perform and does not receive "adequate assurances" when such assurances are sought. See Form N.9 for a model licensor assurances letter.

There are several means for the licensor to address the licensee's concerns without conceding an automatic right of termination. One approach is to allow a right of termination for convenience in the event the licensor's debt rating is reduced to "noninvestment grade." A second approach is to require the licensor to establish a performance bond or other financial guarantee in the event its credit rating is downgraded to "non-investment grade." In negotiating a resolution, it is important to note that the licensor has not breached the agreement or failed to meet its contractual obligations. Further, the licensee has not suffered any harm or incurred any damages. Thus, an absolute right of termination is not justified.

If a licensor is willing to accept a financially related termination right, any such termination should always be considered to be a termination for "convenience" or "without cause" and not a termination for breach. To do otherwise potentially subjects the licensor to significant liability for damages and other costs incurred by the licensee which normally would not be recoverable by the licensee for a termination for its convenience.

(b) Discontinuance of Software

Licensees often seek to provide that in the event the licensor discontinues support or development of the software, the licensee may terminate the agreement. This provision may be appropriate in a short-term license but is not practical if the software is mission-critical and it will be difficult for the licensee to transition to a new software solution. A better approach is for the license to require that the licensor provide the licensee notice well in advance of any discontinuation and then be obligated to provide transition services for an extended period of time.

(c) A Change of Control

Some parties seek to include a provision in the license agreement providing a right of termination in the event there is a change of control in the other party. Licensors should reject provisions to this effect, as a change in control should not justify termination if the licensor is not in breach of the contract. Licensors will occasionally seek the inclusion of a change-of-control provision in the event the licensee is acquired by a competitor of the licensor, as the licensor does not want its software to be accessed by the competitor. In such limited situations, a change-of-control provision may be justified.

4. Termination for Convenience (§ 4.1)

Termination for convenience clauses permit a party to terminate a contract "even in the absence of fault or breach by the other party without suffering the financial consequences of a breach of contract." *See, e.g., Harris Corp. v. Giesting & Associates, Inc.*, 297 F.3d 1270, 1271 (11th Cir. 2002). Often, software development contracts will contain a termination for convenience clause, allowing a licensee to terminate a contract without cause. Usually a licensee terminates an agreement for convenience when its business plans change such that it no longer requires the contracted software or services. Licensors do not favor termination for convenience clauses, as they prevent the licensor from recognizing the full value of the agreement and may disrupt their staffing and development plans. In the event a licensee terminates an agreement for convenience, the agreement should protect the licensor financially as the agreement was terminated on the whim of the licensee.

> *The term of this Agreement shall be effective as of the Effective Date and shall continue through and until __________, 2027, unless earlier terminated in accordance with the provisions of this Agreement; provided that Licensee may terminate this Agreement at any time during the Term subject to the following conditions: (i) Licensee shall provide*

*Licensor with written notice of such intent to terminate by no later than the date that is thirty (30) days prior to the desired termination date (the "**Opt-Out Date**") and (ii) Licensee shall reimburse Licensor for any out of pocket expenses that Licensor (x) has actually incurred for Licensor's obligations under this Agreement prior to the Opt-Out Date, (y) has contractually committed to incur in connection with its obligations under this Agreement prior to the Opt-Out Date, and (z) will reasonably actually incur in connection with the winding down of the performance of the services being provided by Licensor hereunder. Payment of such amounts are to be paid by Licensee to Licensor within thirty (30) days following the Opt-Out Date (subject to Licensee's receipt from Licensor of reasonable supporting documentation and/or invoices evidencing all such amounts.*

For a more detailed discussion, *see* Brown, Kennedy & Martini, *Termination for Convenience Under the Uniform Commercial Code*, Com. Newsltr. (Spring 2014) (http://www.wiggin.com/15008).

(a) Financial Ramifications

Each party should carefully consider the inclusion of such clauses. If included, the parties should ensure the agreed upon language protects each party financially and clearly delineates how any payments due the licensor will be calculated. Too often the parties incorporate such clauses into their agreement without understanding the financial ramifications. By clearly stating how the licensor will be paid for the work performed, the parties will avoid any potential disputes in the future. Many customers seek to limit payment to all work accepted at the time of termination, but this approach fails to compensate the licensor for work that it has performed but has not yet delivered. Further, partially complete work may be ineligible for acceptance as the licensor has not been allowed to complete it. Other customers seek to pay on a percent complete basis; that is, they determine what percentage of the total project was complete at the time of termination and pay the licensor the proportional percentage of the total contract value. This approach, however, does not recognize that in certain projects the licensor's costs may not be directly proportional to the percent of work completed; there may be a significant amount of startup work even before undertaking the development. See the model language below:

Customer may terminate this Agreement and a SOW without cause upon thirty (30) days prior notice to Licensor. To the extent compensation under a SOW which has been terminated without cause is on a time and materials basis, Licensor will be compensated for all Services performed and expenses incurred up to the effective date of termination of the SOW at the rates and expense reimbursement rules specified in the SOW. If a SOW which has been terminated without cause provides compensation for the Services and expenses on a fixed fee basis, Licensor will receive a prorated amount of the SOW compensation equal to the percentage of Services (and Deliverables) completed as of the termination date of the SOW or as otherwise specified in a SOW.

A more equitable approach is to pay the licensor on a time and materials basis for the hours expended provided that in no event will the amount paid to the licensor exceed the total value of the contract or statement of work. The licensor should also insist that if the licensee terminates for convenience, in addition to payment for services rendered, the licensor shall be entitled to recover its termination costs, which may or may not include lost profits and any costs such as the cost of terminating those employees assigned to the project, as well as any travel and expense cost, such as long-term apartment rentals, that cannot be avoided. The model language below is more favorable to the licensor:

> *In the event of premature termination of the Agreement, Customer shall pay Licensor for Deliverables performed, on a prorated basis, and shall pay Licensor for any and all travel, lodging and out-of-pocket expenses incurred by Licensor in accordance with the SOW through the date of termination. In no event shall such amount exceed the amount that would have been payable to Licensor had the SOW not been terminated.*

In the event the licensee seeks to terminate a maintenance contract, the licensee should not be entitled to a refund, as the licensor calculated its pricing based on the licensee purchasing maintenance for the full term of the maintenance agreement.

(b) Legal Ramifications of Termination for Convenience

Where a party properly terminates an agreement for convenience, it is unclear whether it may later maintain a claim for breach of contract. While there is copious authority addressing termination for convenience relating to government contracts, there is very little law addressing termination for convenience in a commercial setting. Existing case law appears to support the proposition that an entity that terminates a contract for convenience cannot sustain a cause of action against the nonterminating party for breach of contract. In the event a party attempts to argue that it in fact terminated for breach, it would likely be found to have wrongfully terminated the contract by failing to provide the nonterminating party any contractually required cure period.

A party who terminates for convenience or wrongfully terminates the contract will have a difficult time bringing a successful claim for breach of contract. Maryland law permits a defendant to introduce evidence that a plaintiff breached the contract first and thus, is not entitled to payment. *Hubler Rentals, Inc. v. Roadway Express, Inc.*, 637 F.2d 257 (4th Cir. 1981) (Roadway's termination of contract did not provide defendant opportunity to cure in accordance with contract and constituted a breach of the agreement. Performance of the contract by the party suing is a condition precedent to recovery.).

New York law appears to prohibit defendants from introducing evidence of nonperformance by the nonterminating party in defense of a claim. *Tishman Construction Corp. v. City of New York*, 643 N.Y.S.2d 589 (1996) (city's termination for convenience entitled contractor to receive amounts due and payable on the date of termination; city precluded from raising a counterclaim for damages due to alleged breach of the contract); *Koppers Company v. Brunswick Corp.*, 303 A.2d 32 (Pa. Super. 1973) (by terminating contract for convenience Brunswick waived its rights to claim breach for defective goods on the part of Koppers); *Fruin-Colnon Corp. v. Niagara Frontier Transportation Auth.*, 180 A.D.2d 222, 585 N.Y.S.2d 248 (1992) (court dismissed defendant's counterclaims as defendant wrongfully terminated the contract, depriving plaintiff of its contractual right to attempt to cure breach. Under the terms of the contract, the wrongful termination of the plaintiff was deemed a termination for convenience. Because the termination was for the convenience of the defendant, it negated the defendant's right to recover payments made to third parties for liquidated damages.) *See also Fruin-Colnon Corp. v. Niagara Frontier Transportation Auth.*, 180 A.D.2d 222, 585 N.Y.S.2d 248 (1992) (counterclaims for liquidated damages dismissed where contract deemed terminated for convenience) and *Paragon Restoration Group, Inc. v. Cambridge Square Condominiums*, 836 N.Y.S.2d 501 (2006) (invoking a termination for convenience clause limits a party's right to recover on a counter-claim for breach, where the terminated party is not provided an opportunity to cure alleged breaches of contract).

Some courts, however, have allowed the terminating party to proceed with a breach of contract counterclaim. *See United States v. TDC Management Corp., Inc.*, 24 F.3d 292 (D.C. Cir. 1994); *Executive Airlines v. Electric Boat Corp.*, 271 F. Supp. 2d 392 (D. Conn. 2003); *G.M. Harston Constr. Co., Inc. v. City of Chicago*, 209 F. Supp. 2d 902, 908 (N.D. Ill. 2002) (rejecting the plaintiffs' absolute contention "that termination for convenience necessarily means that offsets for substandard or delayed performance cannot be considered").

The law does not demand the dismissal of a terminating party's counterclaim when the underlying contract is terminated for convenience. *See, e.g., Lisbon Contractors, Inc. v. United States*, 828 F.2d 759, 769 (Fed. Cir. 1987) (noting that the government had the burden of proving the amount of setoff and refusing to "decide the issue on the legal ground urged by Lisbon that a setoff cannot be made for corrective work where a convenience termination is involved").

Harris explains that where a party properly terminates an agreement for convenience, the terminating party "is entitled to judgment on [the terminated party's] breach of contract claim for [the] contract termination." *Harris Corp.*, 297 F.3d at 1274.

Further, a number of courts have held that a party who terminates a contract for convenience "is not bound by its initial rational for [terminating an agreement] provided that (1) it was not acting in bad faith; and (2) the [terminated party] did not change its position in reliance upon the initial reason given for termination." *Millgard Corp. v. E.E. Cruz/Nab/Fronier-Kemper*, 2004 WL 1488534, at *13 (S.D.N.Y. July 2, 2004). *See also Accart Builder Co., Inc. v. Southwest Concrete Systems, Inc.*, 679 S.W.2d 106, 108 (Tex. App. 1984) (contractor who terminated subcontractor for convenience entitled to present issues of subcontractor's deficient performance to jury).

5. Unjustified Termination

Some licensees seek to include language in their agreements providing that in the event the licensee terminates the agreement for an alleged default which turns out to be incorrect, the termination will be considered to be a termination for convenience. The licensee seeks to do so to avoid any liability from a wrongful termination claim. *See Automated Solutions Corp. v. Paragon Data Sys., Inc.*, 856 N.E.2d 1008 (Ohio App. 2006) (confirming hardware vendor's termination of software vendor's contact improper, as software vendor had not been in breach). In such cases, the licensor will be compensated in accordance with the agreement's termination for convenience provisions. Thus, a prudent licensor should ensure that the agreement's termination for convenience provision protects the licensor's financial interests.

> *If, after notice of termination of the Licensor's right to proceed under this paragraph, it is determined for any reason that the Licensor was not in default under this paragraph, or*

that the delay was excusable under the provisions of Section ___, (Force Majeure), the rights and obligations of the parties shall be the same as if the notice of termination had been issued pursuant to Section __ (Termination for Convenience).

6. Force Majeure (§ 33)

Force majeure clauses are intended to protect against unforeseen events, such as an act of God. Events that are reasonably foreseeable do not excuse performance. Thus, companies purchase business interruption insurance for events like a flood even though they may be seen as an act of God.

The COVID-19 pandemic may or may not qualify as an event of force majeure depending on the language of the underlying agreement and the extent of pandemic. The COVID-19 virus was publicized/discussed for months prior to arriving in the United States, so no one should have been surprised by an outbreak in the workplace. Of course, a court would closely examine a party's efforts to mitigate the effects of any likely force majeure event in reaching a decision. Many force majeure provisions provide that the impacted party (that is, the party who is awaiting performance) may be entitled to terminate the agreement if the event of force majeure continues for a set period of time.

In the event the agreement is terminated as the result of an event of force majeure, neither party should be forced to incur a financial penalty. The licensor should be paid for the work performed but the licensee should not be forced to pay for work it has not received. Under no circumstances should the licensee have the right to exercise the remedy of cover if an agreement is terminated for an event of force majeure as force majeure arises from an unforeseen event outside the control of either party. As such, neither party should receive a financial benefit or be subject to a financial burden. Allowing a licensee to seek cover unfairly places the risk associated with an event of force majeure on the licensor.

See Section 6.D for a more detailed discussion of force majeure.

7. Bankruptcy

Federal Bankruptcy laws prevent a licensor from terminating a licensee in the event the licensee declares bankruptcy. See Chapter 27 for more detailed discussion of the impact of bankruptcy in a licensing transaction.

8. Transition

The parties should plan for transition almost from the time of contract execution to ensure that they are prepared if a termination event occurs. The licensor should create a list of all third-party software used in the solution as well as any consultants and contractors, a description of the services they provide, the duration of their obligations, and any other relevant information. When compiling this information, the licensor should be cognizant of any confidentiality obligations it may be bound by.

The parties should also create a transition plan and meet weekly to update the plan and measure the parties' progress in meeting it. The transition plan will be shaped by the licensee and any incoming vendor. A prudent licensor should disclaim responsibility for any performance results during the transition period and should assume no responsibility for the completion of any activities. The licensor's only obligation should be to support the transition in a professional manner.

9. *PRACTICE POINT*: Checklist for terminating an agreement:

- Was notice properly given?
  - In the proper manner?
  - To the correct address?
  - Within the required time period?
  - With any required description?
  - With the basis for termination?
  - If for breach, is there a cure period?
  - Did the notice contain an effective date?
- Software
  - Will the customer have any post-termination use rights?
  - Will the customer require access rights by any third party?
- Is the payment of a termination fee required?
- Does either party possess the confidential information, data or property of the other party?
  - Has all confidential information and data been returned to the owning party?
  - If such data has been destroyed, has a certificate of destruction been provided?
  - Does the vendor need to return the customer's data?
    - Within what time frame?
    - Does the data need to be returned in a certain format?
    - After what period of time may the vendor destroy the data in its possession?
- Is the vendor required to provide transition/termination assistance?
  - For what services?
  - For how long?
  - At what price?
  - Is the current vendor required to cooperate with the new vendor?
  - Will key resources be made available to the customer?

H. Remedies (§§ 5.2, 5.3)

To protect itself in the event of a breach, each party should seek to include a number of rights and remedies in the parties' contract. The actual rights and remedies included in a particular contract will be dictated by the needs of the parties and the level of protections each party is willing to concede. Given the uncertainty of whether the UCC applies to software licensing transactions, these rights and remedies should supplement any remedies available under the UCC.

The parties should carefully consider the wording related to the stated remedies. Are the stated remedies exclusive? Are other remedies foreclosed? These questions need to be considered and the answers incorporated into the agreement. For example, the inclusion of a liquidated damages provision in an agreement does not prevent a party from seeking other equitable remedies if the agreement did not expressly foreclose such remedies. *Miller v. United States Naval Institute*, 423 A.2d 283 (Md. 1980). Similarly, unless a termination provision for breach is deemed exclusive, it is considered to be cumulative. *Foster-Porter Enterprises v. De Mare*, 81 A.2d 325 (Md. 1951) (contract requiring 10 days' notice specifying nature of default to terminate for breach did not prohibit immediate termination for a material breach).

A stated remedy must declare that it is the sole and exclusive remedy to prevent the licensee from pursuing multiple remedies for a single injury.

1. Remedies under the UCC

The remedies provided under Article 2 of the UCC for a breach of warranty, while potentially applicable, are not easily applied to software due to its intangible nature. Although two states, Maryland and Virginia, have adopted the Uniform Computer Information Transactions Act (UCITA) to address the difficulty of applying the UCC to software licensing, many courts still look to the UCC as a reference. See Chapter 15 for a more detailed discussion of the applicability of the UCC to software licensing.

Under the UCC, damages for breach of warranty may result in merely a reduction in price; that is, the difference in value between what was warranted and what was delivered. UCC § 2-714(2). A customer may also seek rejection under UCC § 2-601 (the "perfect tender rule") or revocation of acceptance under UCC § 2-608. Section 2-601 illustrates the difficulties of applying the UCC to software transactions, as software by its nature is imperfect. In a literal sense, the software deliverable can almost always be rejected under § 2-601 as there will likely be at least one defect, albeit a minor one, in all software.

In cases where the licensor fails to cure a defect, the licensee may recover the amount paid to the seller. UCC § 2-711(2)(a). If the licensor is in breach of the contract, the licensee may, in addition to other potential remedies, purchase reasonable substitute software and recover the difference between the cost of obtaining the substitute software and the contract price as well as any incidental or consequential damages, or, alternatively, the licensee may recover damages for non-delivery equal to the difference between the market price and the contract price of the software at the time when the licensee learned of the breach. UCC §§ 2-712, 2-713.

Both licensees and licensors should understand the difference between general and limited warranties. Under a general warranty, the party providing the warranty is liable upon breach, and the party receiving the warranty has all available remedies. A limited warranty is a warranty in which the remedy is limited, often to repair or re-performance.

For example, purchasers of new automobiles usually receive a limited warranty, normally for several years. If the automobile exhibits problems, the only remedy available to the purchaser is to have the manufacturer repair or replace the automobile.

Thus, a licensee who receives a limited warranty that the software will materially comply with specifications will only be entitled to the specified remedy—normally the repair or replacement of the software. If the warranty were general, the licensee would have all of its remedies available.

2. *Licensee Remedies (§ 5.3)*

(a) Termination (§ 5.3.1)

In the event of a "material breach," the licensee should have the right to terminate the agreement and seek monetary damages under traditional contract law. This remedy is standard in most agreements with a large portion of the negotiations between the parties focused on what constitutes a "material breach."

(b) Equitable Relief

(i) Specific Performance (§§ 5.3.4, 28.A.5)

The licensee should seek to include the right to specific performance. Specific performance protects the licensee from having the licensor cease the performance of its obligations in the event it is no longer profitable to perform. *See, e.g., Metropolitan Life Ins. Co. v. Noble Lowndes Int'l, Inc.*, 643 N.E.2d 504 (N.Y. 1994). The licensor, however, will most likely be unwilling to include such a provision as it creates potentially unlimited liability on its behalf by requiring the licensor to re-perform work on a project until it is completed. Further, given the imperfect nature of software, it gives the licensee significant leverage over the licensor in any dispute.

Many licensees often try to include the remedy of specific performance in their license agreements. Sections 2-711(2)(b) and 2-716 of the UCC specifically identify specific performance as an available remedy. Although the UCC provides that specific performance is available if a party can establish the uniqueness of the software and the contract does not explicitly waive the right, licensees often prefer an affirmative statement of their right to specific performance to remove any uncertainty, especially as it relates to the applicability of the UCC versus the common law.

Some licensees, however, prefer to have the contract remain silent on the issue, and if they later seek to invoke the remedy, argue that specific performance is allowed under the UCC. These licensees believe that seeking an affirmative statement of their right to specific performance will potentially bring the issue to the attention of the licensor, who will in turn seek to contractually exclude specific performance as a remedy available to the licensee.

Licensors are hesitant to contractually agree to specific performance because, if included, a licensee may be able to force the licensor to deliver the software regardless of cost. Given that the risk of a large cost overrun is always present with software development, the risk to the licensor increases if the remedy of specific performance is included. Smart licensees also seek to include a statement that they are entitled to specific performance to force the licensor to comply with the terms of the escrow agreement, including requiring the licensor to place the software in escrow and enforcing the license agreement's indemnification provisions.

Licensors should carefully consider the risks when the licensee seeks to include broad statements such as "the right to obtain equitable relief" in the license agreement. While the equitable remedy of injunctive relief for breach of the agreement's confidentiality provision is important, the phrase "equitable relief" grants the licensee rights to several equitable remedies, not just injunctive relief (e.g., specific performance or reformation). As such, the licensee's rights should be limited solely to injunctive relief. Smart licensors will try to include language in the license agreement that, upon the licensor's breach of the warranty, the licensee shall be entitled to monetary damages only, or licensors will try to specifically state that the licensee is not entitled to obtain an equitable remedy.

There may also be specific aspects of performance for which specific performance is a reasonable remedy. For example, in an application service provider (ASP) arrangement, a licensee may be well advised to seek a right of specific performance for the return of the licensee's data—particularly if a failure to return the data would seriously impact the licensee's ability to conduct its business.

(ii) Right to Set Off (§§ 3.B.2. 5.3.2, 8.7)

Another equitable remedy the licensee should seek to include is the right to set off any damages the licensee incurs against any monies owed to licensor by the licensee. The right of set off can arise from common law, statute and express contractual provisions.

Even if the parties' contract fails to include this right, most licensees will exercise "self-help" by refusing to make payment until the issue has been resolved. While a smart licensor will seek to exclude language acknowledging the licensee's right to set off and perhaps even specifically prohibit the right of set off, there is little the licensor can do to prevent the licensee from withholding any money due the licensor.

Under law, a licensee must specifically state that it possesses the right of set off, as this right is statutorily based and does not exist under common law. 80 C.J.S. Set Off and Counterclaim 4. *See also Stanley v. Clark*, 159 F. Supp. 65, 66 (D.N.H. 1957) (citing C.J.S.); *Carfoss Const. Corp. v. MMSG Ltd. Partnerships*, 904 F. Supp. 450 (D. Md. 1995) (as right of setoff does not exist under Maryland common law it may be exercised only with respect to statutory authority or incident to a courts' equity jurisdiction). Licensors uncertain as to the status of applicable statutory law should insist on an affirmative statement that the licensee may not offset payment to prevent the licensee from gaining additional leverage over the licensor. Removing the right of offset eliminates the licensee's leverage through the ability to withhold payment. In practice, however, a dissatisfied licensee will offset monies owed to the licensor regardless of any contractual prohibition to the contrary or applicable statutory law.

Although setoff may not be allowed under the applicable state law, the licensee should consider whether the closely related doctrine of recoupment has been recognized. Recoupment, a common law remedy, is a form of setoff for damages claimed by the licensee arising from the same transaction for which a party seeks compensation. *See Lee v. Rutledge*, 51 Md. 311, 318 (1878). In short, a defendant in a breach of contract action may, instead of suing, recoup its damages from the plaintiff's breach. *Warfield v. Booth*, 33 Md. 63, 72 (1870).

(iii) Withholding Monies Due

While not truly an equitable remedy, withholding monies due is closely related to set-off. From the licensor's perspective, the contract should be clear that nonpayment can occur only in conjunction with withholding, and withholding can occur only in conjunction with a dispute, and then only when the required contractual protocols are followed; that is, timing, notification and specificity. If there has not been proper notification, there is no dispute. If there is no dispute, there is no right to withhold. If there is no withholding, there is no right to nonpayment. Further, the contract should be clear that only particular and specific charges (i.e., invoice line items) can be disputed, not entire invoices.

(c) Cover (§ 5.3.5)

A smart licensee will seek to include language allowing the licensee to seek "cover" in the event of the licensor's breach. This provision requires the licensor to be financially liable for any costs, in excess of the contract price, incurred by licensee retaining a third party to fulfill the licensor's contractual obligations. Most licensors will not agree to such a provision as it: (i) essentially causes the vendor to invest in its competitors; (ii) removes any incentive for the customer to negotiate the price of the replacement software; (iii) creates a carte blanche for the licensee and the entity that is hired to perform the work; and (iv) may not actually result in the customer obtaining a functionally equivalent software application. The licensee will likely argue that the licensor is under a common-law duty to mitigate its damages and must seek cover. At a minimum, the licensor should include language that limits the licensor's liability to the predetermined limits of liability set forth in the agreement. Under the UCC, the licensee automatically has the right to seek cover. UCC § 2-712. See Section B.6.(b)(v), below, for a further discussion of the duty to mitigate and cover.

Licensors should remember that "cover" is considered to be a form of "direct" or "actual" damages. *See* UCC § 2-712; *U.S. ex. rel. Virginia Beach Mechanical Services, Inc. v. SAMCO Const. Co.*, 39 F. Supp. 661, 673 (E.D. Va. 1999) (direct damages usually equal the difference between the contract price and the cost of purchasing of substitute goods or having a third party covering the work to be performed under the contract); *Hess Die Mold, Inc. v. American Plasti-Plate Corp.*, 653 S.W.2d 927, 929 (Tex. App. 1983). Thus, cover is not necessarily excluded by the licensor's limitation of liability clause. As such, a smart licensor should contractually exclude the licensee's right to obtain cover from its license agreement.

For a discussion of a buyer's right to cover, *see Buyer's Right to Cover*, 264 Com. L. Adv. 1 (Dec. 2009).

(d) Access to Source Code, Documentation, Employees, and Contractors (§§ 5.3.6, 5.3.7)

A licensee should also include language in the contract allowing the licensee to obtain a free or discounted copy of the software's source code and all available documentation in the event of licensor's material breach. While this provision cannot ensure that the licensee will be able to avoid damages from the licensor's breach, it will provide the licensee a means to further limit its risk. The licensee should also insist on language waiving any prohibition on the licensee soliciting and hiring the licensor's employees and contractors in the event of the licensor's material breach. This is important, as without access to the licensor's employees and contractors, possession and use of the source code and documentation will most likely be of little help to the licensee.

(e) Liquidated Damages (§ 3.C)

Liquidated damages clauses are generally enforceable if they represent a good faith attempt by the parties, at the time of contracting, to establish a stipulated amount of damages to compensate the non-breaching party for actual harm suffered by the breach, but which may be difficult or impossible to measure or prove. *Truck Rent-a-Car, Inc. v. Puritan Farms 2nd, Inc.*, 41 N.Y. 2d 420 (1977).

A liquidated damages provision provides an agreement's "exclusive remedy" in that it "precludes any recovery of actual damages." *Federal Realty Ltd. Partnership v. Choices Women's Medical Center, Inc.*, 735 N.Y.S.2d 159, 161 (2d Dept. 2001). "[L]iquidated and actual damages are mutually exclusive remedies," and plaintiffs ordinarily are awarded either actual damages or liquidated damages, but not both when the predicate for the awards is the same. *Wechsler v. Hunt Health Sys.*, 330 F. Supp. 2d 383, 426 (S.D.N.Y. 2004). Liquidated damages, by their nature, are "in lieu of, not in addition to, other compensatory damages." *Levitt Corp. v. Levitt*, 1978 WL 21377 (E.D.N.Y. Aug. 29, 1978).

Liquidated damages provisions are generally enforceable, unless the clause:

(i) acts as an unenforceable penalty;
(ii) permits recovery of both liquidated damages and actual damages;
(iii) seeks to enforce performance rather than making the non-breaching party whole again; or
(iv) goes against public policy.

Licensees, and occasionally licensors, often seek to include a provision for liquidated damages for the late or early delivery of software in development contracts. Often these damages amount to 0.5 percent of the contract value—excluding the value of hardware and third-party software—for each week a delivery is late for up to 10 percent of the contract value.

The parties should carefully consider what triggers payment. Many licensees will try to tie the imposition of liquidated damages to acceptance of the software by a certain date and not the contracted delivery date. This creates significant risk for the licensor as acceptance is totally within the control of the licensee. As such, liability should be based on late delivery of the software and not acceptance of the software by the licensee. A licensee, however, may be hesitant to base such damages on late delivery because the licensor may deliver poor quality software just to avoid paying liquidated damages, believing that the poor quality of the software can be corrected during any cure period. The licensee should include language allowing the right of offset against future progress payments if the licensor does not pay the liquidated damages as required.

Similarly, the agreement's liquidated damages clause should address any potential changes in the delivery date due to changes in the software requested by the licensee. It is rare that the licensee does not request changes to the software as it is being developed. Further, delivery may be delayed by third-party contractors under the control of the customer. As such, the agreement should contain a mechanism to address the impact on the delivery date resulting from any potential changes. If the licensor delivers the software after the delivery date, the licensor often responds that the late delivery was due to changes requested by the licensee. Any material delay caused by the customer will likely result in additional cost to the licensor, for which the licensor should be compensated. To maintain the integrity of the liquidated damages provisions, the parties must include a mechanism to address such changes.

Further, the licensor should ensure that the payment of liquidated damages is in full satisfaction of any liability the licensor may have for late delivery. Further, from the vendor's perspective, liquidated damages should count toward the cap on the vendor's liability. To the extent any delay is caused by the licensee, there should be a one-day extension of the licensor's delivery date for every day the licensee caused delay. The licensee may want to provide further protection by providing for termination of the agreement if the licensor has not delivered the software when the maximum payment amount has been reached to avoid providing the licensor an additional cure period.

The parties should carefully word the liquidated damages provision and set the liquidated damages at a reasonable level to avoid the appearance of a penalty, or if liquidated damages are an exclusive remedy, they should not be set so low that the remedy fails at its essential purpose. *H.M.O. Systems, Inc. v. Choicecare Health Services*, Inc., 665 P.2d 635 (Colo. App. 1983); *Cognifest Corp. v. Riverside Publishing Co.*, 107 F.3d 493 (7th Cir. 1997) (agreed payment of liquidated damages found to be adequate exclusive remedy). Liquidated damages that are out of proportion to the probable loss or grossly in excess of the actual damages may be considered a penalty and thus unenforceable. *Gordonsville Energy L.P. v. Virginia Electric & Power Co.*, 512 S.E.2d 811 (Va. 1999). At least one court has upheld the validity of a contractual waiver of a party's right to attack a liquidated damages provision. *Id.*

The licensee may include a provision providing that if the liquidated damages reach a certain level, the licensor shall be deemed to be in material breach and the licensee may terminate the contract.

Similarly, the licensor should seek to include a combination of liquidated damages and bonuses payable to the licensor in the event of certain licensee actions or inactions. If the customer has certain contractual responsibilities beyond payment, such as site readiness or the obligation to promptly accept the licensor's deliverables, the licensor should insist that the customer pay liquidated damages for the customer's failure to promptly meet its obligations. At the same time, the licensor should receive a bonus for the early delivery of the software or other material deliverables. This bonus counters the damages payable for late delivery and is consistent with the goal of liquidated damages to incent the licensor to deliver on time. Licensors often seek to raise their prices when the licensee asks for liquidated damages, claiming the licensor's initial price did not reflect the additional element the licensee had asked them to assume through the payment of liquidated damages. This argument holds little validity if the customer's initial RFP or the model license contained in the RFP put the licensor on notice that the customer expected the resulting contract to contain a liquidated damages provision. *See generally* UCC § 2-718(1) and Karnezis, *Contractual Liquidated Damages—Provisions under UCC Article 2*, 98 A.L.R.3d 586 (1980).

(f) Legal Fees (§ 5.4)

In the event the licensee brings a successful legal action as a result of a breach of contract by the licensor, the licensee should be entitled to recover its legal fees. This provision provides a disincentive for the licensor to breach the contract or dispute any issue in bad faith. A licensor that agrees to this provision should make sure that it is mutual. By making the provision mutual, both parties are incented to quickly and fairly settle any matter.

(g) Transition Rights (§ 5.3.3)

If the software licensed by the licensee is critical to the operation of the licensee's business, the licensee should require that the licensor provide transition services in the event of any termination of the agreement, regardless of whether the contract was terminated for one party's breach. A contractual transition period reduces the licensor's leverage in those situations where the licensee is in breach, but the services provided by the licensor are important to the continuing business operations of the licensee. Similarly, it requires the licensor to cooperate in the event the licensor is being terminated, where the licensor might otherwise have no incentive to do so. The contract should address the continuation of services or use of the software, knowledge transfer, the cost and duration of such services, as well as the continuation or termination of any collateral services. Regardless of the cause of breach, the licensor should be willing to provide the required services so long as it is compensated accordingly. The price of such services as well as the duration is often determined on the basis of who was in breach.

(h) Monetary Damages

In the event the licensor desires monetary damages based on a refund of monies paid, the licensor should set forth the basis on which they will be determined. The damages may be based on the purchase price, the price paid less any depreciation for actual use, or a predetermined damages (liquidated damages) price. Each of these methods will result in a different amount and could be greatly affected by the nature of the breach.

3. Licensor Remedies (§ 5.2)

(a) Termination (§ 5.3.1)

In the event of a "material breach," the licensor should have the right to terminate the agreement and seek monetary damages under traditional contract law. This remedy is standard in most agreements with a large portion of the negotiations between the parties focused on what constitutes a "material breach." The licensee should carefully consider the licensor's ability to terminate the agreement if the licensee will need to utilize the software on an ongoing basis. The licensor's ability to terminate the agreement gives the licensor significant leverage over the licensee in these situations.

(b) Legal Fees (§ 5.4)

In the event the licensor brings a successful legal action as a result of a breach of contract by the licensee, the licensor should be entitled to recover its legal fees. This provision provides a disincentive for the licensee to breach the contract or dispute any issue in bad faith. A licensee that agrees to this provision should make sure that it is mutual. By making the provision mutual, both parties are incented to quickly and fairly settle any matter.

(c) *Equitable Relief*

(i) Injunctive Relief (§ 28.A.5)

The licensor should include a provision allowing the licensor to obtain injunctive relief in the event the licensee breaches the licensing terms or misuses the software. The ability to obtain injunctive relief is important as the licensor needs to quickly and efficiently prevent the licensee from misusing its software. Requiring the licensor to use traditional dispute mechanisms such as arbitration, mediation, or use of the judicial system may significantly delay the licensor's ability to protect its intellectual property.

Injunctive relief will be granted to the licensor dependent on the individual standards of the jurisdiction in which relief is sought. *See, e.g., Accusoft Corp. v. Mattel, Inc.*, 117 F. Supp. 2d 99 (D. Mass. 2000) (Licensor entitled to injunctive relief due to (i) likelihood to succeed on merits; (ii) significant risk of irreparable harm to licensor; (iii) balance of hardship in favor of injunction; (iv) injunctive relief was in the public interest); *Credit Bureau Connection, Inc. v. Padini et. al.*, 726 F. Supp. 2d 1107 (C.D. Cal. 2010) (temporary restraining order granted upon proof of irreparable harm to business reputation and market share).

In evaluating a motion for injunctive relief, courts are not bound by any affirmative statements within the agreement to the effect that a breach of the agreement will "result in irreparable injury." *Bethesda Softworks, L.L.C. v. Interplay Entertainment Corp.*, 452 Fed. Appx. 351 (4th Cir. 2011) (looking beyond parties' stipulation of irreparable harm was not abuse of discretion by court); *Dominion Video Satellite, Inc. v. Echostar Satellite Corp.*, 356 F.3d 1256 (10th Cir. 2004). *See also Gildor v. Optical Solutions, Inc.*, 2006 WL 4782348 (Del. Ch. June 5, 2006).

(ii) Self-Help (§ 5.2) (§ 29.4)

The licensor should reserve the right to utilize the quasi-equitable relief of "self-help" by retaining the ability to disable the software in the event of the licensee's breach. The licensee, however, will likely seek to include a specific contractual provision prohibiting the licensor from utilizing any self-help until any dispute has been resolved in accordance with the contract's dispute resolution mechanism as self-help provides the licensor with significant leverage in the event of a dispute.

Electronic self-help generally takes one of two forms: the software contains an internal mechanism to automatically prevent the licensee from using the software upon the expiration of the license term, or the licensor electronically terminates the licensee's ability to use the software in the event of the licensee's breach of the license terms. It is the second issue that creates the most concern for licensees, as licensees fear the licensor will unjustly leverage its ability to disable the software in the event of a business dispute.

The use of disabling devices in software is fraught with risk for the licensor as well as the licensee. The presence of such a device creates a significant business risk for the licensee as the licensor has the ability to shut down mission critical software. The licensor also bears substantial risk if it terminates the licensee's ability to use the software, as the licensee will likely bring suit for the licensee's resulting damages. *See Clayton X-Ray Co. v. Professional Systems Corp.*, 812 S.W.2d 565, 567 (Mo. App. 1991) (court upheld award of punitive damages, "Seller had no legal right, or any colorable legal right to lock up [buyer]'s computer system"); *Werner, Zaroff, Slotnck, Stern & Askenazy v. Lewis*, 155 Misc. 2d 558 (N.Y. 1992) (court awarded $25,000 in punitive and compensatory damages to purchaser whose computer system was disabled by consultant through use of a "time bomb"); *State v. Corcoran*, 522 N.W.2d 226 (Wis. 1994) (independent contractor's conviction for computer tampering upheld where he placed time bombs in customer's computer systems over concern of receiving payment for his services). At least one court has found that a "time bomb" may violate the Computer Fraud and Abuse Act. *Kalow & Springnut, LLP v. Commence Corp.*, 2009 WL 44748 (D.N.J. Jan. 6, 2009).

A common law cause of action of conversion may arise from any self-help that goes beyond the limited scope of the law. *Thyroff v. Nationwide Mutual Ins. Co.*, 864 N.E.2d 1272 (N.Y. 2007) (insurance agent permitted to bring conversion action against insurance company which took possession of computer leased to agent that contained work related data as well as agent's personal electronic files). Another court found that a domain name can be converted. *Kremen v. Cohen*, 337 F.3d 1024, 1033–34 (9th Cir. 2003). Massachusetts courts have reached opposite conclusions when considering this issue. *See In re TJX Companies Retail Security Breach Litigation*, 587 F. Supp. 2d 209 (D. Mass. 2007) (Mass. does not recognize cause of action for conversion of intangible records. Court rejected invitation to adopt holding of *Thyroff*). *But see Network Systems Architects Corp. v. Dimitruk*, 23 Mass. L. Rptr. 339 (2007) ("If paper documents can be converted, as they no doubt can, no reason appears that computer files cannot.").

At least one court has upheld a licensor's right to remotely deactivate a licensee's software for breach of the license's payment provisions. *American Computer Trust Leasing v. Jack Farrell Implement Co.*, 763 F. Supp. 1473 (D. Minn. 1991), *aff'd* 967 F.2d 1208 (8th Cir. 1992). *But see Gomar Manufacturing Co. v. Novelli*, C.A. No. 96–4000 (D.N.J. Jan. 28, 1998). The Central District Court of California has held that disabling devices/codes may violate the Computer Fraud and Abuse Act (CFAA), 18 U.S.C. § 1030. *North Texas Preventative Imaging L.L.C. v. Eisenberg*, 1996 WL 1359212 (C. D. Cal. Aug. 19, 1996). *But see Shaw and Moon v. Toshiba et al.*, 91 F. Supp. 2d 926 (E.D. Tex. 1999) (court denied motion for summary judgment as CFAA does not apply to manufacturers inserting disabling codes).

A prudent licensor who desires to retain the remedy of self-help should clearly state in the underlying license that it reserves the right of self-help and/or the right to remotely disable the software in the event of the licensee's breach or the licensor detects unauthorized copying. Further, the license should provide that any attempt by the licensee to circumvent any security/self-help measures within the software is a material breach of the license. The licensor should also retain the contractual right to audit the licensee to ensure its compliance with these terms.

> *In the event of any dispute with Customer regarding an alleged breach of this Agreement or any Statement of Work, or any other agreement, Supplier will not use any means to prevent or interfere with Customer's use of the Software and*

Deliverables or instruct Supplier's employees, agents or subcontractors to shut down, disable, or interfere with the proper operation of the Software and Deliverables without Customer's knowledge and consent. Supplier acknowledges and agrees that, in the event of a breach or threatened breach of this Section, Customer will have no adequate remedy at law and, accordingly, will be entitled to an injunction against a breach or threatened breach.

The Uniform Computer Information Transactions Act (UCITA) places significant restrictions on the use of the disabling devices by the licensor, which in practicality, make their use very risky. See Chapter 15.B.3.(j) for a more detailed discussion. Nonetheless, the licensee should insist on a specific warranty disclaiming the existence of any disabling devices, trap door, or the like (see § 16.L).

For a general discussion, *see* Rowles, *Electronic Software Disablement and Repossession*, 8 E-COMMERCE ADVISOR 7 (Aug. 2001); Roditti, *Is Self-Help a Lawful Contractual Remedy?*, 21 RUTGERS COMPUTER & TECH. L.J. 431 (1995); FRIER & WHITE, THE MODERN LAW OF CONTRACTS 666-749 (3D ED. 2012) (self-help during performance); Symposium, *Property Rights on the Frontier: The Economics of Self-Help and Self-Defense in Cyberspace*, 1 J.L. ECON. & POL'Y 1 (2005).

(d) Monetary Damages

Monetary damages are often difficult to ascertain. Section 504 of the Copyright Act allows a copyright holder to recover either statutory damages or its actual damages resulting from any infringement as well as "any profits of the infringer that are attributable to the infringement and are not taken into account in computing the actual damages." 17 U.S.C. § 504(a)(b). Actual damages are generally "measured by the profits lost due to the infringement or the value of the use of the copyrighted work to the infringer." *Polar Bear Prods., Inc. v. Timex Corp.*, 387 F.3d 700, 708 (9th Cir. 2004). One method of ascertaining the value of the loss is to determine the hypothetical licensee fee that would have been paid had the infringer purchased a license from the copyright owner. *Oracle, USA, Inc. v. SAP AG*, 2010 WL 334446 (N.D. Cal. Jan. 28, 2010) (copyright holder not precluded from seeking damages in the form of a hypothetical license from infringing party). In addition, the licensor should seek interest on license fees which should have been paid and legal costs, if permitted.

In the event the licensor seeks to recover monetary damages for the licensee's breach, the licensee should ensure that the license agreement contains a limit of liability to limit the licensee's liability. Often, licensees are so focused on negotiating the limits on the licensor's liability that they forget to make such limit mutual and limit their own liability.

(e) Duty to Mitigate

All parties have an obligation to mitigate or limit their damages. RESTATEMENT (SECOND) OF CONTRACTS § 350 (1981). This duty forbids an injured party from allowing its damages to balloon when such damages can be limited. *Moran Foods, Inc. v. Mid-Atlantic Market Development Co., LLC*, 476 F.3d 436 (7th Cir. 2007). An injured party is prohibited from recovering any damages that could have been avoided. *Kuhlman, Inc. v. G. Heileman Brewing Co.*, 266 N.W.2d 382 (Wis. 1978). The burden of proof is on the breaching party to prove the injured party could have mitigated its damages. *Id.* Under the law of at least one state, however, a non-breaching party is not obligated to mitigate its damages where the parties' contract contains a valid liquidated damages provision. *Barrie School v. Patch*, 933 A.2d 382 (Md. Ct. App. 2007).

Although implied by law, it is important to include a contractual obligation requiring the parties to mitigate their damages. This is especially important where the parties are utilizing an informal dispute mechanism and are unlikely to discuss implied obligations under the law. If the parties proceed to litigation, the efforts a party took to mitigate its damages will likely become a significant issue in the dispute.

The duty to mitigate includes the ability/right to obtain cover. While the concept of the licensee retaining a third-party vendor to complete the licensor's contractual obligations may be unpalatable to a licensor, it is difficult for a licensor to argue that the licensee cannot do so. The principal concern of the licensor is that the licensee may incur significant costs for which the licensor is responsible. The licensor can limit its risk, however, by ensuring that the license clearly states that the licensee's right to cover is limited by the agreement's limitation on liability. See Section B.7.(a), below.

4. *Cumulative Remedies*

Many agreements contain a cumulative remedies provision in the belief that the failure to do so may limit the injured party's remedy to the listed remedies or if the injured party pursues one remedy, it will be precluded from pursuing any other remedies. The following sentence illustrates this point:

> *Any specific right or remedy provided in this Agreement will not be exclusive but will be cumulative of all other rights and remedies.*

Today, the general principal is that all remedies are considered to be cumulative and such language is unnecessary. STARK, NEGOTIATING AND DRAFTING CONTRACT BOILERPLATE § 9.02[2] (2003). Under UCC 2-719(1)(b) "there is a presumption that clauses prescribing remedies are cumulative rather than exclusive. If the parties intend the term to describe the sole remedy under the contract, this must be clearly expressed." UCC 2-719 cmt. 2. By not stating that a remedy is an exclusive remedy, an injured party may seek any remedy allowed by law. *Consolidation Coal Co. v. Marion Docks, Inc.*, 2010 WL 1337718 (W.D. Pa. Feb. 22, 2010). Thus, if the parties agree that a remedy is an exclusive remedy, the governing agreement should specifically state so.

Some parties seek to include an affirmative statement in their agreement that all remedies are cumulative and that a party may avail itself of any and all remedies available under law and equity. Model language follows:

Rights and Remedies Cumulative. *Except as expressly listed in this Agreement, the parties intend that:*

(a) no right or remedy under this Agreement be exclusive of any other right or remedy,
(b) every other right and remedy be cumulative and in addition to every other right and remedy given under this agreement or existing at Law, in equity, or otherwise now or after the date of this Agreement, and
(c) the assertion or employment of any right or remedy under this Agreement should not prevent the concurrent assertion of any other right.

5. *Sole and Exclusive Remedy*

Unless a contract states otherwise, a remedy is considered to be nonexclusive. As such, vendors should ensure that, if intended, their agreement clearly state that the remedies provided in the agreement are the sole and exclusive remedies available to the customer. *Pulmonary Assoc. of Charleston PLLC v. Greenway Health, LLC*, 508 F. Supp. 3d 1268 (N.D. Ga. 2020) ("Sole" and "exclusive" must be used to indicate a remedy is the sole and exclusive remedy.) The most common use of a sole and exclusive remedy arises in claims related to intellectual property indemnity where the licensor's liability is limited to providing the customer a non-infringing solution or providing the customer a refund, and with service-level agreements where the credits serve as liquidated damages for the failure to meet certain service levels. The following language illustrates this point:

> *The Parties agree that the Vendor will repair or replace, at the Vendor's option, any defective Software for a period of three months from the date of delivery. This remedy is intended to be the sole and exclusive remedy of the Customer under this Agreement. Should this sole and exclusive remedy fail of its essential purpose, however, the Vendor will return the purchase price to the Customer minus the reasonable value of the Customer's use of the Software.*

The first two sentences of the above paragraph provide that the limit of liability is intended as an exclusive remedy and should be made subject to the article, section or paragraph containing the limitation of liability.

The third sentence addresses the remedy's failure of essential purpose, which arises from the Uniform Commercial Code. There is a split among the jurisdictions as to the meaning of "failing of essential purpose." If the contract is governed under New York law, the failure of essential purpose language can be deleted, as a failure of a remedy's essential purpose will not negate the contract's exclusion of consequential damages. *McNally Wellman Co. v. New York State Elec. & Gas Co.*, 63 F.3d 1188 (2d Cir. 1995). However, under the law of other jurisdictions, it is imperative to include this language. Some licensees resist including language to this effect because they lack familiarity with the intent of the wording.

This language does not seek to preclude specific performance, injunctive relief, or other nonmonetary remedies. If service levels are provided for under the agreement, it is appropriate to include service level credits however they may be determined.

> *Unless expressly otherwise provided in this Agreement, no remedy set forth in this Agreement is intended to be, nor shall be, exclusive of, or mutually exclusive with regard to, any other remedy. The remedies provided in this Agreement are cumulative with, and not in lieu of, other remedies available to either Party at law or in equity.*

To the extent the agreement sets forth any cumulative remedies, the sole and exclusive remedy should be carved out from the cumulative remedy provision.

I. Limitation of Liability (§ 17)

A limitation of liability is a risk-benefit analysis for both the licensor and the licensee. Each party assumes a different risk, and each party has a different risk tolerance. The licensee seeks to be compensated in the event the software does not perform as contracted.

The amount of any limit on the licensor's liability will likely be shaped by the size of the license fee and the importance of the software to the licensee's business. Prudent licensors should avoid "betting the ranch" on every contract and seek to limit their monetary liability to the licensee to the amount paid or payable by the licensee.

Some practitioners believe a limitation of liability provisions should be prefaced with: "To the maximum extent permitted by law, . . . " or "Nothing in this Section __ will exclude or limit liability that cannot, as a matter of law, be limited or excluded . . ." They do so in the belief that the failure to include language to this effect runs the risk of an argument that a party in breach was seeking to exclude or limit its liability for death/personal injury, damage to property, fraud, or other items for which liability is not permitted to be limited, and, in an absolute worst case, the whole liability clause could be found to be unenforceable and struck exposing the party to unlimited liability.

While limitations of liabilities usually focus on the licensor's liability, a savvy licensee will also seek to limit its own liability. Each party can limit its aggregate liability by a number of means including limiting its monetary liability; disclaiming special, incidental, consequential, and punitive damages, etc.; and reducing the statute of limitations under which a claim can be made. Each of these means is an integrated part of the party's defenses and is a significant element of any contractual negotiation. Set forth below is an in-depth look at each of these.

For a general overview, *see* Wolfson, *Constructing a Durable Limitations of Liability Clause*, 9 Tools & Tactics Technology Procurement Survival Guide 1 (Issue 9 2002); Wolfson, *Constructing a Durable Limitations of Liability Clause*, Part 2, 9 Tools & Tactics Technology Survival Guide 1 (Issue 10 2002); Shivers & Brunel, *Contractual Limitations of Liability (a/k/a "LOLs" or Why the Other Party Is Laughing Out Loud)*, 19 Computer & Internet L. 7 (May 2002); Hammond, *Limiting and Dealing With Liability in Software Contracts*, 9 Computer Law. 22 (June 1992).

1. Limiting Monetary Liability (§ 17.2)

(a) Limits of Monetary Liability

Every software license should contain a limitation of liability provision protecting both the licensor and the licensee. Limitations of liability in commercial contracts are generally upheld. *Borden, Inc. v. Advent Ins. Co.*, 701 A.2d 255, 262 (Pa. Super. Ct. 1997); *American Nursery Products, Inc. v. Indian Wells Orchards*, 797 P.2d 477 (Wash. 1990). The failure to include a limitation of liability clause potentially subjects the licensor and the licensee to unlimited liability. Although the licensee may not want to accept limits on the licensor's liability, it is unreasonable for a licensor to risk its entire company on a single transaction. The licensor should specifically state that its liability is limited to a set amount regardless of whether the claim is brought under contract, tort, warranty, or otherwise, as many licensees seek to bring claims both under contract and tort. A smart licensee will also limit its own liability, a point many licensees forget to make.

The amount of any cap will vary depending on the value of the underlying contract itself. The licensee will want to set the cap at a level that will create a sufficient financial incentive for the licensor to take the appropriate measures to ensure compliance with its contractual obligations and avoid the liability. A proper set of risk allocations should not be viewed as a means to recoup a party's economic losses as it is unlikely that the offering party will have the financial resources to make the injured party whole even with insurance. Rather, the risk allocation provision should be viewed as a prophylactic attempt to avoid harm in the beginning.

Depending on the type and dollar value of the agreement, licensors often seek to limit their liability to the trailing 12 months' revenue, the dollar value of the license agreement, or the statement of work (SOW) under which the liability arose; the amount of money received by the licensor from the licensee during a set time period (e.g., all revenue received in the 12-month period prior to the claim of liability); or a predetermined amount. In large systems integration agreements that include the development and significant customization of software that will be implemented by the licensor, the parties will often enter into a master services agreement that serves as an overarching "umbrella" containing master terms and conditions. The parties will then execute statements of work for each distinct segment in the overall project that will contain the terms unique to that segment. Many licensors seek to limit their liability to the value of the individual statement of work under which the liability arose, or to the amounts received in a preceding number of months if the statement of work will cover a number of years. *See, e.g., The Colonial Life Insurance Co. of America v. Electronic Data Systems Corp.*, 817 F. Supp. 235 (D.N.H. 1993) (limiting liability to amounts payable in two months prior to event giving rise to liability not unconscionable as a matter of law); *Computerized Radiological Services, Inc. v. Syntex Corp.*, 595 F. Supp. 1495, 1510 (E.D.N.Y. 1984) (limit of liability limiting damages to amount paid is reasonable); *Markborough Cal., Inc. v. Superior Court*, 227 Cal. App. 3d 705 (1991) (no unconscionability found where party had opportunity to negotiate template agreement).

Many licensees will reject this approach, arguing that a structure that limits liability on a statement of work by statement of work basis does not reflect the nature of the underlying transaction and the parties' overall relationship. The licensee is hiring the licensor to develop and systems integrate for the entire project (not an integrator of the work covered by only one statement of work); the agreement's liability structure should reflect the entire relationship of the parties as well as all sums paid by the licensee to the licensor.

A statement of work by statement of work approach may be appropriate for a staff augmentation engagement, but in such a case the licensor's labor rates would be significantly lower than the rates the licensee is likely paying under a license and systems integration agreement.

To the extent that the licensed software is simply an administrative tool, the licensor may argue that it is providing software with certain functionality but is up to the licensee to utilize the tool and the data it generates. In these situations, a statement of work by statement of work approach may be appropriate. For these types of transactions, licensors usually argue that they should be liable for complying with the software's specifications and the like, but not for third-party liability arising from use of the resulting work product.

To the extent that a product is a diagnostic tool, a licensor may have some sympathy with the licensee seeking protection against third-party claims. In these situations, a licensor should only be liable for third party claims to the extent that the licensor established the software's specifications.

If the parties cannot agree on a limitation of liability, a potential solution is for the licensor to purchase insurance to cover the increased liability sought by the licensee and to invoice the licensee for the additional cost. When pricing a project, most licensors assume that the limit of liability will be within industry standard parameters, such as the value of the statement of work or the revenues received by the licensor in the preceding three months. Risk is an element of price and if the licensee wants to shift the burden of risk, it should be willing to pay the cost of doing so.

Like many of the aforementioned issues, licensors often view or will argue that the amount of the cap is an element of price. While most licensors limit their liability to the amount received from the licensee, a few may be willing to increase the limit of their liability in return for an increased license fee from the licensee. A common argument by the licensor against increasing the limit of liability is that the licensor must increase its price in response to the increased risk, as the licensor's original price was based on the initially stated cap.

Some licensees seek the right to terminate the underlying agreement without penalty if the licensee has recovered damages close to the agreement's limitation of liability under the reasoning that the licensee lacks a true remedy because it might be unable to fully recover the extent of its damages in the event of another breach. Licensors should reject this position as it changes the nature of the risk and the nature of the bargain. If the licensor's breach is material, the licensee's remedy is to terminate the contract.

A prudent party should never tie its limitation of liability to the limits of its insurance. First, most insurance is not on a per-claim basis. Second, many insurers do not want to insure entities that simply agree to the entity's policy limits, essentially passing their risk on to the insurer. This is especially true for Errors and Omissions insurance, where insurers carefully evaluate potential customers to ascertain the associated risk.

Considerations and Restrictions on the Ability to Limit Liability:

(i) Reasonableness of Cap

Any cap must be reasonable and not be so low as to be considered unconscionable, or it may not be upheld as failing of its essential purpose. *See Wayne Memorial Hospital, Inc. v. Electronic Data Systems Corp.*, 1990 WL 606686 (E.D.N.C. Apr. 10, 1990) ($4,000 limit of liability on a $2 Million contract is unconscionable). *See also* UCC § 2-719, comment 1. Caps of less than the amounts paid by a licensee, however, may be upheld. *See, e.g., Sch. Dist. of the City of Niagara Falls v. CrossPointe, LLC*, 2011 WL 6208695 (W.D.N.Y. Dec. 12, 2011); *Rob-Win, Inc. v. Lydia Sec. Monitoring, Inc.*, 2007 WL 3360036 (Del Super. Apr. 30, 2007). A provision will likely fail of its essential purpose if the aggrieved party is left without a remedy. *Milgard Tempering, Inc. v. Selas Corp. of America*, 761 F.2d 553 (9th Cir. 1985). But at least one court has held that two commercial entities may agree to waive all liability for a party's breach. *Asch Webhosting, Inc. v. Adelphia Business Solutions Invest., LLC*, 2010 WL 258784 (3d Cir. Jan. 25, 2010) (waiver of liability between two commercial entities enforceable, as limit of liability was neither adverse to public interest nor unconscionable).

On the other hand, some authorities believe that a limitation of liability can never fail of its essential purpose. *Pig Improvement Co. v. Middle States Holding Co.*, 943 F. Supp. 392, 401 & n.14 (D. Del. 1996); Baker et. al., *Special Project: A Tale of Two Warranties in Commercial Transactions*, 64 Cornell L. Rev. 30, 259-261 (1978).

Willful or Wanton Conduct and Fraud

Willful or wanton conduct as well as fraud will also negate an agreement's limitation of liability provisions. *Khulusi v. Southwestern Yellow Pages, Inc.*, 916 S.W.2d 227 (Mo. 1995). The same is true for gross negligence. *Anunziation v. Orkin Exterminating Co., Inc.*, 180 F. Supp. 2d 353, 360 (N.D.N.Y. 2001). *But see Leprino Foods Co. v. Gress Poultry, Inc.*, 379 F. Supp. 2d 659 (M.D. Pa. 2005) (parties may agree to limit their liability for gross negligence in a commercial contract). Many states prohibit contracting parties from limiting their liability for their own fraud, willful injury to a person or property of another or violation of the law. *See, e.g.*, Cal. Civ. Code § 1668; 15 Okla. Stat. Ann. § 212. *Manning v. Brannon*, 956 P.2d 156 (Okla. 1997). Occasionally, vendors seek to exclude liability for "criminal acts" of their employees notwithstanding the exceptions to the cap, arguing that they should not be liable for the illegal acts of their employees which are clearly outside the scope of their employment. See Chapter 5.A.1 above for a discussion of a licensor's potential liability under tort and contract law theories.

(ii) Repair or Replace Remedy

In any license agreement it is also important to include a provision granting the licensee a monetary refund or other remedy if a "repair or replace" remedy fails of its essential purpose. Such remedies should be stated to be exclusive. Whether a remedy fails of its essential purpose is a question of fact for the jury. *Roneker v. Kenworth Truck Co.*, 944 F. Supp. 179, 184 (W.D.N.Y 1996).

According to some but not all courts, if a limited or exclusive warranty is deemed to have failed its essential purpose, the limit on consequential damages may be voided. *McKernon v. United Technologies Corp.*, 717 F. Supp. 60 (D. Conn. 1989); *Caudill Seed and Warehouse Co., Inc. v. Prophet 21, Inc.*, 123 F. Supp. 2d 826 (E.D. Pa. 2000). See Chapter 5.I.2 for a more detailed discussion of the exclusion of consequential damages in the event a remedy fails of its essential purpose. A limitation of a party's liability will likely be upheld even if the agreement's warranty has failed. *Piper Jaffray & Co. v. SunGard Sys. Int'l, Inc.*, 2005 WL 999975 (D. Minn. Apr. 28, 2005). (A license agreement's damages cap is enforceable even if the licensor's warranty to cure the defective software has failed in its essential purpose.) See Chapter 5.I.5 for a more detailed discussion.

In commercial contracts, there is a presumption of conscionability. *Siemens Credit Corp. v. Marvik Colour, Inc.*, 859 F. Supp. 686, 695 (S.D.N.Y. 1995). In determining whether a contract is unconscionable, a court will look at the bargaining power of the parties, whether the terms were actively negotiated and the terms themselves. Adhesion contracts receive greater scrutiny for procedural unconscionability. *Id. See also Johnson v. Long John Silver's Restaurants, Inc.*, 320 F. Supp. 2d 656, 666 (M.D. Tenn. 2004); *American Nursery Products, Inc. v. Indian Wells Orchards*, 797 P.2d 477 (Wash. 1990). At the same time, however, a contract between merchants is rarely found to be unconscionable. *D. S. Am. (East), Inc. v. Chromagrafx Imaging Sys., Inc.*, 873 F. Supp. 786 (E.D.N.Y. 1995).

A court seeks to ensure that the innocent party is made whole. *See Ragen Corp. v. Kearney & Trecker Corp.*, 912 F.2d 619 (3d Cir. 1990). Thus, the smart licensor always includes an alternate remedy in the license, such as refunding the purchase price, to avoid a specified remedy failing of its essential purpose. *See Ritchie Enterprises v. Honeywell Bull, Inc.*, 730 F. Supp. 1041, 1047 (D. Kan. 1990).

(iii) Cap Valid for All Claims

Every limitation of liability clause should clearly provide that the stated limit applies regardless of whether the licensee brings a claim based on contract, tort, or another theory. The failure to do so may result in the licensee seeking to potentially circumvent the cap (and the economic loss doctrine) by bringing a claim under tort theory by arguing that the licensor's liability is limited only in contract. *See generally Committee Reports Tort Theories in Computer Litigation*, 38 REC. ASS'N BAR N.Y. 426 (1983); *Budget Rent A Car Corp. v. Genesys Software Systems, Inc.*, 1996 WL 480388 (D.N. Ill. Aug. 22, 1996) (claims for fraud, fraudulent inducement, and negligent misrepresentation allowed even though contract claims were disallowed under the license's integration clause).

Further, to the extent that a party may agree to a "super cap" for certain breaches such as data privacy, the agreement should clearly state that the super cap encompasses the regular limitation of liability and that there are not two separate and distinct caps, materially increasing the party's liability.

> *The Special Liability Cap in this paragraph is inclusive of and not in addition to the Liability Cap. Any amounts paid under the Special Liability Cap shall reduce the remaining amount, if any, available under the Liability Cap and any amounts paid under the Liability Cap shall reduce the remaining amount available under the Special Liability Cap.*

(iv) Mutuality

Any limitation of liability should be mutual. While the parties often carve out a party's confidentiality obligations from the agreement's limitation of liability, some licensees are hesitant to do so. A viable solution from the licensor's perspective is to accept a limitation of liability on confidentiality but carve out (1) any breach of confidentiality relating to the licensor's intellectual property, or (2) the breach of any of the licensor's intellectual property rights.

(v) Conspicuousness

Any limitation of liability should be conspicuous. While the meaning of "conspicuous" will be determined by state law, at a minimum, the exculpatory language should be in capital letters set off in its own paragraph and be written in plain and clear language. *Morgan Home Fashions, Inc. v. UTI, U.S., Inc.*, 2004 WL 1950370 (D.N.J. Feb. 9, 2004); *Stauffer Chem. Co. v. Curry*, 778 P.2d 1083 (Wyo. 1989). Not all states, however, require a limitation of liability to be conspicuous. *See, e.g., Borden, Inc. v. Advent Ink. Co.*, 701 A.2d 255 (Pa. Super. 1997).

For a detailed discussion of the validity of limitation of liability clauses, *see* West & Lewis, *Contracting to Avoid Extra-Contractual Liability—Can Your Contractual Deal Ever Really Be the "Entire" Deal?* 64 BUS. LAW. 999 (2009); Katz, *Caveat Vendor: Limitation Clauses in Software Agreements May Not Withstand Judicial Scrutiny*, 9 COMPUTER L. ASS'N BULL. 12 (No. 2 1994) and Hammond, *Limiting and Dealing with Liability in Software Contracts*, 9 COMPUTER LAW. 22 (June 1992).

(b) Exclusions to Limitations of Monetary Liability

Licensors and licensees often negotiate a number of commonly accepted exclusions from any limitation of liability. Licensees should insist on excluding breach of the licensor's confidentiality obligations and the licensor's liability under any indemnification obligations (provided the indemnification obligation is limited to intellectual property, personal bodily injury, and tangible personal property, etc.) from any cap. This position should be acceptable to the licensor, provided the indemnification provisions are narrowly drawn. Some licensors seek to limit their liability for intellectual property infringement if the vendor is providing only services. Regardless of whether indemnification is included under the cap, the cost of defending an indemnification claim should never be included under a cap.

Further, many licensees seek to exclude the licensor's failure to comply with any applicable laws. Many practitioners believe it is inappropriate to exclude breach of laws from an agreement's limitation of liability as almost anything can be considered a breach of laws such as intellectual property infringement.

Model language illustrating common exclusions follows:

This Article __ does not exclude or limit liability for:

- *(i) Licensor's termination of this Agreement other than in accordance with the terms of this Agreement;*
- *(ii) for either Party's indemnification obligations with respect to Claims under Section __ ("Intellectual Property Indemnification");*
- *(iii) for either Party's beach of Section __ ("Confidentiality") or any provision of Section __ ("Customer Data and Intangible Property");*
- *(iv) a Party's gross negligence, fraud or willful misconduct;*
- *(v) for Fees owed to Licensor for Services performed;*
- *(vi) Early Termination Fees;*
- *(vii) any intentional breach of this Agreement;*
- *(viii) Customer's misappropriation of the Licensor's intellectual;*
- *(ix) Customer exceeding the scope of the license grant; and*
- *(x) to the extent prohibited by law.*

A licensor should avoid any obligation to indemnify the licensee for general breaches of the contract, as indemnities are traditionally used to protect against *third-party* claims. Further, licensor's indemnification obligations are often excluded from any limitation on liability, potentially negating the licensor's limitation of liability. An intellectual property infringement exclusion should be accepted by the licensor only if the remedies in the intellectual property infringement provision of the license agreement are the "sole and exclusive remedy" of the licensee. If not, the licensor potentially has unlimited liability.

To the extent any limitation of liability is mutual, breach of any payment obligations, the misuse of the licensor's intellectual property, and breach of confidentiality should be excluded from the licensee's cap on liability.

The following section and Chapter 22 for a more detailed discussion of the failure of a party to comply with data privacy provisions and Chapter 6.I for a discussion of the issues associated with compliance with laws.

(i) Confidentiality vs. Data Protection, Data Breach Issues

With the increased legislative focus on data privacy, greater emphasis has been focused on modifying limitations of liability to reflect the risk arising from a data breach. Traditionally, breach of a party's confidential information has been excluded from an agreement's limitation of liability. Data privacy laws differ from the confidentiality provisions contained in most agreements. Confidentiality addresses maintaining the confidential business information and trade secrets of the contracting parties. A breach arises from the wrongful disclosure or misuse of the other party's trade secrets or confidential information.

Data privacy, however, addresses Personally Identifiable Information (PII) and Personal Health Information (PHI) of third parties, usually customers or employees of the licensee, that a licensor may access in performing its obligations under the agreement. PII may include that information which identifies a particular person, such as an individual's name, address, or social security number, while PHI usually encompasses an individual's medical records and information.

For the most part, customers receive the security services for which they have agreed to pay. When pricing the cost to comply with the customer's data privacy and security requirements, the licensor only takes into account the licensor's costs. The licensor usually does not factor into the price (a) the value of the customer's data, (b) the attractiveness of the data to hackers, (c) the monetary benefits the customer will receive from the software, or (d) any other security services or measures the customer is taking to protect its data. The licensor is usually providing services that are tangential to the customer's data privacy obligations. The licensor cannot insure the misappropriation, the loss or destruction of data or the value of the data to the customer. The licensor also does not include in its prices the loss or damage to data even when due to the licensor's own negligence.

Most licensors are unwilling to accept unlimited liability for a breach of a data privacy obligation, as the risks of breach are significantly greater and can arise from actions outside the licensor's control, such as the licensee's negligence, failure to follow the licensor's security protocols, or the licensee being hacked. Most licensees recognize that the risks involved with data privacy are greater than those with confidential information but argue that it is exactly for that reason the licensor's liability should not be limited. These licensees argue that they have unlimited liability to their customers and potentially to governmental agencies for a breach, so the licensor should not be able to limit its own liability for the licensor's breach.

Breach of confidentiality is typically excluded from the consequential damages exclusion as well as any dollar cap. It is important to tie the carve-out to the breach of specific confidentiality provisions in the agreement (i.e., cross reference the specific sections) so it is clear what "breach of confidentiality" means. This should protect the licensor at least as much if not more than the licensee, as the licensor may not have access to much in the way of the licensee's confidential information but the licensee will likely have the licensor's information, although each party should consider who is giving what information to whom on a case-by-case basis.

An Increased Limit of Liability Tied to Specific Standards (Form Q.2.DD).

One potential solution is to create a second, larger limitation of liability for claims related to data privacy and security as well as a party's compliance with applicable laws or the licensor's data security standards. For example, a party's limitation of liability for any such claim may be limited to an amount equal to twice the limitation of liability for other types of claims. Governmental fines should be excluded from the cap. If the value of this increased cap is significant, the licensor may want to negotiate a lower cap equal to the revenue received by the licensor in the six months preceding the event giving rise to the claim.

A licensor's obligations regarding its security and privacy obligations should be tied to specific, objective standards against which it can be measured. For example, the licensor should agree to comply with its data security standards or specific encryption standards as opposed to a more general standard of care, such a duty to use reasonable care in handling confidential customer data and trade secrets. Model language is set forth below:

> *The Liability Cap amount solely with respect to all claims that a party has breached any of its obligations under Section __ (Security and Confidentiality), shall be 24 months (such amount the "Special Liability Cap") instead of 12 months and each reference to 12 months set forth in Section ___ (Limitation of Liability) shall mean 24 months solely for purposes of calculating claims that a party has breached any of its obligations under Section __ (Security and Confidentiality). Except for this modification, all of the provisions of this Article 1 shall be applicable to claims related to Section __. The Special Liability Cap in this paragraph is inclusive of and not in addition to the Liability Cap. Any amounts paid under the Special Liability Cap shall reduce the remaining amount, if any, available under the Liability Cap and any amounts paid under the Liability Cap shall reduce the remaining amount available under the Special Liability Cap.*

See Form Q.DD.2 for additional language illustrative of this point.

Some vendors have sought to create an exclusion of liability for "Zero Day" viruses. Popularized by the book *Countdown to Zero Day*, a Zero Day virus is a virus/intrusion methodology that was previously unknown prior to the event and for which specific antivirus software signatures were unavailable at the time of the attack. In such an event, if (i) the vendor is in compliance with its security standards/requirements, (ii) the vendor has used industry standard virus protection software, and (iii) the virus was unknown prior to the event, the vendor will have no liability for the intrusion. Vendors argue that this exclusion is justified as they should not be held to a higher level than the licensee would be able to achieve itself and that no system, even the federal government's, is impenetrable. Model language is set forth below:

> *Notwithstanding anything to the contrary in the Agreement, Provider shall have no liability for damages resulting from the loss or disclosure of Processed Client Data as and to the extent caused by a Zero-Day Attack on Provider's Systems and Facilities; provided, that Provider has otherwise performed all of its security and confidentiality obligations under this Agreement and has used industry standards to prevent situations such as Zero-Day Attacks from impacting Provider's Systems and Facilities.*
>
> *For purposes of this Section ______, a "**Zero-Day Attack**" means any individual software or hardware vulnerability that is exploited by a third party-attacker (including through use of a "bot" or other automated tool) where there is no prior knowledge of such vulnerability by Provider, leading providers of similar services, or in the general information security community, to the extent that such exploit could not or should not have been detected or prevented using security measures required under this Agreement.*

A related issue is whether any cap is in the aggregate or for each type of claim. For example, an agreement may have a multi-tiered limitation of $10M for general indemnity obligations, a "super-cap" of $20M for indemnity of third-party data privacy breach claims, and unlimited liability for claims related to breach of confidentiality and intellectual property infringement. If there is a breach of confidentiality claim and the vendor pays $20M in damages, does that mean that the general limitation of liability cap has been expended, or is there still $10M of damages available under the general limitation of liability cap for other "generic" contract breaches? Thus, it is very important that any limitation of liability provision clearly provide the interrelationship among the different caps.

(ii) Gross Negligence, Willful Misconduct, and Intentional Acts/ Intentional Breach

Prudent licensees should insist on excluding gross negligence, willful misconduct, and intentional acts from any limitation of liability. In most cases, this exclusion does not significantly increase the licensor's liability as a limitation of liability may not be valid for claims of gross negligence, willful or intentional acts, misrepresentation, or fraud even in a commercial context. *See* Boss & Woodward, *Scope of the Uniform Commercial Code, Survey of Computer Contracting Cases*, 43 BUS. LAW. 1513 (1988). *See also Arthur D. Little International, Inc. v. Dooyang Corp.*, 928 F. Supp. 1189, 1205 (D. Mass. 1996) (under Massachusetts law, a damage limitation clause in a contract does not bar recovery for intentional misrepresentation in the inducement of a contract); *Shelby Mutual Insurance Co. v. City of Grand Rapids*, 6 Mich. App. 95, 148 N.W.2d 260 (1967) (a party may contract against liability for harm caused by its negligence but may not do so for gross negligence); *NMP Corp. v. Parametric Technology Corp.*, 958 F. Supp. 1536, 1543 (N.D. Okla. 1997) (under Oklahoma law, a party may not contractually limit damages resulting from its own gross negligence or fraud); *AGIP Petroleum Co., Inc. v. Gulf Island Fabrication, Inc.*, 920 F. Supp. 1330, 1343 (S.D. Tex. 1996) (under Louisiana law, a party may not limit its liability for gross negligence and intentional conduct); *Kalisch-Jarcho, Inc. v. City of New York*, 448 N.E.2d 413, 416–17 (N.Y. 1983) (exculpatory agreement will not exonerate a party from liability for willful or grossly negligent acts); *Vmark Software, Inc. v. EMC Corp.*, 642 N.E.2d 587 (Mass. App. 1994) (licensor may not limit its liability for misrepresentations based on a contract's limitation of liability clause).

One concern with excluding willful default from the limitation of liability is that if a party repudiates a contract, the damages recoverable against the repudiating party are effectively uncapped.

Several states do allow parties to limit their liability for gross negligence provided that the intent to do so is clearly and unambiguously set forth in the underlying agreement. *Tessler & Son, Inc. v. Sonitrol*, 497 A.2d 530 (N.J. Super. 1985).

(y) Gross Negligence

In many states, the standard for a court to find "gross negligence" is exceedingly high. "Gross Negligence must betoken a reckless influence to the rights of others." *Net2Globe International, Inc. v. Time Warner Telecom of New York*, 273 F. Supp. 2d 436, 450 (S.D.N.Y. 2003), *citing Sommers v. Federal Signal Corp.*, 593 N.E.2d 1365, 1370–71 (N.Y. 1992). A gross negligence standard sets a high threshold. To rise to the level of gross negligence, an act requires special circumstances and particularly egregious conduct. *Colnaghi, USA Ltd. v. Jewelers Protection Services, Ltd.*, 81 N.Y.2d 821, 823–24 (1993) (gross negligence "evinces a reckless disregard for the rights of others or 'smacks' of intentional wrongdoing."). Thus, only rarely will a party be able to demonstrate gross negligence and negate the contractual limitation of liability. *See, e.g., Hunter v. Skate III*, 1999 Mass. App. Div. 274 (1999).

There is usually an express exclusion from the agreement's limitation of liability for gross negligence or willful misconduct. The majority of jurisdictions imply this anyway, as gross negligence does not equate with a right to punitive damages. Any limit of liability for gross negligence will be unlikely to be upheld, as most courts consider the issue to be one of public policy. *Zavras v. Capeway Rovers Motorcycle Club*, 687 N.E.2d 1263, 1265 (Mass. App. Ct. 1997); *but see Rollins, Inc. v. Heller*, 454 So. 2d 580 (Fla. 1984) (limitation of liability applies to gross negligence). Some practitioners argue against carving out gross negligence from an agreement's limitation of liability because there is no agreed definition of gross negligence, and thus the meaning is subject to interpretation by the trier of fact.

Gross negligence will be decided by a jury as it is a question of fact. Most courts do not attempt to define gross negligence but rather simply rule on whether the facts arise to a level of gross negligence. The definition of gross negligence will vary by state. New York law defines "gross negligence" narrowly - a reason for the licensor to select New York law to govern the agreement. California, as may be expected, has adopted a broader definition of gross negligence. *Eastburn v. Regional Fire Protection Authority*, 80 P.3d 656, 662 (2003) ("Gross negligence" long has been defined in California . . . as either a "want of even scant care" or "an extreme departure from the ordinary standard of conduct."). Gross negligence as used in contract law is essentially a contract concept, as opposed to negligence, which is founded in tort. Some attorneys representing licensees suggest that the parties create a definitive list of actions that will be considered "gross negligence" similar to a definition created for direct damages. See, e.g., Form Q.2.DD.7 § 17. Licensors should carefully consider the practicality of such a list as the licensor may not agree with the licensee's proposed list.

(z) Willful Misconduct, and Intentional Acts/Intentional Breach

Licensees should refuse to accept any limit on the licensor's liability for the licensor's intentional breach and should specifically state so in the agreement. As a general principle, parties cannot limit their liability for intentional acts or torts. *Sale v. Slitz*, 998 S.W.2d 159 (Mo. Ct. App. 1999); *ABRY Partners V, L.P. v. F&W Acquisition LLC*, 891 A.2d 1032 (Del. Ch. 2006) (limitation of liability void where representations and warranties included intentional and material misrepresentations); *but see Net2Globe Int'l., Inc. v. Time Warner Telecom*, 273 F. Supp. 2d 436, 451 (S.D.N.Y. 2003) ("economically motivated decision cannot, as a matter of law, rise to the level of malice or intentional wrong-doing necessary to invalidate" an agreement's limitation of liability). At least one court has upheld a limitation of liability where the licensor intentionally failed to perform. *See Metropolitan Life Insurance Co. v. Noble Lowndes Int'l, Inc.*, 84 N.Y.2d 430, 618 N.Y.S.2d 882 (1994). *But see Hosiery Corp. of America, Inc. v. International Data Processing, Inc.*, 1991 WL 30015 (D.N.J. Feb. 28, 1991) (court failed to dismiss breach claim due to factual issue of whether licensor breached agreement by willfully failing to install latest software). *See also* § 14.A.5.

The meaning of willful misconduct varies by state. New York has interpreted this term narrowly. In *Metropolitan Life Ins. Co. v. Noble Lowndes Int'l, Inc.*, the New York

Court of Appeals held that the term "willful misconduct" does not encompass the vendor's intentional failure to perform. In *Metropolitan Life*, Noble delivered the contractually required core software and the functional specifications without incident. After two sets of enhancements were rejected by Metropolitan Life, Noble demanded an increase in the price of the enhancements. When Metropolitan Life refused, Noble stopped performing and Metropolitan Life brought suit against Noble seeking a refund of all monies paid to Noble plus Metropolitan Life's general and consequential damages. *Id.* at 506.

An exception to the limitation of liability provision in the parties' agreement excluded consequential damages except in the case of "intentional misrepresentations, or damages arising out of [Noble's] willful acts or gross negligence." *Id.* at 505–06. The court held that the term "willful acts" should be interpreted as referring to conduct similar in nature to intentional misrepresentation and gross negligence and thus denied Metropolitan Life's claim to recover its consequential damages. *Id.*

If a licensee negotiates a limitation on its own liability, a smart licensor will want to carve out from any such limitation breach of the license grant, violation of the agreement's confidentiality provisions, and the payment of any monies owed the licensor under the payment provisions of the license.

Finally, where the parties are required to insure against potential risks under the license, the license should clearly state that the parties' liability is not limited to the amount of insurance they are required to obtain under the license.

(iii) Tangible Personal Property and Personal Bodily Injury

A licensor should ensure that only its indemnification obligation for tangible personal property damage and personal bodily injuries are excluded from the liability cap. "Personal *bodily* injuries" are usually excluded from any cap, as limiting consequential damages is *prima facie* unconscionable in consumer transactions. UCC. § 2-719(3) prohibits a party from limiting its own liability for personal bodily injury. Most parties are willing to accept these risks, as any loss will likely be covered under a party's insurance policies. See Chapter 6.C for a discussion of insurance issues. Many licensees seek to modify the wording of such exclusions to exclude "personal injury" and "personal property damages" from the agreement's limitation of liability in an effort to expand the limit of the licensor's liability.

By removing the words "tangible" and "bodily," the licensee can potentially seek to hold the licensor liable for any property damage, including intangible property damage. For example, *tangible* personal property damages are unlikely to include erasing a tape, but such an action may be considered personal property damage.

Existing case law supports the proposition that loss of data is considered intangible property damage. *See, e.g., Ward General Insurance Services, Inc. v. Employers Fire Insurance Co.*, 114 Cal. App. 4th 548 (2004) (loss of database is not a direct physical loss); *St. Paul Fire & Marine Insurance Co. v. Nat'l Computer Systems, Inc.*, 490 N.W.2d 626 (Minn. 1992) (trade secrets contained in binders is not damage to tangible property); *Ferrington v. McAfee*, 2010 WL 3910169 (N.D. Cal. Oct. 5, 2010) (software is tangible chattel.); *America Online, Inc. v. St. Paul Mercury Ins. Co.*, 207 F. Supp. 2d 459, 468 (E.D. Va. 2007) ("Computer data software and systems are intangible items stored on a tangible vessel on the computer or a disk."); *Seagate Technology, Inc. v. St. Paul Fire and Marine Ins. Co.*, 11 F. Supp. 2d 1150

(N.D. Cal. 1998) (loss of data alone is not "physical damage to tangible property"). *But see Dechert v. Commonwealth*, 998 A.2d 575 (Pa. 2010) (in tax dispute, canned software found to be tangible personal property). This distinction is important, as increasing amounts of data is being transferred over the internet, as entities move away from using computer tapes to store and transport data. Thus, the data would have to reside on tangible media such as a computer tape or disk to support a claim for "tangible personal property damage." *See, e.g., Retail Systems, Inc. v. CNA Insurance Companies*, 469 N.W.2d 735, 737 (Minn. App. 1991) (Computer tape and resident data "tangible property" as data "was integrated completely with the physical property of the tape.").

Similarly, by removing "bodily," the licensor has assumed significant additional risk. The initial intent of this exclusion was to comply with state law limiting a party's ability to limit its liability for personal bodily injury. The deletion arguably exposes the licensor to any type of personal liability. In essence, these changes significantly dilute or even negate the limitation of liability.

> *Each party agrees to indemnify, hold harmless and defend the other party, its officers, directors, employees, agents and representatives from and against any claim, demand, cause of action, loss, expense or liability, including reasonable attorney's fees, arising on account of any injury to or death of person or* ***damage to personal property*** *to the extent directly or indirectly caused by the acts or* ***omissions*** *of the indemnifying party.*

From the licensor's perspective, the above language provides several reasons for concern. The language fails to expressly reference third-party claims. Many people wrongly believe that by implication indemnification is limited to third-party claims. The licensor should qualify any such language relating to an omission by requiring any omission to be intentional. Some parties are willing to accept that "damage to personal property" provided indemnification is limited to third-party claims. A prudent party will reject this language, as the indemnified party has no onus to limit its liability to the third party. Given that the indemnified party is in contractual privity with the injured party, it has the ability to limit its liability (and thus the indemnifying party's liability) through its contract with the third party. As such, the indemnifying party must ensure that the exclusion is limited to "tangible personal property" to fully protect its interests.

Alternatively, some parties seek to specifically define "tangible personal property" to include data and information which are usually considered to be intangible. The language set forth below seeks to avoid any ambiguity and broaden the licensor's potential liability. By expanding the definition of "tangible personal property" to include intangibles, the licensee is inviting the licensor to strike this expansive language. A savvy licensee is more likely to achieve its goal by deleting "tangible" instead of attempting to redefine "tangible," which emphasizes the licensee's intent to expand the licensor's liability.

> *Licensor shall promptly and fully defend, indemnify and hold harmless licensee and its affiliates and their respective officers, directors, agents and employees (the "Indemnified Parties") against all claims, demands and judgments made or recovered against them for damages to or loss of real or* ***tangible personal property, including Licensee's Confidential Information, data files, web content, software applications*** *or for bodily injury or death to any person arising out of, or in connection with this Agreement, to the*

extent that such damage, injury or death was caused by an action or omission of licensor, its subcontractor or its employees or agents, or on the issue of infringement of any patent, copyright, trade secret, trademark, or trade dress related to a Deliverable or the Services.

2. Disclaimer of Consequential, Incidental, Punitive and Special Damages (§ 17.1)

Most parties agree to limit their damages to direct damages, that is, those damages arising directly from the breach and those which are not unique to the injured party, and disclaim all other damages, such as consequential, incidental, special, and punitive damages.

In drafting a disclaimer, the parties should be careful to physically separate provisions containing a limitation of liability and/or disclaimer of damages from other provisions of the agreement. At least one court has held that a limitation of liability provision included in a force majeure provision applied only to the agreement's force majeure provision. *Therion, Inc. v. Media by Design, Inc.*, 2010 WL 5341925 (E.D.N.Y. Nov. 10, 2010), *accepted*, 2010 WL 5341920 (E.D.N.Y. Dec. 16, 2010).

(a) Consequential Damages

(i) General

Consequential damages constitute "those damages that, although not an invariable result of every breach, were reasonably foreseeable or contemplated by the parties at the time the contract was entered into as a probable result of a breach and were proximately caused by the breach." *Wartsila NSD North America, Inc. v. Hill International, Inc.*, 530 F.3d 269, 277 (3d Cir. 2008). Often, the common-law definition of "consequential" damages is broader than the UCC's, as many common-law interpretations encompass the UCC definition of both "incidental" and "consequential" damages. There is no clear bright-line test for separating direct damages from consequential damages. "[T]he precise demarcation between direct and consequential damages is a question of fact . . . [which] must be left for resolution at trial." *Roneker v. Kenworth Truck Co.*, 977 F. Supp. 237, 240 (W.D.N.Y. 1996). *See also Applied Data Processing, Inc. v. Burroughs Corp.*, 394 F. Supp. 504, 508 (D. Conn. 1975) ("neither in Michigan nor elsewhere does the term 'consequential damages' have a clearly established meaning").

(ii) Failure of Essential Purpose

Under Section 2-719 (1), (3) of the UCC, the parties to a contract may exclude consequential and incidental damages provided such exclusions are not unconscionable and there are no other explicit exceptions. *See, e.g., The Colonial Life Insurance Co. of America v. Electronic Data Systems Corp.*, 817 F. Supp. 235 (D.N.H. 1993). Consequential damages for personal bodily injury cannot be limited in some circumstances. *See* UCC § 2-719 (3), comments 1 and 3.

Unlike Section 2-316 of the UCC, which imposes a conspicuousness requirement for disclaimers of warranty related to merchantability and fitness, Section 2-719 (1), (3) does not contain a conspicuousness requirement. Comment 3 to Section 2-719(3), which discusses the exclusion of consequential damages, also fails to address conspicuousness. Nonetheless, to err on the side of caution, any such disclaimer should be conspicuous to avoid a court imposing such a requirement and potentially voiding any limitation of liability. *See generally Krupp PM Eng'g. v. Honeywell, Inc.*, 530 N.W.2d 146 (Mich. 1995). *See also D. S. Am. (East), Inc. v. Chromagrafx Imaging Systems, Inc.*, 873 F. Supp. 786 (E.D.N.Y. 1995) (the failure to make a limitation of consequential damages conspicuous is one factor in determining whether a limitation is unconscionable).

There is a dichotomy of opinion as to whether a disclaimer of consequential damages is valid if a remedy fails of its essential purpose. Some courts ascribe to the position that UCC Section 2-719 (2) provides that an exclusion of consequential damages will be upheld even if a remedy fails of its essential purpose unless it is unconscionable. Other courts believe that UCC Sections 2-719 (2) and (3) should be read together, negating a disclaimer of consequential damages if a remedy fails of its essential purpose. Compare *Fidelity & Deposit Trust Co. of Maryland v. Krebs Eng'rs*, 859 F.2d 501, 504-05 (7th Cir. 1988) (consequential damages recoverable if remedy fails of its essential purpose (applying Wisconsin law)); *Bishop Logging Co. v. John Deere Indus. Equip. Co.*, 455 S.E.2d 183 (S.C. App. 1995) (permitting consequential damages when remedy failed of its essential purpose), *McNally Wellman Co. v. New York State Elec. & Gas Corp.*, 63 F.3d 1188 (2d Cir. 1995) (allowing consequential damages despite contractual exclusion when remedy failed of its essential purpose) with *Canal Elec. Co. v. Westinghouse Elec. Corp.*, 578 N.E.2d 182, 185 (Mass. 1990) (consequential damages disclaimer valid even though limited remedy failed of its essential purpose); *Caudill Seed and Warehouse Co., Inc. v. Prophet 21, Inc.*, 123 F. Supp. 2d 826 (E.D. Pa. 2000), *Int'l Fin. Serv. v. Franz*, 534 N.W.2d 261 (Minn. 1995) (consequential damage exclusion enforceable notwithstanding failure of remedy's essential purpose).

Still other states have upheld a consequential damages exclusion in the event a remedy failed of its essential purpose where such result was the clear and unambiguous intent of the parties. One court has found that a limitation of consequential damages applies only to a breach of warranty and not for non-performance. *PC COM, Inc. v. Proteon, Inc.*, 906 F. Supp. 894 (S.D.N.Y. 1995).

Two noted commentators believe the two UCC sections operate independently of each other. J. WHITE & R. SUMMER, UNIFORM COMMERCIAL CODE § 12-10 at 526–27 (3d ed. 1988).

The Ninth Circuit upheld an award of consequential damages despite a disclaimer contained in the parties' contract where the seller failed to deliver a working software system and the contract contained an exclusive "repair or replace" remedy. *RRX Indus. v. Lab-Con, Inc.*, 772 F.2d 543 (9th Cir. 1985). In a later case, the Ninth Circuit held that a limitation on consequential damages was inapplicable because the limit was tied to the limited repair remedy contained in the contract. The court concluded that because a working software system was never delivered, the limited remedy and limit on consequential damages never came into effect. *Hawaiian Tel. Co. v. Microform Data Sys.*, 829 F.2d 919 (9th Cir. 1987). *See also Caudill Seed and Warehouse Co., Inc. v. Prophet 21, Inc.*, 123 F. Supp. 2d 826 (E.D. Pa. 2000) (where seller intentionally or negligently stymies buyer's efforts to take advantage of exclusive remedy, damages disclaimer is rendered void and buyer may seek all remedies under UCC including consequential damages).

A limitation on consequential damages will not be upheld where such limitation is unconscionable and contrary to public policy. *Durham v. Ciba-Geigy Corp.*, 315 N.W.2d 696 (S.D. 1982).

To strengthen a disclaimer of consequential damages or other limitation of liability, any limitation of liability provision should be distinct from and in a separate section from the warranty/remedy provisions of a contract. See, e.g., § 17.1 and § 16. The reasoning for such separation is that if the warranty/remedy provisions fail their essential purpose, and such provisions are separate and distinct from the limitation of liability, the court will hopefully view the provisions as unrelated and uphold the limitation of liability. At least one court has held that a limitation of liability provision and a remedy provision contained in different sections of an agreement will be viewed as independent of each other. *Colonial Life Ins. Co. v. Electronic Data Systems Corp.*, 817 F. Supp. 235, 241 (D.N.H. 1993). This philosophy has been endorsed by two leading commentators. *See* Feldman & Nimmer, Drafting Effective Contracts 5.06 [A][2], Aspen Law & Business (2d ed. 2007).

(iii) Lost Profits

To avoid potential disputes, many parties define "direct damages" at the time of contract execution to create certainty, as several courts have found lost profits to be direct damages while others have found lost profits to be consequential damages. *Moore v. Boating Indus. Ass'ns*, 754 F.2d 698, 717 (7th Cir. 1985) ("Lost profits are considered to be general or direct damages in a breach of contract case . . . ."); *Fishman Org., Inc. v. Frick Transfer, Inc.*, 2013 WL 1655984, at *3 (E.D. Pa. Apr. 17, 2013) ("Lost profits are considered a form of consequential damages."). These definitions often include classes of damages that would not normally be considered direct damages. For example, the cost of cover would typically be classified as incidental damages but is often included by the parties in the definition of direct damages.

Prudent parties should not agree, however, to include lost profits or any other material element of consequential loss in the definition of direct damages. Lost profits may under some circumstances be considered outside the scope of direct damages and as such they are often explicitly listed and included in the definition. A prudent licensor should ensure that any exclusionary language does not prevent the licensor from recovering its charges or fees, which may not include future profit. Thus, the agreed upon definition should explicitly provide for the licensor's recovery of such monies. See, e.g., Form B.3.1 § 17.4 for model language. See Chapter 5.I.3 for an additional discussion.

A disclaimer of consequential damages which specifically enumerates lost profits will likely only impact the licensee, as the licensor's lost profits that relate directly to the contract will most likely be considered direct damages that will be recoverable only subject to the agreement's cap on direct damages. To that end, to avoid inadvertently waiving its right to recover lost profits, a prudent licensor should ensure that any disclaimer of consequential damages does not specifically identify lost profits as consequential damages. *See Biotronik A.G. v. Conor Medsystems Ireland, Ltd.*, 11 N.E.3d 676, 677 (N.Y. 2014) ("lost profits were the direct and probable result of a breach of the parties' agreement and thus constitute general damages" and are not barred by the exclusion of consequential damages); *Coremetrics, Inc. v. AtomicPark.com, LLC*, 2005 WL 3310093 (N.D. Cal. Dec. 7, 2005) (lost profits recoverable despite exclusion of consequential damages).

For this reason, Article 2 of the UCC defines consequential damages as those sustained by the buyer. There is no equivalent code section applicable to sellers. Thus, if the licensor intends to collect the profit included in its price, it must ensure the underlying agreement provides that the licensor's fees are an exception to the exclusion of lost profits.

The separate exclusion of profits (as opposed to relying on a general exclusion of consequential damages in a limitation of liability) affects the licensor/seller rather than the licensee/buyer. In some jurisdictions, lost profits will clearly be classified as consequential damages when the lost profits are those sustained by a licensee.

In *Penncro Associates, Inc. v. Sprint Spectrum, L.P.*, 499 F.3d 1151 (10th Cir. 2007), the court considered whether a party could collect its lost profits when the governing master services agreement included a waiver of consequential damages "includ[ing], but . . . not limited to, lost profits, lost revenues and lost business opportunities." The court recognized that lost profits can be considered both direct damages and consequential damages. In this situation, the court allowed the plaintiff to recover its lost profits, finding the disclaimer listed lost profits as a type of consequential damages but did not prohibit the award of direct lost profits. *Id.* at 1155–57.

(iv) Gross Negligence

Prudent licensees seek to exclude consequential damages waivers in the event of gross negligence, willful or intentional acts, or the abandonment of the agreement. From a disclosing party's perspective, an exclusion of consequential damages is not appropriate for a breach of the receiving party's confidentiality obligations, as consequential damages are the principal type of damages that will likely arise from such a breach. From the receiving party's perspective, if consequential damages are not excluded, they should be subject to the agreement's overall limitation of liability cap.

(v) Intellectual Property

Some licensors seek to carve out infringement of a party's intellectual property from the consequential damages exclusion. Licensees often push back, arguing such an exclusion is too broad. Intellectual property infringement is covered under the agreement in two ways: (1) if party A discloses party B's trade secrets, this is usually covered by the breach of confidentiality exclusion discussed above; and (2) if party A is providing intellectual property to party B and a claim arises that party A's intellectual property infringes the intellectual property of a third party, then party B should be covered by an indemnity in the agreement.

(vi) Data Loss

Most damages arising from a data breach will be consequential damages. As such, the parties may want to contractually define such damages as direct damages to allow the injured party to recover its damages.

For a more detailed discussion of consequential damages, *see* West & Duran, *Reassessing the "Consequences" of Consequential Damage Waivers in Acquisition Agreements*, 63 Bus. Law. 777 (2008).

(b) Incidental Damages

A seller's incidental damages are defined under UCC § 2-710(ii) as:

> "any commercially reasonable charges, expenses or commissions incurred in stopping delivery, in the transportation, care, and custody of goods after the buyer's breach, in connection with the return or resale of the goods or otherwise resulting from the breach."

A buyer's incidental damages result "from a seller's breach of contract" and "include expenses reasonably incurred in inspection, receipt, transportation and care and custody of goods rightfully rejected, any commercially reasonable charges, expenses or commissions in connection with effecting cover and any other reasonable expense incident to the delay or other breach."

UCC § 2-715(1).

The UCC definition of incidental damages may not be directly applicable to software licensing as Article 2 does not apply to services, only to "transactions in goods." In any event, the applicable common law definition of incidental damages will likely closely mirror these definitions, and it is likely any court would look to the UCC by analogy.

Some licensees reject any attempt to disclaim incidental damages, arguing that incidental damages, such as cover, are in essence direct damages. Based on the Section 2-715(1) definition, many licensees argue that these types of damages should be recoverable by the licensee in the event of a breach. More importantly, aside from the definition, they argue that if examples of incidental damages were submitted to reasonable business people, they would likely agree that these examples of "reasonable expense incident to the delay or breach" should be recoverable in the event a party breaches the agreement.

In any negotiation from the licensor's perspective, the exclusion of consequential damages is the most important exclusion, much more so than incidental damages. Many licensors generally disagree with the inclusion of incidental damages as recoverable damages, as the exclusion of special and incidental damages is standard in license agreements. If incidental damages cross the line into what are direct damages, they would not be excluded. An alternative position is for the licensor to agree to pay the cost of cover. This solution is especially relevant if the agreement involves third-party suppliers for which the licensor has overall responsibility in its role as a systems integrator, but for which the licensor lacks contractual privity and lacks the contractual right to control their performance.

If a licensor elects to allow the licensee to recover incidental damages, it should ensure that these damages are included in any limit of liability and that the licensee has the obligation to mitigate its damages.

(c) Special Damages

Special damages are "those which are the actual, but not the necessary, result of the injury complained of, and which in fact follow it as a natural and proximate consequence in the particular case, that is, by reason of special circumstances or conditions." *Twin Coach Co. v. Chance Vought Aircraft Inc.*, 163 A.2d 278, 286 (Del. 1960). The Restatement (Second) of Torts § 904 (2) defines special damages as "compensatory damages for a harm other than one for which general damages are given."

Special damages are usually defined by jurisdiction. *See, e.g.*, statutorily: Alabama: ALA. CODE § 15-18-66(2); California: CAL. CIV. CODE § 48(a); Montana: MONT. CODE ANN. § 46-18-243(1)(a); by common law: New York: *Liberman v. Gelstein*, 80 N.Y.2d 429, 434–35 (1992); North Carolina: *Sarda v. City/Cty. of Durham Bd. of Adjust.*, 575 S.E.2d 829, 830–31 (N.C. 2003). *Holtzscheiter v. Thomson Newspapers, Inc., 506 S.E.2d 497, 501, 502 n.4 (S.C. 1998). Ray v. Miller Meester Advertising, Inc.*, 684 N.W.2d 404 (Minn. 2004) (Special damages are those which are the natural but not the necessary and inevitable result of the wrongful act.). Special damages are often equated with consequential damages, *All American School Supply Co. v. Slavens*, 609 P.2d 46 (Ariz. 1980) (and incidental damages), in which case they will be excluded by an agreement's limitation/exclusion on consequential damages. *Wartsila NSD North America, Inc. v. Hill International, Inc.*, 530 F.3d 269, 277 (3d Cir. 2008).

Special damages, if allowed, should come under any limitation on damages.

(d) Punitive Damages

Although an express exclusion of punitive damages (sometimes referred to as exemplary damages) is usually included in most disclaimers, punitive damages are generally not allowed in contract actions. *Purdy v. Consumers Distrib. Co., Ltd.*, 648 F. Supp. 980 (S.D.N.Y. 1986) (punitive damages not available where claim lies solely in contract); *Continental Nat'l Bank v. Evans*, 489 P.2d 15 (Ariz. 1971) (punitive damages not recoverable in contract claims without independent tort). *Splitt v. Deltona Corp.*, 662 F.2d 1142, (5th Cir. 1981) (punitive damages not recoverable under contract claim even where breach is willful, flagrant, or oppressive); *but see General Auto Parts Co., Inc. v. Genuine Parts Co.*, 979 P.2d 1207 (Idaho 1999) (punitive damages may be awarded in contract claims in narrow and compelling circumstances such as fraud and gross negligence.).

In some states, punitive damages may be limited to litigation or other costs. *DiNapoli v. Cooke*, 683 A.2d 603, 609 (Conn. App. 1996) (recovery of punitive damages not recoverable in tort and limited to litigation expenses). Given that many parties bring claims in contract and tort, an express inclusion of punitive damages should be included as there is a trend toward permitting punitive damages where a party's actions have been egregious. Such exclusions have been upheld in at least one case despite the presence of fraud. *Bombardier Aerospace v. SPEP Aircraft Holdings, LLC*, 572 S.W.3d 213 (Tex. 2019) (Court upheld waiver of punitive damages for fraud but stated parties cannot waive all damages for fraud).

3. Deemed Direct Damages (§ 17.4, Form Q.2.DD.7 § 1.2.)

Direct damages are those damages that may be fairly and reasonably considered as arising from a breach and that do not arise from any special circumstances applicable to the non-breaching party. Direct damages would include the cost of purchasing a replacement product or services in the open market, while consequential damages would be the value of lost business due to the breach.

Some licensees seek to specify that certain damages will be "deemed" to be direct damages. This effort arises from consequential damages being disclaimed in an agreement preventing licensees from potentially recovering a significant percentage of their damages. The licensor should closely examine the proposed definition to limit the types of damages that are deemed to be direct damages. The licensor should seek to limit any "deemed" direct damages. In particular, it should be hesitant with respect to reconstructing or reloading data. This liability should be aligned to the related contractual obligations (i.e., this provision would not imply that the licensor has more liability with respect to these items than otherwise set forth in the agreement).

Common examples of damages defined as direct damages include the cost of reconstructing data, expenses associated with replacing damaged equipment, the cost associated with providing work-arounds, and the cost associated with correcting and fixing software errors. Further, the payment of penalties or fines should be limited to be fines and penalties related to the licensor's failure to comply with applicable law. Re-procurement costs would be considered incidental damages. *See, e.g.*, Section 2-715 of the UCC, which defines incidental damages as covering re-procurement costs. Many licensors will also accept a licensee's request to define re-procurement costs as direct damages but seek to exclude any efforts to include lost profits or goodwill. A prudent licensor should seek to limit any expansion of direct damages to those damages that would likely be excluded under the disclaimer of special, incidental and consequential damages.

For a more in-depth discussion of consequential damages, *see* note, *Consequential Damage Limitations and Cross-Subsidization: An Independent Approach to Uniform Commercial Code Section 2-719*, 66 S. Cal. L. Rev. 1273 (1973).

4. Reducing the Statute of Limitations (§ 17.1)

Traditionally, a statute of limitations bars a potential plaintiff from bringing a contract claim after a set period of time after the action that gave rise to the claim. *See, e.g.*, *A.B. Alexander d/b/a A.B. Alexander and Associates v. The Perkin Elmer Corp.*, 729 F.2d 576 (8th Cir. 1984). Most states have statutorily codified this time period as three or four years. *See, e.g.*, California: Calif. Stat. Ann. § 337 (1996) (four years), and Maryland: Md. Code Ann. Cts. & Jud. Proc. § 5-101(2006) (three years). By default, Section 2-725(1) of the UCC provides for a four-year statute of limitations beginning when the cause of action first accrues but allows the parties to reduce the statute of limitations by mutual agreement to a minimum of one year. It is important to remember that the statute of limitations for a contract claim may differ from the statute of limitations for a tort claim. Thus, in agreeing to any reduction of the statute of limitations for a contract claim, the parties need to consider the interrelationship with the statute of limitations for third-party torts vis-à-vis the license's indemnity provisions.

By agreeing to a period less than the statutory time period, the licensor may reduce the time period in which the licensee may bring a claim, thus limiting the licensor's risk and, consequently, its liability. *See Gruet v. Care Free Housing Division of Kennschl Enterprises Inc.*, 759 N.Y.S.2d 276 (2003) (one-year contractual statute of limitations upheld); *Action Mailing Corp. v. Hewlett-Packard Co.*, 2009 WL 3526658 (W.D. Mo. Oct. 26, 2009) (one-year contractual statute of limitations for breach of warranty upheld); *Reengineering Consultants, Ltd. v. EMC Corp.*, 2010 WL 2817228 (S.D. Ohio July 16, 2010).

To be valid, a clause should be clearly and unambiguously written. Some states do not favor contractual agreements to reduce a statute of limitations and will strictly construe such an agreement against the party seeking to enforce it. *Western Filter Corp. v. Argan, Inc.* 540 F.3d 947 (9th Cir. 2008) (ambiguous clause found not to reduce limitation period). Limitations agreed to by sophisticated contracting parties represented by counsel are more likely to be upheld. *Wind Dancer Production Group v. Walt Disney Pictures*, 10 Cal. App. 5th 56 (2017). Further, contractual limitation periods may be waived or estopped. *Id.*

A prudent licensee will want to carefully consider whether to accept any reduction in the statute of limitations and if the licensee chooses to do so, the licensee should make such clause mutual to also reduce its own risk. Given that all states have a statutory statute of limitations for contracts and tort claims, a licensee should resist reducing the statute of limitations to less than the statutory period. Although the contractual statute of limitations may be mutual, in the great majority of instances such limitation will benefit the licensor.

If the statute of limitations is reduced, licensors need to make sure all of their invoices are submitted to the licensee in a timely manner. The licensor should avoid holding invoices in the event of a dispute only to find its collection efforts barred by the statute of limitations. *See, e.g., Ram Systems of LaCrosse, Wis., Inc., v. Wichita Coca-Cola Bottling Co.*, 1994 WL 476528 (D. Kan. Aug. 5, 1994) (licensee alleged one-year statute of limitations barred collection of monies due licensor). Similarly, if the licensee gives notice of a potential breach and the licensor takes over a year to cure, the licensee's claims may be barred by not bringing suit within a year. *See, e.g., Grus v. Patton*, 790 S.W.2d 936 (Mo. App. 1990) (seller's unsuccessful attempts to repair defects over eight-year period did not toll four-year statute of limitations). Thus, a prudent licensee should enter into a tolling agreement while any attempt to cure is under way. See Form N.1 for a model Tolling Agreement.

Licensors should be careful to review the applicable state law to ensure any proposed reduction does not violate the state's law. Texas, for example, prohibits reducing the statute of limitations in most agreements to less than two years. TEXAS CIVIL PRACTICE & REMEDIES CODE § 16.070. The parties should also be careful not to unknowingly extend the statute of limitation. For example, under Maryland law, executing an agreement under seal may extend the statute of limitations from 3 to 12 years. MD. CODE ANN., CTS. & JUD. PROC. § 5-101(2006). See Chapter 6.U for a more detailed discussion. A claim of fraud, however, will not be barred by a contract's statute of limitations. *Invacare Corp. v. Sperry Corp.*, 612 F. Supp. 448 (N.D. Ohio 1984) (seller cannot rely on statute of limitations to bar buyer's claim where alleged contracts were induced by fraud).

Finally, the parties should be cognizant of whether the statute of limitations is tolled by a party's efforts to correct any defect in the software. There is a dichotomy among the courts as to whether efforts to correct a defect will toll the statute of limitations. *Compare Triangle Underwriters, Inc. v. Honeywell, Inc.*, 604 F.2d 737 (2d Cir. 1979) (seller's attempt to repair computer system after malfunction did not toll statute of limitations for breach of contract claim) with *Daley v. Twin Disc, Inc.*, 440 F. Supp. 2d 48, 52 (D. Mass. 2006) (attempts to repair defective goods will not normally extend or toll the statute of limitations, but "purposely prolonging the time for repairs beyond the statute of limitations" may justify extension) and *Waddell v. L.V.R.V., Inc.*, 125 P.3d 1160 (Nev. 2006) (period in which buyer may timely revoke acceptance may be extended when seller repeatedly failed to cure breach despite repeated assurances) and *North Am. Lighting, Inc. v. Hopkins Mfg. Corp.*, 37 F.3d 1253 (7th Cir. 1994) (seller's attempts to cure do not go against buyer's period of timely revocation).

J. Price, Payment, and Revenue Recognition Issues (§ 8)

Price and payment terms will usually depend on the type of license granted and whether the contract requires any software development work to be performed. Both parties need to focus on when payment is due, as the payment terms can affect the licensor's revenue recognition and provide the licensee with the leverage to pay the licensor as each stage of the work is completed.

1. *Pricing Models*

Software licenses can be priced in many different ways including enterprise licenses, seat licenses, user licenses, per processor, per seat, per server, per terabyte/gigabyte etc as well as a blended mix of these methodologies. Occasionally, a vendor may price its licenses on a contingency basis by taking a percentage of cost reductions realized through the implementation of a software solution, such as a percentage of the recovery of improperly paid claims that have been identified by a software solution. Set forth below is a brief explanation of each of these pricing methodologies and the issues associated with each.

(a) Software Licenses

(i) Enterprise/Entity Licenses

"Enterprise" licenses allow an enterprise/entity to install the software or access internet-based resources throughout the entity without limitation. Conceptually, enterprise licenses are the easiest to price and enforce. The vendor charges one fee for the entire licensing entity to utilize the software, regardless of the number of employees accessing the software or the number of computers processing the software. There is no need to audit the customer's use of the software, nor to implement a complicated pricing model. The licensee also receives certainty in that it will not have to pay additional license fees for additional users or when the software is installed on new hardware. Nor does the licensee have the administrative hassle of tracking the number of users and purchasing new licenses when the authorized number of users has been exceeded.

The principal issue for consideration is the extent to which the license includes the customer's affiliates and subsidiaries as well as future acquisitions and divestures. The challenge for both parties is to clearly define the entity which is entitled to use the software. From the licensor's perspective, the license should clearly state the ability of present and future affiliates as well as acquired and divested entities, to utilize the software. In the event the licensor agrees to allow the customer's subsidiaries and affiliates to utilize the software, the underlying license agreement should limit use to those subsidiaries and affiliates set forth on a schedule to the license agreement. In the event the licensee is unwillingly to limit use to a scheduled list of subsidiaries and affiliates, the licensor should carefully define "Affiliates" to quantify/limit the number of entities that can utilize the software.

In the case of a divestiture, the licensor should limit the time in which the divested entity may utilize the software after divestiture before it is required to purchase its own license or cease use of the software. The licensee should require the licensor to provide pricing for any divested entity at the time the license is executed to limit the licensor's leverage at the time of the divesture. The license fee for any divested entity should reflect a significant discount in light of the divested entity's prior use of the software and the fact that the licensor will likely incur insignificant additional costs for training, documentation, and the like. In the event of a divestiture, the licensee's support and maintenance fee should decrease, as the licensor is not responsible for divested business.

As to acquisitions, the licensor should carefully consider whether it will allow the licensee to utilize the software in companies the licensee acquires without the payment of an additional fee. The licensor may be forgoing a significant revenue stream, especially if the licensee acquires a large company. The licensor is also at risk if the licensee merges with another, larger company but the licensee is the surviving entity. Even if the licensor agrees that acquired entities may utilize the software without the payment of an additional license fee, the underlying agreement should clearly provide the licensor the right to increase the relevant maintenance and support fees. Maintenance and support fees should be based on the total number of users which should increase proportionally with the size of the assumed entity. If the licensor negotiates for the right to charge an additional fee in the event the licensee acquires or merges with another entity, the parties should negotiate a pricing schedule at the time the license agreement is executed to limit the licensor's leverage in the event of an acquisition.

A prudent licensor will include language within the license agreement as set forth below to protect itself in the event the licensee acquires or merges with another entity.

> *Customer shall use a single logical production copy of the Licensed System only to process data related to the internal operations or the financial services offerings of itself, excluding businesses, blocks of business, or lines of business acquired thereby from a third party after the effective date of this Statement of Work.*

(ii) Site Licenses

Site licenses grant the licensee the right to use the software at a particular location without limitation on the number of users, individual computers, or their computing power. A variation is to allow a set number of users at a particular site. Licensee fees associated with a site license usually will be lower than an entity license due to the smaller number of users. Site licenses are geared toward large licenses or licensees predicting rapid growth. As most licensees move to a distributed, networked environment, site licenses will likely become less common. Set forth below is model language applicable for use in a site license.

> *[Customer shall install and use the Licensed System only on **[computers]** located at Customer's facilities located at {**[site]**}. All Documentation shall be located and used*

only at such facilities.] ***Option for remote use:*** *[Customer may remotely use the Licensed System only from any facilities within the same country that are controlled, managed, and either owned or leased by Customer.]*

(iii) Seat Licenses (Named Users and Concurrent User Licenses)

Seat licenses are based on the number of users that can access and use the software. These licenses can take several forms, including named user licenses and concurrent user licenses.

With named user seat licenses, the license fee is calculated based on the number of individuals who have access to the software based on a unique personal ID. A licensee must purchase a license for each person who accesses the software. Each person must use his or her own unique ID each time he or she accesses the software. Some licensors provide that the licensee must purchase a "named" seat license. The ID is unique to a particular individual such that if the individual leaves the employ of the licensee, a new employee hired to replace that person will need a new seat license. Under the license agreement, the licensee is unable transfer the old employee's "seat" license to the new employee as each license is "attached" to the named employee.

Concurrent seat license fees are based on the number of concurrent users who are authorized to access the software at the same time. The licensee purchases a number of "seats" which allows the corresponding number of the licensee's employees to access the software at the same time. The employees accessing the software are not identified by name or in any other manner. For example, if the licensee purchased 500 concurrent seat licenses, from one to 500 employees may access and use the software at any one time.

Seat licenses are increasingly favored by both licensors and licensees as more licensors move to a distributed/networked environment. The licensee must carefully negotiate the license terms, as in the sample language below, as questions often arise as to whether the license grant limits the licensee to an agreed upon number of identified users who may access the software or a set number of users who may access the software concurrently. For example, if a licensee purchases 300 seat licenses, can the licensee install the software on 1,000 computers provided only 300 users access the software at one time? Similarly, if the software is installed on only 300 computers, can 900 people working in three shifts utilize the 300 computers to access the software?

Licensee shall pay to Licensor the license and support fee specified in this Schedule 1 (the "License & Support Fee") for Licensor Product licensed to Licensee based on the total number of Licensed Users using the Licensor Products in the amount indicated below:

Number of Unique Users	Per Unique User Cost
0 – 1000	$100
1001 – 2000	$75
2001 – 9999	$50

Licensing is based on a Unique User. "Unique User" is defined as an individual user that utilizes NAME OF SOFTWARE PRODUCT™ as a licensee of the Licensor. Unique Users are individual employees of the Licensee. Unique users will be reported by the Licensor on a monthly basis pursuant to Section X.X of the Agreement.

In *Wall Data, Inc. v. Los Angeles County Sheriff's Dept.*, 447 F.3d 769 (9th Cir. 2006), the Ninth Circuit Court of Appeals found that a licensee who purchased 3,663 licenses but installed the software on 6,007 computers was in breach of the license even though it had configured its computers to limit the total number of users that could access the software to the number of licenses the licensee had purchased. In essence, the court held that the mere presence of a software copy on a computer is an infringement, even though the software is not accessible to a user. The *Wall Data* case was also interesting because the court excluded evidence that the licensee's purchase agreement with the software reseller may have allowed such use because the copyright owner was unaware of the reseller's license terms with the licensee. *Id.* at 782–83. This decision creates significant concern for any company that purchases its software through a reseller. For a more detailed discussion, *see Sheriffs' Over-Installation of Licensed Software was Copyright Infringement, Despite Limited Access or Use of Software*, 23 Computer & Internet Law. 24 (Aug. 2006).

Similarly, in *Thoroughbred Software, Int'l v. Dice Corp., et al.*, the court found a software distributor liable for all unpaid license fees for all unauthorized copies made even though some copies were not accessible to or used by its customers. 488 F.3d 352 (6th Cir. 2007).

The *Wall Data and Thoroughbred Software* cases illustrate the importance of carefully negotiating the terms of use for any seat licenses purchased.

Licensees should avoid the temptation to share passwords as sophisticated licensors track usage and will bring an action against licensees that do not comply with the license terms. *See CoStar Realty Information, Inc. v. Mark Field d/b/a Alliance Evaluation Group*, 2010 WL 5391463 (D. Md. Dec. 21, 2010) (licensor awarded $3.6 Million in damages against defendant who shared passwords).

(iv) Machine, CPU, and Core Licenses

CPU licenses have traditionally been utilized for mainframe solutions. The licensee purchases one license for each computer the software is installed on, each of which is identified by serial number. The price is based on the number of machines and their computing power. If the licensee desires to install the software on a new CPU, it would obtain the consent of the licensor and must usually pay a new license fee or a transfer fee. By requiring the licensee to provide the serial number of all CPUs on which the software is installed, the licensor can easily audit the licensee's compliance with the number of CPU licenses it purchased.

As computers have become more sophisticated, technology has progressed, and licensors have reevaluated their pricing methodologies to reflect these changes. Many mainframe computers today have multiple "logical partitions" or LPARs which allow a computer to simultaneously process data. As a result, many licensors now base their pricing on the number of LPARs and the number of MIPS (or MSUs) processed by each LPAR as opposed to a CPU basis, which reflects that many licensors are using the software on an LPAR basis as opposed to a CPU basis. Many vendors seek to price based on a CPU basis; however, many customers partition their CPUs and do not want to pay for the full CPU if they are not using its entire capacity, especially given the ever-increasing capacity of mainframe CPUs. While many customers prefer pricing based on an LPAR basis as they can license software for use in the required number of LPARs rather than for the entire computer, it can provide more challenges for the licensor to ensure the software is licensed for the applicable number of LPAR MIPs and it is not uncommon for licensors to require licensees to provide a standard report to validate the LPARs and LPAR sizes where the software is installed.

While mainframe CPUs are still used quite heavily, many customers have moved their applications to other mid-range or distributed computers, and these too have evolved to having multiple "cores", which result in more flexible licensing metrics. Customers need to be aware of the different license metrics used by their licensors when planning computer purchases and upgrades. For example, the license fee for a dual core processor may be priced at 125 percent of the license fee for a single-core CPU.

Licensors who utilize long-term master agreements with established pricing during the term should ensure that the agreement addresses or anticipates future technology advances to ensure the sanctity of their pricing methodologies. Otherwise, they risk being limited by the pricing set forth in the agreement and risk losing revenue from more efficient technologies. For example, a master agreement that incorporates a fee schedule with per-CPU pricing would contractually limit a licensor's ability to increase its fees based on the number of cores contained in a CPU. Given that many CPU licenses are perpetual, the licensor would be unable to recoup "lost" fees when the underlying agreement is renegotiated.

(v) Blended Pricing

An increasing number of licensors utilize a blended methodology for determining the relevant license fee. For example, some vendors determine the license fee based on the product of the number of cores by the number of CPUs by the size of the CPUs. Attached to the license agreement is a schedule of all known processors at the time the agreement is executed along with the associated license fee. A prudent licensor will include language stating that the license fee for use of the software on any processor not set forth in the schedule will be negotiated on a case-by-case basis. This protects the licensor from the advent of any technological advances that may impact its license fee stream.

(vi) Alternative Pricing

Occasionally, licensors will propose alternative pricing methods for their software. Usually, the software in question has a limited or special purpose; the degree to which the software will be used by the licensee is uncertain, or the value of such software to the licensee is uncertain, and the licensee is unwilling to pay the licensor what the licensor believes the software is worth. There is no magic to establishing the basis for calculating a license fee. Some licensors base their license fees on industry-specific metrics. For example, a licensor in the healthcare industry may base its license fees on the number of beds in a hospital or the number of insured persons an insurance company covers.

By tying the license fee to a metric other than the number of users, licensors seek to generate greater income. For example, pricing the license on a transactional basis or per-patient/per-insured basis, the license fee is potentially more palatable and justifiable to the licensee as it can be tied to revenue from the patient or the insured.

Another common alternative pricing methodology is "value based," where the licensor's fee is based on the amount of money the software saves the licensee or recovers for the licensee.

An example of this is software that evaluates claims paid by an insurer to identify improperly paid claims. The insurer may be unsure how many claims, if any, were improperly paid. It does not want to pay a license fee if it is unsure it will recover its costs. As such, some licensors are willing to license the software to the licensee for a nominal fee and a percentage of any identified or realized savings. This pricing methodology can be fraught with problems, as the basis for payment and the right to receive payment must be carefully defined, and the licensor must have detailed audit rights. The likelihood of a dispute occurring is high, as the licensor will seek very low thresholds for triggering the licensee's payment obligations, while the licensee will most likely adopt a more conservative approach or interpretation.

For example, in the above illustration, will the licensor be paid on the basis of all claims that have been identified as improperly paid or on the basis of money recovered? The licensee will likely argue that until the licensee has recovered the improper payments it has not benefited from the software. As such, it will only want to pay the licensor a percentage of monies recovered, less the cost of recovery. The licensor will likely argue that it cannot control the actual collection and payment and that the software was successful in identifying improper payments. Thus, it should be paid solely on the basis of the value of improperly paid claims identified by the software. The licensor may further argue that it should not bear the risk if the licensee decides not to seek to recover the improper payments for legal, political, public relations or other reasons. Thus, licensors should carefully consider whether to accept payment on a contingency basis and if they do, clearly set forth the triggers for payment in an unambiguous manner.

(vii) Service Bureau Licenses (Form B.3.2)

Most software license agreements require payment through some form of advance payment and/or milestone payments with final payment due upon installation and acceptance. Service bureau licenses are usually priced and paid on a per "transaction" basis and billed monthly. The actual billing structure is dependent on the type of software involved. For example, with cellular telephone billing software, the license fee may be based on the number of subscriber bills printed, or with electronic medical records, on the number of patients in the database. Service bureau licenses are usually utilized when the software is very expensive, and the licensee wishes to conserve cash flow by paying by the transaction instead of purchasing an outright license. On a long-term basis, a service bureau license is usually less cost-effective, although it may allow a licensee to switch vendors more easily as the licensee has less money "invested" in the software.

(b) Professional Services

Many parties seek to combine software licenses and development contracts and/or maintenance obligations into one agreement. A breach of the development obligations is a breach of the entire agreement. This permits a licensee to make its purchase of the software license contingent upon successful development or customization of the software. However, a risk with this approach is that in the case of the licensor's bankruptcy, the bankruptcy trustee cannot terminate a software license under Section 365(n) if the licensee continues to perform. If the licensee has numerous obligations relating to the license, development requirements, and/or maintenance obligations, it is unclear as to whether a court will allow the trustee to void the license. To avoid this risk, the parties should enter into separate and distinct agreements. For a more detailed discussion of the issues related to bankruptcy, see Chapter 27.

Most license agreements with a software development component provide for payment on a time and materials basis or on the basis of certain pre-agreed milestones. Each structure has certain benefits for both the licensor and the licensee. The ultimate payment structure chosen by the parties will reflect the allocation of risk agreed to by the parties.

(i) Time and Materials (T&M).

Under a time and materials methodology, the vendor charges the customer for each hour a resource/individual works on a matter based on a pre-agreed hourly rate set forth on a schedule/rate card, shifting the cost risk to the customer. Given the fluid nature of services, are usually provided on a time and material basis or a fixed price basis. Occasionally, a licensee may seek to have the licensor provide services on a time and materials basis with a not-to-exceed price. This is not advantageous to the licensor, as the licensor bears all of the risk. If the licensor can deliver the services in an efficient manner, it has no upside, but if the project takes longer than estimated, its fees are capped. T&M contracts provide for payment to the licensor based on direct labor, paid at specified labor rates; and materials paid at cost. In a T&M contract, a prudent license will seek to limit out of pocket costs to 15 percent of the labor costs.

T&M contracts usually are based on a set menu of labor categories and rates. The negotiated rates for labor vary, based on the level of experience and qualifications of each labor category. The customer specifies the work, usually through a statement of work, and the licensor proposes a mix of labor from the labor categories. Materials usually take the form of travel or equipment purchases incidental to the task and are usually estimated with the provision that if they exceed the estimated amount, the customer's prior written consent is required. The licensor is paid the fixed hourly rate for each hour worked, regardless of the cost to deliver that hour, plus materials at cost. Often customers require a monthly/daily rate reflecting a discount off the hourly/daily rate and define a "day" as a minimum of eight hours regardless of the number of hours worked. To prevent being billed more than eight hours a day, revenue is booked on a monthly basis based on the number of hours delivered, multiplied by the labor category for each individual, plus materials at cost. The fee is included in the hourly rates, and all hours and materials are billed monthly in arrears.

A time and materials structure is preferable when the scope of work is not definitive to allow the parties to agree on a fixed price. This places the risk on the customer, as there is no limit on the price charged by the licensor and payment is not tied to the receipt of a deliverable. A prudent customer should be hesitant to enter into a time and materials contract. An estimate of the number of hours or price to complete the work should provide the customer little comfort. Estimates are nonbinding and the customer has no protection in the event the work is not completed within the parameters of the estimate. *See Denniston and Partridge Co. v. Mingus*, 179 N.W.2d 748 (Iowa 1970) (estimated cost is not a fixed price); *Beeler v. Miller*, 254 S.W.2d 986 (Mo. App. 1953) (estimate did not constitute contract to furnish labor and materials for a certain price).

A time and materials structure is appropriate for engagements where the contractor provides expert support personnel to a customer on an ongoing basis and the work is subject to change as time passes. In a time and materials contract, the licensor's risk is in staffing the contract with qualified personnel at rates within the negotiated hourly rates, including indirect costs. The licensee's risk comes from the licensee's lack of a fixed price, placing the licensee at risk if the licensor exceeds its budget/estimate or has unanticipated problems.

(ii) Fixed Price.

Under a fixed-price model, the vendor will perform a specific amount of work/create a specific deliverable for a fixed price. A fixed-price model creates certainty for the customer, as it knows how much it will pay for the contracted services or product. The vendor, bears the risk of any cost overruns.

A licensor can perform work for both services and product deliveries on a fixed-price basis. Services may include items such as help desk responses, software maintenance services, or reports processed. Products may include a system or software deliverable. Revenue is earned based on delivery of specific services to the customer or in the case of a product, as milestones are met.

A fixed price offers the licensor a greater opportunity for profit because the licensor bears a greater share of performance risk, in return for a higher profit opportunity. At the same time, if the licensor significantly underestimates the scope of work, its losses could be significant.

Payment on a time and materials basis is preferred by the licensor, as the licensor is paid as it renders its services, greatly reducing the risk of nonpayment, while, at the same time, eliminating the risk of underestimating the cost of a project. The greatest risk to a developer in a fixed-price contract is that it significantly underestimates the costs involved. If a large contract experiences overruns in the time and labor to finish the project, the overrun can cost the developer tens of millions of dollars. At the same time, without a fixed price, the licensee can never be certain what the cost of the software will be until acceptance. Cynical licensees believe that the developer/licensor has no incentive to limit costs in the absence of a fixed-price contract because it bears no economic risk, thus increasing the cost to the licensee.

The licensee is usually billed on a monthly basis for time and materials contracts. For complex projects, payment on a time and materials basis is not favorable for licensees as the licensee cannot be sure that at the end of the project the services will have been satisfactorily performed. Making substantial contemporaneous or even up-front payments to the licensor greatly reduces the licensee's leverage in the event of a dispute with the licensor.

(iii) Time and Materials with a Cap.

Some licensees seek to implement a time and materials pricing methodology with a fixed cap on price. From the licensor's perspective, this billing mechanism is undesirable. Unlike a fixed-price contract where the licensor can realize additional profit by delivering the project under budget, under this mechanism, the licensor lacks the ability to realize any additional profit because it is being paid on a time and materials basis. Further, unlike a time and materials contract, the licensor assumes the risk that the project cannot be completed on time and on budget. The licensee is protected from any cost overruns by the licensor and receives the financial benefit if the licensor delivers under budget. Like a fixed-price contract, the licensee can budget a definitive amount for the project without any concern of a cost overrun.

2. *Price Indexing (§ 8.4)*

If a license agreement envisions that ongoing services will be provided on a time and materials basis for an extended period of time, both parties will likely seek to limit their pricing risk by establishing an objective basis for increasing the contracted hourly labor rates. This is usually achieved through a pre-agreed annual price increase, i.e., 5% a year, or through indexing the licensor's fees to a government index such as the Consumer Price Index (CPI). Often, the parties will negotiate a cap and a floor on such indexes in the event they experience a dramatic increase, a period of remaining flat or even deflation. When selecting an index, the parties should be careful to correctly identify the chosen index in the agreement and provide an alternative index in the event the chosen index is no longer maintained or applicable. *See, e.g., Seattle-First Nat'l Bank v. Earl*, 565 P.2d 1215 (Wash. App. 1988) (agreed-upon index was non-existent); *Metz Farms v. Fisher Sand & Gravel Co.*, 2006 WL 1047067 (D.S.D. Apr. 17, 2006) (vaguely drafted clause referring to "consumer's price index" litigated for vagueness).

Both parties should carefully choose the appropriate index to use. Many parties simply select the CPI without realizing that the CPI may not reflect the parties' costs. The CPI includes a wide range of costs including gas, real estate food and other expenses that have no bearing on the cost of labor that the licensor will be providing. The recent spike in interest rates and the drastic increase in house prices have impacted the overall CPI. If any price increase is tied to the CPI, the licensor should clearly state that its prices cannot decrease in the event the selected index is negative for the period in question.

A better measurement may be the *US Consumer Price Index: Information Technology, Hardware and Services* which tracks costs associated with the information technology industry, as opposed to consumer products. If the services will be performed outside the United States, the parties should select an index from the relevant country such as the all-India Consumer Price Indices (CPI) on base 2010= for use with Indian labor. Finally, if prices are not quoted in U.S. dollars, the licensor should hedge any currency risk. See § 8.4 for a number of indexes that may be appropriate to determine any cost increase.

For a discussion of the considerations of international licensing, *see* Loza, Chotkowski, Stevens, & Urbanchuk, *Financial Considerations in International Intellectual Property Licensing Transactions*, 23 COMPUTER & INTERNET LAW. 9 (Sept. 2006).

3. *Payment*

(a) Purchase Orders, Invoices and Payment Terms

Many customers issue purchase orders to vendors for administrative or tracking purposes. These purchase orders should not amend or alter the terms of the parties' agreement as usually, purchase orders are issued electronically and may not be reviewed by the vendor once received. Prudent vendors should include language in their agreements stating that any purchase order issued by the customer will not impact or amend the term of the parties' agreement.

> *Any purchase order or other document issued by Customer (including any online terms as part of a required procurement process) is for administrative convenience only and any such terms will not alter or supplement this Agreement, or in any way bind Vendor.*

All payments should be due within 30 days at receipt of the licensor's invoice. Some licensors seek to require payment within 30 days of the date of the invoice, but there is no assurance that the invoice will be properly dated. Many licensees seek to include language to the effect that the licensee's payment obligation matures once it has received a "proper invoice." What constitutes a "proper invoice" is subject to interpretation, and in its most extreme form, a licensee could refuse to make payment based on even the smallest inaccuracy. A more prudent approach from the licensor's perspective is to state that the invoice must be in the proper form and to attach an invoice in the proper format to the agreement as an exhibit.

(b) Credit Concerns

Licensors should place great emphasis on the creditworthiness of any potential licensee. The current recession has placed significant financial stress on many companies. Too often they are unable to pay or refuse to pay after the licensor has provided the contracted deliverable.

Licensors should undertake a number of steps to limit any inherent credit risk in contracting with a particular licensee. The licensor should undertake a detailed examination of the potential licensee's credit history. Some licensors will tailor their contractual terms, requiring more restrictive financial terms, to reflect any increased financial risk. See Form O.5 for a model credit evaluation process.

In addition, the licensor should insist on including language in the underlying agreement allowing it to terminate the agreement without cause in the event the licensee's creditworthiness declines. In addition, the licensor should obtain the ability to increase its prices if the licensee's credit quality slips during the contract term or, in the alternative, require a payment bond at the time of contract signature to ensure payment by the licensee. Finally, the licensor should consider using letters of credit, performance bonds, and guaranties to limit its payment risk

(c) Disputed Fees and the Escrow of Disputed Amounts

A prudent licensor will ensure that the contract allows the licensee to withhold payment if it has notified the licensor of the dispute in advance and if the licensor has had the opportunity to respond to the licensee concerns. In the event of a dispute, the licensee should be obligated to make payment on the undisputed amount, and if the contract is for a significant amount of money, the amount the licensee can withhold should be limited. The failure to pay undisputed amounts should constitute a material breach and a basis for termination. Undisputed fees should never be withheld.

Licensors should insist that in the event of a dispute, the disputed amounts should be placed in an interest-bearing account with a third party, such as a bank. The agreement should clearly state that the licensee is not allowed to simply offset the amount in dispute or allege a dispute and not make payment. Requiring the licensee to place the amount in dispute into escrow will discourage the licensee from specious claims, as it will not retain possession of such amounts. The failure to place the disputed amounts into escrow should be a material breach of the agreement. Otherwise, the licensor lacks any leverage to force the licensee to disgorge the amounts in dispute.

(d) Interest (§ 8.5)

Most agreements provide for the payment of interest in the event a party fails to make timely payment. Usually, the parties include language setting forth the agreed-upon interest rate but provide that in no event should such rate exceed the maximum amount allowed by law (§ 8.5). Most parties insert this phrase to avoid violating any applicable usury laws. Interestingly, at least one court has held that a state's usury laws do not apply to interest on overdue license fees. *Bexer County Ice Cream Co. v. Swenson's Ice Cream Co.*, 859 S.W.2d 402 (Tex. 1993) (absent a loan of money or loan payments, interest charged on IP license did not meet Texas's definition of a usurious transaction). The party seeking to invalidate the interest provision bears the burden of proof to show it is usurious. *Domizio v Progressive County Mut. Ins. Co.*, 54 S.W.3d 867, 874 (Tex. App. 2001).

Some agreements provide that the interest rate shall be the "Prime Rate." Because there is not an agreed-upon Prime Rate, the relevant provision should reference a particular bank—for example, the prime rate offered by Citibank or its successor. Further, because the Prime Rate fluctuates, it is much more complicated to compute the interest due than if the parties used a fixed rate. See Form B.6.1 § 3.5 for model language based on the Prime Rate.

Most licensees will seek to remove any interest provision from the agreement, and some licensors will not resist believing that they will be unlikely to collect interest without going to court and that if they do go to court, the court will impose the state's statutory interest rate on any judgment. If a licensee is willing to agree to a contractually stated interest rate, the interest rate should correspond to the licensor's "cost of funds" when borrowing from a bank. The reason for paying interest is that the licensor is losing use of its funds while the amounts in question are unpaid and thus must borrow. Thus, the licensee should pay interest on the past-due amounts at a rate close to the licensor's cost to borrow.

(e) Foreign Currency Risk

Given the financial uncertainty in Europe, the licensor should consider whether it is prudent to price every sale in U.S. dollars to eliminate currency risk and the possibility that the euro may cease to be a currency. If the euro ceases to be a currency and the contract is priced in euros, how will the correct payment amount be determined?

Acceptance testing should be based on a licensor-determined standard, such as conformance with the licensor's documentation.

Lawyers reviewing a transaction to ensure compliance with ASC 606 should look for a number of warning signs that may indicate an attempt to accelerate revenue recognition in violation of ASC 606. Potential red flags include the provision of road maps to the licensee, backdating contracts to another fiscal period, side letters that alter business terms or obligations, extended warranties, unusual discounts, upgrades or free services, and conditional payment terms such as rebates, payment in advance for uncompleted work, and payment subject to extraordinary events or conditions. To avoid any problems, a prudent lawyer should have all terms reviewed by the licensor's finance department.

For more information on ASC 606, *see* asc.fasb.org.

(b) SaaS Revenue

Even though customers use a software element within software-as-a-service (SaaS) subscription-based arrangements, they generally do not have a contractual right to take possession of the software at any time during the hosting period without significant penalty, or to either run the software on their own hardware or contract with an unrelated third party to host the software. Accordingly, SaaS arrangements, including the fees within the arrangements, are accounted for as subscription services provided all other revenue recognition criteria have been met. The subscription revenue is recognized in a manner reflecting the customer's use of the software, such as on a straight-line basis over the service period.

K. Taxes (§ 8.6)

1. Sales Tax

Often considered boilerplate, the "taxes" provision in license agreements has assumed increasing importance due to continuing changes to federal, state, and local tax laws. Traditionally, software was taxed on the value of media on which it resided (the disk or tape) and services were not taxed. As taxing jurisdictions have encountered tighter budgets, they have sought new sources of revenue, especially in the area of technology licensing.

Today, many jurisdictions tax not only the sale of software, but also ancillary services such as support, customization services and maintenance. *See, e.g., Verizon North, Inc. v. Combs*, 308 S.W.3d 1 (Tex. 2009) (computer software is taxable as tangible personal property); *Dechert v. Commonwealth*, 998 A.2d 575 (Pa. 2010); *TekSystems, Inc. v. Chumley*, 2009 WL 1312835 (Tenn. Ct. App. May 11, 2009). As such, it is very important for both parties to understand where the software will be "delivered." Given that most software is downloaded from the web, the licensee should download the software in a location that will minimize its tax liability.

The applicable structure is ever-changing, creating a significant administrative burden for a licensor without an internal tax department or full-time outside auditor to remain current. As such, the licensor should make sure the license agreement clearly establishes that the licensee is responsible to pay all taxes except those taxes on the licensor's net income. The term "taxes" should be defined as broadly as possible to include any new taxes or form of taxes that may be implemented during the term of the agreement.

From the licensee's perspective, the licensee cannot budget with absolute certainty because it may be unable to anticipate whether new taxes may be imposed over the life of the contract. Nonetheless, in most cases it is the licensee's responsibility to pay such taxes. The licensee can reduce its risk by contractually requiring the licensor to cooperate with it to limit any tax liability and in any appeal of taxes the licensee believes have been wrongly imposed. Further, because it is the licensor's obligation to collect any taxes due, the licensee should seek to have the licensor indemnify it in the event the licensor fails to properly calculate and collect the appropriate taxes. In such case, the licensor should be responsible for paying any interest and penalties due. Given the ever-changing nature of state and local taxes, prudent licensors should avoid any indemnification of the licensee related to taxes or assume any liability for uncollected taxes.

Another manner in which the parties can limit the licensee's tax liability is through the allocation of the consideration among the different products and services provided. Often, taxing jurisdictions have varying tax rates for different types of services and products. Tax rates also vary among different jurisdictions. To the extent they are able to do so, the parties should examine the possibility of delivering the products and services in jurisdictions with lower tax rates and allocating the stated consideration to those aspects of the transaction that are taxed at a lower rate. In seeking to limit the licensee's sales tax liabilities, the licensor should be careful not to increase its own income tax liabilities.

2. *Employee-Related Taxes (Form Q.2.UU.1, 2 and 3)*

The licensor should also include language to address Section 162(a) of the Internal Revenue Code, which requires the licensor to recognize reimbursed expenses such as travel, lodging, and related expenses as taxable income to its employees who remain on an assignment outside of their home state for more than 12 months. *See* I.R.C. § 162(a); IRS Revenue Rulings 93-86 and 99-7. While the licensor must reimburse the employee's living expenses and income taxes, it must also gross up the employee's compensation to compensate for the increased tax burden. On a large project with a significant number of employees working at the licensee's site, these costs can be significant. See § 8.6 for model language addressing this issue.

The licensee should be aware that it will be charged these costs and should budget accordingly. It can limit its risk by contractually limiting the licensor's travel and expense costs to a percentage of its professional fees, such as 15 percent, and defining these additional tax costs as part of the licensor's travel and expense cost, not consulting fees.

3. *Foreign Taxes (Form Q.2.UU.4)*

Some licensors seek to pass on cost of taxes levied by foreign states arising from the licensing of the software in such countries. They do so under the argument that the licensee is responsible for paying all taxes except for taxes on the licensor's net income. Prudent licensees reject this position, arguing that it was the licensor's decision to enter into the particular geographic market and thus the licensor should bear the cost of such taxes. By agreeing to gross up payments to the licensor to negate the financial impact of such taxes, the licensee will likely significantly increase the cost of the software.

In the event the licensee is required by law to withhold any amount from any payment made to the licensor, the licensee should make such withholding and pay the amount withheld to the relevant taxing authority. The licensee should obtain from the taxing authority a certificate of payment of such withholding tax or deduction in such form as shall be acceptable to the tax authorities having jurisdiction over the licensor. and forward it to the licensor. Further, the licensee shall provide to the licensor proof of payment of any tax deduction made by the licensee. The licensor should have the right to have the licensee contest with the taxing authority, at the licensee's expense, any such taxes that the licensor believes are improperly levied.

> *All payments by the Customer shall be made free and clear of any deductions or withholding for taxes, contributions or otherwise and of any liability thereof. In the event the Customer is required by the laws of the territory in which the Software is licensed to withhold any amount from any payment made hereunder, the relevant amount payable shall be increased by such amount as may be necessary in order that the actual amount received by Licensor after such withholding shall equal the amount that would have been received had no withholding been required, and the Customer shall make such withholding and pay the amount withheld to the relevant taxation authority. Customer shall obtain from the competent authorities and forward to Licensor a certificate of payment of such withholding tax or deduction in such form as shall be acceptable to the tax authorities having jurisdiction over Licensor.*

A more practical approach is for the parties to cooperate to limit or lessen the impact of such taxes. For example, jurisdictions tax services, royalties and goods at different rates. To the extent they are able, the parties should allocate the fees paid to the licensor to those categories that are taxed at a lower rate.

> *The Parties agree to reasonably cooperate with each other in good faith to more accurately determine and reflect each Party's tax liability. Each Party shall provide and make available to the other any resale certificates and other exemption certificates or information reasonably requested by either Party. The Parties will also work together to segregate the charges, reimbursements, expenses, and other amounts payable hereunder, into separate payment accounts charged under separate invoices, as appropriate, for Services and the components of the Services (i.e., components that are taxable and non-taxable, including those for which a sales, use, or similar tax has already been paid by Vendor and for which Vendor functions merely as a paying agent for Customer in receiving goods, supplies, or services including licensing arrangements that otherwise are non-taxable or have previously been subjected to tax, components that are capitalized, and components that are expensed).*

L. Third-Party Software and Intellectual Property

Most proprietary software incorporates third-party materials and software into the product. As such, licensors and licensees should understand any licensing restrictions on the use of such third-party software and products as well as any restriction on licensors' ability to allow its licensees to access such software and products. A detailed review should be undertaken of all open-source, third-party commercial software and other non-licensor materials as well as the underlying license terms. The licensor must obtain the appropriate license grants for the uses customers require, and not limit its ability to sell its products. Prudent licensors and licensees will create a Bill of Materials (BOM) for all the licensed products that contain the third-party components and the license terms for such components to ensure that the licensee's use rights are consistent with the license terms of the third-party products. *See* SAP. Further, to the extent the vendor is using a subcontractor to furnish part of the deliverables, the agreement between the vendor and its subcontractor should clearly establish which party is responsible for obtaining the necessary intellectual property rights to allow the customer's use of the deliverables. *See Erickson Products, Inc. v. Kast*, 921 F.3d 822 (9th Cir. 2019).

PRACTICE POINT:

Often a software solution may incorporate third-party software whose license terms require the licensor to pass through the third party's license terms to the ultimate end user, i.e., the licensor's customer. This requirement arises with the use of both commercial and open-source software. Prudent licensors address this requirement by including links to the relevant software licenses. Doing so ensures that the referenced license is current. Licensors should avoid attaching licenses to the document, as such licenses will likely become outdated, potentially placing the licensor in violation of its contractual commitments. Model language is as follows: *This software incorporates third-party software with their own terms and conditions, which you are required to follow [and download and purchase at your own cost/expense]. Attachment A contains links to these third-party terms and conditions.*

M. Purchase of Licenses by Affiliates

Many master agreements define "Licensee" in the heading or preamble of the agreement to include the licensee and all of its affiliates, some of whom may be foreign entities. This arguably allows the licensee's affiliates to utilize the agreement to purchase their licenses, but in the process the licensee/parent entity potentially becomes a guarantor of its affiliates' obligations, which the licensee should seek to avoid. From the licensor's perspective, the agreement should clearly state that the licensee is responsible for its affiliates' breach or non-payment.

Prudent parties should carefully address how affiliates will participate under the license agreement, giving consideration to issues related to financial considerations, the applicability of foreign law, and how the affiliates will license software under the master agreement between a licensor and licensee who are incorporated in the United States. There are several ways for the parties to approach this issue.

The easiest solution is to simply provide in the agreement that affiliates may in the future, on an as-needed basis, enter into separate agreements incorporating the terms of the underlying agreement, deviating only to the extent necessary to capture needed changes in commercial terms (tax, currency, etc.), local business conventions, and local legal constraints (privacy laws, export, etc.). This defers having to negotiate to any local country addendums in advance but allows flexibility in the approach. This is probably the best approach for agreements that, while anticipated to be global, start out as a U.S. agreement only or have only one or two foreign affiliates' needs.

A second method, which poses some risk, is to contemplate that the licensee's affiliates will obtain licenses via a purchase order arising under the master terms, and that the purchase order specific "agreement" will be deemed to be exclusively between the regional entities. The underlying licenses may contemplate some country-specific differences in pricing, or local currency use but at a very high level. The risk of nonbinding terms will be absorbed by both parties. Presumably financial terms (currency, taxes) will be addressed in the price.

A third method for allowing international affiliates to access the software but that entails more effort requires the parties to incorporate terms by country for local participation in the various countries in which they are going to do business. In effect, the parties will create an exhibit that has sub-exhibits containing the local points of deviation by country. The parties will need assistance from each geographic region in defining the list and then more help from local counsel in the region (either in-house or external) in terms of ensuring that the parties address all relevant legal issues. This requires a greater initial effort and extends the length of the negotiations, but when completed, the license agreement is finished and does not need to be revisited at a later date. Extending the length of the negotiation process sometimes benefits the customer as the underlying transaction is held hostage. The level of detail and treatment can be negotiated on a case-by-case basis.

For model Local Country Participation Addendum, see Forms E.4.2 and E.4.3.

N. Licensee Obligations

Too often licensors focus on negotiating the licensor's obligations with the licensee but fail to memorialize the licensee's obligations in the underlying agreement. The licensee's obligations are no less important than the licensor's obligations and should serve as a condition precedent to the licensor's obligations. The licensor should ensure that the underlying agreement sets forth in detail the licensee's obligations. These may include the required hardware and software to operate the licensor's software, as well as any facilities that will be required. If applicable, the license agreement should clearly set out the licensor's ability to access the licensee's facilities and networks.

At the same time, the agreement should provide that the failure of the licensee to meet these obligations will excuse the licensor's performance and, in the event such failure is material, allow the licensor to terminate the agreement for the licensee's breach. Known as "savings clauses," these provisions should clearly state that the licensor's obligation to perform is contingent on the licensee's performance. The licensor should avoid relying on general language stating that the licensee will provide reasonable cooperation to support the licensor's efforts.

See Form B.8.4 for model language setting forth the licensee's obligations.

O. Changes to Features and Functionality; Sunsetting

Prudent customer should consider the likelihood of the vendor sunsetting or stop supporting the software when it develops new products and solutions. At that time, the customer may be faced with the prospect of having to purchase the new solution or having to support and maintain the software itself. To avoid this issue, the customer can protect itself by requiring the vendor:

(i) To provide maintenance and support at a pre-agreed price for x years after the customer purchases the software;
(ii) Require the vendor to provide x months prior written notice before it stops supporting the software,
(iii) To upgrade the customer to the new version without cost if the vendor stops supporting the customer's software within x years of the customer purchasing the software, and
(iv) To make all enhancements backward compatible.

If Licensor deletes any features or functionality from the Software or Services and transfers the same (either directly or through an agreement with a third party) to other or new products or services, the portion of those other or new products or services that contains the features or functionality in question, or the entire product or service, if such features and functionality cannot be separated out, shall be (a) provided to Licensee under the terms of this Agreement at no cost to Licensee and (b) covered under the support and maintenance terms applicable to the Software and/or Services at no additional cost to Licensee.

Licensor agrees to make the Supported Software compatible with upgrades, enhancements, modifications and/or changes in the Third-Party Software and/or in the technology platform, operating system, web-browsers, and databases for which the Software is designed within three (3) months of the general availability of said Third-Party Software, technology platform, operating system, web-browser or databases, as applicable. Licensor shall provide at least twelve (12) months prior written notice before the termination of any Maintenance Services or the end-of-life date of any Software.

CHAPTER **6**

Boilerplate

Unless otherwise indicated, all section references (§) refer to the corresponding sections of the Annotated Software License and Services Agreement set forth in Form B.3.1.

"Boilerplate" has been defined as "standard clauses lifted from other agreements on file or in form books." FARNSWORTH, CONTRACTS § 7.1 at 426 (3d ed. 1999). Many practitioners consider boilerplate those provisions that appear at the end of an agreement. Boilerplate has assumed increasing importance, such that at least one book has been written on the subject, and the University of Michigan Law School held a symposium on boilerplate, "Boilerplate: Foundations of Market Contracts Symposium," at the University of Michigan Law School September 23–24, 2005. *See* 104 MICH. L. REV. (March 2006). *See, e.g.*, STARK, NEGOTIATING AND DRAFTING CONTRACT BOILERPLATE (2003).

Practitioners often pay scant attention to these boilerplate clauses. Subtle nuances in an agreement's boilerplate, however, can have important and unrealized ramifications on the parties. *See* Burr & Tinnen, *Boilerplate Blunders: 12 Mistakes to Avoid When Drafting Commercial Contracts*, 37 ACC DOCKET 52 (Oct. 2019); Weise & Bistrow, *Boilerplate Provisions in Transactional Documents*, 20 CAL. BUS. L. PRAC. 33 (2005). Although parties never enter into an agreement with the expectation of litigation, a skilled lawyer can significantly reduce a client's risk in the event of litigation through thoughtful drafting.

The discussion set forth in this chapter is intended to guide readers through the thought process they should undertake when reviewing and drafting the "boilerplate" provisions of an agreement.

A. Recitals and Headings (§ 53)

1. Recitals

The recitals of an agreement are often viewed as a perfunctory necessity of little importance. While recitals are not mandatory, they can be very important. Recitals give the parties the opportunity to set forth their respective intents for entering into the agreement and provide context to the agreement as well as the factual background. Recitals should not transcend a recitation of the facts to include any terms related to the actual transaction. *Golden West Baseball Co. v. City of Anaheim*, 25 Cal. App. 4th 16, 37 (1994) ("Recital C is not a recital . . . it is not a mere recitation of facts but contains the operative language."). From a litigation perspective, "less is more."

Operative terms such as "will" and "shall" should not be included in the recitals, only in the body of the agreement, as ambiguity and conflict may arise if deal terms included in the recitals conflict with the body of the agreement. Further, a recital should not operate as a representation or warranty or used to define terms.

A properly drafted recital may provide a subtle advantage to a party in the event of a dispute. In general, the recitals are not considered to be a substantive part of the contract, but rather they describe the parties' purposes or objectives and are used in the interpretation and construction of the contract. Depending on the jurisdiction, however, recitals can have a material impact on the interpretation of an agreement. *See people v. Forsyth*, 292 P.3d 1248, 1258 n.95 (Colo. O.P.D.J. 2012) ("Principles of contract law instruct that recitals "should be reconciled with the operative clauses of the contract and given effect as far as possible." *See also* 17A C.J.S. Contracts § 403 ("although 'whereas' clauses do not control over the express provisions of a contract, they may be read in conjunction with the contract's operative portions to ascertain the parties' intention, where the operative clauses are ambiguous") (citations omitted). *Jones v. City of Paducah*, 142 S.W.2d 365, 367 (Ky. 1940).

While each party should be free to set forth their individual intent, licensors should reject any attempt by the licensees to insert overbroad, self-serving statements designed to place the licensor at a significant disadvantage in the event of litigation. Licensors should not agree to statements of fact that essentially serve as additional representations and warranties, such as the following:

> **Whereas** *Licensor is the world leader in the implementation of Enterprise Resource Planning Systems (ERP).*
>
> **Whereas** *Licensor has the expertise and experienced employees to install and support a worldwide, world-class ERP system.*
>
> **Whereas** *Licensee has relied on Licensor's skill in selecting Licensor to implement the system.*

The parties should be especially cautious in those states where recitals involving a statement of fact are considered to be conclusive evidence of the facts stated. *See, e.g., Detroit Grand Park Corp. v. Turner*, 25 N.W.2d 184 (Mich. 1946). *See also* CAL. EVID. CODE § 622. Other jurisdictions, however, have found that recitals are not binding on the contracting parties. *See Int'l Trust Co. v. Palisade Light, Heat & Power Co.*, 153 P. 1002, 1003 (1916) ("Recitals which are general, and not contractual, merely descriptive, are not binding."); *Dornemann v. Dornemann*, 850 A.2d 273, 281 (Conn. Super. Ct. 2004) ("Recitals in a contract, such as 'whereas' clauses, are merely explanations of the circumstances surrounding the execution of the contract and are not binding obligations unless referred to in the operative provisions of the contract.") (quotation omitted).

Prudent parties should ensure that the agreement states that the recitals do not expand a party's obligations under the agreement beyond those set forth in the body of the agreement. If the licensee insists on including self-serving recitals, the licensor should insert a recital stating it is the parties' intent that the licensor make a reasonable profit and that the recitals only be looked to in the event of an ambiguity within the agreement.

2. *Headings (§ 53)*

Practitioners disagree as to the importance of section headings and whether they should be used for assistance in interpretation or used only as finding aids.

Headings are often a single word and are often viewed as clarifying the intent of the parties. *See, e.g., Windsor Sec., Inc. v. Hartford Ins. Co.*, 986 F.2d 655 (3rd Cir. 1993). As such, it is impossible to summarize the intent of a paragraph in one word or even a few words. Headings cannot create ambiguity and cannot be considered operative provisions. *Georgia-Pacific v. OfficeMax Inc.*, 2013 WL 5273007 (N.D. Cal. Sept. 18, 2013).

Courts generally find that headings do not have material effect. *Seidensticker v. The Gasparilla Inn, Inc., et.al.*, 2007 WL 2764872 (Del. Ch. April 24, 2007). At least one court, however, has held that a contractual provision containing a warranty disclaimer set forth under a misleading section heading was void. *See Blankenship v. Northtown Ford, Inc.*, 420 N.E.2d 167 (Ill. App. 1981). As such, the parties should ensure that each section heading clearly reflects the provision it contains and include language that clearly indicates the section headings are for convenience of reference only and are not intended to have any substantive significance.

B. Definitions (§ 1 and Form Q.1)

The "Definitions" section and the definitions contained therein are one of the most important but overlooked parts of an agreement. Creating a definition specific to a contemplated transaction allows the parties to avoid subjecting themselves to the "ordinary" meaning of the word in question as determined by a third party. The failure to create clear definitions by using jargon and knowledge unique to the parties creates uncertainty and ambiguity. A carefully drafted definition may limit or even shift liability. The parties should not use a tradename to identify the software to be delivered to the licensee, as the tradename may transcend many different versions of the software. Further, never define a term using the term itself.

The definitions set forth in § 1 and in Form Q.1 are no exception. Some have been drafted to benefit the licensor and some the customer. A skilled lawyer must read each definition carefully to ensure that it does not place the lawyer's client at a disadvantage. Further, each definition must be read in light of the contemplated transaction as the meaning of each definition may vary with each transaction. Defined terms evolve to recognize the changes in the technology industry. For example, the definition of "source code" used 25 years ago would not necessarily protect the licensee's interests today, as it would likely fail to encompass new technologies such as html, Web browsers, and so on.

The definitions set forth in Form Q.1 serve as examples of how a practitioner should seek to draft definitions to benefit their clients. Further, a review of these definitions may raise issues not initially contemplated by a party or that may have been overlooked. Form Q.1 should serve as a starting point in creating or reviewing a definition. The parties should resist the temptation to utilize a form definition from a prior transaction and instead craft definitions that capture the unique nature of the transaction they are negotiating.

Contracting parties are free to alter the ordinary meaning of a term to better fit the intended meaning employed by the parties, and in the event of a dispute, a court will be bound by this interpretation—assuming the definition is properly written. FELDMAN &

Nimmer, Drafting Effective Contracts: A Practitioner's Guide 2d. ed. (2005 Supp.), § 2.02[L].

The definitions of the "Users," "Authorized Users" and "Affiliates" are especially important, as they serve to limit who may access and use the licensed software. This is especially true if the licensee is incorporating the licensed software into a product which will be accessed by third parties. Further, the licensee will likely want to allow access by its contractors to maintain and support the licensed software. The parties should use caution in "defining" the parties and other entities in the agreement. A party may later claim that such "shorthand" definition modified the parties' intent or could otherwise have unintended consequences. *See, e.g., Roanoke Engineering Sales Co., Inc. v. Rosenbaum*, 290 S.E.2d 882, 884 (Va. 1982) (defendant, who was an officer and director of plaintiff corporation, claimed use of the term "Employee" to identify defendant in his employment agreement and limited the applicability of his non-compete obligations).

C. Insurance (§ 38)

1. General Insurance

The allocation of contractual risk can be achieved through a number of mechanisms, including the assignment of contractual responsibilities, indemnification, limitations of liability and the use of insurance. Insurance is a means to transfer or reduce financial risk, as it allows a third party (the insurer) to assume the risk that otherwise would be borne by one of the contractual parties. It also ensures that a party has the resources to pay any damages, as opposed to indemnification, which is purely a risk-shifting/reimbursement mechanism.

Neither party should assume that a risk can be completely mitigated through insurance, as insurance may be cancelled or inadequate to cover the loss, may become too expensive to maintain, may not cover a claim, and is subject to policy terms, conditions, and exclusions. Further, relying on insurance coverage as the sole remedy will potentially defy public policy by creating potential moral and morale hazards.

(a) Types of Insurance

Most licensees seek to require the licensor to purchase minimum amounts of insurance. Usually, the licensor is required to carry the following coverage:

- Commercial General (public) liability, including products/completed operations coverages, bodily injury, property damage, personal and advertising injury unless otherwise specifically excluded for covered indemnity obligations and negligence. (Note that the breadth of indemnity provisions in most contracts is much broader than the level of coverage in insurance policies is ever intended to cover; i.e., indemnities use language such as "any and all.")
- Automobile liability, which covers third-party bodily injury and property damage from owned, non-owned and hired automobiles as well as covering the commercial entities' own vehicles for damage, subject to comprehensive and collision deductibles and, when elected, Uninsured and Underinsured Liability.

- Workers' compensation (Part A) / employer's liability (Part B), which covers work-related injuries to the licensor's employees. Part A is a statutory coverage and does not have limits; Part B has limits. Coverage Part A is what responds to 99.9 percent of all known claims.
- Umbrella/excess liability insurance, which provides higher limits above the primary limits for general liability, automobile, and employer's liability insurance.
- Crime insurance (fidelity or employee dishonesty insurance) for dishonest acts of employees, including some computer fraud and theft of money or property, including the client's property when third-party crime coverage terms are added. *See G&G Oil Co. of Indiana, Inc. v. Continental Western Insurance, Co.*, 165 N.E.3d 82 (Ind. 2021) (Court evaluated application of commercial crime insurance to the facts of a ransomware attack).
- Professional liability insurance (Errors and Omissions) to respond to claims for wrongful acts and negligence arising out of professional services. Most professional liability policies are "claims-made" policies, which require that a claim be reported during the current policy period. Claims-made policies often include terms requiring that they be continued for a set period of time beyond the term of the license contract. The length is often determined by state-specific statutory reporting time frames. In addition, the ability to purchase Extended Reporting Period coverage varies depending on the carrier's ability to meet coverage requirements after a policy is cancelled or is not renewed by the insured.
- "All risk" property insurance, to cover a licensor's property and the property of clients in a licensee's custody. A licensor may also be required to demonstrate that it has Business Income / Extra Expense coverage to provide a continuation of funds to cover interrupted or ceased revenue to pay for continuing costs and lost profits in the event of a covered cause of loss.

Licensees and licensors may want to purchase/obtain coverage for vicarious liability arising from the sale or distribution of a product designed and manufactured by a third party; this is commonly referred to as Vicarious Liability Coverage under a Commercial General Liability policy.

Commercial General Liability (CGL) policies cover personal injury and property damage as well as loss to tangible property, but not intangible property like software. While many CGL policies exclude coverage for claims arising out of trade secret or intellectual property infringement, the court in *Crum & Foster Specialty Ins. Co. v. Willowood USA LLC*, 696 Fed. Appx. 22 (9th Cir. 2017) found that trade secret theft could potentially trigger coverage under a party's CGL coverage.

Cyber-liability insurance covers two types of claims:

1. Extortion payments made in connection with an attempt to alter or destroy data, misappropriate PII or PHI, denying access to a system or introducing malware; and
2. The costs and expenses arising from responding or preventing an extortion attempt, as these damages are traditionally not covered by professional liability insurance.

Given that the General Data Protection Regulation (GDPR) adopted by the European Union imposes fines and penalties up to 4 percent of a company's gross revenue, prudent customers should explore purchasing cyber insurance. A combined Cyber and Errors and Omissions (E&O) policy is now more prevalent due to the fact that a cyber breach could also be construed an error or omission by the Insured's client.

While some insureds have been successful in recovering for cyber losses under CGL insurance, most insurance companies are unlikely to look favorably on such claims.

Policies are incorporating more restrictive terms and exclusions to make it clear cyber losses are not covered under a General Liability policy. Further, there is no standard policy for cyber insurance, making it difficult to compare policies offered by different insurers, although carriers are now reviewing their competitors' coverage options in order to remain competitive and, where appropriate, adding similar coverages.

Most cyber insurance is issued on a "claims made basis"—i.e., it only covers claims made during the term of the policy. Thus, a "claims made" policy would not cover a claim once the policy has lapsed, although prudent parties can purchase an extended period of indemnity option, the terms of which are included in the policy at inception. Further, most insurers will, upon request, add an additional insured under a cyber policy.

Cyber liability policies offer both first-party coverage for resources and costs related to duties in accordance with local state requirements for notification as well as covering fines and penalties (per policy terms and conditions) and liability brought by third parties related to the breach. It is incredibly important to review a cyber policy for its insuring agreements and exclusions, which can vary widely from carrier to carrier. In particular, the social engineering and cyber-crime coverage carriers range in first-party and third-party coverage offerings; most cyber-crime coverage in a cyber policy carries a sublimit of $100,000 or $250,000 in coverage.

> *Vendor shall, at its own expense, maintain each year during the Term of this Agreement and each Order Form a Cyber Liability insurance policy of no less than $5,000,000 per claim. This limit can be satisfied through a primary policy or a combination of primary and excess/umbrella policies and shall not be construed to relieve Vendor from liability in excess of such limits. Such insurance policies shall include Customer as an additional insured (except workers' compensation and professional liability) and shall be provided by insurance companies that are rated "A-" or better by AM Best or similar local rating agency if not subject to AM Best. Upon written request, Vendor shall provide Customer with proof of insurance in the form of a certificate of insurance.*

In *National Ink and Stitch, LLC. v. State Auto Property and Casualty Insurance Co.*, 435 F. Supp. 3d 679 (D. Md. 2020), the Federal District Court of Maryland found that the insured was entitled to coverage for a ransomware under a property insurance policy based on the loss of software and data as well as the loss of functionality to the computer system itself. The *National Ink* case is important, as the court found an insured may potentially recover on a claim even if it does not have specific cyber insurance.

For a more detailed discussion of cyber insurance, *see* Hathaway, *Everything You Need to Know About Cyber Liability Insurance but Never Knew to Ask*, 34 Comp. & Internet Law. 18 (Apr. 2017); Chesler & Yousef, *Insurance Disputes Over Cyber Claims: Current and Future Flashpoints*, 34 Comp. & Internet Law. 20 (Sept. 2017); Nelson &

Simek, *Cyber Insurance: Necessary, Expensive and Confusing as Hell*, 36 Comp & Internet Law. 19 (Mar. 2019); Johnson, *21st Century Insurance, CYBER Insurance*, 36 Comp. & Internet Law 15 (Aug. 2019); Garczynski, *Protecting Firm Assets with Cyber Liability insurance*, Bus. L. Today (Sept. 2016); Garczynski, *Protecting Against Cyber Threats: A Lawyer's Guide to Choosing a Cyber Liability Insurance Policy* (2d ed. ABA Press 2020).

PRACTICE POINT:

In reviewing a cyber insurance policy, a prudent party should consider the following:

Insurance should cover the following risks:

- Network security
- Privacy liability
- Media communications liability
- Reputation/brand protections
- Data breach
- Data loss – business interruption insurance and contingent business interruption (due to a vendor or third party's business interruption that renders the insured unable to transact business)
- Regulatory response and defense costs
- Systems damage
- Ransomware

The following costs and damages should be covered:

- Notification costs
- Legal fees
- Investigation costs
- Lost or corrupted data recovery
- Ransomware fees
- Loss mitigation (i.e., credit monitoring)
- Public relations/crisis management costs
- Business interruption fees
- Regulatory fines and penalties
- Third-party fines
- Litigation costs

(b) Additional and Named Insureds

During the term of the agreement, many licensees seek to be named as an "additional insured" on the policies the licensor is required to maintain, in the belief that they will receive preference in the payment of any claims. A "named additional insured" is "a person or organization not automatically included as an insured under an insurance policy who is included or added as an insured under the policy at the request of the named insured." https://www.irmi.com/term/insurance-definitions/additional-insured.

The licensor should resist adding the licensee as an additional insured to the licensor's E&O policy unless pressured by the licensee. A licensee can be named as an additional insured under the licensor's general, umbrella and automobile liability insurance policies, but cannot be named under the licensor's workers' compensation policy, as the licensor's employees are not employed by the licensee. An "alternate employer" endorsement is sometimes used on workers' compensation policies to provide limited coverages for the customer. Further, the licensee should not be an additional insured under the licensor's professional liability policy, as the licensee is usually the party bringing the claim.

A licensee should not be a "named insured" or "additional named insured." A named insured can order changes to the policy, is responsible for payment of policy premiums and deductibles, and is obligated to perform certain duties, such as making representations in an application, reporting and cooperating with claims, maintaining records, and allowing audits. Further, if the licensee is named on a policy, the licensee would be unable to claim under the policy, as a named insured cannot seek indemnity under the policy for a claim against itself (or another insured).

While the terms are sometimes used interchangeably throughout the insurance industry, there are often misunderstandings of the obligations involved, so licensors prefer to use "additional insured" for consistency in their contracting practices.

The licensee may be a loss payee under a property insurance policy if the policy holder has custody of the licensee's property. Usually, the governing insurance policy requires the policy holder to report the location and value of the licensee's property in its possession. A party can also be a loss payee under a crime insurance policy if the policy holder's employees hold positions where the client's property could be stolen.

(c) Licensor Obligations

The licensee should also seek to contractually require the licensor to notify the licensee prior to making any material changes in the licensor's coverages or terminating or cancelling any policy. While these demands are reasonable, the licensor should carefully consider any additional demands that may impact the licensor's ability to operate its business in a prudent manner.

Some licensees seek to dictate in detail the parameters of the licensor's insurance coverages, including the type of coverages carried, the dollar amount of such coverages, and the credit rating and financial size of the carrier through which the insurance is purchased, as well as requiring the chosen carrier to be licensed in a particular state. Licensors should not allow the licensee to select the insurer to provide the required coverages or require that the licensor's insurer be licensed to do business in a particular state as long as the insurer is able to pay any claims submitted on the licensee's behalf and is legally authorized to do business in the state in question. Further, licensors should be hesitant to allow the licensee to establish a minimum credit rating that the insurer must maintain.

Prudent licensees should require the licensor to submit proof of insurance prior to execution of the license agreement and again prior to the execution of any statement of work to ensure that the licensor has obtained the required insurance and has maintained the policy in good stead. Licensors should not provide the licensee with copies of its insurance policies, only certificates of insurance, as the insurance policies are the proprietary information of the licensor. The licensee has no need to see the actual policies. Most policies contain similar standard language; thus, the licensor can easily provide a summary of the policy's principal terms in lieu of providing the licensee with a copy of the actual policy. To avoid any unintended cap on its ability to recover from a licensor, licensees should make sure the license agreement clearly states that the licensee's recovery is not limited by the amount of the licensor's insurance. (§ 38)

The licensee should require the licensor to maintain the agreed-upon insurance beyond the termination of the contract. This requirement is inapplicable to "occurrence" policies such as general liability insurance, but is applicable for "claims made" policies, such as E&O insurance.

(d) Coverage

Failure to maintain any required insurance coverages should not be treated as a material breach of the agreement, as the licensee has not suffered an actual loss from the failure to maintain such coverages. From the licensee's perspective, it is faced with the issue of how to enforce its rights if the licensor's failure to comply does not constitute a material breach. Licensors will argue that the licensee is not at risk as long as the licensor has a net worth sufficient to satisfy any claim. In essence, the licensor is self-insuring, and the breach should be treated as immaterial. The licensee is not prejudiced and is essentially in the same position as if the licensor were contractually allowed to self-insure.

Occasionally, in the event of a lapse, a licensee will seek the right to purchase the contractually required coverages and pass on the cost to the licensor or offset the cost of any such premiums against money owed to the licensor. It is unlikely that the licensee would be able to purchase insurance to cover the licensor's non-performance. What insurance company would be willing to insure an unrelated third party's performance? The licensee would be unable to purchase worker's compensation insurance, as the employees in question would not be employed by the licensee. The licensee would also be unable to purchase professional liability insurance for the licensor's performance. Further, to the extent the licensee is able to obtain the desired insurance, this right to "cover" may create a financial risk to the licensor, as the licensee may not act in the licensor's best interest financially. The licensor may mitigate this risk by limiting the licensee to purchasing such insurance from a well-respected broker representing a highly rated insurance company or requiring the licensee to obtain three quotes and accepting the lowest price.

(e) Self-Insurance

Many large companies retain a certain level of their risk either through self-insurance, large deductibles, or retentions. If a licensor seeks to negate any requirement to maintain a certain insurance coverage because it self-insures, the licensee should make sure it understands the nature of the licensor's self-insurance and the licensor's ability to pay any claim. Does the licensor self-insure all of its risk, only a certain portion, or only a certain type of risk? For example, the licensor may self-insure up to $10 Million of liability and purchase third-party insurance for any liability above that amount, or it may self-insure only for its automobile coverage. Only by thoroughly understanding the nature and limits of the licensor's coverages will the licensee be able to quantify the licensee's risks.

> *Vendor may elect to self-insure, in whole or in part, in the amounts and types of insurance required herein* ***subject to the following requirements:*** *Vendor will (i) maintain a separate reserve or trust for its self-insurance, (ii) provide to Customer a copy of the most recent evaluation of its self-insurance funds prepared by an independent actuary, (iii) warrant that its self-insurance fund will comply with applicable Laws and regulations, and (iv) fund its self-insurance funds in accordance with the recommendations of the independent actuary and ensure that funds are available at all times to pay claims in the amounts required by this section. The funding of deductibles and self-insured retentions, if any, maintained by Vendor are the sole responsibility of Vendor, including any deductibles or self-insured retentions applicable to claims involving Customer.*

(f) Subcontractors

The licensee should make sure the licensor flows down all insurance requirements to its subcontractors to ensure the licensee is protected. A licensor should not agree to add its sub-contractors to its own policies and should not name its subcontractors as additional insured.

(g) Indemnity

A licensor should not indemnify the licensee for injuries to the licensor's employees caused by the licensee's negligence. Both parties most likely pay for no-fault workers' compensation. Requiring the licensor to pay the ensuing general liability claim for the licensee, in essence, is requiring the licensor to pay twice. For a more detailed discussion, *see* Gesellschap & Hicks, *The Interplay Between Indemnification Provisions and Insurance Clauses in Contracts for Goods and Services*, 32 ACC Docket. 47 (Mar. 2014).

(h) Subrogation

A waiver of subrogation is a waiver of the common-law right to recover damages from a responsible party. Subrogation allows the insurer to step into the shoes of its insured after paying off the insured for the claim. The insurer can then pursue the claim against the party that caused the loss. Waivers of subrogation can apply to general and automobile liability as well as workers' compensation, crime and property insurance. A waiver causes a party to be responsible for its own loss, which is usually extended to the party's insurers. Any subrogation waiver should be reciprocal.

When the customer demands that the vendor waive rights of subrogation against the customer or, alternatively, obligates that the vendor secure a waiver of subrogation from the vendor's insurer, the customer is essentially attempting to insulate itself from liability caused by its own negligence. For this reason, subrogation waivers are only meaningful in those situations in which the customer could conceivably be the source or cause of the insurable loss.

A request for a subrogation waiver should be carefully considered. Because subrogation is a means by which insurers recoup their losses, most insurance policies require the insured not to take any action that could impair the insurer's subrogation rights. Accepting a waiver of subrogation without consulting the entity's insurance broker or carrier could constitute breach of the insurance policy, providing a basis for denying coverage. Many insurers and brokers are willing to provide an endorsement of subrogation waiver for an additional fee.

Today, most policies (except workers' compensation and some professional policies) now include waiver of subrogation terms automatically with the policy form, as long as it is done in advance of a loss or claim.

(i) Certificates of Insurance

Many agreements require the insured party to provide the counterparty with a certificate of insurance from the insured's insurance company stating that the insured has purchased the required coverages. These certificates are of limited value, as they serve to certify that on the date and time the certificate was issued, the insured carried the required insurance. The insured, however, could have cancelled its insurance shortly after the certificate was issued, rendering the certificate meaningless.

2. Intellectual Property Infringement Claims

(a) Errors and Omissions Insurance

Most errors and omissions (E&O) insurance policies contain very broad and clear exclusions for patent and trade secret infringement. Generally, a licensor's comprehensive or commercial general liability ("GCL") policy includes coverage for "advertising injuries." A claim for intellectual property infringement may fall under the coverage for advertising injury. *See, e.g., Hyundai Motor America v. National Union Fire Insurance*, 600 F.3d 1092 (9th Cir. 2010) (insurer must indemnify patent infringement claim as advertising injury).

A prudent licensor should carefully evaluate its CGL policy and (E&O) policy to ascertain whether its existing policy will provide coverage in the event of a claim of intellectual property infringement, and if not, the licensor should seek an intellectual property endorsement. Insured should carefully examine the definition of a "claim" under its policies to ensure that the definition is broad enough to encompass any potential risks or factual circumstances that may arise. Policies will be read strictly. *See, e.g., FirePond Liquidating Trust v. Vigilant Insurance Co.*, 2007 WL 2695642 (D. Minn. Sept. 11, 2007) (information (E&O) policy does not cover contract dispute). Given the increasing costs to defend such claims, many insurers are modifying their policies to exclude coverage for claims related to intellectual property, advertising and internet-related claims. To the extent the insured lacks the breadth of coverage it desires, it may want to obtain specialized insurance for internet-and cyberspace-related claims.

In the event of a claim, a party should carefully read its policy and promptly place its carrier on notice. The carrier is likely responsible for paying not only any award entered against the insured, but also the cost of defense.

For a more detailed discussion of insurance coverage for claims of intellectual property insurance, *see* Brothers, et al., *Coverage for IP-Related Risks*, 149 INTELL. PROP. COUNS. 1 (May 2009).

(b) Patent Infringement Insurance

Patent infringement insurance is usually segregated into two products: defensive coverage (where the insured is sued) and offensive coverage (where the insurer pays for the insured to enforce its patents against an alleged infringer). Defensive coverage is the most common form, as offensive coverage is often difficult to purchase.

Most policies require the insured to cede significant control to the insurer in managing any defense or claim. The insured should be comfortable with the role and authority of the insurer in any litigation and subsequent settlement. Some defenses, such as defense of the Named Insured, may not be able to be transferred and should not be assumed. In addition, defense provisions within management liability policies (D&O, EPL, Fiduciary, and Professional E&O) are very specific and part of the negotiated terms. Further, the insured should read the terms of its policies carefully and retain outside counsel specializing in insurance law and intellectual property law to assess a policy's actual coverage. Insurance companies often interpret the "metes and bounds" of their coverage obligations narrowly, seeking to deny an insured's claim or severely limit the policy's coverage. The insured should also investigate whether the insurer has a history of litigating with its customers over claims. *See, e.g., Carlson Mktg. Group v. Royal Indem. Co.*, 517 F. Supp. 2d 1089 (D. Minn. 2007).

3. *PRACTICE POINT*: Reviewing and negotiating an insurance provision

In negotiating an insurance provision, the parties should consider the following points:

- Words such as "obtain" and "procure" should be deleted, as each party most likely already maintains coverage.
- Additional insured status should be modified to include "for covered claims to the extent Licensor owes Licensee an indemnity under this Agreement" as well as adding "As Their Interests May Appear Only."
- Limits should be described as "per occurrence (or per claim) and in the aggregate" for general liability, excess, professional, and crime coverage.
- An insured should provide no details or only minimal details describing the scope of its coverage.
- Most parties will not have and will not agree to purchase intellectual property infringement, cyber-liability, or network security/privacy liability insurance unless their business activity specifically includes risk inherent to cyber or breach potential.
- A prohibition on a waiver of subrogation or subrogation should only apply to workers' compensation.
- Evidence of insurance should be provided in the form of certificates of insurance, and a party should not commit to provide copies of its policies or endorsements. There should be no requirement for a licensor to use a licensee-created certificate of insurance document.

- Notice should be provided only in accordance with policy provisions. Insurers or brokers will no longer consistently agree to "endeavor" to provide 30 days' notice of cancellation only.
- Using insurance as a risk transfer strategy should not expand that party's liability by providing coverage (intentional or unintentional) to another party via the terms of a contract.

4. Tying the Agreement's Limitation of Liability to a Party's Insurance Coverage

Some parties seek to tie the vendor's liability to the amount of vendor's insurance coverage. For example, if the vendor is able to recover from its insurance company an amount in excess of the agreement's limitation of liability, the agreement's limitation of liability is increased to equal the amount of the excess recovery. Prudent customers should reject any attempt by the vendor to limit its liability to the amount of its insurance coverage or the amount it recovers from its insurer.

> *Notwithstanding the forgoing, if the coverage amount under any insurance policy Vendor is required to maintain pursuant to Section __ (Insurance) exceeds the amount of the limitation of liability defined in this Article ___, such limitation of liability shall be deemed to equal the amount of such coverage to the extent insurance proceeds in such excess amount are recovered under the applicable insurance policy. Vendor shall vigorously pursue any applicable policy claim as required by Customer.*

D. Force Majeure (§ 33)

1. Overview

Force majeure ("a superior force" in French) clauses are intended to excuse a party's performance in the event the party's ability to perform is thwarted by unforeseen events outside of its control, such as an act of God. The concept of *force majeure* arises under contract, not under common law, although Section 1511 of the California Civil Code does recognize the concept of *force majeure* (a performance obligation is excused "when it is prevented or delayed by an irresistible, superhuman cause, or by the act of public enemies of this state or of the United States, unless the parties have expressly agreed to the contrary."). Thus, in most cases, a party seeking to excuse its performance may only invoke the doctrine of *force majeure* if the parties' agreement contains a *force majeure* clause.

Although there is no generally agreed definition of *force majeure*, *Black's Law Dictionary* defines "force majeure" as "[a]n event or effect that can be neither anticipated nor controlled." BLACK'S LAW DICTIONARY (9TH ed.). *Force majeure* is not limited, however, to the equivalent of an act of God. *Pacific Vegetable Oil Corp. v. C. S. T., Ltd.*, 29 Cal. 2d 228 (1946).

States address *force majeure* differently. There is a split among the different jurisdictions as some will only recognize an event of *force majeure* if the event is specifically identified in the agreement's *force majeure* clause. Others will give meaning to broad catch-all language. *U.S. v. Caterpillar, Inc.*, 277 F. Supp. 2d 73 (D.D.C. 2002). Another dichotomy exists among different jurisdictions as to whether an event must be unforeseeable. Some require that the event must be unforeseeable while others require only that the performance is impracticable, or the event is outside a party's control.

Note that in many European common law countries, *force majeure* is statutorily defined, preventing the parties from contracting around the definition.

To determine whether an event constitutes an event of *force majeure*, a court will examine whether an insuperable interference occurred without the party's intervention that could not have been avoided by the exercise of prudence, diligence, and care. Events that are reasonably foreseeable do not constitute an event of *force majeure* and do not excuse performance. *See URI Cogeneration Partners, L.P. v. Board of Governors for Higher Educ.*, 915 F. Supp. 1267 (D. RI. 1996); *Watson Labs., Inc. v. Rhone-Poulenc Rorer, Inc.*, 178 F. Supp. 2d 1099 (C.D. Cal. 2001).

Foreseeability can be subjective. If an event such as a pandemic has occurred in the past, is it foreseeable? Did the 2009 global avian flu pandemic make COVID potentially foreseeable, and thus not an event of force majeure? What about future pandemics? At least one court has interpreted a force majeure clause that included natural disasters to encompass the COVID 19 pandemic. *JN Contemporary ART LLC v. Philip Auctioneers LLC*, 507 F. Supp. 3d 490 (S.D.N.Y. 2020). Even though a pandemic may itself not constitute an event of *force majeure*, governmental actions in response to the pandemic may constitute an event of *force majeure*.

Under law of many jurisdictions, an "act of god" excuses a party's performance only to the extent the underlying agreement contains a *force majeure* clause. *See e.g., GTPMC, Inc. v. Texas City Ref., Inc.*, 822 S.W.2d 252, 259 (Tex. App. 1990). While in some jurisdictions, performance will be excused if the event causing the "non-performance" is specifically identified. *In re Cablevision Consumer Lit.*, 864 F. Supp. 2d 258, 264 (E.D.N.Y. 2012).

Force majeure clauses are narrowly construed. *Kel Kim Corp. v. Central Markets, Inc.*, 519 N.E. 2d, 295 (N.Y. 1987). To invoke the protections of a *force majeure* clause, the event must be beyond a party's control and not due to its own fault or negligence. *Gulf Oil Corp. v. Federal Energy Regulatory Commission*, 706 F.2d 444 (3d Cir. 1983), *cert. denied*, 464 U.S. 1038 (1984). Because of these limitations, companies carry business interruption insurance even though their injuries may arise from an act of God, such as a flood.

The customer should carefully consider the wording of any clause, as an overly broad *force majeure* clause may undercut any service-level agreements or the vendor's performance obligations. Further, the clause my supersede any common law defences a party may have such as impracticability, impossibility, frustration of purpose. *Commonwealth Edison Co. v. Allied-General Nuclear Services*, 731 F. Supp. 850 (N.D. Ill. 1990). At the same time, the vendor should seek to ensure that the clause is not so narrowly drawn as to restrict the vendor's ability to excuse performance for conditions beyond its control.

Practically speaking, *force majeure* clauses excuse only the vendor's performance, as usually the customer's only affirmative obligation is to pay the vendor. Nonetheless, the customer should insist on making any *force majeure* clause mutual.

The party seeking to excuse its performance "bears the burden of proof of establishing the defence." *Bayou Place Ltd. P'ship. v. Alleppo's Grill, Inc.*, 2020 WL 1235010 (D. Md. Mar. 13, 2020).

PRACTICE POINT:

Depending on the jurisdiction, courts require the following to find an event of *force majeure:*

- *An unforeseeable event;*
- *An express mention of the event in the underlying agreement/a force majeure clause*
- *Which causes a party's non-performance.*

2. Defining Force Majeure

Drafters usually take one of two approaches in defining events of *force majeure*:

Listing those events whose occurrence is deemed to constitute an event of *force majeure, See, e.g., Hearst Commc'ns, Inc. v. Seattle Times Co*, 115 P.3d 362 (2005) (*force majeure* clause provided neither party would be liable to the other for any failing arising from *force majeure* events such as war or labor strikes); or

Utilizing very broad language stating any act outside the control of the parties is deemed to be an event of *force majeure, See, e.g., TransAlta Centralia Generation LLC v. Sicklesteel Cranes, Inc.*, 142 P.3d 209 (2006) (defining *force majeure* as an event that (i) was not within either party's control, and (ii) which could not have been prevented through due diligence).

Each of these approaches has it benefits and drawbacks. With the first, many elements of the list of events may or may not be relevant to a particular transaction. Further, if an event is not listed, does that mean it does not constitute an event of *force majeure*? This is important; given this provision is intended to protect against unforeseen events, how can the parties possibly predict all possible events? For example, very few parties foresaw the COVID-19 pandemic, but it is a safe bet that almost all *force majeure* clauses will include "pandemic" going forward.

If the parties adopt the second approach using broadly drafted language, many events that are not truly events of *force majeure* may fall under the language of the agreement. A lack of specificity results in ambiguity which may lead to a dispute. For example, is an economic downturn or a recession an event of *force majeure*? Is a significant increase in inflation causing the vendor's labor costs to increase beyond what the vendor forecasted an event of *force majeure*? Some courts have held that an event must be unforeseeable to fall under a catch-all force majeure provision. *TEC Olmos, LLC v. Conoco Phillips Company*, 555 S.W.3d 176 (Tex. 2018). Most courts are willing to accept the parties' contractual agreement. *Route 6 Outparcels, LLC v. Ruby Tuesday, Inc.*, 931 N.Y.S. 2d 436, 438 (3d Dept. 2011) ("when the parties themselves defined the contours of force majeure in their agreement, those contours dictate the application, effect and scope of force majeure.")

Many customers are hesitant to include labor strife or strikes within the list of events constituting an event of *force majeure* as theoretically they are within the control of the respective employer. Further, the non-performance of the vendor's subcontractors should also not be considered an event of *force majeure*. Thus, a prudent customer should specifically state that the failure of a vendor's subcontractors to perform shall not excuse the vendor's performance. One way to address this issue is to draft the agreement's *force majeure* clause in such a way that it addresses the different obligations of the vendor. Thus, a vendor may be excused from performing one aspect of a contract but not another upon the occurrence of the same event.

The agreement should address whether presidential decrees, sanctions, tariffs and other unforeseen changes in laws and regulations will constitute an event of *force majeure*. *See Kyocera v. Hemlock Semiconductor, LLC.*, 886 N.W.2d 445 (Mich. 2015) (denying plaintiff 's motion to claim Chinese government involvement in solar panel market which depressed prices an event of *force majeure*).

Customers should carefully consider the definition of *force majeure* in their agreements as some vendors seek to include events such as internet service provider failures, ransomware attacks, data breaches/hackings creating internal delays as well as denial of services attacks. Prudent customers should reject the inclusion of these and similar events as these are not *force majeure* events, but rather internal security failures on the vendor's behalf. This is especially true if the customer has purchased business continuity and disaster recovery services from the vendor, the purpose of which is to ensure there is no interruption of access and services. To avoid a potential dispute, the underlying agreement should explicitly provide that such events are not events of *force majeure*.

Force Majeure shall not include the following occurrences:

a. *A denial of services attack or a hacking resulting in a data breach;*
b. *Late performance by a Subcontractor unless the delay arises out of a force majeure occurrence in accordance with this force majeure term and condition;*
c. *foreseeable events; or*
d. *government imposed shutdowns.*

Each party should carefully review any list of events to ensure that each event is truly an event of *force majeure* and is not simply an effort to expand a party's ability to limit its risk and avoid performance. Some courts will only excuse performance to the extent an event is set forth in an agreement's *force majeure* clause. *Kel Kim Corp. v. Central Markets, Inc.*, 519 N.E. 2d, 295, 296 (N.Y. 1987).

A more prudent approach is tailoring the clause to the governing law and, alternatively, to utilize a combination of approaches to illustrate events the parties believe to be acts of God. See § 33. If a party adopts a hybrid approach, at least one court has held a *force majeure* clause does not relieve a contracting party of the obligation to perform, unless the disabling event was unforeseeable at the time the parties made the contract. *TEC Olmos, LLC v. Conoco Phillips Company*, 555 S.W.3d 176 (Tex. 2018)

Each party shall be excused from performing any of its obligations hereunder, in whole or in part, as a result of delays caused by the other party or a Third Party or by an act of God, war, riot, civil commotion, explosion, fire, government action, epidemic, pandemic, state of emergency, court order, epidemic or other circumstance beyond its reasonable control, but specifically excluding labor and union-related activities and the non-performance of any Vendor subcontractor, regardless of cause. If any of the above-enumerated circumstances prevent, hinder or delay performance of either party's obligations hereunder for more than thirty (30) calendar days, the party not prevented from performing shall have the right to terminate this Agreement without liability or penalty as of the date specified by such party in a written notice of termination to the other party.

3. Notification

A comprehensive *force majeure* provision should detail the requirements of the notice provision including;

- How quickly notice must be given after the event occurred;
- What information must be included in the notice, e.g.:
    - A description of the event of force majeure,
    - A description of how the force majeure impacted the notifying party,
    - How long the event of force majeure is expected to last, and
    - What actions the notifying party is taking to mitigate the delay; and
    - When the event of force majeure is expected to end.

4. Additional Terms

While defining "*force majeure*" is important, it is equally important that the agreement's *force majeure* clause be sufficiently detailed to avoid ambiguity and a potential dispute.

- Will a claim of *force majeure* be time-barred if the claim is not made in a timely manner?
- What actions must the party claiming an event of *force majeure* take to mitigate the impact of the event?
- Must the party claiming an event of *force majeure* continue to perform those obligations that were not affected?
- If a party claims an event of force majeure, is the unaffected party's performance excused as well?
- What rights does the unaffected party have?
    - Disaster recovery
    - Business continuity
    - Step in rights
- How long must the event of force majeure continue before a party may exercise its rights (i.e., terminate the agreement)?
- Which party may terminate the agreement?
- What happens if the parties do not agree that an event of *force majeure* arose?
- What terms of the agreement apply if an event of *force majeure* arises:
    - governing law?
    - dispute resolution?
    - injunctive relief?

5. *Impact on Performance*

Generally, a party's performance is excused only from those obligations impacted by an event of force majeure. *Idaho Power Co. v. Cogeneration, Inc.*, 9 P.3d 1204 (Idaho 2000). For example, the trend toward remote working may limit the ability of a party providing software development services to invoke the doctrine of *force majeure* in the event of a future pandemic as the contracted services may be performed remotely.

An event of *force majeure* does not terminate an agreement but rather excuses a party's performance during the period the event of *force majeure* is in existence. *Commonwealth Edison Co. v. Allied-Gen Nuclear Servs.*, 731 F. Supp. 850 (N.D. Ill. 1990). A party seeking to invoke the protection of a *force majeure* clause can do so only after using its skill, diligence and good faith to perform. *Oosten v. Hay Haulers Dairy Employees and Helpers Union*, 291 P.2d 17, 20–21 (Cal. 1955); CORBIN ON CONTRACTS § 1342.

Both parties should insist on having the right of termination if the event of *force majeure* continues for a set period of time. While this right to terminate may be a hollow right, if every vendor is affected by same the event of *force majeure*, it could be a significant benefit to the customer if a third party could deliver the contracted for software or services. From the vendor's perspective, the vendor does not want to keep a project fully staffed while it waits for the event of *force majeure* to abate. If the vendor is unable to terminate its performance after a set period, it may have to staff a project for which it will not be compensated. The parties should also address whether an event of *force majeure* that continues for a set period of time triggers the release of any source code escrow. Additionally, the customer should include an exclusion of the vendor's disaster recovery obligations from the *force majeure* provision.

The parties should definitively state that a change in the economic conditions underlying a contract's performance, or the economy itself does not constitute an event of *force majeure*. While this position is clearly supported in the case law, it does not hurt to include an affirmative statement to this effect in the contract. *U.S. v. Panhandle Eastern Corp.*, 693 F. Supp. 88, 98 (D. Del. 1988) ("economic hardship due to market fluctuations in the natural gas industry did not constitute a *force majeure* event."); *Chainworks, Inc. v. Webco Indus.*, Inc., 2006 WL 1521946 (W.D. Mich. May 31, 2006); *Marionneaux v. Smith*, 163 So. 206 (La. 1935) (unforeseen economic depression is not an event of *force majeure*).

Model language from the perspective of the party affected by the other's delay:

If any such event of force majeure occurs and such event continues for thirty (30) days or more, the party delayed or unable to perform shall give immediate notice to the other party, and the party affected by the other's delay or inability to perform may elect at its sole discretion to:

(a) terminate this Agreement upon mutual agreement of the parties;
(b) suspend such SOW for the duration of the condition and obtain or sell elsewhere Software or Services comparable to the Software or Services to have been obtained under this Agreement; or
(c) resume performance of such SOW once the condition ceases with the option of the affected party to extend the period of this Agreement up to the length of time the condition endured.

Unless written notice is given within thirty (30) days after the affected party is notified of the condition, option (c) shall be deemed selected.

6. *Other Potentially Applicable Theories*

Beyond *force majeure*, the doctrines of *quantum meruit*, impracticability and frustration of purpose may apply.

To the extent a vendor claims it is excused from performance by an event of *force majeure*, a customer who has paid for undelivered services may be entitled to recover any monies paid to the vendor under the theory of *quantum meruit*. *See Facto v. Pantagis*, 915 A.2d 59 (N.J. Super 2007) (plaintiff entitled to recover monies paid for event cancelled by *force majeure*).

Commercial impracticality may also be applicable. Commercial impracticality is a concept arising under the UCC and the Restatement (Second) of Contracts closely related to the doctrine of *force majeure* that applies in the event a party's performance is thwarted by events outside its control that was not anticipated by the parties. *See* UCC § 2-615; RESTATEMENT (SECOND) CONTRACTS § 261. For a more detailed discussion including the doctrine of commercial impracticality, *see Commercial Impracticality as an Excuse for Contract Performance*, 38 THE LAW. BRIEF 1 (Sept. 15, 2008); Classen, *Judicial Intervention in Contractual Relationships under the Uniform Commercial Code and Common Law*, 42 S.C. L. Rev. 379 (1991).

Commercial frustration is another doctrine that may be applicable. Commercial frustration arises when, after a contract is executed, a party's purpose for entering the agreement is frustrated without its fault by an event the nonoccurrence of which was a basic assumption on which the contract was founded. In such event, the party's performance is excused. RESTATEMENT (SECOND) OF CONTRACTS § 261. *See Howard v. Nicholson*, 556 S.W.2d 477 (Mo. Ct. App. 1977); Bonora & Lipp, *May the Force be With You: Understanding Impossibility, Impracticability and Frustration of Purpose*, ACC DOCKET (Dec. 2020).

7. *PRACTICE POINT*: Checklist for drafting a comprehensive force majeure provision.

- Is *force majeure* limited to a list of identified events or a more conceptual approach, such as "acts of God"?
- Is the definitional approach to defining *force majeure* consistent with the nature of the transaction?
- Are foreseeable events considered *force majeure* events?
- Are economic issues considered *force majeure* events?
- Are certain events carved out from the definition of force majeure?
    - Business continuity obligations,
    - government shutdowns,
    - pandemics
    - foreseeable events,
    - subcontractors
    - labor disputes
    - equipment failures
- What are the parties' obligations upon the occurrence of an event of *force majeure*?

- What is the time period for providing the other party notice of the event of *force majeure*?
- What happens if the party fails to provide notice?
- What must be included in any notice of *force majeure:*
    - a description of the *force majeure*?
    - the expected length of the condition?
    - how is the impacted party seeking to mitigate the impact?
- What if a party disputes that an event of *force majeure* occurred?
- What is the obligation of the party claiming an event of *force majeure* to mitigate the impact?
- Who can terminate the agreement in the event of *force majeure*?
- After what period may they terminate the agreement?
- Will the impacted party be partially or fully excused from performance?
- Will the non-impacted party be partially or fully excused from performance?
- Does the *force majeure* language exclude events arising from the parties' actions or inactions?
- Has the *governing law been reviewed to understand its impact on* force majeure events?

For a more detailed discussion of the doctrine of *force majeure, see* Tanenbaum, *Force Majeure Is Not Just Boilerplate Anymore: Why Combining Force Majeure with Disaster Recovery Provisions Makes Sense*, 18 INTELL. PROP. & TECH. L.J. 17 (Oct. 2006); Klein & Glazer, *The Lowly Force Majeure: Why It Shouldn't Be Neglected*, START-UP & EMERGING COMPANIES 5 (NOV. 2000); *Covid 19 as a Force Majeure, But What is Force Majeure? My Contract Does Not Even Use That Term!*, 22 Under Construction (Summer 2020).

E. Public Disclosures and References (§§ 44, 50)

1. Public Disclosures (§ 44)

Often the licensee seeks to limit the licensor's right to publicize the fact that the licensee is a customer. The reason for doing can stem from a number of reasons including: the licensee's unwillingness to appear to endorse the licensor's product, especially when it is unknown at the time of contract signature whether the software implementation will be successful and the desire to protect the licensee's trademarks and service marks which are valuable assets that require a written license to fully protect and maintain their value. In addition, savvy licensees seek to avoid being associated with a particular licensor product as patent trolls often will sue a licensor's customers to force the licensor to the negotiation table.

On the other hand, the licensor may be required to disclose the existence of the contract if it is a publicly held company. As a result, the parties should carefully negotiate the wording of any publicity clause. The licensee may allow the licensor to publicize the existence of the contract, only to the extent necessary to satisfy any applicable securities laws or retain the right to approve any press release or use of the licensee's marks. Any consent granted by the license should address all applicable uses of the licensee's mark. For example, the agreed upon language should address not only written press releases and filings, but also the use of the licensee's name and marks on websites, product brochures, public speeches, and trade shows.

The licensor should ensure that it obtains the approvals and licenses necessary to use the licensee's name and marks. The failure to do so may result in the licensor's infringement of the licensee's trademarks and service marks. To avoid any potential problems, some licensees prohibit the licensor from disclosing, in any manner, that the licensee has a relationship with the licensor. The licensor should be careful, however, to ensure that it has the right to disclose whatever information is necessary to comply with any applicable laws or regulatory obligations, such as the disclosure obligations placed upon publicly held companies.

To avoid uncertainty, the parties should negotiate a joint press release prior to the execution of the agreement and attach it as an exhibit to the license. This will allow the parties to issue the press release simultaneously with the execution of the license and to surface any wording issues prior to the execution of the license.

2. *References (§ 50)*

Potential customers should ask the vendor for a list of all of the vendor's customers and seek the right to contact them to discuss their level of satisfaction with the vendor. Vendors will usually provide a potential customer with a vetted list of loyal customers who can be counted upon to provide excellent references. Discussions with these customers provide little value to the potential customer. The potential customer should seek to discuss the vendor's capabilities with a variety of customers, including disgruntled customers, to obtain a complete assessment of the vendor's capabilities.

Some customers require the vendor to use them as a reference on all future bids. The reasoning for doing so is that the vendor will likely make sure the customer is satisfied if it is required to use the customer as a reference. While this philosophy is rare, it does create incentive to produce the customer's deliverables on time and on budget. To enforce this obligation, some customers require a vendor to pay the customer a fee each time the vendor fails to use the customer as a reference. Vendors should resist including this language in their agreement as it grants the customer undue leverage.

F. Waiver (§ 31)

All agreements should contain a waiver clause that provides that a party's forbearance in enforcing a provision in an agreement does not prohibit that party from enforcing it in the future. The intent is to avoid a claim by one party that the other's actions or inactions waived that party's right to enforce a particular term of the agreement. *See Klipsch, Inc. v. WWR Technology, Inc.*, 127 F.3d 729 (8th Cir. 1997); *S.H.V.C. v. Roy*, 450 A.2d 351 (Conn. 1982). To avoid disputes, the provision should provide that all waivers must be in writing and that a waiver of one provision does not constitute a waiver of any other provision. *See Hovanian Land Investment Group LLC v. Annapolis Towne Centre at Parole, LLC*, 421 Md. 94 (2011) (party may waive a condition precedent by its action even though underlying agreement provides that all waivers must be in writing). Further, the failure to act or a delay in acting shall not constitute a waiver of any right or remedy.

A party may waive a non-waiver clause including by their conduct. *Bettelhem v. Hagstrom Food Stores, Inc.*, 113 Cal. App. 2d. 873, 878 (1952) ("a waiver clause may be waived by conduct"); *Lee v. Wright.* 485 N.Y.S.2d 543, 544 (N.Y. App. Div. 1985) ("It has long been the rule that parties may waive a no waiver clause . . . ."). Further, a prohibition on oral waivers may be waived. *Aircraft Services Resales LLC v. Oceanic Capital Co. Ltd.*, 586 Fed. Appx. 761 (2d Cir. 2014).

G. Waiver of Right to Jury Trial (§ 32)

With the increase in large jury awards that often include a significant component of punitive damages, many licensors seek to include jury trial waivers in their license agreements. If the parties choose to include a waiver, the waiver should be in a separate paragraph and conspicuous.

Many vendors believe that juries are incapable of understanding complex software/copyright matters and that judges are less likely to award punitive damages. Further, jurors may be influenced by the size of the licensee and its relationship with the community, as well as the number of people the licensee employs in the geographic area. The concern of punitive damages may be overemphasized, as punitive damages are only rarely awarded in contract disputes. Further, the risk of any award of punitive damages can be mitigated by disclaiming such damages in the agreement's limitation of liability clause. See, e.g., § 17.1 and Chapter 5.I.

Customers should carefully consider waiving their right to a jury trial. Many customers would prefer to utilize some form of alternative dispute resolution before waiving their right to a jury trial. Both parties should avoid the temptation to believe they can "shop" for a good judge. An exception may be the recent efforts undertaken by some states to create specialized business and/or technology courts to hear business/technology disputes in the belief such courts will make their states a more attractive place for businesses to locate. *See* Haig, *New York's New Business Court*, 26 COLO. LAW. 65 (May 1997). *See also* http://www.courts.state.md.us/businesstech (Maryland); http://www.ncbusinesscourt.net/final%20rules.htm (North Carolina).

The validity of pre-litigation jury waiver clauses is uncertain, as at least three states have held that prelitigation contractual jury waiver clauses are unenforceable. *See, e.g., Bank South N.A. v. Howard*, 444 S.E.2d 799 (Ga. 1994). The California Supreme Court found that a contractual agreement to waive the right to a jury trial, entered into prior to any dispute between the contracting parties, is unenforceable under the California Constitution and Section 631 of the CALIFORNIA CODE OF CIVIL PROCEDURE. *Grafton Partners LP v. Superior Court*, 88 P.3d 24 (2004), *aff'd*, 116 P.3d 479 (Cal. 2005). Subsequently, the Ninth Circuit Court of Appeals held that jury trial waivers signed under California law will not be enforced in federal court even if they were entered into knowingly and voluntarily. *In re County of Orange*, 784 F.3d 520 (9th Cir. 2015). Further, a choice of forum provision providing the governing law of a forum outside of California is unenforceable against California residents as it deprives the resident of a right to a jury trial which is guaranteed in the California constitution.

William West v. Access Control Related Enterprises, LLC, Case BC642062 (Sup. Ct. Cal. July 29, 2020).

Further, to limit any claim of unconscionability, the parties should make any waiver conspicuous and print such waiver in capital letters.

For a general discussion, *see* McGuire & Belzberg, *Are Jury Trial Waivers Coming of Age?*, 38 Md. B.J. 25 (Nov./Dec. 2005).

H. Governing Law and Venue (§ 28)

1. *Governing Law*

(a) *In General*

Copyright disputes are usually adjudicated under state law, subject to the provisions of federal copyright law. Federal law governs the interpretation of a license where state law conflicts with federal copyright law and policy. *S.O.S., Inc. v. Payday, Inc.*, 886 F.2d 1081, 1088 (9th Cir. 1989); *Foad Consulting Group, Inc. v. Musil Govan Azzalino*, 270 F.3d 821, 827 (9th Cir. 2001). As such, a choice of the law of a particular state may not have a material impact on those disputes involving copyright, patent and other intellectual property rights as opposed to contractual disputes. In recognition of this fact, many savvy practitioners preface their choice of law provision with "Except where governed by federal law . . . ."

Outside of federal copyright law, the laws of a particular jurisdiction could have a material impact on the interpretation of an agreement. As such, the parties should carefully evaluate the impact the laws of a particular jurisdiction may have on their agreement.

Although most parties instinctively seek be governed by the laws and venue of their own jurisdiction, the parties should carefully consider the benefits offered through the election of the governing laws of other jurisdictions. Part of the rationale for the software licensor's home state serving as the exclusive jurisdiction is the licensor's desire that any court rulings related to the licensor's intellectual property be consistent. Doing so guards against inconsistent court rulings in different jurisdictions which cannot always be avoided.

To be enforceable, however, many states require a nexus between the agreement and the choice of law. *See, e.g.*, *Airgo, Inc. v. Horizon Cargo Transport, Inc.*, 670 P.2d 1277 (Haw. 1983); *Navasota Resources Ltd. v. Heep Petroleum, Inc.*, 212 S.W.3d 462 (Tex. App. 2006); Restatement (Second) of Conflicts of Laws § 187 (1) (1971). Under the Uniform Computer Information Transactions Act ("UCITA"), which has been adopted only by Maryland and Virginia, the parties can choose any law regardless of whether there is a nexus to the states with which the parties have a relationship.

The comments to the Virginia code provide:

> In a global information economy, limitations of that type [reasonable relationship] are inappropriate, especially in cyberspace where physical locations are often irrelevant or not knowable. Parties may appropriately wish to select a neutral forum because neither is familiar with the law of the other's jurisdiction.

Va. Code Ann. § 59.1-501.9 cmt. 2a.

See subsection (xii) below for a more detailed discussion of venue and Chapter 15 for a more detailed discussion of UCITA.

In selecting the governing law, the parties should seek the existence of a well-developed body of law relating to software licensing and evaluate the state's other laws, such as whether the state is a contributory or comparative negligence state. A well-developed body of law increases the likelihood of a predictable outcome and in turn reduces litigation costs while increasing the likelihood of settlement. Similarly, some states allow contracting parties to require arbitration and contractually prohibit class action suits, while other states limit their ability to do so. *See Parrish v. Cingular Wireless, LLC*, 2005 WL 2420719 (Cal. App. Oct. 3, 2005), *cert denied*, 547 U.S. 1188 (2006) (arbitration agreement unconscionable because its class-action waiver operated as an exculpatory clause under California law); *Riensche v. Cingular Wireless*, 2006 WL 3827477 (W.D. Wash. Dec. 27, 2007) (court determined that the prohibition against class actions was "unconscionable" and denied the defendant's motion to compel arbitration); *Vasquez-Lopez v. Beneficial Oregon, Inc.* 153 P.3d 940 (Ore. 2007) (prohibition on class actions, in part, rendered the otherwise mandatory arbitration agreement unenforceable).

New York and Delaware are well-accepted governing law, as their well-developed case law provides greater legal certainty. New York is not favored by all attorneys, given it has not adopted the Uniform Trade Secrets Act. At the same time, many parties seek to avoid Maryland and Virginia, which have adopted UCITA, as well as Louisiana, which is a civil-law/code-based jurisdiction. Some vendors with patent portfolios seek to avoid Texas, as the Federal District Court for the Eastern District of Texas has a well-earned reputation as the preferred jurisdiction for patent trolls bringing intellectual property infringement cases. Many software companies prefer California law due to its well-developed body of case law even though California law is considered to be pro-customer, as well as the laws of Washington state due to the significant number of software companies located in those states.

The parties should also consider the impact of the governing law on all aspects of their agreement beyond licensing. For example, some license agreements include non-solicitation restrictions and non-competition covenants. Parties seeking to enforce non-compete agreements should avoid the laws and courts of California, which have held non-compete agreements to be void in almost all cases. California: CAL. BUS. & PROF. CODE ANN. § 16600. The parties should be cognizant of the fact that some states such as Georgia will apply Georgia law to certain aspects of an agreement, such as a covenant of non-competition, even if the parties have contractually agreed to the laws of another state. *See Nasco, Inc. v. Gimbert*, 238 S.E.2d 368, 369 (Ga. 1977).

Many licensors seek to avoid Texas law, as it has strong consumer protection laws and prohibits reducing the statute of limitations to less than two years, while favored jurisdictions include New York, which generally benefits licensors. *See, e.g.*, *Metropolitan Life Insurance Co. v. Noble Lowndes International, Inc.*, 643 N.E.2d 504 (N.Y. 1994) (limitation of liability valid when vendor intentionally fails to perform for its own economic self-interest); *Gruet v. Care Free—Housing Division of Kennschl Enterprises, Inc.*, 759 N.Y.S.2d 276 (2003) (court upheld contract reducing statute of limitations to one year).

For entities licensing their software to consumers, the laws of some states may allow the licensor to contractually prohibit class action lawsuits or to indirectly do so by requiring the parties to resolve all disputes through arbitration. Alabama, Alaska, Georgia, Kentucky, Louisiana, Mississippi, Montana, and Virginia do not permit consumers to assert a class action to enforce their rights. *See* ALA. CODE § 8-19-10(a)(1); ALASKA STAT. § 45.50.531(a); GA. CODE ANN. § 10-1-399(a); KY. REV. STAT. ANN. § 367.170; LA. REV. STAT. ANN. § 51:1409(A); MISS. CODE ANN. § 75-24-15(4); MONT. CODE ANN. § 30-14-133(1); VA. CODE ANN. § 59.1-204(A). The courts are divided as to the legality of class-action exclusions, but a court's willingness to uphold an exclusion may make the laws of a particular state more attractive. *See Johnson v. West Suburban Bank*, 225 F.3d 366 (3d Cir. 2000) (arbitration clause in an agreement enforceable even though it may exclude class action); *Randolph v. Green Tree Financial Corp.*, 244 F.3d 814 (11th Cir. 2001) (contractual provision requiring arbitration enforceable even if it precludes class actions); *Pick v. Discover Financial Service Corp.*, 2001 WL 1180278 (D. Del. Sept. 28, 2001) (arbitration clauses not unconscionable because they exclude class actions).

Finally, selecting a state court as the exclusive forum may prevent the matter from being removed to federal court. *Grand View P V Solar Two, LLC v. Helix Electric, Inc.*, 847 F.3d 255 (5th Cir. 2017) (upholding remand to state court, which has "sole and exclusive" jurisdiction to hear the matter).

For a general discussion, *see* Coyle, *The Canons of Construction for Choice of Law Clauses*, 92 WASH. L REV. 631 (2017).

(b) Specific Issues

Set forth below is a brief overview of several potentially important issues where the laws of the various states vary, and the choice of law could have a material impact on the interpretation of the underlying contract between the parties.

(i) Trade Secrets (§ 28.1.B)

Occasionally, the licensor is flexible as to the choice of governing law but wants to ensure that the law of a particular state governs any trade secret dispute. Given the licensor's trade secrets/intellectual property is its greatest asset; it is understandable that the licensor wants certainty especially when some states have not enacted the Uniform Trade Secrets Act (UTSA). See Chapter 25.B.3 for a detailed discussion of the UTSA and § 28.1.B for model language addressing this issue.

UTSA sets forth the rights and remedies of a trade secret owner when its trade secrets are threatened or exposed. Every state, except for New York, has adopted some version of the UTSA. Because the laws of each state differ, the parties should understand the differences in each state's laws before selecting the agreement's governing law.

In states such as Alaska, trade secrets are tightly protected, and courts may immediately enjoin any actual or threatened misappropriation of trade secrets. ALASKA STAT. § 45.50.910 (2009); *see also* CT. GEN. STAT. ANN. § 35–55 (2009); GA. CODE ANN. § 10-1-765 (2009). Most states, however, fall within the middle ground. In Illinois, for example, to set forth a cause of action for a violation of the Illinois Trade Secrets Act, a plaintiff must assert facts that demonstrate (1) a trade secret (2) was misappropriated and (3) used in the defendant's business. *Arcor, Inc. v. Haas*, 363 Ill. App. 3d 396, 400 (1st Dist. 2005). The *Arcor* court further noted that:

> *[t]here are an additional six common law factors that courts may also consider in determining whether a trade secret exists. These factors are: (1) the extent to which the information is known outside of [the employer's] business; (2) the extent to which it is known by*

> *employees and others involved in [the] business; (3) the extent of measures taken by [the employer] to guard the secrecy of the information; (4) the value of the information to [the employer] and to his [or her] competitors; (5) the amount of effort or money expended by [the employer] in developing the information; [and] (6) the ease or difficulty with which the information could be properly acquired or duplicated by others.*

Id. at 400.

Consequently, in order for the trade secret owner to adequately protect its trade secrets, it must know the law in the various states and employ the necessary safeguards as required by law.

For a more detailed discussion, see Chapter 25.B.

(ii) Limitation of Liability Provisions

Limitation of liability clauses reduce or cap the potential damages that a contracting party may recover in the event the contract is breached. Limitations of liability clauses are becoming more common and enforceable. Joseph C. Faucher, *Limitation of Liability Provisions in Service Provider Contracts*, 32 ASPA J. 6 (2002). *See, e.g., Markborough v. Superior Court*, 227 Cal. App. 3d 705 (1991). In *Metropolitan Life Ins. Co. v. Noble Lowndes Int'l, Inc.*, 643 N.E.2d 504 (N.Y. 1994), the New York Court of Appeals held that the limitation of liability provision contained in a software services contract was valid even when the vendor intentionally failed to perform.

In *Metropolitan Life*, the plaintiff was a national provider of health and life insurance. The defendant, Noble, was a computer software developer. The parties entered into a contract whereby Noble would provide a particular software program as well as enhancements to the program tailored to Metropolitan Life's specific needs. After Metropolitan Life rejected two sets of enhancements, Noble demanded an increase in the price. When Metropolitan Life refused to pay the increase, Noble stopped performing. *Id.* at 506. Metropolitan Life then sued Noble, seeking a refund of the money that it already had paid to Noble, as well as consequential damages.

The contract's limitation of liability provision, however, specifically absolved Noble from liability for "loss of profit, loss of business, or other financial loss resulting from * * * [Noble's] performance or nonperformance[,]" but contained an exception to that limitation "for intentional misrepresentations, or damages arising out of [defendant's] willful acts or gross negligence." *Id.* at 505-06. Thus, Noble claimed that any damages recoverable by Metropolitan Life were limited to a refund of the money already paid. Metropolitan Life disagreed, maintaining that Nobel's conduct fell within the "willful acts" exception to the limitation of liability provision, and therefore, consequential damages were recoverable.

The court found for Noble, interpreting the phrase "willful acts" as conduct similar in nature to intentional misrepresentation and gross negligence, and specifically excluding from the definition of "willful acts" mere intentional nonperformance. *Id.* In so holding, the court looked at the contract as a whole, and concluded that the intent of the parties was to exclude from the limit of liability only "truly culpable, harmful conduct [and] not merely intentional nonperformance of the Agreement motivated by financial self-interest." *Id.* at 508.

To avoid the legacy of *Metropolitan Life*, a customer should include a "specific performance" provision within the governing agreement. By including such a clause, the customer will ensure that the contracted services are performed, and the contracted software delivered. The customer also should include a provision allowing the customer to "cover" its losses by hiring a third party to complete the work if the vendor fails to perform and exclude this right of cover from any limitation of liability contained in the agreement. See Form B.3.1 § 5.3.5 for model language providing the licensee the right of cover.

Finally, the limitation of liability cap contained in the underlying agreement should exclude any willful failure to perform a party's obligations, including any failure to perform based on the lack of profitability of performance.

For a more detailed discussion, see Chapter 5.I.

(iii) Notice and Cure

Licensing and service agreements usually include notice and cure provisions that require the non-breaching party to provide written notice to the breaching party of any breach and permit the breaching party a specific period of time to cure. If the breaching party fails to cure, the non-breaching party may then terminate the contract and enforce its right or remedies.

Jurisdictions interpret notice and cure provisions differently. A number of courts have upheld the principle that "[w]here the contract specifies conditions precedent to the right of cancellation, the conditions must be complied with." *Bausch & Lomb Inc. v. Bressler*, 977 F.2d 720, 727 (2d Cir. 1992) (citing *Consumer Power Co. v. Nuclear Fuel Services, Inc.*, 509 F. Supp. 201, 211 (W.D.N.Y. 1981)). Thus, a non-breaching party in these jurisdictions must be careful to strictly comply with the agreement's notice and cure provisions if the party wishes to terminate the contract and seek recovery for breach. *See Northeast Constr. Group, Inc. v. Deconstruction, Inc.*, 16 A.D.3d 357 (N.Y. App. Div 2005) (The failure to comply with applicable notice and cure provisions in a contract bars recovery on a counterclaim based upon allegations of nonperformance.); *Convergent Group Corp. v. County of Kent*, 266 F. Supp. 2d 647 (W.D. Mich. 2003) (county's failure to comply with notice and cure requirements precluded it from maintaining breach of contract claim); *In re Colony Square Co.*, 843 F.2d 479, 481 (11th Cir. 1988) (litigant's claim of breach rejected because that litigant failed to comply with a contractual "notice and cure" provision).

Some courts also have held that by failing to adhere to a contract's notice and cure provisions, the non-breaching party may find itself in breach of contract and liable for damages, regardless of the other party's initial breaching action. *See National Bankcard Services, Inc. v. Family Express Corp.*, 2006 WL 2480479 (D. Minn. Aug. 29, 2006) (software company that terminated a contract without first adhering to the notice and cure provision breached the contract); *Computrol, Inc. v. Newtrend, L.P.*, 203 F.3d 1064 (8th Cir. 2000) (upholding verdict that company breached contract by failing to follow the termination for cause provision).

A number of other jurisdictions have been less strict when interpreting notice provisions. *See Levi Strauss & Co. v. Esprit US Distribution Ltd.*, 588 F. Supp. 2d 1076 (N.D. Cal. 2008) (the non-breaching party's failure to follow notice and cure provisions did not result in dismissal of claim, but merely a stay until the requisite time had passed); *Hypergraphics Press, Inc. v. Cengage Learning, Inc.*, 2009 WL 972823, at *3 (N.D. Ill. Apr. 8, 2009) (unpublished decision) ("[I]n order for notice and opportunity to cure to be a condition precedent to filing suit on the claim, the contract must so state . . . nothing in the contract suggests that the notice and opportunity to cure clauses are conditions precedent to suing."); *Ixe Banco, S.A. v. MBNA America Bank, N.A.*, 2008 WL 650403, at *11 (S.D.N.Y. March 7, 2008) ("[U]nder this contract, a declaration of default is a condition precedent not to suing for a breach of contract but to being authorized to terminate the contract immediately without liability to the other party.") (citation omitted); *Ariens Co. v. Woods Equip. Co.*, 2006 WL 2597979 (E.D. Wis. Sept. 9, 2006) (failure of plaintiff to provide defendant with notice and opportunity to cure in compliance with contractual notice and cure provision did not preclude plaintiff's claim against defendant for breach).

In instances where the breaching party clearly repudiated or abandoned the contract, and where notice would be futile, courts excuse altogether the nonbreaching party's notice and opportunity to cure obligations. *Wolff & Munier, Inc. v Whiting-Turner Contracting Co.*, 946 F.2d 1003, 1009 (2d Cir. 1991); *Kurabu v. Pension Benefit Guar. Corp.*, 1997 WL 759462, at *11 (S.D.N.Y. Dec. 10, 1997) (noting that "a duty to provide notice and cure may be excused where futile, such as in the face of abandonment or repudiation").

Because jurisdictions vary in their approach to, and enforceability of, notice and cure provisions, it is imperative that each party understand the law in the chosen jurisdiction prior to entering into an agreement.

(iv) Consumer Protection Laws

Most states have consumer protection laws that are intended to protect consumers from unfair business practices and ensure fair competition. Each state defines "consumer" differently, with potentially surprising results. Both a vendor and customer should determine whether their transaction falls under a state's consumer protection laws, as well as what the law entails. Vendors should take particular heed of whether their customers are in fact considered "consumers" under the chosen jurisdiction, especially when the commercial transaction involves two sophisticated parties.

Surprisingly, a number of consumer protection laws apply to business consumers, including sophisticated commercial entities. For instance, Idaho's consumer protection law seeks to "protect both consumer and businesses." IDAHO CODE ANN., § 48-601 (2010). The statute defines a consumer to include any foreign or domestic corporation, trusts, limited and general partnerships, incorporated or unincorporated associations, companies, trusts, or business entities. Under this definition, most, if not all, software licensees would have standing to bring a cause of action under the law.

Still other states create a hybrid consumer protection law, protecting only certain businesses. *See, e.g.*, TEX. BUS. & COM. CODE ANN. § 17.45. For example, the Texas Deceptive Trade Parties Consumer Protection Act (the "Act") applies to some commercial transactions. Under Section 17.45(4) of the Act, an entity is removed from the definition of "consumer" if it "has assets of $25 Million or more, or that is owned or controlled by a corporation or entity with assets of $25 Million or more."

The different approaches to consumer advocacy make it imperative that vendors and customers educate themselves on each state's particular consumer protection law.

(v) Indemnification

(x) Indemnifying Licensors for Their Own Negligence

Increasingly, licensors are seeking to limit their indemnification obligations and liability for third-party claims arising from the licensor's actions. Some licensors even seek to have the licensee indemnify the licensor for the licensor's own negligence. Most licensees argue that this is an unreasonable position to take, as it may leave the licensee with a remedy only in the event of the licensor's gross negligence. Gross negligence is a difficult standard to meet and would likely leave the licensee without a remedy except in the most egregious cases. Given that the licensor controls its own actions and hence its risk, the licensee cannot be expected to insure the actions of the licensor.

It is unclear whether a provision requiring a licensee to indemnify the licensor for the licensor's negligence is enforceable. *See, e.g., Northwest Airlines, Inc. v. Alaska Airlines, Inc.*, 351 F.2d 253 (9th Cir. 1965) (exculpatory and indemnity provision that excuses party from liability for its own negligence is against public policy and invalid). *See also Burns v. N&L Realty Corp.*, 160 F. Supp. 203 (W.D. Pa. 1958) (contract provisions indemnifying lessor for lessor's negligence will be construed strongly against lessor and in favor of lessee). Some jurisdictions, however, permit such indemnification under the express negligence rule, requiring only that any indemnification that releases a party from all liability from its own future negligence "must be expressed in unambiguous terms within the four corners of the contract" and must also be "conspicuous." *Griffin Industries, Inc. v. Foodmaker, Inc.*, 22 S.W.3d 33, 37 (Tex. 2000). See section Z.9 of Form Q.2 for model language requiring the licensee to indemnify licensor for the licensor's negligence.

(y) Implied Indemnification

Indemnification usually arises from a contractual obligation, but it also may be implied by a court. A majority of jurisdictions addressing implied indemnification have found that a contractual relationship under the Uniform Commercial Code ("UCC"), with its implied warranties, provides a sufficient basis for an implied indemnity claim when the buyer incurs liability to a third party as a result of a defect in goods that would constitute a breach of the seller's implied or express warranties.

The following states follow the majority view: California, Maine, Michigan, Minnesota, Missouri, Nebraska, New Hampshire, New York, North Carolina, Pennsylvania, Virginia, and Washington. *See, e.g., Central Washington Refrigeration, Inc. v. Barbee*, 946 P.2d 760, 764 (Wash. 1997); *Carrier Corp. v. Detrex Corp.*, 6 Cal. Rptr. 2d 565, 569 (1992); *Cyr v. Michaud*, 454 A.2d 1376, 1385 (Me. 1983).

Three states follow the minority view: Idaho, South Dakota (*Sheehan v. Morris Irrigation, Inc.*, 460 N.W.2d 413 (S.D. 1990)), and Utah (*Perry v. Pioneer Wholesale Supply Co.*, 681 P.2d 214, 219 (Utah 1984)).

(z) Contributory vs. Comparative Negligence

As of November 1, 2023, only Alabama, the District of Columbia, Maryland, North Carolina, and Virginia apply the doctrine of pure contributory negligence. The failure to include an indemnification provision may limit an injured party's recovery under the laws of those states that have not adopted the doctrine of comparative negligence. The principle of indemnification seeks to ensure that the standard for the allocation of risk is on a comparative risk basis versus a contributory risk basis. Without an indemnification provision, the parties are subject to the uncertainty of where the action is brought and whether that state utilizes a contributory negligence standard. By including an indemnification provision, the parties can limit the impact of the doctrine of contributory negligence while allowing a party to potentially recover legal fees and other damages that would not otherwise be recoverable.

(vi) Statute of Limitations

Traditionally, a statute of limitations requires that a party bring a lawsuit within a specified period of time after the action that gave rise to the claim first arose. *See, e.g., A.B. Alexander d/b/a A.B. Alexander and Associates v. The Perkin Elmer Corp.*, 729 F.2d 576 (8th Cir. 1984). It is important to note that the statute of limitations for a contract claim may differ from the statute of limitations for a tort claim. *See, e.g.*, ARIZ. REV. STAT. ANN. § 12-544(3), 12-548 (six-year statute of limitations for written contracts executed in Arizona; four-year statute of limitations for written contracts executed outside Arizona); 10 DEL. CODE § 8106 (three-year statute of limitations for contract actions in Delaware); *Action Mailing Corp. v. Hewlett-Packard Co.*, 2009 WL 3526658 (W.D. Mo. Oct. 26, 2009) (one-year contractual statute of limitations for breach of warranty upheld); *Gruet v. Care Free Housing Division of Kennschl Enterprises Inc.*, 759 N.Y.S.2d 276 (2003) (one-year contractual statute of limitations upheld).

By default, Section 2-725(1) of the UCC provides for a four-year statute of limitations beginning when the cause of action first accrues but allows the parties to reduce the statute of limitations by mutual agreement to a minimum of one year. Most states have statutorily codified this time period as three or four years. *See, e.g.*, California: CALIF. STAT. ANN. CIV. PRO. § 337 (four years); Maryland: MD CODE ANN., MD. CTS. & JUD. PROC. § 5-101 (three years).

A smart vendor will seek to select the governing law of a state with a short statute of limitations to reduce its risk, because a prudent customer will not agree to contractually reduce the state's statutory statute of limitations. Indeed, a proposed reduction in a state's statutory statute of limitations may violate a state's law. Texas, for example, prohibits reducing the statute of limitations in most agreements to less than two years. TEX. CIV. PRAC. & REM. CODE § 16.070.

The parties also should be careful not to unknowingly extend the statute of limitations. Executing an agreement under seal may extend the statute of limitations. *See, e.g., Whittington v. Dragon Group, L.L.C.*, 991 A.2d 1 (Del. Sup. 2009) (noting that the statute of limitations for a contract under seal is 20 years); *see also* MD. CODE ANN., MD. CTS. & JUD. PROC. § 5-101 and § 5-102(executing agreement under seal will extend statute of limitations to 12 years). In other jurisdictions, fraudulent conduct will extend the statute of limitations. *See Invacare Corp. v. Sperry Corp.*, 612 F. Supp. 448 (N.D. Ohio 1984) (seller cannot rely on contractual statute of limitations to bar buyer's claim where alleged contracts were induced by fraud).

The parties also should be cognizant of whether the statute of limitations is tolled by a party's efforts to correct any defect in the software. There are differences among the courts as to whether efforts to correct a defect will toll the statute of limitations. *Cf. Triangle Underwriters, Inc. v. Honeywell, Inc.*, 604 F.2d 737 (2d Cir. 1979) (seller's attempt to repair computer system after malfunction did not toll statute of limitations for breach of contract claim) and *Grus v. Patton*, 790 S.W.2d 936 (Mo. App. 1990) (seller's unsuccessful attempts to repair defects over eight-year period did not toll four-year statute of limitations) with *Daley v. Twin Disc, Inc.*, 440 F. Supp. 2d 48, 52 (D. Mass. 2006) (attempts to repair defective goods will not normally extend or toll the statute of limitations but "purposely prolonging the time for repairs beyond the statute of limitations" may justify extension) and *Waddell v. L.V.R.V, Inc.*, 125 P.3d 1160 (Nev. 2006) (period in which buyer may timely revoke acceptance may be extended when seller repeatedly failed to cure breach despite repeated assurances) and *North Am. Lighting, Inc. v. Hopkins Mfg. Corp.*, 37 F.3d 1253 (7th Cir. 1994) (seller's attempts to cure do not go against buyer's period of timely revocation).

For a more detailed discussion, see Chapter 5.I.4.

(vii) Jury Waivers

A contractual jury waiver expressly waives the parties' right to a jury should a dispute arise between them. With the increase in large jury awards that often include punitive damages, many vendors seek to include jury trial waivers in their agreements on the belief that juries are incapable of understanding complex delivery matters and that judges are less likely to award punitive damages. Similarly, businesses are replacing arbitration clauses with jury waiver provisions to reduce both cost and time.

Many jurisdictions, such as Texas, have held that jury waivers are permissible under certain circumstances. *See In re Prudential Ins. Co. of Am.*, 148 S.W.3d 124, 129–33 (Tex. 2004). States permitting contractual jury waivers typically have imposed a number of procedural safeguards, including requirements that place on the party seeking enforcement of a waiver the burden of proving the waiver clause was entered into knowingly and voluntarily. Should the vendor and customer agree to a jury waiver, the language must also show that the decision was an informed one. To increase the likelihood that a waiver will be upheld, the waiver should be conspicuous, placed in a stand-alone paragraph and initialled by both parties. Set forth below is model language supporting an informed decision:

> *The parties hereby unconditionally waive their right to a jury trial of any and all claims or causes of action arising from or relating to their relationship. The parties acknowledge that a right to a jury is a constitutional right, that they have had an opportunity to consult with independent counsel, and that this jury waiver has been entered into knowingly and voluntarily by all parties to this agreement. In the event of litigation, this agreement may be filed as a written consent to a trial by the court.*

See Johnson, *Contractual Jury Waiver Is an Alternative to Arbitration*, Ft. Worth Bus. Pr., Nov. 24, 2008.

The validity of prelitigation jury waiver clauses is not absolutely certain. At least two states—Georgia and California—have held that prelitigation contractual jury waiver clauses are unenforceable. *See, e.g., Bank South N.A. v. Howard*, 444 S.E.2d 799 (Ga. 1994); *Grafton*

Partners LP v. Superior Court, 88 P.3d 24 (2004), *aff'd*, 116 P.3d 479 (Cal. 2005). The Georgia Supreme Court held that prelitigation contractual jury trial waivers were not provided for by the Georgia Constitution or Code and, consequently, were not enforceable under the laws of Georgia. *Bank South*, 444 S.E.2d at 800. Similarly, the California Supreme Court found that a contractual agreement to waive the right to a jury trial, entered into prior to any dispute between the contracting parties, is unenforceable under the California Constitution and Section 631 of the California Code of Civil Procedure. *See Grafton*, 88 P.3d at 24. For a general discussion, *see* McGuire & Belzberg, *Are Jury Trial Waivers Coming of Age?*, 38 Md. B.J. 25 (Nov./Dec. 2005); Chuang, *Assigning the Burden of Proof in Contractual Jury Waiver Challenges: How Valuable Is Your Right to a Jury Trial?*, 10 Emp. Rts. & Emp. Pol'y J. 205 (2006).

For a more detailed discussion, see Chapter 6.G.

(viii) Non-solicitation Restrictions and Noncompetition Covenants

The enforceability of non-solicitation and noncompetition covenants is dependent on state law. Although many states have upheld and enforced such provisions, others have not. For example, parties seeking to enforce noncompetition agreements should avoid the laws of California and Georgia, which have held noncompete agreements to be void. California: West's Ann. Cal. Bus. & Prof. Code § 16600 (2007); Georgia: *Jenkins Brick Co. v. Bremer*, 321 F.3d 1366, 1369 (11th Cir. 2003) ("Georgia's courts rarely uphold blanket non-compete agreements.") The parties should also be cognizant of the fact that some states, such as Georgia, will apply Georgia law to certain aspects of an agreement, such as a covenant of noncompetition, even if the parties have contractually agreed to the laws of another state. *See Nasco, Inc. v. Gimbert*, 238 S.E.2d 368, 369 (Ga. 1977).

(ix) Arbitration

Some states allow contracting parties to mandate arbitration and contractually prohibit class action suits, while other states limit their ability to do so. *See Parrish v. Cingular Wireless, LLC*, 2005 WL 2420719 (Cal. App. Oct. 3, 2005), *cert. denied*, 547 U.S. 1188 (2006) (arbitration agreement unconscionable because its class action waiver operated as an exculpatory clause under California law); *Riensche v. Cingular Wireless*, 2006 WL 3827477 (W.D. Wash. Dec. 27, 2007) (court determined that the prohibition against class actions was "unconscionable" and denied the defendant's motion to compel arbitration); *Vasquez-Lopez v. Beneficial Oregon, Inc.* 152 P.3d 940 (Or. 2007) (prohibition on class actions, in part, rendered the otherwise mandatory arbitration agreement unenforceable).

For entities licensing their software to consumers, the laws of some states may allow the licensor to contractually prohibit class-action lawsuits or to indirectly do so by requiring the parties to resolve all disputes through arbitration. The courts are divided as to the legality of class-action exclusions, but a court's willingness to uphold an exclusion may make the laws of a particular state more attractive. *See Johnson v. West Suburban Bank*, 225 F.3d 366 (3d Cir. 2000) (arbitration clause in an agreement enforceable even though it may exclude class action); *Randolph. v. Green Tree Financial Corp.*, 244 F.3d 814 (11th Cir. 2001) (contractual provision requiring arbitration enforceable even if it precludes class actions); *Pick v. Discover Financial Services Inc.*, 2001 WL 1180278 (D. Del. Sept. 28, 2001) (arbitration clauses not unconscionable because they exclude class actions).

For a more detailed discussion, see Chapter 30.D.

(x) Business Courts

Some states have created specialized business and/or technology courts to hear business/technology disputes in the belief that offering parties the ability to have their disputes heard by a jurist experienced in business disputes will make their state a more attractive place for businesses to locate. States that have specialized courts in business or complex litigation include California, Colorado, Delaware, Florida, Georgia, Maryland, Massachusetts, Michigan, Nevada, New Jersey, New York, North Carolina, Ohio, Pennsylvania, and Wisconsin. *See* Mississippi Secretary of State, *A Survey of the Structure of Business Courts by State or Local Jurisdiction* (January 2009); http://www.courts.state.md.us/businesstech (Maryland); https://www.nccourts.gov/courts/business-court (North Carolina). As such, the parties may want to select the laws of a state that has created a business court to improve the likelihood that any dispute that may arise will be heard by an experienced judge.

(xi) Data Protection/Data Privacy Laws

State data protection laws vary widely, with California, Massachusetts and Nevada considered to have one of the most restrictive laws. Thus, many licensees seek to require the licensor to comply with data protection laws of these states. Most states provide that the laws of their state shall govern the access and use of the personal information of their citizens. *See, e.g.*, CONN. GEN. STAT. 36a – 701(b); VT. STAT. TIT. 9 §§ 2430-2445. Consequently, the parties to the agreement must comply not only with the governing law of the agreement but also with the laws of the state of domicile of each person whose personal information is accessed.

For a more detailed discussion, see Chapter 22.

(xii) Uniform Computer Information Transactions Act (UCITA)

If the license is governed by the laws of Virginia or Maryland, the parties need to consider whether to opt out of the Uniform Computer Information Transactions Act, which has been adopted by both states. Proponents of UCITA believe it brings certainty to software licensing transactions, while others believe UCITA is overly pro-licensor. Many parties opt out of UCITA because there are very few court decisions based on UCITA, creating an air of uncertainty. See Chapter 15.B for a more detailed discussion of UCITA and § 28.2 for a UCITA disclaimer.

If the parties elect Maryland or Virginia law but opt out of UCITA, a question arises as to what law governs the transaction. The Maryland and Virginia legislatures superseded existing state laws to enact their respective versions of UCITA. By opting out of UCITA, it is unclear how the contract will be interpreted under Maryland or Virginia law. Thus, it is best to select a governing law other than Maryland or Virginia rather than choosing to opt out of UCITA and retaining Maryland or Virginia as governing law.

UCITA is a model state law designed to regulate transactions in computer information products such as computer software and software access contracts. To date, only two states have enacted UCITA: Virginia in March 2000, effective July 2001 (VA. CODE ANN. §§ 59.1-501.1 *et seq.*), and Maryland, effective October 1, 2000 (MD. CODE ANN., COM. LAW, §§ 22-101 *et seq.*). A number of other states including Arizona, Delaware, the District of Columbia, Illinois, Maine, New Hampshire, New Jersey, Oregon, and Texas have considered but not adopted UCITA. Case law regarding the interpretation of UCITA is not well developed, and as such, many parties are hesitant to agree to be governed by its terms.

To date, the vast majority of states have chosen simply not to enact UCITA. Some states, however, have gone so far as to enact legislation designed to reject the application of UCITA to their residents. The group Americans for Fair Electronic Commerce Transactions ("AFFECT") has published draft legislation termed "bomb shelter" legislation that protects a state's citizens from the application of UCITA.

UCITA permits the parties to choose the law of any state "provided that in a consumer contract[,] such choice does not violate the laws of the jurisdiction whose laws would apply" in certain situations. A concern arises that the parties to a license could specify that Maryland or Virginia law would govern the agreement, even if both parties reside in another state. So-called "bomb shelter" legislation voids any contractual choice of law provision that would result in the application of UCITA to an agreement. Currently, according to AFFECT, "bomb shelter" legislation has been enacted in four states: Iowa (IOWA CODE § 554D.104), North Carolina (N.C. GEN. STAT. § 66-329), Vermont (9 VT. STAT. ANN. § 2463A (2003), AND WEST VIRGINIA (W. VA. CODE § 55-8-15).

See Form B.3.1 § 28.2 for model language waiving the application of UCITA.

For a more detailed discussion see Chapter 15.

(xiii) International Considerations/UN Convention on Contracts for the International Sale of Goods (§ 28.1.C)

Internationally, it is imperative to utilize the laws of the United States, the United Kingdom, Sweden, or other western countries, with well-developed laws and courts with a reputation for impartiality, as most third world countries do not have well-developed software laws or case law for software licensing. If the license is governed by the laws of a country other than the United States, the parties may want to consider binding arbitration as an alternative. Further, the parties should consider opting out of the United Nations Convention on Contracts for the International Sale of Goods ("UN Convention").

If the parties for an agreement for a good (software) are domiciled in two different countries, and both countries are signatories to the UN Convention, the convention automatically applies unless the parties opt out. UN Convention, Article 1. Simply selecting the law of a particular state is not enough to opt out of the convention. *See BP Oil Int'l, Ltd. v. Empresa Estatal Petroleos de Ecuador*, 332 F.3d 333, 337 (5th Cir. 2003). The parties must specifically state that they are opting out of the convention. A choice of law provision selecting the laws of a particular state does not exclude the application of the UN Convention. *Honey Holdings I, Ltd. v. Alfred L. Wolff, Inc.*, 81 F. Supp. 3d 543 (S.D. Tex. 2015). *See Modius, Inc. v. PsiNaptic, Inc.*, 2006 WL 1156390, at *5 (N.D. Cal. May 2, 2006). *But see American Biophysics Corp. v. Dubois Marine Specialties*, 411 F. Supp. 2d 61 (D. R.I. 2006) (UN Convention did not apply to agreement with forum selection clause that contained mandatory venue language).

Many parties opt out believing case law based on the UN Convention is not well developed, creating uncertainty. As a federal treaty, the UN Convention pre-empts any application of the UCC or other applicable law. *De Geofroy v. Riggs*, 133 U.S. 258 (1890).

See http://www.cisg.law.pace.edu for a discussion of the UN Convention and a list of member countries. See also § 28.2 for model language opting out of the Convention. For a more detailed discussion of the UN Convention, see Chapter 26.G.

2. Venue

Venue is equally important as governing law because it is in both parties' interest to have the case decided by a sophisticated, knowledgeable trier of facts and/or jury. Some jurisdictions are known as "rocket dockets" for quickly adjudicating matters. To the extent one party desires to have a dispute quickly resolved, the party should select a jurisdiction such as the Federal District Court for the Northern District of Virginia which has a reputation for quick action. New York is an attractive venue for many parties as it has well-developed commercial case law, an experienced judiciary experienced in adjudicating complex cases, and an established business court. Further, for smaller parties the location of any action or claim can significantly increase the cost of litigation or dispute resolution.

Forum selection clauses "are prima facie valid" and will be enforced unless they are found to be "unreasonable under the circumstances." *The Bremen v. Zapata Off Shore Co.*, 407 U.S. 1 (1972). A forum selection agreement will be honored or enforced by a court "so long as they are procured freely and voluntarily, with the place chosen having some logical nexus to one of the parties or the dispute. . . ." *America On-line, Inc. v. Superior Court*, 108 Cal. Rptr. 2d 699, 707 (2001); *see also AC Controls Co. v. Pomeroy Computer Resources, Inc.*, 284 F. Supp. 2d 357 (W.D.N.C. 2003) (forum selection clause enforceable unless it is unreasonable). New York provides that the parties may select New York law if the contract value exceeds $1,000,000 regardless of whether the parties have a nexus to the state. N.Y Gen. Oblig. Law. § 5-1402. *See also* California Code Civ. Proc. § 410.40.

The party opposed to the forum bears the burden to show why the forum selection clause should not be enforced. *George Jumara and Evangelina Jumara v. State Farm, Inc. Co.*, 55 F.3d 873, 880 (3d Cir. 1995). Further, forum selection clauses will survive termination unless the contract states otherwise. *Payne v. N. Tool & Equip., Co.*, 2013 WL 6019299 at *3 (N.D. Ind. Nov. 12, 2013). Forum selection clauses may be enforced even if selected by accident. *Expresso Disposition Corp. 1 v. Santana Sales and Mkt'g Group, Inc.*, 105 So. 3d 592 (Fla. 2013) (court enforced venue which arose from editing error).

To increase the likelihood that a chosen venue will be upheld if contested, the parties should include language in the residuals stating that the contract was negotiated, executed, and performed within the venue and that the venue was chosen for the convenience of witnesses.

(a) "Sole" or "Exclusive"

The forum selection clause does not need to include the words "sole" or "exclusive" for a court to construe the clause as mandatory. *Scotland Memorial Hospital, Inc. v. Integrated Informatics, Inc.*, 2003 WL 151852 (M.D.N.C. Jan. 8, 2003) ("specific reference to the venue indicates mandatory language").

To avoid any potential dispute, the parties should include a statement of the venue and affirmative consent of the stated jurisdiction. The parties should also include such words as "sole" or "exclusive" to further limit potential disputes over the enforceability of such clauses. *See Hartford Fire Ins. Co. v. Novocargo USA Inc.*, 156 F. Supp. 2d 372, 373–75 (S.D.N.Y. 2001) (provision that disputes "shall" be brought in identified forum not exclusive unless provision provides that claims "shall exclusively" be located in identified forum). Further, the contractual language should state that the forum selection clause applies to "any dispute arising out of or related to the agreement," which would include tort as well as contract claims. *See Terra International, Inc. v. Mississippi Chemical Corp.*, 922 F. Supp. 1334 (N.D. Iowa 1996).

(b) Alternating Venues

To settle any dispute as to the forum prior to entering into a contract, some licensors and licensees include language in their license agreements stating that the forum will be the licensor's choice if the licensee elects to arbitrate or litigate, and that the forum will be the licensee's choice if the licensor elects to bring an action. The benefit is that such language serves to discourage parties from bringing claims. This solution is not viable for the choice of governing law as there must be one pre-agreed governing law to interpret the license agreement prior to any action being commenced. If the parties agree on a mandatory venue, the respective contract language should state that the chosen venue is the "exclusive" venue to avoid any later claim that the language is permissive and not exclusive. In adopting this approach, the parties must ensure that the language is tightly drafted and clearly sets forth the selected venue. *See Micro Focus v. Bell Canada*, 686 F. Supp. 2d 564 (D. Md. 2010) (court declined to enforce "nonsensical" forum selection clause).

(c) Nonexclusive Jurisdiction

Interestingly, it is not uncommon for parties to agree to a "non-exclusive" jurisdiction when the parties cannot agree on an exclusive jurisdiction. From the vendor's perspective, agreeing on a non-exclusive jurisdiction allows the vendor to bring an action in the stated jurisdiction while providing the customer a venue the vendor will accept without a fight, should the customer initiate legal action. This reasoning, in essence, causes a party to waive any claim that the stated non-exclusive jurisdiction is improper. At the same time, it provides a party a semblance of flexibility, while reserving the right to challenge any other jurisdiction. Set forth below is model language reflecting this principle.

> *Customer agrees to the non-exclusive (emphasis added) jurisdiction of the courts of Baltimore County, Maryland, for any action or proceeding arising out of or in relation to this Agreement.*

(d) International

Internationally, an exclusive forum selection clause is also important as many local courts have a bias against foreign licensors and do not always enjoy the same level of competency as the judiciary in the United States.

For a general discussion and sample clauses, *see* Vizy, *Forum Selection Clauses*, 219 Com. L. Adv. (NOV. 2006) and Kobayashi & Ribstein, *Uniformity, Choice of Law and Software Sales*, 8 Geo. Mason L. Rev. 261 (1999) (comparing the choice of law provisions under the UCC, UCITA, and common law).

I. Compliance with Laws (§ 25)

1. General

Many customers seek to include a provision in the underlying license agreement requiring vendors to comply with all "applicable laws." On its face, this statement seems innocuous, as every party has a preexisting duty to comply with valid, applicable laws. A closer examination raises a number of concerns. Most important, from the vendor's perspective, is who is monitoring changes in the laws and regulations (in the US? Globally?), and who will pay for any increases in the cost of performance due to changes in the law arising after contract execution. Customers must recognize that vendors cannot assume unlimited liability for unknown risks and that vendors lack the ability to predict future legislation, preventing them from pricing their products and services to reflect the future costs resulting from future changes. Further, customers cannot expect to outsource their compliance obligations to the vendor and should avoid doing so, as the customer is ultimately responsible if the vendor fails to meet the customer's regulatory obligations.

Outsourcing and hosting agreements usually define the security services and procedures that will be used, and the vendor's obligation is limited to providing the specified services. Most vendors accept this position because the customer chooses the security services the client wants the vendor to implement. For example, the client may choose not to implement robust security in order to save money. If this leads to a security breach, it should be the client's responsibility, not the vendor's.

Many agreements for hosting and outsourcing make a distinction between liability for operational breaches of confidentiality (for example, simple negligence that leads to an unintentional disclosure of data) and intentional disclosures of confidential information. Many vendors accept unlimited liability for the latter but insist that the former remain under the agreement's liability caps.

Many customers seek to tie an agreement's compliance with laws provision to an indemnity, as both parties may bear liability for one party's actions or inactions. Further, a governmental entity may bring both a civil and criminal action against a party, creating serious financial and reputational risk. By tying a party's compliance obligations to an indemnity, the "innocent" party has some redress. Prudent customers should also implement a robust auditing mechanism to ensure that the vendor remains in compliance with all applicable laws. This is especially true for customers in regulated industries, such as the healthcare industry and the financial services industry, or who process personally identifiable information. At a minimum, a compliance with laws provision should be reciprocal. Similar to intellectual property infringement claims, prudent licensors should avoid providing both a warranty and an indemnity for a compliance with laws provision.

The concept of compliance with laws is inherently ambiguous, as it is unclear which laws a vendor must comply with: the laws that apply to the vendor, the laws that apply to the customer, or both? Customers cannot reasonably expect to outsource their compliance obligations to the vendor, as the vendor is not a law firm or an insurance company. Further, the vendor cannot be expected to know and follow the laws applicable to the customer's business and industry. All vendors should, however, be willing to commit to complying with all laws applicable to their business, as they are already subject to those laws, and stating such does not increase their risk.

Many customers seek to include a "compliance with laws" provision in their agreements to ensure that the customer does not incur liability as a result of the vendor's failure to comply with applicable laws. While everyone agrees the parties should comply with the law, the fundamental issue is, what is an "applicable law"? Lawyers often draft broad provisions that require the vendor to comply with all laws applicable to the customer's business, including industry-specific regulations with which the vendor is unfamiliar, creating an expensive and burdensome obligation to track and comply with laws in in the United States, much less globally.

From the vendor's perspective, the vendor is not a law firm and cannot provide legal advice or guidance as to compliance with laws and cannot devote the required resources to track the law, much less changes in the law. The customer is responsible for its own compliance with the laws and regulations affecting its industry, as it is in a much better position to do so. Vendors should explain that their business model and pricing does not support making blanket assurances and that they cannot ensure both parties' compliance with all applicable laws.

The customer should determine if the vendor's products and services are compliant with the law and negotiate the vendor's obligations as opposed to attempting to insert a blanket statement that the vendor will be compliant in the parties' contract. Prudent vendors should resist overbroad provisions, as their products most likely cross many industries and practically cannot be modified for each one. They provide functionality demanded by market forces rather than meeting the compliance requirements of a single industry.

2. A Warranty vs. an Indemnity

Customers and vendors often argue over whether the vendor will provide a warranty or an indemnity or perhaps both.

From the vendor's perspective, a compliance with laws provision should be addressed through reciprocal warranties of compliance rather than as an indemnity, as indemnities are used to address third-party liability, not liability to the counterparty. Customers usually seek to exclude damages arising from a breach of compliance with laws warranty from the agreement's limitation of liability, while vendors, if they are willing to consider a carve-out from the limitation of liability, should expressly limit any carve-out to fines, penalties and levies assessed against the customer by a governmental entity as a result of the vendor's breach. Doing so limits the uncapped damages to a smaller number of claims and avoids liability for non-governmental third-party claims or consequential damages possibly suffered by the customer, such as lost revenue and profits.

Vendors should avoid indemnifying a customer for a violation of law if the customer would also have a breach of contract claim, as indemnities should only be used to address liability arising from third -party claims. To the extent a vendor is willing to agree to an indemnity, the vendor should assume responsibility only for the customer's actual out-of-pocket payments, such fines and penalties to governmental agencies/regulatory agencies.

With an indemnity, the vendor should insist on controlling the defense if it is responsible for any damages assessed in a judgment or settlement. The vendor should not, however, be defending a customer against a governmental entity given the significant financial and reputational risk to the customer.

3. *Utilizing the Change Order Process*

Many licensors seek to qualify their obligations to comply with changes in the law by expressly subjecting any such obligation to the change order process, which allows the licensor to increase its prices if justified. The licensor's remedy in the face of the licensee's rejection of a proposed regulatory-driven change order is to initiate the dispute resolution process, given the licensor most likely lacks the contractual right to refuse the change and terminate the agreement. The licensor is then faced with proceeding to undertake the change at its cost and then seeking to recover such costs from the licensee.

While language proposed by a licensor to make a change in law subject to the change control process may be unacceptable to the licensee, a licensor should look to other provisions in the agreement for protection. One such protection is a covenant by both parties regarding their respective obligations to comply with the law. (See, e.g., § 25) Further, the licensor should seek to include language in the agreement that provides that if the licensee fails to approve a licensor's proposed change required to respond to changes in law, the licensee will hold the licensor harmless from any losses that the licensor incurs in connection with such noncompliance.

In the event of a dispute, the licensor may have to undertake changes to the software and subsequently seek compensation as part of a protracted dispute. To the extent there is ambiguity with respect to the actions the licensor is obligated to undertake at the licensor's cost to respond to changes in the law, the licensor may lose any such dispute and end up financing such changes as well as potentially incurring significant legal costs. Further, to the extent there is any lack of clarity in a statement of work on this issue, such ambiguity may provide additional risk.

Many licensees reject the licensor's position, arguing that the licensor has an existing obligation to comply with all applicable laws, and that the licensee's use of the software cannot be disrupted by a dispute between the licensor and the licensee as to who should pay for the cost of any required changes. They argue that as an industry expert, the licensor is better able to track changes in the law and spread the cost of any required changes across its many customers. A critical factor for the vendor in deciding whether to accept this risk is if the required charges can be made simultaneously, accessing all of its clients, or whether each client's system must be modified individually.

Licensors argue that the licensee would have incurred the cost of any change in the law had the underlying transaction not occurred and thus it is inequitable for the licensee to expect the licensor to assume this cost. Ordinarily, a licensor's remedy in the face of having to absorb costs for which it believes it is not responsible would be to terminate the agreement. Most licensors lack such a termination right, however, and most licensees are unwilling to grant one. Licensees emphasize that the licensor is providing a product that must be current and competitive with market demands (i.e., complying with all laws), and that market forces, that is, the licensor's competitors, will force the licensor to have a compliant product.

See Chapter 7.D for a more detailed discussion of the change order process.

4. Potential Compromises

Many licensees seek to contractually transfer the risk of unknown future changes in the law to the licensor. This is true especially for licensees in regulated industries, such as the healthcare and financial industries, as well as in outsourcing contracts where the licensor may be providing services for a significant period of time during which the applicable laws may change.

Several potential compromises exist to this issue. The first, and perhaps most common, is to have each party assume responsibility for the costs of all changes affecting its industry (e.g., for the vendor, the information technology industry and the customer, the healthcare industry). In this manner, each party is responsible for the costs it would have incurred had a transaction not been entered into. For laws such as the Health Insurance Portability and Accountability Act (HIPAA), the GDPR and Sarbanes-Oxley, etc., the vendor should agree only that it will follow the client's directives set forth in a specific statement of work or other contractual agreement. A common and equitable resolution is for the vendor to warrant that it will comply with all laws that apply to the operation of its business, and the customer is responsible for complying with the regulations and laws applicable to the customer's business. This concept also applies to data protection laws (laws that apply to the provision of the vendor's services, but only to the extent they would apply to the vendor as a data processor for the customer).

A second solution is for customers, using their internal and external counsel, to evaluate the laws applicable to the customer's business and develop a detailed statement of work that governs the vendor's performance. Many vendors will agree to comply with specific detailed obligations related to compliance set forth in a statement of work, as they can quantify the risk and charge for any additional required work. The presumption is that compliance with the statement of work should result in the vendor's performance complying with the laws contemplated under the statement of work. If the vendor assumes responsibility for a finite number of identified laws and regulations, the vendor can factor the cost of complying with these laws and regulations into its fees. Any costs to comply with other laws and regulations would be borne by the customer. The vendor's willingness to accept this approach will likely depend on the services rendered and the industry involved.

Another, but riskier, alternative is for the parties to agree that they will negotiate a price to comply with any new compliance obligations as they arise and execute a change order to memorialize their agreement. From the customer's perspective, the risk arises that if the parties cannot agree on a price, the customer will not be in compliance with its compliance obligations. Model language to this effect follows:

1. Changes in Law and Regulation

1.1 Each Party shall promptly identify and notify the other Party of any changes in Applicable Law under this Agreement, including Customer's Regulatory Requirements, that may relate to the development and use of the Software. Vendor and Customer shall work together to identify the impact of such changes on the development and use of the Software. Vendor shall be responsible for any fines and penalties arising from any noncompliance by Vendor with any Applicable Law relating to the delivery of the Software under this Agreement. In the event Customer suffers any loss, costs, expenses or damages for any noncompliance by Vendor, then Vendor shall promptly reimburse all such costs, losses, and damages, and ensure immediate compliance.

1.2 Vendor shall deliver the Software regardless of changes in Applicable Law, including Vendor's Regulatory Requirements, so long as such performance does not contravene the law. If such changes prevent Vendor from performing its obligations under this Agreement, Vendor shall develop and, upon Customer's approval, implement a suitable workaround, without any increase in Fees or cost to Customer, until such time as Vendor can perform its obligations under this Agreement without such workaround.

1.3 It is agreed between the Parties that any change in Applicable Law, including Customer's Regulatory Requirements, will be discussed and a framework will be developed on mutually agreed terms to enable the Vendor to perform its obligations under this Agreement and any relevant SOW.

1.4 If there will be an increase in any Fees or cost to Customer due to a change in Applicable Law, including Customer's Regulatory Requirements, then such increase in cost will be discussed and mutually agreed between the Parties.

1.5 The failure to achieve a mutual agreement on such changes will provide Customer the right to immediately terminate this Agreement without notice and without liability to Customer for such termination.

5. Contractual Language

As discussed, a licensor should be hesitant to agree that the software and services it provides will be compliant with all future laws, as the cost to do so may be great and difficult to estimate. It should avoid accepting language similar to the following:

> *Licensor, at no additional cost to licensee, shall make all modifications that are recommended, mandated, or required to meet federal and state governmental and quasi-governmental regulatory requirements, statutes, ordinances, policies, edicts, rules, guidelines, or standards related to licensee's use of the software.*

This language creates significant risks for the licensor as the licensor is contractually obligated to bring the software and services into compliance with all future laws without additional compensation. It is very rare, however, to see language that so expressly and comprehensively addresses this issue as set forth above. Vendors are more likely to encounter language that discreetly shifts the burden:

> *Vendor agrees that [or represents and warrants that] the software shall comply with all applicable laws.*

A more balanced approach is to include language similar to that set forth in Section 25 of Form B.3.1. While an improvement over the language set forth in the previous paragraphs, it is ambiguous and will likely lead to a dispute. More equitable language is as follows:

> *Each party hereby agrees to bear the cost of complying with all requirements of its particular industry and each party agrees to equally bear the cost of any subsequent changes in the law outside of each industry such as data privacy laws and security.*

A licensor must consider that without limiting its covenant to the time of delivery, this language may obligate the licensor to deliver updates responsive to future changes in the law. Similarly, a licensee must consider whether it is protected by language to this effect or whether it should seek more explicit language as set forth above in the first example.

In *County of Mercer v. UniLect Corporation*, 612 F. Supp. 2d 638 (W.D. Pa. 2009), the court considered this issue. The County of Mercer brought suit against UniLect, alleging UniLect breached its duty to keep UniLect's voting machines in compliance with state certification standards. The contract between the parties contained the following warranty:

> *"UniLect warrants the products, as delivered, will conform with and perform according to the specifications required by the State of Pennsylvania . . . . If any programs should not so perform, they shall be corrected or replaced by UniLect in a timely manner as mutually agreed."*

The county argued the UniLect breached its obligations to keep the voting machines in compliance with state standards when, three years after delivery date, the machines were found not to be in compliance with new certification standards. The court found that the warranty did not create an express warranty that the machines would meet the specifications beyond the date of delivery, even though the contract stated that the life of the machines was 20 to 25 years. *Id.* at 644–46. The court's decision was founded on the principle that the warranty expired on delivery and did not extend beyond delivery. Thus, the licensor had no ongoing obligation to keep the voting machines compliant with state standards.

From the licensee's perspective, it should clearly state in the license agreement that all representations and warranties shall survive for the desired period and shall identify such representations and warranties in the survival clause.

A prudent licensor should agree only that the software and services will be in compliance with all applicable laws in effect on the date of contract execution or the time of delivery. A licensor may also agree to bring the software and services into compliance with future laws at the licensor's then-existing time and material rates. See Chapter 6.M for a more detailed discussion on survival clauses and § 18.

6. *Monitoring Changes in the Law*

Licensors should neither agree to monitor potential or actual changes in the law nor notify the licensee of any such potential change that may affect the licensee's business, even if the licensee agrees to pay for such compliance monitoring, as the risk to the licensor may be great. Software and technology vendors are not law firms that can opine on legal matters. Further, many licensors provide services across many different industries and lack the ability to track potential legislation for a particular industry. It would be a Herculean task to track legislation nationwide at the local, state, and federal levels, much less internationally. Customers are better suited through their internal legal department, outside counsel, independent auditors, industry trade groups, and consultants to monitor legislation that affects their business. Further, a licensor should not agree to notify the licensee of any changes in the law that it becomes aware of and should never agree to provide its interpretation of the law, as it is not a law firm. Any request for an interpretation of a law or ordinance should be referred to the licensee's law firm.

7. Ensuring Compliance

If a licensor does agree to assume the risk of a licensee's compliance obligations, the licensee should be sure to investigate how the licensor plans to ensure compliance. In the event there is a change in the law that impacts a broad spectrum of a licensor's business, such as HIPAA or identity theft laws, a licensor will likely make its software and services compliant without additional cost to its licensees. Without a HIPAA-compliant product, a licensor would quickly go out of business, as its competitors would almost certainly offer a compliant product. A savvy licensor may ask a licensee to share the licensor's development costs depending on the magnitude of the required changes, given that the licensee will most likely have to pay an even greater amount to migrate to another new, compliant licensor. If a licensee is concerned about assuming the risk of future changes in the law, the licensor can alleviate those concerns by contractually agreeing to amortize the cost of any needed changes across all of the licensor's licensees using the software. See Form Q.2 F.8. for model language allowing a licensee to audit the licensor's obligation to comply with all applicable laws. An alternate approach is for the licensor to assume responsibility for all laws affecting the licensor's industry and for the licensee to assume all liability for those laws affecting the licensee's industry. While this concept appears straightforward, it is often difficult to put into practice because many laws may affect both parties. Shared responsibility is likely to lead to future disputes. Thus, this approach should be avoided unless a strong demarcation can be created dividing the parties' responsibilities.

J. Notices (§ 52)

Notice provisions are not usually highly negotiated but, as electronic communication becomes more prevalent and accepted, the parties should carefully consider to whom notices should be delivered, how "notice" should be delivered, and when notices are given or received. Further, the U.S. mail is increasingly unreliable with the possibility of reducing mail delivery to 5 days a week. The importance of notices cannot be underestimated, as receipt of notice starts the cure period for any breach. Any ambiguity in the notice provision may severely disadvantage one or both parties.

In general, notices should not be addressed to an identified individual but rather directed to a specific position such as "Chief Executive Officer" or "General Counsel."

Doing so will potentially eliminate issues that may arise if the identified individual leaves the company, creating uncertainty as to who the notice should be directed to when leaving or even preventing it from being forwarded to the named individual. To that end, each party should be obligated to promptly notify the other party in the event of a change of address or a change in the recipient of the notice.

Most notice provisions provide for delivery by registered mail or overnight courier or e-mail. Given the challenges with the U.S. mail, prudent parties should avoid using the U.S. postal service to provide notice as mail service may be interrupted due to a pandemic or other national emergency and offices may be closed.

Facsimile notices should be discouraged, as there are significant risks the notice may be received, picked up by an employee other than the recipient, and not delivered to the recipient. Further, the notice may be retained in the machine's memory due to a lack of paper or other errors and never printed out or inadvertently deleted. In each of these instances, receipt could be considered to be contractually satisfied, and the cure period started without the intended recipient ever realizing notice had been received. Finally, privacy issues create additional concerns as a breach notice may be read by any employee passing by the fax, creating a confidentiality issue.

E-mails are equally problematic. The receiving party's spam filter may filter the e-mail after its receipt without the receiving party realizing notice had been received. If the e-mail's heading does not clearly reflect its content, the e-mail may be deleted by the receiving party. Further, the receiving party may leave the company or be assigned a new e-mail address preventing receipt of the message. Companies should consider establishing a single, monitored email address where all notices are sent. In addition, notices should be sent to multiple individuals to increase the likelihood the notice will be received in a timely manner. The sender should be required to use pre-agreed wording in the subject line of any email such as: BREACH NOTICE UNDER THE LICENSE AGREEMENT BETWEEN CUSTOMER AND VENDOR.

Further, the notice provision should provide when notice is effective. For example, all notices should be sent in a manner that requires a signature to confirm receipt. Notices should be effective on the date of signature, or the date receipt is refused.

At a minimum, notice should be effective upon receipt, and the sending party should be obligated to send copies to at least two other individuals, at least one of which should be outside of the receiving party (i.e., their lawyer). Further, if notice is sent electronically, a written confirmation copy should also be sent. This will hopefully ensure the notice is received. The parties should never agree that notice is "deemed" to be received a set number of days after mailing.

Courts will likely hold that an agreement's notice provision must be strictly complied with. *JP Morgan Chase Bank Nat'l. Ass'n. v. Nellis,* 122 N.Y.S.3d 673 (2d Dept. 2020) (plaintiff failed to prove it mailed notice first class mail as contractually required). *But see James Construction Group LLC v. Westlake Chemical Corporation*, 650 S.W.3d 392 (Tex. 2022) (minor deviations from a notice provision that do not severely impair or do not cause prejudice may be allowed).

Despite the strongest precautions, issues will arise. At least one court has found that when parties identify the mode of notification, they are indicating an intention to consider the communication "received" when the notice is dispatched in accordance with such requirement. *United States v. Continental Casualty Co.*, 245 F. Supp. 871, 873 (E.D. La. 1965). Similarly, a Maryland court has found that notice was effective upon its mailing. *Grubbs v. Prince George's County*, 297 A.2d 754 (Md. 1972). As such, the parties should include language that providing notice is effective only upon receipt.

K. Third-Party Beneficiaries (§ 40)

The Restatement (Second) of Contracts and common law recognizes two types of third-party beneficiaries: incidental third-party beneficiaries and intended third-party beneficiaries. *See, e.g.*, RESTATEMENT (SECOND) OF CONTRACTS § 302; *F. O. Bailey Co., Inc. v. Ledgewood, Inc.*, 603 A.2d 466, 468 (Me. 1992). An intended beneficiary is a party who has the ability to enforce the rights and receive the benefits of a contract, while incidental third-party beneficiaries are those who can benefit from a contract but cannot sue to enforce it. *Id.* The Restatement (Second) of Contracts § 302 (2) defines an incidental beneficiary as one who is not an intended beneficiary. Status as a third-party beneficiary may also be inferred from the underlying agreement. *Philadelphia Indemnity Insurance Company v. SMG Holdings, Inc.*, 44 Cal. App. 5th 834 (Cal. 2019).

As a general rule, under common law, a third party who is not an intended beneficiary cannot assert a claim for breach of warranty. *OFW Corp. v. City of Columbia*, 893 S.W.2d 893 (Mo. App. 1995); *see also* RESTATEMENT (SECOND) OF CONTRACTS, Chapter 14 (1979). The determination of whether a party is an incidental or intended beneficiary is made by looking within the "four corners" of the contract. *Pollak v. Federal Insurance Co.*, 2013 WL 6152335 (D. Mass. Nov. 21, 2013).

This general rule has at least three recognized exceptions. The first is for personal injury or tangible damage to property. In such incidences, contractual privity is not required. *See* Prosser, *The Fall of the Citadel*, 50 MINN. L. REV. 791 (1996).

The second is that under Article 2 of the UCC, warranty protection extends under UCC Section 2-318 to one of three classes of persons injured in their person, depending on which alternative the respective state enacted. Two classes are narrow with the third broader. This warranty extension cannot be contractually waived.

The third is created by those states that have abolished privity requirements, even when the loss is only economic. *See, e.g., Dual Building Restoration, Inc. v. 1143 East Jersey Ave. Assocs., Inc.*, 652 A.2d. 1225 (N.J. 1995) (building owner could sue paint manufacturer for peeling paint even though owner's contract was only with his painting contractor).

In many states, the creation of an intended beneficiary is not favored. *MCI Telecommunications Corp. v. Texas Utilities Elec. Co.*, 995 S.W.2d 647 (Tex. 1999).

Except in the case of a sublicense, a licensor should always ensure the license disclaims the creation of any third-party beneficiaries. This is especially important when viewed in light of any representations or warranties granted by the licensor under the license agreement. To be recognized as a third-party beneficiary, the underlying agreement must expressly recognize the third party as an intended beneficiary of the contract. *Sovereign Bank v. BJ's Wholesale Club*, 533 F.3d 162 (3d Cir. 2008). A prudent party may want to provide a limited exception to allow those who claim under an indemnification provision to be recognized as a third-party beneficiary. See the model language below:

> *Nothing in this Agreement, express or implied, is intended to or shall confer upon any Person (other than the parties hereto) any right, benefit or remedy of any nature whatsoever under or by reason of this Agreement; provided, however, that after the Effective Time, the Indemnified Person shall be third-party beneficiaries of, and entitled to enforce, Section ___ (Indemnification of Directors and Officers).*

Occasionally, a licensee will seek to include language in a master agreement, providing that its affiliates are third-party beneficiaries of the agreement and can license software and purchase services under the agreement. While this language serves as a convenient means for related parties to take advantage of an existing contract and pricing structure, the licensor should limit its risk by clearly stating in the agreement that an affiliate is a third-party beneficiary only to the extent that it is a party to a particular work order and then only with respect to that particular work. By doing so, the licensor will hopefully limit the licensee's affiliates' ability to enforce the agreement to only those situations where they are receiving software and services directly from the licensor. To be a third-party beneficiary, the purchaser must prove the manufacturer knew the purchaser's identity and purpose, communicated with the purchaser and delivered the goods to the purchaser. *Johnson v. Metro-Goldwyn-Mayer Studios Inc.*, 2017 WL 3313963 (W.D. Wash. Aug. 3, 2017).

If the licensor is allowing a licensee to sublicense the licensor's software to a third party, the licensor should require the licensee to name the licensor as a third-party beneficiary in the sublicense to allow the licensor to enforce the terms of the license if the licensee chooses not to do so. Without the inclusion of such language, the licensor lacks a meaningful remedy to protect its intellectual property, as monetary remedies are insufficient.

L. Legal Fees (§ 49)

Under the "American rule" of litigation, each party is responsible for paying its own legal fees. *Alyeska Pipeline Svc. Co. v. Wilderness Soc'y*, 421 U.S. 240, 247 (1975). Although some states have enacted statutes and some federal statutes allow for awarding legal fees, they are in the minority. *Alaska Rent-A-Car, Inc. v. Avis Budget Group., Inc.*, 738 F.3d 960 (9th Cir. 2013); Unfair Trade Secrets Act §§22-4; Trademarks: 15 U.S.C. §§1116-1118; Copyrights: 17 U.S.C. §§502-505; Patents: 35 U.S.C. §§ 283-285; *Octane Fitness, LLC v. Icon Health & Fitness, Inc.*, 134 S. Ct. 1749 (2014).

Some parties seek to include provisions in the license agreement allowing the prevailing party in any dispute to recover its legal fees and costs from the losing party in the belief that the threat of an award of legal fees will provide the licensor leverage in the event of a dispute with a smaller licensee. A more aggressive position from the licensor's perspective is to include unilateral language, allowing the licensor to recover its legal costs if it brings legal action to protect its intellectual property. Several states provide that a contractual provision providing for the award of legal fees to only one party shall automatically be made mutual. CAL CIV. CODE § 1717; FLA STAT. ANN. § 57.105; ORE §20.091; TEX. REV.

CIV. STAT. art 38.001. Texas also allows the prevailing party in a contract dispute to recover its legal fees. TEX. REV. CIV. STAT. art 38.001. Many licensees seek to include a prevailing-party clause in their agreement in the belief that the licensee is more likely to bring a claim against the licensor than the licensor bringing a claim against the licensee.

A prevailing-party clause provides the parties an incentive to settle a matter prior to bringing suit, as the cost of litigation can be quite large, thereby increasing the risk in the event a party loses the dispute. Prudent parties should define the meaning of "prevailing," as litigation may not result in a split verdict. *See Desu v. Lewi*, 427 S.W.2d 843, 845 (Mo. 2014) ("This Court has defined a 'prevailing party' for purposes of a contractual award as 'the party prevailing on the main issue in dispute, even though not necessarily to the extent of its original contention.'").

Further, a large number of litigation matters settle before trial without determining a prevailing party. Similarly, most arbitrations are not clearly decided in favor of one party, as it is rare for arbiters to declare one party the prevailing party and award attorney's fees.

To be enforceable, a fee shifting provision must be clear, unequivocable, *Mahani v. Edix Media Grp., Inc.*, 935 A.2d 242 (Del. 2007), in connection with a breach of contract claim with specific language referring to the prevailing party. *Baltimore Pile Driving and Marine Constr., Inc., v Wu & Assoc., Inc.*, 2022 WL 3466066 (Del. Super. Aug. 18, 2022); *Murfey III v. WHC Ventures, LLC*, 2022 WL 214741 (Del. Ch. Jan 25, 2022). To recover legal fees, the fee shifting provision must specifically mention legal fees. *Honeywell Int'l. Inc. v. Opto Electronics Co., Ltd.*, 2023 WL 6367671 (W.D.N.C. Sept. 27, 2023).

Many states disfavor fee shifting and will strictly construe language requiring one party to pay the other party's legal fees. *Baltimore Pile Driving and Marine Constr., Inc., v Wu & Assoc., Inc.*, 2022 WL 3466066 (Del. Super. Aug. 18, 2022). The parties, however, "may contract for the indemnification of attorney's fees and expense." *Blue Citi, LLC v. 5Barz Int'l. Inc.*, 338 F. Supp. 3d 326 (S.D.N.Y. 2018). At least one court has held that an indemnity which included legal fees was not a valid fee shifting arrangement as it applied to third party claims, not claims between the contracting parties. *SARN Energy LLC v. Tatra Defence Vehicle A.S.*, 2019 WL 6525256 (Del. Sup. Ct. Oct. 31, 2019).

A prevailing party's right to collect its legal fees may include any contingency or success fee it has negotiated with its attorneys. *See Johnson Controls, Inc. v. Edman Controls, Inc.*, 712 F.3d 1021 (7th Cir. 2013), as well as reasonable fees associated with an in-house attorney's efforts. *Holland v. Jachmann*, 9 N.E.3d 340 (Mass. 2014). In addition, several courts have awarded electronic discovery costs to the prevailing party. *See, e.g., Jardin v. DATAllegro*, 2011 WL 4835742 (S.D. Cal. Oct. 12, 2011); *Tibble v. Edison Int'l*, 2011 WL 3759927 (C.D. Cal. Aug. 22, 2011).

M. Survival (§ 18)

1. General

A survival clause identifies certain provisions in the agreement as surviving the termination of the agreement for any reason.

There are two philosophies in drafting survival clauses. One is to specifically list those sections that survive by section number and name (e.g., as governing law, the limitation of liability, noncompetition and non-solicitation provisions as well as representations and warranties that must remain true during the term of the agreement). By doing so, the parties avoid any ambiguity and any dispute over whether a particular provision survives termination. The risk in this approach is that the parties fail to include a particular section that should survive. See § 18 for language reflecting this approach.

The second is to use very general language such as "all sections that by their nature should survive the termination of this Agreement shall survive." The lack of specificity avoids the issue of failing to identify a particular section but is potentially problematic as the identity of the surviving clauses is open for interpretation and likely to increase the chance of litigation. Do the warranties survive? The indemnification provisions? In the event of a dispute, it is likely that the parties will have conflicting views as to their intent at the time of contract signature. Typical language reflecting this approach is as follows:

> *Any provision of this Agreement which contemplates performance or observance subsequent to termination or expiration of this Agreement shall survive termination or expiration of this Agreement and continue in full force and effect (provided that if a provision has an express time period that such provision is to be in effect, then such provisions shall survive only for the applicable time periods).*

The above language creates more ambiguity than it resolves. As such, the parties should strive to eliminate ambiguity and should take the time to carefully review the contract and list by section number every clause they want to survive.

See §18, Alternative Language, for additional language reflecting this approach.

Under New York law, a court deciding which terms survive the termination or cancellation of a contract will look at the language of the contract as a whole. *See generally Primex Int'l Corp. v. Wal-Mart Stores, Inc.*, 679 N.E.2d 624 (1997); *Scientific Components Corp. v. Raytheon Co.*, 2005 WL 1561508 (S.D.N.Y. June 21, 2005). The fact that specific terms are not identified in the survival clause does not necessarily mean that they do not survive. *See, e.g., The New York Group, Inc. v. Horizon Casket Group, Inc.*, 2007 WL 2021763 (S.D. Tex. July 11, 2007).

Some courts have adopted a "redundancy" approach as one factor in deciding the intention of the parties. In *Scientific Components Corp. the* court interpreted a manufacturing agreement and its survival clause. *Id.* The agreement included a broad arbitration clause that was not listed as surviving in the survival clause. The court agreed with the arbitration panel and found that the broad arbitration clause already encompassed termination-related issues and that "it would have been redundant to expressly list it in the Survival Clause." *Id.*, at *3.

A Colorado court reached a similar conclusion in *Shams v. Howard*, holding that an arbitration clause survives when a dispute arises under the contract if there is not "clear intent to the contrary." 165 P.3d 876, 879 (Colo. App. 2007). In *Smyx Techs., Inc. v. Stargate Mobile, L.L.C.*, a Michigan court considered the entirety of the contract and held that it would be "strained reading" to suggest that the arbitration clause and other provisions would not survive simply because they were not mentioned in the survival clause. 2006 WL 2943301, at *2 (E.D. Mich. Oct. 13, 2006). However, if the survival of the provisions in *Smyx Techs.* had not been supported throughout the contract itself, the court admitted that the failure to include the provisions in the survival clause could indicate an intent not to survive. *Id.* Thus, even the presence of a survival clause does not necessarily make the identification of the terms that survive termination an easy task. Thus, a court will look to the "four corners" of the document as a guide in determining the intent of the parties.

A dichotomy of opinion exists as to whether a stated survival period for representations and warranties serves as a statute of limitations for bringing a breach claim. *See ENI Holdings, LLC v. KBR Group Holdings, LLC*, 2013 WL 6186326 (Del. Ch. Nov. 27, 2013); *contra*, *Western Filter Corp v. Argan, Inc.*, 540 F.3d 947 (9th Cir. 2008); *Hurlbut v. Christiano*, 405 N.Y.2d 871 (N.Y. App. Div. 1978).

2. *Lack of a Survival Clause*

The intention of the parties also governs when the contract does not contain a survival clause. The lack of a survival clause helps to strengthen the argument that the terms were not intended to survive termination, but it is not conclusive. In *Primex Int'l Corp. v. Wal-Mart Stores, Inc.*, a New York court held that the choice of law provision and arbitration clause in two separate contracts without survival clauses survived the natural expiration and unilateral termination under a notice of cancellation provision or breach. 89 N.Y.2d 594, 598–99 (N.Y. 1997).

If a party can demonstrate, however, that it was the intention of the parties that a clause not survive termination, then the obligation will end with the contract. In *Aberdeen Golf & Country Club v. Bliss Const., Inc.*, a Florida court held that an alternative dispute resolution provision was intended only during performance of a construction contract and terminated when the contract expired. 932 So.2d 235, 241 (Fla. Dist. Ct. App. 2005). The court viewed the contract in light of the entire text, context, structure and performance in order to determine the intention of the parties. *Id.* at 236. The intent not to survive was demonstrated by the facts that performance involved many tasks over a long duration and an alternative dispute resolution provision would postpone litigation for sake of progress on the construction project. *Id.* at 237. Because the contract did not have a survival clause, "the ADR provision went down with the whole." *Id.* at 241.

The *Aberdeen* court's approach is analogous to professional services agreements requiring many tasks over a long duration. Arguably, specific provisions, like an audit clause, were included in the contract for the sake of progress on the entire project and were meant to terminate along with the contract. While *Aberdeen* was decided in Florida, the conclusion reached by the court seems consistent with New York's practice of determining and upholding the intention of the parties.

N. No Construction Against Drafter (§ 51)

As a general principle, ambiguous contractual provisions that cannot be resolved from the four corners of the agreement or through parol evidence are interpreted against the drafter. *Truck Ins. Exchange v. Marks Rentals, Inc.*, 418 A.2d 1187 (Md. 1980). Therefore, most parties seek to include language in their agreement that neither party shall be considered the drafter. A party that has been forced to accept an agreement without material modification should resist agreeing to such language.

Not all courts are in agreement as to interpreting ambiguity against the drafter. At least one court has found that where both parties to an arm's length agreement are sophisticated parties and have been represented by counsel, any ambiguities arising from the agreement should not be automatically construed against the drafter. *Western Sling and Cable Co. v. Hamilton*, 545 So. 2d 29 (Ala. 1989). This potential dichotomy extends to specific industries. *Compare Truck Ins. Exchange v. Marks Rentals, Inc.*, 418 A.2d 1187, 1197 (Md. 1980) (Maryland rejects rule that ambiguous insurance policies are to be interpreted against insurer) and *Lindsay Mfg. Co. v. Hartford Acc. & Indem. Co.*, 118 F.3d 1263, 1269 (8th Cir. 1997) (ambiguous language will be construed against insurer).

To avoid potential problems, the parties should include a clause acknowledging that the parties have been represented by counsel, that they are sophisticated commercial parties, and that any ambiguity should not be interpreted against one party or the other. See § 51. The licensee may reject the notion that it is a sophisticated commercial party as it relates to software licensing and may seek to exclude this provision. If the terms of the license were not broadly negotiated, the licensee may be justified in its position. Notwithstanding the licensee's belief, the licensor should never accept language interpreting any ambiguity against the licensor. See, e.g., Form Q.2.XX.2.

O. Amending Written Agreements Through Online Terms (§ 23)

1. General

An increasing number of parties are seeking to incorporate contractual terms reached through hyperlinks into their contractual agreements and the right to unilaterally amend such terms by posting any changes online.

The following paragraph is illustrative of this issue:

> *The licensing of the Software under this License Agreement is subject to the additional terms of use ("Terms") available on Vendor's website or by clicking the following link: http://www.vendorswebsite.com/legalterms.htm*
>
> *Licensor may modify these Terms at any time by posting a revised version on the Site or by otherwise notifying Customer in accordance with Section ___ (Notices). The modified Terms will become effective upon posting or, if Licensor notifies Customer by email, as stated in the email message. By continuing to utilize the services after the effective date of any modifications to these Terms, Customer agrees to be bound by the modified terms. It is Customer's responsibility to check the Site regularly for modifications to these Terms. Licensor last modified these Terms on the date listed at the beginning of these Terms.*

In a small number of situations, online terms or an online amendment may be appropriate allowing the parties to amend and easily distribute changes to the governing agreement. For example, a cloud provider may need to post changes to its acceptable use policy (AUP) as it would be impractical to execute a written amendment with every customer every time the terms of the AUP changed.

The incorporation of Web-based terms which may be unilaterally amended creates a significant risk for the counter party, usually the customer, as the counter party must continually monitor the website for changes to the contractual provisions to ensure compliance with such provisions. Unless it is notified of any changes by the posting party, a party may never realize that the terms of the parties' agreement have been modified. Problems may also arise if the link links to the party's main web page and not the specific page containing the terms in question. As such, a prudent party should reject any language allowing one party to unilaterally modify the terms initially agreed to by the parties.

2. The Validity of Online Terms and Amendments

The use of a website or hyperlink to incorporate general terms and conditions is generally valid provided the party had notice of the provisions and assented to the agreement. *Kauders v. Uber Techs*, Inc., 159 N.E.3d 1033 (Mass. 2021). *See One Beacon Ins. Co. v. Crowley Marine Services*, 648 F.3d 258 (5th Cir. 2011) (incorporation of terms posted on the internet valid); *Harold H. Higgins Realty, Inc. v. FNC, Inc.*, 575 F. Supp. 2d 696 (D. Md. 2008) (unilateral modification of web-based service contract upheld, as prior agreements permitted modification at any time and provided modifications would be effective after they had been posted for 30 days) and *Patco Construction, Inc. v. peoples United Bank*, 2011 WL 2174507 (opinion of magistrate judge) (D. Me. May 27, 2011), upheld by the district court, 2011 WL 3420588 (D. Me. Aug. 4, 2011) (party bound by online amendment where parties' agreement provided the agreement may be amended at any time effective upon publication); *Lincoln Composites, Inc. v. Firetrace USA, LLC*, 825 F.3d 453, 460 (8th Cir. 2016)("a party is generally charged with knowledge of the contents of a writing he or she signs and cannot avoid a contract just because he or she failed to read the entire writing"); *but see Carey v. 24 Hour Fitness, USA, Inc.*, 669 F.3d 202 (5th Cir. 2012) (arbitration provision unenforceable as employer could unilaterally alter the arbitration provisions).

Traditional contract principals still apply to online contracts. *Wilson v. Huuuge, Inc.*, 944 F.3d 1212 (9th Cir. 2019). For an online amendment to be valid, the affected party must agree to be bound by such changes. *Joe Douglas v. U.S. Dist. Ct.*, 495 F.3d 1062 (9th Cir. 2007) (customer not bound by on-line modification where customer had not agreed to modification of agreement through posting of revised terms online). A party's failure to read the terms does not invalidate them. *Citibank N.A. v. Dalessio*, 756 F. Supp. 2d 1361 (M.D. Fla. 2010).

To increase the changes of the online terms being upheld, the underlying agreement's integration clause should provide that any online terms are incorporated by reference and specifically reference the terms to be incorporated. *See Affinity Internet, Inc. v. Consolidated Credit Counseling Svcs., Inc.*, 920 So. 2d 1286, 1288 (Fla. Ct. App. 2006) (refusing to enforce arbitration clause in on-line terms and conditions because written contract stated only that it was "subject to" the online terms and did not state that the online terms were incorporated by reference in the written contract).

The underlying agreement should also set forth the complete web address where the terms and conditions may be viewed, *Feldman v. United Parcel Service, Inc.*, 2008 WL 800989 (S.D.N.Y. Mar. 24, 2008), and clearly and conspicuously provide that it is governed by and subject to the terms and conditions set forth on the referenced website. To avoid claims of invalidity, a prudent party seeking to incorporate web-based terms should capitalize the language referencing the web-based terms. *See Manasher v. NECC Telecom*, 2007 WL 2713845 (E.D. Mich. Sept. 18, 2007). Finally, if a party desires the right to amend the terms posted on the website, the underlying agreement should clearly reflect this intent.

One practical challenge for both parties is to confirm which version of the agreement the parties agreed to as the referenced website may no longer reflect the terms previously agreed to by the parties. The party seeking to enforce the agreement should archive all versions of the website along with the time periods the archived terms were displayed on the website as well as any periods of time during which terms were not accessible on the web. *See Fu Da Int'l Ltd. v. Kohl's Dep't. Stores, Inc.*, 2009 WL 151727 (S.D.N.Y. Jan. 21, 2009). The failure to do so may impact a party's ability to enforce the agreement, as a court may be unable to determine which terms apply to the parties' relationship. *Morgantown Machine & Hydraulics of Ohio, Inc. v. American Piping Prods., Inc.* 887 F.3d 413 (8th Cir. 2018). If a party is unable to archive the document, it should print the document out and place it in its records.

3. Online Terms under UCITA and the UCC

In mass-market licenses, UCITA requires that the licensee be given a right to terminate the license upon a change. MD. COM. LAW. CODE ANN. § 22-304 ("Continuing Contractual Terms"). In non-mass-market computer information contracts, MD. COM. LAW. CODE ANN. § 22-304 (b) provides: "If a contract provides that terms may be changed as to future performances by compliance with a described procedure, a change proposed in good faith pursuant to that procedure becomes part of the contract if the procedure: (1) Reasonably notifies the other party of the change; and . . . ." Thus, in those states that have adopted UCITA (Maryland and Virginia), a party may be bound by a clause posted on the web provided it is notified of the change.

The use of online terms and conditions to amend an agreement raises the possibility of a "battle of the forms" under Section 2-207 of the UCC. The posting of unilateral online terms and conditions that propose to amend the agreement between the parties clouds the issue of which documents control, as the fundamental issue is whether the online terms and conditions are incorporated into the documents governing the parties' relationship. Thus, a trier of fact must evaluate the online terms and conditions along with the parties' sales documents (i.e., purchase orders, invoices, and other sales documents) to determine the terms of the agreement between the parties.

4. Negotiating Provisions Allowing Online Amendments.

Depending on the customer's negotiating leverage, a customer may be able to negotiate some protections into the agreement to limit its risk from future modifications of any online terms. Set forth below are several solutions that a prudent customer may seek to incorporate.

- Notice of All Changes Required. The vendor should be required to notify the customer in the event of any changes to the online terms. See language to this effect in the following bullet point.
- Termination for Convenience. At a minimum, a prudent customer should seek to insert language to the effect that if the vendor's changes will materially reduce the functionality of the licensed software, the customer may terminate the agreement for convenience without penalty. Model language to this effect follows:

  We reserve our right to amend or supplement this Agreement at any time, at our discretion. When we do so, we will do our best to provide you notice and point out what is different or new. If at any time you do not agree to the terms of this Agreement or any of the terms of any applicable Vendor Contract, please discontinue use of the respective service immediately and close your account. Your continued use of your Vendor Account, the use of www.vendor.com (the "Site"), the Vendor Hosting and any affiliated Vendor's services that redirect or link to this Agreement constitutes your agreement to be bound by the terms of this Agreement and any other applicable Vendor Contract. Notice of any change will be considered given and effective on the date that we update the Site with the change. Please periodically review this Agreement to ensure you are aware of any changes.

- No Modifications for X Years. The customer may seek to have the vendor agree that the terms of the agreement will not change for x years from the date of the agreement's execution.
- Certain Terms May Be Not Be Modified. The customer may want to identify certain important provisions that may not be modified.

  No provisions in any linked document modifying Section ___ (Indemnification) and Section ____ (Limitation of Liability) shall apply, it being the intent of the parties that the terms of Sections __ and ___ in the Master License Agreement shall govern in respect to such provisions.

- Only Specific Terms May Be Modified. Another alternative is to specifically identify those terms which may be modified through an online amendment. Model language to this effect follows:

  Any other provision to the contrary notwithstanding, Customer shall not be bound by any changes made by Vendor to the Terms and Conditions located at www.terms.vendor.com after the date of Customer's signature on this Agreement. The foregoing sentence shall not apply to changes made by Vendor to its Acceptable Use Policy, and Customer shall continue to be bound by such modifications as otherwise set forth in the Agreement.

- No Unilateral Modifications. The customer may seek to incorporate language into the agreement prohibiting unilateral modification.

> *Licensor may not unilaterally modify this Agreement. To the extent any of the Terms of Use permit unilateral modification, such provisions are null and void.*

A variant on this approach is to list those provisions that may not be modified, such as data protection, limitation of liability, confidentiality, and indemnification.

- Only Non-material Terms May Be Modified. The parties may also agree that only non-material terms may be modified.

  > *These General Terms and Conditions, as well as any Order Form, may only be amended in a writing signed by both parties. Notwithstanding the foregoing, Vendor may make non-material changes to these General Terms and Conditions at any time by posting revised General Terms and Conditions at https://www.vendor.com/terms_conditions.htm. A non-material change is any modification that does not have an adverse impact on you, or the Services provided hereunder. You are responsible for regularly reviewing this site to obtain timely notice of such amendments. You shall be deemed to accept the amended General Terms and Conditions by your continued receipt of Services if you do not notify Vendor of your good-faith objection within thirty (30) days after such amended terms and conditions have been posted. If Vendor does not agree to waive the amended terms and conditions to which you object, either party shall have the right to immediately terminate Services without penalty.*

- Require Amendments to Be in Writing and Executed by a Specific Individual. The agreement should provide that any amendment must (i) be in writing, (ii) executed by an authorized executive officer of both parties, and (iii) refer explicitly to the agreement and the particular sections being amended. A party may want to identify by name the single person who has the authority to execute all agreements. *See, e.g., National Auto Lenders, Inc. v. SysLOCATE, Inc.*, 686 F. Supp. 2d 1318 (S.D. Fla. 2010) (licensee not bound by employee acceptance of license terms, as licensee had previously notified licensor that only licensor's executives could accept contractual terms). Some companies (e.g., Oracle and Siemens) specifically provide that all agreements must bear two signatures, one being a member of the legal department, to defeat any ill-advised agreement or an unknown amendment to an agreement.

5. *PRACTICE POINT*: Best practices for creating enforceable online terms and amendments.

To increase the likelihood that online terms/amendments will be held to be enforceable, the party to seeking to do so should adhere to the following best practices:

- Maintain archival copies of the online terms including prior versions as well as the effective date of each version.

- Underline and set off hyperlinks in a different color on the signature page or prominently at the beginning of the agreement so that they are clearly recognizable and identified.
- Highlight sensitive terms (e.g. class action waivers) near the relevant hyperlink.
- Use scroll-wrap or sign-wrap agreements to obtain and document the customer's unambiguous affirmative consent to the terms. Terms should appear on the same page as the consent checkbox or as a pop-up window.
- Provide the contracting party with a copy of the agreed upon terms after acceptance via email.
- Provide conspicuous notice and require affirmative acceptance of a party's ability to undertake unilateral changes to online terms.
- Notify users of updated online terms via an online portal and require user acceptance prior to using such online portal.
- Allow the customer to terminate the agreement and receive a pro-rata refund if the customer does not agree to the updated online terms.

For a general overview of the validity of online contractual terms *see* Kim, *Digital Contracts*, 75 Bus. Law. 1683 (2020); Kim, *Online Contracting*, 72 Bus. Law. 243 (2017), Moringello & Ottauani, *Online Contracts: We May Modify These Terms at Anytime Right?*, Bus. L. Today (May 2016). *See also* the ABA Cyberspace Law Committee's "safe selling" website at http://safeselling.org; Johnson & Tarleton, *Enforceability of Online Terms and Conditions Incorporated into a Written Contract*, http://www.brookspierce.com/news-insights/ enforceability-online-terms-and-conditions-incorporated-written-contract.

See Chapter 11 for a detailed discussion of shrink-wrap, browse wrap, clickwrap and similar licenses.

P. Service of Process

Increasingly, parties are seeking to include provisions in their agreements establishing alternative means of serving the other party in the event of litigation. The intent is to simplify the service of process, eliminating the need to serve the other party's registered agent. Although these provisions are well intentioned, they may be potentially problematic. The language below is illustrative of the attempt to eliminate any requirement to serve a party's resident agent.

> *The Parties agree that service of process may be effected by certified or registered mail, return receipt requested, directed to the other Party at the addresses set forth herein in Section ____, the Notices Provision, and service so made shall be completed when received.*

The parties should clearly provide that the agreement's notice provisions do not apply to the service of process for complaints unless specifically provided for in the notice provision. Parties should be hesitant to allow service by mail or e-mail unless there is a mechanism for confirming receipt. A party wants to avoid failing to realize it has been served and missing any statutory deadlines in which to respond. Some states require that service be transacted through a sheriff or court-appointed processors.

In reality, there is little advantage in providing for an alternative service methodology. Serving a party through its resident agent ensures certainty and protects a party from failing to meet a stator deadline because it did not realize it had been served.

Q. Severability (§ 55)

Severability clauses are intended to save an agreement if one of its provisions is found to be invalid. In such event, the intent is that the invalid clause would be stricken, and the agreement will be read without the clause preventing a court from potentially voiding the entire agreement. *See, e.g., Booker v. Robert Half Int'l, Inc.*, 315 F. Supp. 2d 94, 106 (D.D.C. 2004). This approach, while widely accepted, can have unintended consequences if an important clause is stricken. Therefore, prudent parties should identify those clauses that are essential to the agreement and state that they should not be severed.

> *If any provision of this Agreement shall be found to be illegal or unenforceable in a judicial proceeding, such provision shall be severed and shall be inoperative, and, provided that the fundamental terms and conditions of this Agreement (including, without limitation, Sections __, __, and __) remain legal and enforceable, the remainder of this Agreement shall remain operative and binding on the Parties.*

For a more detailed discussion, *see* Fishman & James, *Drafting a Better Severability Clause*, Corp. Couns. (Oct. 2013).

R. Amendment and Oral Modification

Most agreements provide that they may only be modified by a written amendment signed by both parties to the agreement and that any oral modification is invalid. The following language illustrates this concept:

> *This Agreement may be modified only pursuant to a writing executed by authorized representatives of Customer and Vendor. The parties expressly disclaim the right to claim the enforceability or effectiveness of: (a) any oral modifications to this Agreement; and (b) any other amendments that are based on a course of dealing, waiver, reliance, estoppel or other similar legal theory.*

Prudent parties should be cognizant of subsequent click-wrap terms which a party/employee may agree to, unaware that they are agreeing to supersede a negotiated term in the parties' agreement. Thus, the parties should specifically state that any subsequent click-wrap terms will not override the agreement's negotiated terms.

When drafting amendments, the amendments should:

- be consecutively numbered;
- reference the existing agreement and list all previous amendments;
- use the same nomenclature and defined terms as the overarching agreement; and
- ratify the unmodified provisions.

> *Except as expressly provided in this Amendment, the Agreement shall be unaffected and shall remain in full force and effect and is hereby in all respects ratified and confirmed by each of the parties.*

Some courts have declined to enforce clauses requiring all amendments to be in writing, holding that if a contract may be formed orally, it may be modified or amended orally. *See GE Properties, LLC v. Draggoo*, 370 Wis. 2d 261 (2016). New York has enacted a specific statute stating that agreements with a prohibition on oral modification can only be modified by a writing signed by the party against whom the provision will be enforced. N.Y. GEN. OBLIG. LAW. §15-301(1). Even this prohibition, however, may be waived in certain circumstances. *Aircraft Services Resales LLC v. Oceanic Capital Co. Ltd.*, 586 Fed. Appx. 761 (2d Cir. 2014) (Seller and buyer made enforceable modification to extend closing date of their agreements under equitable estoppel and partial performance exceptions to general prohibition against oral modification of contracts proscribing such modifications.).

See Form O.7 for an annotated amendment agreement.

S. Assignment and Novation of the Agreement (§ 22)

1. *Assignment.*

Prohibitions on assignment will be enforced in accordance with the terms of the assignment clause. Thus, the parties should include any carveouts to any prohibition on assignment in their agreement. *MTA Canada Royalty Corp. v. Compania Minera Pangea, S.A. de C.V.*, 2020 WL 5554161 (Del. Super. Sept. 16, 2020) (Anti-assignment clause prohibiting assignment including by operation of law was breached by merger of contracting party). They should also include language that any attempt to violate the prohibition on assignment will be *void ab initio*. The failure to do so may result in a court upholding the assignment and awarding the injured party monetary damages. See Chapter 4.G for a discussion on the assignment of licenses.

> *Neither this Agreement nor any Order Form nor any right or obligation hereunder or thereunder may be assigned, transferred or delegated, by operation of law or otherwise, in whole or in part, by a Party without the other Party's prior written consent and any attempt to do so shall be void ab initio; provided that (a) such consent shall not to be unreasonably withheld or delayed with respect to a proposed assignment of this Agreement and all Order Forms as a whole and (b) either Party may assign this Agreement and all Order Forms, as a whole, to an Affiliate or in connection with a merger, consolidation, acquisition, sales of all or substantially all of the assets of a Party, or other 'change of control' type transaction (each a "**Change of Control**"), without consent of the other Party; provided the assigning Party provides prompt written notice of assignment to the non-assigning Party following the assignment.*

2. *Novation*

A novation is the creation of a new contractual agreement that extinguishes an existing agreement. *I.W. Berman Properties v. Porter Brothers, Inc.*, 344 A.2d 65, 70 (Md. 1975). A new agreement is created on the same terms and condition with only the parties changing. RESTATEMENT (SECOND) OF CONTRACTS § 280. A novation agreement must clearly evidence the intent of all of parties to "extinguish the old obligations and substitute a new one for it." *Adler v. Walker & Dunlop, Inc.*, 225 A.2d 459, 462 (Md. 1967). By entering into a novation, the assigning party extinguishes its liability or at least limits its liability up to the time of the novation, while the other party releases the novating party from future performance. A novation stands in contrast to an assignment, as an assignment does not generally release the assignor of all its obligations. See Form 0.8 for a model Transfer and Novation Agreement. Thus, a party interested in transferring its obligations, should consider executing a novation instead of an assignment to avoid/limit its future liability.

T. Integration/Entire Agreement (§ 58)

1. General

An "Integration" or "Entire Agreement" clause provides that the entire agreement between the parties is set forth within the four corners of the document and that all provisions, discussions, agreements, statements, etc., not set forth within the agreement shall be of no force and effect. In short, integration clauses limit the rights and obligations of the parties to the actual terms set forth in the license agreement. Negotiations are presumed to be merged into the agreement and oral testimony is inadmissible to explain or vary the agreement. *National Cash Reg. Co. v. Modern Transfer Co., Inc.*, 302 A.2d 486 (Pa. 1973) (integration clause contained in a computer lease agreement prevented the lessee from introducing evidence as to oral representations made by the lessor's agent prior to the execution of the agreement which were not included in the agreement). Integration clauses prevent a party from agreeing in a clearly worded integration clause that it did not rely on statements and representations outside of the agreement then later claiming that it did rely. *ABRY Partners V, L.P. v. F & W Acquisition L.L.C.*, 891 A.2d 1032 (Del. 2006).

Integration clauses protect the licensor from claims that sales "puffery" made by the licensor's sales force in the sales process constitutes fraud. From the licensee's perspective, however, the license agreement needs to ensure that all statements made by the licensor and relied on by the licensee in making its decision to select the licensor are included in the agreement. If these statements are not included, they are moot.

A well-drafted integration clause should contain a statement to the effect that the licensee is not relying upon any written or oral representation or inducement not included or referenced within the underlying agreement. Prudent licensors may want to expand on this concept by specifically providing that the licensee has not relied on any representation not contained within the agreement related to a specific aspect of the agreement. The following language is illustrative of this concept:

> *No representations, promises, or inducements not included or referred to herein shall be binding upon the Licensor. Specifically, Licensee is not relying upon any representations not embodied in this contract, written or oral, concerning [insert specific area of concern].*

The inclusion of an integration clause, however, is not conclusive evidence of an integrated agreement. *United States v. Basin Elec. Power Coop.*, 248 F.3d 781, 809 (8th

Cir. 2001) (two contracts found to be interrelated despite use of integration clause). Most courts will enforce a well-articulated integration clause between sophisticated parties. *MBIA Ins. Corp. v. Royal Indemnity Co.*, 426 F.3d 204, 218 (3d Cir. 2005) ("When sophisticated parties include a broad but unambiguous anti-reliance clause in their agreement, the Delaware Supreme Court will likely indulge the assumption that they said what they meant and meant what they said."). Some courts, however, will strictly interpret such clauses to limit broad exclusions. *Texas Taco Cabana, L.P. v. Taco Cabana of New Mexico*, 304 F. Supp. 2d 903 (W.D. Tex. 2003) (non-reliance clause will bar claims to extent the clause specifically identified statements not relied on but will not always bar claims on other issues not expressly disclaimed in agreement).

An integration clause alone will usually not be sufficient to defeat a fraud claim, *Whelan v. Abell*, 48 F.3d 1247 (D.C. Cir. 1995), but will be considered as one of many factors by a court in reaching its decision. *Dresner v. Utility.com, Inc.*, 371 F. Supp. 2d 476 (S.D.N.Y. 2005).

Prudent licensors, however, will insist on the inclusion of an integration clause to defeat a claim of fraud by the customer arising from the sales process. *See i2 Technologies, Inc. v. DARC Corp.*, 2003 WL 22205091 (N.D. Tex. Sept. 23, 2003). *See also* Houtman & Schmierer, *Walking the Tightrope: Limiting Fraud Claims Based on Extra-contractual Statements and Omissions*, Bus. L. Today (Aug. 2013).

Courts are divided as to whether an integration clause will bar a claim for fraudulent inducement. *Compare Northwest Bank and Trust Co. v. First Illinois National Bank*, 354 F.3d 721 (8th Cir. 2003) (contractual disclaimer ineffective to bar claim for fraudulent inducement) and *Contractor Utility Sales Co., v. Certain-Teed Corp.*, 748 F.2d 1151, 1154 (7th Cir. 1984) ("Integration rule yields to a properly established demonstration of fraud inducing and vitiating the execution of the written agreement.") *with Rosen v. Watermill Development Corp.*, 1 A.D.3d 424 (N.Y. App. 2003) (integration clause must specifically disclaim basis of alleged misrepresentations to defeat claim of fraud). Under New York law, the specificity requirement is lowered where the integration clause resulted from extensive negotiations between sophisticated parties. *Citibank, N.A. v. Plapinger*, 495 N.Y.S.2d 309, 311–12 (N.Y. 1985).

The importance of an integration clause is illustrated by *BSkyB Ltd. v. H.P. Enterprise Sources UK Ltd.*, 2010 WL 20033 (E.W.H.C. B.D. Jan. 26, 2010). Although decided in the United Kingdom, the case provides insight as to the risk that can arise from improper behavior. In *BSkyB*, a company subsequently acquired by HP entered into a contract with BSkyB to design, build and provide systems integrations services for a new Customer Relationship Management (CRM) system. The integration clause in the underlying agreement specifically identified fraudulent misrepresentations as not being excluded by the clause. BSkyB subsequently brought suit against HP for breach of contract in failing to deliver the contractually agreed upon CRM system.

The court found that HP had made fraudulent misrepresentations when HP stated that it had studied BSkyB's requirements and could deliver the required system within the contractually required time frame. HP eventually settled the matter for $459,400,000, an amount more than ten times the contract's $45,294,000 limitation of liability.

To avoid similar claims, licensors should include a statement in the agreement's integration clause to the effect that the licensee has not relied on any representation, warranty or statement other than as set forth in the agreement. The following language is illustrative:

> *Each party acknowledges that, in entering into this Agreement, it has not relied on, and shall have no right or remedy in respect of, any statement, representation, assurance or warranty (whether made negligently or innocently) other than as expressly set out in this Agreement.*

Some vendors seek to include a provision in the integration clause specifically disclaiming reliance on certain identified materials and statements in the belief the court will be more willing to reject a claim of fraud in the inducement based on a specific disclaimer. *See DynCorp v. GTE Corp.*, 215 F. Supp. 2d 308, 311–12 (S.D.N.Y. 2002) (disclaimer provided that seller would have no liability to buyer "resulting from the distribution to Buyer, or Buyer's use of any such information, including the Confidential Offering Memorandum dated July 1999 . . . ."); *Danann Realty Corp. v. Harris*, 157 N.E.2d 597 (N.Y. 1959). Other factors a court may consider when evaluating a fraud claim include the customer's access to information, any provision providing that indemnification is the customer's exclusive remedy, and the inclusion of an "AS-IS" disclaimer in the underlying agreement. *See, e.g., DRR L.L.C. v. Sears Roebuck & Co.*, 949 F. Supp. 1132 (D. Del. 1996).

If the parties are entering into or have entered into multiple agreements, the parties should reference the other agreements in the integration clause to avoid any argument that one agreement superseded another. Another means of avoiding an "unintended consequence" is to include language to the effect that the document reflects the entire agreement between the parties "on the subject matter hereof." *See, e.g., G.M. Persey and Associates v. Britt/Paulk Insurance Agency, Inc.*, 2008 WL 203747 (D. Md. May 6, 2008).

2. Collateral Agreements

To the extent other documents are intended to be included within the terms of the agreement, they should be attached to the agreement as exhibits. The agreement should specifically state that all exhibits and schedules are specifically incorporated into and made part of the agreement. At least one court has held that the "mere reference to another document is not sufficient to incorporate that other document into a contract, particularly where the incorporating document makes no specific reference that it is 'subject to' the collateral documents." *Monfiston v. State of Florida*, 920 So. 2d 1286, 1288 (Fla. 2006). Simply stating that an agreement is subject to a collateral document is not necessarily sufficient to bind a party to a collateral agreement. *Id.* See, e.g., § 53. The parties should ensure that these collateral documents do not in turn reference other documents, such that the effect of the integration clause is effectively mooted by a continuing "daisy chain" of documents.

The parties should be careful when including integration clauses in dependent agreements, that is, agreements that are either incorporated into a separate agreement or attached as an exhibit. At least one court has found that where both an agreement and an exhibit to such agreement contain distinct integration clauses, such agreements should be interpreted as independent agreements. *Baldwin Piano, Inc. v. Deutsche Wurlitzer GMBH*, 2004 WL 46243 (N.D. Ill. Jan. 7, 2004) ("The presence of the integration clauses in each of the agreements therefore indicates the parties' intent that each document should stand on its own and be interpreted as a complete agreement into itself."). Courts will seek to read and construe the various documents together "as evidencing the intention of the parties in regard to a single transaction . . . even though the instruments were executed at different times and do not in terms refer to each other." *Rocks v. Brocius*, 217 A.2d 531, 545 (Md. 1967). Similarly, the parties should ensure that the agreement's integration clause does not impact a party's rights set forth in another agreement, especially if the parties have executed other independent agreements, such a nondisclosure agreement, maintenance agreement, etc. To avoid unintended consequences, the parties often add a clause referring to "the subject matter contained herein". See model language below.

> *This Agreement, the appendices, and subordinate documents referenced in this Agreement constitute the entire agreement between the parties* ***with respect to the subject matter contained herein****, superseding all previous agreements pertaining to such subject matter, and may be modified only by an amendment executed in writing by the authorized officers of both parties hereto.*

U. Seals (Penultimate Paragraph and Signature Line)

The use of seals arises from ancient times when many people could not read and write. Their "seal" indicted their acceptance or endorsement of the relevant document. For a brief history of the use of seals in the legal contract, *see From the History of Seals and Signatures*, Information Security Solutions Europe Conference 2000 (Barcelona, Sept. 28, 2000). Many practitioners often overlook the ramifications of including the word "(SEAL)" after the signature line or including the phrase "executed under seal" in the agreement. It is often believed that such terms are an archaic reminder from earlier times, or that such terms are an acknowledgment that many corporations no longer have a corporate seal.

Sealed instruments or contracts do not require consideration to be binding. RESTATEMENT (SECOND) OF CONTRACTS § 95. *See, e.g., Warten v. Moore*, 366 S.E.2d 666 (Ga. 1988). Further, the use of the term "seal" may significantly extend the statute of limitations and the analogous period for laches. *See, e.g., Whittington v. Dragon Group, L.L.C.*, 991 A.2d 1 (Del. Sup. 2009) (typing word "Seal" on signature line was sufficient to extend statute of limitations and analogous period for laches from 3 to 20 years). Under Maryland law, for example, use of the term "seal" extends the statute of limitations from 3 to 12 years. MD. CODE ANN., MD. CTS. & JUD. PROC. § 5-102(a)(5). The requirements for a sealed instrument vary by state. Under Maryland law, the signature lines need only contain the term "(SEAL)" to be considered sealed. *Warfield v. Baltimore Gas & Electric Co., 512 A.2d 1044 (Md. 1986).* Under New York law, however, the agreement itself must contain an acknowledgment of the parties' intent to have a sealed agreement. *Transbel Inv. Co., Inc. v. Venetos*, 18 N.E.2d 129 (N.Y. 1938).

V. Signatures, Signature Lines, and Signature Pages

Although customary, no specific language is required to precede a signature line. Often the parties include language similar to that set forth in Form B.3.1 to indicate that there are no further contractual provisions and that the signature lines follow.

A party should avoid signing and circulating signature pages that are not attached to the final agreement. Every effort should be made to have the signature lines appear on the same page as the last contractual provisions. Circulating signature pages without the underlying agreement attached creates the possibility of confusion as to which terms were agreed to by the parties and the potential for fraud through the inclusion of additional terms without the knowledge of the other party. *See Kotler v. Shipman Assoc. LLC.*, 2019 WL 4025634 (Del. Aug 21, 2019) (litigating parties circulated signed pages but pages were attached to two different documents). Further, if signature pages are attached to the agreement by a lawyer without the review of the client, the agreement will likely be binding on the client under the theory that the client's lawyer had the actual or apparent authority to approve the agreement and attach the signature pages. While such actions may give rise to a claim of malpractice against the lawyer, a malpractice claim is a hollow remedy for the affected client.

The signature line should clearly state the title of the individual executing the agreement to indicate that he or she is doing so as an employee and not individually. The failure to do so could potentially result in the individual executing the agreement being personally liable. *PMC Chase, LLP v. Branch Structural Solutions, Inc.*, 2020 WL 467791 (Tex. Jan. 28, 2020).

1. Signature Authority

Prudent parties should always confirm that the individual executing an agreement for an entity has the authority to execute the agreement on the entity's behalf and have the contracting entity provide a representation and warranty to that effect. *See Digital Ally, Inc. v. Z3 Tech., LLC*, 2014 WL 1979373 (10th Cir. May 16, 2014).

> ***IN WITNESS WHEREOF**, each Party has duly executed this Agreement on the dates set forth below, effective as of the Effective Date, and the individual signing for each Party certifies that he/she has the authority to bind the Party on behalf of which he/she has signed.*

2. Electronic and Digital Signatures

Since the adoption of the Electronic Signatures in Global and National Commerce Act (E-SIGN) in 2000, 15 U.S.C. § 7001 *et seq.*, and the Uniform Electronic Transactions Act ("UETA") in every state but Illinois, New York and Washington (although each of these states recognize electronic signatures through state legislation), electronic signatures have become widely accepted. Electronic signatures are consummated via third-party vendors such as DocuSign® or AdobeSign®, who validate the identity of the signer via their email and IP address. Under UETA and E-SIGN, electronic signatures have the same legal effect as written signatures.

Electronic signatures, however, are not without their own issues. Among the most common concerns is the need to ensure that the chosen e-signature software allows the parties to authenticate the user's identity/signature and ensure that the "executed" document is the same agreement that the parties had agreed on. Further, the integrity of the document must be guaranteed through a chain of custody so that in the event of a dispute, the document can later be entered into as evidence of the document governing the relationship between the parties. The parties must comply with the compliance obligations set forth in E-SIGN. Thus, prior to agreeing to utilize electronic signatures, the parties should clearly understand the risks and obligations of doing so.

The parties should also recognize that email signatures can create a binding agreement without the need for a written signature, *Cloud Corp. v. Hasbro, Inc.*, 314 F.3d 289 (7th Cir. 2002), as can text messages. *St. John's Holdings, LLC v. Two Elecs., LLC*, 2016 WL 1460477 (Mass. Apr. 14, 2016).

Finally, the parties should ensure that they each maintain proper security for their computer networks, allowing the parties to prove that each executed the agreement electronically. Several courts have refused to enforce an agreement because the party seeking to enforce the agreement could not prove that the other party had electronically executed the agreement. To enforce an agreement, the plaintiff must prove that it had sufficient authentication processes in place to reasonably identify the signer. *See The Prudential Ins. Co. of America v. Dukoff*, 674 F. Supp. 2d 401 (E.D.N.Y. 2009); *Kerr v. Dillard Store Services, Inc.*, 2009 WL 385863 (D. Kan. Feb. 17, 2009).

For a detailed discussion, *see* Brenton & Epstein, *Implementation and Use of Electronic Contracts*, 31 ACC DOCKET 58 (SEPT. 2013).

3. *Facsimile Signatures*

Computer generated facsimile signatures are presumed valid absent evidence to the contrary. *State of Arizona v. Irving*, 797 P.2d 1237 (Ariz. App. 2000).

4. *Manual Signatures*

The agreement should provide that any amendment must be in writing, executed by an authorized executive officer of both parties. A party may want to identify by name a single person who has the authority to execute all agreements and that any signature must be a manual signature. Some companies (e.g., Oracle and Siemens) specifically provide that all agreements must bear two signatures, one being a member of the legal department, to defeat any ill-advised agreement or an unknown amendment to an agreement. To add a further level of protection, some parties explicitly state that amendments executed by individuals in the field are nonbinding.

The agreement should also provide that the agreement cannot be amended electronically and that electronic signatures are invalid. Many parties avoid all electronic amendments, although this may not be practical. Some seek to identify those employees who may accept electronically for the party, as it will likely be very difficult to prove that someone did or did not accept a particular provision/amendment five years after the fact. The person who allegedly accepted for a party will certainly not remember the specific transaction and may have left the party's employ by the time the dispute arises. Further, who will maintain the electronic database necessary to prove the signature is valid?

W. Dating the Agreement

The parties should always date the agreement whether by referencing the date of the last signature or by including a date in the heading of the agreement. The parties should carefully consider backdating an agreement even though it may be permissible in some situations, it may be unlawful if the parties were trying to obscure the compliance obligations or more revenue from one quarter to another. *See U.S. v. Micke*, 859 F.2d 473 (7th Cir. 1988). Backdating may be appropriate in limited situations such as executing an NDA to cover information that has already been disclosed or executing a document that should have been executed at closing but was misplaced.

Some parties seek to backdate an agreement where the licensor may have provided services prior to executing the agreement and the parties contemplate the immediate payment of accrued invoices upon execution. In doing so, the licensee should realize that by backdating the agreement or a SOW, the licensor may have the right to immediately bill the licensee upon contract/SOW execution. Similarly, the licensor, by agreeing to an "effective date" prior to the execution date, may find that it has already missed a deliverable date or may no longer be able to meet the previously agreed-upon milestones. Thus, prior to agreeing to a date, the parties should ensure that the earlier "effective date" does not trigger any liabilities on the part of one or both parties (i.e., the parties' deliverable and payment obligations should be tied to the execution date, not the effective date).

The parties should be careful when stating the date that the contract was executed. While the parties are free to choose an effective date, backdating a contract may be fraudulent and even criminal. As such, the parties should clearly indicate the date on which the agreement was executed and the effective date of the agreement if the parties choose to have different effective dates.

X. Terms/Corporate Policies Incorporated by Reference

In an increasing number of agreements, large multi-national customers often seek to include their corporate policies on a wide range of topics such as child labor, the environment, codes of conduct, travel, diversity, personal background checks, etc., significantly adding to the length of the agreement even though many of these policies are not applicable to the services being rendered by the vendor.

The more cumbersome a policy, the longer the contract cycles will be, and the less capable a party's negotiation team (who may not have any legal contracts training) will be at meaningfully participating in the negotiation and drafting process. Most important, many of these terms will have no impact on the business dealings with the other party (other than to possibly get the parties off to a bad start), and will not provide any meaningful recourse or remedy, outside of litigation, which prudent parties seek to avoid.

To address these concerns, a party needs to reach consensus on how to impose its policies on its customers and vendors. A prudent party should not try to incorporate its policies into its contracts for many reasons:

- Most policies are constantly changing;
- Most policies have been written for internal use and not intended for public consumption in the form written;
- Most policies may not be legally binding and may create a worrisome conflict with binding terms in the underlying agreement and applicable law;
- A party may lack the leverage to impose its policies in important transactions as most sophisticated parties will have their own competing policies and typically will not agree to another party's; and
- Many policies are created using a broad brush to fix a problem that needed to be artfully addressed.

A more prudent approach may be to reference these policies in the overarching agreement. To the extent a party needs to make its policies available to the other party, it should do so outside the contracting process through an "on-boarding" document package or preferably via a URL. In this manner, a party can control the comprehensive updating of its policies and make them universally "known" to all its vendors and customers simultaneously. Model language is as follows:

As part of the on-boarding process, Licensee will provide a supplemental document package to Licensor, which may include additional policies, standards and materials including the Licensee Code of Conduct, and any related forms or tools (collectively, and together with the Responsible Procurement Principles, the "Licensee Responsible Procurement Policies").

Licensors should ensure that the customer's sole remedy in the event the licensor fails to comply with the customer's code of conduct is to terminate the agreement. Model language follows:

Vendor must meet the requirements of Customer's Supplier Code of Conduct, found at www.customer.com. Vendor's agreement to comply with Customer's Supplier Code of Conduct is an agreement exclusively between Vendor and Customer and there are no third-party beneficiaries to such agreement. Customer's sole remedy for Vendor's failure to comply is to terminate any agreements that exist between Customer and Vendor for the license of Vendor's Software. Vendor shall never be liable to Customer for monetary damages of any kind, including but not limited to actual, consequential, special, and punitive damages, for any noncompliance or any termination of any agreement as a result of such noncompliance. Customer shall not be entitled to any equitable relief as respects any noncompliance including, but not limited to, specific performance or any type of injunction.

For a more detailed discussion of the use of online terms, refer to Chapter 6.O.

CHAPTER 7

Other Important Issues

A. The Work Made for Hire Doctrine and Moral Rights

1. Work Made for Hire Doctrine

(a) Works Created by Independent Contractors

United States law generally holds that the copyright in a work is initially vested in the person who creates it. 17 U.S.C. § 201(a). Therefore, an independent contractor, as the "author" of a work, usually retains all copyrights to that work unless he or she assigns its rights to the buyer. 17 U.S.C. § 201(d). Absent any assignment, the buyer is only deemed to hold a nonexclusive license. *See MacLean Associates, Inc. v. Wm. M. Mercer-Meidinger Hansen, Inc.*, 952 F.2d 769 (3d Cir. 1991) (contracting party had obtained an "implied" but limited nonexclusive license); *Effects Associates v. Cohen*, 817 F.2d 72 (9th Cir. 1987), *aff'd*, 908 F.2d 555 (9th Cir. 1990), *cert. denied sub nom. Danforth v. Cohen*, 498 U.S. 1103 (1991). Nonexclusive licenses "may be granted orally or by implication." *Asset Marketing Systems, Inc. v. Gagnon*, 542 F.3d 748, 754 (9th Cir. 2008).

The extent of the license received by the buyer is determined by "the licensor's objective intent at the time of the creation and delivery of the software as manifested by the parties' conduct." *Id.* at 756 (independent contractor's actions manifested intent to grant customer unlimited, nonexclusive, irrevocable license with the right to retain, use and modify the software). The *Gagnon* court created a three- part test for determining a licensor's intent to convey an implied license:

(1) the licensee requests the creation of a work,
(2) the licensor creates the work and delivers it to the licensee, and
(3) the licensor intends for the licensee to copy and distribute the work.

Id. at 754–55.

As such, an implied, nonexclusive license is limited to the scope of use initially contemplated when the buyer commissioned the work, i.e., the number of users, purpose, and the like, and may be terminated by the copyright holder at any time unless the buyer retained other express or implied contractual rights.

Such a limited and nonexclusive license to use the work may place a buyer at a severe disadvantage vis-à-vis its competitors. A contractor, for instance, could potentially disclose a buyer's proprietary information in licensing the work to others and thereby nullify any competitive advantage the employer gained by commissioning the work. In addition, as the "owner" of the copyright in the work, a contractor could limit a buyer's right to use or distribute the work if such use is outside the scope of the original commission. *See Graham v. James*, 144 F.3d 229 (2d Cir. 1990) (creation of a program by an independent contractor remains the property of the contractor and any unauthorized use is actionable).

An independent contractor retaining ownership in software specified and funded by the buyer may seem counterintuitive. A buyer may invest large sums of money and significant technical input in a project only to find that the contractor claims ownership of the work when the project results in a commercially saleable product. The courts have attempted to soften the effect of this result by implying that the employer will have a perpetual, fully paid-up license to use the software for all purposes intended in the contract and, importantly, to modify the software as necessary to support those uses. *See, e.g., Clifford Scott Aymes v. Jonathan J. Bonnelli d/b/a Island Swimming Sales, Inc.*, 47 F.3d 23 (2d Cir. 1995); *LimeCoral, Ltd. v. CareerBuilder, LLC*, 889 F.3d 847 (7th Cir. 2018). *See also Foad Consulting Group, Inc. v. Musil Govan Azzalino*, 270 F.3d 821 (9th Cir. 2001) (party hiring contractor has implied license to use contractor's work product in all ways intended or expected to retain the work's commercial value *unless* the contractor explicitly provides that there is no implied license to use, modify, and assign its rights).

While these interpretations help avoid the harsh results of the rule granting ownership to independent contractors, the courts ultimately hold that, absent an explicit assignment to the employer, the independent contractor owns software produced pursuant to contractual arrangement. *See, e.g., Conwell v. Gray Loon Outdoor Marketing Group, Inc.*, 906 N.E.2d 805 (Ind. 2009). Further, the assignment must be executed prior to the creation of the work. *Estate of Stanley Kauffman v. Rochester Institute of Technology*, 932 F.3d 74 (2d Cir. 2019). Notably, independent contractors rarely demand additional consideration or concessions for such assignments. Failure to secure an assignment from a contractor may result in the loss of a significant asset to the employer, especially where a product may have commercial value apart from the internal use contemplated by the employer. Further, because ownership remains with the contractor, the independent contractor/author may license or assign its rights in a work to a competitor of the party paying for the work.

(b) The Work Made for Hire Doctrine

There are instances where a company will be presumed to be the owner of a commissioned work under the "work made for hire" doctrine. In the United States, an employer is considered the original author of a commissioned work if the work qualifies as work made for hire under the United States Copyright Act. 17 U.S.C. § 201(b). Section 201 of the act provides that "[i]n the case of a work made for hire, the employer or other person for whom the work was prepared is considered the author for purposes of this title, and, unless the parties have expressly agreed otherwise in a written instrument signed by them, owns all of the rights comprised in the copyright." 17 U.S.C. § 201(b). Classifying the work as work made for hire determines not only the initial ownership of copyright, but also the copyright's duration (§ 302(c)), the owner's renewal rights (§ 304(a)) and termination rights (§ 203(a)). *See* 1 MELVILLE B. NIMMER & DAVID NIMMER, NIMMER ON COPYRIGHT, § 5.03[A] at 5–11 to 5–12 (2005).

Work made for hire is defined as: "(1) a work prepared by an employee within the scope of his or her employment; or (2) a work (i) specially ordered or commissioned for use as a contribution to a collective work, (ii) as a part of a motion picture or other audio-visual work, (iii) as a translation, (iv) as a supplementary work, (v) as a compilation, (vi) as an instructional text, (vii) as a test, (viii) as answer material for a test, or (ix) as an atlas, if the parties expressly agree in a written instrument signed by them that the work shall be considered a work made for hire." 17 U.S.C. § 101.

Thus, to be a work for hire, a work must fall into one of the nine categories and there must be an agreement stating that the work is a work made for hire. Several courts have found that the development of software meets the statutory definition of "compilation" or "contributions to collective works" and thus can be a work made for hire. *See Siniouguine v. MediaChase Ltd*, 2012 WL 2317364 (C.D. Cal. June 11, 2012); *Stanacard, LLC. v. Rubard, LLC*, 2016 WL 462508 (S.D.N.Y. Feb. 3, 2016).

To be a "work made for hire" the work in question must also fit under one of nine categories listed in subsection (2) of the definition. "Computer Program" is not listed as a category. However, case law makes clear that nonliteral elements of a computer program are properly considered a "compilation" insofar as the concepts of selection, arrangement and organization, central to the compilation doctrine, are included in the analysis of a computer program's structure. *See Computer Assocs. Int'l, Inc. v. Altai, Inc.*, 982 F.2d 693, 711-12 (2d Cir. 1992); *Harbor Software, Inc. v. Applied Systems, Inc.*, 925 F. Supp. 1024, 1047 (S.D.N.Y.1996).

Software written by a non-employee could qualify as a work made for hire, as a specially commissioned compilation or as a "contribution to a collective work", under the definition of "work made for hire" under section 101 of the Copyright Act. *See e.g.* Garon & Ziff, *The Work Made for Hire Doctrine Revisited: Startup and Technology Employees and the Use of Contracts in a Hiring Relationship*, 12 Minn. J. Law. Sci. & Tech. 489 (2011) ("Software has been argued to be within the nine categories of specially commissioned works either as a part of a collective work in the system as a whole or because the non-literal elements of the program constitute a compilation." (citations omitted)); *iXL Inc. v. AdOutlet.com, Inc.*, 2001 WL 315219 *9 (N.D. Ill. Mar. 21, 2009) (Source code "specially ordered or commissioned for use," qualified as a "contribution to a collective work"); *Logicom Inclusive v. W.P. Stewart & Co.*, 2004 WL 1781009 (S.D.N.Y. Apr. 10, 2004).

In determining whether a work will fall within the employee's "scope of employment," the courts will look at a number of factors including the following:

- the level of skill;
- the source of the instruments and tools for creation of the work;
- the location of the work;
- the duration of the employment relationship;
- whether the hiring party has the right to make additional assignments;
- the hired party's discretion over when or how long to work;
- the method of payment, if any;
- the hired party's role in hiring/paying assistants;

- the location of where the work was created;
- whether the work is part of the hiring party's regular business; and
- the provision of employee benefits.

See, e.g., Siniouguine v. Mediachase Ltd., 2012 WL 2317364 (C.D. Cal. June 11, 2012) (discussing factors for determining whether a software program is a work made for hire); *Avtec Systems, Inc. v. Peiffer*, 67 F.3d 293 (4th Cir. 1995); *Cole v. Control Data Corp.*, 947 F.2d 313 (8th Cir. 1991); *Quin v. City of Detroit* 988 F. Supp. 1044 (E.D. Mich. 1991); *Miller v. CP Chems., Inc.*, 808 F. Supp. 1238, 1242–44 (D.S.C. 1992); Restatement (Second) of Agency § 228.

Performing work at home after hours will not allow an employee to establish copyright ownership and avoid the work made for hire doctrine. *Rouse v. Walter & Associates, L.L.C.*, 513 F. Supp. 2d 1058 (S.D. Iowa 2007). An employee's conduct may be considered within the scope of employment even if it is found in part to benefit the employee or a third party. *Id.* at 1060. Any agreement to alter the employer's ownership in a work under the work made for hire doctrine must be expressly stated. *Id.* at 1061.

Because most computer software will not automatically fall within the nine types of work enumerated earlier in category two, writing a software program will generally qualify as work made for hire only if it was "prepared by an employee, within the scope of his or her employment."

(c) Independent Contractors

An independent contractor, however, will not usually qualify as an "employee" within the meaning of the Copyright Act. In *Community for Creative Non-Violence v. Reid*, 490 U.S. 703 (1989) (CCNV), the Supreme Court declared that an artist, who was commissioned by a nonprofit organization to create a sculpture, was an "independent contractor" and not an employee within the meaning of the copyright act, even though the nonprofit organization directed enough of the sculptor's work to ensure that he produced a sculpture that met their specifications. *Id.* at 753. The U.S. Supreme Court later unanimously generalized *CCNV* as the appropriate standard for defining an employee outside of the copyright area as well. *Nationwide Mutual Ins.* Co. *v. Darden*, 503 U.S. 318, 322 (1992).

If the independent contractor does not qualify as an employee, the employer can only gain title to the work product of the contractor by having the contractor execute an assignment transferring his or her ownership rights in the work to the employer. *CCNV*, 490 U.S. at 750.

Under the Copyright Act, an independent contractor who assigns ownership of a work to a third party can terminate the assignee's ownership rights in the assigned work after 35 years. 17 U.S.C. § 203(a)(3). A work made for hire, however, is not subject to the termination, as there is no underlying transfer, and ownership of the work accrues in the party that commissions the work. Thus, if a work created by an independent contractor qualifies as a work made for hire under the Copyright Act, the commissioning entity will own the copyrighted work in perpetuity.

California Labor Code § 3351.5(c) provides that an individual hired to produce a "work made for hire" is an employee. Further, California Insurance Code (§§ 686 and 621(d)) provides that anyone hiring an individual to produce a "work made for hire" must maintain unemployment and worker's compensation insurance for that individual. Consequently, prudent entities will avoid using the phrase "work made for hire" and instead assign all right, title, and interest in any developments to the hiring party with a fallback of an unlimited perpetual license grant if the assignment should fail for any reason. Model language follows:

> *Except for Consultant's Information as described below, Consultant assigns to Company the title, ownership, and all rights in any deliverables or other work product created by Consultant or Personnel for Company under this Agreement (collectively' "deliverables"). To the extent an assignment is not effective under applicable law, Consultant grants Company an exclusive, perpetual, royalty-free, fully-paid, irrevocable, worldwide, transferable license to use, reproduce, distribute, and commercialize any deliverables to the fullest extent permissible and effective under applicable law. Consultant shall cooperate with Company, at Company's expense and request, as reasonably required to perfect or secure Company's rights, including executing appropriate documents. Deliverables shall not include Consultant's pre-existing proprietary or licensed tools, templates, or methodologies ("Consultant's Information"); however, Consultant grants Company a royalty-free, fully paid, perpetual, irrevocable, worldwide, non-exclusive license to use the Consultant's Information incorporated in the deliverables.*

For a general overview of copyright issues involving independent contractors and employees, *see* Holland, *Copyrights and Consultants*, 36 LAW. BRIEF 2 (May 2006); Brewer, *Who Owns the Invention? Addressing Ownership Claims of Employees and Contractors*, 23 COMPUTER & INTERNET LAW. 17 (Aug. 2006).

(d) Employee Inventions

Although an employer will not receive ownership of any patentable invention created under a general employment context, the employer will receive a nonexclusive, implied license to such patentable material. Known as a "shop right," an employer obtains a nonexclusive limited license to use the patentable invention for its internal purposes if the invention was made on company time with company resources. *United States v. Dubilier Condenser Corp.*, 289 U.S. 178, 188 (1933).

To avoid potential disputes and obtain the intellectual property rights needed to operate their business, most employers require that new employees execute a confidentiality and assignment of inventions agreement, usually in conjunction with a noncompetition agreement upon employment. See Form L.8 for a model Non-competition, Confidentiality, and Inventions Agreement.

Some states, however, limit the intellectual property rights that an employee may be required to assign to the employer where the employee created the intellectual property on his or her own time without use of the employer's assets. California: CAL. LAB. CODE ANN. §§ 2870-72 (West 2010); Washington: WASH. REV. CODE §§ 49.44.140-150 (West 2010).

For a general overview, *see* Pollock, *Who Owns an Employee Invention?*, 34 CORP. COUNS. Q. 345 (Apr. 2018).

(e) Execution of an Assignment

In order to receive sole and exclusive ownership of the copyright, a customer would be well advised to have the contractor execute an assignment transferring to the buyer the contractor's entire right, title, and interest in the work. (Forms C.3.1 and C.3.3 for model Consulting Agreements with an assignment clause.) The author must actually sign the assignment, as a single signature purchase order will not convey ownership to a buyer.

If a contractor previously executed an agreement without an assignment clause, the employer should have a comprehensive assignment agreement executed by the contractor and should be sure to list the consideration that the contractor is receiving for signing the assignment agreement. (See Forms L.2 and L.3 for model Assignment Agreement.) For any such assignment to be valid, it must be in writing and signed by both parties prior to the work's creation. *BancTraining Video Systems v. First American Corp.*, 956 F.2d 268 (6th Cir. 1993); *Schiller & Schmidt, Inc. v. Nordisco Corp.*, 969 F.2d 410 (7th Cir. 1992) (subsequent writing cannot correct the fact that there was no written agreement as required by statute at the time the work was created). *But see Playboy Enters. v. Dumas*, 53 F.3d 549 (2d Cir. 1995), *cert. denied*, 516 U.S. 1010 (1995) (prior oral agreement that work is work made for hire may later be memorialized in writing as the work is created). At least one court, however, has held that a work created by an independent contractor qualified as a "work made for hire" even though the author assigned its rights after the work had been completed. *20th Century Fox Film Corp. v. Entertainment Distributing*, 429 F.3d 869 (9th Cir 2005). In reaching its decision to uphold a lower court decision, the Ninth Circuit emphasized that the work had been created at the "insistence and expense" of the commissioning party and that the parties intended the work to be a "work made for hire." *Id.* at 880–82.

Employers should require a contractor to transfer ownership of all intellectual property created during the period of the relevant project to the employer. If the contractor claims ownership of similar or related intellectual property that exists at the time of executing the relevant consulting agreement, he should list and describe such intellectual property in detail as an exception to the employer's right of ownership. The failure to do so may lead the contractor to claim ownership of related work important to the employer's project. *See, e.g., Fowler v. Bell Helicopter Textron, Inc.*, 2005 WL 548076 (N.D. Tex. Mar. 9, 2005) (denying employer's motion for summary judgment of its claimed ownership of intellectual property created by contractor during term of his consultancy). *See also* Payne, *Departing Employees and "Abandoned" Research*, 23 COMP. & INTERNET LAW. 7 (Jan. 2006).

(f) Independent Contractor or Employee?

In determining whether a party will be considered an employee or an independent contractor, the courts will look beyond how the parties describe *their relationship in their agreement. Alexander v. FedEx Ground Package, Sys., Inc.*, 765 F.3d 981, 989 (9th Cir. 2014). Instead, a court will look at a number of factors, including the following:

- The nature and duration of the assignment. Is the work a discrete project or of a continuous nature?
- The level of skill provided.
- Who provides the *tools* necessary to perform the work?
- The degree of control over the creator and how the work will be performed.

- The length of the contract.
- The duration of the parties' relationship.
- How is the creator compensated?
- Eligibility of the creator for employee benefits.
- The location of the work.
- Whether the work is part of the hiring party's regular business.

The degree of control exercised by the hiring party over the work is perhaps the most critical factor; the greater the control, the greater the likelihood of finding the individual to be an employee. See *CCNV*, 490 U.S. at 75-52.

In *JustMed, Inc. v. Byce*, 600 F.3d 1118 (9th Cir. 2010), the Ninth Circuit Court of Appeals appeared to adopt a more lenient standard for startup technology companies when determining whether an individual is an employee or an independent contractor. In *JustMed*, a small technology start-up brought suit against Byce alleging misappropriation of trade secrets and conversion in relation to certain software source code written by Byce. Byce counterclaimed seeking a declaratory judgment that he was the sole owner of the software under the Copyright Act. The Ninth Circuit found that Byce was an employee despite the following:

- He worked from home in another state.
- He provided his own computer/tools.
- He worked with little supervision.
- JustMed did not issue a W-2 to Byce.
- JustMed did not withhold taxes, pay worker's compensation or pay unemployment insurance for Byce.
- JustMed did not represent Byce as an employee to the state.
- JustMed did not provide Byce any employee benefits.

Despite these indicia of being an independent contractor, the court found Byce to be an employee based on, among other reasons, the nature of the technology industry and JustMed's status as a start-up company. Specifically, the court found that Byce received input and supervision over the phone, recognizing that the nature of computer programming is such that it can be performed remotely without impacting the quality of the work product or the individual's ability to meet the company's needs. The court cited JustMed's status as a start-up company in finding that JustMed's failure to follow all the legal formalities associated with filing the required paperwork associated with its employees was not determinate of an employer/employee relationship. It stated that the failure to comply with applicable employment laws did not justify "denying that firm [Just Med] its intellectual property." *Id.* at 1128. Further, the court provided:

> As a small start-up company, JustMed conducted its business more informally than an established enterprise might. This fact can make it more difficult to decide whether a hired party is an employee or an independent contractor, but it should not make the company more susceptible to losing control over software integral to its product.

Id.

Thus, it appears, at least in the Ninth Circuit, that the courts will examine not only the indicia of an employer/employee relationship but also the nature of the employer's industry and the employer's corporate maturity.

In *Dynamix Operations West, Inc. v. Superior Court of Los Angeles*, 416 P.3d 1 (Cal. Sup. Ct. 2018), the California Supreme Court adopted a new test for determining whether an individual is an employee or independent contractor. Similar to the test utilized in Massachusetts, California adopted a modified "ABC" test. Under the test, an individual is assumed to be an employee unless the individual meets each of the following three prongs:

A. The worker is free from the control and direction of the hiring entity;
B. The worker performs work that is outside the usual course of the hiring entity's business; and
C. The worker is customarily engaged in an independently established trade of the same nature as the work performed.

Under the test, almost all individuals will be found to be employees, creating a significant the risk of misclassification. Thus, prudent employers should carefully evaluate whether their independent contractors meet this standard.

The Internal Revenue Service (IRS) has issued guidelines for determining whether an individual is an employee or an independent contractor focusing on behavioral factors, financial factors, and the nature of the relationship. https://www.irs.gov/Businesses/*Small-Businesses-&-Self-Employed/Independent-Contractor-Self-Employed-or-Employee. See also* Hammerschmidt & Krasnoff, *Employee or Independent Contractor? Historical Perspective, Current Risks, and Practical Tips*, 46 Md. B.J. 53 (Nov. 2013).

(g) Tangential Issues Related to Work Made for Hire

Including work for hire language and an assignment provision into an independent contractor agreement to vest ownership of any intellectual property in the customer raises a number of tangential issues that should be considered. Section 3351.5 (c) of the California Labor Code provides that if the underlying agreement between the parties characterizes the deliverables as work made for hire, the customer must include the independent contractor under the customer's workers compensation coverage. California Labor Code §3351.5(c).

In addition, by characterizing the deliverables as "work made for hire," the copyright for the deliverables will expire the earlier of 95 years from the date of publication or 120 years from the date of creation, as opposed to "work not made for hire," which has a term equal to the life of the author plus 75 years. 17 U.S.C. § 302 (a). Further, the ability of an author to terminate the grant of certain rights after 35–40 years does not exist for works made for hire. 17 U.S.C. § 203. See Chapter 4.B for a more detailed discussion.

Finally, an employer may be held labile for copyright infringement committed by an independent contractor if the employer had the right and ability to supervise the independent contractor. *Hitek Software, LLC v. Timios, Inc.*, 2012 WL 2366368 (C.D. Cal. June 18, 2012).

For a general discussion, *see Employment Issues and Intellectual Property*, Corp. Couns. Q. 343 (Apr. 2020); Holland, *Copyrights and Consultants*, 36 Law. Brief. 2

(May 2006); *Intellectual Property Issues in the Employment Setting,* 120 INTELL. PROP. COUNS. 1 (Dec. 2006).

(h) Sale of a Business

A related issue often arises when a business is being sold and the business cannot show ownership of a relevant work (which may be crucial to its business), because the business failed to obtain ownership through an assignment. Often the author cannot be located, creating hesitancy by the purchaser to expend a significant amount of money when it will not obtain clear title to the software. In such cases, the seller usually must indemnify the purchaser against any third-party claims of ownership or any third-party claims of right of use.

See Form L.2 for a model assignment agreement that may be appropriate in the sale of a business, assigning ownership of all intellectual property created by a contractor to an employer.

2. *Moral Rights*

Moral rights are the right "to claim authorship of the software, to object to or prevent the modification of any software or to withdraw from circulation or control the publication or distribution of any software, and any similar right, existing under judicial or statutory law of any country in the world, or under any treaty, regardless of whether or not such right is denominated or generally referred to as a 'moral right.'" *Managing Risks in Computer Contracts, in* DATA PROCESSING AGREEMENTS § 1.261 (William A. Hancock ed., April 1997).

Under the Berne Convention, "moral rights" in a work may exist in the author regardless of the author's status as an employee or contractor. Moral rights are separate and distinct from any other ownership rights generally provided for under copyright law.

Moral rights encompass several rights: the right of attribution, the right of integrity, paternity, and disclosure rights. The US Copyright Act, however, only recognizes the rights of attribution and the right of integrity and then only for visual arts. *See,* Visual Artists Rights Act. 17 U.S.C. §106

Integrity rights provide that the creator of the work must consent to any change to the work to protect against the derogatory treatment of the work. Paternity rights provide that authorship must be attributed to the author and that a third party cannot falsely attribute development of the work. Further, the author's name cannot be used in association with the work he did not complete. Disclosure rights allow the creator of the work to control the display of his work. For a general discussion *see* Note, *Moral Rights: A Copyright Conflict Between the United States and Canada,* 1 SW. J.L & TRADE IN THE AMERICAS 171 (1994); Kwall, *Copyright and the Moral Right: Is an American Marriage Possible?,* 38 VAND. L. REV. 1 (1985).

The Canadian Copyright Act, for instance, considers moral rights to encompass "paternity rights" (the right of the author to have his or her name appear as the author of the work in all public uses) as well as "integrity rights" (the right of an author that his or her work not be mutilated or altered). Revised Statutes of Canada Chapter C-42

(13), (14), and (15) (1985, as amended). Such rights may prove troublesome in the case of software that is continuously modified or where marketing considerations preclude identification of the author.

Articles 8 and 9 of the Berne Convention establish the author's right of ownership at the time of creation. Under the Berne Convention, an author's moral rights are "inalienable," and thus it is unlikely that such rights could be contractually transferred by a contractor to an employer. Berne Convention Article 6 bis. Furthermore, a waiver of such rights may be difficult or impossible to enforce in some jurisdictions. Some countries allow moral rights to be waived but not assigned. In such countries, an employer hiring a contractor to perform work would be well advised to include a waiver provision in any legal document with the contractor to protect against ownership claims by the contractor at a later point in time. In addition, some lawyers require the contractor to affirmatively state that he or she will not assert his or her moral rights.

A model moral rights waiver is as follows:

> *Consultant hereby irrevocably waives, and covenants not to assert, any and all moral rights in connection with the Services and Deliverables, and shall cause its employees and subcontractors performing services on behalf of Customer to irrevocably waive and covenant not to assert any and all moral rights in connection with the Services and Deliverables.*

While signatories to the Berne Convention are typically required to recognize and comply with the Berne Convention's requirements on an author's moral rights, the United States does not recognize broad moral rights. The United States has enacted legislation affording limited moral rights to prevent mutilation or destruction of visual works of art only, and only under certain circumstances. 17 U.S.C. §§ 106, 113, amended by Pub. L. No. 101-650, § 604, Dec. 1, 1990. The unwillingness of the United States to recognize moral rights is evidenced by its insistence that the General Agreement on Tariffs and Trade (GATT) and North American Free Trade Agreement (NAFTA) specifically provide that the United States is under no obligation to recognize such rights.

The question of whether a U.S. employer would have to recognize an offshore contractor's moral rights under the Berne Convention is closely tied to the issue of how the

Berne Convention is implemented in countries that do not deem treaties to be self-implementing. *See* NIMMER & GELLER, INTERNATIONAL COPYRIGHT LAW AND PRACTICE § 3 pp. 69–76 (1993). The answer to that question is found in Article 36 of the Berne Convention, which provides that:

1. any country party to the Convention undertakes to adopt, in accordance with its constitution, the measures necessary to ensure the application of this Convention; and
2. it is understood that, at the time a country becomes bound by this Convention, it will be in a position under its domestic law to give effect to the provisions of this Convention.

Therefore, the Berne Convention appears to leave the decision about self-implementation of the treaty to each individual member country.

This has also been the position of the United States, which has never viewed the Berne Convention to be self-implementing. The United States acceded to the Berne Convention by means of the Berne Convention Implementation Act of 1988. Pub. L. No. 100–568 (Oct. 31, 1988). In doing so, the United States included an express provision denying the self-implementation of the Berne Convention. *Id.* Because the Berne Convention is not self-implementing, the Berne Convention's provisions are not by themselves enforceable in U.S. courts. Moreover, the United States Copyright Act specifically declares that no right or interest in a work protected under Title 17 may be claimed by virtue of, or in reliance upon, the Berne Convention's provisions or the United States' adherence to the convention. Pub. L. No. 100–568 § 4(c) (Oct. 31, 1988). In other words, neither the Berne Convention itself, nor the fact of adherence to the convention, will affect the current law of the United States. In one of the few U.S. cases addressing moral rights, the Seventh Circuit Court of Appeals rejected their application in the United States. *Vargas v. Esquire Inc.*, 164 F.2d 522 (7th Cir. 1947) (moral rights while recognized by the civil law of foreign countries are not recognized by the laws of the United States).

Because U.S. law does not recognize most moral rights, a U.S. employer hiring an offshore contractor in a jurisdiction that is a signatory to the Berne Convention need be less concerned about the applicability of moral rights if the employer can ensure that U.S. law will govern in case of a copyright dispute between the parties and if the work will only be used in the United States. In an attempt to accomplish this, the U.S. employer may select U.S. law by including in a contract with the offshore contractor a choice of law clause. However, this approach is not entirely free of problems.

3. Patent Rights

As the patenting of software becomes commonplace, employers should have their employees assign ownership in all discoveries and inventions to the employer. The general rule under patent law is that an individual owns the patent rights to the subject matter of which he is an inventor, even though he conceived it or reduced it to practice in the course of his employment. *Banks v. Unisys Corporation*, 228 F.3d 1357, 1359 (Fed. Cir. 2000) (denying summary judgment on implied agreement to assign inventions where employee did not execute assignment agreement and the employer did not pursue the execution of an assignment agreement). Thus, although the copyright act grants the employer ownership as to any copyrights, an employer would not own any resulting patent without an assignment. *Id.* However, if the employee is hired to develop a specific product (e.g., a car engine) the patentable invention belongs to the employer. *United States v. Dubilier Condenser Corp.*, 289 U.S. 178, 187 (1933) (employee employed to make an invention must assign to employer any patent obtained as employee produced what he was hired to invent). This obligation extends to corporate executives as well. *Great Lakes Press Corp. v. Froom*, 695 F. Supp. 1440 (W.D.N.Y. 1987).

Under these guidelines, the IRS has set forth a test involving "categories of evidence." Under this test, a business must divide factors pertaining to a given worker's status into three categories: behavioral control, financial control, and type of relationship.

"Behavioral control" includes facts pertaining to whether or not the business controls how the individual does his or her job (e.g., training and instructions given). "Financial control" comprises evidence related to the business aspects of the worker's job (e.g., the worker's investments and expenses). "Type of Relationship" examines relational indicators (i.e., written contracts and length of association). These "categories of evidence" allow a broader and more flexible examination of an individual's status than the prior 20-point test, as the IRS publication indicates that all evidence about degree of control and independence will be considered. *See* Publication 15-A of the Internal Revenue Service (2020), https://www.irs.gov/pub/irs-pdf/p15a.pdf.

B. Ownership of Software Enhancements (§§ 3.2, 3.5, 12.1)

** Note that this Section discusses software enhancements. See Chapter 16 for a discussion of software development agreements.**

1. General

Ownership of software enhancements created by the licensor for a specific licensee is often a contentious issue. Customization and development should not be confused with software configuration. Configuration refers to structuring existing functionality within a software solution to best serve a customer's needs as opposed to customization, which refers to creating a new functionality that does not presently exist within the solution.

Usually, the licensee claims ownership based upon the fact that it has paid the licensor to enhance the software and that the software enhancement would not have been otherwise created. Further, some licensees are concerned that unless they retain ownership of the intellectual property, they lack standing to bring a claim of intellectual property infringement. Ownership of the created intellectual property may not be of importance to the vendor in certain situations:

- The developed intellectual property is unlikely to create or add to a repeatable solution/product;
- The intellectual property is unrelated to the vendor's industry/product focus; or
- The intellectual property will be a derivative work of existing customer IP.

Conversely, in arguing to retain ownership, many vendors claim they must retain ownership in order to:

- create a solution/product portfolio;
- maintain the integrity of its software (i.e., the licensor does not want its customers owning portions of its proprietary software, especially parts of the program's core code);

- create technological efficiencies and avoid having to create new technical approaches to common problems (there are only so many ways to code a module);
- allow all of the vendor's customers to benefit from improvements made by a few of its other customers;
- increase its profit margins and reduce costs; and
- create a defensive intellectual property portfolio (to protect the vendor from claims of intellectual property infringement by third parties).

Those licensors who consider themselves "consultants," as opposed to product companies, argue that they provide solutions, not deliverables. As such, the licensee is not purchasing a new product but rather is contracting with the licensor to solve an internal technical challenge.

In seeking to resolve any dispute over the ownership of custom developed work, the parties should consider the following questions:

- Why does the customer want to own the technology/technology outside its core competency?
- Is the customer's objective to obtain a competitive advantage/prevent its competitors from using the software?
- Does the customer simply feel it is entitled to own the work having paid for it?
- Is there another, unstated concern?

To determine the relative importance of ownership to each party, the parties should distinguish between a) software that may be reused for other customers and b) software that is created solely for the licensee's environment and is of little or no value to other potential customers. By doing so, all of these concerns can be addressed in the contract while allowing the licensor to retain ownership.

One argument against the licensee owning any intellectual property created by the licensor is that such work product will not be incorporated into the licensor's standard product and thus the maintenance and support of such product will not be included within the licensor's standard maintenance services. By the licensor retaining ownership, the licensee will benefit from any future enhancements and lower maintenance fees, as many other customers will be paying to support and enhance the module in question.

The licensee will likely be unable to independently maintain or support the work product and will be forced to pay an additional fee to the licensor to maintain and support it. Further, if the licensee is concerned that it will lack standing to bring a claim of intellectual property infringement, it can contractually require the licensor to do so. The licensee should carefully consider whether the benefits of owning any work product outweigh the costs of ownership, which includes any additional maintenance and support fees.

The licensee may want to consider alternative restrictions, such as granting the licensor ownership, but prohibiting the licensor from incorporating the work product into its standard product for a set period of time. In return for granting the licensor ownership, the licensor may provide the licensee with free maintenance and support for the period of time prior to the work product being incorporated into the licensor's standard product. This issue is often resolved by having the licensor retain ownership of the custom-developed portion of the licensor's software, but also having the licensor pay the licensee a royalty based on future license fees received by the licensor from relicensing the custom portion. (§ 8.I) Another potential solution is to have the licensee retain ownership of the custom software and grant to the licensor the right to market the custom software, and have the licensor pay a royalty to the licensee for each license sold.

These are not the only solutions. If the licensor is solely concerned with the licensee owning part of the licensor's core code, the licensee can retain ownership of the custom portion without the right of sublicense or assignment. See Form Q.2.CC.3 for illustrative language. The licensee could also be granted an exclusive basis for a set period of time, which would allow the licensee to recoup the benefits of its investment.

For a general overview, *see Ownership of Inventions*, 51 LAW BRIEF 1 (June 30, 2021); Tanenbaum, *Using Business Objectives to Allocate Ownership and License Rights in Custom Software*, 31 COMP. & INTERNET LAW. 15 (May 2014).

2. *Joint Ownership*

Another alternative, but one that is less attractive, is to have the licensor and licensee jointly own the custom software. "Joint Work" is "[w]ork prepared by two or more authors with the intention that their contributions be merged into inseparable or interdependent parts of a unitary whole." 17 U.S.C. § 101. Authors of joint work are "co-owner", and may independently exercise all rights of a copyright owner, *Oddo v. Ries*, 743 F.2d 630, 633 (9th Cir. 1984), including copying, creating and distributing derivative works as well as granting non-exclusive licenses to third parties. *Weissmann v. Freeman*, 868 F.2d 1313, 1318 (2d Cir. 1989).

Joint ownership, however, often creates more issues than it solves, as copyright law imposes a number of restrictions on co-owners. Further, it may be challenging to enforce and exploit the underlying intellectual property. Co-owners of a copyright are treated as "tenants in common with each co-owner having an independent right to use or license the use of a work, subject to a duty of accounting to the other co-owners for any profits." *Davis v. Blige*, 505 F.3d 90, 98 (2d Cir. 2007). "Joint authorship entitles the co-authors to equal undivided interests in the whole work - in other words, each joint author has the right to use or to license the work as he or she wishes, subject only to the obligation to account to the other joint owner for any profits that are made." *Thomson v. Larson*, 147 F.3d 195, 199 (2d. Cir. 1998).

Subject to certain limitations, each "owner" is free to license and use the work as it sees fit, as well as transfer its limited rights in the work to a third party. 1 MELVILLE B. NIMMER & DAVID NIMMER, NIMMER ON COPYRIGHT § 6.11 (Supp. 2006). A co-owner has standing to bring an action for copyright infringement, *Isbell Records v. DM Records*, 2009 WL 3386546 (5th Cir. Oct. 22, 2009), but cannot grant an exclusive license without the consent of all other co-owners, *Sybersound Records v. UAV Corp.*, 517 F.3d 1137 (9th Cir. 2008) and cannot grant a retroactive license. *Davis v. Blige*, 505 F.3d 90 (2d Cir. 2007). Each co-owner must also provide an accounting to all other co-owners for any profits. *Davis, id.* at 98.

Joint ownership allows each party to market the software to whomever it chooses, while at the same time having the right to make modifications and enhancements. This alternative may be detrimental to the licensor as the licensee may license the software to the licensor's direct competitors. Under joint copyright ownership, however, each owner has a duty to account to the other. 1 MELVILLE B. NIMMER & DAVID NIMMER, NIMMER ON COPYRIGHT § 6.12[A] at 36.6 (2005); *see, e.g., Oddo v. Ries*, 743 F.2d 630 (9th Cir. 1984). While the right to an accounting exists for jointly owned copyrights, there is no right to an accounting for a jointly owned software patent. 35 U.S.C. § 262. This dichotomy could likely lead to confusion, and potentially litigation, if the jointly owned software is protected by both copyright and patent. At the same time, this approach is probably unrealistic as most likely the custom portion is of little value unless it is licensed in conjunction with the rest of the software.

If the resulting work product will contain pre-existing intellectual property owned by the vendor and intellectual property owned by the customer, the work product should contain a copyright notice to the following effect:

> *This contains material which is the confidential, unpublished property licensed to Customer. Receipt or possession of it does not convey any rights to divulge, reproduce, use or allow others to use it without the specific written authorization of Customer and use must conform strictly to the license agreement between user and Customer.*
>
> *Copyright © 20__ [Vendor Legal Name]. All rights reserved.*
>
> *Copyright © 20__ [Customer Legal Name]. All rights reserved.*

For a discussion of joint ownership, *see* Johnson, *Avoiding Joint Pain: Treatment of Joint Works of Authorship Conditions*, 43 MD. B.J. 13 (May 2010).
Potential resolutions to the challenges of joint ownership include:

- Assigning sole ownership of the jointly developed intellectual property to one party, with the second party receiving a perpetual, royalty-free, irrevocable, unlimited license to the jointly developed intellectual property. This solution may be acceptable if one party's contribution was significantly greater than the other party, or the second party is willing to accept cash consideration for relinquishing its ownership rights.
- Each party retains joint ownership without an obligation to account to the other party, with one party granting the other an exclusive license to the intellectual property in return for a royalty payment. This structure may or may not include minimum revenue and marketing commitments.

Model Language for joint ownership:

> *All Intellectual Property Rights to the Developed Intellectual Property will be jointly owned by Customer and Vendor in equal undivided interests, with no duty to account to either party, with each party retaining the unrestricted unilateral right and ability to use, develop, disclose, license, modify, enhance, extend, and otherwise exploit the Developed Intellectual Property without the consent or participation of the other. Either party may, in its sole discretion, unilaterally and without the consent of the other party, defend, institute, maintain, and prosecute at its sole expense any lawsuit,*

action, or proceeding in its own name to prohibit, restrain, and recover damages for any infringement of the Developed Intellectual Property, provided that neither party shall be obligated to provide any assistance to or participate in any such lawsuit, action, or proceeding.

Model Language for Joint Ownership with an Exclusive License:

All Intellectual Property Rights to the Developed Intellectual Property will be jointly owned by Customer and Vendor in equal undivided interests, with no duty to account to either party, with each party retaining the unrestricted unilateral right and ability to use, develop, disclose, license, modify, enhance, extend, and otherwise exploit the Developed Intellectual Property without the consent or participation of the other.

Notwithstanding the foregoing, Customer hereby grants Vendor a [fully paid-up, royalty-free,] worldwide, exclusive license to use, sell, offer to sell, import, reproduce, perform, display, modify, improve, extend, make derivative works of, distribute, disclose, and sublicense the Developed Intellectual Property. Customer will not at any time license, sell, convey or distribute, or offer to license, sell, convey or distribute the Developed Intellectual Property, initiate any enforcement actions, or pursue claims against infringers of intellectual property rights in the Developed Intellectual Property, or interfere with any such actions or claims brought by Vendor. Upon Vendor's written request at Vendor's expense, Customer will provide reasonable cooperation and assistance to Vendor in furtherance of such actions or claims.

3. *Other Alternatives*

While the vendor's preferred position is to retain ownership of the developed intellectual property, there are several alternative positions that may be an acceptable compromise to customers:

- Having the vendor give the customer a significant price discount to recognize the intrinsic value the vendor will receive by retaining ownership of the developed intellectual property;
- Having the vendor pay the customer a royalty on future sales of the module;
- Allowing the customer to own the developed intellectual property but grant the vendor an exclusive, non-terminable royalty-free license with the right of sublicense to the developed IP; or
- Allowing the customer to own the developed intellectual property but have the customer issue the vendor a covenant not to sue to allow the vendor to use the developed IP for its internal purposes (from the vendor's perspective, this is not a preferred position).

For a general discussion, *see* Porter, *Negotiating Rights to a Customer's Improvements and Modifications*, 15 Corp. Couns. Q. 14 (April 1999). For a discussion of the licensor's point of view, *see* Gard & Bullock, *What's Wrong With the 'I Paid For It, I Own It' Strategy*, 23 ACC Docket 23 (May 2005).

4. *PRACTICE POINT*: Checklist for negotiating ownership rights in developed intellectual property.

- the level of technical development;
- the level of technological advancement;
- the level of difficulty to develop the technology;
- the ease with which the developed technology can be segregated from the vendor's existing products and solutions;
- the commercial value of the developed intellectual property;
- the existence of any business cases to use the developed intellectual property; and
- the value to be gained by the vendor from reusing the developed intellectual property.

C. Functional Specifications and Technical Specifications (§ 1.7)

1. *Functional Specifications*

The software's functional specifications are the technical architecture that the software must meet once it has been developed to the licensee's requirements, and they are usually set forth in a statement of work (SOW) attached as an exhibit to the agreement.

The functional specifications should be extremely detailed and should be agreed upon prior to execution of the license agreement, as they will determine the cost and extent of the effort exerted by the licensor in the software's development. The functional specifications should set forth any user interfaces, system interfaces, hardware interfaces, software interfaces and communications interfaces. In addition, the functional specifications should discuss such issues as the scalability of the solution. For a more detailed discussion, *see* ISO/IEC/IEEE 29148:2011 "Systems and software engineering—Life cycle processes—Requirements engineering."

If the functional specifications have not been agreed upon in detail, it is impossible for the licensor to determine with confidence the price of the development effort as the scope of the development effort has not been limited or fixed. The licensee is also at risk because it does not have a document describing in detail the deliverable it will receive for the fixed price.

Often the functional specifications and the scope of work—if there is a service component—are not reviewed by the lawyers on the negotiating team. Too often the lawyers believe these are "technical issues" best left to the technical staff, or the technical staff never seeks legal input. This is a serious mistake because the lawyers can enhance the specificity of the applicable document and determine whether legal terms have been included in the specifications or the scope of work, which benefits both parties. Occasionally, the parties enter into an agreement without agreeing on the functional specifications, usually because the customer is seeking to meet an internal deadline and/or the vendor does not want to lose a customer. Doing so can be disastrous, as it invites litigation if the parties cannot later reach agreement on the specifications. *See, e.g., Bubbajunk.com, Inc. v. Momentum Software,* 2004 WL 904081 (Tex. App. Apr. 29, 2004) (unsigned software specification requirements created after contract signature are not part of the contract).

To avoid future problems, the parties should avoid using language such as the following:

> *As soon as mutually practical after the Effective Date, the Parties shall work together diligently and in good faith to reconcile differences between the RFP and the Licensor RFP Response and establish a mutually agreeable document setting forth the technical specifications, functional requirements, project schedule, testing and acceptance procedures (such document being hereinafter referred to as the "Conformed Specification"). Once executed by both Parties, the Conformed Specification shall be automatically incorporated by reference into this Agreement and made a part hereof. In the event that the Parties have not agreed upon and executed a Conformed Specification by [insert date], then either Party may terminate this Agreement [without liability or obligation to the other Party] by providing written notice of such termination to the other Party [in which case Licensor shall invoice Licensee for the time expended by Licensor in developing the Conformed Specification at an hourly rate of $_____].*

By doing so, the parties shift the negotiating leverage to that party with the least incentive to execute an agreement. If the customer has a deadline for the implementation of the system, it is placed in a difficult position. If it walks away from the contract, that customer has to identify a new vendor and quickly negotiate a contract to meet the customer's schedule.

A significant amount of litigation has arisen as a result of agreements being executed containing general language that the "parties shall negotiate in good faith the functional specifications immediately upon execution of this Agreement." After execution, a dispute often arises because the parties are unable to agree on the functional specifications, given that the licensor is usually constrained by a fixed price—a limit with which a licensee is usually not concerned. Several courts have recognized the licensee's obligation to provide the licensor with the needed information to develop a system. *See H/R Stone, Inc. v. Phoenix Business Systems, Inc.*, 660 F. Supp. 351 (S.D.N.Y. 1987) (licensee breached implied covenant of good faith and fair dealing by failing to provide sufficient information to allow licensor to undertake development); *Truktax, Inc. v. Hugh M. Gray & Associates, Inc.*, 1987 WL 13150 (Tenn. App. July 1, 1987) (customer breached contract for computer software by hindering its development and installation and owed developer the remainder of contract price).

Further, by failing to establish definitive specifications, the parties run the risk of having a court disregard the contract's integration clause and include the parties' correspondence and other writings. *See L.S. Heath & Son, Inc. v. AT&T Info. Sys., Inc.*, 9 F.3d 561 (7th Cir. 1993) (if allegedly integrated writing does not, without reference to another document or other coordinating information, reveal what the basic transaction entailed, then the writing is not integrated; where master agreement did not identify prices, products, services, software applications, or configurations).

In the extreme, a court may find the lack of a contract under the theory of contractual indefiniteness, that is, the functional specifications were such a material portion of the contract that the contract could not exist without them. *See generally Rates Technology, Inc. v. New York Telephone Co.*, 1995 WL 438954 (S.D.N.Y. July 25, 1995) and UCC § 2-204. This possibility finds support under the UCC, which requires an agreement to (a) evidence a contract for the sale of goods, (b) be signed by the parties, and (c) specify a quantity in order to be legally enforceable. UCC § 2-201 comment 1.

The prudent methods of contracting are to (1) enter into a two-phase contract with the first phase consisting of a fixed price engagement to draft the functional specifications, and assuming that the parties can agree on the functional specifications, a second phase consisting of the development effort at a fixed price; (2) jointly develop the functional specifications prior to execution of a fixed price contract; or (3) enter into a time and materials contract. The first option is less attractive to the licensor because once the functional specifications have been agreed to, the potential licensee can shop the functional specifications to other potential software developers to obtain the best price. The licensor's concerns can potentially be alleviated by contractually mandating that the jointly developed specifications are the confidential information/intellectual property of both parties and cannot be disclosed to a third party without the other party's prior written consent.

The second alternative is less attractive to the licensor's business people who want to obtain a binding commitment from the licensee and who do not want a long, drawn-out process in order to reach a final agreement, during which time the licensee could select another licensor. From the licensee's perspective, the third option does not provide the price protection needed to protect against cost overruns and necessary for its budgeting process. Finally, the parties must decide whether the licensed software, when delivered or accepted, meets the functional specifications or the current documentation for the licensed software. Often the parties will include language allowing for the termination of the agreement without cause if the specifications developed are not satisfactory to the potential license or not completed within a specified time frame.

The parties should also avoid setting forth a long list of responsibilities for one party and then stating the other party is responsible for everything not set forth on the list. This concept is clearly attractive to the customer as it limits the customer's responsibilities to a finite list, while the vendor is responsible for everything else, including hardware and third-party software whose use may not have been contemplated. The vendor assumes responsibility for the unknown, significantly increasing its risk.

Placing undue risk on one party is likely to lead to a dispute in the future that may prevent the customer from achieving its goal of receiving a system that meets its needs on time and on budget, as well as the vendor's goals of delivering a project on time and on budget.

2. Technical Specifications

The technical specifications describe the physical, programmatic elements of the software including its performance and reliability. Performance should be tied to the licensee's technical environment. The technical specifications should specifically set forth the applicable hardware, operating system, and programming language. While the licensee should seek to insert its intended use of the system into the technical specifications, the licensor should be hesitant to insert such description for fear of creating an implied warranty of fitness for a particular purpose.

D. Change Orders (§ 9.8)

Changes in scope usually arise from the changing needs of the customer over the course of the engagement, which may extend over several years. As the customer's business needs evolve during this period, its information technology needs will likely also change. Occasionally, a change in scope will occur because the vendor proposes a new, more efficient technical approach for achieving the customer's goals. Change orders are used to amend the details related to the deliverables while amendments are used to alter the terms of the governing agreement.

Altering the customer's requirements or a vendor's commitment to complete deliverables during a project is fraught with risk, as the parties have already likely agreed on a fixed price, a specifically defined deliverable, and a definitive delivery date. If the parties are operating on a time and materials basis, an agreement on a change in scope can likely be reached. If the parties cannot agree on the impact of the change order on the price, or agree on a revised delivery date, the parties have opened Pandora's Box as it will likely be difficult for the customer to switch vendors without materially impacting the customer's costs and schedule. Further, the inability of the parties to reach a mutually agreeable resolution may result in litigation, which benefits neither party.

Any change regarding the work to be performed, including a change in the payment terms, the delivery schedule, or the nature of the deliverables themselves should be made through a signed "change order" executed by both parties. Under no circumstances should the customer orally authorize work to be performed, nor should the vendor perform any work, without a written change order. The likelihood of contractual uncertainty and the risk of creating a new, independent oral agreement under the UCC, whose terms may be supplied by the UCC, creates significant risk requiring a written amendment. *See* UCC § 2-204.

Requiring a change order protects the vendor in the event the customer claims the work was not authorized, while limiting any claim by the vendor that the work was performed at the request of the customer or one of its employees. A change order also protects the vendor from having to rely on a *quantum meruit* argument to recover any monies it believes it is entitled to.

1. *Methodology of the Change Order Process*

Any change order provision contained in an agreement should provide a detailed methodology for enacting a change to a work order. A timeline should be included for responding to a proposed change order by one of the parties. The vendor should reject language providing that the failure of the vendor to respond to a change order request within a set period of time (e.g., seven days) is deemed to be acceptance. Silence is generally not deemed to constitute acceptance under contract law, and the parties' contract should adhere to this principle. 2 WILLISTON ON CONTRACTS § 6:53 (4th ed.); *Bowley v. Fuller*, 115 A. 466 (Me. 1921) (mere silence and inaction does not constitute acceptance). The agreed-upon process should also address whether the vendor will be compensated for responding to a change order request if a significant amount of work is involved, such as creating a detailed pricing estimate or undertaking a significant amount of research.

From the vendor's perspective, the vendor should avoid accepting any contractual language requiring the vendor to perform *de minimis* changes without charge. While this language is often proposed by customers, it introduces subjectivity and uncertainty into the contract as to what is meant by "de minimis." See § 9.8 and Form C.2.1 § 2.2.2. Further, it requires the vendor to perform additional work without additional compensation.

2. *The Contents of a Change Order*

A change order should not only clearly state the changes to be made, but it should also clearly identify those segments of the existing statement of work or other governing document that have been superseded. At the same time, the customer should insist on a contractual provision that the vendor cannot perform any work on the customer's behalf without a change order executed by an authorized officer of the customer.

Often, the parties execute a change order delineating the changes in the work to be performed but fail to consider or state how such change order impacts the scope of the overall project and any corresponding change in price. If the parties agree upon a scope change, the resulting change order should clearly state the new deliverable date, if any, as well as the change order's impact on the scope of the project. The parties need to avoid becoming so focused on changes to the functional specifications and price that they fail to consider the impact on the overall project.

3. *The Failure to Agree*

If the parties cannot agree on pricing for the change, the contract should allow the customer to terminate the relevant work order or the contract itself if there are no other work orders. Otherwise, the customer may be forced to pay for work it can no longer use. Thus, the customer should ensure that it has the ability to terminate the contract in the event the parties cannot agree on a change order and, for the maximum flexibility, include a termination for convenience provision—also known as a "termination without cause" provision. *See, e.g.*, § 4.1.A. The customer should also ensure that the agreement provides for termination assistance in the event of such a termination, particularly where the customer anticipates that another vendor, or its internal IT resources, will take over ownership of the project. See Chapter 7.I, below and § 5.3.3. Termination assistance is much more common in the termination of an Application Service Provider ("ASP") relationship, where customer data and proprietary information need to be kept live and accessible right up to the cut-over point.

To protect its expectation interest in the contract, a vendor may wish to minimize the customer's ability to exploit a "failure to agree" termination right, for example, by eliminating the convenience termination—at least in the absence of an early termination penalty payment—or by linking the termination right to the vendor's unreasonable failure to agree. These can be hard to enforce, and most vendors will balk at agreeing to termination solely for disagreement on a change order. This is particularly true in an ASP context where money has already been spent on hardware, or in a large development context where resources have been diverted and may not be capable of being immediately redeployed on another paid project.

In the event the customer elects to terminate the contract without cause, the vendor should ensure the contract provides that the vendor will be paid for all services that have been provided to the customer, not just those services that have been accepted by the customer, as well as the out-of-pocket costs incurred by the vendor as a result of such early termination. These costs may include the cost of terminating any leases for rental housing or office space in the customer's geographic location. Some vendors also seek to have the customer pay the vendor several weeks' salary for each employee working on the customer's project, based on the reasoning that it will take the vendor several weeks to staff these employees on a new project. See, e.g., § 4.1.A.

E. Auditing the Licensor (§§ 9.13, 16.Q; Form Q.2.E)

A software license and services agreement may contain many different types of "audit" provisions allowing the customer to audit the vendor's compliance with its compliance obligations. Some of the most common types include the following:

- Quality audits such as SSAE 18 audits to ensure that the licensor is using appropriate quality assurance mechanisms to deliver a quality product. Forms Q.2.F.1, and 2.
- Compliance audits to determine if the licensor is complying with all applicable laws and the licensee's policies. Form Q.2.F.6.
- Financial audits to ensure any services performed on a time and materials basis are billed correctly by the licensor. Form Q.2.F.5.
- Financial audits to ensure the licensor is paying the licensee any required royalty for software which the licensee paid to develop, and which is licensed to third parties (§ 8.I).
- Security audits to ensure the licensor is safeguarding the licensee's data.

For many practitioners, an agreement's audit provisions are an afterthought which often receives only a cursory review. A prudent party should carefully evaluate a contract's audit provisions to understand the burden and risk they may place on the licensor. Without careful drafting, an audit may, at best, cause the audited party to incur significant costs and expose it to significant penalties and fees and, at worst, provide grounds for termination of the underlying agreement. The burdens imposed by an audit may be felt by both the vendor and the customer depending on the nature of the audit. In some cases, an audit may be impractical. For example, if a vendor has 2,000 clients, it would be impractical to have 2,000 customers audit the vendor each year.

Set forth below is an overview of the issues associated with audits and the different types of audit provisions that may be contained in a software license agreement.

1. General

(a) Establishing the Parameters of an Audit

The provisions for any audit should be carefully negotiated and incorporated into the governing agreement to avoid future disputes. In negotiating the terms of any audit, the parties should carefully consider the parameters of the audit.

(i) Confidentiality

Perhaps the most important issue from the audited party's perspective is the issue of confidentiality. No audit should begin until the auditing party and all members of the audit team, as well as those who will receive the audit report, have executed a non-disclosure agreement requiring each such individual to maintain the confidentiality of all information disclosed during the audit. This is especially true if the auditing party is a competitor of the audited party. If the parties are competitors, the audited party should insist that an independent third party, such as a nationally recognized accounting firm, conduct the audit and that only the final report be provided to the auditing party. If the parties are direct competitors in a highly competitive niche market, the information may be so sensitive that the audited party should insist that the results be provided only to the auditing party's outside attorneys. *See, e.g., Pitney Bowes Inc. v. Broadvision, Inc.*, 2010 WL 3292981 (S.D.N.Y. Aug. 16, 2010).

The auditing party should recognize that the work product of and correspondence with an "independent" third-party auditor hired by its counsel to conduct the audit may not be protected by the attorney-client work product privilege, and any information discovered by the independent auditor may be discoverable by the audited party. *See Columbia Data Products, Inc. v. Autonomy Corp. Ltd.*, 2012 WL 6212898 (D. Mass. Dec. 12, 2012) (Audit results requested by and provided to licensor's attorneys were not prepared in anticipation of litigation and thus were not subject to work product privilege; attorney-client privilege did not apply because audit report was disclosed to the audited party.).

Most parties will not allow their employees to sign a nondisclosure agreement directly with a third party, such as the audited party. Instead, they argue that the employee has already signed a nondisclosure agreement with the auditing party and that the auditing party in turn has signed a nondisclosure agreement with the audited party. While this reasoning may be acceptable for the auditing party's employees, the audited party should require all third-party consultants and contractors to sign nondisclosure agreements directly with the audited party. Use of disclosed information should be limited solely for the purposes of the audit and for no other purpose. For example, if a licensee is being audited to confirm that the licensee is not utilizing more licenses than it has purchased, the audit team should not be permitted to undertake any other activity other than to count the number of licenses in use.

(ii) Scope of the Audit

An audited party should seek to place strict limits on the scope of any audit to limit ill-defined "treasure hunts." A well-drafted audit clause should set forth the time period during which the auditing party can request to conduct an audit. Limitations should be placed on how far back the auditing party can audit and how frequently the auditing party can conduct an audit. For example, the audited party should seek to limit the auditing party's right to request an audit to the term of the agreement and for six months after its termination, while limiting any audit of the vendor's financial records to the period two years prior to the date of the audit request.

To avoid placing an undue burden on the audited party, the audit should take place at the target's place of business during normal business hours or at the location of the relevant records and the auditing party should be required to provide the audited party with at least 10 business days' prior written notice of the audit, be limited to requesting an audit only once in any 12-month period, and limit the type of records that must be made available to the auditing party to those strictly necessary to achieve the stated parameters and agreed upon scope of the audit. Although many licensees seek to require the licensor to conduct the audit during normal business hours, some licensees seek to have the audit conducted outside of normal business hours to limit the impact the audit tools used by the licensor may have on the licensee's information technology systems.

A well-written audit clause will also obligate the audited party to cooperate with the auditing party and set forth how any deficiencies identified by the audit will be addressed. Further, the audited party should seek the contractual right to review and comment on the independent auditor's report prior to the report being sent to the auditing party.

Finally, the audited party should be required to pay any under-payment and fines and penalties within 30 days of a finding of an underpayment. Similarly, in the event the audit finds an overpayment, the customer should be required to refund any such overpayment within 30 days of the completion of the audit.

(b) Reimbursement of Costs

Reimbursement for the costs incurred during an audit can be contentious. The audited party often seeks compensation for the internal costs it incurs in preparing for and supporting the audit. The auditing party often seeks to include language in the audit provision allowing the auditing party to recover its costs in the event it is discovered that the audited party has underreported the revenue due the auditing party by 5 percent or more. Five percent is often considered to be "material" and thus serves as an appropriate threshold for the auditing party to recover its costs. A prudent party, however, will require the underreported revenue to exceed a minimum dollar threshold before the auditing party is entitled to recover its costs. The intent is to avoid a situation where the fees recovered are 5 percent or greater but the cost of conducting the audit significantly exceeds the underreported fees. In the event the audited party intentionally underreports the fees due the licensor, the audited party should pay all costs and fees associated with the audit. Nonetheless, the audited party should insist on an absolute limit on the costs it may be required to reimburse the auditing party, which would typically be stated as a fixed dollar amount in the range of $10,000 to $50,000 depending on the scope of the audit.

See Form Q.2.F.14 for an audit clause illustrating these issues.

2. *Types of Audits*

(a) Vendor Charges to the Customer

Payment audits allow a customer to confirm that it has not been overbilled by the vendor. These audits usually arise in the context of a time and materials contract where the vendor has billed the customer based on the number of hours it has expended on a project as well as for third-party expenses such as third-party hardware and software and out-of-pocket travel and expense charges. The customer seeks to confirm that the vendor has kept accurate time records and has billed all third-party expenses at cost without markup. In agreeing to an audit, the vendor should specifically provide that the customer is not entitled to receive any information related to the vendor's profit margins, overheads, or profitability. The customer should have no right to audit the vendor's fixed price contracts as the price to be paid by the customer is not subject to variation based on time and materials and therefore is not subject to manipulation. See Form Q.2.F.7 for language allowing the customer to audit the vendor's financial records to confirm proper billing by the vendor.

An issue arises as to third-party hardware and software purchased by the vendor on the customer's behalf. Often vendors purchase hardware and software through a Value-Added Reseller (VAR) program where a third-party vendor sells its products at a discount to the vendor who then resells the hardware or software to the customer at a profit. Most vendors do not disclose to the customer that they are marking up the cost of the third-party products and thus are hesitant to submit to an audit of their third-party hardware and software costs. Vendors will argue that the associated rebates and discounts result from the purchasing power of the vendor and that such discounts are reflected in the vendor's pricing. A prudent customer should provide in the underlying agreement that the vendor will not mark up the cost of any third-party goods and services, and will require that all financial benefits associated with the purchase (i.e., rebates, tax benefits, etc.) accrue to it. See Form Q.2.PP.5 for language requiring the vendor to return all rebates received from third-party vendors to the customer.

To protect itself, the vendor should contractually prohibit the customer from retaining an auditor on a contingency basis. An auditor who is paid on a contingency basis has a strong financial incentive to find billing problems and to take an aggressive stance to recover any alleged underpayment.

If the licensee is paying the licensor for software development services on a time and materials basis, or if it is paying for the licensor's travel expenses, it should include an audit provision allowing it to audit the licensor's time and expenses charges. This is a reasonable request for time and material contracts but is inappropriate for a fixed price contract. In negotiating the audit provision, the licensor should limit the rights of the licensee and specifically state that the licensee is not entitled to obtain any information related to the licensor's profit margin. Further, the licensor should insist on including language forbidding the licensee from retaining an auditor on a contingency basis, as the auditor is more likely to take an aggressive position in auditing the licensor's fees, or from retaining a competitor of the licensor to conduct the audit.

A good audit clause will establish the time, location, and length of the audit as well as the obligation of the licensor to cooperate. Further, the clause should provide for the reimbursement of the licensee's audit costs in the event a material discrepancy (5 percent) or a set dollar amount is identified and confirmed.

(b) Payment of Royalties Due Customer (§ 8.I.4)

In those situations where a customer pays the vendor to develop a software module that can be remarketed by the vendor in return for future royalty payments, the customer should negotiate for significantly reduced development costs and retain the right to audit the vendor's future sales of the module to ensure the customer is receiving its negotiated royalties. The customer should contractually require the vendor to automatically provide the customer with quarterly reports setting forth the name of the licensed end user, the license fee charged/received by the vendor from the end user, and the royalty due the customer. If the customer is dissatisfied with the vendor's report or suspects that the vendor is underreporting the royalties due the customer, the customer should have the right to undertake its own audit and audit the vendor's customer contracts as well as the vendor's general ledger. The customer should have the right to audit the vendor's financial records upon 30 days' prior notice at least once a year. Underreporting should result in a penalty and the right to audit the vendor on a more frequent basis.

To the extent the licensee is entitled to receive a royalty from the licensor for software the licensee paid to develop, the licensee should demand the right to audit the licensor's financial records to confirm the licensor has paid the licensee all royalties due the licensee. The language of the audit provision should require the licensor to produce a quarterly statement within 30 days after the end of each calendar quarter. Each such statement should set forth sufficient detail to allow the licensee to confirm that the royalty payment was properly calculated. At a minimum, each such statement should identify the relevant client, the revenue received from the client, and the type of license purchased by the client. The licensee should have the right to audit the licensor's financial records upon 30 days' notice twice a year. The audit provision should include punitive language in the event the licensor underreports the royalty due twice in any two-year period.

See Form Q.2.F.11 for language providing the customer the right to audit the licensor's payments.

For a more detailed discussion of royalty audits, *see* Phillips & Daniel, *Licensing Audit Programs: Issues and Practices*, Advanced Seminar on Licensing Agreements (Chapter 2), Practicing Law Institute (1999).

(c) SSAE 18/ISAE 3402

Effective May 1, 2017, Statement on Standards for Attestation Engagements No. 18 ("SSAE 18"), *Attestation Standards: Clarification and Recodification*, was implemented by the Auditing Standards Board of the American Institute of Certified Public Accountants. SSAE 18 replaces SSAE 16, as the new domestic service organization reporting standard. The International Auditing and Assurance Standards Board's International Standard on Assurance Engagements No. 3402 ("ISAE 3402"), *Assurance Reports on Controls at a Service Organization*, remains the international standard. A prudent customer of hosted software services should require a vendor to undertake an annual SSAE 18/ISAE 3402 audit to ensure the vendor is taking commercially reasonable measures to maintain the controls environment at its data centers in a manner that is consistent with meeting the objectives of these controls. These audits should be performed in accordance with the guidance set forth in SSAE 18, although almost all vendors most likely have their own SSAE 18 and ISAE 3402 audit programs.

SSAE and ISAE audits are conducted on a data-center-by-data-center basis by an independent outside auditor chosen and retained by the vendor. Most vendors conduct these audits as part of their normal quality/compliance efforts and thus the customer should not be charged for these audits. Customers should be provided a copy of the auditor's report annually. The vendor should never allow the customer to select the auditor or undertake the audit itself as doing so potentially allows the customer access to the confidential information of unrelated third parties resident in the data center.

SSAE 18 is intended to provide guidance to auditing firms in response to changes in global assurance standards (e.g., ISAE 3402) and corporate governance and control standards. SSAE 18/ISAE 3402 reports include the service auditor's opinion, a description of the vendor's systems and processes, a description of the vendor's control objectives and controls, and the service auditor's tests of operating effectiveness and results of those tests.

Both SSAE 18 and ISAE 3402 include the following:

(i) Written assertion: SSAE 18/ISAE 3402 reports include the vendor's management's written assertion, as well as the service auditor's opinion and vendor's system description. As management of the service organization, the vendor is required to prepare a written assertion about the description and operation of its system. This assertion includes the following statements:

- The contents of the system description are fairly stated based on certain criteria;
- The vendor has identified the risks that threaten the achievement of the control objectives;
- The controls are suitably designed to provide reasonable assurance that the aforementioned risks are addressed and the control objectives are achieved; and
- The controls were consistently applied throughout the period.

(ii) System Description: Under SSAE 18 and ISAE 3402, the vendor is responsible for providing a "description of its system" as designed and implemented. While the term "system" has many different connotations, a common and useful definition is "the procedures, people, software, data, and infrastructure organized to achieve a specific objective."

(iii) Service Auditor's Opinion: The auditor's opinion on the fairness of the vendor's description and the operating effectiveness of the vendor's controls as well as management's assertion that has been established by the AICPA.

The AICPA provides for three distinct types of Service Organization Controls (SOC) reports:

- *SOC 1* – Reports on a service organization's internal controls that impact a customer's financial information. The reported information is used by the customer's auditors and internal financial teams with responsibility for financial reporting.
- *SOC 2* – Reports on a service organization's controls related to security, availability, processing integrity, confidentiality, or privacy. The reported information is used by the service organization's management, as well as its regulators and customers, usually under protection of a confidentiality agreement.
- *SOC 3* – Reports on a service organization's controls for security, availability, processing integrity, confidentiality, or privacy at a higher level than a SOC 2 report and is publicly available. SOC 3 reports are often used for marketing purposes by the service organization.

SOC 2 reports are issued as either a Type 1 or Type II report. A Type I report provides the auditor's opinion of the relevant controls, whether the controls described are suitably designed to achieve specified control objectives, and whether the controls have been implemented as of a specific date, i.e., January 1. A Type II report offers a greater level of assurance as it covers set period of time, i.e., 12 months, and examines the design of the operational controls and the effectiveness of such controls in meeting the organization's objectives. Type II reports cover the same subject matter as Type I reports but are more expansive in that the auditor opines on the operating effectiveness of the service organization's controls over the covered time period as well as the auditor's testing the controls and the results of such tests.

Prudent vendors should resist a customer's efforts to participate in the planning of such an audit or to have such audits conducted more frequently than annually. *See* § 9.13(i). For vendors who are not required to undertake an SSAE 18 audit, they should agree only to undertake a Type I audit unless the customer itself is required to undertake a Type II audit.

Further, most vendors do not provide copies of the actual reports or their policies but rather certify that they will undertake an audit and resolve any deficiencies.

See Form Q.2.F.1, 2, and 3 for model SSAE 18 audit provisions.

(d) Compliance with Laws (Form Q.2.N.1–5)

Prudent customers should contractually require the vendor to comply with all applicable laws. This is especially important for customers in regulated industries such as the pharmaceutical, financial services, and healthcare industries. The intent of this provision is to protect the customer in the event the vendor fails to comply with any applicable law exposing the customer to potential liability. For example, a customer may be a covered entity under HIPAA and obligated to protect third parties' Protected Health Information (PHI). As a vendor to the customer, the vendor is likely a business associate of the customer and subject to the terms of HIPAA. The vendor's failure to comply with HIPAA when and if it accesses the customer's PHI may in turn expose the customer to liability.

The customer should require the vendor to undertake an annual audit to ensure the vendor is in compliance with all applicable laws. Like data privacy and security audits, compliance audits should consist of both a manual component and an automated electronic assessment component. A customer should be willing to accept a vendor's audit provided it has been conducted by an independent third-party auditor. The vendor should not charge the customer for the audit.

Regardless of the vendor's contractual obligations to the customer, the vendor should undertake an annual audit of its software, solutions, development protocols, processes, and procedures to identify those areas where it is not in compliance with applicable laws. Doing so will hopefully help the vendor avoid any penalties or fees for failing to meet its compliance obligations.

See Form Q.2.F.8 for language allowing the licensee to audit the licensor's compliance with applicable laws and the licensee's policies.

(e) Data Privacy and Security

Comprehensive security and data privacy policies require independent verification for determining the integrity of the vendor's privacy and security practices. The audit should test compliance with industry best practices, which will vary by industry, and may include industry-specific standards such as the Payment Card Industry (PCI) standards. The vendor must have comprehensive control mechanisms in place and have implemented the technology infrastructure to enforce these standards. The audit should reflect compliance with industry standard business practices and tight quality requirements.

Audits are an administrative burden, and penetration tests can create third-party conflicts in a multi-tenant environment. As such, prudent vendors should seek an alternative approach to resolving a customer's concerns. At the same time, vendors should undertake annual data privacy and security audits as part of their annual quality assurance efforts. Audits allow a vendor to identify problems before they arise and hopefully avoid the costs and bad publicity associated with a security incident. A comprehensive security audit should consist of a manual assessment made up of interviews, a review of the audited party's procedures and controls as well as physical security, and automated electronic assessment using the relevant information technology system to monitor compliance and generate exception reports.

Vendors can purchase a number of third-party solutions to monitor compliance with all applicable laws and policies, and automatically identify concerns or potential violations.

See Form Q.2.F.8 for licensee-favorable language addressing compliance with laws and see Form Q.2.F.12 for language allowing the customer to audit the vendor's compliance with its operational and security obligations.

(f) Open Source

Open-source software audits can benefit both the licensor and licensee. An audit can determine how a party's proprietary code has been used historically (not just currently) with open-source software to determine whether the proprietary code has to be made publicly available pursuant to the General Public License (GPL) license. Generally, the

GPL license requires the source code of the combined product to be made publicly available.

From the licensor's perspective, the licensor wants to ensure that no open-source software is included in its product, as the inclusion of certain types of open-source software may potentially place the licensor's software in the public domain. The licensor also wants to avoid unknowingly breaching any representation and warranty it has made to the licensee as to the presence of open-source software in the licensor's software and deliverables. Further, a scan will identify any known security risks associated with the open source software and identify any unlicensed commercial software contained in the code.

Open-source software is accepted by the licensor without protection as to intellectual property infringement, viruses, trapdoors, etc. Most licensees, however, will insist that the licensor represent and warrant that the software will not infringe a third party's intellectual property rights, and be free of viruses and trapdoors. Too often, a licensor's developers incorporate open source into a software deliverable without management's knowledge. Thus, an audit is the only way a vendor can have confidence that the delivered product does not unknowingly contain open-source software.

The licensee also wants to ascertain the existence of open-source software in any deliverables. If the software deliverables are to be included in one of the licensee's products, the licensee wants to avoid potentially placing its products in the public domain through the incorporation of viral open-source software.

In undertaking any audit, the licensee should speak with the licensor's technical staff and, if it has not retained a third party to do so, review the code itself. A licensor should be able to identify all open-source software within its products or deliverables and confirm whether the software has been used in a manner that would require the proprietary code to be made publicly available. If the software has been licensed under a GPL license, the licensor should indicate whether the program qualifies for an exception to the GPL requirements.

The GPL code is protected under copyright law and any violation of the GPL license may subject the breaching party to both civil and criminal penalties. Open-source licenses are conditional copyright licenses. Failure to comply with the conditions may result in copyright infringement claims. *Jacobsen v. Katzer*, 535 F.3d 1373 (Fed. Cir. 2008). Thus, it is in the best interests of both parties to understand the existence, if any, of open-source software in the deliverables and understand each party's contractual obligations under any applicable open-source software license.

An additional benefit of undertaking an open-source audit is that some third-party auditors, such as Black Duck, have the capability to identify not only open-source software in code but also any third-party software in the code for which the licensor may lack a license. They use scanning software to identify open-source software. The audit usually requires a scan of the software in question and a review of the report generated by the scanning software. If the licensee undertakes the audit, the licensor should contractually require that it receive a copy of the audit so that it may address the identified issues, especially if these issues transcend many different customers.

For a more detailed discussion of the issues associated with open-source software, *see* Rehm, *Navigating The Open-Source Minefield: What's a Business To Do?*, 10 W.F. I.P.L.J. 289 (2010).

(g) *Escrow/Source Code*

Some licensors insist on inserting an audit clause in their escrow agreements allowing them to audit the escrow agent to ensure the escrow agent has implemented protections to prevent the improper release of the escrowed materials. A reputable escrow agent should be willing to accept an audit to ensure it is properly managing the risk of an improper release of the escrowed software.

Similarly, the licensee may also want the right to audit the escrow agreement to ensure the escrowed materials are current and complete. Too often, the licensor fails to provide the escrow agent with current versions of the source code after the initial deposit. The escrow agent may also lack the ability to determine whether the deposit software is the most current version and reflects the version in use by the licensee.

See Form Q.2.F.9 for language allowing a licensor to audit the escrow agent to confirm its compliance with the source code release terms.

(g) *Sarbanes-Oxley Act of 2002 (SOX)*

SOX is intended to ensure that companies submit accurate information in their financial reporting and should not involve the licensor. Licensors, however, are increasingly asked to warrant that "the Systems being delivered are 'SOX compliant.'" A licensor cannot warrant that the financial information processed by its system is correct because the information belongs to the licensee. Furthermore, if there is nonconformity in a system that causes incorrect financial information, this is not the licensor's responsibility, since the licensee should be obligated to verify the output of the system. The licensor can warrant that any financial reports issued by the system in accordance with the system's documentation will be verifiable with traceable source data. The following provision should be suggested by licensors to satisfy licensees on this issue:

> *Licensor represents and warrants that any financial reports generated by the System in accordance with the Documentation will be verifiable with traceable source data and that any revisions or modifications to the System will be documented.*

3. *Responding to an Audit Request*

Upon receipt of an audit demand, a party should confirm that its contract permits an audit and any parameters placed on the audit, especially any cost-shifting provisions. The audited party should also confirm with the auditing party how it plans to undertake the audit and what information the auditing party seeks. If the licensor is auditing the licensee's use of the software, such information will usually include who and how many people are using the software, how many licenses the licensee purchased, and the limitations, if any, on the use of such licenses.

Prudent parties will undertake their own audit prior to the auditing party starting its audit so that the audited party can identify any areas of noncompliance and prepare a defense. In the case of a software use audit, the licensee's internal audit should include both the licensee's production and non-production environments. In preparing for an audit, the licensee should review all documents under which the licensee purchased software, including master agreements and any purchase orders.

For an additional discussion, see Chapter 23.D.

4. Disputes

Some audit provisions include dispute resolution procedures applicable solely to the audit to remove disputes relating to audits from the agreement's general dispute resolution provision. Creating specialized dispute resolution provisions related to audits can reduce the time, effort, and expense involved with resolving audit disputes as the amounts in dispute are likely to be small. One method is to require all disputes related to audits to be resolved through an expedited process. Another is to require all audit disputes under a set dollar threshold to be resolved through the expedited dispute process. Establishing a bifurcated approach with an expedited process for disputes under a set dollar level will hopefully allow the parties to quickly and efficiently resolve their disputes. In the event of a large dispute, it may be appropriate to utilize the agreement's general dispute resolution provision.

5. PRACTICE POINT: Checklist for drafting an audit provision.

At a minimum, an audit should address the following:

- The requirement for the parties to execute a nondisclosure agreement
- The obligation of the audited party to cooperate with the audit
- The frequency of audits
- The time period the audit will cover
- The subject matter of the audit
- The aspects of the contract that can be audited
- How much advance notice of the audit must be provided
- The time period of the day during which the audit can take place
- Who may conduct the audit
- What records may be reviewed, i.e., physical and electronic
- How long the party subject to audit must retain the relevant information
- Whether the auditing party can retain or make copies of documents
- Access to third-party records
- The payment of any fees for under- or overpayment
- The payment of interest on under- or overpayments
- Dispute resolution procedures
- The right of the audited party to review and comment on the finding if the audit was conducted by a third party.

See Form Q.2.F.4 for model language limiting the scope of any audit to the purpose of the audit.

F. Business Continuity and Disaster Recovery (§ 35)

1. *Business Continuity*

"Business continuity" refers to the actions that the vendor undertakes, at its cost, to ensure that there is no interruption in the services provided by the licensor to the licensee. A strong business continuity program allows the vendor to get its operations (i.e., data center) back up as quickly as possible for the benefit of all of its customers, if a disaster occurs. These actions may include risk mitigation, security and discount management security, and performance monitoring.

Prudent customers should review the vendor's business continuity plan to ensure that it meets the customer's standards and needs. To the extent it fails to do so, the customer should negotiate a more comprehensive acceptable plan. The agreed upon plan should be attached to the underlying agreement as an exhibit.

The vendor's plan should address three key points:

- The vendor's plan and process to restore its own service delivery locations
- The vendor's plan and process for restoring the customer's facilities and business operations
- Who is responsible for designing and implementing the technology recovery for restoring any data centers, critical technology etc.

For a model business continuity plan, *See* http://web.mit.edu/bcmt/isorecov.htm.

2. *Disaster Recovery*

"Disaster recovery" refers to the actions undertaken by a vendor, at additional cost to the customer, to back up the facilities available to that particular customer in the event of a disaster. Disaster recovery is considered to be a subset of business continuity. For example, the vendor may be paid by the customer to keep a "hot box" live off premises so that all data can be made immediately accessible from the remote site.

Depending on the nature and scope of the ongoing services to be provided by the vendor to the customer, a disaster recovery provision can be the most important provision in the agreement after the license grant.

The goal of any disaster recovery plan or effort is to ensure the continuity necessary to allow a customer to operate its business without interruption The cause of any interruption is likely to come without warning and is difficult to anticipate, such a sudden blizzard, hurricane or fire, or even a terrorist event. A successful plan involves both the vendor and customer working together to ensure a seamless transition in the event of an interruption.

A customer can take a number of actions to protect itself. It should ensure it has alternative power sources, such as emergency generators, at its principal IT sites and that it backs up data nightly. These tapes should be stored offsite, preferably in a different state. Data centers should contain the most up-to-date monitoring systems with Halon fire suppression equipment. The customer should make sure its software licenses allow it to use the software remotely in the event of a "disaster."

To the extent a vendor operates or maintains the customer's data centers or a segment thereof or provides access to business-critical software via an application service provider arrangement, the vendor should be required to establish a formal disaster recovery plan based upon customer requirements. The customer needs to evaluate how critical each of its applications is to its ability to do business and to determine how long the business could operate without access to each application. This will drive the disaster recovery plan. Critical applications may require a "hot" swap capability. A hot site is a site that operates simultaneously with the impacted data center, allowing the applications functions to transfer to the hot site immediately upon a disruption. A customer's business may be able to operate without access to less critical applications for longer periods of time. In this event a "cold" swap may suffice. A cold site is a site that the vendor is required to have operational within a contractually mandated period after a disaster occurs. The cost to maintain a hot site would be significantly higher than a cold site.

Further, the agreement should clearly state the vendor's disaster recovery obligations are not excluded by an event of force majeure and that the vendor is obligated to restore the services and systems within the contractually agreed time period.

Regardless of the support selected by the customer, the customer should visit and audit these sites to ensure the vendor meets its contractual obligations and is prepared for an interruption. Further, the customer and vendor should jointly run tests to ensure that each party's employees are familiar with their responsibilities and that any real disaster will be handled as smoothly as possible. Testing will often expose unanticipated problems with the party's respective plans.

The customer should identify the critical services and the required restoration times. In addition, the parties should establish Recovery Time Objectives (RTOs) setting forth the maximum time each identified critical service may be unavailable and the Recovery Point Objectives (RPOs) establishing the acceptable level of data loss for a system. The vendor's disaster recovery system should be designed to meet each of these metrics and each plan must be tailored to the needs of each particular customer.

In the event the customer's disaster recovery vendor differs from its software vendor, the customer must ensure that its license allows it to operate the software from several locations in order to ensure continual/seamless operations. At a minimum, the license should allow the software to reside at two locations, provided the second location is not using the software simultaneously to process the customer's business needs.

In a cloud environment, disaster recovery costs are usually included in the service fee. Occasionally, vendors offer quicker recovery time objectives for an additional fee. Customers should seek to negotiate quicker recovery time objectives at no additional charge. The terms "disaster recovery" and "business continuity" are both used in cloud services agreements, but the usage of one term or the other does not correspond to any consistently different level or scope of services. Customers should compare their own disaster recovery capability with that offered by a vendor and then identify the position that they would be in under the vendor's plan, both in the case that the proposed recovery time objectives are achieved and in the case they are not.

In outsourcing transactions, disaster recovery is separately rated and priced. If the customer has an existing disaster recovery plan, the vendor will often include the same amount of effort/service in its price to reflect the continuity of the plan after the outsourcing. Many vendors generally agree to provide the same level of disaster recovery that the customer had in place at the time of contract execution, but at a cost.

Regardless of the services or software provided by the vendor, the parties' agreement should set forth the maximum restoration times for critical services and technology with the vendor contractually obligated to meet those times. While service credits may be an appropriate remedy for the failure to meet the requirements for a short term outage, the agreement should also address remedies for outages lasting a significant period of time. Termination for breach, step-in rights, cover/obtaining the services and software from a third party vendor may all be appropriate remedies.

3. *PRACTICE POINT*: Checklist for drafting disaster recovery and business continuity plans.

- Identify the critical services which must be protected and prioritized in the event of a disruption
- Identity those events that may occur and disrupt the critical services
- Conduct a risk analysis including a business impact analysis
- Identify key customer and vendor employees, the skill sets and responsibilities that are necessary for responding to and alleviating a disruption
- Train all employees and contractors on an annual basis
- Review the plan semi-annually to reassess threats and potential disruptions
- Establish recovery Time Objectives and Recovery Point Objectives
- If a disruption occurs, conduct a root cause analysis and a lessons learned exercise to ensure the particular disruption does not reoccur.

G. Future Development/Roadmaps (§ 16K)

When a licensee makes a decision to adopt a certain software platform for a mission critical system, it should receive assurances from the licensor that the licensor will continue to enhance and support the software for some period in the future. The licensee wants to avoid a situation where the licensee adopts a system and the licensor shortly thereafter decides to stop enhancing the system or supporting it, essentially forcing the licensee to purchase a new software system.

The licensee should seek to require that the licensor continue to update and upgrade the software for a set period of time. *See* § 11.3. Some licensees seek to have the licensor commit to invest a certain percentage of the licensor's revenue into the software on an annual basis. *See* § 3.A. This request is usually unacceptable to the licensor as it places the licensee in the position of operating the licensor's business or at least making important business decisions.

The licensee usually seeks these types of commitments to ensure that the licensor does not "sunset" the product in question. The licensee, however, should take comfort from the licensor's support commitment and should base its purchasing decision on the software's functionality at the time of contract execution. If the licensor has committed to the future development of a particular function or module, this commitment should be set forth in the functional specifications or a Statement of Work.

H. Training and Documentation (§§ 11, 13.1)

1. *Training (§ 11)*

A detailed description of the training to be provided by the licensor is important to both the licensor and the licensee. The licensor wants to put distinct limits on the training to be provided to the licensee to fix the licensor's cost. This is especially important when both parties want to use a "train the trainer" approach to reduce costs. The description should set forth absolute time limits, class size, class location, materials to be provided, and the language in which the classes will be taught. A licensor will also want to delineate prerequisite skills the attendees must have to attend the specific training. This is to ensure that the licensor does not spend time teaching basic programming skills that the attendees should already possess. The licensor also wants to carefully state which skills will be taught and which skills the attendees will possess upon completion of the course. For example, training should teach the attendees how to operate the software, but the licensor should not make statements to the effect that the licensee's attendees will be able to maintain the software unless such training will be provided.

At the same time, the licensee wants to clearly state that upon completion of training, the licensee will be able to fully operate the software; that future training will be available at a mutually agreed upon time if the licensee desires to purchase extra training; and that all documentation and training provided by the licensor to the licensee will be accurate and current. Further, the licensee's attendees will receive copies of all documentation used during the course. Smart licensees will distribute the training materials several days before classes begin so that students are familiar with the materials, and in addition they will seek to videotape and audiotape the training sessions to educate other employees. However, some licensors are hesitant to allow the licensees to audiotape or videotape the training if the training incorporates the licensor's trade secrets or if the licensor believes it will lose training revenue.

2. *Documentation (§ 13.1)*

All documentation provided by the licensor should be in sufficient detail to allow a reasonably skilled programmer to operate and use the software. The licensor should warrant that the documentation is the most current version, complete and free from any errors and omissions, and that it corresponds to the licensee's current version of the software installed at the licensee's site and is not a baseline version of the software. Further, the licensor should promptly provide the licensee with updated documentation reflecting any changes made to the software used by the licensee.

Unless the licensor desires to make a profit on duplicating the documentation, the licensee should be free to reproduce the documentation without cost, provided the licensee reproduces the licensor's protective marks (i.e., copyright notices) and does not modify the documentation.

I. Transition/Continuing Services (§ 42.2)

Customers should ensure that the underlying agreement between the parties addresses the vendor's ongoing obligations to provide any ongoing services and support to the customer in the event that the agreement is terminated. By addressing these issues in the agreement, the customer can avoid being held hostage by the vendor.

The biggest concern for the customer is that the vendor ceases to provide support if either the vendor or the customer terminates the contract for breach. The customer should require the vendor to provide support services for no less than six months from the date of termination at the rates set forth in the contract. If the contract is terminated for the vendor's breach, savvy customers seek to have the vendor provide such services at a significant discount from the vendor's existing rates. While a vendor may agree to a discount for its best customers, such a discount is justified by the vendor's breach. In the event of the vendor's breach, the customer should require that the vendor transfer to the customer all necessary licenses needed by the customer to conduct its business, including any third-party licenses.

The vendor should also limit its post-termination obligations to the customer, especially if the vendor has terminated the contract for the customer's breach. In the event the agreement was terminated without cause or for the customer's breach, the vendor should resist providing services beyond 60 or 90 days from the termination date and should charge market rates for its services. If the customer has breached the contract, the vendor will likely want to assign its employees to new accounts as quickly as possible, especially if it can obtain higher rates for their services. Thus, the vendor should not agree to retain specified "key" employees on the account after the termination date. The vendor should also require the customer to pay the vendor's fees monthly in advance to avoid any payment disputes.

J. Benchmarking (§ 8.B)

Closely associated with the concept of "most favored customer pricing" is benchmarking. Benchmarking is the process of evaluating an existing contract and comparing it to the current market environment. Benchmarking usually focuses on pricing and the scope of any applicable service level agreements.

The first issue for consideration is if and when there will be benchmarking. Licensors usually resist benchmarking because it has the effect of increasing their performance metrics while reducing their profit margins. Further, many licensors believe that services are not an easily compared commodities and that the data necessary to make a valid comparison is not easily obtained. Further, cost models are not easily analyzed in great detail. As such, licensors are hesitant to enter into an obligation that will likely lower their margins over the term of the agreement. Licensees, however, usually require benchmarking as a condition to entry into a contract, as they believe they are entitled to receive the benefit of falling prices and increased quality representative of the IT market today. Many contracts require benchmarking every few years depending on the length of the contract. The parties should carefully consider the frequency of any benchmarking, as it is expensive and time-consuming, and it often creates significant tensions between the parties.

The parties should clearly identify the methodology for identifying the third party hired to perform the benchmarking, who pays for the cost of the benchmarking, and how the parties will act on the results. The licensor should avoid having the licensee select the party undertaking the benchmarking. A better solution is to have the licensee identify three well-respected independent vendors, such as Gartner, who perform benchmarking and have the licensor select the actual party to undertake the benchmarking from the three identified vendors. The cost of the resulting study should be divided evenly between the parties.

The licensor should insist that the results of any study be kept confidential. Publishing the results of a study may have a negative impact on the licensor's reputation and/or serve as a floor in any subsequent negotiations with any future client. While this is a reasonable request, the licensee should resist any other restriction on the use of such data by the licensee.

Most licensors generally do not try to restrict use of the benchmark results beyond confidentiality. Each contract is unique in its approach to benchmarking (mandatory, discretionary, frequency, automatic adjustments, guidelines for "acceptable" performance, etc.), but once the licensee receives the results, it is hard to keep it from using the results for whatever purpose it sees fit within the bounds of confidentiality. For example, if the benchmark somehow revealed service level failures not previously known to the licensee, the licensor would be hard pressed to prevent the licensee from assessing any associated credits.

The parties should also clearly delineate the standard against which the licensor's performance will be judged. The two biggest benchmark issues for the licensor are the desire of the customer to use a "best quartile" standard and the desire of the licensee to use "tower-specific" benchmarks. Having benchmark results considered in the aggregate is a material benefit to the licensor in dealing with post-benchmark contractual remedies. When negotiating benchmarking provisions, the licensor should strive to maintain the concept of benchmarking in the aggregate—across all towers and geographies and against a similar scope of services for similarly positioned customers. Otherwise, the vendor runs the risk of having the prices it charges on a small transaction benchmarked against competitors' pricing on a larger-volume transaction. Similarly, benchmarking on cost alone is not fair to the licensor, as contractual terms and service requirements will drive deal costs. Thus, for example, it would be unfair to compare the cost of hosting services between two vendors without making adjustments for the fact that one contract specified 99.999 percent uptime (requiring the vendor to establish redundant hardware), and the other specified only 98.5 percent uptime.

The licensor should also seek to use the concept of the benchmarker's definition of "a good deal" instead of the prevalent "top quartile" standard. Most third-party benchmarking consultants have a "good deal" standard in their benchmark process. If the top quartile standard is to be used, the vendor should still seek to have a materiality standard of 5–10 percent difference before any adjustment in their fees is required.

To fairly assess the benchmarked services, the benchmarker must take into consideration the specifics of the underlying transaction, such as the quality of the service provider, any underlying assets purchased, any employees assumed, the volume of services, and the geographic location of the services being provided. In considering the totality of these requirements, it will be difficult to obtain similar comparators. Thus, the results may be open to interpretation. Likely areas for dispute are the scope and timing of any survey, the sample size of the benchmarked peer group, and where the service provider should fall within the benchmarked comparators.

Given the number of variables in attempting to compare different transactions across different providers, benchmarking can be a complex and expensive process that can lead to a dispute between the parties. Because it is a tool to test the contract against the current market, it is most useful in a long-term arrangement. In shorter-term arrangements, the cost and distraction of benchmarking may not be worthwhile because the market may not have changed significantly.

For model language, see Form E.5.1. The language set forth in Form E.5.1 is well balanced, limiting the list of potential benchmarking companies with performance measured against the mean, and all adjustments are transparent.

For a discussion of benchmarking, *see* Stuckey, *Contractual Items to Consider Before You Outsource Your Company's Data Center*, 25 ACC Docket 70, 79 (Jan./Feb. 2007).

K. Antitrust and Copyright Misuse Issues (§ 3.6)

A licensor may restrict the licensee's use of the licensed product so long as the restrictions imposed on the licensee do not violate antitrust law, constitute copyright misuse, or violate another doctrine. The risk of an antitrust violation/enforcement action increases with the number of end users, especially for operating systems. Katz & Shapiro, *Antitrust in Software Markets*, 22 September 1999: **www.researchgate.net/publication/242429931_Antitrust_in_SoftwaSo_Markets**. Set forth below is a brief discussion of several issues that should be considered in determining the enforceability of any license restrictions.

1. Antitrust Issues

Traditionally, the provision of maintenance, enhancement, and support services has been very lucrative for licensors due to the high margins involved with such services. Licensees often lack the ability to retain alternative providers, as the licensor limits third party access to the software's object code and source code and the necessary proprietary software tools to provide these services. With the advent of outsourcing, the proliferation of competent third parties to maintain proprietary software, and the increasing desire for lower cost alternatives, some licensors have sought injunctions to prohibit third party access to their proprietary software without a license. *See, e.g., Triad Systems Corp. v. Southeastern Express Co.*, 64 F.3d 1330 (9th Cir. 1995), *cert. denied*, 516 U.S. 1145 (preliminary injunction granted and affirmed on appeal); *Independent Services Organizations Antitrust Litigation*, 910 F. Supp. 1537 (D. Kan. 1995) (counterclaim for preliminary injunction against ISO granted). Or they have sought damages for such use. *See Data General Corp. v. Grumman Systems Support Corp.*, 36 F.3d 1147 (1st Cir. 1994) (jury awarded damages for copyright infringement for unlicensed use of diagnostic software). The licensors' actions are based on their claims that their software is a copyrightable, proprietary asset, and that the third party has not purchased a license to use or access the software.

"A software license agreement may reasonably restrict use of the software as long as it does not prevent the development of competing products." *Apple Inc. v. Psystar Corp.*, 658 F.3d 1150, 1159 (9th Cir. 2011).

Similarly, courts have held that the antitrust laws do not negate a patent holder's right to exclude others from licensing a patent. *Intergraph Corp. v. Intel Corp.*, 195 F.3d 1195 (9th Cir 1997). *See also In re Indep. Serv. Org. Antitrust Litig. v. Xerox*, 203 F.3d 1322 (Fed. Cir. 2000) (patent holders' decision not to sell or license patented parts nor to sell or license copyrighted materials and software did not violate antitrust laws).

At the same time, however, a licensor's attempt to exploit its software may be subject to liability based on the antitrust laws. Antitrust claims are usually based on illegal tying or monopolization. Licensees and other third parties have often claimed that licensors "tie" the use of their software to the purchase of maintenance services or hardware from the licensor in a violation of the antitrust laws. *See, e.g., Compuware Corp. v. International Business Machines Corp.*, 366 F. Supp. 2d 475 (E.D. Mich. 2005). A tying arrangement is "an agreement by a party to sell one product only on the condition that the buyer also purchase a different product, *or at least agree not to purchase that product from any other supplier.*" (Emphasis supplied.) *Northern Pacific Ry. v. United States*, 356 U.S. 1, 5–6 (1958).

In order to have a cause of action for tying, the party imposing the tie must have market power in the tying product and use that market power to leverage into the tied products market, creating a competitive disadvantage for the other competitors in the tied product market. *Jefferson Parish Hosp. Dist. No. 2 v. Hyde*, 466 U.S. 2, 16–17 (1984). As always, a key issue is how to define the "market." A patent per se is sufficient to establish market power. *United States v. Loew's, Inc.*, 371 U.S. 38, 45–47 (1962); *United States Steel Corp. v. Fortner Enterprises, Inc.*, 429 U.S. 610, 619 (1977). A copyright is also sufficient to establish market power. *Independent Ink, Inc. v. Illinois Tool Works, Inc.*, 396 F.3d 1342, 1348–49 (Fed. Cir. 2005). One way to avoid a tying allegation is to sell each product separately as well as together. As long as the pricing does not cause an "economic tie," one should avoid violating the law.

In *Data General Corp. v. Grumman System Support Corp.*, 36 F.3d 1147 (1st Cir. 1994), Data General sued Grumman for using its copyrighted diagnostic software that had been provided to Data General's customers on the specific condition that the customers not allow access to a third-party service provider, such as Grumman. Grumman in turn counter-claimed that Data General's actions violated the antitrust laws. The First Circuit held that Data General as a copyright holder had presumptively a valid business reason for refusing to license its copyrighted software. *Id.* at 1187. This holding is consistent with other similar cases in this area. *See MAI Systems Corp. v. Peak Computer, Inc.*, 991 F.2d 511 (9th Cir. 1993), *cert. denied*, 510 U.S. 1033 (1994); *Advanced Computer Services of Michigan v. MAI Systems Corp.*, 845 F. Supp. 356 (E.D. Va. 1994); *but see Electronic Data Systems Corp. v. Computer Associates Int'l, Inc.*, 802 F. Supp. 1463 (N.D. Tex. 1992) (allegation of tying of licenses for certain software to licenses for maintenance software is a valid claim of action). *See also Service and Training, Inc. v. Data General Corp.*, 963 F.2d. 680 (4th Cir. 1992) (refusal of the licensor to license maintenance software, except to computer purchasers who self-maintained, held not to be an antitrust violation or a violation of copyright policy, but rather the right of a copyright owner to exercise control over its copyright).

At least one court has held, however, that the mere refusal to license a patented invention or copyrighted work may give rise to liability if the holder does so with an "anticompetitive" interest. *Image Technical Services, Inc. v. Eastman Kodak Co.*, 125 F.3d 1195 (9th Cir. 1997). *But see Intergraph Corp. v. Intel Corp.*, 195 F.3d 1346 (Fed. Cir. 1999) (termination of advance disclosure agreement by industry leader as a result of customer's suit for patent infringement did not violate antitrust laws as vendor had no obligation to disclose proprietary information).

In January 2017, the Federal Trade Commission and the Antitrust Division of the Department of Justice jointly issued *Antitrust Guidelines for the Licensing of Intellectual Property ("Guidelines")*, which set forth the agencies' antitrust enforcement policy for the licensing of intellectual property. The Guidelines address a broad range of topics, including exclusivity, territorial restrictions, and cross-licenses as well as an analysis of commercial licensing terms.

For a detailed discussion of the issues associated with tying the purchase of computer hardware to the purchase of computer software and maintenance, *see* Chaloupka, *Tying in the Computer Maintenance Context*, 24 Corp. Couns. Q. 395 (July 2008). For an overview of the issues associated with intellectual property licensing and antitrust, *see* Flaton-Origenes & Jones, *On the Road to Innovation and Competition: When Antitrust Laws Intersect with IP Transactional Practice*, 21 ACC Docket 58 (Oct. 2013).

2. Copyright Misuse Issues

A copyright owner may not seek monopolies beyond those granted under the copyright statute. *Broadcast Music, Inc. v. Columbia Broad. Sys., Inc.*, 441 U.S. 1 (1979); *Lasercomb Am. Inc. v. Reynolds*, 911 F.2d 970 (4th Cir. 1990). Copyright misuse arises when the copyright holder seeks an exclusive right or monopoly beyond those granted by copyright law and against public policy. *Lasercomb*, 911 F.2d at 977. A finding of copyright misuse prevents the enforcement of the copyright or any copyright license from such misuse but does not invalidate the copyright itself. *Alcatel USA, Inc. v. DGI Technologies, Inc.*, 166 F.3d 772 (5th Cir. 1999); *DSC Communications Corp. v. DGI Technologies, Inc.*, 81 F.3d 597 (5th Cir. 1996). Thus, a licensor must avoid placing unlawful prohibitions on a licensee.

Courts have been quick to recognize the copyright misuse defense when the copyright owner uses its copyright in a manner that violates public policy. *See, e.g., Alcatel*

USA, Inc. v. DGI Technologies, Inc., 166 F.3d 772 (5th Cir. 1999) (copyright license limiting use of operating software system software to the copyright owner's hardware constituted copyright misuse); *Lasercomb Am. Inc. v. Reynolds*, 911 F.2d 970 (4th Cir. 1990) (prohibition on licensee developing competing software program during term of 99-year license is copyright misuse); *Practice Mgmt. Info. Corp. v. Am. Medical Ass'n.*, 121 F.3d 516, 520 (9th Cir. 1997) (requiring licensee not to buy products that compete with licensed product is copyright misuse).

At the same time, however, courts recognize that a copyright holder has the right to protect its copyright, provided it is done in a way that does not violate public policy. In *Apple, Inc. v. Psystar Corp.*, 673 F. Supp.2d 931 (N.D. Cal. 2009), *aff'd*, 658 F.3d 1150 (9th Cir. 2011) on a motion for summary judgment, the court denied a claim that Apple's practice of requiring that its operating system only be used on Apple computers was misuse. The court noted: "[t]he question is not whether the copyright is being used in a manner violative of antitrust law (such as whether the licensing agreement is 'reasonable'), but the question whether the copyright is being used in a manner violative of the public policy embodied in the grant of a copyright." It emphasized that Apple did not prohibit others from independently developing and using their own operating systems and did not prohibit purchasers of Mac OS X from using competitor's products. Instead, Apple simply prohibited purchasers from using Mac OS X on competitors' products. *See also Oracle USA, Inc. v. Rimini Street, Inc.*, 2010 WL 4386957 (D. Neb. Oct. 29, 2010) (license prohibition on automatic download of support materials and collecting copyrighted materials does not constitute copyright misuse.); *Video Pipeline v. Buena Vista Home Entertainment*, 342 F.3d 191 (3d Cir. 2003) (prohibition on licensee websites from making disparaging comments regarding licensor, motion picture industry or movies not copyright misuse).

A copyright licensor may not continue to collect royalties from the licensee after the copyright underlying the licensed software has expired. *April Productions, Inc. v. G. Schirmer, Inc.*, 126 N.E.2d 283 (Ct. App. N.Y. 1955). Attempts to collect such payments after the copyright has expired may be considered copyright misuse and a violation of the antitrust laws. *See DSC Communications Corp. v. DGI Technologies*, 81 F.3d 597 (5th Cir. 1996). *See also Brulotte v. Thys Co.*, 379 U.S. 29, 33 (1964) (attempts to collect royalties under expired patent constituted an improper use of patent monopoly, analogous to tying purchase or use of patented article to purchase or use of unpatented one).

For a more in-depth discussion, *see* Zinda, *Preserving the Copyright Balance: Why Copyright Misuse Should Invalidate Software Licenses Designed to Prohibit Resale and Oust Service Market Competition*, 48 Hous. L. Rev. 1241 (2012); Holland, *Copyright Misuse*, 87 Intell. Prop. L. Q. 7 (Mar. 2004); Davidson & Enisch, *A Survey of the Law of Copyright Misuse and Fraud on the Copyright Office: Legitimate Restraints on Copyright Owners or Escape Routes for Copyright Infringers?*, Intell. Prop. Antitrust 489 (Practicing Law Inst. 1996).

For a general discussion of the antitrust issues in maintenance, enhancement, and support services, *see* Soobert, *Antitrust Implications of Bundling Software and Support Services*, 21 U. Dayton L. Rev. 63 (1995); Hamilton, *Software Tying Arrangements Under the Antitrust Laws: A More Flexible Approach*, 71 Denv. U. L. Rev. 607 (1994); Johanson & Zollman, *Computer Maintenance Raises Antitrust Issues*, Nat'l L.J., May 20, 1996, at C40; Rosenhouse, *Sufficiency of Copyright Misuse Defense to Allegations of Copyright Infringement Pursuant to Federal Copyright Law*, 185 A.L.R. Fed. 123 (2003).

3. Digital Millennium Copyright Act—Computer Maintenance Competition Assurance Act

On October 28, 1998, Congress enacted legislation known as the Computer Maintenance Competition Assurance Act ("CMCAA"), 17 U.S.C. § 117, to partly overturn the MAI Systems case and make it easier for ISOs to service computer hardware. Incorporated as Title III of the Digital Millennium Copyright Act ("DMCA"), the law is directed solely to the copying of software as part of the act of servicing computer hardware. Under the law, the making of a RAM copy of a computer program by an ISO as part of servicing computer hardware will not be an act of copyright infringement. The law provides a limited immunity to copyright infringement only and does not address the ISO maintaining and modifying the software in and of itself. 17 U.S.C. § 117. As interpreted by at least one court, the CMCAA applies retroactively. *Telecomm Technology Services, Inc. v. Siemens Rolm Communications*, 1999 WL 696011 (N.D. Ga. July 6, 1999).

In a case of first impression, the U.S. Court of Appeals for the Federal Circuit held that an ISO was likely to prevail on its maintenance and repair defense (17 U.S.C. § 117(c)) under the DMCA in an infringement action based on its circumvention of an encryption system of the manufacturer's copyrighted maintenance code, done solely for the purposes of maintenance or repair. Further, the court read the right to "repair and maintain" broadly. *Storage Tech. v. Custom Hardware Engin. & Consult., Inc.*, 421 F.3d 1307 (Fed. Cir. 2005) (absent proof that circumvention of manufacturer's encryption system facilitated copyright infringement, ISO's circumvention to access system codes did not violate DMCA). *See also MGE UPS Systems, Inc. v. GE Consumer and Industrial, Inc., et al.*, 612 F.3d 760 (5th Cir. 2010) (bypassing external hardware security key that prevented user from viewing or using a work did not violate DMCA); *but see Actuate Corp. v. Int'l Business Machines Corp.*, 2010 WL 1340519 (N.D. Cal. Apr. 5, 2010) (unauthorized posting of software license keys and passwords violated DMCA by "circumvent[ing] a technical measure that effectively controls access to a [copyrighted] work.").

The courts are split as to whether simply obtaining, in an unauthorized manner, an otherwise authorized password to gain access to a copyrighted work, constitutes "circumvention." The Third Circuit has held that "misuse of a legitimate password does not fall within the prohibitions of § 1201." *Schork Grp., Inc. v. Choice! Energy Servs., Retail, LP*, 2022 WL 290523 at *10 (E.D. Pa. July 21, 2022), finding that the DMCA requires *both* access "without authorization" and an act that "descrambled a scrambled work, decrypted an encrypted work, avoided, bypassed, removed, deactivated, or impaired the login scheme." *Avaya, Inc. v. Telecom Labs, Inc.*, 2012 WL 13035096 at *6 (D.N.J. May 1, 2012).

The Third Circuit has also found that the DMCA's terms "bypass" and "avoid" "imply that a person circumvents a technological measure only when he affirmatively performs an action that disables or voids the measure that was installed to prevent them from accessing the copyrighted material." *Healthcare Advocates Inc. v. Harding, Earley, Follmer & Frailey*, 497 F. Supp. 2d 627, 644 (E.D. Pa. 2007). Courts have also found that it is reasonable to conclude that "to re-activate software permissions without authority constitutes circumvention," but only where such controls prevent "all forms of access to the protected work." *Avaya, Inc.*, 2012 WL 290523 at *10-11.

Even if bypassing the login limitations using the unauthorized license files did not rise to a DMCA violation, it would still be relevant to show copyright infringement. *Schork Grp., Inc. v. Choice! Energy Servs., Retail, LP*, 2022 WL 290523 at *10-11 (E.D. Pa. July 21, 2022) (noting that "[a]ny potential misuse of the password by unauthorized users" would be "potentially relevant to [plaintiff's] copyright infringement claims").

For an overview of the DMCA, *see Corporate Counsel's Primer on the Digital Millennium Copyright Act*, 39 LAW. BRIEF 1 (July 2009); Lee, *Reverse Engineering Under the DMCA: Recognizing a "Fair Access" Defense*, 20 COMPUTER L. ASSOC. BULL. 133 (No. 4, 2005); Davidson & Axtell, *Reverse Engineering: The DMCA and the Reverse Engineering of Suspected Infringing Products*, 23 COMPUTER & INTERNET LAW. 1 (Feb. 2006).

L. Export/Import Issues (§ 43)

1. General

Under U.S. export regulations, an individual may "undertake transactions subject to the Export Administration Regulations[1] (EARs) without a license or other authorization, unless the regulations affirmatively state such a requirement." 15 C.F.R. § 736.1. The EARs are consistent with the position of many European governments that anything not prohibited is allowed, in contrast to the Bureau of Industry and Security's (BIS) previous position that everything is prohibited unless an exception exists. Under the EARs, licenses are not required for most shipments to Canada and to U.S. territories, possessions, and commonwealths. The export regulations can be found at http://www.bis.doc.gov.

For a general overview, *see* Blageff, *Overview of Export Controls*, 239 COM. L. ADVISOR 1 (Nov. 2007); *Export Licensing Checklist*, 16 FORMS & CHECKLISTS BI-MONTHLY 39 (Mar./Apr. 2012).

2. Definitions

Section 734.13 (a) of the EARs defines "export" as:

"*(1)* An actual shipment or transmission out of the United States, including the sending or taking of an item out of the United States, in any manner . . . ."

Part 772 of the EARs defines technology as:

"Information necessary for the 'development,' 'production,' 'use, operation, installation, maintenance, repair, overhaul, or refurbishing . . . of an item."

Note 1 to the definition of Technology states: "technology" may be in any tangible or intangible form, such as written or oral communications, blueprints, drawings, photographs, plans, diagrams, models, formulae, tables, engineering designs and specifications, computer-aided design files, manuals or documentation, electronic media or information revealed through visual inspection; . . . .

1. The Export Administration Regulations are issued by the Department of Commerce and administered by the Bureau of Industry and Security (BIS) to implement the Export Administration Act of 1979, as amended.

3. *Export of Software and Technology*

The export and re-export of technology and software from the United States is under increasing scrutiny by the U.S. government. Special attention is focused on encryption technology and satellite technology. Exports are controlled by BIS and the Department of State's Directorate of Defense Trade Controls (DDTC). BIS usually governs goods, software, and technology with civilian applications, while the DDTC governs goods, software, and technology with military applications and satellite technology. The first step in exporting any software or technology is to determine whether an export license is needed. Under 15 C.F.R. 736.2(b), the exporter must apply a 10-step process to determine whether the exporter's software or technology requires a license under the EAR. Based on the results, software or technology will fall into one of three categories:

1. *No License Required* (NLR). If software or technology to be exported is either not subject to the EAR or does not require a license as a result of the 10-step process under 15 C.F.R. 736.2(b), it is considered to be "No License Required" or NLR. Software and technology classified as EAR 99 fall into this category.

2. *License Exceptions.* If a determination is made that the software or technology requires a license under the EAR, the exporter must determine whether a "License Exception" is available. A License Exception is the authorization to export under stated conditions that would otherwise require a license. 15 C.F.R. 740.1(a). For software and technology, two potential License Exceptions are available under Section 740:

   (a) *Technology and Software under Restriction (TSR).* Section 740.6 allows export and re-export of software and technology, subject to national security controls, to Country Group B upon receipt of a Letter of Assurance.

   (b) *Technology and Software-Unrestricted (TSU).* Section 740.13 of the EAR provides a License Exception for certain "Operation Technology" and software, software updates, and mass-market software, permitting their export without a license. This License Exception covers certain mass-market software, such as software sold over the counter through mail order transactions and telephone call transactions, sales technology, and software updates. Operation Technology is defined as "the minimum technology necessary for the installation, operation, maintenance (checking), and repair of those commodities or software that are lawfully exported or re-exported under a license, a License Exception or NLR." 15 C.F.R. 740.13(a)(1).

3. If a License Exception does not exist, the exporter must apply for a license under 15 C.F.R. 748.

In addition, the United States and United Nations maintain comprehensive economic embargoes against certain countries. 15 C.F.R. § 746. Sanctioned countries, as of November 15, 2023, include Crimea region of Ukraine, Cuba, Iran, North Korea, and Syria.

For a detailed explanation of the export laws, *see* Bloom & Gibbs, *Common Pitfalls of Export Compliance*, 32 ACC Docket 62 (July/Aug. 2014); Corp. Couns. Guide. To Export Controls (2d ed. 2023).

4. Cloud Computing

Cloud computing raises a number of interesting export issues. Given that the customer's data will be stored in the cloud and can be easily moved around the world, who is responsible for ensuring compliance with U.S. export laws? Further, how can access to data be restricted to U.S. citizens when it resides in the cloud? These issues and others should give both vendors and customers reason to pause. The Department of Commerce has issued three letters attempting to clarify some of these issues. See Chapter 14.A.5 for a detailed discussion of the application of the export laws to cloud computing

5. Deemed Exports

Both parties must be cognizant of the "deemed" export rules. 15 C.F.R. § 734.13(a)(2) of the EARs defines "export" to include:

"Releasing or otherwise transferring "technology" or source code (but not object code) to a foreign person in the United States (a 'deemed export')."

Further, 15 C.F.R. § 734.13(a)(2) defines "reexport" to include:

"Releasing or otherwise transferring "technology" or source code subject to the EAR to a foreign person of a country other than the foreign country where the release or transfer takes place (a deemed reexport)."

Thus, the EARs prohibit the export or release of technology to an entity's foreign offices, employees, customers, and its customer's employees without a valid license or license exception. Except in certain limited situations or with the existence of a license exception, a valid export license is required for foreign nationals to view or access restricted technology in the United States, as this considered is a "deemed" export. This restriction applies to technology and source code provided to foreign nationals inside the United States, whether oral, written, or through other media. Visual inspections also constitute the provision of technology. As such, a party may violate the export laws if it discloses restricted technology to foreign nationals within the United States or to individuals overseas who are employees of the disclosing party.

Further, both parties should not allow IT managers who are foreign nationals to have administration rights that would allow them to access export-controlled files.

Applications for U.S. work visas require a deemed export certification certifying whether the potential employee will be exposed to controlled technology and, if so, a requirement that the employer obtain an export license. If an employer does not routinely address export control issues, the employer should consult with competent counsel to determine whether the individual the employer seeks to hire will have access to controlled technology under the International Traffic in Arms Regulations (ITAR) and EAR. Prudent entities will not overlook this issue, as the penalties can be significant and include both civil and criminal penalties.

6. *Contractual Considerations (§ 45)*

The licensor should ensure the license includes language requiring the licensee to comply with all U.S. export laws, the licensee's acknowledgement that the software and all related materials are subject to U.S. export controls and that the licensee agrees to comply with all applicable laws. The licensor must thoroughly investigate the licensee and confirm it is not on a "Denied Persons List." The failure to do so may subject the licensor to significant liability.

Obtaining an indemnity from the other party for breach of the other party's export obligations will not protect the licensor from criminal actions brought by the government and will not protect the licensor from reputational risk. Further, many foreign indemnitors refuse to stand behind their indemnity obligations, leaving the licensor without a viable remedy.

Most importantly, the license agreement should specifically state that the licensor has no liability for its failure to obtain a U.S. export license to export the software, as the licensor's inability to obtain an export license may be specifically tied to the character of the licensee.

For additional information on export licensing, *see* the Bureau of Industry and Security's website: http://www.bis.doc.gov; the Office of Foreign Asset Control's website: http://www.treasury.gov/about/organizational-structure/offices/Pages/Office-of-Foreign-Assets-Control.aspx; the MIT Technology Licensing Office's website: http://tlo.mit.edu/; and Microsoft's licensing website: http://www.microsoft.com/en-us/exporting.

7. *Customs*

In addition to complying with U.S. export laws, the licensor also needs to be concerned with the custom duty laws of the importing country. And, likewise, U.S. import laws must be abided by when software is imported into the United States. Recently, U.S. Customs and Border Protection issued a ruling that importers must pay duty on the value of royalty payments made in connection with licensing the patented technology incorporated into the goods imported into the United States. HQ W548692 March 2, 2001. These issues are often quite complicated and require serious attention. Not only can there be a significant financial impact as a result of customs duties, but several countries restrict the importation of encryption software or require the source code to be made available to the government. For an overview of the issues involved with customs duties, *see* Jones, *Import Loopholes: Avoiding the Customs Audit*, 29 ACC Docket 58 (Sept. 2011); Lyverse, MacLennan & Apker, *Cracking the Customs Code: How to Export to Europe Effectively*, 24 ACC Docket 40 (June 2006).

8. *PRACTICE POINT*: Checklist for obtaining export approval.

The following diagram provides a high level overview for the steps in reviewing potential exports.

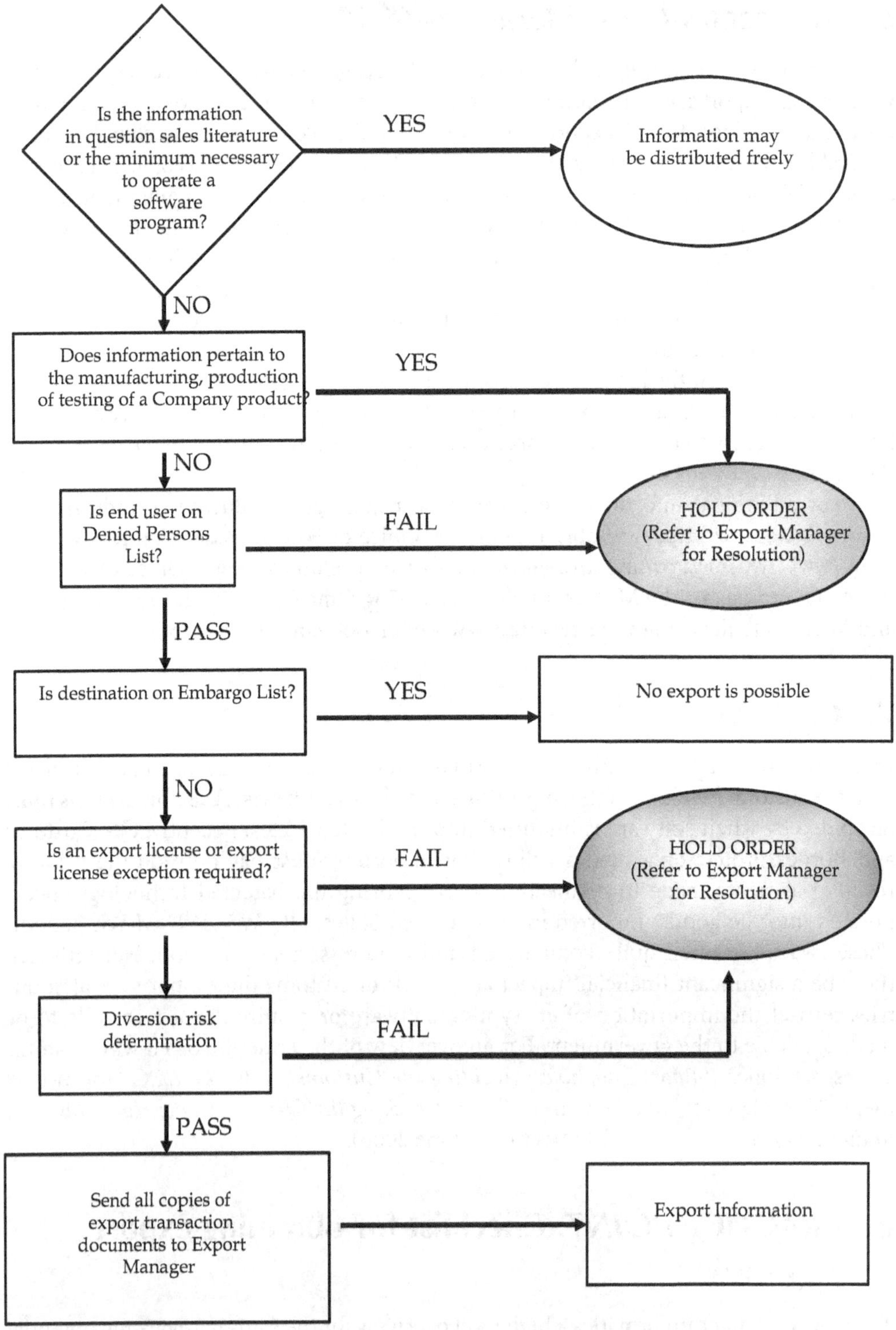
Is the information in question sales literature or the minimum necessary to operate a software program?
YES
Information may be distributed freely
NO
Does information pertain to the manufacturing, production of testing of a Company product?
YES
NO
Is end user on Denied Persons List?
FAIL
HOLD ORDER (Refer to Export Manager for Resolution)
PASS
Is destination on Embargo List?
YES
No export is possible
NO
Is an export license or export license exception required?
FAIL
HOLD ORDER (Refer to Export Manager for Resolution)
Diversion risk determination
FAIL
PASS
Send all copies of export transaction documents to Export Manager
Export Information

M. Bonds, Parent Guarantees, and Letters of Credit (§§ 8.H, Exhibit 8H, 34)

1. *Bonds (§ 34)*

(a) Bid Bonds

Occasionally, a licensee issuing an RFP will require potential bidders to post a bond upon submission of their bid, often equal to 5 percent of the bidder's price. This requirement is to ensure that a bidder is serious about its bid and will enter into an agreement with the licensee if it is selected as the provider of choice. These bonds usually expire once a contract is executed.

(b) Performance Bonds/Payment Bonds (§ 34.1)

Performance bonds and payment bonds are often used when there is concern as to one party's ability to meet its financial obligations. Performance bonds are not favored by licensors as they must be obtained from a bank or insurance company at an additional cost. Payment bonds are often required where there is concern with the ability of the licensee to pay. In such cases, a letter of credit drawn on a U.S. bank payable at sight may be more attractive to the licensor. At a minimum, the party required to obtain a bond should seek to pass the cost of the bond on to the benefiting party and carefully review the terms that instigate payment of the bonds.

For a general overview of performance and payment bonds, *see Performance and Payment Bonds*, 27 Corp. Couns. Q. 481 (Aug. 2011).

2. *Parent Guarantees (§ 8.H, Exhibit 8H, Signature Line) (Form O.1, Q.2.LL.39)*

An alternative to a performance bond or payment bond is a parent guaranty. Parent guarantees are appropriate where there is some concern that either the licensor or licensee may lack the resources to meet its contractual obligations. Guarantees are applicable only where the party in question is the subsidiary of a larger financially solvent parent, and they are attractive to the party required to obtain a guaranty in that they usually do not involve any cost unlike a performance bond or payment bond. In the event the license allows the licensee's affiliates to utilize the software or the licensee can add any of its affiliates to the license as a matter of right, the licensor should insist on a parent guaranty by the licensee.

To limit the parent's risk, the parties should agree that the purpose of the parental guarantee is an obligation from the parent entity to incent its subsidiary to perform its obligations in the underlying agreement. If the parent agrees to give a guaranty, the parent should ensure that it has the right to assert any defenses the affiliate would otherwise have.

The provisions of the underlying license agreement should contain appropriate and mutually agreed procedures for the parties to resolve problems or disputes prior to seeking to enforce the parental guaranty. A common issue arising from parent guarantees is the beneficiary of the guaranty prematurely demanding monetary damages from the guarantor/parent entity without attempting to first resolve the issue or dispute in accordance the terms of the underlying agreement.

Amending an agreement may impact any guaranty associated with the agreement. The beneficiary of the guaranty should ensure the guaranty clearly provides that any amendment of the underlying agreement does not impact the guaranty. Absent such language, the beneficiary should ensure that the parties reaffirm the guaranty. *See Sherwin Williams Co. v. ASBN, Inc.*, 550 S.E.2d 527 (N.C. 2001) (guarantor released due to finding the amended terms constituted a new lease requiring a new guaranty); *Citicorp Leasing, Inc. v. Kusher Family Ltd. P'ship.*, 2006 WL 1982757 (S.D.N.Y. July 14, 2006) (unconditional guaranty precludes affirmative defense by guarantor); *European Amer. Bank v. Lofrese*, 586 N.Y.S.2d 816 (2 Dept. 1992).

3. Letters of Credit (Form Q.2.LL.36)

Another alternative is a letter of credit. Letters of credit can be expensive, and for that reason they are disfavored by parties required to establish such instruments. If the parties do agree to put a letter of credit in place, the party who is the beneficiary should insist that the letter of credit is drawn on a U.S. bank and payable at sight. The use of a U.S. bank is especially important if the issuing party is related to a foreign governmental entity that also holds sway over the bank. To avoid significant delays and perhaps even litigation, the letter of credit should be payable at sight, meaning the beneficiary simply must present a statement—the wording of which has been agreed upon in advance—to the bank to receive payment. The beneficiary should avoid any process that requires the involvement of the other party after the letter of credit has been established. The letter of credit should remain in place well beyond the contemplated completion date of the project to avoid having the letter of credit expire prior to the completion of the establishing party's obligations, due to a delay in the project. Finally, both parties should carefully review the language of the letter of credit to ensure there are not any "surprises."

N. Most Favored Customer (§ 8.A)

1. Overview

Many customers seek to include a "Most Favored Customer" clause in their agreement to ensure that they receive the best price for the software and services purchased from the vendor. Vendors should be hesitant to include such clauses even for their largest customers, as these clauses theoretically lower the vendor's profitability while creating a potentially significant risk in the event the vendor fails to comply with its obligations. This risk rises exponentially if the vendor fails to carefully track the pricing associated with each of its sales. Most Favored Customer clauses, however, have much greater applicability beyond pricing, which can serve as a valuable tool for both the vendor and customer.

In actuality, these clauses can be challenging to enforce unless the obligation is absolute. Some practitioners argue that "Most Favored Customer" provisions are impossible to enforce, as the terms of every agreement are different, thus thwarting a claim by a party that it is entitled to receive a lower price. To that end, vendors that do agree to such provisions seek to insert caveats to limit the applicability of its obligation (e.g., "for similar volumes of similar services"). The customer should limit the number of caveats to the vendor's obligation and ensure that the vendor has a contractual obligation to notify the customer when the vendor offers another customer a lower price. Without an affirmative notification obligation, the customer will never know that the vendor has offered other customers a lower price.

Although challenging to enforce, Most Favored Customer provisions can and will be enforced in court. *JP Morgan Chase Bank, N.A. v. DataTreasury Corp.*, 823 F.3d 1006 (5th Cir. 2016). In 2005, DataTreasury Corporation ("DTC") granted a fully-paid-up patent license to JP Morgan Chase ("JPM") under which JPM agreed to pay a flat fee of $70 million. The license agreement included a most-favored-licensee provision that required DTC:

(i) to notify JPM of any other licenses granted,
(ii) to provide JPM with a copy of the other license agreement, and
(iii) to give JPM the benefit of any more-favorable license terms in those other licenses.

The relevant language of JPM's license agreement with DTC provided:

> "9. *Most Favored Licensee. If DTC grants to any other Person a license to any of the Licensed Patents, it will so notify JPMC, and JPMC will be entitled to the benefit of any and all more favorable terms with respect to such Licensed Patents* . . . ."

In 2012, DTC granted a much smaller company a paid-up license in exchange for a much lower flat license fee. Under the terms granted to the smaller company, JPM's paid-up license fee would have been only $1 million. DTC failed to notify JPM or to provide JPM with a copy of the license agreement until the litigation, causing JPM to sue DTC for breach of contract. The trial court held that DTC owed JPM $69 million (the difference between the license fee that JPM had paid and the license fee it would have paid under the terms granted to the other customer).

The court's decision was not a fluke or a decision by a rogue court. Oracle paid approximately $200 million in 2011 to settle a U.S. Government lawsuit alleging that Oracle had breached an MFC clause in its federal government contract. The whistleblower employee who reported the alleged breach received $40 million.

If successful, an aggrieved party is entitled to recover not only monies overpaid to the licensor but also entitled to benefit from more favorable terms in the future. *Epic. Sys. Corp. v. Allcare Health Mgmt. Sys. Inc.*, 2002 WL 31051023, at * 7 (N.D. Tex. Sept. 11, 2002).

For those agreements involving services, some customers seek the right to terminate the agreement if a third party offers the customer a lower price and the vendor fails to meet it. *See* § 8.B. This provision should be unacceptable to the vendor, who is faced with the potential of continually eroding margins or having its contract terminated at any time.

From the vendor's perspective, these clauses not only have a financial impact but also are an administrative burden. Most vendors lack the ability to administratively track the prices and terms offered to all of their customers to determine their compliance with a most favored customer clause. One solution is to make a breach prospective; in the event a Most Favored Customer clause is triggered, the vendor is only obligated to provide the better price/terms going forward. A customer will likely argue that the vendor has no incentive to comply with its obligations because there is no true penalty for the vendor's breach. Another solution from the vendor's perspective is to offer bundled solutions, making it difficult for customers to compare pricing and claim another customer received more favorable pricing.

Most Favored Customer clauses also provide a potential means for the parties to resolve outstanding impasses. For example, if the vendor refuses to escrow its software, one potential solution is for the vendor to agree that, in the event the vendor escrows source code for another customer, it will provide source code escrow for the customer in question. This solution potentially provides comfort to the customer in that the customer knows that it is on parity with the vendor's other customers. The vendor benefits because it allows the vendor to reach agreement with the customer on the same terms as its existing customers.

See Ettinger & Altman, *Compliance with Most Favored Customer Clauses: Giving Meaning to Ambiguous Terms While Avoiding False Claims Act Allegations*, 90 Notre Dame L. Rev. Online 1 (2015).

2. PRACTICE POINT: Checklist for drafting and reviewing most favored customer provisions.

Checklist for drafting and drafting most favored customer ("MFC") provisions. The parties should consider:

From the customer perspective:

- Whether the customer will be able to enforce the provision and truly benefit.
- Imposing a self-reporting requirement on the vendor.
- Requiring an annual certification of compliance from the vendor.
- Including an audit right within the agreement.
- Rejecting any attempt by the vendor to narrowly draft the governing language to prevent the customer from obtaining the benefit of the bargain.

From the vendor perspective:

- Drafting the MFC provision very narrowly to clearly state when the MFC will apply:
  - for the identical volumes of identical services/products to be provided in the same time frame (DTC argued that such requirements should be implied in its license with JPM, but the court disagreed) or ° for identical terms and conditions.

- Limiting the MFC provision to a set period of time.
- Developing and implementing written internal procedures for complying with the MFC provision.

O. Work for Competitors/Exclusivity (§ 9.12)

In the course of negotiations, some customers in competitive industries seek to contractually restrict the vendor from licensing its software or providing services to the customers' competitors as they believe the vendor's software and services provide a competitive advantage in the market. Customers are also concerned that a vendor may disclose the customers' trade secrets to the customers' competitors.

Conversely, many vendors seek to include a provision in the license agreement stating that they are not precluded from providing services or software competitive with or functionally similar to the products or services provided to the customer. The vendor's ability to do so is limited only by its obligations under the applicable nondisclosure agreement. This reasoning mirrors the "residuals" provision often contained in a confidentiality agreement or license agreement. *See* § 12.7. At least one court has held that corporate agreements not to compete will be evaluated differently from employee covenants not to compete. *Owens Trophies, Inc. f/k/a R.S. Owens & Company, Inc. v. Bluestone Designs & Creations, Inc. and Society Awards*, 2014 WL 126082 (N.D. Ill. Jan. 14, 2014).

Many customers are willing to accept this provision if the vendor's employees assigned to its account do not work for a "competitor." These customers are concerned that by working on a competitor's account, the employees may unintentionally or unknowingly reveal the customer's trade secrets to a competitor. Such reasoning is often based on the "inevitable disclosure" doctrine that an employee will inevitably disclose a company's trade secrets if allowed to provide services to a competitor. *See, e.g., PepsiCo. v. Redmond*, 54 F.3d 1262 (7th Cir. 1995). How the parties define "competitors" is important. Many customers often seek to define "competitor" broadly. For example, members of the beverage industry often define "competitor" to include all beverage manufacturers including alcoholic beverages, non-alcoholic beverages, coffee, teas, and water. By agreeing to such a broad definition, the vendor significantly limits its opportunities to market its industry knowledge, especially in a time of industry consolidation.

From the vendor's perspective, contractual limitations on how it may assign its employees are difficult to accept, as most employers rely on a small group of highly trained employees to manage their development and implementation projects. Utilizing a group of experienced employees allows the vendor to draw upon their significant experience and allows the employees to deliver the contracted services in a shorter time period, saving the customer money. Conversely, having to idle employees because they may not be assigned to competing customers will increase customer costs over time.

Given that the vendor's employees have almost certainly executed nondisclosure agreements protecting the customer's confidential information, the customer should not be worried. Vendors have a strong financial incentive to ensure that their employees abide by their confidentiality agreements, as they do not want bad publicity arising from a claim that the vendor's employee misappropriated a customer's confidential information.

P. Good-Faith Efforts, Best Efforts, and Commercially Reasonable Efforts

1. *General*

Licensees often seek to require the licensor to exercise its "best efforts" in performing the licensor's obligations under the agreement while licensors usually seek to negotiate a "good faith efforts" standard in the belief that "good faith efforts" requires a lesser standard of effort than "best efforts," and that good faith is implied in every contract. *See* Chapter 5.A.1(b)(iii) (Material Misstatements). In practicality, however, these terms are ambiguous without a commonly accepted meaning under the law with some courts finding each of these terms means "reasonable" efforts. Prudent parties should not affix any expectation that one standard dictates a higher level of performance in comparison to the other.

For a general overview, *see* Adams, *Interpreting and Drafting Efforts Provisions: From Reason to Unreason*, 72 Bus. Law. 67 (2019).

2. *Good Faith*

"Good faith" is generally interpreted as requiring the parties to deal openly and honestly with each other and is dependent on the facts of the situation. *Hamlin v. Steward*, 622 N.E.2d 535 (Ind. App. 1993) ("A good faith effort is . . . what a reasonable person would determine is a diligent and honest effort under the same set of facts or circumstances."). "The covenant of good faith and fair dealing does not include the requirement to use best efforts." *Liu v. Beth Israel Med. Ctr.*, 2003 WL 1488081, at *7 (S.D.N.Y. June 26, 2003). Unlike "good faith," which takes on the mantle of dealing fairly with the other party, "best efforts" is generally interpreted as encompassing a performance or diligence standard.

On the other hand, "bad faith" has been defined as the "evasion of the spirit of the bargain, lack of diligence and slacking off, willful rendering of imperfect performance, abuse of a power to specify terms, and interference with or failure to cooperate in the other party's performance." *Foseid v. State Bank of Cross Plains*, 541 N.W.2d 203, 213 (Wis. Ct. App. 1995). Proposing materially different license terms from a term sheet has been found to breach a party's obligation to negotiate in good faith. *Pharmathene, Inc. v. Siga Techs., Inc.*, 2011 WL 4390726 (Del. Ch. Sept. 22, 2011). Accessing computer code to create competitive software has been held to constitute bad faith. *SAS Inst., Inc. v. S&H Computer Sys., Inc.*, 605 F. Supp. 816 (M.D. Tenn. 1985).

The law of most states implies an obligation of good faith in the performance of a party's obligation under an agreement. *See, e.g.*, Cal.: *Kransco v. American Empire Surplus Lines Ins., Co.*, 2 P.3d 1 (Cal. 2000); Penn.: *Fraser v. Nationwide Mut. Ins. Co.*, 135 F. Supp. 2d 623 (E.D. Pa. 2001); Wis.: *Ubelacker v. Paula Allen Holdings, Inc.*, 464 F. Supp. 2d 791 (W.D. Wis. 2006). *See also* Restatement (Second) of Contracts § 205 ("Every contract imposes on each party a duty of good faith and fair dealing in its performance and enforcement."); *but see Creative Dimensions in Management v. Thomas Group, Inc., 1999* WL 225887 (E.D. Pa. Apr. 19, 1999) (Under Texas law "there is no implied covenant of good faith and fair dealing in each contract"). The duty to negotiate in good faith does not prohibit a party from negotiating a contract that is financially advantageous to itself. *Phoenix Mut. Life Ins. Co. v. Shady Grove Plaza Ltd. Partnership*, 374 F. Supp. 118 (D. Md. 1990).

An implied covenant of good faith, however, does not "prohibit a party from doing what is expressly permitted by the agreement itself," even if it is to the detriment of the other party. *Wolf v. Walt Disney Pictures and Television*, 162 Cal. App. 4th 1107, 1120 (2008).

Although state law may infer an obligation of good faith and fair dealing, it does not necessarily create an independent cause of action. *Compare Automed Technologies, Inc. v. Eller*, 160 F. Supp. 2d 915, 925 (N.D. Ill. 2001) (implied duty of good faith "does not create independent duties or give rise to an independent cause of action. It is used more as a canon of construction for interpreting a contract's other terms.") *with MacPhee v. Verizon Communications, Inc.*, 2008 WL 162899, at *7 (S.D.N.Y. Jan. 15, 2008) ("New York courts have recognized a separate cause of action for breach of the covenant of good faith and fair dealing in cases involving efforts by one party to a *contract to subvert a contract to itself.*").

For a general overview, *see* Witz, *The Implied Duty of Good Faith and Fair Dealing*, Practical L. J. 28 (Fall 2020); *Kleinberger, Delineating the Implied Covenant and Providing for "Good Faith,"* Bus. L. Today (May 2017); Burton, *Breach of Contract and the Common Law Duty to Perform in Good Faith*, 94 Harv. L. Rev. 369 (1980) and Summers, *The General Duty of Good Faith – Its Recognition and Conceptualization*, 67 Cornell L. Rev. 810 (1982).

3. Best Efforts

The meaning of "best efforts" has been recognized by many courts as ambiguous. *Martin v. Monumental Life Ins. Co.*, 240 F.3d 223, 233 (3d Cir. 2001); *Carlson Distributing Co. v. Salt Lake Brewing Co.*, 95 P.3d 1171, 1179 (Utah App. 2004) ("'best efforts' is primarily a subjective standard"). Its meaning is generally dependent on the factual circumstances surrounding an agreement. *Carlson Distributing Co.*, 95 P.3d at 1179. At least one court has acknowledged the lack of clarity in distinguishing good faith and best efforts. In *Ashrokan Water Services, Inc. v. New Start LLC*, 111 Misc. 3d 686 (N.Y. 2006), the court stated "[i]t is still unclear . . . the relationship between 'best efforts' and 'good faith' . . . ."

"Best efforts" has been found to require "greater care and diligence than ordinary care and diligence." *Allen v. Williamsburgh Sav. Bank*, 69 N.Y. 314, 322 (1877). It requires more than good faith, which, under UCC § 1-304, is implied in all contracts. *See Accessdata Corp. v. ALSTE Technologies GmbH*, 2009 WL 1743767 (D. Utah June 18, 2009) (court found the sale of unusable software raised the issue of good faith, which could not be addressed in summary judgment); *cf. Fab-Tech, Inc. v. E. I. Du Pont de Nemours & Co.*, 311 Fed. Appx. 443, 447-48 (2d Cir. 2009) (although the UCC does not provide an independent claim for breach of good faith, there may be a common-law action even if the contract is governed by the UCC); *Kroboth v. Brent*, 215 A.D.2d 813, 814 (3d Dept. 1995).

Best efforts generally requires diligence and an elevated duty of good faith. *National Data Payment Systems v. Meridian Bank*, 212 F.3d 849, 854 (3d Cir. 2000). A party is obligated to do the best it can, regardless of the abilities of others. *Carlson Distributing*, 95 P.3d at 1179. The court in *Bloor v. Falstaff Brewing Corp.*, 454 F. Supp. 258 (S.D.N.Y. 1978), *aff'd*, 601 F.2d 609 (2d Cir. 1979), held that "best efforts" requires a party to perform "to the extent of its own total capabilities."

Some courts seek to impose a reasonable efforts standard. "Best efforts" requires "a party to make such efforts as are reasonable in the light of that party's ability and the means at its disposal and of the other party's justifiable expectations." *T.S.I. Holdings, Inc. v. Jenkins*, 924 P.2d 1239, 1250 (Kan. 1996). *Kroboth v. Brent*, 215 A.D.2d 813, 814 (3d Dept. 1995) ("'Best efforts' requires that plaintiffs pursue all reasonable methods for" meeting their contractual obligations); *Timberline Dev. v. Kronman*, 263 A.D.2d 175, 178 (1st Dept. 2000) ("The requirement to employ reasonable efforts or 'best efforts,' as it is generally expressed in the performance of contractual obligations, is deemed to be implicit in every agreement."); *Permanence Corp. v. Kennametal, Inc.*, 908 F.2d 98 (6th Cir. 1990) (the exercise of due diligence or reasonable efforts).

"Best efforts" does not require a party to ignore its own interests. *First Union National Bank v. Steele Software Sys. Corp.*, 838 A.2d 404 (Md. App. 2003); *Macksey v. Egan*, 633 N.E.2d 408, 414 n.16 (Mass. 1994) ("best efforts" requires a good-faith effort to meet a party's obligations with the right to consider its own interests). Further, it does not require success or the "single-minded pursuit of the objective." *Mark Technologies v. Utah Resources Int'l*, 147 P.3d 509, 512 (Utah App. 2006). *See also Triple-A Baseball Club Assocs. v. Northeastern Baseball, Inc.*, 832 F.2d 214, 225–26 (1st. Cir. 1987), *cert. denied*, 485 U.S. 935 (1988) ("best efforts" equates to good faith but does not require every conceivable effort). At least one court has found that the difference between best efforts and reasonable efforts "is merely an issue of semantics . . . ." *Trecom Business Systems, Inc. v. Prasad*, 980 F. Supp. 770, 774 n.1 (D.N.J. 1997).

Several courts held that they will only enforce a "best efforts" provision where the agreement includes an objective definition by which a party's actions can be measured. *DaimlerChrysler Motor Co., LLCZ v. Manuel*, 362 S.W.2d 160 (Tex. App. 2012); *Kevin M. Ehringer Entr. v. McData Serv.*, 646 F.3d 321, 326 (5th Cir. 2011). Given the ambiguity surrounding the concept of best efforts, the parties should avoid adopting a "best efforts" standard unless it is clearly defined. By defining "best efforts," the parties can ensure certainty in the interpretation of their contract. A potential definition is "Reasonable diligence necessary to further the intentions of the parties hereunder."

4. *Commercially Reasonable Efforts*

A common compromise between the use of a "good faith" standard and a "best effort" standard is the use of a "commercially reasonable efforts" standard. Again, the meaning of "commercially reasonable" is ambiguous unless it is defined. General contract law, however, will impose a reasonableness standard unless it is explicitly disclaimed. *Durham v. Warner Elevator Mfg. Co.*, 139 N.E.2d 10 (Ohio 1956); RESTATEMENT (SECOND) OF TORTS § 324A (1965).

A "commercially reasonable standard" is generally thought to be less stringent then a "best efforts" or "reasonable best efforts standards." A commercially reasonable standard has been found to require a party to take all reasonable efforts to obtain the required result. *The Williams Companies, Inc. v. Energy Transfer Equity L.P. et al.*, 159 A.3d 264, 273 (Del. 2017).

For a more detailed discussion, *see* Adams, *Understanding Best Efforts and Its Variants (Including Drafting Recommendations)*, 50 PRAC. LAW. 11 (2014); Farnsworth, *On Trying to Keep One's Promises: The Duty of Best Efforts in Contract Law*, 46 U. PITT. L. REV. 1 (1984); *Best Efforts Clauses*, 236 COM. L. ADVISOR 1 (Aug. 2007); Sergent, *Do Your Best with "Best Efforts": Using Open Contract Terms*, 40 MD. B.J. 49 (Mar. 2007).

Q. Time Is of the Essence

Many licensees seek to include language in the underlying license agreement stating that "time is of the essence" in the licensor's performance of its obligations under the agreement. Such language establishes a party's failure to meet its time-based obligations/deliverables as a material breach of the agreement. *Retrofit Partners I, L.P. v. Lucas Indus., Inc.*, 201 F.3d 155 (2d Cir. 2000) ("Insofar as a time for performance is specified in the contract, failure to comply with the time requirement will be considered to be a material breach of the agreement."). Under New York law, a party's obligation to meet dates in an agreement will be strictly enforced and a court will infer a "time is of the essence" provision. *Towers Charter & Marine Corp. v. Cadillac Ins. Co.*, 894 F.2d 516, 523 (2d Cir. 1990). Any such provision must clearly and unequivocally provide that "time is of the essence" to invoke such a right. *Karapetian v. Carolan*, 188 P.2d 809 (Cal. App. 1948). The remedy for breaching a "time is of the essence" provision is recession. *Id.* (remedy for breach is rescission or to affirm agreement and bring claim for breach of contract); *Cooper v. Klopfenstein*, 185 N.W.2d 604 (Mich. 1971).

Prudent licensors should avoid incorporating a "time is of the essence" provision in their license. Software development by its nature is uncertain and subject to many unpredictable elements. As such, a licensor should avoid subjecting itself to a claim of material breach or recession for a late delivery that may not materially harm the licensee. If a licensee insists on incorporating a "time is of the essence" provision in the underlying agreement, the agreement should provide that the sole and exclusive remedy for the licensor's failure to meet the dates specified in the agreement is the receipt of liquidated damages. Doing so provides an equitable remedy to the licensee without exposing the licensor to significant liability that may arise from a material breach of the agreement. Further, the licensor should select a governing law other than the law of New York or specifically state that time is not of the essence for the stated delivery dates.

From the licensee's perspective, if delivery by a certain date is important, the licensee should seek to include a "time is of the essence" clause. While most licensors will argue against including such a clause in the underlying agreement, at a minimum, the inclusion will generate a frank conversation as to the licensor's confidence in meeting its contractual delivery dates.

See Form Q.2.I.19 for alternative language that allows a party to avoid the punitive nature of a "time is of the essence" clause.

R. Consent Will Not Be Unreasonably Withheld

Many parties seek to qualify any consent requirement by providing that such consent will not be unreasonably withheld or delayed in the belief that this modification will provide an element of protection. In actuality, this modification may not provide the level of protection a party may seek. Courts have interpreted these provisions as requiring any refusal to consent to be reasonable. *Peak-Las Positas Partners v. Bollag*, 172 Cal. App. 4th 101 (2009). Courts will use a reasonable man standard or a reasonably prudent person standard to determine the appropriateness of any withholding of consent. *Broad & Branford Place Corp. v. J. J. Hockenjos Co.*, 39 A.2d.80 (N.J. 1944). In a recent case in the English court system, *Porton Capital Technology Funds and Others v. 3M Holdings Ltd. and 3M Co.* (2011) EWHC 2895 (Comm.), the court found that a party must only show that its decision to withhold consent was reasonable and not that its consent was justified.

In *Speed Play v. Bebop*, 211 F.3d 1245 (Fed. Cir. 2000), the parties entered into an agreement limiting the licensee's right to assign its interests in a license without the consent of the licensor, which consent could not "be withheld unreasonably." The *Speed Play* court concluded that the licensor could only withhold consent if the assignment would impair the licensor's consideration for entering into the license agreement. *Id.* at 1251- 52. Intellectual property owners have the right to withhold consent to maintain the value of their intellectual property. *See, e.g.*, trademarks: *Rey v. Lafferty*, 990 F.2d 1379, 1393 (1st Cir. 1993); copyrights: *Clifford Ross Co. v. Nelvana, Ltd.*, 710 F. Supp. 517 (S.D.N.Y. 1989), *aff'd without opinion*, 883 F.2d 1022 (2d Cir. 1989).

So long as a party has a good-faith basis for withholding consent, even if such reason benefits only that particular party, a court is unlikely to find a party unreasonably withheld consent. As such, a party should not unduly rely on these provisions to protect its interests or ensure an equitable outcome from that party's perspective.

Ken Adams, a well-respected expert on contract drafting, has concluded that the implied covenants of good faith and fair dealing may impose a commercial-reasonableness standard on a party's decision to grant or withhold consent and suggests inserting the phrase "for any reason [or no reason]" to establish the standard for granting or withholding consent. ADAMS, A MANUAL OF STYLE FOR CONTRACT DRAFTING (2d ed.), §§ 2.111–2.126.

S. Third-Party Materials

Some customers seek to prohibit, or at least limit, the vendor's ability to incorporate third-party materials into the vendor's deliverables. They do so for several reasons: (i) to ensure the customer owns the deliverables outright, (ii) to avoid having to pay license fees to any third-party vendor in the future, and (iii) to ensure there are no limitations on their ability to use the deliverables in the future (i.e., the customer is unable to create derivative works, maintain and support the deliverables etc.) A prohibition on the use of third-party materials may cause the vendor to increase its price as the vendor may need to develop a piece of software instead of licensing a readily available third-party off-the-shelf software application.

> *Vendor shall not use any materials owned by or licensed by Vendor from third parties (the "**Third Party Materials**") in the Deliverables unless such materials are ancillary to (and not material to the content provided in) the Deliverables. To the extent that Third Party Materials are included in the Deliverables or provided in connection with the Deliverables, Vendor shall be responsible for obtaining for Customer, at Vendor's sole cost and expense, and hereby grants to Customer, a royalty free, paid-up, transferable, sub-licensable license to copy, publish, display, distribute, perform, use, exploit, create derivative works of (only if derivative works are allowed under the relevant agreement with the licensor of Third Party Materials), advertise, and exhibit such Third Party Materials, for the duration of the Term and in the U.S. and on websites that are registered under U.S. domain names, to the extent it is incorporated in or necessary for the use of any Deliverable delivered to Customer by Vendor hereunder. Vendor shall use commercially reasonable efforts to provide such license to Customer on a perpetual, irrevocable, worldwide basis and with a right for Customer and its affiliates to create derivative works of the Third Party Materials.*

T. Third-Party Access

1. General

Many vendors seek to strictly limit access to their software to the customer's employees in an effort to protect their intellectual property, to ensure the security of their product (i.e., a hacking or viruses being introduced), and increase their profitability. Vendors make a significant investment in their intellectual property and are hesitant to provide access without being compensated.

Many customers seek to allow third parties to access the vendor's intellectual property to allow the third party to provide support and maintenance in an attempt to lower their costs. Many vendors are unwilling to grant access, as they are concerned that once the third party becomes knowledgeable about the vendor's products, they will approach the vendor's other customers in an attempt to gain their business.

Licensees, however, often seek the right to provide third parties access to the licensor's software to allow the third party to operate, support, and/or maintain the software on the licensee's behalf.

Licensees usually do so because they are seeking to lower their IT costs by outsourcing responsibility for their IT systems, or they are seeking cheaper alternatives to purchasing support from the licensor. In most cases, the licensor has no obligation to grant such consent, and in the event the licensor does not provide consent, the licensor has no obligation provide the licensee with the reasons for its decision.

From the licensee's perspective, the licensee should seek the right of third-party access when negotiating the license grant, when it has the most leverage. Many licensees lack leverage after the licensee agreement has been signed and the licensor has little incentive to grant third parties access. Thus, when negotiating the agreement, the licensee should carefully consider the definitions of "Licensee," "Authorized User," "Affiliate," and "Use." See Chapter 4.A for a more detailed discussion.

If the customer requests third-party access rights after the parties' agreement has been signed, the vendor may seek additional compensation, as the original price did not contemplate third-party access. This is especially true if the customer seeks to have a third party host the software or outsource the support and maintenance of the software to a third party.

2. Considering Requests for Third Party Access

In considering whether to grant third-party access rights, a prudent licensor should require the licensee to provide the following information:

- The name of the third-party entity
- The type and level of access needed
- The reason access is required

If the licensor is willing to grant the third-party access, at a minimum, the parties should enter into a tri-party non-disclosure agreement. See Form M.1.8 for a model three-way non-disclosure agreement. From the licensor's perspective, the terms of the nondisclosure agreement should be non-negotiable. The licensor should also require the license to indemnify the licensor for the third party's actions and reserve the ability to terminate the right of access at any time on ten days' notice.

Most licensors will not grant access to a third party if the third party is a competitor or a potential competitor. To the extent the licensee has leverage over the licensor and the licensor believes it must provide some level of access for client relations reasons, the licensor may consider the following:

- Having the third party perform the work as a subcontractor to the licensor;
- Restricting the third party's employees who have access to the licensor's software and intellectual property from providing similar services to other clients of the licensor; and
- Encrypting/protecting the licensor's software/intellectual property to prevent/reduce the risk of unauthorized use/access by the third party.
- Allowing access to only those individuals identified by name;
- Requiring those named individuals to sign a nondisclosure agreement with the vendor that they will be personally liable for any breach;
- Requiring the named individuals to agree not to compete with the vendor; and
- Requiring the named individuals not to provide services to the vendor's competitors or their customers.

Prudent vendors should establish a process for considering customer requests to allow third-party access. By maintaining a set protocol for approving or denying requests, the vendor will likely have greater leverage and bargaining power.

3. *PRACTICE POINT*: Checklist for considering third party access.

- Who is the customer requesting access for?
- Why do they need access?
- What are they accessing? Source code?
- Is the third party a competitor of the vendor?
- Are they willing to execute a separate license agreement with the vendor?
- Is the customer/third party willing to pay the vendor an additional license fee?
- Will the third party execute:
- A nondisclosure agreement with the vendor?
- A noncompetition agreement with the vendor?
- Will the customer indemnify the vendor for any IP infringement claims arising from the third-party actions?
- Will the customer agree not to solicit the vendor's employees?
- Will the customer agree to give the vendor a right of first refusal to perform the work that the customer seeks to have the third party perform?

U. Subcontractor Approval

Many customers seek to impose limits on the vendor's use of subcontractors working on their projects. They do so in an effort to better understand their risk from the vendor's use of subcontractors who fail to deliver as well as subcontractors having access to their systems. Another concern is preventing access to their systems by potential competitors. Vendors argue that any limitations, including obtaining the customer's approval, is unnecessarily bureaucratic given the vendor is responsible for delivering a completed solution and is responsible for the acts of its subcontractors.

While the customer's intent to impose restrictions may be well-meaning, prohibitions on the use of subcontractors may be impractical, as the contracted solution may incorporate a number of disparate services which cannot be provided by a single vendor. For example, a hosted solution may involve a software solution where development and support services may be provided by subcontractors as well as hosting services, security services, call center services, disaster recovery services, etc., each of which is subcontracted.

One compromise is to have the customer approve all subcontractors prior to executing the agreement. A second is to provide that the customer may not unreasonably withhold its consent of any subcontractor. A third is to limit the customer's approval to "material" contractors. A "material" subcontractor is often defined as one who provides a significant portion of the services, those developing important intellectual property and those that have access to the customer's data.

V. Non-disparagement Clauses

Prudent customers should carefully consider the wisdom of agreeing to a non-disparagement clause. While non-disparagement clauses may be appropriate in some cases, such as testing early-stage software/a pilot or beta agreement, there is no reason from the customer's perspective for including a non-disparagement clause in a software license or SaaS agreement. Seeking to include such clauses in an agreement may create the impression the licensor is trying to conceal past or future poor performance. Further, from the customer's perspective, given the ambiguous meaning of "disparagement," the customer should be concerned its employees may make a comment about the licensor's product that could be considered disparaging.

W. Non-solicitation Clauses

The purpose of a non-solicitation provision is to prevent a party from being introduced to an employee of another party through a transaction between the parties and based on knowledge gained during the business relationship between the two parties hiring the employee. It is not meant to prevent a party from hiring an individual unrelated to the transaction between the parties whom the hiring party would have hired anyway.

Vendors who provide integration and installation services often insist on the inclusion of a non-solicitation clause in their agreements as they seek to prevent a client from hiring their skilled employees in an effort to reduce the customer's costs. Customers should also be concerned about the vendor hiring their newly trained employees. Thus, customers should insist on making any such clause mutual.

X. Off-Shore Work

Some customers seek to prohibit the vendor from using off-shore resources to develop the deliverables. They do so for several reasons: (i) the deliverables may be export restricted, (ii) the customer seeks to limit the development team/resources access to sensitive data such as PII/PHI which is required to complete the project; (iii) the customer is concerned about geo-political risks; or (iv) the customer wants the development tam to be in the same time zone.

Restricting off-shore work will likely increase the vendor's price. Thus the customer must balance its concerns against the increased price. One solution may be to allocate sensitive work to the US and the remaining work to an off-shore team.

> *Due to security and identity protection concerns, direct services under any contract shall be performed within the borders of the United States. Any services that are described in the specifications or scope of work that may involve access to secure or sensitive data or personal client data or development or modification of software for the Customer shall be performed within the borders of the United States. Unless specifically stated otherwise in the specifications, this definition does not apply to indirect or "overhead" services, redundant back-up services or services that are incidental to the performance of the Agreement. This provision applies to work performed by subcontractors at all tiers.*

CHAPTER 8

Types of Licenses

There are many types of software licenses, each of which is drafted to reflect the underlying purpose of the license grant. Set forth below is a brief discussion of the principal types of software licenses a practitioner may encounter.

A. End-User Licenses

1. Development Licenses

Development licenses allow the licensee to use the licensed software to develop applications and prototypes based on the licensed software. The licensor usually provides the licensee with a limited license for a reduced license fee, in the belief that any new applications developed by the licensee will increase the sales of the licensor's software, as entities will need to license the licensor's software in order to use the licensee's applications.

(a) License Grant

The license grant usually restricts the licensee's use of the software to developing applications that utilize the licensor's software. Similar to demonstration licenses, most licensees receive limited contractual protections and in turn pay a nominal license fee. If the licensee desires to utilize the software in a production environment to operate its own business as opposed to developing software, it must purchase a production license at market price.

Development licenses usually limit use of the software to the development of commercial applications, service offerings and solutions based on the licensor's software product. In turn, these solutions will be made commercially available to a broad spectrum of customers. Most licensors allow the development and testing of a developed application using customer data as well as providing training to the licensee's employees and those customers who have purchased a production license.

(b) Restrictions

Under the terms of most development licenses, the licensee is required to keep the software on its premises at all times and is prohibited from transferring the software to a customer site. Licensees are usually prohibited from: (i) providing end users access to the software, (ii) providing training to unlicensed end users, and (iii) developing applications or solutions for a particular customer once the licensee has been retained by the customer to develop such application. Further, most licenses prohibit the licensee from distributing or reselling the licensor's software as a stand-alone product and from creating products that directly compete with the licensor's software.

See Forms B.2.1 and I.2.1 for model development licenses.

2. Beta Licenses

Under a "beta" license, the licensee is usually provided with a "pre-production" version of a software product, allowing the licensor to test the software in a production environment prior to commercially distributing the software. A beta version of a software product differs from a release-ready application which has been carefully tested and evaluated for potential bugs, viruses and the potential for third party infringement claims. Beta licenses facilitate the licensor's product development through customer feedback and, based on such feedback, the functionality, look and feel, etc. of the software may be modified and improved. A beta license differs from an evaluation license in that an evaluation license allows a potential customer to test a fully functional software product prior to licensing it, while a beta license allows the evaluation of software that is not yet commercially available or complete. When products are offered for evaluation in "beta" form, licensees can test functionalities before they are commercially available allowing the licensor to incorporate their suggested improvements into the final product. Thus, there is a mutual benefit.

(a) General Terms

Most beta licenses include the term of the beta period and any services that are included (i.e., installation, training, etc.), a license grant setting forth the limitations on use of the software, a warranty/liability disclaimer and a description of what the licensor expects to receive in return.

From the licensor's perspective, the most important aspect is receiving feedback on any issues encountered in the use of the software, the licensee's subsequent participation in a focus group and interviews with the licensee's technical staff, as well as the right to use the licensee's name in the licensor's publicity materials.

Beta agreements also usually allow for the conversion of the beta license to a production license following notice that the product has been commercialized. In recognition of the licensee's assistance in testing the software, the licensor often provides the licensee a discount off the production license fee once the product is ready for commercial use.

The beta process benefits the licensor by having the licensee provide feedback on potential improvements to the software, identifying bugs and creating a market "buzz" through industry discussion of the new product. The licensee receives little benefit outside of the ability to suggest improvements to the software and possibly the ability to guide the development of the software to meet the licensee's needs.

(b) Warranties

Most beta testing occurs in a closed environment, subject to confidentiality and internal use only restrictions. Given the licensee is not paying a licensee fee and the software is still under development, the underlying license usually provides that the software is provided "AS IS," without warranty of any kind. Licensors argue that given the limited use associated with a beta license, the licensee should not require the protections traditionally included in a software license to protect a licensee's interests.

A beta version of a software product is usually not error free, and thus the licensee should not expect to receive a performance warranty from the licensor. The licensee should recognize that the software may not operate properly and may contain numerous bugs. The licensor should, however, warrant that the software is free of viruses, as the licensee has a reasonable expectation that the licensor will test the software for viruses prior to distributing the software. From the licensee's perspective, the software should not corrupt or damage the licensee's information technology system, as the licensee is providing the licensor a tangible benefit by testing the licensor's software.

(c) Intellectual Property Indemnification

One of the principal issues for negotiation in a beta license is the licensor's indemnification of the licensee in the event of a third-party infringement claim. Licensors argue that the risk of a third-party intellectual property infringement claim is remote, as the software is still in the testing phase and is not being commercially distributed. A prudent licensee should think carefully before accepting this risk. If the risk is truly small, the licensor should be willing to indemnify the licensee.

If a licensor does not initially offer an infringement indemnity, the licensee should seek one. From the licensee's perspective, it is reasonable to expect the licensor to indemnify the licensee in the event of a claim of intellectual property infringement. The licensee should not have to defend an infringement action, even if the software is provided without charge, as the licensee most likely received a limited, short term license and received only a minor benefit from the use rights granted by the beta license. The risk to the licensor of indemnifying the licensee is low, as the software is most likely being distributed to only a small number of customers and the licensor has the ability to investigate the risks of infringement prior to distributing the software. If the licensor has not evaluated the software's potential to infringe, the licensor should not release the software, even for beta testing purposes.

(d) Confidentiality

From the licensor's perspective, the parties should execute a confidentiality agreement prohibiting the licensee from disclosing any information about the software, most importantly, its performance. Confidentiality is important to protect such information, not only from the licensor's competitors, but also to protect the reputation of both the software and licensor in the industry if the software's performance is subpar.

(e) Feedback/Publicity

The licensor should insist on the right to publicize the licensee's participation in the trial if the trial is successful. A prudent licensor will contractually require the licensee to provide a positive quote for any publicity materials and require the licensee to serve as a reference in return for granting a discounted license fee for a production license. See Form B.8.3 for a model Discount Addendum, providing the licensee a discounted licensee fee for serving as a reference. The licensor should also have the right to use the results of the beta testing as well as the tester's comments in the licensor's press releases, promotional and marketing materials and other sales and marketing activities without the obligation to compensate the licensee.

Many evaluation agreements provide that all feedback from the licensee is owned by the licensor, potentially transferring valuable intellectual property to the licensor. The feedback may have value beyond the licensor's product or may already be owned by the licensee. Thus, prudent licensees should seek to retain ownership of the feedback but allow the licensor to use the feedback without having to account to the licensee or having to pay the licensee a royalty.

Model language to this effect is as follows:

> *Notwithstanding anything to the contrary, as between the Parties, Vendor retains and shall be the sole owner of all right, title and interest, including all Intellectual Property rights, in, to and under the following (the following being collectively referred to as "**Vendor Property**"): (a) The Software, the Documentation, the Support Services, the Consulting Services and deliverables (if any), usage metrics and similar data ("**Metrics**") regarding Customer's use of the Software, all other software, technology, content and materials provided or prepared by or on behalf of Vendor or used by Vendor in providing the Software, and all other Vendor Confidential Information;*
>
> *(b) any and all suggestions, ideas, enhancement requests, recommendations, modifications, improvements or other feedback provided by Customer or any employee, agent or contractor of Customer relating to any of the foregoing ("**Feedback**"), all rights in which are hereby assigned to Vendor; and*
>
> *(c) all derivative works, customizations, enhancements, modifications, translations, extensions and improvements in or related to any of the foregoing; but in each case of (a) - (c) does not use or rely upon Customer Data and other Confidential Information of Customer.*
>
> *The Parties agree that (i) all Feedback is provided "as is" with no representations or warranty of any kind by Customer, either express or implied; (ii) no Feedback (or any portion(s) thereof) shall be attributed to Customer or identified as originating from Customer; and (iii) Metrics shall be aggregated and de-identified with other customers' de-identified metrics. The foregoing shall also apply to any Feedback or Metrics in connection with the Third-Party Services. Except for the rights expressly granted herein, Vendor does not grant, license or transfer to Customer or any User or other third party any ownership or other rights to any Vendor Property. No implied licenses are granted herein and all rights not expressly granted to Customer herein are reserved by Vendor.*

See Form E.5.2 for a model Feedback Agreement.
See Form B.2.1 for a model Beta License.

3. Demonstration Licenses

Demonstration licenses allow a perspective licensee to evaluate the functionality and performance capabilities of a software solution. It is a risk-free means of testing a software solution without an obligation to purchase a license. In many cases, the software's functionality is demonstrated on a laptop or conducted via an online portal, such as

WebEx® or GoToMeeting®, using dummy data. When software is not being provided to the customer and the customer cannot access the software's object or source code, the parties usually do not sign a license agreement, only a confidentiality agreement.

Where software is provided to the customer for testing in its own environment, the licensee should be required to execute a demonstration license. Because the licensee is not using the software in a production environment, the licensor usually does not charge a license fee. Most demonstration licenses contain minimal provisions beyond the term of the license, the license grant, abbreviated warranties, an indemnification for intellectual property infringement and a governing law provision. Most vendors do not charge a license fee or if they do, it is a token fee as the licensee is only "evaluating" the software not using the software for production use and if the licensee decides to purchase a license for production use, it will then pay the full fee for a production license.

(a) Term

From the licensor's perspective, the term of the evaluation period should be long enough to allow the licensee to become familiar with the functionality of the software, but short enough so that the licensee will not receive a commercial benefit without purchasing a license. From the licensee's perspective, the term should be long enough to allow the licensee to fully test the software in its operating environment prior to purchase, thus reducing the risk of buyer's remorse. Most licenses provide for a 30-90 day term.

(b) Warranty and Warranty Disclaimer

Given the limited purpose of the license and its short duration, the licensor should only provide:

- a warranty of authority to enter into the license agreement,
- a warranty of ownership of the software,
- a warranty as to the inclusion of open source software in the licensed software, and
- a warranty as to viruses, worms, etc.

The license should contain a disclaimer that the software is otherwise provided "AS IS" and limit the licensor's liability to a modest amount. Although the licensee may seek a large limitation of liability and more extensive warranties, the licensor should resist the licensee's attempts to do so, as the risk to the licensee is small, especially given that the software is to only be used for evaluation purposes. Further, it is the licensee that receives the primary benefit of the license, in that it is able to evaluate the software without having to purchase a license first.

(c) Indemnification

Similar to warranties, the licensor should provide the licensee very limited indemnification rights, if any. From the licensor's perspective, an intellectual property infringement indemnity is the only indemnity that may be justified in a demonstration license. Given that the licensee is not utilizing the software for production purposes, the risk of an infringement claim is small, as the licensee has, in most cases, not paid to use the software. Further, the licensee can stop using the software without impacting its business as the software is not in production use. Nonetheless, a prudent licensee should seek an intellectual property infringement indemnity. Because a demonstration license primarily benefits the licensee and the licensee will receive an indemnification if it subsequently purchases a production license, a prudent licensor should resist providing broader indemnity rights.

(d) Confidentiality

The licensor should ensure that the confidentiality agreement between the parties prevents the licensee from releasing the results of any testing that the licensee conducts. The licensor wants to avoid having the licensee provide an unfavorable comparison to other third-party products or publicize the fact that the software failed to meet its stated functionality. The licensor should also require the licensee to provide the licensor with copies of the licensee's test data so that the licensor can evaluate the results and if necessary, correct any short comings.

(e) Feedback

Each party should appoint one individual to serve as the primary point of contact for all issues pertaining to the evaluation and in the case of the licensee, provide feedback to the licensor. The licensee should be obligated to promptly notify the licensor of any problems the licensee encounters and to document the nature of any such problems in reasonable detail. The licensor should have the right to use the results of the evaluation testing as well as the evaluator's comments and the licensor's promotions, press releases, advertisements and other sales and marketing activities without the right to compensation.

In addition, the licensee should agree to serve as a reference and permit the licensor to feature the licensee in case studies evaluating the software's use.

(f) Third-Party Access

Some demonstration licenses allow the licensee to demonstrate the licensor's technology to the licensee's customers and potential customers in connection with the licensee's software or solution. The licensee is usually required to keep the software on its premises at all times and to not transfer the software to a customer location. In addition, licensees are often permitted to provide training to their employees and those customers who have purchased a production license from the licensee. Most demonstration licenses prohibit use of the licensed software for development activities or to provide training to customers or potential customers who have not purchased a production license from the licensee.

See Forms B.1.1, B.1.2, B.1.3 and B.1.4 for model demonstration/evaluation licenses.

4. Evaluation/Pilot Licenses

An evaluation or pilot license usually involves use of the software in a production environment with real data for a short period of time to evaluate the software. Most licensors are unwilling to negotiate the terms of the license agreement. Given the limited use rights granted by the licensor and the short use time (e.g., 90 days), the licensee cannot expect to receive the same level of protection (e.g., representations, warranties, indemnities, and liability caps) it would receive with a production license. Usually the software is provided "AS-IS" without express or implied warranties or an indemnity, and the licensor's liability is usually limited to the amount of the license fee. Licensors usually charge a moderate license fee as well as the cost of any tangential services, such as the cost of any training.

(a) Indemnification

Most licensors are unwilling to provide an indemnity in an evaluation/pilot license, arguing that the licensee's use of the software on a short-term basis for a limited use creates a very low risk for the licensee. Use of software under an evaluation license may carry a low risk to the licensee, but it does not protect the licensee or justify shifting the risk of infringement to the licensee. If the software is a commercial product that is being evaluated in contemplation of the licensee purchasing a production license, the licensor should be willing to assume the risk of infringement, as the licensor is better able to quantify and manage the risk.

Some licensees believe it is important to negotiate an indemnity at the time of entering into an evaluation license to utilize its leverage of a possible sale over the licensor. They believe that by waiting to negotiate an indemnity until the licensee commits to purchasing a production license, the licensee has lost the leverage to negotiate a favorable indemnity.

Some practitioners believe that providing an indemnity for an established product already in production use does not increase the licensor's risk. Because the software is already in production use with other clients, a claim made against one client will likely affect all other clients using the software. Thus, indemnifying additional clients does not increase the licensor's risk and most likely will not materially increase its defense costs. In most cases, however, the licensor possesses significant negotiating leverage over the licensee and will not consider including an indemnity in the evaluation license.

(b) Limitation of Liability

Due to the nature of evaluation licenses, most licensors are usually unwilling to assume more than a token amount of liability, usually equal to the license fee paid by the licensee. Some licensors are willing to assume a higher level of risk if the licensee is using the software solely in a controlled test lab environment where the software is segregated from the licensee's enterprise IT infrastructure, as doing so limits the licensor's risk of a third-party infringement claim.

See Forms B.1.2 and B.1.3 for model Evaluation Licenses.

PRACTICE POINT:

From the licensor's perspective, evaluation licenses should:

- Limit the licensee's usage to a short period of time with the automatic expiration of the agreement at the end of the stated term.
- Provide that if the client uses the software after the end of the evaluation period, the licensor's standard license fees will automatically apply. There

should be clear delineation between the free, or reduced fees, term and any use thereafter.

- Limit the scope of the license rights, i.e., use only by the licensee's employees for purposes of internal evaluation.
- Clearly indicate the software is provided "AS IS" without warranties of any kind.
- Disclaim all liability for all damages including direct damages.
- Not provide indemnities of any kind.
- Expressly state that the licensee disclaims any ownership interest arising from any comments, input, or other feedback provided by the licensee in connection with the software's evaluation.
- Include language providing that if intellectual property ownership of the feedback does not transfer to the licensor for any reason, the licensor will receive an exclusive, perpetual, royalty-free license right to any such intellectual property generated by the feedback.
- State the expectations and requirements relating to the test environment.
- State the parties' rights, roles, and responsibilities.
- Require the licensee to execute a nondisclosure agreement.
- Set forth the parties' termination rights and remedies.
- Allow the licensor to use any endorsements, recommendations, positive comments, etc., in its advertising and marketing. If any feedback comments are negative, consider granting the licensor the discretion to withhold those comments or statements.

5. Production Licenses

A production license grants the licensee the right to use the software in a production environment to process live data including parallel processing for purposes other than software testing or evaluation. The licensee receives the full right to use the software, as opposed to the limited rights granted in a demonstration license, an evaluation license or a beta license. Production licenses are the most common type of license.

See Form B.3.1 for an example of a production license.

6. Sandbox Licenses

Sandbox licenses allow a licensee to set up an identical copy of its organization/org that is distinct and isolated from its production environment, allowing the licensee to use the organization for testing and training purposes while protecting its production servers, data and software from potential harm. Once code has been fully tested in a sandbox it can be merged into the production code without risk. Most software vendors such as AWS and Salesforce sell solutions for establishing partial or full sandbox environments.

B. Specialized Licenses

1. System Integration Licenses

System integrators build and integrate customized solutions for end users using third-party products, managing the installation and customization of the integrated solution with the end user's legacy information technology systems. To do so they often receive a free or discounted development license for the proprietary third-party software products to customize such product for the end user. See model Forms B.1.4 and B.1.5.

System integrators are usually service companies, such as Accenture LLP or DXC Technology Corporation, that do not sell their own proprietary software. Instead, they are usually "technology agnostic," customizing and integrating third-party proprietary products.

See Chapter 17.A for a more detailed discussion regarding system integrators.

2. Sublicenses

Sublicenses arise when a licensee grants a third-party certain license rights it has received from a third-party licensor. Common examples include the licenses granted by resellers/distributors to end users to use a third party's software or when a prime contractor utilizes a subcontractor's software as a deliverable to the prime contractor's customer. In most cases, the licensee accepts the software subject to the terms of both the sublicense granted by the sub-licensor and any mandatory terms passed down from the licensor through the sublicensor.

The sublicensor should be careful to not provide a broader license grant than it receives from the licensor and to ensure its license grant to the sublicense is coterminous with its license grant from the licensor. The licensor should contractually require the sublicensor to provide the licensor notification of all sublicenses granted by the sublicensor including the name of the sublicensee and a copy of the sublicense.

From the sublicensee's perspective, the license should include a representation and warranty that the sublicensor has the right to grant the sublicense in addition to making those representations, warranties and indemnifications commonly found in software license agreements. The sublicensor should also provide maintenance and support consistent with traditional software license agreements. Most importantly, the sublicense should ensure that in the event the sublicensor's relationship with the licensor is terminated for any reason, the sublicensee's rights under the sublicense shall continue undisturbed.

See Forms B.6.1 and B.6.2 for model sublicenses.

3. Outsourcing Licenses

(a) Provision of Outsourcing Services by Licensee to Third Parties

Most traditional software licenses prohibit the licensee from utilizing the software to provide outsourcing services to third parties. From the licensor's perspective, the licensor does not want to allow the licensee to utilize the software without compensating the licensor for the software's full use. To the extent the licensee believes it may utilize the software to provide outsourcing services to third parties, the licensee should negotiate with the licensor at the time the license agreement is entered into to allow use of the software for outsourcing purposes.

See Form Q2.JJ.2 for a model license grant allowing the licensee to utilize software for an outsourcing transaction.

(b) Outsourcing of Licensee by Third-Party Vendor

Licensees should seek to include language in the license grant allowing the licensee to outsource the software to a third-party vendor to allow a third-party vendor to provide professional services to the licensee. Retaining this flexibility will permit the licensee to consider all options for its information technology needs and will not subject the licensee to the whims of the licensor at a later date if it seeks to outsource its information technology functions.

Most traditional licenses prohibit the licensee from allowing any third party to access the software without the licensor's consent and usually prohibit the licensee from assigning or transferring the license without the licensor's prior written consent. See, e.g., Form B.3.1 § 3.6 for illustrative language prohibiting a licensee from providing third-party access to the licensor's software.

See Form C.4.1 for a model Business Process Outsourcing Services Agreement.

CHAPTER **9**

Mobile Applications

A. General

Mobile applications are software applications designed to operate on mobile devices such as tablets and smart phones. Mobile application licenses differ from traditional licenses as they allow users to access information via the internet, capturing the end user's data in the process. End users download the application from the owner's site or a third-party site such as the Apple App Store or Google Play Store.

This Chapter discusses those issues unique to developing mobile applications and licensing end users to use the developed mobile application. It does not revisit those issues related to software development and licensing discussed elsewhere in this book and does not address the process for publishing and distributing an application which vary greatly depending upon the particular App Store.

B. Mobile Application Development Agreements

1. *Native Apps vs Web Apps*

Native applications are applications that are developed for and run on a specific operating system such as Apple iOS, on a specific device. Because native applications are tied to a particular platform, a developer must create a separate application for each operating system, i.e., iOS and Android. As such, developing native applications can be expensive, as a new application must be created for each operating system.

Web applications are developed using languages such as HTML5, are device agnostic, and are compatible with multiple mobile platforms. Because web applications are not device specific, they often lack the ability to access all device functions because they were not developed specifically for that device. Web applications are thought to run slower than native applications and operate at a much lower level, if at all, when not connected to the internet.

2. *The Development Agreement*

Many of the issues that impact traditional software development agreements are present in the development of mobile applications.

The first consideration of the parties is to decide for which mobile platform the application will be designed, i.e., Apple iOS, Android, etc., and where the application will be published. If the application will be published in a third-party store, such as the Apple App Store or the Google Play Store, one gating consideration is to decide the party that is responsible for the publication of the application. If the developer has agreed to publish the app, it should also be responsible for managing the application process, and complying with the publication rules for the applicable App Store, including all security requirements. The party responsible for publishing the application should not contractually commit to a specific timeframe for publication, as the decision to publish an application is often outside the party's control. For example, the Apple App Store has the discretion to reject any application for any reason.

The underlying agreement for the development of the application should clearly allocate ownership of the developed application. It is common for a customer to own all rights, title and interest in the developed application. If the customer will own the developed application, the underlying agreement should provide that the application is a "work made for hire" for copyright purposes, and assign, in perpetuity, to the customer all such worldwide rights, title and interest in and to the application, including the right to sue for infringement.

If the developer will retain ownership of the application, the customer must understand the terms of the license grant and whether those terms meet its needs. The customer will often seek broad transferrable and sublicensable license rights to use the app for any purpose, in a broad territory, or not use it if it so chooses, to modify it, to make derivative works, and to commercialize it in any way it sees fit.

In any event, it is customary for the developer to provide the customer similar representations, warranties and indemnities that are provided by developers of traditional software, including representation and warranties that the application as delivered does not infringe or misappropriate intellectual property rights of a third party, and that the application is free of any lien, claims or encumbrances, and an indemnity for intellectual property infringement or misappropriation, among others.

Many applications incorporate geo-fencing, i.e., the ability to block end users in particular geographies from accessing the application. Common examples are mobile gambling applications limiting the ability of residents of a particular state to place bets, and preventing individuals and entities in embargoed or sanctioned countries from accessing an application.

Because most applications access personal data from the mobile device, including the users' pictures, metadata and contact information, as well as data for anti-fraud activities and mobile payments, the customer or publisher should disclose its data processing practices and make available to users its data privacy policy. The privacy policy should be tailored to the application's functionality and address the applicable data privacy laws. If the application will process personal data, the developer and customer should consider the applicability of all relevant consumer laws, in addition to data privacy laws. Prudent parties should use a *privacy by design* approach in developing the application to limit the amount of personal data collected, and anticipate future uses of the application, to reduce their risk.

As the developer may have access to the confidential and personal information of the customer and/or the end users, the developer should take reasonable steps to protect such information from unauthorized use or processing, and should be contractually prohibited from accessing, collecting, using or sharing the confidential information of the customer and/or end users, as applicable, except as strictly necessary to fulfill its contractual obligations under the development agreement.

Some developers will provide additional services such as hosting the application for the customer once the application has been developed, as well as providing maintenance and support services. In these cases, any collateral services should be addressed in a separate agreement.

3. *Third Party Software and Materials*

One difference from traditional development efforts is the requirement that the customer have the right to distribute any third-party software incorporated into the application to end-users. The agreement should clearly allocate responsibility for obtaining any required licenses for third party software incorporated into the application, and the scope of the third-party license must reflect the intended use of the mobile application. For example, the license cannot be limited to the customer's internal use if the application will be distributed to the public. The developer should also provide a representation and warranty that it will not incorporate any third party software, product or other materials into the application, unless the developer has all the necessary rights, license and consents from such third party. In addition, the party obtaining the required third-party licenses should indemnify the other party for any claims arising from such party's failure to obtain the necessary rights.

All third party licenses obtained by a party should allow the developer, the customer as well as the end users to access and use the software, and the rights should be sublicensable through multiple tiers, as needed. It is important that the license allows the customer to redistribute the software to the end users. See Form B.3.9 for a model license with the right to redistribute the software.

From the developer's perspective, it is preferable that the customer obtain any third party licenses necessary for the development of the application. Doing so relieves the developer of any potential liability if the customer or an end user breaches the license terms or the developer fails to obtain the required use rights. However, this may be impractical due to the fact that the customer may not have visibility into the third-party software or other materials that the developer may incorporate into the mobile applications. If the developer will incorporate its own proprietary software into the application, the customer should obtain a broad license from the developer for such software (which is often defined as background technology) with the right to distribute the software to the end users, and other appropriate representations and warranties that the developer owns all necessary rights into its background technology necessary for the license grant to the customer. In this scenario, such developer background technology would not be included in the provisions addressing the assignment of the application to customer, or the related "work made for hire" language, such that the developer would still maintain ownership of such background technology, if agreed by the parties.

To the extent the customer is required to flow down any license terms to the end users, such as open-source license terms, the developer should design the application in a manner that allows such terms to be embedded in the application or linked via the application. The development agreement should be specific as to what open-source software may not be incorporated or linked to the application, and the developer should maintain a list of open-source licenses for such software.

See Form B.6.1 for a model Mobile Application Development Agreement.

4. End User Agreements

(a) The End User License Agreement

Most mobile applications require the end user to agree to an end user license agreement (EULA) prior to accessing and using the mobile application. End users can indicate their acceptance to the EULA terms through a click-wrap or browse-wrap agreement whereby they must affirmatively agree to be bound by the terms of EULA. See Chapter 11 for a discussion of click-wrap and browse-wrap licenses. The EULA often contains links to other terms such as a data privacy agreement and any third-party license terms, including any open source license terms.

Ther terms of the EULA will be dictated by the nature of the application, the intended audience, and any applicable laws, such as the Children's Online Privacy Protection Act ("COPPA"), governing the access of online applications by children under the age of 13.

Most EULA's include the following provisions which mirror a traditional license agreement:

- The applicable mobile platform.
- A license grant setting forth the end user's use rights and any restrictions.
- Term and termination.
- A limitation of liability and a disclaimer of warranties.
- The vendor's ability to amend the EULA.
- The vendor's privacy policy.
- Any geographic restrictions.
- Any other required terms by Apple or Google, depending on the app store used to publish the application, or other terms required by third parties whose features or content are included or embedded into the application, as further detailed below.

See Forms B.6.2. B.6.3 and B.6.4 for model Mobile Application EULAs.

(b) Collateral Agreements and Terms

Owners of mobile applications should also provide end users with the owner's data privacy policy as well as the license terms and privacy policies for any third-party software, features or content, including open source software, incorporated into the mobile application.

5. *Confidentiality for Mobile Applications*

When licensing mobile applications, some vendors prefer not to execute non-disclosure agreements, as they work with many software and application developers whose products may be similar to or compete with the customer's products, or may compete with in the future. To avoid potential liabilities, these companies will not agree, and expressly disclaim, any confidentiality obligations or use restrictions, express or implied, with respect to any information that a party may provide in or in connection with their product or a product provided by the customer including information about unreleased products. Their agreements often provide that they are free to use and disclose any information learned from the customer on an unrestricted basis, without notifying or compensating the licensee, as long as such information is public, independently developed or otherwise not subject to other confidentiality restrictions.

> *Licensee releases Vendor from all liability and obligations that may arise from the receipt, review, use, or disclosure of all, or any portion, of any information provided by, or learned from, Licensee. Information that otherwise would be deemed Confidential Information but (i) is generally available to the public through no fault or breach of the recipient, (ii) is independently developed by the recipient without the use of any of the other party's Confidential Information, or (iii) was rightfully obtained from a third party who had the right to transfer or disclose it to the recipient without limitation will not be deemed Confidential Information under this Use License.*

C. *PRACTICE POINT*: Checklist for mobile application development agreements.

- Who will own the Application?
  - the customer
  - the developer
  - are ownership rights clearly spelled out in the agreement, including work-for hire, assignment, licenses, moral rights, of any materials developed or incorporated into the application?
- What mobile platforms is the Application designed for?
  - Apple iOS
  - Android
  - Windows
- Who are the intended end users of the Application?
  - adults
  - children
- Who is publishing the Application?
  - the developer
  - the customer
- Who is distributing the Application?
- How will the Application be distributed?

    - directly from the customer's website
    - through a third party site
        - The App Store
        - Google Play Store
        - Microsoft Store
- Who is responsible for ensuring compliance with the rules of the applicable App Stores?
- Who is responsible for ensuring the Application's compliance with applicable laws, including privacy laws and regulations?
- Who is responsible for providing the EULA and privacy policy?
- Who is responsible for licensing any third-party software?
    - the customer
    - the developer
- Has all third-party software (e.g. commercial, freeware or open source) or content (e.g. music, pictures, etc.) been disclosed to the customer (name, what it does and license for review)?
- Has all third-party software and content been approved for usage, and have all necessary rights and consents been obtained?
- Is there detailed acceptance criteria and timelines for the development of the Application?
- Is the customer responsible for end user compliance with all applicable laws and necessary licenses?
- Does the underlying agreement:
    - provide that end users are not third party beneficiaries of the customer's agreement with the developer?
    - indemnify the developer for end user claims, when applicable?
- Who will be hosting the Application?
- Who is testing the Application?
    - what type of data is being tested, production or "test" data?
    - if production data, what is the nature of the data (confidential or sensitive information, health data, financial data, proprietary data) and does the tester have all necessary rights and consents to use such data for the intended purposes?
- Are any third parties involved in the development?
    - if a subcontractor is engaged by the developer, does the relevant agreement transfer ownership of materials created by the subcontractor to the developer?
    - if a subcontractor is engaged by the customer, the customer should grant the developer the right to share information with the subcontractor, and ownership of materials created by the subcontractor should vest to customer directly.
    - The party engaging the subcontractor typically has the responsibility and assumes liabilities associated with the work performed by such subcontractor.

CHAPTER **10**

Free and Open-Source Software

A. Overview

Over the past two decades, free and open-source software ("FOSS") has assumed increasingly greater prominence in commercial software licensing. Any assumptions that FOSS had and would have little commercial value or strategic impact on software vendors or their customers has been proven wrong. Today, many significant applications such as Apache, Firefox, Java and MySQL are distributed under open-source licenses.

With an increasing number of industry leaders developing FOSS products, most vendors using open-source tools to design and develop their products and platforms, and a growing number of for-profit service providers that have founded their business models on developing and supporting FOSS, the fundamental, unavoidable importance and varied and evolving impacts of FOSS can no longer be ignored or disputed. FOSS is a unique blend of law, business, IP innovation, rhetoric, and software engineering processes. Hence, FOSS arguably requires more study or "homework" regarding those "nonlegal" aspects than most other issues in software licensing to achieve individual professional competence or excellence.

FOSS embodies a set of issues arguably more likely to experience change in the coming years than are other areas, given the combination of (i) the frequent latency between facts occurring and later disputes and adjudication and (ii) the relatively recent and arguably accelerating mainstream uptake (by commercial vendors, and hence by mainstream customers) of FOSS components, design, and development practices, marketing messages, and stand-alone products, languages, and tools.

Open-source is developed over the web, via geographically-distributed, predominantly ad hoc volunteers, through a number of means. Common attributes of FOSS creation include:

(i) core developers who determine project direction and approve changes made by others;
(ii) "contributor" coders who supply new coding, fixes, or enhancements (though less often technical or use documentation);
(iii) deployment of source code management ("SCM") tools for tracking development additions and changes over time (sometimes themselves open-source, such as Subversion and Concurrent Versions System (CVS) tools); and
(iv) geographically dispersed "virtual" development teams; occasional staffing, equipment, marketing, and other support from commercial companies; and end users who submit bug reports and enhancement requests.

Open-source software has achieved popularity in many market categories, including user-ready products for operating systems (e.g., Android, Linux, BSD), desktop applications (e.g., Open Office, Firefox Browser), servers (e.g., Apache, Tomcat), software design and development tools, code components (e.g., libraries), and programming languages (e.g., Python and Perl).

Use of open-source software is not without restriction. Once the open-source source code has been reduced to a fixed medium from which it can reproduced, it is entitled to copyright protection like any other software. Although many open-source licenses look and read differently from traditional software license, the breach of the open-source license terms may similarly give rise to claims of copyright infringement and breach of contract.

1. Open-Source Commercial Models

Many open-source software products can be licensed either (i) on an open-source basis or (ii) obtained on a commercial basis, the latter of which may include support, training, and other services. Many users prefer to obtain open-source software through a commercial license, (i) to avoid, depending on the nature of the governing open-source license, the potential of any mandatory (or "viral") terms and potential impacts of the license in the event the licensee wants to integrate the software with the licensee's proprietary software or (ii) to procure confidently technical support resources. Under an open-source license, a licensee will usually not receive an infringement warranty or intellectual property indemnification, placing the licensee at risk that can be avoided by purchasing a commercial license. A commercial license is also sometimes preferred if the licensee is incorporating the open-source software into its own proprietary software program that the licensee intends to further distribute or commercialize since rights and protections, beyond those normally granted in the typical restrictive open-source license, are likely required.

Set forth below are several models through which vendors may provide open-source software and tangential services.

(a) Proprietary Open-Source Software with Maintenance and Updates/Patches

Subscription-based commercial open-source licenses usually provide a licensee access to bug fixes, performance improvements, and security patches, often relatively soon after identification of those issues, without having to wait on the next release of the software like the rest of the open-source community.

One example is Red Hat, which has created a proprietary version of a particular version (or "fork") of Linux and JBoss open-source software.

(b) Proprietary Extensions on Top of Pure Open-source

Some vendors have contributed software to the open-source community and then-sold users proprietary extensions to the contributed software, which the vendor will also maintain. Examples of this model include IBM's proprietary Linux software, upon which IBM has built and sold databases and middleware.

(c) Subscription Maintenance and Consulting Services on Top of Pure Open-source

Another option is to purchase maintenance for the open-source software from a specialized vendor. Purchasing subscription-based support often allows the licensee to provide input as to which features it would like to see included in future releases of the product. This ability to influence future product functionality and timing (known as "roadmap" in the industry) is usually not available as part of commercial software and provides the benefit of being able to incorporate custom features in the software without having to purchase consulting services.

Utilizing a community version of open-source software is more appropriate for trial agreements and exploratory "proof of concept" projects (i.e., conducted by corporate IT departments to assess the feasibility of new software, before committing budget and credibility to deploying it in actual business production). Subscription versions of open-source are more appropriate for software solutions that will be installed as part of the organization's enterprise software.

2. Static vs. Dynamic Linking

Whether a program uses static or dynamic linking may have a significant impact on determining the risk and/or benefits posed by a particular open-source license. Static linking links the various portions of software prior to compiling. Using static linking with open-source and proprietary software modifies the open-source, which under a mandatory or so-called "viral" or "copyleft" license may require all source code that is linked to the open-source software to be disclosed upon distribution. In essence, static linking open-source code with proprietary code is viewed by many as creating a derivative work of the open-source licensed code which may subject the derivative incorporating the proprietary code, to likewise being governed by that viral or copyleft license. Most practitioners believe that static linking is not relevant to "high level languages" such as Java, JavaScript, Python and HTML.

Under dynamic linking, the software is modified only when the program is actually run and dynamically linked to other software. Most commentators believe that there is no "distribution," as the modified software only occurs on the end user's machine. *Lewis Galoob Toys, Inc. v. Nintendo of America, Inc.*, 964 F.2d 965 (9th Cir. 1992) (no derivative work where the underlying source code is not changed).

For a more detailed discussion, *see* Meeker, *Open (Source) for Business: A Practical Guide to Open Source Software Licensing (3d 2020)*; Gue, *Triggering Infection: Distribution and Derivative Works under the GNU General Public License*, 2012 U. ILL. J.L. TECH. & POLICY 95 (2012);

3. Open-Source Tools

The use of open-source tools licensed under copyleft licenses, such as the GPL, usually does not present a risk to the vendor unless code from the tools is incorporated into or statically linked into the application's code and then such application is distributed. Since the licensee/customer usually will not need to utilize the tools, especially in a SaaS environment, the vendor is likely not making any kind of distribution of the tools in association with its own applications, the risk of triggering any copyleft obligations under the GPL is greatly reduced. To be prudent, tools should be kept in a separate file, as there is no need to compile the tools given they are not part of the application.

4. The Right of Attribution

The obligation to provide attribution notice/a copy of the applicable open-source license to all licensees or other recipients of an application is a requirement of nearly all open-source licensees. Most vendors do so by creating a file of the applicable licenses within the source code or by linking to the relevant open-source licenses in the underlying agreement between the vendor and the customer.

B. Free vs. Open-Source Software

While there is no one definitive definition of "open-source software," the term generally refers to software with source code that is made freely available to the public without charge and which may be further distributed under an open-source license. The Free Software Foundation ("FSF") and the Open-source Institute ("OSI"), the two oldest, most influential and longest-active bodies advocating, respectively, free and open-source software, have adopted differing definitions. The OSI (i.e., later, and generally viewed as more business-friendly) definition-sets forth 10 criteria that the software must satisfy. *See* http://www.opensource.org/osd. The FSF (earlier) definition-sets forth four freedoms, and notably requires the software to be licensed under the mandatory "copyleft" license in order to be considered open-source. The four required freedoms are:

1. the freedom to operate the program for any purpose;
2. the freedom to examine how the program works and modify the program for the user's needs;
3. the freedom to redistribute the program; and
4. the freedom to distribute copies of modified versions so that the entire community can benefit from the changes.

In-short, free and open-source software are conceptually similar but philosophically different. Free software focuses on granting users the freedom to run, copy, create improvements, and distribute the software, while open-source software focuses on peer-to-peer development of software and the practical implications of an open-source development model. *See* http://www.fsf.org/licensing/essays/free-sw.html.

Open-source software generally has the following traits:

- The software, including the source code, is made publicly and freely available.
- The licensee is able to use, copy and modify the software.

- The licensee is able to redistribute the software, including its source code.
- The software is subject to a license agreement.
- License terms bind subsequent users without the need for a license to be executed by downstream users.
- Protection is provided through copyright and contract protection, not trade secret protection.
- Licenses are not tied to a specific product, technology or interface.
- Licenses may not place restrictions on the use of the software.

Open-source software differs from other categories of noncommercial third-party software such as shareware, freeware, and public domain software. Shareware is generally considered to be software available in object code that requests the payment of a license fee for its use, often through a so-called "honor system" appeal requesting funding to enable ongoing development and improvement. Freeware is similar to shareware, but the licensor does not require a license fee. Public domain-software is software for which the author has waived or abandoned all rights of ownership, including copyright claims and the right to receive license fees, and is usually distributed in-source code form.

C. Costs Associated with Using Open-Source Software

The belief that open-source software is fully "free" is a misconception, as there are many costs associated with using open-source software. Foremost is the time and resources cost of identifying which open source license governs the use of the applicable piece of software and then complying with that license's requirements and obligations. A prospective licensee is expected to know what open-source their organization is using and then review and understand the associated licensing terms to ensure compliance. It should expect to expend management time and effort (and hence cost), preferably informed by competent counsel, to educate its employees and guide later usage activities (particularly software modification and/or redistribution) impacting the user's compliance obligations.

Many end user organizations also pay support fees to third-party specialist entities that support FOSS (and usually are intimately involved with the prior and ongoing development of some particular application[s] or tool[s]). First-line support is usually provided by the user's in-house development staff. Most users outside very large companies lack the infrastructure or ability to provide complex, higher levels of support.

Further, redistribution of the software is not necessarily free of obligations, as it is subject to the terms of the underlying license. Perhaps the greatest potential cost is under-managed or haphazard use of FOSS modules distributed under more restrictive copyleft or mandatory terms that could impact (or, to some, "infect") proprietary code with unwanted publication and redistribution requirements. Even in cases of permissive licenses where the copyleft potential isn't present, there almost always remains an obligation to include attribution notices or to republish the underlying open-source license itself. These notices obligations can create significant administrative burdens but shouldn't be ignored.

D. Advantages and Risks of Using Open-Source Software

1. Advantages

Open-source software provides a number of potential advantages, depending on a particular prospective user's goals, operating culture, and resources. In addition to the obvious benefit of no monetary fee payment obligations for a software license, with ready access to source code users can quickly obtain enhanced functionality by adding new features to existing development projects and support for new platforms. Utilizing existing software enables faster changes and projects by corporate IT groups, e.g., by allowing the licensee to re-deploy its technology staff to other projects. Platform independence and standardization are other potential advantages, as some long-established FOSS, such as the Apache web server application, has become the de facto standard for certain industries and applications. Further, FOSS may improve consistency and reuse through improved quality, assuming the particular code has enjoyed refinement through many capable individuals and versions.

FOSS advocates believe a large number of contributors results in a higher quality, more stable software. For FOSS projects with active and engaged developer communities behind them, it is arguably the case that a greater number of bugs will be identified and resolved and that there will be more testing and ongoing validation. (Hence the now-famous assertion by open-source advocate and author Eric S. Raymond that "Given enough eyeballs, all bugs are shallow." Raymond, *The Cathedral and the Bazaar* [1999]). Moreover, open source is immediately available as it can be downloaded almost instantaneously from the Internet. Some commentators argue that disclosed deployment of FOSS improves the ability to attract and retain programmer talent, based on the belief that many younger or smarter software engineers enjoy and expect opportunities for working with FOSS development. Finally, open source encourages agreement on common standards and interoperability.

From the customer's perspective, use of open-source software may reduce the customer's dependence on a single vendor (which often arises with proprietary software), as there are usually many vendors supporting open-source platforms. Further, the customer should expect lower prices from those vendors utilizing open-source software.

2. Risks

Open-source software is not the panacea that some FOSS advocates proclaim, and that many programmers hear and believe. There are numerous risks, including the loss of ownership rights in a licensor's intellectual property, the requirement to rewrite the licensor's proprietary code to eliminate use of "copyleft" licenses, having to cease licensing its software in the event of copyright infringement or the threat thereof, embarrassment and reputational risk in the event of discovery and publicizing of non-compliance with applicable FOSS licenses, and, in the case of large OSS licensors, the need to obtain a new license from the source of the open source, such as RedHat or Sun/Oracle.

(a) Compliance with Contractual Obligations

Open-source licenses are non-negotiable, enforceable contracts where use constitutes assent to be bound by the license terms. Licensees must comply with the license terms or risk a breach of contract suit. *See, e.g., Artifex Software, Inc. v. Siemens Product Lifecyle Management Software, Inc.*, Case No.: 4:19-cv-05764-JSW (N.D. Cal. 2019); *Artifex Software, Inc. v. John Wiley & Sons, Inc.*, Case No: 5:20-cv-00665-LHK (N.D. Cal. 2020).

In October 2021, *SFC v. Vizio, Inc.*, the Software Freedom Conservancy, Inc. (SFC) sued Vizio in the Superior Court for Orange County (Case No. 30-2021-01226723) for breach of contract and seeking declaratory relief alleging that Vizio failed to meet the requirements of the General Public License (GPL) and the Lesser General Public License (LGPL) for its smart TVs by not making, or offering to make, certain Vizio source code publicly available. The SFC argues that GPL licensed code was combined by Vizio, in a "copyleft" manner, with the Vizio proprietary code thus creating a derivative of that underlying GPL licensed code. Therefore, the SFC argues, Vizio is contractually compelled by the GPL to disclose the Vizio source code to the SFC or to anyone else who may request such access.

Vizio sought to transfer the case to federal court arguing that the case was not a breach of contract action but, really, a copyright infringement claim which belonged in federal court and thus the SFC had no standing as it was not the copyright holder of the GPL licensed code. The SFC successfully had the case remanded back to state court arguing that the GPL is a valid contract and that the SFC was bringing a breach of contract claim to enforce the public's right under that license, with the SFC essentially acting as a third-party beneficiary of the GPL, to access the Vizio source code. Critically, the SFC is not seeking monetary damages but rather seeks public access to certain Vizio source code that the GPL compels access to and while the SFC is the plaintiff in this particular case, any member of the public could potentially bring forward a similar GPL enforcement action.

Further, open-source licenses are not always compatible with each other, and thus care must be taken to clearly understand the obligations and interactions of each license. Finally, the licensee must ensure that the licensee's contract with its own clients does not prohibit the use of open-source software in the licensee's deliverables to the end user. Problematic areas include the failure to provide a customer/end user with a copy of the underlying open-source license, not providing a complete copy of the source code, not providing attribution notices, and ignoring requests for compliance from the creator of the incorporated open-source software.

Another potential issue arises when the same piece of code appears to have been licensed under multiple open-source licenses. For instance, an open-source component may appear to have been licensed under two distinct licenses such as the BSD and GPL licenses. Resolving this license conflict requires some time and deeper analysis. In such cases, it is important to analyze the pedigree of the particular code at issue to identify the license assigned to that code by its original author. As the original author and copyright holder, that licensor may have released the code under the permissive BSD license, for instance. The BSD license, much like its other permissive counterparts, allows for code licensed under it to be later incorporated with additional code and relicensed under any other type of license including commercial proprietary licenses, the GPL license, and other license which may be totally antithetical to the open and permissive nature of BSD type licenses. If a license compliance analysis stops at only attributing, for example, the GPL license to a certain piece of code and fails to recognize that the original copyright holder released that same code under a permissive license, downstream users may wrongfully stay clear of certain otherwise helpful open-source code based on an incomplete license compliance analysis.

(b) Loss of Intellectual Property Protection

The nature and complexity of software development combined with the challenges of understanding open-source licenses gives rise to the possibility that the licensee may inadvertently lose intellectual property protection for its intellectual property. Loss of intellectual property protection may arise through participation in online open-source communities where the licensee's intellectual property might be disclosed through contributions of binary or source code, or even by discussing concepts and ideas in the open-source community. Inadvertent disclosure may also theoretically occur through the use of open-source that is licensed under a mandatory ("viral") or "copyleft" license; providing a copy of the software to a subsidiary or affiliate, or providing access to the software via a hosting arrangement, can be deemed to be a distribution, triggering the viral provisions of the license. See Section 10.D.3 and Section 10.E.2(b) below.

(c) Security Risk

Open source is inherently no more, or less, secure than other software but does pose some unique challenges based on the very nature of how open-source software is developed. Open-source components are often the product of many contributors and, as with any software, unintentional coding errors are always possible and sometimes exploitable. Detected coding errors in open-source projects are typically well publicized and are often easy fixed. The somewhat unique challenge with respect to open-source, however, is that the onus rests on the user to know what open source they are using and if any of that open source is, or is found to be, subject to any security vulnerabilities. This contrasts with software obtained from commercial vendors who are typically actively monitoring their commercial offerings and are keen to detect and remediate any vulnerabilities or security concerns in their offering.

Users must ensure that they have an accurate and up to the moment list (a bill of materials) of all of the open source components they are using and constantly review that list against lists of publicly disclosed vulnerabilities. Only the user knows what open source it is using, thus it is solely responsible for identifying and mitigating any security risks. The 2017 Equifax data breach, which resulted in approximately 143 million records being stolen, arose from a known security risk in an open-source application that Equifax failed to appreciate that it was using and, hence, failed to patch when a security vulnerability was announced. To reduce the risk of any security vulnerabilities, parties should maintain a constantly updated bill of materials or, at very least, conduct periodic code scans to identify potential security vulnerabilities in addition to license compliance issues.

(d) Lack of Contractual Protection in Open-Source Licenses

Most FOSS comes without a warranty of any kind, including a warranty against intellectual property infringement or any pledge of indemnification made by the licensor. In the event of an intellectual property infringement claim, the user will be forced to defend the claim itself without the benefit of an indemnity (or possibly even knowing the history of how the allegedly infringing code was incorporated into the software). Further, under some license types, owners of proprietary software that integrate FOSS into their product may be required to distribute source code. It is also important to evaluate license compatibility if a party seeks to utilize open-source software licensed through a copyleft license, such as the General Public License, with other open-source code licensed under another license, as the party must ensure the license terms of the two open source licensed programs are compatible with each other as well as with the ultimate commercial license that the party may use.

There is no warranty as to the quality of the code, its suitability for a particular purpose and no guarantee of support for FOSS. As the underlying code usually is the product of many different and dispersed authors, there is little accountability and certainly no service level standards or guarantee of future enhancements. Any enhancements are subject to the evolving degree of interest of the relevant programmers and user community, and the software may be abandoned by its authors, leaving the user on its own with technical "deadwood." In these cases, the user will have to rely on its own in-house support, depend on stale software, or move to a new third-party product. At very least, care should be exercised in choosing what open source to incorporate or build on in the first place and only open source with an active and robust community behind it selected. Finally, both technical (programmer) and user documentation is often weak (as compared to commercial products) with little or no training materials available, depending on the age, level of interest, and style or degree of oversight or management of the particular application, tool, or module.

A vendor is unlikely to provide comprehensive representations, warranties and indemnities, if any, placing the customer at risk in the event of a third-party claim of infringement. Given the nature of open-source software, this risk may be heightened, as the vendor does not know where the open-source software originated from. At a minimum, the vendor should represent and warrant that it is in compliance with the terms of the applicable open-source licenses.

For a more detailed discussion, *see* Determann, Pixley & Shapiro, *Managing Commercial Risks in Open-Source Software Licensing*, 2 J. Intell. Prop. L. & Prac. 770 (2007).

(e) Conflicting License Terms

Another risk when using open-source software applications licensed under different licenses is that the terms of the individual licenses may conflict, making it impossible for the user to comply the terms of both licenses.

3. Legal Concerns

There are many legal issues associated with the use of FOSS. The most prominent is the mandatory (so-called "viral") provisions contained in some licenses, e.g., the GPL and

Lesser General Public License ("LGPL") licenses. The term "viral" refers to the provisions contained in these licenses requiring users who integrate FOSS into their proprietary software or package them together in a manner that creates a derivative work, and then distributes or conveys that resulting work, to offer the combined product as FOSS with the rights of end user further modification and distribution. Often referred to as "copyleft" provisions, in contrast to the protections provided by a copyright, these provisions seek to prevent the redistribution of the integrated FOSS as so-called closed (i.e., no source code available and with traditional proprietary licensing) commercial software.

Open-source licenses may also provide reason for concern as many such licenses (particularly older, influential ones) are not written by lawyers and may be vague, confusing, and contain conflicting terms that are open to interpretation. Licensees should carefully review the license terms for all third-party software that they utilize. For example, some third-party licensors, may prohibit use or combination of their software with open-source products in an attempt to protect their products from viral open source. Many open-source licenses require the user to disclose the existence of FOSS in the user's proprietary product and to provide the end user with a copy of the underlying FOSS license. See Form G.1 § 2 and Form G.2 § 1. For a general discussion, see Bouscaren & Parker, *Notice and Attribution: A Crucial Component of Proper Open Source Software Redistribution*, 27 ACC Docket 66 (Sept. 2009); Murray, *Attribution Requirements in Free and Open-Source Software Licensing*, 25 Computer And Internet Law. 10 (May 2008); Koltun, *Free and Open-Source Software Compliance: An Operational Perspective*, 3 Int'l. Free and Open-Source L. Rev. 95 (2011).

One of the biggest issues and challenges for licensors that incorporate open-source into their proprietary products is attempting to ascertain initial ownership of FOSS and quantifying the associated potential risk of intellectual property infringement, including patent and copyright infringement. Most open-source licenses disclaim any liability for intellectual property infringement and do not provide any accompanying indemnity. The redistributing party's risk is accentuated by the lack of a clear chain of title due to the communal, volunteer-based, and globally-distributed nature of code design, development and testing. Those licensors that accept liability (i.e., the few large corporations that offer enhanced versions of software, usually with extra services, for a subscription or other fee) usually limit their liability to the cost of the software.

The risk of litigation regarding intellectual property allegations over software that is key to the infrastructure and operations of a business may be exploited by a competitor in an effort to discourage the user's potential customers from purchasing the user's products. One of the best-known examples (though not regarding FOSS) is *NTP, Inc. v. Research in Motion, Ltd.*, 418 F.3d. 1282 (Fed. Cir. 2005) where NTP claimed that certain software used by Research in Motion ("RIM") infringed on NTP's patents. NTP sought an injunction to prevent RIM from utilizing the subject, software, which would have shut down RIM's business. At one point in the litigation RIM agreed to pay NTP $450M USD even before the matter was settled.

One risk that is often overlooked when using software licensed through the GPL or Affero General Public License ("AGPL") for internal use is whether use solely within an entity triggers the distributions provision of these licenses. On first impression, there does not appear to be an issue as the code is being used internally and thus should not trigger the distribution provisions. Licensees often fail to recognize, however, that sharing software between two legal entities such as between a parent and a subsidiary or an affiliate, may constitute a distribution. In most cases, however, this will not be a major concern as both companies share an ownership structure and the subsidiary may seek to further distribute the software.

Under the GPL, to "convey" a work means *any type of transfer* that allows other entities to make or receive copies. A subsidiary is a distinct legal entity and thus it is difficult to argue that there is no distribution. In the event the subsidiary is subsequently sold, the existence of the GPL code may be problematic, as the sale of the subsidiary might itself trigger the distribution provisions depending on the nature of the transaction.

To protect against this possibility, all licensees should implement a policy of monitoring and complying with all of the provisions of their open-source licenses (and third-party commercial licenses) even if their immediate intended use is solely for internal purposes, with no current plans for commercial redistribution or external exploitation of the particular code. Further, they may want to consider avoiding and prohibiting the downloading or use, and/or requiring the identification and removal, of all GPL/AGPL/ LGPL software, even for internal use, as a possible risk mitigation tool.

Any use of OSS on client engagements must be properly represented in, and not prohibited by, the client contract and with commercial terms that properly protect the company.

For a more detailed discussion, *see* Meeker, *Open (Source) for Business: A Practical Guide to Open Source Software Licensing* (3d ed. 2020);Van Lindberg, *Intellectual Property and Open Source: A Practical Guide To Protecting Code* (2008); Illardi, *Client Counseling for Common OSS License Problems,* 31 Computer And Internet Law. 1 (Dec. 2014); Gonzalez de Alaiza, *Open Source, Free Software and Contractual Issues,* http://law.bepress.com/cgi/viewcontent.cgi?article=6672&context=expresso; *A Legal Issues Primer for Open Source and Free Software Projects,* http://www.softwarefreedom.org/resources/2008/foss-primer.html (Note that the Software Freedom Law Center is a FOSS advocacy group.).

E. Open-Source License Types

As of October, 2023, there are over 110 different open-source licenses that have been recognized by the Open Source Institute ("OSI"). The great majority of open-source software is licensed under the Apache 2.0, BSD, GPL, LGPL MIT and Mozilla Public License. The plethora of potential FOSS contracts continues, despite an effort in recent years by the OSI to reduce the number of approved licenses in order to reduce complexity and a possible impediment to open-source adoption. Each license reflects the particular goals of the particular license's author(s).

In general, each of these licenses can be placed into one of two categories: permissive licenses and nonpermissive licenses. Set forth below is a general discussion of each of these license types and the issues associated with each.

1. Permissive Licenses ("Nonviral" Licenses)

Permissive licenses are generally defined as those open-source licenses that do not dictate the nature of the license required for further distribution of the permissively licensed code or obligate the licensor to provide source code to downstream users. The licensor may distribute the original open-source software source code or object code if it provides the underlying FOSS copyright notice and license terms (including liability disclaimer) to the end user. Permissive licenses are preferred by many users, as they do not require a user to make the source code of the open-source software available to third parties or to license the user's proprietary software under the open-source license. However, they may impose other obligations, including giving attribution to the open-source developer and granting a release of liability. Modifications and enhancements may be claimed as trade secrets (i.e., if distributed in only object code form) and be owned by the licensor. Further, the user may not represent the software's contributors as endorsing the user's products.

Permissive licenses include, but are not limited to, the Apache License 2.0, MIT License, and BSD License. It is important to note that some FOSS licenses have gone through numerous iterations and are intermittently revised. See Form G.1 for a copy of the MIT license.

2. Nonpermissive Licenses ("Viral" Licenses)

(a) General

Nonpermissive licenses are those that include "copyleft" provisions which require the licensor, in certain circumstances, to make available improvements or enhancements to the underlying FOSS on terms identical to those under which the licensor licensed FOSS. (This potential effect is the historical risk, though risk scenarios possibly are somewhat varied with the GPLv3 license.) This may include making the source code available without charge to end users.

Reciprocal, mandatory, or so-called "viral" provisions in nonpermissive licenses may be activated if the licensor modifies the underlying open-source code and distributes the code as an integrated part of the licensor's proprietary software. *See Wallace v. Int'l Bus. Machines Corp.*, 467 F.3d 1104, 1105 (7th Cir. 2006) ("Copyright law, usually the basis of limiting reproduction in order to collect a fee, ensures that open-source software remains free. Any attempt to sell a derivative work will violate the copyright laws, even if the improver has not accepted the GPL.")

As the creator of a piece of code, the author of that code is the holder of the copyright in that code. One of the rights afforded to a copyright holder is the right to grant others the right to make derivative works. The GPL, in essence, extends the right to make derivative works from the copyright holder to any member of the public who is interested in using the code licensed under the GPL for that purpose. However, the consideration back in exchange for this grant is an obligation on that licensee to, in turn, make any derivative that they create likewise licensed under the terms of the GPL. This includes the obligation to make the corresponding source code of the derivative work available under the GPL.

Determining if a derivative work has been created is a complicated question of engineering fact and license interpretation. If the licensee simply links its software to FOSS without commingling or integration, the viral provisions may not apply because a derivative may not have been created (although the impacts of static versus dynamic linking are debated). The viral provisions in nonpermissive licenses are complicated, and great care should be taken to understand these terms, the technical details of the architecture, the relative degree of integration of FOSS into the proprietary software, and the anticipated distribution strategy for the software.

Copyleft licenses can be divided further into "weak" and "strong" copyleft licenses and have different impacts on proprietary code depending on how they are used. Strong copyleft licenses are typically members of the GPL family (GPLv2, GPLv3, LGPL, Affero GPL/AGPL). These licenses obligate a user to certain treatment of code under these licenses (hereinafter "GPL-licensed code"). The most important obligations are:

- to provide the source code of GPL-licensed code if it distributes the binary of GPL-licensed code and
- the GPL-licensed code and any derivative works cannot be relicensed, which can also include proprietary code depending on the technical manner in which it interacts with the GPL-licensed code. It does not matter if you touch or change the GPL-licensed code. While the actual impact will be based on the reach of copyright's derivative works, community norms may also apply.

Linking a party's proprietary code to AGPL and GPL licenses will likely cause the copyleft effect to apply. LGPL is believed to have lower risk of required and undesired copyleft effects, as it will depend on whether a user dynamically links or statically links to the GPL-licensed code, in which case a user may only have an obligation to share the object code of its proprietary code.

"Weak" copyleft licenses such as the Lesser General Public License (LGPL), Eclipse Public License (EPL) and Mozilla Public License (MPL) require licensors that distribute modifications to the weak copyleft open-source do so under the same weak copyleft license. Copyleft licenses such as the General Public License (GPL) and Affero General Public License (AGPL) require that all open-source software and any proprietary software combined with the open-source software be distributed under the same copyleft license.

Examples of nonpermissive licenses are the GPL license (both v2 and v3), and the LGPL license. *See* Form G.2 for a copy of the GNU license.

Many entities prohibit the use of licensed Affero GPL software when developing software, as the license may require that all software combined with the developed software, even the user's proprietary software, be made available to any third party who accesses the user's software, including accessing the user interface of the software remotely over the internet. See Google's open-source policy: https://opensource.google/documentation/reference/using/agpl-policy

(b) The Inter-relationship of Software as a Service and Nonpermissive Licenses

Under most OSS licenses, accessing open-source software through a cloud model, or software as a service, is not considered by most commentators to constitute "distribution" and does not trigger obligations that accompany the viral licenses. As noted earlier, the copyleft or viral implications of the GPL are triggered upon conveyance or distribution of code licensed under the GPL. Interestingly, accessing GPL licensed code a SaaS deployment model is not considered by the Free Software Foundation as a triggering distribution. Accordingly, many SaaS based organizations consider the use of GPL licensed code to be a relatively low risk matter. Care should be taken, however, in the event that any SaaS deployed software is later converted to a distributed product.

To some, allowing the leveraging of GPL licensed code for commercial use by SaaS based companies without the corresponding obligation to make corresponding source code available is antithetical to the broader purposes of the GPL. The Affero General Public License or AGPL was designed to address the issue of hosting or dispersed software architectures (which arose and become common years after the drafting of, and arguably were not controlled or impacted by, the original GPL). Under the Affero license, accessing the software is the trigger to releasing the source code. ("[I]f you modify the program, your modified version must prominently offer all users interacting with it remotely through a computer network . . . an opportunity to receive the corresponding source code . . . at no charge . . . .") Thus, software developers who create cloud and SaaS available products must clearly understand how the AGPL licensed software interacts with their proprietary software to avoid having to distribute the source code to their proprietary software.

Given the rapid rise in cloud computing, some vendors have altered their licenses to prohibit the distribution of their software by users to third parties or otherwise making it available to third parties. Other vendors require that if a user makes the functionality of the program or a modified version available to a third party, the user must make the source code available for free. *See* https://www.mongodb.com/licensing/server-side-public-license and software vendor MongoDB's explanation of its creation of and shift to that modification in its March 27, 2020 annual 10-K report filed with the U.S. Securities and Exchange Commission (at https://www.sec.gov/ix?doc=/Archives/edgar/data/1441816/000144181620000067/mdb-013120x10k.htm). These vendors do so: (i) to ensure that users give back to the open-source community; (ii) do not benefit financially from the efforts of those vendors that have created new products; and (iii) to prevent these third parties from creating SaaS products that compete with those vendors.

For a more detailed discussion *see*, Strottman, *Open-Source Considerations in the Cloud*, 33 COMPUTER & INTERNET LAW. 17 (June 2016).

See Form G.8 for a heat map identifying the risks associated with particular open-source software licenses.

F. Negotiating Licenses for Software That Incorporates Open-Source Software

Negotiating license agreements where FOSS is incorporated into the licensed application is complex and is presently evolving and arguably relatively immature in the marketplace in commercial negotiations, procurement, and contract precision (as opposed to risk mitigation terms in software company mergers and acquisitions). A prudent licensee will seek an indemnity and warranties flowing to the integrated product, which most licensors are likely hesitant to grant. Some particularly vigilant customers may seek both detailed technical disclosures and specific contractual assurances regarding the particular contents, tools, and development history of the software. For example, such increased transactional diligence and precision may be deemed needed if the application is only available from one vendor, is mission-critical to the customer's entire operations, or implicates regulatory compliance in the customer's industry.

Further, to avoid potential problems, licensors must be ever-vigilant to ensure FOSS is not incorporated into their proprietary software without their knowledge by their employees or subcontractors. Similarly, prudent licensees must be careful to ensure that FOSS is not included into the licensed software without their knowledge. Monitoring the presence of FOSS in a particular program is a challenging task for both licensors and licensees requiring continual vigilance. For a discussion of auditing the presence of open-source software in software code, *see* Madden, *An Overview of Auditing OSS Compliance in Software Products, 29* COMPUTER & INTERNET LAW. 6 (Mar. 2012).

Set forth below is a discussion of several of the issues that licensors and licensees should consider when negotiating a license involving FOSS.

1. *Incoming Licenses*

In evaluating the risks of accepting FOSS in a particular licensed product, licensees can take actions to limit their risk. For example, a licensee should require the licensor to represent and warrant that all FOSS (and the corresponding licenses) is disclosed in a schedule to the underlying software license (i.e., a software bill of materials (SBOM)/notices file). This specification requirement should not be an unreasonable burden for the well-managed, well-informed licensor, as all FOSS licenses recognized by the OSI require users to both attribute authorship of the FOSS contained in their deliverables and provide the licensee with copies of the relevant licenses for the incorporated FOSS.

> *Exhibit ___ sets forth all Open Source Software that is included in or integrated with (including as a programming dependency) the Software. No Open Source Software is incorporated (either directly by the Licensor, or indirectly, by the incorporation of Third Party Technology that itself incorporates Open Source Software) into or distributed with any of the Software: (1) in a manner that would grant or purport to grant to any Person any rights to or immunities under any of the Software, or (2) under any license requiring the Licensor to disclose or distribute the Source Code of any of the Products.*

To protect against unknowingly receiving open-source code, the licensee should also consider scanning of (or requiring scanning by the vendor) the deliverables with a specialized software program designed (and updated) to detect the presence of FOSS. These might include such products and services as those from Black Duck Software (owned by

Synopsys), JFrog, and other vendors or even newer, evolving open-source tools. Proper direction from knowledgeable employees or consultants and specialist counsel is critical.

The scan will not only identify FOSS but may also assist with identifying any unlicensed commercial software and will produce what is commonly referred to as a "software bill of materials" or "SBOM". Many licensors are finding that having an up to date SBOM is not only critical to properly maintaining their own software, but is quickly becoming a business necessity. More and more licensees are requiring that licensors demonstrate sound open source management processes and a readily available and comprehensive SBOM is a cornerstone of that effort. The SBOM is finding its way into other arenas as well. For instance, those licensors seeking business with the United States government may find that sharing an SBOM is a critical selection element and that insurance carriers issuing policies protecting against intellectual property infringement claims may also require an SBOM in underwriting.

Additionally, as further described above in Section 2(a), a comprehensive SBOM may play a critical role in helping to identify any applications (both commercial and FOSS) with known security vulnerabilities. Since many organizations are not aware of the full scope of FOSS being utilized in their organization, when a FOSS component is identified as containing a vulnerability that organization may be slow to react, if at all, with respect to addressing the risk posed by the vulnerability. A comprehensive and up to date SBOM provides the necessary insight into what FOSS an organization is using, and where, and enables an organization to react quickly to remediate known vulnerabilities.

Licensees should also seek to have the licensor represent and warrant that the deliverables do not infringe on any third-party intellectual property. Because FOSS is third-party intellectual property, this would cover, unless expressly disclaimed by the licensor, FOSS. Additionally, the licensee also should seek to have the licensor indemnify the licensee against any ownership disputes, breach of open-source obligations, or third-party intellectual property infringement. However, the licensor may argue that the licensee is receiving a reduced license fee by incorporating FOSS and note that the code was developed by other parties that are one or more tiers or links removed in a supply chain, and thus decline to provide such an indemnity. Licensors incorporate FOSS into their product without any representation, warranty, or indemnity from the community of developers, so they typically will not pass any assurances along to their licensees. However, the licensor is uniquely positions to know what FOSS its developers have included in its products and manage that reuse appropriately. Some licensors may be willing to provide an indemnity for an additional fee. If the licensee is unable to secure proper indemnification, representations, or warranties, then the licensee (with full cooperation from the licensor) should carefully review any incorporated FOSS and associated licenses to assess the risk of future claims. *See* Chapter 5.A, 5.B, and 5.C.

Another approach is to prohibit the licensor from incorporating or utilizing any software licensed under a copy-left license such as the GPL that could require the customer or service provider to make its source code publicly available. Licensors and vendors may be hesitant to agree to any such restrictions on the use of FOSS as in doing so, they are in essence ceding control of their development efforts especially given almost all commercial software incorporated FOSS.

See Form G.4 for a model licensee-oriented warranty applicable to FOSS.

2. Outgoing Licenses

Because most open-source licenses disclaim all warranties, especially the warranty of non-infringement, licensors usually avoid making any representations or warranties to the licensee relating to any FOSS delivered with their product (or software tools used to design and develop the product). Licensors often carefully define "deliverables" or "licensed software" to mean the licensor's proprietary software products and exclude any third-party products (including FOSS) incorporated into the deliverables. By doing so, the licensor can avoid assuming liability arising from third-party products where it cannot accurately identify or quantify its risks.

See Form G.3 for model language limiting the licensor's representations and warranties to its own proprietary software and excluding third-party software including FOSS.

Some licensors will warrant that the deliverables, including any FOSS incorporated therein, will operate in substantial conformance with the delivered documentation. In the event a licensor is willing to make such a warranty, it should clearly limit the licensee's remedy to replacing the nonconforming software with comparable software within a reasonable period of time. The stated time period should reflect the period of time the licensor believes it will take to develop, test, and document a replacement product.

Most open-source licenses require the user to provide its licensees with a copy of the underlying open-source license agreement. *See, e.g.*, Forms G.1 and Form G.2 § 4. To satisfy this requirement, the licensor should capture and maintain accurate records during the software design and development process, and so can attach actual copies of the relevant licenses or provide a link to the relevant open-source licenses in the licensor's license or on the licensor's website. Given today's accelerated pace of software development and the often heavy reliance on FOSS, developers should consider leveraging FOSS tracking tools, like Black Duck, to greatly automate the process of both identifying the FOSS in their products and organizing the necessary attribution notices, licenses and other information that the licensor may need to communicate to third parties.

As indicated earlier, a significant challenge for licensors who utilize FOSS is often the lack of internal management visibility into what FOSS is being incorporated into their proprietary software. Because FOSS normally enters an organizations software development ecosystem outside the purview of normal third-party software acquisition processes, it may bypass the quality assurance and testing mechanisms that an organization exposes other third-party software to. However, FOSS is third party software and should be subject to the same scrutiny that any other third party is exposed to since the licensor assumes the risk that the software is defective, infringes on a third party's intellectual property rights, is FOSS from a poorly supported open-source project or is simply not the right technical solution.

Thus, the licensor should carefully weigh the benefits of utilizing FOSS against the risks of potential liability for intellectual property infringement and the software's failure to operate properly or as expected. Sophisticated software licensors that have incorporated FOSS into their products (or services platforms and tools) in recent years have created, deployed, and often periodically revised detailed procedures to review the need for such formerly nontraditional software, the relevant license terms, and the attendant risks of incorporation. Ideally, as discussed below, these procedures have been co-designed by the legal function of the organization by individuals who have granular, diverse experience in FOSS issues.

Savvy licensees will argue that they are entitled to receive the same representations and warranties as they would under a traditional license, including warranties against infringement and that the software is virus-free as the licensor made the decision to utilize open-source software. Most licensors will respond that the use of FOSS saves the licensee a significant amount of money in development costs and that the licensee must balance the lack of representations and warranties against reduced costs. A compromise may be to have the licensor provide a representation and warranty with a super cap for any breach, as opposed to unlimited liability for a claim of intellectual property infringement.

For well developed, widely used open-source products, tool, or components, the risk may be small, but for unknown products with little or no operating history, the risk could be greater and significant to both the licensor and the licensee. Both the licensor and the licensee should undertake significant due diligence on the product in question before utilizing the software, including an investigation of the modular nature of the software and the relative precision and availability of its documentation to assess the feasibility of future substitution of the FOSS to mitigate risk.

G. Quantifying the Risk

In trying to quantify the risk, licensors and licensees should examine:

- The percentage of the delivered code that is made up of FOSS.
- How is the FOSS linked to the licensor's proprietary product? And how is it anticipated that a licensee is going to use and interact with the licensor's product and the FOSS therein?
- How quickly and effectively could the functionality provided by FOSS be re- created or replaced?
- How important to the operation of the deliverables is FOSS?
- To what extent is the open-source product proven and accepted in the industry, by longevity, iteration to multiple versions, and/or apparent adoption by many organizations?
- Has the licensor used FOSS for a significant period of time?
- What is the licensor's reputation?
- Is the particular open code a "dying tree," with few recent upgrades, bug fixes, or comments at its project base website?
- How closely managed and documented have been code additions, deletions, and revisions over time (given the variety of options in setting up and administering source code "repository" maintenance systems)?
- Has any well-respected corporation provided leadership, resources, and possible code-tracking discipline?
- Do project leaders have significant experience and reputations in FOSS development, recordkeeping, and license compliance?
- What testing regimes, data, tools, and staffing have been deployed and disclosed?

The smaller the impact of open source on the entire product, the smaller the risk. Similarly, if other products are available to replace FOSS, the risk may be relatively smaller.

1. *Establishing an Open-Source Review Board/ Compliance Program for Software Development*

To limit their risks and maintain the integrity of their product, vendors incorporating FOSS into their proprietary product should establish an open-source review board (i.e., multi-disciplinary working committee) to plan, manage, approve, assess and document the incorporation of FOSS into their products and use of FOSS tools and components in software development and/or ecommerce services platforms. Thus, it will allow the vendor to map the "genealogy," "provenance," or "hygiene" of their product and provide a disciplined, possibly evolving, and documented approach to the inclusion of open source. To ensure that a balanced and well-reasoned decision is made, the review board should include diverse, skilled staffing, including representatives of the vendor's software developers; vendor's security team, software licensing lawyer(s) "fluent" in open-source theory, history, culture, concepts and compliance; and businesspeople.

The software developers should determine, in consultation with the vendor's lawyer(s), whether any nonpermissive/viral provisions of the underlying open-source license are triggered based on the nature of incorporation and distribution of FOSS. The businesspeople should periodically evaluate whether the cost savings, speed to market, any marketing benefits, any staffing benefits, or any other resulting benefits achieved through the incorporation of FOSS outweigh the then-perceived risk of incorporating FOSS into the vendor's proprietary software or services platform. Such internal "policy and process" entities are often deployed to handle related issues, such as determining if and when employees may participate in or start open-source projects or identify their employer (related to the employer's business or otherwise). *See* Forms G.5 and G.6.

The Linux Foundation provides a free guide for developing open-source policies, https://www.linuxfoundation.org/resources/open-source-guides/creating-an-open-source-program/. The OpenChain Project, part of the Linux Foundation project, is another resource with policies, training guides and other materials that are free free and licensed under one of the Creative Commons licenses allowing users to republish the materials under their own name. www.openchainproject.org

2. *Evaluating the Risks of Using Open-Source Software*

In evaluating the risks of using open-source software, the potential user should examine how the software will be used and whether it will be distributed outside the company. Based on the type of open-source software that will be used, the user should institute different levels of review and scrutiny.

An entity should carefully consider whether to implement a general prohibition on using FOSS licensed under the GPL ("GPL'd code") when that software will be combined or linked with the entity's proprietary software and then may be distributed or conveyed. Any prohibition would not necessarily apply to other, operational-only, confirmed internal-only uses of FOSS licensed pursuant to a GPL license, as these uses should be evaluated on a case-by-case basis. For example, when a party acquires hardware and equipment for use in its data center, such equipment may include FOSS licensed pursuant to the GPL. Likewise, if there was a FOSS application covered by the GPL that permitted an in-house attorney to track all pending and existing trademark registrations for the entity, then the use of a FOSS product should not present a significant problem.

Nonetheless, the risk of using FOSS, including GPL'd code, should be carefully evaluated particularly in light of the lack of warranties. For example, if the code fails to operate properly, to what extent might the licensee be damaged? Does the software operate a critical function for the entity or merely an incidental function like trademark management? What about infringement issues: is the license potentially exposing its own customers to liability? Finally, would the proposed use of the GPL code result in the combination of different software applications which are licensed by agreements that have conflicting terms?

In cases where the GPL'd code is not involved or associated with the entity's proprietary software, the code will not be modified, the use of the code will not create a conflict between different license agreements, and benefits associated with the use of the software outweigh the risks, such use should not be prohibited. Even if the GPL'd code were to be modified, if the licensee did not have an objection to publishing the modification and had a mechanism for, and a manager responsible to, publish such modification back to the FOSS community (i.e., comply with the obligations that are the conditions to the benefits of such "copyleft" code), the use may be approved.

There are many other situations involving the use of FOSS that may need to be addressed. For example, what if the licensee were providing consulting services for a customer that did not involve or require delivery of its proprietary software and the licensee's programmer wanted to utilize a FOSS application as part of the solution? This situation presents different issues that must be considered, including provisions in the licensee/customer agreement prohibiting the use of FOSS or requiring the licensee to assign title to any deliverable to the customer in addition to the licensee's infringement warranties.

3. *Open-Source Software Audits*

A code audit can determine how proprietary code has been used historically (not just currently) with FOSS to confirm whether the proprietary code has to be made publicly available pursuant to a reciprocal or mandatory license (e.g., the GPL version 2). The GPL license is written not from a legal perspective but from a technical view. Hence, determining the implications of the GPL in each case will require a technical analysis of engineering facts and possible "judgment call" (e.g., regarding whether static vs. dynamic linking was deployed). Typically, GPL licenses require, among other things, that the source code of the combined product, the derivative work, be made publicly available.

If the code has been "combined" with FOSS, then the combined code may become subject to the terms and conditions of the GPL license. This technical analysis will give the licensee the information it needs to decide whether to take a license to the software. The licensee should speak with the licensor's technical staff and actually review the code itself, not just rely on the licensor's technical staff (some of whom may have read and believed incorrect characterizations of open-source licenses or obligations). The licensor should identify each FOSS program, state whether the program has or has not been used in a manner that would require the proprietary code to become open-source code, and explain whether the program qualifies for an exception to the GPL requirements.

Additionally, the GPL code is protected through copyright law. If the licensee were to use it in violation of the terms of the GPL license, it would be considered infringement of copyrighted material, which is illegal and has both possible civil and criminal penalties.

Lastly, all open-source licenses exclude performance warranties, infringement warranties and indemnification obligations. If the licensee were to sublicense code that contains the GPL FOSS with infringement and indemnification warranties, the licensee would be potentially liable to both upstream contributors and downstream users— significant intellectual property exposure.

For more information on conducting a source code audit, visit Synopsys for information on their Black Duck Audit Services, https://www.synopsys.com/software-integrity/open-source-software-audit.html and Flexera, www.revenera.com/sites/default/files/datasheet-sca-software-audit-services.pdf

H. Legal Challenges

An increasing number of legal challenges have been brought by or against authors of FOSS enforcing (or challenging the validity of) the underlying FOSS licenses and the restrictions they contain. These claims have been based both in contract law and copyright law. For an overview of issues that may arise, *see* Williamson, *XimpleWare v. Versata Raised Critical Free and Open Source Software Licensing Issues*, 32 COMPUTER INTERNET LAW. 19 (July 2015).

1. Contract-Based Claims

The FSF acting through its Software Freedom Law Center ("SFLC") has filed a number of complaints against manufacturers of electronics products that incorporated the BusyBox software utility for their alleged failure to comply with the licensing terms contained in the GPLv2 license agreement. Most of these cases were quickly settled by the defendants. In general, the defendants agreed to make a payment to the licensor, contact all prior recipients of the licensor's software to offer them source code, and appoint an open-source compliance officer (a term not required by the GPLv2). See also, *SFC v. Vizio, Inc.* discussed above in Section D.2.(a) above.

2. *Copyright-Based Claims*

In a case of first impression, the U.S. Court of Appeals for the Federal Circuit, in *Jacobsen v. Katzer*, 535 F.3d 1373 (Fed. Cir. 2008), held that open-source software is entitled to the available protections under copyright law. Hearing an appeal from the Federal District Court for the Northern District of California, the *Jacobsen* court was the first court to uphold the validity of open-source software licenses under both contract and copyright law.

Jacobsen bought suit against Matthew Katzer and Kamind Associates alleging, among other claims, that the defendants had failed to include the required notice of attribution required by the open-source license agreement under which they licensed Jacobsen's software. The district court held that open-source licenses were founded on contract law, ignoring the underlying copyright issues, thereby limiting Jacobsen's recovery to monetary damages.

The Federal Circuit court, however, held that "[c]opyright holders who engage in open-source licensing have the right to control the modification and distribution of copyrighted material." *Id.* at 1381. It emphasized that "[t]he choice to extract consideration in the form of compliance with the open-source requirements of disclosure and explanation of changes, rather than as a dollar-denominated fee, is entitled to no less legal recognition." *Id.* at 1382. It distinguished a copyright claim and a contract claim in finding that the restrictions contained in Jacobsen's license were necessary "to accomplish the objectives of the open-source licensing collaboration, including economic benefit." *Id.* at 1381. In reaching its decision, the *Jacobsen* court found that the licensor's terms were conditions on the scope of the license thus giving rise to a claim for copyright infringement. *Id.*

The ruling was the first to recognize that violating the terms of an open-source license could constitute copyright infringement. By doing so, the *Jacobsen* court exposed licensees to potential liability of up to $150,000 per work in statutory damages and the payment of the licensor's legal fees (assuming the plaintiff owner obtained copyright registration before or within three months of the initial publication), as well as allowing licensors the right to seek injunctive relief in addition to monetary damages for breach of contract.

It is interesting to note that the legal foundation for these cases is copyright infringement, and that the plaintiffs resort to the very legal principles designed to protect development on economically advantageous terms by an industry group, which if successful will eliminate the profit element in software development.

For a more detailed discussion, *see* Hines & Robin, *Federal Court Rules that Open Source Licenses Are Enforceable Under Copyright Law*, 143 INTELL. PROP. COUNS. 13 (Nov. 2008).

I. Licenses Masquerading as Open-Source Licenses

Given the ability of software owners to create their own license terms, a number of unique licenses have emerged including the "Beerware" license ("if you see me in a bar, you can buy me a beer"), the "Chicken Dance" license ("to use my software you must perform the chicken dance"), licenses that have restrictions on use in certain industries like meat packing or nuclear and others in a similar vein. These licenses are not recognized by the

Open Source Initiative and, although the software that is licensed under these licenses is in source code form, these licenses are not considered to be true open source licenses due to the consideration required (e.g.; buying a beer or doing a dance) or the discriminative element (no nukes, no meat packing) . See https:/ /en.wikipedia.org/wiki/Beerware

J. Managing Open-Source

Managing the use of open-source software is crucial to the success of a software developer or publisher, as the failure to do so places it at risk of potentially breaching a contractual prohibition on the use of open source in its client deliverables. Or, if the software developer incorporates the open-source code into its proprietary code, it may be prohibited from distributing the combined code solely in its preferred object code only format, and/ or may be obligated to license the combined code including its proprietary code back to the open-source community on the same terms as the open-source code it licensed.

Prudent developers should implement and enforce a detailed, documented approval process for incorporating open-source software into their proprietary code. Many organizations have adopted systems, like that offered by Synopsys, to greatly streamline and automate policy enforcement and the approval process. For those organizations, the approval process is greatly assisted by automated tools that flag open source with licenses or other risks that fall outside the established policies of the organization. These tools have robust data bases and matching technologies that an automatically identify when a developer has utilized a piece of open source, automatically link that piece of open source to the open source license that governs its use and then compare that license against the organization's established policy as it relates to, for instance, that license and the specific intended use for that piece of open source (for instance, internal use, SaaS, distributed, etc.) An automated process allows a high degree of visibility into what open source an organization is using and gives management a significant degree of control over that use.

For organizations using a more manual or paper based process, under a typical approval process, a team of developers, software security specialist, businesspeople and attorneys will meet on such cadence as is dictated by the pace of development at the organization to discuss the need to utilize a particular piece of open-source software, whether there are any viable alternatives (such as using a commercial version of the open-source software), and how the software will be used (e.g., by dynamically or statically linking to the vendor's proprietary software). A written record will be kept of the group's decision, including how the software will be used and any limitations on its use. Doing so allows the employer to hold its employees and contractors accountable in the event they wrongly incorporate open-source software into the company's software and to maintain strict version control. See Forms G.5 and G.6 for a model submission form and a model approval form. Depending on the volume of open-source that the organization is using, relying on developers to flag all of the open-source they are using may not be practical or even possible.

Those developers concerned about the "seepage" of open-source code into their proprietary software can (and do) regularly run open-source code audits in order to determine if any unauthorized open source has been incorporated into their software.

Best practices dictate that the developer should have a process of identifying what open-source they are using very early in the development life cycle where license compliance or other issues can be addressed most effectively and cheaply. However, where vetting has not happened upfront, an organization is wise to undertake periodic code scans. Such scans will identify what open-source has found its way into their software and may also identify an unlicensed third-party commercial code that may have been inserted into the developer's code. Although periodic source code audits can be time-consuming and expensive, they are invaluable in the event unlicensed or unapproved code is identified, allowing the developer to quietly remediate any problems that were not earlier addressed.

K. *PRACTICE POINT*: Open-source best practices

Given the increasing use of open source, customers and vendors alike should create a comprehensive open-source software use policy addressing the use of open-source software and the incorporation of open-source software into a party's products. Prudent parties should:

- Create and implement a comprehensive written policy addressing the use of open source and the incorporation of open-source software into the company's software products;
- Educate all employees routinely on the company's open-source policy including:
    - All compliance obligations, and
    - The risks of incorporating open-source software into the company's proprietary software. Thereafter, it should take publicized actions to enforce the policy, including supplemental internal training.
- Create an open-source committee with experienced technical personnel and legal counsel with open-source experience to identify the risks and benefits of the potential incorporation of open-source software with responsibility for:
    - Reviewing and approving each use of open-source software and the license it is licensed under;
    - Understanding how the application will be used and how any application incorporating open-source software will be distributed;
    - Understanding any interdependencies, i.e. some open-source is incorporated into the open-source software;
    - Evaluating whether there is a commercial version of the open-source software that may be more appropriate to use;
    - For each approved use, identifying the individual responsible for ensuring compliance with the company's open-source policy;
    - Establishing and periodically assessing and improving a well-documented process to approve and map the incorporation of open-source software into the company's proprietary software;
    - Ensuring compliance with all license terms of the utilized open-source software;

  - Confirm that the open-source is not subject to any known security vulnerabilities; and
  - Understanding any export or compliance restrictions.
- Prohibit the use of open source without approval of the open-source committee.
- Require all vendors to:
  - Provide the specific name of all open-source software including the version (including any open-source software incorporated into such open-source software) in their products, including the particular website and page from which both the code and the associated license(s) were downloaded;
  - Identify whether the software is dynamically linked or statically linked; and
  - Identify any modifications made by the vendor to the open-source software.
  - Provide an open-source indemnity to protect against the licensor's failure to comply the terms of the open-source license
- Scan and test all incoming and outgoing software (Black Duck, FlexNet, ScanCode, FOSSology) to identify the incorporation of any unapproved open-source software or unlicensed commercial software into such software.
- When distributing software that incorporates open-source software:
  - List all open-source software in the delivered product;
  - Disclose all compliance obligations to the licensee;
  - Include all copyright notices; and
  - Provide copies of the licenses or the underlying links to the licenses.

For a more in-depth overview of FOSS, *see* Meeker, *Open (Source) for Business: A Practical Guide to Open Source Software Licensing* (3d ed. 2020); Van Lindberg, *Intellectual Property and Open Source: A Practical Guide To Protecting Code* (2008); Bruzzone, Roe & Peterson, *Minimizing Copyright Risks When Using Open Source Software*, 33 ACC Docket 104 (Sept. 2015); Pruger & Zarren, *Open Source Software: Buyer Beware of Custom Development and M&A Transaction Risks*, 47 Md. B.J. 22 (Nov. 2014); Davidson & Kumagai, *Developments in the Open Source Community and the Impact of the Release of GPLv3*, 25 Computer & Internet Law. 1 (Jan. 2008); Falkowski, *Open Source Licensing: An Innovation in Contract Drafting*, 84 Mich. B.J. 30 (May 2005); Kubelka & Fawcett, *No Free Beer — Practice Tips for Open Source Licensing*, 22 Santa Clara Computer & High Tech. L. J. 797 (2006); González de Alaiza Cardona, *Open Source, Free Software, and Contractual Issues*, 15 Tex. Intell. Prop. L. J. 157 (2007); Kennedy, *A Primer on Open Source Licensing Legal Issues; Copyright, Copyleft and Copyfuture*, 20 St. Louis U. Pub. L. Rev. 345 (2001).

CHAPTER **11**

Shrink-Wrap, Click-Wrap, Browse-Wrap, Scroll-wrap, and Sign-in Wrap Licenses

A. Shrink-Wrap Licenses

Shrink-wrap licenses derived their name from the prior-years practice of containing the actual, physical, on-paper licenses on (or currently in) a shrink-wrap package (that also contain3e the software and documentation). The license was visible through the cellophane packaging, and it provides that the purchaser is bound by the terms of the license upon opening the shrink-wrap. Such a license typically stated "If the licensee does not agree with and therefore does not wish to be bound by the terms of the license, it/he/she should return the unopened package to the licensor for a full refund." There is no opportunity to negotiate the terms of the license.

Initially, courts were hesitant to enforce shrink-wrap licenses, citing the Uniform Commercial Code (UCC) as well as other laws to support their decision. *See generally Step-Saver Data Systems, Inc. v. Wyse Technology*, 939 F.2d 91 (3d Cir. 1991) (shrink-wrap license not enforceable under Section 2-207 of UCC, as license terms mutually altered the contract between the parties); *Arizona Retail Systems v. Software Link, Inc.*, 831 F. Supp. 759 (D. Ariz. 1993) (shrink-wrap license not binding under UCC Sections 2-207 and 2-209). *See also Vault Corp. v. Quaid Software, Ltd.*, 847 F.2d 255 (5th Cir. 1988) (provisions of shrink-wrap license unenforceable to the extent their validity is based on Louisiana Software License Enforcement Act that is preempted by federal copyright law).

In *ProCD, Inc. v. Zeidenberg*, 86 F.3d 1447 (7th Cir. 1996), the Seventh Circuit held that "shrink-wrap licenses are enforceable unless their terms are objectionable on grounds applicable to contracts in general" (e.g., unconscionability). The court rejected the applicability of UCC § 2-207, stating that a battle of the forms could not exist if only one form existed. Thus, initially there was a stark dichotomy of opinion as to the enforceability of shrink-wrap licenses. *See also Hill v. Gateway 2000, Inc.*, 105 F.3d 1147 (7th Cir. 1997), *cert. denied*, 522 U.S. 808 (1997) (contract terms in computer box enforceable, including arbitration clause); *M.A. Mortenson Co., Inc. v. Timberline Software Corp.*, 970 P.2d 803 (Wash. 1999), *aff'd*, 998 P.2d 305 (Wash. 2000), *aff'd*, No. 67796-4, 2000 Wash. LEXIS 287 (Wash. Sup. Ct. July 11, 2000); *Bowers v. Baystate Technologies, Inc.*, 320 F.3d 1317 (Fed. Cir. 2003) (Copyright Act does not preempt or narrow contractual prohibition on reverse engineering contained in shrink-wrap license).

Since the *ProCD* ruling, many federal and state courts have upheld the validity of shrink-wrap licenses given to the customer after payment of the license fee provided the licensee has the right to cancel the transaction once it receives the license terms and is unwilling to accept them. *See Meridian Project Systems, Inc. v. Hardin Const. Co.*, 42 F. Supp. 2d 1101 (E.D. Cal. 2006) (shrink-wrap EULA not unconscionable because buyer did not see license prior to purchasing software; EULA not preempted by Copyright Act.). *See also Hill v. Gateway 2000, Inc.*, 105 F.3d 1147, 1149–50 (7th Cir. 1997), *cert. denied*, 522 U.S. 808 (1997); *O'Quin v. Verizon Wireless*, 256 F. Supp. 2d 512 (M.D. La. 2003); *Lozano v. AT&T Wireless*, 216 F. Supp. 2d 1071, 1073 (C.D. Cal. 2002); *i.Lan Systems, Inc. v. NetScout Service Level Corp.*, 183 F. Supp. 2d 328, 337–38 (D. Mass. 2002); *Moore v. Microsoft Corp.*, 741 N.Y.S.2d 91 (2002); *Brower v. Gateway 2000, Inc.*, 676 N.Y.S.2d 569 (1998); *M.A. Mortenson Co. v. Timberline Software Corp.*, 970 P.2d 803, 809 (Wash. 1999).

Given that most shrink-wrapped software is utilized in the consumer market, it is possible that it is subject to the Magnuson-Moss Act. The contrary is also possible. Consequently, to avoid coverage under the Magnuson-Moss Act, and the accompanying limitations, a licensor must be very careful as to the warranties it makes. See Chapter 5.A.3(b) for a detailed discussion of the Magnuson-Moss Act.

Section 209 of the Uniform Computer Information Transactions Act (UCITA) recognizes the validity of shrink-wrap licenses with certain limitations. See Chapter 15.B.3(k) for a more detailed discussion.

Also see Connors, *Dissecting Electronic Arts' Spore: An Analysis of the Illicit Transfer of Copyright Ownership of User-Generated Content in Computer Software*, 4 LIBERTY U. L. REV. 405 (2010).

For a general discussion, *see Shrink-Wrap and Click-Wrap Licenses*, 36 CORP. COUNS. Q. 536 (July 2020); Kim, *Clicking and Cringing*, 86 OR. L.R. 797 (2007); Rowles, *Shrink-Wrap and Click-Wrap Agreements Under the Uniform Computer Information Transactions Act*, 17 E-COMMERCE ADVISOR 3 (May 2001).

See Form B.5.1 for a model shrink-wrap license.

B. Click-Wrap Licenses

Click-wrap licenses "require a user to click on a dialog box, which contains terms and conditions, on a screen in order to proceed. *Ansys, Inc. v. SF Motors, Inc.*, 2021 WL 22453 * n.1 (W.D. Pa. Jan 4., 2021). *See Feldman v. Google, Inc.*, 513 F. Supp. 2d 229, 236 (E.D. Pa. 2007). In *Nguyen v. Barnes & Noble Inc.*, 763 F.3d 1171 (9th Cir. 2014), the court defined click-wrap licenses as agreements in which online users must click on an "I Accept" button after being provided with the terms and conditions of use. Requiring the user to manifest its assent provides a licensor with a stronger argument for enforcing a license than otherwise may be made in the case of shrink-wrap or browse-wrap licenses.

Click-wrap licenses are generally held to be enforceable when the license terms are viewed prior to the software's purchase or installation. *See, e.g., i.LAN Systems, Inc. v. NetScout Service Level Corp.*, 183 F. Supp. 2d 328 (D. Mass. 2002); *Vernon v. Qwest Communications, Int'l, Inc.*, 925 F. Supp. 2d 1185, 1191 (D. Colo. 2013) ("Click-wrap agreements are increasingly common and 'have been routinely upheld.' " (quoting

Smallwood v. NCsoft Corp. , 730 F. Supp. 2d 1213, 1226 (D. Haw. 2010)). *See generally Caspi v. Microsoft Network.*, L.L.C. , 732 A.2d 528 (N.J. Super. Ct. 1999) (forum selection clause in click-wrap agreement was enforceable); *A. V. v. iParadigms, LLC*, 544 F. Supp. 2d 473 (E.D. Va. 2008) (minors bound by terms set forth in click-wrap agreement). A click-wrap agreement will generally be enforced if the user is given the opportunity to read the digital license agreement prior to delivery of the software. *Moore v. Microsoft Corp.*, 293 A.D.2d 587 (N.Y.A.D. 2002). For a general discussion, *see* Rowles, *Shrink-Wrap and Click-Wrap Agreements Under the Uniform Computer Information Transactions Act*, 17 E-COMMERCE ADVISOR 3 (May 2001); Rowles, *Enforceability of Shrink-Wrap and Click-Wrap Licenses—Revisited*, 18 E-COM. ADVISOR 1 (June 2002).

However, licensors must be careful in structuring the click-through process. Licensees should be required to scroll through the license terms prior to being able to assent to the terms. Licensors should not use hyperlinks or scroll boxes allowing the licensee to avoid navigating through the license terms. Prudent licensors should present two options: the option to click "I Agree" and the option to click "I Do Not Agree." With the "I Do Not Agree" box pre-checked, requiring the user affirmatively check the "I Agree" box to access the software. The licensor should not use amorphous terms such as "Continue," "Next Page," or "Process My Order" to indicate assent. At least one appellate court refused to enforce the provisions of a click-wrap agreement when the user had to scroll down below the "download" button to see the license terms and where the "download" button did not indicate unambiguous assent to the terms. *See Specht v. Netscape*, 306 F.3d 17, 35 (2d Cir. 2002). Rather than use language such as "please review and agree to the terms" on the button, the licensor should require the licensee to indicate its assent, by clicking, "I agree to the terms" after the license terms have been displayed.

Users must assent to any amendment to click-wrap terms as continued use of the service is insufficient to indicate assent. *Sifuentes v. Dropbox, Inc.*, 2022 WL 2673080 (N.D. Cal June 29, 2022).

Companies may be bound by an employee's acceptance of clickwrap terms due to the employee's apparent authority or the subsequent ratification of the agreement. *Hugger-Mugger L.L.C. v. NetSuite, Inc.*, 2005 WL 2206128 (D. Utah Sept. 12, 2005). As such, companies should enact strict policies prohibiting employees from purchasing software via online licenses unless they have received the required approvals. Employers should also include in purchase orders and procurement contracts preempting any legal effect of such individual software downloading actions by employees other than specified, designated persons or job titles. Language illustrating typical authority language in online terms follows.

> *If you are accessing and using the Software on behalf of a company (such as your employer) or other legal entity, you represent and warrant that you have the authority to bind that company or other legal entity to this Agreement. If you do not have such authority, or if you do not agree with these terms and conditions, you must not accept this Agreement and may not use the Software.*

Often a court will examine the design and layout of the screen as viewed by the user, if the effectiveness of the purported license contract is challenged. As a result, from the licensor's perspective, all the screens should be uncluttered, clear, easy to read and comprehend. Any hyper-links should be in a different, larger font, underscored, italicized, and/or in a different color such that their presence is apparent to the user.

The licensor should retain all records documenting the licensee's assent, including the terms that the licensee agreed to and the date of the licensee's assent . Further, the licensor should ensure there are no existing agreements between the parties that may cause a conflict among the different written agreements, such as a requirement that any modification of the initial agreement must be in writing signed by authorized representatives of both parties. One court has upheld the right of a licensor to unilaterally modify the license terms as a result of the licensor including a provision in the license permitting the licensor to "modify the agreement at any time by notifying [the licensee] or by posting a new agreement." *Margae, Inc. v. Clear Link Technologies, LLC*, 2008 WL 2465450 (D. Utah June 16, 2008).

Like other breach claims involving traditional software licenses, state law claims involving breach of click-wrap copyright licenses are preempted by federal copyright law. *Microstrategy, Inc. v. Netsolve, Inc.*, 368 F. Supp.2d 533 (E.D. Va. 2005).

For a general overview of the enforceability of click-wrap and shrink-wrap licenses, *see Shrink-Wrap and Click-Wrap Licenses*, 36 CORP. COUNS. Q. 536 (July 2020); Boykin, *Survey of E-Contracting Cases: Browsewrap, Clickwrap, and Modified Clickwrap Agreements*, 68 BUS. LAW. 257 (Nov. 2012); Cunningham & Witkow, *Click with Caution: Liability for Breach of Click-Wrap and Browse-Wrap Agreements*, 23 COMPUTER & INTERNET LAW. 1 (June 2006); Rowles, *Shrink-Wrap and Click-Wrap Agreements Under the Uniform Computer Information Transactions Act*, 17 E-COMMERCE ADVISOR 3 (May 2001); Grierson, *Enforceability of "Click-wrap" or "Shrink-wrap" Agreements Common in Computer Software, Hardware, and Internet Transactions*, 106 A.L.R. 5th 309 (2003); Dessent, *Browse-wraps, Click-Wraps and Cyberlaw: Our Shrinking (Wrap) World*, 25 T. JEFFERSON L. REV. 1 (2002).

See Forms B.5.2 and B.5.3 for model click-wrap licenses.

C. Browse-Wrap Licenses

Browse-wrap licenses are posted on a website that are usually accessed through a hyperlink and that do not require a user to affirmatively indicate his/her acceptance of the license terms. *See Pollstar v. Gigmania, Ltd.*, 170 F. Supp. 2d 974, 981 (E.D. Cal. 2000) ("[A] browse wrap license is part of the website and the user assents to the contract when the user visits the website.").

"The validity of a browse-wrap license turns on whether a website user has actual or constructive knowledge of a site's terms and conditions prior to using the site." *Southwest Airlines Co. v. BoardFirst, L.L.C.*, 2007 WL 4823761 *5 (N.D. Tex. Sept. 12, 2007) (finding defendant had knowledge of Southwest's website terms of use and thus was bound by them). The enforceability of browse-wrap licenses varies by jurisdiction. They often are held unenforceable. *See, e.g., Berman v. Freedom Financial Network, LLC*, 30 F.4th 849 (9th Cir. 2022) (browse-wrap licenses unenforceable in California); *Kauders v. Uber Techs, Inc.*, 159 N.E.3d 1033, 1054 n.26 (Mass. 2021).

For a general overview, *see* Boykin, *Survey of E-Contracting Cases: Browsewrap, Clickwrap, and Modified Clickwrap Agreements*, 68 BUS. LAW. 257 (Nov. 2012); Rambarran &

Hunt, *Are Browse-Wrap Agreements All They Are Wrapped Up to Be?*, 9 TUL. J. TECH. & INTELL. PROP. 173 (Spring 2007); Lemley, *Terms of Use*, 91 MINN. L. REV. 459, 472-76 (2006) (summarizing circumstances under which browse-wrap agreements are valid); Tracy, *Legal Update: Browsewrap Agreements: Register.com v. Verio Inc.*, 11 B.U. J. SCI. & TECH. L. 164 (2005); Kunz et al., *Browse-Wrap Agreements: Validity of Implied Assent in Electronic Form Agreements*, 59 BUS. LAW. 279 (Nov. 2003).

See Form B.5.4 for a model browse-wrap license.

D. Scroll-wrap Licenses

Scroll-wrap agreements are similar to browse-wrap agreements, presenting all of the terms to the user with the user having to click "ACCEPT" to continue using the site. *Berman v. Freedom Financial Network LLC*, 30 F.4th 849 (9th Cir. 2022). Scroll-wrap agreements are generally held to be enforceable. *Sellers v. JustAnswer LLC*, 289 Cal. Rptr. 3d 1 (2021).

E. Sign-in Wrap Licenses

Sign-in wrap agreements require a user to sign up for an internet product or service, with the sign up screen informing the user that acceptance of a separate agreement is necessary to access the service. Users do not have to affirm that they have read the agreements terms before signing up. *Berman v. Freedom Financial Network LLC*, 30 F.4th 849 (9th Cir. 2022).

In evaluating the enforceability of sign-in wrap, courts have used a two-part test:

1. Does the website or app provide reasonably conspicuous notice of the terms to which the user will be bound?; and
2. Has the user taken an unambiguous action to indicate their agreement to be bound by those terms?

Sellers, 289 Cal. Rptr. 3d at 22-23; *Berman*, 30 F.4th at 856. A licensor must satisfy both prongs for a sign-in wrap license to be upheld.

F. *PRACTICE POINT*: Checklist for the enforceability of online agreements.

To increase the likelihood of an online agreement being enforceable, the vendor should:

- Require the user to check or click a box indicating their accent to access or use the site (first click).
- The box they must click should be pre-checked to state "I DO NOT ACCEPT"; requiring the user to affirmatively click the "I ACCEPT" box to proceed. (first click)
- The content, design, and layout of the screen as viewed by the user should be uncluttered, clear, easy to read and comprehend.

- Hyper-links should be in a different, larger font, bolded, italicized, and/or in a different color such that their presence is apparent to the user.
- Hyperlinks should take the user directly to the terms of use.
- The user should be required to review all the terms of use before having the option to click a second box "I ACCEPT" to indicate their acceptance of the terms of use. (second click)

CHAPTER **12**

Service-Level Agreements (SLAs) (§ 3.B)

A. Overview

Service-level agreements (SLAs) set forth mutually agreed performance metrics to measure the vendor's performance. In software transactions, they usually measure whether the software or services meet certain mutually agreed performance standards. SLAs often incentivize the vendor to meet such standards by providing the customer specified financial credits (i.e., reduced fees) for the vendor's failure to do so. Service levels usually are negotiated and documented not regarding every aspect of the vendor's performance, but rather only regarding those aspects of the vendor's performance that have the greatest impact on the customer.

Service level specifications usually measure the most important aspects of the vendor's performance that will determine if the vendor has successfully met its contractual obligations. The accurate monitoring, measuring, and objective verification of the vendor's performance is fundamental to obtaining an accurate snapshot of the vendor's performance. Customers should avoid the temptation to attach service levels to a large measure of areas, overcomplicating the process and time-consuming processes. The service level credit should be large enough to influence the vendor's actions. Such credits should not be characterized as liquidated damages or as the customer's sole and exclusive remedy. A well-drafted agreement will allow the customer to terminate the agreement for cause in the event the vendor repeatedly fails to meet the service levels, even if reduced-pricing credits have occurred. Prudent vendors should insist on any service levels credits be the sole and exclusive financial remedy to avoid allowing the customer to potentially collect service level credits and monetary damages. One compromise may be to allow the customer to terminate the agreement but collect additional damages or allow the customer to terminate the agreement if the vendor fails to meet the service levels for three months in a row or three months in a six month period, or by a significant, large quantity in some particular metric that addresses the customer's ability to maintain and operate its business at all.

SLAs set forth the Service Level Credit (SLC) that a customer is eligible to receive. In some situations where appropriate, the vendor may be entitled to receive a Service-Level Bonus (SLB) for cloud agreements, and from Internet Service Provider agreements (ISPs) and Application Service Provider agreements (ASPs), rather than in general software license agreements. Common metrics covered by SLAs include:

- application availability (i.e., downtime limits),
- response time (i.e., number of seconds for an invoked function to occur or complete),
- time to commence fix (i.e., responsiveness of vendor's customer support team),
- resolution time,
- screen refresh rates,
- maintenance (e.g., frequency during year that vendor releases tested, documented new iterations of its software product[s] with particular, identified new features or functionality),
- help desk response times,
- network availability,
- business/operational processes,
- timeliness of reports/deliverables (e.g., vendor compliance delivering data regarding specified operational data),
- number of errors,
- mean time to report (MTTR).

The nature of the applicable SLAs is dependent on the type of transaction.

From the customer's perspective, the principal purpose of SLAs is to ensure that the customer receives the level of services that it contracted for. Often, however, the customer lacks the necessary information to quantitatively document the level of services it received. To the extent the customer can quantify prior performance levels, the data is often not detailed enough to create meaningful benchmarks. As such, customers often agree to SLAs without a full understanding of the performance standards the vendor should meet or the metrics that should be measured.

From the vendor's perspective, the failure of the parties to agree on whether the Law of Small Numbers (discussed below) should apply to a service level failure within 30 days should form the basis of a "dispute." If the Law of Small Numbers applies to a service-level failure, the results and reporting should be carried over to subsequent month(s) until a sufficient number of total events are recorded in one or more subsequent months to not have the Law of Small Numbers apply to such service level. The achievement of the service level should then be determined for the final such subsequent month (and not for prior months) as though the total number of events all occurred during such month.

From the vendor's perspective, credits should not be cumulative. The vendor can avoid this problem by providing that any failure or success will be determined only within the particular month(s) in which the total number of events exceeds the threshold. Therefore, if a credit accrues, it will only be calculated as if the credit occurred in that month and is not cumulative for all months (i.e., added up over a span of time).

B. The Law of Small Numbers

Licensors should ensure that the service-level agreement provides that service-level failures resulting from violation of the "Law of Small Numbers" will not trigger a performance credit. In short, there must be a meaningful number of events to provide a valid representation of the vendor's performance, as a small sample under the agreement's dispute resolution provision can unfairly skewer the numbers and unfairly penalize the vendor.

The Law of Small Numbers provides that if the measurement of a service level is based on the calculation of a percentage of successful events across a total number of events, a sufficient number of total events must be recorded to permit the reasonable assessment of a service level where there occurs a performance of less than 100 percent (i.e., perfection). For example, if an objective for a service level is 95 percent, there must be at least 20 measured events for the vendor to potentially perform at less than perfection (in this instance, meeting the service level for 19 events and only missing 1) and still achieve the service level. If there are less than 20 events, missing one event will cause the vendor to not meet the SLA.

C. Negotiating Service-Level Agreements

1. Overview

As the old adage suggests: The devil is in the details. So goes the creation of SLAs. The parties must focus not only on the particular metric of an SLA, but also on how the SLA is defined and how it will be calculated.

For example, how often will "availability" be measured? Every 10 minutes, hourly, daily, monthly, yearly? Who is responsible for tracking downtime? Will agreed, reliable, objective technical tools be deployed for such assessments (rather than a vendor or customer employee being required to assess some "grade")? Some vendors seek to have the customer track availability/downtime and have the customer notify the vendor of any downtime even though the vendor is tracking the same information. As to availability, how it is calculated? Scheduled maintenance (i.e., infrequent, pre-announced unavailability, to enable major infrastructure updates within and by a vendor – like a road closing for repair) is usually specifically excluded. But what about unscheduled maintenance, or an event of *force majeure*, or a third-party action or inaction? What if an "upstream" supplier of a key service or component to the vendor announces a cybersecurity flaw or intrusion? In short, a well-written SLA must clearly set forth each party's obligations as well as how the vendor's compliance with the service level will be calculated in great detail.

It is also important to understand the role of "the 9s." How many 9s does the customer truly require to meet the customer's business obligations? While every customer would like to have 100% availability, does the customer really need 100% availability, and is the customer willing to pay for it? The table below indicates "availability" after the inclusion of an additional digit. For example, 99 percent availability means the system may be down seven hours a month and 87 hours a year. *See* Stross, *99.999 Reliable? Don't Hold Your Breath*, *N.Y. Times*, Jan. 9, 2011, Bus. Section, p. 3.

Availability/9s	Annual Downtime
99.999%	5.26 minutes
99.99%	52.56 minutes
99.9%	8.76 hours
99.5%	1.83 days
99%	3.63 days

Finally, as with any transaction there is a "burn in," "ramp-up," or launch-preparation period during which the vendor is implementing the solution or software. As such, service levels should not be measured until the software or solution has been implemented and running for a period of time to allow for an accurate evaluation. Well written contracts will distinguish test-runs, beta-testing usage, and "sandbox" testing within an R&D organization (as differentiated from actual, full "production" utilization.)

2. *Conditions Precedent*

The vendor should clearly set forth any conditions precedent or customer obligations on which the vendor's service-level obligations are predicated. For example, many vendors require the customer to comply with the customer's obligations under the overarching contract, including being current on paying all monies due the vendor. In addition, the vendor may require the customer to maintain certain minimal or specified hardware or technical configurations to receive service-level credits.

3. *Calculating Availability*

(a) Availability

"Availability" or "up-time" is perhaps the most common service level in a Software as a Service (SaaS agreements and services agreements).

The SLA should clearly set forth how availability is calculated. For example, if a system must be down for 15 minutes before it is deemed to be unavailable, a system could be down for 10 minutes every hour but never be considered unavailable. In a multi-device environment, must the entire system/all devices be down to count as unavailable? Further, in multi-device environments, customers should carefully consider definitions that multiply the number of minutes of permitted downtime by the total number of devices being measured. For example, 99.9% availability equates to 41 minutes of downtime per month. If multiplied by 20 devices, the permitted downtime would be almost 15 hours a month.

To avoid these issues, a prudent customer should insist that any time a single device is down, the system will be considered unavailable and the vendor will not be allowed to exclude "*de minimis*" outages. Another approach is to increase availability to 99.99%, or calculate availability by geographic region, both of which will serve to decrease the amount of permitted downtime.

(b) Carve-outs from Availability Calculations

In calculating availability/downtime, vendors exclude "scheduled downtime", i.e., those periods when a system is taken down for scheduled maintenance. Often, maintenance is scheduled for a specific time each month, often when the expected need for or use of the software is minimal, e.g., the third Sunday of each month from 1 am to 4 am Washington D.C. time. Customers should require the vendor to notify the customer at least seven days in advance of any scheduled down time; vendors usually agree, as such events are planned well in advance. If the vendor operates multiple data centers (e.g., for back-up availability protection, in case of geography-specific problems, such as power outage, hurricane, or earthquake), scheduled maintenance should not be an issue, as the vendor should never have downtime.

While most SLAs exclude scheduled maintenance when calculating availability, vendors often try to exclude additional factors that may cause a system to be unavailable. Depending on the product or services provided by the vendor, it may or may not be appropriate to exclude these additional factors from calculating availability. For example, most vendors seek to exclude downtime caused by the customer or by third-party hardware and third-party software, as well as internet access and infrastructure links.

Many vendors also seek to exclude emergency maintenance and events of *force majeure*. Prudent customers should push back on excluding these events. Emergency maintenance should not be required if the vendor's system is stable. Most vendors undertake scheduled maintenance on a regular basis, raising the question of why emergency maintenance is necessary. Further, if a vendor could exclude emergency maintenance from the calculation, it would simply declare all downtime "emergency maintenance," ensuring it always met its SLAs.

Force majeure events should also be excluded, especially if the customer has purchased geo-redundancy services, as the customer is paying the vendor to ensure there is no downtime other than scheduled maintenance. As such, the vendor should have geo-redundant systems to avoid the interruption of its services.

Other common exclusions include downtime due to:

- Third-party hardware, software, or internet vendors
- Issues arising from the customer's actions or inactions including its subcontractors
- Any unauthorized modifications by the customer or its subcontractors of the software or solution
- Any failure arising from a customer dependency (e.g., power or telephony)

Model language favoring the vendor follows:

The service level within Vendor's control is the Service Availability, not, for example, the transmission of data over the public Internet. Service Availability calculations will exclude unavailability arising from any:

(a) scheduled maintenance periods;
(b) emergency maintenance that is necessary to prevent imminent harm to the Service;
(c) force majeure events;
(d) Third-Party Services, Customer application, equipment, software or other technology, or Customer or its User's use of the Service in violation of the Agreement or not in accordance with the Documentation; or
(e) suspension, limitation, and/or termination of Customer's access or use of the Service in accordance with this Agreement.

(c) Period of Time for Measuring Compliance

The SLA should clearly state the time period for measuring compliance, i.e., daily, monthly, quarterly, etc. From the customer's perspective, most customers prefer to have a shorter, more frequent measurement period, such as monthly, as opposed to a longer period (e.g., quarterly), which may allow the vendor to have significant downtime but not violate a service level.

(d) Limitation on Credits

Most vendors seek to cap the amount of credits payable to the customer, arguing that they require a certain level of cash flow to operate their business. Thus, most vendors will not offer a credit greater than 10–15% of the monthly fee payable to the vendor. The model language below favors the customer, allowing the customer to receive a credit up to 100% of the monthly fees.

> *The service credits awarded in any billing month for a particular Service will not, under any circumstance, exceed your monthly service fees for that Service, as applicable, in the billing month.*

4. Reporting

Savvy customers will require the vendor to provide regular reports (e.g., monthly, quarterly, and annual) to the customer. These reports should reflect the quantification of the software or services provided by the vendor, potentially including:

- Downtime/Availability
- Usage Statistics
- Root Cause Analysis, preferably with stated standards regarding degree of specificity and attachment / delivery of related documentation

All reporting should correspond to the measurement metric (e.g., monthly, quarterly). The vendor should be required to implement any tools necessary to obtain and analyze the necessary data to provide the required reports (and perhaps disclose to the customer the provenance, version number, and brands or trademarks of any such tool[s]).

Many vendors require the customer to notify the vendor when the vendor fails to meet the contracted service levels in order to receive a service-level credit. Doing so may be impractical, placing an undue burden on customers, especially small customers. Usually there is no justification for this requirement, as vendors already have this information and thus are aware when they fail to meet the required service levels. Prudent customers should require the vendor to produce a monthly report indicating whether the vendor met the contracted service level and if it did not, require the vendor to automatically apply the earned service-level credit to the vendor's next invoice. Whether the vendor will agree to do so, however, will be dependent on the relative leverage of the respective parties. The following language, favoring the vendor, illustrates this point.

In order for Vendor to consider a fee reduction claim, Customer must submit the claim to customer support at Vendor, including all information necessary for Vendor to validate the claim, including but not limited to:

(i) a detailed description of the Incident;
(ii) information regarding the time and duration of the Downtime;
(iii) the number and location(s) of affected users (if applicable); and
(iv) descriptions of Customer's attempts to resolve the Incident at the time of occurrence.

5. Remedy: Credits vs. Cash Payments vs. Termination

Customers often seek cash payments from the vendor for the vendor's failure to meet the contracted service levels. Vendors, however, are usually unwilling to actually pay the customer, instead preferring to apply a credit to the customer's account against future services. Providing a credit allows the vendor to retain its cash while limiting its cost, as the credit will be applied against an amount that includes the vendor's profit margin, reducing the true cost to the vendor. In addition, by providing a credit, the customer must purchase additional products or software to receive the benefit of the credit. To the extent there is a credit remaining upon the termination of the underlying agreement, the customer should seek to have the credit paid or refunded to the customer in cash; sample text is below

In the event the Vendor fails to adhere to any of the Service Levels, Customer will be credited with an amount equal to the indicated percentage(s) of the monthly amount of Services Fees indicated above on the next invoice for such fees submitted by Vendor. If no further invoices are due under an applicable Cloud Services Addendum, then the full amount of any credit(s) due shall be paid to the Customer within thirty (30) days after the month in which the applicable non-adherence occurred.

6. Exclusive Remedy

From the customer's perspective, service credits are not damages and are not intended to compensate the customer for any overall commercial harm it has incurred as a result of the vendor's inadequate performance. To that end, the service-level credits should not be the customer's sole and exclusive remedy. The customer should always have the right to terminate the agreement in the event the vendor repeatedly fails to meet the service levels. A common methodology is to allow the customer to terminate the agreement if the vendor fails to meet the service levels three times over any six month period.

From the vendor's perspective, the payment of service-level credits should be in full satisfaction of any liability on the vendor's behalf for its failure to meet the stated metrics and the customer's exclusive remedy. Some vendors will argue that allowing the customer to collect service-level credits/payments, as well as collect damages/terminate the agreement, permits the customer to arguably obtain two recoveries for one injury . Prudent customers should not limit their recovery to liquidated damages, as the customer's business damages may far exceed the amount of any credit.

Notwithstanding anything to the contrary in the Agreement, any credits issued under this Service-Level Agreement are cumulative and shall be in addition to any other rights or remedies that Customer may have under the Agreement or at law or in equity.

7. Termination Rights

While most SLAs provide for credits in the event the vendor fails to meet the service level, some vendors provide only a right of termination. See the model language set forth in Paragraph 3(b) above for an example. The customer must determine if this exclusive right of termination provides a meaningful remedy, as the customer may already have the right to terminate the agreement in the event of a breach, and switching vendors may not be practical depending on the nature of the customer's solution.

In the event the Service Availability drops below:

(i) 98.5% for two consecutive calendar months during the Subscription Term, or
(ii) 96.5% in any single calendar month, then

Customer may request to terminate the relevant Service with no penalty. Such termination will be effective as of the end of the then-current billing period and no additional fees will be charged.

As discussed above, prudent customers will insist on the right to terminate the underlying agreement in the event the vendor fails to meet the service levels during a specified number of months within a period of time, such as three months in a six-month period. Cautious customers may negotiate for multiple "out" scenarios, e.g., failure for 5 months in 12 consecutive months, untethered to the contract's annual anniversary. Customers should avoid tying their termination rights to a set number of consecutive months, as the vendor may fix the issue for a short period of time each time the customer's right of termination is about to mature and instead tie their termination rights to a set number of months over a larger period of time such as six months in a year.

8. Model Language

The following language illustrates these points.

*If any Order Form or SOW contains Service levels ("**Service Levels**"), whether specified generally in the Order Form or in a Service Level Agreement ("SLA"), then in addition to any other remedies available to Customer at law, in equity, or otherwise, Vendor will pay to Customer the amount, if any, identified as the Service credit or fees at risk for each failure (the foregoing credits/ refundable fees referred to as "**Service Level Credits**" or "**Service Credits**"). Vendor will deliver to Customer its SLA reports at the frequency specified in the applicable Order Form or SLA, or if no report frequency is specified, then quarterly within 30 days after the end of each calendar quarter, and Vendor's Service Credits will accompany the reports. Vendor's reports will provide* *sufficient detail (such as the Service Level not met, the due date and/or milestone missed, actual versus required time elapsed, etc.) to reasonably facilitate Customer's determination of the correctness of Vendor's Service Credits or payments, as applicable. Customer's acceptance of any report or payment will not be deemed Customer's agreement that the computation is accurate. Should Customer dispute Vendor's report and/or computations, the Parties will promptly work in good faith to reconcile and, if appropriate , adjust the payment or credit. After the Parties' good faith reconciliation attempts, should any disagreement still remain, it may be resolved in accordance with the dispute resolution procedures in this Agreement, either separately, or aggregated with other unresolved discrepancies over the Term of this Agreement or the applicable Order Form.*

Vendor acknowledges that its failure to meet the Service Levels, if any, established in the applicable Order Form or SLA may result in delayed performance and a reduced level of Services to Customer. Customer and Vendor agree that the Service Level Credits are a price adjustment for the relevant period to reflect the reduced level of Service performed by Vendor and (a) reflect a reasonable financial remedy for failure to meet a Service Level in the normal course of business, provided Vendor is otherwise using reasonable effort to perform consistent with the Service Levels and in compliance with this Agreement, and do not constitute a penalty, and (b) do not preclude additional remedies by Customer at law or in equity.

Additionally, if Vendor fails to meet a Service Level, Vendor will:

(i) investigate (via competent technical personnel, provided adequate technical tools and data) and assemble pertinent information (including internal documentation) with respect to, and report on the root causes of, the problem;

(ii) advise Customer of the status of remedial efforts being undertaken with respect to such problem (with periodic, multiple reports if the problem is operationally significant for Customer or extended beyond 24 hours);

(iii) minimize the impact of and correct the problem and begin meeting the Service Level; and

(iv) take appropriate preventive measures so that the problem does not recur.

D. Application to Limitation of Liability

A common issue is whether service-level credits should be applied against the quantitative, financial limit of liability contained in the agreement, or whether they are in addition to any limit of liability. While prudent vendors seek to limit their liability and include any credits paid in the overall monetary cap, the customer has a strong argument that service-level credits represent liquidated damages for prior failure(s) to meet short-term SLAs, and that the overall limit of liability addresses the failure of the project as a whole. Further, "credits" are not cash. The limit of liability goes to the amount of money a customer can recover from the vendor in the event of a breach. As such, the customer should insist that any service credits should not count toward any monetary contractual cap.

Many customers believe that there should not be separate caps on the different types of damages set forth throughout the agreement. This belief is founded on the reasoning that the parties have negotiated a mutually agreeable risk allocation and a cap on direct damages. There should not be separate caps for specific types of failures. By having many "sub" limitations, the parties would be forced to spend a significant amount of time negotiating separate caps for the likely failures of both parties.

Vendors should seek to include a recapture provision in the SLA, allowing the vendor to recover any credits paid to the customer if the vendor performs at a level higher than contractually required either during the period in question or over the term of the contract.

See Forms D.4.1 to D.4.4 for examples of service-level agreements.

E. Service Levels vs. Performance Warranties

Many practitioners believe, depending on the nature of the service offering, it is appropriate for a contract to include performance warranties in addition to SLAs. SLAs usually address the measurable, reportable aspects of performance (e.g., availability, transaction processing time), but that may not capture other qualitative aspects such as performance against documented functional specifications or industry standards. When broader performance warranties are also included, then a question meriting negotiating and clarification is whether SLAs would be the exclusive warranty/remedy for those aspects that it measures.

If the service offering performs only a limited set of functions, then an SLA alone often represents the best measurement of the performance of those functions, and therefore may be the sole standard of performance.

F. *PRACTICE POINT*: Checklist for drafting service level agreements.

Set forth below is a checklist of important considerations when drafting a service level agreement.

- What is/are the particular technical and overall-commercial objective(s) or purpose(s) of the SLA?
- What is the service commitment?
  - Availability
  - Response times
  - Resolution times
  - Performance metrics (i.e., processing times)
  - Degree (granularity) of measurement?
- What is the level of service to be provided?
  - Tied to a metric (e.g., 99.995% Availability)
  - Flow-down or pass-through from a third-party software/services provider (e.g., Amazon Web Services, Microsoft Azure)
- Are there any carveouts from the vendor's obligations/calculating compliance with the SLA?

  - Scheduled maintenance (communicated to customer with agreed amount of advance warning)
  - Non-compliance caused by third party vendors outside the vendor's control
  - Force majeure
  - Customer dependencies
- Are there any reporting obligations?
  - Is the vendor obligated to affirmatively report its results (monthly?, quarterly?)
  - Does the customer need to track results and then notify the vendor of the results, in order to ask for a credit?
- Are there any conditions precedent?
  - The customer is current in all payments due the vendor
  - The customer must maintain certain hardware and software configurations (specified in advance and agreed by the customer)
- Remedies
  - Is the remedy an exclusive remedy?
  - Service credits
    - Will the vendor automatically apply and credits to the vendor's invoice, or does the customer have to request credit?
  - Change in pricing, i.e., a lower price
  - Termination
- Can the vendor recoup services credits/receive a bonus if it exceeds the required service levels?
- Termination Rights
  - Can the customer terminate the agreement if the vendor fails to meet the SLAs: x consecutive months or y times in z months?

CHAPTER **13**

Statements of Work (SOW)

Many license agreements and services agreements are structured as "master" agreements General legal and business terms are set forth in an overarching master agreement, but the actual work to be performed and the particular products or services to be provided are set forth in statements of work or work orders attached to the master agreement. By utilizing a master agreement format, the parties can attach numerous statements of work for many different types of services and products over the life of the master agreement, without having to negotiate a new agreement each time. Moreover, amendments can be negotiated and documented solely for a particular project when there may be multiple simultaneous projects. Because the principal business and legal terms have been agreed to, the parties only need to document the work to be performed, the price for such work, and any terms applicable to that engagement.

A Statement of Work ("SOW") can be the most important operational component of an agreement , as it sets forth the specific services, solutions, and products that the vendor will deliver – and sometimes also (optimally, for a smart customer) the processes and tools that the vendor will deploy. In most cases, executing a master agreement alone without the contemplated SOW will not adequately define or protect the rights and interests of either party.

A. Drafting the SOW

The terms of each SOW will vary based on the particular products and services that will be delivered and rendered. An SOW should set forth in plain, easily understandable language – and in detail - the parties' obligations. Not infrequently an SOW is significantly longer than the base MSA to which it relates.

Prudent parties should avoid merely referencing or substituting a proposal document or an RFP response for the SOW, as these documents usually lack the required level of detail, and may contain outdated deliverables which changed over the course of the procurement process. A SOW should not include sales or marketing language, as doing so is in neither party's best interest. The parties should also avoid the temptation to delegate the entire drafting and approval of SOWs solely to junior employees under the belief the master agreement is the principal document governing their relationship. Too often the vendor is able to dilute its contractual obligations set forth in the parties' master agreement or limit its deliverables through assumptions, creative drafting, omissions, and/or ambiguities in the SOW. At the same time, the vendor should ensure that the customer does not introduce additional terms in the SOW that were not contemplated by the vendor. To that end, each party (including relevant domain experts, and for larger transactions possibly outside technical consultants) and its lawyers should carefully review each SOW prior to its execution.

Depending on the terms of the master agreement, each SOW usually contains a detailed description of the licensed software or services to be provided, the location where and the timing when they will be provided, and ownership of the deliverables, as well as testing and acceptance criteria and payment terms. A SOW should also include any terms unique to the particular deliverables, such as specialized warranties, regulatory compliance, cybersecurity details, and records retention. Most important, a SOW should set forth in detail the functional specifications and technical specifications, the assumptions on which the price and timing of deliverables are based, and what is in scope and out of scope, as well as the responsibilities of each party.

A SOW should not include any legal terms unless the intent is to specifically override a provision in the master agreement. From the perspective of both parties, it is better to err on the side of over-inclusiveness and to avoid the use of vague terms such as "support," "facilitate," and "advise" to describe the vendor's efforts. The parties should avoid including "estimates" and "guesses" while clearly stating any underlying assumption which, if not realized, will negate one party's performance obligations.

To that end, any assumptions should be limited to prevent the vendor from avoiding its performance obligations. At the same time, the parties should avoid using the passive voice and clearly state which party is responsible for each task. Some parties use a detailed spreadsheet with each party's responsibility clearly marked. Best practice is to avoid identifying tasks or roles as "joint." *See* Chapter 7.C for a discussion of the functional specifications and technical specifications.

When drafting a SOW, the parties should use consistent terminology and definitions that flow from the master agreement, so that the master agreement and SOW can be read seamlessly without conflicting definitions and terms.

B. Principal Terms

1. Products and Services

The SOW should address not only the services and products that the vendor will provide, but also the associated:

- functionality,
- features, and
- functional specifications
- version(s) number(s) (where available and technically relevant).

The parties should avoid simply referencing the product or solution by name and attaching a specifications sheet, which will likely lack both the context in which the deliverables will be expected to operate and necessary additional technical details.

See Chapter 16.B.3 for a more detailed discussion.

2. *Ownership of Deliverables*

The SOW should provide who will own the deliverables. If the vendor will own the deliverables, the SOW grants the customer a license for the use of the deliverables.

See Chapter 7.B for a more detailed discussion.

3. *Delivery Timelines*

The SOW should clearly set forth the delivery dates for any milestones and deliverables. Often provisions are negotiated and documented addressing foreseeable delivery delays and associated consequences (sometimes including the impacts of possible, foreseen third party deliveries).

4. *Pricing, Milestones and Payments*

The pricing structure and the pricing itself will be dependent on many factors, such as the nature of the deliverables (i.e., a product or solely services), how the vendor is charging the customer (e.g., fixed price versus time and materials versus some combination), ownership of the deliverables, etc. If pricing is on a time and materials basis, then the SOW should set forth the different labor categories, a specific description of the skill sets associated with each labor category (possibly including required or associated education and/or certification credentials), and the hourly rate associated with the labor category. If the customer will be charged by the day, then the SOW should define what constitutes a "day", 8 hours minimum, 10 hours minimum, etc.

If the customer is making progress payments, then the SOW should also establish milestones which tie to the progress payments to ensure the customer is not paying for vaporware.

See Chapter 5.J for a more detailed discussion.

5. *Duration and Termination Rights*

The parties should contemplate the relationship between the duration of the master agreement and the duration(s) of the SOW(s). Some master agreements permit the term of the SOW to extend beyond the term of the master agreement, with the express proviso that that the master agreement will remain in place until the SOW terminates, and no new SOWs may be executed after the term of the master agreement has expired.

As to termination, is termination for convenience permitted? Will breach of the SOW allow the customer to terminate the SOW and the master agreement or only the SOW? Will termination of one SOW necessarily, or never, cause the termination of another, coterminous project and its SOW?

See Chapter 5.G for a more detailed discussion.

6. *Customer Acceptance and Acceptance Testing*

The acceptance testing procedures are one of the most important aspects of the SOW, as they set forth an objective process for establishing whether the vendor has successfully met its contractual obligations. The acceptance criteria should be set forth in each SOW, not the master agreement, as the deliverables and services performed will differ with each SOW, requiring the acceptance criteria to be tailored to the specific deliverables.

Payment should be tied to acceptance; if the deliverables are not accepted, the vendor should not be paid. The acceptance provisions should set forth in detail how the testing will be conducted, by whom, preferably specifying what testing data and conditions, how many rounds of testing will be permitted, and the ramifications if the deliverables are not acceptable. Frequently a limited number of retesting cycles are negotiated and specified.

See Chapter 16.B for a more detailed discussion.

C. Resolving Conflicts between the Master Agreement and SOW

One potential issue is how to resolve conflicts between the terms of the master agreement and the terms of the SOW. In the majority of agreements, the parties agree that any conflict will be resolved in favor of the SOW, given that the SOW is specific to the unique deliverables, and that the master agreement may have been negotiated prior to a particular SOW even being contemplated.

Some parties believe, however, that the master agreement should prevail in an effort to maintain the sanctity of the broader contractual protections that the MSA contains. They believe that these protections should not be negated in a later SOW, especially where the SOW may be negotiated and executed with less oversight (e.g., by someone who does not understand the risks they are assuming or lacks the authority to do so). This philosophy is problematic if the parties desire to incorporate conflicting terms into the SOW, as they now not only must draft the SOW, but must also amend the master agreement. One compromise is to provide that in the event the parties desire to supersede a provision of the master agreement in the SOW, the SOW must identify by section number the specific provision in the master agreement that will be superseded. By adding this requirement, a concerned party can seek to avoid an unnecessary ambiguity or dispute and/or a significant provision of the master agreement being unknowingly superseded by the SOW.

See Forms E.1.1, E.1.2, E.1.3, and E.1.4 for model SOWs.

D. *PRACTICE POINT*: SOW checklist

- Is the master agreement appropriate for use with the contemplated license or services?
- Does the SOW align completely and accurately with the requirements and commitments of the master agreement?

- Do the terms of the master agreement or the terms of the SOW prevail in the event of a conflict between the two documents?
- Assuming that the master agreement provides that it shall prevail in the event of a conflict, unless the SOW clearly identifies the specific section of the master agreement over which the SOW prevails, does the SOW identify any such sections?
- Does the SOW specifically name (reference) the parties' overarching master agreement?
- What is the duration of the SOW? Does it extend beyond the term of the master agreement?
- Does the SOW include:
    - A detailed description of deliverables?
    - A delivery timetable with the dates linked to "go-live" benchmarks or other requirements, such as milestone payments?
    - The location(s) of the vendor's performance?
    - Where the deliverables will be delivered?
    - A statement of any services that are specifically excluded from the vendor's obligations?
    - A statement of who owns the deliverables?
    - A statement of the customer's obligations?
    - A statement of customer and/or third party dependencies on which the vendor's performance obligations are based?
    - A detailed project implementation plan which should directly relate to the deliverables?
    - Acceptance procedures and testing responsibilities?
    - A statement of the fees for the work performed? A prudent customer will set a fixed price or maximum price/hours, and will tie payment to the vendor meeting well-articulated milestones. The pricing should also describe what, if any, expenses incurred by the vendor are reimbursable.
    - Project assumptions? The SOW should clearly state the assumptions that each party is making when entering into the SOW. For example, is the customer responsible for purchasing all third-party software and hardware? A deviation from the stated project assumptions should result in a change order (drafted with precision) or justify a delay in a party's performance without penalty/or price change.
    - Optional services? The parties should confirm that any "optional" services are listed as being out of scope items. In a fixed-price transaction, the parties need to be absolutely clear as to what is in scope and what is out of scope.
    - The vendor's project management methodologies? These methodologies provide periodic reporting to the customer's designated representative(s) (preferably addressing a specified set of topics, in a specified degree of detail) and advance warnings of problems, escalation, and resolution, which should result in either the avoidance of any schedule problems or the ability to address an expected delay in the spirit of compromise via a change order, pricing adjustment, or amendment.

- A change order process? If the master agreement does not have a change order methodology, then the SOW should include a process for amending the SOW in the event the parties desire to amend their respective obligations. As with an SOW itself, change orders require specificity and often "a second set of eyes."
- The party's termination rights, whether for breach or for convenience?
- A statement addressing how conflicts between the terms of the SOW and master agreement will be resolved? See Chapter 13.C above.
- Key personnel?

- Personally Identifiable Information (PII) or other data between the parties? If so,
  - what data will be exchanged,
  - what will the data be used for, and
  - where will the data be stored?
- Subsequent to the execution of the master agreement, have there been any changes in the law or related mandatory regulations that would impact the terms of the master agreement or that should be incorporated into the master agreement?
- Who on each party's deal team is approving the SOW's terms and conditions?
- Signature lines? Given that the SOW serves as an addendum/amendment to the master agreement, the SOW should be separately signed by an authorized signatory of each party.

See Form E.1.1 for an annotated template Time and Materials SOW and Form E.1.2 for an annotated template Firm Fixed Price SOW.

CHAPTER **14**

Cloud Computing and Hosting

Many, perhaps trending to most, commercial vendors and customers are utilizing delivery models other than the historic on-premise method (i.e., using computer hardware located on the end user's premises) for providing and accessing software applications. Most commonly illustrated through the use of "cloud computing," these delivery models raise many of the same issues involved in traditional software licensing, while at the same time creating issues unique to the respective delivery model. Cloud computing provides on-demand delivery of IT resources and applications via the Internet usually with volume based pricing, allowing customers to reduce initial IT expenses while having the ability to quickly increase or decrease IT resources to meet their varying needs.

Additionally, many software licensors and licensees are delegating the management of their software to third parties who provide server space, web services, and file maintenance for websites on the hosting provider's servers. Hosting refers to providers who host the physical servers providing the service off-site from the user's premises. Access to the services is through a direct connection which may or may not run through the Internet. Also known as "Managed Service Providers" (MSP) or "Application Service Providers" (ASP), these organizations may provide varying services ranging from simple hosting to managing the run time environment to managing the application development environment. The application may be running either on the physical premises of the customer or in the cloud. Cloud services are a subset of hosted services that run through the Internet. "Managed hosting" allows both customers and software vendors to potentially reduce their costs while increasing the efficiency in which the software is utilized. There is disagreement on whether ASPs differ from cloud computing, although the difference lies mainly in how ASP is defined. Both models provide access to software applications over the internet, but ASPs utilize a single tenant on a single instance with the ability to make customizations and modifications but is not easily scalable. Cloud hosting is billed on a consumption basis and is rapidly scalable.

Finally, many licensors distribute and license their software through third-party vendors, resellers, original equipment manufacturers and value-added resellers. The discussion below provides a brief overview of cloud computing and the licensing issues associated with Software-as-a-Service ("SaaS") in particular, as well as, the most common forms of hosting.

A. Cloud Computing

For the purposes of this Section, "licensor" will refer to the owner of the intellectual property being licensed or accessed; "cloud provider" will refer to the party receiving a license, subscription or access to the licensor's intellectual property; and "customer" will refer to the entity that is accessing and using the intellectual property. In some cases, the cloud provider may also be the licensor.

1. Overview of Cloud Computing

Like a true cloud, the parameters of "cloud computing" are somewhat amorphous. The U.S. National Institute of Technology ("NIST") has defined cloud computing as "a model for enabling ubiquitous, convenient, on-demand network access to a shared pool of configurable computing resources (e.g., networks, servers, storage, applications, and services) that can be rapidly provisioned and released with minimal management effort or service provider interaction." http://csrc.nist.gov/publications/nistpubs/800-145/SP800-145.pdf. In essence, "Cloud computing allows businesses and individuals to use the internet to access software programs, applications, and data from data centers . . . . Cloud computing services are not a unitary product but rather a continuum of services which businesses are able to access on an as-needed basis." *IBM Corp. v. Visentin*, 2011 WL 672025 (S.D.N.Y. Feb. 16, 2011).

The NIST definition of cloud computing, while helpful, can be confusing. A more practicable approach is to identify the characteristics of cloud computing:

- On-demand service;
- Broad network access;
- Shared infrastructure and applications;
- Multi-tenant database architecture;
- Rapid scalability;
- Limited equipment provisioning by the end user; and
- Consumption billing.

These characteristics theoretically lower the customer's computing costs by eliminating its fixed and overhead costs for hardware, software and human capital. A customer will only be billed for its actual consumption, creating greater efficiency and reducing costs. Since the customer accesses the software solutions through the web via browser software, unless the customer is committing to a specific platform (also referred to as Platform-as-a-Service or "PaaS"), like Microsoft.NET, it is not constrained by any specific operating system requirements.

A multi-tenant environment allows a vendor to provide the services using one integrated code base that may be delivered simultaneously to multiple customers, creating significant cost efficiencies. In a single-tenant model, the software or services are provided to the customer on an individualized basis, which is inefficient in comparison to a multi-tenant environment and is not easily scalable.

Cloud computing allows cloud providers the flexibility to quickly increase or decrease their infrastructure requirements and potentially lower overall cost when compared to a custom configuration or instance because the cloud is considered to be a commodity. This flexibility leads to greater cost efficiencies. In the situations where the customer is procuring Software as a Service, the cloud provider absorbs the infrastructure costs associated with making the application available to the customer, creating efficiencies for the customer who cares only about its data and business processes, not the enabling infrastructure. In an Infrastructure as a Service model, the efficiencies would be realized by the customer as it is able to quickly and efficiently increase or decrease its infrastructure needs.

Cloud computing also allows a customer to access a software application or computing components through the web and potentially pay only for actual usage rather than paying upfront for all the component parts of the software and hardware needed to make access and computing capacity possible. Some SaaS subscriptions are sold on a per-seat basis with unlimited data, whereas other subscriptions impose data size limitations and overage fees. The actual pricing methodology will depend on the terms of the particular subscription agreement.

(a) Cloud Delivery Models

The NIST has identified four delivery models through which cloud services may be delivered: the public cloud, the private cloud, the hybrid cloud and the community cloud.

(i) Public Cloud

A public cloud places the applicable software applications and the data of many different customers on a common infrastructure allowing customers to realize cost savings by paying for shared infrastructure on a usage basis. The cloud provider is responsible for increasing the infrastructure on an as needed basis in order to maintain acceptable service levels for its customers.

A multi-tenancy environment offers many benefits, including rapid innovation, frequent release of new features and/or other improvements, rapid access through a web browser, real-time scalability, a pay on demand price model and automatic upgrades. While each of these attributes is seen as a benefit, multi-tenancy also comes with risk, including development cycles predicated on collective (i.e., all customers) basis rather than individual user needs and the upgrades to the software, as well as any impact on the customer's legacy system.

The real benefit of a public cloud is the efficient use of resources by the cloud provider allowing it to reduce cost and maintain the application through a "one size fits all" approach. Early on, multi-tenancy was a commonly used term to indicate that the service could be offered at a cost savings, but later the "sticky" nature associated with the degree of difficulty that a customer would endure if it attempted to execute its exit strategy became a concern (i.e., the ability to migrate to another SaaS provider). The real risk arises from data ownership issues and the ease of data extraction, including challenges in transitioning to successor software or a new vendor (e.g., due to possible differences in data schema, preventing a simple "plug and play" replacement).

(ii) Private Cloud

A private cloud provides an individual customer with greater security and control over its data as the customer is, in effect, renting the infrastructure and determining how the software applications are deployed. The customer does not share any common infrastructure with any other customers. As such, the costs associated with a private cloud are usually greater than the costs associated with a public cloud. Some cloud providers keep the usage costs to the customer equivalent to the costs of a public cloud but require a minimum commitment to ensure the cloud provider recovers its fixed costs. Under a private cloud model, the applications and infrastructure may reside at the cloud provider's or customer's facilities.

(iii) Community Cloud

Community clouds allow organizations with common aspects such as similar security risk profiles or similar business models to share infrastructure and applications. For example, community clouds can be used for government agencies and contractors with similar requirements with regard to export control regulations. The community cloud may be more private than a pure public cloud, due to the shared interests of the customers and related controls on their computing but is fundamentally a shared model.

(iv) Hybrid Cloud

A hybrid cloud model incorporates the characteristics of at least two of the three different cloud models (private, community, or public) which remain unique entities while being bound by standardized or proprietary technology that enables data and application portability between the clouds (e.g., cloud bursting for load balancing between clouds). The customer usually seeks the cost advantages of a public cloud but requires some aspect of dedicated resources provided through a private cloud. Hybrid clouds are most commonly used for data storage in the support of web 2.0 applications. More recently, consulting companies are growing via engagements to create hybrid clouds for purposes of driving forth best of breed point solutions as well as to integrate with customers' on-premise solutions that are deemed to be too sensitive (e.g., regarding cyber-security or necessary uptime considerations) to be placed in the cloud.

(b) Service Models

Most cloud computing services fall within one of four service models:

(i) Software as a Service ("SaaS"), which allows a user to access a vendor application on a cloud infrastructure (e.g., Salesforce.com, Gmail, Dropbox);

(ii) Infrastructure as a Service ("IaaS"), which allows a user to access and provision on demand computing power, processing, storage, network capabilities, and other fundamental computing resources to, in essence, create their own data center (e.g., Amazon Web Services (AWS), Rackspace);

(iii) Platform as a Service ("PaaS"), which allows a user to deploy its infrastructure, whether user-created or acquired from a cloud provider, including middleware, the network, servers and storage, which are controlled and managed by the cloud provider (e.g., Salesforce.com, Microsoft Azure, Google App Engine); and

(iv) Business Process as a Service ("BPaaS") offered through a managed service provider allows a user to access an entire business process through the cloud.

(c) *Contracting in the Cloud*

(i) Overview

There are two different types of access and use rights granted in the cloud. In the first: the customer is granted the right to access and use a software application on a SaaS basis usually through a subscription. Because the vendor is providing a service, the customer does not receive a license to utilize a particular application, rather the customer receives the *right to access and use* the services. To avoid implying the customer is licensing software, the vendor sells a *subscription*, not a license, and the customer does not receive a copy of the underlying application. The customer does not need a copy of the application and does not need to install the application on its computers or servers. Instead, it accesses the SaaS.

In the second: the customer purchases capacity (IaaS) and requires a software license for that capacity, i.e., on a virtual machine basis, similar to renting space on a server or data center. An important distinction is that SaaS providers who sell subscriptions generally purchase capacity at the hosting company's data center. PaaS and BpaaS are variations on the IaaS model.

(ii) Subscription Model

Software licensing in the cloud differs from traditional licensing in that the customer is not a licensee and may not have contractual privity with the licensor. Traditionally, in those situations where a licensor granted the licensee the right to utilize the software to support a third-party, most license agreements granted a licensee the right to use the licensed software to support individual customers and perhaps to redeploy software from one customer to another in the event a customer terminated its relationship with the licensee. In the past, usually these licenses did not permit "hosting" or "multi-tenancy" use, i.e., the ability to use one software license to provide multiple different customers simultaneous access to the software. Now, many licenses are obtained by licensees under a cloud business model, placing particular importance on multi-tenancy license rights and on obtaining license grants enabling the use of subscription-based pricing and business models.

Model language granting the customer the right to access and use the application follows:

> *In consideration of Subscriber's payment in full of the applicable Fees and subject to the terms and conditions of this Agreement and the applicable Order Forms, Vendor hereby grants Subscriber the limited, non-exclusive, non-transferable and non-assignable right to access and use, and to permit its Affiliates and Users to access and use, Software and the Documentation for the term identified in the applicable Order Form, by up to the number and type of Users specified in the Order Form(s), for Subscriber's and its Affiliates' internal business purposes only, and in accordance with this Agreement and the Documentation. Subscriber shall use and permit use of Software only for the modules and processes purchased by Subscriber as reflected in an Order Form.*

Consistent with the use of a SaaS model, the vendor should utilize the defined term "Subscriber" to reinforce the notion that the customer is receiving certain identified services from the vendor and is not receiving a license to the underlying software.

Licensing in the cloud raises many issues, as cloud services are usually offered to customers on a subscription basis as opposed to a license basis. Devising a cloud-pricing model presents several challenges for the cloud provider. The cloud provider may be paying the licensor an upfront license fee for usage which may vary by seat, server, etc., but charging the customer on a usage or subscription basis. The flexibility demanded by customers to use the product (for example, surge usage during peak periods) may not be consistent with the licensor's pricing methodology, potentially creating pricing risk for the cloud provider.

The traditional "on-premises" (often described in the industry as "on-prem") licensing model usually provides for a perpetual, up-front, one-time license fee with an additional annual fee for maintenance (e.g., the right to receive upgrades, new versions, etc.) and support (e.g., the right to contact the supplier for technical assistance). Cloud providers, however, usually offer term-based subscriptions for fixed periods of time, such as a year which include both the right to access and use the software as well as maintenance and support.

A subscription licensing model provides the right to use a specified quantity of the software on a pay-as-you-go basis based on actual usage. At the end of each month, the cloud provider submits a report to the upstream licensor detailing the amount of software that the cloud provider actually consumed the prior month. Usage may be measured in various ways, including the number of end users or CPUs accessing the product, aggregate hours of online access, amount of data storage, and/or other metrics. Reports are typically due by the fifteenth day of the following month. The cloud provider is contractually obligated to provide the monthly reports and to allow the upstream licensor to confirm the amount of software that the cloud provider has used. A cloud provider's failure to report its software usage is almost always considered a material breach of the underlying license agreement.

Because the SaaS is not typically a customized solution, acceptance/testing is usually not applicable.

Prudent vendors should not use the term "license" when granting the customer use rights as doing so creates several risks for the vendor. Most importantly, a customer could demand a copy of the software including any third party software incorporated into the application. A customer could also potentially claim a right under any underlying patents. To the extent the application includes open source software, using the term *license* may trigger the copyleft obligations of any viral licenses, requiring the vendor to distribute the source code to the software. Finally, if the vendor were to file for bankruptcy, the customer may claim the right to retain use of the software.

(iii) Risks

Cloud computing is not without risks. Customers/data owners need to be concerned with data privacy and the security of their data, as it is stored in a third-party's facilities and transferred through the web. In some cases, a customer may not know where the software application and its data actually reside, as the cloud provider may store the application and data in multiple data centers, and the data may move between servers located around the world in the course of one day. The customer is simply granted rights to access and use the application as well as the customer data associated with it.

(iv) Updates

Finally, customers are often forced to relinquish flexibility in deciding whether to upgrade or move to a new version of a software application as the cloud provider achieves cost efficiencies through having all customers on a common platform. Having no say in the decision to move to an upgraded system can have an immediate adverse impact on a customer's daily business operations. As such, a customer should seek contractual protections to attempt to ensure that it is not adversely affected by changes imposed on it by the cloud provider. Many providers who release new software into production (i.e., a new version release, bug fix or functionality maintenance) generally do so transparently without a loss of functionality that would impact the customer's business.

Because most customers utilizing a public cloud must accept standard upgrades to the purchased software application, many vendors will provide their customers with a accept notice of any impending material changes to their software along with a description of such changes. Vendors will often create a test environment for customers prior to the change to allow customers to test and demonstrate the new instance. If the customer requires a customized environment, the vendor will usually change the customer for the customized environment to reflect the vendor's labor costs to establish the environment. Similarly, if the customer wants an entire environment, as opposed to a general demonstration, the vendor will most likely be glad to do so but will charge accordingly.

If the customer wants the vendor to create another production instance in the same environment, the cost to do so may not be expensive, as the security procedures are already in existence and do not need to be replicated. If the trial is not set up for the customer's environment and there is a labor cost to customize the demonstration for the environment with the customer's data and production level severity, there will likely be a charge.

Some vendors charge for a temporary environment when a customer is evaluating a potential enhancement and will provide a credit to the customer if the customer decides to implement the enhancement.

The cloud provider should be required to provide the customer 30 days prior written notice before any material software upgrade is implemented and prior to the cloud provider making material changes to the services.

Any related documentation should be provided electronically to the customer's designated IT staff in advance, so the customer can anticipate the changes and prepare for their adoption. Further, from the customer's perspective the underlying agreement should automatically renew upon expiration unless the customer provides the cloud provider written notice of its intent to terminate 30 days (or some other negotiated, specified time frame) prior to the expiration date.

Of greater concern in the case of upgrades and routine maintenance is the loss of data. While a rare occurrence, the risk of data loss as a result of this action. Provisions should be made to have backup copies of data on hand with a workable copy of the executable code to make use of the data. Depending on the service level agreement (SLA), it may be prudent to retain several days/weeks/months of data to fall back to in the event of an unforeseen data loss. This is a precursor to SaaS escrows for customers who mandate high availability as a part of their service level agreement or require such contingencies in place to help them safely migrate to a new solution if they ever needed to do so.

For a general discussion, *see* Kesan, Hayes, &. Bashir, *Cloud Services, Contract Terms, and Legal Rights,* 17 J. INT. L. 3 (Dec. 2013); Hon. Millard, Walder, *Negotiating Cloud Contracts: Looking at Clouds From Both Sides Now,* 16 STAN. TECH. L. REV. 79 (2012); Bradshaw, Millard & Walden, *Contracts for Clouds: Comparison and Analysis of the Terms and Conditions of Cloud Computing Services,* Centre for Commercial Law Studies, Queen Mary Univ. of London (2010); Marotta-Wurgler, *What's in a Standard Form Contract? An Empirical Analysis of Software License Agreements,* 4 J. EMPIRICAL L. STUD. 677 (2007).

2. Licensing from the Perspective of a Third-Party Proprietary Software Vendor

(a) Pricing and Multi-tenancy Licenses

On-premise software licenses traditionally grant a single user the right to access and use the software for its internal use or grant the right to install the software on a single computer. Under a cloud model, a cloud provider may install the software on multiple servers allowing many different customers to access and use the software. Although cloud licensing models continue to evolve in response to market demands for technology access and services, most licensors are willing to grant cloud providers multi-tenancy licenses, provided they are adequately compensated.

Whether a licensor is willing to make its application available in the cloud depends on the licensor's ability to devise a pricing model that aligns with how its product is used. For example, if the licensor's pricing model is based on a per-CPU basis, the licensor will usually want to be paid for the CPUs of the entire infrastructure, even if its software is being used by only one person on one virtual machine.

While some licensors continue to structure their licenses based on the traditional model, many have established alternative pricing methodologies based on usage, the number of users/seats, the number of servers or cores, the quantity of data created and/or processed, or other methodologies that reflect the nature of the cloud provider's business and the customer's business demands. In short, most licensors are willing to grant broad usage rights provided the financial metrics are acceptable.

(b) Pricing Models

Licensors use various pricing models including a flat monthly fee, per seat pricing and a subscription basis (a fee based on actual usage). Most cloud providers prefer a flat fee or per-seat billing model, as they allow for budgetary certainty. A much smaller number of cloud providers prefer a subscription model.

Under a subscription model, cloud providers are invoiced and pay the licensor a license fee based on their actual monthly usage. To reduce the administrative burden, some cloud providers issue an annual not-to-exceed (NTE) or blanket purchase order at the time of contract execution. The licensor then invoices the cloud provider monthly against that purchase order. Cloud providers must monitor the remaining balance on the purchase order to ensure funding is not exhausted, and if low, issue a change order to increase the purchase order's funding to avoid exceeding the value of the purchase order. Administratively, this process is more cumbersome than the past practice of paying the licensor a one-time perpetual license fee based on a per customer basis, enterprise size, CPU, seats or users.

Another issue for cloud providers is allocating costs to the various customer accounts using the cloud provider's cloud services. Unless the application has the ability to track usage on a per user basis, the cloud provider must develop the ability to track usage. Without an automated process, the cloud provider will likely spend significant time and effort to correctly allocate software usage and calculate the proper billing.

See Form Q.2.M.2 for model billing and payment language.

3. *Licensing from the Cloud Provider's Perspective*

(Where the cloud provider is providing customers access to a third-party application)

(a) Access

Historically, most licensees have lacked the right to use licensed software in a hosted or service bureau/multi-tenant environment and could only use the software internally or with identified computer hardware, which may or may not have included the right to later redeploy the software to some different computer(s).

In a cloud environment, the license grant must address muti-tenancy, multi-customer access, as well as the cloud provider's right to redeploy the software. The cloud provider must ensure that it has the right to grant access to the software to multiple customers and, if required, the customer's customers or other third parties. For example, a hospital may purchase access to an application, but non-employee physicians may also need access to the application. Most licensors understand this requirement and are willing to grant the cloud provider the rights it requires, albeit for a larger license fee.

See Form Q.2.M.3 for model language granting the cloud provider the right to provide access to customer customers.

(b) Pricing Models

The cloud provider must understand how the licensor's pricing model maps to the demands of its customers and the underlying payment terms to avoid assuming additional financial risk. For example, if the licensor charges a separate licensee fee for each distinct user on a server, as opposed to charging a per server license fee, the cloud provider must align its pricing model with the licensor's per user pricing to avoid significant financial risk. Similarly, if the licensor charges the cloud provider a significant premium for a subscription-based pricing model and the cloud provider's customers pay the cloud provider on a subscription basis which is terminable on short notice, the cloud provider is assuming the risk that it may be unable to recoup the fees it paid to the licensor from its customers.

Not only will the cloud provider assume the financial risks associated with utilizing two disparate pricing models, the cloud provider may also experience cash flow issues if it is required to pay the licensor on contract signature but collect payment from its customers over time. Instead, the cloud provider should negotiate a pricing structure with the upstream licensor which is consistent with the pricing terms that it negotiates with its customers. Many software vendors have recognized these market driven changes and offer subscription-based pricing with multi-tenancy rights. This increased flexibility comes at a cost to the cloud provider, as the licensor may, for example, charge a cloud provider a significant premium for multi-tenancy rights.

(c) Billing

Another important logistical issue is how the cloud provider's usage will be tracked and how the cloud provider will be billed. If the licensor's fees are based on usage, as opposed to a per user or per machine basis, and the application does not electronically track such usage, how will the usage be determined? How will usage information be transferred to the cloud provider's finance department so that the customer can be billed? How will the information be transferred to the licensor so that the cloud provider can be billed?

Billing is not only a challenge for the cloud provider with respect to the customer, but for the customer as well. If not careful, the customer may lack the ability to ensure that it is billed properly.

- How is the customer's usage being measured?
- How can the customer confirm the accuracy of the reporting?
- Will future license negotiations include end-user rights to audit the licensor's billing practices and accuracy, similar to the customer-audit terms frequently found in on-premises software licenses?

Customers, cloud providers and licensors may prefer different measurement periods as the measurement period can greatly impact the cost to the customer and the fees payable to the licensor and cloud provider. For example, some programs measure use on the last day of the month, while the customer may prefer usage measured hourly. Thus, the level of detail can be challenging for both parties.

As mentioned, most cloud providers offer a number of different billing models, including a flat monthly fee, a per seat basis and a subscription basis. Many customers prefer a flat fee or per seat billing model, as they provide for budgetary certainty.

(d) Third-Party Access

Another important consideration for cloud providers is the ability to grant the customer's customers the ability to access the software if needed. Some customers purchase services to provide a service to their own customers. Others need to allow affiliates to access the software to meet their business needs. Provided that usage by these customers is treated as part of the primary customer's overall usage, the licensor probably will not object to these additional parties accessing the services if it is compensated for their use. *See SAP UK Ltd. v. Diageo Great Britain Ltd.* [2017] EWHC 189 (TCC) Case No: HT-2015-000340 (SAP successfully sought compensation for Diageo's customers' indirect access and use of SAP software). Large or even moderate-scale mergers, acquisitions, or spinoffs, however, may be problematical from the licensor perspective, as they may potentially preclude later desirable new revenue.

Problems may also arise in the agreement between the cloud provider and its customers. For example, if after the agreement between the cloud provider and the customer has been executed, the customer seeks to expand the scope of its access to include additional users. If the cloud provider's agreement with the licensor contains corresponding restrictions, the cloud providers will have no choice but to refuse the customer's request for expanded scope or re-negotiate with the licensor. Thus, a prudent customer should ensure it obtains the right to accommodate any future need for additional capacity including access to an environment running in escrow and managed by the escrow agent at the same or similarly discounted pricing at the time of contract signature. This is especially true if the cloud provider has entered into agreements allowing its customers to resell the application or service.

In some situations, the final end user may not be known to the licensor causing some licensors to be hesitant to grant the cloud provider the right to resell the solution without identifying each party that will or may access the solution. This "identification" concern is compounded if the customer is permitted to allow its own customers and other third parties to use the solution. Thus, many licensors want to know the identity of the customer, especially if the licensor may seek injunctive relief against a customer and would thus need to know their identity. Others are less concerned as they are in contractual privity with the cloud provider and can seek legal recourse against the cloud provider in the event a problem arises.

(e) Third-Party License Terms

Some licensors require the cloud provider to flow down the licensor's terms to each of the cloud provider's customers. A cloud provider may work with dozens of software vendors in establishing its environment, creating an administrative burden for the cloud provider to attach a large number of end-user license agreements (EULAs) to its customer agreements. To avoid this issue, licensors are increasingly permitting the cloud provider's agreement with the customer have terms "no less protective" of the licensor as the terms of the agreement between the licensor and the cloud provider or "terms that are substantially similar to" a set of prescribed terms while retaining the right to audit the cloud provider's compliance. Further, many licensors seek to be a third-party beneficiary of the applicable agreement between the cloud provider and the customer to further protect their interests.

(f) Indemnification

The licensor should indemnify the cloud provider for infringement claims brought against the cloud provider or its customers based on technology or content provided by the vendor. Any such indemnities should be subject to industry standard exclusions such as excluding claims arising from use of the technology in combination with another product. Similarly, the cloud provider should indemnify the licensor against any claims of infringement brought against the licensor arising from technology or content provided by the cloud provider or its customers as well as claims that the customer's storage, use and display for any content violates any third-party right or laws, especially privacy laws. The cloud provider's indemnities should be subject to any applicable limitation of liability, especially foron privacy related claims.

See Chapter 5.B and 5.C for a more detailed discussion of indemnification.

(g) Private Clouds

A cloud provider will require different rights from the licensor if the cloud provider is going to install a separate application on each virtual machine versus loading the application on one machine and allowing access by multiple users.

4. SaaS Contract Terms

(Where the cloud provider is providing access and use of its own proprietary application)

Under a "SaaS" model, access to a software application is provided to the customer as a service. The vendor/cloud provider or another party hosts the software application on its web servers or via a third-party application service provider, allowing customers access to the software using web browser software via a portal and/or the Internet. The customer does not license a copy of the software but accesses the software as a service on an as-needed basis.

(a) Overview

(i) Benefits

From a software cloud provider's perspective, SaaS allows the cloud provider to reduce its support costs by maintaining a single version of its software on a single platform. A SaaS model allows cloud providers to monitor how their customers use the application, bring improvements to the market, and address uniformly for all customers any problem that arises. The cloud provider's support staff is able to evaluate a customer's problem as each customer is using the same application on the same platform. Updates are automatically made available to customers instead of customers having to wait to receive, install, integrate and pay for the newest update. In addition, SaaS allows the cloud provider to sell to customers who may not be able to afford the upfront fees required to procure the software and/or the infrastructure to support it.

From the customer's perspective, the customer is able to reduce its information technology costs by not having to purchase an application license, the hardware required to run it, as well as fees for updates and technical support. All of these costs are built into the fee for accessing the application, allowing the customer to direct its technology budget to those technologies that will provide a competitive advantage in its industry.

For cloud provider owned applications, the customer's cost to access the application should be reduced as the price is amortized among several users and the subscription fee is often based on usage. By paying only for its proportionate share of computing power and other resources that it uses, the customer avoids paying for excess capacity. The usage fee is amortized over the period of the customer's use as differentiated from the purchase of a software license where payment in full is usually due immediately upon acquisition of the license. This payment mechanism evens out the user's payments over the course of a year, potentially helping cash flow.

The customer will also avoid the significant time and cost of installing an application. In essence, application management has been outsourced, allowing the customer's IT staff to focus on other projects. Because the software is already operating on the cloud provider's system, the time to begin using the new application is dramatically reduced. The customer's software usage is fully monitored by the cloud provider, allowing the cloud provider to instantaneously receive "feedback," speeding the pace of improvements to the application, allowing customers to benchmark against their peers. Further, the customer is able to automatically access the most recent updates and enhancements to the application without the risks inherent in transitioning to a new version.

(ii) Limitations

SaaS does have several limitations/reasons for concern. The greatest is that the customer has relinquished control over its IT to a third-party and is totally dependent on the third-party to consistently deliver access without interruption while using a secure environment. See Chapter 14.B.4, below, for a more detailed discussion of the security/risk issues associated with SaaS. Although the customer is purchasing a service not a software license, a customer still needs contingencies that address sudden cessation of the cloud provider's business or an event of force majeure, as application continuity is necessary to enable end-user business continuity (contingency) plans. The customer also lacks the ability to customize the applications for its needs as most cloud providers will only modify the application for very large customers.

Another challenge for customers is that many cloud providers require customers to use the cloud provider's non-negotiable template agreement to purchase the cloud provider's services. These cloud providers argue that pro forma contracts are industry standard and reflect the nature of lower margins and shared services, thus negating the need to negotiate the contract. Although a cloud provider's contract may be non-negotiable, customers should carefully review the agreement to make sure it meets their needs. For example, does the agreement provide the use rights the customer requires, such as allowing the customer, its contractors, and the customer's customers to access and the software?

(iii) Delivery Models

SaaS is usually delivered through one of two models: a hosted application model or a software-on-demand model. In the hosted application management model, a hosting provider hosts the desired application, delivering the application to its customers over the Internet. Under the software-on-demand model, the cloud provider (i.e., the software cloud provider/licensor or cloud provider) provides its customers with network-based access to a single copy of an application modified for SaaS over a network. Software on demand is also known as the "application service provider" model. In both cases, the customer is paying for access to the application. The cloud provider may choose to have someone else host it, but delivery is the same and essentially "on-demand." In most situations, the cloud provider will provide, maintain, and host an application while providing the customer with access to the application. The application may be held in a dedicated environment with its own instance of the application, or alternatively, the application may be hosted in a multi-tenant environment, with a common version of the application running on a logically partitioned environment.

A shared multi-tenant environment uses a single instance of the application to provide access to multiple customers. All customers access and use the same instance of the application, creating an efficient means of implementing patches, upgrades, fixes and maintenance. A single-tenant environment provides access by a single customer, creating a more expensive service that cannot be easily scaled. A shared environment creates greater security risks, as many clients' data may be hosted on a single server. Thus, clients with sensitive data will often insist on dedicated servers. The language below reflects the potential concerns of customers:

> *Dedicated/Partitioned Environment.* *Any time Services are performed at the Customer Facilities, Vendor shall provide the Services using hardware, software and related resources dedicated solely to supporting Customer. Unless otherwise expressly provided in this Agreement, all Services provided from the Vendor's Facilities shall be provided using partitioned or dedicated Equipment. Vendor shall not provide any Services from a shared processing environment unless specifically approved in writing by Customer. The parties agree that a shared processing environment is not a multi-tenant environment; Vendor utilizes a multi- tenant environment.*

The cloud provider may choose to deliver SaaS either by hosting the application itself or by outsourcing the hosting of the application to a hosting provider. See Chapter 14.B for a more detailed discussion of managed hosting. Usually, the cloud provider will use its own proprietary software which it provides to its customers. In some cases, a hosting provider will license a copy of the software from the cloud provider and set up a SaaS model with its own customers. In the latter case, the hosting provider acquires rights from the software cloud provider and provides access and use of the application to customers. This approach is often co-defined through a "reseller" situation. See Chapter 20.C for a more detailed discussion of resellers.

PRACTICE POINT:

The principal means by which a customer can limit its risk when entering into a cloud agreement is to conduct detailed due diligence and a threat assessment on the cloud provider. The customer should explore the cloud provider's capabilities and reputation while at the same time conducting a gap analysis of the customer's needs against the cloud provider's offering. The customer should confirm its security and privacy requirements as well as assess the appropriateness of placing the specific data or applications in the cloud. In doing so, the customer should consider the following:

- Technology Currency and Innovation
- Changes in volume
- Cost
- Functionality
- Ability to decline changes in functionality

- Load demands
- Nature of the information to be placed in the cloud
- Importance to the customer's business
- Data security measures
  - Segregation
  - Location
  - Geo restrictions
- Security standards and commitment
- Architectural control
- Where will the data be stored?
- Dedicated servers vs logical separation
- Is their physical security for the data center/where the data is stored?
- Who has access to the data?
- How is data protected? At rest and during transmission?
- Impact analysis of an extended outage or security breach
- Network dependency
- Data conversion/compatibility
- Scalability
- Regulatory and compliance obligations/risks
- Service levels
- Disaster recovery
- Support and response times
- The need for customization
- Post termination right to technology and personnel
- Transition rights/Assistance
- Employee qualifications
- Limitations on key personnel
- Use of third-party contractors
- Speed to market/time to deliver
- Extent and coverage details of the prospective cloud provider's insurance
- Prospective cloud provider's financial stability
- Prospective cloud provider's management team maturity, adequacy, and stability
- Prospective cloud provider susceptibility to being purchased during the contract term.
- Audit rights
- Risk of bankruptcy

(b) Contractual Provisions

(i) Services

The underlying SaaS agreement between the parties should clearly set forth the cloud provider's obligations and the services it will provide. In a SaaS relationship, most cloud providers will provide:

- Access to an identified application,
- Technology updates,

- Data storage,
- Data backup,
- Data security, and
- User support.

To the extent a service is not listed, the customer should assume it is not included. For example, if data backup is not listed, the customer should assume the cloud provider will not be providing such services and the customer should back up its own data on a regular basis. To the extent the cloud provider desires to implement a material change in the provided services, the cloud provider should be required to furnish the customer advance notice of any material change, and the customer should have the right to terminate the agreement for convenience without penalty.

If applicable, proof of concept or beta testing should be conducted prior to making any long-term commitments to the cloud provider. The customer should ensure that the data created by the application is compatible with the customer's legacy systems (e.g., that the data schema are susceptible to "extract transform and load" ("ETL") modification and injection to other current systems) and thus avoid any potentially costly and time-consuming data migration project. The cloud provider should also be willing to give the customer a written commitment as to the application's future features and functionality that will be made available to customers. A prudent cloud provider may be hesitant to do so, however, to retain the maximum flexibility to operate its business.

(ii) Ownership of Data

From the customer's perspective, the agreement should clearly state:

- the customer owns its data (and all intellectual property rights related thereto);
- the customer will have immediate access to its data without charge upon demand;
- upon termination of the agreement the customer may take its data to a new cloud provider; and
- the format in which the data will be returned to the customer.

The agreement should also describe how and in what format the data will be returned and prohibit the cloud provider from withholding data for non-payment. Return of the data should be prompt and not conditioned on the customer meeting a payment demand by the cloud provider.

Sometimes it is the customer's responsibility to remove the data, i.e., to copy it onto its own system. If this is the case, the customer should make sure that once the data has been copied and the customer has confirmed it has a reliable copy of its data, the cloud provider destroys the data that remains on the cloud provider's systems. Usually, the cloud provider will want to do so in accordance with its own practices, e.g., by overwriting, etc. To the extent any data is contained on backup tapes, the backup tapes should be immediately destroyed, and an authorized officer of the cloud provider should certify that the tapes have been destroyed. Finally, the agreement should set strict time frames for the destruction or return of the data.

Some customers may require the cloud provider to issue a "destruction certificate" as proof of action by the cloud provider. However, there may be issues with respect to multi-tenancy environments where redundant data sets or similar copies of data continue to exist. Unless the relationship is managed in a single tenant database, it may not be possible to assure total destruction of the data. Contrary to the point above, it is also critical from the customer's perspective that the cloud provider be prohibited from destroying the customer's data in the event of non-payment until the customer has provided written instructions to do so.

Prudent cloud providers should develop an internal guidance/checklist setting forth the actions to be completed prior to executing a destruction certificate to avoid unintentionally creating liability on the cloud provider's behalf. To avoid potential problems, the certificate should be signed by the team lead for the team that completed the work, usually a member of the IT department.

(iii) Cloud Provider Access and Use of Customer Data

Cloud providers often seek access to the customer's data for many reasons, including the cloud provider's desire to aggregate and resell the customer's data to third parties. Under no circumstances should the cloud provider be able to sell the customer's data to a third party, even if it has been "cleansed" of any identifying information. The cloud provider should be contractually prohibited from accessing or disclosing the customer and customer data. While prudent customers should seek to limit the cloud provider's use of their data, the cloud provider should have the ability to collect and analyze usage data to improve the quality of the cloud provider's services, including as input for its product/services "road map." The agreement should clearly state that all customer data, including customer data, is confidential regardless of whether it is displayed or accessible by the cloud provider. Allowing the cloud provider to access customer data may raise antitrust issues as well as limit the customer's ability to claim trade secret protection for such data. For a discussion of trade secrets in the cloud, *see* Sandeen, *Lost in the Cloud: Information Flows and the Implications of Cloud Computing for Trade Secret Protection*, 19 VA. J.L. & TECH. 1 (2014).

The customer should not agree to amorphous language such as the cloud provider will "comply with industry standards" or the cloud provider will "use commercially reasonable efforts to protect the customer's confidential information." A prudent customer will also seek to prohibit the storage of users' credentials and passwords by the cloud provider.

Model language favoring the cloud provider:

> *We routinely collect and analyze metadata regarding your usage of the Cloud Services, excluding any personal data. We may use this information to gauge Cloud Services usage levels and application performance, as well as to create anonymized statistics for our own marketing purposes.*

The following language provides the cloud provider even greater leeway to utilize the customer's data.

Vendor may use and reproduce Subscriber Data at the direction of Subscriber (such direction taking the form of the terms of this Agreement and the relevant Schedules) for the limited purposes of providing, operating, and maintaining the Services provided to Subscriber. Subscriber will secure for Vendor the right to use and reproduce Subscriber Data, including any Personal Information therein, solely to the extent necessary to provide the Services to Subscriber, without creating any obligations for Vendor beyond those set forth in this Agreement. Vendor may use usage patterns, trends, and other statistical data derived from use of the Services (but not Subscriber Data itself) for the purposes of providing, operating, maintaining, or improving the Services and any Vendor products and services used to deliver the Services.

Compare the preceding language to the following language, which favors the customer:

Subscriber grants Vendor a limited, royalty-free, non-exclusive, non-transferable and non-sub-licensable license to process the Subscriber Data only in the United States as instructed by Subscriber and only to provide the services for Subscriber's benefit so long as Subscriber uploads or stores Subscriber Data in the System, subject to all terms and conditions of this Agreement.

PRACTICE POINT:

Any provision granting the vendor the right to access the customer's data should address the following:

- The limited purposes for which the vendor may access the customer's data
- The prompt return of the customer's data without charge upon request
- The customer's unfettered access to extract its own data as well as any derivatives of such data
- The allocation of responsibility for backing up the customer's data
- A prohibition on the comingling of the customer's data
- Provisions for recovering and reconstructing data
- The security standard for protecting the customer's data
- Security breach protocols
- The destruction of the customer's data upon the customer's request

(iv) Third-Party Access

Many cloud contracts provide that third parties may not access the solution through the customer. Customers often seek permission for affiliates and contractors (including information technology outsourcing services vendors) acting on their behalf to access and use the application. If the customer intends for its customers, affiliates and or contractors to be able to access and use the solution, the customer should ensure that the underlying agreement clearly provides for such access. This is very important in those situations where the customer is purchasing access to the solution for use by its customers or others. Common examples include a bank utilizing a system to allow its customers to conduct online banking.

(v) Data Retention

Given the significant numbers of customers, relatively short contract lengths, and the commoditized nature of cloud computing, many cloud providers retain customer data for very short periods of time. To the extent the customer has specific concerns, it should ensure the underlying agreement allocates not only responsibility for data retention and backup but also the time period in which data will be retained. The period of retention will depend on RTO/RPO's, requirement for the retention of metadata and the cost of doing so. RTO and RPO are common terms used to measure "Recovery Time Objectives" or how long it will take to recover data and resume using an application that has gone down. "Recovery Point Objectives" speaks to data freshness at the time of recovery. Sometimes, companies can recover data that is a week old meaning all the data from the current week would be lost. For mission critical applications, RPOs of less than one hour are standard.

Another issue for consideration is litigation holds for litigation, including the ability of the cloud provider to retain metadata. A prudent customer will contractually provide how it will notify the cloud provider of any litigation hold and how the cloud provider will preserve the relevant data. The failure to do so may lead to discovery sanctions on the customer in the event of any litigation.

Further to the extent a cloud provider is required to destroy or retain the customer's data, the parties should realize that it is virtually impossible to destroy all data, as customers' data will be inevitably retained in backup tapes and the memory of the servers. As a result, some negotiated transactions include provisions for ongoing but secure storage by the former cloud provider of former customer data for specified, tax, quality control, or other purposes.

(vi) Pricing and Payment

Customers may be charged through various means, including on a per-user per-month basis, on a monthly subscription for the customer's entire company, and results for a customer's use of the application. For example, of the last, infrequent pricing metric, a marketing software company is paid according to the number of solid leads generated through the customer's use of the software.

Customers should carefully evaluate a contract's pricing model to ensure that the pricing structure is clearly delineated and that the customer has the ability to independently verify any amounts that it is billed by the cloud provider. If access is based on the number of seats or users, the definition of "users" will serve as the basis for establishing the aggregate fee paid by the customer. As such, the customer should clearly understand how the application will be used and who will be accessing and using the application.

For example, if a cloud provider defines a "user" as a named individual accessing the system, the "named user" terminates his employment, and a replacement employee is hired, is the customer required to purchase a new license for the new employee, or may it transfer the license from the old employee to the new employee? As with a traditional license, the price should be fixed for a set period of time, and the amount of any future price increases should be capped.

Further, if the customer's customers may be indirectly accessing the application, do they need a license? The customer's failure to obtain the rights it requires or understand its use rights may prevent it from achieving the synergies it expected from using the application, as well as cause the customer to incur significant unforeseen costs. *See SAP UK Limited v. Diageo Great Britain Ltd.* [2017], EWHC 189 (TCC) Feb. 16, 2017 (SAP successfully sought additional compensation for Diageo's customers' access and use of SAP's software.

Many cloud providers require the customer to pay quarterly or annually in advance, eliminating any payment risk.

(vii) Performance Standard/Service-Level Agreements (SLAs)

Service levels are very important as they establish the cloud provider's minimum performance obligations and the degree of access that the customer will have to the application or services, including the customer's own data. Many cloud providers, however, do not offer meaningful SLAs, arguing the application must meet the demands of multiple customers. Most cloud providers will at least offer an availability service levels and some may be willing to provide additional remedies beyond service credits for an additional fee. If appropriate, customers should seek to negotiate additional SLAs, including response times, bandwidth and security breaches, although most cloud providers will only agree to meet minimum legal requirements. SLAs almost never cover failover guarantees or contingencies that address issues beyond the cloud provider's control such as the sudden cessation of the cloud provider's business or an event of force majeure. Cloud providers should avoid being measured on any customer dependent elements such as location processing capability.

(w) Specific Service Levels

Service levels should reflect the usage of the application. For example:

- How is the application being used?
- Where are the employees using the application located?
- What time of day will the employees be accessing and using the application?

A successful service level should be objective, critical to the successful performance of the services, tailored to the services, and achievable by the measured party. Common service levels include:

- Availability (both network and application)
- Remedies (including financial penalties/credits)
- Problem response time
- Issue resolution/Escalation Procedures, including status reporting
- User support
- Data return (Recovery Time/Recovery Point Objectives)
- Simultaneous visitors/users
- Page response times

See Chapter 12 for a more detailed discussion on service levels.

(x) Availability

Availability guarantees, also known as up-time guarantees, must be read carefully as they often exclude maintenance windows (when the system will be unavailable), and other "unforeseen" outages. If the cloud provider has many customers, there will likely be one maintenance window for all its customers as opposed to customer specific maintenance windows. For very large systems, there may not be a maintenance window as the cloud provider may provide for multiple redundancies allowing the customer to access the system from many different servers, a number of which will be available at all times. Where the application will be unavailable due to maintenance, cloud providers should alert users at least one week in advance of planned maintenance (generally undertaken in the middle of the night over the weekend). For many cloud providers, maintenance is consistently performed on all of the servers at one time versus staggering maintenance windows to maintain high-availability which is virtually impossible in a load-balanced environment.

As with many things, the devil is in the details, or in this case the definitions. From the customer's perspective, any "down-time" outside of regularly scheduled maintenance should be counted as down-time. This includes events of *force majeure*, as the customer is paying the cloud provider for availability, and the cloud provider can avoid *force majeure* events through geo-redundancy and other prophylactic measures. In addition, the cloud provider should not be allowed to schedule maintenance on short notice (i.e., less than 5-10 days' notice) and then claim that any such maintenance should not be counted as down-time.

Perhaps the most important metric from the customer's perspective is unplanned outages. Many customers require system availability of 99.99 percent per month and that all maintenance will be scheduled in advance and limited to early morning hours (i.e., 12 a.m. to 4 a.m. on weekends). Unplanned outages are unavoidable, requiring the customer to develop a detailed plan to mitigate its inability to access needed applications and data during any outage. The customer should specifically evaluate any required redundancies to continue operating during a period of outages. Prudent customers will require the vendor to provide historical data on system availability. For a convenient chart converting uptime percentages to minutes, hours and days, *see* http://royal.pingdom.com/2009/03/24/a-handy-uptime-and-downtime-conversion-cheat-sheet/.

It is also important to distinguish between "business" hours and "calendar" hours. Some cloud providers boast of 99.999% uptime (actually, most are more realistic these days at 99.5%), but as a percentage of what? 99.95% of business hours = approximately 25% of calendar hours. Is it specific to one region of the world? In short, there should be one standard of measurement that is clearly stated to provide certainty.

Unlike software vendors, most cloud providers do not have error correction/issue resolution standards. If a service interruption occurs, the contract should also stipulate how quickly the customer will be notified and how quickly the problem will be resolved, especially given that cloud providers may have to look to the underlying licensors to correct problems with the system. To do otherwise, leaves the customer at the mercy of the cloud provider.

(y) Calculating Compliance and Credits

Like many aspects of technology agreements, the parties must clearly and securely establish the cloud provider's obligations. The customer must ensure that the agreement sets forth in detail how the service levels are measured (i.e., what constitutes downtime) and how often they are measured (i.e., every five minutes, daily, monthly). Prudent customers should reject any language that requires the customer to track, identify, measure down-time and to notify the cloud provider in order to trigger any claim for service level credits as the cloud provider already monitors its data centers and its own performance.

The customer should clearly understand how often the service level will be measured. For example, if the service level is measured once an hour and the cloud provider meets the service level for the one minute each hour that the service level is measured but fails to meet the service level for the remaining 59 minutes, the cloud provider will have satisfied its service-level obligation but the customer will be livid. Some cloud providers require the customer to notify the cloud provider when it is not meeting the service level, even though the cloud provider is well aware that it is not meeting its obligations.

Cloud providers should be required to monitor any applicable service levels and provide customers with monthly reports on their compliance with the agreed-upon metrics. To the extent a service-level credit is due the customer, it should be automatically applied by the cloud provider to the next invoice sent to the customer. Prudent customers should demand that the cloud provider provide monthly reports on its performance in meeting the service levels and require the cloud provider to provide the customer with the tools necessary to monitor its performance. Without teeth, a service level is simply aspirational on the cloud provider's behalf.

See Chapter 12 for a detailed discussion of service level agreements.

(z) Remedies

In the event the cloud provider fails to meet an SLA, most cloud providers will only provide future credits instead of refunds to avoid revenue recognition issues. Further, the credit usually must be applied against future services on the customer's monthly bill as opposed to a general credit or allowing the customer the right to terminate the agreement in the event of the failure to meet an SLA. Any under-performance penalties or credits should be carefully delineated. The agreement should include examples of how any such penalties or credits should be calculated and applied.

In addition to service-level credits, the agreement should also set forth an escalation path to address the cloud provider's nonconformance, including an examination of the root cause analysis and the right to terminate the agreement if the cloud provider fails to meet the service level a set number of months in a six-month period.

In agreeing to services levels, the customer should not accept service levels as its sole and exclusive remedy in the event of a breach. It is critical that the customer reserve an exit strategy triggered by a material failure of the cloud provider to meet the SLAs. Such end-user protection should include prior creation and later, if needed, execution of a contingency plan that requires data recovery and migration to a new solution. If the customer does not trust that the cloud provider will cooperate, it should seek a neutral third party who can enable the contingency plan (i.e., SaaS escrow with application continuity and data recovery capabilities).

See Forms D.4.1 and D.4.2 for model availability service levels for IaaS agreements, Forms D.4.3 and D.4.4 for model availability service levels for SaaS agreements.

(viii) Data Security

(p) General

Security is important when utilizing a SaaS model, but it is especially important for those customers utilizing a public cloud. By centralizing a party's data in a secure data center, a party may actually increase its security (e.g., via the greater skills, resources, oversight, and testing that may be enabled by greater scale, i.e., a cloud provider testing and optimizing cybersecurity on behalf of multiple customers and its overall business model, versus a single entity attempting to achieve cybersecurity excellence only on its own behalf and outside its core focus or competencies). On the other hand, the customer has ceded control over its data and now is dependent on the cloud provider for protection.

There are three aspects of security: physical security, technical security and administrative security. Prudent customers should undertake a comprehensive risk assessment that evaluates the scope of the purchased services and seeks to identity any threats and vulnerabilities to customers receiving those services. It should assess the cloud provider's security policies and ascertain the potential risk of a threat triggering a vulnerability, as well as the potential impact if such a threat occurs. Customers will typically address their concerns with the cloud provider and incorporate its security requirements in the underlying agreement—often as a detailed, separate exhibit to the contract. Depending on the value of the contract and the importance of the application, the customer should visit the facility from which the cloud services are provided, if applicable and allowed, and request a written copy of the cloud provider's security protocol for the building's physical security and the security of the network from intrusion and viruses, as well as annual updates. The customer should closely examine and vet the cloud provider's policies, as well as ascertain the specific type of infrastructure used by the cloud provider to provide the hosting services.

The cloud provider should undertake an external and internal security analysis several times a year. The results of these efforts should be provided to the customer without the customer having to request it.

Most vendors will not allow their customers to dictate their security standards and internal policies. Instead, customers should understand the vendor's security standards and different security offerings, and determine if they are sufficient for the customer's needs. At the same time, customers cannot expect vendors to assume the customers' compliance obligations and any accompanying risk.

(q) Definition of "Data"

Most important, however, is the definition of "data," as the definition will establish the cloud provider's security, confidentiality, and privacy obligations. Is "data" limited to information stored by the cloud provider, or does it include data created and collected by the cloud provider in the course of delivering services to the cloud provider? Customers should seek to draft the definition of "data" as broadly as possible to ensure that its data is completely protected.

(r) Competitors

Another concern arises if the cloud provider is a competitor of the customer, later acquired by or enters into a strategic alliance with a customer competitor, or a competitor of the customer's customers. How is the customer's data or the data of the customer's customers protected? The customer must be certain that the cloud provider cannot access or view the data. To that end, both parties should ensure proper security and that strong multi-factor authentication measures are in place (i.e., specified security questions that must be answered to prove a party's identity). The underlying agreement should prohibit the disclosure of data to third parties and prohibit the misuse of data.

If there is a conflict of interest such as the cloud provider is a competitor of the customer or the customer's customer, then the technology should not be placed in the custody of the cloud provider. Rather, the technology should be hosted by a neutral third party, taken on-premises or alternative solutions should be sought to migrate to a new cloud provider. In any event, there should be an exit strategy that contemplates this situation if it arises at any point during the underlying business relationship.

(s) Regulatory Requirements

Dependent on the nature of the data and the customer's business, the customer may require that certain standards apply to the treatment of its data, such as Payment Card Industry (PCI) standards for credit card processing. These concerns, however, may be difficult to address because some specific PCI standards may in fact be under the control of the customer and not the cloud provider. As such, the parties must clearly allocate specific responsibilities between them. For example:

- Who has the ability to grant a new individual access, the cloud provider or the customer, a third-party provider (such as an escrow agent) or a combination?
- Who sets the security standards (e.g., levels of encryption, cadence of reported vulnerability patching, firewall rules, access conditions)—the cloud provider or the customer?

The underlying agreement must clearly allocate these rights and the resulting responsibilities, possibly including resulting periodic reporting obligations. This task is made more difficult by the fact that the application of these standards is essentially a matter of compliance with law, those laws are themselves rapidly evolving, and new legislation arguably does not keep pace with the extent and speed of technology developments.

Security responsibilities will depend on the nature of the cloud services, i.e., whether the cloud provider is providing IaaS or SaaS. Security obligations should be clearly established and not referenced by amorphous or ambiguous language. From the cloud provider's perspective, it should avoid accepting language to the effect that "anything not identified as the customer's responsibility is the cloud provider's responsibility" or "the cloud provider will provide reasonable security." If the customer has PCI obligations, the agreement should clearly state the cloud provider's specific responsibilities with respect to enforcing compliance with those standards.

If the customer is purchasing access to an application, i.e., SaaS, the customer should confirm, and never assume, that the application has the contractually required security and data protection requirements. A prudent customer should conduct due diligence on the cloud provider's security practices and ensure that the cloud provider is contractually obligated to meet certain specified responsibilities for security. Some customers seek to negotiate the right to require periodic penetration testing ("pen tests") of the cloud provider; cloud providers should seek to clarify and constrain the frequency, tools, participants, duration, and circulation of resulting reports.

The customer only has control over who has access to the application, and thus it is appropriate for the cloud provider to assume responsibility for security of the customer's data. If the customer is purchasing capacity, i.e., IaaS, then the customer controls its infrastructure and should have responsibility for security.

(t) Security vs. Confidentiality Obligations

The protections afforded by an agreement's confidentiality obligations differ from the cloud provider's security obligations. Under most confidentiality agreements, a party receiving confidential information agrees to use the confidential information only for the purpose of the disclosure as stated in the agreement and to not otherwise disclose the disclosing party's confidential information. The receiving party also usually agrees to use reasonable or higher efforts to keep the information confidential.

The question arises, does hacking rise to the level of "use" or a "disclosure"? In many cases, hacking may not cause a cloud provider to violate its confidentiality obligations as the cloud provider itself did not disclose the confidential information. Further, the customer may not be the "disclosing party," as the customer may be storing data on behalf of its own customers. In an effort to hold the cloud provider accountable, some customers seek to prohibit any disclosure of information, however caused, but most cloud providers are unlikely to agree to accept this standard, which essentially equates to strict liability for any disclosure.

(u) Security Standards

Multi-tenancy creates significant risks that other customers may be able to access or extract a customer's data, increasing the risk of viruses and malware entering the customer's environment as well as other security lapses. As such, customers should carefully negotiate the agreement's security standards after identifying potential risks and potential approaches to mitigate the identified risks. Such risks, both internal and external, as well as the agreed upon risk mitigation controls, must be continually monitored during the term of agreement.

To avoid ambiguity, the parties should specify the specific security standard the cloud provider must adhere to. The customer should ensure that the data center is ISO compliant as well as SSAE 18/ ISAE 3402 compliant. SSAE 18 SOC 2 and SOC 3 set forth significantly more stringent audit standards and are specifically focused on data centers. ISAE 3402 is the international equivalent of SSAE 18 and should apply and be reported against whenever data is kept in a global environment. See Chapter 7.E for a more detailed discussion of SSAE 18 and its requirements.

The cloud provider should maintain a written comprehensive information security program that includes reasonable security procedures and practices to ensure the security, confidentiality, privacy, availability and integrity of user content and other information if transmitted through or stored in connection with the services. Sophisticated customers seek to negotiate these cybersecurity specifications, attaching the agreed-upon standards as a detailed exhibit to the agreement.

(v) Location of Data

Prudent customers should consider contractually specifying the jurisdiction in which their data must be housed or, alternatively, require that all data remain within the continental United States to avoid subjecting the customer to the laws of those jurisdictions in which the data resides, including the jurisdiction's privacy laws, data transfer laws and jurisdictional discovery rules. The European Union has very restrictive laws as to data protection and prohibits the transfer of data to countries with inadequate data protection laws. To the extent a customer allows its data to be removed from the United States, a customer should monitor the data's location to avoid any potential prohibition by the jurisdiction to which its data was moved from relocating the data back to the United States. Savvy customers will include an audit provision allowing the customer to audit the cloud provider's compliance with its contractual obligations related to data location.

The citizenship of the owners of the data will dictate which state laws govern the vendor's privacy and security obligations.

(w) Physical Security

Physical security should not be overlooked. The cloud provider should be able to furnish the customer with a written security plan setting forth the protections implemented at its data centers, including:

- limiting and segmenting physical access,
- restricting physical access to required personnel,
- personnel background checks,
- badging, and
- training.

The customer should carefully evaluate the cloud provider's security protections. The customer should understand who has access to its confidential information and data and under what circumstances.

- Who has the ability to modify such data?
- What controls are in place to protect the customer from an unauthorized individual accessing and modifying the customer's data?
- Where is the cloud provider's data center located?
- Does the data center have adequate physical and virtual security?
- Does the cloud provider have appropriate virus protection software and appropriate security measures to protect the customer's data and internal systems?
- What particular testing and validation processes and third-party certifications, if any, will be required?
- May the customer initiate periodic "penetration testing," and if so, under what parameters?
- What if any cybersecurity-specific insurance coverage(s) must the cloud provider procure and maintain on the customer's behalf, at what levels, and for what duration? The customer should ensure the required protections are maintained 24×7×365 days a year.

(x) Technical Security

The cloud provider should utilize advanced software to detect any attempted and actual intrusions to its network, as well as eliminate viruses and similar problems. A customer should require that its data be encrypted not only at rest (storage) but also during transmission (i.e., both "at rest" and "in transit"). Not all cloud provider applications are encrypted, making data stored on such applications vulnerable to misappropriation or theft. A customer should insist that the cloud provider comply with specific encryption standards for the encryption of the customer's data. The language below illustrates this point:

> *Subscriber will encrypt the Data using the AES-256 standard and store on Vendor Simple Storage Service (S3) devices within the Vendor east coast and west coast data centers. When needed, the encrypted Data will be replicated to Elastic Band Storage (EBS) devices and made available during the boot process to server instances and associated server user accounts with proper credentials. The credentials will be stored and maintained within the Subscriber-managed data center and presented to the Vendor server instances only during the boot process. No credentials will be stored in the Vendor cloud environment.*

The cloud provider should be required to utilize sophisticated intrusion protection and detection software as well as peripheral equipment and be required to update it on a continuous basis to ensure it remains current with the latest technology. The cloud provider should be contractually obligated to provide detailed reports for any attempted intrusions of material significance as well as any resulting data breaches. The agreement should establish a change-of-custody log and tightly control and restrict access to any data as well as provide an audit procedure for auditing network and user transactions. In cases where the nature of the customer's data warrants it, the parties should also consider the use of a virtual private network (VPN) to further reduce security risks.

The parties should establish stringent requirements for the storage of customer credentials and passwords outside of the cloud, including strong access controls. In addition, the agreement should address other common-sense security controls, such as staff screening, firewall standards, access logs and the ability of third-party contractors to access the system. Priority should also be given to preservation of security controls as part of any disaster recovery plans.

For a more detailed discussion, see Hoover, Compliance in the Ether: Cloud Computing, Data Security and Business Regulation, 8 J. Bus. & Tech. L. 255, 260-66 (2013) (discussing the security risks of cloud computing); Bender, *Privacy and Security Issues in Cloud Computing*, 29 Comp. & Internet L. 1 (Oct. 2012).

(y) Administrative Security

Administrative security refers to the management of operational controls and procedures implemented to protect the system's security including:

- Authentication of HTTP clients
- Administrative console security
- Naming security
- Use of SSL transports
- The common user registry

- The authentication mechanism
- The authentication protocols

(z) Security Breaches and Incidents

The cloud provider should be obligated to notify the customer immediately in the event of a data breach or suspected breach and provide a detailed written explanation of the nature of such breach/suspected breach and the actions it has taken to remedy such breach. The agreement should address the parties' respective responsibilities for complying with all federal, state, and local data breach notification laws, including which party has responsibility for drafting a notice to any affected parties, sending the notice, paying for all costs associated with doing so, and identifying costs the responsible party must assume. In addition, the agreement should address which party must pay for any costs associated with complying with new laws enacted after the execution of the agreement.

The most important aspect in framing the parties' obligations is the definition of "data breach," as the definition will establish the scope of each party's obligations. Both parties should ensure they understand the ramifications of the definition and how it will impact their obligations and potential liability.

The agreement also should set out in detail the necessary response on the part of the cloud provider to a data breach, including, how quickly the cloud provider must contact the customer to disclose the existence of an intrusion or breach, via what means, how much information the cloud provider must provide the customer, what steps the cloud provider must take to investigate, if the cloud provider will interface with law enforcement and how, how often the cloud provider will update the customer on actions taken to mitigate the effects of any breach, and what remedies the cloud provider will offer, if any. From the customer's perspective, the customer does not want the affected individuals or entities or its board of directors and executives to first learn that there has been a security breach involving its data from the media or a third party.

(ix) Disaster Recovery

Disaster recovery differs from business continuity in that business continuity addresses issues that may arise in the ordinary course of business, such as bugs, hacking, general down time and other service interruptions. Disaster recovery addresses incidents more akin to an event of *force majeure*, such as a natural disaster. The cloud provider's disaster recovery plans should be carefully reviewed by the customer and include the level of redundancy for the application, i.e., the availability of the application in the event of a failure of the primary server or application (such as a geographically distant "hot" site), the cloud provider's protocol for backing up data (e.g., what frequency, testing, passwords, chain of custody, etc.), the storage of such data offsite, as well as the duration for which it will retain the backups. See Chapter 7.F for a more detailed discussion of disaster recovery issues. The cloud provider should be able to provide a detailed plan addressing a power outage, natural disaster, equipment failure, the sudden cessation of its business (bankruptcy not withstanding) and so on, as well as service level agreements for uptime and the ability to log onto the application independently of the cloud provider (for more information, see Section A.5 below discussing SaaS Escrow). Finally, the cloud provider should disclose any audit protocols it has adapted to ensure its existing protocols and methodologies are followed. The customer should also ask the cloud provider about any previous security problems or service interruptions.

(x) Customizations and Configurations

In evaluating the use of a potential application, the customer should consider what customizations are required and what required functionality, if any, can be achieved through configuration. Configuration refers to already existing functionality within an application, while customization refers to the creation of new functionality. Customization beyond configuration increases the customer's level of risk, as the customer is now dependent on a third party to modify and implement those modifications.

For those applications that require customization and implementation to meet the customer's needs, the question arises whether the SaaS services and customization services should be addressed in one agreement or in two distinct agreements. Many customers opt for two separate agreements: one with the SaaS provider and one with the implementation services provider, as they believe separate agreements will allow the customer to reach contract quicker by negotiating one contract with the SaaS provider and one with the customization vendor, as opposed to a lengthy master agreement with the cloud provider acting as the prime contractor who then must negotiate a second agreement with the other customization and implementation vendor who acts as a subcontractor to the cloud provider. Two separate agreements may be negotiated faster, especially if the customer starts with the vendors' template agreements as a basis of negotiation.

Conversely, some customers believe this structure adds significant risk if the aggregated solution fails to function properly, as each vendor will likely blame any failure on the other. Conversely, a prime-subcontractor relationship may cause margin stacking, resulting in a higher ultimate cost for the customer, as the prime contractor will likely add a premium onto the subcontractor's price in light of the additional risk the prime contractor has assumed.

Customization also raises the question of when does the cloud agreement's term begin and when does billing start? Does the cloud agreement and billing begin on contract signature or only when the customizations have been completed, accepted, and the customer is using the customized application for productive purposes? Prudent parties should ensure that the agreement clearly states when services commence and when billing commences.

(xi) Indemnification

As with any commercial agreement, indemnification plays an important role in allocating and managing the parties' risk. While indemnities have traditionally addressed third-party claims, both parties should provide a direct cross-indemnity to the other, although the breadth of their respective indemnification obligations will likely differ. Many parties will seek an indemnity for breach of contract, but doing so cannot be justified, as each party's remedy should lie in a breach of contract claim. Further, many vendors argue that an indemnity for the vendor's negligence is not appropriate for SaaS, where vendor personnel are not onsite at the customer's premises.

Customers should seek to have the cloud provider indemnify them for:

- intellectual property infringement claims arising from intellectual property selected and used by the cloud provider;
- compliance with laws;
- breach of confidentiality; and
- breach of the agreement's security obligations and standards by the cloud provider.

In those situations where the cloud provider will not agree to indemnify the customer, the customer should seek to have the cloud provider pay for any costs associated with a party's notification obligations under law or the terms of the contract. These may include investigating the breach, notifying the affected individuals and entities of any breach of security incident, staffing any help desk assisting with questions regarding the breach of security incident, and the cost of any credit monitoring.

Model language for the cloud provider's indemnity obligations follows:

> *Vendor will defend, indemnify and hold Subscriber and its respective officers, directors, employees and agents (each an "Indemnified Party") harmless from and against all liabilities, damages, claims, costs and expenses (including reasonable attorneys' fees and costs and expenses of expert witnesses) or other losses (collectively, "Losses") brought by a third party against an Indemnified Party arising from the acts or omissions of Vendor, its employees, affiliates, subcontractors or agents in the performance of the Services.*

Vendors should seek to have the customer indemnify them for:

- intellectual property infringement claims arising from the customer's content as well as any intellectual property selected and used by the customer;
- compliance with laws;
- breach of confidentiality;
- defamatory statements; violation of law; and
- breach of the cloud provider's acceptable use policy (AUP) including non-compliance with the cloud provider's security policy.

Model language for the customer's indemnity obligations follows: *You agree to indemnify, defend and hold Us, our affiliates and licensors, each of our and their business partners, and each of our and their respective employees, officers, directors and representatives harmless from and against any and all claims, losses, damages, liabilities, judgments, penalties, fines, costs and expenses (including reasonable attorneys' fees) arising out of or in connection with any claim arising out of:*

> (i) *Your use of the Services in a manner not authorized by this Agreement, and/or in violation of the applicable restrictions, AUPs, and/or applicable law,*
>
> (ii) *Your Application, Your content, or the combination of either with other applications, content or processes, including but not limited to any claim involving infringement or misappropriation of third-party rights and/or the use, development,*

design, manufacture, production, advertising, promotion and/or marketing of Your Application and/or Your content,

(iii) *Your violation of any term or condition of this Agreement including, without limitation, Your representations and warranties, or*

(iv) *You or Your employees' or personnel's negligence or wilful misconduct.*

(xii) Representations and Warranties

From the cloud provider's perspective, the underlying agreement should state that the services and documentation are provided "AS IS" without warranty of any kind. In almost every case, the representations and warranties provided in a SaaS agreement will not be as fulsome as those set forth in an on-premise license.

Customers should carefully consider whether a complete disclaimer of warranties is appropriate, as the cloud provider should be willing to warrant its conformance with the documentation during the term of the agreement as well as any implementation and configuration services.

To the extent that it is able to do so, a prudent customer should have the cloud provider represent and warrant that:

- the contracted application will be interoperable with the customer's legacy systems;
- the format of the customer's data will be compatible with the cloud providers' information technology standards;
- use of the cloud provider's services will not infringe on a third party's intellectual property rights;
- the cloud provider will use and update anti-virus software;
- there will be no material reduction in functionality during the term of the service agreement;
- the cloud provider will comply with all appliable laws; and
- the cloud provider will comply with the agreed-upon security standards.

Conversely, many cloud providers seek to have the customer represent and warrant that it will not use the cloud provider's services for illegal purposes or in a manner that infringes on a third party's intellectual property rights.

(xiii) Limitation of Liability

To understand and quantify its risk, the customer should undertake due diligence that includes a review of the cloud provider's technology platform and security practices. Doing so will allow the customer to potentially mitigate any risks associated with the purchased services. By purchasing SaaS services, the customer is outsourcing a service that it did not want to provide itself as well as a set of operational, compliance, and legal risks that it did not want to assume. Thus, a cloud provider should not be expected to assume a risk that the customer itself was unwilling to assume, as the cloud provider is not an insurer of the customer's risks.

It is in both parties' interest to limit risk. The mere fact that personally identifiable information (PII) is exposed does not necessarily mean that the cloud provider (as opposed to the customer or a third party) did anything wrong or that it could have prevented the breach. Some industry commentators assert that no cloud provider (or government agency or nonprofit) can guarantee against sophisticated intrusions and all technology failures. See Chapter 5.I.1 for a discussion of "Zero Day" Events. One solution may be to have the parties share any potential liability. Although the structure of any compromise is subject to negotiation, one compromise may be to have the cloud provider assume liability up to a certain dollar amount, with the customer assuming any excess liability.

Some breaches should naturally result in greater liability on the cloud provider's behalf. If a cloud provider fails to follow its stated security procedures, there is justification to seek a larger or even unlimited liability. In many contracts, intentional actions impose unlimited contractual liability on the cloud provider's behalf, at least after negotiation by knowledgeable customers.

The actual limits of liability will depend on the facts of the underlying transaction:

- What is the nature of the stored/processed data?
- Is the data highly confidential and proprietary or a mere aggregation of data that may be re-assembled from other sources?
- To what extent does the data set include data owned by third parties who have entrusted it to the customer, who may have its own obligations and liability under such arrangements?
- How much revenue is the cloud provider receiving?
- How much risk is arising from the underlying technology platform?
- Is the customer utilizing a public or a private cloud?
- If the cloud provider offers premium services and/or additional security protection at a higher fee, has the customer elected same?

Almost all cloud providers insist on a waiver of any special incident or consequential damages and seek to limit their liability to any service-level credits. Any overarching cap is usually tied to a multiple of the monthly fees received by the cloud provider within a set time period, e.g., three months (though many customers will negotiate longer durations). Common exclusions to the limitation of liability include intellectual property infringement, gross negligence, wilful misconduct, and some indemnification obligations.

Customers should carefully consider whether a disclaimer of indirect damages is appropriate, as in the event of a breach, a significant portion of the customer's damages may be indirect damages. For example, the destruction or loss of data will result in substantial consequential or indirect damages. The sensitively of the data in question will likely determine the importance for a customer to recover its consequential/ indirect damages.

At least one court has voided a limitation of liability where the cloud provider acted in a reckless or grossly negligent manner resulting in a substantial loss of the customer's data. *Clark Street Wine and Spirits v. Emporos Systems Corp., Italy*, 754 F. Supp. 2d 474, 481–82 (E.D.N.Y. 2010) ("In view of great damage to customers and business that breaches of a computer system may cause, a jury may find that the responsible entities, such as [the cloud provider], should take special precautions to protect these systems.").

(xiv) Term

SaaS agreements often have a relatively short term as opposed to on-premise licenses. Given the trend of failing prices over the last several years, a fixed-priced, shorter-term (one-to two-year) cloud agreement is often favored by the customer.

Many cloud providers require buyers of subscription-based services to commit to purchase a minimum volume or dollar amount for a set period of time. In doing so, cloud providers argue that "revenue recognition" rules require the cloud provider to seek revenue minimums and committed term lengths to recognize the associated revenue. Contractual minimums also allow the cloud provider to recover its upfront research, development, infrastructure, and other service-enabling costs incurred in establishing the software availability. From the customer's perspective, minimum commitments create the potential for significant financial risk. Therefore, prudent customers will seek to negotiate shorter minimum terms and favorable termination rights to ensure financial flexibility and avoid limiting their options.

(xv) Suspension and Termination

(x) Suspension

Most cloud providers insist on the contractual right to immediately suspend access or use of the services in the event the customer undertakes any actions that:

- violate the law,
- violate the cloud provider's acceptable use policy (AUP),
- adversely impact the ability of other customers to use the service,
- access other customers' data,
- spam,
- create offensive content,
- cause intellectual property infringement, or
- endanger the security of the system.

See Form D.5.1 and D.5.2 for model Acceptable Use Policies.

While most cloud providers will not relinquish the right of suspension, prudent customers often try to limit suspension solely to material violations of the underlying agreement that threaten the security of the cloud service. In addition, they seek to negotiate a notice-and-cure period for inadvertent violations to avoid an immediate interruption of the customer's access to the services. While some cloud providers will agree to provide notice and a very short cure period, others are unwilling to do so.

(y) Termination for Breach

Some large customers take the position that the cloud provider may not terminate the agreement for any reason, including the customer's nonpayment, arguing that the cloud provider's remedy lies solely in a suit for breach of contract. Further, the customer's access and use rights shall continue during the termination process. They do so in the belief that the services are mission-critical and cannot be easily transferred to a new cloud provider. From the cloud provider's perspective, the requirement to bring a suit delays its remedy and increases its costs while creating a significant administrative and financial burden.

(z) Termination for Convenience

Many customers seek the ability to terminate their agreement for convenience. While termination for convenience provisions are common in many services agreements, the customer's ability to terminate the agreement and the cost to do so will depend on a number of factors, including the pricing model used by the cloud provider and the cost of any capital expenditures the cloud provider made on the customer's behalf.

A SaaS subscription is a *right* to access and use, not *an obligation to use* the services. Thus, the vendor has fully completed its contractual obligations and is entitled to full payment for the entire subscription period as soon as it has provided the customer with access to the SaaS service. From the customer's perspective, there is no contractual justification or obligation for a refund if a customer elects to stop using the service after receiving access. This is a challenging concept for customers who perceive the SaaS service as being delivered monthly, and do not expect to pay for the remaining subscription period after terminating the agreement.

If the cloud provider is providing services under a metered model without a commitment, the customer may have the right to terminate the agreement for convenience but under a subscription model, where pricing discounts are provided based on volume commitments that termination for convenience would negate, cloud providers are unlikely to accept a termination for convenience provision. If the cloud provider purchased hardware and software on the customer's behalf, another factor that will impact the customer's ability to terminate for convenience is the amount of any unamortized capital expenditures. In such cases, cloud providers will most likely require the customer to pay the cost of any unamortized capital expenditures as a condition precedent to any termination for convenience.

Also important from the cloud provider's perspective: revenue is recognized rateably over the life of the contract, and if the contract may be terminated for convenience, the cloud provider will likely be unable to potentially recognize the total contract value to investors, lenders or other constituents.

If the underlying agreement provides the cloud provider the right to make unilateral changes to the parties' agreement or the underlying application, the customer should insist on the right to terminate the agreement for convenience without charge in the event any such change has a material impact on the services purchased by the customer.

Notwithstanding a customer's inability to terminate for convenience under most SaaS agreements, some vendors allow a customer to terminate upon payment of an early termination fee. Model language follows:

> *Subscriber shall have the right to terminate a Service Order under this Agreement at any time during the Term without cause by giving Vendor written notice of such termination, and paying Vendor: (i) fifty percent (50%) of the Service delivery fees remaining under the applicable Service Order(s) if Subscriber terminates the applicable Service Order(s) within twelve (12) months of executing the Service Order(s), thirty-five percent (35%) of the Service delivery fees remaining under the applicable Service Order(s) if Subscriber terminates the applicable Service Order(s) between twelve (12) months and twenty-four (24) months from executing the applicable Service Order(s), and twenty-five percent (25%) of the Service delivery fees remaining under the applicable Service Order(s) if Subscriber terminates the applicable Service Order(s) after twenty-four (24) months, (ii)*

all outstanding invoices, (iii) any work in progress performed but unbilled by Vendor, and (v) if Subscriber was granted a discount or waiver with respect to any recurring or non-recurring charges based on the duration of Subscriber's term commitment, an amount equal to the discount received by Subscriber.

The amount of Service delivery fees remaining shall be calculated by multiplying the number of months remaining in the term of the Service Order by the monthly fee that would have been due based on the greater of: a) the fees associated with the number of Users specified in the Service Order(s); or b) the number of actual Users for the month for which Subscriber was most recently invoiced. It is agreed that Vendor's damages if Services are cancelled prior to the completion of the Term shall be difficult or impossible to ascertain, thus the amounts set forth herein are intended to establish liquidated damages in the event of cancellation and are not intended as a penalty.

(xvi) Transition Rights

Perhaps the most important issue for the customer, but perhaps under-managed, is transition rights. In the event of the early or natural termination of the agreement, the customer wants to ensure an orderly transition of its business to a new cloud provider. Also known as the "Exit Strategy" or "Exit Plan," most good customer Program Management Offices (PMOs) contemplate an exit strategy as a part of their Governance, Risk and Compliance ("GRC") policy—that is, if they have a GRC policy.

The agreement should set out in detail the time period during which the cloud provider must provide transition support to the customer, the cost of such services, and preferably the process for coordinating the parties (possibly including not only the end user and initial cloud provider, but also the successor cloud provider, if2 any). The cloud provider should be contractually obligated to provide services during the transition period at the same service level as it did during the agreement term and to fully cooperate with the customer during the transition of its data to an alternative provider or back in-house. In the event the agreement was terminated due to the customer's breach, the cloud provider should strictly limit the length of any transition period to limit the time and effort required in the transition effort and possibly require pre-payment, including any professional services necessary to extract and migrate data to a new solution.

Finally, a prudent customer should ensure the underlying agreement sets forth in detail the customer's rights upon the termination of the agreement and that any such transition will not interrupt its business. To that end, the customer should obtain:

- a contractual commitment regarding its right to continue to use the services during the transition period,
- the right to the immediate return of its data in the contractually agreed format so that it can be utilized by any subsequent cloud provider,
- an agreement on a rate card establishing the rates for any transition assistance fees, and
- a commitment to cooperate with any new cloud provider, preferably for a specified duration.

At the same time, prudent customers will seek to require the cloud provider to retain their data for some period of time (30-60 days) while they identify a new cloud provider or are in transition. Cloud providers are hesitant to store data for any length of time due to the cost of storage unless they are compensated for doing so. Model language illustrating this point follows:

> *1.1 Upon request, at no additional charge, Subscriber may retrieve Subscriber Data via Subscriber's secure FTP site in the same format in which the Subscriber Data was originally inputted into the Solution. Alternatively, Subscriber Data can be returned in a mutually agreed format at a scope and price to be agreed. Vendor will maintain a copy of Subscriber Data for no more than three (3) months following termination of the Agreement, after which time any Subscriber Data not retrieved will be destroyed.*
>
> *1.2 At the end of the six (6) months all employee data must be purged in a manner compliant with COPPA, HIPAA and FERPA regulations. Upon destruction of the data, Vendor shall represent in writing to the Subscriber that it has destroyed all CDI and no longer has any CDI in its possession or control.*
>
> *1.3 The Subscriber will destroy all physical copies of licensed product or control or terminate access to the Solution.*

In the event the cloud provider is also providing access to a specific application, the agreement should address ownership and use of the license after termination of the agreement. From the cloud provider's perspective, the underlying agreement between the cloud provider and the customer should clearly state that the customer does not receive any rights for future use of the application and that upon termination, the customer's only right is to port its data to a new cloud provider. If the customer purchased a software license as part of the services, the customer should be contractually entitled to transfer the license to the new cloud provider. At the time the agreement is negotiated, the customer should understand its rights, including its transfer rights, if it is "purchasing a license." Although the customer may have paid to "purchase" a license and the cloud provider granted the customer access to use software through a license, the license may terminate with the agreement and prohibit the customer from taking the software to the new cloud provider.

(xvii) Litigation and E-Discovery Considerations

The need to recover data in response to e-discovery obligations is another issue that needs to be specifically addressed in the agreement. The customer must ensure that not only its data will be protected, but also that it will be easily recoverable from the cloud. The parties should set forth in detail how the data will be organized and stored, how it can be searched and, if necessary, extracted. The customer wants to ensure that in the event it must preserve and produce the data, the data can be easily retrieved and searched, i.e., by date, location, custodian, data source, etc. The parties should also determine whether metadata will be preserved, and if so, what type.

An increasing concern is the ability of a party utilizing the cloud to comply with its e-discovery obligations, as a party is required to preserve and disclose all information within its control, even if it resides on a third-party's servers. *Pension Committee of the University of Montreal Pension Plan et al. v. Bank of America Securities, LLC*, 685 F. Supp. 2d 456, 465 (S.D.N.Y. 2010). Courts have interpreted "control" broadly to include not only information in a party's possession, but also information that a party has the right to access or obtain. *See Rock v. Stripling*, 736 F.2d 650 (11th Cir. 1984).

A customer must understand the cloud provider's processes, such as archiving in comparison to the customer's record management policies. For example:

- Will the customer be able to conduct a forensic evaluation to establish the authenticity of any data stored in the cloud?
- Will the customer have the ability to preserve any data in its custody and control?
- Can the cloud provider implement and comply with the customer's document retention policies?
- Will metadata be preserved?
- How frequently does the cloud provider erase or overwrite its storage devices?

A well-drafted provision also will establish the time line in which the cloud provider must produce the data in response to the customer's request, as well as the format in which the data will be produced. To the extent possible, the parties should set forth the cost for identifying and producing the relevant data at the time of contract execution.

Another consideration is the impact of storing data and documents in the cloud on the attorney-client privilege:

- How will storing data and documents in the cloud affect the customer's ability to claim the attorney-client privilege?
- By doing so, has the customer waived the attorney-client privilege?

The model language below protects the customer's interests in regard to e-discovery:

<u>E-Discovery Support</u>

(a) *Within ten (10) business days after the Effective Date, Vendor shall provide to Subscriber such information as may be reasonably necessary to describe, in non-technical terms, the data processing systems, data, databases, computer programs and backup media, and the means available to Subscriber to access, retrieve, search and download all Subscriber data throughout the term of this Agreement, including renewal terms, that comprise the Service in connection with the creation, manipulation, storage, retrieval and use of Subscriber's data.*

(b) *Upon written notice from Subscriber, Vendor shall, within a period of time designated by Subscriber, take all steps necessary to preserve and prevent the destruction and/or alteration of Subscriber data and related metadata, including data that identifies when and by whom Subscriber data was created and how Subscriber's data was formatted, and backup media that contain Subscriber data and metadata, as Subscriber may direct in order for Subscriber to meet legal obligations, including, without limitation, obligations arising from litigation and/or investigations and such other legal obligations that Subscriber may reasonably anticipate.*

(c) *Upon written notice from Subscriber, Vendor shall collect and produce to Subscriber, in a forensically appropriate manner as Subscriber may reasonably specify, at a date and time of Subscriber's designation, Subscriber's data and related metadata created in connection therewith in order to support Subscriber's endeavors to meet legal obligations that arise from, without limitation, litigation and/or investigations and such other legal obligations that Subscriber may reasonably anticipate.*

(d) *In the event of any conflict or inconsistency between the provisions of this Section and any policy that Subscriber may provide to Vendor regarding data retention and disposal, the provisions of this Section shall control.*

(xviii) Export Issues

Both parties should understand the application of U.S. export laws to the remote storage of data and the remote access to applications. In January 2009, the Bureau of Industry and Security ("BIS") issued an advisory opinion on the applicability of the Export Administration Regulations ("EAR") to the transfer of data through cloud computing. The opinion stated that providing computation capacity services through the cloud is "not subject to the EAR, as the service provider is not shipping or transmitting any commodity, software or technology to the user," but that shipping or transferring software that is subject to the EAR would constitute an export. Further, in the event data is transferred via the cloud, the entity that uploads any export-controlled materials is considered to be the exporter and must comply with all export regulations. The cloud service provider is not responsible for inquiring about a user or customer's nationality, and cloud users abroad are not the exporter, as they are outside the United States. https://www.bis.doc.gov/index.php/documents/advisory-opinions/527-application-of-ear-to-grid-and-cloud-computing-services/file.

In January 2011, BIS issued a second advisory opinion confirming that cloud service providers are not exporters, and thus their foreign IT personnel are not deemed export recipients because the cloud service provider is not an exporter. Cloud providers employing foreign nationals are still subject to the deemed export provisions for their own disclosures to foreign nationals. https://www.bis.doc.gov/index.php/documents/advisory-opinions/533-cloud-computing-and-deemed-exports/file. For a more detailed discussion of the deemed export rule, see Chapter 7.L.5.

On November 13, 2014, BIS issued a third advisory opinion providing that cloud providers who provide access to SaaS services where the user cannot download the underlying software but only utilizes the software as a service in the cloud or on a server, does not constitute an export. ttps://www.bis.doc.gov/index.php/documents/advisory-opinions/1098-cloud-based-storefronts/file (("[b]ecause there is no export of software, there is no license requirement").

(xix) Bankruptcy Concerns

One concern for customers is that, in the event of the cloud provider's bankruptcy, the customer may be unable to take advantage of the protections offered under Section 365(n) of the bankruptcy code. Under Section 365(n), if a bankrupt cloud provider rejects an executory contract/license, the licensee retains its license rights to the underlying intellectual property.

SaaS may be considered a service and thus outside the purview of Section 365(n). If the agreement grants access to the software by means of a service contract, the customer will not necessarily receive a license to the underlying intellectual property and will lack the right to continue its use of the software. To protect its interests, the customer should ensure that the underlying agreement includes language stating that the customer is licensing the software and that the "license grant" falls under Section 365(n). *See* Forms Q.2.G.2 and Q.2.G.3. This contingency may not always be contemplated by the customer if they have no intention of moving the software "on premises." Therefore, it should become standard practice to insist upon such provisions in the event that the customer requires application continuity, as is discussed in Section 5 below.

Including such language does not necessarily protect the customer in the event of the cloud provider's bankruptcy and the cloud provider's (or its trustee in U.S. bankruptcy court) subsequent rejection of the license. While the customer would still have rights to the software, the cloud provider would not be obligated to provide hosting, maintenance, and support services. It may be difficult for the customer to obtain such services, much less on short notice. To limit the impact of any interruption, the customer should require the cloud provider to escrow the software and grant the customer the right to host and maintain the software in the event of the cloud provider's bankruptcy. This language also serves to support the customer's position that the underlying agreement is a license of intellectual property, in the event the cloud provider contests the customer's right to access the software. While this is not a perfect solution, it will likely lessen the impact of the cloud provider's bankruptcy and any subsequent rejection of the underlying agreement.

From the cloud provider's perspective, the customer's remedy lies in receiving a refund for the remainder of the agreement's term. Alternatively, a customer utilizing a software solution can purchase the services through a third party other than the software owner, which will hopefully mitigate any risk in the event the software owner ceases to continue as a going concern.

For a more detailed discussion of the issues involved with the bankruptcy of software cloud providers, see Chapter 27. *See* also Form H.1 § 3.1.2.

(xx) Compliance Obligations

Customers often seek to transfer their compliance and regulatory obligations to the cloud provider. Prudent cloud providers will reject the customer's efforts to do so, as the obligation legally rests with the customer, and the customer cannot escape its liability by contractually requiring the cloud provider to assume such obligations. Agreeing to assume such responsibility is very risky for the cloud provider as, in most cases, the cloud provider lacks the requisite industry knowledge to fully understand the risk it is assuming as well as the cost to comply with such obligations. This is especially true with consumer data laws such as HIPAA, where the cloud provider may not know the type of data being stored

Some customers seek to add language obligating the vendor to "co-operate" with the customer in meeting the customer's compliance obligations: "*Vendor will cooperate with Subscriber to enable Subscriber to comply with its obligations under Data Protection Laws as they relate to Personal Data.*" Prudent vendors will reject such language as it is ambiguous, potentially giving the customer the ability to terminate the agreement if the vendor does not "co-operate."

(xxi) Acceptable Use Policies (AUPs)

Acceptable Use Policies (AUPs) are used by cloud providers to establish the parameters of the customer's access and use of the cloud provider's network and services. The customer's failure to abide by these requirements may result in the suspension of the customer's ability to access the cloud provider's network and services and, in extreme cases, the termination of such rights. Cloud providers usually set forth a list of prohibited activities, which may include the following:

- Any activities that are illegal, that violate the rights of others, or that may be harmful to others.
- Content that infringes or misappropriates the intellectual property or proprietary rights of others.
- Content that is defamatory, obscene, abusive, or invasive of privacy.
- Content that may damage, interfere with, surreptitiously intercept, or expropriate any system, program, or data, including viruses, Trojan horses, worms, and time bombs.
- Actions that violate the security or integrity of any network, computer or communications system, software application, or network or computing device.
- Accessing or using the cloud provider's network without permission, including attempting to probe, scan, or test the vulnerability of the cloud provider's network or to breach any security or authentication measures used by the cloud provider's network.
- Forging TCP-IP packet headers, e-mail headers, or any part of a message describing its origin or route.
- Monitoring or crawling of the cloud provider's network that impairs or disrupts the cloud provider's network being monitored or crawled.
- Inundating a target with communications requests so the target either cannot respond to legitimate traffic or responds so slowly that it becomes ineffective.
- Interfering with the proper functioning of the cloud provider's network, including any deliberate attempt to overload a system by mail bombing, news bombing, broadcast attacks, or flooding techniques.
- Using manual or electronic means to avoid any use limitations placed on the cloud provider's network, such as access and storage restrictions.
- Distributing, publishing, sending, or facilitating the sending of unsolicited mass e-mail or other messages, promotions, advertising, or solicitations ("spam"), including commercial.

See Forms D.5.1 and D.5.2 for model Acceptable Use Policies.

5. SaaS Escrow[1] vs. Business Continuity Services

In traditional "on premise" software license agreements, source code escrow creates the opportunity for a customer to maintain and support the licensed application in the event the licensor declares bankruptcy or fails to meet its contractual obligations. The concept

1. The term "escrow" is losing favor to the term "Recovery Services," which is intended to allow customers to continue to utilize the SaaS application (application continuity) as they work to recover their data, migrate and restore their data to a new solution, and resume business operations.

of escrows, however, does not easily translate to cloud computing, as the cloud provider is providing a service (including the technical environment that hosts the application), not software, and the customer did not purchase a license to the underlying software.

In addition, many vendors do not own the software "stack" that underlies the services they provide. In particular, hosting, infrastructure, and SaaS vendors will often partly base their operations on both other vendors and open-source software. As such, the customer most likely lacks access to the source code for all the software in the stack and cannot escrow the software even if it wants to. Even if the customer could access the required software source code, it would need to successfully re-create the SaaS environment, which would likely be prohibitively expensive and technically challenging. In those situations where the cloud provider owns the software, escrow may be more appropriate, but again, a vendor would likely consider it inappropriate given that the customer purchased services, not software. In the event the cloud provider breaches the agreement or declares bankruptcy, the customer will often be able to purchase the same or similar services from another vendor, at least for mainstream IT needs.

A SaaS escrow usually does not address the customer's need to access its data, which can be more important than accessing the application. Prudent customers should ensure that the agreement addresses the escrow and return of the customer's data unless the customer receives frequent downloads to such data.

Cloud providers usually seek to narrowly define "escrowed materials" to avoid being unduly burdened. Can a cloud provider realistically be expected to escrow all ancillary software required to operate a cloud environment, given most of the required software is third-party software?

Another question that arises is: If there is an escrow release, how much should the customer pay the cloud provider to continue to use the application, given the cloud provider is no longer providing the contracted services? Customers will argue that the true value of the cloud provider's services lies in the hosting and support, not access to the application, justifying the payment of a much lower fee. Cloud providers or a bankruptcy trustee will likely argue that the customer is receiving the benefit of using the application and should thus pay the monthly fee charged prior to the release event.

(a) SaaS Escrow vs. Business Continuity Assurances

A SaaS escrow is more complex than a traditional source code escrow, as the elements required to "reanimate" the SaaS application are often not distinct software solutions that can be easily placed in escrow. Contingency planning is critical to consider all of the potential risks associated with the non-availability of the SaaS technology. This includes proper assessments and solutions to address unforeseen problems that can arise during the term of the commercial relationship.

The escrow solution is meant to provide the customer with the luxury of time to extract and migrate its data to a new solution. The transition should only last 30-60 days, so the exposure to risk relative to the rejection of an executory contract may not last longer than a month or two.

Most cloud providers resist any type of SaaS escrow, given that SaaS solutions are often comprised of many distinct elements cobbled together to provide an integrated solution; moreover, the sometimes rapid rate of changes in the SaaS application might render it difficult to update the deposited code. Some cloud providers are willing to provide exports of the customer's data residing on their systems allowing the customer to access its data if the cloud provider ceases to conduct business. To avoid potential issues, the agreement should clearly state the format in which the data will be provided.

Although challenging, a sophisticated escrow agent can provide Recovery Services for a SaaS solution with many different components. Combining the administrative expertise required in traditional escrow arrangement with the disaster recovery component to the SaaS provider's operating environment, the escrow agent will manage and make available the Recovery Environment to the customer upon some occurrence of a Contingency Trigger. Triggering events may include:

- cessation of business or services
- bankruptcy
- *force majeure*
- material breach of the SLAs
- the cloud provider terminating or sunsetting the relevant product(s).

The Recovery Environment is a replicated environment complete with the capability of restoring services based on the last virtualized instance of the software components and related database. This is managed independently of the cloud provider or its hosting supplier. The onus for securing all contractual permits and licenses is borne from the SaaS Provider at the time the escrow arrangement is established.

Essentially, the customer must consider their contingency plan that extends beyond the cloud provider's disaster recovery capabilities or the cloud provider's desire to cooperate with a customer looking to terminate their relationship. There are three potential contingency plans available to the customer:

1. Take the application on-premises and maintain it independently of the SaaS provider;
2. Find a new Managed Service Provider (MSP) to support and host the application; and
3. Keep the services running long enough to source and migrate data to a new solution.

Depending on the variables (investment in the technology, the business impact of an outage and the ability to support applications), any or all of these contingency plans may be employed. The options are not necessarily mutually exclusive, as some customers may elect to implement a sooner-available approach that may lack some desired functionality or not promise long-term viability as an interim, perhaps necessary solution until a better option that may require more time or investment can be invoked. SaaS Recovery Services should enable these contingency plans by providing the customer with application continuity (and precious time) while it executes its plan.

Regardless of the SaaS solution, it is critical that contingency plans are documented in advance of consummating the business relationship. With a SaaS escrow in place, customers can ensure they are capable of executing the contingency plan independently of the SaaS provider. Typical operational guidance can be summarized as follows:

1. Understand, and perhaps rank or prioritize, potential failure points and insist upon a contingency plan that extends beyond the SaaS provider's capabilities;

2. Determine the customer's contingency plan based on the value of the investment and impact to the business;
3. Establish a well-documented SaaS escrow arrangement to facilitate the contingency plan;
4. Test everything to verify viability of the contingency plan; and
5. Adopt a repeatable process for consistently and safely utilizing SaaS.

The key to overcoming the risks of SaaS is to demonstrate that all of these concerns have been adequately addressed. A comprehensive SaaS escrow service is, in essence, a powerful risk management tool for entities involved on both sides of SaaS relationships. By assuring application and data availability, SaaS escrow helps to foster trust between all parties and to accelerate the sales cycle.

For a more detailed discussion of SaaS escrows, *see* Bruno, *Cloud Computing Protection Strategies: SaaS Escrow for Application Continuity*, https://itak.iaitam.org/cloud-computing-protection-strategies-saas-escrow-for-application-continuity-2/.

For a general overview, *see* Denny, *Survey of Recent Developments in the Law of Cloud Computing and Software as a Service Agreement*, 66 Bus. Law.

(b) Business Continuity

Although traditional escrow companies such as Iron Mountain offer SaaS escrow services, many customers prefer that a SaaS provider provide its customers with business continuity assurance using the services of a hosting provider rather than a third-party escrow provider. These customers believe using a hosting provider is more practical and cost-effective than using a third party to provide services that are a core competency of a hosting provider. They also believe using a hosting provider will protect the customer's access to the application and its data in the event of the SaaS provider's bankruptcy.

An alternative approach is for the SaaS provider to operate multiple data centers, allowing the SaaS provider to maintain business continuity rather than outsourcing business continuity to a third party. Not all products lend themselves to this approach. One challenge is that most SaaS providers will not disclose their system's architecture, even if a confidentiality agreement has been signed, to avoid providing competitive information to potential or actual competitors. Thus, the more advanced its system, the more likely the SaaS provider will resist disclosing in detail its architecture.

A second concern is whether another entity can replicate the SaaS provider's services, even if the SaaS provider has disclosed its architecture. In most cases, the answer is probably no. Consequently, even if the SaaS provider selected Iron Mountain or another third-party provider, in most cases, the third party will be unable to meet the requirements of the SaaS provider's customers.

Many SaaS providers operate at least two data centers in locations where the natural disaster profile geographically (i.e., the likelihood of an earthquake or hurricane and consequent unavailability of electricity and/or needed personnel) is different and unlikely to shut down both centers simultaneously. These centers are usually not interchangeable, running in parallel. Thus, in a worst-case scenario, the SaaS provider will have at least one backup center to maintain its operations. If an event is so significant that it shuts down all of the SaaS provider's data centers, the event will probably affect the SaaS provider's customers beyond impacting their system availability.

In those situations where the customer is purchasing IaaS, the customer is purchasing access to an operating system or a virtual server, and thus, there is really no aspect of the service that can be escrowed. Most customers do not see the value in the right to obtain source code as they do not want to maintain and support the code upon the occurrence of a release event. Further, they lack the knowledge, technical personnel or finances to assume responsibility for maintaining a third-party software solution. Practically speaking, the customer wants a working system. If the software fails, the customer still needs a working system and the release of the escrowed software does not resolve the problem.

Some practitioners nonetheless believe that an escrow provision is an important aspect of a cloud agreement. While they agree that customers do not want the underlying source code, they believe that escrows can serve as a strong incentive for service providers to perform. This is especially important in those instances where the cloud service provider owns the computing resource, and there will be no viable alternative provider if the licensor/provider goes bankrupt. While the perception is more so for leverage purposes if the investment is significant enough, a customer may want to consider taking the entire application on premises.

Some attorneys seek to implement a bifurcated approach. First, they seek a grant of an object code license to the cloud provider's system to be run by the customer outside of the cloud and then establish a source code escrow for the licensed software.

This approach is essentially a precursor to the current solution as it is possible to escrow object code and data (release on demand) for customers wishing to replicate the run-time environment. If they want to maintain the technology long-term, they will need the source code managed via a notice release process. Neither this hybrid nor traditional source code-only approach has been well received, and with the evolution of cloud-based technologies application integration, data enrichment has become virtually impossible to support operationally and financially.

For a discussion of why source code escrows are impractical for SaaS agreements, *see* Osei, *Pouring New Wine into Old Wineskins: Why "On Premise" Software Source Code Escrow Arrangements Are Ill-Suited for Remotely Hosted "Off Premise" Software as a Service License Agreement*, 39 J.C. & U.L. 383 (2013).

(c) Release Events

While conceptually an on-premise software escrow and a SaaS escrow are similar, the release events are usually quite different. Under a SaaS agreement, the customer is purchasing services with a clearly stated level of access and performance usually reinforced by service levels. Thus, most release events are focused on the failure of the cloud provider to provide access in conformance with the agreed-upon services levels. See Subsections (v) to (ix) in the model language below. Customers are cognizant that the payment of service-level credits and liquidated damages will not protect the customer's business in the event the cloud provider consistently fails to meet its service-level obligations. As such, a customer should carefully consider those events which are so significant that they justify a release event. Model language follows:

> *The Deposit Materials shall be released to Beneficiary upon the occurrence of any of the following events:*

(i) Depositor's decision to terminate Support Services for the Products;

(ii) Depositor taking any action under law that will cause both the dissolution and the corporate existence of Depositor;

(iii) Depositor has availed itself of or has been subjected to by any third party, a proceeding in bankruptcy in which Depositor is named debtor and which, in the case of a proceeding commenced by a third party, Depositor has not caused to be discharged within 60 days of notice of such proceeding;

(iv) Depositor's material breach of this Agreement to the extent such breach is not cured within 30 days after receipt of written notice of the breach;

(v) A Critical Level Issue occurs which is not resolved within one week after it has been reported by Customer or independently identified by Depositor;

(vi) Depositor's failure to resolve three or more Critical Level Issues in any 12-month period within 72 hours after each has been reported by Customer or independently identified by Depositor;

(vii) Any event, including a Force Majeure Event, occurs that keeps Depositor from providing the hosting services or Support Services required to be performed under the Subscription Agreement for more than 30 days in any 90-day period;

(viii) The Availability Standard is less than 95% for three consecutive months or for more than three months during any 12-month period; and/or

(ix) The Response Standard is more than 1.750 seconds for three consecutive months or for more than three months during any 12-month period.

B. Hosting

1. Overview

In a hosting model, the customer pays the hosting provider for some combination of:

- facilities, network and security,
- hardware and software, and
- management of such hardware and software.

Customers select from a variety of standard components and services offered by the hosting provider. In some instances, the hosting provider may offer custom services. The customer is responsible for managing its own content and for selecting the appropriate level of security for its site and/or hosted applications.

Web hosting and cloud computing are different models, as web hosting provides the customer with a fixed server or a portion of a single server, while cloud computing offers the benefit of many servers all working together as one. Examples of web hosting include allowing small customers to build and operate small websites, and enterprise web hosting, where large businesses contract with large third parties (i.e., internet service providers (ISPs)) to host their sites. Another difference is that cloud hosting offers more flexibility to scale quickly and pay for what the user actually consumes as opposed to having to purchase a fixed amount. Further, cloud hosting relies on multi-tenancy, which drives cost-efficiencies—the hallmark of cloud computing.

The simplest form of hosting is collocation, where the customer retains ownership of all hardware and software, and the hosting provider supplies space for racks of equipment and power within a data center, Internet connectivity, and basic monitoring that the equipment is online—commonly known as "power, pipe, and ping." From a software licensing perspective, the collocation model differs little from the on-premises licensing model between vendor and customer. The hosting provider is merely providing housing for the equipment on which the software resides; the customer is solely responsible for the purchase, maintenance, and use of both the equipment and the software as well as all content the customer places on the site/hosting environment. However, since the hosting provider has physical access to the application, the customer may want this acknowledged in its license agreement with the vendor.

In a managed hosting model, the hosting provider is responsible for managing and maintaining the customer's equipment and/or software in the hosting provider's data center, as well as for providing digital security services (e.g., firewalls, vulnerability testing), high availability services, monitoring services, Internet and/or dedicated access to the customer's hosted sites, physical security (i.e., limited, monitored access to both the overall facility and the customer's rented subset within it), and the like. The hardware may be owned by the hosting provider, or may be supplied by the customer.

The customer is responsible for purchasing the software the customer needs. The customer's hosting environment may consist of equipment and software dedicated to the customer's use, or the customer may purchase segments of a shared physical environment with logical partitioning ("virtual servers").

Additionally, many software vendors and licensees delegate the management of their software to third parties who "host" and maintain the software on the "hosting provider's" servers. Known as "managed hosting," this model allows both customers and software vendors to potentially reduce their costs while increasing the efficiency in which the software is utilized.

The discussion that follows focuses on managed hosting, where the hosting provider has license rights and/or responsibilities with regards to the licensed software that is part of the customer's hosting environment.

2. Dedicated vs. Shared Hosting

The two principal types of hosting are dedicated hosting, also known as outsourced managed hosting, and shared hosting.

(a) Dedicated Hosting

Under a dedicated hosting model, the hardware/server and software architecture provided by the hosting provider is dedicated solely to the use of a particular customer.

The hosting provider may provide a variety of services including security services, monitoring of the hardware and software, technical support, as well as backup services. By leasing the entire server, the customer can exercise greater control over its environment, including selecting the operating system, hardware, and the parameters under which support will be provided. Services offered by a vendor may include updates to the operating system and application, technical support, security, firewall and anti-virus updates, disaster recovery and backups, load balancing among servers (e.g., common to cover multiple physical locations), and database administration.

(b) Shared Hosting

Under a shared hosting model, a hosting infrastructure (network, security, server hardware) is shared by multiple customers. Virtual (i.e., software-created) partitions are created within a shared server ("server virtualization") so that customer data and other software applications can be dedicated to each customer. Because the server is shared, system administrative services are included. This model is attractive for small customers who may not be able to afford a dedicated hosting environment.

3. The Benefits and Drawbacks of Hosting

(a) Benefits

From the customer's perspective, hosting allows the customer to reduce or avoid making a large financial investment in infrastructure technology and IT support staff. The hosting provider is responsible for the support and maintenance of the servers and their software, technical support, security, and disaster recovery and backups. The hosting provider can usually provide a higher level of expertise and technology than the customer would be able to do on its own (e.g., providing highly available, geographically diverse environments, data centers that meet regulatory standards for security, and 24/7/365 support and response to security incidents).

In some scenarios, hosting lowers the cost of technology services as it allows licensees to "share" expensive hardware and software, theoretically allowing the cost to be amortized over a number of licensees. The customer is able to scale quickly up and down as needed, paying only for the services it uses. Even when the customer bears the cost of dedicated hardware and software, the cost may be less than if the customer purchased the required technology itself as the hosting provider often has vendor contracts that provide significant discounts based on volume purchases. Customers who have their own enterprise-wide agreements with the applicable vendors may choose to provide the hardware and/or software themselves.

(b) Drawbacks

One drawback to hosting is that the customer does not "control its destiny." The customer's software applications, which may be critical to the success of the customer's business, are, at least to some extent, under the control of the hosting provider. The customer is now dependent on the hosting provider meeting its contractual obligations. If the hosting provider has significant down time or the hardware or software is not properly maintained, the customer may be left with very few practical remedies. This is especially true if the hosting provider's liability is limited under its contract with the customer.

Hosting does not always result in a lower cost to the customer. Many customers require their own servers for security purposes, requiring the cost of such hardware to be directly borne by the customer, increasing its costs. Further, software licensors are often unwilling to provide discounts beyond those already offered for volume purchases. Unless the customer retains a qualified technology staff, the customer may be forced to use the hosting provider's staff to maintain its site, usually at an increased cost.

4. Issues for Consideration in Hosting Agreements

When entering into a hosting agreement, the parties should ensure that the scope of services to be provided by the hosting provider is clearly delineated. The scope of services should include performance metrics for the hosting provider's services, including: • minimum internet bandwidth,

- availability,
- server response time,
- help desk response time, and
- security.

In addition, the hosting provider should commit to providing additional support as needed, including uploading customer content when requested, creating and storing remote backups on a daily basis with geo-redundancy, ensuring security of the site, and maintaining server activity logs.

Force majeure provisions are usually inappropriate in hosting agreements, as the customer is paying the hosting provider for agreed-upon performance standards, including availability and geo-redundancy. A prudent customer may strive to clarify that any such exculpatory "act of God" "boilerplate" does not remove or immunize the hosting provider's ongoing responsibility to supply and deploy backup power, adequate staff, and current anti-virus software, and should specify whether backup telecommunications supply or bandwidth is expected. If the hosting provider will be accessing the customer's content to maintain and support the site, the provider should be granted a license to access and use such content solely in connection with its obligation to maintain and support the site.

Those events allowing the parties to terminate the agreement should be stated in detail, along with any transition services and the notice period for any termination of services. If the hosting provider has made a significant capital outlay to meet the customer's requirements, the hosting provider is unlikely to allow the customer to terminate for convenience without payment of an early termination fee, usually equating to the hosting provider's unamortized capital expenditure, its wind down costs and an element of profit. Both parties should seek to negotiate a sufficient limitation of liability to protect themselves in the event of a breach, with the hosting provider often seeking to limit its liability to several months' fees.

See Chapter 6.D for a more detailed discussion of force majeure.

5. *Licensing Models*

There are two principal models for a software license used in a managed hosting environment: (i) the hosting provider licenses the software from the third-party vendor, and (ii) the hosting customer licenses the software directly from the third-party vendor for use in the hosting provider's data center.

(a) Hosting Provider Licenses the Software from the Third-Party Vendor

(i) Hosting Provider's Role as Licensee

Under the most common model, the hosting provider licenses proprietary software from a third-party software vendor (e.g., Microsoft) and provides its hosting customers with access to and use of the application in its data centers. The hosting provider obtains from the third-party software vendor the right to sub-license copies of the software to its customers. The hosting provider may receive rights under its license agreement with the software owner that are not passed on to the hosting provider's customers, such as right to copy the software onto different servers.

From the hosting provider's perspective and for most software vendors, the right to re-license required by the hosting provider is different from granting the hosting provider the right to resell the software. The hosting provider is not a sales channel for the software vendor, and the hosting provider's customers do not have the right to the use the software outside of their contract with the hosting provider.

(ii) Hosting Provider's Role as Licensor

In its agreement with its customer, the hosting provider is the licensor of the upstream software vendor's application. The hosting provider grants its customer a limited sublicense to use the software in the hosting provider's data center for the term of the hosting agreement. The underlying software license does not necessarily transfer to the customer upon the termination of the hosting agreement.

(b) The Hosting Customer Licenses the Software Directly from the Third-Party Vendor for Use in the Hosting Provider's Data Center

In this model, the customer obtains the right from the application owner to place its software on the hosting provider's servers. The customer must obtain its own license agreement with the application owner/licensor as the application owner/licensor is not in contractual privity with the hosting provider, which has physical access to the application and may have logical access as well. For applications provided by the customer, the hosting provider relies on the customer to obtain the rights necessary for the hosting provider to fulfil its responsibilities under the hosting contract. Under this model, the customer may also have the hosting provider provide maintenance and/or technical support for the application.

6. Licensing and Contracting Concerns in a Hosted Environment

(a) As between the Software Owner and Hosting Provider

(i) The Software Owner's Perspective

License Grant

Licensors should grant the licensee/hosting provider a nonexclusive, nontransferable license to (1) copy and install the software in object code form only on servers owned or managed by the hosting provider in the hosting provider's data centers (or owned by hosting provider or the hosting provider's customers and installed in hosting provider's data centers), and (2) sublicense copies of the software to its customers under an end-user license agreement. In all cases, the licensor should prohibit reverse engineering, decompiling, or otherwise trying to obtain the source code of the software. The licensor may want to grant the right to transfer the licensed software from one computer to another (e.g., in circumstances of hardware "refresh" or replacement, or "failover" substitution) and/or from one customer to another, provided the number of copies does not increase.

To maintain strict control over its software, the licensor may want to grant a license to use, without the right to copy except for backup and archival copies and without any further right to re-license. In this case, the hosting provider may need to require its customer to license the software directly from the vendor.

Pricing

The license grant is partially dependent on how the software is priced. Is the software licensed:

- per copy?
- per central processing unit (CPU)?
- per user accessing the software (seat license)?
- per named user accessing the software (named seat license)?

The licensor must gauge how to maximize its profitability and/or the desires of its customers to structure both its license and its' pricing accordingly.

If the software is priced on a per user basis, the licensor may grant the hosting provider the right to copy the software on as many computers as it needs. If pricing is on a per copy basis, the licensor may not grant the hosting provider the right to copy and instead grant the hosting provider right to install and use. This way, the licensor controls the number of copies, and the hosting provider must seek the licensor's consent for each additional copy. Alternatively, the licensor may make copies of the software freely available, but production use of the software is subject to a license key, so that the number of copies can be downloaded and used by the licensee/hosting provider can be electronically tracked. Other vendors make their software freely available, but charge for support and maintenance.

Other Contract Terms

In general, most other contract terms follow the same principles as on premises software licensing including the disclaimer of almost all warranties. The hosting provider should insist, however, on a warranty of title or indemnification for infringement. See Chapter 5.C. Like any licensor/licensee relationship, the licensor will likely prefer to give an indemnity instead of a warranty (e.g., to reduce the potential revenue risk that a breached warranty could enable termination for cause by the customer). While an indemnity does not permit the hosting provider to terminate the agreement, it does allow the hosting provider to recover its legal costs.

The licensor should seek an indemnity for any claim arising from the hosting provider's agreement with the customer (e.g., if the hosting provider grants its customer a more favorable warranty than what the licensor has given to the hosting provider or disclaimed in the end-user license, or if the licensor is later involuntarily involved in litigation between the hosting provider and end-user customer).

If the licensor permits the hosting provider to consent to the end user's assignment of the license in the event of the end user's merger/acquisition without the prior written approval of the licensor, the license grant should not allow increased use without appropriate payment. For example, a license grant allowing the software to be copied and used in the hosting provider's two data centers for one fixed fee would potentially allow the purchaser to increase the number of customers without additional payment to the licensor. If a small customer merges with a much larger company, software can potentially be used in many more data centers by many more users without any additional compensation payable to the licensor.

The licensor should provide the hosting provider with an end-user license agreement (EULA) as an exhibit to their contract and require the hosting provider to incorporate such license terms into the hosting provider's contract with its customers as a "flow down" requirement. If the EULA is incorporated into the hosting provider's agreement with its customers, the vendor is in essence dictating the terms that apply to its application. See Forms F.1.1 Schedule 1 and F.1.2 Appendix F for model EULA terms.

The licensor should also require that the hosting provider's agreement with its customers contain at a minimum the following clauses or substantially similar terms:

- identify the licensor as a third-party beneficiary, and
- have the customer acknowledge the proprietary nature of the licensor's software. This point is less important if the licensor's EULA is incorporated into of the agreement between the customer and the hosting provider.

Support

The licensor should carefully consider the level of support it expects to provide. Is the licensor willing to provide support directly to the end user customers? If so, can the customers contact the licensor directly, or does the licensor want the hosting provider to triage calls first?

If the hosting provider is allowed to transfer the license to the customer at the end of the contract between the hosting provider and the customer, does support transfer with the license? Both technical support and basic help-desk support? If so, this could greatly increase the number of calls the licensor may receive.

- Will the licensor provide technical support?
- On what basis?
  - Normal business hours?
  - If so, based on what time zones?
  - 24×7×365? Note: Hosting providers usually require 24×7×365 support.
- Is support included in the license fee, or is it priced separately?

If the licensor grants the hosting provider the right to make derivative works, the licensor should clearly state that support does not include resolving problems caused by the hosting provider's individual customizations, e.g., "bolt on" additional feature, scripts, etc. A prudent licensor will limit its support obligations to avoid being inundated by the hosting provider's customers. The support agreement between the licensor and hosting provider should provide that the hosting provider's customers must direct all calls for technical support to the hosting provider's technical team, who will then filter end-user queries. If help desk/user support will not be provided, the contract should explicitly state so.

(ii) The Hosting Provider's Perspective

License Grant

From the hosting provider's perspective, the license grant from the licensor should allow the software to be installed on multiple servers in different data centers and to be sublicensed to its customers. Doing so avoids the hosting provider having to seek the licensor's permission each time a customer wants to add servers, the hosting provider adds customers or data center locations.

In all cases, the hosting provider should be allowed to make copies for backup and archival purposes at no additional fee as well as obtain additional copies for internal testing purposes at no cost. The right to transfer a copy of the software from one server/computer to another (e.g., if the hardware is replaced or upgraded) is also important to hosting providers. The hosting provider should also have the right to transfer a copy from one customer to another customer without charge. For example, if a customer has paid for a one-year license and the customer leaves the hosting provider, the hosting provider should have the right to use that license for another customer for the balance of the license term. Some licensors do not allow this and require a new fee to be paid for each customer, which is unreasonable from the hosting provider's perspective, as the license fee has already been paid and the licensor will not suffer a financial loss if the number of copies or another metric remains unchanged.

Other Contract Terms

When representing a hosting provider, counsel should ascertain whether the hosting provider (or its customer) wants to write scripts or port the software to a different operating system. Although some licensors expect all derivative works to be owned by the licensor, it makes more sense, from the customer's perspective, if the new code belongs to the party who writes it, subject to the rights of the owner in the original work, which would be the default under federal copyright law, absent a different contractual agreement. *See* 17 U.S.C. § 101. *See also* Chapters 4.C.5, 7.B, and 16.

Licensors are usually unwilling to accept this position, however, as they usually seek to own all enhancements and modifications to maintain the integrity and commercial control of their software. Often licensors are concerned that if third-parties own portions of their software, they will lose their ability to control their software and business destiny. The parties' agreement should clearly provide that the hosting provider (or its customer) is required to deliver the new code to the licensor as sometimes there is an allocation of intellectual property ownership without a corresponding obligation to deliver the material to the licensor.

The hosting provider should seek the right to resell the license to the software (and/or copy and distribute the software in object code form only) to its customers upon termination of the hosting agreement between the hosting provider and customer or initially, so long as the customer will be hosting the software with the hosting provider and they can only use the software on the customer's premises after termination of the agreement between the customer and hosting provider. In practice, however, many licensors are unlikely to allow the hosting provider to resell the license.

For administrative reasons many hosting providers will not want to attach the licensor's EULA to each customer's agreement. Even small hosting architectures can require more than a dozen different applications residing on the customer's servers. Attaching individual EULAs is burdensome and makes the customer's contract unnecessarily long. Instead, the hosting provider should seek the right to not flow-down the EULAs as long as the hosting provider's agreement with the customer contains terms that are no less protective of the licensor's rights than the terms of the hosting provider's agreement with the licensor. This allows the hosting provider to fold the licensor's terms under the general terms of the hosting provider's agreement with its customers and to include a general license grant that will cover all licensor agreements. Thus, the hosting provider's contract should include various references to the provider's "suppliers" to provide the protections desired by those upstream licensors. Alternatively, the hosting provider can include links to all third-party terms by which the customer is bound.

Support

The hosting provider should carefully consider the level of support it expects the licensor to provide and determine what is included in the licensor's fee i.e., upgrades, patches, maintenance, etc. For those services that are likely to be needed but are not included, the license should clearly set forth the applicable pricing to avoid later pricing disputes when the hosting provider lacks leverage.

Since uptime is very important to a hosting provider's customers, hosting providers should insist on access to 24×7×365 support as, from the customer's perspective, the hosting provider is managing the software. If the software crashes, the hosting provider may need immediate support from the licensor in order to meet its uptime service-level agreement with its customer.

(b) As between the Hosting Provider and its Customers

(i) The Hosting Provider's Perspective

Hosting providers usually require the customer to execute the hosting provider's standard form agreement with few, if any, modifications. Its pricing is based on standardized services, process, pricing metrics and shared data centers.

While the hosting provider usually seeks to disclaim all warranties, the customer should insist on a warranty of title or indemnification for infringement, the latter being preferable from the customer's perspective. See Chapter 5.C. Special, incidental, consequential, punitive, and similar damages are usually disclaimed by the hosting provider. The customer's recovery for breach is usually limited to the amount paid by the customer to the hosting provider in the year prior to the event that gave rise to the claim.

The hosting provider must ensure that it flows down the licensor's required terms to the customer. The "license grant" set forth below incorporates a majority of the required flow-down terms typically imposed by licensors:

> *In the event we provide any software to you in connection with the Services, we grant you a personal, nonexclusive, nontransferable license, for the duration of your Service Period, to use such software in object code form only on the hardware on which it is installed for the sole purpose of enabling you to use the Services.*
>
> *We represent and you acknowledge that the software is copyrighted, that title to such software remains with us or our suppliers, and that the content and design of such software are valuable trade secrets. You agree not to (a) disclose or make available to third-parties any portion of such software without our advance written permission; (b) copy or duplicate such software; (c) reverse engineer, de-compile, or disassemble such software; or (d) modify or make derivative works of such software. You agree not to use such software after the Service Period without obtaining a valid license from us or from the third-party supplier.*

From the hosting provider's perspective, it is important to clearly state that the hosting provider is providing the customer a license to use software provided by the hosting provider during the service period, the hosting provider is not purchasing a license on the customer's behalf, the hosting provider will retain the license at the termination or expiration of the agreement, and the hosting provider will provide maintenance for the software it provides while the customer is responsible for maintaining software it provides and manages.

To limit its liability, the hosting provider's agreement usually provides that the customer is responsible for selecting the services it will use and selecting the appropriate level of security. While the hosting provider will often assist the customer in making its selections, the hosting provider does not know the customer's needs and thus, does not want to be held responsible in the event the selected services or security levels do not meet those needs.

From the hosting provider's perspective, the agreement should clearly provide that the hosting provider is not responsible for any data loss, even if due to a service interruption. The hosting provider's pricing is usually based on providing a managed service and not assuming responsibility for operating the hosted site and applications for the customer. The hosting provider should clearly state that it does not guarantee the security of the customer's hosted environment and that the choice of security services and providing secure access to the hosted applications are the responsibility of the customer. Finally, the agreement's limitation of liability provision should be physically separated in a separate, individual header paragraph from those contained in any overarching agreement to strengthen the hosting agreement's disclaimer of liability for loss of data.

The hosting provider should also provide the customer with the hosting provider's Acceptable Use Policy ("AUP") which should provide that any violation of the policy is a material breach of the hosting agreement, allowing the hosting provider to terminate the agreement. See Forms D.5.1 and D.5.2 for model AUPs. The agreement should provide that the customer is solely responsible for all data, software, and images that the customer places on the hosting provider's servers and that the hosting provider does not exercise any control over the content. The customer should indemnify the hosting provider for any claims of intellectual property infringement arising out of the content posted by the customer or the customer's use of the hosting services.

Upon termination of the agreement, the customer should relinquish the IP addresses assigned to it by the hosting provider and upon the hosting provider's request, re-number its IP addresses. Finally, the hosting provider should retain the right to make changes to the services as well as move the customer's hosting environment to another data center without the customer's consent, provided the data center(s) was in the same jurisdiction.

(ii) The Customer's Perspective

From the customer's perspective, the customer should insist that the hosting provider transfer ownership of any application license to the customer upon termination of its agreement with the hosting provider. It may be argued that this position is equitable only if the customer has paid for the license. The hosting provider, however, may consider the underlying agreement a services agreement and thus take the position that the customer is not entitled to assume the software license. While the cost of the software license is considered in pricing the hosting provider's services, the relationship is analogous to an ongoing real estate or equipment lease rather than payment for full ownership. If the parties agree to a transfer, the customer should pay the cost of any transfer fees to the upstream software vendor and the parties should determine whether support and maintenance can be transferred along with the license.

The customer should insist on an indemnification for infringement from the hosting provider, even though the hosting provider is not the owner of the application, as the hosting provider is likely receiving an indemnity from the application owner. From the customer's perspective, it is reasonable to request the IP indemnity be uncapped.

Technical support for the application will usually be provided by the hosting provider, rather than having the customer contact the licensor directly for support. Nonetheless, hosting provider should assume responsibility for the software if the hosting provider causes down-time (i.e., are all problems included for purposes of SLAs), however, the hosting provider should seek an exclusion for defects in the software for which fixes have not been provided by the licensor.

C. *PRACTICE POINT*: Checklist of issues to consider when switching from an on-premise solution to a cloud-based solution:

- Create a gap analysis to identify any gaps in functionality/the customer's technical requirements.
- If there are gaps, determine their importance and the cost/effort/timeline to mitigate any functionality requirements.
- Is there an impact on any legacy third-party technology used by the customer in switching to an SaaS solution?
- Create a transition plan and implementation timeline.
- Establish service levels and remedies.
    - Identify relevant service levels
        - Availability
        - System response time
        - Support response time
        - Disaster recovery time
        - Problem resolution time
        - Call center measurements
    - Remedies for missed service levels
        - Service level credits
        - Reduced pricing
        - Termination
- Include a change order process including the parties rights to require/decline a change
- Confirm the right to receive to releases, additional functionality, and upgrades.
- Clearly set forth the fee schedule for the new service as well as all transition/ancillary costs.
    - Does the pricing include:
        - transition costs,
        - configuration costs,
        - implementation costs,
        - support costs,
        - the cost of porting the customer's data.
    - Are the vendor's fees fixed?
        - Can prices increase during term? at renewal?
        - Can the vendor unilaterally increase prices?
        - How are price increases determined? Tied to the CPI?
    - How often can the vendor increase its prices?
- Where will the servers/hosting environment be located?
- Address security requirements, including:
    - Access and security controls
    - Security incident protocols and responsibilities

  - Ability of contractors and third parties/access to customer data
- Do third-parties including contractors, consultants etc. need/have access and use rights?
- How is the customer's data managed?
  - Can the customer demand the return of its data?
  - Can the vendor withhold the customer's data for any reason?
  - How quickly will the data be returned?
  - How will the data be retuned?
  - In what format?
  - How long must the vendor retain the customer's data at the end of the agreement?
  - Can the vendor destroy the customer's data at the end of the agreement?
- What limitations are placed on the vendor's use of the customer's data?
- Does the vendor obtain any rights in the customer's data? In data that has been:
  - Submitted?
  - Aggregated?
  - De-identified?
  - Anonymized?
- Confirm and review the vendor's business continuity plans/ disaster recovery plans?
- Termination
  - Under what conditions can the vendor suspend or terminate the agreement?
    - Breach of the Acceptable Use Policy (AUP)?
    - Non-payment?
    - Force majeure?
  - Under what conditions can the customer terminate the agreement?
    - The vendor's failure to meet the services levels?
    - Material breach of the agreement?
    - Force majeure?
  - Is the vendor obligated to provide post-termination assistance?
    - For how long?
    - At what cost?
- Obtain copies of the vendor's quality/security certificates/reports.
  - SSAE 18 SOCII reports
  - ISO 9001
  - ISO 27001

CHAPTER 15

Applicability of the Uniform Commercial Code (UCC) and the Principles of Law of Software Contracts

A. Article 2 of the Uniform Commercial Code

Article 2 of the UCC applies to "transactions in goods," and is the fundamental contract law applied in commercial transactions. UCC § 2-102. At the time Article 2 was adopted in 1951, the use of software was not foreseen, and certainly was not a significant part of commercial business transactions as it is today. As such, businesspeople and lawyers have not had a uniform law to look to in commercial transactions involving software, creating uncertainty as to how business disputes involving software should be resolved.

Software is neither fish nor fowl; even though it appears that it is bought, and sold like a good; software is licensed. Nor is it a tangible product. In the past, some courts have looked to whether a software transaction was primarily the sale, or license of software (in which case software has been found to be a good) or the provision of services, such as software development (*See, e.g., Micro Managers Inc. v. Gregory*, 434 N.W.2d 97, 100 (Wis. Ct. App. 1988)) to determine whether UCC Article 2 would apply to a particular transaction. *See also Schroders, Inc. v. Hogan Systems, Inc.*, 522 N.Y.S.2d 404 (N.Y. Sup. Ct. 1987) (substantially customized software considered a good).

If the contract is primarily for the provision of a software program, the UCC will apply. The trend has been to recognize that the UCC governs software transactions, *Wachter Management Co. v. Dexter & Chaney*, 144 P.3d 747, 750 (Kan. 2006) ("without the purchase of the software, the services would have been unnecessary"); *Advent Sys. Ltd. v. Unisys Corp.*, 925 F.2d 670, 674–75 (3d Cir. 1991); *RRX Indus., Inc. v. Lab-Con, Inc.*, 772 F.2d 543, 546 (9th Cir. 1985); *Triangle Underwriters, Inc. v. Honeywell, Inc.*, 604 F.2d 737, 742–43 (2d Cir. 1979), including those transactions involving customized software. *See, e.g., Advent, id.* at 674; *Colonial Life Inc. Co. v. Electronic Data Systems*, 817 F. Supp. 235, 239 (D.N.H. 1993). *But see Mortgage Plus, Inc. v. DocMagic, Inc.*, 2004 WL 2331918 (D. Kan. Aug. 23, 2004) (software worthless without technical services, which were predominant purpose of contract). *See also Computer Software as Sales Law Problem*, 41 UCC L. Letter (No. 6 Aug. 2007); Note, *Computer Software as a Good under the Uniform Commercial Code; Taking a Byte out of the Intangibility Myth*, 65 B.U. L. Rev. 129 (1985), Note, *Computer Programs as Goods under the UCC*, 77 Mich. L. Rev. 1149 (1979).

On the other hand, some courts have also completely ignored UCC Article 2, and have looked to the common law. *DSC Communications Corp. v. Pulse Communications, Inc.*, 170 F.3d 1354 (Fed. Cir. 1999). Other courts have expressly held that UCC Article 2A does not apply, *Rhone-Poulenc Agro, S.A. v. DeKalb Genetics Corporation*, 284 F.3d 1323, 1333 (Fed. Cir. 2002), while at least one court acknowledged that the UCC does not "technically" govern software licenses, but proceeded to apply the UCC. *i.Lan Systems, Inc. v. NetScout Service Level Corp.*, 183 F. Supp. 2d 328, 332 (D. Mass. 2002) ("UCC Article 2 technically does not govern software licenses," but "for the time being, the court will assume that it does." Other courts have questioned the holdings of those courts that assume UCC Article 2 applies. *Specht v. Netscape Communications Corp.*, 306 F.3d 17 n.13 (2d Cir. 2002). This dichotomy is the reason for the development of the Uniform Computer Information Transactions Act discussed in Chapter 15.B below.

The application of UCC Article 2 to software transactions creates significant unforeseen liability for the licensor. *See* Phillips, *When Software Fails: Emerging Standard of Vendor Liability Under the Uniform Commercial Code*, 50 Bus. Law. 151 (1994). Numerous sections of Article 2 on their face appear to be inapplicable to software, or at least fail to recognize the nature of software. For example, the "perfect tender rule" under Section 2-601 would require that the software tendered by the licensor be in total conformity with the contract. In *RRX Industries, Inc. v. LAB-CON, Inc.*, 772 F.2d 543 (9th Cir. 1985), the court looking to the "essence of the agreement" found that the software system in question was a good governed by the terms of the UCC and struck the exclusion of consequential damages.

As a good/product, software is potentially subject to product liability claims, particularly in relation to the healthcare industry. *See Lowe v. Cerner Corp.*, 2022 WL 17269066 (4th Cir. Nov. 29, 2022) (patient brought claim against healthcare software vendor claiming it had a duty to warn about risks in using their software); *but see Rodgers v. Christie*, 795 Fed. Appx. 878 (3d Cir. 2020) (artificial intelligence software not a product for product liability purposes).

For a more detailed discussion as to whether software can be a product, *see* Bexis, *New Decision Directly Addresses the "Is Software a Product Question"*, www.druganddevicelawblog.com/2022/05/new-decision-directly-addresses-the-is-software-a-product-question.html.

To provide certainty, some licensors seek to state definitively that the governing agreement shall not be governed by the UCC. Some licensees, in an effort to take advantage of the protections offered to purchasers by the UCC, seek to affirmatively state that the agreement is subject to the UCC provisions of the applicable governing law. A prudent licensor should avoid at all costs including such a statement in its license agreement as it places the licensor at considerable risk. See § 28.3 for model language opting in and out of the UCC.

For a discussion of how courts analyze whether a transaction involving a software license falls within the purview of Article 2, see Rustad & Kavusturan, *A Commercial Law for Software Contracting*, 76 Wash. & Lee. L. Rev. 775, 792-95 (2019).

See generally Cohn, Kirsh & Nimmer, *License Contracts Under Article 2 of the Uniform Commercial Code: A Proposal*, 19 Rutgers Computer & Tech. L.J. 281 (1994); Brennan, *Why Article 2 Cannot Apply to Software Transactions*, 38 Duq. L. Rev. 459 (2000); *Scope of Article 2 of UCC*, 251 Com. L. Advisor 1 (Nov. 2008).

B. The Uniform Computer Information Transactions Act (UCITA)

1. *History of Attempts to Apply UCC Article 2 to Software Licensing*

(a) Massachusetts Model

In 1990, a committee headed by Stephen Y. Chow in conjunction with the Business Law Section of the Massachusetts Bar Association drafted a model UCC Article 2B to serve as a discussion point for adapting the UCC to software licensing. The committee created a completely new article by modifying those sections of Article 2, which it thought were inapplicable to software, while maintaining the majority of Article 2. Although this article was widely circulated, there was no attempt to adopt it under Massachusetts law, or elsewhere.

(b) Hub and Spoke Approach

As a result of the increasing need for a uniform law for software licensing, the National Conference of Commissioners for Uniform State Laws (NCCUSL) began to create plans to adapt Article 2 to software. The committee discussed utilizing a hub and spoke approach to apply UCC Article 2 to software licensing.

Under a hub and spoke approach, existing UCC Article 2 would serve as a "hub" and from that hub, spokes (i.e., those portions of UCC Article 2 that needed to be amended for software licensing, such as the perfect tender rule), would protrude. In August of 1995, after reviewing several drafts of a revised Article 2 using the hub and spoke approach, the NCCUSL board decided not to pursue the hub and spoke approach but instead to support a totally new Article 2B to directly address software licensing. For a general discussion of the hub and spoke concept, *see* Nimmer, *Intangibles Contracts: Thoughts of Hub, Spokes and Reinvigorating Article 2*, 35 Wm. & Mary L. Rev. 1337 (1994) and Henning, *Amended Article 2: What Went Wrong*, 11 Duq. Bus. L.J. 131 (2009).

(c) UCC Article 2B

In September 1995, the NCCUSL board in conjunction with the American Law Institute (ALI) began discussing a proposed UCC Article 2B. Article 2B was to be a completely new article drafted along the lines of the Massachusetts model. When approved in final form, the Article needed to be voted on by the full NCCUSL board and ALI, and then sent to the individual states to adopt into law. After going through many revisions and being subject to much criticism regarding contract law, consumer law, as well as intellectual property law issues, proposed Article 2B "died" in March 1999 when it became clear that NCCUSL, and ALI lacked a consensus to approve its ratification. On April 17, 1999, NCCUSL announced that there would be no proposed Article 2B of the UCC.

For a more detailed discussion of the history of applying the UCC to software licensing, *see* Rustad & Kavusturan, *A Commercial Law for Software Contracting*, 76 Wash. & Lee. L. Rev. 775 (2019).

2. Present Status of UCITA

NCCUSL decided to move forward without ALI to create a model law (instead of a UCC article) from the proposed UCC Article 2B, the "Uniform Computer Information Transactions Act" (UCITA). NCCUSL approved UCITA in July 1999 and in August 2002, NCCUSL modified certain provisions of UCITA in response to criticism from the American Bar Association, and consumer groups.

As of November 1, 2023, only two states have enacted UCITA: Virginia, effective July 2001 (VA. CODE ANN. §§ 59.1-501.1 *et seq.*), and Maryland, effective October 1, 2000 (MD. CODE ANN., COM. LAW §§ 22-101 *et seq.*). A number of other states, including Arizona, Delaware, the District of Columbia, Illinois, Maine, New Hampshire, New Jersey, Oregon, and Texas, have considered adopting UCITA, but there has not been overwhelming support to adopt it.

NCCUSL believes that a uniform law is needed given the considerable diverse legislative activity within the states regarding electronic commerce issues. The diversity of legislation is particularly troublesome since electronic transactions can, and frequently are, conducted across state lines. NCCUSL views the UCITA as an intermediate step to bring uniformity, and clarity to this area of law until it can develop further. UCITA and the official comments are available at https://www.uniformlaws.org/viewdocument/final-act-with-comments-14?CommunityKey=92b2978d-585f-4ab6-b8a1-53860fbb43b5&tab=librarydocuments.

For a detailed discussion of UCITA, *see* BRENNAN, TOWLE & WOLFSON, THE COMPLETE UCITA, Glasser Legal Works (2004), The Uniform Computer Information Transaction Act, 52 LAW. BRIEF 1 (Oct 15, 2022).

3. Significant Provisions of UCITA (2002 Version)

Section references set forth herein refer to the relevant sections of UCITA.

(a) Scope

UCITA applies to all "computer information transactions," which is defined as "an agreement or the performance of it to create, modify, transfer or license computer information or informational rights in computer information." UCITA §§ 103(a); 102(11). "Computer Information" is defined as "information in electronic form which is obtained from or through the use of a computer or which is in a form capable of being processed by a computer." UCITA § 102(10).

UCITA governs software licenses and sales, computer games, contracts and licenses, online databases, and information systems. It does not govern transactions involving print media, such as printed books, magazines, newspapers, or goods such as television sets, cars, movies, or computers, as well as employment agreements. UCITA § 103(d) comment 3. Where a computer program is imbedded in a good, UCITA will not apply to the imbedded software unless the good is a computer or peripheral or obtaining access, or use of the computer program is a material purpose of the transaction. UCITA § 103(b). Embedded software that is excluded from UCITA cannot be used as a basis to opt into UCITA. UCITA § 103 comment (4)(b)(3).

UCITA provisions are "default," or "background law" provisions that apply only in the event the governing agreement does not contain contrary language (i.e., when the parties are silent as to a topic, UCITA attempts to supply a rule). Except for the provisions set forth in § 115(b) (such as conscionability), UCITA's provision can be varied by agreement. UCITA § 115 comments 2, 3. Under UCITA, the parties to an agreement for computer information may opt out of, or into UCITA. UCITA § 106(b); 115(a). See § 28.2 of the Annotated Software License and Services Agreement in Form B.3.1 for language opting out of UCITA. UCITA provides that any decision to opt into or out of the act does not alter certain obligations, such as the obligations of good faith, diligence, reasonableness, or the limitations on enforceability in the event of unconscionability, or public policy. UCITA §§ 105(b)(c); 115(b). Opting out is often viewed as beneficial by licensees who assume the controversy surrounding UCITA was accurate. In fact, opting out can have significant adverse consequences for licensees.

Any portion of UCITA that is preempted by federal law is unenforceable to the extent of the preemption. UCITA § 105(a). Laws regarding trade secrets, and unfair competition are considered to supplement UCITA, and not preempt it. UCITA § 105(c). Similarly, UCITA does not preempt any consumer protection statute. UCITA § 104(b).

(b) Electronic Contracting

UCITA recognizes the validity of electronic contracts. *See, e.g.*, UCITA § 107; § 202(a); §§ 212-214 ("A contract may be formed in any manner sufficient to show agreement . . ." UCITA § 202(a)). It incorporates the term "record" instead of the word "writing" in recognition of the inclusion of electronic records. UCITA § 102(55). Similarly (and like the revised articles of the UCC, such as revised UCC Article 9), UCITA uses the word "authenticate" in place of the word "signature" to include electronic processes and symbols used to indicate an intent to sign a record. UCITA § 102(6).

(c) Acceptance (§ 203)

UCITA Section 203(4) reverses the mailbox rule for electronic messages by making acceptance effective upon receipt, in contrast to the traditional rule that makes acceptance effective upon deposit of the means of acceptance in the mailbox. See comment 5 of § 203 of The Official Comments to UCITA.

(d) License Terms/Background Rules (§§ 306, 307)

(i) Number of Users

Under UCITA, if the license does not specify the number of users, UCITA holds that the license will be viewed to allow a reasonable number of users "in light of the commercial circumstances existing at the time of the agreement." UCITA § 306.

(ii) Right to Enhancements or Modifications

Section 307(d) provides that a licensee is not automatically entitled to any new enhancements, versions, or modifications. Additionally, any agreement to provide new enhancements, versions, or modifications imposes such duty (as a background law matter) only to those as developed and made generally available from time to time. UCITA § 307(c).

(iii) Right to Source Code

Unless otherwise provided in the agreement, neither party is entitled to receive copies of the other party's source code, schematics, design material, or other similar materials. UCITA § 307(d).

(iv) Term

If a license is silent as to the term of the license, the term will be deemed for a commercially reasonable period. UCITA § 306 comment 2.

(v) Statute of Limitations

Any action for breach of contract must be brought within, "the later of four years after the right of action accrues, or one year after the breach was, or should be been discovered, but not later than five years after the right of action accrues." UCITA § 805(a). Section 805(b)(1) provides that the statute of limitations may be reduced to not less than one year, but cannot be extended. Consumer contracts may not reduce the statute of limitations. UCITA § 805(b)(2).

(e) Assignability (§ 503)

Under § 503(1), a party may generally assign its contractual interest, other than for copyrights, unless (a) the transfer is prohibited by law, or (b) "would materially change the duty of the other party, materially increase the burden or risk imposed on the other party, or materially impair the other party's property or its likelihood or expectation of obtaining return performance." A prohibition on assignment will generally be enforced as a breach of contract and void. UCITA § 503(2). A prohibition on the transfer of a licensee's contractual interest under a mass-market license must be conspicuous. UCITA § 503(4) comment 5.

(f) Choice of Law (§ 109)

Under § 109(a), the parties may choose the governing law of the agreement, provided that in a consumer contract such choice does not violate the laws of the jurisdiction whose laws would apply in the situations below. In the absence of an agreement in the governing contract, UCITA sets forth three rules for determining which jurisdiction's law governs:

1. Internet transactions for the electronic transfer of information are governed by the laws of the state where the licensor was located when the contract was entered into. UCITA § 109(b)(1).
2. Transactions for the physical delivery of a tangible copy in a consumer transaction are governed by the law of the state where the delivery is made. UCITA § 109(b)(2).
3. In all other situations, the transaction is governed by the law of the state with the most significant relationship to the transaction. UCITA § 109(b)(3).

In a case of first impression, a Virginia court has upheld the election of the contracting parties to be governed by the terms of the underlying agreement and not UCITA. *Pilar Services, Inc. v. NCI Information Systems*, 569 F. Supp. 2d 563 (E.D. Va. 2008).

(g) *Choice of Forum (§ 110)*

Under § 110 of UCITA, a choice of an exclusive judicial or arbitral forum will be upheld unless it is considered to be unreasonable or unjust. UCITA § 110(a). To ensure an exclusive judicial forum, the parties must specifically state that the selected venue is the exclusive judicial forum. UCITA § 110(b).

(h) *Survival of Obligations (§ 616)*

Except as set forth in § 616(b) below, all executory obligations of both parties are discharged upon termination of the license. UCITA § 616(a).

Under § 616(b), 11 rights and obligations will survive the termination of a contract:

1. A right based on a previous breach, or performance;
2. Confidentiality, nondisclosure, and noncompetition obligations;
3. Terms applicable to the use of licensed copies, or information not returned to the other party;
4. An obligation to deliver, or dispose of information, documentation, or copies; an obligation to destroy copies; or a right to obtain information from an escrow agent;
5. A choice of law or forum;
6. Arbitration, or alternate dispute resolution obligations;
7. Terms limiting the time for commencing an action, or giving notice;
8. Certain indemnity obligations;
9. A limitation of remedy, modification, or disclaimer of warranty;
10. An obligation to provide an accounting, and make payments due under the accounting; and
11. Any terms that the contract provides will survive.

(i) *Warranties*

(i) Implied Warranty of Non-interference and Non-infringement (§ 401)

Under § 401(a), a licensor who is a merchant dealing in the type of information licensed, "warrants that the information will be delivered free of the rightful claim of any third person by way of infringement or misappropriation . . . ." A licensor will be held harmless for liability arising from its conformance to the detailed specifications, and the method required for meeting such specifications provided by the licensee, unless such claim arises from the licensor's failure to adopt, or notify the licensee of a non-infringing alternative of which the licensor had reason to know. UCITA § 401(a).

Under Section 401(b)(1), a licensor is deemed to warrant that for the duration of the license, except for a claim of infringement, or misappropriation, no person has a valid claim to, or interest in information that arose from an act, or omission of the licensor that will interfere with the licensee's use, or interest. Further, as to an exclusive license, the licensor is deemed to warrant that the "informational rights are valid and exclusive for the information as a whole to the extent exclusivity and validity are recognized by the law applicable to the licensed rights . . . ." UCITA § 401(b)(2)(B).

(ii) Implied Warranty of Merchantability of Computer Program (§ 403)

Unless the warranty is disclaimed, or modified, a merchant that is a licensor of the program type licensed, warrants to the end user that the "program is fit for the ordinary purposes for which such computer programs are used," and that "the program conforms to any promises or affirmations made on the container or label." UCITA § 403(a)(2), (3).

(iii) Implied Warranty of Informational Content (§ 404)

Under UCITA § 404, a merchant in a special relationship of reliance with a licensee who collects, processes, provides, or transmits informational content is deemed to warrant to the licensee that "there is no inaccuracy in the informational content caused by the merchant's failure to perform with reasonable care." UCITA § 404(a).

(iv) Implied Warranty of System Integration (§ 405)

Under UCITA § 405(a), a licensor providing systems integration services is deemed to warrant that the information provided by the licensor is fit, for a particular purpose, if the licensor at the time of contracting has reason to know of the particular purpose, for which the computer information is required, and that the licensee is relying on the licensor's expertise to select, develop, or furnish the needed information.

If the licensor is required to provide, or select a system of computer software, and goods, and the licensor has reason to know that the licensee is relying on the skill of the licensor in making such selections, there is an implied warranty that the components provided, or selected will function together as a system. UCITA § 405(c).

(v) Disclaimer, Modification, or Warranty (§ 406) (§ 16.1.4.A of Form B.3.1)

Section 406 sets forth the language necessary to disclaim the express, and implied warranties set forth in Part 4 of UCITA. The language necessary to disclaim a warranty is different from the UCC, but the use of UCC Article 2 language will suffice. *See* UCITA § 406 comments 1, 2, 4, and 5. In any case, the parties should carefully consider the appropriate language to ensure their intent is met. See § 16.1.4.A of Form B.3.1 for model language.

Any attempt to disclaim an express warranty must be construed wherever reasonable as consistent with language creating the express warranty. To the extent any construction is unreasonable, the disclaimer, or modification is void. UCITA § 406(a). To disclaim, or modify an implied warranty arising under Section 403, the language must include the words "merchantability," or "quality," or words of similar meaning and if contained in a record, must be conspicuous. UCITA § 406(b)(1)(A). To disclaim, or modify an implied warranty arising under Section 404, the language in a record must include the word "accuracy," or similar wording. UCITA § 406(b)(1)(B). To disclaim, or modify an implied warranty under Section 405, the disclaimer or modification must be in a record, and conspicuous. UCITA § 406(b)(2).

A disclaimer is sufficient to disclaim all implied warranties if it individually disclaims each implied warranty, or except for the implied warranty in Section 401, if the following language, or similar language is conspicuously stated: "Except for express warranties stated in this contract, if any, this 'information' 'computer program' is provided with all faults, and the entire risk as to satisfactory quality, performance, accuracy, and effort is with the user." UCITA § 406(b)(3). Unless the facts indicate otherwise, all implied warranties other than the warranty created under Section 401 are disclaimed by the expressions "as is," "with all faults," or other language that calls the licensee's attention to such disclaimer and makes it clear there are no implied warranties. UCITA § 406(c).

If an agreement requires ongoing performance, or a series of performances by the licensor, any proper disclaimer under UCITA is effective as to all subsequent performances. UCITA § 406(f). The parties may limit the remedy for breach of warranty with respect to the limitation of damages and the contractual modification of remedies. UCITA § 406(g). See *Baney Corp. v. Agilysys NV, LLC*, 773 F. Supp. 2d 593 (D. Md. 2011).

(vi) Modification of a Computer Program (§ 407)

A licensee that alters, deletes, or adds code to, or from a computer program, other than by using one of the program's capabilities intended in the ordinary purpose, does not invalidate any performance warranties of the unmodified copies but rather invalidates only those of the modified copy. UCITA § 407.

(vii) Third-Party Beneficiaries of Warranty (§ 409)

A warranty to a licensee extends to any third person for whose benefit the licensor provides the information, or informational rights that rightfully use the information in the manner reasonably expected by the licenser. UCITA § 409(a). A warranty to a consumer extends to the consumer's immediate family, or household if such person's use of the product could be reasonably foreseen by the licensor. UCITA § 409(b).

A licensor may disclaim third party beneficiaries except to a consumer's immediate family in a consumer transaction. UCITA § 409(c). A disclaimer, or modification of a warranty, or remedy that is effective against a licensee is also effective against any third party to which a warranty extends. UCITA § 409(d).

(j) Self-Help (§§ 605, 815, 816)

Three sections within UCITA govern the licensor's use of self-help. Section 605 addresses electronic regulation of performance while Sections 815 and 816 address electronic self-help procedures implemented as a result of the termination of the contract for breach.

Section 605(b) sets forth four situations where a licensor may utilize an "automatic restraint." Automatic restraint is not truly "self-help" because it has nothing to do with breach of the license. A licensor may use an automatic restraint:

1. if the agreement permits the use of a restraint;
2. to prevent a licensee's use inconsistent with a contractual provision;
3. to prevent use of the software after the expiration of the stated duration, or a stated number of uses; and
4. after the contract's termination other than set forth in item three above, and upon reasonable notice to the licensee before preventing access.

The licensor is not required to give prior notice under the first two situations.

An "automatic restraint" is defined as "a program, code, device, or similar electronic or physical limitation the intended purpose of which is to prevent use of information contrary to the contract or applicable law." UCITA § 605(a).

A licensor who meets the requirements set forth in Section 605(b), or (c) is protected from losses due to using the automatic restraint. UCITA § 605(d). A licensor is free to implement an update of a software program that incorporates an automatic restraint to disable an earlier version. UCITA § 605(e). Under Section 605(f), an automatic restraint cannot be used to enforce a remedy for breach of contract, or cancellation for breach. Because UCITA defers to federal law (§ 105(a)), UCITA's rules should be read in light of the rules regarding "technological measures" under the Federal Digital Millennium Copyright Act that imposes fewer burdens on licensors than under UCITA. Sections 815 and 816 of UCITA govern the use of electronic self-help (i.e., use of self-help after breach). Under § 816(b), upon the cancellation of a license, electronic self-help is prohibited. This provision may not be waived, or varied by an agreement before the breach of the license. UCITA § 816(d). Under Section 815(b), a licensor who exercises its rights without judicial process, without breach of the peace, must respect the licensee's information (i.e., it cannot delete the licensee's information).

(k) Mass-Market Licenses (§ 209)

UCITA defines a "mass-market transaction" as a consumer contract, or a transaction with an end-user licensee for information, or informational rights directed to the general public under substantially the same terms for the same information. UCITA § 102(44). This includes transactions in a retail market, such as shrink wrap licenses, but excludes contracts for the display of public works, a contract for information that is customized, a site license, or access contract. UCITA § 102(43). A "mass-market license" is defined as "a standard form used in a mass-market transaction."

To be valid, the license terms must be presented prior to, or at the time the licensee first uses the information, and the licensee manifests its assent. UCITA § 209(a). A term is not part of the license if it is unconscionable, or conflicts with a term that the parties have expressly agreed. UCITA § 209(a)(1), (2). If the licensee refuses the mass-market license after having an opportunity to review the license, the licensee has the right to return the information for a refund, and the reasonable cost of return must be paid by the licensor. UCITA § 209(b). The licensee is also entitled to receive compensation for any actual damages caused by the installation of the information for purposes of reviewing, or removing the software. *Id.* Further, the terms of a mass-market license cannot alter contract terms that have been expressly agreed by the parties. UCITA § 209(a)(2).

4. Rejection of UCITA (Bomb Shelters)

To date, the vast majority of states have chosen simply not to enact UCITA. However, some states have gone so far as to enact legislation designed to reject the application of UCITA to their residents. The group Americans for Fair Electronic Commerce Transactions (AFFECT) has published draft legislation that has been termed "bomb shelter" legislation because it protects a state's citizens from the application of UCITA.

As discussed in Section B.3.(b)(f) of this chapter, UCITA permits the parties to choose the law of any state "provided that in a consumer contract such choice does not violate the laws of the jurisdiction whose laws would apply" in certain situations. AFFECT is concerned that the parties to a license could specify that Maryland or Virginia law would govern the agreement, even if both parties reside in another state. So-called bomb shelter legislation voids any contractual choice of law provision that would result in the application of UCITA to an agreement. As of September 1, 2020, bomb shelter legislation has been enacted in five states: Idaho (IDAHO CODE § 29-116), Iowa (IOWA CODE § 554D.104), North Carolina (N.C. GEN. STAT. § 66-329), Vermont (9 VT. STAT. ANN. § 2463a), and West Virginia (W. VA. CODE § 55815).

C. Principles of the Law of Software Contracts

In May 2009, the American Law Institute approved the Principles of the Law of Software Contracts ("Principles"), which provide many recommendations for reforming the laws applicable to software licensing. Whether these recommendations are ever adopted by the state legislators, or the judiciary remains to be seen

The Principles are perceived as licensee oriented and as incorporating consumer protections into commercial transactions. Many argue the Principles limit the freedom of contract, increasing vendor costs and uncertainty, leading to an increase in litigation.

The Principles focus on the transfer of software, defining "transfer" as "a conveyance of rights in software, or an authorization to access software, including by way of sale, license, lease, or access agreement." Principles § 101(m). The Principles address a number of significant issues that a prudent practitioner should address if, and when the Principles are adopted by the state legislators, or judiciary.

From the licensor's perspective, the most controversial provision addresses a non-disclaimable warranty of no hidden material defects (§ 3.05). Section 3.05 provides that a licensor who receives money in return for use of its software warrants that the software contains no "material hidden defects." This warranty may not be disclaimed. *Id.* The warranty extends "to any party in the normal chain of distribution." *Id.* Thus the licensor could potentially be obligated to correct any defective software regardless of where or when it was purchased.

Another important provision is an implied obligation to indemnify against infringement (§ 3.01). Although most licensors agree to indemnify the licensee against infringement, the indemnification included in the Principles is broader than the indemnification offered by most licensors. Other notable provisions include a disclaimer of warranties (§§ 3.02, 3.06 and 4.01), as well as the "Standard Form of Transfers" (§ 2.02), which likely extends consumer protections to commercial businesses.

As mentioned earlier, it remains to be seen whether the Principles will be adopted. Until the Principles are judicially interpreted, it is difficult to predict their impact on software licensing and the actions a prudent licensor and licensee should take to protect their interests. The controversial nature of the Principles, however, ensures that its provisions will be debated for some time to come.

For a more detailed discussion on the Principles, *see* O'Rourke, *The ALI's Principles of Software Contracting: Some Comments and Clarifications*, 12 J. HIGH TECH. L. 159 (2011); Moringiello & Reynolds, *What's Software Got to Do with It? The ALI Principles of the Law of Software Contracting*, 84 TUL. L. REV. 1 (2010); Hillman, *Contract Law in Context: The Case of Software Contracts*, 45 WAKE FOREST L. REV. 669 (2010); Hillman & O'Rourke, *Principles of the Law of Software Contracts: Some Highlights*, 84 TUL. L. REV. 1519 (2010); Marotta-Wurgler, *Will Increased Disclosure Help? Evaluating the Recommendations of the ALI's "Principles of the Law of Software Contracts,"* 78 U. CHI. L. REV. 165 (2011).

CHAPTER 16

Software Development Agreements

A. Waterfall vs. Agile Development Methodologies

Software has traditionally been developed using a waterfall or sequential methodology, where developers complete one phase of the development and then move on to the next phase. Recently, developers have trended toward the "Agile" methodology, based on the Agile manifesto, for software development. The Agile methodology is considered to offer greater flexibility and often thought to be less expensive than the waterfall approach.

The methodology utilized for a development project impacts more than the development process, and both parties must carefully understand how the chosen methodology will impact the project. The 2019 Standish Group CHAOS report found that projects using the Agile methodology are twice as likely to be successful. Regardless of the development methodology, the developed software should be stable, repeatable and scalable.

1. *Agile*

The Agile methodology is vowed as more customer friendly, as it relies on collaboration and trust between the parties as many crucial elements, such as price and the deliverables, are fluid. Agile has many frameworks for development, including Extreme Programming, Learn, Sprints and Scrum. In the Agile methodology, the delivery approach is rooted in iterative and incremental development, whereby work is performed during time-defined sprints. The work is defined at the beginning of the sprint and undertaken by cross-functional teams. While adding greater flexibility, the deployment of multiple releases can disrupt the customer's business operations.. Work is undertaken on an iterative basis in close cooperation with the client. Agile allows for the constant adaptation of the end deliverable recognizing that the specifications and requirements may change over the development process. Essentially, developers work on several work streams simultaneously, allowing for changes to be continually made based on constant client feedback. As such, the customer should be contractually obligated to cooperate with the vendor during the development process.

Constant client feedback is important to ensure that the client's expectations are met. Supporters argue that the Agile projects produce more accurate and realistic delivery schedules due to client feedback. Further, potential issues are likely to be identified earlier in the development process, avoiding wasted time and effort.

When using an Agile methodology, it is often difficult for a vendor to provide the customer a fixed price, as the requirements are high-level requirements that can change frequently throughout the project due to customer feedback. Customers usually purchase a commitment of resources as opposed to a fixed price. The difficulty in determining a price creates risk for both parties, as the vendor likely prefers pricing on a Time and Materials (T&M) basis, while the customer likely prefers a fixed price for budgeting purposes. Potential compromises include fixed pricing for smaller projects, T&M with a "not to exceed" price, T&M with an incentive for early completion/within budget, and discounted fees if the project exceeds a set number of hours.

In determining and negotiating a price, the parties should develop high-level specifications and agree on the technical architecture. Doing so will hopefully allow the parties to reach consensus on a price estimate from which they can establish the parameters of their pricing which may include "not to exceed pricing" and T&M with a cap. Payment is often tied to deliverables but, given the nature of the Agile approach, many vendors will not commit to delivery milestones.

Under an Agile project, the cost estimate at the time of contract signature may change, requiring a mechanism such as a change order process to address price changes. Delivery dates are also "soft" as a delivery date for a minimally viable product may be established, but other implementation dates will be determined as the project progresses.

Ownership of developed intellectual property using the Agile methodology is more complex given the collaborative nature of the development process. At a minimum, the customer should have a perpetual unrestricted license to use the developed software, and the vendor should be restricted from using any proprietary ideas or confidential information provided by the customer.

Given the parallel development processes underlying the Agile development process, it is important that the vendor represent and warrant that the aggregated deliverables will work in a seamless manner in accordance with the agreed-upon specifications. Customers want to avoid the possibility of having the individual iterations work in isolation but not function correctly together. Further, the vendor should be obligated to deliver comprehensive documentation for the developed software.

Many Agile contracts allow for termination at the end of each Agile iteration or segment. The ability to terminate, however, may not be practical, as early termination may leave the customer without a finished product, and the customer must then identify and contract with another vendor. Vendors are hesitant to assume/complete another vendor's project, potentially creating a challenge for the customer to find a new vendor. To ease any transition, the customer should require the vendor to use software and tools that that the replacement vendor or customer can license and to require the legacy vendor to support the transition and the new vendor, including knowledge transfer. Given that the transition costs may be significant, prudent customers should carefully consider the risks and costs of switching in deciding whether to move to a new vendor.

With multiple internal releases and the customer's and vendor's technical teams intimately involved in the development process, a strong governance process must be implemented. Further, the project manager/scrum manager takes on greater importance. Finally, the parties' agreement should include specific reporting requirements to allow the parties to monitor the project's progress. Common metrics include Velocity,

Defect Density and Sprint Burndown. Other potential solutions to this challenge include specific contractual obligations related to: (i) communications, (ii) the timing, and (iii) effort in refining the development process and delivery schedule for the deliverables during the development process.

Finally, a vendor should ensure that third parties/subcontractors working on an important requirement of the project are also using the Agile development methodology to avoid negatively impacting the development process.

Given the many variables in Agile development projects, the role of the project manager takes on greater importance to manage the project and supervise ongoing development. The underlying agreement should anticipate and address the many issues that can arise. To that end, the parties should craft an agreement tailored to Agile development instead of using a traditional software development agreement.

For more information, *see Agile Practice Guide*, https://www.agilealliance.org/wp-content/uploads/2017/09/AgilePracticeGuide.pdf; www.agilemanifesto.org; Opelt et al., *Agile Contracts: Creating and Managing Successful Projects with Scrum* (2013).

For a template Agile Project Framework Contract, *see* https://www.agilebusiness.org/page/Resource_Templates_contract.

2. *Waterfall*

The Waterfall methodology utilizes a linear approach moving through the different phases of development and, as such, is clearly defined from the start, requiring less input from the customer making changes mid-stream more challenging. The Waterfall methodology traditionally encompasses four phases: Discovery, Design, Development, and Deployment.

As discussed below, each of these phases is undertaken sequentially and can be priced after the preceding phase has been completed. Each phase proceeds from one phase to the next like a "waterfall." By setting the price for the next phase after the previous phase has been completed, each party's risk is substantially reduced. An alternative approach is to fix a price at the beginning of the project based on the vendor's understanding of the customer's desire, creating significant risk for both parties. Because requirements often evolve during the development process, using a waterfall approach can result in additional administrative efforts in negotiating change orders.

The waterfall methodology is best suited for well-defined projects conducive to a linear structure, as the development efforts are less likely to change. It lends itself to traditional contracting with sequential acceptance and payment processes as well as customary representations, warranties and indemnities. Contractual risk may be lowered as the responsibilities of each party and each team member are more transparent.

During the Discovery phase, the vendor seeks to better understand the customer's needs and desires. The Discovery phase allows the vendor to understand the scope of the project and the amount of effort required. Often, the parties will enter into a fixed-price contract for the Discovery phase, as the scope of work and effort are limited. Doing so also reduces both parties' risk, as they are able better determine the price to move forward with the project and the time line to complete the desired deliverables. If the vendor's price for completing the remaining phases exceeds the customer's budget, the customer expenditures are also limited.

During the Design phase, the vendor will, in conjunction with the customer, develop the functional specifications in sufficient detail to provide a fixed price and delivery date for the work. It is important that the customer retain ownership of the resulting work product and functional specifications as it allows the customer to have other vendors bid on the project using the competed functional specifications. Because all vendors are using the same functional specifications to bid on, the customer is also able to review the bids on an "apples to apples' basis.

During the Development phase, the vendor will develop the software based upon the agreed-upon functional specifications. Any changes the customer may request should be addressed though the change order process with an equivalent price adjustment. To ensure the project proceeds smoothly, the vendor should be required to meet certain milestones which will be subject to provisional acceptance. Doing so allows the customer to track the vendor's progress and avoid learning of problems only at the final delivery. Any review of the deliverable must be provisional, as final acceptance should occur only after acceptance testing of the final integrated product.

Some customers seek to include a "Philby" factor during the development phase—i.e., they seek to require the vendor to include members of the customer's technical team on the vendor's development team, or at least grant the customer's technical team unfettered access to the development process. In this way, the customer hopes to establish an early-warning system to learn of any problems early on in the process. See § 10.

During the Deployment phase, the vendor installs and tests the developed software in the customer's environment and runs the software through the agreed-upon acceptance test procedures. The vendor usually undertakes the initial draft of the acceptance test process with the customer's input, as the vendor is usually more familiar with the software. If the software is replacing an existing system, the customer will run the software in parallel with its legacy system, and only once the new software has been proven and accepted will the customer remove the legacy software from production use.

The waterfall methodology has been criticized as being inflexible and unnecessarily rigid. While historically a majority of all development efforts have been undertaken by the waterfall approach, they believe a waterfall approach is inappropriate where the project requirements are uncertain or likely to change. Depending on the parties' contract, unrealistic cost projections or delivery schedules are unlikely to be discovered until much later in the project. Similarly, bugs or functionality issues also may not be discovered until the end of the development process.

The waterfall methodology does, however, make contracting less complicated as the specifications are agreed in advance, allowing the parties to agree on a fixed price and establish milestones and deliverables with payment tied to those milestones. The certainty of price, functionality and schedule are favored by both vendors and customers alike. The vendor can provide a fixed price for its development efforts predicated on a detailed functional specification and the interim and final deliverables. This in turn allows the parties to agree on payments tied to milestones and may potentially include a holdback until the final deliverables have been accepted. Finally, delivery dates, including final implementation, are also usually determined at time of contract signature, providing greater comfort to the customer as to when it will receive the contracted software.

3. *The Development Process*

When developing a software product, as opposed to software development for a particular customer, vendors often utilize a multi-gated development/approval process to ensure the completed product is market ready. Through this process, the development team is required to successfully complete identified tasks to progress through a "gate" to the next level. These tasks are intended to ensure that the product has been fully vetted both from a technical perspective as well as a commercial perspective to avoid any issues once the product is launched. Once the final gate has been cleared, the product is approved for "general availability"/sale to the public without restriction.

Gate 1: Define

- Define business case
- Determine technical feasibility
- Create product description
  - Features and functions
  - Components: application level and platform level
  - Deployment model (e.g., SaaS, on premise etc.)
  - Sales models and channels
  - Risks
- Create product framework, product compliance
- Draft functional architecture
- Undertake security review
- Evaluate product for potential IP protection

Gate 2: Design

- Identify new product features
- User Experience (UX) Solution design
- User Experience (UX) Concept testing
- Functional Architecture finalized
- IP review/validation
- Design review

Gate 3: Develop

- User Experience (UX) Quality Assurance check
- Undertake Third-Party review (open source software, third-party offerings, services0
- Data Governance review
- Security review
- Undertake Privacy Impact Assessment (PIA)
- Regulatory review
- Safety and assurance review
- Product compliance validation
- Coding completed

Gate 4: Deploy

- Curate data for the product demonstration
- User interface analytics configuration

- Draft beta/evaluation agreement
- Develop customer support/operations plan

Gate 5: Limited Availability Launch

- GSM
- Product demonstration for go to market
- Product provisioning
- AIST/PSL approval
- Draft product license

Gate 6: General Availability Launch

- Go to Market IT systems updated (i.e., SAP, Salesforce, etc.)
- Pricing model finalized
- Marketing materials finalized with information on performance, security, privacy and compliance
- Issue press release

Consistent with this approach, vendors create different licenses that track to each gate. Set forth below is a discussion of the different licenses that a vendor may use as the product progresses through the different gates of the development process.
The following flow chart illustrates this process:
Business Requirements Definition ("BRD") Process Flow Diagram

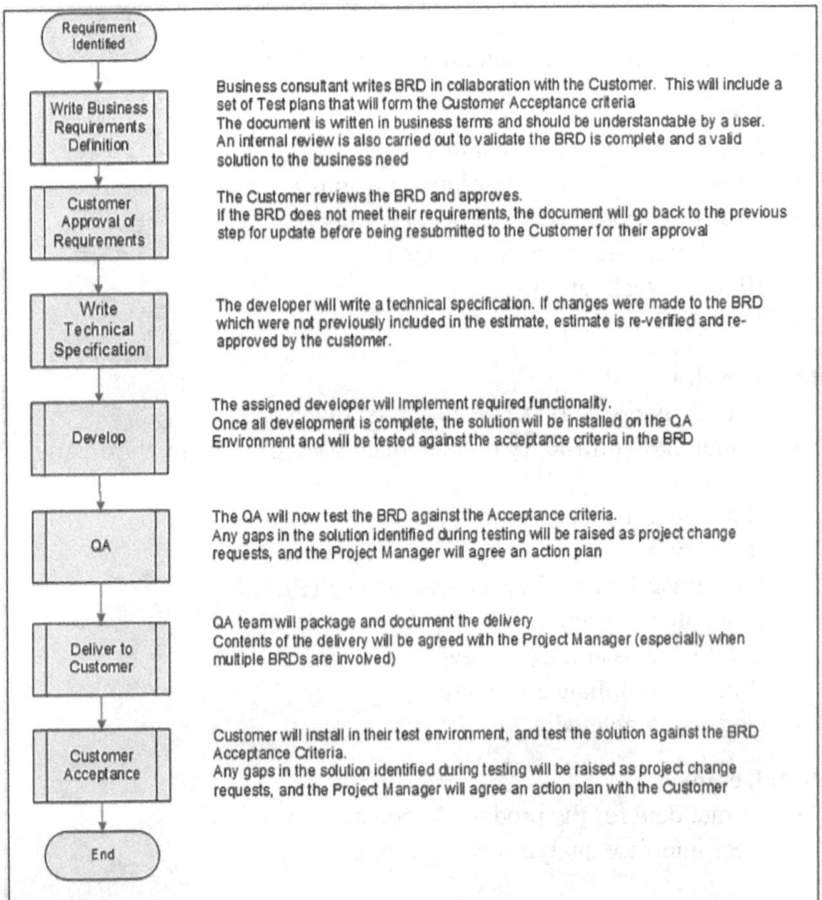

B. Issues to Be Considered in the Development Process

It has often been said that the three principal elements of software development are pricing, functionality and timing, and that a customer can have two of these three elements when developing an application but not all three given their interrelationship and interdependencies. As such, in drafting a software development agreement, it is important to understand the interrelationship of these issues to ensure a successful project. For example, if a party desires significant functionality developed within a short period of time, the price will likely be high. Conversely, if a party desires less functionality without a time deadline, the price will be lower.

1. *Pricing*

(a) Fixed Pricing

Pricing is the issue that is most negotiated, as most customers seek a fixed-price contract to limit their financial risk. Of course, many vendors are hesitant to agree to a fixed-price contract and assume the financial risk. There are many aspects to fixing the price, and the further into the project the price is fixed, the less risk there is for the vendor. Thus, the question becomes at what time in the development process the price can be fixed to allow each party to feel comfortable with the level of risk they are assuming. To that end, many vendors argue that a fixed-price contract usually will cost the client more than time and materials contract, as the vendor will have to include a significant contingency in its price to protect against losing money on the contract.

If the parties have only agreed on business specifications, there is a very high level of risk, as the technical specifications have yet to be agreed on, which in turn will determine the level of effort. Normally the vendor will only fix the price for the production of the functional specifications and will usually include a large contingency to reflect the incumbent risk. See Form C.1.4 for a model Business Requirements Definition.

If the functional specifications have been agreed on, the vendor will usually fix the cost of producing the functional specifications but may include a higher contingency depending on the degree of risk.

If the technical specifications have been completed, the vendor will normally fix the price up to system testing, as the functional specifications allow the vendor to estimate the scope of effort to develop the software with a great deal of certainty.

Under a fixed-price contract, change control must be rigorously enforced for both the vendor and customer to avoid a dispute. Payment is usually made on a percentage-complete basis or on the achievement of key milestones that must be accepted by the customer before payment is made.

(b) Time and Materials

Under a time and materials contract, charges are determined based on the amount of personnel time spent on the project and materials in providing the services in addition to any reimbursable expenses rather than on any results achieved. The client bears the risk of costs that exceed the targeted budget. Payments for time and materials contracts are usually made monthly in arrears based on invoices/time sheets submitted by the vendor.

> *If Vendor provides Customer with an estimate of the cost or timeframe for any services to be provided by Vendor, the estimate will be made in good faith based on the information known to the Vendor. Vendor does not promise that the estimates will be accurate and estimates are not intended as price or performance guarantees.*
>
> *Vendor will provide Customer with the requisite hours of Consulting Services identified within a Statement of Work. The Parties may choose to define a set of deliverables within a Statement of Work, provided that Vendor will not be obligated to provide Consulting Services beyond the total number of hours set forth in the Statement of Work, unless an amended SOW is agreed to by the Parties for additional Consulting Services or a SOW is modified by a change request signed by both Parties. Consulting Services for the implementation of [software product] will include the configuration of requirements in accordance with the approved functional requirement specification ("FRS") and any mutually agreed upon fulfillment criteria during the course of the engagement or as otherwise set forth in the applicable SOW after a Design engagement has been completed and fulfillment criteria has been defined. Should additional configuration be required to meet new or changed requirements from those documented in the approved FRS, Vendor will provide Customer with the estimated Fees, expenses, and requisite Consulting Services hours to complete such additional configuration and, if mutually agreed upon, the Parties will sign a change request to modify the applicable SOW accordingly.*

2. Payment.

Most agreements provide that the vendor will be paid upon achieving certain milestones or in the case of a time and materials agreement, in arrears after receipt of a valid invoice. Prudent customers will reserve the right to withhold payment for the vendor's failure to meet its contractual obligations, obtain credits for the vendor's failure to meet its obligations and to offset monies owed to the vendor under another agreement for the vendor's failure to perform.

3. Scope of Work

The scope of the work is perhaps the most important section of the agreement, as without a detailed scope of work, the parties may have a common understanding of what is being built but not agreement on the specific deliverables. While the parties may agree that the customer is purchasing a car and that the vendor will deliver a car, the customer believes it has purchased a Mercedes, while the vendor believes it is delivering a used Volkswagen. Thus, it is in both party's interests to develop and agree on a detailed scope of work to avoid future disputes which benefit neither party. Only once the parties have discussed and agreed on a detailed scope of work should they discuss and negotiate price.

4. Customer Dependencies

A successful engagement requires active customer participation and involvement, which should be constant through-out the development and delivery process to ensure that any issues are quickly identified and resolved. Once the scope has been finalized and agreed to, the parties should schedule weekly meetings to monitor the project's progress and ensure that the development process is proceeding smoothly. The customer's involvement should include participating in development team meetings as well as developing and approving the acceptance tests.

From the vendor's perspective, the parties' agreement should clearly set forth the customer's obligations, which may include:

- any deliverables to be provided by the customer,
- any information to be provided by the customer,
- a list/description of the customer's relevant hardware and software systems,
- any required customer documentation/materials,
- the customer employees/support staff who will provide services/support the project, including:
  - the skill profiles of the customer employees,
  - the names of customer employees,
- the customer's duty of cooperation,
- the time frames for the performance of the customer's obligations and responses,
- the provision of test data and test cases,
- partial acceptance of deliverables, and
- privacy and data protection obligations.

The agreement should also set forth the vendor's remedies for the customer's failure to meet its obligations, including:

- termination rights,
- relief from vendor's contractual obligations, and
- the extension of delivery dates.

Prudent vendors seek to protect themselves in the event the customer fails to meet its obligations. The following language is illustrative. It protects the vendor from failing to meet its delivery dates in the event the customer fails to promptly provide its feedback.

> *If Customer shall fail to review and provide comments to the Deliverables within 5 business days, the Milestone delivery dates set forth above shall be automatically extended on a day-for-day basis for each business day past such review period that Customer fails to provide its comments of such Deliverable.*

5. Vendor Staffing

Successful development projects are dependent on a skilled development team; constant turnover among team members can negatively impact the project. To that end, many customers seek to identify important team members as "Key Personnel" who the vendor my not remove from the project. Vendors are hesitant to identify too many resources as Key Personnel to avoid limiting their ability to staff projects as they see fit. Further, customers often insist on having the replacement resources work without charge until they are brought up to speed on the project, negatively impacting the vendor's profitability. Two examples of model language follows:

> *Under an applicable SOW, the Parties may identify certain Vendor roles or resources supporting the Consulting Services that are key personnel ("**Key Personnel**"). Before assigning any Vendor personnel to a Key Personnel position, whether as an initial assignment or as a replacement, Vendor shall (i) notify Customer of the proposed assignment, (ii) introduce the individual to appropriate representatives of Customer, (iii) provide Customer with a resume and any other information regarding the individual that may be reasonably requested by Customer, and (iv) obtain Customer's written approval for such assignment, which shall not be unreasonably withheld or delayed. Vendor shall notify Customer promptly if any change becomes necessary to the Key Personnel supporting the Consulting Services. Where reasonably possible, the notice shall be given no later than two (2) weeks prior to the change, during which time the Vendor shall ensure sufficient knowledge transfer. Vendor will use commercially reasonable efforts to not make unscheduled changes to the identified Key Personnel for any phase of the Consulting Services where those particular Key Personnel are deemed critical to that phase. If Customer has any concerns about any Key Personnel, or changes thereto, and their impact on the Consulting Services, Vendor and Customer will promptly meet and discuss in good faith to resolve any concerns related to the Consulting Services impact. If any Consulting Services supported by Key Personnel do not meet with the warranty requirements under Section ____ (**Warranty**) or Customer otherwise becomes reasonably dissatisfied with any of Key Personnel providing the Consulting Services, Customer may notify Vendor of the details of the failure or its dissatisfaction and require the prompt removal and replacement of such Key Personnel with an individual properly licensed, certified, and/or accredited that has sufficient skills, knowledge, and training to support the Consulting Services. Any costs incurred by Vendor due to changes to the Key Personnel shall be borne by Vendor.*

> **Resource Changes.** *Except as otherwise provided in the Agreement, Vendor personnel changes should be communicated a minimum of two (2) weeks in advance to Customer (or as promptly as practicable in the event of unplanned personnel changes, e.g., by reason of a personnel's resignation, death, disability, illness or termination of employment by Vendor).*

> *Any replacement personnel provided by Vendor will have comparable skills and experience as the personnel being replaced. Vendor will use reasonable measures to provide for a smooth transition of Services to the replacement personnel. Upon any replacement of such person, Developer agrees that Client shall not be charged for the initial eighty (80) hours of services provided to Client by such new Developer Team member or Developer Project Executive.*

6. *Milestones and Timelines (§§ 8.2, 8.3).*

Pre-agreed milestones provide greater protection for the licensee while assuring the licensor will receive progress payments necessary to fund its development efforts. This method also provides the licensee greater leverage in the event a dispute arises with the licensor. Most milestones are tied to the licensor's delivery of "value" to the licensee, i.e., completion of a particular work stream or module.

The use of milestones is not without risk, as the parties must agree on what triggers payment (e.g., delivery, acceptance, etc.), which has ramifications on both parties. A licensee should be wary of payment on delivery before the software has been tested, while the licensor must carefully consider accepting payment upon acceptance, as the licensee has greater leverage in not accepting the milestone. A compromise is to have the licensee make payment on delivery, but provide that such payment is only an "advance" and that all such payments are immediately repayable to the licensee if the ultimate deliverable is not accepted. Coupling these payments to the establishment of an advance payment bond in an amount equal to the amount of these "advances" effectively limits the licensee's risks. At the same time, the licensor has complete use of its money, less the minimal cost of the bond.

The customer should insist on tying its payments to the achievement of set milestones with a holdback that is paid upon final acceptance, to ensure that the vendor is paid according to its progress. To the extent the vendor misses a milestone, it should be obligated to assign additional resources to the project to meet the agreed-upon time line. Model language, blacklined to show vendor favorable changes, follows:

> *If a milestone or deadline set forth in the SOW is not met due to reasons attributable solely to Vendor and not due to ~~causes or events caused by~~ reasons attributable to Customer or ~~that are~~ beyond Vendor's reasonable control, Vendor agrees, at no charge to Customer, to make reasonable additional resources available in an effort to ~~ensure~~ mitigate such delay ~~is mitigated~~ as much as possible and ~~does not result I~~ not cause additional delays.*

7. *Reporting*

Prudent customers will require the vendor to provide regular reports on the progress and status of the project to avoid being surprised to learn the vendor will not meet the contractually committed delivery date shortly before such date.

> *On a weekly basis, Developer will provide to Client status reports that (i) correspond to Developer's prior invoice and work-in-process since the last invoice, (ii) for all Services performed, provide detailed descriptions, for each Statement of Work, of progress to date measured against the then-current timelines, and actual fees to date measured against the applicable Budget, (iii) an explanation of any difference between the progress to date versus the then-current timeline and/or between the actual fees versus the applicable Budget and (iv) such other information as reasonably requested by Client (each, a **"Variance Report"**).*

8. Acceptance

Acceptance of the deliverables should be based on pre-agreed acceptance tests created jointly by the vendor and the customer. The deliverables created during each phase of the project should be tested at the end of each phase and conditionally "accepted." Once all phases have been completed, the completed aggregate deliverable should go through acceptance testing. If the aggregate deliverable passes the acceptance tests, a final acceptance certificate should be issued and the holdback released. Customers should always test the aggregate final deliverable because, even though the interim deliverables may pass the interim acceptance tests, when operated together, the aggregate deliverable may not function as contractually required.

See Form E.3.1 and E.3.2 for model Acceptance Certificates.

9. Third Party Materials

Many customer seek to prohibit the vendor from incorporating any third party materials in to the deliverables without their prior written consent. They do so to obtain absolute ownership of the deliverables, free of any restrictions such as the need to acquire licenses for any third-party software incorporated into the deliverables.

C. Development Risks

Development contracts are fraught with risk from the perspective of the vendor as well as the customer, and a successful project requires constant diligence on behalf of both parties.

Listed below are several areas which can lead to failure. Each party should carefully review each list bi-weekly during the development process to ensure that such issues do not arise.

1. ***Customer Risks:***

- Incomplete specifications
- Customer fails to make available to the vendor critical project team members and subject matter experts, as well as customer IT managers of key data sources and application infrastructure.
- Customer makes endless changes to scope/functionality.
- Customer fails to provide test scripts that define the customer's business processes, allowing the vendor to test the business process.
- Unrealistic time schedules
- Customer provides a detailed RFP and insists on an unrealistic period for the vendor to conduct due diligence and to perform.
- Lack of support from the customer's IT staff
- Failure to properly budget for the project
- Inability to make timely decisions
- Lack of proper management by customer to ensure direction and control
- Inadequate change control process

2. ***Vendor Risks:***
- Required/identified staff unavailable to staff project
- Incomplete specifications
- Poor-quality code and poor-quality assurance review
- Inexperienced project management
- Significant staff turnover
- Lack of resources with sufficient skills for new technologies
- Inadequate change control process
- Personality clashes with client staff

D. Ownership of Developed Intellectual Property

Ownership of developed intellectual property is often a contentious issue between vendors and customers. Customers almost always argue that they have paid for the development and thus should own the created work. Vendors often seek ownership to re-use the developed intellectual property as party of their existing products or as part of a new product.

To resolve this dichotomy in a logical and thoughtful manner, the parties should discuss how ownership and license rights will work and then draft the agreement accordingly. Prior to discussing this issue with the opposing party, each party should meet internally to consider a number of factors that will provide guidance as to the importance of the developed intellectual property. Set forth below are several factors a party should consider when determining the importance of ownership.

Industry practice is for each party to retain ownership of the intellectual property it owned prior to entering into the agreement, and usually for the customer to own intellectual property developed for the customer under their agreement. Each party usually retains ownership of all intellectual property they develop independent of the other party or the agreement. Pre-existing intellectual property is often referred to as "Background IP" and newly developed IP as "Foreground IP."

This concept is illustrated as follows:

Background IPR *means, by reference to a Party, all Intellectual Property Rights, excluding Foreground IPR, owned by such Party or any of its Affiliates, or licensed or made available by a third party to such Party and under which such Party is authorised to grant licenses.*

> ***Foreground IP*** *means, by reference to a Party, all Intellectual Property that arises as a result or in the context of any activity pursuant to this Agreement.*

1. ***IP Ownership and Licences.*** The Intellectual Property Rights related to any part of the Work, including any Background IP, Foreground IP and entitlement to all development data, reports and other technical information relating to any part of the Work, shall be owned and licensed as follows:

   1.1 *Each Party shall retain the ownership of its Background IP.*
   1.2. *All Foreground IP shall be owned exclusively by Customer.*
   1.3. *Vendor:*

(a) *shall deliver all models, instructions, algorithms, technology, development data, reports and all other technical information, documentation and other knowhow related to all parts of the Work associated with Foreground IP to Customer;*

(b) *hereby grants to Customer a worldwide, non-exclusive, royalty-free license, with the right to sublicense, under Vendor's Background IP to make, have made, use, import, analyse, test, prepare derivative works of, reproduce, have reproduced, offer to sell, sell or otherwise dispose of such Vendor Background IP, to the extent Vendor incorporates such Background IP into any part of the Work;*

(c) *hereby assigns (and shall cause to be assigned) all Foreground IP to Customer to the extent required under applicable laws; and*

(d) *shall assist Customer, at Customer's expense, in obtaining, registering, perfecting and enforcing all Patents, trademarks and copyrights necessary to protect Customer's interest in the Intellectual Property established pursuant to this Section.*

For a general discussion, *see* Sinninger, *What's Mine Is Mine, What's Yours Is Also Mine,* 23 ACC Docket 12 (Jan. 2005); Porter, *Negotiating Rights to a Customer's Improvements and Modifications,* 15 Corp. Couns. Q. 14 (April 1999). For a discussion of the vendor's point of view, *see* Gard & Bullock, *What's Wrong With the 'I Paid For It, I Own It' Strategy?* 23 ACC Docket 23 (May 2005).

For a more detailed discussion, see Chapter 7.A and B.

1. Factors Influencing Intellectual Property Ownership of Developed Software

In deciding the appropriate position and negotiation strategy, a party should consider the following elements:

- The level of technical development.
- The level of technological advancement.
- The level of difficulty to develop the technology.
- The ease with which the developed technology can be segregated from existing vendor products and solutions.
- The commercial value of the developed intellectual property.
- The existence of an approved business case (including committed investment funds) to re-use the developed intellectual property.
- The value to be gained by the vendor from re-using the developed intellectual property.

Developed code is likely to fall within three categories:

- Routines regularly used on projects which the vendor must retain ownership
- Coding developed for a customer that is inapplicable for future customers
- New coding developed for a current project but not focused on the customer's business and could be used for future customers such that it does not compete with the customer's business.

Developers seek to retain ownership and reuse code with other customers so they do not have to worry that similar code might infringe on code that was transferred to a customer.

In considering the relative importance of ownership, the vendor should distinguish between developed intellectual property that may be re-used for other customers and developed intellectual property that is created solely for the customer's environment and is of little or no value to other potential customers of the vendor.

If the vendor is able to relicense the software to other customers, it will be incentivized to continue to maintain and support the software. Otherwise, the vendor has no incentive to continue to develop or support the software, as it has a single potential customer. The vendor is also incentivized to ensure the developed software is integrated into its existing product. With a large customer base, the vendor will be able to offer lower pricing, as the cost of enhancements and support can be amortized over its entire customer base. Vendors are also more likely to offer more robust SLAs and warranties for a product with a broad customer base than a product with a single customer.

Customers should consider whether the vendor will assign its best technical resources to the project if the customer will own the developed software. Further, will the developed software integrate seamlessly into the vendor's base code, given that the vendor will most likely not be supporting the code it develops for the customer? From the customer's perspective, customers must consider the importance of the developed software to their business. Is the software critical for growing and enhancing customer's business competency or is it a back office application for which there are many similar applications?

For a more detailed discussion see, Tannenbaum, *Using Business Objectives to Allocate Ownership and License Rights in Custom Software*, 31 COMP. & INTERNET LAW. 15 (May 2014).

2. *Ownership Options*

(a) One Party's Ownership of All Developed IP

The cleanest and simplest resolution to the ownership issue is for one party to own all developed intellectual property. Doing so creates a bright line as to ownership and avoids future disputes over which party owns which aspects of the developed intellectual property. Of course, one party is often unwilling to grant exclusive ownership of the developed intellectual property to the other party, requiring the parties to split the baby in a clear and logical manner.

From the vendor's perspective, retaining ownership of the developed intellectual property arguably allows the vendor to maintain the integrity of its products and solutions while ensuring their continued improvement and enhancement. Under the vendor's reasoning, the customer benefits from receiving access to all enhancements and improvements commissioned by other vendor customers as well as reduced development and maintenance costs from the support of a common product.

Vendors argue that a license provides the customer the rights it needs. Ownership does not benefit the customer, as the customer will likely be unable to independently maintain or support the developed intellectual property and will be forced to pay an additional fee to the vendor or a third party to maintain and support it. Vendors remind customers that the benefits of owning any work product are outweighed by the costs of ownership, including the increased maintenance and support fees arising from exclusive ownership of the intellectual property.

In those situations where the vendor is creating intellectual property that will be part of an existing customer-owned product, the customer will likely demand ownership of the intellectual property and will be unwilling to grant the vendor ownership. In these situations, however, ownership of the developed intellectual property will in all likelihood be of little value to the vendor, and the vendor can concede ownership to the customer. Model language granting ownership to the customer follows:

> *Vendor represents, warrants and covenants that all Created Materials shall be free and clear of any liens and encumbrances. Vendor hereby does and will irrevocably assign to Customer or Customer's designee all of Vendor's right, title and interest in and to any and all Created Materials and all associated records, such assignment to occur with respect to each unit of Created Materials at the time such unit of Created Materials is first conceived, made, derived, developed, written or created, and regardless of when the Created Material is first conceived, made, derived, developed, written or created.*
>
> *To the extent any of the rights, title and interest in and to Created Materials cannot be assigned by Vendor to Customer, Vendor hereby grants to Customer an exclusive, royalty-free, transferable, irrevocable, perpetual, worldwide, fully paid-up license (with rights to sublicense through multiple tiers of sublicensees) to fully use, practice and exploit those non-assignable rights, title and interest, including, but not limited to, the right to make, use, sell, offer for sale, import, have made, and have sold, the Created Materials. To the extent any of the rights, title and interest in and to the Created Materials can neither be assigned nor licensed by Vendor to Customer, Vendor hereby irrevocably waives and agrees never to assert the non-assignable and non-licensable rights, title and interest against Customer, Customer's licensors, any of Customer's successors in interest, or any of Customer's customers. If any Created Materials include any work of authorship that qualifies as a "work made for hire" as defined in subclause (2) under Section 101 of the Copyright Law of the United States (Title 17 of the United States Code, as may be amended from time to time), Customer and Vendor agree that Customer or Customer's designee owns such work of authorship as a work made for hire under such section.*
>
> *<u>Assistance</u>. Vendor agrees to perform, during and after the Term of this Agreement, all acts that Customer deems necessary or desirable to permit and assist Customer, at its expense, in obtaining, perfecting and enforcing the full benefits, enjoyment, rights and title throughout the world in the Created Materials as provided to Customer under this Agreement. If Customer is unable for any reason to secure Vendor's signature to any document required to file, prosecute, register or memorialize the assignment of any rights under any Created Materials as provided under this Agreement, Vendor hereby irrevocably designates and appoints Customer and Customer's duly authorized officers and agents as Vendor's agents and attorneys-in-fact to act for and on Vendor's behalf and instead of Customer to take all lawfully permitted acts to further the filing, prosecution, registration, memorialization of assignment, issuance and enforcement of rights in, to and under the Created Materials, all with the same legal force and effect as if executed by Vendor. The foregoing is deemed a power coupled with an interest and is irrevocable.*

(b) Ownership Allocated Based on Characteristics of the Software

While most parties focus on an "all or nothing" approach where one party owns all the developed intellectual property, a more productive approach is for both parties to close look at the functionality of the software and determine if it is possible to allocate ownership based on the characteristics of the software and the needs of the parties.

The first step is to review the schematic diagram for the developed software and determine how, if at all, the developed software interacts with the vendor's solution. For example, the customer may need to pass on certain ownership rights in the developed software to its own customers and cannot do so if the vendor retains ownership of all developed intellectual property. Notwithstanding the parties' seemingly conflicting interests, the vendor's desire to protect the sanctity of its product may not be mutually exclusive with the needs of the customer.

Often the parties negotiating the license may not be technically sophisticated and may not realize that they are negotiating over a particular piece of software that has no value to one party. Thus, it is prudent to review the schematic diagram to ensure that each party understands what the vendor is delivering and the importance of each piece of software, such as an API or interface, to each party. Doing so may provide a common ground for determining ownership, allowing the parties to amicably allocate ownership of discrete portions of the developed software utilizing the schematic diagram. For example, the following language grants the vendor ownership of any developed intellectual property relating to the vendor's core code language while granting the customer ownership of all other developed intellectual property:

> *Vendor's Background IP and any new software developed under this SOW which is part of the Vendor's Platform that requires re-compilation of the software code of the Vendor's Platform in order for such new software to function, any improvements to any of the foregoing, and all intellectual property rights therein shall be owned by Vendor.*

3. Alternative Ownership Options

Many parties are unable to quickly resolve the ownership issue and enter into protracted negotiations around ownership of the developed intellectual property. To reach a resolution, the vendor should explore with the customer the basis for its concern and then craft a response to address the customer's concerns. Set forth below are several possibilities for resolving ownership issues.

(a) The Vendor Retains Ownership of All Developed Intellectual Property but Pays the Customer a Royalty or Provides Discounted Services

If the customer believes that because it paid the vendor to develop the intellectual property, it should retain ownership, the vendor can offer to pay the customer a royalty on future licenses of the developed intellectual property to allow the customer to recoup its fees. Model language is set forth below:

> *In consideration of Customer partially funding the development of the Custom Software, Vendor shall pay Customer a royalty on the future licensing of the Software as set forth in this Section ___. Vendor shall pay to Customer a royalty based on the "Gross License Fee" ("Fee") of the Custom Software for all third-party licenses of Custom Software by Vendor made within (_______) months from the earlier of [Acceptance] or Vendor first licensing such module to any third party.*

While the payment of a royalty is a viable alternative from a business perspective, it may be unwieldy to implement, as the vendor must establish an administrative mechanism to identify, track, and pay royalties to the customer. Further, the customer will most likely insist on a right of audit, which will increase the administrative burden on the vendor. A prudent vendor will seek to limit the customer's right to audit the vendor to limit disruption to its business and the attendant cost.

Unless the vendor has entered, or envisages entering, into a significant number of royalty-generating contracts, the administrative costs of establishing and administrating the royalty payments may outweigh the benefits to the vendor. Before agreeing to pay a royalty, the vendor should ensure that the business has the capability to track the amounts due and to pay the customer. Also, there is a risk that the customer has an expectation of actually receiving royalties which may not come to fruition, especially if the vendor subsequently decides not to continue to invest in the exploitation of the developed intellectual property. To that end, the vendor should never commit to continue to develop and market the software in question.

From the vendor's perspective, the vendor should limit its bad debt risk by calculating the royalty on those funds actually received by the vendor, not the funds payable to the vendor by the customer. Payment should be made only when the relicensed intellectual property has been accepted by the subsequent customer. The vendor should not grant multiple customers royalties from enhancements to the same module or software program. That may cause royalties payable by the vendor to potentially exceed its future revenues from relicensing the intellectual property. From the customer's perspective, royalties should be paid regardless of whether the vendor actually collects payment, as it was the vendor's choice to contract with the client.

To limit its financial obligations, the vendor should place an absolute cap on the royalties payable to the customer from relicensing the developed intellectual property. The cap can be tied to the amount paid by the customer to the vendor, the amount paid by the customer to the vendor plus a reasonable return or tied to a set time period. An alternative is to cap the customer's royalties at a multiple of the fees paid by the customer to the vendor for the developed intellectual property.

From the vendor's perspective, the vendor should not allow the royalty payments to be unlimited in either amount or the period of time in which the customer is entitled to receive them.

One alternative to paying a royalty is to provide the customer free or discounted services to be applied against future development or maintenance and support. Free or discounted services will likely have less of a financial impact on the vendor and will encourage the customer to purchase additional services from the vendor, potentially expanding the relationship between the vendor and the customer.

Offering the customer, a price concession instead of a royalty requires the vendor to assume some risk as under a royalty structure, as the vendor must pay the customer only if the vendor is able to relicense the developed intellectual property. A prudent vendor should not agree to pay a minimum royalty. The benefits of a royalty scheme versus a discount should be balanced against the reduced administrative costs associated with a discount in lieu of a royalty as well as potential cost savings if the discount is less than the projected royalty payments.

(b) The Vendor Retains Ownership of All Developed IP but Agrees to Restrict Future Licenses of the Developed IP

If the customer is focused on obtaining a competitive advantage in the marketplace, the vendor should suggest a means to prevent the customer's competitors from using the developed intellectual property for a stated period of time. The vendor can agree to limit future relicensing of the developed IP in a particular geography, industry, or even a particular customer for a limited time period. The following model language reflects this position.

> *In the event Customer desires Vendor to develop a Modification to the Software for Customer's sole use, Customer must advise Vendor of this restriction prior to development. Upon receipt of such notice, the Modification shall be designated as a "Customer-Specific Modification" and identified as such in the associated Work Order. The parties agree that the Modification shall remain the sole and exclusive property of Vendor; however, Customer shall receive a limited, non-transferable, non-assignable object code license to use such Modification for so long as Customer retains a license to use the Software. Vendor agrees that it shall not license a Customer-Specific Modification to [a third party/named entity or a defined industry] for [a specific time period] after Acceptance.*

Any entity/industry limitation should be tightly drawn and limited in duration. The limitation should be related only to the developed intellectual property and not the provision of all services or solutions in the identified geography, industry, or client.

Further, the vendor should seek to retain the right under the underlying agreement to develop functionally equivalent intellectual property provided the vendor does not use the customer's confidential information. A prudent customer should prohibit the vendor from using the employees and contractors who worked on the developed intellectual property to develop functionally equivalent intellectual property. The customer should also carefully draft the "Residuals" section of the underlying agreement to ensure the customers' interests are protected and that ownership of any business methodologies created by the vendor in the course of the agreement has been addressed. The following language affirms the vendor's right to assign the vendor employees who worked on a customer's project to a competitor's project.

> *Customer recognizes that Vendor's employees performing the Services under this Agreement and the Statements of Work issued hereunder may perform similar services for others, and this Agreement shall not prevent Vendor from providing services or developing materials that are competitive with those developed or provided hereunder regardless of any similarity to such services or materials, provided, however, that Vendor shall*

not use or infringe upon any Confidential Information of Customer, any Deliverable, or any of Customer's other proprietary and intellectual property rights in the performance of such services for others.

Finally, the customer should also insist on including an audit provision allowing the customer to audit the vendor's subsequent licensing of the developed intellectual property. Model audit language is set forth below.

Licensor shall keep all usual and proper books and records pertaining to the licensing and use of the Custom Software. During the Term of this Agreement and for three years thereafter, Customer and/or its designated representatives shall have the right to audit (including by inspecting and copying any such books and records) Licensor, in order to verify its compliance with the terms of this Agreement. Customer shall conduct such audits during the Licensor's normal business hours and in such a manner as not to interfere unreasonably with Licensor's normal business operations. Customer may conduct such audits from time to time as Customer deems necessary, but shall use any information obtained or observed during the course of the audit solely for the purposes of (i) determining whether the Licensor is making the proper royalties in compliance with the terms of this Agreement and is otherwise in compliance with this Agreement and any applicable laws, and (ii) enforcing its rights under this Agreement and any applicable laws. Except to the extent necessary to enforce its rights, Customer and its representatives will hold all such information in confidence.

(c) Joint Ownership of All Developed IP

A "Joint Work" is "[w]ork prepared by two or more authors with the intention that their contributions be merged into inseparable or interdependent parts of a unitary whole." 17 U.S.C. § 101. Joint ownership, however, can create more issues than it resolves, as the rights of joint owners vary depending on the type of intellectual property that is jointly owned.

For example, joint owners of a copyrighted work may independently exercise all rights of a copyright owner but are obligated to share profits from licensing the copyright. Joint owners of a patent have no such obligations. Further, the laws governing the joint ownership of intellectual property varies by country, and the effect of one party's bankruptcy is unclear.

Co-owners of a copyright are treated as tenants in common. *Davis v. Blige*, 505 F.3d 90 (2d Cir. 2007). Subject to certain limitations, each "owner" is free to license and use the work as it sees fit, as well as transfer its limited rights in the work to a third party. 1 MELVILLE B. NIMMER & DAVID NIMMER, NIMMER ON COPYRIGHT § 6.11 (Supp. 2006). A co-owner has standing to bring an action for copyright infringement, *Isbell Records v. DM Records*, 2009 WL 3386546 (5th Cir. Oct. 22, 2009), but cannot grant an exclusive license without the consent of all other co-owners, *Sybersound Records v. UAV Corp.*, 517 F.3d 1137 (9th Cir. 2008) and cannot grant a retroactive license. *Davis v. Blige*, 505 F.3d 90 (2d Cir. 2007). Each co-owner must also provide an accounting to all other co-owners for any profits. *Davis, id.* at 98.

Joint ownership allows each party to market the software to whomever it chooses, while at the same time retaining the right to make modifications and enhancements. This alternative may be detrimental to the licensor, because the licensee may license the software to the licensor's direct competitors. Under joint copyright ownership, however, each owner has a duty to account to the other. 1 MELVILLE B. NIMMER & DAVID NIMMER, NIMMER ON COPYRIGHT § 6.12[A] at 36.6 (2005); *see, e.g.*, *Oddo v. Ries*, 743 F.2d 630 (9th Cir. 1984). While the right to an accounting exists for jointly owned copyrights, there is no right to an accounting for a jointly owned software patent. 35 U.S.C. § 262. This dichotomy could likely lead to confusion, and potentially litigation, if the jointly owned software is protected by both copyright and patent. At the same time, this approach is probably unrealistic as the custom portion most likely is of little value unless it is licensed in conjunction with the rest of the software.

If the resulting work product will contain preexisting intellectual property owned by the vendor and intellectual property owned by the customer, the work product should contain a copyright notice to the following effect:

> *"This contains material, which is the confidential, unpublished property licensed to Customer. Receipt or possession of it does not convey any rights to divulge, reproduce, use, or allow others to use it without the specific written authorization of Customer, and use must conform strictly to the license agreement between user and Customer.*
>
> *Copyright © 2027 [Licensor Legal Name]. All rights reserved.*
>
> *Copyright © 2027 [Customer Legal Name]. All rights reserved."*

For a discussion of joint ownership, see Johnson, *Avoiding Joint Pain: Treatment of Joint Works of Authorship Conditions*, 43 MD. B.J. 13 (May 2010).

With joint ownership, all parties with an ownership right must be a party to any suit to enforce an infringement claim. In essence, both parties have a license, but they must act jointly to enforce their rights.

(d) The Customer Owns All Developed Intellectual Property but Grants the Vendor a Royalty-Free, Perpetual, Non-terminable License to Re-use and Sublicense the Developed Intellectual Property

Receiving a license allows the vendor to "re-use"/sublicense the developed intellectual property, albeit with some restrictions. Under this scenario, the vendor is essentially a reseller. The vendor should seek a royalty-free license so that it may sublicense the developed intellectual property without payment to the customer and seek to retain ownership of all enhancements, improvements, and derivative works made in conjunction with the re-use and sublicensing of the developed intellectual property.

> *Customer hereby grants Vendor a perpetual, non-transferable, non-exclusive, royalty-free license to use and sublicense the Deliverables with the right to create Derivative works.*

See also Checklists for Joint Development Agreements, 90 FORMS & CHECKLISTS BI-MONTHLY 1 (Nov./Dec. 2012)

(e) The Customer Owns the Developed Intellectual Property but Issues the Vendor a Covenant Not to Sue

A covenant not to sue offers minimal rights and protection to the vendor. The vendor receives comfort that it may use the developed intellectual property for its internal purposes without fear of legal action, but it may not sublicense the developed intellectual property nor include the developed intellectual property in any of its products. The customer may bring legal action for any other use or further sublicensing. Thus, the value to the vendor is minimal. In essence, the value lies in the vendor's right to use the developed intellectual property for the vendor's own internal purposes.

E. Customization vs. Configuration

Confusion often arises over the difference between the customization of a software application and the configuration of a software application. Configuration uses the inherent functionality of an application to allow licensees to structure the application to meet a licensee's requirements using tool sets inherent in the software, such as creating fields, creating and modifying drop-down lists, and other similar actions. Utilizing existing configurations allows licensees to avoid the often lengthy, expensive and risky customization process by taking advantage of the flexibility inherent within the application. Configuration carries significantly less risk, as the configurations have most likely been tested by the licensor prior to the public release of the application. As such, configurations are almost always less expensive and less labor-intensive than customization.

Customization, on the other hand, involves modifying the application's source code to create new functionality that does not presently exist within the application. Modification of the underlying code brings with it technical, financial and timing risk, as well as the risk that the modifications fail to achieve the desired result or improved efficiencies. Further, any customization of the source code may impact the implementation of future licensor-developed updates and enhancements of the application if the customizations are not compatible with such updates or enhancements.

F. Funding Options

Many vendors seek to involve their customer in deciding what functionality to develop for their applications. In conjunction with seeking customer input, vendors offer incentives to customers who contribute financially to the development of the new functionality. Therese incentives may include the right to license the new functionality at a discount, the rights to obtain the developed functionality before other customers or even the exclusive right to access such functionality. Model language follows.

> *Vendor may periodically circulate proposals for the development of Shared Cost Enhancements to all customers. Vendor will agree to develop those Shared Cost Enhancements that are sponsored by a minimum number of customers. Vendor will set the minimum number of sponsors for each Shared Cost Enhancement based on Vendor's view of the number of customers interested in the enhancement. The terms for the Shared Cost Enhancement development will be agreed upon by the vendor and the sponsoring customers. Fees for Shared Cost Enhancements are in addition to the base annual license fee.*

Shared Cost Enhancement means a modification to the Software developed by Vendor in conjunction with one or more customers who agree to pay a pro rata share of the development cost. Only customers who contribute to the development cost or subsequently license the enhancement are entitled to use the enhancement.

G. Cloud

Software development for cloud applications is potentially challenging; in a multi-tenant environment, the vendor cannot transfer ownership of any new services or features, as the features are used by all customers. If the customer is in a single tenant environment, the customer may be able to receive ownership of a personalized instance of the software.

H. Starting Work before Contract Signature

Often, project deadlines may lead the parties to consider starting the "Discovery" phase (i.e., the requirements gathering or design work) in parallel with negotiating the services agreement or SOW. Doing so without an agreement creates risk for both parties. The vendor is potentially working without a payment commitment and the customer is unsure the amount it will be paying for the work. From the perspective of both parties, ownership of the work has not been agreed to in writing.

To reduce their respective risks, the parties should enter into a binding, interim agreement, setting forth the minimum terms each party requires to protect its interests. At a minimum, the interim agreement should contain:

- a description of work being performed;
- the fees for such work;
- confirmation that the work product from the Discovery phase is owned by the customer or licensed to the customer with appropriate rights to use the work (including with another vendor) regardless of whether the customer enters into a subsequent agreement with the vendor. The description of Discovery phase work and essential terms should be binding on both parties; and
- from the vendor's perspective, a limitation of liability.

See Form C.1.5 for a model Interim Services Agreement.

I. *PRACTICE POINT:* Checklist for drafting software development agreements.

(a) Deliverables

- Are the deliverables clearly defined, including the functional specifications?
- Who will own the developed software?
- When does ownership transfer?
  - Upon development?
  - Upon payment?

- Is there a work made for hire clause?
- Will the vendor provide any other services?
    - Testing
    - Implementation services
    - Data transfer
    - Porting
    - Maintenance and support

(b) Fees and Payment

- How are the fees be determined?
    - Time and materials
    - Fixed price
    - Time and materials with a "not to exceed" cap
- Is payment contingent on acceptance?

(c) Development

- How will change orders be processed?
- How will the development be managed?
- Can the vendor use subcontractors?
    - Onshore?
    - Offshore?

(d) Acceptance

- Who will draft the acceptance procedures?
- Are the acceptance procedures defined?
- What constitutes acceptance?
    - The failure to reject the deliverables
    - Use of the software in a production environment?
- If rejected, may the vendor cure the non-conformance? If so,
    - How many times?
    - How long does the customer have to resolve the non-conformance?
- Does the customer need to obtain a license to use the vendor's Background IP to use the developed IP?

(e) Remedies

- What remedies does the customer have in the event of the vendor's breach?
    - Specific performance?
    - Cover?

(f) Third Party Materials

- Can the vendor incorporate third party software products into the deliverables?
    - With consent?
    - Open source software?

(g) *Milestones and Service Levels*

- Are there clearly stated consequences for failing to meet the milestones?
- Are to project milestones achievable?
- Are service levels appropriate
- Are service level credits appropriate?

CHAPTER **17**

Services Agreements

Services agreements can take many different forms including support and maintenance agreements, staff augmentation agreements, IT outsourcing agreements, software development agreement, and professional services agreements. Each agreement should be tailored to the nature of the services being provided. Set forth below is a discussion of the principal types of agreements.

A. Professional Services Agreements

Professional services agreements are used when the customer seeks to have the vendor perform specific services, for which the customer lacks the skill set to provide itself.

1. Services and Deliverables (§3)

Professional services agreements vary in how they describe the work to be performed by the vendor. One approach is to set forth the deliverables the vendor is to produce; the other is to describe the services the vendor will provide, usually on an on-going basis. The approach used depends on the nature of the agreement. Is the vendor responsible for providing a specific result such as integrating a software application into the customer's IT systems or providing ongoing services such as support and maintenance services?

The vendor's performance is often measured differently depending on which approach is used. If the vendor is committed to providing ongoing services, the vendor's success is measured/incented through the use of service levels. With specific deliverables, the vendor is measured by whether the vendor provided the deliverables within the required time period and if the deliverables met the stated requirements.

Perhaps the most important aspect of the deliverables provision is how will ownership of the deliverables be allocated between the parties and how will the deliverables be provided. For example, will the customer receive object code or source code for the deliverables?

See Chapter 7.A for a more detailed discussion of the ownership issues associated with developed materials.

2. Warranties (§6)

Most vendors provide limited warranties around professional services, the most common is that the services will be provided in a professional and workmanlike manner. While many customers seek to have the vendor warrant that the services will be provided in accordance with the "highest industry standards", the phrase is ambiguous, as it is unclear which industry standards the warranty is referring to. Model language favoring the customer follows:

Vendor undertakes, warrants and represents that the Services will be:

(i) Performed in a diligent and timely fashion, in accordance with the Specifications and best industry practice, in compliance with any applicable Laws and in a professional and workmanlike manner;

(ii) Performed by adequate numbers of appropriately qualified and trained personnel. With due care and diligence;

(iii) Free from defects as regards their performance;

(iv) Without any loss or corruption of Customer Data;

(v) Provided in such a manner so as not to detrimentally affect the operation of Customer's business;

(vi) Consistent, compatible and interoperable with the services to be provided and the Vendor will use commercially reasonable efforts to maintain such; and consistency, compatibility and interoperability with changes to such services.

3. Remedies (§§6.1, 8)

Most vendors limit their liability to reperforming the services provided the customer notifies the vendor within 30 days of the vendor performing the services.

4. Customer Dependencies (§2.12 (iii))

Prudent vendors should require that the agreement set forth any customer obligations which are conditions precedent to the vendor's obligations and the ramifications if the customer fails to meet its obligations. These dependencies are important as, depending on the particular obligation, the vendor may be unable to meet its obligations unless the customer provides the needed information/support etc. Common dependencies include:

- Providing access to the customer's IT systems
- Providing required information and data
- Providing access to third-party software and hardware
- Providing access to critical customer employees
- Providing necessary approvals and sign-offs within the required time periods

For example, many professional services agreements include milestones by which the vendor must deliver certain portions of the project. The vendor's failure to meet the milestone dates often triggers service level credits, late fees or even constitutes a breach under the agreement. As such, the vendor should insist on including language in the agreement excusing the vendor's performance in the event a delay is caused by the customer. The most common way of addressing this issue is to grant the vendor a day's delay for each day the customer delays the vendor's performance.

> **Day for Day Delay** *If Customer shall fail to review and provide comments to such materials within 5 business days, the Milestone delivery dates set forth above shall be automatically extended on a day-for-day basis for each business day past such review period Customer fails to provide its comments of such SOW Deliverable.*

5. Key Personnel (§4.2)

While it is impractical to require the vendor to assign employees to a particular project for the duration of the project, especially for long-term projects, it is common for customers to ask the vendor to assign certain named "key personnel" to the project for its duration. Prudent vendors should resist demands to make such assignments absolute, as an employee may desire to work on other projects, the vendor may need the employee on other projects and/or it may be impossible to promote the employee if they are required to remain on the project, causing them to resign their employment. Model language follows:

> *Under an applicable SOW, the Parties may identify certain Vendor roles or resources supporting the Consulting Services that are key personnel ("Key Personnel"). Before assigning any Vendor personnel to a Key Personnel position, whether as an initial assignment or as a replacement, Vendor shall (i) notify Customer of the proposed assignment, (ii) introduce the individual to appropriate representatives of Customer, (iii) provide Customer with a resume and any other information regarding the individual that may be reasonably requested by Customer, and (iv) obtain Customer's written approval for such assignment, which shall not be unreasonably withheld or delayed. Vendor shall notify Customer promptly if any change becomes necessary to the Key Personnel supporting the Consulting Services. Where reasonably possible, the notice shall be given no later than four (4) weeks prior to the change, during which time the Vendor shall ensure sufficient knowledge transfer. Vendor will use commercially reasonable efforts to not make unscheduled changes to the identified Key Personnel for any phase of the Consulting Services where those particular Key Personnel are deemed critical to that phase. If Customer has any concerns about any Key Personnel, or changes thereto, and their impact on the Consulting Services, Vendor and Customer will promptly meet and discuss in good faith to resolve any concerns related to the Consulting Services impact. If any Consulting Services supported by Key Personnel do not meet with the warranty requirements under Section ____ or Customer otherwise becomes reasonably dissatisfied with any of Key Personnel providing the Consulting Services, Customer may notify Vendor of the details of the failure or its dissatisfaction and require the prompt removal and replacement of such Key Personnel with an individual properly licensed, certified, and/or accredited that has sufficient skills, knowledge, and training to support the Consulting Services. Any costs incurred by Vendor due to changes to the Key Personnel shall be borne by Vendor.*

6. Staffing Changes

(a) By Vendor (§4.4)

Many customers seek to require the vendor to notify the customer in the event the vendor seeks to reassign an employee working on the project or the employee leaves the project. Prudent vendors should only agree to use their good faith efforts to notify the customer of an employee's departure, as employees may resign on short notice or no notice at all. Thus, vendors should insist on a "as soon as reasonably possible" notice standard.

In those situations where a vendor employee does leave a project, some customers seek to vet and approve any replacements. Prudent vendors should avoid allowing the customer to interview potential replacements to avoid ceding control of their hiring process to the customer. Further, the vendor remains responsible for providing the deliverables.

Some customers seek to have the replacement employee work without charge to the customer while the employee is brought up to speed on the project. Agreeing to a no charge "burn in " period could have a serious impact on the vendor's finances if a significant number of employees leave the project.

> ***Resource Changes.*** *Except as otherwise provided in the Agreement, Vendor personnel changes should be communicated a minimum of 2 weeks in advance to Customer (or as promptly as practicable in the event of unplanned personnel changes, e.g., by reason of a personnel's resignation, death, disability, illness or termination of employment by Vendor). Any replacement personnel provided by Vendor will have comparable skills and experience as the personnel being replaced. Vendor will use reasonable measures to provide for a smooth transition of Services to the replacement personnel. The Vendor objective is to minimize any adverse impact to the Services and Fees hereunder*

For very large engagements some customers require the vendor to provide monthly or quarterly reports on staff turnover, as excessive turnover may impact the ability of the vendor to meet its obligations. To that end, these customers seek to implement service levels to incent the vendor to minimize employee turnover.

(b) Requested By Customer

Some customers seek to review and approve all vendor resources assigned to a project as well as the right to have vendor resources removed from a project. Granting the customer the right to do so potentially impacts the vendor's ability to deliver the contracted for services and deliverables in accordance with the terms of the agreement. Further, if the customer requests the vendor replace a resource in violation of the law, doing so may expose the vendor to potential liability. Thus, the agreement should specifically provide that race, gender, age, religion, national origin, and other legally discriminatory characteristics are not valid grounds for removing a resource.

> *Customer shall have the right to require Vendor to replace Vendor's personnel whom Customer deems to be unfit or otherwise unsatisfactory to perform Vendor's duties hereunder. Race, gender, age, religion, national origin, etc. are never valid grounds for removing a resource.*

7. *Acceptance (§5)*

Unless the vendor is providing staff augmentation services, the agreement should set forth the criteria by which the customer will accept the services. The acceptance criteria should be objective such that a third-party i.e., a judge or a jury, will be able to definitively determine whether the vendor met its obligations. A clear acceptance process will also prevent the customer from wrongfully rejecting the services.

8. *Statements of Work (SOWs) (§8)*

Most services agreements set forth the deliverables and the terms related to the deliverables in a statement of work attached to the agreement. The content and complexity of each statement of work will vary based on the nature of the services to be provided. See Chapter 13 for a detailed discussion of statements of work.

9. *Term and Termination (§8)*

Depending on the nature of the services being provided, services agreements are often terminable by the customer for convenience with prior written notice (i.e., 90 days). The customer may be required to pay the vendor an early termination fee as well as the cost of any non-terminable third-party agreements associated with the provision of the services. The customer's ability to terminate the agreement for convenience will depend on the customer's ability to negotiate such a provision.

10. *PRACTICE POINT*: Checklist for acceptance provisions in services agreements.

- Who is responsible for drafting the acceptance criteria? Usually the vendor drafts the criteria and they are approved by the customer.
- How long does the customer have to review the deliverables/conduct the acceptance tests?
- If the customer fails to notify the vendor of its acceptance or rejection, are the deliverables "deemed" accepted?
- If the deliverables are used in a production environment, are they "deemed" accepted?
- How will the customer communicate to the vendor whether the deliverables are accepted or rejected? If rejected, does the customer have to provide a detailed explanation of why the deliverables failed to meet the acceptance criteria?
- Will the vendor have the right to re-perform the services if they are rejected? If so, how long?

- If the vendor re-performs the services, does the initial acceptance process restart or is there a revised process?
- Is there a limit on the number of times the vendor can reperform the services, attempt to cure any deficiency?

B. System Integration Agreements

System integrators integrate third-party products into a single solution for a customer. For example, a system integrator may integrate a third-party application and a third-party database with a customer's legacy ERP system while customizing the third-party application to meet the needs of the customer. Many systems integrators, such as Accenture LLP and DXC Technology Company, build consulting practices around third-party vendor products like SAP, Salesforce, Cerner and Lawson. There are three common deal structures used by system integrators when structuring their transactions with a customer.

1. The customer contracts with the vendor directly to purchase a vendor's products, and the system integrator operates solely as the system integrator

Under this structure, the customer purchases the vendor's products directly from the vendor, and the client pays the system integrator to integrate the different vendor software/hardware components the customer has purchased. Because the client has purchased the products directly from the vendor, the system integrator assumes no liability for the failure of the vendor's products to meet any contractual requirements in the vendor/client contract, such as performance warranties. This structure is appropriate when the system integrator does not have extensive experience with using a vendor's products or the client seeks to avoid paying the system integrator a premium to assume additional risk if guaranteeing the performance of the integrated/third-party products.

2. The system integrator integrates its products with third-party products, assuming full responsibility for the third-party vendor's products

In this model, the system integrator will charge the customer a premium for assuming the additional risk of guaranteeing the performance of the third-party products and that the integrated solution will work correctly. This structure is commonly used when the system integrator incorporates third-party products into the solution and the system integrator's product is only one component of a fully integrated solution. It is not appropriate where the system integrator is only providing system integration services for third-party products as opposed to its own, as the system integrator does not want to assume liability for a third party's product when the system integrator is not adding value. System integrators should not provide a warranty to the customer that exceeds the warranty provided by the third-party vendor. Adding the system integrator's margin on top of the price of the third-party product may cause the system integrator's pricing to not be competitive.

3. *The system integrator resells the vendor's products to the customer*

Under this structure, the client may benefit from the system integrator's competitive pricing, global sourcing, and a single point of contact for purchases of third-party products. The system integrator acts as a reseller, marking up the purchase price for the vendor's products, thereby making a margin on top of the vendor's sale price. Title and ownership of the vendor's products pass directly from the vendor to the client. In this model, the system integrator assumes no liability, reducing the system integrator's risk, as the system integrator purchases the products and services from the vendor and resells them to the client but takes no responsibility for the products and services or vendor performance. The vendor contracts directly with the client for product performance (including all warranties, indemnities and licenses). The system integrator does not flow-down the vendor terms to the client or sublicense the vendor's licenses and thus has no further obligation to the client after the sale.

See Form C.2.1 for a model Systems Integration Agreement.

4. *PRACTICE POINT*: Checklist for drafting a systems integration agreement.

(a) *Customer Obligations*

- Include a detailed description of customer obligations, including:
  - deliverables to be performed by the customer,
  - information to be provided by customer,
  - customer hardware and software systems,
  - documentation,
  - customer employees/support staff
- skill profiles for customer employees,
- number of employees,
  - customer duty of cooperation,
  - time frames for the performance of customer obligations,
  - customer provision of test data and test cases,
  - partial acceptance of deliverables, and
  - privacy and data protection.
- Describe deliverables with fixed deadlines for customer obligations.
- Compensation/damages recoverable by vendor as a consequence of customer nonperformance, including:
  - termination rights,
  - relief from vendor's contractual obligations, and
  - extension of delivery dates.

(b) Warranty

- The vendor's obligations to correct errors should apply only to deliverables. Staff augmentation agreements where the vendor is providing services at the customer's direction usually do not include performance warranties.
- The warranty period should be for 30–90 days.
- Warranty obligations usually comprise an obligation for error correction. If error correction fails within the appropriate remedy periods, a right to reduce the remuneration or to rescind or terminate the contract may be granted to the customer in addition to an obligation to compensate the customer for damages incurred.
- A rescission or termination for cause should be allowed only for material errors affecting the usability of the entire system.
- The customer should be entitled to exercise its warranty/breach rights only after two cure periods.
- Warranty obligations should apply only to reproducible defects.
- The customer should be obliged to notify the vendor of errors in writing, including the information necessary to detect the errors.
- The customer should support the vendor in remedying the defects as far as is reasonable, e.g., by creating detailed functional specifications.
- The customer should be obliged to undertake acceptance testing for deliverables promptly or lose its warranty rights, excluding hidden defects.
- The warranty should cease to apply if the customer modifies the deliverables unless it can prove the modifications did not cause the defect.
- The vendor should have the right to recover payment for all expenses incurred investigating non-reproducible errors.

(c) Acceptance Procedures

- Acceptance procedures are applicable only for deliverables, not for staff augmentation/pure services.
- Acceptance testing should be performed based on technical specifications and test criteria which have been submitted by vendor and approved by the customer.
- Defects justifying rejection of the deliverables should be defined.
  - An accumulation of minor defects should not justify rejection.
- The acceptance period should be a maximum of four weeks.
- Vendors should avoid agreeing that the acceptance procedures terminate if material errors occur during the acceptance testing with new acceptance testing to follow. Instead, seek an extension of the existing acceptance period upon the occurrence of material errors.
- If the deliverables do not pass the first acceptance test, the vendor should have the right to conduct a minimum of two additional attempts before the customer is entitled to terminate the agreement/receive compensation for its damages.
- If the acceptance period expires without comment from the customer, the deliverables should be deemed accepted.

- Use of any deliverables/software in an production environment should constitute deemed acceptance.
- Partial acceptances should be permitted to allow the project to continue.

(d) Change Requests

- Vendors should not be obliged to perform any change requested by a customer unless it is technically and financially acceptable by the vendor.
- Vendors should have the right to issue change requests.
- Establish a governance structure and escalation/dispute procedures in the event change request issues cannot be agreed to on the project management level.
- Vendors should have the right to decline a request to assess a significant change request if the customer is unwilling to pay the vendor on a time and materials basis for undertaking the assessment effort.
- Project time lines and milestones should be delayed by the equal number of days the vendor is assessing the customer´s change plus a restart period.
- If a change by a customer requires the interruption of the project, the customer should compensate the vendor for its corresponding costs, including labor costs, license fees, etc., if the vendor's employees cannot be reasonably reassigned to a new project.
- Vendor's should reject language deeming the vendor to have accepted any change request where the vendor does not respond within a stated time period.
- The parties should be obliged to perform within the original agreement if the vendor does not accept the requested change or respond within a stated time period.
- The customer should be required to respond to the vendor's change request within a reasonable time period, i.e., 10 days.
- If the customer insists on a right to terminate for convenience in the event a change request cannot be agreed upon, the vendor must be compensated for loss of revenue, profit and/or its wind-down expenses
- All changes should be agreed to in a formal written contract amendment signed by both parties.

(e) Intellectual Property Rights

- Vendors should seek to grant the customer only non-exclusive rights of use to the developed work if the work has value outside the project.
- Vendors may be willing to grant an exclusive right of use if a deliverable is considered to be unique and will not comprise the vendor's products.
- Define "existing software" and "developed software" to maintain ownership rights
- The customer should only be granted a non-exclusive, non- transferable and revocable license to the vendor's "existing software."
- The use of open-source software may require the use of specific wording around the licensing.

- The customer should be responsible for obtaining the right for the vendor to modify and enhance any software licensed by the customer:
  - the vendor must be allowed to grant its subcontractors the agreed rights of use, and
  - the vendor must be indemnified in the event of a claim of intellectual property infringement resulting from the use of such software.
- Many third-party licensors' license terms contain regulations that all IPRs in individual enhancements of their software is owned by them and that the licensee is only granted a non-exclusive right of use in the enhancement.
- A vendor should seek additional compensation if the customer seeks a license for the vendor's intellectual property for the customer's affiliates.

(f) Contractual Penalties for Delay

- Recovery should be limited to those delays caused by the vendor´s sole negligence and exclude delays caused by *force majeure* or the customer.
- Liquidated damages for delay should only relate to the value of the delayed services and include a grace period of two to four weeks.
- Liquidated damages should not exceed 0.1% of the value of the delayed services per each day of delay up to a maximum of 5% of the contract value.
- Contractual penalties should be offset against claims for proven damages.
- Penalties for delay should be offset against penalties for error correction during the warranty period.

(g) Termination

- Vendor's should not agree to termination for convenience.
- In the event of termination for convenience by the customer, the vendor should receive the agreed remuneration less the expenses the vendor would avoid as a consequence of the termination, and the vendor's wind-down costs.
- If termination for convenience is acceptable to the vendor, the vendor should seek 90 days prior written notice to terminate for convenience to permit the vendor to redeploy its resources.
- Each party may terminate the contract for cause if the other party is in breach of a material provision of the contract and fails to cure such breach within 30 days of receiving notice of the breach.
- The vendor should be entitled to terminate for cause for:
  - non-payment or
  - the customer's failure to fulfill its material obligations.

(h) Limitation of Liability

- The vendor should not accept any contract without a limitation of liability.
- Common exclusions from a limitation of liability include:
  - intentional misconduct,
  - gross negligence,
  - breach of confidentiality,

    - death and personal injury, and
    - intellectual property infringement.
- Vendors' liability for negligence should be limited to direct damages, with an aggregate cap equal to the total contract value or the value of the SOW under which liability arose.
- Vendors should seek to limit their liability to the amounts received from the customer, under the SOW that gave rise to the liability.
- Vendors should not agree to a liability cap equal to the value of all contracts with the customer.
- Both parties should disclaim liability for indirect, special, consequential and punitive damages.

C. Staff Augmentation Agreements

Staff augmentation or "body shopping" agreements are used when the customer is purchasing resources or bodies from the vendor and the customer is solely responsible for directing how those resources are used. As such, the vendor makes no representations or warranties other than perhaps that the resources are skilled in a particular computer language and does not indemnify the customer including an indemnity for intellectual property infringement. There are no stated deliverables, as the vendor has no control over how the resources are deployed or managed. The customer owns any created work.

Prudent vendors should review customer agreements carefully as many customers' drafted agreements contain provisions consistent with staff augmentation but yet also contain other terms that are not appropriate for a staff augmentation agreements such as indemnity, and broad intellectual property rights that imply the vendor is making active and independent contributions to product development. Blurring the distinction between staff augmentation and professional services agreements is a lose-lose proposition for the vendor, as the vendor receives lower rates for the work and no real control over the work but yet has the same exposure to risk and liability the vendor would have for much higher priced, independent project engagements.

Some customers seek to have the vendor assume liability for the work created but prudent vendors should reject any responsibility or liability given the customer controls all work performed by the resources.

See Form C.3.5 for a staff augmentation agreement that favors the customer and contains broad terms inappropriate for a staff augmentation agreement.

D. Subcontract Agreements

1. General

Vendors often subcontract some of their obligations under an agreement for cost or expertise reasons. For example, it may be more cost-efficient to have a third-party "partner" provide tangential services, such as training or maintenance, than the vendor's own employees. From the customer's perspective, the customer should ensure the vendor stands behind the subcontractor's work and the subcontractor is experienced in the services it is providing. From the vendor's perspective, the vendor wants to ensure the subcontractor is qualified and that the vendor and subcontractor are 'back to back" with the relevant provisions of the vendor's agreement with the customer.

2. Flow Down Provisions

Many vendors seek to flow down the terms of the prime contract to their subcontractors. They seek to be "back-to-back" with each subcontractor to avoid a potential situation where the subcontractor meets its obligations to the vendor but yet causes the vendor to breach its obligations to the customer. From the vendor's perspective, flowing down these terms is reasonable, as in almost all agreements, non-performance of a subcontractor is not a valid defense in the event of a breach, as vendors are responsible for the acts of their subcontractors. In practice, however, many provisions in the prime contract are not applicable to the sub-contractor (i.e., invoicing and payment terms, dispute resolution) and the subcontractor may lack the resources to comply with every obligation, such as carrying large amounts of insurance, purchasing a performance bond, employee background checks and drug testing.

Many subcontractors reject a vendor's attempt to flow down every provision as too broad. As a result, most subcontractor agreements flow down some but not all terms due to the limited scope of the subcontract or due to negotiating leverage. The customer lacks a direct relationship with the subcontractor, and cannot bring an action against the subcontractor unless the customer requires that it be named as a third-party beneficiary to the subcontract. Model language limiting the subcontractor's obligation to certain provisions in the prime contract follow:

> *The following terms and conditions of the Prime Contract shall apply to this Work Order. With respect to each such provision incorporated herein, references to the Client shall be deemed references to Company, as appropriate, and references to Company shall be deemed references to Subcontractor, as appropriate.*

Customers seek to have their terms flowed down to any subcontractors to ensure: (i) the subcontractor's interests are aligned with the customer's, (ii) the subcontractor is held to the same performance standards, (iii) the subcontractor complies with the customer's internal policies and procedures, (iv) the subcontractor works towards the contractually defined goal, and (v) are subject to the same obligations as the prime contractor. In practice, requiring the terms of the prime contract to be flowed down to the subcontractor does not directly benefit the customer, as the customer lacks contractual privity with the subcontractor, and cannot take recourse against the subcontractor unless the customer is named as a third-party beneficiary in the subcontract.

To avoid any concerns a customer may have with the use of a subcontractor, customers often include "step-in" rights in their agreements permitting the customer to assume the subcontractor's agreement in the event the vendor is terminated. *See Form E.5.3.*

While some vendors may resist "step-in" rights, vendors are not harmed by such clauses, as they should only arise in the event of the vendor's breach. Further, customers often seek the right to approve all subcontractors and the identity of all subcontractors used by the vendor.

Prudent vendors should also reject the obligation that the customer approve all subcontractors, as the vendor is responsible for the overall performance obligations. Further, any absolute obligation to flow all terms down to the subcontractor may expose the vendor to liability in the event it knows the subcontractor is not complying or cannot comply with all of the terms of the prime contract such as the insurance requirements. Instead, the vendor should require the customer to specifically identify those obligations which must be flowed down to the vendor's subcontractor.

To avoid potential disputes with subcontractors, prudent vendors should require their subcontractors to sign a Teaming Agreement (*See Forms A.3.1 and A.3.2*) at the time the vendor is submitting its bid to the customer or negotiating its agreement with the customer, which identifies those provisions of the prime contract that will be flowed down to the subcontractor so that they are agreed prior to the prime contractor being awarded the contract.

Prudent vendors should reject a customer's demand to unilaterally, without cause, require the vendor to terminate a subcontractor. Doing so could impact the vendor's ability to deliver the contracted services, causing the vendor to breach its agreement with the customer because the vendor cannot rely on the subcontractor to perform the contacted services.

3. *Data Privacy Provisions*

Data privacy under the General Data Protection Regulations ("GDPR") is a more complex issue especially when the customer and prime contractor execute a data privacy agreement ("DPA"). Article 28 para. 4 of the GDPR binds subprocessors to the same obligations that apply to a processor/vendor. Thus all data privacy requirements should be flowed down to the subcontractor.

E. Support Agreements

Maintenance and support is usually addressed in a maintenance agreement. Because vendors seek to operate on a product basis as opposed to individual projects to achieve economies of scale, most support and maintenance agreements are not heavily negotiated. Most vendors price maintenance and support as a percentage of the license fee, usually 20%, and cannot achieve economies of scale if every customer has different support terms. Further, uniform terms allow the vendor to staff its support desk in an efficient manner, i.e. uniform operating hours, response time and SLAs. To do otherwise would create a significant burden on the vendor to track and manage its specific obligations to each customer.

See Chapter 21 for a more detailed discussion of support and maintenance agreements.

F. *PRACTICE POINT*: Checklist for drafting professional services agreements.

- Who are the parties?
  - Can the customer's affiliates purchase under the agreement?
- Payment
  - Is payment on a time and materials basis/fixed fee?
  - Has a rate sheet been incorporated into the agreement?
  - Is the vendor required to submit time sheets?
  - Can the vendor increase its rates during the term of the agreement?
    - Are any such increases tied to any metrics such as the CPI?
    - Is there a limit on any such increases?
  - When is the customer required to make payment?
    - Within 30 days of receiving the vendor's invoice?
    - Upon achievement of stated milestones?
  - Can the vendor charge interest on late payments?
  - Can the customer withhold payment for improper invoices?
  - Is the customer obligated to pay the undisputed portions of any invoice
  - Is the customer required to pay all sales taxes, VAT taxes etc.
  - Can the customer audit the vendor?
  - Is there a statement that payment does constitute acceptance
- Is the vendor required to maintain minimum insurance levels?
- Is there a statement that the parties are independent contractors?
- Does the vendor indemnify the customer for any claims by the vendor's employees and contractors claiming they are employees of the customer/ entitled to receive benefits from the customer?
- Are the deliverables set forth in sufficient detail?
- Are the acceptance procedures set forth in sufficient detail?
- Is there a statement that use of the deliverables in a production environment constitutes acceptance?
- Can the customer terminate the agreement for:
  - Breach
  - Convenience
  - Force majeure
- Can the vendor incorporate open source software into the deliverables?
  - With prior written consent?
- Is the vendor required to comply with all applicable laws?
  - Which laws?
    - Laws that govern the customer's performance
    - Laws that govern the vendor's performance
    - Both
- Do any data privacy or security laws apply?:
- Does the agreement contain a limitation of liability?

  - Is it mutual?
  - Are there any exclusions?
- Is the vendor providing any warranties or indemnities?
  - Are the warranties/indemnities tailored to the vendor's obligations/the deliverables?
- What are the likely causes of any dispute?
  - Is there a dispute resolution mechanism?
- May the agreement be assigned?
- Can the vendor subcontract its performance obligations?

CHAPTER 18

Software Development Kit (SDK) Licenses and Application Program Interface (API) Licenses

Software Development Kits (SDKs), and Application Program Interfaces (APIs) are licensed by software owners to developers seeking to build software products that will interact with the owner's software applications. In essence, APIs and SDKs provide the tools, and road maps to guide a developer in creating an interface between one software application and another. It has often been said that you build something with an SDK, and that you use something with an API.

A. Software Development Kit Licenses

1. General

A software development kit (SDK) is a programming package that enables a programmer to develop software applications for a specific platform. SDKs usually include debugging tools, libraries, and other utilities to aid programmers as well as one, or more APIs, programming tools, and documentation. All SDKs are/contain APIs but not all APIs are SDKs. Theoretically, if an API is well documented, an SDK is not needed to build software to use the API; however, utilizing an SDK generally makes the process much easier, and quicker.

Because SDK licenses provide a road map to the licensor's software, and include source code, most licensors are unwilling to materially modify their SDK licenses. Similar to evaluation licenses, SDK licenses often provide minimal protections to the licensee. Because licensees often build the SDKs into their own products, which they will in turn license to their own clients, the licensee should ensure that the SDK license permits the licensee to sublicense the SDK software to its clients, and that the SDK license is compatible with the licensee's own licensing structure.

Prudent licensees will ascertain whether the SDK contains any open-source software, and if it does, conduct an open-source review, inserting any protective language required while making sure to understand how the open source software will impact the proprietary code the licensee is developing.

See Forms I.2.1 and I.2.2 for a model SDK license.

2. *PRACTICE POINT*: Checklist for drafting an SDK license.

- Does the SDK:
  - allow the user to sublicense its rights to its affiliates and clients?
  - permit the use of the information, license, etc. by contractors?
- Are the user's client's rights to use the embedded software terminated if the user's license is terminated?
- Is any prohibition on reverse engineering "subject to any applicable law"? Under EU law a user is allowed to reverse engineer to achieve interoperability.
- Does the license include appropriate export language?
- Does the license include appropriate tax language?
- Does the license prohibit end users from using the user's name, and brand?
- Does the SDK contain open source software? If yes, conduct an open source software review and incorporate any required language.
- Ensure the exclusion of consequential loss is mutual.
- Are there any flow ups that must be passed on to the user's clients?

B. Application Program Interface (API) Licenses

1. Overview

An application programming interface (API) is a set of routines, protocols, and tools for building software applications allowing software applications to communicate, and interact with each other.

An API expresses a software component in terms of its operations, inputs, outputs, and underlying types. APIs often come in the form of a library that includes specifications for routines, data structures, object classes, and variables. APIs are "exposed" and "consumed." "Exposure" means visibility to the API/seeing the API/the ability to write software to consume the API. "Consuming" means using the API or consuming the services of an API.

The "exposed" API contains detailed confidential information regarding the software system that allows other components to connect with the system. The API serves as a map showing how to interact with the solution through the API. By exposing the API, a party can view the layout of the software program with which it seeks to connect.

An API is an interface that specifies how software components should interact by defining a set of rules that should be followed by software programs to communicate, or "call" each other. APIs are a specific method established by an operating system that allows a software application to call, or communicate with the operating system or a third-party application.

APIs can be used to communicate among software applications, libraries, and operating systems, and may come in the form of a library that includes specifications for routines, and data structures. As with any software, APIs vary in complexity from simple specifications to extensive software toolboxes. For example, the JDK (Java Development

Kit) contains the API as well as compilers, run times, and other miscellaneous tools while the Java API contains all the libraries that constitute the core language a programmer can work with out of the box.

APIs also permit a developer to utilize the functions, commands, and procedures of existing applications, saving a developer time and money by eliminating the need to program duplicative functionality. For example, APIs may allow a developer to utilize an existing application's print function instead of having to develop such functionality.

Some APIs include security provisions requiring license keys, authentication, etc., which may prohibit complete use of the API in particular instances. Licensors will provide the licensee with "keys" to allow the licensee to access the licensed materials In such situations, the software must present the right credentials (if required) to use the API.

2. *Negotiating an API License*

The ability of a party to negotiate an API license will depend on the facts and circumstances surrounding the party's need for a license. From the licensor's perspective, the agreement should clearly state the licensee's use rights, such as "to develop, reproduce, and distribute Licensee Applications that interoperate with the Licensor APIs, and to make calls to the Licensor APIs through the Licensee Applications, solely to obtain System Content from, exchange data with, and/or write to the Licensor System, in each case, for each Licensee Application; and use and reproduce Licensor Content only as necessary to format, and display it through the Licensee Applications." See, e.g., § 2.1.1 of Form I.1.3, and to permit the licensee to call the licensor's APIs through the licensee's application.

Most licensors are unwilling to provide representations, warranties and indemnities regarding the licensed APIs if the licensee is not paying for the license. Many licensors consider API licenses to be similar to demonstration licenses; the licensor is providing the API for the convenience of the licensee, and thus is unwilling to assume any risk by providing the API to the licensee. Nonetheless, there is a risk, albeit small, that the licensor's APIs may infringe on a third-party's intellectual property, creating a risk for the licensee. This risk is small, as, in the event of an infringement claim, the licensee can cease use of the API with little impact on its business. At the same time, many licensors seek to have the licensee represent, and warrant as well as indemnify the licensor for any wrongdoing, or infringement. Prudent licensees should provide only limited representations, warranties and indemnities directly related to the licensee's conduct. See, e.g., § 3.2 of Form I.1.3

> *Company shall not (i) translate, decompile, disassemble, or otherwise reverse engineer, or attempt to discover any source code, or underlying ideas or algorithms of the API; (ii) provide, lease, lend, use for time sharing, outsourcing, hosting, or service bureau purposes, or allow others to access or use the API; (iii) modify, incorporate into, or with other software, or services, or create a derivative work of any part of the API; (iv) use the API in ways that violate laws, infringe, or violate the rights of others including, but not limited to third party intellectual property rights, privacy, and publicity rights, or (v) interfere with other users of the API; (vi) introduce in, or to the API any virus, or*

implement a denial of service attack, or introduce, or implement any other code, or routine which results in disruption or damage to, or alter, damage, or delete any data, or retrieve, or record information about the API.

Many licensors limit the number of "calls" a licensee may make, or charge the licensee when the licensee exceeds a stated number of calls, in an attempt to prevent the licensor's system from being overwhelmed. Some licensors seek to pre-certify licensees to ensure security, the performance of the licensee's application, and API connectivity.

Perhaps the biggest issue in many API agreements is data protection, and each party's access to the data of the other party, and their customers. Prudent parties should ensure the license agreement provides that each party will not access, or use any personal information obtained through accessing to the other party's systems other than using de-identified, and anonymized data to improve the operating efficiencies of the parties' applications. To that end, many licensors seek to include language granting the licensor ownership of any feedback provided by the licensee to the licensor.

Prudent licensors will require the licensee to comply with the licensor's data security standards, and the licensee's failure to do so should be a cause for termination of the license.

3. APIs in the European Union

Although the ability to copyright APIs in the United States is uncertain (see Section C below), European Union Software Directive (2009/24/EC) provides that the concepts, and principals underlying computer software, including the related interfaces, are not protected by copyright. In *SAS Institute Inc. v. World Programming Ltd.*, [2013] EWHC 69 (Ch) (Jan. 25, 2013), the court interpreted the Directive, finding "neither the functionality of a computer program, nor the programming language, and the format of the data files used in a computer program in order to exploit certain of its functions constitute a form of expression of that program . . . ." Thus, given the functional nature of APIs, many European practitioners have concluded, based on the *World Programming* decision, that APIs are not entitled to copyright protection in the European Union.

See Forms I.1.1, I.1.2, and I.1.3 for model API licenses.

C. Oracle America, Inc. vs. Google, Inc.

In *Google LLC v. Oracle America, Inc.*, 141 S. Ct. 1183 (2021), the Supreme Court held that Google's copying of the oracle API was "fair use," as Google only used a small amount of the code, and its use was transformative. The decision allows developers to build software that is compatible with other third party software without fear of being sued for copyright infringement. Key to Court's decision was their conclusion that ". . . Google reimplemented a user interface, taking only what was needed to allow users to put their accrued talents to work in a new and transformative program." *Id.* at 1209.

Google used only 11,500 lines of code out of 286 million equating to 0.04% of the total code, with the majority of the implementing code written by Google. The Court assumed the code was copyrightable but did not reach a conclusion as a matter of law. *Id.* at 1205.

For a more detailed discussion of the Supreme Court's decision, see Myers, *Muddy Waters: Fair Use Implications for Google LLC v. Oracle America, Inc.*, 19 Nw. J Tech & Intell. Prop. 155 (2022).

For a general overview of the application of copyright to computer software application interfaces in particular, see Menell, *Rise of the API Copyright Dead? An Updated Epitaph for Copyright Protection of Network and Functional Features of Computer Software*, 31 Harv. J. L. & Tech 205 (2018).

CHAPTER **19**

Tools

A. General

Software tools are used to write, debug, configure, test, or otherwise support other applications. They increase productivity, saving time and effort. In most cases, the term, refers to relatively simple programs which support the development, and installation of an application. Vendors often provide customers with various software tools, and methodologies in conjunction with licensing their application.

Tools are considered to be ancillary to the application, but yet assist the vendor, and the customer in project management, installing, testing, performance analysis, and utilizing the application. Their ability to be used by all customers using a particular application creates intrinsic value for the vendor, and its customers, but on a stand-alone basis most tools lack any meaningful value.

> *"Software Tools" means, with respect to any Software or Embedded Software, any routines, compilers, bootstraps, analyzers, monitors, toolkits, and other software tools used by the licensor of such Software or Embedded Software in connection with the programming, compiling, maintenance, debugging, analysis, configuration, customization, verification, or monitoring of such Software or Embedded Software.*

While tools are tangential to the application's core functionality, and the services purchased by the customer, they provide value by assisting in the implementation, or testing of the application, and generating reports regarding the application's core functionality, such as a dashboard of tasks completed, as well as providing language libraries. These tools are not necessarily required for use of the application, or services, but rather used to supplement the application, or services.

Because most tools can be used across all customer implementations, prudent vendors seek to retain ownership of, and the right to use such tools in future engagements any tools developed in the customer engagement. Vendors also seek to retain ownership of tools, as they serve as a timesaving mechanism, and it is impractical for the vendor to create new tools for each customer engagement, from both a financial and technical perspective. In almost all cases, tools do not contain a customer's confidential information.

In software development engagements, some customers argue that vendors' tools are part of what the customer paid the vendor to create, and thus should be owned by customer. In practice, however, most tools are of little value to the customer, as the intrinsic value arises from their ability to save the vendor time and money by eliminating the need to re-create existing work. As such, the customer is usually not relinquishing anything of material value by allowing the vendor to retain ownership of any tools.

Tools are usually outside the principal focus of the vendor's core competency, and usually are not marketed as stand-alone products. Similarly, customers usually do not see significant value in the tools, and thus, are unlikely to purchase the tools on a stand-alone basis. Because customers place little value on these tools, or may not even be aware of their existence, the price for tools and methodologies provided by the vendor are usually not broken out from the license fee. As such, tools are usually licensed to customers without cost or at a nominal cost. Prudent vendors require the customer to execute a license to access its tools and methodologies to ensure ownership of their tools and methodologies is not inadvertently transferred to the customer. Model language is as follows:

> *As part of the Services throughout the Term, and at no additional cost to Customer, Vendor will implement the measurement, and monitoring tools, and procedures necessary to measure its performance of the Services, and compare such performance to that required by the Service Levels. Such measurement, and monitoring tools are more particularly described in each applicable Statement of Work. Upon Customer's request, Vendor will provide Customer, or its auditors with any information produced by the measurement, and monitoring tools necessary to verify compliance by Vendor with the Service Levels.*

B. Types of Tools

Tools generally fall into two categories: (i) third party development aids which can be purchased by the customer independent of the application, and (ii) those embedded in the application itself. Well known third party applications include GitHub, Jira, bitbucket and HTML5 builder.

C. Ownership of Tools

Ownership should address the technical information, plans, designs, templates, processes, methodologies, procedures, reusable software including source code, object code, routines, and libraries that are commonly used in connection with the typical computer program. Tools are created in the course of performing work for a customer, but have universal application, and usually do not constitute confidential customer information. Their universal application to other customers, and ability to increase productivity creates value for a vendor even though on a stand-alone basis they lack any intrinsic value.

Savvy vendors seek to re-use these tools to avoid having to create new tools for the same tasks in the same way for every customer. If a vendor was faced the creating a tool with the same functionality for each customer, the cost of doing so along with the delay in the project would be great.

The wording of some agreements, makes the re-use or re-creation of such tools a violation of the customer's copyright in the deliverables. Prudent vendors seek to limit the definition of "work product" to work explicitly developed solely for the particular customer during the customer engagement, allowing the vendor to retain ownership of all tools developed out of the customer engagement, and the right to use them in future engagements. Allocating ownership of tools should not be an contentious issue between the parties unless the tools contain a customer's confidential information.

Some customers argue that the tools are part of what the customer paid the vendor to create, and thus the customer should receive ownership of the tools. Practically, most tools are of little value to the customer, and the customer usually receives a perpetual, royalty-free license to use the tools in conjunction with the application. As such, ceding ownership to the vendor does not negatively impact the customer, and can likely be used as a bargaining chip in its negotiations with the vendor.

From the vendor's perspective, there are several approaches to resolve ownership of any tools. One approach is for the vendor to retain ownership of the tools, and grant the customer a non-exclusive license to use the tools solely in conjunction with the licensed technology. Alternatively, if the customer insists on ownership of the tools, the vendor can obtain an exclusive perpetual, royalty-free license with a right of sublicense to use the tools, including, but not limited to the right to make, use, and sell products, and services incorporating the tools, as well as the right to authorize others (e.g., distributors, resellers, etc.) to do the same. Any such license should specifically include the right to make and create derivative works. The following language is an example of a broad license grant from the vendor to the Customer permitting the Customer to sublicense the vendor's tools when incorporated into the customer's products. A mirror image of this language can be used to grant the vendor such rights if the customer is granted ownership of the tools.

> *Vendor hereby grants to Customer, the worldwide, non-exclusive, perpetual, irrevocable, fully paid-up, royalty-free right, and license to the Vendor Tools, in both source code and object code formats, to (i) use the Vendor Tools for Customer's business and administrative purposes, (ii) copy, incorporate, imbed, modify and create derivative works of the Vendor Tools, (iii) compile, and link the source code for the Vendor Tools, both as modified and unmodified, to create object code, and to use, copy, incorporate, imbed, modify, create derivative works of any such object code so created, (iv) publicly perform, and display, import, broadcast, transmit, distribute, license, offer to sell, sell, rent, lease and lend (collectively "**Distribute**") copies of the Vendor Tools (and derivative works thereof); and (v) sublicense to third parties the foregoing rights, including the right to sublicense to further third parties (collectively, the "**Purpose**").*
>
> *Notwithstanding the immediately foregoing sentence, Customer may not (i) Distribute the Vendor Tools (or derivative works thereof) to third parties on a standalone basis (i.e., Customer may only Distribute the Vendor Tools or derivative works thereof as embodied within a Deliverable, as such Deliverable may be modified from time to time.), or (ii) remove any copyright notices, trademarks, or other identifying marks from Vendor Tools, and shall reproduce all such marks on each copy of an Vendor Tool.*

CHAPTER **20**

Distribution Agreements: Reseller, Value Added Reseller, Original Equipment Manufacturer, and Referral Agreements

A. Common Elements

Most Reseller, Value Added Reseller ("VAR"), Original Equipment Manufacturer ("OEM") and Referral Agreements share common contractual elements for the sale or referral of third-party products. While the structure of the agreements may differ, the principal provisions and issues are similar. In drafting and negotiating these agreements, the following provisions should be carefully considered and addressed.

*** *For the purposes of this Section A, "reseller" is used to describe resellers, VARs and OEMs.* ***

1. *Territory*

To the extent sales are limited to a particular "territory," the definition of territory should be clearly defined to avoid ambiguity, especially if the reseller is granted an exclusive right in the territory. Territory can be defined in many ways, including specific countries or regions, industry verticals such as the automotive industry, and size of the targeted customer.

If a territory is defined by geography, specifically list those countries constituting the territory. For example, does North America include Mexico? Does the "United States" include its territories and possessions? Taking the time to eliminate ambiguity when drafting the agreement can avoid potential problems down the road.

2. *Scope of the License Grant*

A reseller license grants a reseller the right to distribute the identified software and grant sublicenses to the reseller's customers. Some reseller licenses grant the reseller the right to modify and enhance the software, as well as the right to support and maintain the software. The licensor's intellectual property is subservient to the reseller's intellectual property as it is engineered by the reseller to work in conjunction with reseller's intellectual property to meet the business needs of the reseller's customers.

The reseller should ensure it receives the license rights necessary for its business model. This includes the required "value-added" components as well as maintenance and support, and the authorization necessary to sublicense the use of the software. To avoid potential disputes, the agreement should clearly list any restrictions on the types of sublicenses a reseller may grant, i.e., can the reseller distribute the product through other resellers and distributors? Further, can the product be bundled or incorporated into any product or only a specific product?

> *Licensor grants to Licensee the non-exclusive and non-transferable right to authorize Affiliates, distributors and/or resellers to further distribute and license the Bundled Solution under an On-Premises License to the same extent and scope as that applied to Licensee, provided that Licensee will ensure that anyone it authorizes to distribute or resell the Software does so only in compliance with, and pursuant to written terms at least as protective of Licensor as the terms of this Agreement.*

PRACTICE POINT:

When negotiating a reseller license to incorporate a third party's software into its own software, the reseller should insure that, at a minimum, it obtains the following rights:

- The right to sublicense and distribute the licensor's software to the reseller's clients and affiliates as well as to other resellers and distributors;
- The right to install the software at any end user location and physically relocate such software as may be needed over time (or to other locations as may be needed over time);
- Access rights to the software for the reseller's and its end users' contractors/consultants, customers, as well as their employees and consultants;
- The rights to redeploy the software;
- The right to assign the licensor's software/transfer the underlying software;
- The right to resell/sub-license the software; and
- The right to provide the "value-added" enhancements.

From the licensor's perspective, the license grant should limit the reseller's rights solely to demonstrating and sublicensing the software to its customers. The license grant should also include any, restrictions on the reseller's ability to resell the software and how the licensor's software can be incorporated into the reseller's products. Except for a pure reseller relationship, most licensors prohibit the reseller from sublicensing the licensor's software on a standalone basis, only permitting the reseller to license the licensor's products in combination with the reseller's products.

3. Term, Termination and Renewal

(a) Term

(i) Term of the Reseller Agreement

Most reseller agreements have a relatively short initial term (i.e., 2 years), as licensors seek to avoid a long term commitment unless the reseller demonstrates that in can generate significant sales for the licensor. To that end, licensors should avoid agreeing to evergreen or automatic renewals.

(ii) Term of any Sublicenses

Sublicenses granted to end users by the reseller usually survive the termination of agreement between the licensor and the reseller, and continue for the stated term under the reseller's sublicense agreement with the end user. End users are unlikely to enter into an agreement with the reseller if they believe they will lose their usage right upon termination of the reseller's agreement with the licensor.

(b) Termination

Unlike a traditional software or services agreement, the parties' obligations are not tied to the successful delivery of software or services. Thus, the parties' termination rights should reflect the nature of the agreement and the reseller's learning curve. The licensor should have the right to terminate the agreement in the event the reseller: (i) fails to sell a minimum volume of the software (e.g., generate a minimum amount of license fees), (ii) breaches the terms of the license grant, (iii) fails to cooperate with the licensor's audit of the reseller's sales of the licensor's software, or (iv) fails to pay the licensor the required fees for the reseller sales.

The reseller should have the right to terminate the agreement in the event: (i) the licensor's software fails to conform to the documentation, (ii) the licensor fails to support the software, or (iii) the licensor otherwise materially breaches the agreement.

(c) Renewal

From the licensor's perspective, any renewal should be dependent on the reseller meeting certain requirements, such as meeting minimum sales targets for an entity to be able to extend the agreement. Licensors should avoid extending an agreement with a party that is not generating revenue for the licensor. Some agreements are structured with a series of hurdles that must be achieved for the agreement to be extended beyond the initial term. Initially, the hurdle may be non-monetary, such as creating marketing collateral, hiring and training a staff, attending trade shows and making a set number of sales calls. Sales targets are often low at first, growing over time as the reseller becomes familiar with the products and develops its sales pipeline. The failure to meet its sales target over a set period of time should be a basis for termination.

4. *Effect of Termination*

The reseller should ensure that the licenses it receives from the licensor allows its end users to continue to use the licensor's technology in the event the licensor terminates the parties' agreement for the reseller's breach. Otherwise, end users will lose their right to utilize the software/products they have licensed from the reseller through no fault of their own. Conversely, end users are unlikely to license the technology if their use may be terminated in the event of the reseller's breach, even if the end user has not breached its agreement with the reseller. If the licensor is unwilling to continue the end users' licenses in the event of the reseller's material breach, an alternative resolution may be for the licensor to assume the reseller's agreements with the end users.

If the termination is due to the licensor's material breach, the reseller may want to negotiate the ability to step in and provide any services that the licensor was providing such as software maintenance and support. Doing so, however, may require a software source code escrow. If the termination is due to the reseller's material breach, then the licensor may want the rights to step into the reseller's shoes to provide maintenance to end users, or to appoint another reseller to assume the reseller's obligations. Most importantly, the end-user licenses should only be terminable if the end user breaches the agreement.

5. Pricing and Fee Structure

(a) Pricing

Pricing between the licensor and the reseller is usually structured on a royalty basis where the licensor receives a royalty for each unit sold. To make the combined product financially attractive, the reseller will usually market the integrated software product at a lower price than the price to purchase the two products separately.

The licensor's pricing to the reseller is often tied to the volume of software purchased; the greater the volume purchased, the lower the price. Prudent licensors should avoid pricing based on projected volumes, as resellers are often overly optimistic or project unrealistically large sales volumes to convince the licensor to provide a lower price. Instead, the licensor should base its pricing on the actual volumes sold and, if the reseller achieves the targeted volumes, the reseller will receive a rebate on previously sold units, allowing the reseller to receive the lower price across all units sold.

Because the reseller often wants to offer the combined product at a lower price than the price of the individual components, and some potential customers may not value every feature, the licensor will often sell its product at a discounted price. From a licensor's perspective, the lower price is often offset by the fact that the reseller will be selling a large volume of the licensor's software and exposing the licensor's software to new customers and markets. To ensure that occurs, prudent licensors will have the reseller commit to a guaranteed royalty.

In recognition of a reseller's ability to price the combined product as the reseller sees fit, including not charging an additional fee for a combined product with the third-party product, licensors may require the reseller to make minimum payments to the licensor for the right to incorporate the licensor's product into the combined product. They do so to avoid situations where a reseller may price the combined product at an artificially low price but reap other benefits through other means such as maintenance and support. The licensor is not financially disadvantaged by the reseller's pricing decisions, as the licensor will receive the contractually committed minimum license fees and/or likely benefit from the broader distribution of its product in the marketplace, as well as receive revenue it would not otherwise receive.

The parties often negotiate a minimum quarterly fee, against which any royalties from a sale will be credited until the reseller's payments exceed the pre-paid quarterly payment.

End-user pricing of any combined product is solely within the purview of the reseller, provided that the licensor receives the contracted-for license fee. The reseller seeks to price the combined product at a price point that will drive sales. Conversely, the end user will compare the price against the software's utility, market pressures, size of the market etc." The reseller may even price the combined product at the same price it charges for its own products on a standalone basis without the third-party product, i.e., with no price increase, to reflect the inclusion of the third-party product in the combined product.

From the licensor's perspective, to avoid potential antitrust issues, pricing discussions should take place solely between the licensor and the reseller. The licensor should not communicate with the end user/customer regarding pricing. The licensor can require the reseller to sell at a certain price, but prices to the reseller should be quoted on a suggested end-user/ customer price (i.e., a percentage of list price) to prevent the reseller from selling below the licensor's suggested price, as the reseller will be responsible for assuming the cost of any discount below that price point. The reseller could charge a price above the recommended price but is unlikely to do so due to competitive market forces.

Another consideration is which party bears the risk of nonpayment in the event an end user fails to pay the license fee. Is the reseller obligated to pay the licensor a royalty if the end user does not pay the license fee? The licensor will argue yes, as the reseller has the ability to manage the risk by undertaking a credit check, requiring payment in advance and bringing legal action to recover any amounts owed to the reseller. If the reseller does not assume the credit risk, it has little incentive to collect the license fees.

Finally, the reseller should seek protection from the licensor against future price increases for the reseller's existing customers. The price protection should extend to the reseller's existing customers only and not new customers, as the reseller has no price risk with new customers.

*As consideration for the license of the Software by the Licensor, the Licensee agrees that it will pay to the Licensor, a one-time royalty payment for each Licensee Product which incorporates the Software that has been activated in a Customer Production Environment (the "**Royalty Fee**"). For the purposes hereof "Customer Production Environment" shall mean each collective group of networks of a Licensee Customer where a finished, user-ready live version of the Licensee Product which incorporates the Software that is activated is deployed and executed. The Parties acknowledge and agree that Licensee Products must be uploaded to multiple networks of each Customer in order to fully function as intended, which in turn will also require the Software to be uploaded to multiple networks of such Customer to function as intended. The Parties agree that each such group of networks of a Customer shall be considered one Production Environment. Under no circumstances shall a Production Environment be considered multiple Production Environments due to the Software being uploaded to multiple networks of the same Customer due to Licensee's Product requiring multiple networks to fully function as intended. The Royalty Fee will be determined in accordance with the table set forth below:[INSERT Table]*

In exchange for the rights granted in this Agreement, for each copy of the Combined Product distributed, Reseller shall remit to Company the following fees:

*10% of the amount paid to Reseller for each copy of the Combined Product licensed, distributed, used or deployed by Reseller to Reseller's Clients, minus any sales, value added, use, property, excise and like taxes, import duties and/or other applicable levies to arrive at the net royalty amount due to Company (the "**License Royalty Fee**")...*

> *"**Combined Product**" shall mean Reseller's Software which incorporates into it ... the object code versions of the Programs. A description of the Combined Product is indicated on Attachment A.*
>
> *"**Reseller Software**" shall mean NAME®, Company's Web-based software...*
>
> *"**Program(s)**" shall mean the software and/or product(s), as listed on Attachment A, Company shall provide...*

(b) Fee Structure

Many agreements require the reseller to commit to the payment of minimum royalties which incentivizes the reseller to sell the licensor's product. These minimum royalties are often paid in advance, are non-refundable and credited against the reseller's sales.

6. Reporting

Most licensors require resellers to provide periodic reports, i.e., quarterly reports on the number of licensor products the reseller has sold and the fees due the licensor. The manner in which sales and payments are reported will vary based on the terms of the agreement and the parties' negotiations as to the level of detail required. *See, e.g.*, Forms F.3.1 and F.3.2. To the extent a specific format is required, the parties often attach a template report to their agreement. *See, e.g.*, Form F.1.1 Schedule 2. Most agreements, however, do not require reports to be in a specific format; usually the agreement includes amorphous language along the following: *All reports must be "in a reasonably detailed form."* Having an officer of the reseller sign the report certifying its accuracy provides the licensor comfort that the report is accurate and that the reseller cannot claim that the reseller's management did not know the contents of the report.

In addition, many licensors require the reseller to provide the licensor with a copy of each end user license agreement under which the end user receives a license to use the licensor's software.

7. Audit

The licensor's agreement with the reseller should require the reseller to maintain detailed records for audit by the licensor and should specifically grant the licensor the right to audit:

(i) the licenses granted by the reseller,
(ii) the fees charged by the reseller, and
(iii) the license agreements between the reseller and its end users.

Usually, the licensor's audit rights extend beyond termination of the underlying agreement for at least a year after the parties' relationship has ended, as end users may continue to purchase additional licenses and maintenance. Thus, the parties' agreement should provide the licensor's audit rights survive termination of the governing agreement.

Some resellers' end users insist on limiting any audits to self-audits conducted to avoid the inconvenience and disruption to their business.

See Chapter 23 for a more detailed discussion on audits.

8. End-User License Agreements (EULAs)

End-user license agreements ("EULAs") are used to protect a licensor's intellectual property when a licensor's software is being resold by a reseller or incorporated into the reseller's product. The licensor protects its intellectual property by requiring the reseller to flow down certain terms to the end user. EULAs are usually attached to the reseller's agreement with the end users or incorporated through a link.

Licensors should be concerned that the reseller may not protect the licensor's intellectual property to the extent the licensor would itself. By requiring certain terms be passed on to the end user, the reseller can ensure that its intellectual property is protected. If the reseller fails to pass on or enforce such terms, the licensor may have a claim against the reseller in addition to the end user. See, e.g., Forms F.2.2 and F.2.3.

Alternatively, the licensor may provide that the reseller cannot grant a sublicensee any rights exceeding those the licensor provided to the reseller. To ensure that the reseller has done so, the reseller should be required to send the licensor a copy of each executed "End User Acknowledgment" as a condition precedent to fulfilling the reseller's orders. Under an End User Acknowledgement, the end user acknowledges that it has received and is bound by certain terms that flow down from the licensor and that the licensor is a third-party beneficiary of the agreement between the reseller and the end user. An "End User Acknowledgment" is signed by each reseller customer to clearly identify the customer by its full legal name and acknowledge that all products and services provided by the vendor are governed by the vendor's EULA.

From the licensor's perspective, the reseller should be jointly and severally liable with the end user for the end user's compliance with the licensor's end-user terms and conditions. Prudent resellers, however, should be hesitant to guaranty the performance of customers over whom they have no control. See Forms F.2.2. and F.2.3.

From the licensor's perspective, resellers should include a scanned or electronically signed copy of the End User Acknowledgment, acknowledging the EULA terms as a condition for fulfilling their orders.

See Forms F.1.1 and F.1.2 for examples of EULAs.

9. Breach of the EULA

Some licensors seek to require the reseller to notify the licensor when it learns an end user breaches the EULA, and to enforce the terms and conditions of the EULA on the licensor's behalf. While it is common to require the reseller to notify the licensor of any actual or suspected breach, prudent resellers should be hesitant to agree to enforce the EULA on the licensor's behalf. Licensor's should also be hesitant to have the reseller enforce the licensor's intellectual property rights as the licensor owns the intellectual property in question and thus has the greatest incentive to ensure that its intellectual property is protected. The reseller is simply a licensee without a long-term vested interest in protecting the licensor's intellectual property.

Further, as a practical matter, the fees received by the reseller from reselling the software do not justify the reseller expending significant time, money and effort to protect the licensor's intellectual property rights, especially when the reseller did not breach the agreement or contribute to its breach.

10 Sales and Marketing Requirements

Prudent licensors should impose specific sales and marketing obligations on the reseller to ensure the reseller aggressively markets the licensor's products, especially when the reseller is receiving an exclusive right. To that end, most reseller agreements impose minimum requirements on the reseller's efforts to promote the software, The licensor does so because it has relinquished certain rights and in turn requires the reseller to meet certain goals to retain such exclusive rights.

The parties should carefully negotiate any minimum requirements and the ramifications for the reseller's failure to meet such requirements. For example, if the reseller fails to meet the minimum sales volumes in a territory in which the reseller has exclusive sales rights, does the reseller lose its exclusivity while retaining the right to resell on a non-exclusive basis, or lose the right to resell in the territory?

These specific sales and marketing obligations may include:

- minimum sales commitments;
- hiring and training a sales staff dedicated to the product in question;
- marketing commitments:
  - attending a specific number of trade shows,
  - purchasing a specific number of magazine advertisements,
  - spending a minimum dollar amount on the sale and marketing of the product,
  - creating and translating marketing collateral, and
  - providing maintenance and support.

The parties should avoid vague commitments to "promote" the product, as there is no objective way to determine if the metric was met.

The licensor should have the right to terminate the reseller for failing to fully meet agreed-upon sales targets and marketing requirements.

See Forms F.1.1 to F.3.2 for model distribution/reseller/OEM licenses.

11. Intellectual Property Use and Ownership

The underlying agreement between the licensor and the reseller should clearly set forth which party owns any newly created intellectual property, such as software code, including APIs, documentation, interfaces, manuals and marketing collateral. As discussed in

Chapters 7.B and 16.D, joint ownership should be avoided, as it presents significant legal challenges for both parties. One alternative is to permit one party to own the intellectual property in question, (most likely the licensor), with the other party receiving royalty free license with the right to make derivative works and to license, sublicense, and authorize others to do so as well.

Use of each party's marks and brands should also be carefully considered. The reseller will most likely want to use the licensor's marks to promote its sales, while at the same, licensors often seek to list the reseller as a member of the licensor's reseller network. If the parties need to use each other's marks, they should enter into a separate licensing agreement to cross-license each other's marks, making sure to require each party to comply with the other party's trademark guidelines.

12. Third-Party Beneficiaries

Some licensors seek to be named as a third-party beneficiary to the reseller's agreement with its end user. Being named as a third-party beneficiary is important, as the licensor lacks contractual privity with the end user and cannot otherwise enforce the license terms in the event the reseller fails to do so or chooses not to do so.

Conversely, some resellers occasionally seek to include language in their agreements designating the reseller's end-user customers as third-party beneficiaries of the agreement between the licensor and the reseller. Licensors should not accept this risk, as the purpose of using a reseller is to have the reseller assume the risk of end-user claims. In any event, the agreement's limitation of liability should limit the licensor's liability to not only the reseller but also any third-party beneficiaries.

13. End User Terms

Occasionally, an end user will seek to flow its terms up to the licensor, which, from the licensor's perspective, undermines the purpose of using a reseller. The licensor allows the reseller to profit from the resale of the licensor's products in return for assuming responsibility for certain administrative costs and risks. If the end user has the ability to pass its terms and the accompanying risk on to the licensor, there is no benefit to the licensor in using a reseller, as the licensor has assumed the risk previously born by the reseller.

14. Indemnification

If the reseller is incorporating the licensor's software into the reseller's own product and then licensing the combined product to end users, the reseller should seek an indemnity from the licensor against claims made against the reseller and reseller's customers. Many licensors, while willing to indemnify the reseller, refuse to indemnify the reseller's customers. They do so arguing that: (i) the reseller can protect itself by disclaiming liability for third-party software, including the licensor's software, in the reseller's contracts with the end users, and (ii) the risk to the reseller is low and within the control of the reseller.

Licensors often operate through resellers to reduce their administrative costs and risks of dealing with end users, allowing resellers to take a percentage of their margin in return for the reseller assuming the risks and effort of the transaction. Thus, licensors are willing to protect the reseller from third-party claims but not the reseller's customers. They believe that if the licensor has to assume responsibilities in relation to the reseller's customers, then it should work directly with those customers and capture the additional margin.

It is important to differentiate indemnifying the reseller's end users and indemnifying the reseller for claims made against the reseller's end users. Licensors are not creating greater liability by indemnifying the reseller for claims made against the reseller's end users, especially if the product is a mature product that has been in the market for some time. If the licensor directly licensed the software to the end user, market forces would require the licensor to indemnify the end user. Further, if the end user brought a claim against the reseller because the end user had been sued for infringement, the licensor would have to indemnify the reseller.

Depending on the wording of the indemnity, another approach, but one less favorable to the reseller, is to have the reseller's customer bring a claim against the reseller and then have the reseller seek indemnification from the licensor.

Prudent resellers should carefully consider the protocol for the licensor's indemnification obligations. For example, clauses requiring the reseller to cede full control of the claim to the licensor may be difficult to satisfy when the reseller incorporated products from several different vendors into its product, and it is unclear which vendor's product gave rise to the claim of infringement.

Ceding over full control of the suit to one vendor may be impractical when the allegedly infringing product is composed of multiple products from multiple vendors. This is also true where more than one component may be infringing or the combination of the products resulted in a potentially infringing solution. In these cases, the reseller may be unable to relinquish control of the matter to the licensor whose product caused the infringement, as the reseller cannot determine which licensor is responsible.

Further, licensors commonly include language in indemnification provisions to excuse their indemnification obligations in the event the licensor's product is combined with other products. Given that most resellers combine the licensor's product with other third-party products to create an integrated product, the licensor may deny the reseller's claim for indemnification even though the vendor's product was the principal cause of the infringement. Finally, a licensor's desire to ensure the long-term viability of its product may conflict with a reseller's desire to quickly resolve any litigation and continue its use of the allegedly infringing product.

15. Potential Risks and Concerns

Except in rare cases where a true legal partnership is intended, the parties should not reference the counter party as a "partner" in the underlying agreement or that the licensor is entering into a "partnership" with the other party. A true legal partnership exists only in those cases where two or more parties come together to conduct business as co-owners of a business, generally for profit. The formation of a true partnership is premised on a sharing of control and ownership responsibilities as well as a sharing of profits and losses. Each party has the imputed authority/ability to contractually obligate its "partner."

Courts have found that certain conduct may lead to the creation of an "implied partnership" based on facts and circumstances associated with the partners' business dealings and behavior, which may or may not be captured in writing. Because reference to the word "partner" and the use of partnership terminology are one set of factors a court will look to determine if an implied partnership exists, a prudent party should avoid using this terminology in its contracts. Prudent parties should be sensitive to these concerns when reviewing agreements for participation in a vendor's referral/reseller program, alliance agreements, or any similar agreement premised on "shared" financial benefits, as opposed to a pure buy/sell business relationship.

Although use of the term "partner" is a convenient and effective means to characterize the intended business relationship between two parties contracting for a united business purpose, best practices dictates: (i) eliminating any references to "partner" or "partnership" in the agreements; and (ii) including express contractual language that defeats any implication that a legal partnership/joint venture is intended by the parties.

While avoiding the terms "partner" and "partnership", the parties may use qualified references to the purpose behind the collaboration such as "VAR Program Partner," or "Alliance Partner" or alternative terminology like "Collaborators," or simply references to the parties by name or function (i.e., company, vendor, reseller), avoiding any reference to role in the nomenclature. These terms should be used consistently throughout the underlying agreement, so that independent references to "partner" alone are not used.

A standard "no partnership/no joint venture" provision is helpful to defeat any implication of a true legal partnership. Model language follows:

> *This Agreement does not create any partnership, franchise, joint venture, agency, fiduciary or employment relationship between the Parties. Neither Party shall have any right or authority to assume or create any obligation or responsibility, express or implied, on behalf of the other Party or to bind the other Party in any way whatsoever.*

This provision should be used in all agreements where the parties:

- co-fund a business undertaking, or share in profits or costs associated with that undertaking;
- establish a joint bank account;
- agree to share in certain tax or other liabilities;
- maintain joint books and records;
- share costs associated with insurance; and
- are authorized to act for another.

B. Reseller Agreements

1. Overview

A software "reseller" acts as a wholesaler purchasing third-party software licenses from the owner and reselling the licenses to end users. The term "reseller agreement" has many different connotations and is often used incorrectly. Further, there is no consistent nomenclature when referring to these types of agreements, as they are often referred to as reseller agreements, marketing agreements, alliance agreements, etc.

Resellers generally purchase software products from a software manufacturer at a discount, often 30-35%, and resell the third-party product as a stand-alone product to end users, marking up the price it paid to the licensor. Essentially they are distributors of the software; licensing the software to end users and potentially assuming the risk of loss. Resellers do not provide value added services and do not bundle the product with other products or services. In most cases, the reseller is in contractual privity with the end user.

Resellers often assume more risk, as they purchase and hold inventory from the licensor. In addition, resellers usually provide promotional, marketing and branding support, maintenance and support and are responsible for marketing the product as well as obtaining government or regulatory approvals if required. As such, they tend to have higher margins, reflecting the additional risk they assume and the efforts they undertake on the licensor's behalf.

In general, resellers have lower margins then VARs, as VARs can increase their margins through the "value-added" portion of the services and products they provide as opposed to the margin on the underlying third-party product.

2. Reseller Licenses

In most reseller relationships, the software owner grants the reseller a license to use the software to support the sale and marketing of the software as well as the right to sub-license the software to end users. The owner and the end user lack contractual privity, although the owner is often identified as a third-party beneficiary in the reseller's sub-license with the end user. *See, e.g.*, Forms F.1.1 § 3.14, F.1.2 § 6.2(c), and F.3.1 § 11.13. Most reseller agreements include a EULA that flows down the licensor's required license terms to the end user in the reseller's sublicense.

The reseller must ensure that the license grant it receives from the owner provides the explicit right to sublicense the software to end users; otherwise, the reseller lacks the right to grant a sublicense to the end user. The right to grant a sublicense must be unequivocally stated, not inferred.

A reseller may or may not provide maintenance and support to end users. Many reseller agreements are structured such that the reseller provides Level 1 support and the licensor provides Level 2 and Level 3 support. See Forms J.1, J.2, and J.3 for model language providing for Level 1, 2, and 3 support.

A reseller is usually free to set its own prices subject to a minimum payment to the owner. As such, the reseller can earn a significant profit by marking up the price of the software while assuming the contractual risk of its contract with the end user. The reseller should obtain an indemnity from the licensor for infringement claims or any material issue with the software. The reseller should ensure the owner has sufficient assets to indemnify the reseller in the event an issue arises. Similarly, the end user needs to ensure that the software will be supported by the reseller or the licensor.

Because a "reseller" is passing through the software to the end user, it should ensure its margins support assuming any accompanying risk for breach of contract, breach of warranty, claims of indemnity, maintenance support, etc. may be best for the end user to purchase a license directly from the licensor.

For a detailed discussion of the issues related to indemnities in VAR/distribution agreements, see English, *Distributors: Tracking IP Indemnity Squeeze in the Supply Channel*, 30 ACC Docket 79 (Oct. 2012).

See Form B.1.4 for model license granting a licensee the right to use the software for non-production purposes.

See Forms F.1.1 and F.1.2 for examples of distribution agreements.

C. Value-Added Reseller (VARs) Agreements

1. Overview

A Value-Added Reseller ("VAR") resells a licensor's products and services to end users in combination with its own services. The VAR usually integrates layered products on top of the third-party software and sells both products as part of an end-user solution. Unlike an OEM arrangement, a VAR usually does not sell the other products on an integrated basis and the licensor's products and branding are disclosed to the end-user. VARs services include creating a turnkey solution, consulting, configuration, customization and implementation services.

Many hardware manufacturers have created VAR programs that allow software companies and system integrators to purchase their hardware at a discount to resell to end users if the hardware is sold in conjunction with a third-party software product in the belief it will incent software vendors to recommend their hardware to their customers. A VAR does not simply resell the manufacturer's hardware or software but rather combines the manufacturer's software or hardware with the vendor's software and services to sell as a bundle. The VAR may not resell the third-party products on a stand-alone basis, only in conjunction with the VAR's software. Thus, the VAR is financially incented to include the hardware vendor's hardware as part of a bundle, increasing the hardware vendor's sales.

VARs usually contract directly with the end-user customer and assume the risk of the sale. Under this model, the licensor sets the price to the VAR, and the VAR sets the price to the end user. In these cases, the VAR is often required to enter into a EULA with its end users, flowing down the licensor's required terms.

In some cases, the licensor may contract directly with the end-user customer, often via a click-wrap license, to avoid providing the VAR with contractual representations and warranties regarding the software's performance and any related indemnities. Doing so also allows the licensor to maintain tighter control over the licenses granted to the licensor's software and the royalties owed by the VAR to the licensor.

See Forms F.2.2–F.2.4 for examples of VAR agreements.

2. Value-Added Reseller Licenses

The VAR should not only receive authorization to use the software, but also sufficient license rights to provide the "value added" services. Many licensors also incorporate additional restrictions in their license grants as illustrated in the bolded language below.

> *Licensor grants you a non-exclusive, limited license to use the technology programs identified in the Licensor's policies for your partner level to: (a) demonstrate, develop or prototype your value added package for the intended commercial use of multiple end users; (b) provide technical support for employees and end users solely in connection with your value added package that you distribute pursuant to a distribution agreement with Licensor that authorizes you to provide technical support for the Licensor programs; and (c) provide training for the value added package to employees and end users to whom you have distributed the value added package pursuant to a distribution agreement with Licensor.* ***Development licenses may not be used to develop or administer your value added package for the exclusive use of a specific end user.***

D. Original Equipment Manufacturer (OEMs) Agreements

1. Overview

An Original Equipment Manufacturer (OEM) licenses a third-party product to incorporate into the OEM's own proprietary product, creating a distinct product, and then markets the combined product under its own name. The licensor's intellectual property is engineered by the OEM to operate in conjunction with OEM's intellectual property to meet the business requirements of the OEM's customers. The licensor's intellectual property and branding is invisible to the end user.

OEM relationships benefit both parties through increased sales of their respective products as the combined product will be more attractive in the marketplace. A combined product benefits the OEM by enhancing features and functionality, thereby allowing OEMs to market and sell a more robust and all-encompassing product It also may provide an OEM a competitive edge over its competitors that cannot offer the functionality of the combined product.

Licensors view OEM agreements as an opportunity to increase their exposure in the marketplace, potentially increase their market share, and receive additional revenue that they would not otherwise receive. Increasing its distribution through bundled sales may also increase product awareness by introducing the product to a broader market. A licensor may also benefit from having its product associated with another company in the same industry that has greater name recognition or marketing power.

Under most OEM agreements, the licensor licenses its product to the OEM in return for a license fee which may require a guaranteed minimum license fee. The OEM sets the price of the combined product to the end user and pays the licensor the negotiated license fee. Prudent licensors should negotiate a set fee for each use of the licensor's software and reject any attempt to tie the license fee to the amounts the reseller receives from the end user. Tying the licensor's fee to the amounts received from the end user places the risk of the end user's non-payment on the licensor and allows the OEM to potentially price the combined product at a low price in an effort to reduce the fee payable to the licensor, and profit from the sale of related services such as integration services as well as maintenance and support which may not require a royalty payment to the licensor.

Prudent licensors should also ensure the underlying agreement specifically provides that the licensor's software may only be distributed as part of a combined product and not on a standalone basis to protect the licensors own sales and margins.

Most OEM agreements allow the OEM to not only market and sell the combined product, but also to allow the parties to continue marketing and selling their legacy products independent of the combined product. This especially true for the OEM, as all potential customers may not want to purchase all the functions of the combined product. Prudent OEMs should resist accepting any limitations on the sale of their products on a standalone basis. in the hope that a combined product may increase sales of those products. Further, the OEM agreement should affirmatively state that the OEM is not required to incorporate the licensor's products into a every sale of a particular product.

Because the OEM is in contractual privity with the end user, the OEM provides the end user a warranty, support, implementation and training. Many licensors take the position that they will indemnify the OEM but will not indemnify the OEM's customers, arguing such indemnification are the responsibility of the OEM. Further, the OEM can limit its risk by carving out claims made against third-party products from any indemnity it provides to its customers, limiting its liability for breach of contract and indemnity claims in its contracts with its customers.

The OEM often commits to train a certain number of its employees in the third party's products to provide sales and support.

See Forms F.3.1 and F.3.2 for examples of OEM agreements.

2. *Original Equipment Manufacturer Licenses*

The OEM licenses with the licensor should not overlook the right to incorporate the licensor's intellectual property into the OEM's product to create an integrated product. The OEM should retain the flexibility to change the way it incorporates the licensor's software into the OEM's underlying product.

From the OEM's perspective, the OEM requires the following rights from the licensor:

(a) The Right of Modification

The right to modify the licensor's software to integrate and bundle it into the OEM's existing software. Prudent licensors will strictly limit how the OEM may modify their software.

(b) The Right of Reproduction

The ability to reproduce the licensor's software as part of the bundled product.

(c) The Right of Distribution

The right distribute the combined product in the marketplace. Model language follows:

Licensor grants to Licensee, and Licensee accepts from Licensor, effective upon Licensee's receipt of the Licensed Software and conditional on payment of the Licensee Fee as per Section __ (Payment) of this Agreement, subject to the terms of this Agreement, a non-exclusive, nontransferable, worldwide license to make the following use of the Licensed Software in order to create the embedded software:

2.1. *Use and copy the Licensed Software and the Documentation only for the internal purpose of developing and creating Modifications of the Licensed Software and embedding the same with Licensee's Products, all only on Licensee's Premises.*
2.2. *Create copies of the Embedded Software in object code and the Documentation to the extent necessary to fully utilize the rights granted herein.*
2.3. *Distribute and sub-license the Embedded Software in object code world-wide directly or indirectly through Distributors, to End Users for the purpose of and to affect the End User's utilization of Licensee's Products.*
2.4. *Authorize Distributors to (a) use, create, and distribute copies of the Embedded Software as part of Licensee's Products and transfer directly to End Users, for the purpose of and to affect the End User's utilization of Licensee's Products, and (b) authorize End Users to create limited copies of the Embedded Software for archival purposes.*

End User shall mean a specific individual authorized directly or indirectly by Licensee to use the Embedded Software regardless of whether the individual is actively using the Embedded Software.

Sublicensing Terms. An End User may be authorized to use the Embedded Software only pursuant to a written agreement between Licensee or a Distributor, as the case may be and an End User. The terms and conditions of such agreement shall be at least as protective of the Licensed Software as part of the Embedded Software as: (i) the terms and conditions Licensee uses for its other software products; (ii) the terms and conditions governing the End User's use of, or marketing of Licensee's Products; and (iii) the terms and conditions contained herein.

See Forms F.3.1 and F.3.2 for model OEM agreements.

E. Referral Agreements

Under a referral agreement, an entity is compensated for referring opportunities to the selling entity, usually the owner of the software. "Referral fees" vary but are often 10-15% of the sale price. The fees can take many forms from an outright cash payment based on a percentage of the sale price to "soft" dollars which the referring party may use for discounted or free products and services including training and maintenance.

Conceptually, a reseller agreement differs from a referral agreement. Under a referral agreement, the referral partner seeks to identify potential customers for the owner's software. The software owner negotiates the terms of the license and enters into a license agreement directly with the end user/customer. The referral partner receives a referral fee/commission but is not involved with the actual licensing of the product or the subsequent support of the product. Further, the referral partner has no liability in the event the vendor subsequently breaches its agreement with the customer. *Young Cheerleaders of America v. Data Specialists, Inc.*, 1987 WL 18581 (N.D. Ill Oct. 13, 1987) (company recommending another company is not a guarantor of the recommended party's performance); *Electro-Matic Products, Inc. v. Prime Computers, Inc.*, 884 F.2d 579 (6th Cir. 1989) (a party recommending a third-party has no obligation to investigate the recommended party's ability to perform).

In most cases, compensation is "earned" from purchases made by an end user or as a result of business obtained directly by the licensor from a referral partner. This compensation structure, while acceptable in a commercial environment, is problematic in the public sector as it can be viewed as a kickback. To that end, prudent parties should provide in the underlying agreement that purchases made by a public sector customer will not generate a fee.

> *No referral and/or influence fees shall be paid or received by the Parties based upon any transaction or sale to a Government Customer under the terms of this Agreement. A Government Customer shall mean a customer or an end user for a customer that is the government of (i) the United States, (ii) any state of the United States, (iii) any city, county, town, territory, or other municipality of the United States, (iv) any corporation, educational institution, or other entity that is owned or controlled by, or subject to the procurement regulations of any entity in subsections (i), (ii), or (iii) above, and (v) any prime contractor who holds a contract with any entity in subsections (i), (ii), (iii), or (iv) above when the fees under this Agreement are related to sales in support of that contract.*

Further, prudent customers/end users should provide in their vendor agreements that all referral fees or discounts received by the vendor from a third-party as a result of the end user's purchase of the vendor's products will be passed through to the customer and that the vendor will not receive or retain any such fees. Customers should also seek a representation and warranty to this effect. Model language follows:

> *If Vendor receives a refund, credit or other rebate for goods, services, or expenses purchased by Vendor or Customer in connection with the Services that has not previously been factored into the Fees, Vendor will promptly notify Customer and will pay such amount to Customer (or, if applicable, provide a credit on the next delivered invoice) within thirty (30) days after receipt thereof.*

Some vendors are hesitant to use referral arrangements for compliance reasons as the vendor lacks transparency into the referral partner's relationship with the customer. The lack of transparency can raise red flags as to the possibility of payments flowing from the referral partner to the customer in return for the customer purchasing the vendor's software and services. To avoid this risk, these vendors enter into reseller agreements as opposed to a referral partner agreements where the reseller/referral partner is in contractual privity with the customer and compliance issues are less likely to arise.

See Forms F.2.2 to F.2.4 for a model Referral Agreements.

F. *PRACTICE POINT:* Checklist for Reseller and OEM agreements.

When drafting and negotiating Reseller and OEM agreements, the parties should ensure the agreement is comprehensive to avoid future disputes. At a minimum, the following terms, to the extent they are applicable, should be addressed:

- Territory
- Product
- Term
- Renewal
- Termination
  - Upon breach, does either party have step-in rights?
    - The reseller to provide software maintenance/support that the licensor previously had been providing.
    - The licensor to provide maintenance or appoint another reseller to provide maintenance.
- Remedies
- Rights of the end users upon termination
- Exclusivity
- License grant. The license grant should authorize the reseller to:
  - resell/sublicense the software
  - use the software to provide the "value-added" services
  - copy and distribute the software
  - the ability to modify/enhance the licensor's code
  - with what restrictions?
    - sublicensing only for the value-added products
    - exclusivity for a geographic area
    - only be bundled or incorporated into specific products the reseller owns or licenses from others.
- Sublicenses
  - Is there a EULA/sublicense agreement which flows down the licensor's mandated "end user terms?"
  - What rights will the sublicensee/end user have upon termination of the agreement by the licensor or VAR*?*
  - Will sublicenses granted to end users continue for the term of the applicable license agreement between the VAR and end user?
  - Does the agreement between the licensor and the VAR address how the EULA/sublicense agreements are managed?
  - Will the reseller/VAR provide the licensor with copies of the end user license agreement or simply maintain adequate records for audits by the licensor?
- Allocation of revenue
- The process for ordering

- Acceptance of the order
- Price/Royalties/Discounts
- Payment and payment risk
- Interest on late payments
- Sales reporting
- Audit rights
    - Do audit rights continue beyond the termination of the license agreement between the licensor and the reseller? If yes, for how long?
    - What if the end user sublicensees continue beyond the termination date or are generating fees for the reseller?.
- Effort level required by reseller/distributor to sell the product
- Quotas/minimum sales performance
- Marketing requirements efforts, trade shows, etc.
- Approval of marketing materials and public statements
- EULAs
- Conflicts of interest
- Confidentiality
- Compliance and Sanctions obligations
- Risk allocation between the parties
- Governing law and venue
- Maintenance
- Delivery of software/electronic keys
- IP Ownership

CHAPTER 21

Maintenance and Support (Forms J.1, J.2, and J.3)/(§§ 11, 16K)

** Section references in this Chapter refer to the sections in Form J.1 – Software Maintenance and Support Agreement **

Maintenance and support are usually associated with perpetual or multiyear term licenses, as maintenance and support are often included in the price of an annual license. When a licensee makes a decision to adopt a certain software solution, it should seek assurances from the licensor that the licensor will continue to enhance and support the software for some period in the future. The licensee wants to avoid a situation where the licensee adopts a mission-critical software solution and the licensor subsequently decides to stop enhancing the software or supporting it, essentially forcing the licensee to migrate to a new software solution.

A. Nomenclature

Fundamental to obtaining a commitment to support and maintain a software solution is understanding the nomenclature used in the governing agreement. Too often the parties fail to understand the other party's obligations and what is encompassed in "maintenance" services. To avoid these issues, the parties should understand the nomenclature of support and maintenance services and ensure that all such services are carefully defined in the underlying agreement.

1. Maintenance vs. Support

Support is considered to be broader in meaning than maintenance and is generally considered to encompass maintenance services. Support refers to all assistance provided by the licensor or a third party to the licensee with any problems related to the operation of the licensed software. It includes training, telephone assistance, installation support, and maintenance. Support is often provided through different tiers or levels, with each tier providing an enhanced level of assistance and a shorter period of time in which the licensor must respond to or resolve the licensee's issues.

Maintenance is generally considered related to modifications, enhancements, and corrections to the licensed software as part of the licensor's efforts to continually improve the licensed software. Maintenance is not limited to correcting defects or bugs but encompasses the continual enhancement of the licensed software's functionality. (§§ 3, 4)

2. Upgrades, Releases, Updates, Enhancements, and Modifications

"*Upgrade*" refers to a new release or version of the software provided to customers who have purchased software maintenance and support from the licensor. If a new release or version of the licensor's software product contains the same core functionality as the software, usually the release or version shall be considered to be an "upgrade." Upgrades include both major and minor releases. (§1.15)

A "Release" is generally considered to mean a redistribution of a software product that contains new features, new functionality, and/or significant performance improvements. A "major release" refers to the introduction of the first release of the software as well as releases with significant new functionality, adaptations for new hardware configurations, and/or the incorporation of new major third-party software. A "minor release" usually means releases of error corrections, additions of minor functionality, minor adaptations for new hardware configurations, and adaptations for new releases of third-party software. To avoid confusion, each major software release is assigned a unique numerical identification utilizing three numbers, separated by periods, such as version 6.3.1.

"Update(s)" refers to the release of error corrections, intermediate releases to maintain conformity with industry standards, and software deliveries not containing increases in functionality. An update typically is identified by a change in a number to the right of the first decimal point in the software's version number (e.g., 6.1 to 6.1.1). (§1.14)

An "Enhancement" adds additional functionality to the existing functionality. (§1.2)

A "Modification" occurs when changes are made to the core code and then functionality is added, which can spawn a major error when upgrading the software.

3. Numbering Protocol

A common protocol for numbering software releases is as follows:

major.minor[.revision[.build]] or major.minor[.maintenance[.build]]

In a numbering scheme consisting of x.y.z, the "x" represents a major release, "y" represents a minor release and "z" represents an update. The first released version of a software product is version 1.0. Numbers below 1 usually refer to alpha or beta versions that have not been publicly released. Traditionally, major releases are numbered as X.0; for example, Microsoft Word 10.0 is a major release, significantly different from any previous version, while Microsoft Word 10.1 has only minor changes and is, thus, only a minor release or revision.

B. Maintenance vs. New Versions

A common issue in the provision of maintenance services is what actually constitutes an "update," which would be considered maintenance and covered under the annual maintenance plan, and what constitutes a new version of the software for which the licensor could levy an additional fee. Given that maintenance is usually charged on an annual basis, licensors have financial incentive to characterize substantial improvements to the software as a new version and outside the scope of maintenance. As such, the licensor would be able to charge the licensee an additional fee. A licensee should seek to clearly define the scope of "maintenance" to ensure that it receives the benefit of what it has paid for and seek to limit the licensor's claim that an "update" is a new version.

See Forms J.1 and J.2 for a description of services usually covered under maintenance.

C. Maintenance

Maintenance is often viewed as an extended warranty. The warranty period and the obligation to perform maintenance address when the licensee begins to pay for support, upgrades and fixes; the shorter the warranty period, the greater the revenue that will likely flow to the licensor from maintenance.

From the licensor's perspective, the maintenance provisions should be separate and distinct from the warranty in the license agreement and should ideally be in a separate agreement. This is important due to the difference in the licensor's liability for breach of the warranty contained in the license agreement and for breach of a separate maintenance agreement. The licensee also benefits from separate agreements as it has the ability to terminate the maintenance agreement while continuing to utilize the software.

Under some license agreements, maintenance begins upon acceptance. Under others, maintenance does not occur until the expiration of the warranty. During the warranty, the licensee may terminate the license agreement if the software does not meet the functional requirements or perform in accordance with the performance requirements set forth in the software license, and may potentially receive a refund of the entire license fee. If the software does not meet the functional specifications during the maintenance period or the licensor fails to maintain the software in accordance with the contractual requirements, the licensee can terminate the maintenance agreement but will usually only be entitled to receive a refund of the maintenance fee, provided the maintenance provisions are contained in a separate agreement. In short, by utilizing separate agreements, assuming industry standard limits of liability—the amount of the license fee for the license agreement and 180 days trailing revenue for the maintenance agreement—the licensor will most likely be able to reduce its liability in the event of a breach, as the warranty under the license agreement will likely be 90 days or less.

The agreement should set forth the process for reporting errors and requesting support. Once a report is received, the vendor will assign a severity level, which determines the timeline for addressing how quickly the vendor will work to resolve the issue. If it the vendor is able to replicate the error, it will begin the process of resolving the error or creating a work around.

A prudent licensor will claim ownership of any modifications, enhancements, or derivative works created by the licensor while performing maintenance for the licensee. **(§3.5)**

1. Principal Terms

(a) Period for Offering Maintenance

Given the complexities of software, the licensee should receive a commitment from the licensor that the licensor will support and maintain the software for a minimum of five years after acceptance. It is not unreasonable to have the licensor agree to a minimum support period, unless the licensor is planning to "sunset" the software and release the employees supporting the software.

Any agreement should address the length and type of notice that must be given to the licensee in the event the licensor stops supporting the software. The maintenance agreement should explicitly state the scope and nature of the support.

Licensees usually require the licensor to agree to offer maintenance for a set period of time, such as five to ten years from acceptance, without committing to actually purchasing maintenance from the licensor. The requirement to offer maintenance for a minimum period is reasonable, as an expensive software system is worthless unless it is properly maintained and most licensees lack the ability to maintain the software themselves. At the same time, a licensee cannot expect the licensor to fix or project its prices 10 years into the future.

(b) Versions Supported (§3.4)

To achieve economies of scale and increase profitability, most vendors will only maintain the two most recent versions of the software. Customers are thus forced to upgrade their software or have to maintain the software themselves, which in most cases is impractical. By essentially forcing customers to use the two most recent versions, the vendor reduces its risk, as any corrections or security fixes passed on to the customer through an upgrade will most likely be implemented.

(c) Term of the Maintenance Agreement (§6)

The term of the underlying software licensee software and the term of the maintenance agreement are usually separate, as the licensee is usually not obligated to purchase maintenance. Most maintenance agreements have a term of one year, with customers having the right to renew for additional one-year terms. Given the significant investment many customers make in their software, they want the comfort of knowing that the vendor will provide maintenance and support for a significant period of time after they purchase the software. At the same time, however, many customers do not want to make a long-term commitment, as their business needs may change. Thus, they often seek the right but not the obligation to purchase maintenance.

Most vendors staff and budget their maintenance teams annually based on the number of customers who have purchased maintenance. Thus, most vendors do not permit customers to terminate their maintenance agreements for convenience. For the same reason, most vendors require customers to purchase an annual maintenance agreement at the expiration of the warranty. If they fail to do so, the vendor (i) may not offer maintenance, or (ii) may require the customer to retroactively purchase maintenance from the date the customer's warranty expired or the date their last maintenance contract expired. Vendors do so to avoid customers waiting until they need maintenance and support before purchasing it. Further, customers who have entered into a 12-month maintenance agreement usually receive priority over customers who seek to purchase support on a time-and-materials basis without entering into a 12-month maintenance agreement.

(d) Cessation/Renewal of Maintenance (§2.4)

Most licensors provide that if the licensee ceases to purchase maintenance and then subsequently seeks to purchase maintenance, the licensee must pay for all maintenance fees from the time it stopped purchasing maintenance until the time it restarts maintenance. They do so to discourage the licensee from staring maintenance when it needs support and stopping maintenance when it does not.

Some maintenance agreements provide that if the licensor ceases to provide maintenance, the licensor will provide the licensee with a copy of the software's source code so that the licensee can maintain the source code itself. In this situation, the licensee should insist on the right to have a third party maintain the software. The parties should distinguish situations where the software has reached the end of its commercial viability or there is no longer a demand for maintenance and support, versus situations in which the licensor simply decides to no longer support the software. If the licensee insists on maintaining the software itself, the licensor may want to consider having the licensee indemnify it for any liability arising from the licensee's continued use of the software and for any claims of intellectual property infringement for any modifications the licensee may make to the software. Licensees should realize, however, that it may be impractical to maintain the software themselves given the complex nature of many large software systems and the large learning curve necessary to master the system. At a minimum, the licensee will need access to the licensor's employees and the documentation necessary to support the software.

Some licensors provide that the failure to purchase annual maintenance negates any warranties related to security, performance, intellectual property infringement, errors, etc. They do so because maintenance includes updates to the software that corrects bugs, errors and security defects.

See Chapter 24 for a more detailed discussion on the issues associated with a software escrow and release.

(e) Level of Support (§§ 2.2, 3.1)

Licensees should insist that the licensor's level of support under the maintenance agreement be the same as the licensor's level of support under the warranty provisions of the license agreement. The licensee should not accept a lesser level of support. This is especially true for any functionality that was not tested or implemented during the warranty period. The maintenance standards should specifically provide the response times and repair times, as well as the licensee's remedies if the licensor fails to properly support the software. Often licensors will implement a "bypass" to correct a problem, as it is often quicker, easier, and cheaper to circumvent an issue than to fix it.

(f) Updates, Upgrades and Enhancements (§3)

Maintenance is a "one to many" model where the vendor seeks to have all customers on the same version of the software to achieve economies of scale and avoid supporting individual "projects" as opposed to a "product." In this manner, errors can be corrected and enhancements can be distributed across all customers at the same time.

Purchasing maintenance and support services allows customers to access enhancements by implementing new versions and releases. The actual enhancements and the timing of the release are determined by the vendor. Although customers are responsible for implementing the new release, they are not contractually obligated to implement any particular enhancement or release.

The agreement should clearly distinguish which the licensee must pay an additional license fee. Maintenance and support usually includes functionality enhancements as well as error and bug fixes when they are made commercially available through releases as well as customer support. Specifically excluded is maintenance support for customer developed code that interacts with the vendor's software and modifications to the vendor's software that results in the customization of the software.

Any new features or enhancements to existing functionality should:

- be compatible with previous versions of the application,
- not degrade the performance or operation of the application, and
- not eliminate any material functions or features of the existing application.

Depending on the nature of the new release, the customer may be required to upgrade any third party dependent software such as the customer's operating system. The customer should have the right to refuse an update, and no update should be installed without the consent of the customer. Finally, many customers insist on retaining the right to remove the update and revert to the previous version if a problem arises that is attributable to the new update.

(g) Product Documentation (§3.2)

The licensor should be required to update the product documentation to reflect any enhancement or alteration to the software to ensure the documentation is consistent with the licensed software. The licensee should require that the licensor's software, as maintained, be compatible with all third-party software and hardware upgrades. This additional requirement creates great risk for the party providing maintenance, given the uncertainty of when such upgrades will occur and the cost to make the licensor's software compatible.

In the event of a dispute between the parties regarding maintenance and support, the governing agreement should provide an escalation procedure to try to resolve the issue.

(h) Error Levels (Appendix A)

Usually, maintenance agreements group errors into three classes based on severity with a shorter response time corresponding to the seriousness of the issue. See Forms J.1 and J.2, which contain illustrative language.

A **Level 1** error usually means that the software will not function and there is no bypass or redundancy available. In such situations, the licensor should respond immediately to the licensee's notification of a Level 1 error. Most licensors will usually not agree to resolve an issue within a set time period but should agree to work continuously until the problem is resolved.

A **Level 2** error usually means that a material aspect of the software's functionality is unavailable and there is no bypass or redundancy available. In such situations, the licensor should commit to work continuously during normal business hours until the issue has been resolved.

A **Level 3** error usually means there is a noncritical "bug" for which a bypass or work-around exists. The licensor usually commits to fix all Level 3 errors in the next update.

Many licensors include language in their agreements limiting their obligation to fix only those errors that can be duplicated. These provisions protect licensors from having to devote substantial time and effort to identify and fix "ghost" errors that are not easily reproducible.

See Form J.3 for an illustration of Error Levels.

(i) Availability

Although licensees seek 24×7 availability, licensors must take their systems down periodically for routine maintenance. Prudent licensees will seek to limit the licensor's ability to do so to a regularly scheduled time period, such as 12 a.m. to 5 a.m. on the third Sunday of each month, or upon 10 days prior notice, to limit any potential disruption of the licensee's business. The licensee should also seek to limit scheduled downtime to a set number of hours a month, such as four hours a month. Licensors usually do not state how long their systems will be down, but instead provide a window of time in which the system may be down. Thus, licensees should recognize there is a difference between a maintenance window and scheduled downtime. In addition, most agreements provide that the licensor may take the system down in an emergency without prior notice. In many cases, the stated downtime is tied to an "Availability" SLA, if applicable. See Form D.4.3.

(j) Service Levels

Maintenance and support agreements should include service levels to incent the vendor to meet the level of services the customer expects to receive. Not all vendors, however, will offer service credits. Several common service levels are discussed below. See Chapter 12 for a more detailed discussion of service levels.

(y) Response Times

Most licensors agree to "respond" to a reported error within a stated time period. The response may come in the form of a return phone call, but more likely the licensor's response will simply be an automated email acknowledging that the licensee reported an error to the licensor's email-based reporting system. The obligation to respond to a reported error is unrelated to resolving the error and should be of little comfort to the licensee other than to know the licensor is aware of the problem. The licensee should ensure that the maintenance agreement provides a set time period corresponding to the licensee's normal business hours when the licensor's help desk will be available to provide telephone support. While most licensors will provide 24×7×365 telephone support for an additional cost, most licensors only provide after-hours support without additional charge for Level 1 errors. The licensee should also require the licensor to attach a list of the licensor's holidays to the maintenance agreement so that the licensee knows the days that support is unavailable.

(z) Error Resolution Times

Although most maintenance agreements provide estimated times for resolving a reported error, most licensors do not commit to resolve an error within a set period of time and simply state that these time periods are aspirational. By accepting this language, the licensee is left without a meaningful remedy.

Similarly, vendors will usually only commit to using commercially reasonable efforts to resolve an issue. Prudent licensees seek to incorporate SLAs into the agreement for the licensor's failure to meet the stated resolution goals. The use of SLAs is reasonable for Level 1 and 2 errors, which severely impact the licensee's use of the software— especially if such errors impact the licensee's ability to provide services to its clients.

See Form J.1 Appendix A and Form J.3 for examples of language illustrating this discussion.

(k) Impact of Customization on Maintenance and Support Fees

To the extent the licensee purchased heavily customized software, the licensor may require the licensee to purchase specialized support at a significantly higher price. Thus, before significantly customizing its software (as opposed to configuration), the licensee should understand how the customization will impact the price of maintenance and support.

(l) Maintenance Windows

Maintenance windows should be regularly scheduled and announced well in advance to allow the customer to plan for any unavailability and avoid any interruption of its business. Vendors should be contractually committed to providing the customer prior written notice, (i.e., ten days), of any maintenance windows during which the software will be unavailable. Maintenance windows should be limited to off times such as weekend evenings when demand is likely low. Any maintenance performed outside these windows should be limited to work that will not have an impact on the availability or functionality of the software.

(m) Remedies (§2.2)

Most vendors provide that the customer's sole and exclusive remedy is to reperform the services. Given the relatively lower cost of the maintenance and support fees, licensors are hesitant to agree to a significant limitation of liability.

2. *Exclusions to Maintenance Obligations (§5)*

A licensor can keep its costs low only by maintaining a standard version of the software and amortizing its costs to do so over a large number of customers. As such, licensors should always state that they will maintain only the last two versions of the software to ensure that previous versions are compatible with all subsequent versions and to avoid increased costs from maintaining too many versions. The licensor should clearly state that while the licensor will support other versions, there will be an additional cost to do so. Further, the licensor should specifically state that maintenance does not include on-site support and is limited to telephonic support.

Most maintenance agreements exclude supporting/correcting errors caused by:

- the licensee or its agents modifying the software without the licensor's prior written consent;
- negligent or unauthorized actions by the licensee;
- the licensee failing to maintain the operating system, hardware or network necessary for the software to function properly;
- use of the software in conjunction with a third-party product that has not been approved by the licensor;
- the failure of the licensee's hardware or software not covered by the maintenance agreement;
- use of software not obtained from the licensor or at the request of the licensor;
- the licensee's failure to comply with the licensor's instructions licensor-provided documentation;
- modifications to the software or configurations that are not set forth in the product description;
- the licensee not using the software in conformance with the specifications or documentation; or
- the licensee's failure to install the most recent versions of the software.

Finally, the licensor should clearly state that any services not explicitly listed as being part of maintenance are outside the scope of maintenance and will be charged on a time and material basis.

3. Pricing and Payment (§ 7)

Maintenance has traditionally been priced at 18 to 20 percent of the undiscounted original license fee and any subsequent enhancements. Some licensors calculate the maintenance fee on the aggregate of the license fee plus the cost of any enhancements or modifications made by the licensor, while others consider any enhancements or modifications to be consulting services or professional services and not included in the base amount for calculating the maintenance fee. From the licensor's perspective, if there is a large price discount, the maintenance fee should be calculated on the list price, not the discounted price, because the scope of effort is the same, and therefore the licensor's cost to provide maintenance remains the same.

Maintenance/support is usually very profitable for a licensor if the software is well written and widely distributed, allowing the cost of support to be amortized over a large number of customers. Some licensors generate margins as high as 85% on software maintenance. The cost/risk of ongoing support rises significantly if the installation becomes more of a project than a product, that is, the software becomes so customized that it cannot be maintained consistent with the versions utilized by other customers.

(a) Pricing

The licensee should seek to have the licensor fix its price for support during an initial five-year period, in which case the licensor will assume the risk of a significant increase in the cost to deliver the support. From the licensor's perspective, the solution is to include language that the licensor will provide such services at "licensor's then-existing price." The licensee should be wary of accepting a commitment to provide support without fixing the price. Without a fixed price, the licensee does not have a true commitment from the licensor, as the licensor may raise its support and prohibitively make the purchase of support services financially unfeasible for the licensee.

A solution that may be mutually agreeable is to increase the cost annually by an escalator. This usually gives rise to an animated discussion as to which index properly reflects the actual increase in the licensor's costs. Two common indexes used are the Consumer Price Index (CPI) and the Employment Cost Index, Civilian Workers, Not Seasonally Adjusted, Compensation Costs (ECI), published by the Bureau of Labor Statistics, U.S. Department of Labor. The CPI is a broad-based index that reflects a large "basket" of goods while the ECI is focused solely on labor costs. The parties should carefully consider whether either index reflects the nature of their agreement or whether they should explore other labor/cost indexes published by the Department of Labor that may more closely mirror the costs incurred in supporting the underlying software. Licensees should seek a mechanism to reduce the licensor's fees if the licensor's costs decrease. This is not unrealistic, as costs in the information technology services industry have historically fallen over time.

Each index carries its own risks. In the 1970s and 1980s, the CPI rose significantly, driven by higher real estate prices, while technology salaries remained constant. In the late 1990s, technology salaries quickly outpaced the rate of inflation, causing many licensors with fixed price obligations to suffer significant losses in providing support. Before agreeing to tie fee increases to the CPI, the licensor should consider the likelihood that the CPI will decline. The recent history has brought the CPI nearly to zero. If the CPI goes negative, will the licensor be obligated to decrease its prices? A prudent licensor should ensure to include language that its prices are not subject to decrease.

A mutually agreeable resolution may be for the licensor to commit to provide support for a period of five to seven years with a fixed price for the first two or three years. For the remainder of the term, the licensor may increase the price annually based on an agreed upon index but with a minimum increase and a maximum cap. Alternatively, the parties may agree after an initial period to tie future price increases to a very specific index, reflecting the licensor's labor costs. See, e.g., § 8.4E. (i.e., the Syntec salary index that tracks technology labor costs in France).

Licensees should also seek to include a most favored customer clause. It is often difficult to have a licensor accept this type of clause except in the case of its largest and best customers. For a detailed discussion of most favored customer clauses, see Chapter 7.N.

(b) Payment

Maintenance fees should be priced on an annual basis, payable annually in advance and nonrefundable. Occasionally, licensees seek to terminate their maintenance agreement for convenience during the stated term and receive a pro rata refund for the remaining term of the agreement. This request is unreasonable from the licensor's perspective because the licensor staffs its help desk based on the number of customers it has and amortizes the cost of such support over those customers. If the licensor loses a customer, it is unable to increase its prices to the remaining customers to cover the lost revenue, as the licensor is usually contractually precluded from raising its prices until each contract is renewed. Thus, from the licensor's perspective, maintenance agreements should be terminable only for cause or upon written notice 90 days prior to the anniversary date of the agreement.

D. Independent Service Organizations (ISOs)

One issue of great concern to licensors is when the licensee seeks to maintain the software through the use of independent service organizations (ISOs). Many licensors are concerned that these independent third parties, who are often their competitors, will learn the licensors' trade secrets or siphon off the licensors' maintenance revenue, which is usually a significant portion of their profits. *See, e.g., Hodge Business Computer Systems, Inc. v. U.S.A. Mobile Communications, Inc.*, 910 F.2d 367 (6th Cir. 1990). Further, any changes made by an ISO may have an unanticipated impact on any future updates or enhancements created by the licensor. See § 14.A.4.(d) for model language limiting the licensor's liability in the event a third party makes changes to the licensor's software.

To limit third-party access to the license or its software and thus prevent the retention of ISOs by the licensee, the license should clearly state that the licensee may not grant a third party access to the software. See § 3.6 for an example of such language. The failure to be explicit may allow a third party to assume responsibility for maintenance of the software. *See, e.g., Hogan Systems, Inc. v. CyberSource Int'l, Inc.*, 158 F.3d 319 (5th Cir. 1998).

In the event the licensee seeks to allow an ISO or other contractor access to the licensor's intellectual property and trade secrets, the licensor should require the licensee to indemnify the licensor for any misuse by the licensee. The issue of third-party access is complex, as the failure to allow third parties to provide maintenance support potentially raises antitrust concerns. For a more detailed discussion of these antitrust issues, see Chapter 7.K. *See* Johanson & Zollman, *Computer Maintenance Raises Antitrust Issues*, NAT'L L.J., May 20, 1996, at C 40. The utilization of an ISO should serve as a basis for terminating an existing warranty relating to intellectual property indemnification as the licensor cannot be responsible for the ISO's actions. The licensor should also be relieved of any responsibility for future enhancements, updates or continuing maintenance, or bug fixes.

Licensees seeking to utilize ISOs to provide maintenance and support services should recognize the risk that the licensor of the proprietary software supported by the ISO may drag the customer into any lawsuit it brings against the ISO, potentially disrupting the customer's business operations. Although the ISO may indemnify the customer against any such risks, in reality, the ISO cannot prevent disruptions to a customer's business. *See Oracle v. Rimini Street Lawsuit: A Guide*, https://www.forbes.com/sites/oracle/2018/12/06/oracle-v-rimini-street-lawsuit-a-guide/#2e4d26578d40; *SAP Verdict Spawns Legal Worries in Software Maintenance Business*, WALL ST. J., Nov. 26, 2010, at B1.

E. *PRACTICE POINT*: Checklist for reviewing maintenance and support agreements.

- Definitions: Have all the key terms been adequately defined? i.e., Error levels?
- Are the vendor's responsibilities clearly stated?
- Are all other activities declared to be out of scope?
- Is pricing for out-of-scope activities included?
- Term: What is the term?
- Termination: What triggers termination?
- What are the customer's remedies in the event of a breach?
- Can the customer terminate for convenience?
- Payment Terms: Must the customer pay annually in advance?
- Are there required times for responding to an issue?
- Are there required times for resolving an issue?
- How will the customer notify the vendor of an issue?
- Is the customer obligated to accept updates/enhancements?
- Is the vendor excused from maintaining a customer application that does not incorporate the most recent updates/version of the software?
- Is there a limitation of liability provision?
- Is there a disclaimer of warranties provision? Does the vendor state that the customer's use/access to the application will not be uninterrupted or error-free?
- Are the support obligations tied to SLAs, such as response times and availability?

CHAPTER 22

Data Privacy, Data Security, Data Use and Ownership

Unlike confidentiality clauses and agreements which traditionally have sought to protect the proprietary trade secrets of the contracting parties, data privacy and data security provisions address the protection of the parties' data, such as Personally Identifiable Information ("PII") (i.e., an individual's name, address, Social Security number, credit card number, bank account information, medical information, etc.), and Protected Health Information ("PHI"), which is a subset of PII. For the purposes of this chapter, all such data and information shall be referred to as "Protected Data."

See Form R.1 for a model Data Privacy/Security Checklist.

A. Data Privacy

1. *Overview*

As states and localities adopt ever-stricter data privacy laws with ever-increasing penalties, the risk to both the vendor and customer is significant. Data security and data protection obligations may arise not only contractually but statutorily. The General Data Protection Regulation ("GDPR"), adopted by the European Union, imposes penalties of up to the greater of 4% of an entity's global revenues and 20M€ for failing to comply with the statute's requirements. Similarly, the California Consumer Protection Act, as amended by the California Privacy Rights Act, imposes significant restrictions and requirements on the use of the consumer data of California residents.

All 50 states and the District of Columbia have enacted data breach notification laws. The nature of these laws varies widely, with some creating a private right of action against companies that fail to comply with a party's obligations to notify affected individuals, certain government officials (including the states' attorneys general), and credit-monitoring agencies in the event Protected Data is disclosed to or accessed by unauthorized persons.

States are also enacting laws that focus on requiring appropriate security safeguards to prevent breaches from happening to begin with (see, for example, Massachusetts comprehensive law that mirrors NIST and ISO standards). Some of these laws create causes of action on behalf of third parties such as the customer's customers and employees who lack contractual privity with the vendor. As such, both parties should carefully negotiate each party's data privacy and security obligations and carefully consider and allocate risk to quantify their risk while limiting the impact of unforeseen consequences.

The underlying agreement should explicitly state which laws the vendor must comply with. Data flows should be traced to identify cross-border flows and hence compliance with international laws.

With the increasing growth of cloud computing, data privacy and data security risks also continue to grow placing even greater emphasis on the importance on privacy and greater security provisions.

2. *Use a Data Protection Addendum (DPA)*

To better ensure the vendor's compliance with the applicable data privacy laws, prudent customer will often seek to have the vendor enter into a Data Privacy Addendum which codifies the vendor's obligations under the applicable data privacy laws. By tying the vendor's obligations to the applicable laws, the customer in turn reduces its risks. Vendors should be careful, however, to not accept responsibility for risks outside their control or accept unreasonable levels of liability.

See Form M.3.3 for a model Data Privacy Addendum.

3. *PRACTICE POINT*: Checklist for drafting Data Privacy Addendums.

A comprehensive data protection addendum should include the following provisions:

- Limits on the vendors use of the data
- A description of how the vendor will access and process the data
- Customer/technical security requirements
- Training requirements for vendor personnel
- The vendor's obligation to assist the customer to carry out data protection impact assessments
- The vendor's ability to audit the customer its compliance with its obligations under the data processing agreement
- The vendor's record keeping obligations
- The vendor's commitment to comply with all laws applicable to the cross-border transfers of personal data such as the GDPR
- The return or destruction of the PII/personal data
- The vendors testing obligations, i.e., penetration testing
- The vendor's requirement to implement appropriate technical and organizational measures to safeguard personal data
- The ability of the vendor to use subprocessors and the details of the applicable subprocessors
- The vendor's commitment to assist the customer for fulfilling the customer's obligation to respond to data subjects' rights under the applicable data privacy laws (i.e., the right of access, the right of rectification under the GDPR)

- The vendor's obligation to promptly notify the customer in the event of a data breach
- The vendor's obligation to undertake any remediation efforts and resolve any issues

B. Data Security

A comprehensive data security program is founded on several fundamental principles:

- Limiting access to the data
- Encrypting the data
- Limiting subcontracting
- The right to audit the vendor's process and procedures
- Implementing a comprehensive business continuity and disaster recovery plans
- Data retention program
- Required data security training for employees at least annually

1. *Identification and Evaluation of the Underlying Risks*

Prior to entering an agreement, both the vendor and customer should evaluate the level of risk and likelihood of a data or security breach. The level of risk is determined by several factors:

- the types and nature of data involved;
- the source of the data;
- the respective responsibilities of the parties related to the data;
- the operational safeguards imposed by the customer; and
- the vendor's own data security safeguards.

(a) Types and Nature of Data the Vendor Will Be Accessing, Transmitting, Processing or Storing

To truly understand the risks associated with the vendor's services, the parties must determine the nature and types of data involved and how it will be accessed:

- What types of data will the vendor be accessing, retaining, selling, transmitting, processing and/or storing? i.e., HR, public company data, financial data, customer data, PII, etc.
- Is the data subject to any regulatory requirements?
- If PII, what is the citizenship of those individuals the PII identifies?
- If they live in the U.S., what is their state of residence?
- Where will the data be accessed and stored? On-site? Remote?
- Has the vendor experienced any previous data security incidents/data breaches?
- Is the vendor involved with any ongoing litigation or government investigations involving a data security incident/data breach?

- Does the vendor conduct regular employee training regarding data privacy?
- Does the vendor have an Incident Response Program ("IRP") in place?

The answers to these questions will dictate the appropriate safeguards that should be implemented to protect the data as well as any statutory/regulatory requirements that must be adhered to. Once the requirements have been identified, the parties can contractually apportion responsibility for each party's compliance obligations.

(b) Respective Responsibilities of the Vendor and Customer for Data Protection

Once the parties have identified the nature and types of data involved, the parties should evaluate the operational aspects of the transaction to assign responsibilities. Each party's responsibilities for protecting any Protected Data should be clearly and unambiguously defined.

The agreement should set forth the contractual standard for the protection of a party's information and data. The contractually agreed upon standard may be the legally required standard, the vendor's standard, the customer's standard or a third-party standard such as the International Organization for Standardization ("ISO") ISO/IEC 270015 – Information Technology – Security Techniques.

Cloud computing (where there are often multiple layers of subcontractors, and environments as well as vendors placing data from multiple customers on the same server) also gives rise to concern. Customers must make risk-based decisions whether to utilize these more cost-effective solutions while contemplating contractually implementing detailed and thoughtful privacy requirements on the vendor. For a more detailed discussion, see Chapter 14.A and http://www.nist.gov/itl/cloud/.

(c) Administrative Safeguards

Each party should have a detailed data security plan that addresses how breaches are detected, how evidence in the event of such a breach should be collected and retained as well as any contractual requirements to notify the customer, the relevant regulatory authorities and any impacted entities or individuals. Comprehensive plans will take into consideration the likelihood of a lawsuit and seek to protect the entity's interests while complying with its contractual obligations. The plan should identify the party responsible for undertaking each action set forth in the plan and should be updated quarterly to reflect changes in the law as well as any changes in the services being provided. For example, a majority of states require businesses to implement reasonable data security practices including secure data disposal. For a 50-state survey, *see* https://www.ncsl.org/research/telecommunications-and-information-technology/data-security-laws.aspx.

(d) Technical/Operational Safeguards

Operational safeguards should also be evaluated including physical security measures for the operation of the vendor's data and service centers, if any, as well as the transfer of data and communications between the parties. Operational safeguards, however, cannot definitively protect against a security lapse. A failure to install an antivirus patch, an unaccounted-for tape, or an employee who makes an inadvertent or intentional disclosure in violation of a party's confidentiality obligations can still occur. Nonetheless, detailed policies and procedures can reduce the level of overall risk.

See Eleftheriou & Garg, *The Rethinking of Data Security: Are You Ready?*, 32 ACC DOCKET 41 (May 2014); also see Chapter 22.B.4 for a more detailed discussion of mitigating risk.

2. *Mitigating the Risk*

Reducing the risks associated with a data breach can be reduced to :

(i) good security practices,
(ii) employee training regarding data privacy and security;
(iii) strong business continuity/disaster recovery processes and capabilities that have been tested thoroughly, and
(iv) recovering any impacted data.

Data breaches often arise from a single user error combined with an escalation of privileges. Strong security processes and practices are critical to minimizing the impact of any breach. Strong security practices provide the operational framework to recover but require specific business continuity and disaster recovery capabilities to quickly react in the event of a data breach.

If the vendor is providing data processing services, information technology support services such as help desk services, or managing and performing general infrastructure services, the vendor may have access to Protected Data. By implementing a comprehensive process for mitigating any identified risks prudent vendors and customers can significantly lower their risk profiles. Set forth below are several actions the parties can take to achieve their mutual goal of preventing a data breach.

(a) Use Clear and Unambiguous Language

Clearly stating a party's obligations will protect both the vendor's and customer's interests. To the extent the parties agree on a data privacy/security standard, it should be clearly identified and stated in an objective manner without ambiguity. The parties should avoid using terms such as "reasonable," "good-faith efforts" and "foreseeable," as they are subjective in nature and increase the likelihood of a dispute over interpretation.

(b) Craft the Definitions with Care

Definitions are an important aspect of establishing each party's obligations and rights. Most parties seek to craft the definitions to their benefit, and thus both parties must carefully consider the meaning of each word in a definition. To that end, each definition should be drafted in a clear, unambiguous manner.

(i) "Protected Data/Confidential Information"

Customers often seek a very broad definition of "protected data," preferably much broader than any applicable statutory definition. They do so to ensure any important or material data and information is protected. Conversely, vendors seek to define protected data narrowly to limit their potential liability in the event of a data breach or security incident.

The agreed-upon definition should include electronic data and tangible data as well as any format such data may subsequently assume, including all data created, stored, processed or transmitted through the vendor's provision of the contracted services.

(ii) Security Incident vs. Security Breach

A *security incident* is a "security event that compromises the integrity, confidentiality or availability of an information asset. A *data breach* is an incident that results in a confirmed disclosure- not just the potential exposure of data to an unauthorized party." While all data breaches are incidents, not all incidents are data breaches.

Incidents can be further segmented into *security incidents* (an event that violates an entity's security policies and procedures) and *privacy incidents* the disclosure of regulated data such as PII and PHI).

https://www.verizon.com/business/resources/reports/dbir/?CMP=OOH_SMB_OTH_22222_MC_20200501_NA_NM20200079_00001

The definition of "Security Incident/Security Breach" is equally important as the occurrence of a Security Incident triggers the parties' respective obligations and responses, including the vendor's obligation to notify the customer of an event.

Customers often seek to define a Security Incident as any attempt to breach the vendor's IT system, any *suspected* intrusion or an actual intrusion. Vendors are hesitant, however, to assume any obligation to act or liability based on a suspected intrusion or suspected breach as opposed to an *actual* intrusion or breach. Many vendors seek to define a Security Incident as an *actual* security breach that arose from the vendor's failure to comply with its security standards, as opposed to any unauthorized access, as vendors do not want to assume liability for any unauthorized access the vendor was not responsible for. Vendors justify this position by arguing that the customer is not purchasing an insurance policy; the vendor should be liable only if it fails to comply with its stated security policy/standards, as opposed to being held to a strict liability standard. The customer may respond, "Why won't you stand behind your product?" but this is not the issue. Rather, the risk of a breach or hacking exists regardless of whether the customer or vendor controls access to the data, and the vendor, like the customer, cannot guaranty that a breach will not occur.

If the parties' agreement requires the vendor to assume the obligation and cost to notify the customer's end user/clients only upon an actual intrusion or breach arising from the vendor's failure to comply with its own standards, the vendor should still be obligated to investigate any incident to determine if an actual breach occurred. At a minimum, a customer should require the vendor to notify it in the event of any suspected intrusion attempt, suspected access to the Protected Data or any suspected use of the sensitive information.

(c) Use of Privacy by Design

Vendors should only have access to the data necessary to perform their obligations under the agreement. In configuring the system and drafting any functional specifications and the services to be delivered, the parties should seek to limit the amount of Protected Data the vendor will have access to, process or store. By limiting the amount of data that will be accessed, stored, or disclosed, the parties can limit the risk of disclosure.

For a more detailed discussion of privacy by design, *see Privacy by Design: Setting a New Standard for Privacy Certification*, https://www2.deloitte.com/content/dam/Deloitte/ca/Documents/risk/ca-en-ers-privacy-by-design-brochure.PDF.

(d) Implement Definitive Security Standards

Prudent parties should avoid generalized, sweeping language such as the following:

> "*. . . . perform the Services at levels of accuracy, quality, completeness, timeliness, responsiveness, resource efficiency, and productivity that are equal to or higher than Industry Standard*"

This language does not benefit either party as it is open to interpretation, which can lead to significant friction between the parties. Even from the perspective of a third party, it is unclear what is the industry standard for data protection. Further, who is the judge of what is the "industry standard"? Generalized commitments, such as "reasonable security precautions," "highest industry standard security," "same security as the recipient's but no less than a reasonable standard of care," and similar expressions that are subjective in nature and should also be avoided.

From the vendor's perspective, a vendor should never agree to comply with a fluid standard or policy set forth in a URL that may change without notice or without compensation for any incremental costs associated with complying with the new standards. *See Margae, Inc. v. Clear Link Technologies, LLC*, 2008 WL 2465450 (D. Utah June 16, 2008) (amendment of contract between two sophisticated parties by one party posting modifications online not unconscionable). See Chapter 6.O for a more detailed discussion of online term and conditions.

Prudent parties should identify and agree on a specific, identified unambiguous definitive standard applicable to the underlying services being provided such as ISO 27001, the NIST Cybersecurity Framework a standard set by the National Institute for Standards and Technology ("NIST"), or an Information Security Management System (ISMS) standard which dictates specific internal controls as well as auditing and an agreement to comply with all applicable laws. ISO 27001 mandates specific requirements allowing an organization's security process to be audited and certified as compliant. The parties should not rely solely on industry guidelines to ensure protection, as these guidelines are usually minimum standards and are not intended to constitute a comprehensive security approach. A comprehensive approach will depend on the nature of the services, the data in question, and a holistic approach to developing "end-to-end protection." Model language is as follows:

> *Vendor contractually commits to implement commercially reasonable administrative, physical, and technical measures. In practice, these include, among others, 256-bit AES data encryption while at rest and in transit, and compliance with ISO 27001, SSAE18/SOC 1 Type II and AT-101/SOC 2 Type II (collectively "Reports") or their recognized substantially equivalent standards. In light of the single back-end support model, Vendor does not agree to individual Customer security policies. All controls set forth in the Reports are conducted by independent third-party auditors or certifications, and Customer can request copies by providing Vendor with a written request on an annual basis.*

Vendors should avoid assuming liability for any data disclosure in absence of its failure to meet the contractually agreed standard. For example, if the vendor was contractually required to ISO 27001 and there is a release of data despite the vendor's compliance with ISO27001, the vendor would have no liability. Conversely, if the vendor failed to meet its compliance obligations, the vendor would be liable. Once agreed, the standard should be then attached to the underlying agreement between the parties. See Form P.1 and Form P.2 for model Security Requirements.

The vendor and its subcontractors should be contractually obligated to encrypt all data at rest and in transmission. This is important as many entities do not encrypt data at rest. Further, vendors should be willing to contractually commit to keep the data within specific geographies. If the agreement does not address the data location, the vendor is free to move the data around the world to those data centers with capacity.

The customer should also undertake an independent assessment of the vendor's security architecture and standard by requiring potential vendors to complete a detailed questionnaire eliciting information regarding their systems and security efforts. The responses can then be benchmarked against the customer's own standards to identify any gaps in the parties' approaches. These questionnaires can be voluminous and may not be applicable for many projects. See Form R.6 and Form R.7 for model Security Questionnaires.

Commitments to follow customers' security rules, processes, policies, and procedures ("customer rules") should be made only after all of the enumerated customer rules have been received, read, and incorporated in the underlying agreement in some fashion. Customer rules, to the extent committed to, should be as in effect and practiced, rather than as written, with any commitment to bring current being treated as a funded project. Changes to customer rules should be subject to a change order process, both for control and funding purposes.

From the customer's perspective, the underlying agreement should clearly require the vendor to comply with the customer's policies and procedures for data protection/privacy and physical protection at the customer's facilities. These standards should supplement the vendor's own security standards. A vendor will likely argue that it can only have one security standard across all its clients, and it cannot agree to be bound by individual client standards.

If applicable, the customer should determine where the mainframe environment, if any, is located and if it or any applicable servers are located inside the customer's firewall perimeter. The customer should ensure the vendor possesses stringent controls and maintains its own firewall perimeter. Further, the parties should ascertain whether the relevant data resides inside the firewall perimeter architected and controlled by the customer. It is important to determine whether there is access by the vendor for remote services, such as reporting, which is outside the customer's firewall perimeter. The services provided by the vendor should be provided over a secure network specified by the customer and approved by the vendor. The agreement should also clearly state which party retains responsibility, if applicable, for security including intrusion detection.

The customer should reserve the right to amend its security standards during the term of the agreement although this right raises the issue of which party bears any increased costs arising from any subsequent amendment. Some vendors seek to attach agreed-upon data privacy/security standards to the agreement to ensure the standards are static, while other vendors decline to disclose their security standards for security reasons and instead will only provide the client with a redacted version. Many cloud vendors will only agree to meet their own security standard to avoid the administrative burden of having to negotiate and comply with different standards in each of its agreements. Regardless, the customer should review the materials provided by the vendor to ensure that the vendor's standards meet the customer's requirements. Finally, to the extent the software is configurable, the customer should configure the software for security, not performance.

(e) *Restrict Access and Use of Data*

A comprehensive security plan will address all aspects of security including physical security as well as contractual and virtual security. Set forth below is an overview of the principal issues that should be addressed.

(i) Physical Security

Any physical location which houses Protected Data including data centers and offices should have 24×7 security with restricted, monitored access. This includes recording ingress and egress as well as the use of badges and escorting visitors. By implementing and maintaining rigorous physical security protections at its offices and data centers, as well as by conducting background checks on its employees who will have access to Protected Data, the vendor can limit its risk from a physical intrusion or the misappropriation of data by an employee or contractor.

In conjunction with addressing physical security, prudent customers should strictly limit how the vendor may access and use any data provided by the customer avoid.

(ii) Ownership and Use

The agreement should clearly state that the customer retains sole and exclusive ownership of its data in all forms (i.e., derivative works, as processed, etc.) and that the vendor has no rights in such data. If the vendor needs to access the customer's data to perform its obligations under the agreement, the customer should grant the vendor a limited license/right to use the data only to the extent necessary to perform the vendor's obligations under the agreement and for no other reason. The vendor should be prohibited from using, disclosing, selling, assigning, or allowing third-party access to the customer's data for any other reason. This includes using any de-identified, anonymized or aggregated data. De-identified data is data where identifying information has been removed, usually replaced by a "key" allowing the data to be returned to its original format. Although anonymized data has had all identifying characteristics removed and cannot be reconstituted, if the data pool is small enough, it may be possible to identify an individual.

(iii) Practical Safeguards

To ensure a secure environment, the customer should require that the vendor's equipment be dedicated solely to the customer and physically or logically separated from those of other customers. Any development, test and production environments should be separated to keep the customer's data from being used in a test environment by mistake. Vendors should be willing to provide dedicated servers/hardware provided the customer is willing to pay the additional cost. A separate data transmission line should be used for transmitting the customer's data. All transmitted data must be encrypted. If such transmitted data will be stored on mobile devices (such as laptops, PDAs, phones, etc.), those devices should also encrypt the data at rest. In addition, the vendor should keep the customer continually updated as to the location of the customer's data, including the location of any backup data. Prudent customers should prohibit the vendor from using offshore technical resources and require the vendor to obtain the customer's prior written consent before moving any data outside of the United States.

If there is a data breach that results from the vendor's breach of its obligations, the customer should be entitled to terminate the agreement for cause.

(iv) Third-Party Access

Employee and subcontractor access should be on a need-to-know basis only. Customers should carefully review their nondisclosure agreement with the vendor to ensure the nondisclosure agreement does not contain any carve-outs limiting the vendor's liability for data breaches.

To the extent the vendor desires to provide a third party with access to the customer's data or system, the vendor should be contractually obligated to identify the third party to the customer and the customer's prior written consent should be required. The third party should be required to disclose its security policy, and if possible, the customer's security policy should be flowed down to the third party. Access should be subject to the third party executing a nondisclosure agreement that restricts the third party's use and access of the data and provides that the customer is a third-party beneficiary to the nondisclosure agreement. The vendor should be obligated to obtain written confidentiality obligations from its subcontractors in addition to its employees. All individuals supplying services, including the vendor's employees and subcontractors, should undergo background checks and, to the extent possible.

For a more detailed discussion, *see* Atchison & Katz, *Data Security and Vendor Agreements: The Chain Is Only as Strong as the Weakest Link*, 33 ACC DOCKET 36 (Dec. 2015).

See Form R.7 for a model Offshore Security Questionnaire.

(v) Off-shore Processing

For customers in the US, the customer should prohibit the vendor from transferring data outside of the United States and should require the vendor to limit any sensitive data to specific locations within the United States. Conversely, all work should be performed in the United States to reduce the risk of misappropriation. To the extent possible, the vendor should ensure Protected Data removed from the United States is properly protected and controlled in the destination jurisdiction. Customers located in other regions (ex. EU) will most likely want their data stored and processed outside of the US.

(vi) Data Management

The agreement should clearly provide how the data in the vendor's possession will be stored and maintained:

- How will the data be stored?
- Where will the data be stored?
- How long will the vendor retain the data?

- When will the data be returned to the customer?
- How will the data be returned to the customer?
- In what format?
- If applicable, how will the vendor destroy the data?

The agreement should also clearly provide for the prompt return of the customer's data at no charge upon the customer's request or upon termination of the agreement. Prudent customers will specify the format and media in which the data must be returned. Finally, the agreement should address the process for reconstructing lost data.

(f) Security Audits

It is essential that the customer retain a right to audit the vendor's compliance with its security obligations to ensure that the customer's data is being protected. While on-site visits are preferable, many vendors are hesitant to provide access to their data centers. Depending on the data and risk, an actual on-site audit may not be practical or necessary, and electronic monitoring and questionnaires may be sufficient. At a minimum, the customer should be entitled to receive an annual SOC II, Type 2 report.

A fully funded security gap analysis must be performed when any substantial security commitments are to be undertaken. Vendors should carefully limit any obligation to provide security audits to the customer and notify the customer of security breaches (other than a restriction to that portion of audits and reports which relate to the customer). Customers should only receive the audit reports directly attributed to them.

Audits need to be scoped, documented, funded, and provisioned to adjust to changing audit requirements.

> *If at any time Vendor fails to complete an unqualified SSAE 18 Type II audit, and fails to properly remediate those items which caused the failure to complete such unqualified SSAE 18 Type II audit within thirty (30) days of the completion of such SSAE 18 Type II audit or other reasonable time thereafter as agreed by the Parties, Customer may terminate the Agreement in whole or in part in accordance with Section ____ (Termination for Cause.).*

For a more detailed discussion on limiting the risks associated with data security, *see* Jett & Sloan, *Once More Unto the Breach: Why and How to Be Ready for a Data Breach*, 33 ACC Docket 36 (Sept. 2015); Dieterich, *Managing the Privacy Risks Associated with Data Outsourcing*, 25 Corp. Couns. (Nov. 2010); *see also* Claypoole & Benoit, *Protecting Data in a Business Failure*, 27 ACC Docket 21 (Sept. 2009).

(g) Use Indemnities

In the current data protection/data privacy climate (and depending on the product or service), prudent parties should seek a specific "data breach/security incident" indemnity that:

(i) is comparative based on each party's fault;
(ii) covers costs of investigation, notification of individuals, responses to regulators; and
(iii) if the data breach/incident potentially involves identity theft, covers the cost an identity protection service for a period of time.

Given that a breach can arise from both the vendor's and the customer's actions, the parties must agree on the breadth of the indemnity and whether the parties will indemnify each other for third-party claims as well as reciprocal claims. The indemnity should be carefully considered and tightly drafted to avoid one party having to indemnify the other for potentially significant costs without knowing with certainty that the indemnitor was responsible for the breach or that there was a breach.

(h) Governing Law

Governing law may have an important impact on the vendor's data security and protection obligations, as the laws of the 50 states vary greatly from state to state, with California, Massachusetts and Nevada considered to have among the most comprehensive and strict data protection laws. Further, although an agreement may be governed by the laws of a particular state, the vendor may be subject to the laws of other states if the vendor has access to the personal data of citizens of other states, creating a challenge for the vendor, as the vendor may not know the nature of the data it possesses or the citizenship of those individuals whose data it possesses.

(i) Insurance

Depending on the size of the proposed transaction and the data involved, the vendor should be required to purchase cyber-insurance of no less than $5M per occurrence.

> *Vendor agrees to purchase and maintain throughout the term of this Agreement a technology/professional liability insurance policy, including coverage for network security/ data protection liability insurance (also called "cyber liability") covering liabilities for financial loss resulting or arising from acts, errors, or omissions, in rendering technology/professional services or in connection with the specific services described in this Agreement.*

See Chapter 6.C for a more detailed discussion of cyber liability insurance. *See also*, Rhodes, Chrisitan, Marcus & King, *Managing Vendor Cybersecurity Risk in IoT Contracting*, 38 COMP. & . INTERNET LAW. 3 (Mar. 2021); Hathaway, *Everything You Need to Know about Cyber Liability Insurance but Never Knew to Ask*, 34 COMP. & INTERNET LAW. 18 (Apr. 2017).

(j) Mandatory Notification of a Breach or Suspected Breach

Most agreements provide that the vendor must promptly notify the customer in the event of a breach or suspected breach. Many vendors push back on the obligation to notify the customer of a suspected breach as many events can be construed as a suspected breach when in actuality they are not. Thus, to avoid creating an administrative burden prudent vendors will only agree to notify the customer of an actual breach.

At any time during the processing of Personal Data, Supplier shall notify Customer without undue delay (and in any event within 72 hours) of any Personal Data Breach involving Personal Data, including any breach at facilities, systems or equipment of Supplier's subprocessors. Supplier agrees to assist and cooperate with Customer concerning any disclosures to affected parties, government or regulatory agencies and with any other reasonable remedial measures requested by Customer or required under any law. Supplier will take such reasonably necessary steps to prevent the continuation or repetition of such Personal Data Breach.

(k) Implement a Comprehensive Business Continuity and Disaster Recovery Plans

Customers should also ensure that the vendor has well-developed business continuity and disaster recovery plans in place. These plans should tie to any service levels that are agreed to between the parties. The customer should review these plans prior to the execution of the agreement and annually thereafter. Monitoring and good record keeping are also important. The customer should require compliance with SSAE18 and have the right to audit the vendor's compliance on an annual basis or, in the alternative, require the vendor to issue a certificate of compliance to the customer if the customer does not conduct an audit. Strong records retention/destruction policies and procedures should be implemented to ensure that all data is destroyed in a safe and controlled environment. Finally, each party should have adequate controls for reporting the enforcement of its obligations.

3. Damages

A breach of the vendor's obligations may give rise to a number of damage claims. Set forth below is a brief discussion of types of the claims that would likely be brought in the event of a data privacy or data security breach.

(a) Direct Damages

A customer whose data or customer's data has been lost or compromised will likely seek to recover the cost of reconstructing the lost data, the loss in value of any secret, technical or other information and the cost of notification of and monitoring any third-party data that was released or lost, as well as all damages directly flowing from the loss. The cost to restore data can be very expensive and the customer must ensure that it is fully protected to avoid a significant disruption of its business or a significant financial loss. Although lost profits are often considered to be consequential damages, they may be considered direct damages if they were foreseeable.

(b) Consequential Damages

The great majority of damages are likely to be consequential damages, i.e., those damages that flow from the vendor's actions. *See Silverpop Systems, Inc. v. Leading Market Technologies,* 641 Fed. Appx. 849 (11th Cir. 2016).

(c) Punitive Damages

Several states have enacted safe harbor laws prohibiting the award of punitive damages in tort class actions alleging the defendant failed to implement reasonable security controls resulting in a data breach of personal information. *See* Connecticut: Public Act

No. 21-119 (enacted October 1, 2021); Ohio: Ohio Rev. Code Ann. §1354.02 (effective November 2, 2018); Utah: Utah Code Ann. §78B-4-703 (effective May 5, 2021).

(d) Governmental Fines

Various federal, state and local agencies such as the Federal Trade Commission ("FTC"), Health and Human Services ("HHS") and the state attorneys general have the ability to impose fines or require enhanced security which may not be contemplated by the vendor at the time the agreement is executed. Governments have been issuing staggering fines for data and security breaches. The U.S. government issued a $575 million fine against Equifax while the British government issued a $230 million fine against British Airways. If liability arises from the vendor's failure to comply with applicable laws, the vendor should assume all liability for all penalties, fines, interest and other costs arising from the breach and there should be no limit on the vendor's liability for government levied fines. For a discussion of the largest fines issued to date, *see* https://www.csoonline.com/article/3410278/the-biggest-data-breach-fines-penalties-and-settlements-so-far.html.

(e) Third-Party Claims by Affected Individuals and Other Third Parties

A significant concern for customers is the possibility of a class-action lawsuit being filed against it for the unauthorized disclosure of personal information. While these types of claims have been largely unsuccessful, the ever-increasing number of federal, state and local laws makes the possibility of success more likely. The likelihood of a third-party claim makes it very important that savvy customers seek indemnification from the vendor for third-party claims without a cap on the vendor's liability.

4. Limitation of Liability

Uncapped liability for direct and consequential damages for breaches of confidentiality has been traditionally accepted in license agreements and professional services agreements. This position remains today, however, as discussed below, the changing landscape for liability related to breaches of data privacy/data protection has caused vendors to re-examine limits of liability and seek to bifurcate those damages arising from the disclosure of a party's trade secrets/confidential information from those damages resulting from a security breach involving Protected Data.

(a) Vendor Perspective

Most vendors believe they should not assume the risk of unlimited liability for the disclosure of customer data when the vendor has otherwise properly performed the services. This belief arises from the fact that the customer and the vendor have mutually agreed on a security standard or the customer has dictated the levels of protection to be used by the vendor (i.e., the number and type of firewalls, level of encryption, password complexity, etc.). If the customer had wanted a higher level of protection (e.g., National Security Agency quality), the customer could have paid for it or modified its processes to reflect its desires. Given the customer almost always retains architectural and/or policy control on levels of security for access to and storage of the customer data, the vendor is simply conforming its technical solution to the customer's demands.

Because the vendor may not have the right to unilaterally decide how customer data is to be protected, and because the technical solution and price dictate an approach based on customer agreement or mandate, it is inequitable for the vendor to bear the entire risk of improper disclosure as a result of the vendor's actually meeting its contractual obligations.

Many vendors also argue that they should not assume unlimited liability for the disclosure of customer data even when the vendor has not properly performed the services. The purpose of limitations on liability is to permit parties to enter into commercial contracts and mutually allocate the risk inherent in the contract. Limitations on liability allow customers to obtain more favorable prices. Unlimited liability will almost always result in higher prices if risk is truly to be priced, regardless of the degree of care assumed to be taken in the performance of the vendor's obligations.

Most vendors resist customer demands for unlimited liability or significantly increased liability for data breaches, as the vendors cannot "bet the company" on a single contract. These vendors argue that the vendor is not an insurance company and the customer cannot outsource its liability by using a third-party vendor. If the customer had an on-premises license, the customer would assume full liability for any data breach. Over time, breaches will occur despite properly implemented best practices and security standards.

Many cloud providers will argue that they do not know what data the customer is storing in their cloud; they cannot see the customer's data, and they do not want to see it. Thus, they should not assume any liability. Further, vendors often argue that liability for its indemnity obligations should be capped, as the customer is able to limit its liability with its own customers by inserting an appropriate limitation of liability in the parties' contract.

Vendors also argue that although some types of customer data (i.e., PII and PHI) may be of greater value, the vendor should not assume unlimited liability for the disclosure of customer data simply because it has greater value. Many customers do not segregate high value data from their other data. From a practical standpoint the vendor is performing services in the same manner for all customer data—high value or not. It is impractical and inequitable to have the disclosure of one type of customer data subject to the contractual limitation of liability and disclosure of another type outside the limitation of liability. This is especially true when the customer-mandated levels and types of protection are the same for each type of data.

Many vendors do not accept uncapped and consequential damages in connection with damage to business data generally, particularly if the breach does not involve a public disclosure. To protect themselves, vendors should limit the carve-out from any applicable limit of liability to tangible personal property (not data), and make sure the terms are (i) not so broad as to constitute every type of business data as confidential information; and (ii) truly limited to public disclosure scenarios, so that negligent use that does not involve disclosure (e.g., loss of data due to a system crash) is not covered.

Thus, in all cases, a prudent vendor should seek a cap on its liability with potentially a "super cap" for a data breach.

> TO THE MAXIMUM EXTENT PERMITTED BY APPLICABLE LAW, NOTWITHSTANDING THE FOREGOING SECTION ____ (LIMITATION OF LIABILITY), BUT SUBJECT TO SECTIONS ____ (DISCLAIMER OF SPECIAL, INCIDENTAL CONSEQUENTIAL DAMAGES), ___ (DISCLAIMER OF LIABILITY ARISING FROM THIRD-PARTY PRODUCTS) AND ____ (EXCLUSIONS FROM LIMIT OF LIABILITY), VENDOR'S AGGREGATE AND CUMULATIVE LIABILITY UNDER OR IN CONNECTION WITH THIS AGREEMENT (A) FOR VENDOR'S BREACH OF (I) SECTION __ (CONFIDENTIALITY) AS IT RELATES SOLELY TO SUBSCRIBER DATA AND (II) THE DATA PROTECTION ADDENDUM (DEFINED IN SECTION __ (DATA PROCESSING AND TRANSFER)) AND (B) UNDER SECTION ___ WITH RESPECT TO A THIRD-PARTY PRIVACY CLAIM (DEFINED IN SUCH SECTION) REGARDLESS OF THE FORM OF ACTION, WHETHER IN CONTRACT, TORT (INCLUDING NEGLIGENCE), BREACH OF STATUTORY DUTY OR OTHERWISE, SHALL IN NO EVENT EXCEED FIVE (5) TIMES THE TOTAL AMOUNT OF THE SUBSCRIPTION FEES PAID BY SUBSCRIBER FOR THE SERVICES HEREUNDER DURING THE 12 MONTH PERIOD IMMEDIATELY PRECEDING THE DATE OF THE EVENT GIVING RISE TO LIABILITY. FOR CLARITY, THE CAP STATED IN THIS SECTION ___ APPLIES TO ALL MATTERS DESCRIBED IN THIS SECTION ___ TAKEN TOGETHER AND NOT ON A CATEGORY-BY-CATEGORY BASIS.

(b) Customer Perspective

Customers increasingly argue that any claims arising from a breach of a vendor's obligations related to Protected Data, especially those in violation of a law, should not be subject to a limitation of liability. They argue that they choose the vendor based on its experience as well as its reputation in the industry, and as an IT expert, the vendor should be able to prevent breaches as well as hacking better than the customer. Thus, the vendor should be held to a higher standard and assume greater liability.

Further, in the event of a data breach or loss, it is likely that the majority of the resulting damages will be consequential damages, not direct damages. To the extent the agreement contains a waiver or limitation on consequential damages, a customer should insist on an exception for data breach or loss. Without such an exception, the injured party may be barred from recovering a significant portion of its damages.

(c) Potential Compromise

As the risk of liability from data breaches rises, vendors are increasingly seeking to negotiate a bifurcated approach based on the nature of the breach with a supplemental cap for Protected Data claims and claims related to compliance with laws that is larger than the cap for other types of claims. While it is unreasonable to expect the vendor to assume unlimited liability in all cases, it is reasonable for the vendor to agree to an increased limit of liability for breaches of its data privacy/security obligations arising from an "operational" breach, as the standard is clearly set and any failure to comply should be able to be proven easily.

"Operational" breaches are often defined to include the following:

- the vendor's failure to follow an agreed upon standard operating procedure;
- the vendor's failure to utilize antivirus software resulting in an infection;
- the inability to account for all tapes in the vendor's possession (often caused by a failure to follow a check-in, check-out procedure);
- a hacker's penetration of a firewall server if vendor personnel failed to perform a duty preventing penetration; and
- the inadvertent disclosure of the customer's business data.

An "operational" breach may also arise from a vendor's employee stealing the customer's data. A theft would most likely not be viewed as an operational error which would expose the vendor to a higher limitation of liability. The theft might also be deemed attributable to gross negligence, which, depending on the terms of the agreement, may expose the vendor to unlimited liability. However, if the theft would not have occurred but for a failure to follow an operational procedure, the vendor could argue that this was an operational error. If the theft was made possible because of a flaw in the customer's security procedures, the vendor would likely argue that the theft would not have taken place but for the security flaw and the liability should remain with the customer.

A two-tiered approach limiting the vendor's liability for data breaches caused by a contracted-for "operational" breach to a multiple of the contract's general limitation of liability is a reasonable compromise. For example, if the agreement contains a limitation of liability equal to 12 months' fees for a general negligence claim, the parties may agree to limit the vendor's liability to an amount equal to 24–36 months' worth of fees for "operational" breaches.

Many vendors seek to disclaim any liability for "Zero Day" events—those disclosures that arose outside the vendor's control through previously unknown viruses or threats—when the vendor has complied with its security standard, used industry standard malware software, and maintained best practices in virus protection and intrusion. See Chapter 5.I.1 for a discussion of Zero Day liability and model Zero Day event language.

For general negligence claims, prudent parties seek to limit their liability to a stated amount, as no entity should risk insolvency over the failure to perform a single contract. See Chapter 5.I for a more detailed discussion on limitations of liability for general negligence.

(d) Exclusions from Limitations of Liability

For breach of a data privacy or data security obligation, the parties usually exclude notification expenses, (i.e., the cost to notify parties whose Protected Data has been wrongly disclosed) from any limitation of liability. That being said, reasonableness should be the standard when negotiating notification processes and determining whether one party will have exclusive say over how the notification should be accomplished.

Claims for breaches of confidentiality, compliance with laws, data security and data privacy are to some degree related and a claim for a data breach or loss will likely be made under one or more of these exclusions. To that end, vendors should ensure that any exception to a limitation of liability is narrowly drafted to avoid an unintended consequence that allows the customer to circumvent the agreement's cap on liability.

5. Responding to a Data/Security Breach

In responding to a data or security breach, it is essential that the vendor and customer cooperate to respond in a timely and comprehensive manner. The parties should not seek to apportion responsibility for the breach until the issue has been addressed and resolved. Too often parties are more focused on assigning blame than addressing the issue, exacerbating the problem.

Following the old adage "an ounce of prevention is worth a pound of cure," prudent vendors and customers should be well-prepared for what commentators say is the inevitable breach. Given the short period in which to respond to a breach, the parties should identify and pre-vet attorneys, technical resources and public relations teams to be ready in the event a breach occurs. The parties should also understand their rights under their insurance policies as well as any limitations in such policies.

Any response should encompass a three-pronged approach:

(i) complying with government requirements and regulations,
(ii) notifying the affected parties, and
(iii) resolving the defects that allowed the problem to arise.

(a) Do Not Wait for a Security Incident

Prudent parties will ensure that their agreement sets forth their respective obligations in the event of a data breach. The agreement should establish:

- When notification is required:
  - A breach?
  - A suspected breach?
- Who is responsible for notifying the affected individuals or entities?
- Who will draft the notification?
- Who assumes the cost of notification?
- Who will select the vendors to support the remediation effort?
- Who will manage the remediation process?
- Who is responsible for the cost of remediation?

(b) Present a Unified Front

It is important that the customer and vendor present a unified front and communicate consistently with any government entities and the affected entities and individuals. Neither party benefits from inter-company squabbling and the resulting bad publicity. The best approach is for the parties to quickly address the issue and then resolve their differences privately. To that end, the parties should select one entity and one person within that entity to be the sole point of contact and communication. All communications should be approved by both parties prior to the communication being issued. That said, some laws require the controller/business/covered entity (GDPR/CCPA/HIPAA--the customer in this chapter) to make all the notices of breach as opposed to the processor/service provider/business advocate--or the vendor in this chapter.

(c) Retain an Experienced Team of Advisors

Most companies have little experience in responding to data and security breaches. As such, the parties should retain an experienced group of advisors to assist in developing and implementing a response plan. Perhaps the most important decision is the selection of an experienced law firm that can guide the parties through the maze of applicable laws addressing data and security breaches as well as the requisite notification obligations. Experienced counsel who have previously addressed these issues are invaluable and may have existing relationships with the various state regulators which can ease the process.

A good public relations firm that can respond to the inevitable news stories and interview requests is also important. It is vital to notify the affected individuals, the public, and investors alike is a forthright manner but at the same time communicate the message that the breach is not catastrophic. Further, the vendor and customer want to undertake all actions necessary to preserve their business reputations.

Companies with an Incident Response Program will already have policies and procedures in place for the Incident Response Team to follow in the event of the security breach/incident.

(d) Identify and Quantify the Harm

The parties should work together to quickly establish a timeline of the breach and identify the extent of the breach, the individuals impacted, the likelihood of harm, and how the breach occurred. Many states provide a "good faith" exception to their notification obligations if the breach/disclosure is unlikely to result in any harm or potential misuse of the information.

(e) Avoid Further Damage and Loss

The parties should jointly implement all changes necessary to ensure that any "gaps" that allowed the data to be compromised have been resolved and that such breach will not happen again. It is important that the parties work continuously until the issue is resolved. All security protections should be reviewed and changed as necessary, including passwords and physical security.

(f) Establish and Implement a Communication Plan

The parties should quickly establish and implement a communication plan. A comprehensive plan may include providing notice to the affected individuals and to the relevant government entities, establishing a help desk to provide information and answer questions from the affected individuals, purchasing credit monitoring services for the affected individuals, and reimbursing the affected individuals for any losses incurred.

The vendor should seek to control the selection of the vendors and the implementation of the plan. Many vendors will argue that because they will most likely be responsible for paying the majority of the costs, they should control the provision of the remediation services. Many customers will argue, however, that because the affected individuals are their customers, the customer should control the decision-making process to ensure its business is not irreparably harmed.

Control of the decision-making process is important as the cost-benefit analysis of undertaking certain actions will vary between the vendor and customer. For example, in the event of a breach, should the parties notify every potential individual who could have been affected or only those individuals who are known to have been affected? Given the significant costs associated with notification, a vendor will often likely seek to notify only those known to have been affected, while a customer, in an effort to protect its customers and its business reputation, may seek to notify every individual who could have been affected. Some customers, however, may not want every non-affected individual to be notified because doing so increases the customer's risk exposure.

(g) Review All Applicable Policies, Procedures, and Contracts

The parties should review all applicable policies, procedures, and contracts to understand their obligations and responsibilities to each other as well as to the affected party's clients and employees.

PRACTICE POINT:

At a minimum, the vendor should have a detailed data breach/disaster recovery policy and plan that addresses the following:

- A specific response
- Remediation
- Mitigation
- A process for assembling and preserving information regarding the breach
- Conducting a "root cause" analysis
- Cooperating with any governmental inquiry or investigation
- A plan for communicating with those impacted by the breach
- Assisting the customer as needed

(h) Resolve the Technical Problems

Most important, the parties must undertake a forensic audit to determine how the breach occurred and how to prevent it from reoccurring. While a single lapse can be forgiven, a second occurrence will likely negatively impact the customer's business and reputation, cause customers to lose faith in the vendor and customer, and potentially expose the parties to significant legal liability.

For a more detailed discussion, *see* Redmon & Ruback, *Actionable Advice in Responding to a Data Breach*, 30 ACC Docket 27 (Sept. 2012).

6. *Insurance*

Data breaches can be very expensive to mitigate and litigate. A prudent customer should ensure that the vendor is financially able to meet its indemnification obligations, and that the customer will be able to collect any judgment it may obtain against the vendor. To that end, prior to execution of the agreement between the parties, the customer and the vendor should ascertain the amount of the vendor's insurance coverage for data breaches under the vendor's errors and omissions policy or general liability policy and ensure that the policy limit is large enough to satisfy any potential claim. The customer should also determine the amount of any retention or deductible to make sure the vendor can satisfy that amount. To the extent the vendor's existing policies do not cover any potential claim and the vendor lacks the financial resources to pay all potential claims, the vendor should be required to obtain insurance in an amount sufficient to cover the customer's likely losses.

For a general discussion of the legal issues associated with data security and data privacy, *see* Westermeier, *Managing the Legal Risks Related to Information Security*, 2 COMPUTER L.R. INT'L. 43 (2008); Cohen & Dieterich, *Five Steps for Managing the Risks Associated with Sensitive Data*, 25 CORP. COUNS. 1 (No. 2 June 2010); Blackmer, *Code or Clear? Encryption Requirements under Information Privacy and Security Laws*, 159 INTELL. PROP. COUNSEL (March 2010); and Claypoole & Benoit, *Protecting Data in a Business Failure*, 27 ACC DOCKET 21 (Sept. 2009).

See Chapter 6.C for a more detailed discussion of cyber liability insurance.

C. Data Ownership and Use

1. *Anonymized vs. De-Identified Data*

While often used interchangeably, there is a significant difference between de-identified data and anonymized data. De-identified data is data from which all personally identifiable information has been removed or obscured so that it does not identify an individual and there is no reasonable basis to believe the remaining information can be used to identify an individual. De-identification of data is reversible.

Anonymized data is data from which all personal identifiers have been permanently and completely removed, such as converting personally identifiable information into aggregated data. Anonymized data can no longer be associated with an individual in any manner because once the data is stripped of personally identifying elements, those elements can never be re-associated with the data or the underlying individual. Anonymization of data is irreversible.

The principal differences between de-identified data and anonymized data are that de-identified data may contain additional information that allows the individual to be associated or re-identified such a through using a key, a code, algorithm, or pseudonym.

2. *Data Ownership*

In almost all cases the customer will be the sole and exclusive owner of its data. The bigger issue is the ability to use the customer's data for analysis purposes and the ownership of data created by the vendor through aggregating and anonymizing the customer's data with the data of other customers. This is increasingly important with the emergence of artificial intelligence (AI)/machine learning technology and the need to train the vendor's AI algorithms. Many licensors argue their manipulation and aggregation of the data creates in essence a "derivative work" which they own. While these vendors claim the derivative data will be used to improve the performance of their product which benefits the customer, they also hope to monetize the data by selling the aggregated data.

The following language illustrates these points:

> *Vendor may (i) compile statistical and other information related to the performance, operation and use of the Subscription Services, and (ii) use, and share data from the Subscription Services environment in aggregated form for security and operations management, to create statistical analyses, and for research and development purposes, and (iii) use this information* ***create anonymized statistics for our own marketing purposes.*** *(clauses (i) and (ii) are collectively referred to as 'Subscription Service Analyses").*
>
> *Subscription Service Analyses will not incorporate any information in a form that could serve to identify Customer or an individual.* ***Vendor retains all intellectual property rights in Subscription Service Analyses.***

Alternative wording:

> *You retain all ownership or other rights over data that you or persons acting on your behalf input, upload, transfer or make available in relation to, or which is collected from your devices or equipment by the SaaS ("***Input Data***"). We and our Affiliates have the right to duplicate, analyze, transfer, modify and otherwise use Input Data to provide, improve or develop our offerings.*

The following language is much more customer friendly and restrictive on the vendor:

> *Without Customer's approval, Customer Data will not be used by Vendor or its subcontractors other than in connection with providing the Services or otherwise complying with Vendor's obligations under this Agreement, nor will Customer Data be commercially exploited by or on behalf of Vendor or its Subcontractors.*
>
> Finally, given the customer may be providing small data set, prudent customers allowing the use of their data place limit use of their data if the data sets are small.
>
> Notwithstanding the foregoing restrictions, Customer agrees that: … (b) Vendor may collect aggregated statistical data regarding Customer's use of the Services and provide such aggregated statistical data to third parties, *provided, that such data shall be aggregated with similar information of at least two (2) or more other customers of Vendor or otherwise anonymized so that it cannot be identifiable as relating to Customer.*

3. Data Output and Reports

Many software applications include reporting functionality which allows the user to analyze and aggregate its data in a specific format and report the results. The methodology, formatting and structure to create the report and the linkage to its process flows are usually copyrighted by the owner of the software application and considered to be a competitive advantage in selling its solution against other vendors. As such, all reports and records generated by the application include the vendor's intellectual property. Customers are often confused when they seek to assert ownership over the reports claiming the reports constitute their proprietary information and data. Vendors reject this position arguing that the reports are their copyrighted intellectual property.

A compromise position is for the vendor to grant the customer a perpetual license to the reports allowing the customer to use the reports for its internal business purposes and retain ownership of its data in the reports. Conversely, the vendor may not use such data without the customer consent.

D. *PRACTICE POINT:* Best practices for vendor data security.

At a minimum, the vendor should:

- Adopt and implement a comprehensive data security and data protection policy which addresses administrative, technical and physical security measures (see Chapter 22.A.3, A.4 and A.5 above), including:
    - Employee background checks
    - Encryption and technology standards
    - Password policies, and single sign-on allowing system administrators to cut off all access to the system quickly
    - Multifactor authentication
    - Employee and contractor training
    - Vulnerability testing
    - Intrusion detection systems
    - Penetration testing on a regular basis
    - Encrypting data both at rest and in transit
    - Incident response procedures and time frames
    - Tracking and time frames for reporting incidents
    - Audits such as Service Organizational Control reports (i.e., SOCII, Type 2)
    - Procedures for disciplining employees for failure to comply with the vendor's security policy
    - Data retention policy including procedures for secure data destruction
    - Have a data inventory and data flow map in place to know the location of all Protected Data in the organization. Knowing where Protected Data is located helps a vendor respond more quickly to a security incident or breach and identify which third parties may be impacted. For companies that must comply with the GDPR, it will be very difficult for the company to comply with the Article 30 compliance obligations without a data inventory and data flow map in place.
- Implementing Encryption Standard 170.302(u)
- Implementing a strong firewall
- Implementing strong network authentication (x.509 certificated)
- Complying with all applicable government regulations (i.e., GDPR and CCPA)

- Complying with all applicable industry standards (i.e., PCI standard)
- Immediately notifying the customer of any actual or attempted intrusion
- Implementing user and data monitoring
- Utilizing a network intrusion prevention and detection system which records all attempts to access the system, whether successful or unsuccessful
- Limiting the number of ports to the absolute minimum
- Utilizing network segmentation with specific Virtual Local Area Network (VLANS)
- Utilizing virtualization technology with appropriate safeguards
- Limiting the number of ports to the absolute minimum
- Data retention and destruction policy

CHAPTER 23

Auditing the Licensee - Software Use Audits

A. Overview

From the vendor's perspective, software audits are an integral part of every software license. Almost all vendors insist on the inclusion of an audit clause to permit a vendor to confirm the customer's compliance with the license's use clause and protect their significant investment in their intellectual property. Vendors believe that many customers either intentionally or unintentionally exceed their license's use rights, and without a right of audit, vendors are unable to enforce their rights. Some customers, however, believe that vendors audit their customers to increase their revenue and margins—a much easier task than finding and closing sales with new customers.

Audits can be "random" (without any probable cause that the customer is not compliant), targeted (e.g. that they are directed towards clients with specific criteria such as a recent merger, recent announcements of global expansion, non-renewal, etc.) or they can be based on infringement information such as "phone home" technology that alerts a vendor of unlicensed software usage at an organization, or a disgruntled employee reports their employer as violating the terms of the underlying license agreement.

Regardless of the reason, audits are occurring with greater frequency. While some customers may intentionally exceed the scope of the license grant, many customers find themselves in violation of the license terms from poor software management, ambiguous contract terms, and ever-evolving licensing models that are inconsistent with the usage contemplated by the license agreement between the parties. Acquisitions, mergers, and spin-offs by customers also create challenges, as the customer must track the license rights of the merged or divested company. Often, software licenses used by the acquired company are mistakenly not renewed even though the licensed software continues to be used by the combined entity or the surviving entity fails to notify the licensor that the software has been transferred to a new location or moved to a different server. Because these licenses were acquired through merger, they are often not included in the acquiring party's software inventory. The failure to provide the licensor with an updated address for invoices and notices may also give rise to a breach as the licensor's invoices are never received or paid by the customer's finance department. Licensees may also run afoul of any "anti-assignment" clause in their license agreement.

Multiplexing and virtualization also make it difficult for a customer to determine and calculate license usage, much less the license fee due. The customer may not understand the financial impact of moving from a per-processor to a per-core-pricing methodology. If a licensor's software is used in a cloud environment and transferred among many "virtual" servers in a server farm, the customer may need to purchase a license for every server in the farm even though the software is resident only on several servers at a time. Similarly, if the licensed software is integrated into a third-party product which will be accessed by the customer's customers, the customer may need a license for each of its customers who will access this product.

Audits involving OEM customers incorporating the vendor's products into their own products can be especially challenging as the vendor may seek access to the OEM's customer. Thus OEMs and VARs should negotiate the audit provisions with the understanding that the vendor may seek to audit their customers' usage. Any end user audit rights should be clearly stated in the OEM/VAR agreement with the vendor but should also be addressed in the agreement with the end user. Most importantly, both agreements should set forth how the information can be collected from the end user, if at all. This is especially important where the end users are in sensitive industries such as national security, healthcare, finance, etc.

To avoid potential issues, OEMs and VARs should include language in their agreements with their end users allowing the vendor to disclose any information in their possession related to the end user's use of the licensed software and require the end-user to cooperate with any third-party audit of the end-user's use of the third party software.

Problems may also arise from employees unlawfully copying an application instead of obtaining a new, licensed copy through the vendor as well as from the purchase of used hardware that, unbeknown to the purchaser, has unlicensed software resident on it or for which the purchaser thought it was obtaining a license as part of the purchase.

1. Use of Software Auditing Tools

Many vendors utilize software tools to monitor customers' compliance with the underlying software license. Prudent customers should resist installing the vendor's audit software within their production environments, primarily due to the nature of audit software's design and operation, particularly the high level of access authority associated with executing the software. To operate effectively, audit software is designed to bypass/circumvent security and access control mechanisms. To assist with this objective, the level of system access granted to the application when it runs is typically considered to be the highest level available. As the audit software is usually installed in the production environment behind the customer's firewalls and behind the intrusion detection systems, the vendor may potentially have access into many areas of the customer's IT environment which could extend well beyond the information required to audit the customer's usage by more traditional means.

Acceding to the vendor's request to install audit software implies the customer's permission for the vendor to execute the software, generally at its sole discretion. While a customer can partition a vendor within its respective environments, in a worst-case scenario, the vendor could gain access to the customer's entire environment. In addition, audit software may also contribute to reduced system performance or other forms of interference with proper system functions.

Prudent vendors should always disclose the fact their software contains a reporting feature as the vendor should obtain the customer's written permission to transfer data from the customer's system to the vendor. Disabling any "phone home" features should be a violation of the underlying the agreement.

At the same time, the customer should request a definitive list of data being transferred to the vendor including the types of data and the possible values that may be transferred. Any consent signed by a customer should limit the data allowed to be transferred.

The vendor should be willing to demonstrate the accuracy of the tool and provide the customer with representations, warranties and indemnities consistent with any other software the customer may license. At a minimum, the vendor should be required to comply with the customer's IT/cybersecurity standards and indemnify the customer in the event of a breach of those standards. Moreover, since some vendors include tools in their software to unilaterally, automatically detect and "report back" apparent or actual unauthorized usage, prudent customers will require the underlying license agreement to state that the tool's use must be concluded upon termination of the license agreement. A customer should seek advice from its network security team and its outside consultants to help define specific technical processes and standards for prior review and authorization of audit-function code. Model language follows:

> *If Licensor-supplied monitoring software is approved for use by Customer in Customer's sole discretion, Customer will have the right to first test it in a non-production environment. Regardless of any prior testing, Licensor shall retain all liability, without limitation, for any problems, damages or losses that directly result from Customer's use of the monitoring tools in Customer's production environment. In any event, Licensor shall not monitor Customer's systems (or the systems of Customer's Clients) in any manner without Customer's prior written approval.*

Many vendors, however, insist on using their own software tools, which are often pre-installed on the software in question. They are unwilling to provide any special warranties or indemnities and see use of the software as a condition precedent to purchasing the underlying license. Because the tool will be running within the customer's IT network, a prudent vendor should disclose the existence of the tool and set forth the terms under which it will operate to avoid any potential legal claims. Model language is set forth below.

<u>License Metering and Auditing</u>

(a) *Licensee acknowledges and understands that the Software has a built-in license metering module. The Software may periodically prompt the user to validate the copies of the Software installed on each computer. Licensee will have fifteen (15) days to respond to a validation prompt. If Licensor does not receive a response to the validation prompt within this 15-day period, the Software will disable itself and will become inoperable.*

(b) *Licensee acknowledges that: (i) the Software may use Licensee's internal network for license metering of installed versions of the Software; (ii) the Software may use licensee's internal network and Internet connections for the purpose of transmitting license-related data to Licensor. Licensee further acknowledges that such information may be used by Licensor for validating the authenticity of the license and monitoring the license-related data, in order to protect the Software against unlicensed or illegal use of the Software. Licensee further acknowledges that license auditing and Software activation is based on the exchange of license related data between Licensee's computers and Licensor's server. Licensee must have an active Internet connection to receive the necessary Installation Upgrade or License Update codes.*

(c) *Licensee acknowledges and agrees that Licensor will automatically receive license metering and compliance information from the built-in metering module set forth in this Section __. Licensee agrees to follow any applicable requirements of this Agreement related to its use of the Software.*

(d) *Licensee acknowledges and agrees that notwithstanding any metering module or other measures put in place by Licensor, Licensee is solely responsible and liable for any and all violations and breaches of this Agreement, whether intentional or unintentional.*

(e) *Licensee acknowledges and agrees that Licensee shall not take any action to circumvent the license metering module or to delete, modify or configure any data so as to prevent the accurate reporting from the license metering module.*

(f) *Licensee agrees that Licensor may conduct on-site audits of Licensee's use of the Software at Licensee's premises for compliance with the terms of this Agreement at any time, upon reasonable notice and during business hours.*

2. *Third Party Auditing Tools*

A number of independent third-party vendors license software that allows customers to audit their compliance with the use limitations set forth in their various license agreements. Known as Software Asset Management (SAM) tools, they provide a mechanism to clarify what licenses are being used, who is using them, to right-size the ongoing license costs by reducing licensing costs where licenses are not being used, and to plan for future growth appropriately. These software tools provide two benefits:

(i) to the extent the audit reveals that the customer is not utilizing all of the licenses it has purchased, the customer can terminate the unused licenses and maintenance to reduce its costs.

(ii) to the extent the customer's use exceeds the number of licenses purchased, the customer can reduce its usage or purchase additional licenses before the licensor potentially becomes aware of such overages, and

B. Elements of an Audit Clause

Prudent practitioners should carefully review and negotiate audit clauses to ensure their clients obtain the rights and protections they need. From the vendor's perspective, the vendor requires the ability to accurately determine the customer's usage of the software/services and confirm that the customer's usage is in compliance with the terms of the underlying agreement. The customer seeks to ensure that its business is not interrupted by an overly intrusive audit and, in the event the customer is found to have exceeded its usage rights, the resulting remedy imposed by the buyer is reasonable in light of the transgression. The outcome will be dictated by the relative negotiating strength of each party.

> *Vendor has the right to verify the installation of, access to, and use of any Offerings by You and Your Authorized Users. As part of any such verification, Vendor or its authorized representative has the right,* **on 15 days' prior notice, to inspect Your records, systems and facilities,** *including machine IDs, serial numbers, Vendor IDs, and other related information,* **on Your premises using a Vendor approved verification tool.** *In addition to Vendor's right to perform a verification on Your premises,* **You shall, within 15 days of such verification request, provide a report to Vendor using a Vendor approved verification tool,** *that contains information relating to the installation of, access to, and use by You and Your Authorized Users of any Offerings including machine IDs, serial numbers, Vendor IDs, and other related information. If Vendor determines that Your installation of, access to, or use is not in conformity with these Terms (including any Additional Agreement, Special Terms or other applicable terms),* ***You will immediately purchase new subscriptions to remedy the noncompliance, and pay Vendor's reasonable costs of the verification. Vendor reserves the right to seek any other remedies available at law or in equity.***

1. *Purpose of the Audit.*

The audit clause establishes the purpose and parameters of the audit, which in turn determines the scope and extent of data collected. From the customer's perspective, the audit scope should be narrowly drawn to prevent the vendor from conducting an unfettered search of the customer's records for unknown problems, searching for potential opportunities to sell additional software, or identifying any competing software used by the customer.

2. *Audit Methodology.*

The methodology by which the audit will be undertaken is the most important aspect of an audit provision.

(i) Self-Certification. The most favorable approach from a customer perspective is for the customer to self-certify that it is in compliance with the license terms. Customers have legitimate concerns regarding the administrative burden audits impose on the customer's technical staff's valuable time and disrupting everyday workflow. A certificate of compliance signed by an officer of the customer avoids the disruption to its business.

However, the vendor is totally relying on the customer's good faith to certify its compliance with its contractual obligations. While a certificate of audit protects the customer from an intrusive third-party audit, vendors may be unwilling to accept a limited audit right and may seek the right to review the raw data in the belief that the customer may not realize it has exceeded its audit rights.

Model language follows.

During the term of this Agreement, upon Vendor's written request, Customer will conduct a review of its books and records solely to the extent necessary to verify Customer's compliance with its payment obligations under this Agreement.

(ii) Self-Audit and Report. A second option is for the customer to undertake a self-audit and provide the vendor a report on its findings, as opposed to a certification, showing that the customer is in compliance with terms of the license. The report can take the form of a summary of the audit findings or the actual audit findings.

During the term of this Agreement, upon Vendor's written request, Customer will conduct a review of its books and records solely to the extent necessary to verify Customer's compliance with its payment obligations under this Agreement Only those Customer facilities that are using Software licenses associated with this Agreement shall be subject to the review. Vendor agrees that if the targeted facilities are found to be in compliance, the entire enterprise shall be deemed to be in compliance. After completion of its review, Customer shall provide a report containing the results of the review. Customer's disclosure of this report and any documents, records or any other information in connection with the review shall be limited to the portion of the documents, records or information that relate to payment obligations set forth in this Agreement, and Vendor shall hold such disclosed information in strict confidence. Nothing contained in this paragraph is intended to allow Vendor to access or review Customer's systems, networks, books or records.

(iii) Third-Party Audit. A third option is to allow a third party to undertake the audit. Most customers seek to prohibit the vendor from using its competitors to conduct the audit to avoid the competitor accessing the customer's confidential information. Customers also seek to prohibit the vendor from using auditors paid on a contingency basis, which incentivizes the auditor to identify as many deficiencies as possible. Customers are also hesitant to allow the Software Publisher Association (SPA) and the Software Alliance (BSA), two software industry associations which conduct audits on behalf of their member entities and often work on contingency, to participate in the audit. Model language to this effect follows:

Upon Licensor's request and subject to Customer's written approval, Licensor may, at Licensor's expense, have an independent third party, reasonably acceptable to Customer, attend the audit ("Auditor"). In no event will organizations such as the Software Publisher Association (SPA) and The Software Alliance (BSA) be involved in the process or used as auditors. Any Auditor shall be required to sign a written nondisclosure agreement with Customer and shall hold all information obtained from such audit in confidence and shall not disclose any such information to any third party, except that the Auditor may disclose information necessary to the purpose of the audit to Licensor in strict confidence. Before beginning any audit, the Licensor and Customer shall use commercially reasonable efforts to agree in writing (via email or otherwise) on the audit process and procedures, including but not limited to (a) what constitutes proof of license, (b) how use will be measured, (c) whether monitoring software will be used, and (d) the number and locations of Customer facilities to be audited as a representative sampling of Customer's enterprise. Only those Customer systems that are using Software licenses associated with this Agreement shall be subject to the audit.

3. *Notice.*

Vendors should provide customers with 30 days prior written notice of the audit and state how the audit will be conducted. All requests for information should be reasonable and the vendor's access to the customer's IT systems should be limited to those segments necessary to conduct the audit.

The audit request should set forth in detail the specific process and nature of the audit as well as the particular software that the vendor seeks to audit. Depending on the nature and types of data requested, the customer should have at least 30 days to respond to the vendor's request. Preparing for an audit and collecting the required data can take several weeks, involving identifying and organizing records of deployment and/or usage, as well as finding and hiring specialized consultants, if needed. Allowing the customer time to prepare should permit the audit to be concluded quickly. The customer should also have the right to delay the audit for good-faith reasons, such as the year-end closing of the customer's financial books, national holidays, or availability of key stakeholders.

4. *Logistics of the Audit.*

Most customers seek to limit the vendor's audit rights to only once in any 12- to 36-month period, arguing that there is no need for a vendor to audit more frequently. Further, non-production instances, backup versions, etc. are usually not subject to audit by the vendor.

Audits should be conducted only during normal business hours, with the location dependent on the nature of the audit. Most audits initially are conducted electronically by running a software tool on the customer's hardware to identify any noncompliance with the license terms. Electronic auditing is often supplemented by on-site visits to validate and/or interpret electronic inventorying results with additional on-site sample testing of selected computer servers, interviewing IT and/or procurement personnel, and/or project team meetings. Prudent customers seek to limit the length of the audit (e.g., 30–45 days) to limit the disruption to their business as well as their operational costs.

Many customers also seek to limit on-site inspections as they are viewed as a distraction to normal business activities. It also is not uncommon for vendors to push back on any involvement by the auditor in the process of collecting data. For example, some customers insist on running any audit software themselves so as to not provide direct access to their production environment to a third-party.

5. *Cost.*

Traditionally, the vendor assumes the costs in undertaking the audit, including the fees of any third-party auditors, unless the audit identifies a specified level of underpayment (e.g., 5%). The vendor usually does not reimburse the customer for its costs in supporting the audit, procuring specialized inventorying software, and/or hiring outside consultants to assist in the audit. Any reimbursement of the vendor should be limited to the vendor's reasonable third-party out-of-pocket fees paid to an outside auditor, excluding vendor staff and overhead.

6. Auditors.

Prudent customers require the vendor to use an "independent" third-party auditor to conduct the audit. In these cases, the third-party auditors should be required to sign a nondisclosure agreement, and the parties should mutually agree on the minimum qualifications an auditor must possess for conducting an audit. As discussed above, customers should exclude third-party auditors compensated on a contingency basis as well as those auditors considered to be competitors of the customer. All auditors should be escorted while on the customer's premises.

7. Compliance with Customer Policies.

The vendor, the vendor's auditor, and their respective employees should be obligated to comply with all applicable customer policies, such as those governing network security and site physical security, in conducting the audit.

8. Compliance with Laws.

Given the ever-increasing focus on data privacy, the vendor and its auditors should be contractually obligated to comply with all applicable laws, including all data privacy laws. This could include, as an example, the masking of personal information that might otherwise be gathered by audit software.

9. Confidentiality/Use of Audit Results.

All aspects of the audit, including the results and the data generated, should be used solely regarding the audit and should not be disclosed publicly in any manner. The customer should ensure that any existing confidentiality agreement or provisions between the parties are sufficient to protect its interests and that the auditor is also subject to an obligation of confidentiality. This is especially important if the vendor or its auditor will have access to protected data. Model confidentiality language is set forth below:

> *Each party agrees to hold confidential (in accordance with Section __ ("Confidentiality") all information learned and determinations made in the course of any inspection or audit under this Section __ ("Audits"), except when it is necessary for a party to reveal such information in order to enforce its rights under this Agreement in arbitration or in court and except when compelled by Law.*

The vendor should be obligated to promptly provide the customer a copy of the audit report and the right to refute any of the auditor's findings.

10. Additional License Fees, Penalties and Interest.

The customer has the strongest negotiating leverage at the time it executes the underlying agreement, and thus it should not wait until it has been found to have exceeded the scope of its use rights to negotiate any fees or penalties the vendor seeks to impose. During the initial license negotiations, prudent customers should seek to incorporate a cushion allowing them to exceed the number of purchased licenses by a specified amount (e.g., 5%) before interest or penalties apply. If the customer is found to have exceeded its use rights, any overage fees will be calculated using the discounted license rate the parties negotiated at the time of the original sale/at a pre-negotiated rate.

Customer-favorable language illustrating this point follows:

In the event any payment discrepancy is uncovered by the review, the parties agree to promptly meet and in good faith resolve the payment discrepancy in a timely and mutually acceptable manner. Unless otherwise mutually agreed by the parties in writing, any discrepancies found in the review will be settled by using the established pricing, discounts and related terms in this agreement and Customer shall not be liable for additional fines, penalties, interest fees or other consequential damages.

From the vendor's perspective, the customer should pay a premium, or at least the vendor's then-existing list price, to incentivize the customer to not exceed the scope of use. Vendors sometimes specifically prohibit the customer from using "true ups" via purchases through a reseller or the application of any prior or current discounts from the software's suggested list price to reduce the cost of any noncompliance. Some vendors seek to require the customer to purchase a new multi-year license to address the prior usage related to non-compliance. For example, a 3 year license term of which the first year covers the previous/current year and the two subsequent years looking forward.

11. Superseding Provisions.

To the extent the parties have negotiated audit provisions, the agreement should clearly state that the negotiated provisions supersede any other licenses or terms to which the customer may be bound, including any on-line terms, click-wrap and browse-wrap terms.

This section shall supersede and have precedence over any provisions relating to review, audit, verification or other similar provisions in any EULA's, click-through licenses, documentation, user information, or any other similar licenses, agreements, or documentation issued, submitted, displayed on websites, or otherwise provided by Licensor in connection with the Software or Services.

12. Resolution of Any Underpayment.

The agreement should provide that any identified noncompliance does not constitute infringement of the vendor's intellectual property and that the vendor's exclusive remedy for the customer exceeding the scope of the license is the collection of monetary damages. Upon payment of any amounts owed, the vendor should execute a release in favor of the customer in full satisfaction of all liability the customer may have to the vendor. Under no circumstances should the vendor be allowed to terminate the license except in the most egregious circumstances.

C. Preparing for the (Eventual) Audit Request

Eventually almost all large customers will be audited at some point. As such, prudent customers should prepare for the day when they receive an audit notice.

1. Implement a Comprehensive Software Procurement and Use Policy

Prudent customers should establish a standing committee consisting of representatives from IT, procurement and legal to oversee the implementation and periodic assessment of the customer's software procurement and use policy. The committee should ensure that employees receive continuing education regarding the customer's policy, the importance of complying with the policy, and the terms of any third-party software licenses. The implementation of a comprehensive policy reinforced by regular training will reduce the customer's risk and, hopefully, limit any damages assessed against the customer in the event the customer is found to have exceeded the scope of the license grant.

To that end, prudent customers should conduct regular self-audits and implement a comprehensive Software Asset Management ("SAM") program. Implementing a strong SAM program can minimize any software misuse and, in the event of a third-party audit, can limit negative findings and the attendant liability. In the event a vendor's audit does uncover non-compliance, the existence of a robust SAM program demonstrates the customer's good-faith efforts to comply with the vendor's license restrictions and may allow it to avoid, or at least mitigate, any fines and penalties.

A strong SAM program should be implemented and administered by a customer's compliance department in conjunction with its procurement group. The program should include a well-developed educational component, as well as an asset-tagging/-tracking methodology, in addition to an audit component. Each business unit must understand the restrictions placed on the use of the software and must be held accountable within the entity for complying with the terms of use. Without accountability, there is no incentive for a business unit to emphasize and ensure compliance, even though the cost to the corporation as a whole can be huge.

Procurement and IT teams should be trained not to respond to vendor audit requests or pre-audit "inquiries," and not to conduct their own self-audits without the involvement of the legal team, as most procurement and IT professionals lack the skills and experience to respond to these issues. Further, any results or actions they take may be subject to discovery in the event the parties end up in litigation. Potentially troublesome inquiries include "business as usual" questionnaires or "usage queries" from software vendors, as the results may serve to justify an audit by the vendor.

2. Conduct Regular Self-Audits

Every entity should conduct annual software use *self*-audits, to assess and hopefully confirm its compliance with its frequently evolving contractual obligations. Identifying potential problems in advance may allow a customer to resolve an issue with less cost, less risk of license termination, less risk of reputational damage (e.g., from litigation), and less disruption prior to the vendor possibly becoming aware of the customer's non-compliance. Further, some vendors look more favorably on customers who self-report their noncompliance. The self-assessment should be undertaken in conjunction with the use of a Software Asset Management (SAM) system. Any self-assessment should involve the customer's legal department to protect the results through the attorney-client privilege, if available.

Some customers retain outside consultants to audit their compliance and assist in preparing a response to a vendor audit request. In doing so, the customer should structure the project to report to and through the customer's legal function. As with audits for possible non-compliance in labor, environmental, securities, or other legal domains, outside specialists should be contracted by the legal department to enable possible protected nondisclosure of potentially unfavorable results or conclusions. Prudent practitioners should check the laws of the governing jurisdiction to determine whether external IT consultants hired by and reporting to outside counsel, rather than the legal department, are necessary in the jurisdiction to obtain protection under the attorney-client privilege.

3. *Create a Protocol for Responding to an Audit Request*

Prudent customers should establish a protocol for responding to audit requests prior to ever receiving one. Waiting to receive an audit request to establish a plan of action puts the customer at a significant disadvantage, as it will be forced to make important decisions in a short period of time. The customer should create a "response" team consisting of representatives from the procurement, legal, IT and finance departments, and train them on the issues associated with conducting a software audit. The team should identify third-party consultants to retain in the event it requires assistance in responding to an audit request. A well-thought-out protocol is important to ensuring that the process goes smoothly and does not disrupt the customer's business operations.

D. Responding to an Audit Request

Upon receipt of a vendor's audit request, a prudent customer should promptly engage with the customer's procurement and legal teams to:

- identify and find applicable license components which likely will have evolved from the initial license agreement, and usually takes more time and effort than initially predicted;
- understand the terms of the applicable license(s) (often a significant, iterative struggle, given the cascade of changing products, pricing terms, and contracts);
- determine the customer's purchasing history with the vendor;

- ascertain how many individuals are using the software and how many licenses were purchased by the customer; and
- confirm the customer's actual, documented compliance with the license terms.

In its initial response, the customer should limit its reply to informing the vendor that the customer is preparing a researched, reasoned response. Savvy customers will research and seek insight on the particular vendor's history and approach in prior audits of other customers. They should also strive to structure the audit and its results to merit the protection of the attorney-client privilege, particularly for litigious vendors, first-time self-audits, and situations of suspected noncompliance. Audits often uncover ambiguities, possible "smoking gun" emails (e.g., staff complaining about software-buying process, record-keeping, or budget constraints) and premature admissions that can and do undermine vendor negotiations and optimal resolution.

Be responsive while at the same time try to narrow the scope of the audit and understand which contracts the vendor would like to audit. For convenience, the output of the audit and any results should be placed on a shared data transfer site or secure FTP to provide transparency, security, and efficiency gains.

Finally, failing to cooperate with a vendor's audit request provides no advantage, as vendor-filed lawsuits often include dramatic, detailed stories of customer "stalling" when contractually required audits have been refused.

E. *PRACTICE POINT*: Checklist for responding to an audit request.

In responding to an audit request, a prudent customer should:

- Understand the scope of the review requested by the vendor and confirm that the vendor is entitled to the requested information under the underlying license agreement. For example, does the license restrict audits to a particular product, entity, business group or geography?
- Establish a process for communicating with the vendor and controlling the flow of information to the vendor.
- Seek to conduct a self-audit in lieu of a vendor conducted audit.
- Reaffirm the vendor's confidentiality obligations and require any third parties involved in the audit process to enter into a confidentiality agreement.
- Comply with the customer's obligations under the agreement's audit clause.
- Seek to limit the scope of the audit, i.e. the products, entities, length of the audit, geographies, users, etc.
- Establish a reasonable timeline for conducting the audit.
- Budget accordingly.
- Set forth a proposal for who collects the data and how it is collected.
- Understand the audit process and how the data will be collected and analyzed.

- Once the data has been collected, the customer should vet the data against the governing license terms.
- To the extent it appears that the customer has exceeded the scope of the license grant, the customer should review the data to validate any alleged overages.
- If the customer agrees it has exceeded the scope of the license, it should seek to negotiate a mutually agreeable settlement. Most vendors are willing to negotiate with the customer, as they recognize litigation is a lose-lose situation and do not want to lose a good customer, especially if any breach was inadvertent.
- Once the cost of any confirmed overages is independently determined or estimated by the customer, the customer should act:
  - defensively based on its internal investigation, and
  - offensively based on leveraging the parties' future relationship, to attempt to ensure a settlement with the lowest possible cost.
- Once an agreement has been reached, the parties should execute a full release.
- After settlement, the customer should conduct a "lesson learned" exercise to ensure that this issue does not arise again with that particular vendor and to determine if disputes with other software vendors can be avoided through better software management practices.

For a more detailed discussion of software audits, *see* Jones et al., *Surviving a Software License Audit*, Forrester Research (Jan. 4, 2010); Scott, *Successfully Defending Software Audits*, 2 Sci. Tech. Law. 18 (Issue 3, 2006); *see also* Raysman & Brown, *How to Avert or Survive a Software Audit*, Acct. Laws., May 13, 2003, at 3. For a more detailed discussion of BSA audits, *see* Sprague & Fish, *Beware of the Watchdog: Responding to the Business Software Alliance*, 84 Mich. B.J. 25 (May 2005).

CHAPTER **24**

Escrow Agreements

Escrow agreements are usually entered into to protect the licensee by providing access to the licensed software's source code in the event of a "release event" or a "release condition," meaning a condition by which the deposit materials would be released to the beneficiary of an escrow agreement. It can also be referred to as a "release trigger" or in the case of a SaaS relationship, a "Contingency Trigger Event."

A. Release Events

1. *General*

(a) Release Events

The most important issues when negotiating an escrow agreement are the release events and related procedures. Release events should not be limited to "failure to function as a going concern" (whatever that means) and "subject to bankruptcy." A licensee should seek much broader rights to include better-defined bankruptcy-related events and an associated early trigger mechanism. The licensee desires the escrow release to occur pre-bankruptcy to avoid complications under bankruptcy laws, as well as default triggers under any service level agreement (SLA) and any other meaningfully linked agreements. The failure to meet an SLA a release event optimizes vendor relationships as the vendor knowing that a beneficiary could access its intellectual property will almost always garner better service levels and response times. From the licensee's perspective, the release should be automatic on the licensee's command and not subject to a complicated submission process subject to the licensor's authorization.

"Notice Release Process" and "Demand Release Process"

Notice Release is the potentially complicated submission process subject to time and potentially dispute resolution, whereas a Demand Release by-passes this authorization. A Demand Release is difficult to obtain when the subject of the deposit material is the Depositor's (licensor's) intellectual property. On the other hand, escrowed materials that represent little risk to the depositor like object code, which is impossible to reverse engineer, or data, then a Demand Release actually is a critical requirement to facilitate the beneficiary's (licensee's or subscriber's) recovery time objectives, especially in an SaaS relationship.

The definition of a release event is one of the most important aspects of a properly drafted escrow agreement. To avoid future disputes and ensure that the licensee is able to promptly access the source code, it is important that the parties clearly define what constitutes a release event. Common release events include:

- a material breach of the license agreement (or SLA) by the licensor;
- the failure of the licensor to properly maintain the software or offer maintenance for a contractually agreed period of time (at least five years);
- the acquisition of or a change in control of the licensor;
- the failure to enhance the software's functionality;
- the vendor is longer in business; and
- the bankruptcy/insolvency of the licensor.

Other potential release events include the time after an announced "de-support" date, the termination or death of a key support resource, and an extended outage for SaaS.

A prudent licensor should ensure that the licensee does not have the unilateral right to declare a release event and trigger the release of the source code but instead the licensee should have a right to file a release request, but under the Notice Release Process. The licensee should not have Demand Release rights for access to the licensor's intellectual property. In the event the licensee believes a release event has occurred, the licensee should be obligated to provide the escrow agent written notice describing the relevant event, and the licensor should have a reasonable time period in which to respond. If the licensor cannot show that a release event has not occurred or the licensor does not contest the licensee's claim, the source code should be released. Conversely, if the licensor can show that a release event did not occur, then it can issue contrary instructions to the escrow agent to block the release. A well-drafted escrow agreement will also establish in detail the dispute resolution process in the event the parties dispute the existence of a release event.

From the licensee's perspective, the licensee should have the automatic right to receive the source code once it files a claim with the escrow agent, without having to arbitrate or invoke the dispute resolution process. Most licensors, however, are unwilling to agree to such an automatic release. *See, e.g., Vemics, Inc. v. Radvision, Ltd.*, 2007 WL 1459290 (S.D.N.Y. May 16, 2007).

A savvy licensor will seek to include a liquidated damages provision in the event the licensee inappropriately uses/releases the source code. *See Mid-Michigan Computer Systems Inc. v. Marc Glassman, Inc.*, 416 F.3d 505 (6th Cir. 2005) (licensee required to pay licensor $50,000 for each site using software in the event source code wrongfully accessed).

(b) The License Grant

To protect itself in the event of the licensor's bankruptcy, the licensee should ensure that the escrow agreement includes an actual license grant to the escrowed materials as opposed to an "agreement to grant" the licensee a license to the escrowed materials.

Subject to the terms of the Software License between the parties, Licensor grants to Licensee a limited, non-transferable, non-assignable license to use the Software solely for Licensee's internal business purposes, provided that the rights granted under this Section x.x shall be exercisable only upon the occurrence of a Release Event.

Providing a present grant strengthens the licensee's argument under Section 365(n) of the U.S. Bankruptcy Code that the licensee can retain its license in the event the licensor seeks to reject such license, as Section 365(n) addresses only licenses in existence at the time of the licensor's bankruptcy filing. An agreement to grant a license as of the time of a future event may be interpreted as a future grant and outside the purview of Section 365(n).

In addition, the escrow agreement should clearly grant the licensee the right to modify, enhance and maintain the software upon a release event.

(c) *Timing of Executing an Escrow Agreement*

The escrow terms are a not insignificant part of the transaction and must be contemplated before the parties agree to enter into the license agreement. Escrow agreements should be pre-negotiated and executed at the same time the overarching license agreement is executed. Obvious concerns that arise during the negotiation of the license agreement (and SLA) should be addressed in the escrow agreement.

Any escrow agreement should be executed prior to or contemporaneously with the license agreement to avoid having the licensor later refuse to execute the escrow agreement, having the parties fail to agree on its terms, or having the licensor fail to escrow the required materials. Too often the parties fail to execute an escrow agreement contemporaneously with execution of the license agreement or it is put-off, soon to become either an abandoned afterthought or noncompliance issue. Unfortunately, once the license has been executed, the licensee has lost much of its leverage and has little ability to require the licensor to enter into an escrow agreement.

2. *In the Event of Bankruptcy*

To the extent the licensee seeks to include the licensor's bankruptcy as a release event, the licensor should ensure that the bankruptcy be in conjunction with a material breach of the licensor's obligations in order for the release to be triggered. It is inequitable to dictate a release solely for the licensor's insolvency if the licensor continues to perform its obligations under the license and is not otherwise in material breach. Further, the ability to enforce an automatic release in the event of bankruptcy is of questionable legality. 11 U.S.C. § 365(e)(i). See Chapter 27 for a more detailed discussion.

It is critical from the licensee's perspective that the escrow agreement includes a "license grant" to use the source code, often referred to "Use Rights" or "Rights to Use Following a Release". Many license agreements grant the licensee an object code license while requiring the escrow of the source code, but yet the license does not address the use of the source code in the event it is released. Without such a license grant and specific terms regarding use of the source code, the licensee may have no "intellectual property right" subject to Section 365(n) of the U.S. Bankruptcy Code as described in Chapter 27. Moreover, the license grant should not be conditioned upon the existence of a bankruptcy related event. Section 365(n) only applies to intellectual property "as such rights existed immediately before the case commenced." 11 U.S.C. § 365(n)(1)(B). Thus, a license grant to the source code, which is conditioned upon the licensor seeking bankruptcy protection, may not be protected by Section 365(n).

From the licensee's perspective, the escrow provision should provide for the release of the source code prior to the licensor declaring bankruptcy. Once an escrow dispute is before a bankruptcy court, it could take up to 18 months to resolve. Even if the licensee ultimately prevails, the release of the source code will likely come too late to be of value to the licensee. See the language in Form H.1 § 3.2, which seeks to avoid having the release of the escrow deposit delayed in the bankruptcy hearings. For a more detailed description of the issues associated with bankruptcy, see Chapter 27.

The licensee should seek to include language in the escrow agreement releasing the source code upon the occurrence of any significant financial warning signs as specifically identified in the license agreement, such as a debt downgrade, the licensor being placed on a credit watch, or the licensor publicly announcing that it has retained an investment bank to explore "strategic options." The licensee should also negotiate a "self-reporting" obligation for the licensor, obligating the licensor to report any warning signs of a triggering event (e.g., the licensor's liabilities exceeding its assets). The licensee should focus on the loss of key support personnel, the erosion of service levels, extended response times leading to the escalation of problem reporting to the C-Level more than twice in any given month.

In short, the licensee should endeavor to include language in the agreement to allow it to avoid appearing before the bankruptcy court to enforce its rights.

3. *Impact of a Release Event*

In the event of a release event, the licensor will most likely consider its representations, warranty and indemnification obligations void, as licensors will not indemnify licensees for third-party infringement claims if the licensee has modified the source code, which will almost certainly occur though the licensee's maintenance and support activities. Further, licensors will usually not honor any representations or warranties regarding the operation or performance of the software, and will most likely refuse to maintain or support the software once the licensee has modified the source code.

B. Use of Third-Party Escrow Agents

1. *General*

Disputes often arise as to whether the software to be "escrowed" must be placed with an independent third party, an escrow agent, or held by the licensor. Occasionally the licensor will agree that the source code can be held by the licensee or made available to the licensee for their perusal. This is especially true with Enterprise Resource Planning (ERP) software providers who after realizing how badly their clients needed help fixing problems the clients caused by modifying the code base, generated significant revenue in professional services. This also increased the popularity of the use of open source by service providers (JBOSS, RedHat, etc.). The potential for infringement claims, however, make access to the code a risky proposition for licensees. The licensor is often hesitant to place its source code in the possession of a third party, where the licensor is unable to control access to the source code and the release of the source code. The licensee should insist on the use of an independent third party as the licensor may wrongfully refuse to release the source code in contravention of the escrow agreement.

In selecting an escrow agent, a licensee and licensor should look for an entity, such as Iron Mountain, specializing in technology escrows with a technical staff to verify the deposit. Experienced escrow agents can provide valuable insight relative to what should be required as a part of the escrow deposit, uncovering potential concerns with respect to the licensor, as well as contingency planning solutions available to the licensee based on those concerns. No reasonable law firm would (or should) agree to assume the responsibilities of the escrow agent. The escrow agent should carry errors and omissions insurance; be ISO 9000 certified; and employ significant security measures both as to the vault and the deposit material. The agent should be financially stable such that it will still be in the business if the licensee ever needs to exercise its rights under the escrow agreement. For a more detailed discussion of the issues involved in escrowing software, *see* http://www.ironmountain.com/ipm/.

Many licensors have a master escrow agreement in place, with their preferred escrow agent adding the licensee to the list of customers entitled to receive a copy of the source code in the event of a release event upon request. Most licensors are unwilling to spend the time and effort to negotiate individual escrow agreements given the cost to do so, the administrative burden of complying with the varying terms of many different escrow agreements, and the small likelihood of a release event occurring. If the licensor is willing to negotiate an agreement, the parties should include the escrow agent in the negotiation process. Escrow agents have their own forms of escrow agreements and often will not agree to terms solely because the licensee and licensor have agreed to them. The escrow agent can potentially be liable for wrongfully releasing the source code, and thus it will want its obligations to be clearly stated, while at the same time seeking to limit its liability.

2. *Verification of Escrowed Materials*

Regardless of whether the source code is escrowed with a third party, the licensee/escrow agent should verify that the licensor has escrowed all the materials it is required to escrow which may include not only the source code but build environment documentation, compilation instructions, use manuals, information regarding third party tools and other collateral materials that would enable the licensee to independently recreate and maintain the licensor's technology. It is important to remember that the licensee, not the escrow agent, is responsible for confirming that the required materials have been deposited by the licensor, although the escrow agent may be willing to do so for a fee.

Licensees should seek to include an affirmative statement granting the licensee the remedy of specific performance to force the licensor to meet its escrow obligations, including but not limited to placing the software in escrow. See Chapter 5.H.2(b)(i) for a more detailed discussion of specific performance.

A prudent licensee will include language in the escrow agreement requiring the licensor to release the software directly to the licensee (or the licensee's support designee) upon the licensee's written request, if the licensor fails to place the required materials including any updates in escrow. The licensee's support designee is usually someone who is familiar with the licensor's code base, and who can help the licensee make quick and effective use of the deposit materials. It could also be a professional services company subject to the same confidentiality standards as the licensee who will provide application services and potentially hosting of the software (aka "Application Service Provider" or "ASP"). *See* § 5.3.6. Although the licensor would likely not comply, such a requirement provides leverage to the licensee in the event it seeks a judicial remedy.

At the time escrowed materials arc deposited, the third party escrow agent should be contractually obligated to verify that the materials are the complete and most recent version, the media is readable and virus free, that the deposited materials duplicate the licensee's development environment with the required information on the relevant utilities, compilers and operating systems. The escrow agent should also verify that the source code can be compiled and that the compiled materials are identical to the licensee's licensed technology. See Section 3 below for a more detailed discussion of the materials to be escrowed.

These duties should be an ongoing obligation, performed on a periodic basis, but no less than quarterly, as the software and escrowed materials are "living" items that will continue to change during the term of the escrow agreement. Because of liability concerns, however, some escrow agents will not agree to evaluate the escrowed materials—they will only report what they are told they received, as well as the results of a visual inspection. A prudent licensee should seek to utilize "full service" escrow agent that can provide verification services.

Escrow agents usually offer several levels of verification. Under the first level, the agent will confirm receipt and take inventory of the software, that the software deposited is what is required to be deposited, and that the source code is readable. The second level requires the agent to confirm that the source code can be compiled into object code and that the software is identical to the software being utilized by the licensee. Under the most comprehensive level, the agent will confirm that the software is functional and will process data in the identical fashion as the licensed software is expected to perform.

Licensors should carefully review the agreement's verification provisions. Licensees occasionally try to include the right to participate in the verification process and thereby obtain access to the licensor's source code. Most licensors, however, are unwilling to allow the licensee to participate in the verification process, unless there is virtually no risk of exposing their intellectual property. There are instances where the licensor will allow the licensee to take the compiled code (object code) from the escrow agent following a verification test for purposes of performing further functionality testing. This is fairly common as the object code released is (or should be) identical to what the licensee's run-time environment.

An escrow arrangement is only as good as the deposit materials are usable. Otherwise, the escrow agreement may be worthless. Verification is critical to ensuring a usable deposit and subsequently strengthening the leverage value of the escrow arrangement. Knowing that the licensee can potentially access the licensor's intellectual property will motivate licensors to provide better service levels and response times.

PRACTICE POINT:

To ensure they receive the current source code upon the occurrence of a release event, the licensee should:

- Verify the escrowed materials are current
- Identify which party pays for the cost of verification
- Plan for the worst

3. *Materials to Be Escrowed*

A prudent licensee will require that the licensor escrow not only the software source code but also the build environment documentation, compilation instructions, use manuals, information regarding third-party tools and other collateral materials (i.e., design documentation, tools, logic diagrams, programmer notes, programmer's personal contact information, encryption keys, compilers, and documentation necessary to operate the software) that would enable the licensee to independently re-create and maintain the licensor's technology. The licensor should be required to update all escrowed materials and software no less than quarterly and warrant that the software escrowed is the current version of the software presently utilized by the licensee. The licensor should also be required to escrow all tools needed by the licensee to operate and support the software if the licensee takes possession of the software. The licensor should provide both the licensee and the escrow agent with a complete and accurate list of all escrowed materials.

In addition, the licensee may want to seek an express right to recruit and hire the licensor's employees in the event the source code is released, as many licenses and employment agreements contain non-solicitation provisions. Of course, if the release arises from the cessation of the licensor's business and the employee no longer works for the licensor, then this should be viewed as an opportunity to benefit both the licensee and the employee, who may be seeking work. Similarly, the licensor should allow the licensee to utilize designees such as third-party contractors (i.e., Managed Service Providers or Application Service Providers) to access and maintain the source code if the original license grant does not allow third party access. Finally, the licensee should require the licensor to escrow the names, phone numbers, and addresses of the licensor's programmers so that the licensee can contact and hire them if need be.

If the software/source code is known to be complex and confusing (the proverbial "spaghetti code"), some licensees seek to have the licensor include a video tutorial with the escrowed materials to explain how the software works. A video can be very valuable if the source code is later released to the licensee and the licensor fails to cooperate with the licensee. Verification testing may also be videoed as well to capture the audit process of the build instructions, not to mention the email records that exist to help answer questions about the build or address gaps in the build instructions.

Each party should appoint one person within its organization to be responsible for the party's obligations under the escrow agreement and to monitor the other party's compliance. The failure to do so will invariably lead to one party's failure to comply with its obligations. A serious issue may arise if the licensee later seeks access to the escrowed materials only to discover that the materials are not current or do not provide the expected level of protection. A best practice is to perform an escrow compliance check upon receipt of the licensor's maintenance invoice and to satisfactorily complete the compliance check before approving any invoices for payment. Model language follows:

Licensor shall submit with the Deposit Materials the following:

(i) Documentation and a licensed copy of all Software tools such as debuggers, assemblers and compilers needed to convert the Source Code into executable form used by the target processors and procedures necessary to transfer executable code to operational systems, as well as configuration Documentation to set up the environment to generate the target for the Source Code;

(ii) hardware devices with their accompanying firmware and Software tools, necessary to transfer the executable programs onto the storage device used by any embedded microprocessor; and

(iii) Documentation that provides for all Source Code the following information:

(a) general descriptions and operations;
(b) architecture schematics;
(c) data flow diagrams;
(d) detailed memory map and listing;
(e) input/output port map; and
(f) the licensing terms for any Open Source software incorporated into or necessary to operate the Software.

4. Escrow Fees

Verification and escrow fees can be quite expensive, sometimes costing tens of thousands of dollars. These costs should be allocated between the parties in the escrow agreement. Usually, the licensee will assume financial responsibility for any third- party escrow fees as the licensee requested that the source code be escrowed. It is inequitable to require the licensor to pay for such fees especially if the licensor has already established a centralized escrow for all of its customers. A licensee should not balk at paying such fees if it believes the source code will be of value if a release event occurs. In the event a software deposit should fail a verification/validation test, the licensor should assume all costs resulting from reperforming such verification or validation.

The licensee should resist the temptation to save money and allow the licensor to "self-escrow" or utilize an escrow agreement such as a two-party agreement signed by the licensor and the escrow agent that does not contemplate the licensee's required terms and conditions (such as required deposit materials, frequency of deposits, release events, release process and verification rights). As a general rule of thumb, if the agreement is not reviewable, modifiable or executable by the licensee, then other escrow arrangements should be made to address the risk.

If the escrow requirement is introduced early enough in the sourcing process, the licensee can require, as a condition of doing business, for the prospective licensor (bidders) to agree to enter into a unique escrow arrangement and to pay for the escrow and verification fees. Obviously if all the bidders are asked before they submit their proposals, the cost of the escrow will be baked into the proposal price. This way the risk is addressed and budgeted for in advance.

Lastly, there is intrinsic value to the licensor in terms of the verification testing exercise, which will assist them instill trust with the current prospect and future prospects. As they embrace the verification opportunity to generate a favorable report from the escrow agent, many licensors have boasted their success by issuing press releases and sharing their verification reports with prospects to instill trust and close deals quicker. Given this reality, the licensor should pay for or share in the cost of verification testing.

C. Use of Escrowed Materials

Use of the licensed software's source code released under an escrow agreement should be subject to the terms of the license agreement, and, depending on the original license grant, the licensee's use of the software should be limited to the usage contemplated in the license. The escrow agreement should contain a specific license grant clearly establishing the limitations on the licensee's use of the software and the licensor's ability to monitor and terminate such source code license in the event the licensee breaches the terms of use. In addition, strict confidentiality restrictions should apply with clearly defined remedies in the event of the licensee's breach.

From the licensee's perspective, the licensee should ensure that it receives the rights it requires to recreate and use the application in the manner it originally contemplated. This includes the right to:

- create derivative works,
- enhance and maintain the software to ensure it continues to meet the licensee's needs,
- make copies, and
- provide third parties access to the software to maintain, enhance and support the software.

To the extent the licensee planned to incorporate the software into its own or a third-party product, the license should clearly grant the licensee the right to do so as well as the right to enhance and maintain the software for the benefit of the licensee's customers. *See Epazz, Inc. v. National Quality Assurance USA, Inc.*, 2021 WL 3808946 (6th Cir.

Aug. 26, 2021) (License did not misappropriate licensor's trade secrets when it obtained licensor's software from a release event and hired a third party to maintain and enhance the software/source code).

Depending on the term of the original license, the licensee should ensure that the term of use for the released source code is sufficient to allow the benefit of application continuity and for enough time to realize its return on its technology investment or to source and migrate to a new solution. In terms of who, how and where it can use the software, the license grant should permit use by the licensee's subcontractors and consultants. Licensees should never seek to use the software for competitive purposes, placing them at great risk of infringement. The following language is illustrative:

> *Licensor hereby grants to Licensee and its affiliates a non-exclusive, worldwide royalty-free fully paid-up, perpetual, non-assignable (except as set forth in Section __ (**Assignment**)), limited, internal-use license to use the Source Materials to support and maintain the Licensed Software to ensure error free operation and operation in compliance with the Specifications. For the avoidance of doubt, the foregoing includes the right to modify and make derivative works of the Licensed Software, in Source Code form, for the purpose of bug fixes, Error corrections, and enhancements to the existing functionality of the Licensed Software as of the date of release ("**Licensee Updates**"). Each Licensee Update shall constitute "Licensed Software" for purposes of the rights and licenses granted under Sections __ (**License Rights**) and __________ (**Sublicense Rights**) above.*

D. Third-Party Software

Another issue for consideration is whether the escrowed software incorporates third-party software and how the incorporation of third-party software may affect the licensee's ability to maintain and support the source code if a release event occurs. To fully utilize the escrowed software, the licensee may need to obtain a license from the third party to use its software. Most third parties have little or no incentive to grant such a license. Some licensees seek to avoid this issue by requiring that the licensor not use any third-party software whose source code cannot be placed in escrow, without the licensee's prior written consent or requiring the licensee to approve the use of any third-party software. See § 5.3.6 for a more detailed discussion.

Third-party tools need not be placed in escrow if the third party does not permit such actions to take place. Of course, an alternative is to have the licensor provide the licensee the information that would allow the licensee to source and procure the licenses when needed.

There is also the matter of using open-source third-party software. If the licensee suspects that open-source software has been intermingled with the licensor's proprietary code, there could be an opportunity to subject use rights to the public license, which potentially compromises the licensor's ability to generate revenue from licensing its proprietary software. Open-source reviews are sometimes required by licensees to ensure that they are legally obligated to pay for what they are receiving. These reviews can be performed with verification testing.

E. Practical Nature of Software Escrow

Escrowing source code is not the panacea many licensees believe it to be. Often a release is delayed by litigation or arbitration over whether a release event has occurred. Even the timely release of the source code may not provide the desired solution for the licensee's problems. Placing fully documented software in escrow does not immediately allow a licensee to support the system. Licensees usually lack the needed expertise to use the source code, and it may take a significant amount of time and investment for the licensee to understand the operation of the software and make the software operational. Further, to utilize the source code, the licensee will need to obtain licenses to all third-party software and tools, including both proprietary software and open-source software, the cost of which will be borne by the licensee. Obtaining these licenses may be time-consuming and further delay the licensee's use of the software while adding an ongoing administrative and financial burden. In short, the cost of transitioning, supporting and maintaining the source code/software will likely be very expensive and impractical from a financial standpoint.

By accessing the source code, the licensee risks unlimited liability in the event the source code is misappropriated or disclosed in violation of licensee's confidentiality obligations either intentionally or unintentionally. Finally, releasing the source code to the licensee may create tax liability implications for the licensee under the laws of some countries.

In actuality, the source code is probably of little value without an employee/programmer of the licensor to support it and explain the software's operation to the licensee's IT staff. Unless the software is extremely important to the operation of the licensee's business, it is unlikely that the licensee will spend the money to understand the code and keep it upgraded and current. The license must also consider the administrative burden on the licensee to ensure that the licensor has indeed placed a current, working copy of the source code and documentation in escrow and has also subsequently escrowed all enhancements, modifications, etc. In considering whether to negotiate a source code escrow, the licensee should consider whether there are alternative products in the marketplace that the licensee could utilize in the event of the licensor's breach. In many cases, the licensee may find that it is easier and more cost-effective to switch to a new product than to try to maintain the licensor's software.

Finally, in the event the parties will not use a third-party escrow agent, the licensee should insist on setting forth the terms related to the release of the software in a separate agreement to protect against the licensor terminating the license in the event of its bankruptcy, potentially leaving the license without a remedy.

In sum, a source code escrow may not provide meaningful protection from the licensor's failure to perform. However, as licensors tend to be extremely concerned as to the possible release of their source code, a well-drafted escrow provision can provide an incentive for a licensor to meet its contracted performance obligations.

For a general discussion of technology escrow, *see* Watzke, *Technology Escrow: Protect Your Company's IP Assets and Technology Investments,* 22 ACC Docket 110 (Apr. 2004); Meeker, *Thinking Outside the Lock Box: Negotiating Technology Escrows,* 20 Computer & Internet Law. 6 (Sept. 2003).

See Forms H.1, H.2, H.3, and H.4 for model Escrow Agreements.

F. *PRACTICE POINT*: Checklist for drafting an escrow agreement.

- Who are the parties to the agreement? The licensor, the licensee, their affiliates?
- What is the term of the escrow agreement?
- What happens upon the escrow agreement's termination?
- What procedures must be followed to undertake a release?
  - Is a release automatic upon the occurrence of a release event?
  - Must the licensor be notified of the pending release?
  - Must the licensor agree to the release?
  - Can the licensor object to an impending release?
  - What happens if there is a dispute over whether a release event occurred?
- Are the release events clearly defined?
- What happens upon a breach of the underlying software agreement?
  - The licensor's failure to provide maintenance and support?
  - A degradation of the licensor's finances?
  - The licensor's bankruptcy?
- Who pays for any fees incurred in escrowing the software?
- What will be escrowed?
  - The source code for the software?
  - The related documentation?
  - Any third-party software?
  - The tools required to support the software?
  - The names and contract information for the licensor's employees who maintain and support the software?
- Who is responsible for confirming the validity of the escrowed materials?
- Who pays the cost to verify the escrowed materials?
- How often will the escrowed materials be updated?
- What limitations are placed on the licensee's use of the escrowed materials upon a release?
- Can the licensee enhance the release software?
- Does the licensee have the right to distributed the code if it is an OEM?
- Can the licensee utilize third parties to maintain, enhance and support the software?
- Is the licensee's use of the software limited by geography, industry, platform, server?
- Are the parties subject to a confidentiality agreement?
- How will any disputes be resolved?

CHAPTER **25**

Confidentiality Provisions and Trade Secret Protection

Protecting a party's confidential information and trade secrets is important if an entity is to enjoy a competitive advantage in the marketplace. The type of protection available and the protections an entity should seek will depend on the nature of the confidential information and the nature of the underlying intellectual property. Set forth in this chapter is a discussion of the different protections offered by proprietary information agreements and trade secret protection as well as the advantages and disadvantages of each.

Customers and vendors often have no choice but to disclose proprietary information to the other in the course of their negotiations. Disclosing such information can, for instance, be incidental to instructing the vendor to the specific requirements a product must meet or to specific functions a product must perform. In such cases, the execution of a proprietary information agreement is imperative to protect each party's proprietary information.

Trade secrets and confidential information are not synonymous. *See, e.g., Warner-Lambert Co. v. Execuquest Corp.*, 427 Mass. 46, 48–49 (1998) (confidential information is protectable even when it does not qualify as a trade secret); *Jet Spray Cooler, Inc. v. Crampton*, 361 Mass. 835, 839–40 (1972) ("confidential information is not limited to technical trade secrets"); *Dynamics Research Corp. v. Analytic Scis. Corp.*, 9 Mass. App. Ct. 254, 273 n.23 (1980). Specifically, trade secrets are a subset of confidential information. While a "trade secret" will always be considered "confidential information," not all confidential information will meet the definition of a trade secret. Common grounds for not satisfying the requirements for being a trade secret include information that may not derive economic value from being kept secret, or the owner may have failed to take reasonable steps to maintain the secrecy of the confidential information.

Many practitioners fail to recognize the difference between a trade secret and confidential information. "Trade Secrets" are usually statutorily defined and relate to a "process or device for continuous use in the operation of a business" while "Confidential Information" is generally considered to relate to a single or ephemeral event that retains its value for a short period of time. *Brown v. Rollet Bros. Trucking Co., Inc.*, 291 S.W.2d 766, 779 (Mo. App. 2009); *see also Dynamics Research Corp. v. Analytic Scis. Corp.*, 9 Mass. App. Ct. 254, 273 n.23 (1980) ("Not every commercial secret . . . qualifies as a trade secret. It is well known that in business most matters are considered as confidential; however, only secrets affording a demonstrable competitive advantage may be properly considered as trade secrets.").

A confidentiality obligation may also arise implicitly through the relationship and interactions of the parties. *See e.g., Burten v. Milton Bradley Co.*, 763 F.2d 463 (1st Cir. 1985); *Daniels Health Sci., LLC v. Vascular Health Sci.*, LLC, 710 F.3d 579 (5th Cir. 2013).

A. Proprietary Information Clauses and Agreements (§ 12)

1. General

(a) Use of Proprietary Information Agreements to Protect Confidential Information and Trade Secrets

Proprietary information agreements, also known as confidentiality agreements or non-disclosure agreements, are essential when dealing with intellectual property. While trade secrets are often protected under state trade secret laws, which are usually based on the Uniform Trade Secrets Act (UTSA), proprietary information agreements provide an added level of protection. In the absence of an express confidentiality agreement, a confidential relationship does not exist between a licensee and licensor. *Seatrax, Inc. v. Sonbeck Int'l, Inc.*, 200 F.3d 358 (5th Cir. 2000).

Proprietary information agreements provide the terms and conditions under which one party's proprietary information will be provided to another party, and the limitations on the use of such information by the receiving party. By executing a proprietary information agreement, the parties may agree upon what information will be exchanged; when the information will be returned to the disclosing party; the period of time during which the information will be kept confidential; and the right of the disclosing party to obtain equitable as well as monetary relief if the receiving party breaches its obligations under the agreement.

A proprietary information agreement may protect information a vendor or customer desires to keep confidential, but which may not constitute a trade secret. These agreements provide a level of contractual protection as opposed to statutory protection under the trade secret laws. Proprietary information agreements allow a party to obtain a level of protection not offered by trade secret laws. While Section 7(a) of the UTSA provides that it "displaces" all conflicting state law providing civil remedies for the misappropriation of trade secrets, Section 7(b) clearly states that it "does not affect contractual remedies, whether or not based upon misappropriation of a trade secret. . . ." *See IDX Sys. Corp. v. Epic Sys. Corp. et al.*, 285 F.3d 581 (7th Cir. 2002) (claim for breach of nondisclosure agreement not preempted by Wisconsin UTSA); *Celeritas Technologies, Ltd. v. Rockwell Int'l Corp.*, 150 F.3d 1354 (Fed. Cir. 1998) (California UTSA does not preempt plaintiff's claim for breach of nondisclosure agreement).

One commentator believes that if the breach of contract/nondisclosure claim simply restates a party's obligation not to disclose trade secrets, the court may view such claim as being preempted by Section 7(a) of the UTSA. Voltchenko, *Software*

Development Outsourcing: NDAs Go Beyond Intellectual Property Laws—but How Far? 20 COMPUTER L. ASS'N BULL. 98, 101 (No. 3, 2005). Thus, a proprietary information agreement can potentially prevent two customers from comparing their respective relationship with a licensor or exchanging any information that falls outside the definition of a trade secret. The breach of a party's confidentiality obligations does not equate to trade secret misappropriation. *See SIS LLC v. Stoneridge Holdings, Inc.et al.*, 2021 WL 2650355 (N.D. Ga. May 28, 2021).

Most vendors insist on using their template nondisclosure agreement, arguing that it will be quicker to do so and allow the vendor to maintain uniformity in its contractual obligations. Vendors often respond to a customer's request to sign the customer's nondisclosure agreement by saying the approval process will take longer because legal will have to review the non-disagreement and potentially negotiate its terms. An exception arises when a customer issues an RFP and the vendor must sign the licensee's nondisclosure agreement to receive the RFP. In such situations, the vendor should ensure that the customer's nondisclosure agreement protects the vendor's information not only during the RFP process but after the contract has been awarded. This is especially important during the RFP process, as the vendor does not want the customer to disclose its confidential information, including its pricing and methodologies, to other bidders in the RFP process.

Prudent parties should only sign nondisclosure agreements when truly needed to avoid creating unnecessary risk from an inadvertent disclosure. Productive conversations can he had exchanging only public information. The parties should never acknowledge that information is confidential unless it is truly confidential.

(b) Practical Considerations

While it is not required that nondisclosure provisions governing the parties' confidentiality obligations be set forth in a separate agreement from the license agreement, it is preferable to utilize a separate and distinct agreement. A separate agreement avoids any claim that the parties' confidentiality obligations do not survive the termination of the agreement which is especially important for the vendor. Further, distinct agreements are usually broader and more comprehensive than the confidentiality language contained in many agreements. A distinct nondisclosure agreement may be appropriate where there will be many stages of a particular project and the parties want to have one agreement govern the relationship throughout the many stages.

To limit the potential for misappropriation of a party's confidential information, the parties should not disclose confidential information at an initial meeting. Only after the parties have determined their interest in entering into a potential transaction should confidential information be disclosed. Doing so will reduce the amount of information disclosed and limit the risk of misappropriation or inadvertent disclosure.

Prudent entities should customize each confidentiality agreement to reflect the nature of the contemplated relationship. For example, a confidentiality agreement with a vendor whose product may be incorporated into a party's own product may grant the receiving party greater leeway to use the confidential information in comparison to a confidentiality agreement executed with a customer, which may contain tighter limits on the use of the confidential information.

(c) Utilizing Unilateral or Bilateral Agreements

Proprietary information agreements may be unilateral or bilateral. A unilateral agreement protects only one party's information, while a bilateral agreement protects both parties' information. (See Forms M.1.3 and M.1.5 for model unilateral and bilateral proprietary information agreements). Given that it is likely that both parties will be exchanging confidential information, it is prudent to sign a bilateral agreement.

Some parties seek to limit their potential liability by only entering into unilateral nondisclosure agreements that protect their confidential information and not the information of the other party. Doing so avoids the risk of being wrongfully accused of using such party's confidential information or improperly disclosing it to others. Thus, a prudent party should accept third party confidential information only when necessary and then only to the extent necessary. At the same time, they should instruct the other party not to provide them with any confidential information. This is often impractical, however as in almost every licensing/SaaS transaction, confidential information will be disclosed by both parties. The vendor will disclose its pricing, methodologies and intellectual property while the customer will likely disclose its business goals, employee names and its own intellectual property.

These parties often proclaim that they do not want to receive the other party's confidential information and that the other party must seek their consent prior to disclosing such party's confidential information. Any information disclosed to such party without its consent will not be considered confidential. Often the party taking this position is a large company that believes that it cannot adequately protect the other party's information. This argument is specious, however, as each party should agree to protect and acknowledge the confidential nature of the other's information. A more likely reason is that these companies want to avoid a claim by a smaller disclosing party that the receiving party's intellectual property was developed from the disclosing party's intellectual property. Prohibiting disclosure reduces the risk of any potential misappropriation claim by the disclosing party.

Another concern in executing a unilateral nondisclosure agreement arises when the disclosing party is disclosing information which is subject to a separate independent nondisclosure agreement with a third party. Such information may lose its confidential status under the third-party nondisclosure agreement as a common exclusion from an obligation of confidentiality if confidential information is disclosed to others without an obligation of confidentiality. See, e.g., Form M.1.5§ 4(d) and Chapter 28.A.2(c) below.

(d) Licensee Concerns

Licensees should be cognizant that a licensor will often disclose trade secrets as part of the deliverable work and that the risk exists that the trade secrets disclosed by the licensor to the licensee may have been misappropriated from a third party. Cases of trade secret infringement or misappropriation arise out of criminal acts, such as trespass and larceny against the premises or property of another, usually a direct competitor. Software engineers and programmers often use tool kits which they have memorized or retain in their personal files. They consider stock routines to handle common programming exercises, such as input/ output, disk access, data capture, and graphics generators, to be the building blocks of their work. The suggestion that such software would be proprietary to the entity that paid the development costs associated with the routines is often a radical departure from what they consider fair and equitable. The fact that they may be subject to confidentiality and invention assignment agreements does not always change their point of view on this issue.

Consequently, licensees should exercise caution when selecting licensors and vendors to avoid unwittingly committing trade secret misappropriation from the licensor's previous customers. The licensor should be interviewed and screened to ensure that its previous engagements did not involve the licensee's direct competitors or products likely to tempt the licensor/contractor into taking shortcuts by replicating prior work. The licensor should be cautioned against using stock routines, and its reputation within the industry should be verified. The licensee should obtain a representation and warranty from the licensor that the deliverables will not include the intellectual property of any third party and that the licensor will indemnify the licensee for all damages incurred by the licensee for the breach of any such warranty. Similarly, if the customer licenses any intellectual property to the licensor for use in the deliverables, the customer should indemnify the licensor for any intellectual property infringement.

(e) Judicial Interpretation

Courts tend to interpret confidentiality agreements strictly. *See Rainbow Nails Enterprises, Inc. v. Maybelline, Inc.*, 93 F. Supp. 808 (E.D. Mich. 2000) (failure to label information "confidential" as required by agreement negates confidentiality obligation); *Confold Pacific v. Polaris Industries*, 433 F.3d 952 (7th Cir. 2006) (claim by plaintiff for unjust enrichment and breach of confidentiality agreement denied where title, preamble, and merger clause all indicated limited nature of NDA and information in dispute was provided to defendant two months after NDA was executed and was not contemplated at time of initial discussions).

For a more detailed discussion, *see* Bowden, *Drafting and Negotiating Effective Confidentiality Agreements*, 14 CORP. COUNS. REV. 155 (Nov. 1995).

(f) Monitoring Compliance

Protection efforts do not end with the execution of the nondisclosure agreement. A disclosing party should send the receiving party annual notices reminding such party of its confidentiality obligations and the requirement that third-party consultants must execute a nondisclosure agreement directly with the disclosing party prior to receiving the disclosing party's confidential information.

(g) Corporate Confidentiality Policies

Both parties should review their internal policies relating to the receipt of confidential information prior to receiving the other party's confidential information. At a minimum, a receiving party must use "reasonable efforts" to protect another party's confidential information. Without the proper standards in place, a receiving party risks significant liability.

A receiving party should have a very specific, detailed written policy regarding the protection of a third party's confidential information. The policy should contain prohibitions on the reproduction of information and the safeguards required to keep the information confidential. These limitations may include limiting dissemination of confidential information toa need-to-know basis; keeping written records of who accessed such information; securing it at all times, not discussing the information in public areas, and limiting access to those areas where the information is stored. Individuals with access to confidential information should be required to reaffirm their agreement to comply with company policies regarding third-party information on an annual basis, and the company should circulate semi-annual reminders to its employees and consultants. Finally, the company should document in writing all of its efforts and policies.

For a general discussion, *see* Barish & Caslin, *Before Signing Your Next Nondisclosure Agreement, Count to 10*, 24 ACC DOCKET 24 (Jan. 2006). For a general overview of proprietary information agreements, *see* Vizy, *Confidentiality Agreements*, 227 COM. L. ADVISOR 8 (Nov. 2006), and for a general checklist for giving, receiving or exchanging confidential information, *see* 88 FORMS & CHECKLISTS BI-MONTHLY 37 (July/Aug. 2012).

(h) Including Trade Secret Protection Under Non-disclosure Agreements

Many entities will not agree to include trade secrets under their non-disclosure agreements, especially when executed in connection with the parties' initial business discussions. They do so in the belief there is no need to disclose trade secrets during preliminary discussions given the obligation to keep trade secrets confidential in perpetuity and significant liability if such trade secrets are disclosed. This is especially true where the proposed non-disclosure agreement does not require the disclosing party to identify the trade secrets being disclosed.

Those entitles that do agree to disclose or exchange trade secrets often insist on executing a separate agreement to address the disclosure of trade secrets (i.e., a technology transfer agreement) with specific provisions governing the disclosure of trade secrets including:

- clearly identifying the trade secrets being disclosed
- restrictions on accessing the trade secrets
- how the trade secrets may be used
- any labeling requirements
- those measures that must be taken to protect the trade secrets disclosed

2. Principal Provisions of a Nondisclosure Agreement

Set forth below is a brief overview of the principal provisions often found in nondisclosure agreements. The actual provisions contained in an agreement will depend on the nature of the transaction and the nature and sensitivity of the information being disclosed.

(a) Defining the Parties to the Agreement

The nondisclosure agreement should carefully define the contracting parties. From the disclosing party's perspective, the disclosing party wants to tightly limit the disclosure of its confidential information. To that end, the definition of the "receiving party" should not include its affiliates, consultants, contractors, agents, directors, etc. Preferably, disclosure should be limited to those employees identified by name or, alternatively, to those employees who need to receive the confidential information to allow the receiving party to achieve the purpose of the disclosure.

Confidentiality agreements that encompass a party's affiliates should be carefully considered in light of any covenants in the agreement or other legal obligations such as sanctions and export laws. For example, if the confidentiality agreement contains a covenant prohibiting the parties from hiring the other party's employees or restricting the reassignment of employees with knowledge of the confidential information, those covenants will apply to each party's affiliates.

If affiliates may receive confidential information, the agreement should clearly provide that the disclosing party may recover its damages from the counter-party for breaches by the counter-party's affiliates.

(b) Defining and Identifying the Confidential Information

The parties should carefully consider what information is considered to be "confidential" under the agreement, as collateral information may also be considered confidential. For example, the vendor may consider its pricing confidential and would not want the customer shopping the vendor's price or approach. The receiving party, however, may want a very narrow definition to limit its risk form an inadvertent disclosure. Similarly, some vendors seek to classify customer feedback and evaluations as confidential information to prevent the publication of negative benchmarking results or information. A licensee, however, may want the right to discuss this information with third parties such as other vendors it is considering working with and thus should resist classifying such information as confidential information.

Some parties seek to include a "catch-all" provision that any information a reasonable person would consider to be confidential will be considered confidential information. Such language creates ambiguity and in the event of a dispute each party will likely argue that a reasonable person should have known that the information it disclosed was confidential even if it was not marked. Thus, many parties require that all confidential information be marked as such to be protected under the agreement. See Chapter 28.A.(2)(c) for a more detailed discussion.

From the disclosing party's perspective, the definition of confidential information should be drafted broadly to include present and future disclosures, derivative works created from the disclosed materials, and information that may not be marked as confidential but which a reasonable person would assume to be confidential. If drafted too broadly, however, a court may not enforce the agreement.

From the receiving party's perspective, the definition should be narrowly drawn, excluding information disclosed prior to the execution of the nondisclosure agreement, as it is difficult for the receiving party to track information that may have been previously disclosed, especially if the receiving party did not realize it was under an obligation of confidentiality. A narrow definition limits the receiving party's risk of a misappropriation claim. To further limit risk, some receiving parties require the disclosing party to receive their consent prior to providing the confidential information to the receiving party.

Many parties seek to use the definition of "trade secrets" under Section 1839(c) of the Economic Espionage Act of 1996 to define confidential information in their confidentiality agreements in the belief that, in the event of a breach of the agreement, they may be able to interest the U.S. Attorney's office in pursuing an action against the breaching party. See Chapter 28.B.5 below for a discussion of the Economic Espionage Act of 1996.

From the licensor's perspective, the nondisclosure agreement should clearly identify the software the licensee (including the licensee's authorized consultants) is authorized to access, examine, or use. Failing to clearly define the confidential information may later hinder the disclosing party's efforts to enforce its rights under the agreement.

(c) Exclusions from a Party's Confidentiality Obligations

Common exclusions from a party's obligation of confidentiality include:

1. Information already known to the receiving party at the time of disclosure;
2. Information independently developed by the receiving party without knowledge of the confidential information, as shown by documentary evidence;
3. Information that is publicly available;
4. Information received from a third party without an obligation of confidentiality; and
5. Confidential Information disclosed pursuant to judicial or governmental order. See the discussion in Section (d) below.

The wording of each of these exclusions should be carefully negotiated to ensure they protect the respective party's interest. For example, if a receiving party is claiming the disclosing party's confidential information was known to it at the time it was received, the receiving party should bear the burden of proof to show, by previously existing writings, that the information was already in its possession. Similarly, a party claiming it independently developed the confidential information should be obligated to prove that the information was developed without the use of the confidential information of the disclosing party.

From the receiving party's perspective, those exclusions requiring documentary evidence can be problematic, as there may not be documentary evidence to support the receiving party's claim. Although a party may be able to provide testimony as to how information may have been independently developed, the failure to provide documentary evidence may doom the receiving party's chances of success.

(d) Disclosures Required Pursuant to Judicial or Governmental Order

While the required disclosure of confidential information by court order or governmental agency is addressed in most nondisclosure agreements, most parties give little thought to these provisions, as they believe the likelihood of a court-ordered disclosure is small. While infrequent, court-ordered disclosures do arise, including through Freedom of Information Act (FOIA) requests. *See, e.g., Workday, Inc. v. Washington State University*, Case 2:19-cv-00433 (E.D. Wash. Dec. 30, 2019) (vendor sought injunctive relief against customer to prevent customer from complying with FOIA request for vendor's confidential information filed by vendor's competitor).

In the case of a judicially required disclosure, the party receiving the disclosure request should be required to:

- promptly notify the disclosing party so that the disclosing party can contest any potential order,
- cooperate with the disclosing party in its defense, and
- minimize any disclosure of the requested information.

While most agreements require the recipient of a court order to notify the disclosing party so that the disclosing party may contest the court order, the obligation to notify the disclosing party should not be absolute. In some cases, the recipient of the order is not permitted to disclose that it has received such a request. Thus, any obligation should be prefaced with the limitation: *to the extent permitted by law . . . .*

Some parties seek to require the receiving party to obtain the opinion of legal counsel that the release is required prior to releasing the requested information. This requirement can be burdensome and expensive; thus, a prudent party should seek to limit its obligations to "consulting" counsel and release such information on the advice of counsel. See model language below.

> *If a receiving party is requested or required to disclose any Confidential Information, then such receiving party shall, to the extent permitted by law, notify the disclosing party promptly of the request or requirement so that disclosing party, at its cost and expense, may seek an appropriate protective order or waive compliance with this Section __. If, in the absence of a protective order or receipt of a waiver hereunder, such receiving party is, on the advice of counsel, compelled to disclose* ***such Confidential Information, such receiving party may so disclose the Confidential Information****, provided that such receiving party shall use commercially reasonable efforts to obtain reliable assurance that confidential treatment shall be afforded to such Confidential Information.*

(e) Reducing Oral Disclosures to Writing

Most agreements provide that for any information to be considered proprietary and confidential, it must be marked as such. Further, any confidential information disclosed orally must be reduced to writing and submitted to the receiving party within x days of its disclosure. The intent of this requirement is to ensure that the receiving party is aware that the disclosing party considers such information to be confidential. An increasing number of parties have sought to include language in the underlying agreement to the effect that any information that the receiving party should have known by its nature to be confidential should be treated as confidential whether or not it has been marked. Many parties reject this broad language as subjective, creating uncertainty as to what is confidential and thus subject to the agreement's obligations.

The obligation to reduce all oral disclosures to writing and submit such writing to the receiving party within a set period of time, (i.e., 30 days) does not reflect the realities of working in a dynamic business environment where an entity's employees may not know or understand the entity's contractual obligations. Oral disclosures are often made by one technical resource to another and documenting the disclosure in a subsequent writing is unlikely to occur. Further, the parties are equally unlikely to remind each other that the information is confidential.

As such, many parties object to including such a requirement as the failure to reduce such disclosure to writing removes any obligation of confidentiality. *See Convolve, Inc. v. Compaq Computer Corp.*, 527 Fed. Appx. 910 (Fed. Cir. 2013) (failure to reduce disclosures to writing as required under the parties' nondisclosure agreement caused confidential information to lose alleged trade secret status). Even if the parties do confirm the confidentiality of the information, the writing will likely not include all aspects of their conversation and may be insufficient if challenged in a dispute.

The possibility of a party's confidential information not being protected because its employees failed to create a writing is a strong argument for convincing most parties to remove the requirement from the nondisclosure agreement. If a party insists on including such a provision, many attorneys include a caveat to the effect that even if a written confirmation is not provided, all information disclosed in such communications shall be considered confidential information. An alternate qualification is to provide that oral information will remain confidential if such information would be considered confidential by a reasonable person.

A related issue is in how much detail must the disclosing party describe the disclosed information? There is often tension between specificity (i.e., to ensure that a particular item is not missed and thus is protected) and generality (i.e., to ensure that everything that was discussed is protected, even if not recorded in notes/minutes of the meeting). Prudent parties will seek a balance that clearly identifies the information requiring protection but avoids the necessity to provide endless detail.

Checklist for oral and visual disclosures:

- Are oral disclosures covered under the agreement?
- Are visual disclosures (i.e., a visual presentation such as a PowerPoint presentation) covered under the agreement?
- If so, how will they be tracked such that the disclosing party can prove that the information was disclosed to the receiving party?
- How should the disclosing party notify the receiving party that an oral or virial disclosures is considered confidential information?
  - Via email
  - Via registered or overnight mail
- Who should the notice be sent to?

(f) Marking Requirements

Many agreements require that any information provided to the other party must be marked "proprietary" or "confidential" in order to receive protection under the agreement. The intent is to place the receiving party on notice as to what information the disclosing party considers to be confidential and which information is not confidential. Marking each document disclosed presents a challenge as employees may not remember to mark every document as "confidential."

To avoid this challenge, many agreements provide that all software shall be considered proprietary and confidential, regardless of whether or not it is marked as such. This is important because, although most agreements require confidential and proprietary information to be marked, the media (CD, DVD, or tape) containing the software is often not marked by the programmer who may be unfamiliar with the confidentiality agreement or the importance of marking the media.). *See also Hoover Panel Systems, Inc. v. Hat Contract Inc.*, 2019 WL 2743589 (N.D. Tex. May 9, 2019) (failure to mark confidential information resulted in dismissal of breach of contract/trade secret misappropriation claim).

To avoid this issue, companies create custom labels preprinted with the term "Proprietary and Confidential, ©Copyright [Company Name YEAR]. All rights reserved," so that the company is protected if its employees fail to properly mark the relevant materials. The disclosing party should ensure that all documents have a watermark or automatically generated footer stating "Proprietary and Confidential" which protects the disclosing party in the event its employees fail to mark each document that is disclosed to the other party.

Further, although counterintuitive, licensors should insist that any open-source software provided to the licensee be considered the confidential information of the licensor, as the licensor may be able to claim copyright protection.

For a detailed discussion, *see* Davidson & Holloway, *Protecting Trade Secrets in an Open Source Environment*, 23 COMP. & INTERNET LAW. 1 (Jan. 2006).

Model language follows:

> *This document contains confidential information belonging to [Vendor/Customer] or one of its subsidiaries. This information is protected by civil and criminal trade secrecy law and such information is intended only for the use of the recipients named above. Disclosure of any information included herein to anyone else is expressly prohibited. If you are not the intended recipient, you are hereby notified that any disclosure, copying, distribution, use, or the taking of any action in reliance on the contents of this information is unauthorized and strictly prohibited.*

Conversely, some parties seek to affirmatively state that they may freely use any information that is not marked "confidential." Agreeing to this language creates a significant risk for the disclosing party in the event it fails to properly mark any information that it considers confidential. The following language illustrates this point.

> *Notwithstanding the foregoing, it is expressly contemplated by the parties to this Agreement that any information, other than Confidential Information, provided, given or made available to the Recipient by the Discloser may be used by the Recipient without any license, fee or charge or obligation of any sort whatsoever, unless otherwise expressly stated in writing. It is the express intent of the parties to protect Recipient from any later claim by the Discloser of any right or claim to compensation for such information. Any compensation for any such information or claim shall be payable only to the extent specifically provided for in writing.*

(g) Method of Disclosure

The agreement should also provide that all information be considered confidential regardless of how it is disclosed (e.g., in writing, electronically, orally, or visually). Some agreements require a disclosing party to identify any confidential information, so that there is not inadvertent disclosure by the receiving party, especially to information that is orally disclosed. In such instances, the disclosing party would be required to identify in writing within a set time period (e.g., 10 days after disclosure) any orally disclosed information as confidential.

(h) Purpose/Use

The nondisclosure agreement should specifically provide that the confidential information may be used solely for the permitted use and for no other purpose. The permitted use should be explicitly stated and narrowly drawn. The failure to restrict the receiving party's use of the confidential information to a clearly stated purpose may allow the receiving party to use the information for any other purposes it deems appropriate, provided it does not disclose the information. *Texas Advanced Optoelectronic Solutions, Inc. v. Renesas Electronics America, Inc.*, 895 F.3d 1304 (Fed. Cir. 2018) (confidentiality agreement limited competitor to evaluating the business and financial condition of the target in potential acquisition; use of information in a "build vs. buy" analysis which resulted in competitor building its own product did not violate confidentiality agreement or constitute trade secret misappropriation). Prudent parties should prohibit the receiving party from reverse engineering the disclosing party's confidential information to understand its products or to create competing products. *See Aqua Connect, Inc. v. Code Rebel, LLC et al.*, 2012 WL 1535769 (C.D. Cal. Feb. 13, 2012) (reverse-engineering software in violation of license agreement did not constitute trade secret misappropriation).

At the same time, the inclusion of a use restriction may prevent the receiving party from pursuing other business opportunities. *See Goodrich Capital, LLC v. Vector Capital Corp.*, 2012 WL 4123401 (S.D.N.Y. June 26, 2012). Therefore, prudent parties should include a provision in their nondisclosure agreements whereby each party acknowledges that the receiving party may be developing similar technology independent of the disclosures contemplated under the nondisclosure agreement and each party is free to continue such development efforts. Subsection (t) below for a further discussion.

A limited purpose will also serve to limit access and use of the information to those employees with the "need to know." To avoid potential disputes associated with a use restriction, the parties may want to include an additional clause providing that nothing in the nondisclosure agreement prohibits the receiving party from entering into other transactions provided it does use the confidential information.

(i) Employee Access to Confidential Information

Some disclosing parties seek to require the employees of the receiving party to execute nondisclosure agreements if they are to access the confidential information. Doing so is not practical, and unnecessary, as in most cases, the receiving party's employees have executed a non-disclosure agreement with their employer as a condition of employment requiring them to keep all information received in the course of their employment confidential. Further, allowing employees into contractual privity with the disclosing party exposes the employee to personal liability. To avoid an undue burden on the receiving party, most parties will accept the confidentiality agreements the employees executed when they began employment with the receiving party as sufficient to protect the disclosing party's interests. Nonetheless, the disclosing party should review the template agreement to make sure it provides adequate protection for its confidential information and request copies of each employee's confidentiality agreement. See, e.g., Form L.8. Another alternative is to have employees who access confidential information acknowledge their confidentiality obligations under their agreement with their employer.

Disclosure to employees should be limited to the employees with a need to know, to limit disclosure of the confidential information.

If the information is highly confidential and provides a competitive advantage in the market, the disclosing party should require that employees of the receiving party with access to the confidential information be prohibited from working on projects for the disclosing party's competitors. This prohibition may be problematic for the receiving party if it has a small number of employees, as it will restrict the receiving party's ability to freely staff its employees in the most efficient manner.

(j) Acknowledgment of Trade Secret Status

Of critical importance to the vendor is an acknowledgment by the customer that the vendor's software is a trade secret and an agreement not to disclose such trade secrets. At the same time, the vendor should be required to protect the confidentiality of the licensee's trade secrets, including the way the licensee operates its computer system and any information about the licensee's own customers. Too often, licensees fail to execute a mutual nondisclosure agreement focusing solely on the vendor's confidential information and not on its own. See Chapter 28.B for a further discussion of this issue.

(k) Standard of Care

Most agreements provide for either a "strict liability" standard or "commercially reasonable" standard for the protection of confidential information; that is, some agreements provide that the receiving party *will not* disclose any confidential information, while others provide the receiving party will use the same standard of care to protect its own confidential information but no less than a reasonable standard of care.

(i) Reasonable Standard of Care

The first creates a strict liability standard, creating liability on the receiving party's behalf if information is disclosed, while the latter requires the disclosing party to prove the receiving party did not exercise a reasonable standard of care to find it liable.

Disclosing parties should carefully consider whether to accept a "reasonable standard of care" standard as it is ambiguous and open to interpretation. *See, e.g., Religious Tech. Ctr. v. Netcom On-Line Commc'n. Servs.*, Inc., 923 F. Supp. 1231, 1253 (N.D. Cal. 1995). ("Reasonable efforts can include advising employees of the existence of a trade secret, limiting access to the information on a 'need to know basis,' requiring employees to sign confidentiality agreements, keeping secret documents under lock.") Any breach of a party's confidentiality obligations should be tied to the respective standard contained in the agreement.

(ii) Strict Liability Standard

A strict liability standard imposes an absolute prohibition on the disclosure of the confidential information:

> *The Receiving Party will not disclose and will not permit the disclosure of the Confidential Information received from the Disclosing Party to any third party.*

From the disclosing party's perspective, anything less than a strict liability standard places the disclosing party at risk. This is especially true in a cloud computing environment. See Chapter 28.A.6 (ii), and (iii). A "commercially reasonable" standard or a "same standard of care" standard is so amorphous that it may be difficult to enforce the agreement except in the most egregious circumstances.

The receiving party, however, must carefully consider accepting a strict liability standard, especially if it is responsible for unauthorized disclosures made by its employees, consultants, or agents. This is especially true in a cloud environment as no system is totally secure; agreeing to such language may create an unintended and unrealized security obligation. Any such breach could create significant liability for the receiving party with little basis for a defense.

(l) Third-Party Access to Confidential Information

From the licensor's perspective, third-party access to the confidential information presents the greatest risk to the disclosure or misappropriation of a party's confidential information. Most licensors seek to prohibit the licensee from disclosing the licensor's confidential information to any person other than those licensee employees that have a need to know. Many licensees are hesitant to accept this position, arguing that third-party consultants are common in the information technology industry and that the licensee will have to make the information available to its third-party consultants.

Many agreements seek to avoid disclosure by prohibiting disclosure to anyone but the receiving party's employees on a need-to-know basis. These restrictions may be unacceptable to a receiving party if its third-party consultants need access to the information. At the same time, the disclosing party has a legitimate concern, as the third-party consultants may be competitors of the disclosing party and may have little incentive not to later disclose or use the confidential information. Thus, the disclosing party should insist that the confidential information not be disclosed to third parties unless they are not competitors and have signed a nondisclosure agreement directly with the disclosing party. See Chapter 28.A.2 below for a more detailed discussion of third-party access to a party's confidential information.

Some parties seek to avoid this issue by including a clause in the license requiring the licensor to acknowledge that the licensee may allow third parties access to the licensor's software or deliverables. See § 41. The licensor should carefully consider whether to accept the inclusion of this type of clause. Licensors should never agree to the disclosure of their confidential information to a third party by their customer without the right to directly enforce their rights against this party (i.e., become a third-party beneficiary to any confidentiality agreement between the customer and third party). See Chapter 6.K. and § 40.

Many licensors insist that all third-party consultants who receive access to a party's confidential information must execute a nondisclosure agreement directly with such party. Doing so places the licensor in direct contractual privity with the third-party contractor and allows the licensor to directly enforce the nondisclosure agreement against the consultant. These agreements should include an acknowledgement that the information disclosed by the licensor to the consultant are the trade secrets of the licensor and must be kept confidential. Some licensors also prohibit the consultant from providing consulting services to any competitor of the licensor or any client of the licensor in the future.

When dealing with third-party consultants, the disclosing party must carefully monitor the consultant's receipt and access to the licensor's confidential information. No information should be disclosed to the consultant until it has signed the disclosing party's nondisclosure agreement. Further, the disclosing party should follow up with the consultant if the consultant has not returned the executed nondisclosure agreement within a short period of time to ensure the consultant has not started work without executing the nondisclosure agreement.

(m) Term of the Agreement and the Period of Confidentiality

(i) Period of Confidentiality

A significant issue for both parties is the period for which the receiving party must keep the information received confidential. This period is different from the term of the agreement, as the obligation of confidentiality should, in most cases, survive the termination of the agreement. To that end, the parties should specifically state that the confidentiality provisions and any other provisions necessary to adjudicate a dispute survive the termination of the confidentiality agreement.

Careful consideration should be given to the length of any confidentiality obligation. Many confidentiality agreements provide for a definitive period of confidentiality, such as three to five years from the date of last disclosure. Some parties impose an artificial term of five or seven years, or until the occurrence of a particular event (i.e., for so long as licensee is using the software) to keep information confidential, when in fact the information may remain confidential well after the expiration of such term or the occurrence of the cited event.

The disclosing party usually seeks a longer confidentiality period while the receiving party seeks a shorter period.

Some agreements, however, do not state a period, preferring that the period of confidentiality be subject to the statute of limitations under the laws of the relevant jurisdiction. This approach, however, may create confusion as to the actual termination date and place greater importance on the agreement's governing law, as the statutes of limitations vary greatly among the different states.

Many agreements provide that either party may terminate the agreement —but not the parties' confidentiality obligations—at any time, and that the parties have no obligation to disclose any confidential information to the other party.

(ii) Trade Secrets

Prudent parties provide that the disclosed information shall remain confidential for a stated period of time but, in the case of trade secrets, for as long as the disclosed information remains a trade secret of the disclosing party. This protects a disclosing party from the risk of losing trade secret protection for its confidential information at the end of the stated term. *See, e.g., Silicon Image, Inc. v. Analogix Semiconductor, Inc.*, 2008 WL 166950 (N.D. Cal. Jan. 17, 2008); *DB Riley, Inc. v. AB Engineering Corp*, 977 F. Supp. 84, 91 (D. Mass. 1997) (Trade secrets protected under confidentiality agreement with 10-year confidentiality obligation lost trade secret status upon expiration of 10-year period, as owner did not exercise reasonable efforts to protect trade secret.); *Structured Capital Solutions, LLC v. Commerzbank AG*, 177 F. Supp. 3d 816 (S.D.N.Y. 2016) (trade secret status does not apply to information disclosed under a time limited non-disclosure agreement); *ECT Int'l, Inc. v. Zwerlein*, 597 NW.2d 479, 484-85 (Wis. Ct. App. 1999) *See also DeVere Co., Inc. v. McColley, et al.*, 2014 WL 6473513 (W.D. Wis. Nov. 8, 2014) (rejecting employer's request to enjoin former employee's use of employer's trade secrets, as employee's nondisclosure agreement had expired). *See, e.g.*, Form M.1.5 § 7 and Form M.1.6 § 10.

A receiving party should carefully consider the risks of agreeing to keep the information confidential for as long as the information remains a trade secret, as a party may not know what information a party considers to be a trade secret and how long a disclosing party considers the information to be a trade secret.

> *The Parties acknowledge that their obligations with regard to the Confidential Information of the Disclosing Party shall remain in effect for the longer of: a)three (3) years after the disclosure of such information to the Recipient, or b) three (3) years after the last day of the period that applicable law shall protect such Confidential Information as a trade secret.* ***However, the Parties acknowledge that their obligations under this Agreement with regard to the trade secrets of the Disclosing Party that are part of any Confidential Information shall remain in effect for as long as such information shall remain a trade secret under applicable law.***

(iii) Other Intellectual Property

While nondisclosure agreements impose certain confidentiality obligations, intellectual property laws impose their own obligations. Intellectual property is still protected after the period of confidentiality expires under the copyright and patent laws and potentially trade secret protection. The owner of the intellectual property can always bring a claim for misuse of its intellectual property, even if it cannot bring a breach of contract claim under the parties' nondisclosure agreement.

(n) Return or Destruction of the Confidential Information

Some disclosing parties seek to include requirements on how the receiving party will store and protect the confidential information. Although uncommon, such provisions may be justified based on the sensitivity of the confidential information.

Most agreements provide that the confidential information must be returned to the disclosing party or destroyed at the end of the term. The parties should carefully consider any requirement to certify that all copies of any confidential information have been returned to the disclosing party or destroyed. See Form M.2.2 for a model certification. In addition to the disclosed information, the agreement should also require the parties to return all derivative information developed from the disclosing party's confidential information and any information stored in an electronic format. It may not be possible for a party to return all confidential information in its possession such as information contained within electronic records that have been retained in the receiving party's backup records. A common exception is to recognize the information contained in electronic records will not be erased but is still subject to the party's confidentiality obligations.

> *Notwithstanding the foregoing, neither Party is required to delete, erase or destroy any electronically stored Confidential Information that has been saved to a back-up file or other electronic medium in accordance with the Party's standard electronic back-up or archive practices; provided, however that any such retained Confidential Information shall remain subject to the terms of this Agreement.*

Some parties believe that it is better to allow each party to retain one copy of the confidential information it received from the disclosing party. The reasons for doing so include the need to meet the receiving party's audit requirements, and the receiving party's desire to know what information it received to defend itself from a subsequent claim by the disclosing party that it misappropriated the confidential information. If copies are retained, they should be kept in a single archive in the office of the party's outside counsel to ensure the information is not later disseminated.

PRACTICE POINT:

If a party is seeking to retain the disclosing party's confidential information after contract termination, it should identify the specific information it proposes to retain and the reason for retaining such information. Model language to this effect follows:

> *At the request of Discloser, Recipient agrees to return to Discloser, or destroy and verify destruction in writing, all written, tangible or otherwise accessible material in any form (including electronic media such as computer diskettes, CD-ROM, electronic copies or any material resident in the hard or external drive of any computer) in its possession containing or reflecting any Confidential Information (including all copies, summaries, excerpts, extracts or other reproductions). Each party may retain copies of the other party's Confidential Information required for compliance with its recordkeeping or quality assurance requirements ("Archival Confidential Information"), provided that*
>
> *(i) Archival Confidential Information shall be limited to emails,*
> *(ii) Archival Confidential Information shall be further limited to Confidential Information collected by periodic and autonomous and security backup functions,*
> *(iii) Archival Confidential Information shall be accessible only by IT (information technology) security teams, and*
> *(iv) Archival Confidential Information shall in any event remain subject to the terms of this Agreement.*

Prior to making this certification, the receiving party must ensure that any "soft" copies have been identified and destroyed. This would include reviewing all archived e-mail files and removing such documents. This could be a burdensome task as most entities back up their e-mail files on a nightly basis and often store these files for months if not years. Thus, to comply, the receiving party would have to review the contents of each of these files. Similarly, if this information was circulated to the receiving party's offices around the world, this search would have to be repeated many times. To avoid this challenge, the receiving party should carefully consider whether to agree to this requirement and should limit the distribution of any confidential information it receives. Further, the parties should carefully consider whether to exchange confidential information in an electronic format. Exchanging information in hard copy will eliminate the problem of identifying and destroying all electronic copies but from a practical standpoint unrealistic.

The language below addresses the issue of the unintentional retention of electronic copies and the difficulty of purging such copies from the receiving party's computer systems.

> *; provided, however, this obligation to return or destroy such Confidential Information and copies thereof does not extend to automatically generated computer back-up or archival copies generated in the ordinary course of Receiving Party's information systems procedures, provided that Receiving Party shall make no further use of such copies.*

> *Notwithstanding the foregoing, to the extent it would be unreasonably costly or cumbersome, the Receiving Party shall not be required to delete intangible copies of Confidential Information that have been made a part of the Receiving Party's (or its representatives') routine systems' back-up files and/or procedures which are not readily accessible to the Receiving Party or its representatives, provided that any intangible copies which are retained pursuant to this sentence shall be deleted or destroyed in accordance with routine procedures and shall remain subject to the obligations of confidentiality and non-use until the date of deletion or destruction.*

(o) Disclaimer of Warranties/Accuracy of Information Disclosed

The disclosing party should include language in the nondisclosure agreement disclaiming any warranties as to the accuracy of the information disclosed and disclaiming any liability for any damages incurred by the receiving party as a result of its reliance on the information disclosed by the disclosing party. To the extent the receiving party is relying on the information, any applicable representations and warranties can be incorporated into the license agreement between the parties. The language below is illustrative of this concept.

> *Although the Confidential Information set forth herein is presented in good faith and believed to be correct as of the date hereof, neither party makes any representations or warranties as to the completeness or accuracy thereof. Confidential Information is supplied upon the condition that the persons receiving same will make their own determination as to its suitability for their purposes prior to use. In no event will either party be responsible for liability or damages of any nature whatsoever resulting from the use or reliance upon the Confidential Information.*

(p) Limitation of Liability

Some parties seek to include limitation of liability provisions, including a disclaimer of consequential damages in their nondisclosure agreement, arguing a waiver of punitive, consequential, special and indirect damages is justified given the possibility of an inadvertent breach where there are no direct damages. From the disclosing party's perspective, the disclosing party should never accept the exclusion of consequential damages, as in the event of a breach, the great majority of its damages may likely be consequential damages. Some parties seek to include a liquidated damages provision, but in most instances, it will be difficult to estimate the damages the disclosing party will incur in the event of a breach.

Because many confidentiality agreements are executed at the beginning of the sales process/a relationship, some parties argue that a consequential damages waiver in a mutual confidentiality agreement is appropriate, as highly confidential information will usually not be disclosed, and any software will be disclosed only after execution of a license agreement, which will most likely include protections for confidential information and trade secrets. If a party is concerned about the risks of receiving the other party's confidential information, it can limit the receipt and disclosure of such confidential information.

(q) Equitable Relief

Proprietary information agreements cannot prevent a receiving party from disclosing proprietary information received from the disclosing party. Rather, proprietary agreements should be viewed as providing a framework for enforcing the disclosing party's rights upon the receiving party's breach.

Every agreement should, therefore, include an acknowledgment of irreparable harm and that contract/monetary damages are an insufficient remedy as well as a provision for equitable relief, which would allow the injured party to obtain injunctive relief without prejudicing its rights to obtain other remedies. The acknowledgment should not be absolute but rather an acknowledgment that any breach *may* cause irreparable harm. Courts have recognized a contractual stipulation of irreparable harm as sufficient to meet the damages requirement necessary to obtain injunctive relief. *See Martin Marietta Materials v. Vulcan Materials,* 68 A.3d 1208, 1226 (Del. 2012) ("contractual stipulations as to irreparable harm alone suffice to establish that element for the purpose of issuing . . . injunctive relief."); *but see Kansas City Southern v. Grupo TMM, S.A.,* 2003 WL 22659332, at *5 (Del. Ch. Nov. 4, 2003) (". . . a contractual stipulation as to the irreparable nature of the harm that would result from a breach cannot limit this Court's discretion to decline to order injunctive relief. . . . If the facts plainly do not warrant a finding of irreparable harm, this Court is not required to ignore those facts, ... ") (citation and internal quotation marks omitted). The availability of equitable relief is very important, as it entitles an injured party to immediate relief when a breach of the proprietary information agreement occurs. This is especially important as monetary damages alone can be inadequate once proprietary information has been widely disseminated.

Most nondisclosure agreements include language that a party seeking injunctive relief will not be required to post a bond. Some parties believe, however, that it is not appropriate for either party to agree in advance to waive a bond based on the economic value of the subject matter, which could let one party try to prevent the other from using its valuable intellectual property based simply on an unsubstantiated claim. They argue that a bond reflects efforts by courts and statutes to create a balance between the rights of a party seeking protection and the rights of the party whose ability to do business could be affected.

> *The Receiving Party understands and acknowledges that any disclosure or use of any Confidential Information that is in violation of this Agreement* ***may*** *cause the Disclosing Party or Customer, as the case may be, irreparable harm, the extent of which would be difficult to ascertain and/or to quantify in monetary damages. Accordingly, the Disclosing Party shall have the right to seek temporary injunctive relief without the posting of a bond to prevent a breach of this Agreement and/or restrain any such further disclosure or misappropriation, until such time as the matter may be heard by a court of competent jurisdiction.*

(r) Indemnification

Some parties seek to include an indemnity in their agreements, which allows a party to recover otherwise unavailable damages, including legal fees, as well as having a lower burden of proof. Indemnification provisions, however, are inappropriate in most cases, as both parties may bring a breach of contract claim against the other. Indemnification is traditionally related to third-party claims brought against a party for which the party seeks indemnification from the indemnitor. Indemnification may be appropriate for those agreements addressing the storage and use of PHI and PII. See Chapter 22 for a more detailed discussion of the issues associated with data privacy and security. With most nondisclosure agreements, the disclosing party is disclosing its own confidential information, so indemnification (which typically addresses a third-party claim against the recipient) is not relevant or needed in a two-party agreement as the receiving party's remedy lies in a breach of contract claim. If the disclosing party is providing a third party's confidential information to the receiving party, an indemnification provision may be appropriate. In those cases, however, there will usually be an underlying agreement that contains both confidentiality and indemnification provisions.

As mentioned, in a number of unique situations an indemnity may be justified, especially where the disclosing party is disclosing a third party's confidential information, such as personally identifiable information (PII), or the information is covered by a nondisclosure agreement with the original discloser. An indemnity will provide an additional remedy distinct from a breach of contract claim.

In the event the parties agree to include an indemnification provision within the agreement, the indemnification should be subject to a cap and carefully drafted to define the nature and scope of the indemnity.

(s) Notification of Suspected Breach

Prudent parties seek to require the receiving party to notify the disclosing party in the event the receiving party believes the disclosing party's confidential information may have been compromised. They do so in the belief that if a potential breach is identified and promptly disclosed, the necessary remedial actions can be taken to mitigate any losses or damage arising from the improper disclosure. The receiving party should also be required to remedy the breach or unauthorized use.

> *Each party will: (a) notify the other party promptly of any material unauthorized possession, use or knowledge, or attempt thereof, of the other party's Confidential Information*

by any person that may become known to such party; (b) promptly furnish to the other party details of the unauthorized possession, use or knowledge, or attempt thereof, and use reasonable efforts to assist the other party in investigating or preventing the recurrence of any unauthorized possession, use or knowledge, or attempt thereof, of Confidential Information; (c) use reasonable efforts to cooperate with the other party in any litigation and investigation against third parties deemed necessary by the other party to protect its proprietary rights; and (d) promptly use reasonable efforts to prevent a recurrence of any such unauthorized possession, use or knowledge of Confidential Information.

(t) Development of Competing Products

One concern in receiving a party's confidential information is that the disclosing party may falsely believe that the receiving party used the disclosed information to develop a competing product or that the confidentiality agreement prohibits the development of a competing product. Thus, if the parties are potential competitors or in the same industry, it is prudent to include language acknowledging that the parties may develop competing products without use of the disclosed information.

The disclosing party acknowledges that the receiving party of the Proprietary Information may currently or in the future be developing information internally, or receiving information from other parties, that is similar to the Proprietary Information. Accordingly, nothing in this Agreement will be construed as a representation or agreement that the Recipient will not develop or have developed for its products, concepts, systems or techniques that are similar to or compete with the products, concepts, systems or techniques contemplated by or embodied in the Proprietary Information, provided that the receiving party does not violate any of its obligations under this Agreement in connection with such development.

(u) Disclosure of Trade Secrets

Given the significant value of trade secrets and the higher standard of protection required to maintain trade secret status, many disclosing parties seek to exclude trade secrets from the period of confidentiality. The receiving party is often unwilling to do so as it has no ability to identify what the disclosing party considers to be a trade secret. To avoid this issue, the parties often agree that trade secrets must be specifically identified in writing as a trade secret prior to disclosure.

A party, as the Discloser, may desire for a particular disclosure to be received by Recipient as a trade secret hereunder, subject to Recipient's advance agreement to accept such a disclosure. Discloser must first notify Recipient and obtain agreement from Recipient that the disclosure will be received as a trade secret in accordance with the process set forth herein. Discloser shall provide Recipient a general description of the information prior to disclosure. Recipient will promptly decide whether to receive the disclosure as a trade secret and respond to Discloser, in writing, within five (5) working days; failure to respond shall mean Recipient will not accept the information as a trade secret. Discloser must (i) obtain written agreement by Recipient that such information is agreed to be received as a trade secret for the purposes of this Agreement, and (ii) the information must be identified as a trade secret with an appropriate stamp or legend ("Received Trade Secret"). In the event any of the preceding conditions are not met, such information will not be considered a Received Trade Secret but will be deemed Confidential Information if disclosed by Discloser.

(v) Dating the Agreement/Effective Date

A common challenge for parties contemplating a relationship is that they often exchange information prior to executing a nondisclosure agreement. To protect the parties' confidential information, the "effective date" of the agreement should be the date the parties first met and exchanged information they believe to be confidential.

Where the parties exchanged information prior to the execution of a confidentiality agreement, some savvy parties seek to include a representation from the receiving party in the subsequent nondisclosure agreement to the effect that it has not disclosed any confidential information of the disclosing party to a third party prior to executing a nondisclosure agreement. They do so to receive confirmation that their information has not been disclosed, as many parties fail to date the nondisclosure agreement to the date information was first disclosed by one party to the other. Model language to this effect is as follows:

> *Each Party represents that it has not disclosed or used any Confidential Information of the other Party before the date of this Agreement, except for any such disclosure or use that would not constitute breach of this Agreement if that disclosure or use were to have taken place upon effectiveness of this Agreement.*

(w) No License

Some nondisclosure agreements include an acknowledgment that the confidential information is the property of the disclosing party and that the disclosing party is not granting the receiving party an express or implied license to the confidential information.

(x) Miscellaneous Clauses

A proprietary information agreement should also include clauses addressing governing law and venue, feedback, attorneys' fees, and the survival of the obligation of confidentiality beyond the termination of the agreement. Some agreements require that individuals who receive the confidential information be prohibited from working for a competing entity for a set period of time. The parties may also want to consider including a prohibition of assignment to prevent their confidential information from being assigned to a competitor and a requirement that any permitted successors to the receiving party be bound by the confidentiality obligations contained in the agreement.

Further, the parties should consider the need for an integration clause if they have executed multiple confidentiality agreements over the course of their relationship. The parties should try to ensure the consistent treatment of their confidential information across the various confidentiality agreements.

Prudent parties will include additional provisions, including a requirement that all confidential information will be encrypted, and the receiving party should agree that it will not remove any confidentiality legends from the confidential information. Depending on the nature of the confidential information, the disclosing party may seek to identify a specific geographic location where the confidential information will be kept and that the confidential information will not be moved without the consent of, or notice to, the disclosing party.

At least one court has held that the statute of limitations for the misappropriation of confidential information or a trade secret is tolled until the owner becomes aware of the misappropriation. *Aspen Technologies, Inc. v. M3 Technology, Inc.*, 569 Fed. Appx. 259 (5th Cir. 2014).

Some agreements grant the disclosing party the right to audit the receiving party's compliance with the terms of the agreement

3. Third-Party Access

A disclosing party should seek to ensure that its confidential information is not disclosed except as is reasonably necessary. It is, of course, necessary for the licensor to disclose its confidential information to its prospects and customers. Customers, however, frequently request that the licensor permit them to disclose the licensor's confidential information not only to their employees, but also to other third parties, such as third-party consultants. Such disclosure is for a variety of purposes but is solely for the benefit of the customer. A licensor has an incentive to work with its customers within certain reasonable boundaries to allow its customers to make such disclosure, provided it does not create an unreasonable risk of loss or misappropriation of the licensor's confidential information or other intellectual property rights.

To protect its information, a licensor may adopt several procedures to provide reasonable safeguards for the continued protection of its confidential information and trade secrets. The first safeguard is that the customer requesting the disclosure must execute a proprietary information agreement and thereby agree to monitor such third party's use of the confidential information; to limit disclosure of such information on a need-to-know basis, and finally to guarantee such third party's compliance with the terms and conditions of the proprietary information agreement. The licensor should also seek to have the third party execute a nondisclosure agreement with the licensor so that the licensor is in contractual privity with the third party.

The guarantee serves several purposes. First, it serves as a measure of how trustworthy the customer believes the third party is. In a case where the customer objects to executing the proprietary information agreement, it is a clear signal the customer views such disclosure as an unacceptable risk. In such a case, the licensor should respond as follows:

(a) the customer (not licensor) selected the third party, has worked with the third party, and therefore is in a better position to judge the risk associated with disclosing the information to the third party;
(b) based on the customer's knowledge and experience with the third party and its business practices, the customer's objections to executing the proprietary information agreement are some of the best evidence of the third party's ability to protect the licensor's intellectual property rights; and
(c) the customer (not the licensor) receives all the benefits from such disclosure and, as such, should bear the risk associated with the disclosure to third parties.

When the customer objects to executing the proprietary information agreement, the licensor should deem the risk to be too great and refuse to allow such disclosure.

The second purpose of the guarantee is to allow the licensor to proceed against both the customer and the third party for a breach of the proprietary information agreement.

The licensor, like most businesses, is not in the habit of suing its customers. However, the customers, who are the paying clients of third parties, are in a better position to get the third parties to cease any wrongful activity. If there is a problem, the licensor will work with its customer to try and get the customer to resolve such breach with its third-party business partner. Without the guarantee, the customer is loath to get involved, making it harder, if not impossible, for the licensor to amicably resolve issues arising out of the proprietary information agreement.

The second procedure or safeguard that the licensor should adopt for the continued protection of its confidential information and trade secrets is that the licensor should not allow disclosure of such information to direct competitors. However, even in this case, a licensor should try to work with its customers to create alternative solutions so that disclosure is not necessary. In very rare circumstances where alternative solutions cannot be created, a licensor may be willing to allow disclosures to direct competitors, subject to the proprietary information agreement including special provisions to ensure the third party employees receiving disclosure to the licensor's confidential information are identified and are not put in a position to use such information for a two-year period. Absent such additional protection, the risk is likely too great, and the disclosure should be prohibited.

4. Residuals

A residuals clause establishes that general knowledge or know-how gained while working on a project that is retained in the *unaided* memories of the receiving party's employees is not covered by confidentiality obligations. Such clauses are common in source code licenses and outsourcing agreements.

Many disclosing parties resist including such clauses in their agreements, arguing that a common exception to the definition of "confidential information" under most nondisclosure agreements is information that is discovered, made, generated, or developed without use of the other party's confidential/proprietary information. They believe that residual knowledge provisions should not open up/negate an agreement's confidentiality provision and are not appropriate in most situations where the nondisclosure agreement was executed to facilitate substantive preliminary discussions.

The following is a model residuals clause:

> *Nothing in this Agreement will be construed to prevent the receiving party's employees who access Confidential Information from using Residuals for any purpose. The term "Residuals" means information of a general nature, such as general knowledge, professional skills, know-how, work experience or techniques, that is retained in the unaided memories (without conscious memorization or subsequent reference to the material in question) of the receiving party's employees who have had access to Confidential Information. Memory will be considered unaided if the employee or contractor has not intentionally memorized the information contained within the Confidential Information for the purpose of retaining and subsequently using or disclosing same.*

Vendors often favor the use of residual clauses, as they allow vendors to work on other assignments without any implied "clean room" obligations.

PRACTICE POINT:

In drafting a residuals clause, a disclosing party should consider:

- excluding trade secrets, patents and copyrights;
- excluding employees working on competitor's projects;
- prohibiting the individual making from refreshing their recollection in anticipation of or in conjunction with the use of the information;
- limiting it to information in an individual's unaided memory; and
- prohibiting the disclosure of information to third parties.

5. *Employees*

(a) *Employees*

(i) Nondisclosure Agreements

Employers should also require their employees to execute nondisclosure agreements as a condition of employment to protect the employer's confidential information, especially in the event the employee leaves the licensor's employment. While preferable that an employee execute a non-disclosure agreement prior to starting their employment, non-disclosure agreements executed after the start of employment may be enforced even if the employee did not receive any additional compensation. *West Shore Home, LLC v. Graeser et. al.*, 2023 WL 2504759 (M.D. Pa. Mar. 14, 2023).

A comprehensive nondisclosure agreement should include an agreement to keep the licensor's and its customers' confidential information confidential; an obligation to return any confidential information upon the termination of the employee's employment; the assignment of any inventions made by the employee to the licensor; an agreement to assist the licensor in obtaining and enforcing any patents or copyrights, and an acknowledgment by the employee of the licensor's right to obtain injunctive and equitable relief in the event of the employee's actual or threatened breach of the agreement.

The licensor may also want to include a covenant of noncompetition and a covenant not to solicit the licensor's employees and customers. The employer should require all of its employees to attend regular training sessions to "refresh" their commitment to abide by their nondisclosure obligations.

An employee's obligation of confidentiality may also arise out of common law. *Jostens, Inc. v. National Computer Systems, Inc.*, 318 N.W.2d 691, 701 (Minn. 1982).

(ii) Civil/Common-Law Actions

At least one court has held that a common-law cause of action of conversion applies to intangible records resident on a computer hard drive. *Thyroff v. Nationwide Mutual Ins. Co.*, 864 N.E.2d 1272 (N.Y. 2007) (insurance agent permitted to bring conversion action against insurance company, which took possession of computer leased to agent that contained work related data as well as agent's personal electronic files). Another found a domain name can be converted. *Kremen v. Cohen*, 337 F.3d 1024, 1033–34 (9th Cir. 2003). Massachusetts courts have reached the opposite conclusion when considering this issue. *See In re TJX Companies Retail Security Breach Litigation*, 587 F. Supp. 2d 209 (D. Mass. 2007) (Mass. does not recognize cause of action for conversion of intangible records. Court rejected invitation to adopt holding of *Thyroff*). *But see Network Systems Architects Corp. v. Dimitruk*, 23 Mass. L. Rptr.. 339 (2007) (If paper documents can be converted, as they no doubt can, no reason appears that computer files cannot).

(iii) Criminal Actions

Licensors may also have the ability to bring a criminal complaint against present or former employees for the theft of trade secrets and numerous employees have received jail time for such thefts. *See* http://www.law360.com/articles/25088/duracell-employee-sentenced-for-trade-secrets-theft; http://money.cnn.com/2007/05/23/news/newsmakers/coke/.

Almost all states have enacted legislation making the theft of a trade secret a crime. For example, Section 499(c) of the California Penal Code (Crimes Against Property) prohibits the theft of trade secrets and broadly defines "theft" to including making copies of trade secrets or using trade secrets without authorization of the owner. Similarly, Section 31.05 of the Texas Penal Code makes the theft of a trade secret and the unauthorized copying of a trade secret a crime. V.T.C.A. PENAL CODE § 31.05. For a listing of state statutes making the theft of a trade secret a crime, *see Protecting Trade Secrets* § 3:21, Thompson* West (2007).

For a general discussion, *see* Gray & O'Rourke, *Preventing Employee Trade Secret Misuse from Derailing Your Company*, 132 INTELL. PROP. COUNS. 1 (Dec. 2007); Newman, *Protecting Trade Secrets: Dealing With the Brave New World of Employee Mobility*, Bus. L. TODAY 25 (Nov./Dec. 2007).

(b) Receiving Party Employee Liability

Some disclosing parties also seek to have the receiving party's employees execute a nondisclosure agreement with the disclosing party. Prudent employers will not allow their employees to sign a nondisclosure agreement directly with the disclosing party to avoid any potential liability on the employee's behalf. To support this position, the receiving party will likely argue that the employee has already signed a nondisclosure with the employer as a condition of employment. Having employees execute an agreement directly with the disclosing party exposes the employee to personal liability in the event of a disclosure, which most employees are unwilling to assume. At the same time, most employees lack the financial assets to fully compensate the disclosing party in the event of a breach.

It is also inequitable for an employer to ask an employee to assume personal liability for a contract through which the employer will financially benefit. Further, under almost all nondisclosure agreements, the receiving party assumes responsibility for any breach of the nondisclosure agreement by its employee. A compromise may be to have employees sign an acknowledgment, acknowledging their confidentiality obligations.

6. Nondisclosure Agreements for Site Visits

Some companies require visitors to execute a non-disclosure agreement prior entering the company's facilities to protect any company confidential information that the individual may observe or receive while visiting the company's facilities. Requiring an individual visiting a site to execute a non-disclosure agreement is controversial as most employees sign a confidentiality agreement with their employer when they begin their employment and the employer in turn signs a confidentiality agreement with the company.

If a company requires visitors to sign a non-disclosure agreement to enter the company's premises, the company should notify the individual and their employer prior to the individual's arrival at the company's facility. The agreement should be sent the employer at least a week in advance to allow the agreement to be reviewed by counsel and to avoid having the employee turned away at the door and the meeting cancelled.

Employees visiting a customer site should be reminded that they lack the authority to sign any agreement related to their employment or which binds their employer, which has not been reviewed and approved by the company's counsel. Further, the company will not support them if they sign any agreement in contravention of those instructions.

7. Overlapping Nondisclosure Agreements

Both parties should be concerned with the execution of potentially conflicting nondisclosure agreements during the course of a business relationship. Often, the parties will execute a new nondisclosure agreement each time they enter into a new transaction, Alternatively, the parties may have entered into a stand-alone nondisclosure agreement, but yet the underlying agreement may also contain a nondisclosure provision. Overlapping nondisclosure agreements create a concern that if there is an issue regarding a breach of a party's confidentiality obligations and there is a variation in terms among the different agreements, the parties may need to resolve the intermediate issue as to which nondisclosure provisions govern the alleged breach. The parties will likely be unable to agree on the governing agreement, as the party in breach will likely select the preferential terms from the different nondisclosure agreements that benefits its position.

A specific purpose nondisclosure agreement is one option but can be problematic as well. A party may have ten projects with a vendor in a year. Negotiating ten different nondisclosure agreements is impractical. Further, if a nondisclosure agreement is limited to a specific proposal, it would not cover ongoing disclosures made in the course of an awarded engagement. The parties will need to enter into a new nondisclosure agreement after executing the underlying agreement. Hence a party may lose protections when it needs them most. If limited to a specific opportunity (by a Statement of Work or service) and another subsequently arises, many parties often fail to execute a second nondisclosure agreement because they believe they have a valid nondisclosure agreement based on an entry in their nondisclosure database.

Creating an electronic database may make it easier to address issues related to renewing nondisclosure agreements, but concern arises with regard to monitoring when a nondisclosure agreement needs to be renewed, when it can be allowed to expire, and how that expiration is effectively communicated to the party's project teams. Ideally, a party should have a companywide nondisclosure agreement program that is orchestrated through a central repository, although such a program is a substantial undertaking and often beyond a party's resources.

To avoid this issue, some entities incorporate confidentiality terms in an agreement or simply reference an existing nondisclosure agreement to avoid the potential for conflict and overlap.

8. Multi-Party Nondisclosure Agreements

Multi-party nondisclosure agreements are intended to facilitate sharing of information among multiple parties with the same interest, such as jointly pursuing an opportunity or supporting a customer. Each party can disclose confidential information it has received from one party to the nondisclosure agreement to all other parties to the nondisclosure agreement without obtaining consent of the disclosing party, as all confidential information exchanged among the parties to the nondisclosure agreement is protected under the terms of the parties' agreement. For example, if a party discloses confidential information to one party in the context of an opportunity, that party can share such information with another party to the agreement without specifically having to ask the disclosing party's permission (even though it may). A disclosing party must be aware of this open exchange, and before providing any confidential information, evaluate/confirm that it wants to have the confidential information exchanged among all the parties.

If a party needs to disclose its information to one party but does not want the information shared with the parties, it will need to indicate to the party it is disclosing to that the information may not be shared with the other parties before providing the confidential information. If a party plans to share one party's confidential information with another, unless it is clear, the party should check with the disclosing party to confirm that the confidential information is meant to be shared.

See Form M.1.8 for a model Three-Party Confidentiality Agreement.

9. Confidentiality and Data Security in the Cloud

Cloud computing is one of the fastest-growing areas in information technology today. While cloud computing provides many benefits such as rapid, flexible, client-managed provisioning along with lower infrastructure, personnel, and software costs, cloud computing is not without its risks, which are principally related to confidentiality, data security, and data privacy.

Many confidentiality agreements do not address the provision of confidential information to cloud services providers. This issue may arise when a disclosing party contracts directly with a cloud provider, or when a vendor stores a customer's data in the cloud via a third-party cloud provider. While most agreements provide that the receiving party will take reasonable steps to protect the disclosing party's confidential information, a prudent party should insist on comprehensive language to protect its confidential information when it is stored in the cloud.

> *The Receiving Party agrees to protect all Confidential Information of the Disclosing Party against* ***disclosure, publication or unauthorized use or access*** *using the same degree of care as it uses to protect its own information of like nature, but no less than a reasonable degree of care.*

If applicable, the receiving party should be contractually obligated to comply with all applicable security standards such as HIPAA, the PCI standards and the GDPR, and should be required to complete a survey of its data security procedures and protocols to protect confidential information under its control.

Where the cloud services provider is a third party under the disclosing party's existing confidentiality agreement with a vendor, disclosure of the disclosing party's confidential information to the cloud services provider, even though the disclosure is solely for the purpose of the cloud services provider hosting the information on the disclosing party's behalf, such disclosure constitutes a breach of most confidentiality agreements, which prohibit disclosures to third parties and for purposes other than the confidentiality agreement's defined "purpose." To avoid this problem, a prudent vendor/receiving party should add an express consent to permit the receiving party/vendor to disclose the confidential information to a cloud services provider for the limited purpose of allowing third parties to perform services on the receiving party's behalf, provided they are subject to confidentiality obligations that are at least as restrictive as those contained in the confidentiality agreement between the disclosing party and the receiving party.

See Chapter 22 for a more detailed discussion.

(a) *Confidentiality in the Cloud*

Confidentiality is of even greater importance in the cloud where a party's confidential information and trade secrets are transferred over the Internet and stored virtually. At a minimum, the cloud services provider must contractually agree not to access or use any of the customer's confidential information other than to maintain and support the cloud services in addition to its obligations to protect and not to disclose the customer's confidential information.

Depending on how the agreement's confidentiality provision is worded, hacking may not cause the service provider to violate its confidentiality obligations. If the confidentiality provision merely says that the service provider will not disclose the confidential information or use it for any purpose other than performing contractual obligations, would hacking rise to the level of a disclosure or use? It is an issue that a service provider would not want to concede and, from the service provider's perspective, one that should be addressed in a contract in a manner that precludes a jury from finding hacking would rise to the level of a disclosure or use. If the agreement includes a provision that specifies the service provider's data security obligations (which it may want to keep separate from its confidentiality obligations, again depending on the applicable remedies and liability limitations), most service providers are not accustomed to agreeing to liability for a data security breach without fault. Service providers usually accept this position in only one of two circumstances: (1) their negotiating leverage is dramatically lower than that of the prospective customer, or (2) they accept any provision that a prospective customer places in front of them. In the latter case, they probably do not have the resources to satisfy the liability to which they are exposed.

The rationale that carries the day in most negotiations, subject to the negotiating leverage of the respective parties, is that the customer cannot make its own environment impervious to hacking, and therefore cannot avoid the consequences of hacking if it retains responsibility for the environment. It cannot expect a service provider to do something that is just as impossible for the service provider to achieve on behalf of the customer as it would be for the customer to achieve for itself. At some point, arguably, when hacking occurs despite the fact that the victim has performed all of its contractual obligations, hacking is a *force majeure* occurrence—an act for which the victim is not responsible and should not have liability to the other contract party.

(i) "Reasonable" Standard of Care

Most confidentiality agreements provide that each party shall use a reasonable standard of care to maintain the confidentiality of the disclosing party's confidential information. So long as the party receiving the information uses its good faith efforts to protect the disclosing party's confidential information, but no less than a reasonable standard of care, the receiving party has met its contractual obligations and cannot be held liable for any disclosure. This would include disclosures resulting from the actions of a third party, such as through hacking. See Form Q.2.O.26 for model language reflecting a 'reasonable" standard of care.

Under the "reasonable" standard of care, the customer assumes the risk of liability for all disclosures other than those arising from the vendor's failure to implement reasonable precautions to prevent a disclosure. While a "reasonable" standard may suffice in most agreements, from the customer's perspective this standard may be inappropriate for cloud-based transactions.

A vendor may implement reasonable, industry-standard protections, such as physical security at its data centers, the use of intrusion detection and reporting software, encryption, passwords, and other protections, yet a hacker may still be able to breach these protections and access the customer's data. The customer will likely be harmed as a result of that breach and may suffer litigation and significant fines, penalties, and notification and credit monitoring expenses. But the "reasonable" standard provided in the parties' agreement leaves the customer without a remedy against the cloud vendor because the vendor did not breach its contractual confidentiality obligations. Accordingly, a savvy customer should reject this language and seek to hold the vendor to a higher standard. At a minimum, the customer should ensure the vendor is held to written security standards and ideally impose the customer's own security standards on the vendor. Depending on the type of services being provided by the vendor and whether the vendor is providing the customer with a private cloud or a public cloud, this may be impractical. Further, most vendors are unwilling to accept the customer's security standards, arguing that they cannot be bound by multiple security standards. For a more detailed discussion of this issue, see Chapter 28.B.2 below.

(ii) Strict Liability "Shall Not Disclose" Standard

Other nondisclosure provisions provide that the vendor "shall not disclose" a customer's confidential information. In the event of a disclosure from hacking or other unauthorized access of the customer's confidential information, a vendor may successfully argue that it did not disclose the customer's confidential information and thus did not breach its confidentiality obligations.

Customers should also reject language to this effect as it may leave them without a remedy in the event of a disclosure. Although most vendors will argue that they should only be liable for their own actions, from the customer's perspective it is reasonable to expect the vendor to assume liability for any disclosure other than those caused by the customer's action or inaction.

See Form Q.2.O.27 for confidentiality language reflecting a "shall not disclose" standard.

(iii) Absolute Prohibition on Disclosure

A prudent customer should insist on an absolute prohibition on the disclosure of the customer's confidential information. It should also insist that the vendor be liable for any disclosure except for those disclosures resulting from the fault of the customer. Under this position, the vendor assumes liability not only for its actions and those of its employees and contractors, but also assumes responsibility for any disclosures resulting from any third-party actions, including those that may be outside the vendor's control.

Customers will argue that this position is equitable, as the vendor controls the environment in which the confidential information resides and thus has the ability to take all actions necessary to protect the confidential information. Vendors will respond that they should have no liability except in those situations where they are at fault. In most cases, the vendor possesses the negotiating leverage to reject the customer's arguments.

See Form Q.2.O.28 for model confidentiality language providing that the vendor assumes liability for all disclosures, including those resulting from the actions and inactions of the customer, its employees, and contractors.

(iv) A Balanced Approach

Both parties must carefully consider contractual language allocating liability for the disclosure of confidential information. Objectively, each party must be responsible for disclosures caused by its employees and contractors. It is more challenging to amicably apportion liability for disclosures that are not the result of a party's own actions.

Most customers will argue that because the vendor controls the security for the system and is providing the services, the vendor should assume the risk of hacking.

A savvy vendor will resist assuming liability for third-party breaches and hacking on the basis that no environment is completely safe, and that the customer would be liable for these risks if it was hosting the data in the customer's own environment. A vendor's willingness to assume this risk will likely depend on a number of factors, including whether the customer is using a public or private cloud, the type of services purchased by the customer (i.e., Infrastructure as a Service (IaaS), Platform as a Service (PaaS), and Software as a Service (SaaS)), pricing, and any limitations of liability set forth in the underlying agreement. IaaS is considered to embody less risk to the customer than SaaS, as the customer retains less control with SaaS. Similarly, a public cloud is considered to be inherently riskier than a private cloud, given the nature of a shared environment.

Beyond identifying the nature of the risk, the parties must balance their risk by allocating liability for breaches without fault against the agreement's limitation of liability and any exclusion of consequential damages as well as the definition of direct damages.

Prudent customers will ensure that the definition of Confidential Information is broad enough to include the information of their customers. Further, the customer should carefully consider what standard the vendor must comply with in protecting the customer's confidential information. The use of a "reasonable efforts" standard may leave the customer without a remedy in the event the vendor is hacked, and the customer's information is stolen or disclosed. See the illustrative language below.

> *Each party will: (a) notify the other party promptly of any material unauthorized possession, use or knowledge, or attempt to gain thereof,* ***of the other party's Confidential Information*** *by any person that may become known to such party; (b) promptly furnish to the other party details of the unauthorized possession, use or knowledge, or attempt to gain thereof, and use reasonable efforts to assist the other party in investigating or preventing the recurrence of any unauthorized possession, use or knowledge, or attempt to gain thereof, of Confidential Information; (c) use* ***reasonable efforts*** *to cooperate with the other party in any litigation and investigation against third parties deemed necessary by the other party to protect its proprietary rights; and (d) promptly* ***use reasonable efforts to prevent a recurrence of any such unauthorized possession, use or knowledge of Confidential Information.***

A prudent customer should consider utilizing a strict liability standard for any disclosure, as illustrated in the highlighted language below.

> ***Vendor shall ensure that no Confidential Information processed or stored by Customer through the Service is (a) accessed*** *or modified by anyone other than a Customer-authorized user or (b) is intentionally or inadvertently deleted, lost or corrupted. Vendor shall indemnify Customer for all losses, damages, costs and expenses incurred by Customer as a result of any breach by Vendor of any of the foregoing obligations.*

(b) Data Security

(i) Liability

Data security is typically a customer's greatest concern when deciding whether to utilize a vendor's cloud services. Customers typically assume that the financial liability for loss, misuse, damage, or destruction of that data falls to the cloud vendor, but that is not necessarily the case. A vendor's data security obligations and liabilities are contractually separate and distinct from its confidentiality obligations and those security obligations may transfer to the customer the responsibility of security for that data. This is especially important if the underlying agreement provides for distinct limitation of liabilities for breaches of confidentiality and data security.

As with confidentiality, most vendors will not agree to liability for a data security breach without fault. Those who do usually lack negotiating leverage over the customer or are unconcerned with the attendant risks. Customers should be concerned if a vendor is blithely willing to accept such liability as the vendor may lack the resources to satisfy any claim made by the customer or any judgment the customer receives against the vendor.

Those vendors unwilling to accept liability without fault usually argue that a customer cannot make its own cloud network environment impervious to hacking and thus the vendor should not be held to a higher standard. Indeed, hacks into government and corporate computer networks by activists and adversarial political governments over the past few years against companies such as Zappos, Sony, and Epsilon have been well-publicized. Why should a vendor be expected to deliver at a level the customer itself is incapable of achieving?

Customers, on the other hand, believe that data security is likely to be higher through a third-party cloud vendor, as the vendor has both the resources to dedicate to that security and the expertise in information technology to detect and confront emerging security threats. In addition, customers rely on the fact that vendors providing cloud services to certain industry sectors know or should know of any mandated minimum standards for data security applicable to those sectors. Accordingly, customers look to the vendor to utilize those resources and that expertise to deliver the services with a higher level of protection than the customer is able to achieve itself. Some vendors, however, argue that because they have undertaken all reasonable efforts to protect against an unauthorized intrusion and that because they have performed all of their contractual obligations, hacking is essentially a *force majeure* event for which the vendor is not responsible and for which it should not have liability.

(ii) Agreeing on Standards

Perhaps the biggest issue related to data security is establishing the data security standards that will govern the provision of the services. Almost all vendors insist on the use of the vendor's own standards to ensure continuity across all of the vendor's customers and data centers. Most of the cost efficiencies that arise in a cloud environment emanate from the use of uniform standards and economies of scale. A vendor cannot achieve these efficiencies if it provides a different standard for each of its customers.

Customers are often concerned, however, that the vendor's standards are not stringent enough and seek to impose their standards on the vendor. While most vendors will not agree to accept the customer's standards, some vendors offer different levels of security and charge accordingly. Thus, the customer can purchase a higher level of security for an increased price. Other vendors do not offer a choice of security levels even at a higher cost in an effort to maintain a consistent standard across their business. A savvy customer should consider whether it truly requires a higher level of security, especially when it is utilizing a private cloud. In most cases, the choice will be driven by the sensitivity of the data in question and whether the customer is utilizing a public or a private cloud.

See Form Q.2.M.16 for model language addressing data security obligations and Form Q.2.M.8 establishing encryption standards for cloud computing.

(iii) Amending the Standards

Another issue for consideration is the vendor's ability to change the security standards during the term of the agreement. Can the vendor unilaterally change the security standards? With prior notice or with written prior notice? Can the customer terminate the agreement in the event the vendor changes its security standards? These are all important issues the customer must understand, and which should be addressed in the agreement.

An increasing number of vendors seek the flexibility to change their security standards, sometimes by posting the new standards on a website, sometimes without notice to the customer. The customer is thus forced to continually monitor the identified site to become aware of any potential changes. This places an undue burden on the customer and alters the basis of the parties' agreement.

At a minimum, the vendor should be contractually obligated to provide the customer 90 days' prior written notice in the event it seeks to change its data security standards. If the customer is contractually obligated to accept such changes and such changes have a material adverse impact on the customer, the customer should have the right to terminate the agreement for convenience and the vendor should be obligated to provide transition services until the customer can transition to a new vendor. The vendor should not provide the customer the right to terminate the agreement if the change does not materially impact the customer or if the changes improve the service.

Prudent customers should not allow the vendor to change their security standards without prior written notice to and the consent of the customer or by posting any such changes on the Internet. The vendor should be required to notify the customer in writing of the proposed changes and be contractually prohibited from unilaterally modifying the agreement without the customer's prior written consent if such changes have a material adverse effect on the customer. As a practical matter, vendors may need to change standards to accommodate new technologies and new threats. The use of an "impact" test provides a practical solution to protect the interests of both parties.

(iv) Compliance with Laws

Compliance with laws is also a point of contention when negotiating data security and privacy provisions as the parties must not only be concerned with the laws in existence at the time of contract execution but also those laws enacted during the term of the agreement. At a minimum, the vendor should agree to comply with all applicable privacy and data security laws in effect at the time of contract signature. The most commonly cited include the Health Insurance Portability and Accountability Act (HIPAA), Gramm-Leach-Bliley and the GDPR. While the customer cannot "outsource" its compliance obligations, it can significantly limit its risk by holding the vendor to the same standards imposed by statute on the customer. Prudent customers want to avoid being held responsible for a vendor error yet be unable to recover any losses from the vendor.

Vendors should be hesitant to assume responsibility for compliance with all applicable laws, especially those laws outside its areas of expertise. Prudent vendors should agree only to comply with those laws applicable to the vendor's industry with the customer assuming responsibility for all other laws. This position is often viewed as an equitable solution as each party is responsible for those laws applicable to its own industry, laws each party is already most likely responsible for complying with. Further, because each party is operating within its industry, the parties are better positioned to address any subsequent changes in the law.

(v) Changes in the Law

The parties must also allocate responsibility/liability for compliance with changes in the law during the term of the agreement. The allocation of this risk is important, as the costs associated with complying with any subsequent changes in the law can be significant. As such, vendors should only agree to comply with those laws in effect at the time of contract signature and those changes in the laws affecting the vendor's industry that arise after contract signature. From the vendor's perspective, customers should be responsible for assuming the risk of all other changes in the law, including those related to the customer's industry. The customer should be prepared to pay for any additional costs incurred by the vendor as a result of complying with such changes.

A more balanced approach is to provide that any changes in the law affecting the parties will be addressed through the change order process and that if the parties cannot agree on a change order, the affected party may terminate the agreement for convenience. Further, in such event, there shall be a transition period during which the parties will cooperate to allow the customer to transition to a third-party vendor.

It is important that, if the agreement provides a termination right in the event the parties are unable to agree on a change order, the termination be designated as a termination for convenience to avoid allowing one party to recover damages for breach. Termination for convenience or without fault usually does not allow the parties to recover damages but rather allows the nonterminating party, usually the vendor, to recover its unamortized/unrecovered costs, while avoiding any punitive measures usually associated with breach.

See Form Q.2.P.24 for sample language requiring compliance with applicable privacy and data security laws.

(vi) Notice of Actual or Attempted Breach

From the customer's perspective, it is very important that the vendor be contractually required to provide the customer prompt notice in the event of any unauthorized access or attempt to access the customer's data. Many vendors seek only to notify the customer in the event of a security breach to avoid raising the customer's ire and perhaps triggering an obligation to notify the customer's customers. Customers, however, should be notified even in the event of an unsuccessful event so that the customer can monitor and track potential security issues, allowing it to correct any defects in its own security standards.

The distinction between "determined" or "verified" breaches and "reasonably suspected" breaches is an important one. Waiting for determination or verification may result in harmful delay. However, notification of attempted, unsuccessful breaches could result in a steady stream of alarming notifications to the customer and its end users. Thus, the parties must carefully consider the type of data at risk and the actual risk of a breach in establishing the notification parameters.

During the negotiations, the parties should carefully negotiate the vendor's obligations in the event there is an actual or attempted breach. Most customers will insist that the vendor bear all costs associated with notifying not only those end users whose data has been accessed, but all end users whose data may have been accessed. Savvy customers will also seek to have the vendor assume the costs of credit monitoring for the customer's clients and the cost to establish and staff a help desk to answer the customer's clients' questions, in addition to assuming liability for all liabilities from claims brought by the customer's clients. The customer should maintain control of retaining and managing all third-party contractors hired to interface with its customers as a result of any actual or attempted breach. The vendor should be responsible for reimbursing the customer for its costs but not the selection or retention of third-party contractors.

The definition of "customers" who must be notified is important, as the larger the pool, the greater the vendor's costs. While prudent vendors may seek to limit their obligations to only those customers whose records were known to be breached and not those who may have been breached, some state laws require notification within a specified number of days after a breach is reasonably believed to have occurred.

See Forms Q.2.P.25 and Q.2.P.26 for model language addressing a vendor's breach notification obligations.

(c) Limitation of Liability

Cloud agreements usually provide that the vendor will retain responsibility for the security, access, and protection of the data placed in the cloud. Users may experience a false sense of security that they will be protected from claims and related business losses resulting from data loss or misuse through data corruption or hacking. The majority of cloud vendors disclaim liability for the significant financial damages that can result from a breach. Given a cloud user is likely to be responsible for the costs associated with responding to a data breach, savvy cloud users should educate themselves on these risks and seek a more balanced allocation of liability. The likelihood of doing so, however, depends on the respective leverage of the parties, which usually resides with the vendor.

(i) Limitation on Direct Damages

A party's willingness to assume risk is closely related to the limitation of liability provisions set forth in the agreement. By the very nature of the cloud hosting services, cloud vendors may assume liability to the individuals whose data resides in the vendor's cloud and to state and federal regulatory agencies for penalties imposed on that vendor for the unauthorized release of the individuals' data. Accordingly, almost all vendors are willing to assume some risk depending on the agreement's aggregate cap on liability, but cloud vendor agreements typically disclaim liability for many of the kinds of damages that a cloud customer is most likely to incur. Very few vendors, however, are willing to assume unlimited liability for breach of their confidentiality/data security obligations, especially when it arises without the fault of the vendor.

A party's risk tolerance will depend on many factors, including which party dictates the data loss prevention standards and backup procedures governing the service, whether those standards and procedures were followed in the event of the loss or destruction of the data, and whether the data storage and access results in a violation of applicable laws or a breach of applicable license terms. A customer who dictates the data security precautions that are applicable to its account, such as the existence and quality of firewalls, the quality of passwords, and the encryption standards used to transmit and store the data, will likely be required by the vendor to assume greater liability for damages arising from deficiencies in those precautions as the customer was responsible for establishing the standards. Similarly, contractual provisions requiring the vendor to segment and back up data, maintain access to it, monitor the account to detect unauthorized access or malware infections, and report in a timely and accurate manner any such intrusions or infections will likely spawn greater liability on the vendor's behalf in the event of its failure to abide by its obligations.

Traditionally, a breach of a party's confidentiality obligations was carved out from the agreement's limitation of liability. This carve-out was based on the reasoning that the breaching party should be subject to unlimited liability for misappropriating and disclosing the disclosing party's trade secrets for its own benefit. This argument does not transcend the cloud, as a disclosure can occur despite the best efforts of the vendor and without the vendor's negligence. Thus, most vendors are unwilling to assume unlimited liability, especially when providing low-margin commodity services such as cloud computing.

One resolution may be to bifurcate the limitation of liability to provide a higher liability for disclosures resulting from the vendor's negligence with lower limits if the disclosure results without fault of the vendor, i.e., hacking. The vendor's liability is lower, arguably, because the vendor did not disclose the information or cause the disclosure. The parties may also explore different limits of liability for different types of disclosure.

Some vendors seek to negotiate a lesser limit of liability for operational breaches of their confidentiality obligations with a higher limit for a nonoperational breach of their confidentiality obligations. For example, a vendor may limit its liability to the value of the services provided in the previous 12 months for a breach of its operational obligations and accept a limit of liability equal to two times the revenue received in the previous 12 months in the event of a general breach of its confidentiality obligations. A small number of vendors may be willing to accept unlimited liability for a traditional breach of a party's confidentiality obligations, but they are definitely in the minority.

Vendors are generally unlikely to assume the liability for damages arising from a cloud user's storage or access of cloud data in violation of applicable industry and regulatory regulations, including export laws, HIPAA/Health Information Technology for Economic and Clinical Health (HITECH) privacy regulations, and applicable trade secret, copyright, or patent laws.

See Form Q.2.DD.2 for model language relating to limitation of liability.

(ii) Consequential Damages

Although most information technology agreements disclaim a party's liability for consequential damages, a customer should carefully consider whether to accept such a disclaimer as it relates to the disclosure of confidential information. The great majority of a party's damages may be consequential damages and the acceptance of such a disclaimer may leave the customer without a meaningful recovery while potentially exposing the customer to significant liability from its own customers. *See Silverpop Systems, Inc. v. Leading Market Technologies*, 641 Fed. Appx. 849 (11th Cir. 2016) (losses associated with a data breach "are best characterized as consequential"). Except for the largest service providers, most service providers are still under significant pressure to carve confidentiality breaches out of consequential damages exclusions.

Vendors do not like to carve confidentiality breaches out of the agreement's consequential damages exclusion, but the weight of history and custom is fairly heavy. To the extent a vendor agrees to do so, it wants to avoid opening the door to all consequential damages resulting from a data security breach, particularly damages for lost profits. Prudent vendors seek to limit confidentiality breaches to unauthorized use and unauthorized disclosure of information so that a data security breach does not breach a confidentiality obligation and expose a vendor to liability for all consequential damages in addition to damages that may be defined as direct damages.

From the perspective of both parties, it may be prudent to include a definition of "direct" damages in the agreement to avoid a subsequent dispute over which damages constitute direct damages and thus are recoverable under the agreement. Defining the "direct" damages the customer may recover should allow both the vendor and the customer to better quantify their risks. Often the definition of "direct" damages will include damages that would traditionally be considered consequential damages; the intent of including a definition is to ensure certainty and thus the definition may not reflect the definition of "direct damages" contained in the Restatement of Contracts. Vendors should embrace the use of a defined term to avoid uncertainty and incurring additional costs to litigate the matter if a dispute arises.

Assuming responsibility for consequential damages may not increase the vendor's aggregate liability as the customer's recovery is still limited by the agreement's overall cap on damages. By assuming liability for consequential damages, the vendor is in essence allowing the customer to potentially reach the agreement's aggregate limit of liability faster without increasing the vendor's aggregate contractual liability. A vendor should be hesitant, however, to accept liability for consequential damages without limiting its aggregate liability as to do so equates to essentially "betting the ranch" on a single contract with a very expansive standard of damages.

See Form B.3.1 §17.4 for model language setting forth a definition of "direct" damages.

B. Trade Secret Laws/Protections

1. General

(a) What Is a Trade Secret?

Whether information is a trade secret must be decided on a case-by-case basis and subject to state law. Computer software has been found to be a trade secret where source code is not easily copied or ascertained. *LinkCo, Inc. v. Fujitsu, Ltd.*, 230 F. Supp. 2d 492, 499 (S.D.N.Y. 2002); *Q-Co Indus., Inc. v. Hoffman*, 625 F. Supp. 608 (S.D.N.Y. 1985). Source code and object code, as well as the concepts and ideas encompassed in the code, can be considered trade secrets. *Trandes Corp. v. Guy F. Atkinson Co.*, 996 F.2d 655 (4th Cir.) *cert. denied*, 510 U.S. 965 (1993); *Integrated Cash Management Servs., Inc. v. Digital Transactions, Inc.*, 732 F. Supp. 370 (S.D.N.Y. 1989), *aff'd*, 920 F.2d 171 (2d Cir. 1990). A software compilation may qualify as a trade secret if the compilation is not generally known. *Decision Insights, Inc. v. Sentia Group., Inc.*, 416 Fed. Appx. 324 (4th Cir. 2011). Further, information derived from public information may be protectable trade secrets. *AirFacts Inc. v. de Amezaga*, 909 F.3d 84 (4th Cir. 2018). Licensing software does not destroy its trade secrets status provided the transaction is subject to a confidentiality agreement. *Cyborg Sys. Inc. v. Management Science Am., Inc.*, 1978 WL 1312 (N.D. Ill. Jan. 30, 1978).

A party may breach its confidentiality obligations but not necessarily misappropriate a trade secret. *SIS, LLC v. Stoneridge Holdings, Inc.*, 2021 WL 2650355 (N.D. Ga. May 28, 2021); *Providence Title Co. v. Truly Title, Inc.*, 547 F. Supp. 3d 585, 609 (E.D. Tex. 2021) ("[B]usiness information is not necessarily a trade secret simply because it is confidential.").

Trade secrets can take many forms including customer lists and information, sales and marketing strategies, pricing, methodologies, functional specifications, technical specifications, object code and source code and employee names.

The prevailing party in a trade secret dispute is entitled to recover its costs. Thus, defendants who successfully defend a claim can recover their costs. *SASCO Rosendin Electric, Inc.*, 207 Cal. App. 4th 837 (2012) (plaintiff ordered to pay defendant's legal costs of $484,543).

While a "trade secret" will always be considered "confidential information," not all confidential information will meet the definition of a "trade secret." Common grounds for not meeting the requirements for being a trade secret include information that may not derive economic value from being kept secret, or the owner may not have taken reasonable steps to maintain the secrecy of the confidential information.

Trade secrets are generally governed by state law in contrast to other intellectual property rights such as copyrights and patents, which are governed by federal law. Trade secret protection encompasses broader protection than is otherwise available for copyright and patent protection. *Salsbury Laboratories, Inc. v. Merieux Laboratories, Inc.*, 735 F. Supp. 1537, 1542 (M.D. Ga. 1987) ("a trade secret does not require the uniqueness and novelty of a patent"). Unlike patent protection, trade secret protection does not prevent other parties from developing similar inventions or reverse engineering the technology in question. Whether a piece of information is in actuality a trade secret is a question of fact to be determined by a trier of fact. *Hoffman-La Roche, Inc. v. Voder*, 950 F. Supp. 1348 (S.D. Ohio 1997).

Common examples of trade secrets include pricing, sales and marketing plans, customer lists, employee lists, road maps for functionality and future development, strategic plans, source code and object code, requests for information (RFIs), requests for proposals (RFPs) and RFP/RFI responses. *Liveware Publ'g., Inc. v. Best Software*, Inc., 252 F. Supp 2d. 74 (D. Del. 2003) (list of customers for licensee's payroll system software a trade secret).

(b) Identifying Trade Secrets

A party must "describe the subject matter of a trade secret with sufficient particularity to separate it from matters of general in the trade or of special knowledge of those persons . . . skilled in the trade." *Imax Corp. v. Cinema Tech., Inc.*, 152 F.3d 1161, 1164-65 (9th Cir. 1998); *TLS Mgmt. & Mktg. Servs LLC v. Rodriguez-Toledo*, 966 F.3d 46 (1st Cir. 2020) (Plaintiff and its attorneys failure to articulate what information were trade secrets from other information required court to deny trade secret protection). "Information alleged to be a misappropriated trade secret must be identified with enough specificity to place a defendant on notice of the basis for the claim being made against ." *Oakwood Laboratories LLC v. Thanoo*, 999 F.3d 892, 906 (3d Cir. 2021).

A party's inability to define its trade secrets with sufficient particularity will cause that party to forfeit trade secret protection. *IDX Sys. Corp. v. Epic Sys. Corp. et al.*, 285 F.3d 581 (W.D. Wis. 2001). *See also, Mallet & Co., Inc. v. Lacy*, 16 F.4th 364 (3d Cir. 2021) (Court vacated injunction against use of trade secrets as the trade secrets not adequately defined).

For an overview of the laws addressing trade secret misappropriation, *see* Vizy, *Trade Secret Update*, 346 Com. L. Advisor 1 (2016); Determann, Schmaus & Tam, *Trade Secret Protection Measures and New Harmonization Laws*, 34 COMP. & INTERNET LAW. 1 (Jan. 2017).

PRACTICE POINT: To avoid having a claim for trade secret misappropriation denied, trade secret owners should:

- clearly and specifically identify the information the party claims as a trade secret
- avoid using broad generalities such as "including but not limited to methodologies for processing insurance claims"
- amend any description if new information becomes available

(c) Reasonable Steps to Protect Trade Secrets

To maintain a concept's or information's status as a trade secret, the owning entity must undertake "reasonable steps" to protect the confidential nature of the information of trade secrets. *Incase, Inc. v. Timex Corp.*, 488 F.3d 46, 52–53 (1st. Cir. 2007) (owner must take reasonable, affirmative steps to maintain secrecy of trade secrets); *Arcor, Inc. v. Haas*, 842 N.E.2d 265 (Ill. App. 2005) (reasonable affirmative steps must be taken to maintain secrecy); An owner is required only to take reasonable steps to protect its trade secrets and is not required to take every conceivable action. *PQ Labs, Inc. v. Qi*, 2014 WL 334453 (N.D. Cal. Jan. 29, 2014). "The more the owner of the trade secret spends on preventing the secret from leaking out, the more he demonstrates that the secret has real value deserving of legal protection . . . ." *Rockwell Graphic Systems, Inc. v. DEV Industries*, Inc., 925 F.2d 174, 179-80 (7th Cir. 1991); *ProExpress Distributors LLC v. Grand Electronics*, 2017 WL 2264750 (Md. May 24, 2017) (storing trade secret in the "cloud" is not a reasonable effort to maintain trade secret status).

The failure to take reasonable steps to protect disclosure of the alleged trade secret will cause the information to lose trade secret protection. *Broker Genius Inc. v. Zalta*, 2017 WL 5991831 (S.D.N.Y. Dec. 4, 2017) (failure to include confidentiality provision in software license terms of use precluded trade secret protection); *CMBB LLC v. Lockwood Mfg., Inc.*, 628 F. Supp. 2d 881 (N.D. Ill. 2009) (employer not entitled to protections of Illinois Trade Secret Act due to its failure to take reasonable protections to protect claimed trade secrets); *nClosures Inc. v. Block and Co.*, 770 F.3d 598 (7th Cir. 2014); *Fire Protection v. Premium Fire & Security*, 2014 WL 897223 (Del. Ch. March 5, 2014) (Password protection alone is insufficient to demonstrate that reasonable measures were taken to protect trade secrets.).

A limited disclosure may not void a trade secret. *Gates Rubber Co. v. Bando Chemical Indus., Ltd.*, 9 F.3d 823 (10th Cir. 1993). *See also, Masimo Corp. v. True Wearables. Inc.*, 2022 WL 205485 (4th Cir. Jan. 24, 2022) (Publication of information in a conference paper cited over 1200 times did not prevent information from being a trade secret). Interestingly, at least one court has held that the posting of a trade secret on the Internet does not necessarily cause a trade secret to lose its protection. *Syncsort, Inc. v. Innovative Routines Int'l, Inc.*, 2011 WL 3651331 (D.N.J. Aug. 18, 2011) (trade secret status not discharged if disclosure is "sufficiently obscure or transient or otherwise limited so that it does not become generally known to the relevant people." *Id.* at 13, *quoting DVD Control Ass'n., Inc. v. Bunner*, 116 Cal. App. 4th 241, 251 (2004). *See also Silicon Image, Inc. v. Analogix Semiconductor, Inc.*, 2008 WL 166950 (N.D. Cal. Jan. 17, 2008); *Data General Corp. v. Digital Computer Controls, Inc.*, 357 A.2d 105 (Del. Ch. 1975) (disclosure of portion of data did not cause information to lose trade secret status).

If a dispute arises, the owner must prove it considered the relevant information to be a trade secret and that it took appropriate action to protect such information. A trade secret does not lose protection if it has been memorized *Al Minor & Assoc., Inc. v. Martin*, 881 N.E.2d 850 (Ohio 2008) but trade secrets are not protected from reverse engineering or accidental disclosure. *See Aqua Connect, Inc. v. Code Rebel, LLC et al.*, 2012 WL 1535769 (C.D. Cal. Feb. 13, 2012) (reverse engineering software in violation of license agreement did not constitute trade secret misappropriation).

A party may be liable for trade secret misappropriation even if it does not comprehend the information or cannot decipher it. *ClearOne Communications, Inc. v. Chiang*, 2007 WL 4376125 (D. Utah Dec. 13, 2007) (party may be liable for trade secret misappropriation even if it cannot understand or decipher object code constituting trade secrets). Further, at least two courts have held that officers, directors and investors of a corporation may be held personally liable for a corporation's misappropriation of a trade secret where the misappropriation was a significant part of the corporation's strategy and the individual had reason to know of the wrongful conduct. *PMC, Inc. v. Kadisha*, 78 Cal. App. 4th 1368 (2000); *Accuimage Diagnostics Corp. v. Terarecon, Inc.*, 260 F. Supp. 2d 941 (N.D. Cal. 2003) *but see Verigy US, Inc. v. Mayder*, 2008 WL 5063873 (N.D. Cal. Nov. 4, 2008) (corporate officer and director cannot be held liable for trade secret misappropriation unless acting outside their scope of employment); *Art and Cook, Inc. v. Haber*, 416 F. Supp 3d 191 (E.D.N.Y. 2017) (employer did not take reasonable measures where it did not ask employee to sign an NDA until three years after their employment and provided employee access to confidential information after the employee refused to sign an NDA).

(d) Actions to Protect Trade Secrets

Actions that demonstrate taking reasonable actions to protect a party's trade secrets include entering into a nondisclosure agreement with the receiving party, identifying all confidential information, and marking all tangible property containing such confidential information, including any disks or tapes, as "Secret" or "Proprietary and Confidential."

Trade secret protection provides an owner with protection for potentially an unlimited duration in comparison to copyright and patent protection. The failure to take reasonable steps to protect a trade secret may lead a court to deny trade secret status for the confidential information. *See Fail-Safe, LLC v. A.O. Smith Corp.*, 674 F.3d 889 (7th Cir. 2012). *See also Hoover Panel Systems, Inc. v. Hat Contract Inc.*, 2019 WL 2743589(N. Tex. May 9, 2019) (failure to mark confidential information resulted in dismissal of breach of contract/trade secret misappropriation claim); *Two Palms Software, Inc. v. Worldwide Freight Management LLC*, 2012 WL 2418913 (E.D. Mo. June 26, 2012) (disclosure of first 50 pages of software code out of 80,000 lines to U.S. Copyright Office did not destroy trade secret status); *Jostens Inc. v. National Computer Systems, Inc.*, 318 N.W.2d 691 (Minn. 1982) (employer failed to take reasonable steps to protect its intellectual property by failing to mark software tapes and documents "secret" or "confidential"). Reasonable protections should be taken for all electronic communications when using conferencing platforms such as Zoom® and Teams®. *Smash Franchise Partners, LLC v. Kanda Holdings, Inc.*, 2020 WL 4692287 (Del. Aug. 13, 2020) (trade secret holder found not to have taken reasonable precautions such as using passwords a waiting room and taking a role call on Zoom® calls even though the parties signing a non-disclosure agreements).

Trade secret protection is especially important in relation to employees as a significant percentage of all trade secret claims involve the alleged misappropriation of an entity's trade secrets by its employees. All employees, consultants, vendors, and customers should execute a confidentiality agreement prior to their access to confidential information. *See MAI Sys. Corp. v. Peak Computer, Inc.*, 991 F.2d 511, 521 (9th Cir. 1993); *C.R.T.R., Inc. v. Lao*, 31 Mass. L. Rptr. 635 (Mass. Sup. Ct. 2014) (company's failure to require independent contractor to execute nondisclosure agreement forfeited claim to trade secret status); *Warehouse Solutions, Inc. v. Integrated Logistics, LLC.*, 610 Fed. Appx. 881 (11th Cir. 2015) (absence of written confidentiality agreement relevant for determining if reasonable steps taken to protect trade secrets; oral statements as to confidentiality insufficient to satisfy reasonable steps requirement). Their confidentiality obligations should be reinforced through regular training and the implementation of comprehensive corporate policies. Upon termination of an employee's employment, the employer should conduct an exit interview to remind the employee of his or her confidentiality obligations and preferably have the employee execute an acknowledgment of his or her confidentiality obligations.

Given the trend toward working remotely, employers should take greater care given employees can access the employer's trade secrets and confidential information remotely. To protect against the increased risk from working remotely, prudent employers should:

- Enhance employee training to reflect the realities of remote work
- Conduct phishing, malware and false flag exercises and training to educate employees
- Establish a "work from home" policy with specific security requirements
- Require employees to only work company provided devices
- Prohibit employees from using personal computers and phones
- Prohibit employees from discussing trade secrets on conference calls
- Prohibit employees from removing trade secrets from the office or printing out trade secrets at home
- Require employees to use the company VPN to access the internet and use two step authentication
- Prohibit employees from leaving devices containing confidential information and trade secrets unattended
- Require employees to immediately report lost or stolen devices containing confidential information or trade secrets

The owning entity should limit the dissemination of the information to a need-to-know basis and limit access to vendors and subcontractors. *Surgidev Corp. v. Eye Technology, Inc.*, 828 F.2d 452, 455 (8th Cir. 1987). Further, the owning entity should secure the business premises with locks, controlled entryways, visitor logs, etc. *Wyeth v. Natural Biologics, Inc.*, 2003 WL 22282371, at *3 (D. Minn. Oct. 2, 2003). All persons and bags entering and leaving a facility should be subject to search.

All documentation should be shredded after use, while all white boards and writing surfaces should be erased and cleaned. Confidential information should not be faxed to unattended machines. Fax machine memories should be purged/cleaned daily. All access to soft copies of all the information should be computer-password restricted with prohibitions on copying or forwarding such information electronically or downloading onto personal digital assistants. All passwords should be required to be reset every 30 days with layered security codes.

Access to network drives should be restricted to those employees with an actual "need to know." Further, users should be required to use separate log-in names and passwords to access any intellectual property or trade secrets. Access to the information should be tracked to record who is accessing the information and why. These logs should be retained to allow the owner to conduct an annual audit of its trade secrets and the strength of its protection. Finally, the owner should utilize penetration testing to further test its protection.

Other potential actions include having all trash shredded, requiring employees to report all solicitations requesting the disclosure of confidential information, limitations on the use of cell phones with cameras on the company's premises, and prohibitions on accessing personal e-mail from company premises and from company computers. The company's technology department should ensure that the appropriate firewalls are in place and that adequate encryption technology is being used. Further, employees should be informed that there is no expectation of privacy for their corporate email.

A company should ensure that all locations where the information is stored are secure, not just the electronic files that may contain the information. *See Nationwide Mutual Ins. Co. v. Mortensen*, 606 F.3d 22 (2d Cir. 2010) (company not entitled to trade secret protection for client information as company failed to take reasonable precautions for all locations where information stored). All trade secrets should be kept in locked rooms, in locked file cabinets.

In addition, the owning entity should have written policies and procedures on protecting and the non-dissemination of its trade secrets/confidential information. Semiannual reminders of this policy should be distributed, and all of the company's efforts should be documented. *Centrol, Inc. v. Morrow*, 489 N.W.2d 890, 894–95 (S.D. 1992). For extremely confidential documents, each document should receive a special tag or footer to allow the company to identify to whom each copy was distributed and provide the ability to trace any copies that are wrongfully circulated. An employee incentive program should be created to encourage the development and maintenance of intellectual property. All intellectual property including trade secrets should be documented and cataloged.

Upon an employee's resignation, the employee's access to the employer's computer networks and intellectual property should be frozen. If technically feasible, the employer should send the ex-employee a "kill e-mail" which, when opened, will automatically delete any of the employer's files on the ex-employee's computer. *See, e.g., Haggard v. Spine*, 2009 WL 1655030 (D. Colo. June 12, 2009) (Employer's protective measures including sending a "kill e-mail" demonstrated the value the employer placed on its trade secrets and the efforts it took to protect them.). The employee's network and computer access for the 90 days prior to resignation or termination should be reviewed to ensure the employee did not improperly access or download any of the employer's intellectual property.

An exit interview should be conducted with all departing employees to remind them of their continuing obligation to maintain the confidentiality of the employer's confidential information. The unauthorized actions of employees will not destroy the employer's confidential information trade secret status if it has taken reasonable precautions. *See E.I. duPont de Nemours & Co. v. Christopher*, 431 F.2d 1012, 1017 (5th Cir. 1970) (A court "should not require . . . a corporation to take unreasonable precautions to prevent another from doing that which he ought not to do in the first place"). An employer should also evaluate whether special protections need to be implemented if a great number of its employees work remotely or use laptops or memory sticks that contain the employer's trade secrets. The employer may want to establish an internal committee to identify potential risks arising from employees who work remotely and seek to implement appropriate safeguards. Appropriate security procedures should be implemented to protect the computer systems accessed by those employees and to address the use of memory sticks.

All actual or potential disclosures should be documented through the execution of a nondisclosure agreement. Execution of a nondisclosure agreement is not, however, per se required to uphold the existence of a trade secret. *Marshall v. Gipson Steel, Inc.*, 806 So. 2d 266, 272 (Miss. 2002).

PRACTICE POINT:

Especially in the event of litigation, an entity should consider the following actions to support its contention that it took reasonable steps to protect its trade secrets.

- Create and maintain an inventory of all information considered to be a trade secret, including the creator, the date of creation, and a description of the trade secret.
- Mark all trade secrets "Confidential and Secret".
- Keep all trade secrets segregated from general information.
- Implement multi-factor authentication/passwords.
- Encrypt all trade secrets.
- Utilize firewalls and anti-virus software to protect all trade secrets.
- Restrict physical access to facilities where trade secrets are kept, including sign-in logs, 24-hour security, etc.
- Require all visitors to a facility to sign a nondisclosure agreement.
- Limit access to trade secrets to a need-to-know basis.
- Track access to each trade secret, including the name of the individual accessing the trade secret, his/her employer, and the date access was provided.
- Require all individuals and entities who have access to trade secrets to execute a nondisclosure agreement prior to accessing the trade secrets.
- Prohibit cameras and phones in the entities' facilities.
- Implement a trade secret policy, including prohibiting employees from bringing/using any confidential information from their previous employer and mark all trade secrets as "Trade Secret – Circulation or Disclosure is Prohibited".

- Require all employees to wear identification badges.
- Use key cards to track employee movement in all facilities.
- Implement a written Bring Your Own Device (BYOD) policy.
- Implement appropriate security procedures when using electronic communications such as Zoom®, Teams® etc.
- Have all employees assign ownership of any intellectual property they create, including trade secrets, to the employer.
- Require all employees to acknowledge the company's trade secret policy and execute a confidentiality agreement as a condition to employment.
- Periodically remind employees of their confidentiality obligations including the use of pop up screens requiring employees to affirmatively acknowledge their obligations under their non-disclosure agreements.
- Monitor and audit compliance with the company's trade secret policy.
- Implement a comprehensive training program to educate employees on the protection of trade secrets.
- Review all public presentations/trade show presentations to ensure that no trade secrets are disclosed.
- Conduct exit interviews with all departing employees and have each employee execute an acknowledgment of their confidentiality obligations.
- Destroy all trade secrets no longer needed.
- Immediately terminate departing employees' access to trade secrets and collect all company property. Have all departing employees certify that they have returned all company property.
- Send departing employees letters reminding them of their confidentiality obligations and that trade secret misappropriation can occur by remembering such information. *First Interstate BancSystem, Inc. v. Hubert*, 615 F. Supp. 3d 1270 (D. Wyo. 2022).

(d) Acknowledgment of Trade Secret Status

To avoid potential disputes over the proprietary nature of their intellectual property, many licensors have the customer acknowledge in their license that the licensor's intellectual property is a trade secret. This may prevent the customer from later claiming the intellectual property was not a trade secret and focuses any dispute on whether the customer breached its confidentiality obligations and the amount of damages suffered. Contractually agreeing, however, that a piece of information is a trade secret will not in and of itself grant trade secret status to such information. *Thompson v. Impaxx, Inc.*, 113 Cal. App. 4th 1425, 1430 (2003) ("Labeling information as a trade secret . . . does not conclusively establish that the information fits this description."). A customer should carefully consider the implications of acknowledging whether something is a trade secret. The customer most likely does not know whether the information in question is a trade secret. A reasonable solution is for the customer to acknowledge that the licensor treats the information as a trade secret. At a minimum, the licensor should also acknowledge that the customer's information is a trade secret.

Having one party acknowledge that certain information is a trade secret is not dispositive. In *Computer Associates International, Inc. v. American Fundware, Inc.*,

831 F. Supp. 1516, 1530 (D. Colo. 1993), the U.S. District Court for Colorado held that the defendant was not estopped from contesting the existence of trade secrets, even though it had signed a license acknowledging that the information in question constituted trade secrets. *See also Gary Van Zeeland Talent, Inc. v. Sandas*, 267 N.W.2d 242, 249 (Wis. 1978) (public policy prohibits estoppel based on contractual acknowledgment of trade secrets in restraint of trade case). Courts have found, however, that where the defendant acknowledged over several years the proprietary nature of the information, estoppel may be appropriate, *In re Uniservices, Inc.*, 517 F.2d 492 (7th Cir. 1975), or where the estopped party had directly developed the trade secrets in question. *Ultra-Life Laboratories, Inc. v. Eanes*, 221 S.W.2d 224 (Mo. 1949).

(f) Ownership Not Required to Bring a Claim

Several courts have held that an entity with a license to use a trade secret but did not own the trade secret, could bring a claim for misappropriation. *Advanced Fluid Systems v. Huber*, 958 F.3d 168 (3d Cir. 2020); *DTM Research, L.L.C. v. AT&T Corp.*, 245 F.3d 327 (4th Cir. 2001); *Gaedeke Holdings VII Ltd. v. Baker*, 683 Fed. App'x. 677 (10th Cir. 2017).

(g) Relationship to Patents

Submission of a trade secret as part of a patent application will cause the trade secret to lose its protection even if the patent is never published, but a unique combination of the elements and process submitted as part of the application is entitled to trade secret protection. *Tewari De-Ox Sys., Inc. v. Mountain States/Rosen, L.L.C.*, 667 F.3d 604 (5th Cir. 2011). Federal patent law does not prevent state trade secret and breach of contract claims where an inventor seeks trade secret protection and not patent protection. *Russo v. Ballard Medical Products*, 550 F.3d 1004 (10th Cir. 2008). *See also Kewanee Oil Company v. Bicron Corp.*, 416 U.S. 470 (1974); *Bonito Boats, Inc. v. Thunder Craft Boats, Inc.*, 489 U.S. 141 (1989). It is important to note, however, that trade secret status is lost only where the trade secret and the patent cover the same subject matter. *Wellogix, Inc. v. Accenture, L.L.P.*, 716 F.3d 867 (5th Cir. 2013). Unlike patent protection, trade secret protection does not protect against a party independently developing the same invention.

For a general overview of data protection and developing confidentiality systems, *see* Catanzariti, *Keeping Secrets—Developing Confidentiality Systems*, ACC DOCKET 24 (Oct. 2006); Spenser, *Tips and Insights on Data Protection*, ACC DOCKET 24 (Oct. 2006); Fine, *7 Steps to Information Protection*, 134 Intell. Prop. Couns. 1 (Feb. 2008).

For a detailed discussion of trade secrets, *see Overview of Trade Secret Protection*, 41 Law. Brief. 5 (Nov. 30, 2011); Halligan & Weyand, Trade Secret Asset Management—An Executive's Guide to Information Asset Management, Including Sarbanes Oxley Accounting Requirements for Trade Secrets, Aspatore Books (2007).

2. Uniform Trade Secret Act

The Uniform Trade Secret Act (UTSA) was approved in 1979 by the National Conference of Commissions on Uniform State Laws and has subsequently been adopted by every state and the District of Columbia, except for New York. For a survey of jurisdictions that have adopted the UTSA, *see* https://www.beckreedriden.com/trade-secrets-laws-and-the-utsa-a-50-state-and-federal-law-survey-chart/.

Section 4 of the UTSA defines a "trade secret" as:

> [I]nformation, including a formula, pattern, compilation, program, device, method, technique, or process, that: (i) derives independent economic value, actual or potential, from not being generally known to, and not being readily ascertainable by proper means by other persons who can obtain economic value from its disclosure or use; and (ii) is the subject of efforts that are reasonable under the circumstances to maintain its secrecy.

This definition is broader than the traditional meaning under common law as, under the UTSA, the trade secret does not need to be presently used in the owner's business. Trade secret status will be granted to information that will be used in a contemplated business activity.

To receive protection under the UTSA, a trade secret must meet three criteria:

- it must have independent economic value as a result of its confidentiality;
- it must not be generally known or readily ascertainable; and
- the owner must take reasonable efforts to maintain its secrecy.

UTSA § 1(4). An owner's efforts to maintain secrecy must be reasonable under the circumstances and need not be extreme. *E.I. duPont de Nemours & Co., Inc. v. Christopher*, 431 F.2d 1012 (5th Cir. 1970).

Some states require that any misappropriation be known. *See, e.g.*, Ga. Code Ann. § 101-761. *See Southern Nuclear Operating Co., Inc. v. Electric Data Systems Corp.*, 2008 WL 1700204 (11th Cir. April 14, 2008).

Under the UTSA Section 3(a), an injured party is entitled to recover monetary damages for lost profits and unjust enrichment. *See, e.g.*, *Ice Corp. v. Hamilton Sundstrand Corp.*, 615 F. Supp. 2d 1256 (D. Kan. 2009) (plaintiff in successful misappropriation claim entitled to recover lost profits). In the alternative, the UTSA also allows the aggrieved party to receive a royalty. A party is also entitled to injunctive relief for both actual and threatened misappropriation. Injunctive relief remains in place until the affected party seeks its removal, because the information in question is no longer a trade secret. Further, in the event of a willful and malicious misappropriation, an injured party can receive exemplary damages equal to two times its actual damages. UTSA § 3(b). Finally, the prevailing party may also obtain lawyer's fees. UTSA § 4. *See, e.g.*, *FLIR Systems, Inc. v. Parrish*, 174 Cal. App. 4th 1270 (Cal. 2009) (affirming award of legal fees under California UTSA).

Any claim for misappropriation of a trade secret must be brought within three years after the misappropriation has been discovered. UTSA § 6. Many states have adopted their own statute of limitations. *See e.g.*, Alabama, two years, Ala. Code Ann. § 8-27-5; Georgia, five years, Ga. Code Ann. § 10-1-766; Ohio, four years, Ohio Rev. Code § 1333.66. California courts have interpreted the statute of limitations as beginning to run "when the plaintiff has any reason to suspect that the third party knows or reasonably should know that the information is a trade secret." *Cypress Semiconductor Corp. v. Superior Court*, 77 Cal. Rptr. 3d 685, 687 (Cal. 2008).

A dichotomy exists among the courts as to whether the UTSA preempts a right of recovery under common law. The majority holds that the UTSA preempts all common-law and statutory recovery rights for theft, including unfair competition, conversion, breach of fiduciary duty, tortuous interference with a contractual relationship, and *quantum meruit. See, e.g., Thomas & Betts Corp. v. Panduit Corp.*, 108 F. Supp. 2d 968, 971 (N.D. Ill. 2000); *AutoChannel, Inc. v. Speedvision Network, LLC*, 144 F. Supp. 2d 784, 788–89 (W.D. Ky. 2001) (allowing both common-law and UTSA claims to be asserted "would undermine the uniformity and clarity that motivated the creation and passage of the Uniform Act."); *K.C. Multimedia, Inc. v. Bank of America Tech. & Oper., Inc.*, 171 Cal. App. 4th 939, 958 (Cal. 2009), quoting *Digital Envoy, Inc. v. Google, Inc.*, 370 F. Supp. 2d 1025, 1035 (N.D. Cal. 2005) (California UTSA "prevents common law claims that are based on the same nucleus of facts as the misappropriation of trade secret claims for relief"); *Composite Marine Propellers, Inc. v. Van Der Woude*, 962 F.2d 1263, 1265 (7th Cir. 1992) (Illinois Trade Secrets Act abolished all common-law theories of misuse of confidential information). The minority holds that the UTSA preempts common-law causes of action for misappropriation of trade secrets but allows a party to seek remedies based in tort for the theft of a trade secret. *See, e.g., Accuimage Diagnostics Corp. v. Terarecon, Inc.*, 260 F. Supp. 2d 941, 953–54 (N.D. Cal. 2003) (common-law trade secret misappropriation claim preempted); *Mortgage Specialists, Inc. v. Davey*, 904 A.2d 652, 666 (N.H. 2006) (UTSA preempts conversion).

Independently developing know-how that constitutes a trade secret is recognized by the UTSA as a defense to a claim of trade secret misappropriation. One means of utilizing this defense is to show that the allegedly infringing know-how was developed in a "clean room" by individuals without knowledge or access to the trade secret in question. Such efforts are not always enough, however, to prevent a preliminary injunction from being issued. *See, e.g., Computer Associates International v. Quest Software, Inc.*, 333 F. Supp. 2d 688 (N.D. Ill. 2004).

For a more detailed discussion of the Independent Development Defense, *see* Katz, *The "Independent Development" Defense under the Uniform Trade Secrets Act*, 140 Intell. Prop. Couns. 1 (Aug. 2008); Kahnke & Burdy, *Clean Rooms Are Not Just for Kids: How to Demonstrate Independent Development to Avoid a Trade Secret*, http://www.faegrebd.com/files/12645_Trends%20March%20and%20April%202008.pdf.

Interestingly, the UTSA recognizes that independent parties who develop the same trade secret can own the rights to the same trade secret and both parties are entitled to trade secret protection for the same information. Only the party from whom the information was misappropriated, however, can collect damages. Comment Sections 1 and 3 to UTSA. Further, a party is free to disclose the secret to the public, thus destroying its value. In the event a trade secret becomes public, a licensee's obligation to pay royalty fees is not necessarily negated. *See Warner-Lambert Pharmaceutical Co. v. John J. Reynolds, Inc.*, 178 F. Supp. 655 (S.D.N.Y. 1959), *aff'd*, 280 F.2d 197 (2d Cir. 1960), but a hybrid trade secret-patent would be invalid. *Meehan v. PPG Industries, Inc.*, 802 F.2d 881 (7th Cir. 1986); *Pitney Bowes, Inc. v. Mestre*, 701 F.2d 1365 (11th Cir. 1983).

3. *Computer Fraud and Abuse Act (CFAA)*

The Computer Fraud and Abuse Act (CFAA), 18 U.S.C. § 1030, offers another means for an employer to bring an action against a former employee. The CFAA prohibits the theft of computer data, the unauthorized access to protected computer information, and the knowing transmission of a command that intentionally damages an employer's computer. 18 U.S.C. § 1030(a). An injured party must prove that it suffered a "loss" of at least $5,000 in damages. 18 U.S.C. § 1030(a)(4).

Courts are divided as to whether an employee still employed by the employer violates the CFAA when he steals information from the employer or damages the employer's computer hardware or software. See Chapter 28.F for a more detailed discussion of the CFAA and its application to employee misconduct.

4. *Restatement (Third) of Unfair Competition*

Section 39 of the Restatement (Third) of Unfair Competition sets forth two factors to determine whether a concept or information is a trade secret: (1) the extent to which the information can be used in the operation of a business or other enterprise, and (2) whether it is sufficiently valuable and secret to afford an actual or potential economic advantage to others. Thus, the determination of whether a piece of information is a trade secret depends on whether it meets these requirements. The definition of "trade secret" under the Restatement is consistent with the definition of trade secret in § 1(4) of the UTSA.

5. *Economic Espionage Act of 1996*

The Economic Espionage Act of 1996 ("Act") makes certain misappropriations of a trade secret a federal crime and provides enhanced penalties for the theft of trade secrets. 18 U.S.C. § 1831 *et seq.* The Act has two principal objectives, to prevent the theft of trade secrets by an agent of a foreign government or instrumentality or a person acting on behalf of a foreign government, and the protection of trade secrets from theft in general.

Under the Act, anyone who seeks to steal a trade secret related to or included in a product that is produced for or placed in interstate or foreign commerce that injures the owner of that trade secret shall be subject to a fine of not more than the greater of $5 million or three times the value of the trade secret to the organization. 18 U.S.C. § 1832(b). In addition, the guilty party may be subject to imprisonment of not more than 10 years, or both. 18 U.S.C. § 1832(a). The requirements of the Act are similar to the requirements of UTSA, with the added requirement that the trade secret be related to a product placed into interstate commerce.

The Economic Espionage Act defines "trade secrets" broadly as:

> all forms and types of financial, business, scientific, technical, economic, or engineering information, including patterns, plans, compilations, program devices, formulas,

> designs, prototypes, methods, techniques, processes, procedures, programs or codes, whether tangible or intangible, and whether or how stored, compiled or memorialized physically, electronically, graphically, photographically, or in writing if - (A) the owner thereof has taken reasonable measures to keep such information secret; and (B) the information derives independent economic value, actual or potential, from not being generally known to, and not being readily ascertainable through proper means, by another person . . . .

18 U.S.C. § 1839(3). The Act defines "trade secrets" more broadly than common law or the Restatement. *See United States v. Martin*, 228 F.3d 1 (1st Cir. 2000) (Act defines "trade secret" broadly to include tangible property and intangible information). This law is also applicable to anyone who receives, buys, or possesses such information knowing that it has been stolen or appropriated, obtained, or converted without authorization. 18 U.S.C. § 1832(a)(3). The Economic Espionage Act does not preempt or displace any other remedies, whether civil or criminal, provided by U.S. federal, state, commonwealth, or territory law for the misappropriation of trade secrets. 18 U.S.C. § 1838.

While the Economic Espionage Act contains criminal penalties unlike the UTSA, a plaintiff under the Act must prove guilt "beyond a reasonable doubt." Further, the due process requirements for criminal acts must be satisfied.

For a general overview of potential criminal liability for the staff of software and electronic data, *see* Gross, *Criminal Liability for Theft of, Interference with, or Unauthorized Use of Computer Programs, Files or Systems*, 51 A.L.R. 4th 971 (1987).

6. *The Defend Trade Secrets Act*

The Defend Trade Secrets Act ("DTSA"), 18 U.S.C. § 1836(b)(1), amends the Economic Espionage Act of 2016 by expanding federal law to include protection for trade secret theft. The DTSA created a new federal cause of action for trade secret theft allowing aggrieved parties to bring a claim under federal law, supplementing existing state law protections. The DTSA increased the maximum penalty for trade secret theft while creating the right to *ex parte* seizures to prevent the further dissemination of the misappropriated trade secrets where injunctive relief is inadequate. *See Mission Capital Advisors LLC v. Romaka*, 2016 WL 11517104 (S.D.N.Y. July 29, 2016); *but see OOO Brunswick Rail Mgmt. v. Sultanov*, 2017 WL 67119 (N.D. Cal. Jan. 6, 2017) (*ex parte* seizure denied). The DTSA also provides for the recovery of attorney's fees in the event of a bad faith claim of misappropriation and the award of exemplary damages up to two times the amount of compensatory damages in the event of willful and malicious appropriation.

Employees who disclose confidential information in conjunction with reporting suspected violations of the law are immune from liability, including in any lawsuit or any retaliation proceeding brought by the employee. Further, employers must amend their employee nondisclosure agreements to inform their employees of this exclusion

For an overview of the DTSA *see* Meyer, *The Defend Trade Secrets Act Creates a Federal Option for Addressing Misappropriation*, 34 COMP. & INTERNET LAW. 24 (May 2017); Campbell, *The Federal Defend Trade Secrets Act – Keeping Secrets Secret*, 35 COMP. & INTERNET LAW. 9 (Feb. 2018).

7. *State Laws*

Employers may also be entitled to protection from an employee's theft of the employer's trade secrets under various state laws. *See, e.g., New Jersey: New Jersey Computer Related Offenses Act*, N.J.S.A. 2A:38A-3; Georgia OCGA § 16-9-93 (Computer Theft), *DuCom v. State*, 654 S.E.2d 670 (Ga. App. 2007). These laws vary by state, and their applicability will depend on the location of the employer and whether the employee is a resident of the relevant state or working in an office in such state. A prudent employer must understand the impact of the various state laws, as they may have a significant impact on the trade secret owner. For example, under Massachusetts, New York, and Texas law, the trade secret must be in continual use, while many states have established their own statute of limitations distinct from the UTSA.

A number of states have held employers liable under the doctrine of *respondeat superior* when an employee acting within the scope of his employment misappropriates trade secrets for the benefit of his employer. *Newport News Indus. v. Dynamic Testing, Inc.*, 131 F. Supp. 2d 745 (E.D. Va. 2007); *Hagen v. Burmeister & Assocs., Inc.*, 1999 WL 31130 (Minn. App. Jan. 26, 1999); *but see Infinity Products, Inc. v. Quandt*, 810 N.E.2d 1028 (Ind. 2004).

For a list of states and the corresponding state statutes that criminalize the theft of trade secrets, *see Criminal Unfair Competition in Intellectual Property*, 45 The Law. Brief 10 (June 2015).

For a further discussion, see Chapter 28.D, E, and F.

8. *The Inevitable Disclosure Doctrine*

The inevitable disclosure doctrine arises when a former employee with the confidential information of a former employer accepts a position with a competitor of the former employer. Under the doctrine, it is "inevitable" that the employee will disclose the former employer's trade secrets if he or she accepts employment with a competitor, thus permitting the former employer to obtain injunctive relief preventing the former employee from starting employment with the new employer. *See PepsiCo., Inc. v. Redmond*, 54 F.3d 1262 (7th Cir. 1995) (unless the employee "possesses an uncanny ability to compartmentalize information," he would be making decisions at his/her employee based on knowledge of his former employer's trade secrets. *See also Strata Marketing, Inc. v. Murphy*, 740 N.E.2d 1166 (Ill. 2002); *Merck & Co., Inc. v. Lyon*, 941 F. Supp. 1443 (M.D.N.C. 1996); *Uncle B's Bakery, Inc. v. O'Rourke*, 920 F. Supp. 1405 (N.D. Iowa 1996); *B.F. Goodrich Co. v. Wohlgemuth*, 192 N.E.2d 99 (Ohio Ct. App. 1966); *Allis-Chalmers Mfg. Co. v. Continental Aviation & Eng'g Corp.*, 255 F. Supp. 645 (E.D. Mich. 1966); *E.I. du Pont de Nemours & Co. v. American Potash & Chem. Corp.*, 200 A.2d 428 (Del. Ch. 1964).

Not all states recognize the doctrine of inevitable disclosure. In *Marrietta Corp. v. Fairhurst*, 754 N.Y.S.2d 62 (N.Y. App. 2003), a New York court refused to apply the doctrine, stating, "The doctrine of inevitable disclosure is disfavored." *See also Whyte v. Schlage Lock Co.*, 101 Cal. App. 4th 1443 (2002) (rejecting inevitable disclosure doctrine); *Government Tech. Services, Inc. v. IntelliSys Tech. Corp.*, 51 Va. Cir. 55, 56 (1999) ("Virginia does not recognize the inevitable disclosure doctrine."); *Le Jeune, Inc., v. Coin*

Acceptors, Inc., 849 A.2d 451, 470 (Md. 2004) (court "declines" to adopt doctrine of inevitable disclosure).

For an overview of the doctrine of inevitable disclosure, *see* Godfrey, *Inevitable Disclosure of Trade Secrets: Employee Mobility v. Employer Rights*, 37 High Tech. L. 16 (2004); Comment, *An Overview of Individual States' Application of Inevitable Disclosure: Concrete Doctrine or Equitable Tool?*, 55 SMU L. Rev. 621 (2002); Murphy, *Managing the Risk of Inevitable Trade Secrets Disclosure*, 26 CORP. COUNS. Q. 58 (Jan. 2010).

For a discussion of employee confidentiality and trade secret obligations, see Chapter 28.B.

CHAPTER **26**

Representing the Global Entity

Although this book focuses on the issues arising in the domestic software licensing and cloud computing, counsel must consider whether the underlying license or services agreement raise any international issues. These issues may arise even when both parties are incorporated and headquartered in the United States. The consideration of these issues assumes greater importance as more software development and information technology services are performed outside of the United States. If the underlying license and related services transaction are considered to be a consumer transaction, the licensor must also consider the implications of the various consumer laws of each applicable country.

The issues that may arise and thus require consideration will depend on the type of software being licensed and the services being provided. The parties must ascertain where the software will be used; whether the software and technical data will be accessed by the customer from outside the United States; and where the services will be performed, as the failure to comply with U.S. export laws may lead to criminal penalties, civil penalties, and the revocation of the vendor's export privileges. See Chapter 7.L for a more detailed discussion of export related issues. Customers should ascertain where the software will be used, whether the customer will access the software from outside the United States and what, if any, services will be provided from outside of the United States. Services may include development services, application support and maintenance services, help desk/call center services and data processing, as well as database management.

To quantify the level of risk involved, the customer should require the vendor to represent and warrant to the customer where the services will be performed. See Chapter 5.A. This representation and warranty should be accompanied by a mirrored indemnification, indemnifying the customer for any claims or liability arising from work performed outside of the United States. If all work is to be performed within the United States, the licensor should make a representation and warranty to that the effect. Further, from the customer's perspective, the contract should provide that no work may be performed outside of the United States without the prior written consent of the customer. See § 16.AB.

Set forth below is a brief overview of some of the specific issues that prudent parties should consider when entering into a contract where services will be or may be performed outside of the United States, where software may be developed outside the United States, or where a customer may access or use the vendor's software and technical data outside of the United States.

A. Access and the Scope of Use

As discussed in Chapter 7.L, U.S. export/import laws, rules, and regulations may have an important impact on transferring or accessing software and technical data internationally. From the vendor's perspective, it is important to ascertain what rights the customer requires (such as the ability/right to access the licensed software remotely from outside of the United States) and to draft the license grant accordingly. While software licenses often restrict where the software can be installed (i.e., at a facility/ data center within the United States) to the extent the software is accessible by the licensee from outside the United States, the applicable license should address this contingency. The licensor must be careful not to grant the customer rights that would violate U.S. export laws.

The first issue for the licensor to consider is whether the software will be accessed remotely. For instance, certain software is used in facility-based applications, without the need to be remotely accessed. For many administrative and production systems serving the global needs of organizations, however, companies need to provide remote access to these systems for their employees.

The second issue is whether the software application, or portions of it, is required to reside on a laptop or other portable electronic device (known sometimes as "fat client" architecture). If the software, or portions thereof, is required to reside on a computer in order to facilitate remote access, then an export event will occur when the laptop or other portable device is taken out of the United States. In that event, U.S. export laws would apply and must be adhered to. In addition, other import laws may apply as well. For example, if the software is situated on computer servers located in the United States with Internet access capabilities, the question arises whether accessing and displaying the software on a laptop or another portable device is an "export" for purposes of compliance with U.S. export laws. On a theoretical basis, since the software is being displayed remotely, one could argue that the export laws apply. In practice, however, many practitioners do not believe that such access triggers the applicability of U.S. export laws. The correct answer will depend upon whether the source code or technical data is accessible from outside of the United States.

U.S. export authorities take an expansive view of the applicability of U.S. export laws, particularly if the software has capabilities that are considered sensitive. For example, if a customer in Russia sends data to a location in the United States and later accesses pieces of software located in the United States, such actions are likely to be considered an "export" and subject to U.S. export controls, even though the software does not leave the United States. The trigger is the customer's access to the software. If the Russian customer simply provides the data that is processed in the United States and the Russian customer later receives only the processed data, the transaction is unlikely to be considered an export.

When drafting a software license agreement where the customer will be accessing the software from outside of the United States, a prudent vendor should incorporate a "scope of use" clause that recognizes that the software may be accessed remotely from outside of the United States, and, to the extent compliance with U.S. export laws is required, require the customer to comply with all applicable laws. A sample license provision protecting the vendor's interests is as follows:

> *Licensor grants to Customer a nonexclusive, perpetual, non-assessable, fully paid, unlimited user type, multi-site and nontransferable license for Customer to use and install the Software in the United States, and to permit its Affiliates and other Authorized Users to use the Software and Documentation in accordance with the Agreement, and by remote access worldwide provided that Customer shall be responsible for compliance with any applicable laws, rules and regulations related to access of the Software outside of the United States.*

B. Provision of Technology to Non-U.S. Citizens

The U.S. export laws apply to the "export" of technology whether it is an actual export to a location outside of the United States or a "deemed" export where a foreign national accesses the technology from within or outside of the United States. *See* 15 C.F.R. § 734.13. If the work is performed by an individual who is not a Unites States citizen, export control law issues need to be considered. Under U.S. export control laws, all technology exported from the United States to any country that does not fall under a license exception generally requires an export license. 15 C.F.R. § 736.2. This includes technology provided by an employer to an alien who is not a permanent resident of the United States, regardless of his or her location (i.e., even if the alien is in the United States when receiving the information) and regardless of whether the alien is an independent contractor or employee.

Section 734.13(a)(2) of the Export Administration Regulations defines "export" to include: *Releasing or otherwise transferring "technology" or source code (but not object code) to a foreign person in the United States (a "deemed export")*. Further, Section 734.14 defines "reexport" to include: *Releasing or otherwise transferring "technology" or source code subject to the EAR to a foreign person of a country other than the foreign country where the release or transfer takes place (a deemed reexport).*"

"Technology" is defined broadly as *"[i]nformation necessary for the 'development,' 'production,' 'use,' operation, installation, maintenance, repair, overhaul, or refurbishing . . . of an item. Technology "may be in any tangible or intangible form, such as written or oral communications, blueprints, drawings, photographs, plans, diagrams, models, formulae, tables, engineering designs and specifications, computer-aided design files, manuals or documentation, electronic media or information revealed through visual inspection."* 15 C.F.R. § 772.1

Thus, the customer and vendor must determine not only whether the work will be performed outside of the United States, but whether any technology will be accessed by a foreign national from outside as well as inside the United States and if so, obtain any required export licenses before disclosing the restricted technology to those individuals.

The approval period for an export license may be many months depending on the type of information to be exported. Furthermore, the United States maintains comprehensive trade sanctions against certain countries. The export of technology to citizens of certain countries, including Cuba, Iraq, Iran, North Korea and Syria, regardless of its use, may be impermissible. *See* 15 C.F.R. § 746. In order to avoid any potential violations of U.S. export control laws, a party who provides technical information to another party should ascertain the citizenship of the individuals who will have access to such information. The disclosing party should require the receiving party to represent and warrant the receiving party's compliance with U.S. export laws. Further, the disclosing party should keep detailed records of exactly what technical information is provided to the recipient. To protect its interest, the disclosing party may want to have each of its subcontractors verify the nationality of each of its employees with access to the disclosing party's technical information.

See Chapter 7.L for a more detailed discussion of the issues created by U.S. export laws.

C. Ownership of Developed Work

Ownership of the work to be developed is a significant concern for the customer. To ensure that it obtains ownership of the developed intellectual property, the customer must understand the laws of the jurisdiction in which the work will be performed. Many countries recognize moral rights under the Berne Convention. Unlike an author's rights under the "work made for hire" doctrine, which can be assigned, moral rights can only be waived. Thus, the customer should ensure that the vendor obtains the necessary waivers from its employees and subcontractors to validly transfer ownership to the customer.

D. Taxes and Import/Export Duties

Both parties should determine what foreign taxes and/or import/export duties may be applicable to the provision of the services and/or licenses contemplated under the agreement. Given that most agreements require the customer to pay any such levies, the customer should exert its best efforts to quantify the amount of such levies and should not rely on any claims by the licensor that no duties or taxes are payable. Foreign customers should reject any attempt by a U.S. vendor to have the customer pay any local income taxes levied on the licensor's income when the licensor is licensing and installing its software outside of the United States. See § 8.6. If the customer agrees to pay any such taxes on the licensor's income, it should require the licensor to provide the customer with a valid receipt to allow the customer to receive a tax deduction.

Many countries tax royalties, dividends, services, software, and hardware at different rates. As such, the agreement between the parties should require the parties to cooperate to limit the amount of such duties or taxes and agree on the allocation of any consideration payable to the vendor among royalties, dividends, services, software, and hardware. See § 8.6.A.3. Further, the contract should obligate the vendor to contest any such duties or taxes on the customer's behalf and at the customer's expense if the customer requests the vendor to do so.

E. Governing Law and Venue Provisions

1. *Governing Law*

It is a generally accepted principle of international law that intellectual property rights are governed by the laws of the country in which the work is created or used. *See* MELVILLE B. NIMMER & PAUL E. GELLER, INTERNATIONAL COPYRIGHT LAW AND PRACTICE § 1 (1993). *See also* MELVILLE B. NIMMER & DAVID NIMMER, NIMMER ON COPYRIGHTS § 17.02 (1990). A choice of law provision may be effective in selecting U.S. law to govern an agreement between a U.S. entity and a foreign entity and may thereby help minimize an offshore software developer's claim of ownership in the commissioned work, but it may not be adequate to override local statutory intellectual property law. NIMMER & GELLER, INTERNATIONAL COPYRIGHT LAW AND PRACTICE § 6, p.189 (1993).

In *Bragance c. Michel de Grece*, an author asked a French court to enforce a French copyright law provision that makes moral rights inalienable and grants to authors a share of the proceeds from exploitation of their work. The author had signed a contract under which the parties agreed to have U.S. law govern the contract. The court granted relief to the author on the basis that moral rights set out a French law copyright rule, which overrode the otherwise valid U.S. contract. The court then distinguished French statutory provisions governing moral rights from provisions assuring authors a share of the proceeds for use of their product. It found the latter to constitute a French law contract rule, which did not override the U.S. contract insofar as the contract stipulated terms of payment for the transfer. *Bragance c. Michel de Grece*, Paris, 1 ere ch., Feb. 1, 1989, 142 R.I.D.A. 301 (1989). For a more in-depth discussion of this case, see NIMMER & GELLER, INTERNATIONAL COPYRIGHT LAW AND PRACTICE § 6, p.188 (1993).

In light of the *Bragance* decision, contracting parties should recognize the possibility that a choice of law clause may not always guarantee the application of U.S. law, especially in the intellectual property area, and that "no over-riding choice of law system determines which copyright-contracts rules are subject to which conflicts principles worldwide." NIMMER & GELLER, INTERNATIONAL COPYRIGHT LAW AND PRACTICE § 6, p.189 (1993).

Licensors should recognize that even if the court does recognize the applicability of U.S. law, a local court may lack experience in interpreting and applying U.S. law. As such, any outcome may be uncertain.

Finally, to the extent possible, the parties should contemplate potential geopolitical changes to minimize risk and uncertainty. For example, the United Kingdom's withdrawal from the European Union may have unforeseen consequences on contracting parties who chose their agreement to be governed by the laws of England and Wales, believing their agreement would also be subject to the laws of the European Union. Today, given Brexit, the laws of the European Union likely no longer apply, creating uncertainty as to how a dispute may be resolved. Thus, the uncertainty inherent in foreign laws provides an added incentive to select the laws of the United States to govern any transaction.

2. Venue

An important consideration in selecting a venue for resolving international disputes is the ability to enforce the resulting decision. As a first step, a party must identify the country or countries where it will likely seek to enforce a decision and then confirm that the resulting decision is, in fact, enforceable in that jurisdiction. In addition, a party should consider the cost to utilize a particular body, such as the London Court of Arbitration or the International Chamber of Commerce (ICC) to resolve a dispute. Many entities utilize the ICC and its arbitration rules to resolve disputes as ICC arbitration decisions are enforceable under treaties between the United States and most prospective U.S. trading partners. Further, the laws of individual U.S. states are acceptable in ICC arbitrations.

F. Reverse Engineering in the European Union

Local laws may also have a significant unforeseen impact on the contract as these laws may not be well known and may increase the parties' costs as well as potentially place the vendor's intellectual property at risk. Set forth in the subsequent paragraphs are several examples of laws that a customer and vendor must consider when licensing software and providing services internationally.

(a) European Council (EC) Directive 91/250/EEC

Under EC Directive 91/250, a licensee is deemed to have the right to create such copies as are necessary to utilize a software program for the licensed purpose and to revise the program within its licensed purpose for the correction of errors. (Art. 5.) Further, similar to the Digital Millennium Copyright Act, 17 U.S.C. § 1201(f), the licensee may reverse engineer the software, but only as strictly necessary to ensure interoperability with the licensee's other software. (Art. 6.) The licensee may not, however, reverse engineer the software for any other purpose.

(b) European Council (EC) Directive 2009/24/EC and European Council (EC) Directive 2001/29/EC

Based on EC Directives 2009/24/EC (April 23, 2009) and 2001/29/EC (May 22, 2001), the United Kingdom's High Court of Justice in *SAS Institute Inc. v. World Programming, Ltd.* [2013] EWHC 69 (Ch.), Case No. HC09C03293, held that a licensee can reverse engineer licensed software to create a competing product. See Chapter 17.B.3 for a more detailed discussion.

G. UN Convention on Contracts for the International Sale of Goods

The parties should also be cognizant of the potential application of the United Nations Convention on Contracts for the International Sale of Goods ("UN Convention"), as it automatically applies to all contracts for the sale of goods between two parties who are domiciled in different countries, both of which are signatories to the UN Convention.

The UN Convention, adopted by the United States on January 1, 1988, provides a substantive framework for the formation of international contracts for the sale of goods and governs the rights of the buyer and seller. Even though the UN Convention does not define the term "good," it is written broadly enough to potentially include services for the development of software rendered by an independent contractor.

Computer software is not specifically included in the UN Convention, but is also not identified in the exclusionary provisions. UN Convention Arts. 2 and 4. The UN Convention does provide that if a "good" is regulated by a signatory country, the UN Convention will not govern its sale, because such action would interfere with the domestic laws of that particular country. UN Convention Art. 4. In the United States, the development and sale of software may be considered a "good" within the meaning of the Uniform Commercial Code (UCC) and may also be considered to be part of a nonregulated industry. *See, e.g., RRX Industries, Inc. v. Lab-Con, Inc.*, 772 F.2d 543, 546 (9th Cir. 1985); *Communications Group, Inc. v. Warner Communications, Inc.*, 527 N.Y.S.2d 341, 343–44 (1988); *Schroeders, Inc. v. Hogan Systems, Inc.*, 522 N.Y.S.2d 404 (1987). Thus, in the case of software development, a court could use the UCC definition of a "good" to justify the applicability of the UN Convention to the agreement.

If the parties wish to ensure that U.S. domestic law governs their agreement, the agreement must specifically opt out of coverage by the UN Convention. UN Convention Art. 6. At the same time, the parties are free to opt in to the UN Convention based on the premises of contractual freedom recognized by the laws of many countries. *Asante Technologies, Inc. v. PMC-Sierra, Inc.*, 164 F. Supp. 2d 1142 (N.D. Cal 2001) (Specifying the laws of a US state as the governing law does not exclude the application of the UN Convention).

Whether it is advisable to opt out of the UN Convention depends on the particular circumstances surrounding the contract. The fact that domestic courts are often unfamiliar with the UN Convention due to the lack of a fully developed body of case law (particularly as to its potential application to the software field) may prompt the contracting parties to opt out of its coverage. It may not be prudent for a party to subject itself to a legal regime that is still largely untested. However, if a party in a developing country will not agree to select U.S. law as the governing law of the agreement, the UN Convention may provide an acceptable alternative to both parties. In such cases, the UN Convention may be preferable to the uncertainties resulting from the application of conflict-of-laws rules or the risk of being subjected to less developed legal systems.

In sum, the parties must first determine if the country where the work will be performed is a signatory to the UN Convention. The party should then determine whether the UN Convention would cover the services/software to be provided under the relevant contract. If the parties wish to avoid any uncertainties resulting from the application of the UN Convention, the parties should opt out of the UN Convention and specify which country's laws govern the contract. See § 28.1 model language opting out of the UN Convention. The agreement should specifically exclude the application of any conflicts of laws principles. It should be noted that it is not entirely clear under U.S. law whether parties can choose to "opt in" to the UN Convention where the convention does not otherwise apply to the transaction in question.

In some instances, it may be technically unnecessary to opt out of coverage by the UN Convention. The United States implementing legislation adopting the UN

Convention contains a reservation limiting its applicability to situations where the contracting U.S. party has a place of business in the country of the other party. Isaak Dore, *Choice of Law under the International Sales Convention, a U.S. Perspective*, 77 Am. J. Intl. L. 521, 525–26 (1980). If the U.S. party has no place of business in the country in which the other party is domiciled, an opt-out clause may not be required, although it would be prudent to include one whenever possible for the sake of certainty.

For a more detailed discussion, *see Guide to the International Sale of Goods Convention*, Thompson Reuters (2020); Karambelas, *United Nations Convention on International Sale of Goods: An International Law as Domestic Law*, Wash. Law. 27 (April 2009); Nicholas, *Teach an Old UCC Dog New Tricks - An Overview of the UN Convention on International Sale of Goods*, Bus. L. Today 39 (Sept./Oct. 2008).

H. The Foreign Corrupt Practices Act

The U.S. Foreign Corrupt Practices Act ("FCPA") is a federal criminal statute enforced by the U.S. Department of Justice (the "DOJ") and the U.S. Securities and Exchange Commission (the "SEC"). The FCPA contains separate "anti-bribery" provisions and "books and records" provisions.

1. *Anti-Bribery Provisions*

(a) Statutory Elements

The FCPA's anti-bribery provisions prohibit certain entities and individuals from "corruptly" offering or paying anything of value to a foreign official for the purpose of influencing an act or decision in his or her official capacity or securing any improper business advantage in order to obtain or retain business. *See* 15 U.S.C. §§ 78dd-1(a)(1), 78dd-2(a)(1), 78dd-3(a)(1).

Because the FCPA prohibits only payments or offers made "*corruptly*," an offer or payment is unlawful only if made with wrongful intent to influence the recipient. *See* 15 U.S.C. § 78dd-1(a). According to the FCPA's legislative history, a payment is made "corruptly" if it is "intended to induce the recipient to *misuse his official position* . . . ." S. Rep. No. 95-114, 95th Cong., 1st Sess., at 10 (1977) (emphasis added); *see also United States v. Liebo*, 923 F.2d 1308, 1312 (8th Cir. 1991) (citing Senate Report). The legislative history also suggests that the domestic bribery statute, 18 U.S.C. § 201, may be useful in interpreting the FCPA. *See* H.R. Conf. Rep. 100-576, 95th Cong., 1st Sess., at 918 (1977). Under the domestic bribery statute, the evidence must show that the bribe was made as part of a *quid pro quo* for a tangible benefit from the government. It is not sufficient to show that a party conferred something of value upon an official simply because of his or her official position. The value must be offered or given in connection with a specific action from that official. *See United States v. Sun-Diamond Growers of California*, 526 U.S. 398, 414 (1999).

"Anything of value" is broadly construed to encompass currency, securities, and currency equivalents (such as coupons or gift cards), tangible items, and intangible benefits (including travel, entertainment, and valuable favors). The FCPA does not contain any exception for *de minimis* expenditures; accordingly, giving or offering things of little value for an improper reason may create liability.

The FCPA defines the term "foreign official" to include "any officer or employee of a foreign government or any department, agency, or instrumentality thereof." *See* 15 U.S.C. §§ 78dd-1(f)(1), 78dd-2(f)(1), 78dd-3(f)(1). This broad definition encompasses employees of state-owned businesses.

The FCPA prohibits not only payments intended to obtain business directly from government, but also efforts to obtain favorable legal or regulatory treatment. *See, e.g., United States v. Kay,* 359 F.3d 738 (5th Cir. 2004) (payments allegedly made to Haitian government officials for purpose of reducing corporation's customs duties and taxes were potentially within the FCPA's prohibition against payments to foreign officials to secure an "improper advantage" in order to "obtain or retain" business).

The FCPA also prohibits "corruptly" giving anything of value to "any person" while "knowing" that all or a portion of such thing of value will be given, directly or indirectly, to a foreign official for the purpose of influencing an act or decision in his or her official capacity or securing any improper business advantage in order to obtain or retain business. *See* 15 U.S.C. § 78dd-1(a)(3). The FCPA defines a "knowing" state of mind as being aware or having a firm belief that a result is substantially certain to occur. *See* 15 U.S.C. § 78dd-1(f)(2)(A). Specifically, knowledge of circumstances "is established if a person is aware of a high probability of the existence of such circumstance, unless the person actually believes that such a circumstance does not exist." *See* 15 U.S.C. § 78dd-1(f)(2)(B). Accordingly, conscious disregard of indications that a third-party intermediary is making prohibited payments may give rise to liability, even absent actual knowledge of such payments.

(b) Affirmative Defenses

The FCPA allows two affirmative defenses for conduct that might otherwise satisfy the elements of an offense. Under the "local law defense," payments to government officials that are lawful under the "written laws and regulations" of the recipient's country do not violate the FCPA. *See* 15 U.S.C. § 78dd-1(c)(1). Under the "promotional expenses defense," payments to government officials do not violate the FCPA if they constitute "reasonable and bona fide expenditures" that "directly relate" to the "promotion, demonstration, or explanation" of products or services or performance of contracts. *See* 15 U.S.C. § 78dd-1(c)(2). As these are affirmative defenses, a party defending against FCPA allegations bears the burden of establishing their elements.

(c) Penalties

Criminal penalties for violating the anti-bribery provisions of the FCPA include, for individuals, a fine of up to $100,000 and/or five years in prison. 15 U.S.C. §§ 78dd-2(g)(2) (A). Corporations are subject to fines up to $2 million per count. 15 U.S.C. §§ 78dd-2(g) (1)(A). Civil penalties include fines of guilty corporate entities and individuals of up to $16,000 for each violation. Entities: 15 U.S.C. §§ 78ff(c)(1)(B); 17 C.F.R. § 201.1005 and 17 C.F.R. Pt 201, Subpt. E, Tbl. v. (effective March 5, 2013); Individuals: 15 U.S.C.

§§ 78ff(c)(2)(B), 17 C.F.R. § 201.1005 and 17 C.F.R. Pt 201, Subpt. E, Tbl. v. (effective March 5, 2013). Companies are prohibited from paying fines and penalties assessed on the employees and agents. 15 U.S.C. §§ 78dd-2(g)(3), 78dd-3(e)(3), 78ff(c)(3). Public companies are subject to fines of $2 million per count, permanent injunctions, cease and desist orders, and a disgorgement of profits.

In addition, under the Alternative Fines Act, courts may impose a maximum alternative fine equal to twice the amount of improper financial gain received from the activity. 18 U.S.C. § 3571.

2. *Books and Records Provisions*

(a) Statutory Elements

The FCPA's books and records provisions contain two components, an accounting component and an internal controls component, both flowing from the Securities Exchange Act of 1934 (the "Exchange Act"). The books and records provisions apply only to "issuers" of U.S. securities.

The FCPA's accounting provisions require issuers to "make and keep books, records, and accounts, which, in reasonable detail, accurately and fairly reflect the transactions and dispositions of the assets of the issuer." *See* 15 U.S.C. § 78m(b)(1)(A). This requirement mandates that all reported information be "reasonably current" and "in reasonable detail" or maintained at "such level of detail and degree of assurance as would satisfy prudent officials in the conduct of their own affairs." *See* 15 U.S.C. § 78(b)(7). Essentially, this provision makes it illegal to falsify, misrepresent, or omit information in the records kept under the FCPA. Records are "inaccurate" and violate the Act if they fail to record illegal or even improper transactions or falsify or disguise such transactions. There is no materiality threshold.

The internal-controls component of the FCPA requires a U.S. issuer to implement a system of controls to prevent and detect improper accounting for transactions. Specifically, the provision requires issuers to "devise and maintain a system of internal accounting controls sufficient to provide reasonable assurances" that transactions are executed according to management's general or specific authorization, that transactions are recorded as necessary to permit preparation of financial statements according to generally accepted standards; and that the recorded accountability for assets is compared with the existing assets at reasonable intervals, and appropriate action is taken with respect to any differences. *See* 15 U.S.C. § 78m(b)(2)(B).

Because the books and records provisions apply only to U.S. issuers, the SEC has primary enforcement authority over these provisions. However, the DOJ enforces the sections of these provisions that provide criminal liability for U.S. issuers who "*knowingly* circumvent or *knowingly* fail to implement a system of internal accounting controls or knowingly falsify any book, record, or account." *See* 15 U.S.C. § 78m(b)(5) (emphasis added). The legislative history for the 1988 amendments to the FCPA make clear that "criminal penalties shall not be imposed for failing to comply with the FCPA's books and records or accounting provisions. This provision is meant to ensure that criminal penalties would be imposed where acts of commission or omission in keeping books or records or administering accounting controls have the purpose of falsifying books, records, or accounts, or of circumventing the accounting controls set forth in the Act. This would include the deliberate falsification of books and records and other conduct calculated to evade the internal controls requirement." Summary of Legislative History of the 1988 Amendments to the FCPA, *available at* http://www.justice.gov/criminal/fraud/fcpa/history.

(b) Penalties

Criminal penalties for willful violations of the Books and Records/Internal Controls provisions of the FCPA are significant. Individuals are liable for fines of up to $5 million and/or 20 years in prison for each violation while corporations are liable for fines of up to $25 million per count.15 U.S.C. § 78ff(a) Civil penalties include civil fines, disgorgement of profits, permanent injunctions, and barring guilty officers and directors from serving in other corporations. Liability is based on a strict liability standard with no knowledge required to find guilt. 15 U.S.C. §§ 78u(2)(b), 17 C.F.R. § 201.1005 and 17 C.F.R. Pt 201, Subpt. E, Tbl. v. (effective March 5, 2013).

In addition, under the Alternative Fines Act, courts may impose a maximum alternative fine equal to twice the amount of improper financial gain received from the activity. 18 U.S.C. § 3571.

3. Applicability of Foreign Corrupt Practices Act

(a) Jurisdictional Limits

The jurisdictional limits of the anti-bribery provisions and the books and records provisions (and the extent of their applicability to foreign subsidiaries) differ.

The anti-bribery provisions of the FCPA are predicated on a variety of possible jurisdictional bases linking the conduct to the United States. First, the anti-bribery provisions apply to U.S. issuers, or officers, directors, employees, agents or stockholders of an issuer acting on behalf of a U.S. issuer. *See* 15 U.S.C. § 78dd-1(a). Second, the anti-bribery provisions apply to "domestic concerns," or a domestic concern's officers, directors, employees, agents or stockholders. *See* 15 U.S.C. § 78dd-2(a). Domestic concerns include U.S. citizens, nationals or residents, or corporations that are incorporated in, or have their primary place of business in, the United States. *Id.* at § 78dd-2(h)(1). Third, any action by any other person within the United States in furtherance of improper activity triggers the anti-bribery provisions. *See* 15 U.S.C. § 78dd-3. Merely transferring funds to, from, or through the United States may be sufficient to confer jurisdiction under this provision. In addition, the FCPA applies whenever a "United States person" commits any act, anywhere in the world, in furtherance of a prohibited payment. *See* 15 U.S.C. § 78dd-3(i). Thus, the applicability of the FCPA anti-bribery rules in specific circumstances requires analysis of the involvement of U.S. issuers and U.S. persons (both natural and corporate) as well as a determination of whether there was U.S. activity.

On its face, the FCPA does not make a U.S. issuer directly liable for improper payments by its foreign subsidiaries. However, the Department of Justice has interpreted expansively the three jurisdictional links outlined above and has been willing to assert corporate liability on the basis of virtually any nexus with the United States. Under a literal reading of the statute, a foreign subsidiary of a U.S. company does not appear to fall within the anti-bribery provisions of the FCPA, provided that its principal place of business lies overseas, it is not itself a U.S. issuer, and it does not act within the United States or make use of U.S. mail or wires. However, U.S. enforcement authorities take the position that a parent company in the United States may be held liable for the acts of its foreign subsidiary if it "authorized, directed, or controlled the activity in question." *See In re United Industrial Corp.*, 2009 WL 1507586 (May 29, 2009). More often, however, the U.S. enforcement authorities simply rely on evidence that directors, officers, or employees of the parent company knew about the foreign subsidiary's illicit payments or ignored clear evidence that the foreign subsidiary was violating the anti-bribery provisions of the FCPA.

Unlike the FCPA's anti-bribery provisions, the books and records provisions of the FCPA explicitly apply to majority-owned subsidiaries. *See* 15 U.S.C. § 78m(b) (6). Thus, when U.S. issuers own a majority of shares, foreign subsidiaries must comply with the FCPA record-keeping requirements in the same manner as their parent corporations, who effectively face strict (civil) liability for any violations by their subsidiaries.

4. *Risks under FCPA Anti-Bribery Provisions*

(a) Business Gifts, Travel, and Entertainment

The principal risk with respect to the FCPA related to the anti-bribery provisions is the practice of providing extensive travel, gifts, and entertainment for employees of state-owned enterprises and government agencies.

Such recipients would qualify as "foreign officials" for purposes of the FCPA, even if they do not qualify as public officials for purposes of, for example, Chinese law. Providing travel, gifts, and entertainment to foreign government officials thus constitutes the provision of "things of value" to foreign officials. The entertainment of employees of customers and prospective customers is usually undertaken to "assist" in "obtaining or retaining business."

Providing gifts, travel, and entertainment for government officials may be consistent with the FCPA to the extent that either: (1) the other elements of an anti-bribery offense requiring corrupt intent to influence improperly the official conduct of a government official in connection with the company's business are not satisfied; or (2) the conduct qualifies for the affirmative defense for as a "reasonable and bona fide" expenditures "directly related" to the promotion or demonstration of products and services of the performance of a contract. Evidence of "corrupt intent" or of the "reasonable and bona fide" nature of an expense may be inferred from the circumstances. U.S. enforcement authorities are likely to conclude that any gifts or entertainment for employees of state-owned customers which are *not* reasonable and bona fide promotional expenses constitute corrupt payments intended to influence the recipient to act improperly.

(i) Relevant Enforcement Actions and DOJ Guidance

The FCPA itself does not define acceptable promotional activities or business entertainment, and there are no judicial decisions that do so. Indeed, there have only been two enforcement actions brought on grounds that payment of travel and entertainment expenses alone violated the anti-bribery provisions of the FCPA.

(x) SAP SE.

In April 2021, SAP settled claims by the Department of Justice, the Treasury's Office of Foreign Asset Control and the Department of Commerce Bureau's Office of Industry and Security alleging that between 2010 and 2017, SAP engaged in thousands of transactions including downloaded software, upgrades and patches with Iran, directly and indirectly, through resellers in violation of the law. SAP agreed to pay the Department of Justice $5.14 million, OFAC $2.13 million and the Department of Commerce $3.29 million to settle the investigation.

(y) U.S. v. Lucent

Lucent entered settlements with the SEC and DOJ to resolve allegations that it had violated the FCPA in connection with travel and entertainment practices involving employees of Chinese state-owned telecommunications companies.

In a civil complaint filed in the U.S. District Court for the District of Columbia, the SEC alleged that Lucent, a global communications solutions provider, paid for Chinese government officials to travel to the United States and elsewhere for sightseeing, entertainment, and leisure purposes. According to the government, Lucent hosted approximately 315 trips and spent over $10 million on travel and entertainment expenses from 2000 to 2003 for approximately 1,000 employees of state-owned or state-controlled telecommunications enterprises in China that were prospective or existing Lucent customers. Although many of the approximately 315 trips were ostensibly to provide training or to allow inspection of Lucent's factories, the foreign officials spent little or no time in the United States visiting Lucent's facilities. Instead, they visited tourist destinations, such as Hawaii, Las Vegas, New York City, Niagara Falls, the Grand Canyon, Disney World, and Universal Studios. Some visits had only a day or half-day of business activities, followed by up to two weeks of tourist activities.

One visit described in the complaint involved five days of visiting Lucent facilities followed by nine days of traveling and sightseeing across the country at Lucent's expense. Another visit included five days of training in Florida followed by sixteen days of sightseeing in California, Nevada, Arizona, New York, Washington D.C., and Hawaii, again, at Lucent's expense. In addition, Lucent was alleged to have paid per diems of $500 to $1,000 per day, even though it was already paying for all lodging, transportation, food, and entertainment expenses. The SEC Complaint noted Lucent's apparent focus on the capacity of trip participants to influence the award of specific contracts in approving or declining requests for travel, and also highlighted evidence that Lucent personnel were aware of the impropriety of the trips (e.g., by providing itineraries overstating the business purpose of the trips in connection with visa applications).

The government also alleged that Lucent improperly recorded the expenses in its books and records. For example, over 160 trips were charged to Lucent's "factory inspection account," even though the officials did not visit a Lucent factory at any time during their trips. Indeed, during much of the time period at issue, Lucent did not have any factories in the United States. Similarly, expenses were often recorded as "Service Rendered - Other Services," an expense account that Lucent normally used for crediting "other service" expenses rather than as a repository for travel expenses. Another set of expenses was recorded as "Transportation International," which Lucent normally used for international freight transportation costs where a product crosses country borders. In addition, the government alleged that Lucent lacked internal controls to detect and prevent trips intended for sightseeing, entertainment, or leisure, rather than business purposes.

The SEC filed a settled complaint, alleging that Lucent had violated the recordkeeping and internal controls provisions of the FCPA. Lucent did not admit or deny the allegations as part of the settlement, but consented to the entry of a final judgment ordering it to pay a $1.5 million civil penalty and permanently enjoining it from future violations of Sections 13(b)(2)(A) and 13(b)(2)(B) of the Securities Exchange Act of 1934. Lucent also entered into a non-prosecution agreement with the DOJ. Lucent agreed to pay a $1 million fine and to implement more rigorous internal controls to ensure compliance with the FCPA. The DOJ agreed not to prosecute Lucent if it complied with the terms of the agreement over the next two years.

(z) DOJ Opinion Releases

In addition to these two published enforcement actions, the DOJ has issued a series of "Opinion Releases" addressing promotional activities and business entertainment for foreign officials. Through the Opinion Releases, the DOJ provides prospective guidance on the DOJ's intent to take enforcement actions with respect to future activities based on facts and circumstances as represented by the requesting party. Opinion Procedure Releases are available at https://www.justice.gov/criminal-fraud/opinion-releases-index.

In each instance the DOJ indicated that it would not bring an enforcement action in light of the commercial circumstances, the business purpose for the activity, and the precautions taken to promote transparency and avoid impropriety (or the appearance thereof). Together, these Opinion Releases suggest a set of best practices for promotional activities and business entertainment for government officials.

In each of these Opinion Releases, the proposed activity was directly related to a demonstrably legitimate business activity. Opinion Release 07-02 involved a tour of a U.S. company's operating facilities to demonstrate its operations and capabilities and help establish the company's business credibility. The other Opinion Releases involved educational tours for foreign regulators to learn about relevant U.S. regulatory practices.

5. *PRACTICE POINT:* Checklist for export and sanctions compliance.

To avoid potentially violating U.S. export laws and sanctions requirements, prudent vendors should:

- Undertake due diligence on all third party resellers, etc. and all end users of the vendor's products
- Implement disciplinary measures for the failure to comply with the vendor's policies

- Screen all end users through the use of their IP addresses and use geo-fencing technologies to prevent access from sanctioned countries, entities and individuals
- Ensure all internal compliance teams are funded and empowered to undertake all required reviews and implement all necessary controls and reviews
- Continually evaluate all compliance functions, practices and procedures to ensure adherence to industry best practices

Where the proposed activity has a legitimate business purpose at its core, the following practices can further reduce the risk of improper payments:

- Limiting covered expenses to lodging, meals, local transport, and airfare directly related to the legitimate activity.
- Not funding, organizing, or hosting any entertainment or leisure activities for the officials, apart from meals and receptions connected to substantive meetings, speakers, or events. Any such entertainment or leisure activities should be incidental and proportionate to the core business activity. (For example, the DOJ approved a "modest four-hour city sightseeing tour" incidental to a five-day education seminar).
- Allowing the government entity to select individual participants rather than inviting specific government officials to participate.
- Limiting participation to relevant personnel with legitimate business purpose for participating in the activity.
- Not paying for any expenses for spouses, family, or other guests of the officials.
- Funding appropriate expenses through direct payment to the vendor (e.g., hotel, airline, restaurant) rather than to the government entity or to the individual government official.
- Where reimbursement of appropriate expenses is necessary, limiting reimbursement to modest amounts upon presentation written receipts and paying reimbursements through means other than cash (e.g., check, wire transfer).
- Limiting souvenirs or gifts to items of nominal value (hats, shirts, tote bags) featuring the host company's name and logo.
- Not compensating or paying foreign officials to participate.
- Not providing any per diems or pocket money to foreign officials.
- Obtaining written assurances for a reputable law firm that the sponsorship of the event and payment for disclosed expenses is not contrary to the law of the foreign country.
- Obtaining written assurances from the government entity that the sponsorship of the event and payment for disclosed expenses is not contrary to the law of the foreign country.

While a promotional event need not necessarily conform to each of these practices in order to qualify as a reasonable and bona fide business expense, following these practices reduces the risk of an actual or apparent violation of the anti-bribery provisions of the FCPA.

Additionally, these Opinion Releases suggest that promotional activities involving foreign officials are less likely to raise concerns under the FCPA when the host company either has no current or planned business (e.g., bids, product approvals, license applications) before the relevant agencies or its current or planned business before the relevant agencies is limited to routine activities involving little or no discretionary action by government authorities.

From an FCPA perspective, it is prudent to obtain certifications of compliance with the FCPA from foreign contractors and agents—especially sales agents and distributors. A prudent vendor should require local contractors and agents to complete a questionnaire that demonstrates that it is a valid and qualified contractor and agent and is not simply a conduit for funneling funds to the local government in violation of the FCPA. See Form R.4 for a model FCPA questionnaire.

For a general overview, *see* Gordon & Guerra, *FCPA: Drilling Down on Declinations, Hefty Fines, Disgorgements, and Monitors, Partnering Perspectives* (Eversheds Sutherland, Summer 2019). For a detailed overview of the FCPA, *see* TARUN & TOMCZAK, FOREIGN CORRUPT PRACTICES ACT HANDBOOK (5th ed. 2018); DEMING, DESIGNING AN EFFECTIVE ANTI-BRIBERY COMPLIANCE PROGRAM: A PRACTICAL GUIDE FOR BUSINESS (ABA Press 2018).

I. The USA Patriot Act (Public Law 107-56)

On October 26, 2001, President George W. Bush signed into law the Uniting and Strengthening America by Providing Appropriate Tools Required to Intercept and Obstruct Terrorism Act ("Patriot Act") as a direct result of the September 11, 2001 terrorist attacks. The Patriot Act expands the federal government's ability to access customer data maintained by Internet service providers (ISPs) as part of their business operations. The Patriot Act was amended in 2006 in two ways that create greater transparency over this process of obtaining evidence from companies. The amendments provide for congressional oversight by requiring the U.S. Department of Justice to report to Congress every six months about how many business record subpoenas it seeks. They also permit companies that receive these subpoenas to challenge any government order to keep the request secret.

Many non-U.S. companies operating outside of the United States fear that by using a vendor incorporated in the United States, the U.S. government will have unfettered access to their customers' data under the Patriot Act. In reality, U.S. law enforcement does not have unfettered access to data under the Patriot Act, and even under its broadest provision, the Foreign Intelligence Surveillance Act (FISA) business records ex parte subpoena must still follow a legal process in obtaining information and must swear to the issuing court that the information is "sought for an authorized investigation conducted accordance with [Department of Justice guidelines] . . . to obtain foreign intelligence information . . . or to protect against international terrorism or clandestine intelligence activities." 50 U.S.C. § 1861(b)(2). In fact, this authority is comparable to the powers of law enforcement authorities in many European jurisdictions.

Many customers seek to limit the U.S. government's access to their data by requiring the vendor to store their data outside of the United States. While the desire of the vendor to protect its clients' data is understandable, there is little a U.S. company can do to limit governmental access pursuant to lawful process, short of challenging the constitutionality of the Patriot Act. *See, e.g., Doe v. Ashcroft*, 334 F. Supp. 2d 471 (S.D.N.Y. 2004); *Doe v. Gonzales*, 386 F. Supp. 2d 66 (D. Conn. 2005), *aff'd*, 449 F.3d 415 (2d Cir. 2006).

Section 215 of the Patriot Act enables U.S. authorities to seek a court order directing the production of books, records, and other tangible items that are relevant to an authorized national security investigation. Further, Section 215 allows the U.S. government to obtain the same types of records that can be obtained pursuant to a grand jury subpoena in an ordinary criminal investigation, though unlike a grand jury subpoena, a Section 215 order must be issued by the court following a government showing of necessity. Thus, IT service providers who are subsidiaries of U.S. companies could potentially be forced to disclose customer data to their U.S. parents who would in turn disclose the information to the U.S. authorities under such an order or subpoena.

Many customers are concerned that Section 215 of the Patriot Act may allow U.S. authorities to gain access to the customer's data held by a vendor's foreign subsidiary as a result of the vendor providing services to the customer.

Many vendors argue that it is highly unlikely that a foreign subsidiary could be forced to turn over the customer's data and that the customer's concerns are ill-founded.

The likelihood that U.S. authorities would seek to use the Patriot Act as the vehicle to obtain terrorist-related information is small. Under most bilateral mutual legal assistance treaties, U.S. authorities typically work with local law enforcement who in turn initiate local processes to issue subpoenas and data requests to the data owner (i.e., the customer). Involvement of local authorities helps ensure that the U.S. request is harmonized with local laws and regulations. The most likely scenario is that the customer would receive a subpoena or order from local authorities requiring disclosure of data, which subpoena, or order was originally requested by U.S. authorities.

Most vendors argue that in the unlikely event the vendor receives a subpoena or order under the Patriot Act relating to a customer's data, the vendor (both in the United States and its subsidiary in the host country) will use all legal means to inform the customer of the subpoena/order so that the customer can fight it. In the event the vendor is not permitted to inform the customer of the subpoena/order, the vendor would likely endeavor to utilize any appropriate privacy, civil liberty, and other human rights laws to prevent disclosure.

J. Anti-Boycott Regulations

Foreign engagements require that counsel be aware of U.S. Anti-boycott Regulations. The Anti-boycott Regulations (15 C.F.R Part 760 and 26 U.S.C. § 999) ("Regulations") address all boycotts, but primarily are directed toward the Arab boycott of Israel. The Regulations are enforced through two independent regulatory provisions administered by the Treasury Department and Commerce Department.

All United States companies and their "controlled in fact" foreign subsidiaries are subject to the Regulations, regardless of whether the transactions occur in the United States. The Treasury Department administers United States companies' compliance. In addition, all entities conducting "activities in the interstate or foreign commerce of the United States" are subject to the Regulations, which the Commerce Department regulates.

The term "activities in the interstate or foreign commerce of the United States" is broadly defined. 15 C.F.R. § 760.1(d). Entities subject to the law are prohibited from refusing to do business with Israel, taking discriminatory actions, furnishing information to any individual or entity about business relationships with boycotted countries or black listed persons, and furnishing information to any individual or entity about its association with charitable and fraternal organizations. 15 C.F.R. § 760.2 Further, they are prohibited from providing a "negative certificate or statement of origin" as well as implementing letters of credit containing prohibited conditions or requirements. 15 C.F.R. § 760.2.

A negative certificate or statement of origin is a statement by a manufacturer that the goods or services in question were not created in a particular country or location. While a negative certificate or statement of origin in conjunction with a boycott request is illegal, the manufacturer may positively state where the goods were manufactured. Further, an entity may not implement a letter of credit with prohibited conditions, such as specifying that a party does not do business with a boycotted country, or that the goods shipped did not originate in a boycotted country.

Entities subject to the law are required to report all requests, written or oral, including requests to furnish information or to implement an agreement. 15 C.F.R. § 760.5. Reporting is made through the quarterly filing of Forms BXA-621P or BXA-6051P (for multiple boycott requests) with the Bureau of Export Administration of the Department of Commerce, and the annual filing of Form 5713 with the Internal Revenue Service. Furthermore, entities are required to retain records of all transactions involving the restrictive trade practices or boycotts described above for five years. 15 C.F.R. §§ 762.1, 762.6.

Failure to comply with the Commerce Department's Anti-boycott Regulations or failure to file the appropriate forms can result in criminal fines of up to the greater of $50,000 or five times the value of the export and imprisonment of up to five years per incident, as well as civil penalties, including loss of the exporter's export privileges. Criminal penalties: 15 C.F.R. § 764.3(b); Export privileges: 15 C.F.R. § 764.3(a). Under the Treasury Department's Anti-boycott Regulations, a company could also lose foreign tax credits. 26 C.F.R. § 7.999-1.

For an overview, *See Overview of U.S. Antiboycott Laws Part I*, 53 Lawyer's Brief 1 (October 15, 2023); *Overview of U.S. Antiboycott Laws Part II*, 53 Lawyer's Brief 1 (October 31, 2023); *Overview of U.S. Antiboycott Laws Part III*, 53 Lawyer's Brief 1 (November 15, 2023).

K. Availability of a Meaningful Remedy

When entering into an agreement with a foreign entity, a party must consider whether it will have a meaningful remedy in the event of a breach of contract by the foreign entity. Many parties that are domiciled outside of the United States have only a small sales operation in the United States with the great majority of their assets outside of this country. The ability to obtain a meaningful remedy is especially important in the event of a third-party claim of intellectual property infringement or if a party breaches its confidentiality obligations. If a customer has retained an Indian company to develop an important piece of software, and the Indian entity fails to deliver, will the customer have the ability to obtain an adequate remedy for such breach? Similarly, if a licensor licenses its software to the United States subsidiary of a foreign company and the subsidiary breaches the license agreement, does the licensor have a meaningful recovery? In these situations, the domestic party should ensure that the foreign entity has sufficient resources in the United States in the event of a breach of contract. If the foreign entity lacks sufficient assets, the domestic entity should require the foreign entity to establish a performance bond or establish a letter of credit for the benefit of the domestic party.

To avoid these types of issues, prudent customers include language in their agreements and/or a Request for Proposal (RFP) to the following effect:

> *Customer requires that the Vendor entity that is party to the Agreement be a U.S. entity. If the services required under the Agreement will be provided by an entity other than the Vendor's ultimate Parent Company, the Vendor must provide a guarantee from its ultimate parent company in a form and substance satisfactory to Customer, which irrevocably and unconditionally guarantees the complete and proper performance of the contract and the financial liabilities of the Vendor. If the Parent Company is not a U.S. entity, Customer requires Parent Company to provide a performance bond acceptable to Customer.*

CHAPTER **27**

Bankruptcy Issues[1]

Software has assumed an omnipresent existence in our society. It is so pervasive and intertwined with the operation of most businesses that it would be impossible to successfully operate without it. At the same time, software companies rely on their contracts to protect the sanctity of their ownership interests.

The present economic uncertainties require that both licensors and licensees place greater emphasis on protecting their rights under their existing software licenses and focus on mitigating any potential risks when negotiating a new license. This chapter examines the risks and liabilities that may arise from the financial instability or bankruptcy of a licensor or a licensee. It discusses several means by which licensors and licensees can reduce their potential exposure to business risk or financial liability.

For a general discussion of the treatment of intellectual property licenses in bankruptcy, *see* Cook, *Connecticut Supreme Court Defines Bankruptcy Effect on Contracts*, 35 Bankr. Strategist 3 (Jan 2018); *Intellectual Property and Bankruptcy Law*, 35 Corp. Couns. Q. 318 (Apr. 2019); Agin, *Bankruptcy and Intellectual Property Deskbook* (2016).

A. The Treatment of Software Licenses in Bankruptcy

The treatment to be accorded a software license when the licensor or licensee files for bankruptcy depends upon whether the license is executory or nonexecutory. 11 U.S.C. § 365. Title 11 of the United States Code (the "Bankruptcy Code") treats executory agreements very differently from nonexecutory agreements. Section 365 of the Bankruptcy Code, which governs the treatment of executory agreements, generally permits a debtor to do one of three things: (1) assume the agreement, (2) assume and assign the agreement to a third party, or (3) reject the agreement. *Id.* Generally speaking, a debtor may not enjoy the full benefits of an executory agreement unless it assumes all of the obligations under the agreement, including the curing of all prepetition defaults under the agreement. *Id.* The same is not true with respect to a nonexecutory agreement.

---

1. An earlier version of this chapter was published as Classen & Sullivan, *Software Licensing in a Troubled Environment*, 19 Bus. L. Today 23 (No. 2, Nov./Dec. 2009). Mr. Sullivan is a partner in the law firm of Windels Marx and can be reached at jsullivan@windelsmarx.com.

Although the Bankruptcy Code does not define the term "executory," most bankruptcy courts use the definition formulated by Professor Vern Countryman:

> . . . a contract under which the obligations of both the bankrupt and the other party to the contract are so far unperformed that the failure of either to complete performance would constitute a material breach excusing the performance of the other.

Countryman, *Executory Contracts in Bankruptcy, Part I*, 57 MINN. L. REV. 439, 460 (1973). Thus, where performance has been substantially completed by one or both parties to the contract, the license is nonexecutory.

Whether a bankruptcy court will find a software license to be executory will depend upon a very fact-based analysis of the license agreement and the remaining obligations of each party under the license agreement. Although most software licenses with ongoing payment obligations by the licensee will likely qualify as an executory contract, the courts will look to the substance of the license agreement rather than the form in determining whether a contract is executory. *See Waterman v. Mackenzie*, 138 U.S. 252, 256 (1891) (differentiating between nonexclusive license of patent rights and exclusive assignment of such rights); *Microsoft Corp. v. Dak Indus.*, 66 F.3d 1091, 1095 n.2 (9th Cir. 1995). Thus, a royalty-free or fully paid-up license of software may not in fact be a license at all, but an assignment of a property interest that is nonexecutory. *See, e.g., Chesapeake Fiber Packaging Corp. v. Sebro Packaging Corp.*, 143 B.R. 360, 374–75 (Bankr. D. Md. 1992), *aff'd*, 8 F.3d 817 (4th Cir. 1993); *In re Stein*, 81 B.R. 263, 266–67 (Bankr. S.D.N.Y. 1988); *In re Monument Record Corp.*, 61 B.R. 866, 868–69 (Bankr. M.D. Tenn. 1986).

Some examples of types of continuing obligations that may render a software license executory are continuing obligations to account for and pay royalties; duty to notify licensor or licensee of infringement suits; duty of licensor to defend licensee against infringement claims; obligation to forbear from making sales or licenses of the software to others; obligation to forbear from engaging in certain activities in certain territories or markets; duty to pursue infringement claims against third parties; obligations to provide maintenance and software upgrades; obligation to cross-license software or other intellectual property; indemnity and warranty obligations; training obligations; obligation to maintain records and permit inspections; confidentiality obligations; duty to pay fees for maintenance or ancillary services; obligations to provide most-favored nation treatment; and development and commercialization obligations. *See, e.g., Lubrizol Enters., Inc. v. Richmond Metal Finishers, Inc.*, 756 F.2d 1043, 1045 (4th Cir. 1985); *Fenix Cattle Co. v. Silver*, 625 F.2d 290, 292 (9th Cir. 1980).

B. The Licensor's Bankruptcy

1. Nonexecutory License

When a licensor files for bankruptcy, a licensee may be left in a precarious position, especially if its license agreement is nonexecutory. That is because the licensor may seek to breach the license by refusing to provide necessary support or software upgrades, or even worse by relicensing the software to a third party. The Bankruptcy Code offers little protection to a licensee that is a party to a nonexecutory contract with a debtor.

In fact, a licensee's sole recourse may be to file a general unsecured claim against the debtor. Accordingly, a licensee should seek to protect itself from a licensor's bankruptcy to the greatest extent possible. Some techniques include getting a security interest in the licensed software, getting a technology escrow, drafting the license in such a way to ensure that it will be treated as an executory contract entitled to the protections of Section 365(n) of the Bankruptcy Code, and/or drafting the license to include equitable remedies that will survive the licensor's bankruptcy. See Section B.3 below for a description of these drafting techniques.

2. *Executory License*

In response to the concern of the software industry and licensees in particular, the federal bankruptcy laws were rewritten in 1987 to protect licensees in the event of a licensor's bankruptcy. Section 365(n) of the Bankruptcy Code (11 U.S.C. § 365(n)) ("Section 365(n)"), provides that in the event the debtor/licensor rejects the license agreement, the non-debtor/licensee has two options. First, it can bring a claim for damages to the extent the rejection caused the licensor to fail to meet the licensor's obligations under the license agreement. 11 U.S.C. § 365(n)(1)(A). Under this option, the licensee forgoes any right to use the licensed technology/software in the future. *Id.* Second, it can retain the rights to use the software/intellectual property for the period provided for under the license and any contractual extension periods. 11 U.S.C. § 365(n)(1)(B).

The trustee in bankruptcy can still reject the license agreement causing any executory provisions to become null and void, but the licensee can elect to retain its rights under the software license. If the licensee elects to retain its intellectual property rights, it must continue to pay the license fees due the licensor and must forego certain remedies otherwise available under the Bankruptcy Code (e.g., rights of setoff or to assert a § 503(b) administrative priority claim). Under Section 365(n), the licensee does not need to affirmatively elect to retain its intellectual property rights to preserve its license. 11 U.S.C. § 365(n)(1)(B). *But see In re E.I. International*, 123 B.R. 64, 67 (Bankr. D. Idaho 1991) (failure of licensee to elect to retain benefits of license caused license to be treated as terminated).

Most licensees elect the second option, to continue using the software. Although the licensee may continue using the software, it cannot compel the licensor to perform other contractual obligations except for any exclusivity provisions in the contract. The licensor is relieved of its obligations to provide any ancillary services, such as training, maintenance, support, documentation, or updates. The licensee is able to require the trustee to turn over any embodiments of the licensed technology, provided they were stated in the license, including any exclusivity right. 11 U.S.C. §§ 365(n)(1)(B) and 365(n)(3). The licensee must continue, however, to pay all royalties due the licensor. 11 U.S.C. § 365(n)(2)(B). This is a good reason to have separate agreements or payment schedules for the software license and any ancillary obligations, such as development as well as maintenance and support services. Utilizing a single contractual document rather than multiple documents will make the agreement appear executory in nature because of the existence of long-term ongoing obligations. Separate agreements or payment schedules lessen the risk of an agreement being rejected because each obligation is compartmentalized and associated with a specific payment and a licensor will not be entitled to receive the separate fee unless it performs the separate service.

Other executory provisions of the contract are not enforceable by the licensee, such as maintenance and any unfinished development work. The licensee is able to require the trustee to turn over any embodiments of the licensed technology, provided they were stated in the license, including any exclusivity right. 11 U.S.C. §§ 365(n)(1)(B) and 365(n)(3).

3. Drafting Techniques

To ensure the protections of Section 365(n) are available to the licensee, the licensee should make sure the license specifically provides that the licensed software is "intellectual property" under § 101(56) and that the license is governed by Section 365(n) in the event the licensor files for bankruptcy protection.

Set forth below is model language that a licensee should include in its license agreement to ensure that it may avail itself of the protections set forth in Section 365(n).

> ***Affirmation of Rights.*** *All rights and licenses granted pursuant to any section of this Agreement are, and will otherwise be, for purposes of Section 365(n) of the U.S. Bankruptcy Code and/or any similar or comparable section of the U.S. Bankruptcy Code (as such sections may be modified, amended, replaced, or renumbered from time to time), executory licenses of rights to "intellectual property," as defined under* ***Section 101 (35A)*** *of the U.S. Bankruptcy Code and/or any similar or comparable section of the U.S. Bankruptcy Code (as such sections may be modified, amended, replaced, or renumbered from time to time). The parties will retain and may fully exercise all of their respective rights and elections under the U.S. Bankruptcy Code. Accordingly, the licensee of such rights shall retain and may fully exercise all of its rights and elections under the U.S. Bankruptcy Code. Upon the commencement of bankruptcy proceedings by or against either Party under the U.S. Bankruptcy Code, the other Party shall be entitled to retain all of its license rights and use rights granted under this Agreement.*

Under the Bankruptcy Code, "intellectual property" is defined as "(A) trade secrets; (B) invention, process, design or plant protected under title 35; (C) patent application; (D) plant variety; (E) work of authorship protected under title 17; or (F) mask work protected under chapter 9 of title 17; to the extent protected by applicable non-bankruptcy law." 11 U.S.C. § 101 (56). It is clear that software will fall under this definition. As such, software will usually be governed by Section 365 of the Bankruptcy Code.

In addition, to further ensure that Section 365(n) is available to the licensee, the licensee should be sure to include sufficient continuing obligations in the license by both sides. See Section A above for examples of such obligations, to ensure that the license will be deemed an executory agreement. A licensee should also clearly state the contractual obligations that are deemed material, such that the breach by one party of such provision would excuse continued performance by the other party. Doing so will assist a bankruptcy court in applying the *Countryman* standard for determining whether an agreement is executory or the point at which an executory agreement becomes nonexecutory.

To limit its financial risk, the licensee should delineate the payments made for collateral obligations, such as training and support, from general royalty/license fees. The licensee should seek to have such collateral obligations contained in a separate agreement or payment schedule. By lumping all fees together, the licensee could be obligated to pay for collateral services that the licensor is no longer providing.

Many licensees seek to further limit their risk in the event of a licensor bankruptcy through the use of a source code escrow. Such an escrow will ensure that the licensee will have access to the source code for the licensed software if the licensor rejects the license and refuses to perform its obligations under the license agreement. Set forth below is model language than a licensee should include in its escrow agreement to ensure that it may avail itself of the protections set forth in Section 365(n).

> ***Supplementary Agreement****. This Escrow Agreement is "supplementary" to the License Agreement within the meaning of § 365(n) of the U.S. Bankruptcy Code (11 USC § 365 (n)) and/or any similar or comparable section of the U.S. Bankruptcy Code (as such sections may be modified, amended, replaced, or renumbered from time to time). If this Escrow Agreement and/or the License Agreement are/is rejected by Licensor as a debtor in possession or a trustee or by any other person or entity under the U.S. Bankruptcy Code, then the Licensee may elect to retain its right as provided in § 365(n). The Parties intend that no bankruptcy or bankruptcy proceeding, petition, law or regulation (and no other proceeding, petition, law or regulation of a similar nature in any state or foreign jurisdiction) will impede, delay or prevent the release of Deposit Materials to Licensee in accordance with the provisions of this Agreement, and the Licensor hereby conveys to Escrow Agent such rights (including intellectual property rights) as are necessary to allow Escrow Agent to lawfully make such release and perform this Agreement.*
>
> *Any licenses granted under this Agreement or which are provided pursuant to this Agreement are intended to be executory licenses of rights in intellectual property as contemplated by Section 365(n) of the U.S. Bankruptcy Code, 11 U.S.C. § 365(n), and/ or any similar or comparable section of the U.S. Bankruptcy Code (as such sections may be modified, amended, replaced, or renumbered from time to time). In the event that Licensor becomes a debtor under the U.S. Bankruptcy Code, it is the intent of the Parties that Licensee shall have all benefits granted to licensees under the provisions of the U.S. Bankruptcy Code including, without limitation, Section 365(n) of the U.S. Bankruptcy Code (11 U.S. 365(n)) and/or any similar or comparable section of the U.S. Bankruptcy Code (as such sections may be modified, amended, replaced, or renumbered from time to time).*

Even though the licensee does not have access to the source code pre-bankruptcy, the licensee should incorporate language into the license agreement providing the licensee the right to support and maintain the software as well as create derivative works, as upon the licensor's bankruptcy, the bankruptcy court will not grant the licensee any additional rights beyond those set forth in the original license.

Another option is for the licensee to obtain a security interest in the licensor's software. In addition to protecting the licensee's interest in the software, the security interest will also secure any rejection damages claim available to the licensee in the event the debtor rejects the license agreement. Because the security interest will limit the benefits available to a debtor upon rejecting the license, it will incentivize the debtor to assume the license agreement. In order to perfect a security interest in a licensor's software, the licensee must comply with both the Uniform Commercial Code and copyright law, which require that a notice be filed with the Copyright Office. The grant of a security interest is considered to be the transfer of copyright ownership. *In re Avalon Software, Inc.*, 209 B.R. 517 (Bankr. D. Ariz. 1997).

Finally, the licensee should include equitable remedies in the license agreement, such as the right to enforce any exclusivity provisions in favor of the licensee with an injunction against infringement. Such remedies are particularly important where the license is not executory and thus not entitled to the remedies available under Section 365(n). The majority of courts will enforce such a provision where such remedy is not an alternative or substitute for money damages. *See, e.g., Kennedy v. Medicap Pharmacies, Inc.*, 267 F.3d 493, 497 (6th Cir. 2001) (holding that an equitable remedy for breach of an agreement that is not an alternative to monetary remedy is not a "claim" that can be discharged in bankruptcy); *In re Udell*, 18 F.3d 403 (7th Cir. 1994) (same); *In re Gilpin*, 391 B.R. 210 (Table) (6th Cir. BAP 2008) (same). *But see, e.g., In re Ward*, 194 B.R. 703, 709–15 (Bankr. D. Mass. 1996) (holding that equitable remedies can be discharged if breach of agreement can be remedied with monetary damages, even where equitable remedies are also available); *In re Brown*, 1997 WL 786994 (Bankr. E.D. Pa. Nov. 26, 1997) (adopting middle-ground approach that requires the court to consider the nature of relief available under applicable state law in determining whether equitable remedies should be discharged). One method that can be used to increase the likelihood that a court will enforce the equitable remedies is to include a provision in the agreement that the parties agree that a breach cannot be adequately addressed through monetary damages and an agreement that equitable relief, such as an injunction, is needed to protect the licensee's rights in the software.

For a more detailed discussion, *see* Agin, *Reconciling Commercial Law and Information Technology: An Essay on Bankruptcy Practice During the Next Business Cycle*, 4 J. of Internet L. (October 2000) and Kupetz, *Beware When Dealing With Licensors of Intellectual Property: Avoiding Potential Pitfalls Facing Licensees and Lendors When Bankruptcy Intervenes*, 17 Computer Law. 21 (Jan. 2000); Kupetz, *Dealing with Issues in Chapter 11 Cases Filed by Licensors of Intellectual Property*, 16 E-Commerce & Strategy 1 (Jan. 2000). *See also* Sommer, *Bankruptcy and Intellectual Property Contracts*, 21 Licensing J. 11 (Jan. 2001); Bartlett, *Effects of Bankruptcy on Licensing under 11 U.S.C. § 365(n)*, 5 J. Proprietary Rts. 20 (July 1993); *The Protection of Intellectual Property Rights of a Licensee When a Licensor Goes into Bankruptcy under the Amended 11 U.S.C. 11 § 365*, 73 J. Pat. & Trademark Off. Soc'y. 893 (1991); Brown, Hansend & Salerno, *Technology Licenses under Section 365(n) of the Bankruptcy Code: The Protections Afforded the Technology User*, 95 Com. L.J. 170 (1990).

For a detailed discussion of the application of 365(n) on international licensors, *see* Groshong, Petrich & Voth, *Intellectual Property Licenses and Bankruptcy: the Latest Word*, Bus. L. Today (August 2014); *Jaffé v. Samsung Elec. Co.*, 737 F.3d 14 (4th Cir. 2013).

It is important to note that Alternative Service Provider ("ASP") licenses do not receive the same protection under the Bankruptcy Code as other software licenses. *See* Raymond T. Nimmer & Holly K. Towle, Law of Electronic Commercial Transactions, § 8.14 (Thompson* West 2003).

C. The Licensee's Bankruptcy

1. *Nonexecutory License*

A software licensor's primary concern when a licensee files for bankruptcy is payment. If the license is considered to be nonexecutory, for example where the licensor has already substantially performed its obligations under the agreement, then the licensor's sole recourse may be to assert a general unsecured claim against the licensee's estate. Accordingly, a licensor should seek to protect itself from a licensee's bankruptcy to the greatest extent possible. One technique is obtaining a security interest in the licensed software and/or other assets, which will incentivize the licensee to honor its commitments under the license agreement. Another technique is to draft the license in such a way to ensure that it will be treated as an executory contract, which may make it difficult for the licensee to assume or assign the license without the licensor's consent and thus provide the licensor with greater leverage. See Section B.3 above for a description of these drafting techniques. Although the restrictions on assignment of an executory software license may also apply to the assignment of a nonexecutory software license, a court might treat a nonexecutory license as a sale or assignment of the software rather than a license, in which case the court may not be inclined to apply the exception to assignment provided for under Section 365(c) of the Bankruptcy Code.

2. *Executory License*

(a) Termination of License

Many licensors include language in their license agreements automatically terminating the license agreement upon a licensee's bankruptcy even though such provisions, sometimes referred to as *ipso facto* clauses, are not enforceable once a debtor declares bankruptcy. 11 U.S.C. § 365(e). Section 365(e) (1) of the Bankruptcy Code provides that an executory contract of the debtor may not be terminated or modified after a bankruptcy filing because of a provision in the license agreement that is conditioned on the insolvency or financial condition of the debtor or the commencement of a bankruptcy filing. 11 U.S.C. § 365(e)(1). Any attempt by the non-bankrupt party to unilaterally terminate a contract covered by the provisions of the Bankruptcy Code without first seeking relief from the automatic stay may expose such party to significant liability. *See, e.g.*, *In re Computer Communications, Inc.*, 824 F.2d 725 (9th Cir. 1987) (unilateral termination of agreement to buy hardware and software from bankrupt debtor violates bankruptcy code as ability to terminate stayed by bankruptcy filing; debtor awarded over $4 million in damages).

Although *ipso facto* clauses are generally not enforceable, their inclusion in a license agreement may provide a party leverage in the event the other party is insolvent and does not declare bankruptcy or a bankruptcy court rejects the insolvent party's bankruptcy petition. To the extent a party has received a parent guaranty for the performance of the other party and the parent declares bankruptcy, the beneficiary of the guaranty would be able to terminate the agreement. Some practitioners include *ipso facto* clauses, as prior to the Bankruptcy Code being codified in 1979, such clauses were enforceable and they believe the Bankruptcy Code may be amended in the future to recognize the validity of such clauses. Section 365(e)(2) of the Bankruptcy Code provides an exception, however, allowing for the enforceability of *ipso facto* clauses in the case of personal services by an individual with a special knowledge, skill or ability.

To provide a greater level of protection, a licensor can include certain performance requirements in the license agreement that will allow the licensor to terminate the license agreement if the licensee fails to abide by such requirements. These may include requiring the licensee to continue operating, maintain a minimum amount of sales, or expend a minimum amount on marketing or promotion, maintain a set credit rating or receiving a qualified opinion from an external auditor. These rights are separate and distinct from those provisions typically placed in a license agreement allowing the licensor to terminate the license for the licensee's bankruptcy.

The language below illustrates a potential basis for terminating a license without violating the *ipso facto* prohibitions of the Bankruptcy Code. Only covenants that do not relate solely to the financial condition of the debtor are capable of being enforced.

a) *If Licensee (i) fails to continue operating its material businesses; (ii) fails to maintain monthly sales of $__________; or (iii) fails to expend at least $__________ per month on marketing and promotion of [product name].*

b) *then Licensor may by giving written notice to Licensee, terminate this Agreement in whole or in part and without charge, as of the date specified in such notice of termination.*

In addition, a licensor may terminate a license prior to a licensee's bankruptcy filing provided the termination is effectuated prior to the licensee's bankruptcy filing. *See, e.g., Moody v. Amoco Oil Co.*, 734 F.2d 1200 (7th Cir. 1984). The fact that the effective date of any notice of termination does not occur until after the licensee files for bankruptcy should not affect the result so long as the termination is complete and not subject to cure or reversal, either under the terms of the contract or under state law. *Id.* at 1213 (holding that automatic stay does not toll mere running of time under contract and does not prevent automatic termination of contract, nor does it give debtor greater rights under contract, and debtors could not rely upon it to prevent termination of contracts as to which 90-day notice had been given before filing of petition). Where the termination is subject to cure or reversal at the time of the bankruptcy filing, however, the licensee will have an opportunity to cure the default under Section 365 of the Bankruptcy Code and prevent the termination from occurring. *Id.* at 1215 (where debtors filed for bankruptcy before expiration of 15-day cure period allowed by termination notice, debtors could elect to assume the contract, and, if they did so determine, they could cure default at any time prior to the assumption).

(b) Assumption or Assignment of Executory License

Under Section 365(b) of the Bankruptcy Code, a software licensee who declares bankruptcy and desires to assume an executory license agreement must cure all breaches, fully perform its obligations under the license agreement, and provide adequate assurances that it will perform in the future. If the licensee fails to do so, it must reject the license agreement and relinquish all rights to the underlying intellectual property. *In re*

Chapin Revenue Cycle Management, LLC, 343 Bankr. 728 (M.D. Fla 2006), the court held that in the event of a non-monetary incurable default, "the debtor is precluded from assuming an executory contract only if the default was material or if the default caused 'substantial economic detriment.'" *Id.* at 731.

Furthermore, there is a limit on a debtor licensee's ability to assign a software license to a third party. For example, it appears that a debtor licensee cannot assign a nonexclusive software license to another entity without the licensor's consent even where there is no prohibition to such assignment under the license agreement. *See, e.g., In re Alltech Plastics, Inc.*, 71 B.R. 686 (Bankr. W.D. Tenn. 1987) (holding that patent licenses cannot be assigned by licensee under Section 365 of the Bankruptcy Code without licensor's consent because under federal common law the duties and obligations of a licensee are personal and nondelegable and thus not assignable without the licensor's consent); *In re CFLC, Inc.*, 89 F.3d 673, 679 (9th Cir. 1996) (prohibiting assignment of nonexclusive patent license without licensor's consent); *In re Patient Educ. Media, Inc.*, 210 B.R. 237, 242–43 (Bankr. S.D.N.Y. 1997) (prohibiting nonexclusive copyright license without licensor's consent); 11 U.S.C. § 365(c) (providing exception to assignment of contracts under Section 365 of the Bankruptcy Code where "applicable law" excuses a nondebtor party to an executory contract from accepting its assignment).

The same limitations may not apply to the assignment of an exclusive software license, which may be characterized as an assignment of a property interest rather than the license of limited rights to use the software. *See In re Golden Books Family Entertainment, Inc.*, 269 B.R. 311 (Bankr. D. Del. 2001) (assignability of copyright license turns on whether it is exclusive or nonexclusive; exclusive copyright license of children's book character was assignable by debtor); *In re Supernatural Foods, L.L.C.*, 268 B.R. 759 (Bankr. M.D. La. 2001) (holding that trustee could assume and assign exclusive patent license, despite provision to contrary in agreement because generally applicable law did not prohibit assignment). *But see Gardner v. Nike, Inc.*, 279 F.3d 774 (9th Cir. 2002) (holding that licensee did not have right to transfer its rights in exclusive copyright license without licensor's consent); *ProteoTech, Inc. v. Unicity Intern., Inc.*, 542 F. Supp. 2d 1216 (W.D. Wash. 2008) (holding that licensee did not have right to transfer its rights in exclusive patent license without licensor's consent); cf. *In re Hernandez*, 285 B.R. 435 (Bankr. D. Ariz. 2002) (holding that licensee could not assume exclusive patent license notwithstanding lack of debtor's intention to transfer license).

Similarly, at least one court has held that a licensee cannot use a nonexclusive license after its bankruptcy reorganization absent the licensor's consent. *In re Catapult Enter., Inc.*, 165 F.3d 747, 754–55 (9th Cir. 1999) ("Where applicable non-bankruptcy law makes an executory contract non-assignable because the identity of the non-debtor is material, a debtor in possession may not assume the contract absent consent of the non-debtor party."). *But see Institut Pasteur v. Cambridge Biotech Corp.*, 104 F.3d 489 (1st Cir. 1997) (holding that debtor is not to be prevented from assuming license unless it actually intended to assign license to third party); *In re Hernandez*, 287 B.R. 795 (Bankr. D. Ariz. 2002) (holding that exclusive patent license need not be assumed or rejected by debtor but may "ride through" the bankruptcy case).

Licensees also need to be concerned about their right to assume a license in the event of their bankruptcy as there is a dichotomy among the federal circuit courts. In *In re Sunterra Corporation*, 361 F.3d 257 (4th Cir. 2004), Sunterra licensed certain software and cross-licensed any enhancements Sunterra made to the software back to the licensor. Prior to declaring bankruptcy, Sunterra spent approximately $38 million to enhance the software. When Sunterra later declared bankruptcy and subsequently tried to assume the license, the licensor claimed that under 11 U.S.C. § 365 (c), the licensee was precluded from assuming the contract without the licensor's consent even though the license agreement permitted the debtor to assign the license.

The Fourth Circuit Court of Appeals held that Section 365(c) of the Bankruptcy Code precluded the debtor licensee from assuming the contract without the licensor's consent even though the license agreement permitted the debtor to assign the license. *Id.* This position, which emphasizes the literal meaning of the statutory language to evaluate the assumption of executory contracts (also known as the "hypothetical test") has been adopted by the Third, Fourth, Ninth and Eleventh Circuits. The hypothetical test provides that the courts should follow the plain meaning of the statute (§ 365(c)) when the terms of the statute are unambiguous. Third: *In re West Elec., Inc.*, 852 F.2d 79, 83 (3d Cir. 1988); Fourth: *In re Catron*, 158 B.R. 629, 633–38 (E.D. Va. 1993), *aff'd without op.*, 25 F.3d 1038 (4th Cir. 1994); Ninth: *In re Catapult*, 165 F.3d at 750; Eleventh: *In re James Cable Partners*, 27 F.3d 534, 537 (11th Cir. 1994) (in dicta).

The First Circuit along with a majority of bankruptcy courts, however, has adopted the "actual" test, which it believes represents the intent of Congress. *Institut Pasteur v. Cambridge Biotech Corp.*, 104 F.3d at 493; *In re Footstar, Inc.*, 323 B.R. 566, 569 n.2 (Bankr. S.D.N.Y. 2005). *See In re Footstar*, 323 B.R. at 569 n.2 and *In re Catapult*, 165 F.3d at 749 n.2 for a summary of bankruptcy courts that have adopted the "actual" test. Under the "actual test," a court will examine, on a case by case basis, whether the non-debtor would be required to accept performance from a party other than the party with which it initially contracted. Further, a debtor is not to be prevented from assuming a license unless it actually intends to assign the license to a third party.

Thus, a prudent licensee should include language in its license that in the event of the licensee's bankruptcy, and subsequent decision to assume the license, the licensor agrees that it will consent to and accept the assumption. The ramifications of not having such a provision in the license agreement may be so big that it ultimately could affect a licensee's decision on where to file for bankruptcy protection or whether to file for bankruptcy protection at all. A licensor who agrees to such a provision may wish to limit a consent to assumption provision to situations that do not involve a change in control of the licensee.

In addition, a personal services contract cannot be assigned or assumed by a debtor under the Bankruptcy Code. 11 U.S.C § 365(c); *In re Catron*, 158 B.R. 624 (Bankr. E.D. Va. 1992), *aff'd*, 158 B.R. 629, *aff'd*, 25 F.3d 1038. *But see In re Fastrax, Inc.*, 129 B.R. 274 (Bankr. M.D. Fla. 1991) (subcontract for installation of storage, retrieval, and distribution computer center not a personal service contract and could be performed by another computer software company).

For a more detailed discussion, *see* Brown-Edwards & Murphy, *Assigning Intellectual Property in Bankruptcy: Is the Licensor's Consent Necessary?*, Bloomberg Law Rep. (Jan. 12, 2012); Agin, *Reconciling Commercial Law and Information Technology: An Essay on Bankruptcy Practice During the Next Business Cycle*, 4 J. of Internet L. (October 2000).

For a general overview of the bankruptcy process in the event of a customer's bankruptcy, *see* Sullivan & Ravert, *A Vendor's Guide to Bankruptcy*, 1 Bloomberg Corp. L.J. 494 (2006).

CHAPTER 28

Employee Issues

A tangential but important consideration in software licensing is ensuring that appropriate safeguards have been taken by the licensor in relation to its employees and contractors. These actions are important not only to protect the licensor's business but also the interests of the licensor's customers.

A. Assignment of Intellectual Property Rights

From the employer's perspective, it is important to ensure that the employer owns its employee's work product in order to maintain the integrity of the licensor's products and to ensure that the licensor has the right to transfer ownership of any intellectual property it creates, particularly if it is contractually obligated to do so.

1. *The Employer's Ownership of Employee Inventions*

Generally, an employer has an interest in the inventions of an employee by an implied contract if the employee is "employed to invent." *See Standard Parts Co. v. Peck*, 264 U.S. 52, 59–60 (1924). The meaning of "employed to invent" is a matter of state law and will vary by state. For example, some states require only that the employee's job description generally include innovation or improvements. In other states, however, the employee must be employed to invent specific innovations or improvements that must be detailed in advance. *Standard Parts Co. v. Peck*, 264 U.S. 52, 59–60 (1924); *Teets v. Chromalloy Gas Turbine Corp.*, 83 F.3d 403 (Fed. Cir. 1996); *Cahill v. Regan*, 157 N.E.2d 505 (N.Y. 1959). Other states provide that an employer cannot claim ownership of an invention unrelated to the employee's employment. *See, e.g.*, MINN. STAT. § 181.78. Thus, the choice of law governing a person's employment contract or related confidentiality and inventions agreements signed upon hiring is a very important consideration. *See* Van Slyke & Friedman, *Employer's Rights to Inventions and Patents of Its Officers, Directors and Employees*, 18 AM. INTELL. PROP. L. Q. 127 (1990).

2. *Documenting the Employee's Existing Intellectual Property*

An employer must carefully document its ownership of an employee's work product to avoid future disputes. At the time the employee begins his/her employment, he/she should be required to execute an agreement assigning ownership of all work created during the scope of his/her employment to the employer. To the extent the employee claims to own intellectual property existing at the time of employment, all such intellectual property should be listed in detail on a schedule attached to the agreement. See, e.g., Form L.11. The agreement should provide that the failure to identify and list any such intellectual property is conclusive evidence that the employee lacked any intellectual property at the time of his/her employment. Some employers seek to state that *all* intellectual property created by an employee during the period of his/her employment with the employer or within a set period of time following the termination of the employee's employment will be owned by the employer. Given that this intellectual property may be created outside of the scope of the employee's employment, it is unclear whether or not this language is enforceable. *See Applied Materials, Inc. v. Advanced Micro-Fabrication Equip. Co.*, 630 F. Supp. 2d 1084 (N.D. Cal. 2009) (assignment clause assigning ownership of employee work created outside of employment unenforceable).

An employer should carefully define the inventions and other materials that are being assigned to the employer to avoid any ambiguity as to what is being transferred. The description should be as broad as possible. The failure to clearly describe the nature of what is being assigned to the employer may provide the opportunity for the employee to claim that he or she did not assign all ideas and concepts related to such materials to the employer, and in fact retained certain "ideas." *See, e.g., Mattel v. MGA Entertainment, Inc.*, 616 F.3d 904 (9th Cir. 2010) (employment agreement did not unambiguously require assignment of employee's idea for a new doll to employer).

3. *Executing a Proper Assignment*

Employers also should pay careful attention to the language used to transfer ownership of an employee's work to the employer to ensure that it creates an immediate assignment of intellectual property rights at the time the intellectual property is created as opposed to the employee agreeing to assign his or her rights in the future. If the employee later fails to assign his or her rights in the future or assigns these rights to another party, the employer's remedy is to bring a breach of contract claim against the employee. While the employer may be able to obtain specific performance through such a suit, the employer would not have sufficient title to enforce a patent in the interim. Further, the employee may be "judgment proof," negating the benefits of any monetary award. See Form L.8 § 5 for model assignment language.

In *DDB Technologies, L.L.C. v. MLB Advanced Media L.P.*, 517 F.3d 1284 (Fed. Cir. 2008), the United States Court of Appeals held that if an employee agreement grants the employer all rights in future inventions, the assignment arises automatically upon creation of the work, and the transfer occurs by operation of law. The court focused on the fact that the agreement contained an actual assignment, not an agreement to assign. *Id.* at 1287, 1290. ("Employee agrees to and does **hereby grant and assign** to Company or its nominee his entire right, title and interest in and to ideas, inventions and improvements . . . .") (emphasis supplied). It contrasted the language contained in the employee agreement to an *agreement to transfer* any future invention, which does not automatically vest title in the employer since it requires the execution of an assignment in the future. *Id.*

Similarly, in *Board of Trustees of Leland Stanford Junior University v. Roche*, 583 F.3d 832 (Fed. Cir. 2009) *aff'd*, 563 U.S. 776 (2011), the court found that the language used by Stanford University in its employment agreement was inadequate to assign ownership in an employee's invention to the University. In *Roche*, an employee executed an employment agreement which provided: "I agree to assign or confirm in writing to Stanford . . . that right, title and interest in . . . such inventions as required by Contracts or Grants." *Id.* at 837. The employee entered into a subsequent agreement with Cetus as part of Stanford's collaboration with Cetus. As a condition to accessing Cetus's confidential information, he executed a Visitor Confidential Agreement ("VCA"), which provided that he "will assign and do[es] assign to Cetus, my right, title, and interest in each of the ideas and improvements" developed as a result of his work at Cetus.

A dispute subsequently arose as to the ownership of patents developed by the employee. Stanford claimed ownership as a result of the employee executing the Stanford agreement, while Cetus claimed ownership based on the VCA. The United States Court of Appeals found that the language of the Stanford agreement did not assign ownership to Stanford, as it was only an agreement to assign and thus Stanford did not immediately gain title to the invention. One the other hand, the court found the Cetus VCA effected an immediate assignment of the researcher's invention to Cetus. *Id.* at 841–42. Thus, ownership vested in Cetus, not Stanford.

To avoid potential disputes and ensure ownership of its employee's work, a prudent employer should ensure that its employment agreement includes a present assignment of all of the employee's rights in all copyrights, patents and other intellectual property created by the employee rather than an agreement to assign such sights in the future.. See Form L.8 § 5 for model language. *See also, Omni Medsci, Inc. v. Apple, Inc.*, 7 F.4th 1148 (Fed. Cir. 2021) (language of assignment found to be a statement of future intention).

To the extent the employer seeks to have the employee execute an agreement after the start of his employment, the employer should provide the employee additional consideration beyond the employee's continued employment to ensure such agreement will be binding. *See, e.g., Lucht's Concrete Pumping, Inc. v. Homer*, 224 P.3d 355 (Colo. App. 2009).

B. Protection of Employer and Customer Confidential Information

As a condition of employment, all employees also should be required to sign an employee confidentiality agreement that is tailored to the employee's state of residence. These agreements should provide that during and after the termination of his or her employment, the employee will treat all employer and customer information as confidential and that the employee will not disclose any such confidential information other than is required in the performance of his or her duties for the employer. The confidentiality provisions should be narrowly written to protect the parties' actual confidential information and specifically identify and limit the use of any confidential information. Employers should avoid overly broad language, limiting an employee's confidentiality obligations to actual confidential information and trade secrets. *See Marsh USA, Inc. v. Alliant Ins. Servs., Inc.*,

49 Misc.3d 1210 (N.Y. Sup. Ct. 2015) (confidentiality provision that encompassed all client information and personal information unenforceable as overbroad and unnecessary to protect trade secrets and confidential information). Doing so will protect the parties in the event an employee misuses the information. *Marketing Technology Solutions, Inc. v. Medizine LLC*, 2010 WL 2034404 (S.D.N.Y. May 18, 2010) (employee's access of employer's computer system exceeded authorized use under employee's employment agreement).

Unlike covenants of noncompetition, which must be of reasonable duration, courts do not generally restrict covenants of confidentiality to a set time period. *See Ashland Management Inc. v. Altair Investments NA, LLC*, 869 N.Y.S.2d 465 (N.Y. 2008) (court enforced confidentiality agreement of unlimited duration). Further, all states recognize an employer's right to protect its confidential information. *See, e.g., Majestic Marketing, Inc. v. Nay*, 2010 WL 338966, at *5 (Cal. App. Jan. 29, 2010) ("Despite California's broad prohibition against noncompetition agreements, covenants not to compete may be enforced to the extent that enforcement is necessary to protect a company's trade secrets."). Employers may obtain a recovery from employees even if the information is considered confidential information and not a trade secret. *Orthofix v. Hunter*, 630 Fed. Appx. 566 (6th Cir. 2015).

Some customers seek to have the vendor's employees sign a confidentiality agreement directly with the customer. Vendors should not agree to have their employees execute a confidentiality obligation directly with the customer, as it exposes the employee, personally, to potential liability for breach. Instead, the underlying license agreement between the vendor and customer should provide that the employees will sign a confidentiality agreement with the vendor that is as restrictive or more restrictive than the agreement between the vendor and the customer.

1. Ethics and Training

All employees should be informed of the employer's Code of Ethics and Standards of Conduct with the expectation they will be adhered to. At the start of each new customer project, all employees working on the project should complete an "on-boarding" process during which the employee team is briefed on the project, including any requirements of confidentiality particular to such project. To the extent possible, the employer should keep a record of those in attendance and have employees sign an acknowledgement of their obligations.

Employees also should be required to complete annual online ethics training, and the employer's human resources department should circulate periodic ethics related articles to all of the employer's employees. These should include reminders of each employee's obligations in regard to the customer's confidential information. Additionally, if the employer publishes an employee newsletter, the employer should include an ethics and confidentiality reminder in the newsletter.

Employers should only bring a good-faith claim against an employee and should refrain from bringing a claim solely to have a chilling effect on its employees, especially those employees seeking to leave the employer's employ. Employers should only bring a claim in the event of an actual trade secret misappropriation and should avoid the tendency to sue first and develop facts to support their case afterwards. *See FLIR Systems, Inc. v. Parrish*, 174 Cal. App. 4th 1270 (Cal. App. 2009) (court awarded ex-employees $1.6M for claim brought in bad faith by former employer alleging trade secret misappropriation under doctrine of inevitable disclosure, despite the fact the doctrine had been rejected in California. Court found suit had been brought to stifle competition and there was no evidence of trade secret misappropriation.); *but see Bimbo Bakeries, USA, Inc. v. Butticella*, 613 F.3d 102 (3d Cir. 2010) (injunction on starting new position appropriate if misappropriation of former employer's trade secrets likely).

See Chapter 25.B.8 for a more detailed discussion of the Inevitable Disclosure Doctrine.

2. *Confidential Information of Employee's Former Employer*

Employers can be held liable if a new employee uses his or her former employer's confidential information in their new role to their new employer. *See, e.g., William A. Graham Co. v. Haughey*, 484 F. Supp. 2d 324 (E.D. Pa. 2007) (use of former employer's copyrighted templates brought by ex-employee to new job constituted copyright infringement by new employer). The potential damages can be significant. *See, e.g.*, Gullo, *SAP to Appeal $306 Million Judgment in Oracle Lawsuit*, http://www.bloomberg.com/news/2012-09-15/sap-to-appeal-306-million-judgment-in-oracle-lawsuit-1-.html.

To that end, employers should, during the interview process, inform all candidates that they should not bring with them or use any confidential information from their former employer when they begin their new employment. This requirement should also be included in the employee's offer letter. All new employees should also execute an acknowledgment, acknowledging their obligation to abide by any agreements entered into with former employers and requiring the employee to provide the new employer with a copy of any such agreement. Finally, if a former employer believes an employee is potentially taking the employer's confidential information to their new employer, company should provide the new employer a copy of the employee's confidentiality agreement with the former employer and inform the new employer that it expects the employee and the new employer to abide by the terms of the agreement. See Form L.6 for a model acknowledgment.

For a general discussion of trade secret misappropriation by employees, *see* Feldman& Stamm, *How Employers Can Stop Trade secret Misuse Before it Happens*, ACC Docket 26 (April 2020); Gray & O'Rourke, *Preventing Employee Trade Secret Misuse from Derailing Your Company*, 24 Corp. Couns. Q. 205 (April 2008); Weller & Shaffer, *Employee Theft of Trade Secrets*, 26 ACC Docket 87 (Oct. 2008); Starr & Franciose, *Disloyalty and the USTA*, Nat'l L.J. Apr. 20, 2009, at 13.

3. *PRACTICE POINT*: Checklist for employee confidentiality agreements.

To increase the likelihood of an employee nondisclosure agreement being enforceable in the event of a dispute, prudent employers should undertake the following actions:

- Execute a single purpose nondisclosure agreement that has been tailored for use with the employer's employees. Resist the temptation to use a business to business nondisclosure agreement that the employer uses with its customers and vendors.
- Ensure that the agreement clearly defines "confidential information" to include the employer's confidential information as well as its customers' confidential information in whatever form it may exist, including tangible and intangible as well as information that resides within the employee's memory.
- Include the whistleblower immunity language required under the Defend Trade Secrets Act (DTSA).("*Nothing in this Agreement prohibits Employee from reporting possible violations of law or regulation to any governmental agency or entity, or making other disclosures that are protected under the whistleblower provisions of law. Employee does not need the prior authorization of the Law Department to make any such reports or disclosures and Employee is not required to notify the Company that he/she has made such reports or disclosures.*")
- Create a corporate culture of protecting trade secrets and confidential information, including requiring annual employee training which documents the employee's participation.
- Place confidentiality legends on all confidential documents, including its customer lists and lists of prospects and limiting access to all confidential information.
- Execute nondisclosure agreements with all vendors, customers, and third parties with whom it exchanges confidential information.
- Make all offers of employment subject to the employee's execution of the employer's confidentiality agreement.
- Clearly state in the employee handbook and any document employees sign as part of the onboarding process that the employer owns all confidential information generated through the employment relationship. If possible, have the employee execute an acknowledgment to this effect.
- To the extent the employer has a Bring Your Own Device (BYOD) policy and/or provides corporate-owned mobile devices for employee use, clearly state the employer's right to access such devices and/or the data resident on such devices.
- Ensure that both the employee and the employer actually sign the agreement and the employee is provided a copy of the executed agreement.
- Store all executed original copies of the agreement in a locked cabinet and in the cloud. If the employee asks to review his or her personnel file, allow the employee to access only a copy.

- During employee exit interviews, provide employees with a copy of their confidentiality agreement and remind them of their confidentiality obligations. See, e.g., Form L.12.

C. Non-solicitation of Employees by Former Employees (§§ 5.3.7, 9.14)

As part of the hiring process, prudent employers should require employees to execute a covenant of non-solicitation, prohibiting an employee, upon departure, from soliciting his or her former co-workers to leave the employment of the employer. Prohibitions on soliciting co-workers protect an employer's interest in its employees, as employers make a significant financial investment in training and developing their employees.

Practically, non-solicitation provisions are difficult to enforce, but they do provide the employer with some leverage in the event a former employee tries to entice a former co-worker to leave the employer. Enforcement is difficult, as both the soliciting employee and the solicited employee will likely deny one solicited the other. It is almost impossible to prove solicitation without a paper trail or an admission.

Employee referral programs may provide the necessary paper trail and a motivation. Many employers have an "employee referral program" that provides existing employees a "referral fee" for referring potential candidates for open positions. Employees often seek to encourage their former co-workers to join them at the new employer to receive a referral fee. By subpoenaing the new employer's records, the former employer will be able to determine if the employee received a referral bonus, and thus by implication, violated his non-solicitation covenant.

A less confrontational means of addressing the issue is to send the employee a letter reminding the employee of his non-solicitation obligation and copying his new employer. It puts both the employee and the new employer on notice that the prior employer plans to enforce its rights in the event of a breach. For the same reason, every employee leaving the company should be required to have an exit interview. During the exit interview the employee should be given a copy of his/her noncompetition agreement and reminded of his/her obligations under the agreement. To the extent it can, the employer should have the soon to be ex-employee execute an acknowledgement, acknowledging his/her obligations. See Form L.10 for model language.

To avoid potential problems, a new employer should have each employee represent and warrant that he or she is not subject to any contractual obligation that would prohibit him or her from accepting employment with the employer, and that there are no limitations on the employee fulfilling his or her duties as an employee. The new employer should remind the employee not to bring any materials or information from the employee's previous employer to the new job. All electronic media from the employee's personal equipment should be deleted/erased. See Form L.6 for a model certification requiring the prospective employee to disclose any actual or potential conflict. *See Southwest Stainless L.P. v. Sappington*, 582 F.3d 1176 (10th Cir. 2009) (finding that former employee and new employer tortuously interfered with ex-employer's contractual relationship with its employees by soliciting an employee known to be subject to a non-competition agreement). Employers should carefully select the governing law for any non-solicitation agreement, as some courts have found covenants of ex-employees not to solicit former co-workers to terminate their employment an illegal restraint of trade. *Schmersahl, Treloar & Co., P.C. v. McHugh*, 28 S.W.3d 345 (Mo. App. 2000).

D. Non-solicitation of Employees of Vendor/Customer

Many vendors include language in their license/services agreements prohibiting the customer from soliciting their employees for employment. They do so to protect their investment in their employees and to protect their revenue stream. A well-worded prohibition will prevent the customer from hiring only those employees who provided services to the customer for a set period of time, or alternatively, proscribing liquidated damages in the event the prohibition is breached.

Non-hire provisions are difficult to enforce if the customer is a large or profitable customer and the enforcement of the provision may damage the business relationship. In the event of a dispute with a customer over a non-solicitation provision, most vendors are hesitant to enforce such provisions to avoid alienating the customer. Many customers recognize the leverage they hold over the vendor, and thus seek to negotiate an "exception" to any non-hire prohibitions. Often the customer will seek to include an exception granting it the right to hire the employee after the employee has been assigned to the customer's project for a minimum period of time, such as three months, or include a liquidated damages provision that provides for reduced payments the longer the employee provides services to the customer.

If the customer is willing to accept a non-solicitation clause, it should seek to negotiate any desired exceptions for which it would need to hire the vendor's employees, such as in the event of the vendor's breach of the contract, the vendor declaring bankruptcy or the vendor ceasing support of the software. Many customers exclude from any prohibition hiring an employee through a general solicitation, such as an advertisement or job posting, or employees involuntarily terminated by the vendor. A general solicitation exclusion creates a loophole, as any claim that a customer specifically targeted a desired employee can be readily refuted by reference to the advertisement and any screening of responses received in connection with the advertisement.

The customer should insist that any non-hire provision in the license agreement be mutual to protect its own employee population, especially for those employees with hard-to-find expertise. Very few customers seek to include a non-solicitation provision in their agreements, which is a serious oversight. For vendors, a customer's employee population is a fertile recruiting ground for employees with scarce skill sets, especially if the vendor has trained the employees at the customer's expense as part of the implementation. Further, many customer employees are underpaid in comparison paid by vendors, making the opportunity to join the vendor financially attractive.

> *For a period of 180 days from the termination of this Agreement, neither party shall solicit for employment or hire employees of the other party who have been directly*

> *involved in rendering or receiving services under this Agreement without obtaining the prior written consent of the other party; provided, however, nothing in this Section shall restrict or preclude either party from: (a) making generalized searches for, and hiring, employees by use of advertisements in the media (including trade media), (b) continuing its ordinary course hiring practices that are not targeted specifically at employees of the other party (including use of internal or external recruiters who are not directed based upon information learned through this Agreement), (c) hiring any employee of a party who was in discussions with the other party prior to the Effective Date, or (d) responding to and hiring any employee of a party who contacts the other party seeking employment on his or her own initiative without any direct solicitation by the other party (other than any generalized search or ordinary course practice referred to in clause (a), (b) or (c) above).*

E. Noncompetition Agreements

Most software vendors require their employees to execute a covenant of noncompetition, prohibiting the employee from competing with the employer for a period of time after the employee leaves the employer's employ. To increase the likelihood that the covenant will be upheld by a court, prudent employers will draft the limitation narrowly, limiting the employee from working directly or indirectly for, or providing services to, those customers with whom the employee interacted or had access to their confidential information in the 12 months prior to the termination of his or her employment and require only senior level employees to execute a non-competition agreement. *See Unisource Worldwide, Inc. v. Carrara*, 244 F. Supp. 2d 977 (C.D. Ill. 2003). The prohibition on soliciting customers and employees should be limited to no more than two years and limited to those customers with whom the employee was involved in the two years prior to the termination of his or her employment. The underlying agreement should provide that the period of noncompetition will be tolled for a stated period of time each time the signatory violates the restrictive covenant. *See, e.g., Proudfoot Consulting Co. v. Gordon*, 576 F.3d 1223 (11th Cir. 2009). Employers should draft any prohibition on solicitation broadly enough to prevent any contact or solicitation of the employer's customers through social media such as Facebook® or LinkedIn®.

The enforceability of any covenants of noncompetition and any non-solicitation covenants will depend on the governing law and venue of the underlying agreement. *See Down-Lite International, Inc. v. Chad Altbaier. et al.*, 821 Fed. Appx. 553 (6th Cir. 2020) (Ohio court upheld application of Ohio law to California based employee in employee non-competition agreement.).

In January 2023, the Federal Trade Commission issued a notice of proposed rulemaking on a federal ban on post-employment non-competition agreements which it viewed as a violation of federal antitrust law The potential rule that would ban any "contractual term between an employer and a worker that prevents the worker from seeking or accepting employment with a person, or operating a business after the conclusion of the worker's employment with the employer." See. FTC, Notice of Proposed Rulemaking: Non-compete Clause Rule, 2023 WL 255956 (Fed. Rules Jan. 19, 2023).

To be upheld, a non-compete provision should be:

- limited to a small number of key employees,
- reasonably and narrowly drawn, and
- accompanied by consideration such as a job offer, a promotion, cash consideration or stock options, etc. *See Lycos, Inc. v. Lincoln Jackson,* 18 Mass. L. Rptr. 256 (2004) (a promotion may void an employee's noncompetition agreement because the terms of employment changed as a result of the employee's new role).

Recently, an increasing number of states, including Illinois, Maine, Maryland, New Hampshire and Washington, have banned noncompetition agreements altogether, while Massachusetts has significantly restricted their enforceability. In July 2021, President Biden signed an Executive Order to address laws and entities that unfairly limit worker mobility. www.whitehouse.gov/briefing-room/presidential-actions/2021/07/09/executive-order-on-promoting-competition-in-the-american-economy/ Employers should avoid having the agreement governed by the laws of California, which has held non-compete agreements in most cases to be void. California: CAL. BUS. & PROF. CODE ANN. § 16600; *Edwards v. Arthur Anderson LLP,* 189 P.3d. 285 (Cal. 2008) (restrictive covenant of limited duration prohibiting solicitation of specific client unenforceable); *but see Pyro Spectaculars North, Inc. v. Souza,* 861 F. Supp. 2d 1079 (E.D. Cal. 2012) (court issued preliminary injunction against salesman soliciting former employer's customers); *Richmond Technologies, Inc. v. Aumtech Business Solutions,* 2011 WL 2607158 (N.D. Cal. July 1, 2011) (granting motion for temporary restraining order barring former employee from utilizing former employer's confidential information and from calling on former employer's customers). Many states will enforce noncompetition provisions to protect trade secrets. *Muggill v. Reuben H. Donnelley Corp.,* 62 Cal. 2d 239 (1965). Other states limit enforcement to certain categories of employees, COLO. REV. STAT. ANN. § 8.2-113 (2)(d) (covenant not to compete enforceable as to executives and management personnel); HAW. ACT 158 (non-compete and non-solicitation agreements unenforceable against technology workers).

Texas courts will enforce a choice of venue provision against a Texas resident where the venue is outside of Texas, but they will not enforce the choice of another state's law against a Texas resident. *See In re AutoNation, Inc.,* 228 S.W.3d 663 (Tex. 2007) (enforcing Florida venue in matter to enforce noncompetition agreement against a Texas resident); *DeSantis v. Wackenhut Corp.,* 793 S.W.2d 670 (Tex. 1990) (Texas law, rather than contractually selected Florida law, used to interpret noncompetition agreement signed by Texas resident). To ensure certainty, an employer should always select the state of the employee's residence to govern the interpretation of the agreement, but the employer may select its desired venue to hear any dispute.

The courts of some states will "blue pencil" any overly broad provision, allowing courts to strike those overly broad provisions and enforce the remaining provisions. Thus, these states should be viewed favorably in comparison to those that will void the entire agreement. *See, e.g., Fowler v. Printers II,* 598 A.2d 794 (Md. 1991), *cert.* denied,

602 A.2d 710 (Md. 1992); *Duong v. Fielden Hanson Isaacs Miyada Robison Yeh Ltd.*, 478 P.3d 380 (Nev. 2020) (Nevada courts may blue pencil a non-competition agreement if the agreement contains a blue pencil provision). Georgia enacted legislation allowing courts to "blue pencil" overbroad employer covenants not to compete but not to completely rewrite contracts by supplying new material terms. GA. CODE. ANN. § 13-8-53(d). Model language follows:

> *If any of the terms contained in Sections __ and ___ shall be deemed to be unenforceable by reasons of their extent, duration, geographical scope or any other reason, then the parties hereto agree that a court of competent jurisdiction may reduce such extent, duration, or geographical scope or appropriately modify the other provisions hereof and enforce such Sections in their reduced form for all purposes in the contemplated hereby.*

Some employers will waive a covenant of noncompetition if the employee is involuntarily terminated, as it is difficult to argue that the employee should be prohibited from working for another employer or that the employee's subsequent employment is a threat to the former employer's business when the employer did not deem the employee worthy of being retained.

A tangential question that often arises is whether a noncompetition agreement may be assigned by the employer without the employee's consent. A dichotomy of opinions exists on this issue. Ohio and Minnesota courts have held that noncompetition agreements without an assignment clause may be assigned by the employer. *Haughen v. Sundseth*, 118 N.W. 666 (Minn. 1908); *Artomick Int'l, Inc. v. Koch*, 759 N.E.2d 385 (Ohio Ct. App. 2001). Hawaii and Virginia, among others, prohibit the assignment of noncompetition agreements. *UARCO Inc. v. Lam*, 18 F. Supp. 2d 1116 (D. Haw. 1998); *Reynolds & Reynolds Co. v. Hardee*, 932 F. Supp. 149, 153 (E.D. Va. 1996) ("contracts for personal services are not assignable unless both parties agree to the assignment").

Pennsylvania, however, has adopted a more tempered approach interpreting the right of assignment narrowly but allowing assignment in some cases. *All-Pak, Inc. v. Johnston*, 694 A.2d 347, 351 (Pa. Super. 1997) ("absent an explicit assignability provision, courts should be hesitant to read one into the contract"). Those agreements requiring the employer to obtain the employee's consent to assignment likely will be strictly construed. *Guy Carpenter & Co. v. John B. Collins & Assocs.*, 2006 WL 2502232 (D. Minn. Aug. 29, 2006) (failure of employer to obtain employees' consent prior to assignment of noncompetition agreement rendered noncompetition provision unenforceable).

Based on the disparate holdings of the different jurisdictions, a prudent employer should include an explicit assignment clause permitting the employer to assign an employee's noncompetition agreement. See, e.g. Form L.8 § 11.

For a general overview, *see* Kalogredis, Cochran & Steinberg, *Addressing Increasing Uncertainty in the Law of Non-Competes*, 36 ACC DOCKET 34 (Apr. 2018).

For an overview of covenants not to complete *see, Antitrust and Employment Part II*, 51 LAW BRIEF (Apr. 30, 2021); Belcher & Gullickson, *Fencing the Herd: Protecting Your Company's Proprietary Interests with Restrictive Covenants*, 27 ACC DOCKET 55 (Dec. 2009).

PRACTICE POINT: Checklist for protecting employer confidential information.

Although the trend is toward limiting or outright banning non-compete agreements, in most cases employers may take the following actions to protect their interests:

- Ensure all employees and contractors enter into non-disclosure agreements which provide for injunctive relief
- Require all employees to notify the employer if they subsequently accept a position with a competitor
- Limit employee access to confidential information and trade secrets to a need to know basis and block employees from having access to all areas of the employer's IT systems
- Understand the employee's rights under the Defend Trade Secrets Acts and which claims can be brought under the Defend Trade Secrets Act.

F. Theft/Destruction of Employer Property—Computer Fraud and Abuse Act

1. Overview

The Computer Fraud and Abuse Act, 18 U.S.C. § 1030 ("CFAA") potentially provides an employer a means to bring an action against a former employee who has stolen or destroyed employer property through the use of a computer. An employer may seek civil damages and criminal penalties. The CFAA prohibits intentionally accessing computer data without authorization or accessing computer data that exceeds the individual's authorized access. 18 U.S.C. § 1030(a). Success in bringing a CFAA claim depends on the court's interpretation of "authorized."

The CFAA is more favorable to employers as it provides access to the federal courts in commercial matters that are usually heard in state court. Further, the elements proof of a CFAA claim are less than those required for most state law claims.

2. The Meaning of "Loss"

To prevail in a CFAA claim, an injured party must prove that it suffered a "loss" of at least $5,000 in damages. 18 U.S.C. § 1030(c)(4)(A)(i)(l). The CFAA has adopted a broad definition of "loss" allowing a plaintiff to recover for a broad array of damages. "Loss" is defined as:

> *[a]ny reasonable cost . . . including the cost of responding to an offense, conducting a damage assessment, and restoring the data, program, system, or information to its condition prior to the offense, and any revenue lost, cost incurred, or other consequential damages incurred because of interruption of service.*

18 U.S.C. § 1030(e)(8)(11)(emphasis supplied).

Notwithstanding the potentially broad remedy the CFAA might otherwise have provided, courts are divided as to whether an interruption of services is a condition precedent to recovering damages.

In *Southern Parts & Engineering Co. v. Air Compressor Services LLC*, 2014 WL 667958 (N.D. Ga. Feb. 20, 2014), the court found that an interruption of service is not a prerequisite to recovering damages. *ResDev v. Lot Builders*, 2005 WL 1924743 (M.D. Fla. Aug. 10, 2005); *Nexans v. Sark-USA, Inc.*, 319 F. Supp. 2d 468 (S.D.N.Y. 2004).

Other courts have limited the reach of the CFAA more literally by reading the definition of "loss" very strictly. *American Family Mut. Ins. Co. v. Rickman*, 554 F. Supp. 2d 766 (N.D. Ohio 2008) (losses incurred from employee's theft of data do not constitute "losses" as defined under CFAA). *See also Modis Inc. v. Bardelli*, 531 F. Supp. 2d. 314 (D. Conn. 2008). The CFAA "treats lost revenue as a different concept from incurred costs," and permits recovery of lost revenue only when connected to "an interruption in service." *Nexans Wires S.A. v. Sark-USA, Inc.*, 166 Fed. Appx. 559, 562 (2d Cir. 2006); *CustomGuide v. CareerBuilder, LLC*, 813 F. Supp. 2d 990 (N.D. Ill. 2011) (lost sales from unauthorized access not a loss under CFAA if they are unrelated to interruption of computer services).

Losses under the CFAA are not required to be "cash" losses. The costs of internal investigations, as well as employee time associated with these investigations, are recoverable as qualifying losses under the CFAA. *Animators at Law, Inc. v. Capital Legal Solutions, LLC*, 786 F. Supp. 2d 1114, 1121–22 (E.D. Va. 2011) ("[P]erpetrators of unauthorized access should forsee that their actions may result in significant investigations and costs far exceeding the actual damage to the system.") "[T]he costs of responding to the offense" are recoverable, regardless of whether there is an interruption in service, and federal courts have sustained actions based on allegations of costs to investigate and take remedial steps in response to a defendant's misappropriation of data. *P.C. Yonkers, Inc. v. Celebrations! The Party and Seasonal Superstore, L.L.C.*, 2007 WL 708978 (D.N.J. March 5, 2007); *Animators at Law, Inc. v. Capital Legal Solutions, LLC*, 786 F. Supp. 2d 1114 (E.D. Va. 2011) (cost of forensic company hired to investigate theft may constitute "loss" under CFAA); *Mobile Mark, Inc. v. Paskosz*, 2011 WL 3898032 (E.D. Ill. Sept. 6, 2011) (cost of company investigation into alleged employee data theft is "loss" under CFAA).

3. "Unauthorized Access"

In *Van Buren v. United States*, 141 S. Ct. 1648 (2021), the Supreme Court resolved a dichotomy among the circuit courts in holding an employee who accessed a data base in violation of his employer's policy did not exceed his authorized access. The Court found that "an individual 'exceeds authorized access' when he accesses a computer with authorization but then obtains information located in a particular area of the computer-such as files, folders and databases – that are off-limits to him." *Id.* at 1662. Because the employee was authorized to access the database, but accessed for a forbidden purpose, he did not exceed his authorized access codified under the CFAA 18 U.S.C. 1030 (e)(6).

It is clear, however, that the CFAA does apply to ex-employees who wrongfully access a former employer's computer system. *Multiven, Inc. v. Cisco Systems, Inc.*,

725 F. Supp. 2d 887 (N.D. Cal. 2010) (Court granted summary judgment on CFAA claim against ex-employee who used an employee's password to gain access to Cisco's computer systems.). Further, only the system owner may grant authorization to access a system, not a legitimate user. *United States v. Nosal,* 844 F.3d 1024, 1028 (9th Cir 2016*)* ("[O] nce authorization to access a computer has been affirmatively revoked, the user cannot sidestep the statute by going through the backdoor and accessing the computer through a third party."*)*.

4. Contractual Protections

To avoid problems related to unauthorized systems access, the employer should insert language to the following effect in any employment agreement its employees may sign:

> ***Authorized Access.*** *I understand that the Company maintains information systems for business purposes and that my authorization to access and use the Company's business information stored on the Company's information systems is limited to such business purposes for the benefit of Company. I agree that any access to the Company's information on the Company's information systems that I undertake for my personal use or for any third-party for other than the Company's business purposes exceeds my authorization to access and use the Company's information systems. I agree I am not entitled to obtain or alter any Company information that I access, or assist others in accessing, in excess of the limited scope of my authorized access as set forth in this Agreement.*

Language to this effect will strengthen a case against an employee who steals his employer's valuable information. At least one company was able to obtain a preliminary injunction for violation of the CFAA against former employees who violated their confidentiality agreements. *EF Cultural Travel B.V. v. Explorica, Inc.*, 274 F.3d 577 (1st Cir. 2001).

Under *United States v. Nosal*, 676 F.3d 854 (9th Cir. 2012), violation of an employer's use policy is not a violation of the CFAA; however, violation of an employer's access policy may constitute a violation; *Weingand v. Harland Financial Solutions, Inc.* 2012 WL 2327660 (N.D. Cal. June 19, 2012). *See also Accenture, LLP v. Sidhu*, 2010 WL 4691944 (N.D. Cal. Nov. 9, 2010) ("[A]ccess is not established by employer's policies, but by the extent the employer makes the computer system available to the employee." *Id.* at *10.)

5. Corporate Policies

Any policies for accessing and using the employer's information and data should specifically prohibit any use other than for the employer's direct benefit. Access should be limited to a "need to know" basis and be compartmentalized to limit access to only those areas that the employee needs to know. Security protocols should be reviewed and updated regularly. Upon termination of employment, an employee's access should immediately be revoked, and the employee's hard drive and email scanned for any unusual activity.

An employer should include language in its employee handbook explaining the company's expectations as to the protection of its confidential information, and state that employees have no expectation of privacy in the use of their computers. In *Bank v. Mario*

Industries of Virginia, Inc., 650 S.E.2d 687 (Va. 2007), an employer brought suit against two ex-employees who left to start a competing business. Prior to leaving, one employee wrote a memo to his attorney on the employer's computer, which included the employer's confidential information. The employer sought to introduce the memo into court and the employee objected, claiming the protection of the attorney-client privilege. The Supreme Court of Virginia found that the memo was not protected by the attorney-client privilege, as it was written on the employer's computer, and the employer's handbook clearly stated that while its employees could use work computers for personal matters there was no expectation of privacy. *See also Sims v. Lakeside School*, 2007 WL 2745367 (W.D. Wash. Sept. 20, 2007) (relying on school policy, court concluded school employee did not have reasonable expectation of privacy as to emails created on school laptop).

For a more detailed discussion, *see* Kopeikin, *Employee Liability Under the Computer Fraud and Abuse Act for "Exceeding Authorized Access" to a Computer*, 29 COMPUTER & INTERNET L.J. 15 (April 2012); Eichten, *The Computer Fraud and Abuse Act—A Survey of Recent Cases*, 66 BUS. LAW. 231 (2010); Kerr, *Vagueness Challenges to the Computer Fraud and Abuse Act*, 94 MINN. L. REV. 1561 (2010).

6. Other Theories of Recovery

Some commentators have suggested that employers and others can bring claims for wrongful access under the theories of trespass and conversion. These theories are not well developed, however, and thus the likelihood of success is uncertain. *See, generally*, Trespass: Urwin & Wagman, *The Digital Pendulum: Conforming or Mutating the Parameters of Trespass Theory to Address the Act of Wrongfully Accessing a Computer System*, 21 INTELL. PROP. & TECH L.J. 1 (Jan. 2009); *Miller v. International Business Machines Corp.*, 2006 WL 2792416 (N.D. Cal. Sept. 26, 2006); Conversion: *Ali v. Fasteners for Retail, Inc.*, 544 F. Supp. 2d 1064 (E.D. Cal. 2008).

For an overview of the CFAA, *see* Porvaznik, *Navigating the Contours of the Civil Provisions of the Computer Fraud and Abuse Act*, 31 COMPUTER & INTERNET L.J. 12 (Jan. 2014); Vizy, *The Computer Fraud and Abuse Act*, 42 LAW. BRIEF 1 (Aug. 31, 2012).

CHAPTER **29**

When Problems Arise

Parties to a contract can be so focused on signing the agreement that they are unprepared for problems that may arise thereafter. The ability to anticipate and quickly address potential problems is essential for ensuring a successful project. Too often, a lack of foresight creates a downward spiral resulting in litigation which benefits neither party as it creates additional expense without satisfying the original goals of the parties. The Standish Group's 2018 *CHAOS Report* found that only 36 percent of IT projects were deemed successful. *See also* McConnell, *Rapid Development—Taming Wild Software Schedules*, p. 81, MICROSOFT PRESS ("The odds of a large project finishing on time are close to zero. The odds of a large project being cancelled are an even-money bet").

For a helpful checklist of actions to take to avoid litigation, *see Checklist for Avoiding Litigation in Commercial Procurement*, 94 FORMS & CHECKLISTS BI-MONTHLY 1 (July/August 2013).

A. Addressing Issues That May Arise

Problems usually arise in one of three areas:

- failure by the vendor to meet the agreed-upon project milestones;
- failure of the deliverables to meet the agreed-upon specifications; and
- cost overruns by the vendor in a fixed-price environment and by the customer in a time and materials engagement.

Frequently problems in one area trigger problems in one or both of the other areas. For example, failure of deliverables to meet agreed-upon specifications will often delay the delivery schedule both of which generate unanticipated project costs.

While each of these issues may have a different genesis, they all should be addressed in the same manner.

1. Be Proactive

The first step to a successful relationship is for each party to closely monitor the progress of the contract and each party's performance from the date the contract is signed. Each party should appoint a project manager, who monitors compliance with the contract. The vendor for its part should insist on change orders when the customer requests features/functions not covered by the contract. See Chapter 7.D for a discussion of change orders. A strong change order procedure will avoid "scope creep" and hopefully limit any potential disputes among the parties. The parties should hold weekly meetings to ascertain their progress and to identify potential issues before they mature. By proactively monitoring the project, the likelihood of problems arising is reduced and the impact of those problems is minimized. Early identification of problems also allows the parties greater time to resolve the issue, develop work-arounds, and maintain the parties' original delivery schedule.

2. *Maintaining the Attorney-Client Privilege/Attorney Work Product Doctrine*

The Attorney-Client Privilege and Attorney Work Product doctrines are designed to protect legitimate exchanges of information between attorney and client from disclosure to an opposing party in litigation. If a party cannot keep a truthful and probing assessment of its performance, or a plain discussion of its legal rights and obligations, protected from potential claimants, it would present an almost insurmountable impediment to forthright communications between a client and their attorney.

See Form R.8 for a checklist for maintaining the attorney-client privilege and the attorney-client work product privilege.

Often, there is confusion among lawyers as to the differences between the Attorney Work Product doctrine and the Attorney-Client Privilege generally. Set forth below is a brief overview of each.

(a) Attorney-Client Privilege

The Attorney-Client Privilege (Legal Professional Privilege in the United Kingdom and Canada) is a long-standing legal concept that was created to protect from disclosure confidential communications between lawyers and their clients. The privilege is based on several fundamental considerations:

- Clients are encouraged to be completely open, honest and truthful with their attorneys so that the attorney's legal advice can be based on all relevant facts; and
- Clients would be reluctant to seek an attorney's advice if they feared that their communications would be revealed to others such as opposing parties.

Communications between a client and an attorney are privileged whether oral or written, irrespective of whether litigation is anticipated or in progress at the time. However, not all communications between attorneys and clients are protected—only communications made between privileged persons that are intended to be confidential and which are for the purpose of seeking or rendering legal advice. RESTATEMENT (THIRD) OF THE LAW GOVERNING LAWYERS § 68; *Georgia-Pacific Corp. v. GAF Roofing Manufacturing Corp.*, 1996 WL 29392 (S.D.N.Y. Jan. 25, 1996) (in-house attorney acting as negotiator found to be in an advisory capacity and could not claim protection of attorney-client privilege; *United States v. Int'l Board of Teamsters*, 119 F.3d 210, 214 (2d Cir. 1997). The Attorney-Client Privilege applies to corporations as well as individuals.

Thus, communications between employees and a company's in-house and external counsel that are made in confidence for the purpose of seeking legal advice concerning corporate legal matters are protected by the Attorney-Client Privilege. In this context, legal advice is not confined to receiving pure legal advice regarding legal rights and obligations (e.g., whether a party is in breach of a contract or other legal obligation); it can, include practical, strategic advice as to what actions can and should be done in the relevant legal context.

For example, not every internal report can be protected by the Attorney-Client Privilege. A draft of a project report could be protected if, upon completion, it is sent to a party's attorneys for the genuine purpose of legal review with a request for legal advice as to content, legal risks arising for the party from the findings, etc.

The applicability of the Attorney-Client Privilege is dependent on the facts of the situation, but protection will result only if a party is sincerely seeking legal advice and not simply trying to protect its communications from being discoverable.

It is important to remember that confidentiality is the key to preserving the privileged nature of the communication. If the substance of an attorney-client communication is disclosed to people outside of the company (other than external legal counsel) or even to people within the company who are not directly involved in a specific legal matter, the privilege may be lost. "The inclusion of a third party in attorney-client communications does not destroy the privilege if the purpose of the third party's participation is to improve the comprehension of the communications between attorney and client." *United States v. Ackert*, 169 F.3d 136, 139 (2d Cir. 1999). Therefore, confidential communications with a company's attorneys must not be discussed with anyone outside of the company or with individuals within the company who are not involved in the specific matter nor have a business need to know.

For the privilege to exist, the communication must be to, from, or with a licensed attorney with a company's legal department or the company's outside law firm. Discussing a matter with a company employee who has a law degree but is not part of the company's legal department will not be privileged. The only exception is a company employee or law firm paralegal working under the direction of counsel. Moreover, in-house counsel often have dual responsibilities: one legal and one business. If the communication with in-house counsel was for a business rather than legal purpose, or if in-house counsel was acting in his role as a business person rather than lawyer, the communications may not be protected.

Vendors should carefully consider asserting any claim of privilege, as placing "privilege" on a document may have no impact at all. A careful examination of the applicable state laws on privilege, which usually require a communication be made in seeking legal advice, is essential. By placing "privilege" on a document and subsequently producing it, under the laws of some states a party may waive the privilege for all lawyer-client communications related to the matter. As such, a party should carefully consider the ramifications of its actions before asserting any claim of privilege. For a more detailed discussion on the subject of preserving privilege in connection with internal investigations, *see Preserving Attorney-Client Privilege in Internal Investigations*, at www.faegredrinker.com/en/insights/publications/2006/6/preserving-attorneyclient-privilege-in-internal-investigations. *See also Upjohn Co. v. United States*, 449 U.S. 383 (1981).

An investigation that a vendor's quality assurance group undertakes at an attorney's request should be protected by the attorney-client privilege. While expanding the disclosure of the content of these reports unnecessarily is not desirable, any such materials should be used for the legitimate purpose of addressing delivery issues on a client account and remedying the issues, which may prevent litigation from arising.

The parameters listed below should be adhered to in facilitating any exchange between a party's quality assurance team examining contractual compliance and the use of best practices and the business people associated with the account:

- Only those portions of the quality assurance investigation reports that are relevant to the efforts of the account team should be shared.
- All information provided to the account team is provided on a confidential basis and should be kept confidential. The account team should be advised as to the requirements of the confidentiality agreements they signed at the time of their employment.
- Any reports generated by quality assurance team should be marked "Confidential."
- Only those members of the account team necessary to the further investigation who need access to the quality assurance report should be provided with a copy. Such copies should not be further distributed by them to anyone.
- Information in the quality assurance report should not be shared with the customer, and if possible that information should not be brought to the customer site.

Every entity should have a well-established policy on when and how it uses Attorney-Client Privilege/Attorney Work Product legends in its correspondence. Consistent and appropriate uses of the legends are necessary to ensure the underlying doctrines will be held enforceable, at least where the law allows for their enforceability. These concerns are now heightened in an e-discovery context where access to electronic communications is so pervasive and immediate, as well as by employees who have a law degree and claim protection under the doctrine but who are not employed in the capacity of an attorney for the company.

Prudent actions include placing the appropriate legends in the "subject" line so that theoretically the e-mail is never opened by anyone but the intended recipient. The subject text should be typed in all caps so that the legends are conspicuous. Finally, add a "DO NOT FORWARD" statement in an effort to defeat any diminishment of the doctrines by a non-lawyer sharing the communication with a larger audience.

(b) Attorney Work-Product Doctrine

The Work Product Doctrine is more expansive than the Attorney-Client Privilege as it applies to materials created in anticipation of litigation, at which time an obligation to maintain a party's documents may arise. The Work-Product Doctrine is not limited to communications between an attorney and his/her client, but rather encompasses documents created by any person in preparation of potential litigation. It also encompasses interrogatories, materials acquired to bring or defend a matter, as well as any documents, records or information created by an attorney. *Hickman v. Taylor*, 329 U.S. 495 (1947). The intent of the doctrine is to allow a client and his attorney to "prepare and develop legal theories and strategy 'with an eye toward litigation,' free from unnecessary intrusion by his adversaries." *United States v. Adlman*, 134 F.3d 1194, 1196 (2d Cir. 1998) (quoting, in part, from *Hickman v. Taylor*, 329 U.S. 495, 510–11 (1947).

The Work-Product Doctrine provides in general that "a party may not discover documents and tangible things that are prepared in anticipation of litigation or for trial by or for another party or its representative." Rule 26(b)(3) of the Federal Rules of Civil Procedure. Unlike the Attorney-Client Privilege, the Work Product Doctrine is not absolute. Rule 26(b)(3) permits the discovery of documents, even if they otherwise would be protected by the work product privilege, if the moving party can show that it has substantial need for the requested documents and that it cannot obtain the needed information by other means without undue hardship. Rule 26(b)(3)(A). However, "mental impressions . . . opinions, or legal theories" receive heightened protection. Rule 26(b)(3).

However, the doctrine applies only to work done *in contemplation* of or preparation for litigation or another formal dispute resolution mechanism. Documents prepared in the ordinary course of business are not protected. What, precisely, is meant by litigation being "in contemplation" has never been clearly and objectively defined, but case law indicates it is clear that there has to be a "reasonable prospect" of litigation, but that "reasonable prospect" does not necessarily mean greater than a 50 percent chance. The party's lawyer always should advise on this issue in light of the relevant circumstances in each case.

Proper preparation by an attorney for litigation requires that they assemble information, review that information to determine what is relevant, prepare legal theories, plan strategy, and present the case. This work is reflected in interviews, statements, memoranda, technical expert evaluations, correspondence, briefs, mental impressions, personal beliefs, and many other tangible and intangible ways.

As mentioned previously, although "factual" work product may be discoverable upon a showing of substantial need for the information sought, the protection afforded to "opinion" work product—which reflects counsel's subjective beliefs, impressions, and strategies regarding a case—is nearly absolute. Thus, to the extent that work product reveals the opinions, judgments, and thought processes of counsel, it receives some higher level of protection, and a party seeking discovery must show extraordinary justification.

The doctrine also protects material prepared by the attorney, whether or not disclosed to the client, and it protects material prepared by the attorney's agents, such as paralegals and technical experts. When an employee is asked to work under the direction of an in house or external attorney to support litigation, that person becomes an agent of the attorney. As such, the work the employee performs in this capacity is subject to the same protection as if the attorney performed the work him or herself.

It is important to distinguish between collecting existing data for an attorney, and creating original documents that analyze the data for the attorney. In the former situation, the data collected from the files or computer systems of a party is not attorney work product. The data existed before a litigation case was ever conceived. For example, if an attorney asks an employee to extract financial data from a company computer system, the data that he or she extracts and provides to the attorney is not protected. However, if the attorney asks an employee to extract and analyze the data—providing the attorney with a memorandum containing an analysis of the data in the context of the case—the memorandum to the attorney is subject to the attorney work product doctrine.

If a party is retaining an outside consultant, it is imperative to demonstrate that the consultant was retained at the direction of counsel to support and ongoing legal investigation and not for generic consulting work to avoid having to disclose any resulting report. *In re Capital One Data Security Breach Litigation*, 2020 WL 13609410 (E.D. Va. Dec.10, 2020) (Capital One required to disclose a third-party report analyzing a 2019 data breach as it would have been prepared regardless of the litigation, not because of the threat of litigation).

To ensure the protection of the doctrine, all documents should contain a header that reads: "SUBJECT TO THE ATTORNEY WORK-PRODUCT DOCTRINE." Distribution of any documents should be limited to only those who need to know relative to the impending litigation or mediation, and all distributions should in all instances include an attorney representing the party's interests.

For a more detailed discussion, *see* Villa, *Work Product Protection for Document Collections: A Quarter Century After Sporck v. Peil*, 28 ACC DOCKET 106 (May 2010).

3. Keep Lines of Communication Open

Once a potential issue has arisen, the parties immediately should meet to discuss the issue in detail. The parties should agree on the specific nature of the problem, including its cause; its impact on the project from a cost, time, and functionality perspective; as well as a resolution or a course of action to fix it. The proposed solution should receive "buy in" from both parties, and both parties should be responsible for its implementation.

At the same time, both parties should identify a single point of contact to communicate with the other party. Doing so will ensure that a consistent position is communicated to the other party while avoiding unintentionally making a concession or an admission against interest. The parties should carefully consider their actions, as an act taken in good faith may have a negative implication if litigation ensues.

It is important that both parties communicate their positions to preserve their rights in the event of litigation. The failure to raise an issue may compromise the party's ability to raise the issue at a later date.

Managing a customer's expectations and maintaining a strong relationship with the customer is critical for a successful project. In every discussion, the vendor should be forthright about explaining to the customer the nature of the challenges the vendor faces in trying to resolve the problem. Failing to address the problem honestly and openly only creates larger problems later, particularly if the customer concludes that the vendor was not forthright about the extent of the problems and the project is delayed or has greater costs than previously anticipated.

Although it is critical to consider involving legal counsel early in the process (as discussed later), the parties' lawyers alone will not be able to resolve most problems. Resolution of the problem and maintenance of the customer relationship only can be accomplished by the parties themselves. It is best to have the parties' technical staff meet first to define the problem and undertake a root cause analysis. The business owners should then join the discussion to evaluate potential solutions. Both of those meetings should focus on the problem and resolution without assigning blame. The nature of software requires that the parties be as specific and detailed as possible in defining the problem and the solution.

4. *Document the Process*

Both parties should document their meetings, the actions agreed to be taken by the parties, and their progress in resolving the issue. Minutes of all meetings should be kept. These minutes should be reviewed, approved, and signed by both parties. A written record ensures that at a later date an independent third party can evaluate whether each party undertook to meet its responsibilities under the agreements of the parties and how diligent and timely each party was in seeking to resolve the problem. Further, by communicating in writing, the parties can avoid any misinterpretation of their position that may arise through verbal communications. The parties should remember that these documents and records are discoverable if litigation arises and are often some of the most critical pieces of evidence in determining which party will bear the cost of the problem.

Given that litigation may arise, each party may want to retain their own legal counsel early in the process to review any minutes or other documents prior to execution, and otherwise establish protocols for the creation and maintenance of documents. The parties also may want to agree that, in order to foster an open atmosphere that is crucial to address the issue, their discussions and any documents produced by the parties may not be used in any subsequent litigation, and they should execute a confidentiality agreement to cover their negotiations. Any such agreement should be in writing, and it is important to remember that the agreement only binds the parties to it. A third-party subcontractor who may provide software or services is not bound by an agreement between the vendor and the customer, and would be free to use any and all documents should either the customer or vendor bring a claim against it.

5. *Quality Assurance Audits*

The parties' contract often requires the vendor to undertake quality audits of the project's status and provide the customer with any resulting reports. See, e.g., Chapter 7.E and §§ 8.B, 9.3. The vendor's quality assurance team is charged with identifying actual or potential problems in the vendor's development process so that they may be corrected prior to delivery.

These quality audit reports frequently support the customer's breach of contract claims and undercut the vendor's defense that the software met the contract requirements. The requirement to produce the audit reports places the vendor in a quandary: it needs to undertake quality audits to ensure a quality product, but at the same time it wants to avoid creating a report that is critical of its development efforts and may be used against it in any litigation.

Similarly, some customers seek to require the vendor to notify the customer in the event the vendor becomes aware of a problem or anticipates that a problem is likely to arise. See, e.g., Chapter 7.E and § 9.13. A broad reading of this obligation may require the vendor to notify the customer of any issues identified by the vendor's quality audits. Savvy customers also will seek to review the vendor's quality audit reports to determine when the vendor realized that a problem existed.

To avoid such problems, some vendors seek to have their quality audit reports prepared under the direction of the vendor's lawyers and claim protection under the lawyer-client privilege and the lawyer-client work product doctrine. See, e.g., Form N.4, for a model memo requesting the production of internal confidential information. It is unclear whether privilege would protect the report, and moreover if the reports are provided to the customer, the vendor is unlikely to prevail in any dispute over a claim of privilege.

6. *Prepare for the Possibility of Litigation*

Although the parties seek to avoid litigation, they should be prepared for that possibility. First and foremost, the parties should carefully review the underlying agreement to ensure they understand their contractual and legal rights as well as their obligations. The non-breaching party should seek to minimize its damages, as it has a duty to mitigate its damages. The non-breaching party should also evaluate whether the breach is a material or a non-material breach, as in some states only a material breach excuses future performance by the non-breaching party.

In addition, the party allegedly in breach should prepare to respond to a breach notice by assembling all relevant documentation and conducting interviews with the party's employees who have knowledge relevant to the dispute. If a breach notice is issued, the party allegedly in breach should be prepared to have frank discussions with the other party under the protection of a confidentiality agreement to explore the basis for the party's claim, its expectations, and potential resolutions.

Litigation counsel should be contacted as soon as a party suspects a dispute cannot be amicably resolved. Counsel can assist the client in undertaking an unbiased assessment of the dispute and assess the risk as well as the likelihood of success. As part of the process, counsel should interview the relevant employees who are more likely to speak open and honestly to a third party the company's management or legal staff. Counsel should also identify potential claims and provide advice on contractual provision.

Legal counsel should notify all employees and consultants associated with the project to retain all documents regarding the project whether written, electronic, or oral (voice mail). See Form N.5 for a model Document Preservation memo. There is not a consensus as to when legal counsel should send such notice. Some believe that notice should be sent when a party believes it may sue another party, while others argue that notice should be sent when a notice is received from the other party. The party's information technology department should be notified to retain all emails that may otherwise be destroyed as part of the company's document retention policy.

Counsel also should consider placing the other party on notice that it may be bringing a legal claim and remind the other party of its obligation to preserve all documentation related to the project, given that litigation is contemplated. Consideration also should be given as to whether to recommend that the other party notify its insurance carrier regarding a potential claim. Although this may cause the other party to take a more aggressive position (possibly including bringing a lawsuit for a declaratory judgment), early notification may be advantageous if a party believes the other may not otherwise retain documentation that may support the party's case.

B. Responding to a Deficiency Notice

In the event the customer receives a deficiency notice (usually related to the vendor seeking additional license fees, service fees or maintenance fees) the customer should undertake several actions to strengthen its negotiating position. First, and foremost, the customer should ensure that the parties' relationship remains strong and that any differences are resolved through an amicable business negotiation. The customer should not assume a hostile, contentious posture, causing both sides to assume inflexible positions.

In responding to a deficiency notice, a prudent customer should undertake the following actions:

- Thoroughly examine the audit data with the goal of validating the overages and attendant costs presented by the vendor. The customer must confirm whether the vendor's calculations are correct. As the customer's users are closest to the data, the user's operational team should produce this information.
- Once the totals/alleged costs have been confirmed, the customer should assemble supporting data internally to determine how the overages occurred. This is important not only to avoid future claims but also to potentially reduce the customer's exposure in the existing situation. Being able to discuss the facts giving rise to the overages may help. For example, was the overage due to the failure of the vendor to accurately report the number of actual users, the failure of the vendor's software to prevent the addition of users beyond the number of licenses purchased, a simple oversight by the customer, a flaw in the software, a one-time occurrence, etc.?
- Using the internal data collected on usage patterns and other factors, the customer should vet the results against the governing contract language which may provide some "excuse" for improper use. The customer may uncover a lack of clarity in the governing language that may work to the customer's advantage in seeking further concessions.
- Leverage its existing business relationship with the vendor. If the customer purchases other products and services from the vendor, the customer should provide the vendor with the customer's current expenditures on the vendor's products and services as well as the customer's anticipated future purchases. Vendors may be more willing to compromise if the customer is a significant customer who is likely to make large purchases in the future.
- Upon independently determining the amount/cost of any alleged overages, meet with the vendor, combining its defensively aimed investigative work related to the actual overages with offensively aimed relationship-based arguments, to reach a settlement with the lowest possible cost to the customer.

Once a settlement has been agreed in principle, the parties should execute a release, vetted by the customer's litigation counsel, to bring the matter to a close.

See Chapter 23 for a more detailed discussion of software use audits.

C. Potential Claims, Defenses, and Counterclaims

Information technology litigation is often like kabuki, the ritualized Japanese theatre. Although the nature of every dispute is different, most disputes are related to: (i) the vendor's delivery obligations (both quality and timeliness), costs, functionality of the software to be delivered, and scope creep, or (ii) the customer's failure to pay the proper use fees. An experienced practitioner will recognize an atmosphere of *déjà vu* with information technology disputes as the vendor and customer exchange common claims and defenses that often repeat from one dispute to another.

1. Customer Claims

Most customer claims arise from disputes over the vendor's failure to provide the deliverables in accordance with the agreed upon specifications in a timely manner. As such, most claims are based on breach of contract, fraud, or similar claims. Occasionally, customers will "up the ante" by bringing specious claims, such as RICO claims to force the vendor into a settlement. *See, e.g., County of Marin v. Deloitte Consulting LLP*, 836 F. Supp. 2d 1030 (N.D. Cal. 2011).

(a) Breach of Contract

(i) Failure to Deliver Required Functionality

Perhaps the most common problems alleged by customers are that the software lacks the required functionality, fails to operate in a stable manner, fails to perform the required functions in a timely manner, and/or is filled with bugs.

Disputes over functionality often arise when the technical specifications have not been drafted in sufficient detail. Although each party may have had a thorough understanding of what it expected would be delivered at the time the contract was entered into, the failure to include detailed technical specifications in the agreement may result in a product that does not meet the customer's expectations or needs. If the specifications included in the agreement are not detailed, the vendor may be able to correctly claim that it met its contractual obligations. This scenario benefits neither the customer nor the vendor as the parties likely will enter into a lengthy, time-consuming, and expensive dispute resolution process to resolve the issue.

Most of these issues are identified through acceptance testing procedures. Once identified, the vendor likely will have a "cure period" in which to make any allegedly necessary corrections. If the vendor is unable to do so, the customer is left with little recourse but to bring a claim under the contract's dispute resolution provision. An inability of the vendor to satisfy the contractually agreed-to acceptance tests provides a strong incentive for the vendor to reach a settlement with the customer. Failure to be able to meet the acceptance tests is rare. However the typical response by the vendor is that it has met the contractually required functionality and that the demands of the customer are outside the scope of the contract.

See, e.g., Activant Solutions, Inc. v. Notoco Industries, LLC, 2011 WL 5079490 (N.D. Cal. Oct. 26, 2011).

(ii) Failure to Deliver in a Timely Manner

Customers seek to implement their technology solution as quickly as possible. During the negotiation process, they often encourage the vendor to compress the proposed development schedule to meet the desired delivery date. Although many customers realize the problems that may arise by shortening the development and delivery cycle, they believe that these problems are the vendor's issue and that the customer should not be concerned. Fearing that it may lose the business, vendors often accept a tight schedule that leaves little room for error. Although, the customer may be happy in the short term, this strategy can be catastrophic, with the customer missing its published implementation date, resulting in litigation with the vendor. When the inevitable delay occurs, both the vendor and customer are placed in a difficult spot. To meet the required delivery date, the vendor may be forced to expend additional resources/labor that was not contemplated, creating cost overruns that must be absorbed by the vendor. A rush to complete the project will likely increase the number of bugs in the software, which will cause further delays when the software needs to be rewritten. In turn, the customer suffers by receiving the late delivery of an unstable product, which may harm its business. Customers are better served by accepting a realistic delivery schedule, with agreed-upon incentives to encourage the vendor to deliver early. Depending on the terms of the agreement, the vendor may be subject to liquidated damages for failure to deliver on time, in addition to absorbing the additional labor costs necessary to complete the project. See, § 3.C. The vendor is confronted with the options of delivering late, asking the customer for additional funds to pay for additional resources, or reducing the functionality of the deliverables. These options are unlikely to be well received by the customer.

To mitigate the efforts of any potential delay, most savvy customers contractually obligate the vendor to promptly notify the customer if the vendor foresees any delay in the delivery schedule. See § 9.6.4.

(iii) Failure to Deliver for Contracted Price

In a fixed-price contract, the parties contractually agree on both the scope of the deliverables and the price to be paid. Vendors usually seek to avoid fixed-price contracts as they allocate the risk of cost overruns to the vendor. Customers often require that the contract have a fixed price in order to estimate the project cost and to place the burden on the party that should have better knowledge of what is necessary to develop and implement the software.

If a vendor has underestimated the work effort involved, its only option under a fixed-price contract, other than to assume the loss or be held in default, is to approach the customer to seek an increase in the contract price. Most customers, however, are unlikely to accept an increase in the contract price, leaving the vendor to bear any loss.

(b) Fraud

Customers often allege fraud, usually by the licensor's salespeople during the sales process, in an attempt to void the contract's limitation of liability. *See, Enercon v. Global Computer Supplies, Inc.*, 675 F. Supp. 2d 188 (D. Me. 2009); *Neoris de Mexico S.A.de C.V. v. Ariba, Inc.*, 2004 WL 2445237 (N.D. Cal. Aug. 2, 2004). Fraud is one of the few claims that will allow a court to negate a carefully negotiated limitation of liability. *See Vmark Software, Inc. v. EMC Corp.*, 642 N.E.2d 587 (Ct. App. Mass. 1994) (vendor's misrepresentation voided contract's limitation of liability). While "fraud in the inducement" is easily alleged, it is difficult to prove, as comprehensive integration clauses and trial periods often undercut the customer's ability to prevail on a misrepresentation claim. *See IBM Corp. v. Lufkin Industries, LLC*, 573 S.W.2d 244 (Tex. 2019) ("contractual declaimers bar the buyer from recovering in tort for misrepresentations the seller made . . . to induce the buyer to enter into the contract . . . ."). Further, customers run the risk that the licensor and its sales representative may file a counterclaim alleging defamation. *See* Blair, *A Matter of Trust: Should No Reliance Clauses Bar Claims for Fraudulent Inducement of Contract?*, 92 MARQ. L. REV. 423 (2009) for the challenges of prevailing on a fraudulent inducement claim.

If it is unable to void the agreement's limitation of liability, a customer often is contractually limited to a refund of the monies it has paid under the statement of work under which the liability arose. For statements of work (SOWs) with a large dollar value, the vendor's liability often is limited to a percentage of the full contract price. For example, those monies received by the vendor under the relevant statement of work in the 90 days prior to the event giving rise to the claim of breach.

A fraud claim is usually founded on allegations that the vendor made a misrepresentation to induce the customer to enter into the agreement, or that the vendor knew at the time the agreement was executed that it could not meet a particular contractual obligation (such as a delivery date) or that the vendor misrepresented the software's functionality or capabilities. Although fraud cases are very difficult to win, the fear of negating the contract's limit of liability may cause the vendor to settle. The *BSkyB Ltd. v. H.P. Enterprise Sources UK Ltd.* case in the United Kingdom, 2010 WL 20033 (E.W.H.C. B.D. Jan. 26, 2010), illustrates this issue. By bringing a claim for fraud, BSkyB was able to defeat the agreement's limitation of liability and receive a judgment in excess of $450M. See Chapter 6.S.1 for a more detailed discussion of the *BSkyB* case.

To bring a successful claim for actual fraud, a party must demonstrate the following:

1. False representation or concealment of a material fact;
2. Knowledge of its falsity;
3. The intent to induce reliance;
4. Justifiable reliance; and
5. Damages to the misled party.

See, e.g., Davis v. Marshall Homes, Inc., 576 S.E.2d 291, 297 (Va. 2003). Any reliance must be reasonable, as a party "cannot blindly rely on . . . oral representations to the exclusion of written disclosures in a contract." *Wright Therapy Equipment LLC v. Blue Cross and Blue Shield of Alabama*, 991 So. 2d 701, 706 (Ala. 2008). A party may also bring a claim for constructive fraud in those situations where the wrongful actor does not have knowledge of the falsehood. *Economopoulos v. Kolaitis*, 528 S.E.2d 714, 719 (Va. 2000).

A vendor should carefully consider a choice of law provision in the contract that (i) explicitly applies to any fraud claims arising out of the execution or performance of the contract, and (ii) selects a forum whose laws are unfriendly to fraud in the inducement claims, such as New York. In addition, a carefully worded merger clause is important in defending against a fraud claim. Finally, a vendor should never misrepresent the status of a project by assuring the client that a project is on track when in actuality the project is behind schedule.

(c) Breach of Fiduciary Duty

Often a customer will ask the vendor to evaluate and recommend a software product or solution or the vendor will provide a third-party software product in connection with the deliverable. Many times, the vendor will receive a referral fee or a VAR fee for recommending or reselling the third-party product in question. If the vendor fails to disclose to the customer that it is receiving a referral fee, it risks the customer bringing a claim based on the breach of the vendor's alleged fiduciary duty or fraud. See Forms Q.2.LL.22 and Q.2.PP.5 for model language addressing this issue.

2. Customer Actions

(a) Setoff and Recoupment

Setoff and recoupment are types of counterclaims that may be asserted by a defendant in response to a plaintiff's initial complaint seeking recovery. *Stulz v. Boswell*, 307 Pa. Super. 515, 520 (1982) ("A counterclaim is defined as a claim presented by a defendant in opposition to, or deduction from, the claim of the plaintiff; a counterclaim encompasses both set off and recoupment.") (internal quotation marks omitted); *see also J.B. Hunt Transport, Inc. v. Falcon Transport, Co.*, 723 F. Supp. 359, 361 (W.D. Pa. 1989) ("Pennsylvania law draws a distinction between a counterclaim that seeks affirmative relief (known as a "setoff") and a counterclaim that 'involves only the claims averred by the plaintiff and raises no possibility of affirmative relief' (known as 'recoupment')") (quoting *Harmer v. Hulsey*, 321 Pa. Super. 11 (1983)).

A defendant's counterclaim does not turn the plaintiff into a defendant. *See Shuman v. Colasono*, 1978 WL 283 (Pa. Ct. Com. Pl. Dec. 6, 1978) (rejecting the plaintiff's contention that they should be treated as "defendants" since they are responding to a counterclaim, because "the rules . . . do not countenance such an interpretation"). By invoking the doctrines of setoff and recoupment, the plaintiff seeks to assert a counterclaim to the defendant's counterclaim. "There is, however, no provision for a reply containing a counter-counterclaim." *Id.*

(i) Setoff

Setoff arises under common law allowing "every creditor to apply the appropriated moneys of his debtor, in his hands, in extinguishment of the debts due him." *Boers v. United States*, 44 Fed. Cl. 725, 733 (1999). The common-law right of setoff is not forfeited in the absence of language to the contrary or the absence of a reservation of rights clause. *Applied Companies v. United States*, 144 F.3d 1470 (Fed. Cir. 1998).

In the case of bankruptcy, the debtor's claim against the creditor and the creditor's claim against the debtor must both arise pre-petition. A party cannot set off a post-petition payable against a pre-petition receivable and cannot exercise its right of setoff without first obtaining relief from the automatic stay in the bankruptcy court by filing a motion. The bankruptcy code recognizes the existence of a creditor's setoff rights. 11 U.S.C. § 553.

(ii) Recoupment

Recoupment is "not in the nature of a cross demand, but rather it lessens or defeats any recovery by the plaintiff." *Algrant v. Evergreen Valley Nurseries Ltd. P'ship*, 126 F.3d 178, 184 (3d Cir. 1997). Recoupment is a defensive claim that "must be related to the nature of the demand brought by the plaintiff." *Id.*

Like the doctrine of setoff, the doctrine of recoupment allows a creditor that owes a debt to a debtor to reduce the amount of its debt by the amount of a debt owed by the debtor to the creditor. The doctrine of recoupment only exists where the two debts arise out of the same transaction (i.e., the same contract). For recoupment to apply, the defendant's claim must arise from the same transaction. *See Koken v. Legion Ins. Co.*, 900 A.2d 418, 428 (Pa. Commw. 2006) (discussing the "same transaction" requirement for recoupment); *see also Cohen v. Goldberg*, 554 Pa. 201, 205 (1998) ("Recoupment is the setting up of a demand arising from the same transaction as the plaintiff's claim or cause of action, strictly for the purpose of abatement or reduction of such claim.") (internal quotation marks omitted). The "same transaction" requirement has been narrowly construed. *Cohen*, 554 Pa. at 205. The same transaction requirement exists because recoupment originated as an equitable remedy, intending that "a transaction which is made the subject of a suit by a plaintiff . . . be examined in all aspects and a judgment rendered that does justice in view of the one transaction as a whole." *Stulz*, 307 Pa. Super. at 521.

Unlike setoff, the right of recoupment is not limited to pre-petition debts. The right of recoupment is not codified in the Bankruptcy Code and was established through case law.

(iii) Preclusion/Waiver of Rights

Although recoupment and waiver may be available to a party at common law, the party may contract away its rights to setoff or recoupment. *Lytle v. CitiFinancial Service, Inc.*, 2001 WL 34644548 (Pa. Com. Pl. Mar. 6, 2001); *see also Pearce v. Utah Athletic Foundation*, 179 P.3d 760, 765 (Utah 2008) ("In two recent cases, we reaffirmed our position with the majority of states that people may contract away their rights to recover in tort for damages caused by the ordinary negligence of others."); *CPI Phipps, LLC v. 100 Park Avenue Partners, L.P.*, 654 S.E.2d 690, 693 (Ga. App. 2007) ("[I]t is clear that two parties may contract away or extend their rights as they please so long as public policy is not violated."). It is not against public policy to contract away those rights.

In evaluating a party's ability to exercise the common law remedies of set off and recoupment, a party must examine whether they are precluded by the contractual terms of the underlying license agreement. Although a license agreement may address equitable remedies, that language in and of itself does not preclude the rights of set off or recoupment. *See Bender*, 493 A.2d at 760, 763 (refusing to read exclusion of all remedies into a contract). An integration clause that provides that the contract represents the "entire agreement and understanding between the licensee and licensor relating to the subject matter herein" does not exclude a remedy. *Id.* A party may not read language into the agreement that is not included within its plain terms. The question of whether the parties intended to contract away their equitable remedies is a question of fact for the court to interpret.

(b) Laches

In those situations where the vendor is claiming the customer failed to pay the appropriate license fees, a laches defense may be available to the customer. *See ExperExchange, Inc. v. Doculex, Inc.*, 2009 WL 3837275 (N.D. Cal. Nov. 16, 2009) (licensor's copyright claims barred by laches due to licensor's failure to bring claim for eight years).

3. Vendor Defenses

(a) Desired Functionality Is Out of Scope

In response to a customer's claim that the vendor did not deliver the contracted functionality, the vendor often will respond that it has met the requirements of the contract, and that the customer is seeking functionality outside the scope of the contract. In short, the customer is seeking to increase the scope of the deliverables without paying for the vendor's increased costs.

To avoid disputes, a vendor should never agree to change in functionality, or scope without a written agreement. A vendor that acts otherwise is inviting a customer to claim that the work done was in scope because otherwise, a new agreement would have been executed.

(b) Vendor's Failure to Perform Caused by Customer's Breach

In response to a customer's allegations that the vendor breached the contract by its failure to deliver in a timely manner, the vendor often will respond that any such delay was, in fact, caused by the customer. Delivery delays may arise from many factors, including customer-demanded changes in scope; the failure of the customer to promptly approve the functional specifications; the failure of the customer to provide access to its third party legacy software systems; the failure of the customer to provide qualified employees; the failure of the customer to provide necessary assistance; and the failure of the customer to perform any other contractual obligations.

Under a fixed-price contract, if the customer fails to meet its contractual obligations, the contract should provide for financial compensation to the vendor for the impact of any delay caused by the customer. See, e.g., § 21.

Customer-caused delays also can arise from the failure of third-party vendors retained directly by the customer to meet their contractual obligations. For example, when the vendor's performance is contingent on the successful performance of such third parties. Because the other vendors have contracted directly with the customer and the vendor lacks the ability to control their performance, the customer must be contractually responsible for their impact on the vendor.

To protect the vendor's interests, the contract should set forth the customer's obligations and provide that they are conditions precedent to the vendor's obligations. The customer's obligations should include assigning knowledgeable employees to the project and promptly responding to any requests by the vendor. See, e.g., §§ 9.5, 21, 37. Too often, customers claim that their only obligation is to pay the vendor. That is never true in major technology contracts, and vendors should ensure during negotiation of the agreement that the customer's responsibilities are defined clearly.

Customers frequently fail to address the impact of their other vendors on the vendor's obligations. A prudent customer will retain a prime contractor, requiring all third-party vendors to contract directly with the prime contractor to avoid any potential liability on the customer's behalf when a vendor other than the prime contractor fails to perform. A prudent vendor should identify specifically those third parties on whom the vendor's performance is contingent, and specify that the vendor is excused from performing in the event the customer's other vendors fail to perform.

Finally, when faced with customer-caused delays or nonpayment, a vendor should notify the customer, in writing, in conformance with the contract's notice provisions that the vendor is ready, willing, and able to perform. See, e.g., § 52. This will protect the vendor when seeking compensation for any such delay and will provide protection in the event the customer claims the vendor was unable to perform or that the vendor was not materially harmed. See Form N.9 for a model letter stating the vendor's ability to perform.

(c) The Gist of the Action Doctrine

Plaintiffs often bring multiple claims against defendants based in contract and tort in an effort to maximize their recovery. The tort claims are often founded on negligent and/or intentional misrepresentation. These multiple claims are usually duplicative, and under the laws of many states violate the gist of the action doctrine. Specifically:

> [T]he [gist of the action] doctrine bars tort claims: (1) arising solely from a contract between the parties; (2) where the duties allegedly breached were created and grounded in the contract itself; (3) where the liability stems from a contract; or (4) where the tort essentially duplicates a breach of contract claim or the success of which is wholly dependent on the terms of the contract.

Etoll, Inc. v. Elias/Savion Advertising, Inc., 811 A.2d 10, 19 (Pa. Super. 2002) (internal citations and quotations omitted); *Caudill Seed & Warehouse Co. v. Prophet 21, Inc.*, 123 F. Supp. 2d 826 (E.D. Pa. 2000).

Many plaintiffs' tort claims fall within all of the categories set forth in *Etoll*. It is clear that a plaintiff's misrepresentation claims all alleged statements or omissions supposedly made by the defendant during the course of the project and about the performance on the project. Those are exactly the types of claims that are barred by the gist of the action doctrine because they are directly related to the contractual obligations of the parties.

Second, the allegations in support of the negligent and/or intentional misrepresentation claim are the same allegations that form the basis for plaintiff's breach of contract claim.

Third, any liability stems from the underlying contract. The only relationship between most parties is their contractual relationship. Without the contract, most defendants would have no duty whatsoever to plaintiff. In *Etoll*, 811 A.2d at 23, the court affirmed the dismissal of the plaintiff's complaint, in part because it held that no special relationship existed that would create a duty outside of the parties' contract. The court reasoned: "If parties to routine arm's-length commercial contracts for the provision of needed goods or services were held to have a 'special relationship,' virtually every breach of such a contract would support a tort claim." *Id.* The court refused to permit tort claims to usurp the law of contracts.

Fourth, the success of a plaintiff's tort claims is wholly dependent upon the terms of the contract.

The law is clear, allegations that stem from the performance under a contract, regardless of whether they are couched in terms of misrepresentation, properly can be brought as breach of contract claims, but not as tort claims. As such, the plaintiff's tort claims must be dismissed.

(d) The Economic Loss Rule

The economic loss rule similarly bars a plaintiff's misrepresentation claim. *Werwinski v. Ford Motor Co.*, 286 F.3d 661, 675 (3d Cir. 2002). The economic loss doctrine provides that a party who suffers purely economic loss as a result of another's conduct cannot recover that loss under tort law, but must seek to redress under contract law. *Apollo Group, Inc. v. Avnet, Inc.*, 58 F.3d 477, 479 (9th Cir. 1995). Economic loss is a term of art used to distinguish commercial injury from physical or personal injury. *Rich Products Corp. v. Kemutec, Inc.*, 66 F. Supp. 2d 937, 968 (E.D. Wis. 1999). A claim to recover commercial injuries must be brought as a breach of contract action, whereas a claim for personal injuries may be brought in tort.

Usually, the damages sought by the plaintiff are for economic loss only and are based upon the plaintiff's allegations that the defendant failed to perform its contractual obligations.

(e) Professional Negligence Is Not a Recognized Cause of Action

Although plaintiffs often allege "professional negligence," no such tort exists for providers of computer consulting services. *Avazpour Networking Servs. v. Falconstor Software, Inc.*, 937 F. Supp. 2d 355 (E.D.N.Y. 2013); *Rapidigm Inc. v. ATM Mgmt. Servs. LLC*, 2003 WL 23146480 (Pa. Com. Pl. July 10, 2003) (dismissing claim for professional negligence against a computer consultant because Pennsylvania law does not recognize such a cause of action). *See also Ferris & Salter, P.C. v. Thomson Reuters Corp.*, 819 F. Supp. 2d 667 (E.D. Mich. 2011) (computer engineers and technicians are not "professionals" under Michigan and Minnesota law as required to state claim for professional negligence); *RKB Enterprises, Inc. v. Ernst & Young*, 582 N.Y.S.2d 814 (1992) (no cause of action for malpractice arising from computer services); *Chatlos Systems, Inc. v. National Cash Register Corp.*, 479 F. Supp. 738 (D.N.J. 1979) (declining to find tort for computer malpractice).

4. Vendor Claims/Counterclaims

In almost all disputes that reach litigation, the vendor will bring counterclaims against the customer, if for no other reason than to gain leverage in any settlement negotiation, or to "muddy the waters" if the matter ultimately goes to trial. Vendors should avoid bringing a claim against a customer unless it lacks any other option, as suing a customer likely will have a chilling effect on the vendor's business. The three most common claims are breach of contract, *quantum meruit*, and copyright infringement.

Copyright infringement claims form the basis of many breach actions. These claims often fall into two categories:

(i) unauthorized use—i.e., in a divestiture where the successor entity is not the licensee, and does not have a license, and
(ii) excess use—i.e., the licensee purchased a license but exceeded the license's usage restrictions.

In the case of excess use, a licensee would likely defend the licensor's claim by arguing it purchased a license but exceeded its usage rights. Therefore, damages are a matter of contract law, with damages determined based on the software's list price multiplied by the number of excess unlicensed users, or valued at the licensee's pro-rata cost if it had purchased the additional licenses, which may have been at a discount to the licensor's list price. In nearly all cases, the damages recovered are much lower than the statutory damages allowed under the Copyright Act of 1976, as amended.

(a) Breach of Contract

Like the customer, the vendor will respond to the customer's claim with a counterclaim alleging a breach of contract by the customer. Such claims can encompass a broad range of factual theories, including the customer's failure to pay the vendor's invoices; the failure of the customer to provide needed hardware and software; the failure of the customer to provide the vendor access to the customer's third party legacy systems; and the failure of the customer to make decisions critical to the success of the project in a timely fashion. Further, an aggressive vendor may consider filing a declaratory judgment action seeking to have the customer's demands declared outside the scope of the contract. Seeking a declaratory judgment likely will irreparably harm the relationship. Nonetheless, this strategy may be attractive to a vendor who believes that the customer is planning to sue for breach of contract and believes the relationship cannot be salvaged. The exact nature of these claims will depend on the requirements of the contract, but the essence of the vendor's claim is that the customer failed to meet its contractual obligations, or that what the customer is demanding is outside the scope of the contract.

Vendors must think carefully before bringing suit against a customer who fails to make payment because of the vendor's failure to successfully deliver a working system. Many customers with a legitimate claim have successfully countersued the vendor. *See, e.g., Vmark Software, Inc. v. EMC Corp.*, 642 N.E.2d 587 n.7 (Ct. App. Mass. 1994) ("Experienced lawyers often caution clients not to sue customers who refuse to pay an invoice because of a reasonable complaint about the product. This case may be cited as an illustration of the soundness of that advice.").

Customers often fail to limit their own liability in their contracts. See, e.g., § 17.2. In these cases, the vendor will seek to leverage this oversight by seeking a significant recovery including its full profit. The vendor hopes to cause the customer to rethink its suit, given the customer's unlimited liability and the vendor's contractually limited liability.

(b) Quantum Meruit

The vendor may bring a counterclaim under the quasi-contract doctrine of *quantum meruit*. *Quantum meruit*, is an equitable remedy that attempts to prevent unjust enrichment. Under this theory, the vendor seeks to recover the value of the services it provided to the customer. The vendor is alleging that the customer has been unjustly enriched by receiving services for which the customer has not paid. To bring a successful *quantum meruit* claim, the vendor must demonstrate the following:

1. The vendor provided services or materials of value
2. To the person or entity from whom the vendor seeks to collect.
3. The services or materials were accepted by such person who used such services or materials; and
4. Under circumstances where the beneficiary of such services or materials was aware that the vendor expected to be paid for such services or materials.

Vortt Exploration Co. v. Chevron USA Inc., 787 S.W.2d 942, 944 (Tex. 1990). *Quantum meruit* usually is not available as a remedy if there is an existing agreement between the parties. *Truly v. Austin*, 744 S.W.2d 934 (Tex. 1988).

From the customer's perspective, a *quantum meruit* argument may seem specious if the customer does not want to continue using the deliverables/software because the vendor failed to meet its contractual obligations. A *quantum meruit* claim is likely to be successful where the vendor successfully delivered the deliverable (or some independently valuable portion thereof) and the customer lacks a valid basis for its failure to pay. In many jurisdictions, however, a *quantum meruit* claim is not viable if there is a valid contract. *See, e.g.*, Georgia: *Blue Soft Inc. v. Advanced Computing Technologies, Inc.*, 616 S.E.2d 816 (Ga. 2005); Ohio: *Daniels v. National Employee Ben. Services, Inc.*, 877 F. Supp. 1067 (N.D. Ohio 1995); South Dakota: *Mooney's v. South Dakota Dept. of Finance*, 482 N.W.2d 43, 47 (S.D. 1992) ("Quantum meruit does not provide a basis for recovery when a valid express contract exists."); Texas: *Sherman Acquisition II, LP v. Garcia*, 229 S.W.2d 802 (Tex. 2007). In such a case, breach of contract is the proper claim. Nevertheless, the *quantum meruit* counterclaim provides a potentially valuable defensive countermeasure to the customer's fraud claim, because if the fraud claim voids the contract, then the *quantum meruit* claim may survive and may provide the vendor with damages to offset the customer's claims.

(c) Copyright Infringement

A vendor also may respond by filing a copyright infringement claim against the customer. Under U.S. law, copyright is created in the name of the author at the time a written work is created. *In re World Auxiliary Power Co.*, 303 F.3d 1120, 1125 (9th Cir. 2002).

Because computer software frequently (though not always) fails to meet one of the nine enumerated exceptions of the "work made for hire" doctrine, the deliverables typically are owned by the vendor until, and unless ownership is assigned to the customer. See Chapter 7.A.1 for a more detailed discussion of the work made for hire doctrine. Although, the agreement between the vendor and the customer most likely will contain an assignment transferring ownership of the deliverables created under the agreement to the customer, it is not uncommon for customers to start negotiations by insisting that ownership vests in the customer at the time of creation. A prudent vendor, however, should insist on language that ownership not transfer to the customer until the vendor has been paid in full.

If the governing agreement provides that the vendor shall retain ownership, the customer's continued use of the software without a license is potentially a copyright infringement and provides the vendor leverage in the event there is a dispute (including the possibility of an injunction against the customer's continued use of the software. *See, e.g.*, §§ 5.2, 29.5). This is true even if the vendor did not register its copyright in the work, although remedies for infringement are limited if the infringement arose before registration. *See Conwell v. Gray Loon Outdoor Marketing Group, Inc.*, 906 N.E.2d 805 (Ind. 2009). See Chapter 3.A.2(c) for a more detailed discussion of copyright law. The licensor must distinguish, however, between a breach of contract claim and a copyright infringement claim. A licensor may bring a copyright infringement claim only when the licensee acts outside the scope of the license. *Quest Software v. Direct TV Operations*, 2011 WL 4500922, * at 4 (C.D. Cal. Sept. 26, 2011).

To prove copyright infringement, the licensor must prove the licensee violated a condition to the license, as opposed to a covenant, which is governed by state contract law. *MDY Indus., LLC v. Blizzard Entm't, Inc.*, 2011 WL 538748 (9th Cir. Feb. 14, 2011). "Stated somewhat circularly, conditions are 'contractual terms that limit a license's scope . . . the breach of which constitute[s] copyright infringement.' All other license terms are 'covenants,' which the Ninth Circuit has defined to mean a 'contractual promise, i.e., a manifestation or intention to act or refrain from acting in a particular way.'" *Quest Software, * at 4* (citing *MDY Indus., LLC v. Blizzard Entm't, Inc.*). Covenants are considered to mean a "contractual promise," i.e., a manifestation or intention to act or refrain from acting in a particular way.

(d) Amount of Vendor Claim

Often in the event of a dispute, vendors seek to recover the value of all services performed for a client including the value of unbilled services. Many times, the vendor has not billed the customer for services it performed for a variety of reasons, including trying to placate the customer, the contract was a fixed-price contract, or the contract limited the vendor's employees to billing eight hours a day. Courts usually are unpersuaded by a vendor's efforts to recover for unbilled services, questioning why the vendor is entitled to recover when it never planned to bill for such services.

A savvy vender may be more likely to recover such fees if it bills the client for all work performed, and notifies the customer that it will issue a credit for the fees in question upon the customer's acceptance of the software, or services. This approach should strengthen a vendor's claim, as it has not reduced the amount of its claim. If the customer never accepts the deliverables, the licensor will be able to bring a claim for the total value of its services.

(e) Injunctive Relief

A savvy vendor will seek injunctive relief to prevent the licensee from using its software while the dispute is being resolved. Doing so not only protects the vendor's intellectual property rights, but also increases the vendor's leverage over the licensee, as the licensee can no longer use the vendor's software. In *Salinger v. Colting*, 607 F.3d 68 (2d. Cir. 2010), the Second Circuit, citing *eBay, Inc. v. MercExchange*, 547 U.S. 388 (2006), found that the party seeking injunctive relief must demonstrate irreparable injury. Prior to *Salinger*, the courts utilized a "presumption of harm" standard, which set a much lower hurdle for seeking an injunction.

5. Termination for Convenience (§ 4.1.A)

In some situations, a customer may consider terminating an agreement or statement of work for "convenience" instead of breach to avoid expending the effort and cost to prove the vendor's breach. This option exists only if the underlying agreement contains a termination for convenience provision. Although that strategy may appear to be the best solution in the short term, it can cause the customer significant problems. "Termination for convenience" or "without cause" means the vendor is without fault.

Once the customer provides written notice that it is terminating the agreement or statement of work for convenience, it is difficult for the customer to later claim that the vendor failed to meet its performance obligations. A savvy vendor will point out the inconsistency of the customer's earlier statement that the vendor was not at fault.

Termination for convenience potentially allows the vendor to claim payment not only for the services rendered, but also for the vendor's costs of winding down the project, which may be significant if the vendor has entered into long-term agreements with subcontractors in connection with the customer's project. The customer usually lacks a contractual basis for making a counterclaim, as termination for convenience reflects that the customer seeks to terminate for its own convenience, not the vendor's breach. Thus, the customer is limited to negotiating the amount of compensation due the vendor. As such, customers should carefully consider terminating the agreement for convenience if they believe the vendor is at fault.

See Chapter 5.G.4 for a more detailed discussion.

D. The Negotiation Process

A more fruitful approach to litigation, which at best is usually a break-even proposition, is to contact the vendor, and try to negotiate an early termination-upon-payment termination fee. At a minimum, the vendor should be willing to accept the net present value of the future license fees. Often, vendors are willing to provide disgruntled customers a credit against future services or products in an effort to settle any dispute.

1. Tolling Agreement

One of the first actions the parties should take when seeking to settle a dispute is to execute a tolling agreement to preserve their respective rights. See, e.g., the model Tolling Agreement set forth in Form N.1. Settlement negotiations may take a significant period of time and will likely last longer than expected. A tolling agreement is especially important if the parties have agreed to contractually limit the time to bring litigation. *See generally* Chapter 5.I.4, Section C.1 in this chapter, and § 17.1. The vendor should ensure that the tolling agreement is mutual as its claims should remain viable as well as those claims that could be asserted by its customer.

2. Settlement Negotiations

(a) Deciding to Settle

In almost all situations, a negotiated settlement is preferable to entering into litigation or an alternative dispute resolution process. The dispute process can be lengthy as well as expensive and prevent the parties from achieving the goals each party hoped to achieve at the time the agreement was signed.

Prior to meeting with the other party, each party should decide whether it wants to terminate the agreement and enter into a settlement agreement, or whether it wants to renegotiate the original agreement and continue the relationship. Parties usually renegotiate an agreement when both parties bear some culpability, and the customer believes the vendor can successfully complete the project.

In considering whether to enter into a settlement, the customer must first determine whether it wants to continue its relationship with the vendor. If the vendor failed to successfully meet its initial contractual obligations, what makes the customer believe that the vendor will meet the new commitments?

(b) Structuring the Settlement

In negotiating a settlement, vendors are generally loath to make a cash payment to the customer. More often, the vendor will offer a discount on, or a credit against future work. These structures are favored by vendors because the vendors usually will not have to take a write-off. By offering a discount or a credit, the vendor also ensures a continuing working relationship with the customer. The cost to the vendor is limited as the offered discount is often less than the vendor's margins. Further, the customer may not use the full credit, especially if the vendor has imposed a limited time period in which the customer may use the credit.

If the vendor offers a credit against or a discount on future services, the customer should make certain that it will be able to receive the full benefit of its bargain. Is the future discount offered by the vendor of value to the customer? Will the customer be able to fully use any credit offered? After the discount, are the vendor's services priced lower or higher than other similar vendors?

In exploring the possibility of a settlement, a party should discuss the parameters of any proposed settlement with not only their lawyers, but also their accountants, and businesspeople to avoid any unintended consequences, including an unforeseen financial impact, especially as to previous financial reporting periods. The businesspeople will advise on whether any credit, or discount given to the customer would violate the terms of any agreement with any other customer, such as a most favored nation clause, and the accountants will be able to advise whether the credit, or discount will impact prior, current, or future period financial statements.

The terms of any resulting settlement agreement should reflect the needs, and goals of the parties. The agreement may combine the elements of both a settlement and a termination, where the customer retains a license to the deliverables, and will perhaps employ the services of a third party to complete the vendor's work as well as a cash payment in return for releasing the vendor from all liability. In short, the structure is limited only by the imagination of the parties.

(c) Leverage

(i) Customer Leverage

The customer's principal leverage is the ability to withhold payment or set-off monies due the vendor. Withholding payment, however, usually will not incent the vendor to complete the work on time. *See* Chapter 5.H.1 and §§ 5.3.2, 8.7. The customer may express its dissatisfaction with the vendor in the marketplace, which may impact the vendor's ability to obtain future work. In doing so, the customer should be mindful of defaming the vendor.

(ii) Vendor Leverage

Although the customer possesses the ability to withhold payment, the vendor also may hold significant leverage if the customer continues to use the deliverables after the dispute has ripened. Savvy vendors usually provide in the agreement between the parties that ownership of the deliverables only transfers to the customer upon full payment. Thus, even if the vendor does not exercise the remedy of self-help (see Chapter 5.H.3(c)(ii)), the vendor has the ability to bring a claim against the customer for copyright infringement, and seek injunctive relief to prevent the customer from using the deliverables. See, e.g., §§ 5.2, 29.5. For more detailed discussion, see section C.4.(c) in this chapter. If successful, injunctive relief may seriously impact the customer if the software is critical to its business.

To avoid this problem, savvy customers should refuse to include language transferring ownership to the customer only upon full payment, or include language in the contract requiring the vendor to continue to provide services, and allow the customer to use the deliverables while any contract dispute is adjudicated. See, e.g., §§ 5.5, 8.7. *See, e.g., IKL, Inc. v. Adoutlet.com, Inc.*, 2001 WL 315219, at *10 (N.D. Ill. March 29, 2001) (court denied motion for preliminary injunction where agreement did not provide customer "will be considered the author of the source code and the owner of its copyright only after full payment . . . .") Most vendors will accept language allowing the customer to continue to use the deliverables, but many are hesitant to continue working if they believe they may not be paid. Prudent vendors should provide that nonpayment by a customer is a contractually permitted basis for ceasing work. Even without explicit language, unexcused nonpayment is a basis for claiming material breach.

An additional area of vendor leverage is withholding maintenance and support. Even if the customer retains the right to use the deliverables, without support and maintenance the deliverables may be useless.

(d) The Settlement Agreement

Once the parties have reached a settlement, the resulting agreement should set forth the concessions made by each party. If the vendor is going to provide a credit or discount to the customer, the settlement agreement should provide specific examples of how such credit or discount will be applied. See, e.g., the model Settlement Agreement and Mutual Release set forth in Form N.2.

The parties should make sure that any release is carefully drafted to avoid releasing the parties from obligations that were meant to survive. See §§ 1, 4(b) of Form N.2. At the same time, if a party is settling a claim for less than it is owed, the release should provide that if the party making the payment declares bankruptcy, and the payment is found to be a preference, the party receiving payment may file a claim for the full amount it was owed, not the amount it settled for. See Form N.3.

Of equal importance is the confidentiality provision. Most licensors seek to publicize any settlement as a warning to others that may be in violation of their licenses. The Business Software Alliance, which pursues copyright violations on behalf of its members, who are principally large software companies, will include a confidentiality provision in its settlement agreements only if the offending party agrees to pay a significantly higher settlement fee.

Licensees who have brought a claim against the licensor are less concerned with publicity, as their primary concern is to be compensated for damages. In these situations, the licensor should insist on including a confidentiality provision in any settlement agreement to protect its image in the market. In addition, it should not admit guilt in any settlement, as the settlement agreement may ultimately become a public document. The agreement simply should state that a disagreement arose between the parties and that the parties are settling their dispute to avoid the cost of litigation.

Finally, in drafting the settlement agreement, the parties should remember that the general words of a release are limited by the recital of a particular claim. *Camperlino v. Bargabos*, 946 N.Y.S.2d 814 (N.Y. A.D. 2012).

3. Renegotiating the Contract

If both parties bear some responsibility for the problem in question, the parties may seek to renegotiate the contract. A renegotiation may be as simple as a one-page contract amendment or as complicated as a complete redrafting of the agreement. Regardless of which approach is taken, the parties should keep in mind a number of issues when undertaking the renegotiation.

Each party should form a "well-rounded" team experienced in renegotiating contracts. A typical team should include the business sponsor, the relevant information technology employees, an experienced information technology lawyer, and a finance person. Each person's perspective is necessary to ensure that neither party negotiates a contract that best serves its interests. The failure to field a well-rounded team creates the risk that the resulting contract will neither meet the needs of the party, nor will be approved by management. The new agreement should address the prior actions of the parties under the original agreement, and if appropriate, release one or both parties for actions taken prior to the date of the amended contract. Further, if appropriate, it should release the parties from their duties to perform their obligations under the previous contract. See, e.g., the model Settlement Agreement and Mutual Release set forth in Form N.2. If consideration is given for the release of obligations under the original agreement, the new agreement should clearly state such consideration. The vendor should avoid making a concession while being held to its original obligations under the old contract.

E. If Litigation Arises

If litigation is unavoidable, the parties should retain litigators with extensive information technology (IT) litigation experience. IT litigation differs from other litigation in that the facts of the case must be viewed in light of the underlying technology, and industry practice. It is extremely difficult, if not impossible, for a lawyer without a background in technology litigation to obtain the requisite knowledge quickly enough to successfully represent a party in a complicated IT dispute. In addition, litigators with experience in IT disputes know the patterns of failure (on both sides) in such projects, and know what "rocks to look under" to uncover the weak points of the other side's case. They also will have experience working with the kinds of experts who are necessary in such cases which may help to advance the case, and make it understandable to a judge or jury without the significant learning curve (and associated cost) that litigators without IT experience often face.

Ideally, the parties should seek to have as part of their legal team lawyers who were computer programmers prior to practicing law, or who at least have a degree in computer programming. Many IT lawyers started their careers as computer programmers. An experienced IT lawyer will be able to quickly judge the strength of a party's case, and spot the weaknesses in its opponent's case. The value of an experienced IT practitioner cannot, and should not be underestimated.

Finally, if applicable, the parties should place their insurance carriers on notice as to the likelihood of a potential claim. The parties should make sure they understand the required procedures under their insurance policy for making a claim. Further, if a party believes it is entitled to make a claim for indemnification, it should understand and follow the procedures for doing so.

For a more detailed discussion on how to effectively litigate a matter, *see* Peters, Cahill-Boley & Lauer, *Disputes and Litigation: Tame the Two-Headed Beast*, 32 ACC Docket 38 (May 2014); Bonora & Lipp, *The In-house Checklist of Steps for New Litigation*, 32 ACC Docket 27 (May 2014); Churay, Bedell, English & O'Malley, *Case Studies in Settlement Counsel: Best Practices for Litigation Strategies*, 33 ACC Docket 50 (October 2015).

CHAPTER **30**

Dispute Resolution (§§ 29, 30)

Given the large number of disputes arising in the development, and installation of complex computer systems, each party should carefully consider incorporating a multi-tiered dispute resolution process to resolve any disputes that may arise between the parties. This approach can take many forms, including, but not limited to, escalating the dispute within the different management levels of the parties, mediation, arbitration, mini-trials, and neutral evaluation. Each has its benefits and drawbacks, which can be magnified in intellectual property disputes. Given the ever-increasing expense of litigation, the uncertainty of juries, and the diversion of corporate resources even when a party prevails, an increasing number of parties are focusing on resolving disputes extrajudicially.

For a general overview, *see* Christopher, *Confessions of a Former Litigator: How to Craft Truly Business Friendly ADR*, 35 ACC DOCKET 77 (October 2017); Molina & Benton, *Resolving Tech Disputes Internationally*, 34 ACC DOCKET 50 (May 2016); Jamar, *Resolving Intellectual Property License Disputes Out of Court*, 24 COMPUTER & INTERNET LAW. 24 (Sept. 2007).

A. The Causes for Disputes

Disputes can arise for a myriad of reasons, but most have the same genesis. According to an international consultancy, the following issues are among the most common reasons for disputes.

1. Failing to understand/manage client expectations of the solution/product:
   - Missing scope, requirements, complexity, or expectations
   - Poor client relationship management
   - An agreement that fails to define expectations
   - Failing to document or properly communicate expectations
   - Unrealistic expectations as to cost-savings, profitability, efficiencies achieved

2. Ongoing scope management issues:
   - Vague scope definitions
   - Failing to enforce scope control processes
   - Failing to update the agreement to reflect scope/schedule changes
   - Poor change control processes
   - Providing free services to the client
   - Avoiding difficult discussions with the client/failing to address issues promptly

3. Failing to understand the complexity of a solution:
    - Missing scope, requirements, or complexity
    - Lack of industry skills/knowledge
    - Making overly aggressive estimates
    - Pressure to win/sell other deals

4. Flawed solution assumptions and inputs:
    - Missing or incorrect solution inputs or complexity
    - Aggressive schedule or estimates
    - Misestimating the skill levels of needed resources
    - Underestimating the solution

5. Ineffective delivery management:
    - Lack of risk/issue management
    - Poor client relationship management
    - Poor program management

6. A one-sided deal structure

B. Internal Dispute Resolution (§ 29)

To be successful, an internal dispute resolution process should be tailored to the nature of the underlying contract, and the parties should avoid using boilerplate language that ignores the contract's realities. The dispute resolution process should be closely aligned with the agreement's governance provisions. If timely delivery is very important to the customer, the dispute resolution process should be focused on quickly resolving any potential dispute.

A standing meeting should be scheduled on a regular basis (e.g., every two weeks) to discuss any potential issues that may have arisen since the previous meeting, and any existing issues. Each party should submit a position statement for each outstanding issue setting forth their understanding of:

- the issue,
- the cause of the issue, and
- a proposed resolution.

The parties should assign specific individuals from each side to investigate, and resolve each issue within an agreed time period. Minutes should be kept of every meeting, and circulated to all parties.

If an issue is not resolved within a set time period (e.g., 10 days) it should be elevated to the next level of management, and then to the next level if the issue is still unresolved after 20 days. By escalating to more senior levels, the upper-level management will be less emotionally attached to the issue, and will hopefully be able to reach agreement with their counterpart from the other party.

C. Mediation (§ 29)

Mediation is an attractive alternative in those cases where:

- the relationship between the parties can be repaired or continued;
- the law is well settled and there is no need for additional discovery;
- the positions of both parties have merit, making the outcome difficult to predict; and
- the cost of litigation is likely to be great.

Mediation is unlikely to be a viable alternative where:

- one party has a significant advantage;
- there is no factual issue in dispute;
- one party seeks to delay resolution of the issue;
- a vital corporate interest is at stake; or
- the dispute is emotionally charged, with each party's position being irretractable.

Mediation is usually a much quicker process than arbitration due to limited, if any, discovery, and the desire of the parties to move quickly through mediation because of its nonbinding nature. This is extremely important if the nature of the dispute is time sensitive. Mediation is usually used as a last step prior to litigation or during litigation if the parties believe a compromise can be reached. Many parties include an informal mediation process to allow the escalation of disputes, thereby permitting the parties to continue working constructively while the dispute is addressed at higher levels in their respective organizations.

Mediation does not impact the ability of either party to pursue litigation. Rather, it allows the parties to attempt to resolve their differences at a number of different levels prior to initiating the litigation process. At the same time, each party can educate itself as to the strength of the other party's case. The parties must be mindful, however, of the statute of limitations and, if applicable, execute a tolling agreement to preserve their rights to bring a claim. See Form N.1 for a model Tolling Agreement.

The absence of discovery avoids potentially damaging admissions, the production of damaging documentation, and the costs associated with discovery. Further, the use of a qualified expert as the mediator ensures a decision maker well versed in the law governing the issues in dispute who will provide an independent assessment of the respective strengths, and weaknesses of each party's position. Mediation also offers lower costs, and greater confidentiality due to the limited discovery, and the fact that any decision is not publicly reported. Finally, the often-acrimonious nature of litigation is usually avoided due to the more relaxed nature of the proceedings.

To increase the likelihood of resolving the matter in questions, the parties should choose an experienced mediator with significant experience in mediating intellectual property/software disputes. A skilled mediator can assist the parties in clarifying the issues in dispute, evaluate the strengths, and weaknesses of their respective positions, and drive them to settlement.

If the parties are successful in reaching a resolution through mediation, they should carefully consider any documents memorializing their agreement at the end of the mediation session prior to execution, as they may be considered a complete, and final settlement of the dispute. *Hill v. Hutchinson Care Center, L.L.C.*, 357 P.3d 313 (Kan. App. 2015).

For a discussion of mediation, and how to select a mediator, *see* Lampert, *What Mediators Want*, ACC DOCKET (May 2021); Cohen, *Meditate Before You Mediate: 12 Ways to Position Yourself for Success*, 30 ACC DOCKET 74–78 (Sept. 2012).

For a more in-depth discussion of international mediations, *see* Rogers & Dawson, *Chartered Waters: Ten Considerations to Crafting the International Mediation Clause*, 26 ACC DOCKET 78 (Oct. 2008).

D. Arbitration (§ 30)

1. General Benefits and Drawbacks

Like most things in life, arbitration has its advantages and disadvantages. Arbitration is, generally, quicker than the court system, but may provide an ineffective means of resolving certain legal issues. For example, a customer would not want to arbitrate whether a vendor must indemnify the customer for an alleged intellectual property infringement since the passage of time involved in reaching the decision could be highly damaging to the customer's financial position. Alternatively, a court can quickly issue an injunction in the vendor's favor if the customer breaches the terms of the license grant. For a discussion of the issues involved in obtaining an injunction, *see* Friedman & LaMotta, *When Protecting Software Through an Injunction, How Do You Spell Relief?*, 11 COMPUTER LAW. 18 (March 1994).

While there is strong public policy in favor of arbitration, a court cannot compel the parties to arbitrate a matter that they did not agree to submit to arbitration. *Shopsmith Woodworking Promotions, Inc. v. American Woodworking Academy, Inc.*, 1995 WL 614355 (Ohio App. Oct. 18, 1995). As such, if the parties desire to arbitrate, the governing agreement should clearly indicate that intent.

Arbitration is often advantageous in terms of cost, particularly when used in smaller disputes. Many parties will agree on a single arbiter if the dispute is less than an agreed-upon amount, i.e., $5 million, and three arbiters if the dispute exceeds that amount. With large matters, cost savings may be achieved by avoiding an extensive, and protracted discovery process, and eliminating any appeals process through a well-drafted arbitration provision. Often, there is no need for hiring court reporters for depositions or expert witnesses, as most arbiters are themselves experts in the field. Arbiters are not bound by legal precedent and need not articulate a rationale for their decision. Thus, arbitration may result in an outcome much more efficiently, without the time, and expense associated with having to address every legal nuance than a court would.

Vendors often prefer arbitration, as it allows for the selection of a subject matter expert to adjudicate the dispute instead of potentially having the dispute decided by someone who lacks an in-depth knowledge of the technology underlying the dispute. Further, because the arbitration is specific to an individual dispute, an adverse ruling will not invalidate the vendor's intellectual property, and will not serve as precedent for claims made by the vendor's other customers.

Large arbitrations can take years to reach their conclusion, during which time each party will incur significant expense. Because the outcome of arbitration is not dictated by legal precedent, and therefore less predictable, arbitration may not be a prudent choice if the dispute is one commonly dealt with by the courts. There are no evidentiary rules in arbitration. If there is crucial evidence in the dispute that would not likely be admissible in court, and would negatively impact the party in question, a court may be the better choice. Further, many arbiters are reluctant to rule on pre-hearing dispositive motions. Another disadvantage is that the non-breaching party may be prohibited from bringing a claim in court.

Arbitration may benefit a breaching party due to the potentially greater time period needed to reach a resolution, and the fact that there is no possibility of summary judgment. Furthermore, an entity must disclose its claims in arbitration, which puts a vendor at a disadvantage assuming the customer is in breach. Finally, under arbitration all actions must be by mutual agreement, allowing one party to potentially delay the proceedings if it chooses.

Another consideration is the business relationship between the parties to the dispute. An ongoing relationship, such as the performance of long-term contracts, is often more likely to be preserved through an arbitration proceeding than by litigation. Arbitration is less stressful on the parties, and is confidential. Prudent parties should specifically state that the arbitration, and its result are confidential. The lack of public exposure can help protect the present, and future business relationship between the parties as well as their relationships with other clients or vendors.

A common complaint about arbitration is that the arbiters will often try to "split the baby" without a real resolution of the issue, leaving neither party satisfied.

Another potential benefit of arbitration arises in the context of enforcement of an injunction in a foreign jurisdiction. Most courts are hesitant to enter a court order for injunctive relief based on a decision of a foreign jurisdiction. On the other hand, a court may be more likely to support an arbitral award for injunctive relief. It requires courts of member states to recognize the validity of arbitration agreements, and reject a party's efforts to litigate a matter that is subject to a contractual agreement to arbitrate. Further, the courts of member states are required to recognize, and enforce foreign arbitral decisions. Under the NY Convention, judicial review of the merits of an award is prohibited. As a result of the widespread acceptance of the NY Convention, arbitration in some situations may be preferable to a judicial decision for injunctive relief.

In pursuing non-binding arbitration, the parties must be cognizant of the applicable statute of limitations, as contractually mandated arbitration that is a condition precedent to litigation will not toll the statute of limitations. *Kumar v. Dhanda*, 43 A.3d 1029 (Md. 2012).

In consumer transactions, a properly drafted arbitration clause may allow a vendor to eliminate the ability of a customer to bring a class-action suit, or to serve as a class representative. See Chapter 6.H.1 for a more detailed discussion.

For a comparison of the benefits of arbitration to litigation, *see* Freeman & Wilson, *Arbitration or Litigation?* 24 ACC Docket 37 (Oct. 2006). For a general overview of the pros and cons of arbitration, *see Commercial Arbitration*, 27 Corp. Couns. Q. 812 (Oct. 2011).

2. *Legal Concerns*

Federal policy favors arbitration as a means to resolve disputes. *Shearson/American Express, Inc. v. McMahon*, 482 U.S. 220, 225–26 (1987). Any challenges to the underlying agreement, and not specifically the arbitration clause within such agreement must be resolved by the arbiter(s). *Buckeye Check Cashing, Inc. v. Cardegna*, 546 U.S. 440, 449 (2006). *See also Qualcomm v. Nokia*, 466 F.3d 1366, 1374 (Fed. Cir. 2006) (If parties indicated intent to delegate authority to arbiter, any claim for arbitral relief that is not wholly groundless must proceed.). A party may waive its right to arbitration through its conduct. *Worbes Corp. v. Sebrow*, 78 Misc. 3d 1212 (Sup. Ct. 2023).

For any arbitration clause to be enforceable, it cannot be procedurally and substantively unconscionable. Even if the agreement is procedurally unconscionable, it may be enforceable if the substantive terms are reasonable. *Comb v. PayPal, Inc.*, 218 F. Supp. 1165 (N.D. Cal. 2002). The procedural aspect requires the parties to have equal bargaining positions, and to avoid terms reflective of an adhesion contract. *Id.* at 1172. The substantive aspect looks to whether the agreement is one-sided, and "shocks the conscience." *Id.* To be enforceable, the terms of the arbitration agreement cannot be so one sided that the agreement is unconscionable. Unequal bargaining power alone, however, will not cause an agreement to be found procedurally unconscionable. *Zimmer v. Cooperneff Advisors, Inc.*, 523 F.3d 224 (3d Cir. 2008). The parties should avoid agreements where (i) one party must pay a significant portion of the arbitration costs; (ii) the forum for the arbitration is inconvenient for one party; (iii) the obligation to arbitrate is not mutual; and (iv) there is a prohibition against the consolidation of claims. An arbitration clause should be broadly drafted so that it encompasses all of the parties' potential claims, not simply a portion of their claims. *See, e.g.*, *Tres Jeanee v. Brolin Retail Systems Midwest, Inc.*, 2007 WL 3118482 (W.D. Ky. Oct. 22, 2007) (software licensor's motion to compel arbitration under clause requiring mandatory arbitration of software disputes denied because dispute involved software and hardware issues); *Holt Co. v. Ohio Machinery Co.*, 2007 WL 1674023 (Ohio App. June 12, 2007).

When drafting a mandatory arbitration provision, the parties should carefully consider the language of the arbitration provision to ensure their intent will be fulfilled. *See NCR Corporation v. Korala Associates, Ltd.*, 512 F.3d 807 (2008) (6th Cir. 2008) (resolution of plaintiff's copyright infringement claim was not dependent on reference to, or interpretation of the license agreement, thus claim not arbitrable under provision requiring arbitration of "any controversy or claim arising out of or related to this contract"). To avoid a court adopting the reasoning of the *Korala* court, prudent parties should draft the arbitration provision broadly so that it addresses all intellectual property issues arising from the agreement except for injunctive relief. Model language follows:

> *Any controversy, claim or dispute between the parties arising out of or relating to this Agreement, the Licensed Software, Support Services, or Intellectual Property Rights, including controversies, claims or disputes involving the validity or infringement of Intellectual Property Rights, will exclusively be resolved by binding arbitration conducted in accordance with the rules of the American Arbitration Association's Rules. Nothing in this section will be construed to preclude the right and ability of either party to pursue injunctive or provisional relief at any time in any court of competent jurisdiction.*

For a general discussion of the arbitrability of a potential dispute, *see* Polichar, *Hanging by a Thread: Finding Arbitrability Without Clear Evidence of a Contract*, Bus. L. Today (July 2011).

3. Practical Concerns

To avoid any potential problems that arbitration may create, the parties should set forth specific language in the contract to assuage such problems. See § 30, for model language addressing some potential concerns.

To be effective, the language should provide that the arbitration is the *exclusive* means to resolve any dispute. Any exceptions should be specifically listed. By specifically stating the scope of the disputes to be arbitrated, the parties can avoid further disagreements when seeking arbitration. At least one court has declined to enforce an arbitration clause in the underlying license agreement that provided "[a]ny controversy or claim arising out of or relating to this contract, or breach thereof, shall be settled by arbitration . . . ," determining that a party's copyright infringement claim was not dependent on the license agreement, and thus the dispute could proceed in court. *NCR Corporation v. Korala Associates, Ltd.*, 512 F.3d 807 (6th Cir. 2008). Further, courts will strictly interpret the scope of an agreement's arbitration provision. *Evans v. Bldg. Materials Corp. of America*, 858 F.3d 1377 (4th Cir. 2017).

The location of the arbitration should be stated along with the governing law. To ensure prompt action, the parties should include the time period in which an action must be filed, and the period in which the action must be resolved. This will prevent the arbitration from extending for an indefinite period. The parties should also clearly identify the arbitration rules under which the arbitration will take place. In addition, the parties should state any parameters for the use and protection of the parties' confidential information.

The parties should limit the number of witnesses, document requests, interrogatories, and depositions and their length. By setting forth such restrictions in detail, the parties can significantly reduce future costs and any potential disputes. The agreement should also establish the number and qualifications of the panel member(s). For example, do the panel member(s) need to be lawyers, or have experience in software licensing or a particular industry? By requiring the panel to have specific, relevant experience and expertise, the arbitration will move quicker, and more likely result in a well-reasoned decision. Some parties include language as follows: "*Such arbitrators shall be recognized experts in the computer software field.*"

The parties should avoid identifying a specific arbiter, or arbitral body if they cannot ensure that the identified individual, or body will be able to hear the dispute. At least one court has refused to enforce an arbitration agreement where the arbitral body identified in the agreement no longer heard the type of dispute in question. *See Carr v. Gateway*, 944 N.E.2d 327 (Ill. 2011) (court denied motion to compel arbitration where designated arbitral body no longer heard consumer disputes) *but see Khan v. Dell*, 669 F.3d 350 (3d Cir. 2012) (Federal Arbitration Act required the appointment of a new arbiter to hear matter when designated arbitral forum unavailable, as selection of arbiter not integral to agreement.).

Many agreements require three arbiters, one chosen by each party, and a third "neutral" arbiter chosen by mutual agreement of the parties. The use of three arbiters, however, significantly increases the cost of the arbitration, principally as a result of the arbiter's collective fees. Further, coordinating the schedule of three arbiters can significantly delay any resolution of the matter. The parties may want to consider the retention of a single, neutral arbiter as a means to reduce bureaucracy and costs.

Finally, the parties should enumerate any limitation on the awarding of damages. Many entities select arbitration to avoid large, punitive damages awards. The arbitration agreement should clearly set out any limits on the arbiters' ability to award damages and any limits on the types of damages that may be awarded. It is unclear whether punitive damages can be awarded when the overarching agreement is silent as to punitive damages. See *Mastrobuono v. Shearson Lehman Hutton*, 514 U.S. 52 (1995); *Garity v. Lyle Stuart, Inc.*, 40 N.Y.2d 354 (1976). To avoid any uncertainty and to eliminate the possibility of the arbiters awarding punitive damages, the parties should include language to the following effect:

> *In any arbitration arising out of or related to this Agreement, the arbiter(s) are not empowered to award punitive damages or other damages in excess of compensatory damages, except where required by statute, and the parties waive any right to recover any such damages.*

The arbitration agreement should clearly set forth the form any decision will take. For example, is a signed opinion sufficient, or do the parties want a detailed explanation of the arbiters' rationale, and the basis for the decision? The parties may want the arbiters to set forth their findings of fact. The lack of a detailed opinion may make it more difficult to challenge any decision that is clearly erroneous as to law. Nonetheless, arbitration agreements are subject to judicial review in only a limited number of situations. *See Hall Street Associates, LLC v. Mattel*, 552 U.S. 576 (2008).

4. *PRACTICE POINT*: Checklist for drafting a domestic arbitration clause.

- The administering institution (i.e., AAA, JAMS, ICC, etc.)
- The location of the arbitration (Make sure the administrating institution has an office in the chosen location).
- The governing law
- The number of arbiters
- The arbiters' qualifications
- Selection of the arbiters (by the parties, by the administrating institution, strike and rank)
- The scope of matters subject to arbitration
- Language of the arbitration
- Scope of discovery
- The availability of judicial review
- Payment of arbitral costs and legal fees

- The arbitration is confidential
- The remedies available to the arbitrators (e.g., the award of punitive damages)
- The requirement for a reasoned decision
- Injunctive relief/interim relief
- Scope of remedies
- Specific performance
- The format of the opinion issued by the arbiters (e.g., an order, a detailed opinion)

Inclusion of an arbitration provision in a license may impact other collateral agreements. At least two courts have held that an arbitration provision in a license agreement is enforceable as to a separate services agreement. *See Armed Forces Insur. Corp. v. Allenbrook, Inc.*, 2001 WL 699735 (D. Kan. June 11, 2001); *LDS, Inc. v. Metro Can. Logistics, Inc.*, 28 F. Supp. 2d 1297 (D. Kan. 1998) (arbitration clause in license agreement encompasses all matters in dispute including maintenance agreement).

For a comparison of relative advantages and disadvantages of arbitration and litigation, see Freeman & Wilson, *A Tale of 2 Cases: Arbitration or Litigation?*, 24 ACC DOCKET 24, 36–46 (Oct. 2006). The parties should carefully consider the impact of ancillary documents having conflicting dispute resolution mechanisms to avoid a protracted, and expensive resolution of the collective dispute. *See, e.g., Brennan v. Global Safety Labs.*, 2008 WL 2234830 (N.D. Okla. May 29, 2008).

For a general discussion on the arbitration of disputes, *see* Greenspan &Weiner, *Reassessing Commercial Arbitration: Making It Work For Your Company*, 35 ACC DOCKET 52 (March 2017); Arnold, *Suggested Form of Contract to Arbitrate a Patent or Other Commercial Dispute Annotated*, 2 TEX. INTELL. PROP. L.J. 205 (1994).

5. The Risks Associated with a Bifurcated Approach

The benefits of arbitration are not necessarily applicable to all types of disputes. The use of arbitration to resolve intellectual property disputes is often impractical, given the potential sensitivity of the dispute and the need to quickly reach a resolution. To avoid the challenges associated with arbitration, but still take advantage of its benefits, some parties adopt a bifurcated approach—agreeing to arbitrate some aspects of their agreement while litigating other aspects.

(a) Intellectual Property Disputes

For intellectual property disputes, a delay in resolving an issue can have serious consequences, especially if one party has misappropriated another party's intellectual property or is infringing on the other party's intellectual property rights. To mitigate this concern, many parties that select arbitration to settle their disputes have incorporated an additional provision allowing the aggrieved party to seek injunctive relief through the court system without having to go through arbitration. Simply stated, they have carved out disputes relating to intellectual property from arbitration. This bifurcated approach allows the aggrieved party to quickly seek judicial protection to preserve its intellectual property rights. The model language below illustrates this point.

> *The Parties agree that any action related to or arising from this Agreement that cannot be resolved by the good faith efforts of the parties shall be referred to, and finally resolved by arbitration in New York, New York. Such arbitration shall be decided pursuant to the Rules of the American Arbitration Association from time to time in force. Notwithstanding any provision in this Agreement, in no event shall any claims, disputes, or controversies between the Parties which potentially concern the validity, enforceability, infringement, or misappropriation of any Intellectual Property rights, including any rights protectable under Intellectual Property law anywhere throughout the world such as patent, copyright, trade secret, and trademark law, be subject to resolution by arbitration.*

This solution is not perfect, as many parties end up litigating the aggrieved party's right to seek judicial relief, or simply litigating the entire matter, defeating the intent of the arbitration clause. Further, as discussed below, the parties' intent to seek certainty in resolving their disputes will often be frustrated.

(b) Judicial Interpretation

Several cases have addressed bifurcated dispute resolution provisions. In *Oracle v. Myriad Group AG*, 2012 WL 146364 (N.D. Cal. Jan. 17, 2012), Oracle initiated a claim in the Federal District Court for the Northern District of California against the Myriad Group, alleging that Myriad infringed on Oracle's trademarks and copyrights. Myriad filed a motion to compel arbitration, and subsequently submitted a demand for arbitration in accordance with the underlying agreement's dispute resolution provision.

The license agreement between Oracle and Myriad provided:

> Any dispute arising out of or relating to this License shall be finally settled by arbitration as set out herein, *except that either party may bring any action, in a court of competent jurisdiction which jurisdiction shall be exclusive), with respect to any dispute relating to such party's Intellectual Property Rights . . . .*

Id. at *1.

The *Myriad* court emphasized that the clear intent of this provision is to establish either party's contractual right to file a lawsuit in a court where Oracle's intellectual property rights, or compliance with the license were at issue. Moreover, the provision granted the court "*exclusive*" jurisdiction to decide intellectual property disputes.

The court cited *Bridge Fund Capital Corp. v. Fastbucks Franchise Corp., 622 F.3d 996, 1000 (9th Cir. 2010)* for the position that the arbitrability of a particular dispute is a threshold issue to be decided by the courts, unless that issue is *explicitly assigned to the arbitrator*. It concluded that it, not the arbitrator, had responsibility for determining whether Oracle's claims were subject to arbitration, and found that Oracle's intellectual property claims were not subject to the agreement's arbitration clause, allowing Oracle to seek injunctive relief.

Similarly, in *Pharmacia & Upjohn Co. v. Elan Pharmaceuticals, Inc.*, 781 N.Y.S.2d 95 (2004), the parties entered into an agreement that contained the following provision:

> Any dispute arising out of or relating to this Agreement which does not involve intellectual property rights which is not resolved pursuant to Articles 15.1 or 15.2 shall be resolved by final and binding Arbitration conducted in New York ... and, except as provided for in this Article 15.3, under the then current Rules of the American Arbitration Association ("AAA").

A dispute arose and Elan filed a demand for arbitration. Pharmacia filed suit seeking to stay the arbitration, and contended the dispute must be litigated given that the agreement's arbitration clause specifically excludes disputes related to intellectual property. Only eight months after Elan's initial demand for arbitration did the court rule that the question of whether the matter was subject to arbitration was a decision for the courts and remanded the matter to a lower court to determine a number of facts. Thus, in *Pharmacia*, the parties were no closer to reaching a resolution eight months later than when the initial demand for arbitration had been filed. From the perspective of a party whose intellectual property is at risk, such a delay is totally unacceptable.

Similarly, in *McKesson Corp. v. Health Robotics, S.R.L.*, 2011 WL 3157044 (N.D. Cal. July 26, 2011), the parties agreed to resolve any disputes through binding arbitration in Switzerland, but allowing the parties to seek injunctive relief for disputes related to intellectual property rights. After a dispute arose as to Health Robotics's right to grant the license in question, the parties spent significant time, effort, and money litigating whether the disputed was required to be arbitrated.

The risks of a bifurcated approach are even greater internationally where case law and the local judicial system may not be as developed as in the United States. See, American Super Conductor Company's dispute with Sinovel Wind Group Co., Ltd, and Dalian Guotong Electric Co., Ltd. https://www.bloomberg. com/news/articles/2012-03-15/china-corporate-espionage-boom-knocks-wind-out- of-u-s-companies.

(c) Is a Bifurcated Approach Prudent?

As the use of arbitration has become more prevalent, many parties are questioning its advantages over litigation, and whether arbitration is preferable to resolve intellectual property disputes. Some parties have utilized a bifurcated approach: selecting arbitration, but carving out intellectual-property-related disputes, potentially requiring the parties to resolve the proper means for resolving the dispute before deciding the issue in question. With a bifurcated approach, the risk arises that each party will seek to enforce the approach (e.g., arbitration/litigation) that best promotes its interests. As the *Myriad, Elan, and Health Robotics* cases illustrate, often this delays justice while increasing legal expenditures, and animosity between the parties.

From a licensor's perspective, there seems to be little benefit in a bifurcated approach. Litigation will likely be quicker while providing greater certainty and consistency. The ability to obtain a preliminary injunction resulting in a prompt resolution of the dispute is important for allowing the licensor to maintain the value of its intellectual property. Arbitration alone holds little promise, as obtaining immediate injunctive relief through arbitration is at best very difficult to obtain. Given that a party will likely have to obtain judicial protection to enforce compliance with certain aspects of the governing contract's provisions, the value of having any remaining portions of the dispute resolved through arbitration is questionable.

Another risk of a bifurcated approach is that a court may improperly interpret the dispute resolution provision of the underlying agreement. In the case of a licensing dispute, a fundamental issue is often whether the dispute relates to a breach of contract or a breach of the underlying license grant. Breach of a party's intellectual property rights, such as a copyright infringement, should be addressed in the federal court system, which has exclusive jurisdiction over such matters. Breach of contract claims, however, may be addressed either through arbitration or litigation.

As illustrated by the *Myriad* case, each party will try to frame the issue in a manner that serves its own interests, potentially causing each party to expend a significant amount of time, effort, and money to resolve the issue. Utilizing a bifurcated approach adds another potential issue to be resolved before the principal issue in dispute can be adjudicated.

The principal benefit of arbitration is confidentiality. When selecting a dispute resolution process, both parties should contemplate the importance of confidentiality. The licensor may prefer that the dispute not be kept confidential to serve as a warning to other licensees that the licensor plans to aggressively enforce the terms of its license. On the other hand, if the dispute involves an interpretation of the contractual terms of the license, and the court rules against the licensor, the licensor may not want a record in the public domain, as it may impact all of the licensor's licenses.

From the licensor's perspective, other than confidentiality concerns, there is no reason not to resolve all disputes through litigation. The licensor's intellectual property assets have significant value, and should not be placed at risk. There is very little downside to contractually requiring that all disputes be litigated. This consistency creates certainty, and potentially eliminates the risk of specious disputes delaying the licensor from enforcing its intellectual property rights.

From the licensee's perspective, the licensee may not care whether disputes are arbitrated, or litigated as there does not appear to be strong evidence that one means of dispute resolution would benefit the licensee over the other. For a detailed discussion of the advantages and disadvantages of arbitrating intellectual property disputes, see Fox & Weinstein, *Myth Busting: Arbitration Perceptions, Realities and Ramifications*, American Bar Association, 14th Annual Spring Conference, April 19, 2012, http://www.micronomics.com/articles/Arbitration_and_Intellectual_Property_Disputes.pdf.

Some parties believe that intellectual property disputes should not be litigated as the judiciary, and the juries will not understand the often-complicated intellectual property issues they have been charged with resolving. These parties argue that arbiters, who are chosen by the parties, are much more likely to understand the issues before them as the parties have the flexibility to review, and select the arbiters who have extensive experience in understanding, and resolving intellectual property disputes. Further, in the case of a three-party arbitration panel, each party will be able to select an experienced IP attorney who will be able to "educate" the third independent arbiter in the issues before the panel.

To the extent a party is concerned that a judge hearing the matter may not be knowledgeable on intellectual property matters, the parties may want to designate a business court as the exclusive venue for resolving their disputes. Many states have established business courts to hear business disputes in the belief that these courts will develop an expertise that will allow them to quickly and expeditiously resolve business disputes while providing the parties with the confidence that the judges assigned to the court possess the requisite knowledge to understand the issues before them. See Form Q.2.Y.7 for model language providing for the exclusive venue of the business courts of the state courts of New York to hear any disputes.

For an additional discussion of this issue, see Hu & Zammit, *Arbitrating International Intellectual Property Disputes*, 24 MEALEY'S INTERNATIONAL ARBITRATION REPORT 1 (June 2009) and Garcia, *Scope of Arbitration Clauses and Carve-Out Clauses: Erring on the Side of Caution or on the Side of Daring?*, http://kluwerarbitrationblog.com/blog/2012/05/25/scope-of-arbitration-clauses-and-carve-out-clauses-erring-on-the-side-of-caution-or-on-the-side-of-daring/.

(d) Avoiding the Problem

To avoid the problems associated with a bifurcated approach, the parties should agree to either litigate, or arbitrate all disputes arising from the underlying agreement. Providing for a consistent approach to resolve all disputes arising from the underlying agreement provides certainty, avoids fragmenting the resolution of the dispute, likely reduces costs, and reduces the time to definitively resolve the dispute.

Whether the parties ultimately agree to arbitrate, or litigate their dispute is less important than selecting a process that provides certainty. Both parties, but especially the licensor, rely on certainty when entering into an agreement to ensure the protection of their rights. It is the need for certainty that drove many licensors to exclude intellectual property disputes from an agreement's arbitration provisions. This is especially true in intellectual property disputes where the value of the intellectual property in question may be large, and is the principal asset of the licensor.

Avoiding a fragmented approach is also important. The concept of judicial economy should factor into any decision when selecting a particular means of dispute resolution. The parties want to limit the time, and effort spent resolving an issue. The prospect of bouncing back, and forth between the court system, and an arbitral body does not lend itself to an efficient, and cost-effective resolution. Many arbitration panels will be unable to act while a related matter is winding its way through the court system. Further, no decision by the panel will be considered definitive if the parties can always appeal that decision to the judiciary.

If the parties still desire to utilize arbitration to resolve certain aspects of their relationship but remove intellectual property disputes from the arbitration panel's authority, the parties should ensure that the language removing intellectual property disputes is broadly, and clearly worded so that these issues will not be subject to arbitration and the parties will not end up litigating whether a particular issue must be arbitrated or litigated. In this manner, the parties will hopefully create certainty, and eliminate any preliminary disputes that will delay the resolution of the fundamental issues between them.

A unified approach in most cases will also reduce the time and cost of reaching a resolution, not only for resolving the ultimate dispute, but any effort to seek injunctive relief as well. As the previously discussed cases have illustrated, a bifurcated approach often delays a resolution which in turn affects both parties and increases their costs.

For a more detailed discussion, *see*, American Arbitration Association, *Drafting Dispute Resolution Clauses: A Practical Guide.* https://www.adr.org/sites/default/files/document_repository/Drafting%20Dispute%20Resolution%20Clauses%20A%20Practical%20Guide.pdf.

E. International Arbitration

1. General

International arbitration offers an alternative to subjecting a U.S. domiciled party to the uncertainty of a foreign court proceeding, and may be an attractive alternative, given increasing global hostility toward the United States, and the judicial corruption that exists in many developing countries. By carefully selecting the arbitral body, the arbiters, the venue of the arbitration, and the governing law, a U.S. entity can avoid many risks inherent in international disputes.

International arbitration may also be attractive to a foreign entity that is reluctant to adjudicate a matter in the United States due to significant legal costs, and the potential for "hometown" prejudice. The most popular venues for international arbitration are England, France, Singapore, and Switzerland. Choosing the venue is one of the most important decisions a party will make as some countries may not enforce the arbiter's decision. Thus, it is important that the country chosen for the venue is a signatory to the NY Convention.

From the perspective of a U.S. entity, the arbitration should be conducted in English, and specify a governing law at the time of contract signature. It is advantageous to a U.S. entity to have a dispute resolved in an English-speaking country with a common legal law system which will hopefully be fair and impartial. A party selling goods should also consider the applicability the United Nations Convention on Contracts for the International Sale of Goods ("CISG").

Initiating an overseas arbitration is usually only financially justified in the event of a significant dispute, as the cost of retaining foreign counsel combined with global travel costs for U.S.-based witnesses, and employees can be prohibitive. Further, arbitration in civil law countries may be more expensive than litigating the matter. The significant costs associated with international arbitration may cause some companies to not pursue small disputes, or to reach a quick resolution with a larger, well-financed adversary. As such, it may be more advantageous to arbitrate in a more cost-efficient venue, such as New York or Washington.

The parties may want to consider a dispute resolution process utilizing a tiered approach to resolve the issue. The first step may be direct, personal conversations between top executives of the parties followed, if needed, by mediation of the dispute, with arbitration as a last resort. A multistep process arguably increases the overall cost of the dispute, but it provides the parties multiple opportunities to reach resolution. Further, during this process, the parties may likely recognize the time, distraction, and costs involved in prolonging the dispute and reach a settlement.

Model language to address this issue is as follows:

Any dispute under or related to this Agreement including with respect to the execution, performance, or termination thereof shall be settled by means of arbitration by the London Court of International Arbitration in compliance with the Court's Organizational and Operation Rules, the Court's Procedural Rules and Article 4 of the European Convention on International Commercial Arbitration signed on April 21st, 1961. The number of Arbitrators shall be three (3), and the venue of arbitration shall be London, United Kingdom. The language for hearings and documents submitted to Court shall be in the English language only, and the verdict of the Arbitration panel shall be final and binding on both parties.

The selection of the arbiter(s) is an equally important decision as the arbiters should have a thorough understanding of the industry from which the dispute arises as well as the area of law in question. The arbiters' schedule should be flexible so that the arbitration may be held promptly, and a decision rendered quickly. It is important that the arbiters are fluent in the language of the arbitration, not only conversationally, but also in the technical terms of the industry. If possible, the agreement should contain a requirement for impartial arbiters who were previously unaware of, and not otherwise impacted by, the dispute.

2. *PRACTICE POINT*: Checklist for drafting an international arbitration provision.

A comprehensive arbitration provision will address the following:

- The scope of the arbitration (i.e., the specific disputes subject to arbitration)
- The venue (including the physical location of the arbitration)
- The parties subject to the arbitration (entities, directors, officers, employees, etc.)
- The governing law
- The administering institution (i.e., ICC, LCIA, etc.)
- The qualifications of the arbiters
- The number of arbiters
- The parties' confidentiality obligations
- The scope of discovery (i.e., the number of depositions, interrogatories, third party subpoenas
- The time frame for completing discovery
- The use of experts
- The scope of testimony
- The scope of the panel's authority
- The rights and powers of the arbiters
- The rules that govern the arbitration
- The language in which the arbitration will be conducted
- The remedies available to the arbitrators (e.g., the award of punitive damages)
- The requirement for a reasoned decision

- The finality of the decision
- The availability of injunctive relief/interim relief
- The enforcement of any decision through the NY Convention.

For a more detailed discussion, see Sherby, *A Checklist for Drafting an International Arbitration Clause*, Bus. L. Today, September 20, 2010.

Set forth below is model language that bifurcates the terms, and location of the arbitration based on the customer's location.

(1.1) Customer in the United States of America, and Its Territories. This License Agreement shall be governed by and construed in accordance with the laws of the State of New York without reference to conflict of laws principles, except that US federal law shall govern in matters of intellectual property, and for US government agency use. Any dispute arising out of, or relating to this License Agreement, or the breach thereof that cannot be settled through negotiation shall be finally settled by confidential arbitration administered by the American Arbitration Association under its Commercial Arbitration Rules. All aspects of the arbitration, including any results, shall be confidential. If the total amount claimed as damages by either party, or the financial impact of the asserted claims is $5 million or greater, the dispute shall be decided by three arbitrators, with each party choosing and arbitrator and those two arbitrators choosing the third arbitrator who will serve as chairperson. If the total amount claimed as damages by either party, or the financial impact of the asserted claims is less than $5 million, the dispute shall be decided by one arbitrator agreed to by the parties. The arbitration shall take place in [New York] unless the parties agree in writing on a different location. Judgment on the award rendered by the arbitrator(s) may be entered in a court of competent jurisdiction. This License Agreement shall not be governed by the United Nations Convention on Contracts for the International Sale of Goods, the application of which is expressly excluded.

(1.2) All Other Customer Locations. Except as provided in Section ___ (Equitable Relief), any dispute arising out of, or relating to this License Agreement, or the breach thereof that cannot be settled through negotiation shall be finally settled by confidential arbitration under the Rules of Arbitration of the International Chamber of Commerce by one (1) arbitrator appointed in accordance with said rules. The language of the arbitration shall be English. The seat of the arbitration shall be [London] and all hearing will be conducted in [London] unless the parties agree in writing on a different location. This License Agreement shall not be governed by the United Nations Convention on Contracts for the International Sale of Goods, the application of which is expressly excluded. Either party shall, at the request of the other, make available documents or witnesses relevant to the major aspects of the dispute.

There are a number of well-respected arbitral organizations outside the United States, including the International Chamber of Commerce (ICC), the London Court of International Arbitration (LCIA), the Singapore International Arbitration Centre, and the Stockholm Chamber of Commerce. While the American Arbitration Association

(AAA) has a division devoted to international arbitration, the International Centre for Dispute Resolution (ICDR), it is not as well known, or utilized to the extent of the other arbitral organizations. Each of these organizations has its own rules and procedures. As such, a potential party should familiarize itself with the rules and procedures of the different organizations before agreeing to be bound by the decisions of a particular arbitral organization. For a comparison of the rules of the AAA, ICC, and LCIA, see Horn, *Choosing the Right Form of International Arbitration in London*, TRENDS 7 (May 2007); Chaloupka, *International Distribution and Licensing*, 70 DISTRIBUTION COUNS. 1, 9–12 (Oct. 2006). Shanks, Chedid & Chao, *Tools that Create Successful Resolutions in International Arbitration*, 25 ACC DOCKET 50 (June 2007).

For an overview of the advantages, and disadvantages of international arbitration, including instruction on drafting an international arbitration clause, see *International Arbitration*, 52 LAW. BRIEF 1 (Sept. 30, 2022); Wilburn, *Mix and Match: Divergent Legal Traditions in International Arbitration*, 53 MD. B.J. 4 (July 2010); Constable, *International Commercial Arbitration*, 53 MD. B.J. 12 (July 2010). Swanton, *A Survival Guide to International Arbitration*, INSIDE COUNS. 43 (Jan. 2008); Shanks, Chedid & Chao, *Tools that Create Successful Resolutions in International Arbitration*, 25 ACC DOCKET 50 (June 2007); *The Neutral Zone: A Practical Guide to International Arbitration*, 24 ACC DOCKET 64 (June 2006).

F. Settlement Agreements

1. *Possible Compromises*

(a) Customer Claims

In seeking a solution to any customer claim, vendors often seek to avoid making a cash payment to the customer and instead, offer non-cash consideration such a credit for future services including free or reduced fees for maintenance, software development, or software licenses. These credits can be offered as an outright credit, or with dependencies such as the credit must be used by a set date, the credit may only be used for certain services, or the credit may be used only to off-set a percentage of new services, i.e. 50% of the cost of any additional services.

From the customer's perspective, a credit only has value if the customer plans to continue working with the vendor, and has a need for future services. If the customer suspects the vendor will not provide quality services, or does not require additional services, the offer is worthless.

(b) Vendor Claims

If the customer has exceeded the scope of the license grant, and the vendor has brought a claim against the customer, the customer may seek to negotiate the amount owed or offer to purchase additional services in return for the vendor eliminating or reducing the amount the vendor claims the customer owes. Alternatively, the vendor may require the customer to purchase additional licenses, and/or extend the length of the customer's license.

2. *Settlement Agreements*

Careful consideration should be given to the terms of any agreement settling a dispute. While the terms of any settlement agreement will be driven by the nature of the dispute, prudent parties should ensure there are no unintended consequences, as a result of executing the agreement. For example, if the settlement calls for the forgiveness of certain debts of the licensee, the release should specifically identify by invoice number those invoices that are being credited or forgiven, as opposed to simply stating a dollar value. If there are multiple agreements between the parties, such as a software license agreement, and a maintenance agreement, the parties should identify which agreement a release relates to, and state that all other agreements will continue unchanged. In the event the underlying agreement will be terminated by a release, the parties should identify any rights that will survive the termination of the underlying agreement such as, any outstanding payment obligations, the return of equipment or continuing license rights. See Form N.2 §3 for model language addressing these issues.

In the event of a non-payment claim, the creditor, usually the vendor, should insist on the inclusion of language protecting its claim for payment in the event the debtor, usually the customer, declares bankruptcy, and the amount paid or payable to the creditor is considered to be a preference. If the claim is considered to be a preference, and the creditor settled the dispute for less than the full amount of its claim in return for payment, the creditor should be entitled to submit its full claim to the bankruptcy trustee, not the reduced amount agreed to in settling the claim prior to bankruptcy. See the language below and Form N.3 for a release with model language seeking to protect the creditor's claim in the event of the debtor's bankruptcy.

> *This Settlement Agreement and the obligations of the Parties derived hereunder will be void, and have no force or effect, and the Parties will each be entitled to enforce all of their respective rights, and remedies against each other if the transactions referred to in this Settlement Agreement are set aside, cancelled or voided by a court of law, equity or bankruptcy (collectively, a "Set Aside") at any time. Set Aside shall include, without limitation, set aside, cancellation or avoidance of this Settlement Agreement, and/or the payments made thereby in any proceedings involving any of the parties such that Vendor is required to disgorge any funds or is requited to make any payment to the estate of Customer or to a trustee for Customer in bankruptcy, insolvency, or other proceeding involving Customer.*

Finally, in executing a release, the releasing party should carve out fraud and any other unknown claims that may later arise. *ADM Alliance Nutrition, Inc. v. SGA Pharm. Lab, Inc.*, 877 F.3d 742 (7th. Cir. 2017) (unambiguous release released seller from all claims arising out of its supply contract, whether known, or unknown, including claims for breach of contract and fraud).

3. *PRACTICE POINT*: Checklist for drafting a release agreement.

In the event the dispute arises over the customer exceeding the license's scope of use, the vendor should ensure the release addresses the following points:

- Payment for all past due license fees
- The adoption of a Software Code of Ethics by the licensee (See Form P.10)
- Enforcement of the licensee's Software Code of Ethics
- A requirement that the customer conduct annual training on its employees' obligations to comply with the Software Code of Ethics
- On an annual basis, the provision of a certificate to the vendor from an authorized officer of the customer certifying the customer's compliance with the obligations set forth above
- An annual audit by vendor of the customer's compliance with its Software Code of Ethics and the terms of the underlying license agreement

CHAPTER **31**

Best Practices for Contract Drafting and Successful Implementation

One means of limiting contractual risk is to implement a quality assurance program to ensure the entity's internal standards are consistent with industry best practices. A robust program will include creating uniform terms and conditions, eliminating ambiguity in the agreement, implementing peer review, using an authority matrix, and auditing compliance with these best practices after contract execution. Set forth below is a discussion of these methods and the benefits that may be achieved through their use.

A. It All Begins with Marketing and Sales

A strong relationship between the parties starts with the marketing and sales process allowing the parties to develop a strong level of trust through the process. To that end, the vendor should avoid making misleading statements, including statements that are misleading by omission, make promises that it cannot keep such as delivery dates, or functionality that is still under development. It is extremely important to manage the client's expectations especially issues that are important to the client such as, the software's functionality, and the timeline for delivery

1. Marketing

Depending on a party's intellectual property portfolio marketing may involve an entity's copyrights, trademarks, patents, trade dress, and rights of publicity. Both parties will most likely have policies, and procedures for the use of their intellectual property. The parties should ensure that they have received the appropriate approvals for the use of their own intellectual property as well as the intellectual property of the counter party.

PRACTICE POINT: **Checklist for avoiding issues arising from the vendor's marketing efforts:**

- Use the most precise words to describe accurately the vendor's products and services being careful to not mislead the customer.
- Confirm all factual statements are current, specific, accurate, and true

- Obtain all required consents for all price quotations
- Describe how the offering will help customers instead of stating an alleged fact. For example, instead of "Vendor's Software will reduce costs by 25%.," state "Vendor's Software can help Customer reduce costs" or "Vendor's Software will support Customer's cost reduction efforts."
- Do not make promises with respect to:
  - The vendor's future products, and/or services
  - The benefits of using the vendor's products, and/or services
- As to third party trademarks, branding, logos, or references:
  - Confirm generalized third parties referenced cannot be identified from the context of the reference
  - Obtain written consent to use such third-party materials in all marketing materials
  - Ensure use of all third-party materials contain appropriate notations and attribution
- Document all marketing claims with evidence from a reputable source (there must be a reasonable basis for claims) and retaining such evidence
- Carefully review the wording, and context of all marketing materials and claims

As to third party partners:

- Ensure all partners' claims are being made by (and clearly attributable to) them. When possible, reference their online statements, and the applicable URL
- Prohibit third parties from using a party's trademarks, logos, or references without approval from the party that owns such marks, logos, branding etc.
- Ensure all third-party confidential information has been removed

Special attention should be given to the marketing, and sale of cyber-security products as no product can completely prevent a cyber-security incident or data breach. No software product should be advertised as completely secure as there are significant risks with describing a product as "secure" in an unqualified manner. *See Ohanian v. Apple Inc.*, 2021 WL 5331753 (S.D.N.Y. Nov. 16, 2021) (consumer claim allowed to proceed against Apply for making representations regarding secure nature of iMessage and FaceTime). *See also, In re Intel Corp. CPU Marketing, Sales Practices and Prods. Liability Litig.*, 2020 WL 1495304 (D. Or. Mar 27, 2020) (Intel's statements regarding "cutting edge security," and consumers being "safe and secure at home" were actionable as misrepresentations).

The FTC has made online security a priority, and there is proposed rulemaking under consideration. The FTC has made clear that it does not require "perfect" security, and the fact of a breach does not necessarily mean that a company's security was unreasonable. Avoiding advertising of products as completely secure will limit the vendor's risk in the event of a security incident or breach.

2. *Sales Commitments*

While salespeople are compensated to close deals, they must be careful in how they communicate with potential customers, and the statements they make. All communications should be accurate, and truthful, using precise language to communicate the functionality of the vendor's products and services. Vendors should never denigrate, criticize competitors, or repeat unflattering information they may have heard about the competitor or its products. Instead, vendors should emphasize the superior quality, and functionality of their products and services in comparison to their competitors.

B. Focus on Creating a Long-Term, Mutually Beneficial Agreement

The amount of effort that goes into negotiating one-sided agreements takes away from the creation of a long-term positive relationship between the parties. Avoid imposing unrealistic terms, or time lines on the other party, such as seeking guaranteed savings. Creating a true partnership will make it much easier to resolve disputes, and develop a strong business relationship. A strong relationship will likely result in additional business, and higher profit margins for the vendor.

C. Carefully Craft and Understand the Definitions

The failure of the parties to clearly define, and understand the relevant terms in an agreement creates a significant risk. A definition should stand on its own, providing a clear meaning to the defined word, and should not include contractual provisions, or use the defined term in the definition. Incorporating terms of the agreement in the definition will likely create conflicts in interpretation, while including the defined term in the definition creates a circular meaning. To avoid these types of issues, the drafting parties should focus on making the definition clear, succinct, and unambiguous without using adjectives.

The parties are free to define terms as they see fit, and are not bound by common understandings in the industry. The definitions set forth in the license agreement will control the interpretation of the agreement irrespective of whether they conform to common usage in the industry. Thus, the parties should carefully draft the definitions, and make sure they understand the impact those definitions will have on the interpretations of the agreement. *See Accusoft Cor. v. Quest Diagnostics Inc.*, 2012 WL 1358662 (D. Mass. Apr. 18, 2012) (definition of "concurrent user" agreed to by the parties differed from common industry understanding, giving rise to claim of breach of the license).

D. Create Uniform Terms, Conditions, and Processes

A second means in reducing contractual risk is to create a standard set of terms, and conditions that can be used as a starting point for all negotiations throughout the contracting entity. Utilizing standard terms ensures that the entity's employees are starting the negotiation process with terms that are favorable to the entity, and have been approved by the entity's legal counsel. Through repeated use, the entity's employees will gain familiarity with an agreement's terms, and the risks involved in accepting alternative language. Further, the entity can update its terms to reflect lessons learned from other negotiations, and projects as well as changes in the law. Prudent parties should review their templates annually to ensure their template agreements reflect current market terms, and best practices. Ideally, all employees involved in the contracting process should understand the meaning, and purpose of the agreement's contractual terms. Detailed knowledge of an agreement's terms will allow the employees to better assess the risks involved.

Realistically, it is unlikely that a licensor, or licensee will be able to utilize its preferred terms at the start of every negotiation. In many situations, but particularly in large transactions, the customer has greater leverage, and thus is able to require the vendor to use the customer's terms as a starting point. It is unlikely; however, that the customer will have standard terms for every contemplated transaction, as cost and time considerations will dictate the creation of standard terms only for those transactions that arise on a frequent basis, such as nondisclosure agreements.

To the extent practical, a licensor, or licensee should create a playbook/matrix setting forth its acceptable, preferred, and minimum positions for all material terms in an agreement. The preferred position is the position a party seeks to allow it to meet its contractual obligations with a comfortable margin of error, and thus a small amount of risk. The acceptable position is the position that is acceptable to a party although the level of risk is higher than the party would like to accept. The minimum position represents the maximum level of risk a party is willing to accept before walking away from the contract. Providing a guideline as to acceptable, and preferred positions allows a licensor's, or licensee's negotiation team to know their limits of authority. While there will always be the tendency to accept the "minimum" position to get the deal done, a minimum position ensures that the individuals negotiating the agreement can only promote a position acceptable to the entity.

In creating a matrix, it should be clearly stated that an individual negotiating an agreement cannot accept a term less favorable than the minimum position without obtaining prior approval from a higher authority. While the licensor, or licensee may ultimately accept a position less favorable than the stated minimum position, the matrix ensures that the decision to do so will be made outside of the negotiating sales team, which may have a financial incentive to assume an unacceptable amount of risk.

See Section K. below for a discussion on the use of authority matrices and Form O.4 for a model authority matrix.

E. Use Plain Language and Choose Your Words Carefully

1. Choice of Words

As the court in *Neon Enterprise Software, LLC v. International Business Machines*, 2011 WL 830737, * at 6 (W.D. Tex. Feb. 17, 2011), so clearly stated:

A party who fails to properly protect itself in a contract must suffer the consequences of poor drafting; ideally, the plain meaning of a contract will reflect the circumstances surrounding the contract's creation and embody the parties' reasonable expectations.

Similarly, every word and clause in a contract is presumed to have meaning, and to have a purpose. *Reyes v. Metromedia Software, Inc.*, 840 F. Supp. 2d 752, 755 (S.D.N.Y. 2012) ("a court must evaluate the disputed language 'in the context of the entire agreement .... [to] safeguard against adopting an interpretation that would render any individual provision superfluous.'").

While the risk of having a contract interpreted against the drafter can be avoided by including a mutual drafting language (see Form B.3.1 § 51), the parties should choose their words carefully to avoid open-ended interpretations, and to ensure that every statement is unambiguous. Open-ended, ambiguous wording benefits neither party, as each party seeks certainty, and to avoid the cost and distraction of entering into the dispute resolution process. *See, e.g., Primary Investments, LLC v. Wee Tender Care III, Inc.*, 746 S.E.2d 823 (Ga. App. 2013) (failure to carefully define the "seller" of day-care business limited purchaser's ability to enforce accompanying covenant of non-competition).

Prudent vendors should avoid superlatives, such as "best," "most," "proven," "greatest," "largest," "world class," "success," "best of breed" and "leading edge," which may give rise to claims of an implied warranty by the customer in the event of a dispute. At the same time, vendors should emphasize the pro-competitive aspects of their products, such as reducing of costs, while avoiding anti-competitive terms, such as "dominant" or "pricing or margin leverage."

Too often the parties draft important provisions, such as the license grant, in broad flowing terms without considering the implications of doing so. From the licensor's perspective, the licensor should seek to succinctly, and clearly define not only the licensee's rights but also the limitations of its rights. Utilizing broad language will likely give rise to future problems if a dispute arises over the licensee's rights. *See, e.g., Edgenet, Inc. v. Home Depot U.S.A., Inc.*, 658 F.3d 662 (7th Cir. 2011) (broad unrestrictive license grant permitted licensee to copy copyrighted materials and create derivative works).

To avoid ambiguity, the parties should use an active voice when drafting the parties' obligations. Further, drafting should be in the present tense.

In particular, the following words and phrases should be avoided:

All: The use of the word "all" in some contexts is imprecise. As the context dictates, best practices are to establish a definitive list or otherwise limit the meaning to a finite set. Every effort should be made to avoid the use of "all" in a contractual context that allows the parties to adopt different connotations of its meaning.

As necessary: Who decides what is necessary, and on what basis?

Authorized: Who decides if an action is "authorized"? On what criteria is an action "authorized"?

Best in Class or **World Leader:** Any such statement must be validated by an independent third-party such as Gartner. Alternatively use *highly effective*.

Cutting Edge: Is subjective and should be avoided. *See, In re Intel Corp. CPU Marketing, Sales Practices and Prods. Liability Litig.*, 2020 WL 1495304 (D. Or. Mar 27, 2020) (Intel's statements regarding "cutting edge security" and consumers being "safe and secure at home were actionable as misrepresentations).

Easy: Use *easier* instead, and describe why a process is easier as *easy* is subjective.

Eliminate: Use *lower, reduce* or *mitigate.*

End-to-end solution: Use this phrase only if it is factually accurate.

Ensure: "Ensure" can be construed to equate to a guarantee. Depending on the context, "validate," "verify," "confirm," "improve," "enhance," "support," or "test" are preferable, and will hopefully limit any connotation that a party is guaranteeing a result. In the few instances where it is difficult to eliminate the word "ensure," the parties may want to consider utilizing the phrase "in an effort to ensure."

Equal to or **Higher than the Industry Standard:** This phrase in relation to performance, or service levels is open to interpretation, leading to potential friction between the parties. For example, often an industry standard will not exist, i.e., there is no "industry standard" for data protection. Thus, the parties should avoid any similar language as well, including "a reasonable standard," "highest industry standard," "the same security as the recipient but no less than a reasonable standard of care," etc.

Expert: Use *experienced professional.*

Foreseeable: "Foreseeable" is subjective, and will likely be interpreted differently by the parties. *See Nissan North America, Inc. v. Schrader Electronics, Ltd.*, 2014 WL 5410296 (M.D. Tenn. Oct. 23, 2014).

Improve: Use *enhance.*

Includes/Including: References to the words "include" or "including" will likely be construed as meaning "without limitation." With the exception of the phrase "only includes" or the use of similar restrictive or limiting language, the use of "includes/including" suggests that a list is not definitive, and that there are additional responsibilities or obligations other than those listed. Prudent parties should use the following alternative language:

- are;
- consists of;
- comprises;
- the following;
- includes only; and
- is as follows.

Relevant: "Relevant" is also subjective by nature, leaving it open for interpretation by the parties, increasing the potential for dispute. Who is to say what is relevant? When used to reference compliance with a law, "applicable" is a preferred substitute, as the law dictates when it applies and when it does not.

Resolve or **Remedy**: Potentially create a legal obligation to resolve or fix. Use *address*.

Secure: No software system is ever secure. Use *improve/enhance security*. See the discussion above in Section 31.A regarding the use of the term "secure" in relation to modifying and selling cyber-security products.

Shall/Will: Avoid as these can be interpreted as a covenant or promise.

Other words and phrases that should be avoided include:

- "as necessary"
- authorized
- best practices/best efforts/best
- complete
- crucial
- free
- fully responsible/personally responsible
- highest quality/highest standard
- immediately
- industry standard
- increase margins/enhance profitability
- maximize
- meet/fully meet/exceed requirements or expectations
- minimize
- optimum
- partner/partnership – potentially infers profit sharing
- prevent
- proven/prove
- satisfaction – too subjective
- specialized in
- state-of-the-art/cutting-edge
- success/successful (e.g., "We are committed to your success." Can be interpreted as a warranty or covenant)
- total satisfaction – too subjective
- uniquely qualified
- will/will result in
- world-class
- works for hire

2. *Terminology Harmonization*

Ambiguity in agreements often arises because the negotiation process is bifurcated among different functional groups within each party, such as legal, finance, technology, etc. Often these functional groups negotiate their respective portions of the underlying agreement without the active participation of the other functions. As a result of this disjunctive approach, each function may use different terminology, or ascribe different meanings to the same terminology. Both parties should ensure that their negotiating teams contain representatives from all functional areas to ensure consistency in approach throughout the underlying agreement. Further, both parties should carefully review the completed document prior to execution to ensure the consistent use of terminology throughout the agreement, and consistency of the definitions ascribed to the terminology.

In a larger sense, this issue extends beyond terminology. Each function should be familiar with all significant aspects of the transaction to avoid potential problems during the delivery phase. If each function focuses solely on its responsibilities, an issue will likely "fall between the cracks," potentially causing a problem later in the relationship.

3. Avoid Creating New Obligations

The vendor should avoid creating new obligations through the execution of an earlier agreement, or by reference in another obligation. Any earlier iteration of the underlying agreement should be disclaimed through the agreement's integration clause, which should be comprehensive to disclaim any previous agreements or oral statements. See Form B.3.1 § 58. Service providers, and subcontractors to whom client data is provided should maintain a comprehensive data security program, which should include reasonable and appropriate technical, organizational, and security measures against the destruction, loss, unauthorized access, or alteration of client data.

Any generalized commitment that is subjective should be avoided, for example: "Vendor will perform *appropriate* security audits." To the extent the vendor agrees to abide by a customer standard, a "gap analysis" should be undertaken to quantify any additional effort the vendor must take to bring the vendor's standards into compliance with the customer's standards, and the cost of doing so.

Unintended contractual commitments can also arise through the exchange of emails, and electronic documents. The parties should carefully respond to electronic communications, especially those containing offers, or negotiated terms. *See Cunningham v. Zurich Am. Ins.* Co., 352 S.W.3d 519, 530 (Tex. App. 2011) (declining to hold that signature block satisfied signature requirement); *but see Williamson v. Bank of New York*, 947 F. Supp. 2d 704 (N.D. Tex. 2013) (rejecting *Cunningham* and holding that signature block satisfied signature requirement).

> *This e-mail neither constitutes an agreement to conduct transactions by electronic means nor creates any legally binding contract or enforceable obligation in the absence of a fully signed written contract. [Contract terms contained in this e-mail are subject to approval by [PARTY] and are not binding until [PARTY] provides such approval in writing.]*

4. Headings and Formatting

Headings and formatting can make an agreement easier to read and understand, thus eliminating potential ambiguity. To the extent possible, headings should be used to clearly communicate the subject matter of the paragraph and its contents.

Formatting through the use of shorter paragraphs with the use of numbered subparagraphs as well as bullets allows the reader to more easily comprehend the intent of the written words. In the event of an ambiguity, the meaning of the ambiguous language will be decided by a third party who will have no knowledge of the parties' intent. Thus, the formatting is important to help convey the parties' intent, and ideally eliminate any ambiguity.

5. *Eliminate Legalese*

Too often parties use overt legalese where the use of plain English can avoid potential misinterpretations and challenges in the future. Terms such as *heretofore, to wit, and except as otherwise provided in this Agreement* are likely to spawn confusion. Prudent parties should use simple, easy to understand language that can be clearly understood by non-lawyers who may be called to interpret the language in the event of a dispute. Instead, of providing "Except as provided in this Agreement…", the parties should instead state "Except as provided in Sections 11 and 17 of this Agreement, …." to avoid a potential misinterpretation. Make sure to be specific!

F. Eliminate Ambiguity

A contract is considered to be ambiguous "when it is reasonably susceptible to more than one reading." *Reyes v. Metromedia Software, Inc.*, 840 F. Supp. 2d 752 (S.D.N.Y. 2012), *citing U.S. Fire Ins. Co. v. Gen. Reinsurance Corp.*, 949 F.2d 569, 572 (2d Cir.1991). Conflicting contractual provisions may create ambiguity in an agreement. *Fraternal Order of Police v. City of Fairmont*, 468 S.E.2d 712 (W.Va. 1996).

Eliminating ambiguity is perhaps the most important element for reducing risk in an agreement. Disputes usually do not arise from a limitation of liability provision, or a disclaimer of warranties but rather from ambiguity relating to a definition, the license grant, pricing, a statement of work, or other fundamental terms related to what the licensor will deliver. Both parties should strive to create a contract that is clear, concise, and easily understandable, as well as one that can be easily adjudicated by an unrelated third party, such as a judge or an arbiter. One way to do so is to create concise, single subject paragraphs free of compound sentences that will allow an unrelated third party (i.e., a judge, juror, arbiter) to understand the parties' intent.

Further, do not "overdraft" the language, repeat a term multiple times or repeat prohibitions to avoid gaps or inconsistencies in the language that may create ambiguity. The trend toward using "we", "us", "you", "your" also increases the risk of ambiguity and should be used only in consumer agreements, if at all.

Too often, parties draft a contract based on their common understanding of the underlying transaction, which arises through many months of negotiations, and meetings without providing sufficient contractual detail or clarity. In some cases, the licensee may not understand the rights it needs to utilize the software as contemplated, or realize that it did not receive the use rights required to operate its business. *See SAP UK Limited v. Diageo Great Britain Ltd.* [2017] EWHC 189 (TCC).

Ambiguity can arise in many forms:

- The failure to clearly define terms, leading each party to ascribe their own definition to terms in question. *See, e.g., JA Apparel Corp. v. Abboud*, 568 F.3d 390 (2d Cir. 2009) (agreement ambiguous as term "name" could be interpreted in two different manners).
- The failure to use the correct terminology in the license grant, *Vernor v. Audodesk, Inc.*, 621 F.3d 1102 (9th Cir. 2010) (agreement granted limited license, and was not a sale).
- The failure to clearly state license restrictions. *See Creative Minds v. FedEx Office and Print Services, Inc.*, 886 F.3d 91 (2d Cir. 2018) (express prohibition in license required to restrict non-exclusive licensee exercise of license).
- The failure to clearly establish their rights upon termination, including ownership, use, and access to data. *See, e.g., DRL Software Solutions, LLC v. JourneyPure, LLC*, 2018 WL 6407616 (S.D.N.Y. Dec. 6, 2018).
- The failure to contemplate and address potential future problems/issues.
- The failure to clearly state the contractual requirements. *Weinberg .v Waystar, Inc.*, 294 A.3d 1039 (Del. 2023) ("and" meant "or" in the context of the document).
- The failure to address in detail the parties' rights upon termination. *See, e.g., Topps Co., Inc. v. Cadbury Stani S.A.L.C.*, 526 F.3d 63 (2d Cir. 2008) (license agreement ambiguous as licensee's rights upon termination open for interpretation).
- The failure to use precise language in the agreement, change orders, and the statement of work. *Honeywell International, Inc. v. Opto Electronics Co., Ltd.*, 2023 WL 6367671 (W.D.N.C. Sept. 27, 2023) (Failure to include the word "legal" in fee recovery provision precluded the recovery of legal fees.); *Midwest Medical Solutions, LLC v. Exactech U.S., Inc.*, 21 F.4th 1002 (8th Cir. 2021) (manufacturer required to pay representative 7.5% of the total sales from the trailing 12-month period each month for six months, instead of 7.5% of sales paid in six monthly installments as it intended).
- Lack of detail in eliminating conflicting terms within the agreement. Rey *v. Lafferty*, 990 F.2d 1379, 1384 (1st Cir. 1993) (contract language "usually considered ambiguous "where "an agreement's terms are inconsistent on their face . . . . ")
- The failure to establish clear lines of communication.
- The failure to ensure adequate levels of accountability.
- The failure to catch typos. *See Fetch Interactive Television v. Touchstream Technologies, Inc.* 2019 WL 193921 (Del. Ch. Jan. 15, 2019) ("[FetchIT] shall cure such default within *fifteen (30)* days or immediately if deemed to be incurable.") (UCC-3-114: "words prevail over numbers").
- The failure to appreciate the importance of punctuation. *See O'Connor v. Oakhurst Dairy*, 851 F.3d 69 (1st. Cir. 2017) (absence of comma created ambiguity); *Gibraltar Private Bank & Tr. Co. v. Bos. Private Fin. Holdings, Inc.*, 2011 WL 6000792 (Del. Ch. Nov. 30, 2011) (lack of a comma created ambiguity).

One means of reducing ambiguity is to include, if appropriate, diagrams, or examples. Examples may be appropriate in illustrating the calculation of license fees, and royalty payments. The inclusion of these aids may not eliminate a dispute, but they will guide a third party adjudicating any dispute in ascertaining the parties' intent. Generic examples also provide a means to define general terms. Matrices indicating each party's responsibilities may also serve to reduce ambiguities. Outsourcing agreements commonly use matrices to assign responsibility for various activities to the vendor, the customer, or both parties jointly. For a more detailed discussion, *see* Jones, *Envisioning Visual Contracting: Why Non-Textual Tools and Content Will Improve Your Contracting*, 2 CONTRACTING EXCELLENCE 27 (No. 6 Aug. 15, 2009), International Association for Contract and Commercial Management (IACCM), available at www.worldcc.com/Resources/Content-Hub/View/ArticleId/7402/Envisioning-visual-contracting-why-nontextual-tools-will-improve-your-contracting.

Another means of avoiding ambiguity is through the use of checklists. A checklist allows a party to apply best practices to its contracting processes, and is a useful means to ensure a particular provision, or concern has not been overlooked. See the forms in Section R for several checklists setting forth best practices.

A third method of eliminating ambiguity is through the implementation of a robust education program to train all employees involved with the contract negotiation and drafting, on issue-spotting and best practices. One of the most effective means of educating employees is by using examples where a party's expectations were not met, because of the use of ambiguous language.

See, e.g., Practice Point for Avoiding Scope Creep in Section 31.N below.

Often in the event of a dispute over a contract's interpretation, or the parties' intent after a contract's execution, the parties find that the contract does not clearly address the issue in question. The likelihood of a dispute is foreseeable, as the parties often enter into extended negotiations, the result of which is that each party clearly understands the desires of the other party, and the deal at the time of contract signature. While each party previously understood the issues at the time of contract execution, problems can arise when the individuals involved in the negotiation are no longer involved in the transaction, and their successors lack the detailed knowledge of their predecessors. *See, e.g., Upper Deck Co., LLC v. BreaKey Int'l*, 2004 WL 2980190, at *3 (S.D.N.Y. Dec. 22, 2004) (language requiring developer to deliver source code "necessary to enable consumers to use the product . . . in the same manner as the Product is presently operated" is ambiguous).

The parties' relationship is usually strongest at the time of contract signature. After execution, the individuals involved usually transition from the negotiation team to a new group of individuals that is responsible for delivering the deliverables, and managing the contract. Often, the new individuals lack the historical knowledge arising from the negotiation. Thus, the parties should make every effort to document all aspects of the transaction in minute detail and resist the temptation to address and document an issue after contract signature.

Whether a contract is ambiguous is a question of law to be resolved by a court. *Leprino Foods Co. v. Gress Poultry, Inc.*, 379 F. Supp. 2d 659 (M.D. Pa. 2005). A court interpreting a contract must first assess whether the contract is ambiguous. "To answer the ambiguity question, the court must first examine the language of the contract by itself, independent of extrinsic evidence concerning the drafting history or the intention of the parties." *Bank v. Thermo Elemental Inc.*, 451 Mass. 638, 648, 888 N.E.2d 897 (2008). "Ambiguity is not created merely because the litigants disagree about the meaning of a contract." *Nicolaci v. Anapol*, 387 F.3d 21, 26 (1st Cir. 2004). Rather, "a contract is only ambiguous where an agreement's terms are inconsistent on their face, or where the phraseology can support reasonable differences of opinion as to the meaning of the words employed and obligations undertaken." *Bank v. Int'l Bus. Machs. Corp.*, 145 F.3d 420, 424 (1st Cir. 1998) (quotations and citations omitted). The meaning of an unambiguous contract term is a question of law, while the meaning of an ambiguous contract term is a question of fact. *Seaco Ins. Co. v. Barbosa*, 435 Mass. 772, 779, 761 N.E.2d 946 (2002); *see also Fairfield 274-278 Clarendon Trust v. Dwek*, 970 F.2d 990, 993 (1st Cir. 1992). "Should the court find the contract language unambiguous, we interpret it according to its plain terms." *Den Norske Bank AS v. First Nat'l Bank of Boston*, 75 F.3d 49, 52 (1st Cir. 1996).

Ambiguity will usually be resolved through the use of a "four-corners" approach where the court will seek to determine the intent of the parties from reading the agreement as a whole. *Scungio v. Scungio*, 6713 N.W.2d (Okla. 2012). In a minority of jurisdictions, the court will allow the introduction of intrinsic evidence to determine the intent of the parties. *Lietz v. Hansen Law Offices, P.S.C.*, 271 P.3d 899 (Wash. App. 2012).

Individual clauses will be subordinated to the overall intent of the parties by reading the contract as a whole. RESTATEMENT (SECOND) OF CONTRACTS §§ 202(2), 230, 233. Courts will look to commercial reasonableness in attempting to interpret an ambiguous contract, and will examine the conflicting interpretations of the parties to ascertain which "interpretation fits both the language of the contract and the contract's commercial setting . . . ." *Sutter Insurance Co. v. Applied Systems, Inc.*, 393 F.3d 722, 726 (7th Cir. 2004). The intent of the parties must be ascertained from the entire agreement. *Waldman v. Shoemaker*, 80 A.2d. 776 (Pa. 1951). Greater weight will be placed on the specific terms of the agreement over general language. *County of Suffolk v. Alcorn*, 266 F.3d 131 (2d Cir. 2001); RESTATEMENT (SECOND) OF CONTRACTS § 203(c) (1981). Terms will be interpreted to give "the meaning that would be ascribed to it by a reasonably intelligent person who was acquainted with all of the usages and circumstances surrounding the making of the writing." *Unihealth v. U.S. Healthcare, Inc.*, 14 F. Supp. 2d 623, 633 (D.N.J. 1998).

If the court is unable to resolve the ambiguity, it will be construed against the drafter, or the person who supplies the words and meanings. *See Wiser v. Enervest Operating, L.L.C..*, 803 F. Supp. 2d 109 (N.D.N.Y. 2011) (contract will be interpreted against the drafter as the drafter is responsible for the ambiguity). *Current Tech. Concepts v. Irie Enterprises*, 530 N.W.2d 539 (Minn. 1995); RESTATEMENT (SECOND) OF CONTRACTS §§ 206, 261(c). As such, the party drafting the agreement should include language to the effect that each party was involved in the drafting and negotiation of the agreement, and that neither party should be deemed to be the drafter of the agreement. See § 51.

For an excellent discussion of drafting ambiguity-free contracts, *see* FELDMAN & NIMMER, DRAFTING EFFECTIVE CONTRACTS: A PRACTITIONER'S GUIDE, 4th ed. (2023).

See also Adams, *Making a Mess of Ambiguity: Lessons from the Third Circuit's Opinion in 'Meyer v. CUNA Mutual Insurance Society,'* at https://www.adamsdrafting.com/wp/wp-content/uploads/2014/07/Making-Mess-Ambiguity.pdf.

PRACTICE POINT:

In conducting a final review of the document, each party should:

- Check the definitions whenever a defined word is used to ensure that it is actually defined, and it's use is correct;
- Not copy and paste clauses from other agreements without checking for ambiguity in the new context;
- Assume that even if a word has appeared before, it may still be considered ambiguous in its present context.
- Ensure terminology is used consistently. For example, if you refer to attachments as schedules, or exhibits in the agreement do not alternate in how you refer to them.
- Not agree to provisions it does not understand;
- Avoid latent ambiguities by understanding the underlying transaction;
- Review the document after putting it aside for some period of time to proof it with a clear mind;
- Check the interrelationship of each part of the agreement against the remainder, particularly as structural integrity is weakened by changes to the original form;
- Know the general rules of construction, e.g., terms should be interpreted so that all terms have effect. These rules or guidelines should be used only to test whether there is ambiguity if they were to be applied, and they should not be relied on in countenancing ambiguity.
- If using a template agreement as a starting point, ensure the template is modified to reflect the terms of the transaction.
- Ensure the agreement grants the customer the rights it needs while protecting the vendor's interests.
- Establish and understand the vendor's performance standards
- Consider privacy and security issues.
- Consider the basis for, and implications of termination.

G. Clearly Document the Parties' Obligations ("Never Agree to Agree")

All obligations between the parties should be agreed to, and documented at the time of contract execution. The parties should never defer negotiating contractual obligations, "agree to agree" at a later date, or defer executing ancillary agreements, such as escrow agreements, service levels, or services agreements until after execution of the principal agreement. Kicking the can down the road does not further the interests of either party and may put the parties' agreement at risk. *See, e.g., Warner Bros. Int'l. T.V. Distrib. v. Golden Channels & Co.*, 522 F.3d 1060, 1070 (9th Cir. 2008) ("Failure to agree was not a breach because as agreement to agree is not a contract."). If the parties cannot avoid utilizing "agreement to agree" language, the agreement should set forth the impact of the parties not agreeing at a later date, e.g., either party may terminate the agreement without liability if the agreement cannot be reached in 30 days.

During the life of the agreement, all changes, and modifications should be contemporaneously documented through the change-order process in the underlying agreement, including any notices, waivers, consents, or resolutions of disputes agreed to by the parties. Further, the parties should maintain, and distribute internally records of all such agreements. To the extent the parties undertake a remedial plan, the documents setting forth, and confirming the plan should clearly state whether the plan constitutes a waiver of past noncompliance, and whether or not the action is precedential..

Finally, all change orders should be undertaken in conformance with the agreement's change order process. See Chapter 7.D.

H. Do Not Ignore the Exhibits and Schedules

Many parties fail to use skilled and knowledgeable writers to draft, and review an agreement's exhibits and schedules. Skilled writers possess extensive industry knowledge, and are experienced in drafting clear, unambiguous, technical documents. A technical resource may have great technical skills but is not necessarily qualified to draft, and negotiate a statement of work, or the functional specifications. It is the rare person who can understand the technical requirements of a transaction, and clearly express those obligations on paper.

Too often, the parties view the schedules and exhibits as an afterthought, yet in reality the schedules, and exhibits are often the most important aspect of a contract. The schedules and exhibits are one of the most important aspects of an agreement because they set forth what will be delivered as well as the obligations of both parties. Both parties should ensure that they carefully review the schedules and exhibits prior to contract execution, and that these documents clearly establish the obligations of the parties that reflect both parties' understanding of the transaction.

I. Use A Playbook

Playbooks set forth responses, and fallback positions when responding to the opposing party's proposed terms, which help to ensure users understand the purpose of the clause in question. They also explain why a party takes a particular position. They allow a party to respond with consistent terms/positions. Most playbooks set forth when an issue must be elevated to a higher level (i.e., finance, compliance, risk management, privacy, tax etc.) for approval ensuring the risk has been approved at the appropriate level, and creating accountability. Using a playbook shortens negotiations resulting in cost savings, and a reduced time to contract. Playbooks also allow a party to funnel lower value work to para-professionals, freeing lawyers to work on high value matters.

See Form M.3.2 for a model playbook for non-disclosure agreements.

J. Use an Authority Matrix

Every entity should create an authority matrix to ensure that any agreement receives the appropriate level of scrutiny prior to execution, as well as any amendments, or change orders executed after execution of the underlying agreement. A prudent entity will require the agreement to be approved by all functions involved with the delivery, or acceptance of the deliverables to ensure all aspects of the agreement meet the entity's requirements. The level of approvals will usually depend on the dollar value of the contract, and the risk involved. From the licensor's perspective, risk is usually an element of cost, functionality, and the time in which the deliverables must be provided. As such, at a minimum, representatives from the following areas should be required to review, and/or approve the agreement: finance, project management/information technology, delivery assurance/quality assurance, and the business sponsor. Members of the sales team should be prohibited from signing sales contracts, as doing so is a direct conflict of interest.

Ideally, depending on the size of the deal and the size of the company, the division president, or the division CFO should be the only party who can execute an agreement. It is important that there should be clear guidance as to who is authorized to sign an agreement. Requiring a senior officer to sign the agreement will increase accountability by having the senior person accept responsibility for the terms of the agreement. Too often when a problem arises, managers are quick to point the finger at others. Having a senior person execute the agreement will likely cause that person to implement quality measures, and have the authority to enforce them. The matrix may also provide that modifications to terms such as warranties, indemnification, and limitation of liability may not be agreed to without approval from the legal, and finance departments. Certain terms, such as returns, future discounts, credits, and road mapping, may not be agreed to without approval from an identified level of management, as such changes may impact the vendor's ability to recognize revenue.

To the extent the parties execute a change order, authority matrices should clearly indicate who has authority to execute such changes. Although the dollar value of a change order may be small, the change order may have a significant impact on the deliverables, finances, and each party's performance obligations under the agreement.

Finally, many companies have issues with document control, and often cannot locate a contract after it has been executed. If signature authority is vested in only a small number of people, it is much easier to track the executed contracts after contract signature. Creating a central repository to which all executed agreements must be sent will help eliminate document control issues.

See Form O.4 for a model Authority Matrix.

K. Use a Deal Desk

A deal desk acts as a final checkpoint to ensure all transactional risks have been identified, and addressed prior to contract signing. During a deal desk review, the project sponsor presents the benefits and risks of the proposed transaction to a cross-functional group who probe, and then ultimately approve or reject the proposed transaction based on the merits of the deal. If rejected, the project sponsor is usually asked to address those risks the group believes were not adequately addressed, and mitigated, and to bring the deal back for approval after the requested changes have been negotiated with the counter-party. To avoid potential issues with having to reopen negotiations with the counter-party, a deal desk review is usually held prior to the parties finalizing their negotiations, but when the negotiation is in its final stages.

Most deal desk reviews consider the following points:

- Opportunity Overview
- Product and Solution Overview
- Product / Execution Risk
- Investment Commitments
- Legal / Contract Risk
- Pricing Model
- Financials
- An Approval Log and Any Conditions to Approval

See Form O.12 for a model Deal Desk Approval Presentation.

L. Manage the Relationship/Contract

1. General

Managing the contract's lifecycle is important for both the customer, and the vendor to ensure the parties are meeting their contractual obligations. To that end, many entities utilize Contract Lifecycle Management (CLM) software to manage the process. CLM software allows a party to track its obligations, and the obligations of the counter-party including delivery dates, invoicing, auto renewals, payment terms, penalties, etc. allowing users to quickly search its contracts to identify those agreements with certain attributes, such as all contracts where it has a limitation of liability in excess of $5,000,000 or those agreements expiring in December 2026. As such, CLM software is a valuable tool for entities that have a large number of agreements.

Managing to the terms of the agreement, and maintaining an open dialogue between the parties are of the most important steps in ensuring a successful relationship.

The failure to communicate in a forthright, and open manner will lead to distrust, and long-term problems. During the development, and delivery phase, the parties should agree to meet weekly to discuss the project's progress, and to raise any issues or concerns. Once the parties have entered the testing phase, they should meet several times a week to ensure no unanticipated problems arise. Constant communication will significantly reduce the risk of a material problem and ongoing friction. A vibrant, healthy communications plan requires a significant investment in time and effort, and cannot be implemented without commitment by both parties.

A customer should be contractually required to promptly notify the vendor of any potential problems, or basis for dispute as soon as it becomes aware of any such non-performance, or potential breach. It should not be allowed to remain silent while the seriousness of the problem grows. Receipt of prompt notice will potentially allow the parties to address the problem in an expeditious fashion and restore their contractual relationship.

The parties also need to ensure that decision-making processes have been established, and that the individuals who are accountable for success have been identified. A clear escalation ladder must be established and circulated so that both parties understand how and to whom a dispute should be escalated for resolution. Further, any such escalation ladder should include short time frames for the issue in question to be resolved before it is escalated to the next higher level.

A collaborative approach allows each party to reap the benefit it bargained and will lead to a long-term mutually beneficial relationship; the transaction will be profitable for the vendor while the customer will hopefully achieve the greater operating efficiencies it seeks.

2. *PRACTICE POINT*: Checklist for avoiding problems and resolving issues.

To avoid problems and resolve issues, the parties should:

- Be proactive
    - Identify potential business concerns, and seek to resolve such concerns.
    - Identify, and escalate issues to remove roadblocks.
    - Propose practical solutions.
    - Drive matters to completion. Do not wait for others to act.
    - Follow through on all responsibilities. Do not let matters languish.
- Be solution-oriented
    - Think critically to identify the most important issues confronting the business, and the most efficient solutions.
    - Think creatively to identify multiple solutions; choose practical, efficient solutions tailored to the parties' needs.
- Ask the proverbial Second Question
    - Focus on the most important aspects of the issue.
        - What issue is causing concern?
        - What caused this issue to arise?
        - What are the other party's concerns?
        - Does the proposed path forward make practical and business sense?
- Communicate
    - Communicate in a clear, concise, easily understood manner.
    - Ensure that all individuals with a need to know are kept current on the status of all material matters.
    - Provide prompt updates in the event of a material change in a matter's status.
    - Include all relevant parties in all communications.
    - Create easily accessible written records using email chains.

M. Avoid Scope Creep

1. *Managing Scope Creep*

Scope creep is the extension of functionality or services beyond the vendor's contractual obligations without the extension being contractually documented or providing for payment of additional compensation to the vendor. Scope creep is a constant concern to the vendor, as it causes the vendor to expend additional resources without receiving additional compensation. It may also cause the vendor to incur substantial administrative costs through the vendor's subsequent attempts to document the additional services rendered at the time it becomes aware of the scope creep. Undocumented services may also contribute toward the creation of additional ill-defined short- or long-term obligations on the vendor's behalf, as well as negatively impacting the vendor's existing delivery services, including delivery dates.

Both parties should undertake a concerted effort to avoid scope creep. Vendors have a financial incentive to avoid providing services for which they are not contractually entitled to be compensated. At the same time, customers want to avoid potential disputes with the vendor or having the vendor seek compensation under a theory of *quantum meruit*. See Chapter 29.C.4 for a more detailed discussion of *quantum meruit* claims. Even if the vendor does not bring an actual claim, prudent customers will want to avoid expending the time, and effort to resolve any dispute that may in turn threaten the contractually agreed delivery schedule.

Factors that can contribute to scope creep include the following:

- The scope is not well defined in the underlying statement of work or project plan.
- Personnel performing the services do not understand that the services being provided are out of scope.
- Personnel performing the services do not understand the process they should follow to obtain authorization to perform out-of-scope work.
- Managers are not aware that out-of-scope work is being performed.
- Vendor personnel want to satisfy a demanding or disgruntled customer.
- Account management makes a deliberate decision to perform out-of-scope work without compensation.

2. *PRACTICE POINT:* Checklist for preventing, detecting, and mitigating scope creep.

- Create clearly defined and detailed contractual descriptions of the scope of work. To the extent possible, avoid adjectives, and include as much detail as reasonably possible.
- Develop, and distribute to all employees assigned to the project a concise summation of the existing scope of work.

- Educate all employees assigned to the project, including subcontractors, on the existing scope of work as well as the importance of executing a change order when new work is contemplated, or when the nature of the existing work is modified.
- Conduct due diligence prior to contract execution to clearly understand the development and delivery environment as well as the work to be performed
- Establish a strong internal governance process to address out-of-scope work issues.
- Implement a well-defined change order/amendment process and clearly communicate this process to all employees assigned to the project, including that all change orders/amendments must be executed by an authorized executive officer of each party.
- Clearly state in the agreement that the parties have no obligation to provide, or pay for out-of-scope services without a signed change order.
- Implement audit mechanisms to compare the contracted deliverable against the work being performed to assist in identifying out-of-scope work.
- Require all employees assigned to the project to promptly report any requests from the other party to perform out-of-scope work or to alter the project plan, or contracted services.
- Ensure that scope-related knowledge is transferred to new employees assigned to the project, or when there is a change in responsibility for managing the delivery of the contracted deliverables.
- Promptly notify account management, and if appropriate, consult legal counsel to assist in developing a mitigation strategy when a party becomes aware that scope creep is occurring or has occurred.
- Manage the underlying agreement's finances strictly to provide visibility into ongoing labor costs.
- Conduct frequent financial, and operational audits to identify, and correct any deviations from a party's policies, and procedures.

N. Implement Peer Review

Peer review is perhaps the best defense against ambiguity. A careful, thorough review of the documentation by a group of individuals who have not been involved in negotiating, and drafting the agreement will create a higher likelihood that any significant ambiguities, or inconsistencies will be identified. Peer reviews are also valuable for reviewing form agreements, not just negotiated transactions based on another party's forms. If time, resources, and the political climate permit, peer reviews should be mandatory for all significant transactions.

A robust Institutional Review Team ("IRT"), consisting of cross-functional employees, is crucial to providing an independent opinion on the risks inherent in a particular transaction. IRTs should be involved early on in the process. If the IRT is engaged only at the end of the process, the parties' negotiation may be too developed to allow a change in position, or the identified problem may be unable to be fixed without alienating the other party, or causing the other party to walk away from the transaction.

The delivery of a successful project requires the involvement of many functions, each of which has its own perspective. It is important that IRTs contain a broad cross-section of functions to ensure a well-rounded review. All functions that will be involved in the delivery process should be included. To ensure an unbiased review, the IRT members should be independent of the negotiation team. For example, IRT members should not have a reporting relationship to members of the negotiating team, members of the sales team, or those with a financial incentive to close the transaction. At a minimum, legal, contracts, finance, delivery assurance, project management, and technology should be included to ensure the transaction receives a thorough vetting. As an independent group, unrelated to the negotiation process, IRTs also limit "second guessing."

Peer review by employees not associated with the pursuit provides a reliable tool to avoid problems. Too often, the pursuit team uses unrealistic assumptions in order to meet customer demands which may, in and of themselves, be unrealistic. This is especially true for vendors trying to meet tight delivery deadlines. As Fred Brooks stated in his book *The Mythical Man Month: Essays on Software Engineering*, software development is linear, and delivery times cannot be shortened by simply adding resources. The "Brooks Rule" provides that adding resources at a late stage actually delays delivery.

O. Audit Compliance after Contract Execution

After the contract has been executed, both parties should audit the delivery team's compliance with its internal standards on a regular basis. For example, the vendor's finance department should undertake regular audits to ensure statements of work, project plans, change orders, and/or other contractually required documentation necessary to authorize, and be paid for work have been executed for all work being performed by the vendor, and that the customer is billed in accordance with the contract's milestones. Large unbilled, or unpaid receivables are often a sign of problems. In such an event, the finance team should question the project management team to understand why the customer has not been billed for, or paid the invoices. Further, the auditors should confirm the vendor's delivery team is utilizing the contract's change order process to capture any changes.

During the audit process, the auditors should examine the following questions:

- Have all contractual documents (License Agreement, Statements of Work, Program Definitions, Change Orders, etc.) been signed by both parties?
- Have all contractual agreements been scanned, and/or filed in the appropriate locations (e.g., central repository)?
- Is the vendor performing work without a signed statement of work, a signed change order, or other contractually authorizing document?
- Have any deliverables been rejected due to quality, or content issues?
- Has vendor's/customer's project sponsor, or vendor/customer's senior executives changed?
- Has a project review been conducted within the past 90 days, and have the results been reviewed with senior management?
- Has the project team received any negative indications (verbal, email, letter, etc.) from the customer?

- Are all invoices being paid consistent with all payment terms?
- Have any project milestones, or other time-sensitive items been missed, or are any forecasted to miss, the contractual delivery dates?
- Has the project exceeded, or is it forecasted to exceed, time schedule estimates by more than 5 percent?
- Has the project exceeded, or is it forecasted to exceed, the budget/cost estimates by more than 5 percent?
- Are there any evergreen renewal provisions requiring notification in a limited window to terminate the agreement?

Regular technical reviews should be scheduled to track the delivery team's progress against the deliverable timeline. The vendor wants to avoid any deviation that will create significant risk and additional cost. Similarly, the customer wants to avoid waiting until the delivery date to learn that there is a delivery problem. As such, the customer should monitor the vendor's progress to ensure the vendor is meeting the timeline to provide the deliverables within the contractually required time. Further, the vendor should be obligated to promptly inform the customer if the vendor knows, or suspects that the project is behind schedule, or that the deliverables will be late (§ 9.6.4).

P. Create an Early Warning System

The licensor should create an "early warning system" to monitor its progress in completing the deliverables within the parameters of the contract. The intent of an early warning system is to identify problems before it is too late to fix them. The licensor should establish a process to identify contracts with the following traits:

- Significant costs in excess of revenues during the initial phases
- Significant proposed cost deferrals
- Large billed and unbilled receivables
- Pricing modifications
- Proposed capitalization of software development costs
- Ongoing losses
- Legal disputes/settlements
- Write-offs
- The licensing of software/provision of services in overseas locations
- Corporate reports, such as delivery assurance, internal audit, or Sarbanes-Oxley that identify material deficiencies
- Potential regulatory changes that may impact the cost of delivery
- Change in management impacting relationship

A cross-functional team of legal, finance, delivery assurance, and business representatives should meet on a monthly basis to review, and resolve any potential issues that have been identified by the early warning system. Each issue should be coded red, yellow, or green to indicate the severity of the issue, and allow the members of the team to easily track the progress of the issue from month to month. The team should be careful not to include any attorney-client privileged information within the matrix to avoid potentially waiving any claim of privilege. See Form N.10 for a model Early Warning Report.

Most important, senior management should be notified promptly as soon as a material issue arises.

Q. Address Issues Promptly

To ensure a successful, positive relationship, each party's employees should thoroughly understand both parties' contractual obligations. Information technology agreements are high value agreements that address mission critical customer needs. A failed project may have a significant impact on the customer's business creating the likelihood of a costly and time-consuming distraction. Thus, both parties have a significant incentive to quickly resolve disputes before they trigger the dispute resolution process. Each party's implementation team should carefully monitor the other party's obligations, and immediately notify their management team if the other party fails to meet any of its contractual obligations, or if the party is in danger of not meeting one of its own commitments.

Bad news does not get better with age, and potential issues should be addressed as soon as they arise, or are identified. Potential issues should not be allowed to fester, but rather should be carefully documented, and promptly discussed with the other party. By carefully tracking each party's obligations, and raising potential issues in a timely manner, the parties can avoid a small issue becoming a large, and costly problem. The parties should not rely on the agreement's dispute resolution provisions to resolve the issue, as once the formal dispute resolution process is initiated, the parties' relationship may be irreparably damaged.

The parties should address those areas of the governing contract that may be ambiguous. Terminology such as "reasonable efforts," and "agree to cooperate" are subject to interpretation, potentially exacerbating a difficult issue. These issues should be addressed, and resolved before a problem arises. The best way of doing so is to establish a formal governance process whereby the parties meet on a regular basis to discuss any actual, or potential issues.

Many parties are hesitant to raise actual, or potential issues to avoid antagonizing the other party, especially if an issue has not come to fruition. In addition, a party may lack the resources to closely monitor the parties' obligations. The failure to address a potential issue may materially negatively impact a party's position, and likelihood of prevailing if a problem later arises.

To limit its risk, a party should implement detailed processes addressing document control, changes in scope, and obligation management. The failure to document changes, and issues is one of the leading causes of disputes. On the other hand, carefully documenting and managing each party's obligations, changes in scope, and issues that arise can reduce, or eliminate risk, and protect the party in the event a dispute arises.

Often agreements provide that a party must notify the other party within a stated period of time if it becomes aware of an issue. The failure to do so in essence effectively acts as a waiver. Prudent parties should include language to this effect in their agreements, as it forces a party to acknowledge an issue instead of waiting to disclose it at a later time. Forcing an issue to be disclosed allows the parties to address it in a timely manner before it becomes unmanageable, and prevents a party from failing to disclose a problem in an effort to strengthen its position.

Before raising an issue with the other party, the disclosing party should be well prepared. The party should understand the issue in question, and its genesis. The party should understand those provisions of the underlying agreement that govern its resolution, and how the risk has been allocated between the parties, if at all. The parties should discuss the issue in a frank, open manner. All communications should be managed to avoid making an admission against the party's interest, or taking an inconsistent position. Internal communications should also be managed to avoid creating a paper trail of damaging documents that will later harm the party's interest. In particular, the party should seek to have all communications circulated in a manner that maintains the attorney-client privilege.

To the extent the issue threatens the parties' relationship, the parties should consider whether the dispute resolution provisions set forth in the governing agreement are appropriate for the nature of the dispute. The parties may want to consider another mechanism to resolve the dispute outside of the agreement's contractual provisions, such as mediation.

In considering a resolution, a prudent party should carefully consider the contractual provisions governing the dispute resolution process. For example, are there any unique provisions provided for by the governing law that will provide an advantage to one party, or the other? Is the contractually identified venue favorable to the plaintiff or defendant? Is the prevailing party entitled to recover its legal fees? Each of these facts will influence how the parties move forward to resolve the issue.

R. The Role of Delivery Assurance

Delivery assurance has an important role in ensuring the vendor's successful delivery. To eliminate risk, and the cost of nonconformance, the vendor's delivery assurance team should undertake the following:

- The implementation of comprehensive tools, and processes for use with SOWs:
    - Create interactive electronic templates that guide users through the process for creating new agreements, with explanations of the need for importance of potential terms—e.g., on-demand training.
    - Review the process of who is responsible for drafting various agreements: Should the sales/delivery team draft SOWs? Should RFPs be used as the source of SOW text? What processes exist for ensuring the proper input and review?
    - Create a legal and delivery assurance deal review process and sign-off sheet for any SOWs above a certain dollar threshold (e.g., $100K), with provisions for legal escalation points.
- Enhanced accountability:
    - Whose fault is it when a deal fails during delivery? What responsibility does delivery assurance have if contractual commitments exceed the

vendor's capabilities, e.g., staffing was wrong, the delivery timetable could not be achieved, etc.? (not for failures in individual team member performance, but more conceptual level failures)

- What leverage does delivery assurance have to terminate a transaction when the transaction does not support staffing models, pricing, etc.?
- Create an "escalation" path for delivery assurance to seek assistance when the task of negotiating a SOW exceeds delivery assurance's internal resource capability or greater technical expertise is required beyond mere legal intervention.

FORM B.3.1

Software License and Services Agreement (Annotated)

The model license that follows is not intended to be used verbatim. Instead, it is intended to be used as a guide to potential clauses that may be included in an agreement while providing an explanation of the ramifications of including such clauses.

CONTENTS

7. Acceptance of Software and Services
    - 7.1 Acceptance Tests
    - 7.2 Failure to Comply
    - 7.3 Deemed Acceptance

8. Price and Payments
    - 8.1 Price
        - 8.1.A Remote Network Connectivity
    - 8.2 Cash Advances
    - 8.3 Payments to be Made with Respect to Deliverables
    - 8.4 Adjustment of Prices
        - 8.4.A Fees Charged by Licensor
    - 8.5 Interest
    - 8.6 Taxes
        - 8.6.A Taxes
            - 8.6.A.1 Responsibility
            - 8.6.A.2 Taxes on the Services
            - 8.6.A.3 Cooperation to Minimize Tax Liability
    - 8.7 Disputed Amounts
    - 8.8 Discounts
        - 8.A Most Favored Customer
        - 8.B Benchmarking
            - 8.B.1 Benchmarking Procedures
            - 8.B.2 Licensor Review of Benchmarking Results
            - 8.B.3 Customer's Acceptance or Rejection of Licensor's Plan
        - 8.C CPU License
        - 8.D CPU Upgrade
        - 8.E Transfer Fees
        - 8.F Service Fees
            - 8.F.1 Fixed Fee Services
            - 8.F.2 Time-and-Materials Services
        - 8.G Customer Credit Risk
        - 8.H Parent Company Guarantee
        - 8.I Customer Royalty
            - 8.I.1 Fee
            - 8.I.2 Fee Cap
            - 8.I.3 Payment
            - 8.I.4 Audit
        - 8.J Reports, Payments, Accounting, and Inspections
            - 8.J.1 Periodic Accounting Reports
            - 8.J.2 Payments
            - 8.J.3 Books and Records
            - 8.J.4 Audit
            - 8.J.5 Inspections by Licensor

9. Personnel, Management, New Projects, and Testing
    - 9.1 Cooperation with Customer
    - 9.2 Licensor Personnel
        - 9.2.1 General
        - 9.2.2 Licensor Services Manager
        - 9.2.3 Licensor Services Support Team
        - 9.2.4 Licensor Technical Support Team
    - 9.3 Selection and Continuity
        - 9.3.1 Selection
        - 9.3.2 Continuity
        - 9.3.3 Succession Plan
    - 9.4 Replacement
    - 9.5 Customer Personnel
    - 9.6 Meeting and Reports
        - 9.6.1 On-site Readiness Meetings
        - 9.6.2 Contract Management Meetings
        - 9.6.3 Planning/Review Meetings
        - 9.6.4 Reports
    - 9.7 Administration of the Agreement
    - 9.8 Change Order Procedure
        - 9.8.A Mandatory Changes
            - 9.8.A.1 Commencement of Required Changes
            - 9.8.A.2 Significant Event
            - 9.8.A.3 Changes in Law
    - 9.9 New Projects
    - 9.10 Testing Process
    - 9.11 Time Tracking
    - 9.12 Competitors
    - 9.13 Audit/Quality Control
    - 9.14 Non-solicitation of Employees
    - 9.15 Approval of Subcontractors
    - 9.16 Screening of Licensor Personnel
    - 9.17 Licensor Management
    - 9.18 Technology Changes

10. Involvement of Customer Employees in Licensor's Team
    - 10.1 Involvement of Customer Employees/Consultants in Licensor's Development Team
    - 10.2 Involvement of Customer Personnel in Licensor's Integration and Acceptance Team
    - 10.3 General

11. Support and Maintenance Services
    - 11.1 Training Services
    - 11.2 Installation Services
    - 11.3 Hardware and Software Support Services
    - 11.4 Additional Support Services

12. Proprietary Rights, Confidentiality, and Security
    - 12.1 Ownership of Intellectual Property
    - 12.2 Confidential Information
    - 12.3 Privileged Information
    - 12.4 Return of Confidential Information
    - 12.5 Notification Obligation
    - 12.6 Non-Aggregation of Data
    - 12.7 Residuals
    - 12.8 Employee/Agent Acknowledgment
    - 12.9 Survival; No Limitation of Liability
    - 12.10 Customer Information
    - 12.11 International Privacy Laws

13. Reproduction of Documentation, Object Code, and Source Code
    - 13.1 Documentation
    - 13.2 Object Code
    - 13.3 Source Code

14. Patent and Other Proprietary Rights Indemnification
    - 14.1.A Language that Favors Licensor
        - 14.A.1 Third Party Infringement Claims
        - 14.A.2 Conditions
        - 14.A.3 Licensor's Options
        - 14.A.4 Exclusions
        - 14.A.5 Entire Liability
    - 14.1.B Language that Favors Licensee
        - 14.B.1 Indemnification
        - 14.B.2 Exclusions
        - 14.B.3 Defense of Third Party Suits
    - 14.2 Assumption of Defense
    - 14.3 Cessation of Fees
    - 14.4 Licensee Indemnification of Licensor

15. General Indemnity
    - 15.1 Indemnity
    - 15.2 Assumption of Defense

16. Warranty and Warranty Disclaimer
    - 16.1 Licensor Warranties
        - 16.1.1 General Warranties
        - 16.1.2 Operation of Software
        - 16.1.3 Remedy
        - 16.1.4 Warranty Disclaimer
        - 16.1.5 Voiding of Warranties
    - 16.A System

31. Waiver of Breach

32. Waiver of Right to Jury Trial

33. Force Majeure

34. Bonds
    34.1 Performance and Payment Bonds
    34.2 Requirements

35. Business Continuity Plan (Disaster Recovery) [If Applicable]

36. Covenant of Good Faith

37. Time Is of the Essence

38. Insurance

39. Third Party Software

40. Third Party Beneficiaries

41. Outsourcing

42. Divestiture and Transition
    42.1 Divestiture
    42.2 Transition

43. Export

44. Publicity and Use of Customer Marks
    44.1 Publicity
    44.2 Use/License of Customer Marks

45. Appointment of Agent for Service of Process

46. Electronic Transfer of Intellectual Property

47. Electronic Documents and Transmissions

48. Liens

49. Legal Fees

50. Mandatory Reference

51. No Construction against Drafter

52. Notices

53. Background, Enumerations, and Headings

54. Incorporation of Appendices and Exhibits
55. Severability
56. Counterparts
57. Facsimile Execution
58. Entire Agreement
59. Contingent Agreement

APPENDICES AND EXHIBITS REFERENCED IN SOFTWARE LICENSE

Appendix 1.2	Affiliates
Appendix 1.5	Custom Software
Appendix 1.6	Deliverable(s)
Appendix 1.11	Functional Specifications
Appendix 1.12	Hardware
Appendix 1.21	Software Acceptance Plan
Appendix 1.23	Standard Software
Appendix 3.1	Central Processing Units
Appendix 3.B	Service Level Standards and Credits
Appendix 3.C	On-site Inspection Certificate
Appendix 5.3.6	Source Code License Terms
Appendix 8	Model Pricing Schedule for Time and Materials Contracts
Appendix 8.C	CPU License Fees
Appendix 9.2	Key Personnel
Appendix 9.2.3	Information Technology Support and Maintenance Services
Appendix 9.6.1	Expense Guidelines
Appendix 9.6.4	Performance Reports

Appendix 9.9	Project Terms and Conditions
Appendix 11.2	Installation Services
Appendix 11.3	Hardware and Support Services
Appendix 16.Q	Quality Standards
Appendix 35	Disaster Recovery
Exhibit 7.1	Certificate of Acceptance
Exhibit 8.H	Form of Parent Guarantee
Exhibit 9.15	Confidentiality and Nondisclosure Agreement
Exhibit 16.C	Standards of Conduct
Exhibit 34	Form of Performance Bond and Payment Bond
Exhibit 43	Letter of Assurance
APPENDIX A	Customer Affiliates
APPENDIX B	Price Schedule

Software License and Services Agreement

THIS SOFTWARE LICENSE AND SERVICES AGREEMENT is made this _____ day of _____, 20__ by and between ____________________, a ______________ corporation with its principal address at______________ (hereinafter "Licensor") and __________, a __________ corporation with offices located at ______________ (hereinafter "Customer").

- ***Who are the appropriate contracting entities?***
- ***Who is the Customer? Is the Customer financially stable and able to pay the Licensor, or is a parent guarantee needed? (See Section 8.H, the signature line and Form O.1)***
- ***Is a parent guarantee or performance bond needed to ensure the Licensor's performance? (See Sections 8.H and 34)***
- ***Consider the Licensor's and the Customer's addresses as they may have income tax implications for the Licensor, sales tax implications for the Customer, and impact any dispute over venue and governing law.***

BACKGROUND

Licensor has developed and owns certain proprietary software for use in the __________ industry. Customer desires to obtain a license to use such software and have Licensor develop certain modifications and enhancements for such software. Licensor desires to license such software to Customer and perform the services on the terms and conditions set forth herein.

- ***Think carefully about the wording contained in any recital, as the laws of some states such as Michigan treat recitals involving a statement of fact as conclusive evidence of the facts stated. See,*** **Detroit Grand Park Corp. v. Turner, 25 N.W.2d 184 (Mich. 1946).**
- ***Avoid incorporating by reference the Customer's RFP or the Licensor's RFP response as this may create an internal conflict with the terms of the Agreement and the functional specifications contained in the Agreement.***

IN CONSIDERATION of the foregoing and the mutual covenants set forth herein, and intending to be legally bound, the parties agree as follows:

Alternatively:

NOW, THEREFORE, in consideration of the foregoing Recitals, **which shall be deemed to be a substantive part of this Agreement**, and the mutual covenants, agreements, representations, and warranties hereinafter set forth, the parties hereto do hereby agree, as follows:

- ***Licensors should be hesitant to accept language acknowledging the recitals to be a substantive part of the agreement. From the Customer's perspective if the Licensor is willing to acknowledge the facts of the recitals, it should be willing to stand behind such statements. The risk to the Licensor is that the recitals are now part of the agreement even in those states that have not adopted the position of Michigan.***

1. Definitions

Whenever used in this Agreement, any Schedules, Exhibits, or Addenda to this Agreement, or the Source Code Escrow Agreement, the following terms shall have the meaning ascribed to them below. Other capitalized terms used in this Agreement are defined in the context in which they are used and shall have the meanings ascribed therein. The terms defined in this Schedule include the plural as well as the singular.

- ***See Form Q.1 for additional and/or alternative definitions that may be more applicable for your transaction.***

1.1 **Acceptance** for the System shall occur only when: (a) Licensor has provided to Customer all Deliverables required to be provided to Customer; and (b) (i) Customer notifies Licensor in writing that all testing for the System has been completed successfully in accordance with the terms of this Article, or (ii) Licensor provides to the applicable Customer Project Manager a written notice of completion stating that all Critical Defects and Medium Defects have been corrected. Nothing else, including Customer's use of the System, or any portion thereof, in a live, operational environment, shall constitute Acceptance (under contract law or the Uniform Commercial Code of [STATE]) of any portion of the applicable system.

1.2 **Affiliate(s)** or **Affiliate Company** shall mean those companies that are initially listed on Appendix 1.2 attached hereto, which may be amended from time to time with the prior written consent of an authorized executive officer of Licensor.

- ***Think about who is going to be able to use the software and how the usage by those entities may affect the Licensor's revenues and pricing. The Customer may want to provide software to all of its "Affiliates" including those overseas. The Licensor will often seek to restrict the license to the Customer alone or to the Customer's then existing "Affiliates" who are listed on an attached Appendix. By listing the Affiliates, the Licensor is able to limit the license to a finite number of entities avoiding any***

potential misunderstanding as to who is included. The Customer may not add an entity to the list of Affiliates without Licensor's permission. The breadth of this definition is often an element of price. In addition to pricing concerns, the Licensor may want to limit use of the software to ensure compliance with U.S. export laws.

1.2.A **Affiliate** shall mean, as to a Party, any other Person that directly or indirectly controls or is controlled by such Party. The term "control" (including, with correlative meanings, the terms "controlled by" and "under common control with") as applied to any Person means the possession, direct or indirect, of the power to direct or cause the direction of the management and policies of such Person, whether through the ownership of voting securities or other ownership interest. For the purposes of this definition, "Person" means any individual, partnership, corporation, limited liability company, unincorporated organization or association, any trust, or any other business entity.

- ***The definition of "Affiliate" set forth in Section 1.2.A offers greater flexibility to reflect the ever changing nature of a large corporation's relationship with its affiliates. The definition of "Affiliate" is not fixed as of a particular time allowing additional users without modifying the agreement. This definition more closely tracks the definition of affiliates used under the securities laws and from a Securities and Exchange Commission perspective.***

1.3 **"Consolidated Net Worth"** means, at any time, (a) the total assets of the Customer [and its Affiliates] that would be shown as assets on a consolidated balance sheet of the Customer [and its Affiliates] as of such time prepared in accordance with GAAP, after eliminating all amounts properly attributable to minority interests, if any, in the stock and surplus of Affiliates, minus (b) the total liabilities of the Customer and its Affiliates that would be shown as liabilities on a consolidated balance sheet of the Customer and its Affiliates as of such time prepared in accordance with GAAP.

1.4 **Critical Error(s)** shall mean a failure of the Software that severely impacts Customer's ability to provide service or has a significant financial impact on Customer for which an alternative temporary solution or work around [acceptable to Customer] may not be accomplished.

- ***This definition favors the Customer as it includes not only those errors that impact the Customer's ability to provide services but also any that have a "financial impact" on the Customer.***

1.5 **Custom Software** means those Deliverables that are classified in Appendix 1.5 hereto as Custom Software, as well as the documentation related thereto; an exhaustive list of Custom Software is set forth in Appendix 1.5 hereto.

1.6 **Deliverable** means the Hardware, Software, and Documentation to be delivered hereunder; an exhaustive list of all Deliverables is set forth in Appendix 1.6 hereto.

1.7 **Direct Damages** means the damages incurred by the claiming Party to this Agreement directly resulting from a breach of this Agreement by another party to this

Agreement and specifically excludes: (a) loss of interest, profit, or revenue; failure to achieve cost savings or business interruption and (b) any incidental, consequential, punitive, multiple, or indirect damages of any kind or nature. Direct Damages include by way of example but without limitation, (i) the costs incurred by Customer to obtain software or services that are the same as or substantially similar to (but not broader in scope than) the Software or Services being replaced, that is, the charges to be paid to another services provider(s) to the extent such costs are commercially reasonable and exceed the Fixed Charges hereunder for such Software or Services; (ii) the costs to correct any deficiencies in the Software or Services rendered that result in a failure of the Deliverables to meet Service Levels or the specifications set forth in the applicable Statement of Work, after Licensor has failed or refused to correct such deficiencies; (iii) the costs incurred to transition the Software or Services to another provider(s) of services; (iv) any payments, fines, penalties, or interest imposed by a governmental body or regulatory agency for failure to comply with requirements or deadlines; and (v) the reasonable out-of-pocket costs and fees incurred by Licensor to collect from Customer any fees payable to Licensor under the Agreement.

- ***Alternatively the parties may want to include a section similar to Sections 17.3 and 17.4***

1.8 **Divested Business** means any business unit, as determined by Licensee, that Licensee sells or of which it otherwise transfers the assets or ownership. The term "Divested Business" shall mean such business unit or the acquirer thereof, as applicable.

1.9 **Documentation** means collectively: (a) all of the written, printed, electronic, or other format materials published or otherwise made available by Licensor that relate to the functional, operational, and/or performance capabilities of the ABC System and/or any Software; (b) all user, operator, system administration, technical, support, and other manuals and all other written, printed, electronic, or other format materials published or otherwise made available by Licensor that describe the functional, operational, and/or performance capabilities of the ABC System and/or any Software including but not limited to the Functional Specifications and Software Acceptance Plan; and (c) any other Deliverable that is not Hardware or Software. Documentation shall not include Source Code.

1.10 **Error(s)** shall mean a failure of the Software to substantially conform to the Documentation or the Functional Specifications, which materially impacts the Software's operational performance or functional performance.

- ***The definition of "Error" is drafted to recognize that software by its nature is imperfect. The Customer, however, may require a tighter definition to ensure the software's performance meets the Customer's needs.***

1.11 **Functional Specifications** shall mean those specifications to which the Software shall conform as set forth Appendix 1.11.

- ***The Functional Specifications should be set out in detail prior to execution of the Agreement to avoid later disagreements. Agreement in advance may not be feasible depending on the nature of the development undertaken***

by Licensor. Without agreeing upon the Functional Specifications, the Licensor cannot give the Customer a fixed price for any software development. At the same time, it is unwise for either party to agree to a fixed price with the intent on negotiating the Functional Specifications later.

1.12 **Hardware** means those Deliverables that are classified in Appendix 1.5 hereto as Hardware, as well as the documentation furnished therewith in the normal course of business; an exhaustive list of Hardware is set forth in Appendix 1.12 hereto.

1.13 **License(s)** shall mean any personal, nonexclusive, nontransferable, non-assignable license or licenses for Customer's internal use only granted by Licensor to Customer to use the Software under this Agreement.

1.14 **Object Code** shall mean the binary machine-readable version of the Software.

1.15 **"Open Source Materials"** shall mean any software, library, utility, tool, or other computer or program code (collectively, **"Code"**) that is licensed or distributed as "free software," "freeware," "open source software," or under any terms or conditions that impose any requirement that the Code or any software using, linked with, incorporating, distributed with, based on, derived from or accessing the Code: (i) be made available or distributed in source code form; (ii) be licensed for the purpose of making derivative works; (iii) be licensed under terms that allow reverse engineering, reverse assembly or disassembly of any kind; or (iv) be redistributable at no charge. Open Source Materials include without limitation any Code licensed or distributed under any of the following licenses or distribution models or similar licenses or distribution models: the GNU General Public License (GPL), GNU Lesser General Public License or GNU Library General Public License (LGPL), Mozilla Public License (MPL), BSD licenses, the Artistic License, the Netscape Public License, the Sun Community Source License (SCSL) the Sun Industry Standards License (SISL) and the Apache License).

- ***Licensees and Licensors need to ensure the definition of "open source" reflects the contemplated use of the software and any changes in technology. The parties should not ignore the risk of utilizing language such as "includes without limitation" or "including but not limited to."***

1.16 **Performance Standards** means collectively the warranties and performance standards set forth in Section 16 and all associated Exhibits, Appendixes, Attachments, and Addenda referenced therein.

1.17 **Regulatory Requirements** is defined in Appendix 3.B "Service Level Standards and Credits," Attachment 8 "Information Technology Support."

1.18 **Services** shall mean the work done by Licensor in support of the Software, including but not limited to development services, installation services, training, consulting, support, telephone support, and such other services.

1.19 **Site** shall mean a Customer's computer facility located in one specific geographic location.

1.20 **Software** means the aggregate of the Standard Software and the Custom Software including all physical components that are provided by Licensor, including but not limited to, magnetic media, job aids, templates, and other similar devices; an exhaustive list of all Software is set forth in Appendix 1.20.

1.21 **Software Acceptance Plan** shall mean that plan set forth in Appendix 1.21.

- ***The Software Acceptance Plan should be set out in detail prior to execution of the Agreement to avoid later disagreements. Agreement in advance may not be feasible, however, depending on the nature of the development undertaken by Licensor. Any plan should be objective in nature to protect both parties.***

1.22 "**Source Code**" means computer software in the form of source statements for the Software (excluding all Third Party Software) including, without limitation, all software in the form of electronic and printed human-readable, mnemonic or English-like program listings, including printed and on-line descriptions of the design of such software including, without limitation, data definition models, indices, structure tables, system flow charts, program flow charts, defined terms, file layouts, program narratives, global documentation (including global variables) and program listings.

1.23 **Standard Software** means those Deliverables that are classified, in Appendix 1.23 hereto as Standard Software, as well as the documentation furnished therewith by Licensor or its subcontractors in the normal course of business; an exhaustive list of the Standard Software is set forth in Appendix 1.23.

- ***The "Definitions" section of any agreement is very important, as this is where the Customer or Licensor may try to insert a definition, which has a favorable implication later in the Agreement, based upon its use. For example, many Customers try to define the "Agreement" to include the RFP. This is dangerous as the deliverables may have changed from the RFP or Licensor may never have intended to meet certain requirements of the RFP by listing such requirements in the "Exceptions" portions of Licensor's RFP response. Further, if the RFP and RFP response are incorporated in the Agreement, the two documents may be inconsistent, leading to internal inconsistencies and potential problems of interpretation.***

2. Scope of This Agreement

2.1 **Scope.** This Agreement defines the terms and conditions under which Licensor will design, develop, integrate, deliver, install, and support the Software and the Deliverables.

2.2 **Turn-key Basis**. The Parties hereto acknowledge that the performance by Licensor of its obligations hereunder is to be done on a "turn-key" basis." This expression is understood to mean that Licensor is fully responsible, pursuant to the terms and conditions hereof, for the delivery of the Deliverables in full conformity with the terms and conditions hereof, and that the said Deliverables shall function in conformity with the performance criteria stipulated herein upon delivery and up to and including the date on which the acceptance certificate is issued.

- ***From the Customer's prospective, it is important that the Licensor be responsible for providing the entire software system. Otherwise, if there is a defect each individual vendor will affix blame for the problem on the other vendors. The Customer wants to place the responsibility on the Licensor to deliver a complete, integrated working system and if required fix any problem that arises regardless of whether it arises from the hardware, operating system, proprietary software, data base software, etc. For assuming this additional risk, the Licensor should be entitled to receive a higher fee.***

2.3 **Modification of Delivery Date.** Either Party hereto may submit a request to the other to modify the delivery date for one or more Deliverable(s) if it believes that such a modification of a delivery date is necessary or appropriate given circumstances external to this Agreement or the failure of the other Party to perform in strict conformity with the terms hereof. It is nonetheless acknowledged that the other party shall have full power and authority to accept or reject such a request.

3. Software and Services

3.1 **License Grant.** Subject to the provisions of this Agreement as well as the payment of all applicable license fees for the term of such license, Licensor grants Customer and Customer accepts a limited, personal, nonexclusive, nontransferable, non-assignable Object Code [Source Code] license to use the [Standard] Software for Customer's internal use only in the United States [on the Central Processing Units (CPUs) listed on Appendix 3.1.]

- ***Customer—Who is the Customer?***
- ***License—Licensor "licenses" its software; Licensor does not "sell" it. "Selling" indicates a transfer of ownership, meaning the Customer could potentially "resell" the software to a third party.***
- ***Limited—The Customer has only limited rights in the software.***
- ***Personal—Use of the software is "personal" to the Customer only.***
- ***Nonexclusive—Other customers may receive a license to use the same software.***
- ***Nontransferable—The software cannot be transferred to other entities.***
- ***Non-assignable—The software cannot be assigned to other entities.***
- ***Object code—Unless source code is being licensed, the Customer will receive object code only.***
- ***Internal use—The software cannot be used for outsourcing, timesharing, service bureaus, etc.***
- ***United States—To avoid export issues and the potential diversion of the software, the Customer may use the software only in the United States.***
- ***This Section assumes that the Licensor shall own all Software including the custom software in contradiction of Sections 6.4 and 12.1, which***

assume that the Customer will own the custom software. Section 3.1.A below provides additional language, which allows the Licensor to retain ownership, but grants the Customer an exclusive license to use the custom software.

- ***The entire license grant is preceded by the clause "Subject to the provisions of this Agreement," which allows Licensor to terminate the license grant if the Customer breaches any other terms of the Agreement.***
- ***The scope of the license grant is directly related to pricing. For example, while the Licensor may not initially grant a source code license that could potentially limit the Licensor's ability to earn revenue from maintaining the software or developing enhancements, licensors will often license source code for an appropriately larger license fee.***

Additional Language Granting the Customer an Exclusive License in Return for Funding Development

3.1.A **Exclusive License Grant.** In consideration of the Customer funding the development of the Custom Software, the Customer is hereby granted the exclusive license and right to utilize the Custom Software for five years from the date Customer accepts the Software (the "Exclusivity Period"). During the Exclusivity Period, Licensor shall not license or sell the Custom Software or allow any other individual or entity to utilize the Custom Software. Further, the Licensor shall not develop, create, or license any other software functionally equivalent to the Custom Software.

- ***This language provides a compromise to the Customer claiming ownership of the custom software. It allows the Licensor to retain ownership of the custom software while providing the Customer with the benefit of any competitive advantage that the custom software may provide. This language is too broad from the Licensor's perspective. Not only does it provide the Customer with an exclusive license, but it also prohibits the Licensor from developing any functionally equivalent software. This prohibition may severely impact the Licensor's ability to sell future work. Section 8.H provides alternative language allowing the Customer to recoup its investment in funding the development of the custom software from royalty payments for future licenses of the custom software granted by the Licensor.***

Additional Language Granting the Customer the Right to Copy the Software

3.1.B **Right to Copy**. Customer may copy the Software only in so far as strictly necessary for the intended use of the Software. Customer explicitly agrees that in the foreseeable future the intended use of the Software does not require copies of the Software other than for archival and/or backup purposes should at any time occur that the intended use of the Software implies the necessity of copies for other purposes than archival and/or backup purposes, Customer shall immediately notify Licensor in writing and provide Licensor with all information necessary in order to enable Licensor to evaluate the actual necessity of such copies.

3.2 **Software Related Materials.** All Software used in, for, or in connection with the software, parts, subsystems, or derivatives thereof (the "ABC System"), in whatever form, including, without limitation, source code, object code, microcode, and mask works, including any computer programs and any documentation relating to or describing such Software, such as but not limited to logic manuals and flow charts provided by Licensor, including instructions for use of the Software and formulation of theory upon which the Software, is based are furnished to Customer only under a personal, nonexclusive, nontransferable, non-assignable Object Code license solely for Customer's own internal use.

3.3 **No Licenses.** Except as explicitly provided in Section 3.1 of this Agreement, no license under any patents, copyrights, trademarks, trade secrets, or any other intellectual property rights, express or implied, are granted by Licensor to Customer under this Agreement.

3.4 **Reverse Engineering.** Customer shall not and shall not permit its Affiliates or any third party to translate, reverse engineer, decompile, recompile, update, or modify all or any part of the Software or merge the Software into any other software.

Additional/Alternative Language Benefiting Customer

Customer shall not otherwise, in whole or in part, sublicense, copy, rent, loan, transfer, prepare derivatives of the Software or any copy of the Software. Customer shall not decompile the Software for other purposes than creating interoperability of the Software and Customer shall not create interoperability without having approached Licensor in order to obtain from Licensor the necessary information and data to do so, provided that Licensor does not provide Customer with such information and data within a reasonable time, Customer shall have the right to decompile the Software.

Customer shall not modify the Software for other purposes than correcting errors of the Software. Customer acknowledges that all Improvements and Modifications, not made contrary to the terms of this Agreement, of the Software or any part thereof (whether developed by Licensor, Licensor, Customer or any third party acting on behalf of them at any time during the term of this agreement) shall be deemed to be part of the Software and shall be and remain the sole and exclusive property of Licensor, subject to the terms and conditions of the Agreement and any additional agreements concluded and maintenance contracts permitted by this Agreement.

- ***Section 3.4 restricts the Customer from modifying or enhancing the software. It is essential this paragraph remain in the agreement, otherwise the Customer (and potentially the Customer's other vendors) would under the* Sega, Atari, *and* Bateman *decisions have the right to reverse engineer the software to create its own interfaces, etc. It is also important that the Customer is forbidden from merging the software with other software, which in turn may create a new work, which could be copyrighted in the Customer's name.***

3.5 **Ownership of Materials.** All patents, copyrights, circuit layouts, mask works, trade secrets, and other proprietary rights in or related to the Software are and will remain the exclusive property of Licensor, whether or not specifically recognized or perfected under the laws of the jurisdiction in which the Software is used or licensed. Customer will not take any action that jeopardizes Licensor's proprietary rights or acquire any right in the Software or the Confidential Information, as defined in Section 12 herein below. Unless otherwise agreed on a case-by-case basis, Licensor will own all rights in any copy, translation, modification, adaptation, or derivation of the Software or other items of Confidential Information, including any improvement or development thereof. Customer will obtain, at Licensor's request, the execution of any instrument that may be appropriate to assign these rights to Licensor or perfect these rights in Licensor's name.

- ***Section 3.5 provides that even if the Customer creates a derivative work or a modification or enhancement, in contradiction to Section 3.4, Licensor will have sole and exclusive ownership of such work. The Licensor needs to be careful that any restrictions placed on the Customer do not amount to copyright misuse.***

3.6 **Third Party Access.** Customer shall not allow any third party to have access to the Software without Licensor's prior written consent. Further, Customer shall neither engage in nor permit any use of the Software such that a copy would be made of such Software solely by virtue of the activation of a machine containing a copy of the Software.

- ***Section 3.6 prevents the Customer from utilizing outside contractors and consultants to utilize, maintain, or support the software. This protects the Licensor from the Customer hiring Licensor's competitors or outsourcing the software and its maintenance. The second sentence seeks to negate the effect of The Computer Maintenance Competition Assurance Act, 17 U.S.C. § 117.***

3.7 **Service Locations.** To the extent applicable, each specific Statement of Work shall identify (i) the Customer Locations that shall receive Services under such Statement of Work, and (ii) the Licensor Service Locations that shall provide such Services. Customer acknowledges that Licensor may utilize non-U.S. based operations in connection with the performance of this Agreement. Licensor shall be entitled, upon obtaining prior written consent from Customer (such consent to be granted or withheld in Customer's sole discretion) and subject to compliance with all applicable Laws, including all Data Protection Laws, to move the Services and related obligations from a Licensor Service Location to another location and, if such move is from one country to another country, from one Local Agreement to another Local Agreement. Notwithstanding Customer's approval of such transfer of Services, Licensor shall remain liable and responsible for the performance of all Services by it and all its Affiliates hereunder and Licensor shall be responsible for any expenses and price increases (including, but not limited to additional taxes) resulting from any transfer from one Licensor Service Location to another Licensor Service Location unless expressly otherwise agreed by Customer in a Change Order.

"**Data Protection Laws**" shall mean any data protection or privacy Laws.

"**Local Agreement**" shall mean a separate agreement between (i) Customer or a customer Affiliate, and (ii) Licensor or a Licensor Affiliate in a jurisdiction in which the Services shall be provided by Licensor or an Affiliate of Licensor that shall modify the terms and conditions of this Agreement as necessary to address the requirements of local laws. A Local Agreement for a particular jurisdiction shall govern the Statement of Work under which Services are provided in such jurisdiction.

- ***See Section 16.AB for a representation and warranty as to the location of where the services will be performed.***

3.8 **Improvements and New Technology.**

3.8.1 **Continuous Improvement**. Licensor will explore opportunities on an ongoing basis to reduce Customer's total cost of receiving the Services (including but not limited to the charges) and to improve Licensor's performance of the Services and Service Levels and shall be required, throughout the Term, to implement such measures. Such opportunities may include economies of scale and greater efficiencies developed by Licensor and technological changes and other developments affecting delivery of the Services. Prior to the execution of a Statement of Work hereunder, Licensor will present a continuous improvement program with respect to the Services to be provided under such Statement of Work. The continuous improvement program will include short-term initiatives (0-6 months) with detailed business cases and demonstrable business benefit to Customer, medium-term initiatives (6-12 months) with high-level business cases, and long-term initiatives (12 months on).

3.8.2 **New Technology and Reengineering**. During the Term, Licensor shall keep itself informed of new technology and improvements in current technology that may facilitate or improve the Services to result in cost savings, improvement in Licensor's performance of the Services and Service Levels, and other benefits to Customer. Licensor shall promptly advise Customer of such new technology or improvements about which it is aware and promptly advise Customer of their prospective benefits to Customer. In addition, Licensor shall review the operations required to support Customer and shall recommend to Customer certain reengineering procedures, processes and tools. In the event that the reengineering opportunity would require Customer to modify its methods, practices or policies, Licensor shall (i) present the changes to Customer, (ii) discuss with Customer the requirements of implementation, and (iii) identify the projected benefits to both Customer and Licensor. The Parties shall work in good faith to determine the costs, benefits, and proper level of commitment by both Customer and Licensor for implementing such reengineering projects. Either Party may request implementation of any of the foregoing in accordance with the procedures for Changes set forth in Article ___, and Licensor shall not implement any of the foregoing without Customer's prior written consent.

3.9 **Customer Authorized User Satisfaction**

3.9.1 **Baseline Customer Authorized User Satisfaction Survey**. In the time frames set forth in Exhibit _____ (Critical Deliverables), an independent third party selected by Customer shall conduct a baseline Customer Authorized User satisfaction survey for affected users at each Customer Service Location and/or Customer Site Approved by Customer measuring their satisfaction with their receipt of the Services. This Customer Authorized User Satisfaction Survey shall be mutually agreed upon by the Parties, and shall be administered as determined by the selected organization and shall be the initial baseline for measurement of user satisfaction improvement described in Section ____ (Customer Authorized User Satisfaction Survey).

3.9.2 **Customer Authorized User Satisfaction Survey.** Every six (6) months during the first four (4) years of the Term and annually thereafter (unless otherwise agreed in writing by the Parties), an independent third party selected by Customer shall conduct a Customer Authorized User Satisfaction Survey for each Customer Service Location and/or Customer Site. The survey shall, at a minimum, cover at least the following classes of users: (1) sample of end users of the Services, and (2) all senior management of Customer. The content, scope, and method of the survey shall be consistent with the baseline Customer Authorized User Satisfaction Survey conducted pursuant to Section ____ (Baseline Customer Authorized User Satisfaction Survey) and the timing of the above surveys are subject to Customer's Approval. It is the goal of Licensor to increase Customer Authorized User satisfaction for each class of Customer Authorized Users. The baseline for determining the initial gap shall be the results of the surveys conducted pursuant to Section _____ (Baseline Customer Authorized User Satisfaction Survey). The baseline for determining subsequent gaps will be the results of the Customer Authorized User Satisfaction Survey compared to the immediately prior Customer Authorized User Satisfaction Survey. Licensor agrees that increasing measured Customer Authorized User satisfaction shall be a key performance incentive for compensation for key executives assigned to Customer's account. The costs for all Customer Authorized User Satisfaction Surveys shall be borne solely by Customer. Notwithstanding the foregoing, in the event that any Customer Authorized User Satisfaction Survey fails to meet the applicable Service Level, the cost of all surveys following such failure shall be borne solely by Licensor until the Service Level failure has been remedied by Licensor (after a survey Service Level failure is remedied Customer again shall bear the costs of the subsequent survey); provided, however, that the first Customer Authorized User Satisfaction Survey immediately following any Service Level failure shall be conducted no earlier than six (6) months, and no later than seven (7) months, after such failure.

3.10 **Data Maps**

Licensor shall provide current data dictionaries and maps to Licensee both with the initial installation and with each Update of the Licensed Software, so that all data managed by the Licensed Software can be readily located, searched, extracted, and exported in whole or in part by Licensee personnel as Licensee deems appropriate, with or without the use of tools provided by Licensor.

Alternative/Additional Language

3.A **Commitment to Research and Development.** Licensor acknowledges that research and development is an integral part of being able to continue to improve functionality and meet the increasing business needs of the [name of] industry in the future. Having acknowledged the foregoing, Licensor shall invest on a yearly basis a minimum of [XX] percent (XX%) of the gross revenues it collects from all customers using and receiving services related to the Software into research and development efforts related to the Software. In the event that Licensor fails to invest the required amount into the research and development of the Software, Customer shall: (a) have the right to migrate to the new services or system that Licensor offers to its customers, which migration shall be at no additional cost to Customer and shall include the retro-fitting of all custom programming, or (b) have the right, at any time, to terminate this Agreement and: (i) obtain all Source Code and other deposit material to all Software and/or to provide Services to Customer; and/or (ii) transition to a new software vendor, pursuant to Customer's rights under Section 5.3.3. [Transition Rights in the event of Licensor breach.] All Services provided by Licensor during any such transition period shall be provided at no cost to Customer.

- ***When purchasing a mission critical software system, the Customer should obtain a commitment from the Licensor that the Licensor will continue to invest in the software to keep the software competitive during the term of the Customer's license. This protects the Customer from the Licensor's "sunsetting" the software by failing to invest in the software and keep the software competitive with market requirements. The language set forth above provides the Customer the right to migrate to any new product the Licensor offers to replace the software at no additional cost, or to terminate the agreement and obtain the source code and/or transition to a new vendor. This clause provides complete protection in the event the Licensor creates a new product shortly after the Customer enters into the agreement. At the same time, the clause creates significant risks for the Licensor and will likely be hotly negotiated in most licensing negotiations.***

3.B **Service Level Standards**

3.B.1 **General.** Licensor shall provide the Software, and any other Services, as applicable, according to the performance criteria and at the service level standards ("Service Level Standards") set forth in Appendix 3.B. Licensor and Customer shall meet on a semi-annual basis to discuss whether changes to the Service Level Standards are necessary due to any changes business needs of Customer. Any changes to the Service Level Standards agreed upon in writing by both parties shall replace the then existing Appendix 3.B.

- ***Almost all license agreements from the Customer's prospective should include service level standards. Service level standards establish the minimum level of acceptable performance such as response times and refresh rates. While a general warranty may include broad generalizations as to the software's performance, service level standards provide specific standards that the Licensor's software must meet. This creates greater risks for the Licensor but the Customer is only asking the Licensor to commit in writing to the standards the Licensor has most likely already agreed to or stated in its marketing materials.***

3.B.2 **Service Level Credits.** In the event Licensor fails to meet the Service Level Standards, Customer shall be entitled to receive from Licensor service level credits ("Service Level Credits"), which shall be: (a) in the amounts and according to the terms set forth in Appendix 3.B, all of which shall be based on Licensor's monthly performance as set forth in the monthly performance reports prepared by Licensor pursuant to Section X.6.3 (attached as an alternative section); and/or (b) in the amount imposed upon Customer by [Regulatory Agency] for failing to comply with a State standard where such failure is caused by a Licensor failure to meet the Service Level Standards or any other performance standard or requirement set forth in this Agreement. Customer shall have the right to set off any undisputed amounts owed to Licensor against any Service Level Credits assessed by Customer against Licensor.

- ***Service Level Credits flow directly from the failure of the software to meet the service level standards. The Customer has invested significant money and effort in the implementation of the software. Termination of the agreement for the failure of the software to meet the service level standards is not always a practical solution. Further, a regulatory agency or end-user may have imposed penalties on the Customer causing the Customer to incur out-of-pocket costs. Consequently, service level credits provide the Customer with a way to incent the Licensor short of terminating the Agreement. The Customer should provide, however, that if the service level credits exceed a certain threshold, the Customer shall have the right to terminate the Agreement (See § 5.1(d)). The Licensor should ensure that the level of credits is acceptable and that the service level standards are achievable and fair. Further, the Licensor should insist that each set of credits be capped in the aggregate, and calculated on a monthly basis.***

3.C **Liquidated Damages**

3.C.1 **Liquidated Damages Payable by Licensor.**

(a) In the event that Customer refuses, as per the provisions of Appendix 3.C hereto, to issue the On-Site Acceptance Certificate on or before a day which is twenty (20) calendar days after the Delivery Date for Milestone Nos. ___ or ___ (On-Site Acceptance Certificates), respectively (hereinafter referred to as the "LD Date"), liquidated damages shall be payable by Licensor pursuant to the conditions set forth in Section 3.C hereof. Such liquidated damages shall be imposed on a daily basis, as from and including the day immediately following the LD Date up to and including the date on which the aforesaid On-Site Acceptance Certificate is issued. The amount of such liquidated damages shall be __________ (____) per calendar day, subject to a maximum amount of __________ (____).

(b) In the event that Customer refuses, as per the provisions of Appendix 3.C hereto, to issue the Provisional Acceptance Certificate on or before a day which is twenty (20) calendar days after Milestone Nos. ____ or __ (Provisional Acceptance Certificates), respectively (hereinafter referred to as the "LD Date"), liquidated damages shall be payable by Licensor pursuant to the conditions set forth in Section 3.C hereof. Such liquidated damages shall be imposed on a daily basis, as from and including the day immediately following the LD Date up to and including the date on which the aforesaid

Provisional Acceptance Certificate is issued. The amount of such liquidated damages shall ______ (___) per calendar day, subject to a maximum amount ____ (_____).

(c) Notwithstanding the provisions of Sections 3.C.1 (a) hereof, in the event that the On-Site Acceptance Certificate is issued on a date that is more than twenty (20) calendar days after Milestone No. ___ (On-Site Acceptance Certificate), Milestone No. ___ (Provisional Acceptance Certificate) shall be deemed to be moved forward in time by the number of calendar days equal to a number of calendar days between Milestone No. _____, plus twenty (20) days, and the date on which the On-Site Acceptance Certificate is issued, provided, however, that in no event shall the number of days by which the aforesaid Milestone No. ___ shall be moved forward in time exceed one hundred (100).

3.C.2 **Liquidated Damages Payable by Customer**

(a) In the event that Licensor refuses, as per the provisions of Appendix 3.C hereto, to issue the Acceptance Test Cases Acceptance Certificate on or before a day which is twenty (20) calendar days after Milestones Nos. __ or __ (Acceptance Tests Cases Certificates), respectively (hereinafter referred to as the "LD Date"), liquidated damages shall be payable by Customer pursuant to the conditions set forth in Section 3.C.3 hereof. Such liquidated damages shall be imposed on a daily basis, as from and including the day immediately following the LD Date up to and including the date on which the aforesaid Acceptance Test Cases Acceptance Certificate is issued. The amount of such liquidated damages shall be ________ (________) per calendar day, subject to a maximum amount of _____ (___).

(b) In the event that Licensor refuses, as per the provisions of Appendix 3.C hereto, to issue the Site Ready Acceptance Certificate on or before a day which is twenty (20) calendar days after Milestone No. ___ (Site Ready Acceptance Certificate) (hereinafter referred to as the "LD Date"), liquidated damages shall be payable by Customer pursuant to the conditions set forth in Section 3.C.3 hereof. Such liquidated damages shall be imposed on a daily basis, as from and including the day immediately following the LD Date up to and including the date on which the aforesaid Site Ready Acceptance Certificate is issued. The amount of such liquidated damages shall be ___ (___) per calendar day, subject to a maximum amount of _____ (_____).

(c) Notwithstanding the provisions of Section 3.C.2 (a) hereof, in the event that the Acceptance Tests Cases Acceptance Certificate is issued on a date that is after Milestone No. ___ (Acceptance Tests Cases Acceptance Certificate), Milestones Nos. ___, ___ and ___ (On-Site Delivery, On-Site and Provisional Acceptance Certificates) shall be deemed to be moved forward in time by a number of calendar days equal to the number of calendar days between Milestone No. ___ and the date on which the Acceptance Tests Cases Acceptance Certificate is issued, provided, however, that in no event shall the number of days by which the aforesaid Milestones Nos. ___, ___ and ___ shall be moved forward in time exceed one hundred (100). Notwithstanding the provisions of Section 3.C.2 hereof, in the event that the Site Ready Acceptance Certificate is issued on a date that is after Milestone No. ___, subsequent impacted Milestones shall be deemed to be moved forward in time by a number of calendar days equal to the number of calendar days between Milestone No. ___ and the date on which the Site Ready Acceptance Certificate is issued, provided, however, that in no event shall the number of days by which the aforesaid subsequent impacted Milestones shall be moved forward in time exceed one hundred (100).

3.C.3 **Payment of Liquidated Damages.** If Customer is entitled to receive liquidated damages pursuant to Section 3.C.1 hereof, it shall notify Licensor thereof in writing and Licensor shall cause a credit to appear on the next invoice it issues hereunder. If Licensor is entitled to receive liquidated damages pursuant to Section 3.C.2 hereof, it shall notify Customer thereof in writing and shall cause a debit to appear on the next invoice it issues to Customer hereunder.

3.C.4 **Termination in Lieu of Liquidated Damages.** In the event that the maximum amount of liquidated damages prescribed by Sections 3.C.1 or 3.C.2 is reached, the Party that would otherwise be entitled to receive liquidated damages shall have the right, but not the obligation, to terminate this Agreement pursuant to the provisions of Section 5 hereof by sending a notice to that effect to the other Party.

- ***Liquidated damages are a predetermined good faith estimate of damages the Customer will incur as a result of the Licensor's breach or that the Licensor will incur as a result of the Customer's breach. Agreeing on liquidated damages eliminates the necessity that the injured party prove its damages. For example, once the Customer demonstrates that the Licensor breached its obligations, it is entitled to collect the pre-agreed damages. If there are concerns about the ability to collect payment, each party can require the other to establish an irrevocable bond or letter of credit.***
- ***Any provision for liquidated damages should be mutual as the Licensor may also suffer damages, for example if the Customer's performance is delayed.***
- ***To the extent one party's performance is delayed by the action or inaction of the other party and as a result it is liable for liquidated damages, the party whose performance has been delayed shall be entitled to one extra day for each day its performance has been delayed by the other party.***

4. Term of Agreement and License

4.1 **Term of Agreement.** The term of this Agreement shall commence upon the execution of this Agreement, and shall continue for ____ years unless terminated upon the breach of this Agreement by either party [or as otherwise provided herein].

- ***This "term" relates to the term of the agreement although the term of individual licenses granted under the agreement may be different.***

Additional Language Allowing Customer to Terminate for Convenience

4.1.A **Termination without Cause.** Upon written notice to Licensor, Customer shall have the right to terminate this Agreement without cause. In such event: (a) Licensor shall discontinue its Services with respect to this Agreement, and (b) Customer shall be obligated to pay to Licensor a termination fee in an amount equal to the Services Fees paid or payable for the two (2) month period immediately preceding the effective date of such termination.

- ***This clause usually benefits the Customer as it allows the Customer to terminate the agreement at the Customer's convenience and depending***

on the wording it may not allow the Licensor to recover its termination costs, investment, etc. The Licensor should make sure that if the Licensor accepts such a clause that the negotiated termination fee allows the Licensor to recover its investment, expenses, and the cost of money. The Licensor may have significant termination costs including employee termination costs, subcontract termination costs, leases, travel, etc. The language set forth above does not favor the Licensor as the termination fee is not specifically stated and is tied to revenues. This creates the risk of an unanticipated event that reduces the agreement's revenues and in turn lowers the termination fee the Licensor is entitled to receive.

- ***This clause must be carefully worded to clearly state how any termination fee will be calculated. Usually the Customer must pay for work completed, the Licensor's termination costs*** **and** ***the Licensor's lost profit. The Licensor must determine whether the Customer should compensate the Licensor for work performed based on the Licensor's costs (a cost plus model) or on a percent complete (of the project) basis. In either case, the agreement should provide that the Licensor is entitled to recover the Licensor's lost profit or at least a pro rata portion of its lost profits.***

4.1.B **Termination upon Acquisition by XYZ Software Company**. Upon written notice to Licensor, Customer shall have the right to immediately terminate this Agreement if Licensor is acquired by XYZ Software Company of one of its Affiliates. In such event: (a) Licensor shall discontinue its Services with respect to this Agreement; and (b) Customer shall be obligated to pay to Licensor a termination fee in an amount equal to the Services Fees paid or payable for the two (2) month period immediately preceding the effective date of such termination.

4.2 **Term of Licenses.** Subject to the limitations contained in this Agreement, the term of each individual License granted under this Agreement begins on the date of delivery of the Software, and shall terminate on the date set forth herein, unless earlier terminated as provided in this Agreement.

- ***The term of the "License" should begin on "delivery" not on "acceptance", otherwise the Customer would have no legal obligations as to the use of the Software prior to "acceptance." Binding the Customer to the terms of the license upon delivery does not indicate the Customer's acceptance or create an obligation for the Customer to pay the applicable license fee.***

5. Events of Default and Remedies

5.1 **Events of Default.** Licensor and Customer acknowledge and agree that the following shall constitute events of default ("Events of Default") and that the occurrence of one (1) or more of such Events of Default shall constitute a material breach of this Agreement, which shall allow a party, as applicable, to seek the rights and remedies set forth in this Section:

(a) Licensor's failure to deposit the Deposit material as required by the Source Code Escrow Agreement within the time frames specified therein;
(b) Licensor's breach of the Regulatory Requirements warranty set forth in Section 16.M, and in no event shall such failure be subject to a cure period;
(c) Except for breaches that constitute a Section 5.1.(d) Event of Default, Licensor's material breach of any license obligation as provided in Section 3 provided that such breach is not cured within thirty (30) calendar days following written notice of such breach;
(d) Licensor's failure to materially conform to the Service Level Standards set forth in Appendix 3.B, or the occurrence of Service Level Credits for any three months during a twelve (12) month period in the amount of ________________ ($) or more per month; provided that Customer shall have provided Licensor with written notice of Licensor's non-compliance after the second month of non-compliance with such written notice being provided to Licensor within thirty (30) calendar days of the second month of Licensor's non-compliance of Service Level Standards;
(e) Licensor's continuous failure to timely provide to Customer monthly performance reports regarding Licensor's performance in relation to the Service Level Standards as set forth in Section 9.6.4.;
(f) Licensor's failure to maintain insurance coverage as specified in Section 36, provided that such failure is not cured within thirty (30) calendar days following receipt of written notice of such failure;
(g) Customer's failure to timely pay any undisputed amount owed to Licensor, provided that such failure is not cured within thirty (30) calendar days following receipt of written notice of such failure;
(h) Customer's breach of Sections 3, 12, or 13 or if Customer otherwise misuses the Software in contravention of this Agreement;
(i) Either party's material breach of any representation or warranty set forth in this Agreement, provided that such breach, if curable, is not cured within the time frames specified in Section 16, if applicable, or if such Section 16 does not apply to the breach, then within thirty (30) calendar days following receipt of written notice of such breach;
(j) Failure of a party to perform any other material obligation under this Agreement, provided that such failure is not cured within thirty (30) calendar days following receipt of written notice of such failure;
(k) The institution of bankruptcy, receivership, insolvency, reorganization, or other similar proceedings by or against either party under any section or chapter of the United States Bankruptcy Code, as amended, or under any similar laws or statutes of the United States or any state thereof, if such proceedings have not been dismissed or discharged within thirty (30) calendar days after they are instituted; or the insolvency or making of an assignment for the benefit of creditors or the admittance by either party of any involuntary debts as they mature or the institution of any reorganization arrangement or other readjustment of debt plan of either party not involving

the U.S. Bankruptcy Code; or any corporate action taken by the Board of Directors of either party in furtherance of any of the above actions;

(l) Appointment of a receiver for all or substantially all of either party's assets or any corporate action taken by the Board of Directors of either party in furtherance of the above action; and

- ***While many parties include language similar to the language set forth in subsections (k) and (l) in their agreements, these provisions are unenforceable as contrary to the provisions of the U.S. Bankruptcy Act, which provides that an executory contract may not be terminated solely because of a party's seeking protection under the bankruptcy laws.***

(m) If, but for the application of Section __ [Limitation of Liability] Licensor would be liable for damages in excess of the applicable Cap, Customer may terminate for material breach of this Agreement upon not less than thirty (30) days notice; provided, however, that if Licensor agrees in writing, within thirty (30) days after receiving notice of Customer's intention to terminate this Agreement, to reset such Cap to an amount equal to the payments made by Customer to Licensor for Services during the twenty-four (24) months prior to the occurrence of the first event that is the subject of the first claim with respect to any liability arising after receipt of such notice, Customer may, at its option, choose not to terminate the Agreement and the Cap shall be so reset.

- ***Some Customers seek to insert language allowing them to terminate the agreement if the Licensor's maximum liability under the agreement has been reached unless the Licensor agrees to increase its limit of liability. This demand is unreasonable as the parties previously negotiated a limit of liability that was agreeable to both parties. The Customer should not be allowed to unilaterally renegotiate the agreement or otherwise be allowed to terminate the agreement if the Licensor does not agree to amend it.***
- ***A Customer should carefully consider what actions or inactions on the Licensor's behalf should constitute a material breach. Some issues such as (e) and (f) are not as important as the failure to deliver a working product. At the same time, the Licensor should seek to limit the number of events of default to limit its risk.***
- ***Licensor must have the* immediate *right to terminate the agreement without granting a cure period if the Customer misuses or misappropriates the software as a cure period cannot "absolve" the breach.***
- ***Licensor must have a time period in which to "cure" any defaults. The time period must be long enough to allow Licensor to be able to cure the default. Given the nature of software, this period should be no less than 30 days.***

5.2 **Rights and Remedies of Licensor upon Default of Customer.** Upon the occurrence of an Event of Default by or with respect to Customer, subject to Customer's rights set forth in **Section 5.3.3**, Licensor shall be entitled to any of the following remedies:

(a) terminate, in whole or in part, this Agreement; and/or

(b) subject to the terms of Section 17, seek to recover damages from Customer; and/or

(c) if applicable, seek to obtain the additional rights and remedies set forth in Section 29.5 [Equitable Relief]; and/or

(d) [exercise the right of self-help]

Notwithstanding anything contained herein to the contrary, Licensor expressly waives and disclaims any right or remedy it may have to discontinue the performance of the Services or any portion thereof or terminate the License without due process of law.

- ***This clause seeks to prevent the Licensor from exercising any form of "self help," such as stopping the delivery services or disabling its software without following the dispute resolution procedure set forth in Section 29. Note that Section 5.3.2 specifically allows the Customer to exercise a form of self-help. This limitation conflicts ideologically with Customer's right of setoff in Section 5.3.2. and 3.B.2. Consequently, the Licensor should insist on parity for self-help.***

5.3 **Rights and Remedies of Customer upon Default of Licensor**

5.3.1 **General.** Upon the occurrence of an Event of Default by or with respect to Licensor, Customer shall be entitled to any of the following remedies:

(a) terminate, in whole or in part, this Agreement; and/or

(b) subject to the terms of Section 17, seek to recover damages from Licensor; and/or

(c) if applicable, obtain the additional remedies described in Sections 5.3.2–5.3.7; and/or

(d) if applicable, seek to obtain the additional rights and remedies set forth in Section 29.5 [Equitable Relief].

5.3.2 **Right to Set Off.** Customer shall have the right to set off any undisputed amounts owed to Licensor against any damages or charges including, without limitation, Service Level Credits, assessed by Customer against Licensor.

- ***Note that this section allows the Customer to set off only*** **undisputed** ***amounts owed to Licensor.***
- ***The parties should specifically state and agree as to whether they have the right of set off against the other. The common law of many states allows the right of set off even if it is not set forth in the contract. The Licensor is more likely to be concerned, as the Customer will want to offset any payments due the Licensor in the event of the Licensor's breach.***

5.3.3 **Transition Rights**

(a) **Termination by Customer**. In the event Customer terminates this Agreement pursuant to the terms of this Agreement in whole or in part, Customer shall provide to Licensor a written notice of transition ("Transition Notice"), setting forth the target date on which Customer plans to cut-over from Licensor's system to a new system or otherwise not require the future services of Licensor (the "Target Cut-Over Date"). At least thirty (30) days prior to the actual cut-over date ("Actual Cut-Over Date"), Customer shall provide Licensor with written notice of the Actual Cut-Over Date. Licensor shall continue to provide to Customer all Services required by Customer ("Transition Period"). Services provided by Licensor during the Transition Period shall include all conversion and other Services necessary for an orderly transition to another system. Customer shall place the Services Fees that accrue from and after the date of Transition Notice to the Actual Cut-Over Date into a Customer reserve account, and such reserved funds shall be disbursed as follows: (i) fifty percent (50%) of the reserve funds shall be distributed to Licensor on a pro-rata monthly basis over the first twelve (12) months after the Actual Cut-Over Date, and (ii) the remaining fifty percent (50%) of the reserve funds shall be paid to Licensor in one lump sum upon the completion of all Outsourcing Services obligations under this Agreement relating to the Prior Claims.

(b) **Termination by Licensor**. In the event Licensor terminates this Agreement pursuant to the terms of this Agreement, and provided Customer pays all undisputed amounts owed to Licensor, Licensor shall provide to Customer a minimum of twelve (12) months of all Services. Services provided by Licensor during this period shall include all conversion and other Services necessary (at Licensor's Service Rates) for an orderly transition to another system.

- ***In both 5.3.3(a) and (b), the parties should carefully negotiate the payment terms. In the event of 5.3.3(b), the Licensor may want to require the Customer to make payment in advance. At the same time, the Licensor may want to soften the payment terms in Section 5.3.3(a).***

Alternative Language Benefiting the Customer

Termination/Expiration Assistance Services

Termination/Expiration Transition Plan. Licensor understands and agrees that Customer's business operations are dependent on the Services, and that Customer's inability to receive the Services would result in irreparable damages to Customer. Therefore, upon the expiration of this Agreement or its termination by either Party for any reason, including the breach of this Agreement by the other Party, Termination Assistance Services shall be provided as set forth in this Section ___ (Termination/Expiration Assistance Services). If no Termination Transition Plan has yet been agreed to at the time of termination, the rights of Customer upon any expiration or termination of this Agreement shall be as set forth in this Section ___ (Termination/Expiration Assistance Services). If a Termination Transition Plan has been agreed to, then the rights of Customer upon any expiration or termination of this Agreement shall be as set forth in the most recent approved Termination Transition Plan, and also as set forth in this Section ____ (Termination/Expiration Assistance Services). In the event of any inconsistency between this Section ____ (Termination/Expiration Assistance Services) and the applicable

Termination Transition Plan, this Section shall govern. If no Termination Transition Plan has been agreed to by the Parties at the time of any termination of this Agreement, then Licensor shall provide the professional services staff necessary to provide (1) the Services (as requested by Customer in accordance with Section ____ (Termination Transition Period) at performance standards and Service Levels in effect at the time of termination or expiration, and (2) the Termination Assistance Services.

Performance of Services. Licensor and Customer acknowledge and agree that their mutual cooperation is important to an effective transition of technology services provided by Licensor to Customer or its designated provider(s). As requested by Customer in accordance with Section ___ (Termination Transition Period), Licensor shall provide Customer with all of the Services, including all of the Termination Assistance Services set forth in this Section ___ (Termination/Expiration Assistance Services) and in the then most recent version of the Termination Transition Plan. Licensor shall have no right to withhold or limit any of the Services (including the Termination Assistance Services) on the basis of any alleged breach of this Agreement by Customer, other than a failure by Customer to timely pay the amounts due for the Services (including Termination Assistance Services) rendered during the Termination Transition Period (as set forth in Section ___ (Termination Transition Period). Customer shall have the right to seek specific performance of this Section ___ (Termination/Expiration Assistance Services). In addition to the Services as set forth in this Agreement, the Termination Assistance Services shall include, at a minimum, (i) converting data; (ii) providing parallel services until transition to a new system; (iii) providing on-site technical support; (iv) cooperating with Customer or its designated vendor in developing required interfaces; (v) meeting with Customer as soon as practicable after a notice of termination or notice of a decision to not extend this Agreement has been given, to discuss any potential modifications to the then most current Termination Transition Plan; (vi) using all commercially reasonable efforts to assist Customer in effecting a transition of the Services, in accordance with best practices, to Customer or another vendor chosen by Customer; (vii) providing the number and types of resources necessary to complete the transition in accordance with the Termination Transition Plan; and (viii) such other services as shall be necessary or appropriate to facilitate, without interruption to the Services, the orderly transition of the Services to Customer or its new provider of services in accordance with best practices. If Licensor is providing any Services hereunder at the time of such transition utilizing any software license from a Third Party Vendor, the responsibility for obtaining and paying for the transfer of such licenses shall be in accordance with Section ___ (Consents). Notwithstanding anything in this Agreement to the contrary, Customer shall be entitled to increase and/or decrease the scope of the Services and Termination Assistance Services in its sole discretion during any Termination Transition Period. Licensor shall be compensated on a time and material basis or fixed fee basis (as agreed by the Parties) for all Termination Assistance Services by payment by Customer, with respect to time and materials charges, in accordance with the rates set forth in this Agreement or, if applicable rates for time and materials charges are not contained in this Agreement, and for all fixed fee charges, at commercially reasonable rates, it being understood that the charges for the Termination Assistance Services are not included in the Charges.

Termination Transition Period. Unless otherwise directed by Customer, commencing: (i) six (6) months prior to the expiration of the Agreement; (ii) upon any notice of termination or non-renewal of the Agreement; or (iii) six (6) months prior to any other ceasing of Service under the Agreement, and continuing for a period defined in the Termination Transition Plan but in no event less than twelve (12) months following the expiration or termination of this Agreement (unless a shorter time period is requested by Customer), Licensor will continue to provide the Services (including the Termination Assistance Services) as requested by Customer. After such twelve (12) month period (or such shorter time period as requested by Customer), unless otherwise directed by Customer, Licensor shall provide extensions of the Services (including the Termination Assistance Services) as requested by Customer in serial thirty (30) day extension terms for up to an additional six (6) months (such period, the "Termination Transition Period"). The total Termination Transition Period shall not exceed eighteen (18) months.

In addition to the Services as set forth in this Agreement, the Termination Assistance Services shall include, at a minimum, converting data, providing parallel services until transition to a new system, providing on-site technical support, cooperating with Customer or its designated vendor in developing required interfaces, and such other services as shall be necessary or appropriate to facilitate, without material or extended interruption to the Services, the orderly transition of the Services to Customer or its new provider of services in accordance with Licensor's best practices. Customer shall have the same rights to Software and such other intellectual property rights as provided in Section ____ (Intellectual Property) during the transition period as it does during the Term.

Transition Services. Licensor will provide the following Termination Assistance Services at Customer's request:

A. Licensor shall (i) assist Customer in developing a written transition plan for the transition of the Services to Customer or Customer's designee, which shall include capacity planning, facilities planning, human resources planning, and data transport/telecommunications planning necessary to effect the transition; (ii) perform programming and consulting services as requested to assist in implementing the transition plan; (iii) train personnel designated by Customer in the use of any Equipment, Software, materials, or processes to be transferred; (iv) catalog all Software, Customer Data and Equipment used to provide the Services, provide machine readable and printed listings of source code for Software in accordance with Section ____ (Intellectual Property) to the extent such source code is generally made available for such Software, and assist in its reconfiguration; (v) analyze and report on the space required for the Customer Data and the Software needed to provide the Services; (vi) assist in the execution of a parallel operation, data migration, and testing process until the transition to Customer or Customer's designee has been successfully completed; (vii) create and provide copies of the Customer Data in the format and on the media reasonably requested by Customer and, when directed by Customer to do so, delete (and certify in writing such deletion) all Customer Data in Licensor's possession or control from any tapes or other data storage media, including written records, in Licensor's possession or control except archival records as necessary for documentation of Licensor's engagement with Customer;

(viii) provide a complete and up-to-date, electronic copy of the Policy and Procedures Manual, in the format and on the media reasonably requested by Customer; (ix) identify, and assist Customer in Provisioning, a suitable functionally equivalent replacement for any shared hardware or software then used by Licensor to provide the Services, and (x) provide other technical assistance as requested by Customer.

B. Customer or Customer's designee shall be permitted to undertake, without interference from Licensor or Licensor Affiliates (including counter-offers), to hire, effective after the later of the termination of the Term or completion of any Termination Assistance Services, any employees of Licensor or Licensor Affiliates primarily assigned to the performance of Services within the twelve (12) month period prior to the expiration or termination date by providing Licensor with written notice of its intent to hire any such employees no later than the latter of (i) forty-five (45) days prior to the expiration of the Term, or (ii) forty-five (45) days prior to the completion of any Termination Assistance Period. Licensor shall waive, and shall cause its Affiliates to waive, their rights, if any, under contracts with such personnel restricting the ability of such personnel to be recruited or hired by Customer or its designee. Customer or its designee shall have reasonable access to such employees of Licensor or Licensor Affiliates for interviews, evaluations, and recruitment. Customer shall conduct the above-described hiring activity in a manner that is not unnecessarily disruptive of the performance by Licensor of its obligations under this Agreement or any of the Implementation Agreements.

C. To the extent Customer or its designee is entitled under Section ____ (Intellectual Property) to a license, sublicense, or other right to use any Software or other IP utilized in performing the Services, Licensor shall provide Customer or its designee with such license, sublicense, or other right, including, Source Materials (where Customer has the right to such Source Materials), Object Code and Documentation related to Software (where Customer has the right to such Documentation), in Licensor's possession or control in a form reasonably requested by Customer. Notwithstanding anything in this Agreement to the contrary, Licensor shall have no obligation to provide Customer any Software that is Source Materials other than where the Source Material is Custom IP.

D. Customer or its designee shall have the right (but not the obligation, except as set forth in Sections ____ (Failure to Comply with the Transition-In Plan), _____ (Change of Control), ____ (Termination for Insolvency), or ____ (Termination for Convenience)) upon reasonable notice to purchase any Equipment owned by Licensor and which, on the date of expiration or termination of this Agreement, Licensor is using on a dedicated basis to perform the Services. In addition, at Customer's request, Licensor shall use commercially reasonable efforts to provide Customer with the right to either (i) lease directly from the applicable third party lessor (other than a Licensor Affiliate) any leased Equipment that on the date of expiration or termination of this Agreement Licensor is using on a dedicated basis to perform the Services; or (ii) assume Licensor's lease for any such Equipment (other than as to Equipment provided by a Licensor Affiliate), provided that Licensor shall use commercially reasonable efforts to minimize any costs associated with the exercise of any such right by Customer and any transfer, assumption or termination fees or expenses associated with the exercise of any such right shall be the responsibility of, and paid for by, Customer. Customer shall assume such lease obligations (or pay for the applicable lease buy-out) if obligated to do so in accordance with Exhibit ___ (Fees). Customer shall execute such documents as necessary for Licensor to be relieved of Licensor's obligations under such assumed leases after the transfer date. In the case of leases entered into specifically to provide the Services, Licensor shall use commercially reasonable efforts to obtain such rights in advance and shall not enter into any such lease not offering such rights without Customer's prior written consent, which shall not be unreasonably withheld or delayed (provided that the withholding of consent shall not preclude Licensor from then using a lease not entered into specifically for this engagement to acquire such Equipment). In all cases, such owned or leased Equipment shall be transferred in good working condition, reasonable wear and tear excepted, as of the expiration or termination date or the completion of any Services associated with such Equipment requested by Customer under this Agreement, whichever is later. In the case of Licensor-owned equipment, Licensor shall grant to Customer a warranty of title and a warranty that such Equipment is free and clear of all liens and encumbrances. Such conveyance by Licensor to Customer shall be at net book value (not to exceed fair market value at the time placed in service) calculated in accordance with generally accepted accounting principles using the depreciation schedule customarily used by Licensor for the applicable type of equipment (including equipment dedicated to Licensor internal use, used at shared Licensor service facilities and dedicated to specific Licensor customers). In the case of leased Equipment, Licensor shall represent and warrant that the lease is not in default and that all payments thereunder have been made through the date of transfer.

E. Licensor shall return to Customer, if not previously returned, all Customer Equipment, in condition at least as good as the condition thereof on the Reference Date, ordinary wear and tear accepted. Such Equipment shall be returned at the expiration or termination date or the completion of any Services or Termination Assistance Services associated with such Equipment requested by Customer under this Agreement, whichever is later.

F. Licensor shall inform Customer of Subcontracts or Third Party Vendor contracts primarily dedicated by Licensor, Licensor Subcontractors or Licensor Affiliates to perform the Services. Customer shall retain the right to contract directly with any such Subcontractor or Third Party Vendor. In addition, Licensor shall use commercially reasonable efforts to provide Customer with the right to contract directly with any Subcontractor or Third Party Vendor previously utilized by Licensor to perform any Services or to assume Licensor's contract with such Subcontractor or Third Party Vendor.

In the event that Licensor is able to obtain the right for Customer to assume such Subcontracts and Third Party Vendor contracts in accordance with the Subsection (F) above, Licensor shall assign the designated Subcontracts and Third Party Vendor contracts to Customer or its designee as of the expiration or termination date or the completion of any Services associated with such Subcontracts or Third Party Vendor contracts, whichever is later. There shall be no charge or fee imposed by Licensor on Customer related to such assignment and Licensor shall use commercially reasonable efforts to minimize or eliminate any such charges or fees imposed by any Subcontractors or Third Party Vendor. To the extent charges or fees are imposed by any Subcontractors or Third Party Vendor, such costs shall be paid by Customer. Licensor shall (i) represent and warrant that it is not in default of such Subcontracts and Third Party Vendor contracts; (ii) represent and warrant that all payments have been made thereunder through the date of assignment; and (iii) notify Customer of any defaults by Subcontractors or Third Party Vendor contractors with respect to such Subcontracts and Third Party Vendor contracts of which Licensor is then aware. Subject to Licensor's compliance with the requirements of this subsection, Customer shall represent and warrant to Licensor that, from the date of assumption, it will assume all contractual responsibilities and liability associated with such Subcontracts and Third Party Vendor contract assigned to Customer hereunder.

5.3.4 **Specific Performance.** Licensor acknowledges that, in the event it breaches (or attempts or threatens to breach) its obligation to provide [the services and software contemplated under this Agreement][termination/expiration assistance] as provided in Section 6.6.3, Customer will be irreparably harmed. In such a circumstance, Customer may proceed directly to court. If a court of competent jurisdiction should find that Licensor has breached (or attempted or threatened to breach) any such obligations, Licensor agrees that without any additional findings of irreparable injury or other conditions to injunctive relief, it shall not oppose the entry of an appropriate order compelling performance by Licensor and restraining it from any further breaches (or attempted or threatened breaches).

- ***See Form Q.2.NN.4 and 5 for language allowing both parties to utilize the remedy of specific performance.***
- ***A Licensor should carefully consider the risks before including any language that allows the Customer to invoke the remedy of specific performance. Specific performance may have a significant impact on the Licensor's profitability and may serve to circumvent the limits of liability set forth in the agreement.***

5.3.5 **Cover.** In the event that this Agreement is terminated in whole or part for Licensor's breach, Customer shall have the right, at Licensor's expense, to engage third parties to correct Licensor's breach and to deliver any software or services that Licensor failed to deliver. Licensor shall continue performance of this Agreement to the extent not terminated.

- ***The Licensor should limit its liability for cover to the overall limit of liability of the agreement and seek to prevent the Customer from retaining the Licensor's competitors to complete the work.***

5.3.6 **Access to Source Code.**

- ***Each of the clauses set forth below seeks to address the release of source code to the Customer, albeit each in a different way. A Customer***

should review each clause to determine which best fits its needs. Often, a Customer will utilize a combination of these approaches.

In the event that this Agreement is terminated for Licensor's breach, Customer shall have the right to obtain, and Licensor shall have the obligation to grant to Customer, [upon payment to Licensor by Customer of a fee of ________________ U.S. Dollars (U.S.$ __________),] such nonexclusive, [royalty-free], non-transferable, personal, Source Code license for the Software as may be necessary in order to permit Customer to complete the development, installation, deployment, operation, and maintenance of the Software system as contemplated hereby. Set forth in Paragraph X of Appendix 5.3.6 is the terms and conditions of the Source Code license contemplated by this Section 5.3.6.

- ***This provision grants the Customer a source code license in the event of the Licensor's breach. It provides the option of requiring the Customer to purchase the license, which is unreasonable given the fact the Licensor has breached the agreement. This language is fairly standard but the Customer need to carefully review the terms of any agreement to ensure such terms meet its needs.***

Alternatively:

In the event that this Agreement is terminated for Licensor's breach, all rights, title, and interest and all copyrights and other intellectual property rights including the right to use, reproduce, adapt, enhance, and commercialize the same, in and to the Custom Software or any part thereof, therefore developed pursuant hereto, shall immediately vest in Customer upon the effective date of termination agreed between the parties.

- ***This language transfers actual ownership of the custom software to the Customer as opposed to simply granting the Customer a license to use the source code. This provision would be utilized when the Licensor developed custom applications to the Licensor's core software and retained ownership of such enhancements under the term of the license. It would also be applicable in the unlikely event the Licensor custom developed a new application for the Customer and retained ownership under the terms of the development agreement.***

and/alternatively:

Direct Access to Licensor Source Code. If the parties do not conclude an agreement with a Escrow Provider, of if Licensor fails to deposit conforming Source Materials including updates as required, then upon the occurrence of the conditions described in Section 5.3.6 above, Licensor shall provide Customer with all Source Materials immediately upon Customer's written request, subject to the same limitations on use set forth in Section 5.3.6.

- ***This provision addresses the issue of what happens if the parties fail to reach agreement on the terms of an escrow agreement or if the Licensor***

fails to deposit the required materials with the escrow agent. It seeks to provide a remedy outside of those set forth in the escrow agreement. In reality, however, if the Licensor breaches the terms of the escrow agreement, the Licensor will likely not provide the source code to the Customer as required under this language.

and/alternatively:

Third Party Software. If Licensor is providing Third Party Software to Customer and the applicable third party license does not provide Customer with rights to Source Code, Licensor shall obtain an appropriate software escrow agreement from the third party licensor for Customer's benefit, or if unable to do so, shall obtain Customer's prior written consent that the Third Party Software may be provided without such an escrow agreement.

- ***This language seeks to ensure the Customer will have access to the source code for any third party software. By requiring the Licensor to obtain the Customer's consent prior to utilizing any third party software, the Customer will be aware and can ascertain the risks it faces in the event of the Licensor's breach.***

and/alternatively:

Customer Completion of Payment: Access to Software and Equipment. Customer shall have the right to obtain, and Licensor shall have the obligation to grant to Customer, such nonexclusive, world-wide, permanent licenses as may be necessary or appropriate in order to permit Customer, or a third party engaged by Customer for such purpose, to complete the development, installation, deployment, operation, and maintenance of the Software system as contemplated hereby. The licenses so granted shall (a) be to all such Standard Software and other software, tools, and materials, in object and/or source form, as may be necessary and appropriate as aforesaid, and (b) be limited to the exclusive purposes of the completion of the obligations assumed by Licensor hereunder. The royalties payable by Customer with respect to the licenses so granted shall be equal to fifty percent (50%) of the royalties charged by Licensor in the normal course of business. At Customer's request, Licensor shall: (a) obtain any required consents from third parties and thereafter assign to Customer or its designee leases for some or all of the Equipment that was used primarily in providing the Services as of the date of termination/expiration of this Agreement, and Customer shall assume all obligations under such leases that relate to periods after such date, and (b) sell to Customer or its designee, at the lower of Licensor's then current book value, unrecovered capital payments, or fair market value, some or all of the Equipment owned by Licensor that was used primarily in providing the Services as of such date. Licensor shall also provide all user and other documentation relevant to such Equipment which is in Licensor's possession. Customer will assume responsibility under any maintenance agreements for such Equipment to the extent such responsibilities relate to periods after the date of termination/expiration of this Agreement. Licensor shall obtain any necessary rights and thereafter make available to Customer or its designee, pursuant to reasonable terms and conditions, any third party services then being utilized by Licensor in the performance of the Services including services being provided through third party service or maintenance contracts on Equipment and Software. Licensor will be entitled to retain the right to utilize any such third party services in connection with the performance of services for any other Licensor Customer.

- ***This language favors the Licensor, as it requires the Customer to pay royalty for use of the software in the event of the Licensor's breach.***

5.3.7 **Licensor Employees and Contractors.** In the event that this Agreement is terminated for Licensor's breach, Customer or Customer's designee shall be permitted to undertake, without interference from Licensor, to hire any Licensor employees primarily performing the Services as of the date Licensor receives notice of termination, or, in the case of expiration, within the six (6) month period (or longer period requested by Customer) prior to expiration. Licensor shall waive, and shall cause its subcontractors to waive, their rights, if any, under contracts with such personnel restricting the ability of such personnel to be recruited or hired by Customer. Customer or its designee shall have reasonable access to such personnel for interviews and recruitment. If Customer is entitled pursuant to this Agreement to a sublicense or other right to use any Software owned or licensed by Licensor and utilized in performing the Services, Licensor shall provide such sublicense or other right.

- ***In the event of the Licensor's breach, it is important that the Customer have access to the Licensor's employees and contractors. Access to the source code alone will usually not permit the Customer to maintain, support, or modify the software. The Customer's ability to do so will be significantly greater if it is allowed to hire the Licensor's employees and contractors. Thus, any prohibition on their solicitation should be waived in the event of the Licensor's breach.***

5.4 **Attorneys' Fees**. In the event of an alleged breach of this Agreement, the prevailing party shall be entitled to reimbursement of all of its costs and expenses, including reasonable attorneys' fees, incurred in connection with such dispute, claim, or litigation, including any appeal therefrom. For purposes of this Section, the determination of which party is to be considered the prevailing party shall be decided by the court of competent jurisdiction or independent party (i.e., mediator or arbitrator) that resolves such dispute, claim, or litigation.

5.5 **Services Not to Be Withheld**

5.5.1 **Prohibition**. Licensor shall not "Abandon" the Services. Unless otherwise specified in a Statement of Work, for the purposes of this Agreement, "Abandon," or "Abandonment" means: Licensor's actual willful non-performance of any material aspects of the Services in breach of the Agreement, and which results in a material adverse effect on (i) the ability of Customer to timely and properly receive and/or use the Services including the Services Transfer Assistance, or (ii) critical aspects of Customer's internal operations or financial reporting requirements, to be performed and provided by Licensor for Customer. For avoidance of doubt, an Abandonment will not have occurred, if Licensor has properly terminated, or has the right to terminate this Agreement, or if Licensor's performance is excused by Force Majeure Event in accordance with Section 33.

5.5.2 **Termination.** In the event of an Abandonment, Customer may, but shall not be required to, (i) terminate this Agreement for cause upon notice to Licensor pursuant to Section 12.1(a) (without observing the cure period set forth therein) and (ii) require Licensor to provide Services Transfer Assistance for a period of up to twelve (12) months from the effective date of the termination effected pursuant to this Section 5.5.2., provided that such Services Transfer Assistance is fully paid for by Customer in accordance with the terms of this Agreement. The exercise of Customer's right to require Licensor to provide the Services Transfer Assistance under this Section 5.5.2. shall not waive or release any rights, claims, or remedies that Customer may have for the Abandonment of the Services for the entire remaining portion of the Term.

5.5.3 **Injunctive Relief.** If Licensor breaches or threatens to breach Section 5.5.1., Licensor agrees that Customer will be irreparably harmed and shall be entitled to apply to a court of competent jurisdiction for an injunction compelling specific performance by Licensor of its obligations under this Agreement without the necessity of posting bond.

- ***As the result of Metropolitan Life Insurance, Co. v. Noble Lowndes Int'l, Inc., 643 N.E.2d 504 (NY App. 1994), which held that an intentional failure to perform did not pierce the limitation of liability, many cautious customers have insisted on including clauses similar to Section 5.5 above to mitigate their potential damages in such event. See Chapter 6.H for a discussion of the issues involved in the selection of a governing law.***

6. *Delivery of Deliverables—Risk of Loss—Title*

6.1 **Delivery by Licensor of Deliverables.** Licensor shall deliver the Deliverables to Customer at ____________ ("Delivery Place") on the Delivery Dates.

6.2 **Risk of Loss of Deliverables.** The risk of loss appurtenant to all Deliverables shall be transferred to Customer upon the issuance of an Acknowledgment of Receipt with respect thereto at the Delivery Place.

6.3 **Title to Standard Software.** It is hereby acknowledged and agreed that Customer shall not obtain title to any Standard Software. In lieu thereof, Customer shall obtain the license rights relating thereto stipulated in Section 3 hereof.

- ***Generally, the Customer does not have a legitimate basis for claiming ownership of the Licensor's core software that the Licensor owned prior to entering into the agreement. It is common, however, to negotiate ownership of any custom developed software as discussed in Section 6.4 below.***

6.4 **Title to Custom Software.** Without prejudice to the provisions of Section 3 hereof, Customer shall obtain good and clear title in and to the Custom Software upon the due payment by Customer of the sums relating thereto. Licensor hereby agrees to provide to Customer, upon its written request, with such title certificates, acknowledgments, and other documents as may be necessary or appropriate to establish Customer's good and clear title in and to the Custom Software.

- ***Section 6.4 and Section 12.1 assume that the parties have agreed that the Customer will own any custom software. See Sections 3.1 and 3.1.A, which assume the Licensor will retain sole ownership of all software.***
- ***Ownership of any custom software is often one of the most negotiated sections in a software license. The Licensor usually insists on retaining ownership to ensure the sanctity of its product while the Customer usually believes that because it has paid for the development, it should own the resulting product. A compromise can usually be reached based upon the needs of each party. For example, if the Licensor wants to retain ownership to ensure it owns its products, the Customer may be willing to accept royalty payments for future licenses granted by the Licensor as a tradeoff to ownership. If, however, the Customer wants to own the custom software to ensure its competitors do not receive a license to the software, the Customer may be willing to accept an exclusive license to the custom software and allow the Licensor to retain ownership. This exclusive license may or may not be limited to a set time period. See Section 3.1.A for an example of an exclusive license.***

6.5 **Title to Hardware.** Customer shall obtain good and clear title in and to the Hardware upon the payment in full by Customer of the sums relating thereto. Licensor hereby agrees to provide to Customer, upon its written request, with such title certificates, acknowledgments, and other documents as may be necessary or appropriate to establish Customer's good and clear title in and to the Hardware.

6.6 **Title to Documentation, Contractual Documents, and Deliverables Other Than Those Prescribed by Sections 6.1–6.5 Hereof.** It is hereby acknowledged and agreed that Customer is, and shall remain, the owner of (a) all Documentation other than [list exceptions], (b) the Functional Specifications hereto, and (c) any and all information contained therein. Licensor shall obtain the license rights relating thereto stipulated in Section 12.1 hereof.

- ***This section assumes that the Customer will own the intellectual property rights developed by Licensor.***

7. Acceptance of Software and Services

7.1 **Acceptance Tests.** Licensor and Customer shall jointly conduct Software and Services acceptance tests in accordance with the Software Acceptance Plan during the installation process at a Customer designated location(s) during a thirty (30) day acceptance period. The acceptance period will commence once the Software is operational in the Customer designated location(s). The Software and Services shall

(1) materially comply with the Functional Specifications; (2) function substantially in accordance with Licensor's specifications; (3) be compatible and substantially conform to the Documentation; and (4) substantially comply with the Software Acceptance Plan. Upon Acceptance, the Customer shall immediately execute a Certificate of Acceptance, substantially in the form attached hereto as Exhibit 7.1.

- ***Because the Licensor has greater familiarity with its own software, the Licensor should create the first draft of the software acceptance plan. The Licensee should then modify it to make sure the plan reflects the parties' intent.***

7.2 **Failure to Comply.** If, during the acceptance period, Customer determines that the Software and/or Services do not substantially meet the above requirements, Customer shall so notify Licensor in writing, specifying in detail the area of noncompliance. Licensor shall use its good faith efforts to correct all conditions that prevent the Software and/or Services from substantially meeting the requirements within fifteen (15) calendar days following receipt of notice from Customer. If all Customer reported conditions that prevent the Software and/or Services from substantially complying with the acceptance criteria are not corrected by the end of acceptance period, the Customer will notify the Licensor, in writing, within two (2) calendar days following the end of the acceptance period identifying the specific areas of noncompliance. Failure to notify Licensor in writing will constitute acceptance of the Software and/or Services. Upon receipt of written notice of noncompliance, an extension period of sixty (60) calendar days begins, which will supply Licensor with the time necessary to correct the deficiencies identified in the notice. Within five (5) days after such sixty (60) day period, the Customer will provide written notice to Licensor indicating Customer's acceptance of the Software and/or Services, Customer's desire to extend the "extension period" or the Customer's intent to terminate this Agreement without penalty or further financial obligation.

7.3 **Deemed Acceptance.** Notwithstanding anything contained herein, Customer shall be deemed to have accepted the Software or Services if Customer uses the Software or Services in the operation of Customer's business prior to accepting the Software.

- ***From the Licensor's perspective, the agreement must provide that use of the software in the operation of the Customer's business constitutes acceptance. Otherwise, there is no incentive for the Customer to start or complete acceptance test procedures. If the Customer is using the software in conducting its business, the software most likely meets the Customer's requirements. Note that the definition of "Acceptance" under Section 1.1 disclaims any "deemed" acceptance.***

Alternative Language Benefiting the Customer

Nothing else, including Customer's use of the Services and/or Software, or any components thereof, in a live, operational environment for limited testing-related purposes, shall constitute Acceptance (under applicable state contract law, the Uniform Commercial Code (UCC) or the Uniform Computer Information Transactions Act

(UCITA), as adopted by any state) of any portion of the Services and/or Software, and/or the applicable Statement of Work.

- ***This language protects the Customer from any claim by the licensor that the Customer has constructively accepted the software while testing the software in a live environment or while the Software is being operated in parallel with the legacy system.***

The language set forth below is additional language, albeit in more detail to be considered for inclusion.

Certification Testing Provision for Software

Pre-live testing for the Software ("Pre-Live Testing") shall commence on the date specified in the applicable Implementation Work plan, including the execution of the test suites as provided for in the applicable Test Plan. Customer shall have a period of thirty (30) calendar days (the "Pre-Live Testing Period") to conduct Pre-Live Testing pursuant to the Test Plan and the provisions of this Section. In order for Customer to determine whether the Software operates in accordance with the testing criteria set forth in the Test Plan, Pre-Live Testing shall include the following types of testing:

(a) Functionality Testing—the Software shall be tested on an individual basis for functional capabilities and characteristics;
(b) Integration Testing—the Software shall be tested for integration by testing the information flows to and from the Software and between and among the various modules of such Software; and
(c) Stress Testing—the Software shall undergo load testing by transmitting and processing high-volume operational data in a production-simulated environment to verify and confirm that the Software is integrated into the operating environment.

If any Defects are discovered as a result of Pre-Live Testing, Licensor shall promptly correct such Defects. When all Defects identified during Pre-Live Testing have been corrected by Licensor, Customer shall give Licensor written notice thereof and the Software shall thereafter be ready for Live Testing. Customer shall have a period of not less than sixty (60) calendar days following successful completion of all Pre-Live Testing (the "Live Testing Period") to test the Software under actual, everyday operating conditions to assess whether such Software operates in accordance with the applicable Documentation, Specifications, Performance Standards, and Regulatory Requirements ("Live Testing"). (Defects defined as "High" and "Medium" defects.)

Defect Correction Provision

In the event any Defects are discovered during the Pre-Live Testing Period or Live Testing Period, Customer shall report such Defects to Licensor, and Licensor shall promptly correct all such Defects. Upon Licensor's receipt of notice from Customer of any Defects, the Pre-Live Testing Period or Live Testing Period (but not Customer's use of the Software) shall be suspended temporarily and shall recommence upon Licensor's receipt of written notice from Customer that such Defects have been corrects; provided, however, that Customer shall in no event have less than fifteen (15) calendar days to verify any correction provided by Licensor. Subject to the terms of Section [____] (the failure to achieve project acceptance section), such process shall repeat as often as necessary until all Defects have been corrected. Successful Live Testing shall occur when the Software: (a) has been operating for the Live Testing Period and all High Defects and Medium Defects have been corrected, and (b) has been operating during the last ten (10) calendar days of the Live Testing Period without experiencing any High Defects or any Medium Defects.

Post-Acceptance Remedy

Following Acceptance, if Customer discovers that the Software fails to comply with any of the functional or performance representations and warranties, within ten (10) calendar days of Customer's notice to Licensor of such breach, Licensor shall repair, replace, or correct the applicable Software and/or provide corrective equipment and/or software without any cost to Customer as required to repair, replace, or correct such defective Software. If Licensor is not able to repair, replace, or correct the Software with such ten (10) calendar day period, Customer shall be entitled, in its sole discretion, to: (a) seek monetary damages from the Licensor; (b) terminate in whole or part the Agreement and or the applicable Statement of Work for such Software; (c) receive a refund of all monies paid to Licensor for the defective Software; and/or (d) seek any other legal and equitable rights and remedies Customer may have.

8. *Price and Payments*

8.1 **Price.** Without prejudice to the other provisions of Section 8, in consideration of the development and delivery by Licensor of the Deliverables and the provision of the Support Services pursuant to Section 11 hereof, Licensor shall invoice Customer and Customer shall pay Licensor, pursuant to the terms and conditions of this Section 8, the following aggregate sums:

U.S. Dollars
For Hardware:
For Standard Software:
For Custom Software:
Grand Total:

The aforesaid aggregate sums shall be paid in _______ (___) installments, ____ (___) of which are to be made pursuant to Section 8.2 hereof and _______ (___) of which are to be made pursuant to Section 8.3 hereof.

Additional Language that May Be Applicable for Overseas Development

8.1.A **Remote Network Connectivity.** Licensor's offshore rates include only Licensor's standard VPN "Client-to-Site" remote connectivity, in which (1) VPN software is installed directly on the individual developer's desktop computer in India and (2) a secure VPN network connection is established, utilizing the Internet, between the desktop and Customer's VPN network termination point. Additional remote networking components are available at additional cost. For the avoidance of doubt, such additional components include but are not limited to:

- ***A scalable, site-to-site VPN network connection between Licensor's Global Network and Customer,***
- ***Design, installation, and testing of the above,***
- ***Managed firewall services,***
- ***India-based printers,***
- ***Additional network equipment, and user authentication tokens or certificates.***

8.2 **Cash Advances.** The Parties have agreed that Customer is to make the following cash advances in order to provide Licensor with some of the working capital necessary to perform hereunder:

Cash Advance Number	Event Giving Rise to the Cash Advance	Amount of the Cash Advance
1	Letter of Intent	
2	Contract Signature	
3	Milestone 1	
4	Milestone 2	
5	Delivery	
TOTAL		

All cash advances so paid by Customer shall not, when paid, be deemed to have been earned by Licensor, either for accounting purposes or for purposes of this Agreement. Consequently, each cash advance shall be deemed to constitute an advance payment for the Deliverables to be delivered by Licensor subsequent thereto and shall be deemed to be "earned," in part or in full, if and when the payment against which it is taken as a credit is made pursuant to said Section 8.3 hereof. In the event that this Agreement is terminated, by Licensor, Customer, or operation of law, Licensor shall forthwith place in escrow, pursuant to the terms and conditions of the Escrow Agreement attached hereto and made a part hereof as Appendix 8.2, that portion of the cash advances theretofore paid which have not then been earned.

- ***Section 8.2 characterizes progress payments or milestone payments as "advances." By characterizing these payments as an "advance," the Customer seeks to undercut any claim by the Licensor that the Licensor is entitled to retain any monies in the event Licensor breaches the agreement. The advances are matched against the payment schedule set forth in Section 8.3.***

- ***Section 8.2 provides a mechanism for the Customer to advance money to the Licensor for cash advances to help the Licensor eliminate cash flow problems.***

8.3 **Payments to Be Made with Respect to Deliverables.** Licensor shall issue invoices for the amounts set forth in the following table upon the occurrence of the following events, at which time the payments corresponding to such events shall be deemed "earned"; Customer shall remit the net payment stipulated in said table pursuant to the provisions of Sections 8.1 and 8.2 hereof:

Payment Number	Event Giving Rise to Payment	Amount of Payment	Credit from Cash Advance Earned	Net Payment
1	Deliverable A	X	Cash Advance A and B	X – (A+B)
2	Deliverable B	Y	Cash Advance C	Y – C
3	Final Acceptance Certificate	Z	N/A	Z
TOTALS				

- ***The amounts in the foregoing table that are marked with an asterisk (*) are subject to adjustment pursuant to the provisions of Section 8.4 hereof.***
- ***Section 8.3 corresponds with Section 8.2. Section 8.3 provides the mechanism to vest payment in the Licensor after Licensor's successful performance.***

8.4 **Adjustment of Prices.** The amounts expressed in Payments Number ____, in the table set forth in Section 8.3 hereof that are marked with an asterisk (*) shall be subject to adjustment pursuant to the following formula:

$$P = P_0 (0.15 + 0.7 * S_1/S_0 + 0.15 * Psdc_1/Psdc_0)$$

P	Amount of Net Payment after adjustment
P_0	Amount of the Net Payment prescribed in the table set forth in Section 8.3 hereof prior to adjustment
S_1	Syntec salary index value for the month of invoicing
$Psdc_1$	Syntec products and services index value for the month of invoicing
S_0	Syntec salary index value for MONTH 2011
$Psdc_0$	Syntec products and services index value for MONTH 2011

Notwithstanding the foregoing, in the event that Licensor is obligated to pay liquidated damages with respect to the late issuance of the Acceptance Certificates or the Provisional Acceptance Certificates, the payment to be made upon the issuance of one of the aforesaid Acceptance Certificates shall not be adjusted pursuant to this Section 8.4 with respect to the period extending from the Delivery Date for the issuance of the

Acceptance Certificate in question up to and including the date on which the invoice for the said payment is issued.

This section is illustrative of a mathematical formula to adjust the Licensor's prices to reflect the impact of inflation. The actual methodology adopted should reflect the geographic region where the majority of the licensor's employees will be located or employed. The formula above is specific to France as the "Syntec salary index" is a salary index compiled by "Syntec Informatique," a French consortium of software services companies (including many U.S. companies) established in 1970 to track French technology salaries, products, and services. Two common indexes used for the United States are the Consumer Price Index (CPI) and the Employment Cost Index, Civilian Workers, Not Seasonally Adjusted, Compensation Costs (ECI), published by the Bureau of Labor Statistics, United States Department of Labor. The CPI is a broad based index that reflects a large "basket" of goods while the ECI is focused solely on labor costs. The parties should carefully consider which index best reflects the nature of their agreement. See Chapter 5.J.2

For transactions involving international cost/pricing, refer to the Foreign Labor Statistics section of the U.S. Department of Labor, Bureau of Labor Statistics website (http://www.bls.gov/fls), and/or (http://www.bls.gov/bls/other.htm#International).

Currently, consumer price indices are available on this site for the following countries outside the United States: Canada, Australia, Japan, Austria, Belgium, Denmark, France, Germany, Italy, Netherlands, Norway, Spain, Sweden, Switzerland, and the United Kingdom. If you require a country that is not on this list, there are links on the website to the various statistical agencies around the world. Two other sources on the Internet where international inflation data can be found are http://www.oecd.org, which publishes inflation data for its member countries, or http://laborstat.ilo.org/ which provides consumer price indices for almost every country in the world.

Examples of some of the common indices are provided below:

- *For work performed from India:*
  The all-India Consumer Price Indices (CPI) on base 2010.
- *For work performed from North America:*
  Employment Cost Index (ECI), Not Seasonally Adjusted, Total Compensation, Professional, Specialty, and Technical Occupations, Private Industry (U.S. Department of Labor, Bureau of Labor Statistics)
  or
  Consumer Price Index (ECI) ECU 12132A: The Total Compensation Index for Service Providing Industries: White Collar Occupations (U.S. Department of Labor, Bureau of Labor Statistics)
- *For work performed from Germany:*
  Index of Collectively Agreed Wages of Wage Earners (Federal Statistical Office—Germany)
- *For work performed from Switzerland:*
  Index of Real Wages Adjusted for est. Inflation (Swiss Federal Statistical Office)
- *For work performed from the United Kingdom:*
  Average Earnings Index: Service Industries (National Statistics Office)

- ***For work performed from Canada:***
  Statistics Canada, Canadian Statistics, The Economy, Latest Indicators, Labour (Employment by major industry groups, and province, seasonally adjusted)
  For work performed in the Philippines: National Capital Region Index

Alternative Language to Section 8.4

8.4.A **Fees Charged by Licensor.** The fees charged by Licensor for the Services may be increased by Licensor once annually commencing on the date one (1) year from the Effective Date; provided, however, that such annual increases shall not exceed the percentage increase in the ECI for the applicable Service period. In no event shall such increases exceed the following percentages over the previous year rates, nor shall such increases be cumulative from year to year:

Date	Maximum Percentage Increase
September 1, 2024 to August 31, 2025	X%
September 1, 2025 to August 31, 2026	X%
September 1, 2026 to August 31, 2027	X%
September 1, 2027 to August 31, 2028	X%

On or after September 1, 2027, Licensor shall have the right to request a meeting between the parties to propose a fee adjustment. If the parties cannot agree upon a fee adjustment within ten (10) business days of the request, Customer shall have the right to: (a) terminate this Agreement and Customer shall have no termination fee obligations, or (b) continue this Agreement by paying Licensor adjusted Service fees based on the actual ECI increase for the fiscal years commencing September 1, 2028 and September 1, 2028, respectively and as applicable. Any invoice relating to fees for any Services shall detail: (a) the Services performed (i.e., each activity, task, and/or milestone), (b) the identity of the Licensor personnel performing the Services, and (c) the number of hours and corresponding fees attributable to each such person's performance of the Services.

If you use this Section 8.4.A, insert this definition in the "Definitions" Section of your agreement: " 'ECI' shall mean the official Employment Cost Index, Civilian Workers, Not Seasonally Adjusted, Compensation Costs, published by the Bureau of Labor Statistics United States Department of Labor."

alternatively:

Renewal Pricing Terms. No more than once every twenty-four (24) months, but in no event earlier than twenty-six (26) months from the Effective Date, Licensor may propose an increase in the fees listed on Schedule __. Such proposed increases must be negotiated by the parties in good faith, with any resulting increases not exceeding the lesser of (a) 105 percent of the applicable fee charged by Licensor for comparable services during the immediately preceding twenty-four (24) month period, or (b) percentage increases in the Consumer Price Index (Workers) (CPI-W) of the U.S. Department of Labor for the relevant geographical area of the position for the relevant time period.

8.5 **Interest.** Licensor may charge Customer a one and one-half percent (1½%) monthly finance charge to be calculated monthly with respect to all outstanding amounts not paid within thirty (30) days following the date of Licensor's invoice(s), but in no event shall any finance charge exceed the maximum allowed by law.

- ***The Licensor must have the right to charge interest on unpaid balances, otherwise the Customer will not have a motivation to pay its bills on time. If a dispute occurs, the Licensor may be unable to charge the Customer interest while the dispute is being resolved or afterwards unless the Licensor is successful in its claim. The interest rate should be high enough so that the Customer does not view the Licensor as a bank. At the same time, the Customer should include a provision allowing the Customer to charge interest on any unpaid amounts the Licensor owes the Customer.***

8.6 **Taxes.** There shall be added to the charges provided for in this Agreement amounts equal to any taxes, whether federal, state, or local, however designated, that may be validly levied or based upon this Agreement or upon the Software, Hardware, and Services furnished hereunder, excluding, however, taxes based on or measured by Licensor's net income, and any taxes or amounts in lieu thereof paid or payable by Licensor in respect of the foregoing. Taxes payable by Customer shall be billed as separate items on Licensor's invoices and shall not be included in Licensor's prices. Customer shall have the right to have Licensor contest with the imposing jurisdiction, at Customer's expense, any such taxes that Customer deems are improperly levied.

- ***The Customer as the purchaser is required by law to pay sales taxes where applicable. Traditionally, sales taxes were not collected on services but as states look for additional sources of revenue they have sought to tax services. To protect against unanticipated costs or changes in the law, Licensors should insist on including language requiring the Customer to pay all taxes except taxes on Licensor's income. If the Customer claims a tax exemption, the Customer must produce the appropriate documentation to prove its exemption.***

As to Licensor personnel that ultimately remain or have intent to remain on the assignment for more than 12 months, or who perform services in states/countries other than where they are permanently assigned, or in other certain limited situations, there may be an increased tax burden pursuant to home and work jurisdiction tax laws. Customer will be responsible for, and will pay, the increased expenses related to federal, state, and local tax assistance provided by Licensor to the affected Licensor personnel. Application of the appropriate tax rules will be determined by Licensor in accordance with Internal Revenue Service guidelines. The charges will be billed, when appropriate, with the travel and living expenses affected and incurred in the performance of the Services detailed in this Agreement or a Work Order attached hereto. In the case of services performed outside the individual's permanent work country, there may be additional charges as a result of the international assignment program.

Licensor will invoice Customer for Services and applicable taxes directly where appropriate and may provide estimated payment schedules in advance to address the potential tax impact. In addition, Licensor will invoice Customer monthly for actual travel and living expenses, applicable taxes, and other reasonable expenses incurred in connection with the Services. Invoices are payable upon receipt.

Alternatively:

Customer shall also reimburse Licensor for any incremental taxes incurred by the employee due to Customer's requirements that the Licensor employee provide Services from another tax jurisdiction other than Licensor's employee's domicile.

- ***Section 162 of the Internal Revenue Code requires an employer to include as income on an employee's W-2 any monies paid to such employee for travel and living expenses for any assignment in which the employee provides services in a location outside if its home state for more than 12 consecutive months. The employer in most instances will "gross up" such payments to the employee to mitigate the financial impact to the employee. The employer needs to include the language set forth above to avoid incurring significant un-reimbursable costs in the provision of the services. The parties can limit their exposure to such costs by rotating the employees assigned to a project and having the employees work remotely.***

Alternative Language Benefiting Customer

8.6.A **Taxes**

8.6.A.1 **Responsibility.** The charges described in Section 8.1 to be paid by Customer are inclusive of all applicable income, sales, use, gross-receipts, excise, personal property, real property, intangibles, or other similar taxes based upon or measured by (i) Licensor's cost in acquiring or providing Equipment, materials, supplies, or services furnished to or used by Licensor in providing and performing the Services; (ii) the value or cost or use of all Licensor Equipment, Licensor Software, and other Licensor resources however described; and (iii) Licensor's revenues, income, and/or profit. Licensor shall be solely responsible for remitting all the applicable taxes to the appropriate taxing authority in each jurisdiction. Each Party shall bear sole responsibility for all taxes, assessments, and other real or personal property-related levies on its owned or leased real or personal property, for franchise or similar taxes on its business, for employment taxes on its employees, and for intangible taxes on property it owns or licenses.

8.6.A.2 **Taxes on the Services.** Notwithstanding Section 8.6.A.1, if a value added tax or tax on services is assessed solely and directly with respect to Charges to Customer for the provision of the Services by Licensor to Customer under this Agreement, Customer shall be responsible for and pay the amount of any such tax to Licensor, or as the law otherwise requires, in addition to the Charges.

8.6.A.3 **Cooperation to Minimize Tax Liability.** The Parties agree to reasonably cooperate with each other in good faith to more accurately determine and reflect each Party's tax liability. Each Party shall provide and make available to the other any resale certificates and other exemption certificates or information reasonably requested by either Party. The Parties will also work together to segregate the Charges, reimbursements, expenses, and other amounts payable hereunder, into separate payment accounts charged under separate invoices, as appropriate, for Services and the components of the Services (i.e., components that are taxable and non-taxable, including those for which a sales, use, or similar tax has already been paid by Licensor and for which Licensor functions merely as a paying agent for Customer in receiving goods, supplies, or services including licensing arrangements that otherwise are non-taxable or have previously been subjected to tax, components that are capitalized, and components that are expensed).

8.7 **Disputed Amounts.** If an invoiced amount is disputed in good faith by Customer then, until resolution of the dispute occurs pursuant to Article 29, Customer may suspend disputed payments and toll the running of time for default by: (a) paying the undisputed amount, if any, and (b) sending a written statement of exceptions to Licensor. All of Licensor's obligations shall continue unabated during the duration of the dispute resolution. In the event that, as a result of the dispute resolution process, Customer is found to have inappropriately withheld payment two (2) times in any twelve (12) month period, Customer shall pay interest to Licensor on the second withheld payment and any subsequent withheld payments at a rate equal to the then-applicable Prime Rate plus ____ percent as published in the *Wall Street Journal.*

- ***To protect against the Customer wrongfully withholding payment from the Licensor, the Licensor should include language allowing the Licensor to charge interest for any amounts wrongfully withheld. See also Section 8.5 providing for interest on undisputed amounts.***

8.8 **Discounts**

All fees paid by customer or any of its affiliates to supplier, regardless of the agreement governing the services, shall be aggregated for the purpose of calculating discounts under this agreement. Unless expressly prohibited by a separate agreement, the existence of such separate agreement shall not preclude any customer business unit or affiliate from obtaining services under this agreement. All services provided by supplier, regardless of the line of business, business unit, or the legal relationship between supplier and the entity/unit that is providing the service, shall be governed by the terms of this agreement, and to the extent separate implementation agreements are approved in writing by customer, such implementation agreements shall not change, alter, or modify any term of this agreement, except as required by the law of the country in which services are to be provided under such implementation agreement or as set forth in Section ___ (terms and conditions). Other than modifications required to comply with the law of the country in which services are to be provided under such implementation agreement or as set forth in Section ____ (terms and conditions), no negotiation or counter proposals by supplier of terms contained in this agreement is permissible in connection with the execution of an implementation agreement. Supplier commits to acting as the sole interface with customer in connection with the negotiation of implementation agreements, regardless of the nature of the legal relationship between supplier and an "in-country" affiliate. This provision is specifically intended to eliminate efforts to renegotiate the terms of this agreement in the context of executing implementation agreements.

Additional Language Favoring Customer

8.A **Most Favored Customer.** Licensor represents and warrants to Customer that all of the pricing terms set forth in this Agreement are comparable to or better than the equivalent pricing terms being offered by Licensor to any present customer of Licensor of the same or lesser [insert limiting factors] as customer licensing similar Software and Services. If, during the term of this Agreement, Licensor enters into arrangements with any other customer of the same or lesser [insert limiting factors] as Customer to receive similar Software and Services and provides such customer more favorable pricing terms than those set forth herein, Licensor shall immediately provide Customer with a detailed written notice of such terms (without disclosing Licensor's customer) and, upon such notice, this Agreement shall be deemed amended to provide the same pricing terms to Customer.

or

Most Favored Customer. In no event shall Customer pay a fee for any Services, whether such Services are provided on a Fixed Fee basis or on a time and materials basis, which exceeds the fees paid by any of Licensor's other customers for services comparable to the Services. On an annual basis Licensor's auditor shall certify in writing that (1) no Fixed Fee arrangement and no rate or price set forth in Exhibit D exceeds this limitation, and (2) any fee that would exceed this limitation has been reduced to be the same as or less than the lowest price charged to any of Licensor's other customers for comparable services. Licensor's compliance with this provision shall be subject to audit pursuant to Section ___. [***Insert Cross Reference to relevant audit language.***]

- ***Customers usually desire "Most Favored Customer" wording to ensure they receive the best price offered by the Licensor. The Licensor, however, should avoid including this language to avoid having its prices ratcheted down to the lowest common denominator. Licensors often seek to dilute the effect of such language by inserting qualifying language (i.e., "if Customer purchases like quantities, under similar terms and conditions") that makes it difficult for the Customer to successfully claim the benefit of its bargain. The language set forth above is self-initiating and favors the Customer as it requires the Licensor to take the affirmative step of notifying the Customer that the Customer is entitled to a lower price/refund rather than having the Customer have to claim the benefit from the Licensor.***

8.B **Benchmarking.** On the first anniversary of the Effective Date and each anniversary thereafter, Customer shall be entitled at its option to select a third party (the "Benchmarker") to compare Licensor's Services and fees with other arrangements of Licensor or other consultants of a similar nature, size, and significance ("Similar Arrangements") to ensure that (i) Licensor is providing the Services at a level equal to or greater than the level at which Similar Arrangements are performed, and (ii) Licensor's fees are competitive with the fees for which Similar Arrangements are performed. Customer shall attempt in good faith to select a Benchmarker agreeable to both parties, but if the parties are not able to agree upon a Benchmarker within a reasonable amount of time then Customer shall have sole discretion to select the Benchmarker, provided that Customer shall not select a Benchmarker that is a direct competitor of Licensor without Licensor's express written consent. Each party shall pay half of the cost for the services of the Benchmarker. In the event the Benchmarker determines Customer is not receiving (a) Services at a level equal to or greater than the level at which Similar Arrangements are performed, or (b) fees that are competitive with the fees for which Similar Arrangements are performed, then the parties shall revise the Services or adjust the fees, as applicable, in accordance with such determination, provided that in no circumstance shall the level of Services be diminished or decreased nor shall the fees payable by Customer be increased.

Alternative Language Favorable to Customer

Benchmarking

8.B.1. **Benchmarking Procedure.** Licensor shall improve the quality of the Services during the term of this Agreement. Customer shall have the right, at any time during the Term and at its cost, to benchmark any of the Services to ensure that the Services are competitive with respect to price, quality, service, performance standards, and technology. Customer shall consult with Licensor in advance concerning the definition and specifications of each Service provided by Licensor that Customer desires to subject to the benchmarking process, but the final decision on such definition and specifications shall be made by Customer. Licensor shall, at Customer's request, prepare and provide, or cooperate with Customer's reasonable requests, given the nature of the Services pursuant to the applicable Work Process Agreement, in the preparation of comparative competitive information and data verifying the competitive nature of the Services delivered or offered in such frequency, methodology and detail as required by Customer. The benchmark procedure shall be performed by a third party selected by Customer. Such third party shall not be a direct competitor of Licensor. The benchmarker will deliver the benchmark results to Customer in a written report. If the results of the benchmark show, in Customer's reasonable judgment, that Services provided by Licensor are not competitive with respect to price, quality, service, performance standards and technology, then Customer shall provide Licensor with a copy of the benchmark results.

8.B.2 **Licensor Review of Benchmarking Results.** Upon receipt of the benchmarking results, Licensor shall be given a thirty (30) day period (or such other period as may be agreed in writing) to review the results and discuss with Customer any disagreement with the benchmark results. At the end of such review period, Licensor shall be given the opportunity to propose a plan to address any or all of the benchmark results that Licensor agrees show Licensor not to be competitive. Such plan will be delivered to Customer within thirty (30) days of the end of the review period specified above or such other period as shall be agreed between by Customer and Licensor in writing.

8.B.3 **Customer's Acceptance or Rejection of Licensor's Plan.** Customer must accept or reject the plan within thirty (30) days of receipt. If accepted, Licensor must implement the plan in strict accordance with its terms. If Customer accepts the plan and Licensor fails to deliver in line with the plan, or if Customer does not accept the plan, Customer may terminate the Services upon sixty (60) days' written notice and such termination shall be deemed to have occurred pursuant to Section [Termination for Convenience].

Additional Language Where Appropriate

8.C **CPU License.** The machine class of each Software License, where applicable, shall be determined at the time of execution of this Agreement, **in accordance with Licensor's then current price list as may be amended from time to time [and initially set forth in Appendix 8.C]**. Unless Customer moves the Software to a higher class Central Processing Unit (CPU), said machine class shall not change for any existing License and Licensor shall not restructure machine classes or License fees in any way that will cause an increase in any License fees for Licenses already acquired by Customer, other than in accordance with this Section.

- ***Pricing should be determined by the type of license granted.***
- ***Depending on the type of pricing utilized by the Licensor paragraphs 8.B, 8.C, 8.D, or 8.E may not be applicable.***
- ***The Licensor must have the ability to amend its pricing, otherwise the Customer may claim the price is fixed for the duration of the license or the Agreement.***

8.D **CPU Upgrade.** If Customer moves the Software to a higher machine class CPU, Customer shall notify Licensor in writing thirty (30) days prior to the move and shall incur and pay an upgrade charge that will be the difference between the License fee charged for functionally identical Software placed on the higher class CPU, after any associated discounts are applied, and the License fee paid by Customer for the Software being moved.

8.E **Transfer Fees.** If Customer desires, subject to obtaining Licensor's prior written consent, to operate the Software subsequent to a change in control of Customer, other than with the designated CPU's or other than at Customer's site identified in this Agreement, Customer will be required to pay Licensor a transfer fee according to Licensor's then-existing fee structure.

- ***Section 8.E allows the Licensor to charge the Customer a transfer fee for a change of control. See Section 22.2 for alternative language for the Customer's rights upon a change of control.***

8.F **Service Fees.**

8.F.1 **Fixed Fee Services.** All Services identified in a purchase order or statement of work as Services to be paid at a fixed rate shall be invoiced according to the following:

% of Services Fee	Event
25%	Execution of the Purchase Order/ Statement of Work
50%	Spread equally among no less than two (2) Critical Path Milestones
25%	Project Acceptance

8.F.2 **Time-and-Materials Services.** All Services identified in a purchase order or statement of work as Services to be paid on a time-and-materials basis shall be invoiced in accordance with the terms set forth in this Section. Licensor shall invoice Customer for an amount equal to eighty-five percent (85%) of the fees for all Services rendered by Licensor as such Services are rendered. The remaining fifteen percent (15%) of such fees shall be invoiced by Licensor upon Acceptance.

8.G **Customer Credit Risk.** If in Licensor's reasonable judgment, Customer's financial condition does not justify the terms of payment specified above, unless Customer immediately pays for all Software, Software Products, and Services that have been delivered, and pays in advance for the balance of Software, Software Products, and Services remaining to be delivered during the term of this Agreement, Licensor may terminate this Agreement without further liability to Customer.

8.H **Parent Company Guarantee.** [Concurrently with the execution of this Agreement,] Licensor/Customer shall within twenty-one (21) days from the date hereof provide a guarantee from its parent company [**List Name**] and in the form of Exhibit 8H. The cost of obtaining the guarantee shall be at the sole expense of Licensor/Customer. The parent company guarantee shall be valid from the date of this Agreement until [**final payment**] [**thirty (30) days after the expiry of the warranty period of the software**].

8.I **Customer Royalty.** In consideration of Customer partially funding the development of the Custom Software, Licensor shall pay Customer a royalty on the future licensing of the Software as set forth in this Section 8.I. Licensor shall pay to Customer a royalty based on the "Gross License Fee" ("Fee") of the Custom Software for all third party licenses of Custom Software by Licensor made within ________ ( ) months from the earlier of [**Acceptance**] or the Licensor licensing such module to any third party.

8.I.1 **Fee.** Subject to the limitations of Section 8.I above, Customer shall receive five percent (5%) of the Fee received by Licensor for all licenses of the Custom Software licensed by the Licensor.

- ***Both parties should carefully review any language describing the Customer's right to receive a royalty. For example, the Licensor would want to revise the above language to limit the Customer's right to receive a royalty on those funds actually received by the Licensor. The above language places the risk of a bad debt on the Licensor, as the Licensor may be obligated to pay the Customer a royalty on license fees the Licensor invoiced but did not receive.***

8.I.2 **Fee Cap.** Notwithstanding anything contained in this Section 8.I, Customer shall not be entitled to receive royalties once it has received an aggregated ______________ ($ ________) in royalties from Licensor's licensing of the Custom Software.

- ***The Licensor should seek to place an absolute cap on the royalties payable to the Customer. The Customer should be willing to agree to limit its recovery to an amount equal to the fees it paid to the Licensor. An alternative is to cap the Customer's recovery at a multiple of the fees paid by Customer to the Licensor for the module's development. In no event should the Licensor agree to unlimited royalty payments in either dollar amount or the period of time during which the Customer is entitled to receive royalties.***

8.I.3 **Payment.** On or before the last business day of the first month following the end of each calendar quarter, Licensor shall generate a report that shall document the number of licenses of the Custom Software granted by the Licensor in the previous calendar quarter and all license fees received by the Licensor from the licensing of the Custom Software in the previous calendar quarter. Licensor shall calculate the fees, if any, that are due to Customer under the terms of this Section 8.H. and within thirty (30) days of such date, Licensor shall pay to Customer all such monies due Customer.

8.I.4 **Audit.** Licensor shall keep all usual and proper books and records pertaining to the licensing and use of the Custom Software. During the Term of this Agreement and for three years thereafter, Customer and/or its designated representatives shall have the right to audit (including by inspecting and copying any such books and records) Licensor, in order to verify its compliance with the terms of this Agreement. Customer shall conduct such audits during the Licensor's normal business hours and in such a manner as not to interfere unreasonably with Licensor's normal business operations. Customer may conduct such audits from time to time, as Customer deems necessary, but shall use any information obtained or observed during the course of the audit solely for the purposes of determining (i) whether the Licensor is making the proper royalties in compliance with the terms of this Agreement, and is otherwise in compliance with this Agreement and any applicable laws, and (ii) of enforcing its rights under this Agreement and any applicable laws. Except to the extent necessary to enforce its rights, Customer and its representatives will hold all such information in confidence.

- ***In agreements where the Customer is entitled to receive a royalty or is being charged on a time and materials basis, the agreement should always provide for the Customer's right to audit the Licensor even if the Customer never plans to invoke it. Audit clauses are not appropriate for fixed price contracts under which the Customer is not entitled to a royalty or is paying a fixed price for the software or services.***

8.J **Reports, Payments, Accounting, and Inspections**

8.J.1 **Periodic Accounting Reports.** On or before the last business day of the first month following the end of each calendar quarter, Licensee shall generate a report using functionality provided by the system that shall document Licensee's user count. If the user count provided by the report is greater than the current license limitation, Licensee shall report the current user count to Licensor. Licensor shall determine what fees are due to Licensor under the terms of this Agreement and Licensor shall invoice Licensee for the appropriate amount.

8.J.2 **Payments.** Within thirty (30) days of receipt of any invoice referenced in the preceding Paragraph, Licensee shall pay to Licensor all payments due and payable pursuant to Article Y of this Agreement.

8.J.3 **Books and Records.** Licensee shall maintain at its principal place of business full, accurate, and complete books of account and records reflecting all activities and transactions subject to or covered by this Agreement. Licensee shall keep such books and records in at least sufficient detail as will permit the written reports provided for in this Agreement to be made and the licensee fees payable hereunder to be determined. These books and records shall be open to inspection and/or audit during usual business hours, from time to time, upon reasonable advance notice, by Licensor or by Licensor's designated representatives, who shall be entitled to copy extracts therefrom. Licensor's right to inspect shall include any of Licensee's records reflecting information either provided to or maintained for any regulatory agencies or authorities or industry associations pertaining to the Software or to Licensee's operations under the License. Such books and records shall be maintained for at least three (3) years after the period to which they pertain for the purposes, e.g., of verifying the accuracy of the payments by Licensee. Licensee shall cause its appropriate employees and agents to cooperate with Licensor in connection with such inspections or audits.

8.J.4 **Audit.** In the event that Licensor requests an independent audit of Licensee's books and records pursuant to this Agreement, all audit expenses shall be borne by Licensor. However, should such audit reveal a deficiency in the licensee fees paid by Licensee of greater than five percent (5%) of any payment thereof, then Licensee shall bear the entire cost of the audit.

8.J.5 **Inspections by Licensor.** Licensor shall have the right at any time during normal business hours, upon reasonable advance notice, to visit and inspect Licensee's facilities, and all operations by Licensee conducted under the License, and all equipment and materials utilized by Licensee in so doing. Licensee shall cause its appropriate employees and agents to cooperate with Licensor and to provide reasonable facilities and assistance to Licensor in connection with such visits or inspections.

9. *Personnel, Management, New Projects, and Testing*

- ***The Sections set forth below generally favor the Customer in that the Licensor is contractually obligated to commit certain Customer employees to the project. By doing so, the Licensor potentially limits its ability to operate and manage its overall business. Consequently, the Licensor may want to delete some of the provisions set forth below.***

9.1 **Cooperation with Customer.** Licensor shall cooperate fully with Customer as necessary to provide the Services and shall disclose such information to Customer relating to Licensor, the ABC System, and Software as may be required or necessary to provide the Services. The parties agree that joint planning and experienced personnel are critical factors for successfully providing the Services.

9.2 **Licensor Personnel**

9.2.1 **General.** Licensor shall provide sufficient qualified personnel to perform Licensor's obligations hereunder, which personnel shall have a minimum of twelve (12) months of experience similar or related to the tasks to which they are assigned to perform. All Licensor personnel described in this Agreement shall be intimately familiar with Customer, its networks, operations, needs, and requirements. Additionally, all such personnel shall be intimately familiar with [industry] functions and the regulatory requirements of the [Regulatory Agency] with respect to [industry] functions. Such individuals shall be equipped with all necessary infrastructure in terms of tools, networks, and documentation regarding the ABC System and the Services and shall be sufficiently mobile to allow on-site assistance at Customer's location at any time. The individuals described in Sections 9.2.2, 9.2.3, and 9.2.4 below are designated as key personnel ("Key Personnel") and are identified in Appendix 9.2.

- ***The Licensor should limit the number of individuals identified as key personnel to retain the greatest degree of flexibility in allocating its employees among the many different projects it is performing. The Customer, however, should insist that any Licensor employee who is important to the project be identified as a key employee. This prevents the Licensor from transferring an important member of the production team to another client's project if that Customer's project were to need assistance. A complete listing of all important employees will give the Customer greater leverage if the Licensor seeks to reassign those employees to another project.***
- ***NOTE: Appendix 8 sets forth a model Pricing Schedule for Time and Materials Contacts.***

9.2.2 **Licensor Services Manager**. The Licensor manager for the Services ("Licensor Services Manager") is identified in Appendix 9.2. The Licensor Services Manager shall act as a liaison between Licensor and Customer for all matters related to this Agreement and shall have overall responsibility for ensuring Licensor's performance of its responsibilities and obligations as set forth in this Agreement.

9.2.3 **Licensor Services Support Team**. The individuals identified in Appendix 9.2 shall serve as a designated group of experts experienced with the ABC System and Licensor's Services who shall be available via telephone or pager continuously (twenty-four (24) hours per day, seven (7) days per week, three hundred sixty-five (365) days per year) for Customer to consult with regarding issues related to the ABC System and/or the Services ("Licensor Services Support Team"). The Licensor support representative identified in Appendix 9.2 ("Licensor Services Support Representative") shall serve as the liaison between Customer and Licensor with respect to Support matters, which shall include attending all Planning/Review Meetings. The Licensor Services Support Team shall provide the Information Technology Support and Maintenance Services described in Appendix 9.2.3, which shall include, without limitation:

(a) Answering ABC System related technical, functional, and operational questions and resolving all ABC System problems reported by Customer;
(b) Coordinating all activities of Licensor personnel and Third Party personnel to implement appropriate actions and resolve ABC System problems;
(c) Serving as the single point of contact for any Equipment-related problems;
(d) Providing any on-site Support and Maintenance Services, and
(e) Such other items and/or matters as may be requested by either Customer or Licensor.

9.2.4 **Licensor Technical Support Team**. The individuals identified in Appendix 9.2 shall serve as a select number of highly qualified technical staff to assist Customer in all technical matters related to the ABC System and/or the Services ("*Licensor* Technical Support Team"). The Licensor technical support representative identified in Appendix 9.2 ("Licensor Technical Support Representative") shall serve as the liaison between Customer and Licensor with respect to technical support matters, including providing input at all Planning/Review Meetings. The Licensor Technical Support Team shall be knowledgeable about and capable of discussing with Customer the following subjects, without limitation:

(a) The design and architecture of the ABC System;
(b) Licensor's current research and development efforts and activities;
(c) Suggestions made by Customer representatives as to future Licensor research and development efforts;
(d) Changes to Licensor's preferred equipment platforms for the ABC System;
(e) Emerging technologies and the role such technologies can and should play in future research and development efforts;
(f) Licensor short-term and long-term business strategies vis-à-vis Licensor's decisions to invest in the development of certain products or services over others;
(g) Licensor's internal research and development budget proposals (before finalized) for the future fiscal year, and
(h) Such other items and/or matters as may be requested by either Customer or Licensor.

9.3 **Selection and Continuity**.

9.3.1 **Selection**. For any new or additional Licensor personnel, Licensor shall provide Customer with a listing of the qualifications required of the personnel who will be assigned to accomplish the tasks described in this Agreement and a list of the personnel Licensor proposes to assign to perform such tasks. Licensor shall notify Customer if any of the proposed individuals have less than twelve (12) months' experience related to such tasks. The list shall include the professional qualifications of each individual, along with their proposed role. Customer shall have the right to review the qualifications of the proposed Licensor personnel, interview all such personnel and reject any personnel whom Customer reasonably determines to be unqualified to perform the tasks assigned to them under this Agreement. Any Licensor personnel who are assigned or designated to perform such tasks who have less than the required twelve (12) months of experience shall be clearly identified by Licensor to Customer as "Trainees." Licensor shall obtain Customer's written consent prior to deploying any Trainees to work under this Agreement and shall not charge Customer for the services of any such Trainees.

9.3.2 **Continuity**. Except for changes in personnel due to resignation, termination, promotion, geographic transfers, or leaves of absence, Licensor shall maintain the same Licensor Services Manager and other Key Personnel throughout the term of this Agreement. Licensor shall not reassign away from Customer the Licensor Services Manager or any member of the Licensor Services Support Team or the Licensor Technical Support Team. Licensor shall not promote an employee for the purpose of avoiding its obligations under this Section. For any transfers approved by Customer, any required transitions will be accomplished in an orderly and businesslike manner upon four (4) weeks advance written notification and with on-going telephone consultation with the departing individual in order to achieve a seamless transition and minimize any disruption that may be experienced by Customer as a result of such transitions.

- ***Although the Customer may seek to limit the transfer of certain key employees it is unreasonable to prevent the Licensor from operating its business in the normal course. Consequently, the agreement should allow the Licensor to replace certain key employees in certain situations.***

9.3.3 **Succession Plan**. Licensor will maintain detailed written substitution and succession plans and replacement procedures for the Licensor Services Manager in such a manner so as to assure an orderly succession if the Licensor Services Manager takes a leave of absence or must be replaced. Upon request, Licensor will make such plans and procedures available to Customer.

9.4 **Replacement.** Customer shall have the right to require Licensor to replace the Licensor Services Manager and other Key Personnel whom Customer deems to be unfit or otherwise unsatisfactory to perform Licensor's duties hereunder. In the event Customer requests that Licensor replace any such Licensor personnel, Licensor promptly shall replace such personnel with qualified replacement personnel. For the purpose of this Section, "qualified" means that the proposed replacement personnel possess comparable experience and training as the Licensor personnel being replaced. At no additional cost to Customer, such replacement personnel shall work with the replaced Licensor personnel for a transition period that will be specified by Customer, the duration of which shall be based upon the duties and responsibilities of the person being replaced and any other applicable criteria. In addition to the foregoing, and provided the replaced Licensor personnel remain in the employ of Licensor, such personnel shall continue to be available by telephone to answer any project-related questions in order to achieve a seamless transition and minimize any disruption that may be experienced by Customer as a result of such replacement. The cost and expenses associated with the replacement of any Licensor personnel shall be paid by Licensor. Race, gender, age, religion, national origin, and other legally discriminatory characteristics shall not be valid grounds for any such request by Customer.

9.5 **Customer Personnel.** Customer shall provide personnel to perform its responsibilities under this Agreement, including a manager for the Services (the "Customer Services Manager"), who shall act as a liaison between Licensor and Customer, coordinate Customer resources, coordinate Customer personnel and have overall responsibility for meeting Customer's responsibilities and obligations.

9.6 **Meetings and Reports**

9.6.1 **On-site Readiness Meetings**. On a bi-weekly basis, the Licensor Services Manager and the Customer Services Manager shall be available to meet at Customer's facility to review the status of Licensor's performance under this Agreement including, without limitation, the timely and accurate generation of all required reports as set forth in Attachment ___ to Appendix 9.6.1. Customer shall reimburse Licensor for all reasonable travel and out-of-pocket expenses incurred by the Licensor Services Manager in connection with such meetings, provided that such expenses conform to Appendix 9.6.1.

9.6.2 **Contract Management Meetings.** On a monthly basis, or more often if Customer requests, the Licensor Services Manager and other applicable Key Personnel, the Customer Services Manager, other appropriate representatives of the parties and any necessary Third Parties shall meet at a Customer-designated site to discuss Licensor's compliance with the terms and conditions of this Agreement, and to review, without limitation, the following items:

(a) All financial arrangements; including invoices submitted by Licensor;
(b) A detailed status report as described in Section 9.6.4, including, without limitation, reporting on Licensor's compliance with all Service Level Standards and the status of any Project;
(c) Any specific difficulties or issues that may exist; including any personnel issues and any proposed changes to the Agreement or any Service Level Standards, and
(d) Such other matters as may be requested by either party.

Licensor shall keep minutes of all Contract Management Meetings in form and substance reasonably satisfactory to Customer, and Licensor shall issue copies of the minutes to all meeting attendees within forty-eight (48) hours of each meeting.

9.6.3 **Planning/Review Meetings.** On a quarterly basis, or more often if Customer requests, the Licensor Services Manager, the Customer Services Manager, the Licensor Technical Support Representative, the Licensor Technical Support Representative, any other appropriate representatives of the parties and any necessary Third Parties, shall meet at a Customer-designated site to review Licensor's compliance with the terms and conditions of this Agreement and to plan for Customer's acquisition of any new services and to discuss, without limitation, the following items:

(a) Performance of the ABC System and plans for improving Licensor's performance;
(b) Performance of the Licensor Services Support Team and plans for improving Licensor's performance;
(c) Performance of the Licensor Technical Support Team and plans for improving Licensor's performance;
(d) The status of any Projects, including Custom Programming Projects;
(e) A description of any change in recommended Equipment platforms, and
(f) Such other matters as may be identified for discussion by either party.

The parties jointly shall prepare and distribute a meeting agenda for each quarterly Planning/Review Meeting at least ten (10) calendar days prior to the date of the Planning/Review Meeting. Each party shall be responsible for its own travel or out-of-pocket expenses incurred in connection with attending the Planning/Review Meeting.

9.6.4 **Reports.** Licensor shall provide to Customer the specific reports listed in Attachment ___ to Appendix 9.6.4 in accordance with the terms and conditions set forth therein. In addition, at least five (5) business days before each monthly Contract Management Meeting, Licensor shall present to Customer written reports of the performance of the ABC System and the Services in forms substantially similar to the forms attached as Appendix 9.6.4. The report shall include a summary, in such detail as Customer shall reasonably request, of: (a) the monthly performance of the ABC System and Services in relation to the Service Level Standards, (b) any accomplishments and difficulties encountered during the prior reporting period, (c) suggestions and proposed actions for dealing with and resolving any identified difficulties and the anticipated results during the next reporting period, and (d) a comprehensive and consolidated log of all outstanding support and technical problems identified by Customer and Licensor that remain to be resolved. Customer shall have the right to assume that Licensor does not know of any problems, difficulties, or issues that may have an adverse impact on the Services (whether from a timing, cost, or performance standpoint) unless Licensor specifically identifies such problems, difficulties, or issues in its written performance reports. Licensor's failure to provide such reports within the time frames set forth in this Section shall result in a $1,000/day per report late charge to be paid by Licensor to Customer.

9.7 **Administration of the Agreement.** The Customer Services Manager and the Licensor Services Manager shall administer the Change Order process set forth in Section 9.8 and all decisions requiring the consent and/or approval of the other party, except for those decisions requiring the consent and/or approval of Customer pursuant to the terms set forth in Sections 22 and 40, which consent and/or approval shall be effective only upon a written notice signed by a Vice President or higher-level officer of Customer. All consents and/or approvals made in contravention of the terms set forth in this Section shall be void and of no force and effect. Such Managers shall be responsible for identifying within their respective organizations the individual(s) authorized to sign a Change Order based on the dollar value of such Change Order.

9.8 **Change Order Procedure.** If either party believes that a change in the Services and/or a Project (whether in time frames, costs, or deliverables) is necessary or desirable, such party shall submit a written change request to the other (a "Change Request"). Licensor represents to Customer that it has factored into Licensor's fee adequate contingencies for *de minimis* change orders. Accordingly, if Change Requests are made, they will be presumed not to impact the fees under this Agreement; provided, however, that if the Change Request consists of other than a *de minimis* deviation from the scope of the Services and/or Project, Licensor shall provide Customer with written notification of such other deviation within five (5) business days after receipt of the Change Request. If agreed to by Customer, a change in the fee shall be made. In the event of a Customer-initiated Change Request, within five (5) business days of Licensor's receipt of such Change Request, Licensor shall provide to Customer a written statement describing in detail: (a) the impact on the ABC System performance, if any, and the modifications to the ABC System that will be required as a result of the Change Request including, without limitation, Change in Software, Equipment, if any, and Services, and (b) an estimate of the cost to implement each Change Request (collectively, the "*Change Response*"). If Licensor submits a Change Request to Customer, such Change Request shall include the information required for a Change Response. Customer shall accept or reject any Change Response or Licensor-initiated Change Request, as applicable, within five (5) business days after receipt of same from Licensor. If Customer accepts a Change Response or Licensor initiated Change Request in writing, such Change Response, together with Customer's Change Request or such Licensor-initiated Change Request, shall be deemed to be a "*Change Order*" and shall become part of this Agreement. If Customer rejects Licensor's Change Response or Licensor-initiated Change Request, Licensor shall proceed to fulfill its obligations under this Agreement.

- ***The change order procedure provisions are one of the most important sections in any agreement, but yet they often receive little attention in the negotiation process. Many disputes that arise under a software license are directly related to "scope creep," changes to the functional specifications or other delivery obligations. The process for implementing these or other similar changes should be clearly documented to eliminate the potential for future disagreements. Licensors should avoid language like that above, which allows the Customer to make*** **de minimis** ***changes without additional cost to the Customer. This subjective standard can create many problems of interpretation potentially leading to litigation.***

9.8.A **Mandatory Changes.**

9.8.A.1 **Commencement of Required Changes.**

If the Parties have not agreed in writing on the terms of a Change Request that consists primarily of modified or additional services that are of a type that is the same as or similar to the Services, and Customer determines that the Change is a Required Change, then Customer may, by written notice, **require** Licensor to commence with such Change prior to reaching agreement on the applicable Change Request. Customer shall reimburse Licensor for reasonable costs, if any, that Licensor incurs in implementing such Change at the rates set forth in Exhibit __ until the Parties agree on Licensor's charges for such Change, if any, through the Change control procedures set forth in this Article 9.8.

9.8.A.2 **Significant Event**

Customer shall notify Licensor as soon as reasonably possible with respect to any event or set of events that Customer believes constitutes a Significant Event, subject to Customer's obligations relating to confidentiality and any applicable Laws. If, as a result of a Significant Event, Customer requires Licensor to perform Significant Event Additional Services, Licensor shall provide the Significant Event Additional Services as soon as reasonably possible. To the extent there is a charging methodology or pricing metric for such additional Services in the applicable Work Process Agreement, Licensor shall charge Customer for the Significant Event Additional Services at such rate. In the event there is no such charging methodology or pricing metric for such additional Services in the applicable Work Process Agreement, the Parties shall agree upon any pricing changes to reflect adequately and equitably such Significant Event Additional Services in accordance with the procedures set forth in this Article 9.8. Notwithstanding the foregoing, if such Significant Event Additional Services are included in the scope of Services set forth for the then-current pricing in the applicable Work Process Agreement, Licensor shall provide such Significant Event Additional Services at no additional cost to Customer. To the extent that the Significant Event Additional Services adversely affect Licensor's ability to meet the applicable Service Levels, Licensor shall notify Customer, in advance, of such adverse effect and shall use its best efforts to mitigate such effect. Licensor shall not be subject to affected Service Level Credits for such length of time as is reasonably necessary for Licensor to accommodate the Significant Event Additional Services so as to meet the affected Service Levels, which period may be specified in a Change Order to be approved in connection with, or subsequent to, the commencement of the Significant Event Additional Services. Such Change Order may also set forth new Service Levels intended to apply to Licensor's provision of Significant Event Additional Services.

9.8.A.3 **Changes in Law.**

If Customer reasonably determines that a Change is necessary or advisable due to a change in applicable Law, Licensor shall, promptly upon notice from Customer regarding the necessity of such a Change, implement any such Change. Licensor shall, promptly upon becoming aware of any change in Laws applicable to the Services, notify Customer of such change in Law and promptly implement any Change that Customer reasonably determines is necessary or advisable due to such change in Law. Licensor shall be financially responsible for any Change required due to changes in Laws (i) that apply to Licensor's principal business as a service provider, (ii) that apply to Licensor's customers generally, or (iii) that Licensor makes available to any other customer without charge. The Parties shall negotiate in good faith with respect to the allocation of costs, if any, associated with a Change required due to a change in Law other than the types set forth in the preceding sentence. If the scope of Services set forth in the applicable Work Process Agreement includes adequate resources to implement a Change required by changes in Law or otherwise allocates the costs associated with such Change to Licensor, Licensor shall bear the costs associated with such Change.

- ***The Licensor should be careful about committing to pay for any modifications necessary due to changes in the law without knowing the potential cost. A more practical solution is to agree to amortize the cost over all of the Licensor's customers and charge the Customer its pro rata portion.***

"Significant Event" shall mean a circumstance in which an event or discrete set of events has occurred or is planned with respect to the business of Customer that results or shall result in a significant change in the scope or nature of the Services that shall be required from Licensor. By way of illustration and not limitation, examples of the kinds of events that might cause such significant changes are: (i) changes in the method of Customer's service delivery, or (ii) a substantial acquisition or divestiture.

9.9 **New Projects.** Licensor shall provide any new product and/or functionality to Customer as part of a project (each a "Project") to be implemented and managed pursuant to the terms and conditions set for in Appendix 9.9.

9.10 **Testing Process.** Customer shall have the right to test all new Services, Software and Custom Programming obtained or licensed from Licensor, as applicable, and shall have the right to test any and all Enhancements thereto in accordance with the terms set forth in Appendix 9.10.

9.11 **Time Tracking.** At the end of each week during which Licensor provides Services on site at a Customer location, Licensor shall report in a Customer time tracking system all hours that it and its employees worked pursuant to this Agreement and any individual project during such week. Customer shall review such reports and notify

Licensor of its acceptance of such reports or its good faith dispute of any of the information provided in such reports. Customer shall not be obligated to pay Licensor for any of Licensor's time that is the subject of such a dispute, and the provisions of Section 8.7 relating to disputed invoices shall also apply to any disputes under this Section 9.11. The parties may agree that employees of Licensor who provide Services from a location other than a Customer location will have access to the time tracking system and, in such event, such employees' use of the time tracking system shall be governed by the provisions of this Section 9.11.

9.12 **Competitors.** Licensor acknowledges that any work performed by Licensor for competitors of Customer could implicate the proprietary rights of Customer. In order to avoid disputes concerning infringement of Customer's proprietary rights, during the term of any Project Agreement and for a period of one (1) year thereafter, Licensor shall not, without the prior written consent of Customer, provide consulting services to any company or entity whose business competes with any [describe product] product of Customer or whose interests are adverse to those of Customer.

Alternative Language Benefiting Vendor

Licensor shall not be precluded by this Agreement from rendering services or developing work products that are competitive with, or functionally comparable to, the services rendered and Deliverables provided hereunder. Licensor shall not be restricted in its use of ideas, concepts, know-how, and techniques acquired or learned in the course of activities hereunder. The provisions of this Section 9.12 shall not be construed to alter Licensor's obligations under the [Nondisclosure Agreement **or** Section 12. Proprietary Rights, Confidentiality, and Security].

9.13 **Audit/Quality Control.**

(a) **Contract Records**. Licensor shall, and shall cause its Subcontractors and suppliers to, maintain complete and accurate records of and supporting documentation for all Charges, all Customer Data and all transactions, authorizations, changes, implementations, soft document accesses, reports, filings, returns, analyses, procedures, controls, records, data, or information created, generated, collected, processed or stored by Licensor in the performance of its obligations under this Agreement ("**Contract Records**"). Licensor shall maintain such Contract Records in accordance with applicable Laws. Licensor shall retain Contract Records in accordance with Customer's record retention policy (as such policy may be modified from time to time and provided to Licensor in writing) and in all events in compliance with Internal Revenue Code Section 6001 and regulations and revenue procedures issued thereunder, and successor provisions, during the Term and any Termination Assistance Services period and thereafter through the end of the second full calendar year after the calendar year in which Licensor stopped performing Services (including Termination Assistance Services requested by Customer under Section ______) (the "**Audit Period**"); provided, however, the Audit Period shall in all events not be shorter than the records retention period provided under federal or other governmental programs applicable in Customer's or the Eligible Recipients' business operations.

(b) **Operational Audits**. During the Audit Period (as defined in Section ________), Licensor shall, and shall cause its Subcontractors and suppliers to, provide to Customer (and internal and external auditors, inspectors, regulators, and other representatives that Customer may designate from time to time, including customers, vendors, licensees, and other third parties to the extent Customer or the Eligible Recipients are legally or contractually obligated to submit to audits by such entities) access at reasonable hours to Licensor Personnel, to the facilities at or from which Services are then being provided and to Licensor records and other pertinent information, all to the extent relevant to the Services and Licensor's obligations under this Agreement. Such access shall be provided for the purpose of performing audits and inspections to (i) verify the integrity of Customer Data; (ii) examine the systems that process, store, support, and transmit that data (including system capacity, performance, and utilization); (iii) examine the internal controls (i.e., financial controls, human resource controls, organizational controls, input/output controls, system modification controls, processing controls, system design controls, and access controls) and the security, disaster recovery and back-up practices and procedures; (iv) examine Licensor's performance of the Services; (v) verify Licensor's reported performance against the applicable Service Levels; (vi) examine Licensor's measurement, monitoring and management tools; and (vii) enable Customer and the Eligible Recipients to meet applicable legal, regulatory, and contractual requirements (including those associated with the Sarbanes-Oxley Act of 2002 and the implementing regulations promulgated by the United States Securities and Exchange Commission and Public Company Accounting Oversight Board). Licensor shall (A) provide any assistance reasonably requested by Customer or its designee in conducting any such audit, including installing and operating audit software; (B) make requested personnel, records, and information available to Customer or its designee; and (C) in all cases, provide such assistance, personnel, records, and information in an expeditious manner to facilitate the timely completion of such audit. If an audit reveals a breach of this Agreement, Licensor shall promptly reimburse Customer for the actual cost of such audit and any damages, fees, fines, or penalties assessed against or incurred by Customer or an Eligible Recipient as a result thereof.

(c) **Financial Audits**. During the Audit Period (as defined in Section ______), Licensor shall, and shall cause its Subcontractors to, provide to Customer (and internal and external auditors, inspectors, regulators, and other representatives that Customer may designate from time to time, including customers, vendors, licensees, and other third parties to the extent Customer or the Eligible Recipients are legally or contractually obligated to submit to audits by such entities) access at reasonable hours to Licensor Personnel and to Contract Records and other pertinent information to conduct financial audits, all to the extent relevant to the performance of Licensor's obligations under this Agreement. Such access shall be provided for the purpose of performing audits and inspections to (i) verify the accuracy and completeness of Contract Records; (ii) verify the accuracy and completeness of Charges and any Pass-Through Expenses and Out-of-Pocket Expenses; (iii) examine the financial controls, processes, and procedures utilized by Licensor; (iv) examine Licensor's performance of its other financial and accounting obligations; and (v) enable Customer and the Eligible Recipients to meet applicable legal, regulatory and contractual requirements, in each case to the extent applicable to the Services and/or the Charges for such Services. Licensor shall (A) provide any assistance reasonably requested by Customer or its designee in conducting any such audit; (B) make requested personnel, records, and information available to Customer or its designee; and (C) in all cases, provide such assistance, personnel, records, and information in an expeditious manner to facilitate the timely completion of such audit. If any such audit reveals an overcharge by Licensor, and Licensor does not successfully dispute the amount questioned by such audit in accordance with Article ___, Licensor shall promptly pay to Customer the amount of such overcharge. In addition, if any such audit reveals an overcharge of more than one percent (1%) of the audited Charges in any Charges category, Licensor shall promptly reimburse Customer for the actual cost of such audit (including auditors' fees).

(d) **Audit Assistance**. Customer and certain Eligible Recipients may be subject to regulation and audit by governmental bodies, standards, or certification or accreditation organizations, other regulatory authorities, customers, payors, or other parties to contracts with Customer or an Eligible Recipient under applicable Laws, rules, regulations, standards, and contract provisions, including certification or accreditation requirements of JCAHO. If a governmental body, standards or certification or accreditation organization, other regulatory authority or customer, payor, or other party to a contract with Customer or an Eligible Recipient exercises its right to examine or audit Customer or an Eligible Recipient pursuant to such Laws, rules, regulations, standards or contract provisions, Licensor shall provide all assistance (including such assistance as contemplated in Sections _____ and ___ requested by Customer or the Eligible Recipient in responding to such audits or requests for information and shall do so in an expeditious manner to facilitate the prompt closure of such audit or request.

(e) **General Procedures**.

(i) Licensor shall obtain audit rights equivalent to those specified in this Section 9.13 from all Subcontractors and will cause such rights to extend to Customer.

(ii) Notwithstanding the intended breadth of Customer's audit rights, Customer shall not be given access to (A) the proprietary information of other Licensor customers; (B) Licensor locations that are not related to Customer, the Eligible Recipients or the Services; or (C) Licensor's internal costs, except to the extent such costs are the basis upon which Customer is charged (i.e., reimbursable expenses, Out-of-Pocket Expenses, Pass-Through Expenses, or cost-plus Charges) and/or are necessary to calculate the applicable variable Charges.

(iii) In performing audits, Customer shall endeavor to avoid unnecessary disruption of Licensor's operations and unnecessary interference with Licensor's ability to perform the Services in accordance with the Service Levels.

(iv) Following any audit, Customer shall conduct (in the case of an internal audit), or request its external auditors or examiners to conduct, an exit conference with Licensor to obtain factual concurrence with issues identified in the review.

(v) Customer shall be given adequate private workspace in which to perform an audit, plus access to photocopiers, telephones, facsimile machines, computer hook-ups, and any other facilities or equipment needed for the performance of the audit.

(f) **Licensor Internal Audit**. If Licensor determines as a result of its own internal audit that it has overcharged Customer, then Licensor shall promptly pay to Customer the amount of such overcharge.

(g) **Licensor Response**. Licensor and Customer shall meet promptly upon the completion of an audit conducted pursuant to this Section 9.13 (i.e., an exit interview) and/or issuance of an interim or final report to Licensor and Customer following such an audit. Licensor shall respond to each exit interview and/or audit report in writing within thirty (30) days, unless a shorter response time is specified in such report. Licensor and Customer shall develop and agree upon an action plan to promptly address and resolve any deficiencies, concerns and/or recommendations identified in such exit interview and/or audit report and Licensor, at its own expense, shall undertake remedial action in accordance with such action plan and the dates specified therein to the extent necessary to comply with Licensor's obligations under this Agreement.

(h) **Licensor Response to External Audits**. If an audit by a governmental body, standards organization or regulatory authority having jurisdiction over Customer, an Eligible Recipient or Licensor results in a finding that Licensor is not in compliance with any applicable Law or standard, including any generally accepted accounting principle or other audit requirement relating to the performance of its obligations under this Agreement, Licensor shall, at its own expense and within the time period specified by such auditor, address and resolve the deficiency(ies) identified by such governmental body, standards organization, or regulatory authority, in the manner approved by Customer.

(i) **SSAE 18 Audit**. In addition to its other obligations under this Section 9.13, Licensor shall cause a Type II Statement on Standards for Attestation Engagements (SSAE) No. 18, ("SSAE 18") audit (or equivalent audit) to be conducted on an annual or more frequent basis for each Licensor shared services facility at or from which the Services are provided to Customer and/or the Eligible Recipients. Licensor shall permit Customer to participate in the planning of each such audit, confer with Customer as to the scope and timing of each such audit, and accommodate Customer's requirements and concerns to the extent practicable. Unless otherwise agreed by the Parties, each **SSAE 18** audit shall be designed and conducted to facilitate periodic compliance reporting by Customer and the Eligible Recipients under the Sarbanes-Oxley Act of 2002 (and implementing regulations promulgated by the United States Securities and Exchange Commission and Public Company Accounting Oversight Board) and comparable Laws in other jurisdictions. To the extent the resulting audit report is relevant to Customer and/or the Eligible Recipients, Licensor shall provide a copy of such report to Customer and its independent auditors for review and comment as soon as reasonably practicable and in all events within thirty (30) days of completion. Licensor shall respond to such report in accordance with Section _____.

To the extent Customer provides reasonable notice and requests that, in addition to the Type II **SSAE 18** audit described above, Licensor conduct a Customer-specific Type II **SSAE 18** audit, Licensor shall do so and Customer will be financially responsible for the third party auditors fees and expense for such audit (provided, Licensor notifies Customer of such fee and expense, obtains Customer's approval, and uses commercially reasonable efforts to minimize such fees and expense). If, however, Licensor undertakes additional or different Type II **SSAE 18** audits (or equivalent audits) of Licensor Facilities at, from or through which Services are provided to Customer and/or the Eligible Recipients (other than customer-specific audits requested and paid for by other Licensor customers), Licensor shall accord Customer the rights described in the preceding paragraph with respect to such audits.

(f) **Audits Costs.** Licensor and its Subcontractors and suppliers shall provide the Services described in this Section 9.13 at no additional charge to Customer.

Alternative SSAE 18 Language Benefiting Customer

SSAE 16 COMPLIANCE:

A. Each year during the Term (and the Termination/Expiration Assistance Period) Licensor shall obtain the **SSAE 18** Type 2 Report applicable to Services being rendered under this Agreement. Licensor shall provide Customer with a copy of the **SSAE 18** Type 2 Report within 15 days of Licensor's receipt thereof from the Service Auditor. Licensor shall bear all costs and expenses associated with obtaining and delivering each **SSAE 18** Type 2 Report.

B. If any Services are provided or related systems are operated by a Licensor subcontractor, and if such Services or Systems (or any controls or other aspects of such Services or Systems) would fall within the scope of the **SSAE 18** Type 2 Report had such Services or Systems been provided directly by Licensor, then Licensor shall cause each such subcontractor to comply with the requirements of Section ____ and, if applicable, Section ____.

C. As requested by Customer, Licensor shall either (1) certify to Customer in writing that during the applicable **SSAE 18** Gap Period no changes have been made to the Services or the Systems, the manner in which the Services or Systems are provided or operated, applicable controls, or the Control Objectives that could reasonably be expected to have any impact on the contents of, or opinions set forth in, the applicable **SSAE 18** Type 2 Report; or (2) provide Customer with a written description of any such changes.

D. The **SSAE 18** Type 2 Report shall be Confidential Information of Licensor (or the applicable Licensor subcontractor); provided, however, that notwithstanding the foregoing or the confidentiality provisions of this Agreement, Customer (and Customer's independent auditors) shall be permitted to disclose the **SSAE 18** Type 2 Report (or any of the content thereof) to any person, entity or governmental authority as necessary for Customer to comply with the Sarbanes-Oxley Requirements or any other applicable Law.

E. As of the Effective Date, the Control Objectives include those set forth in Exhibit __ to this Agreement. Customer may update the Control Objectives set forth in Exhibit __ to this Agreement at any time during the Term (or the Termination/Expiration Assistance Period) provided that, subject to the Change Control Procedure, Customer shall be responsible for any additional costs incurred by Licensor in complying with the updated Control Objectives to the extent that such updated Control Objectives apply only to Customer and not to any other customer of Licensor. To the extent that such updated Control Objectives apply to other customers of Licensor, then the costs associated with compliance with such updated Control Objectives will be, subject to the Change Control Procedure, equitably allocated among Customer and such customers.

Alternative Language Benefiting Licensor

Licensor shall provide all Work Products and Services in conformance with any quality control requirements Customer may provide to Licensor from time to time and shall provide to Customer such documentation as Customer may request, demonstrating that such Work Products and Services have been provided in conformance with such requirements. Customer may visit Licensor's facilities to audit Licensor's adherence to any such quality control requirements provided by Customer.

- ***Licensors should avoid language as set forth immediately above as it leaves the Licensor's obligation open ended. Instead, Licensors should commit to meet certain industry standard requirements such as SSAE 18 or ISO 9001. See § 16.Q.***

9.14 **Non-solicitation of Employees.** During the term of this Agreement and for a period of 180 days thereafter, neither party shall solicit for employment or hire employees of the other party and its subcontractors who have been involved in rendering or receiving services under this Agreement without obtaining the prior written consent of the other party; provided, however, that this restriction shall not prohibit either party from conducting general solicitations in newspapers in connection with its hiring. Accordingly, if either Licensor or Customer, at any time during the term and 180 days thereafter, hires any employee of the other party and its subcontractors who has been involved in rendering or receiving services hereunder, the hiring party shall pay to the other party a fee, equal to one hundred percent (100%) of the annualized gross compensation, reportable on a Form W-2 to the Internal Revenue Service, that was most recently earned by such person as an employee of the other party. The provisions of this Section 9.14 shall not restrict the hiring of any person who: (a) has not been involved in rendering or receiving services, on behalf of Licensor or Customer, under this Agreement; or (b) has not been an employee of the other party for one hundred eighty (180) or more days. This Section 9.14 sets forth the exclusive remedy of Licensor and Customer in each instance in which a party hires a present or former employee of the other. The parties expressly agree that a fee calculated in accordance with this Article is reasonable and adequate compensation for the costs that would be incurred in each such instance. Further, Licensor shall provide Customer with written notice before hiring any person who has been employed by Customer at anytime in the 12 months prior to such notice.

- ***Both parties should insist on the inclusion of a non-solicitation clause or the execution of a separate nondisclosure agreement as both parties have made significant investments in their employees. The Licensor does not want the Customer hiring its employees directly to save money or create internal expertise. At the same time, the Customer does not want the Licensor hiring its employees after they have been trained. Agreeing upon a liquidated damages amount serves as a significant deterrent. See Chapter 5.H.(b)(v).***

9.15 **Approval of Subcontractors.** Licensor shall obtain Customer's prior written consent, which Customer may withhold in its sole discretion, before entering into an agreement with any subcontractor who may be retained by Licensor to supply any Software, Services, or provide any Deliverables hereunder. Customer shall not be bound by the terms of such agreements entered into by Licensor and such agreements shall not contain any obligation with respect to Customer including, without limitation, a guarantee of payments to such subcontractor. Any approval of Licensor's right to use a subcontractor shall be conditioned upon Customer's ability to obtain a full assignment of such agreement upon written notice by Customer to Licensor and the subcontractor following any default by Licensor under this Agreement including, without limitation, any warranties contained therein. Licensor agrees that assignment of any subcontractor agreement to Customer shall in no way diminish, reduce, modify, or affect Licensor's duties or warranties to Customer hereunder, except with respect to the future performance of the subcontractors subsequent to such assignment. All subcontractors and their representatives, agents, and employees must sign a Confidentiality and Nondisclosure Agreement, in substantially the form set forth in Exhibit 9.15.

9.16 **Screening of Licensor Personnel.** Licensor acknowledges that Customer must comply with VCCA and the OFAC SDN Requirements. Licensor shall, at Licensor's expense and prior to assigning any Personnel to provide Services hereunder, perform all background checks and any other applicable testing on its Personnel as necessary or desirable to ensure compliance and, in addition, such checks and testing as indicated on the applicable Statement of Work. Such background checks and testing shall include, at a minimum, an initial review and subsequent periodic reviews of the SDN Lists against its Personnel lists. Upon Customer's request, Licensor shall provide Customer information regarding the methods and safeguards utilized when conducting such background checks and screening Licensor shall not bring upon Customer premises, or assign to provide the Services, any Personnel or Third Party Personnel whose background check revealed: (i) the appearance of such individual's name on, and/or such individual's association with, persons, companies, other entities or countries on the SDN Lists; (ii) a felony (or equivalent) conviction; or (iii) any other pertinent information indicating that such individual poses a significant risk to the health or safety of others.

Upon determining that any of the foregoing conditions apply to any Personnel or Third Party Personnel, Licensor shall: (i) not assign such Personnel or Third Party Personnel to provide the Services, if such Personnel or Third Party Personnel has not yet been assigned to provide Services hereunder; or (ii) immediately notify Customer of the existence of such conditions and provide relevant information concerning the role of such Personnel or Third Party Personnel in providing the Services to date and such other information as Customer may reasonably request, if such Personnel or Third Party Personnel had previously been assigned to provide Services and such conditions were found to exist pursuant to a subsequent background check.

Additional Language Relating to the Screening of Licensor Personnel in Compliance with U.S. Export Laws.

Prohibited Persons and Entities. All Licensor personnel performing the Services, regardless of their location, shall be validated by Licensor upon assignment, to have not been on any list published and maintained by the government of the United States of

America of persons or entities with whom any U.S. person or entity is prohibited from conducting business. Presently, the lists of such persons or entities include without limitation the following websites: (i) Denied Persons List on the Bureau of Industry and Security at http://www.bis.doc.gov/dpl/default.shtm, or (ii) the Specially Designated Nationals and Blocked Persons List of the Office of Foreign Assets Control Department of Treasury at http://www.ustreas.gov/offices/enforcement/ofac/sdn/index.html. In the event of either Party becoming aware of any Licensor Personnel involved in providing Services being included in the list of prohibited persons or entities, Licensor shall promptly remove such personnel from the provision of Services under this Agreement. Licensor shall conduct a quarterly review of the lists mentioned above and shall provide to Customer results of such reviews. Licensor shall report to Customer immediately if the name of any of Licensor Personnel is placed on any list published by the government of the United States of America of persons or entities with whom any U.S. person or entity is prohibited from conducting business and shall immediately, at Licensor's sole expense, remove such person(s) from performing any Services and as soon as possible and replace such person(s) with qualified person(s) whose names do not appear on such lists.

9.17 ***Licensor Management***. In Customer's sole discretion, Customer may elect to use a third party Licensor management company ("Management Company") to administer certain activities on Customer's behalf (i.e., time collection, expense reimbursement and fee and invoice management, collectively "Licensor Management Services"). Licensor acknowledges that in order to supply Services to Customer, it may be required to enter into an agreement with Customer's Management Company and Licensor will timely do so upon Customer's request. SUCH LICENSOR MANAGEMENT SERVICES AGREEMENT BETWEEN THE LICENSOR AND MANAGEMENT COMPANY MAY INCLUDE A FEE TO BE PAID BY LICENSOR TO THE MANAGEMENT COMPANY FOR THESE SERVICES. As between this Agreement and the Licensor's Management Company agreement, for any conflicting terms other than those concerning Licensor Management Services, this Agreement shall supersede. "Statement of Work" as defined herein shall include any "job description" documentation received by Licensor from either Customer and/or the Management Company that outlines, in lieu of a Statement of Work, the Licensor's expected duties and services hereunder.

- ***While many Customers are outsourcing their contracts administration function and requiring their vendors to underwrite the cost of doing so, a Licensor should never agree to do so, especially if it has a unique solution in the market. The language set forth above is more applicable to the provision of temporary labor or "body-shopping."***

9.18 **Technology Changes.** If a Technology Change (defined below) occurs, Customer and Licensor will identify the efficiencies, economies, and net savings resulting from such Technology Change and will, in good faith, evaluate the affected Services including Charges and negotiate equitable adjustments (including, as applicable, increases or decreases) to the Charges specified in Exhibit ___ (Fees) as to the affected Service(s). "Technology Change" shall mean a material change to the Customer IT Environment resulting from the implementation of (1) planned efficiencies (e.g., server consolidation); (2) process improvements; or (3) new technology advances, Customer investments or delivery model changes that result in demonstrable and material reductions in Licensor's cost of providing the Services. For purposes of this Section 9.18 (Technology Changes), an increase in Licensor Personnel providing Services off shore or near shore by ten (10) or more shall be deemed a delivery model change. The Parties agree that delivery by Licensor of the technology solutions detailed in Exhibit ____ (Transition/Transformation Projects Overview), including server consolidation and the global resourcing solution shall not be deemed a Technology Change under this Section.

10. Involvement of Customer Employees in Licensor's Team

10.1 **Involvement of Customer Employees/Consultants in Licensor's Development Team**

10.1.1 In order to permit a transfer of know-how relating to the Custom Software, Customer shall have the right, but not the obligation, to cause up to three (3) of its employees and/or consultants to work at Licensor's offices in [Location] as part of each of the Licensor teams that develop the Custom Software and Licensor hereby agrees to welcome such Customer employees/consultants into such teams pursuant to the terms and conditions of Sections 10.1.1–10.1.3 and 10.3.1–10.3.6 hereof. If Customer wishes to avail itself of this possibility, it must notify Licensor, no later than thirty (30) calendar days before the date on which the said Customer employees/consultants will join the Licensor development team(s). The said employees/consultants shall join Licensor's development team(s) no earlier than the date of issuance of the Functional Specifications Acceptance Certificate, as the case may be, and shall cease to work with Licensor no later than the date on which the Acceptance Certificate is issued.

10.1.2 Customer shall ensure that its aforesaid employees/consultants possess a minimum level of engineering competence in (a) the general field of software and documentation development, in particular, as concerns UNIX systems, telecommunications protocols, local area networks (LANs), and wide area network systems (WANs), and (b) Type B technology or EDI or 9.400 technologies.

10.1.3 During the time of involvement of the aforesaid Customer employees/consultants, Licensor shall have full authority to direct such employees/consultants.

10.2 **Involvement of Customer Personnel in Licensor's Integration and Acceptance Team.**

10.2.1 In order to permit the training of Customer employees/consultants with respect to the use and operation of the Deliverables, Customer shall have the right, but not the obligation, to cause up to two (2) of its employees/consultants to work at Licensor Licensor's offices in the [Location], or at the Site, as part of each of the Licensor integration and acceptance teams. Licensor hereby agrees to welcome such Customer employees/consultants into such teams pursuant to the terms and conditions of Sections 10.2.1–10.3.6 hereof. If Customer wishes to avail itself of this possibility, it must notify Licensor, no later than fifteen (15) calendar days before the date on which Licensor commences the factory tests at its premises with respect to the project on which the said employees/consultants will work; in this connection, Licensor hereby agrees to give Customer no less than thirty (30) calendar days prior written notice of the date on which it intends to commence its factory tests. The said Customer employees/consultants will join Licensor's integration and acceptance team(s) no earlier than the date on which Licensor commences its factory tests for the project in question and shall cease to work with Licensor no later than the date on which the Delivery Acceptance Certificate is issued.

10.2.2 Customer shall ensure that its aforesaid employees/consultants possess a minimum level of engineering competence in (a) the general field of software integration and acceptance, in particular, as concerns Unix systems, telecommunications protocols, local area networks (LANs), and wide area network systems (WANs); (b) Type B or 9.400; or (c) the content of the Acceptance Tests.

10.2.3 During the time of involvement of the aforesaid Customer employees/consultants, Licensor shall have full authority to direct such employees/consultants.

10.3 **General**

10.3.1 Notwithstanding the foregoing, Licensor shall have the right, (a) prior to Customer employee's/consultant's relocation to Licensor, to reject said employee/consultant on the basis of his credentials, or (b) subsequent to an employee's relocation to Licensor, to require Customer to recall the said employee on the basis of his job performance. In the event of a rejection or recall of a Customer employee/consultant, Customer shall have the right but not the obligation to provide a replacement for such employee/consultant. In no event shall any such rejection or recall diminish or void Customer's assurance relating to the technical competence of its employees/consultants, as aforesaid.

10.3.2 Each of the aforesaid Customer employees/consultants shall, before commencing any work, execute and deliver to Licensor and Customer a Nondisclosure Agreement in the form of Appendix 10.3.2 attached hereto. Customer acknowledges that a material breach by one of its employees/consultants of the aforesaid Nondisclosure Agreement shall, for the purposes of this Agreement, constitute a breach by Customer under Section 5 of this Agreement.

10.3.3 Licensor shall be responsible for any and all work performed by the aforesaid Customer employees/consultants; in no event shall Licensor be relieved of any of its obligations hereunder, as a result of (a) any rejection/replacement of a Customer employee/consultant pursuant to Section 10.3.3 hereof; (b) the activities of Customer employees/consultants, except where such activities are in direct opposition to instructions given by Licensor or constitute intentional or grossly negligent acts or omissions that affect Licensor's performance hereunder; or (c) the election by Customer not to cause any of its employees/consultants to be integrated into the Licensor team. In no event shall Licensor be liable for the tortuous acts or omissions of any Customer employee/consultant and Customer shall indemnify and hold harmless Licensor from any third party claims, actual losses, costs (including reasonable attorneys fees), and direct damages or liabilities arising therefrom.

10.3.4 The Parties hereto expressly agree that the Customer employees/consultants relocated to Licensor as per above shall not be considered to be employees/consultants of Licensor. Customer shall, at all times, be responsible for any compensation, insurance, or other employee benefits to which such employees/consultants are, or may become, entitled and, under no circumstances, shall Licensor be required to make payment of any kind to any such employee/consultant on Customer's behalf.

10.3.5 The Parties hereto further expressly agree that said Customer employees/consultants shall not have the authority (a) to make representations on behalf of or to otherwise bind Customer or Licensor in any manner whatsoever, and (b) to convey any information or Deliverable to Licensor for or on behalf of Customer. Consequently, if Licensor relies on any representations and statements of the aforesaid Customer employees/consultants, it shall do so at its own risk.

- ***A Customer should insist on including language similar to that set forth in this Section 10 to avoid the Licensor selling a project with its experienced personnel and later staffing the Customer's project with less experienced people. It is unlikely, however, that a Licensor would accept the language as written.***
- ***The language set forth above allows the Customer's employees to participate in the development process. The Customer's goal is two-fold. The first is to allow the Customer's employees to become educated in the operation and development of the software. This will reduce the Customer's dependency on the Licensor's employees. To some extent, it will also allow the Customer's employees to provide maintenance, potentially reducing the Customer's maintenance costs. The second is to allow the Customer to keep closer track of the development process. If problems develop, the Customer will have an unbiased view of the nature of the problem and its significance. It will avoid any lack of candor on behalf of the Licensor if a problem arises. The Licensor may have concerns about including this language, but there are no legitimate reasons for not including it if the Customer's employees sign appropriate nondisclosure agreements and the Customer's assumes responsibility for any delays caused by its employees.***

11. Support and Maintenance Services

11.1 **Training Services.** In addition to the training prescribed by Section 10 hereof, Licensor undertakes to provide training services to Customer personnel with a view to permitting them to operate, administer, and maintain the ABC System. In the event that Customer wishes to obtain such training services, Customer and Licensor shall agree upon a statement of work pursuant to the provisions of Section 11.4 hereof. Customer shall designate, in this regard, such members of its personnel that are sufficiently qualified and skilled to participate in such training, and the said training shall take place in compliance with the conditions to be defined at a later date by mutual agreement between the Parties.

11.2 **Installation Services.** It is hereby acknowledged and agreed that Licensor shall provide such installation services as are classified, pursuant to the provisions of Appendix 11.2 hereto, as prerequisites for the appropriate Acceptance Procedures. In the event that Customer wishes to receive installation services above and beyond same, Customer and Licensor shall agree upon a statement of work pursuant to the provisions of Section 11.2 hereof.

11.3 **Hardware and Software Support Services.** Provided Customer is not then in default of its obligations under this Agreement, Licensor agrees to make Hardware support services, Standard Software support services, and Custom Software support services available to Customer on an annually renewable basis **for a period of ______ (__) years from [the Effective Date, the date of this Agreement, or an event such as acceptance]** pursuant the terms and conditions of Appendix 11.3 hereto.

Alternative Language Benefiting Licensor

Maintenance support may be ordered by Customer and upon payment of Maintenance Fees, will be provided under Licensor's Customer Support Programs policies in effect at the time the services are ordered. Following the first anniversary of the Agreement date, as long as Licensor is offering Maintenance, Customer may at Customer's option renew Maintenance. In the event Customer allows Maintenance to lapse, it may thereafter renew such support for the affected Software by paying, in addition to the then current annual Maintenance Fee, an amount equal to the aggregate Maintenance Fee that would have been payable for the affected Software during the period of lapse. Licensor agrees that the Maintenance support will be conducted from the Licensor location, which is geographically closest to the Customer location eligible for such Maintenance support.

Alternative Language Benefiting Customer

Maintenance Commitment. Subject to the provisions of this Agreement allowing for suspension or termination of Maintenance or this Agreement, Licensor agrees to make Maintenance available to Licensee for at least five (5) years beyond the date of this Agreement.

No Automatic Installation of Updates. Licensee may elect to defer or decline installation of Updates or to install Updates in a test environment before applying them in its production systems. Licensor shall not install or attempt to install any Update on any Licensee system without Licensee's prior written consent.

Obsolescence. Licensor acknowledges that Licensee is making a significant resource commitment to acquire the Licensed Software and that it does not want to move involuntarily to a new system or a new hardware or operating environment in order to be able to continue using the Licensed Software. Accordingly, provided that Licensee continues to purchase Maintenance and Support from Licensor, and subject to Sections ___ (Maintenance Commitment) and ___ (Support Commitment), Licensor shall continue to make Maintenance and Support available to Licensee for each version, release, or Update of the Licensed Software installed by Licensee for at least five (5) years after the installation date. Within that time period, Licensor shall not require Licensee to migrate to a new version, release, or Update of the Licensed Software or new versions, releases, or Updates of third party Software or database platforms, as a condition of continued Maintenance or Support.

- ***Most software is of little value if it is not supported and maintained. The Customer is usually unable to provide such support and maintenance as it lacks access to the software's source code and the Customer lacks the requisite knowledge to provide such support. As such, the Customer***

should require the Licensor to commit to provide support for a set number of years for a set price. Without a set price, the Licensor has significant leverage over the Customer as the Customer has no practical choice but to purchase support regardless of price.

11.4 **Additional Support Services.** In the event that Customer wishes to receive services above and beyond those contemplated by Section 11.1–11.3 hereof, Customer and Licensor shall agree upon a statement of work pursuant to the provisions of Appendix 3 hereto.

12. Proprietary Rights, Confidentiality, and Security

12.1 **Ownership of Intellectual Property.** Pre-existing intellectual property and all improvements thereto that Licensor uses in connection with performing the Services, providing any Deliverables and performing any other Services hereunder shall remain the sole and exclusive property of Licensor, and Licensor shall mark any such written materials as "confidential" and/or "proprietary." Any Custom Programming, including all source code and materials developed by Licensor, all intermediate and partial versions thereof, as well as all specifications, program materials, flow charts, notes, outlines, and the like created in connection therewith (collectively, "Custom Programming Materials") shall be the sole and exclusive property of Customer. All written reports, requirements documents (including newly created technical and non-technical data embodied therein), specifications, program materials, flow charts, notes, outlines, and the like that are developed, conceived, originated, prepared, or generated by Licensor in connection with Licensor's performance under this Agreement including, without limitation, all copyright, trademark, trade secret, and all other proprietary rights therein and derivative works created therefrom (collectively, "Written Deliverables"), shall be the sole and exclusive property of Customer. Such ownership of Custom Programming Materials and Written Deliverables shall inure to the benefit of Customer from the date of the conception, creation, or fixation of the Custom Programming Materials and Written Deliverables in a tangible medium of expression, as applicable. All newly created copyright aspects of the Custom Programming Materials and Written Deliverables shall be considered a "work-made-for-hire" within the meaning of the Copyright Act of 1976, as amended. If and to the extent the Custom Programming Materials and Written Deliverables, or any part thereof, are found by a court of competent jurisdiction not to be a "work-made-for-hire" within the meaning of the Copyright Act of 1976, as amended, Licensor agrees that all exclusive right, title, and interest in and to those newly created copyrightable aspects of the Custom Programming Materials and Written Deliverables, and all copies thereof, are hereby expressly assigned automatically to Customer without further consideration. Any agreement entered into by Licensor and a Third Party in connection with Services related to Custom Programming Materials and Written Deliverables under this Agreement shall require the prior consent of Customer as set forth in Section 12.3, and shall further include substantially the same terms as those appearing in this Section to ensure that Customer obtains the same rights in the Custom

Programming Materials and Written Deliverables generated under such Third Party agreement as those set forth in this Section. Licensor agrees to assist Customer in obtaining and enforcing all rights and other legal protections for the Custom Programming Materials and Written Deliverables and to execute any and all documents that Customer may reasonably request in connection therewith, including any copyright assignment document(s). Licensor shall ensure that all Custom Programming Materials and Written Deliverables created hereunder (including each page of any document produced) will be marked as follows:

Confidential and Proprietary
© Copyright ***[20__/Year Developed]*** *Customer*
All Rights Reserved

Licensor shall not reuse the Custom Programming Materials or Written Deliverables, or any intermediate or partial version thereof, or any derivative work based upon the Custom Programming Materials or Written Deliverables without Customer's express written consent, which consent may be withheld by Customer in its sole discretion.

- ***This language assumes that the Customer will own the work product created by the Licensor under the agreement. The Licensor should think carefully before agreeing to relinquish ownership rights as this decision may limit the Licensor's ability to perform similar work in the future, impact the Licensor's future profit margins by limiting its ability to reuse the code or impact the sanctity of its product..***
- ***Alternately, allow the IP rights to be assigned according to statute / common law and provide as follows:***

Nothing contained in this Agreement will restrict either party from using any ideas, concepts, know-how, methodologies processes, technologies, algorithms, or techniques relating to the Services that either party, individually or jointly, develops or discloses under this Agreement, provided that in doing so the party does not breach its obligations under Section 12 (Proprietary Rights, Confidentiality, and Security) or infringe the intellectual property rights of the other party or third parties who have licensed or provided materials to the other party. Nothing in this Agreement will prevent either party from independently developing any software that is the same or similar to any software owned by the other party so long as the developing party does not infringe or misappropriate any intellectual property rights of the other party.

12.2 **Confidential Information.** "Confidential Information" means any material, data, or information in whatever form or media of a party to this Agreement that is provided or disclosed to the other, except for any information that is: (a) publicly available or later becomes available other than through a breach of this Agreement; (b) known to the Receiving Party or its employees, agents, or representatives prior to such disclosure or is independently developed by the Receiving Party or its employees, agents, or representatives subsequent to such disclosure; or (c) subsequently lawfully obtained by the Receiving Party or its employees, agents, or representatives from a Third Party without obligations of confidentiality. Confidential Information shall include the following categories of information whether disclosed orally or not marked as confidential: Written Deliverables, network configurations, network architecture, Services rendered by Licensor to Customer, financial and operational information, and other matters relating to the operation of the parties' business, including information relating to actual or potential customers and customer lists, customer usage or requirements, business and customer usage forecasts and projections, accounting, finance or tax information, pricing information, and any information relating to the corporate and/or operational structure of Customer and its Affiliates, Software, Equipment, Deliverables, or Services rendered under the Letter Agreement and any amendments thereto, any information exchanged between the parties pursuant to the Nondisclosure Agreement, and all information and materials relating to Third Party vendors, systems integrators, or consultants of Customer that have provided or that may provide in the future any part of Customer's information or communications infrastructure to Customer. The party that has received Confidential Information (the "Receiving Party") shall exercise the same degree of care and protection with respect to the Confidential Information of the party that has disclosed Confidential Information to the Receiving Party (the "Disclosing Party") that it exercises with respect to its own Confidential Information and shall not directly or indirectly disclose, copy, distribute, republish, or allow any Third Party to have access to any Confidential Information of the Disclosing Party. Notwithstanding the above: (i) Customer may disclose Licensor Confidential Information to Authorized Users who have a need to know; (ii) Licensor may disclose Customer's Confidential Information to its employees and agents who have a need to know, provided that for Licensor's agents, such agent is acceptable to Customer in its sole discretion and the agent has previously executed the Confidentiality Agreement as set forth in Exhibit 2 ("Confidentiality Agreement"); and (iii) either party may disclose Confidential Information if so required by law (including court order or subpoena), provided that such disclosure is made in accordance with the terms of Section 12.5.

12.3 **Privileged Information.** Licensor shall keep and maintain all Privileged Information in strict confidence and shall protect all such Privileged Information from disclosure to third parties without the prior written consent of Customer.

12.4 **Return of Confidential Information.** Unless otherwise authorized, upon the earlier of termination of this Agreement or request of the Disclosing Party, with respect to the Disclosing Party's Confidential Information and/or Privileged Information (except for any Software licenses and related Documentation paid for by Customer, which Customer shall have the right to retain) the Receiving Party shall promptly either: (a) return such Confidential Information and/or Privileged Information and provide certification to the Disclosing Party that all such Confidential Information and/or Privileged Information has been returned; or (b) destroy such Confidential Information and/or Privileged Information and provide certification to the Disclosing Party that all such Confidential Information and/or Privileged Information has been destroyed.

12.5 **Notification Obligation.** If the Receiving Party becomes aware of any unauthorized use or disclosure of the Confidential Information and/or Privileged Information of the Disclosing Party, the Receiving Party shall promptly and fully notify the Disclosing Party of all facts known to it concerning such unauthorized use or disclosure. In addition, if the Receiving Party or any of its employees or agents are requested or required (by oral questions, interrogatories, requests for information or documents in legal proceedings, subpoena, civil investigative demand, or other similar process) to disclose any of the Confidential Information and/or Privileged Information of the Disclosing Party, the Receiving Party shall not disclose the Confidential Information and/or Privileged Information without providing the Disclosing Party at least twenty-four (24) hours prior written notice of any such request or requirement so that the Disclosing Party may seek a protective order or other appropriate remedy and/or waive compliance with the provisions of this Agreement. Notwithstanding the foregoing, the Receiving Party shall exercise its best efforts to preserve the confidentiality of the Confidential Information and/or Privileged Information including, without limitation, by cooperating with the Disclosing Party to obtain an appropriate protective order or other reliable assurance that confidential treatment will be accorded the Confidential Information and/or Privileged Information by such tribunal.

12.6 **Non-Aggregation of Data.** Licensor shall not compile and/or distribute statistical analyses and reports utilizing aggregated data derived from information and data obtained from Company; provided that upon Company's written request and direction, Licensor may compile Company data for the sole and exclusive purpose of preparing statistical analysis for Company and Licensor shall be prohibited from sharing, directly or indirectly, any data, whether compiled or non-Company specific, with any third party.

- ***The Licensor should think carefully before including language similar to Section 12.6 in the agreement as it prevents the Licensor from compiling data that may help the Licensor later in the development or enhancement of the software. The Customer should have no objection if the compilation is undertaken in such a way that the Customer's proprietary information and/or identity are not disclosed.***

12.7 **Residuals.** Licensor will not be precluded by this Agreement from rendering services or developing work products that are competitive with, or functionally comparable to, the services rendered and Deliverables provided hereunder. Licensor shall not be restricted in its use of ideas, concepts, know-how, methodologies, and techniques acquired or learned in the course of activities hereunder. The provisions of this Section 12.7 shall not be construed to alter Licensor's obligations under any nondisclosure agreements between the parties.

***Alternatively*:**

Residuals. Notwithstanding anything herein to the contrary, either party may use Residuals resulting from this Agreement for any purpose, including without limitations use in the development, manufacture, acquisition, promotion, sale, or maintenance of the party's products and/or services; provided, however, that this right to Residuals does not represent the grant of any license under any valid patents, copyrights, or other intellectual property rights of the disclosing party. The term "Residuals" shall mean any information that is retained in the unaided memories of the receiving party's employees who have had access to the disclosing party's information pursuant to the terms of this Agreement. An employee's memory is unaided if the employee has not intentionally memorized the information for the purpose of retaining and subsequently using or disclosing it.

- ***The Licensor will want to include language similar to Section 12.7 into the agreement so that the Licensor may utilize the intangible knowledge that it obtains during the project on future projects. If the agreement provides that the Licensor retains ownership of all deliverables this section is moot.***

12.8 **Employee/Agent Acknowledgment.** Licensor and Customer shall not disclose Confidential Information or Privileged Information to any of their employees, agents, or representatives unless and until such employee, agent, or representative has been made aware that his or her obligations under this Agreement are subject to confidentiality restrictions and unless such employee, agent, or representative is the subject of a written confidentiality or nondisclosure agreement and has executed the Confidentiality Agreement.

12.9 **Survival; No Limitation of Liability.** The terms of this Article shall survive the expiration or termination of this Agreement. Notwithstanding anything contained in this Agreement to the contrary, the terms of any limitation of liability set forth in this Agreement shall not apply to any breach by a party of its confidentiality obligations under this Article.

- ***Additional language for use when the Licensor will be performing services internationally or will have access to personal data for individuals who reside outside of the United States.***

12.10 **Customer Information.** Licensor shall comply with all U.S. and international Laws governing or relating to privacy, data security and the handling of data security breaches. All information pertaining to a former or current customer or applicant of Customer, including but not limited to such person's address, telephone number and other contact information, image, gender, age, social security number, account or other identifying numbers or attributes, and financial, health and insurance information, and other information about an individual, including the fact that the individual is or was a customer or applicant of Customer ("Customer Information"), shall be deemed to be Confidential Information, subject to the obligations and restrictions set forth in this subsection and Customer's Health Insurance Portability and Accountability Act of 1996 (HIPAA) requirements, attached hereto as Schedule 12.10.

12.11 **International Privacy Laws.** In addition to the above, if any country where Services are to be rendered under the Agreement has or enacts a data protection-related law that requires the execution of a data export agreement, then Licensor shall, upon Customer's request, execute and cause any subcontractors to execute such supplemental agreement promptly on such terms and conditions as shall be mutually agreed.

Alternative Language for Use When the Parties Desire to Have an Independent Nondisclosure Agreement

Notwithstanding the previous paragraphs, all information provided by either party to the other under this Agreement shall be kept confidential in conformance with and subject to the terms of a certain Proprietary Information Agreement dated ___________, 20__ by and between the parties hereto.

- ***The parties may want to execute a separate proprietary information agreement to eliminate any survivability issues arising upon the termination of the license agreement.***

Additional Language Setting Forth Specific Security Requirements

Security Procedures. Licensor shall employ reasonable security measures for itself and the Licensor Personnel, which shall include, but not be limited to:

A. Prohibiting of the disclosure of Proprietary or Confidential Information within Licensor's organization except to individuals identified as requiring access to such information to perform Licensor's obligations under this Agreement pursuant to Section __ hereto;

B. Precluding access to Proprietary and Confidential Information by any Licensor Personnel until such individual has been trained with regard to the handling of the Proprietary or Confidential Information, and use of security measures identified herein;

C. Requiring all new Licensor Personnel who are not employees of Licensor to execute a confidentiality agreement with terms no less restrictive than those in Section __;

D. Providing each individual authorized to access Proprietary or Confidential Information with a unique access code and notifying such individual that disclosure of any password, access code, or security device shall result in disciplinary action, including termination;

E. Promptly canceling any password or security access code when Licensor Personnel is terminated or transferred;

F. Locating display screens, keyboard devices, and other desktop devices in a way that access and visualization is restricted to authorized users only;

G. Physically safeguarding all telecommunication switches, computer rooms, and tape libraries, as well as restricting access to such sites to authorized personnel through card access system (CAS) badges or comparable security mechanisms;

H. Ensuring audit trails are maintained with regard to access to all Licensor premises and computers. Without limitation, Licensor shall utilize sufficient access control applications to enable it to identify and authenticate Licensor's users with access to Licensor's or Customer's data, and to record and investigate security related events and data. Licensor shall investigate any security breach in Licensor's premises and computers resulting in unauthorized access to such data, and provide additional security protections, at no additional charge to Customer;

I. Reporting to Customer immediately any breaches of security or unauthorized access to Customer's systems that Licensor detects or becomes aware of. Licensor will use diligent efforts to remedy such breach of security or unauthorized access that is caused by Licensor in a timely manner and deliver to Customer a root cause assessment and future incident mitigation plan with regard to any such breach of security or unauthorized access affecting Protected Health Information; and

J. Understanding that Licensor may receive access to Customer's computers and electronic communications systems ("Communication Systems"), including, but not limited to, voicemail, email, customer databases, and Internet and intranet systems. Such Communication Systems are intended for legitimate business use related to Customer's business. Licensor acknowledges that Licensor does not have any expectation of privacy as between Licensor and Customer in the use of or access to Customer's Communication Systems and that all communications sent over, received by or from, or stored in any such systems by or on behalf of Licensor are subject to Customer's scrutiny, use and disclosure (subject to the protections of Proprietary and Confidential Information herein), at Customer's sole discretion. Customer reserves the right, for business purposes, to monitor, review, audit, interpret, access, archive, and/or disclose (subject to the protections of Proprietary and Confidential Information herein) materials sent over, received by or from, or stored in any of its Communication Systems. This includes, without limitation, email communications sent by users across the Internet and intranet from and to all domain names maintained by Customer. This also includes, without limitation, any electronic Communication Systems that has been used to access any of Customer's systems. Licensor further agrees that Licensor will use all appropriate security, such as, for example, encryption and passwords, to protect Customer's Proprietary or Confidential Information from unauthorized disclosure (internally or externally) and that the use of such security does not give rise to any privacy rights in the communication as between Licensor and Customer. Customer reserves the right to override any security passwords to obtain access to voicemail, email, computer (and software or other applications), and/or computer disks in connection with its Communication Systems. Licensor also acknowledges that Customer reserves the right, for legitimate business purposes, to search all work areas on Customer Sites (for example, offices, cubicles, desks, drawers, cabinets, computers, computer disks, and files) and all personal items brought onto Customer property.

13. Reproduction of Documentation, Object Code, and Source Code

13.1 **Documentation.** Customer shall have the right, at no additional charge, to reproduce solely for its own internal use, all Documentation furnished by Licensor pursuant to this Agreement regardless of whether such Documentation is copyrighted by Licensor. All copies of Documentation made by Customer shall include any proprietary notice or stamp that has been affixed by Licensor. Licensor shall furnish for each License purchased by Customer, and at no additional charge to Customer, one (1) copy of the Documentation sufficient to enable Customer to operate the Software. All Documentation shall be in the English language.

- ***Licensors usually do not profit from reproducing their documents and manuals; thus Licensors should not be concerned that the Customer makes copies so long as the Customer reproduces the Licensor's protective notices.***

Licensors should not include language in the documentation that the documentation will allow the Customer to successfully operate the software. At the same time, the Customer should insist on the inclusion of language that provides that the level of detail of the documentation is sufficient to allow a reasonably qualified Customer employee to operate the software.

13.2 **Object Code.** One copy of the Object Code may be reproduced by Customer, at no additional charge, only for backup or archival purposes. Customer shall notify Licensor in writing of its methods and procedures for archiving the Object Code prior to doing so.

13.3 **Source Code.** Upon purchase of a Source Code license, one additional copy of the Source Code may be reproduced by Customer, at no additional charge, only for backup or archival purposes. Customer shall notify Licensor in writing of its methods and procedures for archiving the Source Code prior to doing so.

- ***When a Customer purchases a source code license it should receive only one copy of the source code with the right to make one backup copy for archival purposes. The Customer must purchase a second copy of the source code if it wants to modify the source code while using the original copy of the source code in the Customer's production environment.***
- ***The Customer is prohibited under Section 3.4 from reverse engineering the software.***

14. Patent and Other Proprietary Rights Indemnification

14.1.A **Language that Favors Licensor**

14.A.1 **Third Party Infringement Claims.** Licensor will defend at its own expense any action against Licensee brought by a third party to the extent that the action is based upon a claim that the Software directly infringes any U.S. copyright or misappropriates any trade secret recognized as such under the Uniform Trade Secret Law, and Licensor will pay those costs and damages finally awarded against Licensee in any such action that are specifically attributable to such claim or those costs and damages agreed to in a monetary settlement of such action.

- ***This language favors the Licensor as the Licensor's obligations are extremely limited. The Licensor is obligated only to defend a third party claim and not to indemnify the Licensee.***
- ***The Licensor's obligation to defend is limited only to third party claims that the software directly infringes on any U.S. copyright or the misappropriation of "trade secrets" as the Uniform Trade Secret Law defines such term. This language does not address patent claims or claims made under any laws other than those of the United States.***
- ***"Finally awarded" limits the Licensor's obligation to pay for the costs and damages incurred until all appeals have been exhausted. Further, it only addresses "monetary settlements" and not other types of settlements.***

- ***The infringement is limited to U.S. copyrights. With foreign transactions, indemnification should be limited to the United States and the country in which the software will be used.***

14.A.2 **Conditions.** Licensor's obligations under the preceding paragraph with respect to an action are conditioned on (a) Licensee notifying Licensor promptly in writing of such action; (b) Licensee giving Licensor sole control of the defense thereof and any related settlement negotiations; and (c) Licensee cooperating with Licensor in such defense (including, without limitation, by making available to Licensor all documents and information in Licensee's possession or control that are relevant to the infringement or misappropriation claims, and by making Licensee's personnel available to testify or consult with Licensor or its attorneys in connection with such defense).

14.A.3 **Licensor's Options.** If the Software becomes, or in Licensor's opinion **is likely to become, the subject of an infringement or misappropriation claim**, Licensor may, **at its option** and expense, either (a) procure for Licensee the right to continue using the Software; (b) replace or modify the Software so that it becomes non-infringing; **or** (c) terminate Licensee's right to use the Software and give Licensee a refund or credit for the license fees actually paid by Licensee to Licensor for the infringing components of the Software less a reasonable allowance for the period of time Licensee has used the Software.

- ***This language gives the Licensor significant leeway as it allows the Licensor to modify the software if, in the Licensor's opinion, the software may potentially infringe a third party's intellectual property. Further, the Licensor maintains control over the remedy chosen. If the software is mission critical, the Licensee should retain the right to select the appropriate remedy.***

14.A.4 **Exclusions**. Notwithstanding the foregoing, Licensor will have no obligation or otherwise with respect to any infringement or misappropriation claim based upon (a) any use of the Software not in accordance with the Agreement or for purposes not intended by Licensor; (b) any use of the Software in combination with other products, equipment, software, or data not supplied by Licensor; (c) any use of any release of the Software other than the most current release made available to Licensee; or (d) any modification of the Software made by any person other than Licensor.

- ***The Licensor's stated exclusions should only be effective to the extent that one of the enumerated events causes a claim of infringement or misappropriation. The Licensor should not be excused from its obligations if one of the enumerated events occurs but the claim of infringement or misappropriation does not arise as a result of such excluded event.***
- ***The Customer should indemnify the Licensor if an infringement claim arises from modifications or uses undertaken by the Customer that were not authorized by the license which cause any actual or alleged infringement.***

14.A.5. **Entire Liability.** This section states licensor's entire liability and licensee's sole and exclusive remedy for infringement and misappropriation claims and actions.

- ***The language set forth in 14.A.5 protects the Licensor from unlimited liability and should be contained in any agreement where intellectual property indemnification is excluded from the limit of liability.***

14.1.B **Language that Favors Licensee**

14.B.1. **Indemnification.** Licensor will indemnify and hold Licensee harmless from and against any and all claims, losses, liability, damages, costs, and expenses (including attorney's fees, expert witness fees, and court costs) directly or indirectly arising from or related to any actual or alleged infringement (including contributory infringement), misappropriation, or violation of any third party's patents, copyrights, trade secret rights, trademarks, or other intellectual property or proprietary rights of any nature in any jurisdiction in the world, resulting from the use of the Software by Licensee. If Licensee's continued use of the Software is restricted or prohibited as a result of any such infringement, misappropriation, or violation of third party rights, Licensor shall, at Licensee's option and at no charge to Licensee, and in addition to Licensee's other rights and remedies, (a) secure for Licensee the right to continue using the Software as allowed under this Agreement, (b) modify or replace the infringing components of the Software so that they are non-infringing with no loss or degradation of features, functionality, or performance, or (c) refund to Licensee all amounts paid by Licensee for the Software.

- ***This language favors the Licensee, as the Licensor must indemnify the Licensee for any claim directly or indirectly related to any actual or alleged infringement. Further, it grants the Licensee the option to select the remedy that meets the Licensee's business needs, including a full refund of all amounts paid, not a pro-rated refund.***
- ***The Licensor must be careful to limit indemnification to a specific entity and not a broad class of entities, i.e., all Affiliates of the Licensee.***
- ***Including "attorney's fees" allows the indemnified party to collect attorney's fees, which are usually not recoverable under common law.***
- ***The Licensor always needs the option to refund the Licensee's money if the Licensor cannot alter the software to make it non-infringing or obtain a license for the Licensee to use the Software. Otherwise, the Licensor could potentially be obligated to provide a software fix/license regardless of cost or the Licensor's ability to do so.***
- ***The Licensee should include language providing that if the Licensee must move off the Licensor's software to a third party system, the Licensor will pay all costs incurred by the Licensee in such conversion.***

14.B.2 **Exclusions.** Notwithstanding the foregoing, Licensor will not be obligated to indemnify Licensee to the extent that an infringement or misappropriation claim is based upon (i) use of the Software in breach of this Agreement, if such infringement or misappropriation would not have occurred but for such breach; (ii) use of the Software in combination with other products not supplied or recommended by Licensor or specified by Licensor as being compatible with the Software, if such infringement or misappropriation would not have occurred but for such combined use; (iii) use of any release of the Software other than the most current release made available to Licensee, if the most current release was furnished to Licensee specifically to avoid such infringement or misappropriation and if such infringement or misappropriation would have been avoided by use of the most current release; or (iv) any modification of the Software made by Licensee (other than at Licensor's direction), if such infringement or misappropriation would not have occurred but for such modification.

14.B.3 **Defense of Third Party Suits.** Licensee will use reasonable efforts to notify Licensor promptly of any third party claim, suit, or action (a "Claim") for which Licensee believes it is entitled to indemnification under this Section 14 and which Licensee desires Licensor to defend. However, Licensee's failure to provide such notice or delay in providing such notice will relieve Licensor of its obligations under this Section 14 only if and to the extent that such delay or failure materially prejudices Licensor's ability to defend such Claim. If Licensee tenders the defense of a Claim to Licensor, Licensor will have the right and the obligation to defend such Claim with counsel of its choice; however, Licensee may participate in the defense of the Claim with its own counsel and at its own expense. Once Licensor assumes defense of a Claim, it will be conclusively presumed that Licensor is obligated to indemnify Licensee for such Claim, and Licensee will cooperate with Licensor, at Licensor's reasonable request and at Licensor's expense, in the defense of the Claim. No settlement of a Claim will be binding on Licensee without Licensee's prior written consent.

- ***This language favors the Licensee in that the Licensee must only use reasonable efforts to promptly notify the Licensor of any third party claim. Further, the Licensee may notify the Licensor of those claims "which Licensee desires Licensor to defend" regardless of the Licensor's legal obligation to actual defend the Licensee. Further, the Licensee's failure to give prompt notice to the Licensor will only excuse the Licensor's obligation to defend the Licensee to the extent the Licensor's interest have been materially prejudiced, which will be difficult to prove.***
- ***Further, once the Licensor assumes defense of a claim, the Licensor is conclusively presumed to be obligated to defend such claim. This prevents the Licensor from later claiming it did not have a legal obligation to defend such claim, significantly increasing its risks.***
- ***The Licensor may bind the Licensee under any settlement without the Licensee's consent. From the Licensee's perspective, this is imprudent, as the Licensee cannot allow its business interests to be determined by the Licensor.***

[***Alternative Language Dependant on Prior Language Accepted***]

14.2 **Assumption of Defense.** If the indemnifying party fails to assume the defense of any actual or threatened action covered by this Section 14 within the earlier of (a) any deadline established by a third party in a written demand or by a court, and (b) thirty (30) days of notice of the claim, the indemnified party may follow such course of action as it reasonably deems necessary to protect its interest and shall be indemnified for all costs reasonably incurred in such course of action; provided, however, that the indemnified party shall not settle a claim without the consent of the indemnifying party.

- ***This language allows a party to undertake its own defense if the indemnifying party fails to do so.***
- ***Although intellectual property indemnification is usually excluded from any limit of liability, in actuality the Licensor is protected by the limits set forth in subsections (a), (b), and (c).***
- ***Traditionally, there is no limitation of liability for intellectual property indemnification claims.***

14.3 **Cessation of Fees.** In no event shall Customer be liable to Licensor for any charges after the date that Customer no longer uses the item because of actual or claimed infringement.

14.4 **Licensee Indemnification of Licensor.** Except as otherwise expressly provided in Section 14.1 of this Agreement, Customer shall indemnify and defend Licensor, its directors, and its officers, and shall hold such parties harmless from and against any and all claims, liabilities, damages and expenses, including reasonable attorneys' fees, arising from any third party claim in connection with (a) any Customer supplied intellectual property, (b) any Functional Specifications supplied by Customer, or (c) Customer's transaction of business through the use of any web page or website. The provisions of this Section 14.4 shall not apply to any third party loss or damage caused by Licensor's gross negligence or willful misconduct.

15. General Indemnity

15.1 **Indemnity.** Subject to the limitations contained in this Agreement, Licensor agrees to indemnify and hold harmless Customer, and Customer agrees to indemnify and hold harmless Licensor respectively, from any liabilities, penalties, demands, or claims **finally awarded** (including the costs, expenses, and **reasonable attorney's fees** on account thereof) that may be made **by any third party** for **personal bodily injuries, including death, resulting from the indemnifying party's gross negligence or willful acts or omissions or those of persons furnished by the indemnifying party, its agents, or subcontractors or resulting from use of the Software, Software Products, and/or Services furnished hereunder**. Licensor agrees to defend Customer, at Customer's request, and Customer agrees to defend Licensor, at Licensor's request, against any such liability, claim, or demand. Customer and Licensor respectively agree to notify the other party promptly of any written claims or demands against the indemnified party for which the indemnifying party is responsible hereunder. The foregoing indemnity shall be in addition to any other indemnity obligations of Licensor or Customer set forth in this Agreement.

- ***Indemnification by its nature acts as a risk-shifting device usually with respect to third party liability. As such, it usually addresses intellectual property infringement, personal bodily injury, and property damage. In some cases, indemnification may include damages resulting from intentional acts and willful misconduct.***
- ***Many Customers seek to have the Licensor indemnify the Customer for any liability arising from or related to the agreement. The Licensor***

should strictly limit its indemnification obligations to addresses intellectual property infringement, personal bodily injury, and property damage as the Customer has a remedy for the Licensor's breach through a breach of contract claim.

- ***The alternative language below favors the Customer by significantly expanding the nature of the Licensor's indemnification obligations and hence the Licensor's risk. The first clause limits Licensor's liability to the amounts set forth in Section 16 (i.e., to the amount of money received from the Customer). Most licensees will want to exclude indemnification from any limit of liability.***
- ***"Finally awarded" limits Licensor's obligations to pay the Customer until all appeals have been exhausted.***
- ***An indemnification clause may also allow a recovery in those states that recognize the doctrine of contributory negligence and not the doctrine of comparative negligence. It also allows for the recovery of attorneys' fees, which are usually not recoverable.***

Alternative Language Benefiting the Customer

Indemnification. Licensor hereby agrees to indemnify and hold Customer and its Representatives harmless from and against all claims, liabilities, losses, damages, and expenses (including reasonable attorneys' fees and expenses) incurred or suffered by any of them as a result of or in connection with (a) any breach by Licensor or any of its Representatives of any of their obligations under this Agreement or any Representative Agreement, or (b) the negligence or willful misconduct of Licensor or any of its Representatives.

or:

Indemnification. Licensor shall indemnify, defend and hold Customer's (its directors, officers and employees) harmless from and against any and all suits, proceedings at law or in equity, claims, loss, liabilities, costs, payments, injury, damage and expenses of any nature (including attorney's fees and court costs) to the extent such damages result from or arise out of (1) failure of Licensor or its Personnel, servants or subcontractors to comply with the terms and conditions of this Agreement; (2) failure of Licensor or its Personnel, servants or subcontractors to comply with applicable laws; (3) negligent acts or willful misconduct of Licensor or its Personnel, servants or subcontractors; (4) any obligation of Licensor to its Personnel, servants or subcontractors including any payment or worker's compensation claim; (5) claims of intellectual property infringement arising from the Services performed hereunder; or (6) any injury or death to any person or damage to property caused by or sustained by Licensor its Personnel, servants, or subcontractors as a result of being on, at or in Customer's facility or entering or leaving therefrom.

15.2 **Assumption of Defense.** If the indemnifying party fails to assume the defense of any actual or threatened action covered by this Section 15 within the earlier of (a) any deadline established by a third party in a written demand or by a court, and (b) thirty (30) days of notice of the claim, the indemnified party may follow such course of action as it reasonably deems necessary to protect its interest and shall be indemnified for all costs reasonably incurred in such course of action; provided, however, that the indemnified party shall not settle a claim without the consent of the indemnifying party.

- ***This language allows a party to undertake its own defense if the indemnifying party fails to do so.***

16. Warranty and Warranty Disclaimer

- ***Because Section 2-316 of the UCC requires that warranty disclaimers be "conspicuous" this paragraph is broken into several shorter paragraphs to allow ease of reading and comprehension. Further, Section 16.1.4, which contains the actual disclaimer, is in block letters.***

16.1 **Licensor Warranties**

16.1.1 **General Warranties.** Licensor warrants that it owns all rights, title, and interest in and to the Software, or that in the case of any third party software that it has the right to grant a sublicense to use such third party software, that all Software shall substantially conform to the Functional Specifications, and that the Software and Services shall be free from material defects in workmanship and materials that prevent them from substantially meeting the aforementioned criteria. Licensor further warrants that any Services provided by Licensor under this Agreement shall be performed in a workmanlike manner and in accordance with the prevailing professional standards of the software industry. This warranty coverage shall include any modifications made to the Software by Licensor. Such warranty shall extend for sixty (60) days from acceptance and shall survive inspection, test, acceptance, use, and payment.

- ***Licensors should carefully limits what they warrant. Here, the Licensor only warrants that (1) Licensor owns the software or has the right to license the software, (2) the software substantially conforms to the Functional Specifications, and (3) the software is free from material defects in workmanship and materials. By using the phrases "substantially conforms" and "material defects," the Licensor allows itself a small level of error as software by its nature is imperfect.***
- ***The Licensor's warranty is sixty (60) days. Warranty is an element of price. If the Customer wants a longer warranty, the Licensor can provide one at an increased price although the length of the warranty may impact the Licensor's ability to recognize revenue..***
- ***Avoid stating "Licensor represents and warrants . . . ." A breach of a "representation" gives rise to a claim under tort while warranties give rise to contract claims with a substantially smaller risk of a large recovery.***

16.1.2 **Operation of Software.** Licensor does not warrant that the operation of the Software or the operation of the Software Products will be uninterrupted or error free.

- ***The Licensor should always state that the operation of the software will be neither error free nor uninterrupted to avoid creating any implied warranties.***

16.1.3 **Remedy**. In the event of any breach of the warranties set forth in this Agreement, Licensor's sole and exclusive responsibility, and Customer's sole and exclusive remedy, shall be for Licensor to correct or replace, at no additional charge to Customer, any portion of the Software or Services found to be defective; provided, however, that if within a commercially reasonable period Licensor neither corrects such defects nor replaces the defective Software or Services, then Customer's sole and exclusive remedy shall be to receive direct damages not to exceed the license fees paid to Licensor for use of the defective Software or Services. In the event of any breach of any provision of this Agreement other than the warranties set forth in this Agreement, Customer's sole and exclusive remedy shall be to receive direct damages not to exceed the amounts received by Licensor pursuant to this Agreement. For the avoidance of doubt, Customer's monetary remedies for any breaches of any provision of this Agreement (including, without limitation, the warranty provisions) shall not, in the aggregate, exceed an amount equal to the amounts actually received by Licensor from Customer.

16.1.4 **Warranty Disclaimer.**

EXCEPT AS SET FORTH **IN THIS SECTION 16**, LICENSOR MAKES NO EXPRESS OR IMPLIED REPRESENTATIONS OR WARRANTIES WITH RESPECT TO THE SOFTWARE, OR SERVICES OR THEIR CONDITION, MERCHANTABILITY, FITNESS FOR ANY PARTICULAR PURPOSE OR USE BY CUSTOMER. LICENSOR FURNISHES THE ABOVE WARRANTIES IN LIEU OF ALL OTHER WARRANTIES, EXPRESSED OR IMPLIED, INCLUDING THE WARRANTIES OF MERCHANTABILITY AND FITNESS FOR A PARTICULAR PURPOSE.

- ***UCC Section 2-316 requires all warranty disclaimers to be "conspicuous." Therefore the disclaimer should be in capital block letters.***
- ***From the Licensor's perspective, it is important to specifically reference the section(s) of the agreement that contains the representations and warranties being made by the Licensor. The failure to do so may result in the inclusion of certain implied representations and warranties that may be located elsewhere in the agreement that were never intended to be part of the agreement. The Customer, however, should insist on more general language, such as "Except as set forth in this Agreement," or should carefully review the agreement to ensure all representations and warranties are included and referenced by section number. For example, Section 35 contains additional representations and warranties related to disaster recovery, which may be excluded by the reference to "Section 16" set forth above.***

To avoid any attempt to limit the Licensor's warranties to a specific section, some Customers seek to include language to the following effect:

Representations and Warranties throughout Agreement. It is understood and agreed by the Parties that Supplier's representations and warranties are et forth

throughout this Agreement and are not confined to this Section ___ (Representations, Warranties, and Covenants).

- ***If Licensor does not disclaim all other warranties, Licensor may be liable for certain implied warranties including the failure of the software to function as the Customer thought it would.***

Alternative Language to Meet UCITA Requirements

16.1.4.A **UCITA Warranty Disclaimer.**

The Parties hereby agree that, in respect of information and computer programs provided by one Party to the other Party under this Agreement, and except for the express warranties set forth in Section 16.1 of this Agreement: THERE ARE NO WARRANTIES (A) AGAINST INTERFERENCE WITH ENJOYMENT OF INFORMATION, (B) AGAINST INFRINGEMENT, (C) THAT INFORMATON, EITHER PARTY'S EFFORTS, OR SYSTEMS, AS EACH MAY BE PROVIDED UNDER THIS AGREEMENT, WILL FULFILL ANY OF EITHER PARTY'S PARTICULAR PURPOSES OR NEEDS, AND (D) WITH RESPECT TO DEFECTS IN THE INFORMATION OR SOFTWARE THAT AN EXAMINATION SHOULD HAVE REASONABLY REVEALED. THE PARTIES HEREBY EACH DISCLAIM IMPLIED WARRANTIES OF MERCHANTIBILITY, QUALITY, AND ACCURACY. THE INFORMATION AND COMPUTER PROGRAMS PROVIDED UNDER THIS AGREEMENT ARE PROVIDED "AS IS" WITH ALL FAULTS, AND THE ENTIRE RISK AS TO SATISFACTORY QUALITY, PERFORMANCE, ACCURACY, AND EFFORT IS WITH THE USER OF SUCH INFORMATION AND COMPUTER PROGRAMS.

- ***Language similar to that set forth in Section 16.1.4.A should be used in those agreements governed by the laws of those states that have adopted UCITA. UCITA's warranty disclaimer requirements are different then the UCC, thus the parties must carefully evaluate whether UCITA applies and ensure that the disclaimers included in the agreement are appropriate for the type of damages the Licensor seeks to limit.***

16.1.5 **Voiding of Warranties.** Any and all warranties and indemnifications shall be void as to Services or Software where the non-compliance is caused by or related to (1) the acts or omissions of non-Licensor personnel, its agents, or third parties; (2) misuse, theft, vandalism, fire, water, or other peril; (3) moving or relocation not authorized by Licensor; (4) any alterations or modifications made to any Software by the Customer, it representatives, or agents; (5) use of the Software other than in the operating environment specified in the technical specifications; or (6) coding, information, or specifications created or provided by client.

- ***The Licensor should not be held liable for a breach of warranty or an indemnity if the Customer was the cause of any such breach.***
- ***While the Licensor wants to limit its liability in the event the Customer modifies the software, the Customer should insist or more limiting/exacting language that excuses the Licensor's performance only to the extent***

any failure was caused by the Customer's modifications (i.e., to protect against those cases where the infringement was not caused by the modification but rather by the Licensor's existing code). The limiting language should mirror the language for any intellectual property infringement set forth in Section 14.1.

- ***The Customer may also take exception to language voiding of the warranty arguing that the warranty does not apply in the identified situations but not be totally voided.***
- ***It is important to note that there is a difference between warranty and maintenance. Warranty is much more comprehensive including modifying the software to make it work. Maintenance involves only maintaining an ongoing software system, a lesser standard. Breaches of the maintenance obligations will usually result in a refund of the maintenance fees paid to the Licensor, but a breach of a warranty may allow the Customer to recover all license, development and services fees paid to the Licensor, which usually significantly exceed the maintenance fees amount. As such, maintenance should always be addressed in a separate and separate agreement to limit the Licensee's ability to recover its license and development fees.***

Additional Warranties Benefiting the Customer

16.A **System.** Licensor represents and warrants to Customer that the ABC System shall function without Critical Error in accordance with the applicable Specifications, Performance Standards, Documentation, and Regulatory Requirements.

- ***This warranty ties together all of the appropriate items that set forth the performance of the software system as a whole. This warranty is much broader and goes to the collective operation of the hardware, the Licensor's proprietary software, and any third party software. This warranty presents a significant risk for the Licensor as it is essentially warranting the operation of the system as a whole as well as any third party components over which the Licensor potentially has no control. By tying together the specifications, performance standards, documentation, and regulatory requirements, if any, the Customer has guaranteed that is will receive the complete benefit of its bargain.***

16.B **Software Performance.** Licensor represents and warrants to Company that the Software or System, as applicable, shall meet the Performance Standards set forth in this Agreement when operating in the operating environment described therein, including the maximum response times and availability ("Operating Environment"). Licensor shall correct any failure of the applicable Software and/or System to operate in accordance with the performance warranties set forth in this Section by providing all additional software, equipment, and/or services to Company at no additional cost to Company. In the event Licensor is unable to correct such failure within a forty-eight (48) hour period [an event of "Default" shall be deemed to have occurred.] **OR** [Customer shall receive from Licensor credits in the amounts set forth in Appendix 3.B.2. In the event Licensor is unable to correct such failure within thirty (30) calendar days, an Event of Default shall be deemed to have occurred.]

Customer and Licensor shall jointly assess, on an annual basis commencing on the first anniversary of Project Acceptance, or more frequently if necessary, whether Customer is operating the Software and/or System in accordance with the Operating Environment. In the event the parties determine that (a) the Operating Environment has changed so that Customer is no longer operating the Software and/or System in accordance with the Operating Environment; and (b) Customer wants to continue the performance warranties set forth in this Section, Licensor shall make such adjustments and recommendations that it deems reasonably necessary to ensure that the Software and/or System will continue to operate in accordance with the warranties set forth herein while operating within the re-established Operating Environment including, without limitation, a recommendation that Customer purchase additional equipment and/or license additional software from Licensor or a third party. If Customer implements such recommendations, the warranties set forth in this Section shall remain in effect. The process described in this Section shall, at Customer's option, repeat for as long as Customer continues to receive Support and Maintenance Services and wants to maintain the performance warranties set forth in this Section. Licensor represents and warrants to Customer that the Software provided under this Agreement shall function without Defect in accordance with the applicable Specifications, Performance Standards, Documentation, and Regulatory Requirements (Defect being defined as a "High" and/or "Medium" Defect).

- ***The warranty contained in Section 16.B contains an additional remedy if the Licensor fails to meet the performance standards. In addition to the Customer's right to receive service level credits and to terminate the agreement, the Licensor has the obligation to purchase all necessary hardware, software, and services necessary to meet the performance standards placing significant risks and a financial burden on the Licensor.***

16.C **Services.** Licensor represents and warrants to Customer that it shall perform the Services and provide the Deliverables required by this Agreement in a workmanlike manner, in accordance with the standards of care and diligence and the level of skill, knowledge, and judgment normally practiced by nationally recognized information technology services firms in performing services of a similar nature, and in accordance with the standards of conduct attached hereto as Exhibit 16.C provided, however, that where this Agreement specifies a particular standard or criteria for performance, this warranty is not intended to and does not diminish that standard or criteria for performance. Further, Licensor represents, warrants, and covenants that it shall provide the Services or create any Deliverables using only proven current technology or methods unless otherwise mutually agreed by the parties [in a particular Statement of Work].

16.D **Documentation.** Licensor represents and warrants to Customer that it has provided to Customer all Documentation for the ABC System and that such Documentation is detailed and complete and accurately describes the functional and operational characteristics of the ABC System. Licensor further represents and warrants that it will provide to Customer updated versions of all such Documentation when it provides to Customer Enhancements to the ABC System and that all such updated Documentation will be complete and accurate and will be at least as detailed as the Documentation issued to Customer with the initial version of the ABC System. The warranty and commitments contained in this Section shall remain in full force and effect for as long as Company continues to receive Support and Maintenance Services from Vendor.

Additional Language that Benefits Licensee

Licensee represents and warrants that it shall at all times document the operation of the Software in a manner consistent with the best practices of the software development industry, and such Documentation shall accurately reflect the operation of the Software and enable a person reasonably skilled in computer programming and in possession of the Software source code to use and maintain the Software fully and completely. Licensee further represents and warrants that it shall control and identify all adaptations, upgrades, and enhancements of the Software by means of a version number, and all lesser modifications by means of a release number.

- ***The Licensor should warrant that not only is the initial documentation detailed and complete but that the documentation should reflect any customizations or modifications made to the Customer's system. The Licensor should also warrant that any subsequent documentation delivered with any modifications or enhancements is complete and accurate and as detailed as the documentation initially delivered to the Customer.***

16.E **Defects.** Licensor warrants that the Software will be free of defects in design, materials, and workmanship.

- ***A prudent Licensor should avoid making any warranty regarding the software's design. System architecture/design is a very complex area and thus creates a significant level of risk for the licensor who makes this type of warranty.*** **See USM Corp. v. Arthur D. Little Systems, Inc.,** ***546 N.E.2d 888 (Mass. 1989) (warranty against defects in design required that computer system be able to perform necessary functions in a reasonable time period).***

16.F **Interfaces.** Licensor acknowledges that Customer is working with a number of third parties in developing, maintaining, and supporting Customer's various systems and that Customer's use of the Software may involve the development and/or use of one or more application programming interfaces (APIs) between such third party systems and the Software. Licensor agrees that it will fully cooperate with the Customer and third parties to develop, maintain, and support such APIs. Licensor further agrees that Licensor shall communicate to Customer the industry-standard APIs that Licensor is evaluating and/or implementing, and shall reasonably cooperate and work with Customer and such third parties in good faith to identify industry-standard APIs and, if mutually agreed to by the parties, develop such APIs using as many industry-standard protocols as possible.

[***Optional—where Licensor does not create or publish APIs***]

Licensor acknowledges and agrees that Customer shall be entitled, for Customer's internal use only, to reverse engineer, disassemble, or decompile the Software licensed hereunder for the purpose of creating interoperable computer programs that facilitate interoperability between Licensor's Software and third party software products.

16.G **Open Architecture/Open System.** Licensor represents and warrants to Customer that the Software systems are designed and shall continue to be designed to operate in an Open Architecture environment and, as such, all external Licensor interface specifications shall be published and generally available. For purposes of the foregoing, an "Open Architecture" is an architecture that adheres to a publicly known set of interface specifications so that any applications that have been implemented to those interface specifications shall be able to interoperate with any other third party applications that adhere to the same interface specifications.

16.H **Compatibility.** Licensor represents and warrants to Customer that the Software is fully operational on the Equipment. Licensor further represents and warrants that non-Licensor supplied third party software is capable of being loaded on the Equipment with no upgrades or modifications to the Equipment or any Software (operating system or otherwise) relating to the Equipment.

Additional Language that Benefits Licensee

Licensor warrants that the Software will be compatible with the Licensee's technical environment, including hardware, operating system(s), software application(s), CPUs, and networks specified by Licensee in the applicable Request for Proposal or Work Order.

16.I **Future Compatibility.** Licensor warrants that all updates, upgrades, and revisions to the Software furnished hereunder will be implemented in such a manner as to maintain backward compatibility with the previous version or release of the Software furnished hereunder, under the Agreement, or under any other agreement issued pursuant to this Agreement, so that such previous versions or releases shall continue to be operable with the Software as updated, upgraded, or revised, in materially the same manner and with materially equivalent performance.

16.J **Data Integrity.** Licensor represents and warrants to Customer that all data types, structures, formats, and content will be converted completely and accurately such that the Customer will be able to reconcile the original data with the converted data without any loss to or deviation from the original data. **In the event of data loss caused by the Software or Software failure, including, but not limited to, a Software failure resulting from an error, malfunction, or overloading, Licensor shall undertake its best efforts to restore or recover any data or results at no cost to Customer within a commercially reasonable time.**

- ***The highlighted language benefits the Licensor as the Licensor is required to use its "best efforts" to remediate any problem, but it is not definitively obligated to resolve the problem.***

Alternative Language Benefiting Customer

In the event that Customer's data is corrupted or lost as a result of any action by the Licensor, Customer may, in addition to the other remedies that may be available to it, require the Licensor at the Licensor's expense to restore or procure the restoration of Customer's data by whatever means necessary to ensure its integrity.

- ***Licensors should be hesitant to make this warranty or to convert data in general. Data conversion can be very expensive and result in corrupted data. Thus, it is prudent to have the Licensee convert its own data.***

16.K **Software Obsolescence.** Licensor acknowledges that Customer is making a significant resource commitment in order to acquire the Software and that Customer does not want to move involuntarily to a new system *[at a later date OR prior to a specified date]*. Having acknowledged the foregoing, Licensor represents and warrants to Customer that it will continue to enhance the Software (meaning adding new features and functionality, in addition to ordinary course defect corrections), as long as Customer continues to receive Software support services from Licensor.

additionally/alternatively:

Latest Versions. All Software as delivered will be the most current release or version that Licensor has made commercially available to its customers, unless Customer, after being advised by Licensor of the availability of a newer release or version, expressly elects to acquire and deploy and older one.

- ***The Customer should ensure that the Licensor commits to continually enhance the software. Otherwise, the Customer may make a significant investment only to find that the Licensor plans to "sunset" the software requiring the Customer to purchase a new software system.***

16.L **Disabling Code.** Licensor represents and warrants to Customer that in connection with the licensing of the Software, Customer will not receive or experience any virus, worm, trap door, back door, timer, clock, counter, or other limiting routine, instruction, or design that would erase data or programming or otherwise cause any Customer system to become inoperable or incapable of being used in the full manner for which it was designed and created (collectively, a "Disabling Code"). In the event a Disabling Code is identified, Licensor shall take all steps necessary, at no additional cost to Customer, to restore and/or reconstruct any and all data lost by Customer as a result of such Disabling Code.

- ***This warranty favors the Customer in that it is impossible for the Licensor to ensure that the software is free of viruses, etc. Virus detection is reactive, not pro-active. It is updated periodically, addressing the latest identified viruses. Thus a prudent Licensor should only state is that it will use commercially reasonable virus detection software prior to delivering the software to the Customer. The language set forth below provides a more balanced language, which the Licensor should be willing to accept.***

alternatively

Viruses. Licensor warrants that it will use commercially reasonable virus detection computer software programs to test the Software licensed hereunder for viruses prior to delivery to Customer and that Licensor will continue to take such step with respect to any code delivered to Customer to correct any identified error. Customer hereby warrants that it will use commercially reasonable virus detection computer software programs to test the Software licensed hereunder for viruses prior to installation and that Customer will continue to take such step with respect to any code delivered to Customer to correct any identified error. Licensor warrants that it will maintain a copy of the current version and the one (1) immediately preceding version of the Software, which have been tested as set forth herein. Upon Customer's request, Licensor agrees to make such copy of the Software available to Customer, for Customer's comparison with Customer's copy of the Software. Licensor further warrants to Customer that it is not the policy of Licensor to intentionally include disabling mechanisms or computer viruses into software provided to its customers and that should such policy change, Licensor will advise Customer in advance and, upon Customer's request, will provide Customer with the code(s) necessary to defeat any such disabling mechanisms or computer viruses, intentionally inserted by Licensor or its employees into the Software.

Unauthorized Code. Unauthorized Code means computer instructions that alter, destroy, or inhibit the Customer's processing environment, including, but not limited to, data storage and computer libraries. Unauthorized Code includes, but is not limited to, programs that self-replicate without manual intervention, instructions programmed to activate at a predetermined time or upon a specified event, and programs purporting to do a meaningful function but designed for a destructive function. During the Term, Licensor warrants that it shall take reasonable steps to test all releases furnished to Customer for the presence of Unauthorized Code. The determination of "reasonable tests" shall be based on then current industry standards for testing for such Unauthorized Code on the applicable hardware platform. However, Customer may not use said releases until Customer has similarly tested all releases on Customer's computers after delivery. If Customer notifies Licensor in reasonable detail of a breach of the foregoing warranties that occurred in the sixty (60) days prior to such notice, then Licensor shall provide a release conforming with this warranty as soon as reasonably possible but within ten (10) business days. THIS SHALL BE CUSTOMER'S Sole REMEDY FOR ANY SUCH BREACH, TO THE EXCLUSION OF ALL OTHER REMEDIES, EVEN IF SUCH LIMITATION CAUSES THIS WARRANTY OR ITS REMEDY TO FAIL OF THEIR ESSENTIAL PURPOSES.

- ***This warranty should be mutual, as it is possible that the Customer's employees or consultants may introduce a virus into the system.***

16.M **Regulatory Requirements.** Licensor represents and warrants to Customer that the Software meets and satisfies all Regulatory Requirements. Licensor further warrants that the Licensor, its employees, agents, and subcontractors shall comply with the Regulatory Requirements [set forth in the Business Associate Addendum] attached hereto as Exhibit 16.M.

- ***To the extent the Customer is subject to any regulatory requirements such as in the healthcare, insurance, or telecommunications industries, the Licensor should warrant that the software meets and satisfies all applicable regulatory requirements.***

16.N **Media.** Licensor warrants that for a period of 90 days from the date of delivery of the Software that the media used to store and deliver the Software to the Customer shall be free from defects in manufacture and material. Should the media fail to be free of defects in manufacture or material during the 90-day warranty period, Licensor shall replace the defective media. Defective media shipped to the Licensor with a shipping date within the 90-day warranty period will be replaced at no charge including shipping.

16.O **Intellectual Property.** Licensor represents and warrants to Customer that Customer's use of the Software does not and shall not infringe upon any [U.S.] patent, trademark, copyright, trade secret or other intellectual property, or proprietary right of any Third Party, and there is currently no actual or threatened suit against Licensor by any Third Party based on an alleged violation of such right. This warranty shall survive the expiration or termination of this Agreement.

- ***Given the explosion of patent infringement suits involving software, many Licensors no longer want to make a representation or warranty as the intellectual property infringement arguing that because the Licensor agrees to indemnify the Customer as the result of such infringement (See Section 14), the Customer does not need a warranty. While a Customer may insist on a "belt and suspenders" approach, the Customer does not usually gain a significant level of greater protection.***
- ***If the Licensor does give such a warranty, the Licensor will want to reduce its potential risks by limiting liability to the infringement of U.S. intellectual property rights.***

16.P **Third Party Warranties and Indemnities.** For any Third Party Software provided by Licensor to Customer, Licensor hereby assigns to Customer all end user warranties and indemnities relating to such Third Party Software. To the extent that Licensor is not permitted to assign any of such end user warranties and indemnities through to Customer, Licensor shall enforce such warranties and indemnities on behalf of Customer to the extent Licensor is permitted to do so under the terms of the applicable Third Party agreements.

16.Q **ISO 9001.** Licensor warrants that during the term of this Agreement, Licensor shall utilize a quality system in accordance with Appendix 16.Q. This quality system shall also be in accordance with ISO 9001.

16.R **Authority.** Each party represents and warrants to the other that it has the right to enter into this Agreement. Licensor further represents and warrants that there are no outstanding assignments, grants, licenses, encumbrances, obligations, or agreements (whether written oral or implied) that are inconsistent with this Agreement and the rights granted or transferred herein. This warranty shall survive the expiration or termination of this Agreement.

16.S **Pending Litigation.** Licensor represents and warrants to Customer that there is no action, suit, claim, investigation or proceeding pending, or to the best of Licensor's knowledge, **threatened** against, by or affecting Licensor or the ABC System which, if adversely decided, might adversely affect Licensor's ability to enter into this Agreement, Licensor's performance of its obligations herein, or Customer's use of the Software. As of the date hereof, Licensor further represents and warrants that it does not know of any basis for any such action.

- ***This warranty protects the Customer by requiring the Licensor to disclose any threatened or pending litigation that may interfere with the Customer's license rights. This is especially important with regard to any third party intellectual property infringement claims. A prudent Licensor should not agree to this warranty because it is too broad.***

16.T **Change of Control.** Licensor represents and warrants to Customer that no Change of Control with respect to Licensor is being considered, planned, or pending by the Board of Directors, shareholders or management of Licensor or by any Affiliate of Licensor.

- ***A prudent Licensor should not agree to this warranty because it is so broad and may place the Licensor in the position of inadvertently violating the securities laws or breaking the agreement.***

16.U **Material Misstatements or Omissions.** No representation or warranty by Licensor that is contained in this Agreement or in any Appendix, Exhibit, or other Attachment hereto contains any untrue statement of a material fact or omits to state a material fact necessary to make the statements and facts contained herein or therein not materially misleading.

- ***A prudent Licensor should not agree to this warranty, as it is too broad creating a significant level of risk for the Licensor.***

16.V **Fitness for a Particular Purpose.** Licensor warrants that the Software will be fit for [describe purpose] by the Customer under normal use and service.

- ***A prudent Licensor should avoid giving this warranty as it creates a significant risk of liability on the Licensor's behalf by promising the software will be fit for the Licensee's intended use or purpose.***

16.W **Privacy/HIPAA.** Licensor acknowledges that the Licensee Data may contain personal data, health data, and/or medical records data, the use of which data is subject to various Privacy Laws, including all state, federal, and international laws and regulations and state, federal, and national government agency orders and decrees to which Licensee may be subject ("Privacy Laws"), as well as certain restrictions imposed on the Licensee Data by the data subjects or other third party data providers. Licensor agrees to strictly abide by all such restrictions pertaining to the Licensee Data, as they are promulgated and applied, currently and in the future. Furthermore, Licensor shall in good faith execute any and all agreements that Licensee is required to have Licensor execute in order that Licensee may comply with any Privacy Laws. If Licensor's use (whether directly or indirectly) of the Licensee Data is contrary to any Privacy Law, or contrary to any of the restrictions set forth in this Agreement, Licensee shall have the right to (i) terminate this Agreement for cause if such breach has not been cured within five (5) days of receipt by Licensor of written notice, and (ii) pursue any other legal and equitable remedies.

16.X **Data Transfer.** Licensor represents and warrants that it will only transfer (including internal Licensor transfers that occur beyond the internal firewalls of Licensor) Licensee Data in a secure and confidential manner, including at a minimum, encrypting the data with no less than 128 bit encryption or through establishing a virtual private network with Licensee and shall comply with all security provisions and procedures set forth in Licensee's Information Asset Protection Policies and Licensee's Consumer Data Protection Policies and Procedures.

16.Y **Gifts and Gratuities.** Licensor, its employees, and agents shall not give or offer to give any material gifts or gratuities of any kind whatsoever to any Licensee employee or members of their families. In the event that Licensor is approached by anyone suggesting fraudulent or unethical behavior with regard to Licensor's business activities with Licensee, or if any request is made to Licensor, its employees, or agents by any Licensee employees or members of their families for gifts or gratuities of any kind, Licensor agrees to immediately notify Licensee's legal department. Licensor certifies by execution of this Agreement that it knows of no material gifts or gratuities, or any kind whatsoever, paid to Licensee employees or members of their families by Licensor, Licensor's employees, or agents during the past two (2) years, except as otherwise set forth in writing to Licensee's legal department as an exhibit to this Agreement. Licensor agrees to immediately notify Licensee legal department in writing of any violations of this subsection.

16.Z **Customer Complaints.** There is no existing pattern or repetition of customer complaints regarding the Programs or Services, including functionality or performance issues, and that Licensor's engineers have not currently identified any repeating adverse impact on the Programs or Services, including functionality or performance, for which the root cause is believed to be a flaw or defect in the Programs or Services. The foregoing warranty shall not extend to any specifications provided by Customer.

16.AA **Open Source Materials.** Except as set forth in Schedule 16.AA, Licensor represents and warrants to Customer that Licensor has not (i) incorporated Open Source Materials into, or combined Open Source Materials with, the Deliverables or Software, (ii) distributed Open Source Materials in conjunction with any Deliverables or Software, or (iii) used Open Source Materials, in such a way that, with respect to the foregoing (i), (ii), or (iii), creates obligations for the Licensor with respect to any material Deliverables or grant, or purport to grant, to any third party, any rights or immunities under any material Deliverables (including, but not limited to, using any Open Source Materials that require, as a condition of use, modification and/or distribution of such Open Source Materials that other material software included in Deliverables incorporated into, derived from or distributed with such Open Source Materials be (A) disclosed or distributed in source code form, (B) be licensed for the purpose of making derivative works, or (C) be redistributable at no charge).

Alternatively:

Open Source. Licensor represents and warrants to Customer that the Work Product provided pursuant to this Agreement shall not contain any "Open Source." For purposes of this Agreement, "Open Source" means any software code that: (a) contains, or is derived in any manner (in whole or in part) from, any software that is distributed as free software, open source software, shareware (e.g., Linux), or similar licensing or distribution models; and (b) is subject to any agreement with terms requiring that such software code be (i) disclosed or distributed in Source Code or Object Code form, (ii) licensed for the purpose of making derivative works, and/or (iii) redistributable. Open Source includes, but is not limited to, software licensed or distributed under any of the following licenses or distribution models, or licenses or distribution models similar to any of the following: (A) GNU's General Public License (GPL) or Lesser/Library GPL (LGPL); (B) the Artistic License (e.g., PERL); (C) the Mozilla Public License(s); (D) the Netscape Public License; (E) the Berkeley Software Design (BSD) license including Free BSD or BSD-style license; (F) the Sun Community Source License (SCSL); (G) an Open Source Foundation License (e.g., CDE and Motif UNIX user interfaces); (H) the Apache Server license; and (I) any licenses listed at http://www.opensource.org/licenses.

16.AB **Location of Performance.** Licensor further warrants that all Services shall be performed and rendered within the continental United States.

- ***See Section 3.7 for language acknowledging that the Licensor will be performing services offshore.***

16.AC **Usability of Source Code.** Licensor represents and warrants that the Source Code is and shall be understandable and useable by a trained computer-programming contractor who is familiar with similar systems, though not necessarily those incorporating the Software. Licensor further represents and warrants that the Software does not involve any proprietary languages or programming components that such contractor could not reasonably be expected to understand, except to the extent the source code contains sufficient commentary to enable such contractor to understand and to use such languages or components. Licensor further represents and warrants that the source code includes all of the devices, programming and documentation necessary for the maintenance of the Software by the Customer upon release of the source code pursuant to this Escrow Agreement, except for devices, programming and documentation commercially available to the Customer on reasonable terms through readily known sources other than the Licensor.

16.AD **Security.** Licensor warrants and represents to Customer and its Affiliates that (i) the provision of the Services shall not permit any unauthorized access to or cause any loss or damage to Customer Systems, Customer Pre-existing Intellectual Property, any Work Products (where such Work Products are owned by Customer in accordance with this Agreement) or Confidential Information belonging to Customer; and (ii) it shall comply with any Customer Security Policies in place from time to time during the term of this Agreement.

16.AE **Representations Made in RFI and RFP.**

Licensor represents and warrants that all statements and representations made in Licensor's response to each of Customer's Request for Information dated as of_______, 20__ and Customer's Request for Proposal dated as of _____, 20__ were true and correct at the time made and remain true and correct as of the date of this Agreement.

The Following Clauses Are Typical of Those Used in the Pharmaceutical and Healthcare Industries

16.AF **Debarment.** Licensor represents and warrants that Licensor and its officers, directors, employees, and agents have not been debarred under any federal, state or local law, regulation, rule, or order, including, but not limited to, the Generic Drug Enforcement Act of 1992. In the event any pending proceeding or threatened debarment of Licensor or its officers, directors, employees, or agents, Licensor shall immediately notify Licensee of such proceeding or threatened debarment.

16.AG **Recording Devices.** Licensor, subcontractors, and their respective employees shall not bring video or audio recording devices, including, but not limited to, cameras, PDAs, or similar devices with video or audio capabilities into Licensee's facilities without the express written permission of Licensee's security department. Licensor, subcontractors, and their respective employees shall not make audio or video recordings inside Licensee's facilities without the express written permission of Licensee's security department.

16.AH **Drug Testing/Criminal Background Investigation.** Licensor represents and warrants that all Licensor personnel and its subcontractor personnel that will be providing services at a Licensee facility have received and passed a pre-assignment drug test within thirty (30) days of beginning an assignment at a Licensee facility and at least annually thereafter. Licensor represents and warrants that Licensor personnel and its subcontractor personnel used to perform services for Licensee under this Agreement have not been convicted of the following crimes: felony or misdemeanor fraud conviction, felony or misdemeanor theft conviction, felony drug conviction, felony firearms conviction, or felony convictions of crimes of a violent or serious nature (e.g., battery, sexual offenses, robbery). In addition, Licensor shall not use Licensor personnel or subcontractor personnel on the Licensee project that have multiple convictions (i.e., three or more) for offenses less serious than those listed above (other than minor traffic offenses) during the last five years.

Other Warranties to Consider

- ***A Licensee should consider whether any other warranties are required depending on the nature of the underlying transaction. These may include complying with future regulatory changes and scalability, etc.***

16.2 **Customer Warranties**

- ***The Licensor should also insist on the inclusion of certain representations and warranties by the Customer, the most important of which are the Customer's representation that it has the authority to enter into the agreement and that it has the ability to pay the license fee. The Licensor***

should consider whether any special representations or warranties are needed i.e., in international transactions, that the Customer has received approval for the Licensor to repatriate any fees received by it.

16.2.1 **Authority**. Customer represents and warrants to the Licensor that Customer has all requisite power and authority to execute and deliver this Agreement and to perform the Customer's obligations hereunder. This Agreement has been duly and validly executed and delivered by the Customer, and constitutes a valid and binding obligation of the Customer, enforceable against the Customer in accordance with its terms.

16.2.2 **Conflict with Other Agreements.** Customer represents and warrants to the Licensor that neither the execution and delivery of this Agreement by the Customer nor the consummation by the Customer of the transactions contemplated by this Agreement will (i) conflict with or violate any provision of the Certificate of Incorporation or bylaws of the Customer; (ii) require on the part of the Customer any filing with, or any permit, authorization, consent, or approval of, any court, arbitrational tribunal, administrative agency or commission, or other governmental or regulatory authority or agency (a "Governmental Entity"); (iii) conflict with, result in a breach of, constitute (with or without due notice or lapse of time or both) a default under, result in the acceleration of, create in any party the right to accelerate, terminate, modify, or cancel, or require any notice, consent, or waiver under, any agreement, instrument, contract, or arrangement to which the Customer is a party or by which the Customer or any of its properties is bound; or (iv) violate any order, writ, injunction, decree, law, statute, rule, or regulation applicable to the Customer.

16.2.3 **Financial Ability**. Customer represents and warrants to the Licensor that it presently has sufficient funds and will have sufficient funds available to timely pay Licensor all amounts due or that will come due under this Agreement. The Customer further represents and warrants to Licensor that Customer will not, at any time, permit its Consolidated Net Worth to be less than $[___].

17. Limitation of Liability

17.1 **DISCLAIMER OF LIABILITY**.

LICENSOR SHALL NOT BE LIABLE FOR ANY (A) SPECIAL, INDIRECT, INCIDENTAL, PUNITIVE, OR CONSEQUENTIAL DAMAGES, INCLUDING LOSS OF PROFITS, ARISING FROM OR RELATED TO A BREACH OF THIS AGREEMENT OR ANY ORDER OR THE OPERATION OR USE OF THE SOFTWARE AND SERVICES INCLUDING SUCH DAMAGES, WITHOUT LIMITATION, AS DAMAGES ARISING FROM LOSS OF DATA OR PROGRAMMING, LOSS OF REVENUE OR PROFITS, FAILURE TO REALIZE SAVINGS OR OTHER BENEFITS, DAMAGE TO EQUIPMENT, AND CLAIMS AGAINST CUSTOMER BY ANY THIRD PERSON, EVEN IF LICENSOR HAS BEEN ADVISED OF THE POSSIBILITY OF SUCH DAMAGES; (B) DAMAGES (REGARDLESS OF THEIR NATURE) FOR ANY DELAY OR FAILURE BY LICENSOR TO PERFORM ITS OBLIGATIONS UNDER THIS AGREEMENT DUE TO ANY CAUSE BEYOND LICENSOR'S REASONABLE

CONTROL; OR (C) CLAIMS MADE A SUBJECT OF A LEGAL PROCEEDING AGAINST LICENSOR MORE THAN TWO YEARS AFTER ANY SUCH CAUSE OF ACTION FIRST AROSE.

- ***Licensor should disclaim all "speculative" and "third party" damages. Damages recoverable by the Customer should be limited to Customer's actual direct damages. The Uniform Commercial Code does not require that any disclaimer be "conspicuous" although the courts may impose this requirement. Therefore this section should be in large block letters.***
- ***Licensor will not be liable for any damages suffered by the Customer's customers or any other third party.***
- ***By requiring claims be brought within two years, Licensor limits its risk/liability by shortening the statute of limitations which may be up to 12 years.***

17.2 LIMITATION OF LIABILITY.

NOTWITHSTANDING ANY OTHER PROVISION OF THIS AGREEMENT, BUT EXCLUDING ANY CLAIMS FOR INDEMNIFICATION UNDER SECTION 14.1 LICENSOR'S LIABILITIES UNDER THIS AGREEMENT, WHETHER UNDER CONTRACT LAW, TORT LAW, WARRANTY, OR OTHERWISE SHALL BE LIMITED TO DIRECT DAMAGES NOT TO EXCEED THE AMOUNTS ACTUALLY RECEIVED BY LICENSOR [**UNDER THIS AGREEMENT OR IN THE _______ MONTHS PRIOR TO THE DATE OF THE ACTION GIVING RISE TO THE CLAIM**].

Additional Language Benefiting Customer

NOTWITHSTANDING THE FOREGOING, IF ANY CLAIM AGAINST LICENSOR IS A CLAIM COVERED BY ANY INSURANCE POLICY MAINTAINED BY LICENSOR, ANY RECOVERY OF PROCEEDS UNDER SUCH POLICY SHALL BE PAID TO CUSTOMER TO THE EXTENT CUSTOMER'S DAMAGES EXCEED THE FOREGOING LIMITATION OF LIABILITY.

- ***Licensor seeks to limit its liability under both contract and tort theories, which have different statues of limitations, and different bases for which a recovery can be made.***
- ***The customer should seek to carve out a number of claims from the licensor's limit of liability including patent indemnification, personal bodily injury and personal property damage, breach of the licensor's confidentiality obligations, gross negligence, and intentional misconduct. For public policy reasons, many jurisdictions forbid tortfeasors from limiting their liability for personal injuries arising from consumer goods. See UCC § 2 719(13).***
- ***Licensor should limit its liability (to the amount received from the Customer) or it could potentially be liable for Licensor's entire net worth. (Traditionally, there is no limitation of liability for patent indemnification claims and in consumer transactions, for personal bodily injury). The Licensor will want to limit its liability to the amount received so that***

it is never out of pocket, while the Customer will want to ensure that it recovers its actual losses, which may exceed the amounts paid to the Licensor. The Customer may want to agree to limit the Licensor's liability to a multiple of the amount paid to the Licensor or a multiple of the value of the contract regardless of the amount paid. To protect itself during the early periods of the agreement when it is likely that only a small amount of money has been paid to the Licensor, the Customer may want to insist that the Licensor's liability is limited to the greater of a set dollar amount or the value of the contract.

- ***Limitation of liability is an element of price. Licensor has based its pricing on limiting Licensor's liability at the amount received from the Customer or alternatively the contract value. If the Customer wants a higher limitation of liability, Licensor can raise its limit of liability but: (a) the license fee must increase because Licensor is now bearing more risk; or (b) Licensor must buy errors and omissions insurance and charge the Customer for the cost.***
- ***It is important to retain a default remedy provision, otherwise a court may find Licensor's warranty "failed of its essential purpose" (i.e., did not provide the Customer with an adequate remedy) and void Licensor's limitation of liability and disclaimer for consequential damages.***

17.3 **Items Not Considered Damages.** The following shall not be considered damages subject to, and shall not be counted toward the liability cap specified in, Section 17.1:

(i) amounts withheld by Customer in accordance with this Agreement due either to incorrect Charges by Licensor or nonconforming Services; or
(ii) amounts paid by Customer but subsequently recovered from Licensor due either to incorrect Charges by Licensor or nonconforming Services.

17.4 **Acknowledged Direct Damages.** The following shall be considered direct damages and neither Party shall assert that they are indirect, incidental, collateral, consequential, or special damages or lost profits to the extent they result directly from either Party's failure to perform in accordance with this Agreement:

(a) Reasonable costs and expenses of recreating or reloading any lost, stolen, or damaged Customer data;
(b) Reasonable costs and expenses of implementing a work-around in respect of a failure to provide the Software or Services or any part thereof;
(c) Reasonable costs and expenses of replacing lost, stolen or damaged equipment, software, and materials;
(d) Reasonable costs and expenses incurred to procure the Software or Services or corrected Software or Services from an alternate source to the extent in excess of Licensor's Charges under this Agreement;
(e) Reasonable straight time, overtime, or related expenses incurred by either Party, wages and salaries of additional employees, travel expenses,

overtime, expenses, telecommunication charges, and similar charges due to failure of Licensor to provide all or a portion of the Software or Services incurred in connection with (a) through (d) above;

(f) Reasonable costs and expenses incurred to bring the Services in-house or to contract to obtain the Software or Services from an alternate source, including the costs and expenses associated with the retention of external consultants and legal counsel to assist with any re-sourcing; provided that, with respect to external consultants and legal counsel, Customer shall act and in a manner consistent with that historically used by Customer or customarily used by other customers in procuring similar services in similar transactions;

(g) Payments, fines, penalties, or interest imposed by a governmental body or regulatory agency for failure to comply with requirements or deadlines;

(h) Liquidated damages assessed under (Transition Services); or

(i) Service Level Credits assessed against Licensor.

18. Obligations that Survive Termination (Chapter 6.M)

The parties recognize and agree that their obligations under Sections 8, 12, 14, 15, 17, 28, 30, 34, and 35 of this Agreement survive the cancellation, termination, or expiration of this Agreement or the License granted under Section 3.1.

- ***The obligations of the parties that will survive termination of the agreement, i.e., payment to the Licensor, confidentiality, limitation of liability, governing law etc., should be specifically identified by section number because these obligations would otherwise "terminate" with the agreement. As a result, the Licensor may be unable to recover monies owed to it or protect its proprietary information since the agreement is no longer in existence and the Customer is no longer bound by the agreement's terms. The parties should avoid use of broad language such as "Any terms of this Agreement that would, by their nature, survive the expiration or termination of this Agreement shall so survive" to avoid disputes over the intent or meaning of this or similar language.***

Alternative Language

The terms, provisions, representations and warranties contained in this Agreement shall survive completion or other termination of this Agreement unless otherwise provided.

- ***The above language creates more ambiguity than it resolves. As such, the parties should strive to eliminate ambiguity and should take the time to carefully review the agreement and list by section number every clause they want to survive.***

19. Error Correction under Warranty

19.1 **Notification of Errors.** During the warranty period, Customer will notify Licensor verbally of Errors and provide written notification to Licensor within seventy-two (72) hours of such verbal notification. Licensor shall provide Customer with a telephone number that is answered from 9:00 a.m. to 6:00 p.m. Washington, D.C. time, Monday through Friday, except for Licensor holidays, a list of which is set forth on Appendix 19.1. Customer shall have access via this telephone number to individuals who shall accept Error reports and are qualified to assist Customer with the verification of suspected Errors and who may provide solutions for said Errors. Customer shall be provided with a telephone number that is answered for all hours outside of Monday through Friday, 9:00 a.m. to 6:00 p.m. Washington, D.C. time by individuals who shall accept Error reports.

19.2 **Correction of Errors.** During the warranty period, Licensor shall use its good faith efforts to immediately correct any Critical Errors affecting Customer's continued business use of the Software after Licensor's notification of the Error. Licensor will use its good faith efforts to correct all other Errors within twenty (20) days after Licensor's notification of the Error.

20. Right to Move [If Applicable]

Any Software License may be temporarily transferred to a backup computer while the licensed computer is inoperative or for emergency testing purpose. The backup computer may be at the same Customer Site, another Customer Site, or an off-site location under emergency conditions and after sufficient advance notice has been given to Licensor of the name and location of the off-site operator. Customer may re-designate the Site or the CPU on which the Software will be used for on-going operations with Licensor's consent. Customer shall be permitted concurrent operation at the new and old Site or CPU for not more than thirty (30) days and such operation will require no additional fees. Customer shall provide Licensor written notice of the re-designation within a reasonable length of time of the Software being moved to the new Site or CPU. In the event Licensor consents to the Customer moving the Software to another Customer Site or CPU, or Customer assigning the Software licensed under this Agreement, Licensor agrees that it shall continue the warranty and assist in its transfer to such other Site, CPU, or assignee.

21. Customer Preparation

If the Software is to be installed by Licensor, the Customer shall have all things in readiness for installation, including, but not limited to, other equipment, connections, and facilities for installation at the time the Software is delivered. In the event the Customer shall fail to have all things in readiness for installation on the scheduled installation date, the Customer shall reimburse Licensor for any and all expenses caused by Customer's failure to have things in readiness, unless Customer has notified Licensor at least thirty

(30) business days prior to the scheduled installation date. Customer agrees to provide and bear the cost of all communications costs incurred by Licensor from the Customer site and the costs of a dedicated dial-up communications facility equipped with 56KB Hayes compatible modem for the purposes of remote access and support by the Licensor consultant or phone support group. In addition, Customer shall fully cooperate with Licensor during the term of this Agreement.

- ***The agreement should set forth in detail any actions the Customer is obligated to undertake to prepare for the installation of the software. This list should be very detailed and include any physical requirements such as air conditioning, internet access, etc. The Customer should be subject to liquidated damages for its failure to meet these obligations.***

22. Assignment and Transfer (Chapter 4.H)

22.1 **Prohibition on Assignment.** Customer may not assign or transfer its interests, rights, or obligations under this Agreement by written agreement, merger, consolidation, **operation of law**, or otherwise, without the prior written consent of an authorized executive officer of Licensor. Any attempt to assign this Agreement by Customer shall be null and void. Furthermore, for the purposes of this Agreement the acquisition of an equity interest in Customer of greater than 25 percent by any third party shall be considered an "assignment."

- ***The Licensor must limit the ability of the Customer to assign the agreement to avoid losing potential license fees. In a merger or acquisition, the entity being acquired will seek to assign its pre-merger contracts to the acquiring party to avoid paying a transfer or license fee. By stating that any assignment is "void" a court will not allow the assignment. In the absence of such language the court will permit the assignment and allow the Licensor to seek recovery of monetary damages.***
- ***To protect itself in the event that it believes it may be acquired, the Customer may want to include language to the following effect:***

Notwithstanding the foregoing, Customer may assign its rights and obligations under this Agreement, in whole or part, without the approval of Licensor to (a) an entity acquiring, directly or indirectly, Customer through a Change of Control of Customer; (b) an entity into which Customer is merged; or (c) an entity acquiring all or substantially all of Customer's assets to which this Agreement relates, in any case provided the acquirer or surviving entity agrees in writing to be bound by the terms and conditions of this Agreement. Without limiting the generality of the foregoing, the phrase "by operation of law" shall include a Change of Control.

Additional Language Benefiting Customer

22.2 **Remedy.** In the event that Licensor, with Customer's written consent, assigns, or otherwise transfers this Agreement, or any part hereof, or delegates any of its duties hereunder, whether by operation of law or otherwise, to any Third Party or Affiliate and, within eighteen (18) months after such transfer, Customer, in its sole discretion, is not satisfied with the level of service provided under this Agreement, Customer shall have the right to terminate this Agreement and, pursuant to Customer's rights under Section 4.1.A, [Termination/Termination for Convenience] transition to a new software vendor. All Services provided by Licensor's transferee during the Transition Period shall be provided at no cost. Customer may assign this Agreement to any Affiliate at any time upon written notice to Licensor. Any rights granted to Customer under this Agreement to use the Software and Documentation shall inure to the benefit of any acquirer of, or successor in interest to, Customer, whether by merger, consolidation, purchase, operation of law, or otherwise.

- ***This language attempts to protect the Customer in the event that a new entity provides services or software in the Licensor's stead. While the language as written gives the Customer broad discretion as to whether the quality of services has degraded under the new provider a more objective standard should be selected such as a material increase in the failure to meet the service level standards.***

22.3 **Transfer.** Licensee may assign or transfer the License, in whole or in part, to any Affiliate or Divested Business that agrees in writing to be bound by the terms of this Agreement; provided such transferee's primary business is not licensing similar software. After any such assignment or transfer and with respect to such portion of the Software assigned or transferred, (i) Licensee will not continue to use that portion of the Software; (ii) Licensor will have recourse only to the transferee and will not have recourse to Licensee or Affiliates, and the transferee will be solely responsible and liable, for breaches by the transferee with respect to any such transferred rights, the License, or this Agreement.

23. Amendments, Modifications, or Supplements (Chapter 6.R)

Amendments, modifications, or supplements to this Agreement shall be permitted, provided all such changes shall be in writing signed by the authorized representatives of both parties, and all such changes shall reference this Agreement and identify the specific articles or sections of this Agreement or the particular order that is amended, modified, or supplemented.

24. Independent Contractor (Chapter 7.A)

All work performed by Licensor in connection with the Software and/or Services described in this Agreement shall be performed by Licensor as an independent contractor and not as the agent or employee of Customer. All persons furnished by Licensor shall be for all purposes solely Licensor's employees or agents and shall not be deemed to be employees of Customer for any purpose whatsoever. Licensor shall furnish, employ, and have exclusive control of all persons to be engaged in performing Services under this Agreement and shall prescribe and control the means and methods of performing such Services by providing adequate and proper supervision. Licensor shall be solely responsible for compliance with all rules, laws, and regulations relating to employment of labor, hours of labor, working conditions, payment of wages and payment of taxes, such as employment, Social Security, and other payroll taxes including applicable contributions from such persons when required by law.

25. Compliance with Laws/Changes in Laws (Chapter 6.I)

Licensor and Customer each shall comply with the provision of all applicable federal, state, county and local laws, ordinances, regulations, and codes [as of the date of this Agreement] including, but not limited to, Licensor's and Customer's obligations as employers with regard to the health, safety, and payment of its employees, and identification and procurement of required permits, certificates, approvals, and inspections in Licensor's and Customer's performance of this Agreement.

- ***It is unclear whether this language requires the Licensor to conform its software and services to any applicable changes in the law. Both parties should agree on which party will bear the responsibility and cost for ensuring that the software and services will comply with all applicable laws. Most Licensors will accept responsibility to ensure all software and services comply with all laws applicable to their industry in effect as of the date of the agreement. Licensors should be hesitant to agree to comply with all laws in the future without additional compensation as the Licensor cannot quantify the price of ensuring its compliance with unknown future changes. A reasonable compromise is to require the Licensor to make all such changes at the Customer's expense unless the cost of such changes can be amortized over all of the Licensor's customers. See the language set forth in Section 9.8.A that specifically addresses this issue.***

Alternative Language that Benefits the Customer:

Changes in Law and Regulations.

Licensor represents warrants and agrees that it shall identify the impact of changes in Licensor Regulatory Requirements on its ability to deliver the Services and perform its obligations under the Agreement. Licensor shall notify Customer of such Licensor Regulatory Requirements within ten (10) days after it learns of the enactment of any such Licensor Regulatory Requirements and shall work with Customer to identify the impact of such changes on how Customer uses the Services or on how Licensor delivers the Services. Customer and Licensor shall promptly make any resulting modifications to the Services as reasonably necessary as a result of changes in such Licensor Regulatory Requirements. Licensor shall comply with changes to all Licensor Regulatory Requirements and shall implement any necessary modifications to the Services prior to the deadline imposed, or extensions authorized by, the regulatory or other governmental body having jurisdiction for such Licensor Regulatory Requirements. All costs associated with identification and compliance with Licensor Regulatory Requirements shall be borne by Licensor. Upon Approval by Customer of an applicable change request pursuant to the Change Control Procedures, Licensor shall (i) implement Customer Regulatory Requirements, and (ii) shall implement any necessary modfications to the Services, in accordance with Customer's Policies and Procedures and/or an applicable Statement of Work, as applicable. Except as provided in this Section, Licensor shall have no obligation to identify regulatory changes.

Alternative Additional Language that May Be Appropriate Depending on the Customer's Business

For Customers subject to SEC regulation:

SEC Requirements. Licensor hereby undertakes to furnish promptly to the U.S. Securities and Exchange Commission ("Commission"), its designees or representatives, any self-regulatory organization of which Customer is a member, or any State securities regulator having jurisdiction over Customer, upon reasonable request, such information as is deemed necessary by the staffs of the Commission, any self-regulatory organization of which Customer is a member, or any State securities regulator having jurisdiction over Customer to download information kept on electronic storage media for Customer to any medium acceptable under Rule 17a-4. Furthermore, Licensor hereby undertakes to take reasonable steps to provide access to information contained on such electronic storage media, including, as appropriate, arrangements for the downloading of any record required to be maintained and preserved by Customer pursuant to Rules 17a-3 and 17a-4 under the Securities Exchange Act of 1934 in a format acceptable to the staffs of the Commission, any self-regulatory organization of which Customer is a member, or any State securities regulator having jurisdiction over Customer. Such arrangements will provide specifically that in the event of a failure on the part of Customer to download the record into a readable format and after reasonable notice to Customer, upon being provided with the appropriate electronic storage medium, the Licensor will undertake to do so, as the staffs of the Commission, any self-regulatory organization of which Customer is a member, or any State securities regulator having jurisdiction over Customer may request.

With respect to any books and records maintained or preserved on behalf of Customer, Licensor hereby undertakes to permit examination of such books and records at any time or from time to time during business hours by representatives or designees of the Securities and Exchange Commission, and to promptly furnish to said Commission or its designee true, correct, complete and current hard copy of any or all or any part of such books and records.

Licensor further represents that the media with which the books and records of Customer are maintained by the undersigned meet the requirements of Rule 17a-4(f) (2).

For a publicly held company:

Sarbanes-Oxley Requirements: Licensor recognizes that Customer will be subject to Sarbanes-Oxley Requirements. Licensor shall provide whatever assistance is necessary to ensure Customer is able to comply with such requirements with respect to its outsourced information technology functions. Licensor will comply with Customer's financial reporting process as set forth in the Policies and Procedures Guide (and as such process is revised from time to time by Customer) and provide Customer with copies of all related records, reports and data as necessary for Customer to satisfy Sarbanes-Oxley Requirements. Licensor shall recommend and, subject to Customer approval, implement compliance measures to satisfy Sarbanes-Oxley Requirements.

26. Security, Access, and Safety Requirements

Licensor shall instruct its employees, agents, and subcontractors that they shall comply with Customer's security, access, and safety requirements for the protection of Customer's facilities and employees while on Customer's premises.

27. Releases Void

Neither party shall require waivers or releases of any personal rights from representatives of the other in connection with visits to Licensor's and Customer's respective premises. No such releases or waivers shall be pleaded by Licensor or Customer or third persons in any action or proceeding against an employee.

28. Governing Law and Venue (Chapter 6.H)

28.1 **Governing Law and Venue.** The validity, construction, interpretation, and performance of this Agreement shall be governed by and construed in accordance with the domestic laws of the State of [________] except as to its principals of conflicts of laws and the parties hereto irrevocably submit to the exclusive jurisdiction and venue of the Federal District Court for the District of [________] to resolve any disputes arising hereunder or related hereto.

The parties hereto hereby (a) submit to the exclusive jurisdiction of any state or federal court sitting in [______________] for the purpose of any Action arising out of or relating to this Agreement brought by any party hereto, and (b) irrevocably waive, and agree not to assert by way of motion, defense, or otherwise, in any such Action, any claim that it is not subject personally to the jurisdiction of the above-named courts, that its property is exempt or immune from attachment or execution, that the Action is brought in an inconvenient forum, that the venue of the Action is improper, or that this Agreement may not be enforced in or by any of the above-named courts.

The parties may bring any actions seeking specific performance, equitable relief or other non-monetary remedies in any state or federal court of competent jurisdiction.

Alternative Language for Alternating Choice of Venues

28.1.A **Alternating Venue.** The validity, construction, interpretation, and performance of this Agreement shall be governed by and construed in accordance with the domestic laws of the State of [________] except as to its principals of conflicts of laws, and the parties hereto irrevocably submit to the exclusive jurisdiction and venue of the Federal District Court for the District of [**Licensee's desired venue**] if the Licensor shall bring an action hereunder or related hereto provided, however, Customer agrees to submit to the exclusive jurisdiction of [**Licensor's desired venue**] for any action brought by Licensor alleging a violation by Customer's confidentiality obligations hereunder. If the Licensee shall bring an action hereunder or related hereto, the parties hereto irrevocably submit to the exclusive jurisdiction and venue of the Federal District Court for the District of [**Licensor's desired venue**] to resolve any disputes arising hereunder or related hereto.

Alternative Language for Differing Venues Based on Trade Secret Concerns

28.1.B. **Governing Law.** This Agreement shall be deemed to have been entered into and executed in the State of (**CUSTOMER'S REQUESTED STATE**) and shall be construed, performed, and enforced in all respects in accordance with the laws of that State, except as to the definition and protection of trade secrets and confidential information which shall be determined pursuant to the laws of the State of (**LICENSOR'S REQUESTED STATE**).

Alternative Language for Opting Out of the United Nations Convention on Contracts for the International Sale of Goods

28.1.C. **The United Nations Convention on Contracts for the International Sale of Goods** The United Nations Convention on Contracts for the International Sale of Goods shall not govern or be used to construe this Agreement. OR

It is hereby stipulated that the "Convention Relating to a Uniform Law on the International Sale of Goods" shall not apply to this Agreement. OR

The application of the United Nations Convention on Contracts for the International Sale of Goods is expressly excluded.

- ***If the parties to the agreement are incorporated under the laws of two different countries, both of which are signatories to the UN Convention, the UN Convention automatically governs the agreement unless the parties affirmatively opt out of the UN Convention. Given that case law interpreting the UN Convention is not well developed and its impact on software licenses is unclear, the parties should opt out.***

28.2 **UCITA Disclaimer.** Pursuant to Md. Code Ann. Section 21-104, the parties hereby expressly agree to opt out of application of the Maryland Uniform Computer Information Transactions Act (MUCITA), Md. Code Ann. Commercial Law Sections 21-101 through 21-816, except to the extent that Section 21-104(2) of the Act applies. The parties further agree that this Agreement shall be governed by the common law of

Maryland relating to written agreements and Maryland statutes other than MUCITA which may apply.

Alternative Language to Address UCITA Where It Has Not Been Adopted

The parties agree that, in the event that the Uniform Computer Information Transaction Act, any version thereof or a substantially similar law (collectively UCITA) is enacted as to be applicable to a party's performance under the Agreement and this Addendum, said statute shall not govern any aspect of the Agreement and this Addendum, any license granted hereunder, nor any of the parties' rights and obligations arising pursuant to the Agreement and this Addendum. The applicable law shall be the law as it existed prior to the enactment of UCITA.

- ***Most licensors would like the agreement to be governed by the laws of the state where they are headquartered although there is some flexibility as to the particular state law. It is also important to have the venue (the location of any trial) be in the same state. Some states such as Texas favor the Customer while others such as New York favor the Licensor. To ensure the choice of law is upheld, there must be a nexus between that state and one of the parties. Usually, it is where one of the parties is headquartered, the Customer site is located or where a majority of the work is performed.***
- ***Make sure to review the law of the state chosen and understand its ramifications. For example, has the state in question adopted UCITA? (see Section 28.2 if to avoid having the contract governed by UCITA. Make sure to include language opting out of UCITA) and to utilize the UCITA required warranty disclaimer (see Section 16.1.4.A.)***
- ***Be certain to use the word "exclusive" to ensure that the relevant venue is the exclusive venue and the identified venue is not interpreted to be the "permissive" venue.***
- ***The Licensor wants to avoid arbitration or alternative dispute resolution (ADR) because arbitrators tend to "split the baby." In addition, it may be very difficult to get an immediate injunction to halt the misuse of the Licensor's software. Advantages of arbitration are quicker resolution, lower cost, and lower profile.***

Potential Language to Resolve Any Question as to the Applicability of the UCC

Favoring Licensee:

28.3 **Applicability of Uniform Commercial Code.** To the extent this Agreement or any SOW entails the delivery of Software or Software Products, such Software or Software Products shall be deemed "goods" within the meaning of Article 2 of the Uniform Commercial Code, except when deeming services as "goods" would cause an unreasonable result. This Agreement or an SOW shall control where there is a conflict with the UCC.

Favoring Licensor:

28.3 **Applicability of Uniform Commercial Code.** The parties agree that this contract is not a contract for the sale of goods; therefore, this Agreement shall not be governed by any codification of Article 2 or 2A of the Uniform Commercial Code, or any codification of the Uniform Computer Information Technology Act (UCITA), or any references to the United National Convention on Contracts for the International Sale of Goods.

- ***Occasionally, Licensees will seek to include language "declaring" software to be a good in an attempt to create certainty in the event of a dispute and to take advantage of the protections the UCC offers to the purchasers of goods. This language often has the opposite effect as the language itself is unclear and adds further uncertainty. The applicability of the UCC, as opposed to UCITA, places the Licensor at a significant disadvantage.***

29. Non-Binding Dispute Resolution (Chapter 30.C)

Additional Language Related to Dispute Resolution

29.1 **Manager Level Performance Review.** The applicable Licensor Manager and Customer Manager shall meet as often as shall reasonably be required to review the performance of the parties under this Agreement and to resolve any disputes. Written minutes of such meetings shall be kept by Licensor for review and approval by Customer. If these representatives are unable to resolve a dispute within ten (10) calendar days after the initial request for a meeting, then the dispute shall be submitted to an executive level performance review as described in Section 29.2.

29.2 **Executive Level Performance Review.** Face-to-face negotiations shall be conducted by senior executive officers of Customer and Licensor. If these representatives are unable to resolve the dispute within ten (10) calendar days after the representatives have commenced negotiations, or twenty (20) calendar days have passed since the initial request for negotiations at this level, then the parties may agree in writing to submit the dispute to mediation.

29.3 **Voluntary, Non-binding Mediation.** If executive level performance review is not successful in resolving the dispute, the parties may, but shall not be obligated to, mutually agree in writing to submit the dispute to non-binding mediation. Mediation must occur within five (5) business days after the parties agree to submit the dispute to mediation, and the duration of the mediation shall be limited to one (1) business day. The parties mutually shall select an independent mediator experienced in commercial information systems contract disputes, and each shall designate a representative(s) to meet with the mediator in good faith in an effort to resolve the dispute. The specific format for the mediation shall be left to the discretion of the mediator and the designated party representatives and may include the preparation of agreed-upon statements of fact or written statements of position furnished to the other party.

29.4 **Continued Performance.** Except where clearly prevented by the area in dispute, both parties shall continue performing their obligations under this Agreement while the dispute is being resolved under this Section unless and until the dispute is resolved or until this Agreement is terminated as provided herein. Except for disputes relating to the payment of Licensor invoices as described in Section 8.7, the time frame for a party to cure any breach of the terms of this Agreement shall not be tolled by the pendency of any dispute resolution procedures.

29.5 **Equitable Relief.** Notwithstanding anything contained in this Agreement to the contrary, the parties shall be entitled to seek injunctive or other equitable relief whenever the facts or circumstances would permit a party to seek such equitable relief in a court of competent jurisdiction.

- ***The language set forth above in Section 29.5 favors the Customer and should be limited. While injunctive relief is commonly accepted, other potential equitable remedies including specific performance are not. Thus, the language set forth above should be narrowed to limit equitable relief solely to injunctive relief. See Section 5.3.4 for a discussion of specific performance.***

30. Arbitration (Chapter 30.D)

Alternative Language When the Parties Agree to Arbitration

30.1 **Binding Nature.** Any claim or controversy arising out of or relating to this Agreement or the alleged breach hereof must be submitted and settled as set forth in this section.

30.2 **Escalation Procedure.** If any party to this Agreement alleges that any other party to this Agreement has breached [**or may breach**] any of the terms of this Agreement, then the party alleging breach shall inform the other party or parties of their breach in writing pursuant to the notice provisions of this Agreement. Upon receipt of such notice, the allegedly nonperforming party shall have ten (10) days to cure the alleged breach. If the parties do not agree that effective cure has been accomplished by the end of the ten (10) day period, then the parties' Project Coordinators shall meet in person and confer in good faith to resolve the dispute within fifteen (15) days of the expiration of the prior ten (10) day period. If the parties do not agree that effective cure has been accomplished by the end of the fifteen (15) day period, then upon written request of any party Licensor's Chief Operating Officer and Customer's Chief Financial Officer shall meet in person and confer in good faith to resolve the dispute within fifteen (15) days of the expiration of the prior fifteen (15) day period. If the parties do not resolve the dispute through a meeting of Licensor's Chief Operating Officer and Customer's Chief Financial Officer, then the parties agree jointly to retain a mediator from a professional mediation organization (such as the American Arbitration Association, JAMS/Endispute, or the CPR Institute for Dispute Resolution) and to mediate the dispute within the next thirty (30) days.

30.3 **Filing of Claim.** If, after the above procedures, the dispute remains unresolved, then the dispute shall be submitted to the office of the American Arbitration Association located closest to [City, State], and shall be settled by arbitration to occur in

[City, State], said arbitration to be administered by the American Arbitration Association in accordance with its Commercial Arbitration Rules in effect at the time of the arbitration and the laws of the State of __________ governing such arbitrations. Such arbitration must be filed within twelve (12) months of the first accrual of the cause of action, and the parties agree that the statute of limitations for any cause of action brought pursuant to, in connection with, or relating to the provision of the Services or any other subject matter of this Agreement shall be twelve (12) months from the first accrual of the cause of action.

30.4 **General Rules.** The arbitration shall be heard and decided no later than seven (7) months after the notice of arbitration is filed with the American Arbitration Association. The arbitrators shall hear and determine any preliminary issue of law asserted by a party to be dispositive of any claim, in whole or in part, in the manner of a court hearing a motion to dismiss for failure to state a claim or for summary judgment, pursuant to such terms and procedures as the arbitrators deem appropriate. No witness or party may be required to waive any privilege recognized under [State] law. The hearing shall not last longer than four (4) days unless all parties agree otherwise, with time to be divided equally between Licensor and Customer. In the event of such arbitration each party shall select an impartial arbitrator and the parties' impartial arbitrators shall select a chief arbitrator from a list provided by the American Arbitration Association.

30.5 **Discovery.** For good cause shown, the arbitrators may permit each side to serve no more than fifteen (15) document requests (including subparts) and ten (10) interrogatories (including subparts) on the opposing parties. For good cause shown, the arbitrators may permit each side to subpoena no more than two (2) third party witnesses for testimonial depositions (each deposition not to exceed two (2) hours of examination by __________ and not to exceed two (2) hours of examination by __________) if the witnesses cannot be compelled to attend the arbitration, and no more than two (2) current (at the time of the subpoena) employees of each opposing party for testimonial depositions (each deposition not to exceed two (2) hours of examination by __________ and not to exceed two (2) hours of examination by __________) if the witnesses cannot be compelled to attend the arbitration. Any discovery as set forth above shall be governed by the Federal Rules of Civil Procedure and the precedents applicable to cases brought in the United States District Court for the __________ District of [State]. No other discovery shall be permitted except by written agreement of all parties. The parties and the arbitrators shall treat all aspects of the arbitration proceedings, including, without limitation, discovery, testimony and other evidence, briefs, and the award, as strictly confidential and not subject to disclosure to any third party or entity, other than to the parties, the arbitrators, and the American Arbitration Association. The arbitrators must give full effect to the applicable law and to all terms of this Agreement, and are specifically divested of any power to render decisions in derogation thereof or *ex aequo et bono*.

30.6 **Decision.** The arbitrators shall issue written findings of fact and conclusions of law, the decisions of the arbitrators will be binding and conclusive upon all parties involved, and judgment upon any decision of the arbitrators may be entered in the highest court of any forum, federal or state, having jurisdiction thereof.

31. Waiver of Breach (Chapter 6.F)

No waiver of breach or failure to exercise any option, right, or privilege under the terms of this Agreement or any order on any occasion or occasions shall be construed to be a waiver of the same or any other option, right, or privilege on any other occasion.

- ***This provision provides that if the Licensor fails to enforce any of its rights, the Licensor is not prohibited from enforcing such rights at a later date.***

32. Waiver of Right to Jury Trial (Chapter 6.G)

THE PARTIES HEREBY UNCONDITIONALLY WAIVE THEIR RESPECTIVE RIGHTS TO A JURY TRIAL OF ANY CLAIM OR CAUSE OF ACTION ARISING DIRECTLY OR INDIRECTLY OUT OF, RELATED TO, OR IN ANY WAY CONNECTED WITH THE PERFORMANCE OR BREACH OF THIS AGREEMENT, AND/OR THE RELATIONSHIP THAT IS BEING ESTABLISHED AMONG THEM. The scope of this waiver is intended to be all encompassing of any and all disputes that may be filed in any court or other tribunal (including, without limitation, contract claims, tort claims, breach of duty claims, and all other common law and statutory claims). THIS WAIVER IS IRREVOCABLE, MEANING THAT IT MAY NOT BE MODIFIED EITHER ORALLY OR IN WRITING, AND THE WAIVER SHALL APPLY TO ANY SUBSEQUENT AMENDMENTS, RENEWALS, SUPPLEMENTS, OR MODIFICATIONS TO THIS AGREEMENT, AND RELATED DOCUMENTS, OR TO ANY OTHER DOCUMENTS OR AGREEMENTS RELATING TO THIS TRANSACTION OR ANY RELATED TRANSACTION. In the event of litigation, this Agreement may be filed as a written consent to a trial by the court.

Each of the parties hereto (a) certifies that no representative, agent, or attorney of any other party has represented, expressly or otherwise, that such other party would not, in the event of litigation, seek to enforce that foregoing waiver, and (b) acknowledges that it and the other parties hereto have been induced to enter into this Agreement, as applicable, by, among other things, the mutual waivers and certifications in this Section 32.

Alternatively:

EACH PARTY ACKNOWLEDGES AND AGREES THAT ANY CONTROVERSY WHICH MAY ARISE UNDER THIS AGREEMENT IS LIKELY TO INVOLVE COMPLICATED AND DIFFICULT ISSUES, AND THEREFORE IT HEREBY IRREVOCABLY AND UNCONDITIONALLY WAIVES ANY RIGHT IT MAY HAVE TO A TRIAL BY JURY IN RESPECT OF ANY LITIGATION DIRECTLY OR INDIRECTLY ARISING OUT OF OR RELATING TO THIS AGREEMENT AND ANY OF THE AGREEMENTS DELIVERED IN CONNECTION HEREWITH OR THE TRANSACTIONS CONTEMPLATED HEREBY OR THEREBY. EACH PARTY CERTIFIES AND ACKNOWLEDGES THAT (A) NO REPRESENTATIVE, AGENT OR ATTORNEY OF ANY OTHER PARTY HAS REPRESENTED, EXPRESSLY OR OTHERWISE, THAT SUCH OTHER PARTY WOULD NOT, IN THE EVENT OF LITIGATION, SEEK TO ENFORCE EITHER OF SUCH WAIVERS, (B) IT

UNDERSTANDS AND HAS CONSIDERED THE IMPLICATIONS OF SUCH WAIVERS, (C) IT MAKES SUCH WAIVERS VOLUNTARILY, AND (D) IT HAS BEEN INDUCED TO ENTER INTO THIS AGREEMENT BY, AMONG OTHER THINGS, THE MUTUAL WAIVERS AND CERTIFICATIONS IN THIS SECTION 32.

- ***Before agreeing to a contractual waiver to a trial by jury, confirm that a pre-litigation jury waiver clause will be upheld under the governing law chosen by the parties as at least two states have held that pre-litigation contractual jury waiver clauses are unenforceable.* See Bank South N.A. v. Howard, *444 S.E.2d 799 (Ga. 1994);* Grafton Partners LP v. Superior Court, *88 P.3d 24 (2004), aff'd 116 P.3d 479 (2005).***

33. Force Majeure (Chapter 6.D)

Neither party shall be responsible for any delay or failure in performance of any part of this Agreement to the extent that such delay or failure is caused by fire, flood, explosion, war, embargo, government requirement, civil, or military authority, act of God, act or omission of carriers, or other similar causes beyond its control. If any such event of force majeure occurs and such event continues for ninety (90) days or more, the party delayed or unable to perform shall give immediate notice to the other party, and the party affected by the other's delay or inability to perform may elect at its sole discretion to (a) terminate this Agreement upon mutual agreement of the parties; (b) suspend such order for the duration of the condition and obtain or sell elsewhere Software or Services comparable to the Software or Services to have been obtained under this Agreement; or (c) resume performance of such order once the condition ceases with the option of the affected party to extend the period of this Agreement up to the length of time the condition endured. Unless written notice is given within thirty (30) days after the affected party is notified of the condition, option (c) shall be deemed selected.

Alternatively:

Except for monetary obligations hereunder, neither party shall be liable for any failure or delay in performance due in whole or in part to any cause beyond the reasonable control of such party or its contractors, agents or suppliers, **including but not limited** to utility or transmission failures, failure of phone lines or phone equipment, power failure, strikes or other labor disturbances, acts of God, acts of war or terror, floods, sabotage, fire, natural or other disasters ("Force Majeure").

- ***The parties should always exclude monetary obligations from a force majeure event to avoid having a party claim it cannot perform (pay any monies due) due to an economic downturn and thereby be excused from making payment.* See e.g., *Marionneaux v. Smith,* 163 So. 206 (La. 1935) *(unforeseen economic depression is not an event of force majeure).***
- ***The Licensee should ensure that the list of force majeure "events" is narrowly drawn such that the Licensor cannot invoke the clause to avoid***

meeting its service level agreements or other obligations. Usually, the agreed upon events only pertain to the entity's day-to-day operations. While the Licensee may desire to agree upon a specific list that will excuse nonperformance, force majeure clauses by their nature are designed to protect against an unanticipated contingency and should not be limited to a list of specific events. The Licensee should specifically exclude the Licensor's subcontractor's nonperformance. Given the nature of the agreement, it may be appropriate to have different force majeure provisions for different events.

- ***All force majeure clauses must be carefully reviewed to ensure that the Customer cannot automatically terminate the Agreement. It is preferable that the Agreement be put on hold until the force majeure dissipates.***

34. Bonds (Chapter 7.M)

Licensor shall provide Customer with the bonds set forth in this Section. The bonding companies providing such bonds must be acceptable to Customer, in its sole discretion, and be authorized to do business in the State of_________. In the event the bonding company providing such bonding does not have an A.M. Best rating of A or better, Customer may require Licensor to obtain bonds required under this Section 34 from another bonding company. The premium for all bonds required below shall be paid solely by Licensor.

34.1 **Performance and Payment Bonds**. Licensor shall obtain, or cause to be obtained, a performance bond (a "Performance Bond") and a payment bond (a "Payment Bond"). The Performance Bond shall continue through the term of the Agreement and the Payment Bond shall continue until the earlier to occur of the following: (a) when Licensor has obtained all applicable releases from all subcontractors (and provided copies of such releases to Customer); or (b) when Licensor has satisfied in full any and all obligations and amounts due and owing to all subcontractors for work performed pursuant to this Agreement and provided Customer with satisfactory evidence of such payment. Licensor shall secure a Payment Bond and Performance Bond, each in an amount equivalent to the value of the Agreement. Licensor shall deliver such Performance Bond and Payment Bond to Customer on or prior to the Effective Date hereof and such Performance Bond and Payment Bond shall be attached as Appendix 34.

34.2 **Requirements**. Unless otherwise agreed to by the parties, the Performance Bond and Payment Bond shall: (a) name Customer as obligee; (b) be in a form, and be issued by, a licensed surety satisfactory to Customer, its sole discretion, and not subject to mediation or arbitration; and (c) be in the amounts described in Section 34.1 above.

35. Business Continuity Plan (Disaster Recovery) [If Applicable] (Chapter 7.F)

Upon the Commencement Date for Services to be performed by Licensor under certain Statements of Work, Licensor shall apply Licensor's business continuity and disaster recovery plans (as approved by Customer and as modified pursuant to this Agreement) to such Services. An outline and executive summary of Licensor's Business Continuity Plan shall be exchanged. The Business Continuity Plan for all such Services shall (i) be designed (a) to continue all Licensor business operations that are critical to the overall operation and functionality of such Services, and (b) to ensure Licensor's compliance with the information security requirements set forth in Exhibit __ notwithstanding the occurrence of a Crisis; (ii) specify procedures and frequency of testing; (iii) be compatible with Customer's own business continuity and disaster recovery plans, as such plans are provided and amended from time to time by Customer, and ensure business reasonable integration with such Customer plans in the event of a Crisis; and (iv) be, and shall be maintained, consistent with then-current highest generally accepted industry standards and Customer's then-current business continuity plan. The Business Continuity Plan shall specifically address the ability of Licensor to provide each such Service in the event of a Crisis. The Business Continuity Plan shall provide, among other things, a mechanism for the redundancy or backup of business operations designed to keep such Services from becoming unavailable for a significant amount of time due to a Crisis and to permit the related business operations of Customer to be re-instituted in a time period that permits the ongoing operation and functionality of Customer's business to which such Services relate. Without limiting the generality of the foregoing, the Business Continuity Plan shall address all of the computer software, computer hardware (whether general or special purpose), telecommunications capabilities (including all voice, data and video networks) and other similar or related items of automated, computerized, and/or software system(s) and any other network(s) or system(s) that are used, or relied on, by Licensor in the provision of such Services and the manner in which Licensor will re-institute the processing of relevant information in a time period that permits the ongoing operation and functionality of Customer's business to which such Services relate. Notwithstanding the foregoing, if a Crisis prevents Licensor from providing such Services to Customer, Licensor shall allocate its efforts and resources to restoring Customer's Services no less favorably to Customer than it allocates to any of its other customers affected by the Crisis.

Upon the occurrence of a Crisis and at vendor's sole expense, Licensor shall promptly (but in any event in less than twenty-four (24) hours) implement the Business Continuity Plan. The occurrence of a Crisis (including any Force Majeure Event) will not relieve Licensor of its obligation to implement the Business Continuity Plan and to provide disaster recovery Services. If the Services are not restored within the period specified in the Business Continuity Plan, Customer may terminate the applicable Work Process Agreement and such termination will be deemed to have occurred under Section ___.

"**Crisis**" shall mean (i) any extraordinary event affecting Licensor that requires emergency response measures to be taken, including any event that may result in the Services becoming unavailable for a significant amount of time, or (ii) any event that, **in the Customer's reasonable determination**, requires emergency measures to be taken.

- ***The Licensor should avoid agreeing to perform any services or take any action based on the Customer's sole determination regardless of whether it is subject to a reasonableness standard unless the Customer has agreed to pay for such services.***

Alternatively:

> ***Disaster Recovery:*** As part of this Agreement, if Licensor maintains any Customer information on its computer system or in databases, Licensor will maintain a Disaster Recovery plan that defines the tasks and timeframes to expeditiously overcome any disability that causes a system outage. The Disaster Recovery plan will adequately address the backup of hardware, software, and facilities during a service outage. Licensor agrees that the Disaster Recovery Plan will provide, without limitation, the following: (i) in the event of any incidence of system failure (other than a catastrophic system failure as determined by Customer), Licensor will define the problem and present a plan of resolution to Customer within four (4) business hours of identification of the system failure; and (ii) Licensor will use its best efforts to correct any system failure in no more than eight (8) business hours and to ensure that multiple incidents of system failure will occur no more than twice in a single calendar month. Supplier must provide Customer with a written Contingency Plan, which outlines how the Supplier will provide continuity of Products in the event of a disaster, catastrophe or pandemic. Supplier will provide an update once per year or as often as changes are made whichever is more frequent. In the event that Supplier fails to provide a plan or provides a plan which does not meet Customer's approval, Customer reserves the right to take its own measures to ensure continuity of Product. Such measures may include contracting with alternate suppliers for backup supply, altering the volume allocation previously given to Supplier, and/or termination of this Agreement.

- ***The Customer should make certain that the Licensor provides reasonable assurances as to the Licensor's disaster recovery plans. These plans should be set forth in detail in an exhibit. If the Licensor is unwilling to do so, the Licensee should retain another vendor.***

36. Covenant of Good Faith (Chapter 7.P.2)

Each Party agrees that, in its respective dealings with the other Party under or in connection with this Agreement, it shall act in good faith.

- ***This section is important as it imposes a duty of good faith in those jurisdictions that do not already do so. The implementation of such a duty may create additional obligations and risks for the parties. See §16.U.***

37. Time Is of the Essence (Chapter 7.Q)

The Parties hereto acknowledge that the performance by Licensor and Customer of their obligations hereunder is to be done on a "time is of the essence" basis. This expression is understood to mean that Licensor and Customer are to deliver their respective Deliverables no later than the Delivery Dates therefore and that any delay in connection therewith will cause the other Party damage; it is for this reason that the Parties have agreed, pursuant to Section 3.C hereof, that liquidated damages will be imposed if delays are experienced.

Alternatively:

Time is of the essence with respect to Licensor's performance of all of its obligations under License/Service Schedules, SOWs, and implementation plans. ***Licensor shall not be entitled to any increase in fees or any other adjustment caused by delay attributable in whole or in part to Licensor, or any delay as to which Licensee did not receive timely notice. Licensor agrees to make no claim for damages for delay occasioned by an act or a failure to act by Licensee or any of its representatives.*** Licensor's sole remedy for such delay shall be an extension of its deadlines for performance, provided such extension is otherwise agreed to in advance in writing by the parties.

- ***The first clause provides that Licensor will deliver the Software on time. If Licensor is even one minute late, the delay is considered material allowing the Customer to terminate the Agreement and collect damages from Licensor. Consequently, the Licensor should think carefully before including this language. Licensor should clearly state that any times lines are good faith estimates and contingent on licensee timely meeting all of its obligations. At a minimum, the language should be made mutual.***
- ***The second clause seeks to limit the Licensor's ability to collect additional fees or hold the Customer liable for any delay caused by the Customer.***

38. Insurance (Chapter 6.C)

Licensor shall maintain in effect at all times during the term of this Agreement insurance with a carrier with an A.M. Best rating of A or better. Such insurance shall include, without limitation, worker's compensation in statutory amounts, and products/completed operations liability, errors and omissions, business interruption, comprehensive general liability, and automobile insurance in amounts not less than $10 million per occurrence and $25 million annual aggregate for all claims against all losses, claims, demands, proceedings, damages, costs, charges, and expenses for injuries or damage to any person or property arising out of or in connection with Licensor's performance or non-performance under this Agreement and shall designate Customer and its Affiliates as "additional insureds" on such insurance policies. Licensor shall, on or before the Effective Date and thereafter upon Customer's reasonable request, provide Customer with certified copies of all applicable endorsements and certificates of insurance, both evidencing such coverage, which shall also state that Customer shall be provided a minimum of thirty (30) calendar days prior written notice of any proposed cancellation, or expiration without renewal, and five (5) business days prior written notice of any proposed change in carriers or material terms of coverage. Upon Customer's request, Licensor shall also provide Customer with certified copies of the involved insurance policy or policies within fifteen (15) calendar days of such request. Licensor shall obtain or otherwise arrange for appropriate levels of insurance coverage for all subcontractors. Licensor shall maintain, in its files, evidence of all subcontractors' insurance coverage and shall provide proof of such coverage to Customer upon Customer's request. In the event coverage is denied or reimbursement of a properly presented claim is disputed by the carrier for insurance provided as described above, upon written request, Licensor shall provide Customer with a certified copy of the involved insurance policy or policies within ten (10) business days of receipt of such request. Customer may withhold an amount equal to fifty percent (50%) of all monies due and to become due to Licensor under this Agreement should Licensor not comply with any terms of this Section. The terms of this Section shall not be deemed to limit the liability of Licensor hereunder, or to limit any rights Customer may have including, without limitation, rights of indemnity, or contribution.

- ***Most Customers require the Licensor to provide a certificate of insurance evidencing the Licensor has the required insurance from an insurance company acceptable to the Customer. Language should be included allowing the Licensor to self-insure. Do not waive Licensor's/Licensor's insurer's right of subrogation (the right of Licensor or its insurer to sue any co-tortfeasor for their pro rata portion of any damages award) as the waiver of this right may raise the Licensor's insurance rates. This section should be mutual if the Licensor is working on the Customer's premises as the Licensor's employees may be injured by the Customer's employees, agents, or contractors. The Licensor should never accept language that allows the Customer to purchase insurance for the Licensor or allow the Customer to offset money due Licensor for the Licensor's failure to obtain insurance.***

39. Third Party Software (Chapter 5.L)

Customer shall have sole responsibility to obtain and pay for any third party software necessary or desirable to operate the Software or ABC System.

- ***The Licensor should not provide any third party software unless the cost of such third party software was included in Licensor's pricing.***

40. Third Party Beneficiaries (Chapter 6.K)

This Agreement is entered into solely for the benefit of Licensor and Customer. No third party shall have the right to make any claim or assert any right under it, and no third party shall be deemed a beneficiary of this Agreement. The foregoing notwithstanding, the Parties acknowledge and agree that [**list exception**] is the intended third party beneficiary of this Agreement and, as such, [**list exception**] is entitled, subject to the terms and conditions of this Agreement, to all remedies entitled to third party beneficiaries under law.

- ***A Licensor must be careful to disclaim any third party beneficiaries to avoid a third party claiming the benefit of a warranty granted under the agreement. This is especially important when the software will process information or tasks for a third party.***

and/or

The parties acknowledge that the Software may include software licensed by Licensor from Licensor's licensors. Licensor's licensors may be direct and intended third party beneficiaries of this Agreement and may be entitled to enforce it directly against Customer to the extent (a) this Agreement relates to the licensing of Licensor's licensors' software products, and (b) Licensor fails to enforce the terms of this Agreement on their behalf.

41. Outsourcing

Licensor acknowledges that Customer has entered into information technology services agreements with International Business Machines Corporation ("IBM") for the provision of information technology, data processing, and related services, to Customer. Licensor hereby agrees that, at no additional charge to Customer, (i) Customer may disclose to IBM all hardware, software, and related products and documentation that are licensed or transferred to Customer pursuant to this Agreement (the "IT Systems"); (ii) IBM shall have the limited right to use the IT Systems for the sole purpose of delivering information technology, data processing, and related services to Customer; and (iii) upon notice to Licensor, all or part of the IT Systems may be installed or relocated to a facility controlled by IBM. Notwithstanding clauses (i) or (ii) above, IBM shall not use the IT Systems in a manner that is inconsistent with Customer's rights under this Agreement.

Licensor further acknowledges that Customer may at any time during the term of this Agreement enter into an arrangement with other third parties ("Outsourcer(s)") for the provision of information technology, data processing, and related services. Customer shall notify the Licensor of the name and location of the Outsourcer(s), and the Licensor consents to the use of the IT Systems by the Outsourcer(s) at any time during the term of this Agreement for the purpose of providing information technology, data processing, and related services to Company so long as use of the IT Systems by the Outsourcer(s) is not inconsistent with the other terms of this section.

42. Divestiture and Transition

42.1 **Divestiture.** In the event of an assignment or transfer to a Divested Business, Licensor shall enter into a separate agreement with the Divested Business upon the same terms and conditions (including fees) as this Agreement.

42.2 **Transition.** Licensee shall have the right to use Software to provide services to Divested Businesses as part of any such divestiture, as Licensee directs, for a period of two (2) years after the completion of each such divestiture, at no additional cost other than the compensation provided for in this Agreement. In addition, Licensee shall have the right to use Software to provide such services for an additional one (1) year period (or any longer period as Licensee and Licensor agree), subject to reasonable terms and license fees to be agreed upon.

43. Export (Chapter 7.L)

Licensor and Customer each shall comply with the provision of all applicable federal, state, county, and local laws, ordinances, regulations, and codes including, but not limited to, Licensor's and Customer's obligations as employers with regard to the health, safety, and payment of its employees, and identification and procurement of required permits, certificates, approvals, and inspections in Licensor's and Customer's performance of this Agreement.

Customer and Licensor acknowledge that the Software and all related technical information, documents, and materials are subject to export controls under the U.S. Export Administration Regulation. Customer and Licensor will (i) comply strictly with all legal requirements established under these controls; (ii) cooperate fully with the other party in any official or unofficial audit or inspection that relates to these controls; and (iii) not export, re-export, divert, transfer, or disclose, directly or indirectly, any Software or related technical information, document, or material or direct products thereof to any country so restricted by the U.S. Export Administration Regulations, as modified from time to time, or to any national or resident thereof, unless Customer has obtained the prior written authorization of Licensor and the U.S. Commerce Department and any relevant local governmental authority. Furthermore, Customer recognizes and agrees that concurrently with the execution of this Agreement it shall provide Licensor with a Letter of Assurance, substantially in the form of Exhibit 43 attached hereto. Customer agrees Licensor shall have no liability for the failure to obtain a U.S. export license to export the Software to **[COUNTRY NAME]**.

- ***Both parties should ensure that the agreement provides the necessary protections under the U.S. export laws. The U.S. Commerce Department has taken an aggressive position to ensure compliance and the failure to include the appropriate language, especially in an agreement with a foreign entity, may expose the Licensor to significant liability.***

44. Publicity and Use of Customer Marks

44.1 **Publicity**

Both parties hereby agree to make best endeavors to issue a mutually agreed press release or similar publicity statement within six (6) weeks of the date of this Agreement. Thereafter, neither party shall issue a press release or other similar publicity of any nature regarding this Agreement without the other party's prior written approval, which shall not be unreasonably withheld. Notwithstanding the foregoing, each party hereby agrees the other party may use its name, URL, and logo on its website and in its customer and partner lists for corporate and financial presentations.

Alternatively:

Neither party shall issue a press release or similar public announcement of any kind regarding the Parties' relationship established hereunder without the prior written approval of the other Party. Other than expressly set forth herein, neither Party shall use publicly the other Party's name or refer to the other Party in any way in or with the media, including, but not limited to, in advertising, without the other Party's prior written consent as required herein, provided, however, that either Party may make disclosures or filings required to comply with applicable laws, including filings with regulatory agencies, such as the United States Securities and Exchange Commission, or disclosures or filings required to comply with the rules of a national securities exchange or automated quotations systems such as the National Association of Securities Dealer's Automated Quotations. A VIOLATION OF THIS PROVISION SHALL CONSTITUTE A MATERIAL BREACH OF THIS AGREEMENT.

***Alternatively*:**

Without the prior written consent of the other Party, neither Party shall issue or release any statement, article, advertisement, public or private announcement, media release or other similar publicity relating in any manner to: (a) any aspect of this Agreement, including Statement of Works; (b) any aspect of any Services and/or Deliverables; or (c) the fact that the Parties have engaged in any discussions or negotiations regarding any of the foregoing. Neither Party shall use the name or any business name, trade name, trademark, service mark or logo of the other Party without the prior written consent of the other Party.

***Alternatively*:**

Promotions Referring to Customer. Licensor agrees that Customer shall be entitled to review and Approve any and all promotional materials that contain a reference to Customer as contemplated herein before publication or distribution of same. No public disclosures by Licensor relating to this Agreement, except for internal announcements or disclosures required to meet legal or regulatory requirements, shall be made without the prior written approval of authorized representatives of the other Party.

Demonstration and Promotions Not Warranties. In no event shall any demonstration or any promotional materials pursuant to this Section constitute an endorsement, representation or warranty, express or implied, by Customer. In the event of a dispute between Customer and Licensor, Customer's agreement to participate in promotions and demonstrations under this Section and all statements made by Customer in connection with such activities shall not be deemed an admission or declaration against interest of Customer in any trial or dispute resolution proceeding between the Parties.

- ***Set forth above are four examples of potential "publicity" clauses reflecting differing degrees of restrictions on publicizing the underlying agreement. Publicly held companies must, at a minimum, have the right to disclose any information necessary to comply with any applicable securities laws. The Licensor usually wants to publicize its client list especially if it has prestigious clients. A Customer may not want to have the Licensor use the Customer's name in the Licensor's marketing campaign to avoid giving the appearance that the Customer is endorsing the***

Licensor's products. If the Customer does grant the Licensor the right to use the Customer's name and trademark/service marks in the Customer's marketing and sales activities, the Customer should ensure that it clearly delineates the terms under which the Licensor may use the Customer's name and marks.

- ***Set forth below is model language to license the Licensor to use the Customer's trademarks and service marks.***

44.2 **Use/License of Customer Marks.**

44.2.1 Subject to the terms and conditions specified in this Agreement, Customer hereby grants to Licensor (and Licensor's Affiliates), for the term of this Agreement, a non-exclusive, non-transferable license to use the Customer licensed marks setforth in Exhibit __ ("the Customer Licensed Marks") exactly as depicted in the graphic configuration or as subsequently modified by Customer. Customer may, in its sole discretion, at any time add to or delete from the Customer Licensed Marks and change the graphic configuration of the Customer Licensed Marks.

44.2.2 Licensor agrees that the style of use of the Customer Licensed Marks shall be in the form and style conforming to the trademark usage guidelines as provided to Licensor in writing. Licensor shall not use any of the Customer Licensed Marks as part of its corporate name, trade name, business name or Internet domain name.

44.2.3 Licensor shall submit to Customer for review and approval, at least ten (10) business days prior to proposed use, any web pages or other Internet locations, and all marketing, advertising, press releases or other Promotional Materials in which the Customer Licensed Marks are used. Customer shall approve or disapprove such materials at least five (5) business days after its receipt of such materials; Customer will not unreasonably withhold or delay the granting of its approval thereof. Licensor shall not publish, distribute or use any such web pages or other Internet locations, or any such marketing, advertising, press releases or other Promotional Materials in which the Customer Licensed Marks are used, without the prior written approval of Customer.

44.2.4 Notwithstanding the foregoing, Licensor may designate at the time of submission that the requested approval is for multiple/repetitive, identical uses on the same medium. Customer may request approval for such multiple/repetitive, identical use through the end of the Initial Term or any Renewal Term of this Agreement, or six (6) months, whichever is less. Such multiple/repetitive, identical use shall be in accordance with this Agreement and shall be subject to revocation by Customer upon written notice to Licensor.

44.2.5 Licensor further acknowledges and agrees that all use of the Customer Licensed Marks by Licensor and all goodwill developed therefrom shall inure to the benefit of and be on behalf of Customer except for the goodwill associated or derived from the Licensor Licensed Marks.

44.2.6 Licensor agrees that nothing in this Agreement shall give Licensor any right, title, or interest in or to the Customer Licensed Marks other than the right to use the Customer Licensed Marks in the manner contemplated by this Agreement, and only for so long as this Agreement is in force or as otherwise permitted under this Agreement (unless such Customer Licensed Marks are licensed pursuant to a separate agreement).

44.2.7 Infringement.

44.2.7.1 Licensor agrees to use commercially reasonable efforts to notify Customer promptly of any unauthorized use of the Customer Licensed Marks by others, to the extent Licensor has actual notice of such use. Customer and its parent and affiliated companies shall have the sole right to engage in infringement or unfair competition proceedings involving the Customer Licensed Marks.

44.2.7.2 Any recovery obtained in connection with or as a result of any infringement action contemplated under this section, whether by settlement or otherwise, shall be retained by Customer.

45. Appointment of Agent for Service of Process (Chapter 6.P)

During the Term of this Agreement and for a period of two (2) years thereafter, Licensor shall maintain, for each Affiliate rendering Services under this Agreement, registered agents authorized to receive service of process within the State of _______, and shall provide the name and street address of such registered agents to Customer within thirty (30) days of the date of this Agreement and any change during the Term.

46. Electronic Transfer of Intellectual Property

Whenever practical, Licensor agrees to deliver any Software deliverable under this Agreement including any updates or patches, via download, file transfer protocol (ftp), or through the use of Licensor's copy of the tangible Software media. Notwithstanding anything to the contrary in Section _____ (Documentation), upon completion of such delivery, Licensor shall remove the tangible Software media and not provide any of the tangible Software media to Customer.

47. Electronic Documents and Transmissions

Each party, at its own expense, provides and maintains the equipment, software, services, and testing necessary to send and receive electronic documents effectively and reliably and shall maintain audit trails with respect thereto. Electronic documents shall not be considered to have been properly received, and no document shall give rise to any obligation, until accessible to the receiving party at such party's receipt computer. Posting of information by Customer on any Licensor discussion boards, user groups or online forums does not place any material associated with this Agreement in the public domain nor constitute any waiver by any part of any Customer Intellectual Property in such material, nor grant any express or implied right or license to Licensor. Licensor is responsible for data backup and recovery of data held by, or on, facilities or hardware under Licensor's control, and shall ensure that processing can be properly resumed in the event of failures, which include but are not limited to power, mechanical, electronic or communication failure.

48. Liens

Licensor agrees to keep customer, all of the real and personal property of customer, and the services free and clear of all liens or lien claims. Should any lien or lien claim be asserted for any reason, customer may, at its sole discretion (i) pay the amount of such lien or lien claim; (ii) deduct such amounts from payments due to Licensor; and/or (iii) require Licensor to obtain a properly executed release of lien satisfactory to Customer.

49. Legal Fees (Chapter 6.L)

In the event of litigation relating to the enforcement of this Agreement, the prevailing party shall be entitled to recover its reasonable attorneys' fees from the non-prevailing party.

50. Mandatory References

Effective at the beginning of the second calendar quarter after the Reference Date, Customer will be provided the option to be a reference for new Licensor offshoring business of significant value to Licensor (determined by anticipated annual fees of $50 million or more, or in the event that there is not a Licensor transaction of such size to provide as a reference in a calendar quarter, then Licensor shall use the transaction that most closely approximates the $50 million anticipated annual fee requirement as a reference) within the United States. At a minimum, the Customer Applications Partnership Executive and Customer Chief Information Officer will be afforded this opportunity on a calendar quarterly basis. If Licensor elects not to provide the reference opportunity to Customer in any calendar quarter ("Non-Referral Quarter"), Customer shall be entitled to withhold one percent (1%) of the amount of invoices to be paid subsequent to such Non-Referral Quarter. In the event Customer is provided the option to be a reference as required in this Section in the calendar quarter subsequent to a Non-Referral Quarter, the accumulated withhold amount attributable to that Non-Referral Quarter under this Section shall be paid to Licensor with the payment of the next invoice, without interest. In the event Customer is not provided the option to be a reference as required in this Section in the calendar quarter subsequent to the Non-Referral Quarter, the withhold amounts under this Section shall be retained by Customer and converted from a withhold to an applied credit to undisputed amounts owed by Customer to Licensor in the next invoice.

51. No Construction against Drafter (Chapter 6.N)

The parties agree that any principle of construction or rule of law that provides that an agreement shall be construed against the drafter of the agreement in the event of any inconsistency or ambiguity in such agreement shall not apply to the terms and conditions of this Agreement.

52. Notices (Chapter 6.J)

All notices, demands, or other communications herein provided to be given or that may be given by any party to the other shall be deemed to have been duly given when made in writing and delivered in person, or upon receipt, if deposited in the United States mail, postage prepaid, certified mail, return receipt requested, as follows:

Notices to Licensor:	*Notices to Customer:*
____________________	____________________
____________________	____________________
____________________	____________________
Attn:______________	Attn:______________

With a required copy to:

____

____

____

____

Attn: General Counsel

or to such address as the parties may provide to each other in writing from time to time.

- ***All notices should be effective upon receipt, not mailing, because the notice may get lost in the mail or delayed, potentially allowing the one party to terminate the agreement without the other party ever knowing it was in breach.***
- ***Always require the parties to give notice to the appropriate business person and a party's legal department to avoid any notice "falling through the cracks." By requiring that a second copy be delivered to each party's legal counsel, each party limits the risk that a notice could be misplaced or lost.***
- ***Notices should not be given by fax or email to limit the possibility of a notice being lost or not received by the party to whom it is addressed.***

53. Background, Enumerations, and Headings (Chapter 6.A)

The "Background," enumerations, and headings contained in this Agreement are for convenience of reference only and are not intended to have any substantive significance in interpreting this Agreement.

54. Incorporation of Appendices and Exhibits

Appendices [list] referred to in this Agreement and attached hereto are integral parts of this Agreement and are incorporated herein by this reference.

55. Severability (Chapter 6.Q)

If any of the provisions of this Agreement shall be invalid or unenforceable under the laws of the jurisdiction where enforcement is sought whether on the basis of a court decision or of arbitral award applicable to the entire Agreement, such invalidity or unenforceability shall not invalidate or render unenforceable the entire Agreement but rather the entire Agreement shall be construed as if not containing the particular invalid or unenforceable provision or provisions and the rights and obligations of Licensor and Customer shall be construed and enforced accordingly.

56. Counterparts

This Agreement and any Appendix hereto, may be executed simultaneously in two (2) or more counterparts, each of which will be considered an original, but all of which together will constitute one and the same instrument.

57. Facsimile Execution (Chapter 6.V)

The parties agree that transmission to the other party of this Agreement with its facsimile signatures shall suffice to bind the party transmitting same to this Agreement in the same manner as if an original signature had been delivered. Without limitation of the foregoing, each party who transmits this Agreement with its facsimile signature covenants to deliver the original thereof to the other party as soon as possible thereafter.

58. Entire Agreement (Chapter 6.T)

This Agreement, the appendices, and subordinate documents referenced in this Agreement constitute the entire agreement between the parties with respect to the subject matter contained herein, superseding all previous agreements pertaining to such subject matter, and may be modified only by an amendment executed in writing by the authorized officers of both parties hereto. All prior agreements, representations, warranties, statements, negotiations, understandings, and undertakings are superseded hereby **and Customer hereby represents and acknowledges that in entering into this Agreement it did not rely on any representations or warranties other than those explicitly set forth in Section 16 of this Agreement**. Both parties hereto represent that they have read this Agreement, understand it, agree to be bound by all terms and conditions stated herein, and acknowledge receipt of a signed, true, and exact copy of this Agreement.

- ***This statement prevents the Customer from trying to hold the Licensor to any statements made by the Licensor's salespeople or those contained in the Licensor's RFP response that are not specifically included in the Agreement.***
- ***The acknowledgment that the Customer did not rely on any representations or warranties other than those set forth in Section 16, attempts to***

avoid any liability for tort claims as well as contract claims arising from implied representations or warranties.

- ***Avoid incorporating by reference the Customer's RFP or the Licensor's RFP response as this may create an internal conflict with the terms of the Agreement including the functional specifications.***

59. Contingent Agreement

The parties agree and acknowledge that this Agreement has been signed by an officer of Customer subject to the approval of the Board of Directors of Customer (the "Board"). The parties agree that neither party will be bound by the terms of this Agreement until the Board approves this Agreement and that upon such approval, this Agreement will be binding against both parties. Customer agrees to give Licensor prompt written notice of the Board's approval or rejection of this Agreement.

- ***This language should be used when one party requires Board consent or the consent of a third party prior to executing the agreement. While such language may be acceptable, the other party must be careful to impose a strict time limit for receiving such approval to ensure that such consent or rejection is quickly received and does not interfere with the other party's business.***

IN WITNESS WHEREOF, the parties have executed this Agreement **under seal** as of the day and year first written above.

- ***An actual corporate "seal" is not necessary, as the word (seal) is legally valid because many corporations no longer have actual "seals." The use of a "seal" may have a beneficial impact. For example, in Maryland, the use of a "seal" extends the statute of limitations from the three to twelve years.***

ATTEST: CUSTOMER:

__________________ By: __________________ (SEAL)

ATTEST: LICENSOR:

__________________ By: __________________ (SEAL)

[USE IN LIEU OF SECTION 8H]

The performance of the Licensor's\Customer's obligations under this Agreement, including the Statements of Work, is hereby guaranteed by:

NAME OF COMPANY MAKING GUARANTY

By:__________________

or

Parent hereby (i) guarantees the payment and performance by Licensor\Customer of all its liabilities and obligations under this Agreement and all documents, instruments, and agreements delivered hereunder, and (ii) consents to the jurisdiction of the U.S. District Court for the _______ District of _______ with regard to any claim under this guarantee as provided in Section 12(h) of this Agreement. This guarantee is a guarantee of payment and not of collection and shall continue to be effective or shall be reinstated if any payment of a guaranteed obligation is rescinded or must otherwise be returned by Licensor\Customer because of the insolvency, bankruptcy, or reorganization of Parent, all as though such payment had not been made.

PARENT/ NAME OF COMPANY MAKING GUARANTY

By:_______________________________

Name: _______________________________

Title: _______________________________

- ***Always sign the agreement in non-black ink so that original versions are clearly identifiable.***
- ***To be legally binding, persons signing for the Customer and the Licensor must be authorized and have "signing authority."***
- ***Always use "By" and a person's title to indicate they are signing in their corporate capacity to limit/avoid personal liability.***
- ***"Attest" is used for a corporate signatory, "Witness" for an individual signatory.***
- ***See the agreement's preamble for issues as to when a corporate guarantee may be appropriate.***
- ***Check the date of the template to make sure the template used to start drafting is most recent and the "original" template, not an existing contract which was negotiated with another customer.***

SCHEDULES

The Appendixes are very important as they contain the crucial details of the agreement, including payment terms, deliverables, acceptance test procedures, etc. The deliverables should be set forth in great detail and avoid incorporating the deliverables in a high level requirements document.

DO NOT UNDER ANY CIRCUMSTANCE FAIL TO READ OR UNDERSTAND THE SCHEDULES

[The business team must decide whether the Licensor will provide pricing in advance or whether all prices will be at the Licensor's then-existing rates.]

APPENDIX 8

Model Price Schedule For Time and Materials Contracts

Prices as of __________, 20__

I. SOFTWARE

A. LICENSES

1. TERM OF LICENSES AVAILABLE: Licensor may offer Customer a Software License for any term listed in this Section. Such License shall continue for the period of time indicated, so long as Customer is not in default under this Agreement. The provisions for each term are as follows:

i. **Perpetual.** For payment of a one-time perpetual License fee, Customer shall be granted a perpetual License to use the Software for ninety-nine (99) years or until discontinued by Customer in accordance with this Agreement.

ii. **Annual.** For payment of an annual License fee, Customer shall be granted a one (1) year License to use the Software. Customer shall notify Licensor in writing at least thirty (30) days in advance of the pending expiration if Customer desires to discontinue said License. Otherwise, said annual License will be automatically renewed for another term of one (1) year until discontinued by Customer in accordance with this Agreement. If perpetual Licenses are offered by Licensor, Customer may elect to convert an annual License to a perpetual License by providing Licensor thirty (30) days written notice in advance of the perpetual License effective date and Customer shall receive a credit in the amount of fifty percent (50%) of all annual license fees already paid for the particular License being converted. Such credit shall be applied toward payment of the perpetual License fee then currently in effect under this Agreement.

iii. **Monthly.** For payment of a monthly License fee, Customer shall be granted a License to use the Software on a monthly basis until discontinued by Customer in accordance with this Agreement. If Customer elects to convert a monthly License to a perpetual or annual License, Customer shall so notify Licensor in writing by providing Licensor thirty (30) days written notice in advance of the perpetual or annual License effective date. Customer shall receive a credit in the amount of fifty percent (50%) of all monthly License fees paid for the particular License being converted. Such credit shall be applied toward payment of the perpetual or annual License fee then currently in effect under this Agreement.

2. TYPES OF SOFTWARE LICENSES AVAILABLE: The types of Licenses that may be offered by Licensor to the Customer are as follows:

i. **Corporate License.** A Corporate License grants Customer, including all Affiliated Companies listed, the right to duplicate the Software and Software Products for use at as many Customer locations and on as many leased Central Processing Units (CPUs) as Customer desires. Customer shall pay only one (1) Corporate License fee for this type of license. If Customer orders Software Maintenance for Software under a Corporate License, then Customer shall pay only one (1) Software Maintenance fee for said Software.

ii. **Site License.** Each Site License grants Customer the right to use the Software on any or all CPU's located at the facility indicated on the Order as the Site License address. Customer must obtain a separate Site License for each site where the Software is located.

iii. **CPU License.** Each CPU License grants Customer the right to use the Software on a single CPU designated by type and serial number. A separate CPU License is required for each CPU on which the licensed Software will be used.

3. LICENSE FEES: A one-time perpetual "Right To Use" Site License for ____________. **[FILL IN PRICE SCHEDULE]**

II. SERVICES

A. **System Installation:** This support service option provides initial Software installation as follows:

Prices for system installation include instructor and training materials. Licensor's reasonable and customary travel expenses will be billed separately.

Installation Charges. The installation cost for the Customer is a one time fee of $____________ exclusive of all reasonable and customary travel charges. An invoice for this fee will be sent once Licensor begins the installation process. Should the installation exceed the time period specified herein, due to elements beyond Licensor's control, an additional charge of $__________ per week will be applicable.

B. **Telephone Support:** Licensor maintains a group of highly trained phone support specialists who will be familiar with your application. If there is a problem or even a question that requires our attention, we can remotely access your system through the telephone line and modem that was installed with the system. This capability allows us to assist you as if we were sitting locally in the service center. Licensor's phone support specialists can resolve system problems, answer questions, dispatch a hardware support team, or assist your field consultant in support activities.

This support service provides a reasonable number of calls to Licensor's telephone support organization from a single point of contact at each installed location. This group will assist Customer in testing, evaluating, diagnosing, and directing Customer personnel via telecommunication to make the Software function substantially in accordance with the installed generic release specification. The phone support group will report all Software bugs to the appropriate. Licensor personnel and can report suspected hardware problems to the appropriate Customer Contact.

Under this support service option, Licensor will receive phone calls from Customer representatives during the hours of 8 AM to 7 PM Eastern Standard Time, Monday through Friday excluding Licensor holidays.

Telephone Support Charges: The Telephone Support cost for the Customer is a one time fee of $__________ exclusive of all reasonable and customary travel charges. An invoice for this fee will be sent once Licensor begins the Telephone Support process. Should the Telephone Support exceed the time period specified due to elements beyond Licensor's control, an additional charge of $__________ per week will be applicable.

C. **Consulting Support:** This support service option provides a dedicated consultant to assist the Customer with Software questions, work with local users on establishing site specific operational procedures, assume all table maintenance responsibility, discuss system enhancement alternatives, provide follow up training, and work with Customer to prepare Software user guides.

After initial training is completed and daily on-site support is no longer needed, Licensor will continue to be responsive to Customer's needs by maintaining a Licensor consultant dedicated to your account. The consultant will answer any questions that arise, assist in problem resolution, and make any necessary table modification. Customer will have up to thirty (30) hours a month of consultant availability included in the basic monthly charge. Consultant hours used in excess of thirty per month will be billed at the rate of $__________/hour. All reasonable and customary travel expenses incurred by Licensor in rendering such services will be billed separately.

Customer Support Charges: The Customer Support charges for the Customer is a one time fee of $__________ exclusive of all reasonable and customary travel charges. An invoice for this fee will be sent once Licensor begins the Customer Support process. Should the Customer Support exceed the time period specified due to elements beyond Licensor's control, an additional charge of $__________ per week will be applicable.

D. **Follow-up Training:** This support service option will provide follow up training to assist Customer in the use of Software and Software Products. Two classes of follow up training are available.

[DESCRIBE TRAINING] Training $__________/year.

E. **Enhancements:**

i. Generic Releases: Licensor will price Generic Releases consisting of Customer requested software enhancements in accordance with the price schedule specified in this Appendix C. Once a Generic Release has been priced, Customer will receive a proposal for the release which will be valid for thirty (30) days. The proposal will consist of a price quote and a delivery interval from the time the Licensor receives written approval to begin work from Customer. Licensor will not begin work on any Generic Release until receiving written authorization from Customer to proceed with the development activity. Licensor will use the lowest rate possible when multiple enhancements are requested for a specific generic release. Licensor's reasonable and customary travel charges will be invoiced separately.

ii. Generic Release Charges: Licensor will provide prices for all Enhancement requests in accordance with the following schedule of charges:*

(a) Hourly rate: $______ per hour. This applies to anything less than eight hours. The minimum is four hours.

(b) Daily rate: $______ per day. This applies to anything less than forty hours. The minimum number of hours at this rate is eight.
(c) Weekly rate: $______ per week. This applies to anything less than 160 hours and greater than 39 hours.
(d) Monthly rate: $______ per month. This rate is for 160 hours; anything beyond 160 hours will be billed at the rate of $______ per hour.

* *Licensor will use the lowest rate possible when multiple enhancements are programmed at one time.*

III. HARDWARE

A. **System Hardware:** Customer will supply all necessary system hardware to run the Software in Customer designated locations. The selection of system hardware will be contingent upon Licensor approval. This includes, but is not limited to, computer hardware, peripheral devices, modems, and cables. Licensor agrees to assist Customer in the selection of suitable system hardware necessary to operate the Software. Customer will acquire all hardware maintenance services necessary to support the Software implementation. Licensor agrees to work with Customer to provide all Software modifications necessary to support upgrades or changes to Customer owned hardware within a mutually agreed upon time frame.

B. **Hardware Maintenance**: Customer is responsible for all ongoing maintenance charges for all system hardware.

IV. SYSTEM SOFTWARE

A. **System Software:** Customer will supply all necessary system software to run the Software in Customer designated locations. The selection of system software will be contingent upon Licensor approval. This includes, but is not limited to, operating system software, communications software, and firmware, and other system software that may facilitate the use of the Software. Licensor agrees to assist Customer in the selection of suitable system software necessary to operate the Software. Customer will acquire all system software maintenance services necessary to support the Software implementation. Licensor agrees to work with Customer to provide all Software modifications necessary to support upgrades or changes to Customer supplied system software within a mutually agreed upon time frame.

B. **System Software Maintenance:** Customer is responsible for all system software maintenance.

V. NETWORK COMMUNICATION

A. **Network Communications:** Customer will supply all networking required to implement the Software. All networking will be contingent upon Licensor approval. This includes, but is not limited to, data circuits, communications equipment, modems, and cabling. Licensor agrees to assist Customer in the determination of network communication requirements necessary to implement the Software. Customer agrees to provide all network communications maintenance services required to support the Software implementation. Licensor agrees to work with Customer to provide all Software modifications necessary to support upgrades or changes to Customer supplied Networking within a mutually agreed upon time frame. All Software modifications will be provided as part of a Generic Release for a fee that is calculated based upon the price schedule listed in this Appendix B as amended from time to time. The Generic Release programming activity will begin upon receiving written authorization from Customer complete with all necessary technical information on the new network architecture..

B. **Network Communications Maintenance:** Customer is responsible for all network communications maintenance.

VI. MISCELLANEOUS

A. **Price Changes:** All prices set forth in this Appendix B are subject to change upon thirty (30) days prior written notice to Customer.

B. **Other Costs:** Customer agrees to pay all of Licensor's reasonable, actual, out of pocket costs, including but not limited to travel expenses incurred by Licensor in project management, system analysis, and consulting during the term of this Agreement, such expenses will be billed to Customer separately at cost.

APPENDIX 3.B

Service Level Standards and Credits

The Services consist of the terms and conditions set forth herein and in the Attachments identified below.

Attachment 1	Benefit Plan Administration
Attachment 2	Member Eligibility Administration
Attachment 3	Provides/Capitation Management
Attachment 4	Claims Processing
Attachment 5	Case Management
Attachment 6	Reporting
Attachment 7	Customer Service
Attachment 8	Information Technology Support

The Service Level Standards and Credits identified in Attachments 1 through 8 represent the basic service levels and credits provided by Licensor to Customer. In the event Customer negotiates a contract with a substantial customer with increased Service Level Standards and/or Credits, Customer shall communicate such increased service level standards and/or credits to Licensor thirty (30) calendar days prior to the effective date of such standards and credits and such standards and credits for such Customer shall become effective at the end of the thirty (30) day period.

ATTACHMENT 1

Benefit Plan Administration

1. **Licensor Obligations.** Licensor shall establish and maintain the integrity and accuracy of the Customer benefit plans by timely processing routine updates and performing quality control audits. Licensor's Services shall include the following:

(a) Define with Customer the data requirements for benefit plan definition. Licensor will identify system requirements for benefit plan data.

(b) Develop source format requirements and submission procedures for benefit plan maintenance.

(c) Perform benefit plan maintenance:

(i) Establish new lines of business.

(ii) Establish and verify new benefit plans.

(iii) Log, track, process, and verify routine plan updates.

(iv) Initiate and drive resolution of benefit plan maintenance issues.

(d) Perform quality control audits on benefit plan. Initiate and drive resolution of discrepancies identified through results of regular claims processing sampling audits.

(e) Correct all errors and inaccuracies in the benefit plan database and validate, on a monthly basis, the information contained therein.

(f) Validate the completeness of the benefit plan data provided by Customer.

(g) Participate with Customer in developing Test Data and a Test Plan pursuant to Schedule ____ in order to validate the accuracy of the Customer benefit plans. The Test Plan for the benefit plans shall include various benefit plan scenarios, which shall be updated and refined from time to time.

2. **Customer Responsibilities.** Customer shall cooperate with Licensor in the performance of Licensor's above-listed obligations by performing the tasks set forth below; provided, however, that in no event shall any failure by Customer to act as described below be construed as or result in a breach of this Agreement:

(a) Define with Licensor the data requirements for benefit plan definition. Customer will identify their requirements for benefit plan data.

(b) Define benefit plans for Members.

(c) Provide benefit plan source documents, communicate completeness criteria to Licensor.

(d) Participate in the verification of benefit plan maintenance.

3. Service Level Standards/Credits.

Standard	Credit
Successfully process fully tested routine benefit plan update within three (3) calendar days of receipt of complete maintenance request.	$1,000/day for the first seven (7) calendar days past due. $2,000/day for each day thereafter.
Successfully process up to twenty-five (25) new benefit plans loaded in the system within thirty (30) calendar days of receipt of complete source documents. At Customer's option, additional plans will be either (i) processed in the current period for an additional fee, or (ii) processed in the next period.	$2,000/day for the first seven (7) calendar days that standard is not met. $5,000/day for each day thereafter.

ATTACHMENT 2

Member Eligibility Administration

[Customer to Provide Descriptions]

1. **Licensor Obligations.** Licensor shall ______________________________. Licensor's Services shall include the following:

(a)

(b)

2. **Customer Responsibilities.** Customer shall cooperate with Licensor in the performance of Licensor's above-listed obligations by performing the tasks set forth below; provided, however, that in no event shall any failure by Customer to act as described below be construed as or result in a breach of this Agreement.

(a)

(b)

3. **Service Level Standards/Credits.**

ATTACHMENT 3

Provider/Capitation Management

1. **Licensor Obligations.** As requested by Customer and at no additional charge or expense to Customer, Licensor shall establish providers within the system, create and maintain provider fee schedules, price rules, generate capitation reports, reconcile with payer, and perform periodic quality assurance on capitation models. Licensor's Services shall include the following:

(a) Define with Customer the data requirements for provider fee schedules. Licensor will identify system requirements for provider fee schedule data.

(b) Develop source format requirements and submission procedures for provider fee schedule maintenance.

(c) Perform provider fee schedule maintenance:

(i) Establish and verify new provider fee schedules and institutional pricing as submitted,

(ii) Log, track, process, and verify provider fee schedule and institutional pricing updates as submitted;

(iii) Initiate and drive resolution of provider fee schedule and institutional pricing maintenance issues.

(d) Provide notice to Customer within two (2) business days of any incompleteness in source document information.

(e) Perform quality control audits on provider fee schedules and reimbursement formulas. Initiate and drive resolution of discrepancies identified through results of regular claims processing sampling audits.

(f) Process withholds in accordance with contractual arrangements.

(g) Provide retroactive processing.

2. **Customer Responsibilities.** Customer shall cooperate with Licensor in the performance of Licensor's above-listed obligations by performing the tasks set forth below; provided, however, that in no event shall any failure by Customer to act as described below be construed as or result in a breach of this Agreement:

(a) Define and provide provider reimbursement plans/fee schedule methodologies for providers and hospitals.

(b) Participate in the verification of reimbursement formulas and follow-up with the appropriate source documents for missing information.

(c) Define financial requirements (bank accounts, etc).

(d) Receive payments from payers for reconciliation.

3. **Service Level Standards/Credits.**

Standard	Credit
Successfully process routine participating provider fee schedule updates and price rules within three (3) calendar days of receipt of maintenance request.	$250/day per provider schedule or provider contract for which standard is not met.
Successfully establish up to fifty (50) new participating provider fee schedules and price rules in system within fourteen (14) calendar days of receipt of complete source documents.	$250/day per provider schedule or provider contract for which standard is not met.

ATTACHMENT 4

Claims Processing

1. **Licensor Obligations.** Licensor shall administer the processing and adjudication of claims to ensure that submitted claims are processed in a timely manner. Licensor's Services shall include the following:

(a) Define with Customer the claims format and procedures for claims receipt, routing, and verification.

(b) Define with Customer the procedures for fixing holes in pricing, forwarding unclean claim information to Customer for resolution, handling COB, and resolving denied claims.

(c) Define with Customer the procedures for management of third party liability, subrogation processes, and pre-existing conditions.

(d) Log, track, and process submitted claims.

(e) Adjudicate claims for payments, which shall include DRG Grouper processing.

(f) Resolve pended claims.

(g) Receive Remittance Advice (RAs) and explanation of benefits (EOBs) and process accordingly. Produce claims checks, process weekly or as requested by Customer and distribute to Customer within 24 hours.

(h) Respond to customer service personnel inquiries.

(i) If requested by Customer, print RAs with checks.

(j) Administer HPR Code Review to detect and correct claim unbundling and fraudulent billing.

(k) Processing of unique requirements, i.e., special turnaround time for large clients.

(l) Maintain physical copies of claims for a minimum of seven (7) years unless otherwise required by Customer.

(m) Produce copies of microfilm images for Customer on a monthly basis.

(n) Identify and correct voided checks, refunds, and claim overpayment recoveries.

(o) Maintain sufficient internal payment audit process to ensure claims payment accuracy, to include the development and implementation of corrective action plans.

(p) Accept and process electronic data interchange ("EDI") transmissions.

(q) Define EOBs text.

(r) Verify and distribute withholds.

(s) Verify and approve checks and EOBs.

(t) Provide financial report/statement and/or data files for close-of-period (including annual) reconciliation.

2. **Customer Responsibilities.** Customer shall cooperate with Licensor in the performance of Licensor's above-listed obligations by performing the tasks set forth below; provided, however, that in no event shall any failure by Customer to act as described below be construed as or result in a breach of this Agreement:

(a) Define with Licensor the claims format and procedures for claims receipt, routing, and verification.

(b) Assist Licensor with the procedures for correcting pricing issues, forwarding unclean claim information to Licensor for resolution, handling COB, and resolving denied claims.

(c) Define correspondence text for claims, EOB/request, and or letters.

(d) Verify and approve claims checks/RAs.

3. **Service Level Standards/Credits.**

Standard	Credit
Produce checks within two (2) business days of Customer sign off.	
Enter new claims into ABC System within two (2) business days of receipt.	
Adjudicate 99 percent of claims within fifteen (15) calendar days of receipt. Adjudicate 99 percent of claims within thirty (30) calendar days of receipt. Adjudicate 99 percent of claims within sixty (60) calendar days of receipt. Licensor shall produce a detailed written explanation as to why any claims are not adjudicated by the thirty (30) day mark, which explanation shall include, without limitation, the reason(s) for such delay and the individuals responsible for and necessary to achieve adjudication.	$100 per claim not adjudicated within sixty (60) calendar days.
Provide resolution to "Hot Claim" issue within three (3) business days from date of input for Licensor attention, unless information provided is incorrect, then Licensor shall provide response within three (3) days.	If less than 99 percent of issues are not resolved or responded to, as applicable, in a given thirty (30) day period, Customer shall receive from Licensor $2,500 for that period.
Complete online or daily processing of HPR within twenty-four (24) hours of adjudication and make adjustments prior to next check run.	

Standard	Credit
9 percent random of experienced examiners. Audit and correct prior to claims payment or audit plan acceptable to Customer.	
9 percent manager review of all claim payments in excess of $10,000 billed Customer prior to payment.	
Process held claims within forty-eight (48) hours of client direction.	
9 percent error-free clerical accuracy on claims processed.* For purposes hereof, "clerical accuracy" shall mean data entry that does not cause a financial impact. *Based on Customer's internal audit	If Licensor does not meet required standard in a given thirty (30) day period, the following credit structure shall apply for that period: Licensor Performance Credit 95% to 100%: $0 91% to <95%: 5,000 81% to <90%: 10,000 <80%: 20,000
99 percent financial accuracy.* For purposes hereof, "financial accuracy" shall mean data entry that causes any adjudication resulting in an over or under payment. *Based on Customer's internal audit	If Licensor does not meet required standard in a given thirty (30) day period, the following credit structure shall apply for that period: Licensor Performance 99% to 100% $25,000 bonus (to Licensor) 98% to <99%: 0 96% to <98%: 25,000 credit 91% to <95%: 50,000 credit <90%: 100,000 credit

ATTACHMENT 5

Case Management

1. **Licensor Obligations.** Licensor shall establish and maintain remote system access to allow Customer personnel to perform required case management responsibilities. Licensor's Services shall include the following:

(a) Provide access to claims history and utilization history files, both online and archived files for ad hoc reporting and case management.

(b) Provide capability to develop screening criteria and protocols online.

(c) Define and develop with Customer interfaces with critical resource directories.

2. **Customer Responsibilities.** Customer shall cooperate with Licensor in the performance of Licensor's above-listed obligations by performing the tasks set forth below; provided, however, that in no event shall any failure by Customer to act as described below be construed as or result in a breach of this Agreement:

(a) Define case management requirements for all functionality (e.g., CM responsibilities, pre-certification validation criteria, screening criteria, protocols, and reports).

(b) Define and develop with Licensor interfaces with critical resource directories.

(c) Create authorizations for service.

ATTACHMENT 6

Reporting

1. **Licensor Obligations.** Licensor shall assist Customer in the development and on-going generation of necessary reports and downloaded files. Licensor's Services shall include the following:

(a) Provide/download the necessary files to generate ad hoc reports, labels, and correspondences, as requested.

(b) Provide ad hoc reporting capabilities to support Customer requests. [______] Ad hoc reports shall be provided to Customer per month at no additional charge.

(c) Restart printer queues following any scheduled or unscheduled reboot of system.

(d) Provide management, performance, and other reports to Customer at the frequencies specified below to include the following:

(i) Management Reports: **[TBD]**

(ii) Performance Reports: See Schedule 4.6.4.

(iii) Other Reports: **[TBD]**

(e) Assist Customer in downloading of data for Customer internal reports at mutually agreed-upon frequencies.

(f) Provide the capabilities to run month-end financial reporting by the third working day after month end.

(g) Facilitate Customer's downloading of data from ABC System into report formats.

2. **Customer Responsibilities.** Customer shall cooperate with Licensor in the performance of Licensor's above-listed obligations by performing the tasks set forth below; provided, however, that in no event shall any failure by Customer to act as described below be construed as or result in a breach of this Agreement:

(a) Define membership profile reporting requirements.

(b) Define capitation reporting requirements.

(c) Develop format with Licensor and define frequencies for generation of reports.

3. **Service Level Standards/Credits.**

Standard	Credit
Complete report request within five (5) business days of sign-off of report specifications.	
Complete closing schedule within three (3) business days from end of month.	
Provide monthly performance reports on data specified.	$1,000/day per report late charge
Report data accuracy and consistency.	$5,000/day per finance report from date of discovery to date of correction

ATTACHMENT 7

Customer Service

1. **Licensor Obligations.** Licensor shall establish and maintain remote system access to allow Customer personnel to perform required Customer Service responsibilities. Licensor's Services shall include the following:

(a) Develop with Customer a mechanism to report back to Customer Service the results of processing events.

2. **Customer Responsibilities.** Customer shall cooperate with Licensor in the performance of Licensor's above-listed obligations by performing the tasks set forth below; provided, however, that in no event shall any failure by Customer to act as described below be construed as or result in a breach of this Agreement:

(a) Develop with Licensor a mechanism to report back to Customer Service the results of processing events.

(b) Log provider/Member inquiries, complaints, and grievances.

ATTACHMENT 8

Information Technology Support

1. **Licensor Obligations.** Licensor shall provide Services and otherwise maintain the ABC System (including all Custom Programming) so that such services and system function without Material Defects in accordance with the Specifications, Performance Standards, Documentation, and Regulatory Requirements, and Licensor shall provide the following additional Support and Maintenance Services to Customer:

1.1 Telephone Hotline/Help Desk. Licensor shall continuously (twenty-four (24) hours per day, seven (7) days per week) provide a telephone number for Customer personnel to call for all purposes regarding Support and Maintenance Services for the ABC System. Customer's help desk shall be monitored exclusively by members of the Licensor Support Team. At Customer's option, Licensor shall only provide such telephone hotline support from 7 AM to 7 PM, Eastern Time (i.e., business hours); provided, that if Customer elects such option: (a) the Support and Maintenance Services fees attributable to continuous 24–7 telephone hotline support shall be decreased on a pro-rata basis according the hours of support provided; (b) Licensor shall make call-out support services available during non-business hours, which services shall be charged at the Services Rates designated in Schedule _____, and Customer shall be charged only for call-out services that Licensor actually provides to Customer (i.e., no "on-call" charges); and (c) Customer may revert back to continuous 24–7 telephone hotline support at any time upon notice to Licensor.

1.2 Modem Support. Licensor shall provide modem support to Customer twenty-four (24) hours per day, seven (7) days per week. Customer shall maintain a dial-up modem with unique dial back identification passwords for each individual assigned by Licensor to provide modem support to Customer. Customer may disconnect the dial-up modem, at its sole discretion, during the hours of operation. Customer acknowledges that disconnection of its modem may adversely affect the Defect resolution time frames.

1.3 Support and Maintenance History and Tracking System. Licensor shall maintain a current record of Customer's Support and Maintenance Services history. Upon Customer's request, Licensor shall provide a detailed history of all Support and Maintenance Services performed by Licensor. Customer shall own all such records. On a monthly basis, Licensor shall provide to Customer a report detailing: (a) the number of calls to the support center received by Licensor during the reporting period; (b) the date, time, day of the week, and duration of each call; (c) the subject matter of each call; and (d) the resolution of the matter.

1.4 Software Information Network. Customer shall have online access to Licensor's software information network, if any, for online software information and questions. Licensor shall provide to Customer phone number for purposes of accessing Licensor's software information network. Customer shall not be charged an access fee to such network, but Customer shall be responsible for any connect-time charges to the public telecommunications carrier.

1.5 Enhancements and New Features. Licensor shall provide all Enhancements to the ABC System including, without limitation, all Enhancements necessary to operate the ABC System on the current versions of the Equipment and all Enhancements necessary to maintain compatibility with all Embedded Third Party Software. Enhancements requested by Customer shall be performed by Licensor by the Programmers at no additional cost to Customer.

1.6 Regulatory Requirements. Regulatory modifications to the ABC System shall be provided by Licensor, at no additional cost to Customer, whenever such modifications are recommended, mandated, or required to meet federal and state governmental and quasi-governmental regulatory requirements, statutes, ordinances, policies, edicts, rules, guidelines, or standards related to Customer's use of the Services or the functions of the ABC System including, without limitation, all standards or guidelines established by committees, agencies, or other standard-setting organizations implementing regulatory requirements, policies, or operating standards adopted by the [name] industry and any other such modifications or changes that may be required to meet the then-current, industry-accepted specifications or standards for Third Party Software with which the ABC System interfaces and all federal, state, and regulatory requirements that relate to Customer's provision of [industry] services (collectively, "**Regulatory Requirement**"). Without limiting the generality of the foregoing, Regulatory Requirements shall mean those requirements as set forth in the State Contract and shall include, without limitation, all federal and state standards and regulations regarding electronic data interchange transactions (including, without limitation, 45 CFR Part 142 and any other standards or regulations addressing the mandates of Section 262 (Administrative Simplification) of the Health Insurance Portability and Accountability Act of 1996). Before the date on which Customer is required to comply with such Regulatory Requirements and with sufficient time in which to test, Licensor shall provide to Customer and install and test all such Regulatory Requirements modifications. Licensor represents to Customer that the ABC System and Services currently operate in accordance with all Regulatory Requirements and that the ABC System and Services and all future Enhancements to the ABC System will operate in accordance with all Regulatory Requirements. Licensor shall provide to Customer all Regulatory Requirements, including, without limitation, Regulatory Requirements for components of the ABC System and Services that currently are not regulated but that may, in the future, be regulated by Regulatory Requirements prior to the date on which Customer is required to comply with such Regulatory Requirements.

1.6.1 Annual Updates. For changes required to the federal DRG Grouper, the ICD9CM Codes and the CPT Codes on an annual basis, Licensor shall ensure delivery within fifteen (15) business days of receipt of third party software from 3M (DRG Grouper), HCFA (DRG Pricer), HCIA (ICD9CM Codes), and AMA (CPT Codes) or other electronic provider, except that, when annual regulations require major Licensor system revisions to accommodate major federal changes, such as for century date compliance, reimbursement methodology revisions, or massive coding system alterations, Licensor will ensure that all personnel responsible for applicable regulatory programming changes are assigned to provide the changes in a timely manner, as their highest priority project.

1.6.2 DRG Window Rule. Licensor shall cause its software to comply with the federal regulations set forth in Fed. Reg. 63 No. 28, February 11, 1998 (**"DRG Rule Regulations"**). Any changes needed to Licensor Software to implement changes associated with the DRG Rule Regulations will be provided by Licensor at no additional charge to Customer.

1.6.3 EDI Regulations. The Licensor Software shall comply with all Federal and State standards and regulations regarding electronic data interchange (**"EDI"**) transactions (including 45 CFR Part 142). If any of the Licensor Software currently does not comply with any newly enacted Federal and/or State regulations, Licensor shall ensure that such Software does comply within the time frames/windows for compliance allowed by such regulations.

1.7 Obligation to Generally Improve the ABC System. Licensor shall generally enhance and improve the ABC System for as long as Customer elects to receive and pays for the Services.

1.8 Documentation and Specifications. Licensor shall provide any and all updated Documentation and/or Specifications, as applicable, for the ABC System, any Enhancements or Custom Programming provided to Customer in accordance with the Agreement as such Documentation and/or Specifications are generally released, or more frequently if significant errors and/or discrepancies are discovered in such Documentation and/or Specifications.

2. Customer Responsibilities. Customer shall cooperate with Licensor in the performance of Licensor's above-listed obligations by performing the tasks set forth below. Provided however, that in no event shall any failure by Customer to act as described below be interpreted as or result in a breach of this Agreement:

(a) Assist Licensor in the development of support procedures.

(b) Define with Licensor process for submission, qualification, approval, and implementation of functionality modification requests.

(c) Ensure end users follow established support procedures.

(d) End users will employ reasonable efforts to solve problems/address requests before calling the Help Desk.

(e) Work with Licensor to define and establish telecommunication links necessary to exchanges data electronically among all parties for enrollment, eligibility, benefit plans, encounters for PCPs claims, back-end files, and reconciliation.

(f) Maintain local network and devices.

(g) Work with payers to define file formats for required/desired interfaces.

(h) Assist in the development of disaster recovery plan per item (k) above.

(i) Assist in development of system capacity planner.

(j) Assist in development/modification of backup and archive strategy.

3. Resolution of Defects

3.1 Defect Levels. Customer shall classify, or reclassify, as applicable, all Defects as Critical Defects, Medium Defects, and Low Defects pursuant to the definitions set forth below in **Section 3.3.**

3.2 Reporting of Defects. Reports of Defects (an "Incident Report") will be made through Licensor's Customer Support Center via telephone, fax, or email at numbers to be provided by Licensor to Customer. Licensor shall provide to Customer Support Center coverage twenty-four (24) hours per day, seven (7) days per week, as follows:

(a) Customer Support Center Peak Coverage Hours: 6 AM to 6 PM, Eastern Time, Monday through Friday, excluding New Year's Day, Memorial Day, July 4, Labor Day, Thanksgiving Day, and Christmas Day, or the days on which Licensor observes any of these holidays. Calls of a non-emergency nature (requests not involving a Critical Defect or a Medium Defect) should be reserved to peak coverage hours. During peak coverage hours, a member of the Licensor Support Team will answer the call. Incident Reports of Critical Defects and Medium Defects should be made by telephone during peak coverage hours to facilitate a timely response.

(b) Customer Support Center On-Call Coverage Hours: All periods not included as peak coverage. During on-call coverage hours, an on-call support contact will contact Customer within thirty (30) minutes after Customer's report of a Defect. Incident Reports of Critical Defects and Medium Defects should be made by pager number during on call coverage hours to facilitate a timely response.

The Licensor Customer Support Center will log the reported Defect and provide Customer with an incident tracking number to refer to when making follow-up inquiries. The Incident Report shall contain, to the extent known, applicable and/or possible: (c) the name/type of affected equipment; (d) Customer contact name, email address if available, telephone number, and fax number; and (e) the nature of the Defect, a description of the Defect and Customer's classification of the Defect. Customer will exercise commercially reasonably efforts to limit Incident Reports concerning Low Defects to peak coverage times. If Customer makes a call to the Customer Support Center during on-call coverage hours, Customer personnel shall remain available to receive a reply from Licensor's personnel. Customer will provide Licensor with as much information as possible to enable Licensor to investigate and attempt to identify and verify the reported maintenance issue. Customer will work with Licensor support personnel during the problem isolation process, as reasonably needed. Customer will notify Licensor of any configuration charges, such as network installation/expansion, upgrades, relocations, etc.

3.3 Response Procedures. Based upon a Defect's severity level, Licensor shall correct such Defect in accordance with the procedures set forth in this Section.

Severity of Defect	Response
"**Critical Defect**" means any Defect that severely impacts Customer's ability to receive or Licensor's ability to provide Services, or any Defect that has a significant financial impact on Customer or a direct impact on Customer's managed care services, or the failure of any network element, such as a printer, to be operable.	Licensor shall: (i) Provide a Defect Analysis for a Critical Defect within one (1) hour of receipt of an Incident Report; (ii) Provide an Interim Resolution for a Critical Defect as soon as possible, and in no event later than four (4) hours of receipt of an Incident Report, and Licensor shall provide progress reports every one (1) hour; and (iii) Provide a Final Resolution for a Critical Defect within five (5) calendar days after notice thereof.
"**Medium Defect**" means any Defect that adversely affects Customer's ability to receive or Licensor's ability to provide Services but for which an alternative temporary solution or workaround acceptable to Customer may be accomplished.	Licensor shall: (i) Provide a Defect Analysis for a Medium Defect as soon as possible, but in no event later than four (4) hours of receipt of an Incident Report; (ii) Provide an Interim Resolution to a Medium Defect within forty-eight (48) hours after notice thereof; and (iii) Provide a Final Resolution for a Medium Defect within thirty (30) calendar days of notice thereof.
"**Low Defect**" means any Defect that is of de minimis nature.	Licensor shall respond to a Low Defect within forty-eight (48) hours of receipt of an Incident Report and resolve a Low Defect in the next release of the affected Software.

For purposes of this Section:

"Defect Analysis" means a fax, email, or telephone call from Licensor acknowledging that an Incident Report has been received, details on what Licensor has learned about the Defect as of the time of communication that appropriate technical personnel have been assigned to work on the Defect, and Licensor's initial analysis of and action plan for resolving the reported Defect.

"Final Resolution" means Licensor provides a correction or modification of the ABC System that corrects the Defect.

"Interim Resolution" means Licensor: (a) reinitiates or restarts, as applicable, the ABC System, or affected part thereof, if the reported Defect caused the ABC System to be inoperative; (b) enables Customer to access the ABC System, if the reported Defect caused Customer to be unable to access the ABC System; or (c) provides Customer with an acceptable workaround that solves or mitigates a reported Defect, which workaround can be provided with minimal Customer inconvenience.

4. Time-and-Materials Support.

4.1 General. Customer shall have the right, at any time upon thirty (30) calendar days written notice to Licensor, to obtain Support and Maintenance Services on a time-and-materials basis ("Time-and-Materials Support") at the Service Rates set forth in an applicable purchase order, which rates shall not exceed the Service Rates set forth in Schedule ____. In the event Customer elects to obtain Time-and-Materials Support: (a) Licensor shall credit any pre-paid, but unearned Support and Maintenance Services fees, which fees shall be applied against any amounts invoiced for Time-and-Materials Support; and (b) Customer shall have the right, at any time upon thirty (30) calendar days written notice to Licensor, to return to obtaining Support and Maintenance Services on an annual basis for the Support and Maintenance Services fees set forth in an applicable purchase order, which fees shall not exceed the Support and Maintenance Services fees set forth in Schedule ____.

4.2 Enhancements. At the time of Customer's election to obtain the Time-and-Materials Support, the parties shall negotiate in good faith a fixed fee, if any, for Customer to obtain Enhancements under Section 1.5 of this Attachment 8.

FORM J.1

Software Maintenance and Services Agreement

THIS SOFTWARE MAINTENANCE AND SERVICES AGREEMENT is made this ________ day of ______________, 20__ by and between __________ a __________________ corporation, with its principal place of business at ______________________________ (hereinafter "Company") and __________, a ____________ corporation, (hereinafter "Customer"), with offices located at _____ ______________________________________.

BACKGROUND

Company has licensed Customer Company's proprietary __________ software as modified to meet Customer's needs in accordance with the Software License and Services Agreement dated ________________, 20__ by and between Company and Customer (the "Software License Agreement"). Customer desires to have Company maintain and support such software and Company desires to maintain and support such software for Customer under the terms and conditions set forth herein.

IN CONSIDERATION of the foregoing and the mutual covenants set forth herein, and intending to be legally bound, the parties agree as follows:

1. Definitions

The following words shall have the following means when used in this Agreement:

1.1 "**Bypass**" shall mean a procedure communicated by Company to Customer, which permits Customer to avoid Error(s) by implementing the same when using the Software.

1.2 "**Enhancement(s)**" shall mean a modification to the Software that alters the functionalities described in the Functional Specifications without materially degrading the functionalities or performance of the Software prescribed by the Functional Specifications.

1.3 "**Error(s)**" shall mean a failure of the Software to conform to the Functional Specifications.

1.4 "**Error Report**" shall mean the document to be created by Company, pursuant to Article 3 hereof, each time that Customer reports an Error.

1.5 "**Fix(es)**" shall mean the document to be created by Company pursuant to this Agreement in order to correct Errors.

1.6 "**License(s)**" shall mean any license or licenses granted by Company to Customer to use the Software under the Software License Agreement.

1.7 "**Object Code**" shall mean the binary machine readable version of the Software.

1.8 "**Maintenance Services**" shall mean the services to be provided under this Agreement.

1.9 "**Optional Maintenance Services**" means the services that Customer may elect to receive from Company pursuant to the provisions of Article 4 hereof; it is hereby agreed that if Customer elects to receive any Optional Maintenance Services, the said Optional Maintenance Services shall thenceforth be deemed to constitute Maintenance Services.

1.10 "**Severity Level**" shall mean the level of severity assigned to a reported Error with the Software, in accordance with the Severity Level definitions set forth in Appendix A to this Agreement.

1.11 "**Site**" shall mean a Customer computer facility located in one specific geographic location.

1.12 "**Software**" shall mean Company's proprietary __________ software as modified with Customer's specified enhancements, including Bypasses, Fixes, Enhancements, Updates, and Upgrades. The term "Software" includes Software Products.

1.13 "**Software Products**" shall mean all physical components, other than program codes that are offered by Company, including but not limited to, manuals, documentation, magnetic media, job aids, templates, and other similar devices.

1.14 "**Update**" shall mean a compendium of Fixes that Company releases to the users of the Software from time to time and which Company shall supply to Customer pursuant to the terms of this Agreement.

1.15 "**Upgrades**" shall mean a new release or version of the Software constituting a compendium of Enhancements.

Any capitalized terms not defined in this Agreement shall have the meaning set forth in the Software License Agreement.

2. *Company's Obligations*

2.1 In consideration of Customer's performance hereunder, Company shall, in addition to the other obligations imposed on Company hereby, render the Maintenance Services pursuant to Article 3 hereof, and render such Optional Maintenance Services as Customer may elect to purchase pursuant to the provisions of Article 4 hereof.

2.2 All Maintenance Services performed by Company under this Agreement shall be performed by Company in a professional manner in accordance with industry standards. If Company receives notice of defects in the Maintenance Services, Company shall re-perform said Maintenance Services. Company does not warrant that the Maintenance Services or Software will be uninterrupted or error free.

2.3 The parties acknowledge and agree that, notwithstanding anything to the contrary herein contained, Company shall not maintain the Hardware or the Third Party Software.

Optional language:

2.4 In the event Customer allows Maintenance to lapse, it may thereafter renew such support for the affected Software by paying, in addition to the then current annual Maintenance Fee, an amount equal to the aggregate Maintenance Fee that would have been payable for the affected Software during the period of lapse. Company agrees that the Maintenance support will be conducted from the Company location that is geographically closest to the Customer location eligible for such Maintenance support.

3. Maintenance Services

3.1 By rendering the Maintenance Services, Company shall correct all Errors, regardless of how such Errors are brought to the attention of Company, in accordance with this Agreement, and, in particular, Appendix A hereto. During the term of this Agreement, Company shall provide the following types of Maintenance Services:

3.1.1 Telephone Support. Company telephone support representative(s) shall be available to receive Customer telephone calls between the hours of 8:30 a.m. and 5:30 p.m., Washington, D.C. time, Monday through Friday, excluding public holidays. Company shall provide Customer with a telephone number that is answered at all other times by an individual who will accept Error Reports. Such telephone support representative(s) shall serve as the Customer's interface with Company and shall ensure that reported Errors are handled in a timely manner as specified in Appendix A hereto. Company shall provide to Customer in writing, the name(s) and telephone number(s) of such telephone support representative(s) within ten (10) days of the later of the execution of this Agreement or the acceptance of the Software by Customer under the Software License Agreement. All Errors shall be investigated and if the Error relates to the Software, or is directly caused by the Software, (a) an Error Report shall be opened, (b) the Error shall be assigned a Severity Level as per the provisions of Exhibit A hereto, and (c) the Error shall be resolved in accordance with the procedures and processes set forth in Appendix A hereto.

3.1.2 Installation Assistance. Company shall provide to Customer telephone assistance for the implementation or installation of Bypasses, Fixes, and Updates between the hours of 8:30 a.m. and 5:30 p.m., Washington, D.C. time, Monday through Friday, excluding public holidays.

3.1.3 Bypasses. Company shall provide to Customer such Bypasses as are necessary to ensure the resolution of Errors that can be resolved by a Bypass.

3.1.4 Fixes. Company shall provide to Customer such Fixes as are necessary to ensure the resolution of Errors that can be resolved by a Fix.

3.1.5 Updates. Company shall, as soon as they are made available, provide to Customer such Updates as it provides to the users for the Software from time to time.

3.1.6 Enhancements. Company shall provide to Customer such Enhancements as it provides to the users for the Software from time to time.

3.1.7 Upgrades. Company shall provide, as soon as they are made available, to Customer such Upgrades as it provides to the users for the Software from time to time.

3.2 Other Software Products. Company shall provide to Customer, at no additional cost, any Software Products relating to the Software made generally available to other Software users without charge. Any Software Products so made available at a given cost to the other Software users shall be offered to Customer at Company's then-existing rates.

3.3 Regular Activity Reports. Upon written request by Customer, Company shall provide: (a) a status report of Error resolution activities; and (b) a status report of all outstanding Error Reports. Such status reports shall contain Company's tracking number, Error description, Error resolution status, and a definitive resolution time frame and release number for all Errors.

3.4 Limitation on Maintenance Services. Notwithstanding any other provisions in this Maintenance and Services Agreement, Company shall provide Maintenance Services only with respect to the two (2) most recent Upgrades of the Software.

3.5 Intellectual Property Rights. Title to all Bypasses, Fixes, Updates, Enhancements, and Upgrades shall remain solely and exclusively with Company. It is hereby acknowledged and agreed that the former shall be deemed to constitute Software for purposes of the application of the Software License Agreement.

4. Optional Maintenance Services

4.1 Customer shall be entitled to purchase from Company the following Optional Maintenance Services at the rates set forth in Appendix B of this Agreement:

4.1.1 Consultant Support. Software Maintenance can be extended to include up to eighty (80) hours per month of on-site or off-site consultant support to assist with the operations and support of the Software. Such consultant shall offer training, support, and consultation to optimize the Software system and the Customer's practices. The consultant will also act as liaison between Customer and Company. All travel and expenses arising from consultant support shall be billed to the Customer at Company's actual cost, provided all such travel and expenses shall be approved by Customer in advance.

4.1.2 Dedicated Telephone Support. Company shall provide the number of any dedicated telephone representatives ordered by Customer. Such dedicated telephone representative(s) shall be available between the hours 8 a.m. and 6 p.m., Washington, D.C. time, Monday through Friday, excluding public holidays. Such dedicated telephone representatives shall, in addition to telephone support services, answer application questions (i.e., how to run reports, etc.) and system questions (i.e., what system precautions should be taken during month end processing, UNIX-related questions, etc.).

4.1.3. Proactive System Checks. Should Customer purchase the services of a dedicated telephone representative, such representative shall perform weekly proactive system checks. The dedicated telephone representative shall check the Software for possible problems (i.e. runaway processes, dbspace, file system space, etc.). If problems are found they shall be reported to the Customer's designated system administrator at the affected Site within two (2) hours.

5. *Out of Scope Problems*

5.1 Any time incurred by Company in diagnosing or fixing problems that are not caused by the Software, or are not covered by this Agreement are billable to the Customer at Company's then-existing rates that are initially set forth in Appendix B of this Agreement, with a one-hour minimum per call.

5.2 Any travel and expenses incurred in conjunction with out of scope maintenance and support shall be billed to Customer at Company's actual costs, provided all such travel and expenses shall be approved by Customer in advance.

6. *Term of Agreement*

This Agreement shall become effective ______________ and continue for a ________ (__________) year term (the "Initial Term"). Thereafter, it shall continue on a year-to-year basis, until terminated by either party ninety (90) days prior to the anniversary date of this Agreement.

7. *Fees for Maintenance and Services*

7.1 During the Initial Term, Customer shall pay Company for the Maintenance Services set forth in Section 3 an amount calculated as follows: an annual fee equal to 15 percent of the sum of (i) the undiscounted RTU Fee, as set forth in Section ______________ of the Software License Agreement; (ii) the price of the development work as set forth in Section __________ of the Software License Agreement; and (ii) the price of any other enhancements or modifications to the Software undertaken by Company at the written request of Customer, including any change orders received under the Software License Agreement (collectively, the "Agreed Maintenance Fee").

7.2 Company shall charge Customer its then existing rates for all optional services. Such rates are initially set forth in Appendix B of this Agreement.

8. *Designated Customer Personnel*

The Customer shall identify by name and location all Customer personnel who may contact the Company representatives as set forth in Sections 3 and 4. The personnel identified shall have authority to authorize an investigation of software problems and have knowledge of the rules of engagement for maintenance and support. The list of authorized Customer contact personnel is set forth in Appendix C of this Agreement, provided that such list may be revised by Customer at any time as long as Company is informed in writing and such list does not exceed a maximum of fifteen (15) Customer contact personnel.

9. Confidentiality

Information provided by either party to the other under this Agreement shall be kept confidential in conformance with and subject to the terms of the Nondisclosure Agreement dated __________________, 20__ by and between the parties hereto.

10. Reproduction of manuals, documentation, and object code

10.1 Customer shall have the right, at no additional charge, to reproduce solely for its internal use, all manuals and documentation furnished by Company relating to the Software, regardless of whether such manual or documentation is copyrighted by Company. All copies of manuals or documentation made by Customer shall include any proprietary notice or stamp that has been affixed by Company. Company shall furnish to Customer and at no additional charge to Customer, one (1) hard copy of the relevant documentation sufficient to enable Customer to maintain and operate the Software. All documentation shall be in the English language.

10.2. One (1) copy of the Object Code may be reproduced by Customer, at no additional charge, only for back up or archival purposes. On written request by Company, Customer shall notify Company in writing of its methods and procedures for archiving of Object Code software prior to doing so.

11. Limitation of Liability and Disclaimer of Warranty

11.1 In no event shall Company be liable for any special, indirect, incidental, punitive, or consequential damages, including loss of profits arising from or related to the breach of this Agreement, even if Company had been advised of the possibility of such damages.

11.2 NOTWITHSTANDING ANY OTHER PROVISION OF THIS AGREEMENT, IN THE EVENT ANY REMEDY FAILS OF ITS ESSENTIAL PURPOSE, COMPANY'S LIABILITIES UNDER THIS AGREEMENT, WHETHER UNDER CONTRACT LAW, TORT LAW, OR OTHERWISE, SHALL BE LIMITED TO DIRECT DAMAGES NOT TO EXCEED THE AMOUNT ACTUALLY RECEIVED BY COMPANY PURSUANT TO THIS AGREEMENT.

11.3 EXCEPT AS SET FORTH IN SECTION 2.2, COMPANY MAKES NO EXPRESS OR IMPLIED REPRESENTATIONS OR WARRANTIES WITH RESPECT TO THE SOFTWARE OR MAINTENANCE SERVICES OR THEIR CONDITION,

MERCHANTABILITY, FITNESS FOR ANY PARTICULAR PURPOSE, OR USE BY CUSTOMER. COMPANY FURNISHES THE WARRANTIES IN SECTION 2.2 IN LIEU OF ALL OTHER WARRANTIES, EXPRESSED OR IMPLIED, INCLUDING THE WARRANTIES OF MERCHANTABILITY AND FITNESS FOR A PARTICULAR PURPOSE.

11.4 No action, regardless of form, arising under this Agreement, may be brought more than one year after the cause of action has arisen, except that an action for non-payment may be brought within two (2) years after the date of the most recent payment.

12. *Independent Contractor*

All work performed by Company in con-nection with the Software and/or Maintenance Services described in this Agreement shall be performed by Company as an independent contractor and not as the agent or employee of Customer. All persons furnished by Company shall be for all purposes solely the Company's employees or agents and shall not be deemed to be employees of Customer for any purpose whatsoever. Company shall furnish, employ, and have exclusive control of all persons to be engaged in performing maintenance services under this Agreement and shall prescribe and control the means and methods of performing such maintenance services by providing adequate and proper supervision. Company shall be solely responsible for compliance with all rules, laws, and regulations relating to employment of labor, hours of labor, working conditions, payment of wages, and payment of taxes, such as employment, Social Security, and other payroll taxes including applicable contributions from such persons when required by law.

13. *Force Majeure*

Neither party shall be responsible for any delay or failure in performance of any part of this Agreement to the extent that such delay or failure is caused by fire, flood, explosion, war, embargo, government requirement, civil, or military authority, act of God, act or omission of carriers, or other similar causes beyond its control. If any such an event of force majeure occurs and such event continues for ninety (90) days or more, the party delayed or unable to perform shall give immediate notice to the other party, and the party affected by the other's delay or inability to perform may elect at its sole discretion to: (a) terminate this Agreement or the affected order solely upon mutual agreement of the parties; (b) suspend such order for the duration of the condition and obtain or sell elsewhere Software, Software Products, or Maintenance Services comparable to the Software, Software Products, or Maintenance Services to have been obtained under the order; or (c) resume performance of such order once the condition ceases with the option of the affected party to extend the period of this Agreement up to the length of time the condition endured. Unless written notice is given within thirty (30) days after the affected party is notified of the condition, option (c) shall be deemed selected.

14. Assignment

This Agreement shall be binding on the successors and assigns of both parties, provided, that neither party may assign or transfer its interests, rights, or obligations under this Agreement or any order by written agreement, merger, consolidation, operation of law, or otherwise without the prior written consent of an authorized executive officer of the other party, which consent shall not be unreasonably withheld. It shall be reasonable to withhold consent to such assignment or transfer if the assignee or transferee is in direct competition with the other party. Any purported assignment of this Agreement in violation of this Section 14 shall be null and void.

15. Amendments, Modifications, or Supplements

Amendments, modifications, or supplements to this Agreement shall be permitted, provided all such changes shall be in writing signed by the authorized representatives of both parties, and all such changes shall reference this Agreement and identify the specific articles or sections of this Agreement that is amended, modified, or supplemented.

16. Notices

All notices, demands, or other communications herein provided to be given or that may be given by any party to the other shall be deemed to have been duly given when made in writing and delivered in person, or upon receipt, if (a) deposited in the U.S. mail, postage prepaid, certified mail, return receipt requested, or (b) sent by reputable overnight courier addressed as follows:

Notices to Company:	**Notices to Customer:**
With a required copy to:	With a required copy to:

or to such address as the parties may provide to each other in writing from time to time.

17. Obligations that Survive termination

The parties recognize and agree that the obligations of the other party under Sections 9, 11, 16, and 19 of this Agreement, shall survive the cancellation, termination, or expiration of this Agreement.

18. Export Regulations

Customer and Company acknowledge that the Software and all related technical information, documents, and materials may be subject to export controls under the U.S. Export Administration Regulations and, to the extent applicable, Customer and Company shall

(a) comply with all requirements set forth in such regulations, and (b) cooperate fully with each other in any official or unofficial audit or inspection that relates to such export requirements.

19. Governing Law

The validity, construction, interpretation, and performance of this Agreement shall be governed by and construed in accordance with the domestic laws of the State of __________ except as to its principles of conflicts of laws. The parties acknowledge and agree that the United Nations Convention for the Sale of Goods shall not apply to this Agreement. The parties irrevocably submit to the jurisdiction of the Federal District Court for the District of __________ to resolve any disputes arising under or related to this Agreement.

20. Background, Enumerations, and Headings.

The "Background" enumerations and headings contained in this Agreement are for convenience of reference only and are not intended to have any substantive significance in interpreting this Agreement.

21. Entire Agreement

This Agreement shall constitute the entire agreement between the parties hereto and replaces and supersedes all prior agreements, written and oral, relating to the subject matter hereof, between the parties to this Agreement.

IN WITNESS WHEREOF, the parties have executed this Agreement under seal as of the day and year first written above.

ATTEST:	[CUSTOMER]
____________________________	By: ____________________ (Seal)
ATTEST:	[COMPANY]
____________________________	By:____________________ (Seal)

APPENDIX A

Escalation Procedures and Processes for Software Error Resolution

Classification of Errors

All Errors reported by Customer to Company shall be assigned a Severity Level jointly agreed upon by Customer and Company. The point of contact throughout this initial Error reporting procedure shall be the applicable Company support representative available to Customer under the terms of this Agreement. Reported Errors shall be classified as follows:

Severity Level 1—Severity Level 1 implies that the Software is not functioning. Some examples of Severity Level 1 Errors are as follows:

1. Production System down and will not restart;
2. Production Software not able to communicate with external systems (including the network control center) that halts online and other processing and no Bypass is available; and
3. Production Software is generating a data corruption condition that halts online and other processing and no Bypass is available.

Severity Level 2—Severity Level 2 implies that the Software is running but that Customer is unable to use major portions of the Software, and no Bypass is available. Some examples of Severity Level 2 Errors are as follows:

1. Intermittent Error in a live, production system that continues processing with no Bypass; and
2. Major functional component is unavailable with no Bypass.

Severity Level 3—Severity Level 3 implies that the Software is operating close to normal, but there is a non-critical Error for which an operational Bypass exists for such Error. Severity Level 3 Errors will be fixed in the next scheduled Update.

Severity Level 4—Severity Level 4 includes purely cosmetic Errors and documentation anomalies.

Out-of-Scope—A reported problem is out-of-scope when it is determined not to be related to the Software and is beyond the bounds of Company's responsibility. Examples of such unrelated problems include, but are not limited to, Customer host or applications software, Customer hardware and cabling, power or environmental conditions, and human error.

Severity Level 1

Error Resolution—Immediate steps shall be taken toward solving the Error. Company shall work to resolve Severity Level 1 Errors on a twenty-four (24) hour basis until the Error is resolved. If required, Company staff shall be moved off of lower Severity Level Errors to service Severity Level 1 Errors.

Resource Commitment—When a Severity Level 1 Error is reported, Company shall assign all resources required to correct the Error. Work on the Error shall be continuous until a Fix is found. If system access is required, Customer shall provide a contact available to Company and access to its system and software for the duration of the Error correction procedures.

Completion Goal—The completion goal shall be to resolve 100 percent of all Severity Level 1 Errors with a Fix or Bypass within eight (8) hours of receipt of the Error Report.

Escalation and Status Thresholds—When a Severity Level 1 Error Report is opened, the following escalation and status procedures shall be followed.

Hour 1–Hour 3

1. The Error shall be resolved by Company first line support; or
2. The Error will be referred to the maintenance engineering group. All log files and a description of the work done by Company will be transferred to this group. The report will receive an Error Report number that will be entered into the SMS. The error will be passed to the maintenance engineering group via the SMS as well as by email.

The Customer will be notified of the status of the Error.

Hour 3

1. The maintenance engineering point of contact will resolve the Error; or
2. It will be decided that more resources are required to work on the Error.

The Customer will be notified of the status of the Error.

Hour 4–Resolution

1. Company shall continue to work on the Error, on a twenty-four (24) hour basis, until a resolution is found. All available resources shall be used to assist the person who is responsible for the resolution of the Error; and
2. The Project Manager and Operations Support Manager shall be notified that a Severity Level 1 Error has reached a critical time frame.

Severity Level 2

Error Resolution—Severity Level 2 Errors will be analyzed in the order that they are reported. Severity Level 1 Errors will take priority over Severity Level 2 Errors.

Resource Commitment—Appropriate technical resources will be assigned to Severity Level 2 issues as long as Severity Level 1 Errors are not open.

Completion Goal—The completion goal will be to resolve 100 percent of all Severity Level 2 Errors with a Fix or Bypass within forty-eight (48) hours of receipt of the Error Report. If it is a Bypass, a Fix will be applied within sixty (60) days.

Escalation and Status Thresholds—When a Severity Level 2 Error Report is opened, the following escalation and status procedures will be followed.

Hour 1–Hour 24

1. The Error shall be resolved by Company; or
2. The maintenance point of contact person will be contacted. All log files and a description of the work done by Company will be transferred to this group. An Error Report number will be assigned and entered in the trouble tracking system.

The Customer will be notified of the status at this stage.

Hour 25–Hour 48

1. The maintenance engineering point of contact will resolve the Error; or
2. The maintenance engineer will continue working the Error until it is fixed.
3. A date will be estimated upon when this Error will be fixed.

The Customer will be notified of the status at this stage.

Severity Level 3

Error Resolution—Severity Level 3 errors shall be researched after Severity Level 1 and Severity Level 2 Errors. The majority of the Severity Level 3 Errors shall be scheduled for correction and be resolved as part of the next scheduled Update.

Resource Commitment—Severity Level 3 Fixes shall be included in the next scheduled Update.

Completion Goal—The completion goal and objective shall be to correct Errors in the next scheduled Update.

Escalation and Status Thresholds—The status of Severity Level 3 Errors shall be available on demand. A monthly report will be distributed that will reference any uncorrected Errors that are over ninety (90) days old.

Severity Level 4

Error Resolution—Severity Level 4 Errors shall be addressed at Company's discretion after Severity Level 1, Severity Level 2, and Severity Level 3 Errors are corrected. All Severity Level 4 Errors shall be scheduled for correction and be resolved as part of the next scheduled Update.

Resource Commitment—Severity Level 4 Fixes shall be included in the next scheduled Update.

Completion Goal—The completion goal and objective will be to correct issues in the next scheduled Update.

Escalation and Status Thresholds—The status of Severity Level 4 Errors shall be available on demand.

APPENDIX B

Optional Services and Standard Rate Schedule Effective Through [DATE]

(all prices are in U.S. Dollars)

BILLING RATES	
Classification	$ Monthly
Senior Consultant	
Consultant	
Project Manager	
Project Leader	
System Analyst	
Training Manager	
Trainer	
Senior Programmer	
Programmer	
Documentation Specialist	

Travel and Expenses are not part of the standardrate and are to be paid by the Customer.

OPTIONAL SUPPORT SERVICES
Consultant Support $/year
Dedicated Telephone Support $/year
Off-Hour Support $/year
Consultant Support/Annual Maintenance Fee Adjustment Reduction

If any one individual or combination of the Consultant Support, Dedicated Telephone Support, and Off-Hour Support options listed above is ordered by Customer simultaneously with the Annual Software Maintenance and Software Support Fee, the Annual Software Maintenance and Software Support Fee will be reduced to __% of the Delivered Software per Annum for that particular year.

Out-Of-Scope / Secondary Authorized Rate $/hour

To be used in conjunction with support delineated under Sections 2, 3, and 4.

Training $/program

A comprehensive training program to "train the trainers" shall be offered to Customer by Company. This instructor led program requires a total of fifteen (15) days to complete and will accommodate up to five (5) attendees. Training shall be conducted at a designated Customer location. An outline of the "train the trainer" program shall be provided by Company on request. Reasonable travel and expenses are not part of the training fee and shall be billed to Customer at Company's actual cost.

APPENDIX C

Designated Customer Personnel

The following Customer personnel shall be designated by Customer to contact Company in accordance with the terms of this Agreement and shall have authority to authorize an investigation of software errors and have knowledge of the terms and conditions set forth therein:

FORM H.1

Source Code Escrow Agreement (Annotated)

THIS SOURCE CODE ESCROW AGREEMENT ("Escrow Agreement"), is made and entered into this ____ day of ____________, 20__, ("Effective Date") by and among ________________ (hereinafter, "Licensor"), ________________ (hereinafter, "Licensee"), and __________, as escrow agent (hereinafter, the "Escrow Agent").

WHEREAS, Licensor and Licensee have entered into a Software License Agreement dated as of ______________, 20__ (the "Services Agreement"), which provides for, among other things, the provision of certain services to Licensee utilizing Licensor's computer software programs ("Computer Programs") in accordance with the terms and provisions thereof; and

WHEREAS, the availability and provision of such services utilizing Licensor's Computer Programs is critical to Licensee in the conduct of its business and, as a consequence, Licensor has agreed to deposit in escrow a machine-readable copy of source code, object code, source code specifications, and other items required by Licensee and identified and defined in Attachment A to this Escrow Agreement, to operate, support, and maintain the Computer Programs without reliance on or support from Licensor (such items referred to in Attachment A shall individually be referred to as a "Deposit," and collectively referred to as the "Deposits" or "Deposit Materials"); and

- ***Licensors should avoid agreeing to self-serving statements with no relationship to the agreement itself.***

WHEREAS, the Deposits are to be held by the Escrow Agent in accordance with the terms and conditions of this Escrow Agreement.

NOW, THEREFORE, in consideration of the promises and the mutual covenants contained herein, the parties agree to the foregoing and as follows:

ARTICLE 1
CREATION AND MAINTENANCE OF ESCROW; ESCROW AGENT OBLIGATIONS

1.1 Creation and Maintenance of Escrow. Licensor hereby agrees to deposit with Escrow Agent the current release of the Deposits for the Computer Programs ("Initial Deposits") **within thirty (30) calendar days following the Effective Date**. Licensor further agrees that it shall deposit current copies of the items described in Attachment A ("Supplemental Deposits") with Escrow Agent thirty (30) calendar days after the close of each calendar quarter, provided that the parties may mutually agree in writing to have the Supplemental Deposits deposited less frequently. Licensor shall package the items comprising the Deposits separately and label each package in accordance with the definitions in Attachment A so that each of the items can be separately and easily identified by Escrow Agent and Licensee. Along with each Deposit, Licensor shall prepare and submit to Escrow Agent a Description of the Deposit Materials in the form attached hereto as Attachment B.

- ***The licensee should require the licensor to deposit the Deposits at the time of the executing of the Escrow agreement or on the date the software is accepted. By allowing the licensor to deposit the software 30 days after the Escrow Agreement was signed creates the risk of breach and having to sue the licensor to require it to deposit the software.***
- ***Licensee should set forth in detail the manner in which the deposits will be delivered. By setting forth the licensor's obligations, the escrow agent will be more likely able to determine if the required deposits have been delivered and help the Licensee utilize the deposits in the event of a release.***

1.2 Escrow Agent Obligations. In addition to the other duties and obligations imposed upon Escrow Agent in connection with the terms of this Escrow Agreement:

(a) Escrow Agent shall notify Licensee as to the receipt of the Deposit or Deposits described in Attachment A according to the procedures specified in Section 1.2(b). Escrow Agent's responsibilities under this provision shall be limited to checking the label and quantity of the Deposits that are shipped to identify whether the items described in Attachment B have been received, and shall not include determining whether the purported contents of such boxes or packages actually contain the necessary information Licensor is required to submit as part of the Deposits; provided that Escrow Agent's responsibilities under this provision shall not be reduced or diminished by Licensor's submission of a Description of Deposit Materials as described in Attachment B.

(b) Upon the acceptance of the Initial Deposit and each Supplemental Deposit, Escrow Agent shall notify Licensee and Licensor by issuing an executed copy of Attachment B within ten (10) calendar days of such acceptance. If no quarterly Deposit has been made by Licensor, Licensor shall certify to Licensee that the Deposit Materials contain the current copies of the items identified in Attachment A. Licensor shall use the form attached hereto as Attachment B for such notification.

- ***To avoid having the quarterly deposits "fall through the cracks," the referenced form will allow the Licensee/escrow agent to track the licensor's actions even if a deposit does not need to be made.***

(c) Escrow Agent shall separately identify the Deposits through a deposit account number and shall segregate the Deposits from any of Licensor's other materials that may be in the possession of Escrow Agent.

(d) Escrow Agent shall store the Deposits in defined units of space ("Storage Units"). The cost of the first Storage Unit is included in the Deposit Fee. Costs for additional Storage Units are detailed in Attachment D.

(e) Escrow Agent shall safeguard, safekeep and maintain the Deposits in accordance with industry standards applicable to an escrow company. Escrow Agent shall secure insurance covering its obligations to safeguard, safekeep, and maintain the Deposits and shall, upon request of Licensee, procure reasonable evidence of such insurance. The parties agree that under no circumstances shall the Escrow Agent be liable for breach or delay in performance due to hostile or warlike action in time of peace or war, including action in hindering, combating or defending against an actual, impending or expected attack, military action or governmental action or other peril not ordinarily covered by typical property insurance maintained by a trust company in accordance with industry standards and not covered by the insurance actually maintained by Escrow Agent. The parties agree that the amount of liability insurance that the Escrow Agent shall secure for the Deposits shall be at least One Million Dollars ($1,000,000), and that such insurance shall: (i) cover Licensee against damages incurred as a result of the destruction of the Deposits (which Deposits cannot be replaced), and (ii) name Licensee as an additional insured. Licensee shall notify the Escrow Agent in writing of any need to increase the amount of such insurance, which may be required after the date hereof. The cost for such additional insurance shall be borne by Licensee.

(f) Except as provided in this Escrow Agreement, Escrow Agent agrees that it will not divulge or disclose or otherwise make available to any third person whatsoever, or make any use whatsoever, of the Deposits, without the express prior written consent of Licensor.

1.3 Limitation of Liability. ESCROW AGENT SHALL NOT BE Liable TO LICENSOR OR LICENSEE UNDER THIS ESCROW AGREEMENT FOR ANY INDIRECT, CONSEQUENTIAL, INCIDENTAL, SPECIAL OR PUNITIVE DAMAGES.

ARTICLE 2
TERM OF ESCROW AGREEMENT

Upon payment of the initial fee, this Escrow Agreement shall remain in full force and effect for an initial period of seven (7) years unless earlier terminated by the Licensor and Licensee upon a joint, written notice to the Escrow Agent or otherwise as provided herein. This Escrow Agreement shall be renewed automatically thereafter on an annual basis, provided Escrow Agent receives the renewal fees prior to the last day of the initial period or any subsequent renewal period ("Expiration Date"). Escrow Agent may, however, extend the period of the Escrow Agreement to cover the processing of any outstanding instruction made during any period of the Escrow Agreement. Licensee shall pay renewal fees and other related fees in accordance with Article 10. In the event Licensor is of the opinion that a renewal should not occur, Licensor may so notify Escrow Agent and Licensee in writing; provided, however, that Escrow Agent may not terminate this Escrow Agreement based on Licensor's notice that the renewal should not occur. If the Escrow Agreement is not renewed or is otherwise terminated in accordance with the terms and conditions set forth herein at the end of any initial or renewal period: (a) all duties and obligations of Escrow Agent to Licensor and Licensee will terminate; and (b) if Licensor requests return of the Deposit, Escrow Agent shall return the Deposit to Licensor only after any outstanding or due and payable invoices and the Deposit return fee as provided in Attachment D are paid by Licensor. Escrow Agent's obligations to hold and maintain the Deposits shall immediately cease upon delivery of the Deposits to Licensee or to Licensor in accordance with the provisions of this Escrow Agreement.

ARTICLE 3
DISCLOSURE EVENTS

An event requiring the release of the Deposits to Licensee ("Disclosure Event") shall be deemed to have occurred under this Escrow Agreement in the event of:

3.1 An Licensor Event of Default as set forth in the Software License Agreement; or

3.2 Licensor's uncured material breach of any of its support and maintenance obligations under the Software License; or

3.3 Licensor's discontinuation of any part of the Software or support and maintenance services under the Software License Agreement for any reason other than Licensee's uncured material breach of its obligation to pay Licensor for such services; or

3.4 The institution of bankruptcy, receivership, insolvency, reorganization, or other similar proceedings by or against Licensor under the Federal Bankruptcy Code, if such proceedings have not been dismissed or discharged within thirty (30) calendar days after they are instituted; the insolvency or making of an assignment for the benefit of creditors or the admittance of any involuntary debts as they mature by Licensor; or the taking of any action by the Board of Directors of Licensor in furtherance of any of the foregoing.

3.5 [LIST ANY "WARNING SIGNS" applicable to the Licensor's business, the existence of which would trigger a deposit release and hopefully allow the licensee to avoid being subjected to bankruptcy court proceedings to obtain access to deposited materials.]

- ***The Licensee should include a "laundry list" of potential concerns that will trigger the release of the source code and deposit materials. The Licensee should seek to identify those events that are likely to occur not only in the near future but in the distant future as it is unlikely the Licensor will agree to amend the escrow agreement once it has been executed. The Licensor should seek to limit this list to avoid having the source code released and potentially lose the ability to control its dissemination.***

ARTICLE 4
NOTICE OF DISCLOSURE EVENT AND DELIVERY OF DEPOSITS

4.1 In the event Licensee believes that a Disclosure Event has occurred, Licensee shall provide written notice of such Disclosure Event to Licensor. Within seven (7) calendar days after receiving such notice, Licensor shall either: (1) cure the Disclosure Event; or (2) provide a written explanation and corrective plan to Licensee that is satisfactory to Licensee in its sole discretion explaining why the Disclosure Event has not occurred. If Licensor fails to either cure the Disclosure Event or provide an explanation and corrective plan to Licensee that is satisfactory to Licensee as provided in this Section 4.1, Licensee may, by written notice to Licensor and Escrow Agent (the "Notice"), demand that the Deposits be delivered to Licensee by Escrow Agent. Such demand shall be accompanied by an affidavit signed by an officer of Licensee attesting:

(a) To a full description of the Disclosure Event; and
(b) That the specific Disclosure Event has occurred and, in the case of a material breach by Licensor of its support and maintenance obligations under the Services Agreement, that the breach has continued for more than thirty (30) calendar days from Licensor's receipt of written notice from Licensee and that the breach is continuing; and
(c) That Licensee is not in breach of the Services Agreement; and
(d) That the Deposits shall continue to be the sole property of Licensor and shall be subject to the confidentiality provisions of the Services Agreement; and
(e) That the Deposits shall be used solely for Licensee's support and maintenance, modification or correction of the Computer Programs used by Licensor to provide services to Licensee; and
(f) That Notice and said affidavit has been provided to Licensor in accordance with the provisions of this Escrow Agreement.

Said affidavit must be dated and sworn to within the seven (7) calendar-day period prior to receipt of the Notice by the Escrow Agent. Escrow Agent shall send Licensor a copy of each request and any related materials received from the Licensee (including the affidavit) within three (3) business days of receipt.

4.2 Unless Escrow Agent receives an original order or certified copy of an order of a court of competent jurisdiction as described in Section 4.3 restraining Escrow Agent from making delivery of the Deposits to Licensee, then Escrow Agent shall deliver the Deposits to Licensee on the twenty-first (21st) calendar day after the date of the Notice;

provided that Escrow Agent shall not be required to deliver the Deposits until Licensee has made all payments to Escrow Agent for any fees described under Section 10.1 that remain unpaid at the time the Deposits are due to be delivered to Licensee. In no event shall Licensee be required to pay for any legal fees incurred by Escrow Agent except as stated in Article 6.

4.3 Licensor's exclusive and only right to challenge Licensee's demand for delivery of the Deposits shall be through: (a) instituting an appropriate action in a court of competent jurisdiction; and (b) within the twenty (20) calendar day period after the date of the Notice, causing the delivery and receipt by Escrow Agent of an order of such court to Escrow Agent restraining Escrow Agent from making delivery of the Deposits to Licensee. Licensor and Licensee agree that the sole basis for the entry of such an order shall be the absence of a Disclosure Event as described in Sections 3.1 or 3.2 or Licensor's cure of a Section 3.3 Disclosure Event within the time provided.

* ***Section 4.3 seeks to limit the licensor's ability to wrongfully delay or challenge a release of the deposit materials.***

4.4 In the event Licensee receives the Deposits pursuant to the provisions of this Article 4, Licensee agrees that it shall maintain the confidentiality of the Deposits and shall use the Deposits in accordance with the terms of this Escrow Agreement and the Services Agreement.

- ***The Licensor should include language to ensure that the terms of the license grant in the original license agreement govern the Licensee's use of the source code. The failure to do so may grant the Licensee unlimited rights.***

4.5 Escrow Agent's sole responsibility is to review the affidavit from Licensee for execution in accordance with this Escrow Agreement. Escrow Agent shall have no duty to investigate the facts set forth in the affidavit including, without limitation, whether a Disclosure Event and lack of cure as described in Section 3.3 exists, or any other document, and may act upon receipt of a properly executed affidavit.

ARTICLE 5
TERMINATION OF SOFTWARE LICENSE AGREEMENT

In the event the Software License Agreement is terminated by Licensee in accordance with the terms of the Software License Agreement, Licensor may by written notice to Escrow Agent and Licensee demand return of the Deposits by Escrow Agent to the Licensor, and Escrow Agent shall deliver said Deposits to Licensor on the thirtieth (30th) calendar day following receipt of such notice, unless Escrow Agent has received a second notice from Licensor canceling the first notice or a notice from Licensee stating that Licensee is entitled to an extension in accordance with its transition rights as set forth in the Services Agreement. Such notice and demand for return of the Deposits by Licensor shall include written acknowledgment or other instructions satisfactory to the Escrow

Agent that the Services Agreement has been terminated. Such notice shall also be accompanied by the Deposit return fee.

ARTICLE 6
INDEMNIFICATION OF ESCROW AGENT

Escrow Agent, by reason of its execution of this Escrow Agreement, shall not assume any responsibility or liability for any transactions between Licensor and Licensee other than for the performance of Escrow Agent's obligations with respect to the Deposits held by it in accordance with this Escrow Agreement. The party on whose behalf, or pursuant to whose direction, Escrow Agent acts, shall indemnify, defend and hold harmless Escrow Agent from any and all liability, damages, costs or expenses, including reasonable attorneys' fees, which may be sustained or incurred by Escrow Agent as a result of taking such action. Absent any such direction, the parties hereto shall jointly and severally indemnify and hold harmless the Escrow Agent from any and all liability, damages, costs or expenses, including reasonable attorneys' fees, except for any liability, damages, costs or expenses that may be sustained or incurred by the gross negligence or willful misconduct on the part of Escrow Agent, its employees or agents, and except for the breach by Escrow Agent of Escrow Agent's duties under Section 1.2. Escrow Agent is not a party to, or bound by, any provisions contained in the Services Agreement, and with respect to the Deposits acts as a depository only and is not responsible or liable in any manner whatever for the sufficiency, correctness, genuineness or validity of the Services Agreement, or with respect to the form or execution of the same, or the identity, authority or right of any person executing the same or depositing the Deposits. This indemnification shall survive the termination of this Escrow Agreement.

ARTICLE 7
COMPLIANCE WITH ORDERS OF COURT

Escrow Agent is hereby expressly authorized to comply with and obey any and all orders, judgments or decrees of any court of competent jurisdiction as determined by counsel of the Escrow Agent's choosing, and in case the Escrow Agent complies with any such order, judgment or decree, it shall not be liable to the parties hereto or to any other person or entity by reason of such compliance. In complying with the foregoing, if Escrow Agent becomes or is made a party to any court proceeding that affects this Escrow Agreement or the parties hereto or the Deposits, Escrow Agent shall promptly give notice of such order or directive to Licensor and Licensee and comply therewith. Licensor or Licensee, as the case may be, shall hold the Escrow Agent harmless from any loss or expense incurred by the Escrow Agent as a result of following the instructions given by Licensor or Licensee. To the extent possible in any such proceedings, Escrow Agent shall interplead Licensor and Licensee, and Licensor and Licensee shall take all actions necessary to assume complete responsibility for such proceedings.

ARTICLE 8
LOCATION AND CONDITION OF DEPOSITS

The parties hereby acknowledge that the Deposits will be stored in accordance with Escrow Agent's standard escrow operating procedures. Escrow Agent shall maintain the environmental conditions within the vault within normal operating temperatures and humidities. For purposes of this Escrow Agreement, normal operating temperatures and humidities shall mean temperatures and humidities at or near the range usually maintained for ordinary computer media storage. Licensor and Licensee hereby agree not to hold Escrow Agent liable for any damages or claims resulting from loss of data that may occur: (a) solely as a result of self-destruction or disintegration of a tape or disk; (b) solely because of defects of the tapes or disks on which the data is stored; or (c) solely because such tapes or disks are sensitive to the normal operating temperatures and humidities in the vault.

** **Both licensor and licensee should insist on incorporating the Escrow Agent's "standard operating procedures" into the Escrow Agreement.***

ARTICLE 9
RESIGNATION OF ESCROW AGENT

In the event the Escrow Agent wishes to resign for any reason, it shall give the other parties sixty (60) calendar days prior written notice of such resignation and within said sixty (60) calendar day period Licensor and Licensee, jointly shall appoint and designate a successor Escrow Agent to stand in the place and stead of the Escrow Agent under this Escrow Agreement, and following such appointment and designation, Escrow Agent shall forthwith deliver the Deposits to the successor Escrow Agent. If the parties do not appoint a successor Escrow Agent within said sixty (60) calendar day period, the Escrow Agent may apply to a court of competent jurisdiction for the appointment of a successor Escrow Agent and any costs incurred in connection therewith shall be borne by Licensee and Licensor equally. This Escrow Agreement shall terminate when the Escrow Agent delivers the Deposits to the successor Escrow Agent.

ARTICLE 10
FEES AND EXPENSES OF THE ESCROW AGENT

10.1 Licensee hereby agrees to pay Escrow Agent in accordance with this Article 10 and the fee schedule set forth in Attachment D or the then-current fee schedule of Escrow Agent, which such new fee schedule shall be in accordance with the terms set forth in Attachment D and shall be provided to Licensor and Licensee ninety (90) calendar days prior to any fee change. Such fees are subject to periodic review by the management of the Escrow Agent in accordance with its pricing policies.

10.2 Notwithstanding anything in this Escrow Agreement to the contrary, except for any acts taken by Escrow Agent at the direction of Licensee or Licensor pursuant to Article 6, Licensor and Licensee shall each reimburse the Escrow Agent for fifty percent (50%) of any extraordinary costs which Escrow Agent may incur including, without limitation, the costs of hiring or retaining any agents or attorneys; provided, however, that Escrow Agent shall provide written notice to Licensor and Licensee before incurring any extraordinary costs.

10.3 Initial fees shall be invoiced by Escrow Agent upon the Effective Date. In the event the initial fees are not paid within thirty (30) calendar days of the Effective Date, Escrow Agent shall notify Licensee and Licensor with a notice in the form of Attachment C. Such notice shall be sent in accordance with the notice procedures specified herein. If the initial fees are not received within thirty (30) calendar days following Licensee's and Licensor's receipt of such notice, Escrow Agent may terminate the Escrow Agreement without further notice or liability to Licensor or Licensee.

10.4 Yearly renewal fees are due in full upon the receipt of invoice, unless otherwise specified in the invoice. Each year during the term of this Escrow Agreement, Escrow Agent shall invoice Licensee for the renewal fees ninety (90) calendar days prior to the anniversary of the execution date of this Escrow Agreement. In the event the renewal fees are not received thirty (30) calendar days prior to the anniversary of the execution date of this Escrow Agreement, Escrow Agent shall notify Licensor and Licensee that the renewal fees have not been received by providing Licensor and Licensee with a notice in the form of Attachment C. Such notice shall be sent in accordance with the notice procedures specified herein. If the renewal fees are not received by the anniversary of the execution date of this Escrow Agreement, Escrow Agent may terminate the Escrow Agreement without further notice or liability to Licensor or Licensee.

- ***In general, the Licensee usually agrees to pay for the cost of the escrow as the escrow benefits the Licensee.***

ARTICLE 11
ANNUAL REPORTS

Escrow Agent agrees to keep records of the activities undertaken and materials prepared pursuant to this Escrow Agreement. Escrow Agent shall issue to Licensor and Licensee an annual report profiling the Deposit account or otherwise make the information described in this Article available to Licensor and Licensee. Such annual report shall identify the Licensor, Licensee, the current designated contacts, selected special services, and the Deposit history which includes all Initial Deposits, Supplemental Deposits and/or releases of the Deposits and any instructions related thereto. Upon reasonable notice, during Escrow Agent's normal business hours and during the term of the Escrow Agreement, Licensor or Licensee shall be entitled to inspect the records of Escrow Agent pertaining to this Escrow Agreement. The Deposit may not be changed during the audit period.

ARTICLE 12
VERIFICATION RIGHTS

Licensor grants to Licensee the option to verify the Deposit for accuracy, completeness, and sufficiency and upon reasonable notice during Escrow Agent's normal business hours, Licensee shall be entitled to inspect the physical status and condition of the Deposit. Further, Licensor agrees to permit Escrow Agent and/or at least one (1) employee or agent of Licensee to be present at Licensor's facilities to verify, audit and inspect the Deposit held by Escrow Agent to confirm the quality and/or content of the Deposit for the benefit of Licensee. If Escrow Agent is present or is selected to perform the verification, Escrow Agent will be paid by Licensee according to Escrow Agent's then-current verification service hourly rate and any out-of-pocket expenses; provided, however, that in the event that such inspection indicates that Licensor has failed to keep the Deposits current in accordance with the terms of this Escrow Agreement, then Licensor shall be solely responsible for the payment of Escrow Agent's verification fees as set forth herein.

- ***The right of verification is the most important right the licensee has. The licensee should make sure to use it.***

ARTICLE 13
MISCELLANEOUS

13.1 **Further Assurances.** Each of the parties hereto shall from time to time execute and deliver all such further documents and instruments and do all acts and things as any other party may reasonably require to effectively carry out the intent and meaning of this Escrow Agreement.

13.2 **Amendments and Waiver.** No modification of or amendment to this Escrow Agreement shall be valid or binding unless set forth in writing and duly executed by the parties hereto. No waiver of any breach of any term or provision of this Escrow Agreement shall be effective or binding unless made in writing and signed by the party against whom enforcement is sought and, purporting to give the same and, unless otherwise provided, shall be limited to the specific breach waived.

13.3 **Assignment.** This Escrow Agreement shall not be assigned by any party except with the written consent of the other parties and any such attempt shall be null and void. This Escrow Agreement shall inure to the benefit of and be binding upon the respective successors and permitted assigns of the parties hereto.

13.4 **Notices.** Any demand and/or notice to be given in connection with this Escrow Agreement shall be given in writing and may be given by ordinary mail, except for demands and/or notices required to be given in connection with Sections 4 and 5 of this Escrow Agreement, which shall be given by registered or certified mail, or by overnight courier addressed to the recipient as follows:

If to Licensee:

Attention:
Telecopier:

If to Escrow Agent:

Attention:
Telecopier:
email:

If to Licensor:

Telecopier:
email:

or to such other address or individual as may be designated hereafter from time to time by notice given by any party to the other parties. Any demand, notice or other communication given by personal delivery shall be deemed to have been given on the business day of actual delivery thereof or, if given by overnight courier, the next business day, or if given by registered, certified or ordinary mail, on the third (3rd) business day following the deposit thereof in the mail.

13.5 **Severability**. If any provisions of this Escrow Agreement shall for any reason be held illegal or unenforceable, such provision shall be deemed separable from the remaining provisions of this Escrow Agreement and shall in no way affect or impair the validity or the enforceability of the remaining provisions of this Escrow Agreement.

13.6 **Headings**. The division of this Escrow Agreement into Sections and the insertion of headings are for convenience of reference only and shall not affect the construction or interpretation of this Escrow Agreement. The terms "this Escrow Agreement," "hereof," "hereunder" and similar expressions refer to this Escrow Agreement and not to any particular Section or other portion hereof and include any agreement supplemental hereto. Unless something in the subject matter or context is inconsistent therewith, references herein to Sections are to Sections of this Escrow Agreement.

13.7 **Attorneys' Fees**. In the event that Licensor or Licensee shall commence a proceeding or bring an action to enforce the provisions of this Escrow Agreement, the prevailing party shall be entitled to be reimbursed for its reasonable attorneys' fees, disbursements and all applicable court costs.

From the Licensee's perspective, this may be a moot point if the Licensor is in bankruptcy. Nonetheless, it serves as a deterrent against the Licensor filing frivolous motions to prevent the release of the deposit materials.

13.8 **Governing Law; Exclusive Jurisdiction**. This Escrow Agreement, and all the rights and duties of the parties arising from or relating in any way to the subject matter of this Escrow Agreement or the transaction(s) contemplated by it, shall be governed by, construed, and enforced in accordance with the laws of the State of ______ (excluding any ________ conflict of laws rules that would refer to and apply the substantive laws of another jurisdiction). Any suit or proceeding relating to this Escrow Agreement shall be brought only in the courts, state and federal, located in ____ County, _____ and the parties hereby consent to the exclusive personal jurisdiction and venue of such courts.

13.9 **Attachments**. The following are Attachments annexed hereto and incorporated by reference and deemed to be part hereof:

Attachment A – Deposits
Attachment B – Description of Deposit Materials
Attachment C – Notice
Attachment D – Escrow Fees

13.10 **Counterparts**. This Escrow Agreement may be executed in any number of counterparts, each of which shall be deemed to be an original and all of which taken together shall be deemed to constitute one and the same instrument.

13.11 **Defined Terms**. As used in this Escrow Agreement, capitalized terms shall have the meanings specified in this Escrow Agreement or as specified in <u>Definitions Section</u> of the Software License Agreement.

13.12 **Supplementary Agreement.** This Escrow Agreement is "supplementary" to the License Agreement within the meaning of § 365(n) of the U.S. Bankruptcy Code (11 USC § 365 (n)). If this Escrow Agreement and/or the License Agreement are/is rejected by Licensor as a debtor in possession or a trustee or by any other person or entity under the U.S. Bankruptcy Code, then the Licensee may elect to retain its right as provided in § 365 (n). The Parties intend that no bankruptcy or bankruptcy proceeding, petition, law, or regulation (and no other proceeding, petition, law, or regulation of a similar nature in any state or foreign jurisdiction) will impede, delay, or prevent the release of Deposit Materials to Licensee in accordance with the provisions of this Agreement, and the Licensor hereby conveys to Escrow Agent such rights (including intellectual property rights) as are necessary to allow Escrow Agent to lawfully make such release and perform this Agreement.

13.13 **Entire Agreement**. This Escrow Agreement constitutes the entire agreement between the parties hereto with respect to the subject matter hereof and cancels and supersedes any prior understandings and agreements between the parties hereto with respect thereto. There are no representations, warranties, terms, conditions, undertakings or collateral agreements, express, implied, or statutory, between the parties other than as expressly set forth in this Escrow Agreement.

IN WITNESS WHEREOF, the parties have executed this Source Code Escrow Agreement on the day and in the year as set forth above.

LICENSOR:

____

By: ____________________________

Title: ____________________________

LICENSEE:

____

By: ____________________________

Title: ____________________________

ESCROW AGENT:

____

By: ____________________________

Title: ____________________________

ATTACHMENT A

Deposits

- ***The Licensee should carefully review this list to ensure that it is a comprehensive list of the materials and information the Licensee needs to operate and maintain the software in the event of the Licensor's breach.***

A. Description of Deposits

1. All Licensor-developed or owned source code for the Computer Programs used to provide services to Licensee under the Services Agreement, including all source code listings in human-readable and machine-readable form.

2. All Custom Programming modifications to the Computer Programs and all Documentation associated with such Custom Programming modifications.

3. All Enhancements to the Computer Programs and Custom Programming modifications thereto to which Licensee is entitled under the Services Agreement, to the extent the source code for such Enhancements is not provided to Licensee pursuant to the terms of the Services Agreement.

4. All available sub-programs, routines, program files, data files, file and data definitions and relationships, data definition specifications, data models, program and system logic, interfaces, algorithms, program architecture, design concepts, system designs, program structure, sequence and organization, screen displays and report layouts related to interacting with or a part of the Computer Programs and Custom Programming modifications thereto, whether in human-readable or machine-readable form (collectively, "Additional Programs").

5. All initial program load and start-up instructions, directions, information, and material that will enable a reasonably skilled programmer to load and execute (including compiling if necessary), the source code without the assistance of Licensor or any other person or reference to other materials (collectively, "Load Instructions").

6. Licensor-developed or owned maintenance and support tools, utilities, diagnostic programs, and supporting programs used or utilized by Licensor internally in the support or maintenance of the Computer Programs, or externally in connection with supporting other customer locations, whether or not such items are made available to Licensees generally or at an additional fee, whether in human-readable or machine-readable form (collectively "Support Tools").

7. All documentation and source code specifications including, without limitation, a list of all the names and business addresses and telephone numbers of key programmers or authors currently employed by Licensor, of any portion of the Computer Programs and the items referenced in paragraphs 2, 3, 4, 5 and 6 above ("Programmer List").

8. A complete list of third party products, including versions, incorporated in the Computer Programs and Custom Programming modifications thereto.

9. Third party system utilities (compiler and assembler descriptions). A description of the system/program generation, and descriptions and locations of programs not owned by Licensor that are required for use and/or support of the Computer Programs and Custom Programming modifications thereto.

10. Any other information and technical materials in Licensor's possession that are required for a reasonably skilled computer programmer to maintain, modify or enhance the Computer Programs and Custom Programming modifications thereto without the aid of Licensor or any other person and without reference to any other materials.

B. Usability of Source Code

Licensor represents and warrants that the source code is and shall be understandable and useable by a trained computer-programming contractor who is familiar with similar systems, though not necessarily those incorporating the Computer Programs. Licensor further represents and warrants that the Computer Programs do not involve any proprietary languages or programming components that such contractor could not reasonably be expected to understand, except to the extent the source code contains sufficient commentary to enable such contractor to understand and to use such languages or components. Licensor further represents and warrants that the source code includes all of the devices, programming, and documentation necessary for the maintenance of the Computer Programs by the Licensee upon release of the source code pursuant to this Escrow Agreement, except for devices, programming, and documentation commercially available to the Licensee on reasonable terms through readily known sources other than the Licensor.

ATTACHMENT B

Description of Deposit Materials

Licensee Name and Address

Re: Account No. [**Account No.**]; Computer Programs of ____________

Ladies and Gentlemen:

This writing is to inform you of the receipt of the following items of Deposit under the terms of that certain Escrow Agreement by and among ____________________ ________, __________________ and __________________, as Escrow Agent, dated as of __________, 20__ ("Escrow Agreement"). All capitalized terms herein shall have the meanings ascribed to them in the Escrow Agreement and the Attachment(s) attached thereto. The items marked or checked below have been received as of the dates indicated below:

Received	*Label Description Item of Deposit*	*Quarterly Updates*	*Date Received*
______	1. Source Code	______	__________, ____
______	2. Custom Programming	______	__________, ____
______	3. Enhancements	______	__________, ____
______	4. Additional Programs	______	__________, ____
______	5. Load Instructions	______	__________, ____
______	6. Support Tools	______	__________, ____
______	7. Specifications including Source Code Specifications and Programmer List	______	__________, ____
______	8. List of third party products	______	__________, ____
______	9. Third party system utilities	______	__________, ____
______	10. Other information and materials Please check as applicable:	______	__________, ____

Deposit Type: Initial _____ Supplemental ______

Environment: ____

Special Instructions: ____

____

I received and deposited the above described Deposit Materials pursuant to the terms and conditions of this Escrow Agreement.

Escrow Agent

By: ____

Title: ____

Date: ____

I certify that the above described Deposit Materials were forwarded to Escrow Agent.

Licensor

By: ____

Title: ____

Date: ____

ATTACHMENT C

Notice

____

____

____

Attention:______________________________

RE: Escrow Agreement #

Dear Sir or Madam:

In accordance with your escrow agreement, the [**SPECIFY EITHER "INITIAL" OR "RENEWAL"**] fees are due by [**INSERT APPLICABLE DUE DATE**]. If such fees are not received by the date set forth above, [Escrow Agent] may terminate the escrow agreement without further notice or liability to you.

If you have any questions, please contact me at (__)-____________.

Sincerely,
Escrow Agent

____

Name

____

Title

____

Date

ATTACHMENT D

Escrow Fees

Initialization fee (one time only)	$ _____
Annual maintenance/storage fee • Includes four (4) Deposit Material updates • Includes one (1) cubic foot of storage space	$ _____
Additional Updates (above four (4) per year)	$ _____
Additional Storage Space	$ _____ /cubic foot
Due Upon Licensee's Request for Release of Deposit Materials	$ _____ for initial 2 hrs

A 10 percent discount is credited towards the initialization fee for current Escrow Agent clients. Fees due in accordance with **Article 10** and shall be paid in U.S. Dollars. Fees shall be subject to then-current pricing, provided that the prices set forth above shall not increase by more than 10 percent per year. An invoice for all renewal fees will be issued on the anniversary of the initial invoice. If other currency acceptance is necessary, please contact your Account Manager to make arrangements. For any service not listed on this fee schedule, Escrow Agent shall provide a quote prior to rendering such service.

FORM M.1.5

Bilateral Proprietary Information Agreement (Annotated)

THIS PROPRIETARY INFORMATION AGREEMENT is made this ________ day of ____________, 20___ by and between ____________, a ____________ corporation, with its principal place of business at __________ ("Company"), and ________, [a __________ corporation][individually], with [its][his][her] principal place of business at ______________ ("Covenantor").

- ***The parties should consider whether their subsidiaries and affiliates should be parties to this agreement. The answer will depend on whether the confidential information of any affiliate will be disclosed and whether any affiliate will receive any confidential information disclosed under this agreement. From the Furnishing Party's perspective, the prudent approach is to limit the number of entities receiving its confidential information and thus it should prohibit disclosure to the receiving party's affiliates unless there is a compelling business reason to do otherwise. If information will be disclosed to a party's affiliates, the receiving party should be contractually obligated to keep written records of which of its affiliates received what information.***

BACKGROUND

1. Company has extensive expertise in the creation and development of technical information, ideas, and concepts relating to the ________ industry including consulting, pricing, marketing, and implementation and system designs for such software, including without limitation, copyrights, trade secrets, plans, source codes, object codes, prototypes, working models, and production models (the "Confidential Information").

2. Covenantor has extensive expertise in ______________________ (collectively referred to with Company's expertise as the "Confidential Information").

- ***The parties should ensure that the definition of "Confidential Information" is broad enough to encompass all information that will be disclosed. The definition should be drafted in such a manner to include all reports,***

analysis and derivative works encompassing the confidential information. The definition should be modified in each agreement to reflect the actual information that will be disclosed in that transaction. The parties should be careful to make sure the definition is not so broad and amorphous that it is unenforceable.

3. The parties desire to exchange the Confidential Information in conjunction with ____ **[give detailed description as to why the parties are exchanging information]**.

- ***The parties should narrowly define the purpose for exchanging information as the description establishes the limitations as to who may access such information and what purposes the information may be used for. See e.g., Section 2(d) below.***

4. The "Furnishing Party" will be furnishing the other party, the "Recipient," with information and or other materials, in writing, orally, and in other tangible form, regarding the Furnishing Party. **Such information, in whole or in part, together with any analyses, compilations, studies, or other documents prepared by the Recipient, the Recipient's agents or employees, which contain or otherwise reflect such information and Recipient's review or interest in the Furnishing Party, shall be considered Confidential Information.**

- ***The Furnishing Party should ensure that the definition of "Confidential Information" includes "derivative" works to avoid later disputes over what constitutes confidential information and whether all such information has been returned or destroyed by the Recipient.***

5. The Confidential Information of Company and Covenantor is proprietary, secret, and confidential and is only being disclosed to the other party in conjunction with Company's business relationship or potential business relationship with Covenantor and for no other reason.

NOW THEREFORE, in consideration of the mutual covenants herein contained, the parties intending to be legally bound, agree as follows:

1. Company and Covenantor shall disclose to the other such Confidential Information as such party deems appropriate.

2. Company and Covenantor shall review and maintain the Confidential Information in accordance with the following terms and conditions:

(a) Company and Covenantor agree to treat all Confidential Information as defined above as confidential **and not to disclose the same to any third party. The documents containing such information should be designated "Confidential" or "Proprietary" and shall be so marked by the Furnishing Party provided, however, that all software provided to Covenantor hereunder shall be deemed to be proprietary and confidential regardless of whether it is marked "Confidential" or "Proprietary."**

- ***Nondisclosure agreements usually provide for one of two standards for the disclosure of confidential information. This agreement creates a strict liability standard by providing that the Recipient will not disclose the Furnishing Party's confidential information to a third party. Other agreements provide that the Recipient will use the same standards to protect the Furnishing Party's confidential information as it does to protect its own but no less than a reasonable standard of care. This "reasonable" standard provides a much lower level of protection to the Furnishing party and thus should be avoided if possible.***
- ***The Furnishing Party should ensure that the Recipient may not disclose its Confidential Information to third parties without the Furnishing Party's consent. The Recipient is likely to argue that it needs to disclose the Furnishing Party's Confidential Information to its third party contractors and consultants but the Furnishing Party needs to ensure that these third parties are not competitors of the Furnishing Party.***

(b) No copies of the Confidential Information shall be made, unless agreed to in writing by the Furnishing Party.

(c) All of the Confidential Information shall be kept and maintained in a safe and secure place with adequate safeguards to ensure that unauthorized persons do not have access to the Confidential Information. Company and Covenantor shall, at all times, keep the other informed in writing of the location of the Confidential Information.

(d) **Only representatives of Company and Covenantor whose review of the Confidential Information is necessary and appropriate for the purpose set forth in Paragraph 3 of the Background above shall have access to the Confidential Information. The Confidential Information shall be used by the Receiving Party solely for the purpose stated in Paragraph 3 of the Background above.**

- ***The Furnishing Party should ensure the agreement limits who may have access to its Confidential Information. Some parties seek to include language to the effect that the receiving party's employees must execute non-disclosure agreements equally restrictive to the overarching proprietary information agreement prior to accessing the confidential information. Under no circumstances should the receiving party agree to have its employees execute a proprietary information agreement directly with the disclosing party as such action potentially exposes its employees to personal liability.***

(e) Any oral discussions between Company and Covenantor that relate to the Confidential Information shall be kept secret and confidential and are deemed to be Confidential Information.

- ***Some nondisclosure agreements require the Furnishing Party to reduce to writing all oral disclosures and to provide such writing to the Recipient within 30 days of the disclosure in order for the disclosure to be considered Confidential***

Information. The likelihood of the Furnishing Party's employees remembering to do so after each disclosure is small. Thus, the language set forth above protects the Furnishing Party. The Recipient will argue, however, that unless the Confidential Information is reduced to writing and provided to the Recipient, the Recipient will have no way of knowing which disclosures are confidential.

(f) Upon the request of the Furnishing Party or after the termination of this Agreement, the Recipient shall promptly return all of the Confidential Information to the Furnishing Party **or destroy all such Confidential Information including all work products of the Recipient containing Confidential Information. The returning party shall certify that all Confidential Information and copies or extracts thereof have been returned or destroyed.**

- ***Some parties request the right to retain one copy of the Confidential Information for their records on the belief that if a dispute arises in the future, the Recipient will have no means to show what Confidential Information it received from the Furnishing Party. If the Furnishing Party allows the Recipient to keep a copy, the Recipient should be required to keep such information in a locked file in the General Counsel's office.***

(g) The Recipient agrees to immediately notify the Furnishing Party in writing of any misuse or misappropriation of the Confidential Information or violation of this Agreement that may come to its attention.

3. **Neither party, its agents, employees, representatives, subsidiaries, affiliates, or parent companies shall, for themselves or for the benefit of any person or entity other than the Furnishing Party,** use or disclose the Confidential Information of the other whether written or oral, software technology or otherwise for any purpose, at any time or in any place, without the express prior written approval of the Furnishing Party.

- ***The Furnishing Party should ensure that the Confidential Information should be used only for the purposes contemplated under the Agreement and that any restrictions bind not only to Recipient but also its agents, employees, representatives, subsidiaries, affiliates, or parent companies.***

4. Notwithstanding anything to the contrary herein, the Recipient shall have no obligation to preserve the confidentiality of any information that:

(a) Was previously known to the Recipient free of any obligation to keep it confidential as shown by the Recipient's written records, so long as the Recipient did not receive such information directly or indirectly from the Furnishing Party; or

(b) Is or becomes publicly available, by other than unauthorized disclosure; or

(c) Other than for patents, is independently developed by Recipient without knowledge of the Confidential Information as shown by the Recipient's written records; or

(d) Is disclosed to third parties by the Furnishing Party without restriction; or

(e) Is lawfully received from a third party whose disclosure would not violate any confidentiality or other legal obligation.

5. No liability shall arise under this Agreement due to the Recipient's disclosure of Confidential Information made pursuant to judicial or governmental order, provided the Recipient notifies the Furnishing Party as soon as possible and in any event prior to such disclosure and cooperates with the Furnishing Party in the event the Furnishing Party elects to legally contest and avoid such disclosure.

6. Company and Covenantor agree that neither party acquires any title, ownership, or other intellectual property right or license under this Agreement.

7. The obligations of this Agreement with respect to the disclosure of Confidential Information shall survive for a period of seven (7) years from the date of last disclosure or for as long as Company or Covenantor is commercially marketing the Confidential Information, whichever is longer.

- ***The Furnishing Party should not agree on an artificial period of time for the Recipient's Confidential Information to survive. Often the parties agree on a period of two to three years but yet at the end of such period, the Confidential Information is still considered to be a trade secret of the Furnishing Party. To that end, the Furnishing Party should insist on the inclusion of language to the effect that the Recipient's obligations of confidentiality shall continue so long as the Furnishing Party considers the Confidential Information to be a trade secret.***

8. Company and Covenantor recognize and agree that their obligations under Sections 2, 3, and 7 of this Agreement shall survive the termination of this Agreement and Company and Covenantor shall be bound by such obligations after termination hereof.

- ***It is important that the parties state that their obligations of confidentiality survive any earlier termination of the non-disclosure agreement.***

9. This Agreement may be terminated by either party upon thirty (30) days prior written notice provided, however, that this Agreement may be terminated immediately and the return of all Confidential Information may be demanded upon written notice in the event that the other party breaches any material term of this Agreement, is declared bankrupt, creates, or permits an assignment for the benefit of its creditors, is dissolved, or ownership and control of said party is transferred to a third party.

- ***If the amount of information disclosed is voluminous, some parties agree that the receiving party may destroy the information instead of physically returning it to the disclosing party. In such event, an officer of the receiving party should certify in writing that the information has been destroyed.***

10. Company and Covenantor acknowledge their obligations to control access to technical data under the U.S. Export Laws and Regulations and agree to adhere to such laws and regulations with regard to any technical data received under this Agreement.

11. In the event either party breaches, or threatens to breach any of the covenants expressed herein, the **damages to the non-threatening or non-breaching party** will **be great and irreparable and difficult to quantify**; therefore, the non-threatening or non-breaching party may apply to a court of competent jurisdiction for injunctive or other equitable relief to restrain such breach or threat of breach, without disentitling such party from any other relief in either law or equity.

- ***Both parties should be hesitant to acknowledge in advance that any damages "will" be great. Instead, prudent parties should provide that the damages "may" be great. Further, the party seeking an injunction should not be required to post a bond to do so.***

12. Covenantor and Company agree they will **indemnify and hold harmless the other party from all losses, damages, causes of action, and attorneys' fees** incurred by the other party arising from the breach of this Agreement by Covenantor or Company as the case may be.

- ***The parties should consider whether they want to indemnify each other as they already have a breach of contract claim. An indemnity claim will allow the aggrieved party to recover a greater level of damages that would otherwise be allowed under a contract claim.***

13. This Agreement merges and supersedes all prior Agreements between the parties hereto ***as to the subject matter hereof,*** and shall be governed by and construed in accordance with the domestic laws of the state of ______________________________, of the United States of America, excluding its principles of conflicts of laws. The parties hereto agree that any action related to this Agreement shall solely be venued in the Federal District Court for the Eastern District of ____________________ and the parties hereby irrevocably submit to the jurisdiction and venue of said court.

- ***To the extent the proprietary information agreement is executed in conjunction with another agreement such as a master services agreement, the parties should clearly provide that the agreements are separate and distinct and that the proprietary information agreement will survive the termination of the other agreement.***

14. This Agreement shall not be assigned by any party hereto without the express prior written consent of the other party. Any attempted assignment in contravention of this Section 14 shall be void.

- ***The parties need to state that any attempted assignment is void; otherwise, a court will allow the assignment to occur but award the non-consenting party monetary damages. See Chapter 4.G for a more in-depth discussion.***

15. In the event that the Confidential Information is or becomes the subject of a patent application, patent, copyright application, or copyright, the Recipient agrees and understands that the Furnishing Party will have all the rights and remedies available to it under the law as a result of said patent applications, patents, copyright applications, or

copyrights, and that disclosure of such Confidential Information to the Recipient does not in any way effect those rights and remedies.

16. It is understood by the Recipient that the Confidential Information disclosed hereunder may relate to products that are under development or planned for development. THE FURNISHING PARTY DISCLAIMS ANY IMPLIED WARRANTY OF MERCHANTABILITY, ANY IMPLIED WARRANTY OF FITNESS FOR A PARTICULAR PURPOSE, ANY IMPLIED WARRANTY OF NON-INFRINGEMENT, AND ANY EXPRESS WARRANTY WITH RESPECT TO ANY OF THE CONFIDENTIAL INFORMATION AND DOCUMENTATION DISCLOSED HEREUNDER. The Furnishing Party accepts no responsibility as a result of any expenses, losses, damages, or actions incurred or undertaken by the Recipient as a result of the Furnishing Party's receipt or use of any Confidential Information or Documentation.

17. The waiver by either party hereto of any breach of the terms and conditions hereof will not be considered a modification of any provision, nor shall such a waiver act to bar the enforcement of any subsequent breach.

OPTIONAL

18. Covenantor acknowledges and agrees that Company has outstanding publicly traded shares, and that the Confidential Information disclosed hereunder may constitute material non-public information. Covenantor agrees to treat any such Confidential Information in accordance with the requirements of the United States securities laws, including Rule 10b-5 under the Securities Exchange Act of 1934, as amended.

- ***If one of the disclosing parties is a publically traded company, it may want to include the above language to protect itself from any claim that the information provided under the Agreement violated any applicable securities laws, including but not limited to Regulation FD.***

IN WITNESS WHEREOF, the parties have executed this Proprietary Information Agreement under seal effective the date first written above.

ATTEST:	**COMPANY**
______________________	**By:**______________________**(SEAL)**
WITNESS/ATTEST:	**COVENANTOR**
______________________	**By:**______________________**(SEAL)**

- ***If the party executing the agreement is signing in his/her corporate capacity, they should always use the designation "By:" prior to their signature. Further, the witness should always sign under the title "ATTEST." If the person signing is signing in their individual capacity, then the term "WITNESS" should be used.***

APPENDIX **1**

Technology Acronyms

AAA	American Arbitration Association
ACV	Annualized Contract Value
ADM	Application Development and Maintenance
ADR	Alternative Dispute Resolution
AI	Artificial Intelligence
AES	Advanced Encryption Standard
AFFECT	Americans for Fair Electronic Commerce Transactions
AICPA	American Institute of Certified Public Accountants
ALI	American Law Institute
AO	Application Outsourcing
API	Application Programming Interface
API	Application Protocol Interface
APM	Application Performance Management
ARC	Additional Resource Charge
ARS	Approval Rating System
ASP	Application Service Provider or Alternative Service Provider
AUP	Acceptable Use Policy
AWS	Amazon Web Services
ARR	Annual Recurring Revenue
BAA	Business Associate Agreement
B2B	Business to Business
BPaaS	Business Process as a Service
BPO	Business Process Outsourcing
BSA	Business Software Alliance
BSI	Bureau of Industry and Security
BXA	Bureau of Export Control
C2B	Consumer to Business
C2C	Consumer to Consumer
C2M	Consumer to Merchant

CAB	Customer Advisory Board
CAD/CAM	Computer Aided Design/Computer Aided Manufacturing
CCL	Commerce Control List
CFAA	Computer Fraud and Abuse Act
CGI	Common Gateway Interface
CISG	United Nations Convention on Contracts for the International Sale of Goods
CLI	Command Line Interface
CMMI	Capability Maturity Model Integration
CMS	Content Management System
CAP	Corrective Action Plan
CAPA	Corrective and Preventive Action
CO	Central Office
COE	Consistent or Common Operating Environment
COE	Center of Excellence
COLA	Cost of Living Adjustment
COPA	Child Online Protection Act
COTS	Commercial Off the Shelf (as it relates to software)
CPI	Consumer Price Index
CPU	Central Processing Unit
CRM	Customer Relationship Management (software)
CSP	Cloud Service Provider
Db	Database
DBA	Database Administrator
DBMS	Database Management System
DFAR	Defense Federal Acquisition Regulations
DMCA	Digital Millennium Copyright Act
DMS	Desktop Managed Services
DPA	Data Privacy Agreement
DSD	Digital Solution Design
DSL	Digital Subscriber Line
E2E	End to End
EA	Enterprise Architecture
EAR	Export Administration Regulations
EEA	European Economic Area
ECCN	Export Control Classification Number

ECI	Employment Cost Index
EDI	Electronic Data Interchange
ELA	Enterprise License Agreement
EMEA	Europe, Middle East and Africa
ERP	Enterprise Resource Planning (software or systems)
ESB	Enterprise Service Bus
ETL	Extraction, Transformation and Loading
EULA	End User License Agreement
FAR	Federal Acquisition Regulations
FCPA	Foreign Corrupt Practices Act
FFP	Firm Fixed Price
FME	Force Majeure Event
FTC	Federal Trade Commission
FTE	Full-Time Equivalent
FTP	File Transfer Protocol
4GL	Fourth Generation (computer) Language
GA	General Availability
GAAP	Generally Accepted Accounting Principles
Gb	Gigabyte
GDPR	General Data Protection Regulation
GLB	Gramm-Leach-Bliley Act
GTM	Go To Market
GUI	Graphical User Interface
HIPAA	Health Insurance Portability and Accountability Act
HITECH	The Health Information Technology for Economic and Clinical Health Act
HTML	Hyper Text Markup Language
HTTP	Hyper Text Transfer Protocol
IaaS	Infrastructure as a Service
IDS	Intrusion Detection System
IMEI	International Mobile Equipment Identifier
IPS	Intrusion Protection System
ISO	Independent Sales Organizations or Independent Service Organizations
ISP	Internet Service Provider
ISV	Independent Software Vendor
IT	Information Technology

ITO	Information Technology Outsourcing
IP	Intellectual Property
ISDN	Integrated Services Digital Network
KPI	Key Performance Indicator
LA	Limited Availability
LAN	Local Area Network
LOI	Letter of Intent
LAWN	Local Area Wireless Network
LOL	Limitation of Liability
LPAR	Logical Partition (virtual computing platform)
Mb	Megabyte
MDE	Managed Desktop Environment
MDM	Mobile Device Management
MDP	Mobile Device Protection
MEAP	Mobile Enterprise Application Platform
MHS	Managed Hosting Services
MIP	Million Instructions per Second
MOE	Managed Operating Environment,
MSA	Master Services Agreement
MSP	Managed Service Provider
MTTR	Mean Time to Report
NDA	Non-Disclosure Agreement
NIST	National Institute of Standards
NLR	No License Required
NTE	Not to Exceed
OEM	Original Equipment Manufacturer
OCR	Optical Character Recognition
OEM	Original Equipment Manufacturer
OKR	Objective and Key Results
OS	Open Source
OS	Operating System
OSA	Outsourcing Agreement
OSI	Open Source Initiative
PaaS	Platform as a Service
PDF	Portable Document Format
PHI	Protected Health Information

PIA	Privacy Impact Assessment
PII	Personally Identifiable Information
QBR	Quarterly Business Review
QOS	Quality of Service
RAS	Route Access System
RFI	Request for Information
RFP	Request for Proposal
RRC	Reduced Resource Credit/Charge
RPO	Recovery Point Objectives
RTO	Recovery Time Objectives
RTU	Right to Use
SaaS	Software-as-a-Service
SCM	Supply Chain Management
SDE	Standard Desktop Environment
SDLC	Systems Development Life Cycle
SIIA	Software and Information Industry Association
SL	Service Level
SLA	Service-Level Agreement
SLB	Service-Level Bonus
SLC	Service-Level Credit
SME	Subject Matter Expert
SMTP	Simple Mail Transfer Protocol
SOC	Statement of Organization and Control
SOE	Server Operating Environment or Standard Operating Environment
SOP	Standard Operating Procedure or Statement of Position
SOW	Statement of Work
SOX	Sarbanes-Oxley Act
SQL	Structured Query Language
3GL	Third Generation (computer) Language
TIA	Transfer Impact Assessment
T&M	Time and Materials
TCV	Total Contract Value
TSR	Technology and Software under Restriction
TSS	Technical Support Services
TSSG	Technical Support Guidelines
TSU	Technology and Software–Unrestricted

UAT	User Acceptance Testing
UCC	Uniform Commercial Code
UE	User Experience
UI	User Interface
UCITA	Uniform Computer Information Transactions Act
UETA	Uniform Electronic Transactions Act
UTSA	Uniform Trade Secret Act
VAR	Value Added Reseller
VLAN	Virtual Local Area Network
VPN	Virtual Private Network
WAN	Wide Area Network
WSDL	Web Services Description Language
XML	eXtensible Markup Language
XSD	XML Schema Definition

APPENDIX **2**

Glossary

Acceptable Use Policy (AUP)—a policy setting forth permitted and prohibited uses of a software system by users, often in conjunction with a cloud-based application. The AUP supplements the applicable information security policy.

Acceptance Testing—formal testing to determine whether a system works according to specifications and should be accepted.

Actual Business Run Test—use of the software in the licensee's business environment during a test period in which the software vendor corrects all identified errors.

Additional Resource Charge (ARC)—the charge for an additional resource that is above and beyond the fee associated with the services baseline. Usually used in conjunction with an outsourcing contract. Resources are typically measured in units of full-time equivalents (FTE).

Advanced Encryption Standard (AES)—a symmetric key encryption standard adopted by the National Institute of Standards (NIST) consisting of three block ciphers: AES-128, AES-192 and AES-256.

Agile Methodology)—a software development methodology with limited initial definition and budgeting. The Agile methodology values constant collaboration, frequent deliverables, and continuous evolution of requirements. See Chapter 16.A for a detailed discussion.

Alpha Testing—internal testing conducted by a software developer; the first of two pre-release phases.

Application Program Interface (API)—is a set of specifications, tools, libraries and routines for building software applications. APIs have been compared to building blocks that allow a software developer to build a program. Software Development Kits (SDKs) often include APIs.

App—short for software application.

Application Service Provider (ASP)—a service provider who provides shared access to proprietary software through a hosted environment.

Applications Software or **Applications**—a software program, or in the case of outsourcing those programs and programming—including the supporting documentation, media, online help facilities, and tutorials—that perform, in the conduct of the services, specific user-related data processing and telecommunications tasks.

Authentication—The process of verifying the identity of an individual user, machine, software component, or other entity.

Baseline—a specific quantity of resources for a resource category included within an annual base charge when pricing an outsourcing agreement.

Benchmark(ing)—the process of comparing the vendor's service levels, results, and pricing against a pre-agreed industry standard.

Best Efforts—a standard of performance that is typically thought to be the highest and hardest to satisfy. Best efforts are generally interpreted to require more effort than merely reasonable efforts or good faith efforts. Effort-based clauses can be useful in dealing with situations where a party is uncertain as to their ability to meet a specific objective.

Best Practices—the process of identifying the practices, processes, and standards that are utilized in a particular industry (i.e., the information technology industry) and considered to be the gold standard of the industry. The vendor is subsequently obligated to adopt such practices in delivering its services/products.

Beta Software—software which is under development and has not been released to the general public. Beta software is often distributed on a limited basis for customer testing and to obtain customer feedback.

Beta Testing—testing conducted by select users of the software under normal operating conditions; the second phase of pre-release testing.

Blade Server—means an all-inclusive computing system with a design optimized to minimize physical space and heat. Blade servers contain only the core computing components: processor and memory. They rely on a blade enclosure to provide the non-core computing components: power, storage, network switch, and basic I/O.

Bot—(also known as a web bot, web crawler or spider - "a computer program which operates across the Internet to perform searching, copying and retrieving functions on the websites of others." *eBay, Inc. v. Bidder's Edge, Inc.*, 100 F. Supp.2d 1058, 1060 (N.D. Cal 2000).

Business Continuity—the concept of ensuring that an entity's critical business processes continue to operate in the event of a disruption or are quickly restored to normal functionality.

Business Continuity Plan—a process that defines how a business will respond in the event of a disruption to ensure that its essential business functions/processes continue during and after a disruption.

Business Process Outsourcing (BPO)—the transfer of discrete business functions, such as billing, claims processing, etc., to an external vendor.

Call Center—an organization that provides customer support usually over the phone, although their support services may be provided over the Internet.

Central Processing Unit (CPU)—the principal processing unit of a computer that processes the computer application in question. Many license agreements will limit the number of CPUs that can be used to access a particular computer program at one time. Some license agreements may be CPU specific.

Change Control Procedure—the procedure that the parties follow to implement a change order.

Change Order—a change to a party's contractual obligations, such as deliverable, time of delivery, or price, that may be requested by either the vendor or customer.

Clean Room—a process by which software development is undertaken by individuals who are removed from outside influences and information (i.e., a "clean" room") in an effort to avoid claims that the finished product incorporated another party's intellectual property.

Cloud Computing—allows a user to access an application, data storage and processing power from any computer with a web browser, eliminating the need to provide applications and the attendant hardware. Data is accessed and transferred over the internet instead of through a fixed transmission line.

Community Cloud—a cloud infrastructure that is provisioned for exclusive use by a specific community of consumers from organizations that have shared concerns (e.g., mission, security requirements, policy, and compliance considerations). It may be owned, managed, and operated by one or more of the organizations in the community, a third party, or some combination of them, and it may exist on or off premises.

Core—a single "**Core**" is (a) a physical processing core located in a CPU or (b) a virtual processing core, in whole or in part as the case may be, each part counting as a core, within a virtual machine, in each case, that contains or executes the software. Originally, every processor had a single core but today, processors can have many cores, allowing for faster processing as the cores can work independently of each other.

Customer Relationship Management (CRM) Software—the generic name for proprietary software that can manage an entity's relationship with its customer, such as billing, shipping, payments, etc.

Data Migration—the transfer of data from one computer system to another.

Database (Db)—a collection of records that are organized in such a manner as to be easily searchable, sortable, and updatable. There are many commercially available database products. There are many different types of databases, but relational databases are the most commonly used. Relational databases use a specific set of instructions referred to as Structured Query Language (SQL).

Data Warehouse—a data store or series of data stores used to support reporting and analysis. The data stored in the warehouse may come from multiple sources, based on the master data management rules. Focused on historical data, it provides processes for collecting, aggregating, matching, consolidating, quality-assuring, and persisting such data throughout an organization to ensure consistency and control in the ongoing maintenance and use of this information.

Derivative Work—"a work based upon one or more preexisting works, such as a translation, musical arrangement, dramatization, fictionalization, motion picture version, sound recording, art reproduction, abridgment, condensation, or any other form in which a work may be recast, transformed, or adapted. A work consisting of editorial revisions, annotations, elaborations, or other modifications which, as a whole, represent an original work of authorship, is a 'derivative work.' " 17 U.S.C. § 101. Some derivative works may include relatively minor derivations from the original work on which the derivative work is based, while other derivative works may include substantial derivations from the original work.

Disabling Device—a piece of computer code that disables a user's ability to use a software application. Often inserted by a vendor to allow the vendor to prevent the end user from using the software after the license has expired. It may also refer to a virus, spider, worm, etc., that disables the software. Disabling code is often referred to as malicious code.

Disaster Recovery—the process by which an entity's data systems are returned to operating order in the event of a disruption.

Disentanglement Services—the provision of services by the vendor to provide customer assistance and services in the event of termination of the applicable agreement and to facilitate the orderly transition and migration of the services. May require the vendor to continue to provide services until all of the customer's data files have been completely converted and transferred to the customer's alternative system provider. The vendor usually provides for the prompt and orderly conversion of all the customer's data files on the vendor system and the conclusion of all work—as the customer may reasonably direct—including completion or partial completion of some projects, documentation of work in process, and other measures to ensure an orderly transition to the customer. The work is usually performed by the vendor at no additional cost to the customer beyond what the customer would pay for the services absent the performance of the disentanglement services. For services provided after the expiration date of the contract, the vendor may charge the customer a premium to the amounts normally charged.

Dual Core Processor(s)—two independent computer processors on a single computer chip enhancing the computer's performance.

Emulated App—an application that is translated into the machine language of the computer at run time and is thus slower than a native app.

End User—the user of the vendor's services or the application software, such as an employee, agent, and authorized third party of the customer, as well as other users of similar services.

End User License Agreement (EULA)—a contract between an end user and the manufacturer or distributor of an application software product. End user license agreements can be executed in a variety of nontraditional ways, such as communicating acceptance to the agreement by clicking on an "I Accept" button on a computer screen.

Enhancements—any new software releases, versions, improvements, modifications, upgrades, updates, fixes, and additions to the software that the applicable vendor markets or makes available to its customers who are eligible to receive maintenance support services. Enhancements usually include any re-platformed software, whether on different operating systems or equipment, except, however, that enhancements do not include new, separate product offerings.

Enterprise Resource Planning (ERP) Software—the generic name for proprietary software that can manage an entity's infrastructure needs, such as its accounting system, payroll, sales pipelines, purchasing, human resources, and inventory management.

eXtensible Markup Language—a simplified version of SGML that is used to facilitate the exchange of documents on the World Wide Web. XML allows for the marking of a document according to content rather than by format.

Extranet—an intranet that is accessible to authorized outsiders.

Firewall—a set of software programs located at a network gateway server that protects the network from unauthorized access.

Firmware—software embedded on a computer chip or hard disc, often referring to the computerized element in consumer electronics and other programs.

Flat Files—a file for which there is no embedded structure used to manage information and govern relationships between records. A flat file database uses a single table, in contrast to a relational database that utilizes different tables with different columns and data relationships.

Flow Downs—contractual provisions that "flow down" from a customer to a vendor's subcontractors. Usually used in connection with a systems integration project where certain customer terms such insurance requirements are required to be "flowed down" or included into the vendor's subcontracts.

Flow Ups—contractual provisions that "flow up" from a subcontractor to the end user customer. Usually used in connection with a systems integration project where a subcontracting software licensor requires the system integrator to "flow up" or pass on the licensor's license terms to the end-user customer.

Forking—the creation of an independent branch of software code that "forks" off from the original program.

Freeware—software that is licensed to the licensee for free. Although the license agreement for freeware does not involve the payment of a fee, the license agreement will often include limitations and restrictions similar to those found in fee-based licensing arrangements.

Functional Specifications—the specifications to which the developed/licensed software must contractually conform.

Functionality—the capabilities of a program.

Gigabyte (Gb)—a measurement of digital data. A gigabyte equates to 1,000 megabytes.

Good Faith—honest intentions without any intent to defraud. In Section 1-201 of the Uniform Commercial Code (UCC) good faith is defined generally as "honesty in fact in the conduct or transaction concerned."

Gramm-Leach-Bliley Act (15 U.S.C. §§ 6801-6810)—regulates the sharing of personal information about individuals who obtain financial products or services from financial institutions. It attempts to inform individuals about the privacy policies and practices of financial institutions so that consumers can make choices about financial institutions with which they wish to do business. The law gives consumers limited control, via opt out provisions, over how financial institutions use and share the consumers' personal information.

Graphical User Interface (GUI)—a visual computer environment that uses visual representations and tools, such as menus, icons, and buttons, to represent programs, files, and options.

Help Desk—a vendor-maintained technical support usually offered over the phone and Internet.

Hosting (a/k/a Managed Hosting Services)—See ***Managed Hosting Services.***

Hybrid Cloud—a cloud infrastructure is a composition of two or more clouds (community, private, or public) that remain unique entities but are bound together by standardized or proprietary technology that enables data and application portability.

Hyper Text Transfer Protocol (HTTP)—the communications protocol used on the World Wide Web to carry requests from a web browser to a web server, and to transport pages from web servers back to the requesting browser.

Infrastructure as a Service (IaaS)—the capability provided to the consumer to provision processing, storage, networks, and other fundamental computing resources where the consumer can deploy and run arbitrary software, which can include operating systems and applications. The consumer does not manage or control the underlying cloud infrastructure but has control over operating systems, storage, deployed applications, and possibly limited control of select networking components (e.g., host firewalls).

Integrated Databases—facilitating the ability of multiple databases to exchange information with each other. The phrase is typically used in the context of integrating non-relational databases with relational databases.

Interfaces—software that allows two, third party software applications to "interface" or communicate with each other (i.e., an Oracle Database and another third-party proprietary application).

Instance—a cloud instance is a virtual server in a cloud computing environment. It is built and delivered by cloud platforms such as Amazon Web Services. For example - AWS currently offers nearly 400 different instances with choices across storage options, networking, and operating systems.

Intranet—an IP network that resides behind a firewall and is accessible only to people who are members of the same organization.

Intrusion Detection System (IDS)—a security inspection system for computers and networks that can allow for the inspection of systems activity and inbound/outbound network activity, allowing for the identification of suspicious activity or patterns that may indicate a network or system attack.

Intrusion Protection System (IPS)—a more sophisticated Intrusion Detection System that allows administrators to configure predefined actions to be taken if suspicious activity is detected.

Load Testing—the process of testing how much traffic a software application can simultaneously support.

Local Area Network—a communications network within a closed environment such as a building connecting various hardware devices to facilitate the sharing of software applications and data.

Local Network System—multiple, interactive user terminals connected to a single-processing or multi-processing, micro-computing unit that is owned, leased, or operated by the customer.

Maintenance—the continued support provided by a software licensor after it has delivered its product. Maintenance may or may not include enhancements, a help desk, and new editions of the software.

Malware—software designed to secretly access a computer system without the owner's informed consent, such as computer viruses, worms, Trojan horses, spyware, dishonest adware, ransomware, and other malicious and unwanted software or programs.

Managed Hosting Services (MHS)—a service in which software applications that would otherwise be hosted on the servers of a particular organization are instead hosted by a third-party provider, such as a vendor of IT outsourcing services.

Megabyte (Mb)—a measurement of digital data. A megabyte equates to 1,048,576 bytes.

Metered Service—the ability of cloud systems to automatically control and optimize resource use by leveraging a metering capability at some level of abstraction appropriate to the type of service (e.g., storage, processing, bandwidth, and active user accounts). Resource usage can be monitored, controlled, and reported, providing transparency for both the provider and consumer of the utilized service.

Methodology—refers to a party's proprietary methodology that is used in implementing the deliverables.

Milestone—a scheduled event, accomplishment, or achievement (including delivery of a deliverable) as specified in a contract.

Mobile app—a computer program designed to run on smartphones, tablet computers and other mobile devices.

Multi-core Processor(s)—multiple independent computer processors on a single computer chip enhancing the computer's performance. For example, a quad core processor has four independent computer processors on a single computer chip.

Multi-factor Authentication—a security approach using two or more of the three categories of factors: (i) something the user knows (e.g., password), (ii) something the user has (e.g., secure token), and (iii) something the user is (e.g., a biometric characteristic, such as a fingerprint).

Native App—a locally installed application that is compiled at run time. Because the application is written for a specific hardware platform, a native app will run faster than a web app as no translation is required.

Network Configuration—the hardware and software arrangements that define a computer or telecommunications system, such as LAN and WAN, and thus determine what the system will do and how effectively and efficiently it functions.

Object Code—the machine-readable version of the source code after it has been compiled.

Off-the-Shelf Software—Pre-built software that is installed and configured with no original development, as opposed to custom developed software.

On-Demand Self-Service—the ability of a consumer to unilaterally provision computing capabilities, such as server time and network storage, as needed without human interaction with the service provider.

Open Source (Software)—a framework for licensing software in which the source code is made free to interested users and developers, even though they were not involved in creating the original product and do not have a relationship with the originator of the software. An open-source license is typically embedded within the source code. The underlying exchange in many open-source licenses is that the licensee is given free access to software, in exchange for the licensee agreeing not to charge a license fee to a third-party sublicensee for any software applications made by the licensee using the open-source code components. Many open-source licenses are referred to as copyleft licenses because they utilize copyright laws to prevent open-source licenses from charging a license fee to third parties.

Operating System (OS)—the underlying computer software on which a computer's operation is founded, such as Linux® and Windows®. Operating systems control the interactions between the underlying software and the various hardware peripherals such as keyboards, printers and modems, acting as the interface between the software applications and the computer itself.

Original Equipment Manufacturer (OEM)—with respect to computers and software, this term is used interchangeably with VAR and ISO. An OEM generally purchases computers and customizes them with software applications for end users.

Parallel Run Testing—running a process concurrently using the old and new software, and then comparing the results.

Patch—a piece of software that is incorporated into an existing piece of software to address a bug or enhance the functionality of the existing piece of software.

Penetration Testing—an authorized simulated attack on a computer system that seeks to identify security weaknesses.

Performance Standards—the quantitative and qualitative performance standards and commitments for the vendor's services, including the service levels, which are usually contained in the applicable agreement.

Personally Identifiable Information (PII)—any information that allows the identification of a specific individual. PII includes date and place of birth, full name, Social Security number, driver's license number, bank account number, passport number, and email address.

Physical Node—a physical system on which an entity installs or executes all or a portion of the software including, without limitation, a server, work station, laptop, blade or other physical system, as applicable. Subscriptions based on Physical Nodes may contain additional entitlements for software running as virtual instances on such Physical Node.

Pipes—a temporary software connection between two applications or commands, usually in connection with a Unix operating system.

Platform as a Service—provides the ability to the consumer to deploy onto the cloud infrastructure consumer-created or acquired applications created using programming languages, libraries, services, and tools supported by the provider. The consumer does not manage or control the underlying cloud infrastructure, including network, servers, operating systems, or storage, but has control over the deployed applications and possibly configuration settings for the application-hosting environment.

Prime Rate—a particular rate of interest charged by a particular bank from time to time.

Private Cloud—cloud infrastructure is provisioned for exclusive use by a single organization comprising multiple consumers (e.g., business units). It may be owned, managed, and operated by the organization, a third party, or some combination of them, and it may exist on or off premises.

Product Roadmap—a plan for the future development of a software application including a timeline for the release of functionality, features, patches, and updates.

Protected Health Information (PHI)—individually identifiable information relating to the past, present, or future health status of an individual that is created, collected, or transmitted, or maintained by a HIPAA-covered entity in relation to the provision of healthcare, payment for healthcare services, or use in healthcare operations.

Provisioning Profile—a collection of digital entities that uniquely ties developers and devices to an authorized iPhone development team and enables a device to be used for testing.

Public Cloud—cloud infrastructure that is provisioned for open use by the general public. It may be owned, managed, and operated by a business, academic, or government organization, or some combination of them. It exists on the premises of the cloud provider.

Push Message—any notification from a smartphone app that displays while that app is not actively in use. Push messages are common on apps for iPhone and Android, and they frequently appear as pop-up dialogs, banners and small badges on each app's icon.

Reduced Resource Credit/Charge (RRC)—a credit to be provided by a vendor to a customer in the event a customer uses fewer resources than the vendor is contractually obligated to provide. Usually used in conjunction with a contract for outsourced services.

Regression Errors—bugs or flaws that are introduced into a software application as a consequence of fixing other bugs or adding features.

Regression Testing—software testing to identify regression errors.

Remote Access—the ability to access a computer or networked computer from a remote location.

Residuals—the vendor's general knowledge, skills, and experience, and any ideas, concepts, know-how, methodologies, and techniques that are not protected or susceptible of protection under U.S. patent or copyright laws, but that are used by the vendor within the scope of the vendor's business practice and may be used by it in the course of providing the services. Residuals usually do not include any work product, customer data, or customer confidential information.

Response Time—the time it takes for a computer to process a particular transaction once the "Enter" button is pressed.

Reverse Engineering—with respect to software, the process of recreating, extracting, decompiling, or otherwise determining the source code of a software program from the object code or machine code form.

Right to Use—a license grant that allows the end user the right to use the software.

Root Cause Analysis—the formal process used by a vendor to diagnose the underlying cause of problems at the lowest reasonable level so that corrective action can be taken to eliminate repeat failures.

Sample Data Test—testing conducted by running typical and atypical functions on a sampling of user data.

Scope Creep—gradual small changes in a project's scope that, when aggregated, can add up to a large project impact in time and budget.

Seat—in a multi-networked environment, a client computer from which a user can access or utilize, directly or indirectly, an application. In a single user or standalone environment, a seat means a computer that has an application installed for use by a single user.

Seat License—a means of calculating the license fee charged to a licensee based on the number of users accessing the application, i.e., on a per seat basis. The fee may be calculated based on the number of concurrent users or on the aggregate number users with access to the system; i.e., each individual would be required to purchase a license even though they are all not accessing the application at the same time.

Server or **Servers**—a computer connected to a local- or wide-area network serving one or more desktop devices or peripherals, including application servers, domain servers, file servers, print servers, fax servers, and data servers.

Service Bureau—another name for hosting.

Service Level—contractual technical standard that a service provider must meet in the provision of its technical services. For example, the time in which a vendor must answer a call to a help desk or the time in which a computer must process a particular transaction once the "Enter" button is pressed.

Service Level Agreement (SLA)—an agreement setting forth the standards to which the vendor's services must comply.

Service Level Credit (SLC)—a credit that may be granted to a customer in the event the vendor does not meet a contractual obligation to provide its services at a certain level. Usually used in conjunction with an outsourcing contract.

Shareware—software provided on a trial basis without charge. If the customer decides to use such software on a continuing basis, the customer will then pay for a license.

Simple Mail Transfer Protocol (SMTP)—the de facto standard for email transmissions across the Internet.

Socket—provides a mechanical and electrical connection between a microprocessor and a printed circuit board permitting the central processing unit (CPU) to be installed or replaced without soldering.

Software as a Service (SaaS)—the capability provided to the consumer to use the provider's applications running on a cloud infrastructure. The applications are accessible from various client devices through either a thin client interface, such as a web browser (e.g., web-based email), or a program interface. The consumer does not manage or control the underlying cloud infrastructure including network, servers, operating systems, storage, or even individual application capabilities, with the possible exception of limited user-specific application configuration settings.

Software Development Kit (SDK)—a programming package that enables a programmer to develop software applications for a specific platform. SDKs usually include debugging tools, libraries, and other utilities to aid programmers as well as one or more APIs, programming tools, and documentation. All SDKs are/contain APIs but not all APIs are SDKs.

Software key(s)—a piece of software used to certify that a software program is original. A software key may also be used to activate a software program and prevent multiple users from using the same copy of the software.

Source Code—computer software in the form of electronic and printed human-readable, mnemonic or English-like program listings. Printed and online descriptions of the design of such software, including data definition models, indices, structure tables, system flow charts, program flow charts, defined terms, file layouts, program narratives, global documentation (including global variables), and program listings.

Specifications—in software development, a written statement or outline for the development of software, indicating the functions or tasks that the software should accomplish and/or the hardware, programming techniques, or algorithms that must be used.

SSAE 18—an auditing standard created by the American Institute for Certified Public Accountants in response to the requirements of the Sarbanes-Oxley Act. See Chapter 7.E and Form B.3.1 § 9.13 for a more detailed description of SSAE 18.

Statement of Work (SOW)—a detailed explanation of the work to be performed by the vendor and the standards it must meet for acceptance, as well as any related contractual obligations of the vendor and customer.

Subject Matter Expert (SME)—an individual with expertise in a particular area.

Systems Administrator—the individual responsible for the ongoing upkeep, maintenance, and reliable operation of a software system or application.

System Integrator—a vendor responsible for combining a customer's hardware, software, and network into an integrated working system.

Terabyte—a measurement of digital data. A terabyte equates to 1,000 gigabytes.

Termination/Expiration Assistance—assistance provided by a vendor when a customer is transitioning from one vendor to another or as the contract is terminated.

Third-Party Software—applications software and systems software used by a systems integrator to provide the services under license to the customer or vendor by a third party. They often include ongoing services (e.g., maintenance and support services, upgrades, subscription services) provided by third parties (e.g., vendor, manufacturer, lessor) in the same license covering such software.

Threads—virtual components or codes which divide the physical core of a CPU into multiple virtual cores. A single CPU core can have up-to 2 threads per core.

Tools—reusable code components used by software developers to develop software applications and customizations to software applications.

Transition Plan—a plan between a service provider and a customer to transition the customer to or from the service provider's products or services.

Turn-key System—a complete hardware and software system, preassembled and preconfigured for the user, so that the user does not need to program or configure the system in order to use it.

Updates—a compendium of "fixes" that the licensor releases to the users of the software.

Upgrades—a new release or version of the software constituting a compendium of enhancements.

User Acceptance Testing (UAT)—testing undertaken by a customer/end user to ensure an application meets the contractually agreed requirements/functionality before using the application in a production environment.

User Experience (UX)—encompasses all aspects of the end-user's interaction with the company, its services, and its products.

User Interface—In information technology, the user interface (UI) is everything designed into an information device with which a human being may interact — including display screen, keyboard, mouse, light pen, the appearance of a desktop, illuminated characters, help messages, and how an application program or a website invites interaction and responds to it.

Value Added Reseller (VAR)—a reseller of a third party's products after having improved them. For example, a software vendor may resell third-party hardware after having installed its proprietary software on the hardware. The VAR usually buys the third-party products at a discount and marks them up. See, e.g., Forms.in Section F.2.

Virtual Machine—a software computer that, like a physical computer, runs an operating system and applications. The virtual machine is composed of a set of specification and configuration files backed by the physical resources of a host.

Virtual Node—an instance of the software executed, in whole or in part, on a virtual machine.

Virtual Private Network (VPN)—a communication tunnel running through a shared network, such as the Internet, which uses encryption and other security mechanisms to ensure the data cannot be intercepted and that the data senders and receivers are authenticated.

Virus—a program code, programming instruction, or set of instructions intentionally constructed with the ability to damage, interfere with, or otherwise adversely affect computer programs, data files, or operations.

Vulnerability Scan—a systematic review process to search for and map systems for weaknesses in an application, computer or network. The intent is to determine if there are points of weakness in the security control system that can be exploited from outside the network.

Waterfall—a traditional method of software development whereby projects are completed in a sequential series of steps including initial gathering of requirements, developing of software according to those requirements, testing, and delivering. See Chapter 16.A for a detailed discussion

Web App—application software that runs in a web browser and is created in a browser-supported programming language (such as the combination of JavaScript, HTML and CSS) and relies on a common web browser to render the application.

Web Browser—a software application for retrieving, presenting and traversing information resources on the World Wide Web. Popular web browsers include Firefox, Internet Explorer, Google Chrome, and Safari.

Web Services Description Language (WSDL)—an XML format for describing network services as a set of endpoints operating on messages containing either document-oriented or procedure-oriented information. The operations and messages are described abstractly, and then bound to a concrete network protocol and message format to define an endpoint. Related concrete endpoints are combined into abstract endpoints (services). WSDL is extensible to allow description of endpoints and their messages regardless of what message formats or network protocols are used to communicate. However, the only bindings described in this document describe how to use WSDL in conjunction with SOAP, HTTP GET/POST, and MIME.

Wide Area Network—a communications network connecting various hardware devices to facilitate the sharing of software applications and data.

XML Schema Definition (XSD)—specifies how to formally describe the elements in an Extensible Markup Language (XML) document. This description can be used to verify that each item of content in a document adheres to the description of the element in which the content is to be placed.

APPENDIX **3**

Recommended Resource Materials

Charles Bieneman, The Software IP report, www.b2ipreport.com/blog/

Jeff C. Dodd, Robert A. Feldman & Raymond T. Nimmer, Drafting Effective Contracts: A Practitioner's Guide, (2023).

Stuart H. Deming, Designing an Effective Anti-Bribery Compliance Program, (2018).

Michael A. Epstein & Frank L. Politano, Drafting License Agreements, 4th ed. (2023).

Kurtis A. Kemper, Computer and Information Law Digest, 2d ed. (2018).

Intellectual Property Misuse: Licensing and Litigation 2d ed. (2020).

Lisa R. Lifshitz & John A. Rothchild (editors), Cloud 3.0: Drafting and Negotiating Cloud Computing Agreements (2019).

Mark G. Malven, Technology Transactions: A Practical Guide to Drafting and Negotiating Commercial Contracts (2023).

Susan A. Maslow & David V. Snyder, Contracts For Responsible and Sustainable Supply Chains (2023).

Heather A. Meeker, Open Source For Business, 3d. ed. (2020).

Raymond T. Nimmer, Law of Computer Technology, 4th ed. (2023).

Raymond T. Nimmer & Jeff C. Dodd, Modern Licensing Law (2023).

Henry A. Perritt, Jr., Trade Secrets: A Practitioner's Guide, 2d ed. (2022).

Peter C. Quittmeyer, Clarence H. Ridley, & John Matuszeski, Computer Software Agreements: Forms and Commentary, 3d ed. (2023).

Margaret Jane Radin, Boilerplate: The Fine Print, Vanishing Rights, and the Rule of Law (2014).

Brian Rogers, The Contract Guy, https://thecontractsguy.net/about-2/

Vladimir R. Rossman & Morton Moskin eds., Commercial Contracts: Strategies For Drafting And Negotiating 2d ed. (2021).

Michael L. Rustad, Software Licensing, Cloud Computing Agreements, Open Source, And Internet Terms of Use: A Practical Approach To Information Age Contracts In A Global Setting (2016).

Michael D. Scott, Scott on Information Technology Law, 3d ed. (2023).

W. Stanford Smith, Guide To Privacy (2022).

Tina L. Stark, Negotiating and Drafting Contract Boilerplate (2003).

THOMSON* REUTERS EDITORIAL STAFF, CORPORATE COUNSEL'S GUIDE TO SOFTWARE TRANSACTIONS (2023).

THOMSON* REUTERS EDITORIAL STAFF, INTELLECTUAL PROPERTY COUNSELOR (2023).

D.C. TOEDT, ON CONTRACTS, WWW.ONCONTRACTS.COM.

DAVID W. TOLLEN. THE TECH INDEMNITIES POCKET GUIDE: INDEMNITIES IN SOFTWARE AND OTHER IT CONTRACTS for LAWYERS AND BUSINESS PEOPLE (2020).

Index of Cases

A

D

E

F

H

K

L

M

N

Q

R

S

T

W

Y

Z

Index

M

N

O

Q

R

T

About the Author

H. Ward Classen is Vice-President and General Counsel of Honeywell Connected Life Sciences. He has over 35 years' experience negotiating complex information technology agreements and has practiced with many of the world's leading technology companies, including Computer Sciences Corporation (now DXC Technology Corporation), Accenture plc, and InterDigital, Inc.

A graduate of Trinity College in Connecticut, Mr. Classen received his Juris Doctor from The Catholic University of America in Washington, D.C., and a Master of Business Administration from the Wharton School of the University of Pennsylvania. While in law school, Mr. Classen was a member of the *Catholic University Law Review* and editor-in-chief and founder of *The Journal of Contemporary Health Law and Policy.*

Mr. Classen serves on a number of business, professional, and civic boards, including The Maryland State Fair & Agricultural Society, Inc., The Board of the Maryland Race Track Employees' Pension Fund, and the board of advisors of The *Computer & Internet Lawyer*. Mr. Classen has been widely published in legal journals and spoken extensively before professional groups, both domestically and internationally. His recent articles address technology licensing and cloud computing. Mr. Classen welcomes any thoughts on this book or suggestions on how it may be improved. He can be contacted at ward.classen@gmail.com.

Additional Contents on https://ambar.org/softlic8edcloud

Model Forms

(The Model Forms in this publication are available in electronic format and may be downloaded and customized for your practice. Please visit https://ambar.org/softlic8edcloud.)

A. RFI and RFP Related Documents

A.1 RFI Related Documents

Form A.1.1: Request for Information (RFI)
Form A.1.2: Request for Information—Alternate Form

A.2 RFP Related Documents

Form A.2.1: Request for Proposal (RFP)
Form A.2.2: RFP Response Matrix
Form A.2.3: RFP Nondisclosure Agreement
Form A.2.4: RFP Nondisclosure Agreement – Alternate Form
Form A.2.5: Contractual Provisions RFP Response Form
Form A.2.6: RFP Terms and Conditions
Form A.2.7: RFP Terms and Conditions - Alternate Form
Form A.2.8: Model RFP Responses
Form A.2.9: RFP Representations and Warranties
Form A.2.10: Declaration of Conflict of Interest
Form A.2.11: Customer Use of Vendor Proposal
Form A.2.12: Supplier Authority Statement

A.3 Teaming Agreements

Form A.3.1: Teaming Agreement
Form A.3.2: Teaming Agreement – For federal contract with restrictive employee disclosure provisions

A.4 Memorandums of Understanding

Form A.4.1: Memorandum of Understanding

B. Software Licenses and Related Agreements

B1. Demonstration, Evaluation and Training Licenses

Form B.1.1: Demonstration License Agreement
Form B.1.2: Evaluation License Agreement
Form B.1.3: Evaluation License – Blacklined with Customer comments
Form B.1.4: Non-Production Use Software License – For reseller internal testing and training
Form B.1.5: Build Server License – For software compilation and testing

B.2 Beta Licenses
Form B.2.1: Beta Development Agreement

B.3 Production Licenses
Form B.3.1: Software License and Services Agreement (Annotated)
Form B.3.2: Software License, Maintenance, and Subscriber Billing Services Agreement
Form B.3.3: Hardware Purchase, Software License, and Related Services
Form B.3.4: Software License and Support Agreement – Seat License – Informal Tone
Form B.3.5: Software License – Seat License
Form B.3.6: Software License and Support Agreement – Named Users
Form B.3.7: Software License Agreement – for ITO Outsourcing
Form B.3.8: End User License Agreement – Blacklined with Customer comments
Form B.3.9: Software License Agreement - Redistributables – Blacklined with Customer comments
Form B.3.10: Software License and Services Agreement

B.4 Source Code Licenses
Form B.4.1: Source Code License Agreement

B.5 Click-wrap, Shrink-wrap and Browse-wrap Licenses
Form B.5.1: Shrink Wrap License
Form B.5.2: End User License Agreement (Click-wrap Agreement)
Form B.5.3: End User License Agreement – Click-wrap – Alternate Form
Form B.5.4: Browse-wrap License Agreement

B.6 Mobile Applications
Form B.6.1: Mobile Application Development Agreement
Form B.6.2: Mobile Application EULA
Form B.6.3: Mobile Application EULA – non iOS
Form B.6.4: Mobile Application EULA – iOS
Form B.6.5: Mobile Application Front End Terms and Conditions

B.7 Sublicenses
Form B.7.1: Software Sublicense Agreement – Per core license fee (Annotated)
Form B.7.2: Software Sublicense Agreement

B.8 Miscellaneous Licenses
Form B.8.1: ABA Model Software License Provisions with Commentary and Ancillary Agreements
Form B.8.2: Inter-company Software Distribution License Agreement

B.9 Miscellaneous
Form B.9.1: Customer Intake Questionnaire
Form B.9.2: Notification of Audit Letter
Form B.9.3: Reference Discount Addendum – Discount given to Licensee for serving as reference
Form B.9.4: Licensee's Support Obligations to Licensor Performance
Form B.9.5: License Retirement Acknowledgment

C. Software Development and Related Services Agreements
C.1 Software Development Agreement
Form C.1.1: Software Development Agreement – Time and Materials Basis – Favors Customer
Form C.1.2: Shared Cost Enhancement Sponsorship Exhibit
Form C.1.3: Shared Cost Enhancement Sponsorship Exhibit – Alternate Form – Greater Detail
Form C.1.4: Business Requirements Definition